# THE INDIAN TRILOGY

V.S. NAIPAUL was born in Trinidad in 1932. He went to England on a scholarship in 1950. After four years at University College, Oxford, he began to write, and since then has followed no other profession. He has published more than twenty books of fiction and non-fiction, including *Half a Life*, *A House for Mr Biswas*, *A Bend in the River* and, most recently, a collection of correspondence, *Letters Between a Father and Son*, and *The Masque of Africa*. In 2001, he was awarded the Nobel Prize in Literature.

## Also by V.S. Naipaul

FICTION

*The Mystic Masseur*
*The Suffrage of Elvira*
*Miguel Street*
*A House for Mr Biswas*
*Mr Stone and the Knights Companion*
*The Mimic Men*
*A Flag on the Island*
*In a Free State*
*Guerrillas*
*A Bend in the River*
*The Enigma of Arrival*
*A Way in the World*
*Half a Life*
*Magic Seeds*

NON-FICTION

*The Middle Passage*
*The Loss of El Dorado*
*The Overcrowded Barracoon*
*The Return of Eva Perón*
*Among the Believers: An Islamic Journey*
*Finding the Centre*
*A Turn in the South*
*Beyond Belief*
*Letters Between a Father and Son*
*The Writer and the World: Essays*
*Literary Occasions*
*A Writer's People: Ways of Looking and Feeling*
*The Masque of Africa*

Praise for *The Indian Trilogy*

'Brilliant . . . tender, lyrical, explosive' *Observer*

'His narrative skill is spectacular. One returns with pleasure to the slow hand-in-hand revelation of both India and himself' *The Times*

'A devastating work, but proof that a novelist of Naipaul's stature can often define problems quicker and more effectively than a team of economists and other experts' *The Times*

'It is a long and angry stare at the obvious; it is humbling . . . because it seems chasteningly right' *New Statesman*

'Indispensable for anyone who wants seriously to come to grips with the experience of India' *New York Times Book Review*

'Brilliantly enjoyable . . . Everyone should read him' *Sunday Telegraph*

'With this book he may well have written his own enduring monument, in prose at once stirring and intensely personal, distinguished both by style and critical acumen' *Financial Times*

# THE INDIAN TRILOGY

AN AREA OF DARKNESS

A WOUNDED CIVILIZATION

a million mutinies now

V.S. NAIPAUL

PICADOR INDIA

Reprinted 2023

*An Area of Darkness* first published 1964 by André Deutsch
First published by Picador 1995
First published in paperback 2002 by Picador
Published with a new preface 2010 by Picador


*India: A Wounded Civilization* first published 1977 by André Deutsch
First published in paperback 1979 by Penguin Books
First published by Picador 2002
Published with a new preface 2010 by Picador


*India: A Million Mutinies Now* first published 1990 by William Heinemann
First published in paperback in 1991 by Vintage, a division within
The Random House Group
First published by Picador 2010


This edition first published 2016 by Picador India
an imprint of Pan Macmillan Publishing India Private Limited

707 Kailash Building
26 K.G. Marg, New Delhi 110001
www.panmacmillan.co.in

Pan Macmillan, The Smithson, 6 Briset Street, Farringdon, London EC1M 5NR
Associated companies throughout the world
www.panmacmillan.com

ISBN 978-93-82616-90-0


3 5 7 9 8 6 4

A CIP catalogue record for this book is available from the British Library



Printed and bound in India by Thomson Press India Ltd.

FSC www.fsc.org
MIX
Paper | Supporting responsible forestry
FSC® C010615

# CONTENTS

# INTRODUCTION

## Naipaul's India

IN A SPIRIT of inquiry, V.S. Naipaul sailed in 1962 to India, a country he had never seen, but a place that had been on his mind since childhood. He was twenty-nine years old. His work was praised in England, but his great literary reputation was yet to be made. He spent a year in India and on his return, after a period of muddle ('overwhelmed by the distress I saw'), he wrote *An Area of Darkness* (1964). The book was acclaimed. He returned to India in 1975, in a period of national anxiety during the Emergency declared by the authoritarian government of Prime Minister Indira Gandhi. He travelled widely and wrote a series of essays on the situation he experienced, and these became *India: A Wounded Civilization* (1977). Fifteen years later he went back, with a particular strategy in mind, that in order to understand India better he would need to spend more time with individuals and know their stories in depth. The result was *India: A Million Mutinies Now* (1990), more ambitious than his first two books, both in the complexity of its themes and the ways in which he tackled them, through portraiture and an extensive series of encounters, lengthy interviews that might better be described as interrogations.

That last book contains one of Naipaul's wisest observations: 'I believe that the present, accurately seized, foretells the future.'

Three books, one thousand pages of text, written over thirty years, a work that could be described as *India: A Chronicle.* But still he was not done. He travelled a number of times to India after that, always inquisitive, often writing, sometimes speaking, now an honoured and garlanded guest rather than an anonymous traveller. His last visit in January 2015 was to Rajasthan to speak at the Jaipur Literary Festival. He was then eighty-two, in a wheelchair because of ill-health, but the wheelchair propelled by his wife Nadira was less like a medical expedient than a portable throne. In his public presentations Naipaul was funny, friendly, benign, reflective – hardly the fierce young man of a half-century earlier who reported in *An Area of Darkness* on the times he'd lost his temper, or denounced 'the fat, impertinent Anglo-Indian girl and the rat-faced Anglo-Indian manager' at his Bombay hotel – a litany of his exasperations. People said he was much mellower.

Then, after one of his talks, a woman in the Jaipur audience hectored him in an aggrieved tone, asking him why he did not regard India as a singular place of piety, its problems of poverty and social justice receiving insufficient sympathy from the wider world.

There came a flash of the old Naipaul, bristling in his chair: 'What makes you think' – and he rose slightly from his seat in temper – 'what makes you think India deserves more compassion than other countries?'

Later that same week, being driven to Amber Fort, Naipaul looked out the side window as the car was delayed in traffic at a crowded intersection. I was beside him, our friendship had been restored a few years earlier. A small boy, no more than four or five, was seated on a triangular section of broken pavement between two busy roads. The boy was neatly dressed, in a shirt and shorts, cross-legged on a folded square of cloth, at risk amid the confusion of traffic and pedestrians, sadhus, box-wallahs, beggars, hawkers with baskets on their head, school children, bus fumes, pushcarts, and motorbikes and honking horns. The child was animated by the scene, yet he was alone – no adult near him, no one attending to him. Very odd, symbolic and unlikely.

Naipaul stared sadly at him and the scene for a long moment, and as our car began to move on he said to me, 'I see myself in that child.'

*

He had been raised in a traditional Indian household in Trinidad. He wrote, 'I had no belief; I disliked religious ritual; and I had a sense of the ridiculous. I refused to go through the *janaywa*, or thread ceremony . . . A pleasing piece of theatre. But I knew we were in Trinidad, an island separated by only ten miles from the South American coast'.

Still, he has stayed true to the world he knows. Indians have populated nearly all his fiction – his heroes, his central characters, from Pundit Ganesh in his earliest novel, through Mr Biswas and the mimic man Ralph Singh, and Salim in *A Bend in the River*, to Willie Chandran of his last two novels, *Half a Life* and *Magic Seeds*.

But India remained a mystery. He explains in *An Area of Darkness* that 'The India . . . which was the background to my childhood was an area of the imagination' – stimulated by books, films, conjecture, and religious rituals. 'I was without belief or interest in belief; I was incapable of worship, of God or holy men; and so one whole side of India was closed to me.'

Later, in *India: A Wounded Civilization*, he wrote: 'India, which I visited for the first time in 1962, turned out to be a very strange land', adding: 'India is for me a difficult country. It isn't my home and cannot be my home; and yet I cannot reject it or be indifferent to it; I cannot travel only for the sights . . . It has taken me much time to come to terms with the strangeness of India'.

Deepening his intention, he speaks of his sense of alienation and 'neurosis' on his previous journeys and wrote in *India: A Million Mutinies Now*, that in order to fulfil himself as a writer, to understand the currents of history and his place in the world, he had to create a new way of seeing, and, 'In the practising of this new way I had to deal first of all with my ancestral land, India. I was not an insider, even after many months of travel; nor could I consider myself an outsider: India and the idea of India had always been important to me. So I was always divided about India, and found it hard to say a final word.'

'Travel in itself for a book about a journey doesn't interest me,' he told me once, long ago. 'My intention has always been to travel with a theme in mind.' These three books Naipaul says are non-fiction 'but they are as personal and varied and deeply felt as any work of fiction could be'.

You could say that India has been Naipaul's obsessive, almost lifelong subject, a way of evaluating the world, a way of understanding his origins; and it is clear from his first experiences that India is maddening. Many would admit that it would take at least a lifetime to understand India. Naipaul persisted, and this perhaps accounts for the fact that though these books are different in form, and in structure, and set years apart, they overlap in subject matter, always going deeper, distrusting appearances. Naipaul notices the physical world, the stinks, the sewers, the slums, but nowhere in these books are the mock ordeals of the conventional travel books; mentions of meals and hotels are made in passing, and there is no sightseeing, no account of ruins or temples unless they are related to his argument. The dinner parties are often occasions for combat. A thousand pages about India with no mention of the Taj Mahal, tiger hunts, or chicken biryani.

The Harijans ('Children of God') – or untouchables – figure, though, and so do the Naxalite rebels, the paradoxes of the caste system and the conflicts in Indian marriages. The long shadow of Indian history with the legacies of empire is a theme throughout, Gandhi a recurring personage, the failures of government, urban life and architecture, the disclosures in Indian novels, the notion of cleanliness, the implications of ruins, the imperatives of Hinduism (but without any recitation of the attributes of gods or goddesses), the plight of the poor, the oppression of poverty, the intrusions of outsiders, Indian vision and the Indian sense of self.

Naipaul said that his difficulty in writing *An Area of Darkness* was that he had been bewildered or enraged by much of what he saw on his first experience of India. He was not a prodigal son but a foreigner, who looked Indian ('one of the crowd') but who did not speak the language or have the support of any local relatives. He was on his own, with limited resources, staying in the more modest hotels and as a paying guest with Indian families (Mrs Mahindra's stands out, with her chant that she is 'craze, just craze for foreign'). Intent on making the most of his year, he spent a good part of the time in a small hotel in Srinagar, writing his London novel, *Mr Stone and the Knights Companion*. He says he did not keep a diary, and had only scraps of notes.

But his memory served him – and it is important to point out that none of the thousand pages of this India trilogy were written with the aid of a tape-recorder. Naipaul has maintained that, in all his non-fiction, he practised the mental discipline of remembering in detail what someone had said to him. He has also said that, wishing to verify what someone told him, he might revisit the person and ask him or her to repeat the story.

*An Area of Darkness* is closer to what we think of as a traditional travel book, although unlike most others it is personal and passionate. The traveller arrives, is bewildered, battles bureaucracy, begins to make finer distinctions, discovers contradictions and the repetition of certain national habits, compares appearance with reality, and is subjected to a certain amount of harassing detail, and at last finds an oasis of peace in which to work (the hotel in Srinagar). In the end, he makes a sentimental visit to the village of his ancestors – and is appalled, and sums up his experience. In the beginning, India was a darkness. For a period of his travel he felt the shadows lift. And then with his departure the darkness closes in again.

What makes this book unusual (and this is true of the two which follow) is the unsparing eye of the traveller, the originality of his thought, the vividness of his physical description – of people and places; and the vitality of the dialogue. Naipaul is first a novelist, and he brings to his non-fiction a power to recreate a person's physical presence, a manner of speech, or the look of a landscape.

Indians generally were upset by the book when it appeared. Naipaul had expected this, because one of its repeated themes was that Indians had lived so long with contradictions and received wisdom that they had lost the ability to see things as they are.

'Indians defecate everywhere. They defecate, mostly, beside the railway tracks. But they also defecate on the beaches; they defecate on the hills; they defecate on the river banks; they defecate on the streets; they never look for cover.'

These three sentences, with their Churchillian rhythms, drove Indian reviewers mad. And there is more, a whole closely printed page, in which Naipaul offers the quaint image of 'These squatting figures – to the visitor, as eternal and emblematic as Rodin's Thinker', and he makes his point: they are never spoken of, written about, or mentioned, because he says with the emphasis of italics '*Indians do not see these squatters*.'

Naipaul uses this as an example of a fundamental Indian deficiency, the inability or unwillingness to see things as they are. 'There is little subtlety to India. The poor are thin; the rich are fat.' Naipaul's India of 1962 was moribund, characterized by decay and dereliction, and the confinement of the caste system. 'Class is a system of rewards. Caste imprisons a man in his function.' There is a sweeper caste, but sweepers are not required to clean, only to *be* sweepers. In a powerful paragraph that begins 'Study these four men washing down the steps of this unpalatable Bombay hotel', Naipaul presents the reader with a ritualized instance of caste.

Gandhi 'saw India so clearly because he was in part a colonial', returning to India having spent twenty years in South Africa. And the implication is that Naipaul himself, with his colonial childhood, brought this clear-sightedness to India and to his book, which is much more than a condemnation of Indian faults. It is a series of discoveries and examinations, but here the traveller is on the move in a spirited way – confronting obstinacy or fraudulence, weighing Indian explanations. There is more landscape in this book than the others, and (though it ends in futility) Naipaul recounts the bittersweet experience of a pilgrimage he took. Naipaul is physically more present and opinionated in this book than in any other – losing his temper, arguing, being happy and humorous, as well as exhausted and dispirited. In the end, he sees that it is no homecoming; he has no place in this static and self-deluded country.

You assume he won't go back. But new events, and dramatic changes, brought him again to India years later to re-examine the 'difficult country', and to reassess his memories. He is in a more confident mood, more detached, better informed. Bombay – each of these books begins in Bombay – has its charms and, though one particular slum is 'a hellish vision' of wasted-looking people living in filth, among skinny cows and excrement, the rest of the city is improved. Or has the mood of the traveller improved? I like this teasing observation of the rats below the Gateway of India, 'mingling easily with the crowd, and at nightfall as playful as baby rabbits.'

Vijayanagar now 'seemed less awesome than when I had seen it thirteen years before'. India has become a destination for hippies and other foreign wanderers, but 'theirs is a shallow narcissism'. Foreigners and returning Indians do not come out well in this book. They are fantasists, parasites, romancers, not to be trusted; they see nothing.

This idea, that India is blind to itself – already apparent in the first book – is enlarged and developed here and in the next book. This inability to see is partly complacency or obstinacy, but more profoundly a function of caste, the blindness having 'its roots in caste and religion'.

'A caste vision: what is remote from me is remote from me. The Indian press has interpreted its function in an Indian way. It has not sought to put India in touch with itself; it doesn't really know how, and it hasn't felt the need.' In this examination of the crisis the Emergency has brought about, Naipaul puts the point powerfully: 'When men cannot observe, they don't have ideas; they have obsessions. When people live instinctive lives, something like a collective amnesia steadily blurs the past.'

Along with this devastating insight, Naipaul discovers that something has improved. The press has failed, but some Indian writers have become more observant. One of those is Vijay Tendulkar, whose play *The Vultures* had recently been staged in an English version. This drama resonated with Naipaul, who saw that India had become 'a land of vultures'. Hearing that Tendulkar had been awarded a fellowship to travel throughout India, Naipaul makes an effort to see him. Their talk encourages Naipaul; some Indians have begun to see the country as it is. Tendulkar becomes one of the telling portraits in the book (and it must be said that subsequent to his meeting with Naipaul, Tendulkar went on to a long, well-rewarded literary career, dying in 2008 at the age of eighty).

There are many such portraits in the book, not all of them flattering. There is the man described as 'a magnate' – 'There was a risen-dough quality about the magnate's face and physique which hinted at a man given to solitary sexual excitations.'

And the portrait of a sarpanch or chairman of a village council: 'He was a plump man, the sarpanch, noticeably unwashed and unshaved; but his hair was well-oiled. He was chewing a full red mouthful of betel nut and he wore correctly grubby clothes'. Any other writer would leave it there, but Naipaul examines the motive, elaborating that unexpected pair of words 'correctly grubby'.

'The grubbiness was studied, and it was correct because any attempt at greater elegance would have been not only unnecessary and wasteful but also impious, a provocation of the gods who had so far played fair with the sarpanch and wouldn't have cared to see the man getting above himself.'

Gandhi reappears, not 'the colonial' here but a more dynamic figure, who awakened India. But his message became blurred in his deification. 'Gandhi took India out of one kind of *Kal Yug*, one kind of Black Age; his success inevitably pushed it back into another.' The result is the 'decadent Gandhianism' of his followers.

The reason for Naipaul's trip was the Emergency, the stages of which he describes, but along the way he speaks of the conflicts and pressures, among them the Maoist Naxalites, and the persistence of poverty and the Indian reaction to it, extolling it as an ideal of humility, though Indian poverty, 'more dehumanizing than any machine,' in this decaying civilization, wounded, 'without an ideology'. This closely argued book is not a travel book, more an extended essay, which required travel for testimony: travel with a theme.

'But the alarm has been sounded', Naipaul writes in it. 'The millions are on the move. Both in the cities and in the villages there is an urgent new claim on the land; and any idea of India which does not take this claim into account is worthless.'

This statement is a preview of *India: A Million Mutinies Now*, the account of another revisit, this one sixteen years later. He speaks of his previous work, saying, how it 'had taken the writer all that time to go beyond personal discovery and pain, and analysis, to arrive at the simple and overwhelming idea that the most important thing about India, the thing to be gone into and understood, and not seen from the outside, was the people.'

This, Naipaul's biggest and perhaps most important book on India, is also his most compassionate, most patient and forgiving. He puts himself in the hands of the people; he records, he interrogates, asks for clarification. He spends a great deal of time in people's houses – parlours, kitchens, and sometime-shacks. But more than a book of interviews, it contains landscape and weather, train journeys, hikes through slums, visits to the poorest, to Dalits, and Indian royalty, and the pundit of a maharaja, and senior officials, such as Mr Prakash, a minister in the state government of Karnataka. It contains a four-page account of a delay at an airport, an analysis of Portuguese colonialism ('haters of idolatry, haters of all that was not the true faith . . .'), a lengthy reflection on the fate of Indian women, the complexity of the family: 'Cruelty, yes: it was in the nature of Indian family life.'

'The eternal conflict of Hindu family life [is] a ritualized aspect of the fate of women', he writes. 'To be tormented by a mother-in-law was part of a young woman's testing, part, almost, of growing up. Somehow the young woman survived; and then one day she became a mother-in-law herself, and had her own daughter-in-law to torment, to round off a life, to balance pain and joy.'

These are not chance encounters but extensive meetings in which he sees the inner life of the people: Papu the stockbroker, who says, 'I am sure there's going to be a revolution.' Mr Patil, the Shiv Sena leader: 'The paunch looked new, something he was still learning to live with'. Mr Ghate the Sena official in Dharavi slum, Subroto the scriptwriter in his small room: 'He stood up and raised both arms . . . and looked at the ceiling. The gesture filled the little room. He said, "This is my room. This is my only room under the sun."' He offers us a portrait of Periyar (1879 –1973), the rationalist and anti-Hindu social activist: 'There is no God. There is no God. There is no God at all. He who invented God is a fool' – and of Mr Gopalakrishnan who agrees with this and tells his story. And Parveen and Kala, valiant women, and many more. There are, among these people, footnotes to his first book in the form of unexpected reunions. He meets a man, Rajan, whom he had last met in 1962, and 'Sugar' (now well-known, but 'a prisoner of his reputation') another man who'd accompanied him on the pilgrimage that same year.

Much had happened to India since his earliest visit – the assassination of Mrs Gandhi, the occupation of the Golden Temple (which Naipaul analyses, again with the stories of Sikhs who were peripherally involved). The rise of Indian manufacturing and successes in industry are new: India has modernized, though not all have shared in the prosperity. The concluding episode is a revisit to Mr Butt's hotel in Srinagar, Aziz, and Mr Butt still alive and reminiscing, the best of endings, a reunion of friends.

This human document is a chain of voices that evokes the beating heart of India. In these witnesses, some of them potential mutineers, Naipaul sees a new way in India – growth, self-awareness, restoration, the development of a vision.

'A million mutinies, supported by twenty kinds of group excess, sectarian excess, religious excess, regional excess: the beginnings of self-awareness, it would seem, the beginnings of an intellectual life, already negated by old anarchy and disorder. But there was in India now what didn't exist 200 years before: a central will, a central intellect, a national idea.'

2016

Paul Theroux

# AN AREA OF DARKNESS

*To Francis Wyndham*

# PREFACE

THE TRAVEL FOR *An Area of Darkness* followed immediately on the writing of *The Middle Passage*. I was living at the time, very happily, in South London, and the complicated arrangements for the travel out to India – by train and by ship – were made by the Streatham branch of a travel agency. The dates were not easy to rearrange, and I hurried through *The Middle Passage* not to lose the bookings for the later book. The idea of doing a book like *An Area of Darkness* had come to me during the writing of *A House for Mr Biswas*. That was a two-year labour, and at that period when things moved more slowly for me it began to seem that I had been engaged for too long in fiction. The idea of the other form, non-fiction, began to seem like a liberation, and I arranged with André Deutsch to do a book on India – although at this time I had done very little non-fiction and couldn't be said to know my way around the special difficulties of the form.

At last I was ready to go. I remember a winter journey across France by rail and I remember the achingly romantic sight of a big white horse ploughing. The rest of that journey to India is recorded in these pages. I had tried before leaving England to place a piece or two with an English paper. I had no success; I had no reputation. I remember only a letter from a newspaper telling me that India was 'inexhaustible', and that they would be happy in due course to see what I could come up with.

India was inexhaustible perhaps, but my India was not like an

English or British India. My India was full of pain. Sixty years or so before, my ancestors had made the very long journey to the Caribbean from India, six weeks at least, and though this was hardly spoken about when I was a child, it worried me more and more as I got older. So, writer though I was, I wasn't travelling to Forster's India or Kipling's. I was travelling to an India which existed only in my head. The India I found in those early days was sad and simple and repetitive, too repetitive for a book, and I began to feel that André Deutsch wasn't going to get his book. I was saved by the deeper anxiety that had been with me throughout the journey to India. This anxiety was that after *A House for Mr Biswas* I had run out of fictional material and that life was going to be very hard for me in the future; perhaps the writing career would have to stop. This anxiety took various forms, some mental, some physical, some a combination of the two. The most debilitating anxiety was that I was losing the gift of speech. It was at the back of everything I did, at the back of everything that is recorded in the early pages of *An Area of Darkness*. India was physically like a blow. I exaggerated the heat, the squalor, everything that might make me unhappy. I wondered how I was going to last the year which I had thought of spending in the country. And all the time, as I have said, was the pressing need to get started on a novel – not that I had a subject, but merely to do something to reassure myself that I still had a career.

I went to Kashmir. I found a rough but friendly hotel in the Dal Lake in Srinagar. It was cooler; I could think more rationally; the reader of these pages will find out how I arranged my life there. And then I had some luck. An idea for a novel came to me and for three months I settled down to write that novel. That bit of work was a blessing. It gave me a point of rest; it enabled the life of India to flow slowly around me, giving me material for an Indian narrative, which developed even as the matter in my typewriter grew. Without that piece of work, that point of rest, I would not have been able to last in India; I would have been too unhappy; I might even have had to go back to England – a failure in every way. And it is strange to recall that it was that small fiction, that little piece of luck, which made the rest of my time in India possible, and led to the fruitfulness and growth of the next two or three years.

After that piece of good fortune *An Area of Darkness* wrote itself. I could be as flexible as I wished. I could go back to the beginnings of the journey itself or into my own family story. The travel I did after Kashmir was like a filling in, and an addition to a country already half known. I could deal with the large or the small; everything could be made to fit; it was a dazzling experience; and though a new fiction didn't come easily afterwards, yet the memory of this writing ease stayed with me, gave a measure of possible things, and made later essays or projects manageable.

2010

# CONTENTS

# TRAVELLER'S PRELUDE: A LITTLE PAPERWORK

AS SOON AS our quarantine flag came down and the last of the barefooted, blue-uniformed policemen of the Bombay Port Health Authority had left the ship, Coelho the Goan came aboard and, luring me with a long beckoning finger into the saloon, whispered, 'You have any cheej?'

Coelho had been sent by the travel agency to help me through the customs. He was tall and thin and shabby and nervous, and I imagined he was speaking of some type of contraband. He was. He required cheese. It was a delicacy in India. Imports were restricted, and the Indians had not yet learned how to make cheese, just as they had not yet learned how to bleach newsprint. But I couldn't help Coelho. The cheese on this Greek freighter was not good. Throughout the three-week journey from Alexandria I had been complaining about it to the impassive chief steward, and I didn't feel I could ask him now for some to take ashore.

'All right, all right,' Coelho said, not believing me and not willing to waste time listening to excuses. He left the saloon and began prowling light-footedly down a corridor, assessing the names above doors.

I went down to my cabin. I opened a new bottle of Scotch and took a sip. Then I opened a bottle of Metaxas and took a sip of that. These were the two bottles of spirits I was hoping to take into prohibition-dry Bombay, and this was the precaution my friend in the Indian Tourist Department had advised: full bottles would be confiscated.

Coelho and I met later in the dining-room. He had lost a little of his nervousness. He was carrying a very large Greek doll, its folk costume gaudy against his own shabby trousers and shirt, its rosy cheeks and unblinking blue eyes serene beside the restless melancholy of his long thin face. He saw my opened bottles and nervousness returned to him.

'Open. But why?'

'Isn't that the law?'

'Hide them.'

'The Metaxas is too tall to hide.'

'Put it flat.'

'I don't trust the cork. But don't they allow you to take in two bottles?'

'I don't know, I don't know. Just hold this dolly for me. Carry it in your hand. Say souvenir. You have your Tourist Introduction Card? Good. Very valuable document. With a document like that they wouldn't search you. Why don't you hide the bottles?'

He clapped his hands and at once a barefooted man, stunted and bony, appeared and began to take our suitcases away. He had been waiting, unseen, unheard, ever since Coelho came aboard. Carrying only the doll and the bag containing the bottles, we climbed down into the launch. Coelho's man stowed away the suitcases. Then he squatted on the floor, as though to squeeze himself into the smallest possible space, as though to apologize for his presence, even at the exposed stern, in the launch in which his master was travelling. The master, only occasionally glancing at the doll in my lap, stared ahead, his face full of foreboding.

*

For me the East had begun weeks before. Even in Greece I had felt Europe falling away. There was the East in the food, the emphasis on sweets, some of which I knew from my childhood;

in the posters for Indian films with the actress Nargis, a favourite, I was told, of Greek audiences; in the instantaneous friendships, the invitations to meals and homes. Greece was a preparation for Egypt: Alexandria at sunset, a wide shining arc in the winter sea; beyond the breakwaters, a glimpse through fine rain of the ex-king's white yacht; the ship's engine cut off; then abruptly, as at a signal, a roar from the quay, shouting and quarrelling and jabbering from men in grubby jibbahs who in an instant overran the already crowded ship and kept on running through it. And it was clear that here, and not in Greece, the East began: in this chaos of uneconomical movement, the self-stimulated din, the sudden feeling of insecurity, the conviction that all men were not brothers and that luggage was in danger.

Here was to be learned the importance of the guide, the man who knew local customs, the fixer to whom badly printed illiterate forms held no mysteries. 'Write here,' my guide said in the customs house, aswirl with porters and guides and officials and idlers and policemen and travellers and a Greek refugee whispering in my ear, 'Let me warn you. They are stealing tonight.' 'Write here. One Kodak.' He, the guide, indicated the dotted line marked *date*. 'And here,' pointing to *signature*, 'write no gold, ornaments or precious stones.' I objected. He said, 'Write.' He pronounced it like an Arabic word. He was tall, grave, Hollywood-sinister; he wore a fez and lightly tapped his thigh with a cane. I wrote. And it worked. 'And now,' he said, exchanging the fez marked *Travel Agent* for one marked *Hotel X*, 'let us go to the hotel.'

Thereafter, feature by feature, the East, known only from books, continued to reveal itself; and each recognition was a discovery, as much as it had been a revelation to see the jibbah, a garment made almost mythical by countless photographs and descriptions, on the backs of real people. In the faded hotel, full, one felt, of memories of the Raj, there was a foreshadowing of the caste system. The old French waiter only served; he had his runners, sad-eyed silent Negroes in fezzes and cummerbunds, who fetched and cleared away. In the lobby there were innumerable Negro pages, picturesquely attired. And in the streets there was the East one had expected: the children, the dirt, the disease, the undernourishment, the cries of *bakshish*, the hawkers, the touts, the glimpses of minarets. There were the reminders of imperialisms that had withdrawn in the dark, glass-cased European-style shops, wilting for lack of patronage; in the sad whispering of the French hairdresser that French perfumes could no longer be obtained and that one had to make do with heavy Egyptian scents; in the disparaging references of the Lebanese businessman to 'natives', all of whom he distrusted except for his assistant, who, quietly to me, spoke of the day when all the Lebanese and Europeans would be driven out of the country.

Feature by feature, the East one had read about. On the train to Cairo the man across the aisle hawked twice, with an expert tongue rolled the phlegm into a ball, plucked the ball out of his mouth with thumb and forefinger, considered it, and then rubbed it away between his palms. He was wearing a three-piece suit, and his transistor played loudly. Cairo revealed the meaning of the bazaar: narrow streets encrusted with filth, stinking even on this winter's day; tiny shops full of shoddy goods; crowds; the din, already barely supportable, made worse by the steady blaring of motor-car horns; medieval buildings partly collapsed, others rising on old rubble, with here and there sections of tiles, turquoise and royal blue, hinting at a past of order and beauty, crystal fountains and amorous adventures, as perhaps in the no less disordered past they always had done.

And in this bazaar, a cobbler. With white skullcap, lined face, steel-rimmed spectacles and white beard, he might have posed for a photograph in the *National Geographic Magazine*: the skilled and patient Oriental craftsman. My sole was flapping. Could he repair it? Sitting almost flat on the pavement, bowed over his work, he squinted at my shoes, my trousers, my raincoat. 'Fifty piastres.' I said: 'Four.' He nodded, pulled the shoe off my foot and with a carpenter's hammer began hammering in a one-inch nail. I grabbed the shoe; he, smiling, hammer raised, held on to it. I pulled; he let go.

The Pyramids, whose function as a public latrine no guide book mentions, were made impossible by guides, 'watchmen', camel-drivers and by boys whose donkeys were all called Whisky-and-soda. *Bakshish! Bakshish!* 'Come and have a cup of coffee. I don't want you to buy anything. I just want to have a little intelligent conversation. Mr Nehru is a great man. Let us exchange ideas. I am a graduate of the university.' I took the desert bus back to Alexandria and, two days before the appointed time, retreated to the Greek freighter.

Then came the tedium of the African ports. Little clearings, one felt them, at the edge of a vast continent; and here one knew that Egypt, for all its Negroes, was not Africa, and for all its minarets and jibbahs, not the East: it was the last of Europe. At Jeddah the jibbahs were cleaner, the American automobiles new and numerous and driven with great style. We were not permitted to land and could see only the life of the port. Camels and goats were being unloaded by cranes and slings from dingy tramp steamers on to the piers; they were to be slaughtered for the ritual feast that marks the end of Ramadan. Swung aloft, the camels splayed out their suddenly useless legs; touching earth, lightly or with a bump, they crouched; then they ran to their fellows and rubbed against them. A fire broke out in a launch; our freighter sounded the alarm and within minutes the fire engines arrived. 'Autocracy has its charms,' the young Pakistani student said.

We had touched Africa, and four of the passengers had not been inoculated against yellow fever. A Pakistan-fed smallpox epidemic was raging in Britain and we feared stringency in Karachi. The Pakistani officials came aboard, drank a good deal, and our quarantine was waived. At Bombay, though, the Indian officials refused alcohol and didn't even finish the Coca-Cola they were offered. They were sorry, but the four passengers would have to go to the isolation hospital at Santa Cruz; either that or the ship would have to stay out in the stream. Two of the passengers without inoculations were the captain's parents. We stayed out in the stream.

It had been a slow journey, its impressions varied and superficial. But it had been a preparation for the East. After the bazaar of Cairo the bazaar of Karachi was no surprise; and *bakshish* was the same in both languages. The change from the Mediterranean winter to the sticky high summer of the Red Sea had been swift. But other changes had been slower. From Athens to Bombay another idea of man had defined itself by degrees, a new type of authority and subservience. The physique of Europe had melted away first into that of Africa and then, through Semitic Arabia, into Aryan Asia. Men had been diminished and deformed; they begged and whined. Hysteria had been my reaction, and a brutality dictated by a new awareness of myself as a whole human being and a determination, touched with fear, to remain what I was. It mattered little through whose eyes I was seeing the East; there had as yet been no time for this type of self-assessment.

Superficial impressions, intemperate reactions. But one memory had stayed with me, and I had tried to hold it close during that day out in the stream at Bombay, when I had seen the sun set behind the Taj Mahal Hotel and had wished that Bombay was only another port such as those we had touched on the journey, a port that the freighter passenger might explore or reject.

*

It was at Alexandria. Here we had been pestered most by horsecabs. The horses were ribby, the coachwork as tattered as the garments of the drivers. The drivers hailed you; they drove their cabs beside you and left you only when another likely fare appeared. It had been good to get away from them, and from the security of the ship to watch them make their assault on others. It was like watching a silent film: the victim sighted, the racing cab, the victim engaged, gesticulations, the cab moving beside the victim and matching his pace, at first brisk, then exaggeratedly slow, then steady.

Then one morning the desert vastness of the dock was quickened with activity, and it was as if the silent film had become a silent epic. Long rows of two-toned taxicabs were drawn up outside the terminal building; scattered all over the dock area, as though awaiting a director's call to action, were black little clusters of horsecabs; and steadily, through the dock gates, far to the right, more taxis and cabs came rolling in. The horses galloped, the drivers' whip hands worked. It was a brief exaltation. Soon enough for each cab came repose, at the edge of a cab-cluster. The cause of the excitement was presently seen: a large white liner, possibly carrying tourists, possibly carrying ten-pound immigrants to Australia. Slowly, silently, she idled in. And more taxis came pelting through the gates, and more cabs, racing in feverishly to an anti-climax of nosebags and grass.

The liner docked early in the morning. It was not until noon that the first passengers came out of the terminal building into the wasteland of the dock area. This was like the director's call. Grass was snatched from the asphalt and thrust into boxes below the drivers' seats; and every passenger became the target of several converging attacks. Pink, inexperienced, timid and vulnerable these passengers appeared to us. They carried baskets and cameras; they wore straw hats and bright cotton shirts for the Egyptian winter (a bitter wind was blowing from the sea). But our sympathies had shifted; we were on the side of the Alexandrians. They had waited all morning; they had arrived with high panache and zeal; we wanted them to engage, conquer and drive away with their victims through the dock gates.

But this was not to be. Just when the passengers had been penned by cabs and taxis, and gestures of remonstrance had given way to stillness, so that it seemed escape was impossible and capture certain, two shiny motor-coaches came through the dock gates. From the ship they looked like expensive toys. They cleared a way through taxis and cabs, which closed in again and then opened out to permit the coaches to make a slow, wide turn; and where before there had been tourists in gay cottons there was now only asphalt. The cabs, as though unwilling to accept the finality of this disappearance, backed and moved forward as if in pursuit. Then without haste they made their way back to their respective stations, where the horses retrieved from the asphalt what grass had escaped the hurried snatch of the drivers.

All through the afternoon the cabs and taxis remained, waiting for passengers who had not gone on the coaches. These passengers were few; they came out in ones and twos; and they appeared to prefer the taxis. But the enthusiasm of the horsecabs did not wane. Still, when a passenger appeared, the drivers jumped on to their seats, lashed their thin horses into action and rattled away to engage, transformed from idlers in old overcoats and scarves into figures of skill and purpose. Sometimes they engaged; often then there were disputes between drivers and the passengers withdrew. Sometimes a cab accompanied a passenger to the very gates. Sometimes at that point we saw the tiny walker halt; and then, with triumph and relief, we saw him climb into the cab. But this was rare.

The light faded. The cabs no longer galloped to engage. They wheeled and went at walking pace. The wind became keener; the dock grew dark; lights appeared. But the cabs remained. It was only later, when the liner blazed with lights, even its smoke-stack illuminated, and hope had been altogether extinguished, that they went away one by one, leaving behind shreds of grass and horse-droppings where they had stood.

Later that night I went up to the deck. Not far away, below a lamp standard, stood a lone cab. It had been there since the late afternoon; it had withdrawn early from the turmoil around the terminal. It had had no fares, and there could be no fares for it now. The cab-lamp burned low; the horse was eating grass from a shallow pile on the road. The driver, wrapped against the wind, was polishing the dully gleaming hood of his cab with a large rag.

The polishing over, he dusted; then he gave the horse a brief, brisk rub down. Less than a minute later he was out of his cab again, polishing, dusting, brushing. He went in; he came out. His actions were compulsive. The animal chewed; his coat shone; the cab gleamed. And there were no fares. And next morning the liner had gone, and the dock was deserted again.

Now, sitting in the launch about to tie up at the Bombay pier where the names on cranes and buildings were, so oddly, English; feeling unease at the thought of the mute animal crouching on the floor at his master's back, and a similar unease at the sight of figures – not of romance, as the first figures seen on a foreign shore ought to be – on the pier, their frailty and raggedness contrasting with the stone buildings and metal cranes; now I tried to remember that in Bombay, as in Alexandria, there could be no pride in power, and that to give way to anger and contempt was to know a later self-disgust.

*

And of course Coelho, guide, fixer, knower of government forms, was right. Bombay was rigorously dry, and my two opened bottles of spirit were seized by the customs officers in white, who summoned a depressed-looking man in blue to seal them 'in my presence'. The man in blue worked at this manual and therefore degrading labour with slow relish; his manner proclaimed him an established civil servant, however degraded. I was given a receipt and told that I could get the bottles back when I got a liquor permit. Coelho wasn't so sure; these seized bottles, he said, had a habit of breaking. But his own worries were over. There had been no general search; his Greek doll had passed without query. He took it and his fee and disappeared into Bombay; I never saw him again.

To be in Bombay was to be exhausted. The moist heat sapped energy and will, and some days passed before I decided to recover my bottles. I decided in the morning; I started in the afternoon. I stood in the shade of Churchgate Station and debated whether I had it in me to cross the exposed street to the Tourist Office.

Debate languished into daydream; it was minutes before I made the crossing. A flight of steps remained. I sat below a fan and rested. A lure greater than a liquor permit roused me: the office upstairs was air-conditioned. There India was an ordered, even luxurious country. The design was contemporary; the walls were hung with maps and coloured photographs; and there were little wooden racks of leaflets and booklets. Too soon my turn came; my idleness was over. I filled in my form. The clerk filled in his, three to my one, made entries in various ledgers and presented me with a sheaf of foolscap papers: my liquor permit. He had been prompt and courteous. I thanked him. There was no need, he said; it was only a little paperwork.

One step a day: this was my rule. And it was not until the following afternoon that I took a taxi back to the docks. The customs officers in white and the degraded man in blue were surprised to see me.

'Did you leave something here?'

'I left two bottles of liquor.'

'You didn't. We seized two bottles from you. They were sealed in your presence.'

'That's what I meant. I've come to get them back.'

'But we don't keep seized liquor here. Everything we seize and seal is sent off at once to the New Customs House.'

My taxi was searched on the way out.

The New Customs House was a large, two-storeyed PWD building, governmentally gloomy, and it was as thronged as a court-house. There were people in the drive, in the galleries, on the steps, in the corridors. 'Liquor, liquor,' I said, and was led from office to office, each full of shrunken, bespectacled young men in white shirts sitting at desks shaggily stacked with paper. Someone sent me upstairs. On the landing I came upon a barefooted group seated on the stone floor. At first I thought they were playing cards: it was a popular Bombay pavement pastime. But they were sorting parcels. Their spokesman told me I had been misdirected;

I needed the building at the back. This building, from the quantity of ragged clothing seen in one of the lower rooms, appeared to be a tenement; and then, from the number of broken chairs and dusty pieces of useless furniture seen in another room, appeared to be a junk-shop. But it was the place for unclaimed baggage and was therefore the place I wanted. Upstairs I stood in a slow queue, at the end of which I discovered only an accountant.

'You don't want me. You want that officer in the white pants. Over there. He is a nice fellow.'

I went to him.

'You have your liquor permit?'

I showed him the stamped and signed foolscap sheaf.

'You have your transport permit?'

It was the first I had heard of this permit.

'You must have a transport permit.'

I was exhausted, sweating, and when I opened my mouth to speak I found I was on the verge of tears. 'But they *told* me.'

He was sympathetic. 'We have told them many times.'

I thrust all the papers I had at him: my liquor permit, my customs receipt, my passport, my receipt for wharfage charges, my Tourist Introduction Card.

Dutifully he looked through what I offered. 'No. I would have known at once whether you had a transport permit. By the colour of the paper. A sort of buff.'

'But what is a transport permit? Why didn't they give it to me? Why do I need one?'

'I must have it before I can surrender anything.'

'Please.'

'Sorry.'

'I am going to write to the papers about this.'

'I wish you would. I keep telling them they must tell people about this transport permit. Not only for you. We had an American here yesterday who said he was going to break the bottle as soon as he got it.'

'Help me. Where can I get this transport permit?'

'The people who gave you the receipt should also give you the transport permit.'

'But I've just come from them.'

'I don't know. We keep on telling them.'

'Back to the Old Customs,' I said to the taxi-driver.

This time the police at the gates recognized us and didn't search the car. This dock had been my own gateway to India. Only a few days before everything in it had been new: the sticky black asphalt, the money-changers' booths, the stalls, the people in white, khaki or blue: everything had been studied for what it portended of India beyond the gates. Now already I had ceased to see or care. My stupor, though, was tempered by the thought of the small triumph that awaited me: I had trapped those customs officers in white and that degraded man in blue.

They didn't look trapped.

'Transport permit?' one said. 'Are you sure?'

'Did you tell them you were leaving Bombay?' asked a second.

'*Transport* permit?' said a third and, walking away to a fourth, asked, 'Transport permit, ever hear of *transport* permit?'

He had. 'They've been writing us about it.'

A transport permit was required to transport liquor from the customs to a hotel or house.

'Please give me a transport permit.'

'We don't issue transport permits. You have to go to –' He looked up at me and his manner softened. 'Here, let me write it down for you. And look, I will also give you your code-number. That will help them out at the New Customs.'

The taxi-driver had so far been calm; and it seemed now that my journeys had fallen into a pattern that was familiar to him. I began to read out the address that had been given me. He cut me short and without another word buzzed through the thickening afternoon traffic to a large brick building hung with black-and-white government boards.

'You go,' he said sympathetically. 'I wait.'

Outside every office there was a little crowd.

'Transport permit, transport permit.'

Some Sikhs directed me round to the back to a low shed next to a gate marked *Prohibited Area*, out of which workers came, one after the other, raising their hands while armed soldiers frisked them.

'Transport permit, transport permit.'

I entered a long corridor and found myself among some Sikhs. They were lorry-drivers.

'Liquor permit, liquor permit.'

And at last I reached the office. It was a long low room at ground level, hidden from the scorching sun and as dark as a London basement, but warm and dusty with the smell of old paper, which was everywhere, on shelves rising to the grey ceiling, on desks, on chairs, in the hands of clerks, in the hands of khaki-clad messengers. Folders had grown dog-eared, their edges limp with reverential handling; and to many were attached pink slips, equally faded, equally limp, marked URGENT, VERY URGENT, or IMMEDIATE. Between these mounds and columns and buttresses of paper, clerks were scattered about unimportantly, men and women, mild-featured, Indian-pallid, high-shouldered; paper was their perfect camouflage. An elderly bespectacled man sat at a desk in one corner, his face slightly puffy and dyspeptic. Tremulous control of the paper-filled room was his: at his disappearance the clerks might be altogether overwhelmed.

'Transport permit?'

He looked up slowly. He showed no surprise, no displeasure at being disturbed. Papers, pink-slipped, were spread all over his desk. A table fan, nicely poised, blew over them without disturbance.

'Transport permit.' He spoke the words mildly, as though they were rare words but words which, after searching for only a second in the files of his mind, he had traced. 'Write an application. Only one is necessary.'

'Do you have the form?'

'No forms have been issued. Write a letter. Here, have a sheet of paper. Sit down and write. To the Collector, Excise and Prohibition, Bombay. Do you have your passport? Put down the number. Oh, and you have a Tourist Introduction Card. Put down that number too. I will expedite matters.'

And while I wrote, noting down the number of my Tourist Introduction Card, TIO (L) 156, he, expediting matters, passed my documents over to a woman clerk, saying, 'Miss Desai, could you start making out a transport permit?' I thought I detected an odd pride in his voice. He was like a man still after many years discovering the richness and variety of his work and subduing an excitement which he nevertheless wished to communicate to his subordinates.

I was finding it hard to spell and to frame simple sentences. I crumpled up the sheet of paper.

The head clerk looked up at me in gentle reproof. 'Only one application is necessary.'

At my back Miss Desai filled in forms with that blunt, indelible, illegible pencil which government offices throughout the former Empire use, less for the sake of what is written than for the sake of the copies required.

I managed to complete my application.

And at this point my companion slumped forward on her chair, hung her head between her knees and fainted.

'Water,' I said to Miss Desai.

She barely paused in her writing and pointed to an empty dusty glass on a shelf.

The head clerk, already frowningly preoccupied with other papers, regarded the figure slumped in front of him.

'Not feeling well?' His voice was as mild and even as before. 'Let her rest.' He turned the table fan away from him.

'Where is the water?'

Giggles came from women clerks, hidden behind paper.

'Water!' I cried to a male clerk.

He rose, saying nothing, walked to the end of the room and vanished.

Miss Desai finished her writing. Giving me a glance as of terror, she brought her tall bloated pad to the head clerk.

'The transport permit is ready,' he said. 'As soon as you are free you can sign for it.'

The male clerk returned, waterless, and sat down at his desk.

'Where is the water?'

His eyes distastefully acknowledged my impatience. He neither shrugged nor spoke; he went on with his papers.

It was worse than impatience. It was ill-breeding and ingratitude. For presently, sporting his uniform as proudly as any officer, a messenger appeared. He carried a tray and on the tray stood a glass of water. I should have known better. A clerk was a clerk; a messenger was a messenger.

The crisis passed.

I signed three times and received my permit.

The head clerk opened another folder.

'Nadkarni,' he called softly to a clerk. 'I don't understand this memo.'

I had been forgotten already.

It was suffocatingly hot in the taxi, the seats scorching. We drove to the flat of a friend and stayed there until it was dark.

A friend of our friend came in.

'What's wrong?'

'We went to get a transport permit and she fainted.' I did not wish to sound critical. I added, 'Perhaps it's the heat.'

'It isn't the heat at all. Always the heat or the water with you people from outside. There's nothing wrong with her. You make up your minds about India before coming to the country. You've been reading the wrong books.'

*

The officer who had sent me on the track of the transport permit was pleased to see me back. But the transport permit wasn't enough.

I had to go to Mr Kulkarni to find out about the warehouse charges. When I had settled what the charges were I was to come back to that clerk over there, with the blue shirt; then I had to go to the cashier, to pay the warehouse charges; then I had to go back to Mr Kulkarni to get my bottles.

I couldn't find Mr Kulkarni. My papers were in my hand. Someone tried to take them. I knew he was expressing only his kindness and curiosity. I pulled the papers back. He looked at me; I looked at him. I yielded. He went through my papers and said with authority that I had come to the wrong building.

I screamed: '*Mr Kulkarni!*'

Everyone around me was startled. Someone came up to me, calmed me down and led me to the adjoining room where Mr Kulkarni had been all along. I rushed to the head of the queue and began to shout at Mr Kulkarni, waving my papers at him. He got hold of them as I waved and began to read. Some Sikhs in the queue complained. Mr Kulkarni replied that I was in a hurry, that I was a person of importance, and that in any case I was younger. Curiously, they were pacified.

Mr Kulkarni called for ledgers. They were brought to him. Turning the crisp pages, not looking up, he made a loose-wristed gesture of indefinable elegance with his yellow pencil. The Sikhs at once separated into two broken lines. Mr Kulkarni put on his spectacles, studied the calendar on the far wall, counted on his fingers, took off his spectacles and returned to his ledgers. He made another abstracted gesture with his pencil and the Sikhs fell into line again, obscuring the calendar.

Upstairs again. The clerk with the blue shirt stamped on Mr Kulkarni's sheet of paper and made entries in two ledgers. The cashier added his own stamp. I paid him and he made entries in two more ledgers.

'It's all right,' the officer said, scanning the twice-stamped and thrice-signed sheet of paper. He added his own signature. 'You're safe now. Go down to Mr Kulkarni. And be quick. They might be closing any minute.'

# PART ONE

I

# A RESTING-PLACE FOR THE IMAGINATION

> These Antipodes call to one's mind old recollections of childish doubt and wonder. Only the other day I looked forward to this airy barrier as a definite point in our journey homewards; but now I find it, and all such resting-places for the imagination, are like shadows, which a man moving onwards cannot catch.
>
> Charles Darwin: *Voyage of the Beagle*

YOU'VE BEEN READING the wrong books, the businessman said. But he did me an injustice. I had read any number of the books which he would have considered right. And India had in a special way been the background of my childhood. It was the country from which my grandfather came, a country never physically described and therefore never real, a country out in the void beyond the dot of Trinidad; and from it our journey had been final. It was a country suspended in time; it could not be related to the country, discovered later, which was the subject of the many correct books issued by Mr Gollancz and Messrs Allen and Unwin and was the source of agency dispatches in the *Trinidad Guardian*. It remained a special, isolated area of ground which had produced my grandfather and others I knew who had been born in India and had come to Trinidad as indentured labourers, though that past too had fallen into the void into which India had fallen, for they carried no mark of indenture, no mark even of having been labourers.

There was an old lady, a friend of my mother's family. She was jewelled, fair and white-haired; she was very grand. She spoke only Hindi. The elegance of her manner and the grave handsomeness of her husband, with his thick white moustache, his spotless Indian dress and his silence, which compensated for his wife's bustling authority, impressed them early upon me as a couple who, though so friendly and close – they ran a tiny shop not far from my grandmother's establishment – as to be considered almost relations, were already foreign. They came from India; this gave them glamour, but the glamour was itself a barrier. They not so much ignored Trinidad as denied it; they made no attempt even to learn English, which was what the children spoke. The lady had two or three gold teeth and was called by everyone Gold Teeth Nanee, Gold Teeth Grandmother, the mixture of English and Hindi revealing to what extent the world to which she belonged was receding. Gold Teeth was childless. This probably accounted for her briskness and her desire to share my grandmother's authority over the children. It did not make her better liked. But she had a flaw. She was as greedy as a child; she was a great uninvited eater, whom it was easy to trap with a square of laxative chocolate. One day she noticed a tumbler of what looked like coconut milk. She tasted, she drank to the end, and fell ill; and in her distress made a confession which was like a reproach. She had drunk a tumbler of blanco fluid. It was astonishing that she should have drunk to the end; but in matters of food she was, unusually for an Indian, experimental and pertinacious. She was to carry the disgrace till her death. So one India crashed; and as we grew older, living now in the town, Gold Teeth dwindled to a rustic oddity with whom there could be no converse. So remote her world seemed then, so dead; yet how little time separated her from us!

Then there was Babu. Moustached, as grave and silent as Gold Teeth's husband, he occupied a curious position in my grandmother's household. He too was born in India; and why he should have lived alone in one room at the back of the kitchen I never understood. It is an indication of the narrowness of the world in which we lived as children that all I knew about Babu was that he was a *kshatriya*, one of the warrior caste: this solitary man who, squatting in his dark-room at the end of the day, prepared his own simple food, kneading flour, cutting vegetables and doing other things which I had always thought of as woman's work. Could this man from the warrior caste have been a labourer? Inconceivable then; but later, alas, when such disillusionment meant little, to be proved true. We had moved. My grandmother required someone to dig a well. It was Babu who came, from that back room where he had continued to live. The well deepened; Babu was let down in a hammock, which presently brought up the earth he had excavated. One day no more earth came up. Babu had struck rock. He came up on the hammock for the last time and went away back into that void from which he had come. I never saw him again and had of him as a reminder only that deep hole at the edge of the cricket ground. The hole was planked over, but it remained in my imagination a standing nightmare peril to energetic fielders chasing a boundary hit.

More than in people, India lay about us in things: in a string bed or two, grimy, tattered, no longer serving any function, never repaired because there was no one with this caste skill in Trinidad, yet still permitted to take up room; in plaited straw mats; in innumerable brass vessels; in wooden printing blocks, never used because printed cotton was abundant and cheap and because the secret of the dyes had been forgotten, no dyer being at hand; in books, the sheets large, coarse and brittle, the ink thick and oily; in drums and one ruined harmonium; in brightly coloured pictures of deities on pink lotus or radiant against Himalayan snow; and in all the paraphernalia of the prayer-room: the brass bells and gongs and camphor-burners like Roman lamps, the slender-handled spoon for the doling out of the consecrated 'nectar' (peasant's nectar: on ordinary days brown sugar and water, with some shreds of the tulsi leaf, sweetened milk on high days), the images, the smooth pebbles, the stick of sandalwood.

The journey had been final. And it was only on this trip to India that I was to see how complete a transference had been made from eastern Uttar Pradesh to Trinidad, and that in days when the village was some hours' walk from the nearest branch-line railway station, the station more than a day's journey from the port, and that anything up to three months' sailing from Trinidad. In its artefacts India existed whole in Trinidad. But our community, though seemingly self-contained, was imperfect. Sweepers we had quickly learned to do without. Others supplied the skills of carpenters, masons and cobblers. But we were also without weavers and dyers, workers in brass and makers of string beds. Many of the things in my grandmother's house were therefore irreplaceable. They were cherished because they came from India, but they continued to be used and no regret attached to their disintegration. It was an Indian attitude, as I was to recognize. Customs are to be maintained because they are felt to be ancient. This is continuity enough; it does not need to be supported by a cultivation of the past, and the old, however hallowed, be it a Gupta image or a string bed, is to be used until it can be used no more.

To me as a child the India that had produced so many of the persons and things around me was featureless, and I thought of the time when the transference was made as a period of darkness, darkness which also extended to the land, as darkness surrounds a hut at evening, though for a little way around the hut there is still light. The light was the area of my experience, in time and place. And even now, though time has widened, though space has contracted and I have travelled lucidly over that area which was to me the area of darkness, something of darkness remains, in those attitudes, those ways of thinking and seeing, which are no longer mine. My grandfather had made a difficult and courageous journey. It must have brought him into collision with startling sights, even like the sea, several hundred miles from his village; yet I cannot help feeling that as soon as he had left his village he ceased to see. When he went back to India it was to return with more things of India. When he built his house he ignored every colonial style he might have found in Trinidad and put up a heavy, flat-roofed oddity, whose image I was to see again and again in the small ramshackle towns of Uttar Pradesh. He had abandoned India; and, like Gold Teeth, he denied Trinidad. Yet he walked on solid earth. Nothing beyond his village had stirred him; nothing had forced him out of himself; he carried his village with him. A few reassuring relationships, a strip of land, and he could satisfyingly re-create an eastern Uttar Pradesh village in central Trinidad as if in the vastness of India.

We who came after could not deny Trinidad. The house we lived in was distinctive, but not more distinctive than many. It was easy to accept that we lived on an island where there were all sorts of people and all sorts of houses. Doubtless they too had their own things. We ate certain food, performed certain ceremonies and had certain taboos; we expected others to have their own. We did not wish to share theirs; we did not expect them to share ours. They were what they were; we were what we were. We were never instructed in this. To our condition as Indians in a multi-racial society we gave no thought. Criticism from others there was, as I now realize, but it never penetrated the walls of our house, and I cannot as a child remember hearing any discussion about race. Though permeated with the sense of difference, in racial matters, oddly, I remained an innocent for long. At school I was puzzled by the kinky hair of a teacher I liked; I came to the conclusion that he was still, like me, growing, and that when he had grown a little more his hair would grow straighter and longer. Race was never discussed; but at an early age I understood that Muslims were somewhat more different than others. They were not to be trusted; they would always do you down; and point was given to this by the presence close to my grandmother's house of a Muslim, in whose cap and grey beard, avowals of his especial difference, lay every sort of threat. For the difference we saw as the attribute of every group outside our own was more easily discernible in other Indians and more discernible yet in other Hindus. Racial awareness was to come; in the meantime – and until how recently – for the social antagonisms that give savour to life we relied on the old, Indian divisions, meaningless though these had become.

Everything beyond our family had this quality of difference. This was to be accepted when we went abroad and perhaps even forgotten, as for instance at school. But the moment any intercourse threatened, we scented violation and withdrew. I remember – and this was later, after this family life had broken up – being taken to visit one family. They were not related. This made the visit unusual; and because it became fixed in my mind, no doubt from something that had been said, that they were Muslims, everything about them had a heightened difference. I saw it in their appearance, their house, their dress and presently, as I had been fearing, in their food. We were offered some vermicelli done in milk. I believed it to be associated with some unknown and distasteful ritual; I could not eat it. They were in fact Hindus; our families were later joined by marriage.

Inevitably this family life shrank, and the process was accelerated by our removal to the capital, where there were few Indians. The outside world intruded more. We became secretive. But once we made an open assault on the city. My grandmother wished to have a *kattha* said, and she wished to have it said under a pipal tree. There was only one pipal tree in the island; it was in the Botanical Gardens. Permission was applied for. To my amazement it was given; and one Sunday morning we all sat under the pipal tree, botanically labelled, and the pundit read. The crackling sacrificial fire was scented with pitch-pine, brown sugar and ghee; bells were rung, gongs struck, conch-shells blown. We attracted the silent interest of a small mixed crowd of morning strollers and the proselytizing attentions of a Seventh Day Adventist. It was a scene of pure pastoral: Aryan ritual, of another continent and age, a few hundred yards from the governor's house. But this is a later appreciation. For those of us at school at the time the public ceremony had been a strain. We were becoming self-conscious, self-assessing: our secret world was shrinking fast. Still, very occasionally, some devout Hindu of the few in Port of Spain might wish to feed some brahmins. We were at hand. We went; we were fed; we received gifts of cloth and money. We never questioned our luck. Luck indeed it seemed, for immediately afterwards, walking back home in trousers and shirt, we became ordinary boys again.

To me this luck was touched with fraudulence. I came of a family that abounded with pundits. But I had been born an unbeliever. I took no pleasure in religious ceremonies. They were too long, and the food came only at the end. I did not understand the language – it was as if our elders expected that our understanding would be instinctive – and no one explained the prayers or the ritual. One ceremony was like another. The images didn't interest me; I never sought to learn their significance. With my lack of belief and distaste for ritual there also went a metaphysical incapacity, this again a betrayal of heredity, for my father's appetite for Hindu speculation was great. So it happened that, though growing up in an orthodox family, I remained almost totally ignorant of Hinduism. What, then, survived of Hinduism in me? Perhaps I had received a certain supporting philosophy. I cannot say; my uncle often put it to me that my denial was an admissible type of Hinduism. Examining myself, I found only that sense of the difference of people, which I have tried to explain, a vaguer sense of caste, and a horror of the unclean.

It still horrifies me that people should put out food for animals on plates that they themselves use; as it horrified me at school to see boys sharing Popsicles and Palates, local iced lollies; as it horrifies me to see women sipping from ladles with which they stir their pots. This was more than difference; this was the uncleanliness we had to guard against. From all food restrictions sweets were, curiously, exempt. We bought cassava pone from street stalls; but black pudding and souse, favourite street-corner and sports-ground dishes of the Negro proletariat, were regarded by us with fascinated horror. This might suggest that our food remained what it always had been. But this was not so. It is not easy to understand just how communication occurred, but we were steadily adopting the food styles of others: the Portuguese stew of tomato and onions, in which almost anything might be done, the Negro way with yams, plantains, breadfruit and bananas. Everything we adopted became our own; the outside was still to be dreaded, and my prejudices were so strong that when I left Trinidad, shortly before my eighteenth birthday, I had eaten in restaurants only three times. The day of my swift transportation to New York was a day of misery. I spent a frightened, hungry day in that city; and on the ship to Southampton I ate mainly the sweets, which encouraged the steward to say when I tipped him, 'The others made pigs of themselves. But you sure do like ice-cream.'

Food was one thing. Caste was another. Though I had quickly grown to see it as only part of our private play, it was capable on occasion of influencing my attitude to others. A distant relation was married; it was rumoured that her husband was of the *chamar*, or leather-worker, caste. The man was rich and travelled; he was successful in his profession and was later to hold a position of some responsibility. But he was a *chamar*. The rumour was perhaps unfounded – few marriages are not attended by disparagement of this sort – but the thought still occurs whenever we meet and that initial sniffing for difference is now involuntary. He is the only person thus coloured for me; the marriage took place when I was very young. In India people were also to be tainted by their caste, especially when this was announced beforehand, approvingly or disapprovingly. But caste in India was not what it had been to me in Trinidad. In Trinidad caste had no meaning in our day-to-day life; the caste we occasionally played at was no more than an acknowledgement of latent qualities; the assurance it offered was such as might have been offered by a palmist or a reader of handwriting. In India it implied a brutal division of labour; and at its centre, as I had never realized, lay the degradation of the latrine-cleaner. In India caste was unpleasant; I never wished to know what a man's caste was.

I had no belief; I disliked religious ritual; and I had a sense of the ridiculous. I refused to go through the *janaywa*, or thread ceremony of the newborn, with some of my cousins. The ceremony ends with the initiate, his head shaved, his thread new and obvious, taking up his staff and bundle – as he might have done in an Indian village two thousand years ago – and announcing his intention of going to Kasi-Banaras to study. His mother weeps and begs him not to go; the initiate insists that he must; a senior member of the family is summoned to plead with the initiate, who at length yields and lays down his staff and bundle. It was a pleasing piece of theatre. But I knew that we were in Trinidad, an island separated by only ten miles from the South American coast, and that the appearance in a Port of Spain street of my cousin, perhaps of no great academic attainment, in the garb of a Hindu mendicant-scholar bound for Banaras, would have attracted unwelcome attention. So I refused; though now this ancient drama, absurdly surviving in a Trinidad yard, seems to me touching and attractive.

I had contracted out. Yet there is a balancing memory. In the science class at school one day we were doing an experiment with siphons, to an end which I have now forgotten. At one stage a beaker and a length of tube were passed from boy to boy, so that we might suck and observe the effects. I let the beaker pass me. I thought I hadn't been seen, but an Indian boy in the row behind, a Port of Spain boy, a recognized class tough, whispered, 'Real brahmin.' His tone was approving. I was surprised at his knowledge, having assumed him, a Port of Spain boy, to be ignorant of these things; at the unexpected tenderness of his voice; and also at the bringing out into public of that other, secret life. But I was also pleased. And with this pleasure there came a new tenderness for that boy, and a sadness for our common loss: mine, which he did not suspect, the result of my own decision or temperament, his, which by his behaviour he openly acknowledged, the result of history and environment: a feeling which was to come to me again more strongly and much later, in entirely different circumstances, when the loss was complete, in London.

I have been rebuked by writers from the West Indies, and notably George Lamming, for not paying sufficient attention in my books to non-Indian groups. The confrontation of different communities, he said, was the fundamental West Indian experience. So indeed it is, and increasingly. But to see the attenuation of the culture of my childhood as the result of a dramatic confrontation of opposed worlds would be to distort the reality. To me the worlds were juxtaposed and mutually exclusive. One gradually contracted. It had to; it fed only on memories and its completeness was only apparent. It was yielding not to attack but to a type of seepage from the other. I can speak only out of my own experience. The family life I have been describing began to dissolve when I was six or seven; when I was fourteen it had ceased to exist. Between my brother, twelve years younger than myself, and me there is more than a generation of difference. He can have no memory of that private world which survived with such apparent solidity up to only twenty-five years ago, a world which had lengthened out, its energy of inertia steadily weakening, from the featureless area of darkness which was India.

That this world should have existed at all, even in the consciousness of a child, is to me a marvel; as it is a marvel that we should have accepted the separateness of our two worlds and seen no incongruity in their juxtaposition. In one world we existed as if in blinkers, as if seeing no more than my grandfather's village; outside, we were totally self-aware. And in India I was to see that so many of the things which the newer and now perhaps truer side of my nature kicked against – the smugness, as it seemed to me, the imperviousness to criticism, the refusal to *see*, the double-talk and double-think – had an answer in that side of myself which I had thought buried and which India revived as a faint memory. I understood better than I admitted. And to me it is an additional marvel that an upbringing of the kind I have described, cut short and rendered invalid so soon, should have left so deep an impression. Indians are an old people, and it might be that they continue to belong to the old world. That Indian reverence for the established and ancient, however awkward, however indefensible, however little understood: it is part of the serious buffoonery of Ancient Rome, an aspect of the Roman *pietas*. I had rejected tradition; yet how can I explain my feeling of outrage when I heard that in Bombay they used candles and electric bulbs for the Diwali festival, and not the rustic clay lamps, of immemorial design, which in Trinidad we still used? I had been born an unbeliever. Yet the thought of the decay of the old customs and reverences saddened me when the boy whispered 'Real brahmin', and when, many years later, in London, I heard that Ramon was dead.

*

He was perhaps twenty-four. He died in a car crash. It was fitting. Motor-cars were all that mattered to him, and it was to continue to handle them that he came to London, abandoning mother and father, wife and children. I met him almost as soon as he had arrived. It was in a dingy Chelsea boarding-house whose façade was like all the other façades in that respectable, rising street: white, the area railings black, the door an oblong of vivid colour. Only milk bottles and a quality of curtaining betrayed the house where, in a passageway, below the diffused, misty glow of a forty-watt bulb, I first saw Ramon. He was short, his hair thick and curling at the ends, his features blunt, like his strong stubby fingers. He wore a moustache and was unshaved; and in his pullover, which I could see had belonged to someone else who had made the pilgrimage to London from Trinidad and had taken back the pullover as a mark of the voyager to temperate climes, he looked shabby and unwashed.

He was of a piece with the setting, the green grown dingy of the walls, the linoleum, the circles of dirt around door handles, the faded upholstery of cheap chairs, the stained wallpaper; the indications of the passage of numberless transients to whom these rooms had never been meant for the arranging of their things; the rim of soot below the windowsill, the smoked ceiling, the empty fireplace bearing the marks of a brief, ancient fire and suggesting a camping ground; the carpets smelly and torn. He was of a piece, yet he was alien. He belonged to unfenced backyards and lean-tos, where, pullover-less and shirtless, he might wander in the cool of the evening, about him the unfading bright green of Trinidad foliage, chickens settling down for the night, while in a neighbouring yard a coalpot sent up a thin line of blue smoke. Now, at a similar time of day, he sat choked in someone else's pullover on a low bed, how often used, how little cleaned, in the dim light of a furnished room in Chelsea, the electric fire, its dull reflector seemingly spat upon and sanded, making little impression on the dampness and cold. His fellow voyagers had gone out. He was not bright, as they were; he cared little about dress; he could not support or share their high spirits.

He was shy, and spoke only when spoken to, responding to questions like a man who had nothing to hide, a man to whom the future, never considered, held no threat and possibly no purpose. He had left Trinidad because he had lost his driving licence. His career of crime had begun when, scarcely a boy, he was arrested for driving without a licence; later he was arrested for driving while still banned. One offence led to another, until Trinidad had ceased to be a place where he could live; he needed to be in motorcars. His parents had scraped together some money to send him to England. They had done it because they loved him, their son; yet when he spoke of their sacrifice it was without emotion.

He was incapable of assessing the morality of actions; he was a person to whom things merely happened. He had left his wife behind; she had two children. 'And I believe I have something else boiling up for me.' The words were spoken without the Trinidad back-street pride. They recorded a fact; they passed judgement neither on his desertion nor his virility.

His name was Spanish because his mother was part Venezuelan; and he had spent some time in Venezuela until the police had hustled him out. But he was a Hindu and had been married according to Hindu rites. These rites must have meant as little to him as they did to me, and perhaps even less, for he had grown up as an individual, had never had the protection of a family life like mine, and had at an early age been transferred to a civilization which remained as puzzling to him as this new transference to Chelsea.

He was an innocent, a lost soul, rescued from animality only by his ruling passion. That section of the mind, if such a section exists, which judges and feels was in him a blank, on which others could write. He wished to drive; he drove. He liked a car; he applied his skill to it and drove it away. He would be eventually caught; that he never struggled against or seemed to doubt. You told him, 'I need a hubcap for my car. Can you get me one?' He went out and took the first suitable hubcap he saw. He was caught; he blamed no one. Things happened to him. His innocence, which was not mere simpleness, was frightening. He was as innocent as a complicated machine. He could be animated by his wish to please. There was an unmarried mother in the house; to her and her child he was unfailingly tender, and protective, whenever that was required of him.

But there was his ruling passion. And with motor-cars he was a genius. The word quickly got around; and it was not unusual some weeks later to see him in grease-stained clothes working on a run-down motor-car, while a cavalry-twilled man spoke to him of money. He might have made money. But all his profits went on fresh cars and on the fines he had already begun to pay to the courts for stealing this lamp and that part which he had needed to complete a job. It was not necessary for him to steal; but he stole. Still, the news of his skill went round, and he was busy.

Then I heard that he was in serious trouble. A friend in the boarding-house had asked him to burn a scooter. In Trinidad if you wished to burn a motor-car you set it alight on the bank of the muddy Caroni River and rolled it in. London, too, had a river. Ramon put the scooter into the van which he owned at the time and drove down one evening to the Embankment. Before he could set the scooter alight a policeman appeared, as policemen had always appeared in Ramon's life.

I thought that, as the scooter hadn't been burnt, the case couldn't be serious.

'But no,' one man in the boarding-house said. 'This is conspiracy.' He spoke the word with awe; he too had been booked as a conspirator.

So Ramon went up to the assizes, and I went to see how the case would go. I had some trouble finding the correct court – 'Have you come to answer a summons yourself, sir?' a policeman asked, his courtesy as bewildering as his question – and when I did find the court, I might have been back in St Vincent Street in Port of Spain. The conspirators were all there, looking like frightened students. They wore suits, as though all about to be interviewed. They, so boisterous, so anxious to antagonize their neighbours in the Chelsea street – they had taken to clipping one another's hair on the pavement of a Sunday morning (the locals washing their cars the while), as they might have done in Port of Spain – now succeeded in giving an opposed picture of themselves.

Ramon stood apart from them, he too wearing a suit, but with nothing in his face or in his greeting to show that we were meeting in circumstances slightly different from those in the boarding-house. A girl was attached to him, a simple creature, dressed as for a dance. Not anxious they seemed, but blank; she too was a person to whom things difficult or puzzling kept happening. More worried than either of them was Ramon's employer, a garage-owner. He had come to give evidence about Ramon's 'character', and he again was in a suit, of stiff brown tweed. His face was flushed and puffy, hinting at some type of heart disorder; his eyes blinked continually behind his pink-rimmed spectacles. He stood beside Ramon.

'A good boy, a good boy,' the garage-owner said, tears coming to his eyes. 'It's only his company.' It was strange that this simple view of the relationships of the simple could hold so much force and be so moving.

The trial was an anti-climax. It began sombrely enough, with police evidence and cross-examinations. (Ramon was quoted as saying at the moment of arrest: 'Yes, copper, you got me now, sah.' This I rejected.) Ramon was being defended by a young court-supplied lawyer. He was very brisk and stylish, and beside himself with enthusiasm. He showed more concern than Ramon, whom he had needlessly encouraged to cheer up. Once he caught the judge out on some point of legal etiquette and in an instant was on his feet, administering a shocked, stern rebuke. The judge listened with pure pleasure and apologized. We might have been in a nursery for lawyers: Ramon's lawyer the star pupil, the judge the principal, and we in the gallery proud parents. When the judge began his summing up, speaking slowly, in a voice court-house rich, sombreness altogether disappeared. It was clear he was not used to the ways of Trinidad. He said he found it hard to regard an attempt to burn a scooter on the Embankment as more than a foolish student's prank; however, an intention to defraud the insurance company was serious . . . There was an Indian lady in the gallery, of great beauty, who smiled and had to suppress her laughter at every witticism and every elegant phrase. The judge was aware of her, and the summing up was like a dialogue between the two, between the elderly man, confident of his gifts, and the beautiful, appreciative woman. The tenseness of the jury – a bespectacled, hatted woman sat forward, clutching the rail as if in distress – was irrelevant; and no one, not even the police, seemed surprised at the verdict of not guilty. Ramon's lawyer was exultant. Ramon was as serene as before; his fellow conspirators suddenly appeared utterly exhausted.

Soon enough, however, Ramon was in trouble again, and this time there was no garage-owner to speak for him. He had, I believe, stolen a car or had pillaged its engine beyond economic repair; and he was sent to prison for some time. When he came out he said he had spent a few weeks in Brixton. 'Then I went down to a place in Kent.' I heard this from his former co-accused in the boarding-house. There Ramon had become a figure of fun. And when I next heard of him he was dead, in a car crash.

He was a child, an innocent, a maker; someone for whom the world had never held either glory or pathos; someone for whom there had been no place. 'Then I went down to a place in Kent.' He was guiltless of humour or posturing. One place was like another; the world was full of such places in which, unseeing, one passed one's days. He was dead now, and I wished to offer him recognition. He was of the religion of my family; we were debased members of that religion, and this very debasement I felt as a bond. We were a tiny, special part of that featureless, unknown country, meaningful to us, if we thought about it, only in that we were its remote descendants. I wished his body to be handled with reverence, and I wished it to be handled according to the old rites. This alone would spare him final nonentity. So perhaps the Roman felt in Cappadocia or Britain; and London was now as remote from the centre of our world as, among the ruins of some Roman villa in Gloucestershire, Britain still feels far from home and can be seen as a country which in an emblematic map, curling at the corners, is partly obscured by the clouds blown by a cherub, a country of mist and rain and forest, from which the traveller is soon to hurry back to a warm, familiar land. For us no such land existed.

I missed Ramon's funeral. He was not cremated but buried, and a student from Trinidad conducted the rites which his caste entitled him to perform. He had read my books and did not want me to be there. Denied a presence I so much wished, I had to imagine the scene: a man in a white dhoti speaking gibberish over the corpse of Ramon, making up rites among the tombstones and crosses of a more recent religion, the mean buildings of a London suburb low in the distance, against an industrial sky.

But how could the mood be supported? Ramon died fittingly and was buried fittingly. In addition to everything else, he was buried free, by a funeral agency whose stalled hearse, encountered by chance on the road only a few days before his death, he had set going again.

*

The India, then, which was the background to my childhood was an area of the imagination. It was not the real country I presently began to read about and whose map I committed to memory. I became a nationalist; even a book like Beverley Nichols's *Verdict on India* could anger me. But this came almost at the end. The next year India became independent; and I found that my interest was failing. I now had almost no Hindi. But it was more than language which divided me from what I knew of India. Indian films were both tedious and disquieting; they delighted in decay, agony and death; a funeral dirge or a blind man's lament could become a hit. And there was religion, with which, as one of Mr Gollancz's writers had noted with approval, the people of India were intoxicated. I was without belief or interest in belief; I was incapable of worship, of God or holy men; and so one whole side of India was closed to me.

Then there came people from India, not the India of Gold Teeth and Babu, but this other India; and I saw that to this country I was not at all linked. The Gujerati and Sindhi merchants were as foreign as the Syrians. They lived enclosed lives of a narrowness which I considered asphyxiating. They were devoted to their work, the making of money; they seldom went out; their pallid women were secluded; and all day their houses screeched with morbid Indian film songs. They contributed nothing to the society, nothing even to the Indian community. They were reputed among us to be sharp businessmen. In so many ways, as I now see, they were to us what we were to other communities. But their journey had not been final; their private world was not shrinking. They made regular trips to India, to buy and sell, to marry, to bring out recruits; the gap between us widened.

I came to London. It had become the centre of my world and I had worked hard to come to it. And I was lost. London was not the centre of my world. I had been misled; but there was nowhere else to go. It was a good place for getting lost in, a city no one ever knew, a city explored from the neutral heart outwards until, after years, it defined itself into a jumble of clearings separated by stretches of the unknown, through which the narrowest of paths had been cut. Here I became no more than an inhabitant of a big city, robbed of loyalties, time passing, taking me away from what I was, thrown more and more into myself, fighting to keep my balance and to keep alive the thought of the clear world beyond the brick and asphalt and the chaos of railway lines. All mythical lands faded, and in the big city I was confined to a smaller world than I had ever known. I became my flat, my desk, my name.

As India had drawn near, I had felt more than the usual fear of arrival. In spite of myself, in spite of lucidity and London and my years, and over and above every other fear, and the memory of the Alexandrian cab-driver, some little feeling for India as the mythical land of my childhood was awakened. I knew it to be foolish. The launch was solid enough and dingy enough; there was a tariff for fair weather and foul weather; the heat was real and disagreeable; the city we could see beyond the heat-mist was big and busy; and its inhabitants, seen in other vessels, were of small physique, betokening all the fearful things that had soon to be faced. The buildings grew larger. The figures on the docks became clearer. The buildings spoke of London and industrial England; and how, in spite of knowledge, this seemed ordinary and inappropriate! Perhaps all lands of myth were like this: dazzling with light, familiar to drabness, the margin of the sea unremarkably littered, until the moment of departure.

*

And for the first time in my life I was one of the crowd. There was nothing in my appearance or dress to distinguish me from the crowd eternally hurrying into Churchgate Station. In Trinidad to be an Indian was to be distinctive. To be anything there was distinctive; difference was each man's attribute. To be an Indian in England was distinctive; in Egypt it was more so. Now in Bombay I entered a shop or a restaurant and awaited a special quality of response. And there was nothing. It was like being denied part of my reality. Again and again I was caught. I was faceless. I might sink without a trace into that Indian crowd. I had been made by Trinidad and England; recognition of my difference was necessary to me. I felt the need to impose myself, and didn't know how.

'You require dark glasses? From your accent, sir, I perceive that you are perhaps a student, returned from Europe. You will understand therefore what I am about to say. Observe how these lenses soften glare and heighten colour. With the manufacture of these lenses I assure you that a new chapter has been written in the history of optics.'

So I was a student, perhaps returned from Europe. The patter was better than I had expected. But I didn't buy the lenses the man offered. I bought Crookes, hideously expensive, in a clip-on Indian frame which broke almost as soon as I left the shop. I was too tired to go back, to talk in a voice whose absurdity I felt whenever I opened my mouth. Feeling less real than before behind my dark glasses, which rattled in their broken frame, the Bombay street splintering into dazzle with every step I took, I walked, unnoticed, back to the hotel, past the fat, impertinent Anglo-Indian girl and the rat-faced Anglo-Indian manager in a silky fawn-coloured suit, and lay down on my bed below the electric ceiling fan.

2

# DEGREE

THEY TELL THE story of the Sikh who, returning to India after many years, sat down among his suitcases on the Bombay docks and wept. He had forgotten what Indian poverty was like. It is an Indian story, in its arrangement of figure and properties, its melodrama, its pathos. It is Indian above all in its attitude to poverty as something which, thought about from time to time in the midst of other preoccupations, releases the sweetest of emotions. This is poverty, our especial poverty, and how sad it is! Poverty not as an urge to anger or improving action, but poverty as an inexhaustible source of tears, an exercise of the purest sensibility. 'They became so poor that year,' the beloved Hindi novelist Premchand writes, 'that even beggars left their door empty-handed.' That, indeed, is our poverty: not the fact of beggary, but that beggars should have to go from our doors empty-handed. This is our poverty, which in a hundred Indian short stories in all the Indian languages drives the pretty girl to prostitution to pay the family's medical bills.

India is the poorest country in the world. Therefore, to see its poverty is to make an observation of no value; a thousand newcomers to the country before you have seen and said as you. And not only newcomers. Our own sons and daughters, when they return from Europe and America, have spoken in your very words. Do not think that your anger and contempt are marks of your sensitivity. You might have seen more: the smiles on the faces of the begging children, that domestic group among the pavement sleepers waking in the cool Bombay morning, father, mother and baby in a trinity of love, so self-contained that they are as private as if walls had separated them from you: it is your gaze that violates them, your sense of outrage that outrages them. You might have seen the boy sweeping his area of pavement, spreading his mat, lying down; exhaustion and undernourishment are in his tiny body and shrunken face, but lying flat on his back, oblivious of you and the thousands who walk past in the lane between sleepers' mats and house walls bright with advertisements and election slogans, oblivious of the warm, overbreathed air, he plays with fatigued concentration with a tiny pistol in blue plastic. It is your surprise, your anger that denies him humanity. But wait. Stay six months. The winter will bring fresh visitors. Their talk will also be of poverty; they too will show their anger. You will agree; but deep down there will be annoyance; it will seem to you then, too, that they are seeing only the obvious; and it will not please you to find your sensibility so accurately parodied.

Ten months later I was to revisit Bombay and to wonder at my hysteria. It was cooler, and in the crowded courtyards of Colaba there were Christmas decorations, illuminated stars hanging out of windows against the black sky. It was my eye that had changed. I had seen Indian villages: the narrow, broken lanes with green slime in the gutters, the choked back-to-back mud houses, the jumble of filth and food and animals and people, the baby in the dust, swollen-bellied, black with flies, but wearing its good-luck amulet. I had seen the starved child defecating at the roadside while the mangy dog waited to eat the excrement. I had seen the physique of the people of Andhra, which had suggested the possibility of an evolution downwards, wasted body to wasted body, Nature mocking herself, incapable of remission. Compassion and pity did not answer; they were refinements of hope. Fear was what I felt. Contempt was what I had to fight against; to give way to that was to abandon the self I had known. Perhaps in the end it was fatigue that overcame me. For abruptly, in the midst of hysteria, there occurred periods of calm, in which I found that I had grown to separate myself from what I saw, to separate the pleasant from the unpleasant, the whole circular sky ablaze at sunset from the peasants diminished by its glory, the beauty of brassware and silk from the thin wrists that held them up for display, the ruins from the child defecating among them, to separate things from men. I had learned too that escape was always possible, that in every Indian town there was a corner of comparative order and cleanliness in which one could recover and cherish one's self-respect. In India the easiest and most necessary thing to ignore was the most obvious. Which no doubt was why, in spite of all that I had read about the country, nothing had prepared me for it.

But in the beginning the obvious was overwhelming, and there was the knowledge that there was no ship to run back to, as there had been at Alexandria, Port Sudan, Djibouti, Karachi. It was new to me then that the obvious could be separated from the pleasant, from the areas of self-respect and self-love. Marine Drive, Malabar Hill, the lights of the city at night from Kamala Nehru Park, the Parsi Towers of Silence: these are what the tourist brochures put forward as Bombay, and these were the things we were taken to see on three successive days by three kind persons. They built up a dread of what was not shown, that other city where lived the hundreds of thousands who poured in a white stream in and out of Churchgate Station as though hurrying to and from an endless football match. This was the city that presently revealed itself, in the broad, choked and endless main roads of suburbs, a chaos of shops, tall tenements, decaying balconies, electric wires and advertisements, the film posters that seemed to derive from a cooler and more luscious world, cooler and more luscious than the film posters of England and America, promising a greater gaiety, an ampler breast and hip, a more fruitful womb. And the courtyards behind the main streets: the heat heightened, at night the sense of outdoors destroyed, the air holding on its stillness the odours of mingled filth, the windows not showing as oblongs of light but revealing lines, clothes, furniture, boxes and suggesting an occupation of more than floor space. On the roads northwards, the cool redbrick factories set in gardens: Middlesex it might have been, but not attached to these factories any semi-detached or terrace houses, but that shanty town, that rubbish dump. And, inevitably, the prostitutes, the 'gay girls' of the Indian newspapers. But where, in these warrens where three brothels might be in one building and not all the sandal-oil perfumes of Lucknow could hide the stench of gutters and latrines, was the gaiety? Lust, like compassion, was a refinement of hope. Before this one felt only the fragility of one's own sexual impulses. One hesitated to probe, to imagine; one concentrated on one's own revulsion. Men with clubs stood guard at the entrances. Protecting whom from what? In the dim, stinking corridors sat expressionless women, very old, very dirty, shrivelled almost to futility; and already one had the feeling that people were negligible: these were the sweepers, the servants of the gay girls of the Bombay poor, doubtless lucky because employed: a frightening glimpse of India's ever receding degrees of degradation.

Degrees of degradation, because gradually one discovers that in spite of its appearance of chaos, in spite of all the bustling white-clad crowds which by their number would appear to defy or to make worthless any attempt at categorization, this degradation is charted, as the Indian landscape itself which, from the train no more than a jumble of tiny irregularly shaped fields, private follies of which no official organization would take cognizance, has yet been measured and surveyed and sketched and remains recorded in all its absurdity in the various collectorates, where the title deeds, wrapped in red cloth or yellow cloth, rise in bundles from floor to ceiling. This is the result of an English endeavour answering the Indian need: definition, distinction. To define is to begin to separate oneself, to assure oneself of one's position, to be withdrawn from the chaos that India always threatens, the abyss at whose edge the sweeper of the gay girl sits. A special type of hat or turban, a way of cutting the beard or a way of not cutting the beard, the Western-style suit or the unreliable politicians' khadi, the caste mark of the Kashmiri Hindu or Madras brahmin: this gives proof of one's community, one's worth as a man, one's function, as the title deed in the collectorate gives proof of one's ownership of part of the earth.

The prompting is universal, but the Indian practice is purely of India. 'And do thy duty, even if it be humble, rather than another's, even if it be great. To die in one's duty is life: to live in another's is death.' This is the Gita, preaching degree fifteen hundred years before Shakespeare's Ulysses, preaching it today. And the man who makes the dingy bed in the hotel room will be affronted if he is asked to sweep the gritty floor. The clerk will not bring you a glass of water even if you faint. The architecture student will consider it a degradation to make drawings, to be a mere draughtsman. And Ramnath, the stenographer, so designated on the triangular block of wood that stands on his desk, will refuse to type out what he has taken down in shorthand.

*

Ramnath was a clerk in a government department. He earned 110 rupees a month and was happy until Malhotra, a 600-rupee-a-month officer, came to his department. Malhotra was an Indian from East Africa; he had been educated at an English university, and had just returned from a European posting. Ramnath and his 110-rupee colleagues secretly scoffed at Europe-returned Indians, but they were all a little frightened of Malhotra, whose reputation was terrifying. He was supposed to know every paragraph of the Civil Service code; he knew his privileges as well as his responsibilities.

Soon enough Ramnath was summoned to Malhotra's office, and there a letter was dictated to him at speed. Ramnath was happily able to catch it all and he returned to the desk marked 'Steno' with a feeling of satisfaction. No further summons came that day; but one came early next morning and when Ramnath went in he found Malhotra quite pale with anger. His neatly trimmed moustache bristled; his eyes were hard. He was freshly bathed and shaved, and Ramnath could feel the difference between his own loose white trousers and open-necked, long-tailed blue shirt and Malhotra's European-tailored grey suit set off by the university tie. Ramnath remained composed. The anger of a superior, for whatever reason, was as natural as Ramnath's own abuse of the sweeper who twice daily cleaned out his tenement privy in Mahim. In such relationships anger and abuse were almost without meaning; they merely marked proper distinctions.

'That letter you took yesterday,' Malhotra said. 'Why wasn't it returned for signature yesterday afternoon?'

'It wasn't? I am sorry, sir. I will see about it now.' Ramnath took his leave and presently returned. 'I have spoken about it to the typist, sir. But Hiralal has had quite a lot of work these last few days.'

'Hiralal? Typist? Don't you type?'

'Oh no, sir. I am a steno.'

'And what do you think a steno is? In future you type out the letters I give you, do you hear?'

Ramnath's face went blank.

'Do you hear?'

'That is not my job, sir.'

'We'll see about that. Take another letter now. And I want this one back before lunch.'

Malhotra dictated. Ramnath made his squiggles with a dancing pen, bowed when the dictating was over, and left the room. In the afternoon Malhotra buzzed for him.

'Where is that letter you took this morning?'

'It is with Hiralal, sir.'

'And yesterday's letter is still with Hiralal. Didn't I tell you that you must type out the letters I give you?'

Silence.

'Where is my letter?'

'It is not my job, sir.'

Malhotra banged the table. 'But we went through all that this morning.'

This was what Ramnath also felt. 'I am a steno, sir. I am not a typist.'

'I am going to report you, Ramnath, for insubordination.'

'That is your right, sir.'

'Don't *talk* to me like that! You won't type my letters. Let me have it from you like that. Say, "I won't type your letters".'

'I am a steno, sir.'

Malhotra dismissed Ramnath and went to see the head of his department. He was made to wait a little in the ante-room before he was called in. The head was tired, tolerant. He understood the impatience of a man like Malhotra, fresh from Europe. But no one before had required a steno to type. Of course, a steno's duties might be said to include typing. But that would be extending the definition of the word. Besides, this was India, and in India it was necessary to take people's feelings into consideration.

'If that is your attitude, sir, then I am sorry to say that you leave me with no alternative but to take the matter to the Union Public Service Commission. I shall report Ramnath for insubordination to you. And through you I shall ask for a full-scale inquiry into the duties of stenos.'

The head sighed. Malhotra wasn't going to get far in the service. That was clear; but he had his rights, and a demand for an inquiry would at some time, though not immediately, create a good deal of trouble: papers, questions, reports.

'Try a little persuasion, Malhotra.'

'I take it, sir, that this is your last word on the subject?'

'Last word?' The head was vague. 'My last word . . .'

The telephone rang: the head seized it, smiling at Malhotra. Malhotra rose and withdrew.

There was no letter awaiting signature on Malhotra's desk. He buzzed for Ramnath and very promptly Ramnath appeared. His triumph could scarcely be concealed by his excessive gravity, his bowed shoulders, his pad pressed to his blue-shirted breast, his gaze fixed on his shoes. He knew that Malhotra had been to see the head, and that not even a rebuke had resulted.

'A letter, Ramnath.'

Pad fell open; pen squiggled above and below ruled lines. But as he squiggled, Ramnath's assurance gave way to terror. What he was taking down was Malhotra's request for his sacking, for insubordination, for inefficiency as a stenographer, and for insolence. This committing of a thing to paper was threatening enough. What was worse was that the letter would have to be typed out by Hiralal. For Ramnath now there seemed only a choice of humiliations. Controlling his terror, he took the letter down, waited with bowed head to be dismissed, and when dismissal came, fled to the office of the head of the department. He waited a long time in the ante-room; he went in; and in no time he came out again.

At five that afternoon Ramnath tapped at Malhotra's door and stood in the doorway. In a trembling hand he held some typewritten sheets; and as soon as Malhotra looked up, Ramnath's eyes filled with tears.

'Ah,' Malhotra said. 'Hiralal has been catching up with his work, I see.'

Saying nothing, Ramnath shot to the side of Malhotra's desk, placed the typewritten sheets on the green blotting pad and, in a continuation of this downward action, dropped to the floor and touched Malhotra's polished shoes with his clasped palms.

'Get up! Get up! Did Hiralal type this?'

'I did! I did!' Ramnath was sobbing on the worn floor mat.

'Treat you people like people, and the net result is that you get insubordinate. Treat you like animals, and then you behave like this.'

Sobbing, embracing the shoes, polishing them with his palms, Ramnath agreed.

'You will type my letters from now on?'

Ramnath struck his forehead on Malhotra's shoes.

'All right. We'll tear this letter up. This is how we get through our work in this department.'

Sobbing, banging his forehead on Malhotra's shoes, Ramnath waited until the interleaved scraps of top copy and carbon fell into the wastepaper basket. Then he rose, his eyes dry, and ran out of the room. The day's work was over; now, with the great jostling crowds, home to Mahim. He had yet to accustom himself to the humiliations of the new world. He had been violated in the tenderest area of his self-esteem, and fear of the abyss alone had given him the strength to endure such a violation. It was a little tragedy. He had learned to obey; he would survive.

Countless such tragedies are marked on the hearts of those whom one sees in those brisk white-clad crowds, hurrying to and from their homes like city-workers in every city of the world, people for whom all the advertisements are meant, all the electric trains run, to whom the film posters are directed, all the extravagantly coloured women with big breasts and big hips, descendants of those figures of old Indian sculpture which, until separated from the people who created them, are like a tragic folk longing.

*

For Malhotra, too, with his Italian-styled suit and English university tie, the society and its violations were new. East Africa, the English university and the years in Europe had made him just enough of a colonial to be out of place in India. He had no family to speak of. He was only a 600-rupee-a-month man, and his place was therefore with 600-rupee-a-month men. But at that level there were no outsiders, no one who, like Malhotra, had rejected the badges of food and caste and dress. He wished to marry; it was also what his parents wished for him. But his colonial eye made him aspire too high. 'Don't call us. We will call you.' 'We thank you for your interest, and we will let you know as soon as the numerous applications have been gone through.' 'We don't appreciate 600 rupees a month.' This was what the son of one family said. And below that there was, in Malhotra's view, little more than village society. No marriage, then, for him; and the years were going by, and his parents were breaking their hearts. He could only share his bitterness with his friends.

Malik was one of these. He too was a 'new man'. He and Malhotra were bound only by their common bitterness, for Malik was an engineer and earned 1,200 rupees a month. He lived in a well-appointed flat in one of the finer areas of Bombay. By the standards of London he was well off. By the standards of Bombay he was overprivileged. But he was miserable. European engineers less qualified than himself earned three times as much for their services as experts and advisers; the mere fact that they were Europeans commended them to Indian firms. This was his story. A new man, he remained a stranger in Bombay, more of an outsider than any visiting European technician, to whom many doors were open. Malik's qualifications for the young business executive or 'box-wallah' society seemed high, but at our first meeting he told me of the probing by which he was continually rejected. He was an engineer; that was good. That he was Scandinavia-returned was impressive. That he worked for an established firm with European connexions made him more than promising. Then: 'Do you own a car?' Malik didn't. The probing was abandoned; no one was even interested in his parentage.

He spoke sadly in his passé modernistic flat, which he was beginning to let go: the irregular bookshelves, the irregular ceramics, the irregular coffee table. For all this there was no audience, and it was like the scrupulous preparation for going out of a girl whom no one will notice. It is with contemporary furniture as with contemporary clothes: sad unless there is someone who notices and cares. On the irregular coffee table there was a large photograph in a gilt frame of a pretty white girl with dark hair and high cheekbones. I asked no questions, but Malhotra told me later that the girl had died years before in her Northern land. While we talked and drank the tape-recorder played songs Malik had recorded in his student days in Europe, songs which even I could recognize as old. And in that Bombay flat, surrounded by the dramatic squares of light and darkness of other metropolitan blocks, below us the glittering arc of Marine Drive, in that room with the central photograph of the dead girl and the sour background of dead songs, we looked through the well-thumbed photograph albums: Malik in overcoat, Malik and his friends, Malik and the girl, against snow- or pine-covered mountains, against open-air cafés: Malik and Malhotra sharing the past (Ibsen in the original on the irregular bookshelves), 600-rupee-a-month and 1,200-rupee-a-month men temporarily forgetting their humiliations in memories of a past acceptance, when to be a man and a student was enough, and to be Indian gave glamour.

*

Jivan was thirteen or fourteen when he left his village to look for work in Bombay. He had no friends in the city and nowhere to go. He slept on the pavements. At last he found a job in a printery in the Fort area. He earned fifty rupees a month. He did not look for lodgings; he continued to sleep on that stretch of pavement which custom had now made his. Jivan could read and write; he was intelligent and anxious to please; and after some months he was chasing advertisements for a magazine his firm printed. His wages steadily rose and it seemed he was set for success and high responsibility in the firm. Then one day, without warning, he went to his employer and gave notice.

'It is my luck,' his employer said. 'I can never keep good people. I train them. Then they leave me. What's this new job you've found?'

'I have none, sir. I was hoping you would find one for me.'

'Oho! It's another rise you're after.'

'No, sir. It isn't money I want. It's this cycling about. It was all right when I was younger. But now I would like an office job. I want a desk of my own. I will even take less money if I can get an office job. I hope you will help me find one.'

Jivan's mind was made up. His employer was a kind-hearted man and he recommended Jivan for a clerkship in another firm. Here, as a clerk, Jivan rose fast. He was as loyal and hard-working as he had been in the printery; and he had the magic touch. Soon he was almost running the firm. After some time he had saved eight thousand rupees, slightly more than six hundred pounds. He bought a taxi and hired it out at twenty rupees a day: Malhotra's salary. He still worked for his firm. He still slept on the pavements. He was twenty-five years old.

*

Vasant grew up in a Bombay slum. He was very young when he left school to look for work. He took to hanging around the stock exchange. His face became familiar and the stockbrokers sent him on little errands. They began to use him as a telegraph-runner. One day a stockbroker gave Vasant a message but no money. 'It's all right,' the stockbroker said. 'They'll bill me at the end of the month.' So Vasant discovered that if you sent telegrams in some number the telegraph office gave you credit for a month. He offered a service to stockbrokers: he would collect all their telegrams from their offices, file them, and he would ask for money only at the end of the month. He charged a small fee; he made a little money; he even managed to rent a little cubby-hole of a 'telegraph office'. He read all the stockbrokers' telegrams: his knowledge of the market grew. He began to deal himself. He became rich. Now he was old and established. He had a respectably furnished office in a suitable block. He had a receptionist, secretaries, clerks. But this was mainly for show. He continued to do all his important work in his cramped little 'telegraph office'; he could think nowhere else. When he was poor he had never eaten during the day. The habit remained with him. If he ate during the day he became sluggish.

*

The worker in leather is among the lowest of the low, the most tainted of the tainted, and it was unusual, especially in the far South, where caste distinctions are rigid, to find two brahmin brothers making leather goods. Their establishment was small and self-contained: house, workshops and vegetable gardens on a plot of four acres. One brother, lean, nervous, hunted orders in the town and with his quick eyes observed foreign designs in briefcases, diary bindings, camera cases; the other brother, plump, placid, superintended the work. The greatest praise, which made both of them smirk and squirm with pleasure, was: 'But you didn't make this here. It looks foreign. American, *I* would say.' They both had progressive views about what the lean brother, in khaki shorts and vest on this Sunday morning, referred to as 'labour relations'. 'You've got to keep them happy. I can't do the work. I can't get my children to do it. You've got to keep them happy.' An 'ar-chin', picked off the streets, got one rupee a day; when he was fourteen or fifteen he could get four rupees a day; the 'maistry' got one hundred and twenty rupees a month, with a yearly bonus of about two hundred and forty rupees. 'Yes,' the other brother said. 'You have to keep them happy.' They were proud that everything in their workshops was made by hand, but their ambition was to create an 'industrial estate' which would bear their name. They had come from a poor family. They had begun by making envelopes. They still made envelopes. In one corner of the workshop a boy was standing on a neat stack of envelope sheets; a 'maistry', wielding a broad-bladed chopper, chopped the paper close to the boy's toes; elsewhere boys were folding up the paper that had been cut to the pattern required. The brothers were worth seventy thousand pounds.

*

Adventure is possible. But a knowledge of degree is in the bones and no Indian is far from his origins. It is like a physical yearning: the tycoon in his cubby-hole, the entrepreneur clerk sleeping on the pavement, the brahmin leather-goods manufacturers anxious to protect their children against caste contamination. However incongruous the imported mechanics of the new world – stockbrokers, telegrams, labour relations, advertisements – might seem, they have been incorporated into the rule of degree. Few Indians are outsiders. Malik and Malhotra are exceptional. They are not interested in the type of adventure the society can provide; their aspirations are alien and disruptive. Rejecting the badges of dress and food and function, rejecting degree, they find themselves rejected. They look for Balzacian adventure in a society which has no room for Rastignacs.

'When unrighteous disorder prevails, the women sin and are impure; and when women are not pure, Krishna, there is disorder of castes, social confusion.' This is the Gita again. And in India there is no social confusion, no disorder of castes, no adventure, in spite of the bingo on Sunday mornings in the old British clubs, in spite of the yellow-covered overseas editions of the *Daily Mirror* which the ladies in their graceful saris seize with eager manicured hands, and the copy of *Woman's Own* which the dainty shopper, basket-carrying servant respectfully in her train, presses to one breast like a badge of caste; in spite of the dance floors of Bombay, Delhi and Calcutta: those sad bands, those sad Anglo-Indian girls at the microphone, and the air full of dated slang. 'Oh, just bung your coat down there.' 'I say, by Jove!' And the names fly: Bunty, Andy, Freddy, Jimmy, Bunny. They are real, the men who answer to these names, and they answer them well: their jackets and ties and collars and accents do make them Bunty and Andy and Freddy. But they are not wholly what they seem. Andy is also Anand, Danny Dhandeva; their marriages have been strictly arranged, their children's marriages will be arranged; the astrologer will be earnestly consulted and horoscopes will be cast. For every man and woman on the dance floor is marked by destiny, on every one Fate has its eye. The Parsis, perhaps Freddy's lesser friends or relations, in their enclosure between decks on the holiday steamer from Goa, might loudly sing, their pleasure heightened by the confusion of the native crowd, *Barbara Allen* and *The Ash Grove* and *I Don't Have a Wooden Heart*. But that little corner of merry England which they have created in Bombay is also Druidical. It worships fire; its ways are narrow and protective, and at the end lie the Towers of Silence and the grim rites behind those walls whose main portals are marked with a symbol from the ancient world.

The outer and inner worlds do not have the physical separateness which they had for us in Trinidad. They coexist; the society only pretends to be colonial; and for this reason its absurdities are at once apparent. Its mimicry is both less and more than a colonial mimicry. It is the special mimicry of an old country which has been without a native aristocracy for a thousand years and has learned to make room for outsiders, but only at the top. The mimicry changes, the inner world remains constant: this is the secret of survival. And so it happens that, to one whole area of India, a late seventeenth-century traveller like Ovington remains in many ways a reliable guide. Yesterday the mimicry was Mogul; tomorrow it might be Russian or American; today it is English.

Mimicry might be too harsh a word for what appears so comprehensive and profound: buildings, railways, a system of administration, the intellectual discipline of the civil servant and the economist. Schizophrenia might better explain the scientist who, before taking up his appointment, consults the astrologer for an auspicious day. But mimicry must be used because so much has been acquired that the schizophrenia is often concealed; because so much of what is seen remains simple mimicry, incongruous and absurd; and because no people, by their varied physical endowments, are as capable of mimicry as the Indians. The Indian Army officer is at a first meeting a complete English army officer. He even manages to look English; his gait and bearing are English; his mannerisms, his tastes in drink are English; his slang is English. In the Indian setting this Indian English mimicry is like fantasy. It is an undiminishing absurdity; and it is only slowly that one formulates what was sensed from the first day: this is a mimicry not of England, a real country, but of the fairy-tale land of Anglo-India, of clubs and sahibs and syces and bearers. It is as if an entire society has fallen for a casual confidence trickster. Casual because the trickster has gone away, losing interest in his joke, but leaving the Anglo-Indians flocking to the churches of Calcutta on a Sunday morning to assert the alien faith, more or less abandoned in its country of origin; leaving Freddy crying, 'Just bung your coat down there, Andy'; leaving the officer exclaiming, 'I say, by Jove! I feel rather bushed.' Leaving 'civil lines', 'cantonments', leaving people 'going off to the hills'; magic words now fully possessed, now spoken as of right, in what is now at last Indian Anglo-India, where smartness can be found in the cosy proletarian trivialities of *Woman's Own* and the *Daily Mirror* and where Mrs Hauksbee, a Millamant of the suburbs, is still the arbiter of elegance.

But room has been left at the top, and out of this mimicry a new aristocracy is being essayed, not of politicians or civil servants, but of the business executives of foreign, mostly British, firms. To them, the box-wallahs, as they are called, have gone the privileges India reserves for the foreign and conquering; and it is to this new commercial caste that both Malik, the engineer 'drawing' twelve hundred rupees a month, and Malhotra, the government servant drawing six hundred, aspire with despair, and, despairing, seek to ridicule. We are now as far above them as they are above Ramnath, with his flapping Indian-style white cotton trousers, boarding the crowded suburban electric train to get to his tenement room in Mahim; as far above them as Ramnath is above the sweeper of the 'gay girl' in Forras Road. We have left even the lower-class Parsis far below; we can hardly hear them singing *Flow Gently, Sweet Afton* on the holiday steamer from Goa.

Bunty the box-wallah. He is envied and ridiculed throughout India. Much is made of the name, and even Bunty, from the security of his aristocracy, sometimes pretends to find its origin in the box of the street pedlar, though it is more likely that the name derives from the Anglo-Indian office box, the burden in the old days of a special servant, of which Kipling speaks so feelingly in *Something of Myself.* Bunty is envied for his luxurious company flat, his inflated salary and his consequent ability, in an India which is now independent, guiltlessly to withdraw from India. For this withdrawal he is also ridiculed. He is an easy target. He is new to the caste, but the caste is old and, though essentially engaged in trade, it has been ennobled by the glamour of the conqueror, the rewards of trade, and now by Bunty himself, whom these two things in conjunction have attracted.

Bunty comes of a 'good' family, Army, ICS; he might even have princely connexions. He is two or three generations removed from purely Indian India; he, possibly like his father, has been to an Indian or English public school and one of the two English universities, whose accent, through all the encircling hazards of Indian intonation, he strenuously maintains. He is a blend of East and West; he is 'broad-minded'. He permits his name to be corrupted into the closest English equivalent, like place names in the mouth of the conqueror. So Firdaus becomes Freddy, Jamshed Jimmy, and Chandrashekhar, which is clearly impossible, becomes the almost universal Bunty or Bunny. Bunty knows it will count in his favour, as a mark of his broadmindedness, though at this level it requires a minimum of heroism, if he makes a mixed marriage; if, say, as a Punjabi Hindu he marries a Bengali Muslim or a Bombay Parsi. Freed of one set of caste rules, he obeys another, and these are as nice: to introduce Jimmy, whose air-conditioned office is shared and has hard furnishings, into the home of Andy, who has an office to himself with soft furnishings, is to commit a blunder.

Bunty's grandfather might have conducted his business over a hookah or while reclining on bolsters in a dreadfully furnished room. Bunty discusses business over drinks at the club or on the golf course. There is no need for the golf course: the box-wallah circle is tiny. But it is a condition of Bunty's employment that he play golf, in order to make suitable 'contacts', and on the golf courses of clubs all over the country he can be seen with an equally unhappy Andy, who, as he goes out into the drizzle of Bangalore, might remark that it is rather like the rain of England. There are other traditions, which vary from city to city. In Calcutta there is the Friday afternoon revelry at Firpo's restaurant on Chowringhee. In the days of the British this celebrated the departure of the mail boat for England and marked the end of the four-and-a-half-day week. Letters to England now go by air; but Bunty is caste-minded; he maintains the tradition, unembarrassed by its origin.

It is easy for Indians to make fun of Bunty for being called 'daddy' by his English-speaking children; for his imitated manners: he rises when ladies come into a room; for his foreign interest in interior decoration; for the spotless bathroom and adequate towels he provides for his guests (such attentions in India being beneath the notice of all but the latrine-cleaner: the Indian lavatory and the Indian kitchen are the visitor's nightmare). But Bunty is no fool. He has withdrawn from India, but he does not wish to be a European. He sees the glamour of Europe; but, being in almost daily contact with Europeans, he is compelled by his pride to be Indian. He strives too hard perhaps to blend East with West; his patronage of Indian arts and crafts is a little like that of the visitor. In his drawing-room, hung with contemporary Indian fabrics, the odd sketch from Kangra, Basohli or Rajasthan or a piece of the bright bazaar art of Jamini Roy stands beside the Picasso lithograph or the Sisley reproduction. His food is a mixture of Indian and European; his drink is wholly European.

But this mixture of East and West in Bunty's home tells more of the truth about Bunty than either his friends or enemies believe. For Bunty is only pretending to be a colonial. He sees himself as every man's equal and most men's superior; and in him, as in every Indian, the inner world continues whole and untouched. Bunty might relish the light, attractive complexions of his wife and children. He might be at especial pains to draw your attention to the complexions of his children, and he might do so by some flippant denigratory assessment. But their paleness is not a European paleness, which to Bunty is reminiscent of the Indian albino; and indeed about the European, however to be imitated, fawned upon and resented, there still remains some stigma of the *mleccha*, the unclean. Bunty's caste is European; but Bunty carries within himself a strong sense of Aryan race and ancientness as exclusive possessions. It is for this reason that the Anglo-Indian half-breed, however pale, however anglicized, can form no respectable part of Bunty's society unless graced by some notable family connexion; for this group there can be no room in India except as outsiders and not at the top. (Nor would they wish there to be room. Their dream is of England; and to England they come – the paler go to Australia, white – and they congregate in sad little colonies in places like Forest Hill, busy churchgoers in short dresses which, in India anti-Indian, in London are un-English and colonial; and they read *Woman's Own* and the *Daily Mirror* on the day of publication: a dream of romance fulfilled.) Towards Europe Bunty is like the puritan seducer: he despises even while he violates.

On Sunday morning Bunty entertains his friends to drinks in his flat. This might be on Malabar Hill if it is in Bombay; if in Calcutta, it will be well hidden from the *bustees* which provide factory labour.

'I had a round of golf yesterday with the Deputy Director . . .' This is from Andy.

'Well, the Director told me . . .'

Bunty and Andy are not discussing business. They are talking of the Chinese invasion. Even now, however, they appear to be taking delight in their new closeness to power. It is not for this reason alone that their gossip is disturbing. It is a unique type of gossip. How can it be described? It is unslanted; it states facts and draws no conclusions. It makes one long to shake them by the shoulder and say, 'Express your prejudices. Say at least, "If I had the power I would do this". Say that you are on the side of this and against that. Don't just go on calmly reporting unrelated little disasters. Get angry. Get excited. Get worried. Try to link all that you have been saying. Make some sort of pattern out of it, however prejudiced. Then at least I will understand. Right now you are behaving as though you are talking of well-known history.'

It is with this gossip that one begins to doubt what Bunty and Andy show of themselves and one begins to feel that they are not what they seem, that there are areas to which they can retreat and where they are hard to get at. The flat now seems to hang in a void. India is a stone's throw away, but in the flat it is denied: the beggars, the gutters, the starved bodies, the weeping swollen-bellied child black with flies in the filth and cowdung and human excrement of a bazaar lane, the dogs, ribby, mangy, cowed and cowardly, reserving their anger, like the human beings around them, for others of their kind. The decoration of the flat is contemporary; many of its ingredients are Indian; but it is based on nothing. On the shelves there are novels that might be found on shelves in a dozen other countries: vulgarity nowadays is international and swift. But novels imply an interest in people. This flat holds a rejection of concern. And did not that educated brahmin read the romances of Denise Robins, which lay on his shelves next to the bulky volumes of ancient astrological prophecies published by the Madras Government? Did not that young man, a student at Punjab University, read the paperbound volumes of the School-girl's Own Library for relaxation? Will not Bunty's wife fall on the *Daily Mirror* and *Woman's Own* in the club? Will she not consult her astrologer?

Somewhere there has been a failure of communication, unrecognized because communication seems to have been established. In the cafés there are earnest groups of the young who talk about 'theatre' and the need for bringing theatre to the 'people'. They are like their counterparts in England, whom, like the army officers, they even manage physically to resemble; and like their counterparts in England, by theatre they mean *Look Back in Anger*, professionally abbreviated to *Look Back*. A willingness to accept, an underlying, unwitting rejection of the values implied: in Bunty's rooms, the irritating gossip going on, the Chinese about to break through into Assam, the mimicry is no longer as funny as the sight on that first day in Bombay, after the exhaustion and hysteria, of the banner hung across the hot, squalid street advertising the Oxford and Cambridge Players' production of *The Importance of Being Earnest.*

*

Withdrawal, denial, confusion of values: these are vague words. We need more direct evidence; and a little, I feel, is provided by a recent Indian novel, *The Princes*, by Manohar Malgonkar, published in London by Hamish Hamilton in 1963. *The Princes* is the medieval tragedy of a medieval Indian petty prince who loses power with Independence and feels the humiliation of his fall so deeply that he goes out unarmed after a wounded tiger and is killed. It is an honest book, and the writing is not without skill. Malgonkar has a feeling for outdoor life and his descriptions of hunting and shooting can convey the enchantment of these pastimes even to those who do not practise them.

The Prince is descended from casteless Deccani bandits who, when they acquired political power, surrendered a lakh of rupees to the pundits in exchange for caste privileges. The treasures they amassed remain in the state treasury, objects of almost religious awe, guarded by a special group of retainers. For the ruling house these treasures are a private delectation, a reminder of the past; it is unthinkable that they should be used to improve the impoverished state. The Prince is opposed to progress. He states the view quite bluntly; and when the British decide to build a dam in territory adjacent to the state, he persuades his aboriginal subjects who live in the area to be affected to vote against the scheme. The Prince gives five annual scholarships, each worth £70, to deserving boys. On himself he is more lavish. He has two palaces, thirty motorcars and annual pocket money of £70,000. To spend £1,500 to bring down a courtesan from Simla is nothing. He has much time to devote to his hobbies. He is an excellent shot and a fearless tracker of wounded tigers. 'I am rich and well-born,' he says, quoting the Gita. 'Who else is equal to me?' He matches words with action. When the nationalists of the state occupy the administration building in 1947 he goes in alone, ignoring the crowd, and hauls down the Indian flag. He is unable to accommodate himself to the handsome terms of the Home Ministry in Delhi, and when he sees that it is too late to save his state and his powers he is heart-broken. He does not rage or weep. Quoting that line of the Gita, he goes out unarmed after a wounded tiger and is killed. He was rich and high; he has fallen.

It is a medieval concept of tragedy.

> Reduce we all our lessons unto this:
> To rise, sweet Spenser, therefore live we all.
> Spenser, all live to die, and rise to fall.

But what is puzzling is that it should be so presented to us by the Prince's son, who is the narrator. He was born in 1920, educated at an English-style English-staffed public school for the sons of princes, and served as an officer in the army during the war. 'Indeed it seems to me,' he says, 'that with the passing of the years I have come to identify myself more and more with (my father's) values.' After the public school which sought to root out snobbery between princes of big states and princes of little states; after the army; after the love affair with an Anglo-Indian girl, encountered in Simla:

> The British certainly knew all about resisting change. It was spring in the Himalayas, and Simla was exactly as it had been fifty years ago or a hundred, and Mrs Hauksbee might have been living just around the corner.
>
> 'I like your perfume, whatever it is.'
>
> 'Chanel number five. I had just a scrap left, but I had to wear it – for going out with a prince.'
>
> 'Why, thanks! I'll buy some more.'

After the clubs of Delhi:

> 'Rumpus?' I exclaimed. 'Why not? Of course we can have a rumpus. One is not a father every day, dammit! What sort of a rumpus had you in mind?' I was certainly learning to handle conversation, now that I had been in New Delhi for nearly two years; meaningless, insincere, but light. You had to keep it frothy, that was all that mattered.

This is how far we will appear to move from the Prince and his derelict principality and the local primary school where, at the beginning of the story, the narrator, Abhayraj, and his half-brother Charudutt are pupils. They are kept separate from the untouchables, who sit on the floor at the back. One morning during the break a game of mango-seed football starts in the veranda. The untouchables watch from a distance. One joins in, trips Charudutt. The caste boys, Abhayraj included, abuse the untouchables: 'Cow-eaters, stinkers, cow-skinners.' And they throw the offending untouchable boy and his satchel into the pond. 'Bastard!' the boy shouts from the pond at Charudutt. 'You are no prince. You are a whore's son.'

It is this word, bastard, which interests Abhayraj. He asks his English tutor, Mr Moreton, what the word means. Mr Moreton hesitates. 'I could understand his embarrassment. He was a sensitive man, and he knew about Charudutt and about the numerous *upraja* sons in our family – children born to rulers out of wedlock.' This is the sensitivity of Mr Moreton. Neither tutor nor pupil speaks of the scene in the school grounds.

The untouchable boy, Kanakchand, has no books the next day. He is put out of the class and in the afternoon Abhayraj sees him 'miserable and downcast, still squatting on the wall'. He is still there the following morning. Abhayraj speaks to him and finds out that he cannot stay at home because he will be flogged if his father gets to know that his books have been destroyed; he cannot go into the class because he has no books and no money to buy new ones. Abhayraj gives Kanakchand all the books in his own satchel. Among them, however, is the *Highroads Treasury*, which is not a school book but a gift from Mr Moreton. Mr Moreton, by some chance, asks after the book that day; the truth is told him; he understands. The next morning Kanakchand comes to Abhayraj and returns the *Highroads Treasury*. 'It was a present. Here, I have brought it back.'

It is a brutal but touching episode, rendered with fidelity, from the taunting to the forgetting to the impulse of pity and generosity. Now comes the sentence which distorts it all, which cuts the ground from under our feet. 'He was as sound as a silver rupee when he began,' Abhayraj comments. 'What made him turn so sour and twisted in later life?' Kanakchand sound as a silver rupee! Kanakchand, untouchable, cow-eater, stinker, squatting on the floor at the back of the class, sitting on the fountain wall for two days because he has lost his books! Did his soundness lie in his acceptance of degree? Did it lie in his refusal to steal from someone who had made him a valuable gift?

The friendship develops. One day Kanakchand makes a gift to Abhayraj of enormous bean seeds, good for nothing except looking at and holding in the hands, and Abhayraj is 'vaguely distressed at my first contact with the playthings of the poor, bean seeds found on the floor of the forest'. And more is to come. 'I did not realize it then, but Kanakchand was my first direct contact with the quivering poverty of India.' It is a singular word, this *quivering*. At first it seems unnecessary; then it seems theatrical yet oddly matter-of-fact; then it seems a concession to a convention of feeling.

Kanakchand's poverty is certainly theatrical. His lunch is one black roti, chillis and an onion.

> It seemed that even the onion was something of a treat, and that bajra or millet bread and chilli powder mixed with groundnut oil formed his main meal of the day. I watched with fascination as he

> ate, hungrily and with relish . . . He wolfed the very last crumb, biting alternately on the charred bajra roti and the onion. And when he finished the very last mouthful, he licked his fingers clean.

It is like a description of the feeding habits of a rare animal. Poverty as occasional spectacle: this is our poverty. Abhayraj offers Kanakchand a chocolate. Kanakchand throws it, wrapper and all, into his mouth. Abhayraj exclaims. Kanakchand spits it out and – sound as a silver rupee, remember – makes this curious statement: 'Oh, I didn't know. I thought Bal-raje was playing some kind of joke on me – making me eat green paper.'

Kanakchand is intelligent but his English is poor. To win one of the Prince's five scholarships to a high school he has to write an English essay. Abhayraj writes the essay for him; Kanakchand wins the scholarship; and the day arrives for the Prince to make the presentation. Kanakchand's parents are present, 'deliriously happy'. 'Truth, honesty, faith in God and above all, loyalty,' the Prince begins his speech, 'add up to far more than the gaining of worldly rewards.' With this he raises his riding crop and strikes Kanakchand to the floor, strikes him twice again and 'wiped his hands delicately on a handkerchief'. Abhayraj is horrified. He persuades his mother to provide for Kanakchand's education. But Abhayraj notes that Kanakchand never shows any 'gratitude'; and Abhayraj is tormented, not by Kanakchand's humiliation, but by 'the guilt of turning a high-spirited, ambitious boy into a malevolent revolutionary': again that distorting gloss, that cutting of the ground from under our feet.

The years pass. Kanakchand becomes important in the nationalist movement. He wishes to be avenged, and with Independence vengeance is his. He is now presented to us as physically repulsive and contemptible, overbearing at one moment, instinctively cringing at the next. The Prince's little principality disappears. Kanakchand, adding insult to injury, leads a demonstration through the streets, chanting, 'The raj is dead!'

> That, I thought, was the one thing I would never forgive Kanakchand. He was hitting at a man who had already fallen but was putting up a brave front. He was humiliating someone who still held that he had no equal among men. That, truly, was the vengeance of sheep, as my father had said.

The stiff upper lip reinforcing a medieval conception of degree, public school fair-play stimulating an opposed passion: the confusion is now apparent. It is with more than public school righteousness, though it might seem that in its name alone action is being taken, that Abhayraj makes a vow. He will avenge his father. He will do so by inflicting an old humiliation – in retrospect how deserved, answering how apt an assessment of degree – on Kanakchand. He will flog him in public; he will flog him with a riding crop. 'He was one of those who would always squeal, one of those unfortunates who had not learned to take their punishment without showing it.' This is the action with which the book ends. This is what is presented for our approval; this is what, after the tragedy of the Prince's fall, restores calm of mind to the narrator and is meant to restore it to us.

The poverty of India is *quivering*. The guilt Abhayraj carries for his father's flogging of Kanakchand, not public school material in the final analysis, is only the guilt of turning a high-spirited boy into a revolutionary. And all the cruelty of India is magicked away in textbook Western phrases which are as empty as that *quivering*: the narrator sees his father denying 'basic rights' to 'the people', he talks of the 'collective wish of the people'. Nowhere do I see the India I know: those poor fields, those three-legged dogs, those sweating red-coated railway porters carrying heavy tin trunks on their heads. 'The mountains were rainwashed, the sky was a bright blue and the air was stiff with the scent of pine and flowers and charged with an almost electric silence broken by the sharp warnings of the rickshaw pullers.' It is so the rickshaw puller appears, beast of burden more degrading than degraded: unseen, the source only of a holiday sound, part of the atmosphere of a Simla romance. This is the Indian withdrawal and denial; this is part of the confusion of Indian Anglo-India.

*

So too it comes to the traveller. The poor become faceless. Then all the rest, the dance floors, the Western mimicry, might be subjects for gentle satire. But first the background, the obvious, must be ignored.

# 3
# THE COLONIAL

Well, India is a country of nonsense.
M.K. Gandhi

THE MAN MOVES briskly among the passengers on the crowded suburban train, distributing leaflets. The leaflets are smudged and dog-eared; in three languages they tell of the misfortunes of a refugee family. Some passengers read the leaflets; many more don't. The train comes into a station. The leaflet-distributor goes out through one door and a woman and a boy enter through another. The leaflet didn't promise this. It promised an impoverished Bengali woman and her six starving children, not this small boy, blind, thin, half-naked, scaly with dirt, whining at a low, steady pitch, tears streaming out of raw red eyes, his arms held aloft in supplication. The boy is manoeuvred and propelled through the coach by the woman, who weeps and whines and briskly, without acknowledgement, collects the small coins which the passengers, barely looking up, hand to her. She does not pause to plead with those who don't give. By the time the train stops she and the boy are at the door, ready to change coaches. They go out. Another man comes in. He too is in a rush. He pushes through the coach, retrieving what leaflets he can before the next station.

It has been swift; everyone, passengers included, is well-drilled; there has been little stir. Stencilled notices in three languages on the grimy woodwork warn against alms-giving, as they warn against accepting cigarettes from strangers since 'these may be doped'. But it is good to give to the beggar. He follows a holy calling; he can exercise the pity and virtue of even the poor. Possibly the boy had been blinded to work this suburban route; and the organization was certainly at fault in issuing the wrong leaflets. But this is not important. What matters is the giving to the beggar, the automatic act of charity which is an automatic reverence to God, like the offering of a candle or a spin of the prayer-wheel. The beggar, like the priest, has his function; like the priest, he might need an organization.

But here is an observer who dissents:

> If I had the power, I would stop every *sadavrata* where free meals are given. It has degraded the nation and it has encouraged laziness, idleness, hypocrisy and even crime. Such misplaced charity adds nothing to the wealth of the country, whether material or spiritual . . . I know that it is . . . much more difficult to organize an institution where honest work has to be done before meals are served . . . But I am convinced that it will be cheaper in the long run, if we do not want to increase in geometrical progression the race of loafers which is fast overrunning this land.

It is the attitude of the foreigner who does not understand the function of the beggar in India and is judging India by the standards of Europe. He is too radical to succeed and of course in this matter of beggary he has failed.

*

Shankaracharya Hill, overlooking the Dal Lake, is one of the beauty spots of Srinagar. It has to be climbed with care, for large areas of its lower slopes are used as latrines by Indian tourists. If you surprise a group of three women, companionably defecating, they will giggle: the shame is yours, for exposing yourself to such a scene.

In Madras the bus station near the High Court is one of the more popular latrines. The traveller arrives; to pass the time he raises his dhoti, defecates in the gutter. The bus arrives; he boards it; the woman sweeper cleans up after him. Still in Madras, observe this bespectacled patriarch walking past the University on the Marina. Without warning he raises his dhoti, revealing a backside bare save for what appears to be a rope-like G-string; he squats, pisses on the pavement, leisurely rises; the dhoti still raised, he rearranges his G-string, lets the dhoti fall, and continues on his promenade. It is a popular evening walk, this Marina; but no one looks, no face is averted in embarrassment.

In Goa you might think of taking an early morning walk along the balustraded avenue that runs beside the Mandovi River. Six feet below, on the water's edge, and as far as you can see, there is a line, like a wavering tidewrack, of squatters. For the people of Goa, as for those of imperial Rome, defecating is a social activity; they squat close to one another; they chatter. When they are done they advance, trousers still down, backsides bare, into the water to wash themselves. They climb back on to the avenue, jump on their cycles or get into their cars, and go away. The strand is littered with excrement; amid this excrement fish is being haggled over as it is landed from the boats; and every hundred yards or so there is a blue-and-white enamelled notice in Portuguese threatening punishment for soiling the river. But no one notices.

Indians defecate everywhere. They defecate, mostly, beside the railway tracks. But they also defecate on the beaches; they defecate on the hills; they defecate on the river banks; they defecate on the streets; they never look for cover. Muslims, with their tradition of purdah, can at times be secretive. But this is a religious act of self-denial, for it is said that the peasant, Muslim or Hindu, suffers from claustrophobia if he has to use an enclosed latrine. A handsome young Muslim boy, a student at a laughable institute of education in an Uttar Pradesh weaving town, elegantly dressed in the style of Mr Nehru, even down to the buttonhole, had another explanation. Indians were a poetic people, he said. He himself always sought the open because he was a poet, a lover of Nature, which was the matter of his Urdu verses; and nothing was as poetic as squatting on a river bank at dawn.

These squatting figures – to the visitor, after a time, as eternal and emblematic as Rodin's Thinker – are never spoken of; they are never written about; they are not mentioned in novels or stories; they do not appear in feature films or documentaries. This might be regarded as part of a permissible prettifying intention. But the truth is that *Indians do not see these squatters* and might even, with complete sincerity, deny that they exist: a collective blindness arising out of the Indian fear of pollution and the resulting conviction that Indians are the cleanest people in the world. They are required by their religion to take a bath every day. This is central; and they have devised minute rules to protect themselves from every conceivable contamination. There is only one pure way to defecate; in love-making only the left hand is to be used; food is to be taken only with the right. It has all been regulated and purified. To observe the squatters is therefore distorting; it is to fail to see through to the truth. And the ladies at the Lucknow Club, after denying that Indians defecate in public, will remind you, their faces creased with distaste, of the habits of Europe – the right hand used for love-making, toilet paper and food, the weekly bath in a tub of water contaminated by the body of the bather, the washing in a washbasin that has been spat and gargled into – proving by such emotive illustrations not the dirtiness of Europe but the security of India. It is an Indian method of argument, an Indian way of seeing: it is so that squatters and wayside filth begin to disappear.

But here is that observer again:

> Instead of having graceful hamlets dotting the land, we have dung-heaps. The approach to many villages is not a refreshing experience. Often one would like to shut one's eyes and stuff one's nose; such is the surrounding dirt and offending smell.

> The one thing which we can and must learn from the West is the science of municipal sanitation.
>
> By our bad habits we spoil our sacred river banks and furnish excellent breeding grounds for flies . . . A small spade is the means of salvation from a great nuisance. Leaving night-soil, cleaning the nose, or spitting on the road is a sin against God as well as humanity, and betrays a sad want of consideration for others. The man who does not cover his waste deserves a heavy penalty even if he lives in a forest.

The observer is seeing what no Indian sees. But he has now declared his foreign inspiration. The celebrated Indian daily bath he frequently dismisses as 'a kind of bath'. He is unwilling to see beyond the ritual act to the intention, and in the intention to find reality. Sanitation is one of his obsessions. And just as in London he had read books on vegetarianism and clothes-washing and in South Africa books on bookkeeping, so he has read books on this subject.

> In his book on rural hygiene Dr Poore says that excreta should be buried in earth no deeper than nine to twelve inches. The author contends that superficial earth is charged with minute life, which, together with light and air which easily penetrate it, turn the excreta into good soft sweet-smelling soil within a week. Any villager can test this for himself.

It is the characteristic note of this observer. His interest in sanitation, which is properly the concern of the latrine-cleaner, is not widely shared. The briefest glimpse of the lavatories at New Delhi's international airport is sufficient. Indians defecate everywhere, on floors, in urinals for men (as a result of yogic contortions that can only be conjectured). Fearing contamination, they squat rather than sit, and every lavatory cubicle carries marks of their misses. No one notices.

*

In Europe and elsewhere the favoured bunk in a railway sleeper is the top bunk. It is more private and less liable to disturbance from dangling feet or opening doors. In India, however, where the top bunk has the added advantage of being freer of dust, the lower bunk is preferred, not because it is easier to spread one's bedding on it – there are porters and servants to do that – but because climbing to the top bunk involves physical effort, and physical effort is to be avoided as a degradation.

On this express to Delhi my sleeper had been booked by a high railway official and I was naturally given the lower bunk. My travelling companion was about forty. He wore a suit; he might have been a senior clerk or a university teacher. He was not happy about the top bunk. He complained about it first to the porter and then, after the train had started, to himself. I offered to change with him. His sourness vanished. But he simply stood where he was and did nothing. His bedding had been spread for him on the top bunk by the porter, and he was waiting until we got to the next station, two hours distant, so that he might get a porter to take it down for him. I wished to settle down. I began to do the porter's job. He smiled but offered no help. I lost my temper. His face acquired that Indian expressionlessness which indicates that communication has ceased and that the Indian has withdrawn from a situation he cannot understand. Labour is a degradation; only a foreigner would see otherwise:

> Divorce of the intellect from body-labour has made of us the shortest-lived, most resourceless and most exploited nation on earth.

The observer, the failed reformer, is of course Mohandas Gandhi. Mahatma, great-souled, father of the nation, deified, his name given to streets and parks and squares, honoured everywhere by statues and *mandaps* and in Delhi by Rajghat, which the visitor must approach barefooted over scorching sand, his portrait garlanded in every *pan*-shop, hung in hundreds of offices, bare-chested, bespectacled, radiating light and goodness, his likeness so familiar that, simplified to caricature and picked out in electric lights, it is now an accepted part of the decorations of a wedding house, he is nevertheless the least Indian of Indian leaders. He looked at India as no Indian was able to; his vision was direct, and this directness was, and is, revolutionary. He sees exactly what the visitor sees; he does not ignore the obvious. He sees the beggars and the shameless pundits and the filth of Banaras; he sees the atrocious sanitary habits of doctors, lawyers and journalists. He sees the Indian callousness, the Indian refusal to see. No Indian attitude escapes him, no Indian problem; he looks down to the roots of the static, decayed society. And the picture of India which comes out of his writings and exhortations over more than thirty years still holds: this is the measure of his failure.

He saw India so clearly because he was in part a colonial. He settled finally in India when he was forty-six, after spending twenty years in South Africa. There he had seen an Indian community removed from the setting of India; contrast made for clarity, criticism and discrimination for self-analysis. He emerged a colonial blend of East and West, Hindu and Christian. Nehru is more Indian; he has a romantic feeling for the country and its past; he takes it all to his heart, and the India he writes about cannot easily be recognized. Gandhi never loses the critical, comparing South African eye; he never rhapsodizes, except in the vague Indian way, about the glories of ancient India. But it is Gandhi, and not Nehru, who will give as much emphasis to the resolutions passed at a Congress gathering as to the fact that the Tamilian delegates ate by themselves because they would have been polluted by the sight of non-Tamilians, and that certain delegates, forgetting that there were no excrement removers at hand, used the veranda as a latrine.

It is a correct emphasis, for more than a problem of sanitation is involved. It is possible, starting from that casual defecation in a veranda at an important assembly, to analyse the whole diseased society. Sanitation was linked to caste, caste to callousness, inefficiency and a hopelessly divided country, division to weakness, weakness to foreign rule. This is what Gandhi saw, and no one purely of India could have seen it. It needed the straight simple vision of the West; and it is revealing to find, just after his return from South Africa, how Gandhi speaks Christian, Western, simplicities with a new, discovering fervour: 'Before the Throne of the Almighty we shall be judged, not by what we have eaten nor by whom we have been touched but by whom we have served and how. Inasmuch as we serve a single human being in distress, we shall find favour in the sight of God.' The New Testament tone is not inappropriate. It is in India, and with Gandhi, that one can begin to see how revolutionary the now familiar Christian ethic must once have been. Hindus might try to find in this ideal of service the 'selfless action' of the Gita. But this is only Indian distortion, the eternal Indian attempt to incorporate and nullify. The Gita's selfless action is a call to self-fulfilment and at the same time a restatement of degree; it is the opposite of the service which Gandhi, the Indian revolutionary, is putting forward as a practicable day-to-day ideal.

The spirit of service, excrement, bread-labour, the dignity of scavenging, and excrement again: Gandhi's obsessions – even when we remove non-violence, when we set aside all that he sought to make of himself, and concentrate on his analysis of India – seem ill-assorted and sometimes unpleasant. But they hang together; they form a logical whole; they answer the directness of his colonial vision.

*

Study these four men washing down the steps of this unpalatable Bombay hotel. The first pours water from a bucket, the second scratches the tiles with a twig broom, the third uses a rag to slop the dirty water down the steps into another bucket, which is held by the fourth. After they have passed, the steps are as dirty as before; but now above the blackened skirting-tiles the walls are freshly and dirtily splashed. The bathrooms and lavatories are foul; the slimy woodwork has rotted away as a result of this daily drenching; the concrete walls are green and black with slime. You cannot complain that the hotel is dirty. No Indian will agree with you. Four sweepers are in daily attendance, and it is enough in India that the sweepers attend. They are not required to *clean*. That is a subsidiary part of their function, which is to *be* sweepers, degraded beings, to go through the motions of degradation. They must stoop when they sweep; cleaning the floor of the smart Delhi café, they will squat and move like crabs between the feet of the customers, careful to touch no one, never looking up, never rising. In Jammu City you will see them collecting filth from the streets with their bare hands. This is the degradation the society requires of them, and to this they willingly submit. They are dirt; they wish to appear as dirt.

Class is a system of rewards. Caste imprisons a man in his function. From this it follows, since there are no rewards, that duties and responsibilities become irrelevant to position. A man is his proclaimed function. There is little subtlety to India. The poor are thin; the rich are fat. The petty Marwari merchant in Calcutta eats quantities of sweets to develop the layers of fat that will proclaim his prosperity. 'You look fat and fresh today' is a compliment in the Punjab. And in every Uttar Pradesh town you might see the rich and very fat man in cool, clean white sitting in a cycle-rickshaw being pedalled by a poor and very thin man, prematurely aged, in rags. Beggars whine. Holy men give up all. Politicians are grave and unsmiling. And the cadet of the Indian Administrative Service, when asked why he has joined the service, replies after some thought, 'It gives me prestige.' His colleagues, who are present, do not disagree. It is an honest reply; it explains why, when the Chinese invade, the administration in Assam will collapse.

Service is not an Indian concept, and the providing of services has long ceased to be a concept of caste. The function of the businessman is to make money. He might wish to sell shoes to Russia. He therefore sends good samples; the order obtained, he sends a shipload of shoes with cardboard soles. Overcoming foreign distrust of Indian business practices, he gets an order from Malaya for drugs. And sends coloured water. It is not his duty as a merchant to supply genuine drugs or good shoes or any shoes or drugs at all; his duty is, by whatever means, to make money. The shoes are sent back; there are complaints about the coloured water. This is the merchant's luck; these are the trials he has to endure. He hops from enterprise to enterprise, from shoes to drugs to tea. A tea plantation is a delicate organization; he soon works it to ruin. Short-sightedness and dishonesty do not enter into it. The merchant is simply fulfilling his function. Later, fulfilling another aspect of his function, he might give up his money altogether and end his days as a mendicant sadhu.

The tailor in Madras will give you trousers with a false hem. At the first shrinking the trousers are useless. But his label is in the waistband and he begged you to give his name to others. He can make money only if he gets customers; and he will get customers, not by making good trousers, but by getting his name known. And here is a shirtmaker distributing leaflets to announce the opening of his establishment. The Japanese have driven him out of West Africa. 'Their finish was better.' He speaks without rancour; that defeat was just part of his luck. His response to it is not to improve his finish but, abandoning 'the black Negro savages of Africa', to start afresh in this Indian town. The shirt he makes you is atrocious. The cuffs are an inch too narrow, the tail is several inches too short; and after the first wash the whole thing shrinks. He has made a little extra money by saving on material; for this reason he remains warm towards you and whenever he sees you he presses you to have another shirt made. (If you had gone to him with an introduction and had therefore been represented to him as someone capable of doing him harm, it would have been in his interest to be extravagantly generous; the shirt might even have been a little too large.) Every morning he pauses at the door of his shop, bows and touches the dust of the threshold to his forehead. This is how he guards his luck; his enterprise is a contract between God and himself alone.

'After acceptance she should please him; when he is infatuated with her she should suck him dry of his wealth and at last abandon him. This is the duty of a public woman.' The *Kama Sutra*, it might be said, reveals a society in undress; and no Indian manual is so old that it has ceased to be relevant. It is perhaps inevitable that a religion which teaches that life is illusion should encourage a balancing pragmatism in earthly, illusory relationships. The duty of the public woman – and mark that word duty – resembles the duty of the businessman: if you want to find sharp practice and monopolies preached as high virtues you can do no better than read some of the tales of the Indian classical period. The cow is holy. It is to be reverenced by being allowed to live, even if it has to be turned out into grassless city streets; even if it has been knocked down by a lorry on the Delhi-Chandigarh road and lies dying slowly in its blood for a whole afternoon, it remains holy: the villagers will stand by to see that no one attempts to take its life. The black buffalo, on the other hand, creature of darkness, is always fat and sleek and well looked after. It is not holy; it is only more expensive. The *Kama Sutra* lists fifteen situations in which adultery is permissible; the fifth situation is 'when such clandestine relations are safe and a sure method of earning money'; and at the end of the list comes the warning that 'it must be distinctly understood that it (adultery) is permitted for these purposes alone and not for the satisfaction of mere lust'. This moral ambiguity is in keeping with what the *Kama Sutra*, like other Indian manuals, lays down as the duties of the cultured man: 'to engage in activities that do not endanger one's prospects in the other world, that do not entail loss of wealth and that are withal pleasant'.

In the introduction to *Tales of Ancient India*, a selection of translations from the Sanskrit, published by the University of Chicago Press in 1959, J.A.B. Van Buitenen writes:

> If I have toned down the 'spiritual', it is because sometimes one wishes to protest against the image of Indian spirituality – here as well as in India. The classical civilization was not overly spiritual. Even its skull-bearing hermits and vagrant saints had the zest to find humour in a funeral pyre. The homely Buddha of history becomes a towering pantheon of tier upon tier of beings teeming with a restless splendour that owes little to resignation. For a brief span even free will could be an issue. There was a spirit abroad that fleetingly allowed itself to be captured in a living form before it lost itself in formless spirituality. It is hard to believe that so much life would die even in a thousand years.

Caste, sanctioned by the Gita with almost propagandist fervour, might be seen as part of the older Indian pragmatism, the 'life' of classical India. It has decayed and ossified with the society, and its corollary, function, has become all: the sweeper's inefficiency and the merchant's short-sighted ruthlessness are inevitable. It is not easy to get candidates for a recently instituted award for brave children. Children do not wish their parents to know that they have risked their lives to save others. It isn't that Indians are especially cowardly or have no admiration for courage. It is that bravery, the willingness to risk one's life, is the function of the soldier and no one else. Indians have been known to go on picnicking on a river bank while a stranger drowned. Every man is an island; each man to his function, his private contract with God. This is the realization of the Gita's selfless action. This is caste. In the beginning a no doubt useful division of labour in a rural society, it has now divorced function from social obligation, position from duties. It is inefficient and destructive; it has created a psychology which will frustrate all improving plans. It has led to the Indian passion for speech-making, for gestures and for symbolic action.

Symbolic action: tree-planting week (seventy per cent of the trees planted die from lack of attention after the speeches), smallpox eradication week (one central minister is reported to have refused to be vaccinated for religious reasons, and vaccination certificates can be bought for a few shillings from various medical men), anti-fly week (declared in one state before the flies came), children's day (a correct speech by Mr Nehru about children on the front page of the newspaper and on the back page a report that free milk intended for poor children had found its way to the Calcutta open market), malaria eradication week (HELP ERADICATE MALARIA daubed, in English, on the walls of illiterate Hindi-speaking villages).

When action is so symbolic, labels are important, for things and places as well as for people. An enclosed open space, its purpose made clear by its fixtures, nevertheless carries a large board: CHILDREN'S PLAYGROUND. Another open space with a stage at one end has the sign: OPEN AIR THEATRE. The jeep that leads a state governor's cavalcade is marked in white: PILOT JEEP. New Delhi is a jumble of labels; the effect is of a civil service bazaar. Even ancient and holy buildings are disfigured. The eighth-century temple at the top of Shankaracharya Hill in Srinagar is hung at the gateway with a multi-coloured sign which would serve a haberdasher's shop. Set into the ancient stonework of one of the temples at Mahabalipuram near Madras is a plaque commemorating the minister who inaugurated the work of restoration. The Gandhi Mandap in Madras is a small colonnaded structure; carved on it are the names of the members of the committee that put the mandap up; the list is taller than a man.

The machinery of the modern state exists. The buildings exist; they are labelled; they sometimes anticipate need, and such anticipation can often be its own sufficient fulfilment. Consider the credits at the bottom of a Tourist Department leaflet: *Designed and produced by the Directorate of Advertising and Visual Publicity, Ministry of Information and Broadcasting, for the Department of Tourism, Ministry of Transport and Communications.* The structure is too perfect, too well labelled. It is not surprising that sometimes it proclaims no more than good intentions. The copies of *Family Planning News* that I saw contained little news of families that had been planned and many photographs of charming ladies in those wonderful saris, planning family planning. Traffic lights are part of the trappings of the modern city. Lucknow therefore has them; but they are only decorations, and dangerous, because ministers are required by their dignity never to halt at lights; and there are forty-six ministers in this state. The sweetshops of Gorakhpur are required to have glass cases; the cases accordingly stand, quite empty, next to the heaps of exposed sweets. There is that fine new theatre at Chandigarh; but who will write the plays?

When a crisis occurs, as during the Chinese invasion, the symbolic nature of the structure is made plain. Speeches are made and reported at length. Many gestures – the woman Minister of Health giving blood, somebody else giving jewellery – are given publicity. Various services are suspended. Then no one seems to know what to do next. Perhaps a Defence of the Realm Act? Dora, everyone calls it, adding a comforting familiarity to a correct label; and for a few days it is spoken like a magic word. The British proclaimed Dora in 1939. Now the Indian Government does the same. The British dug trenches. So they dig trenches in Delhi, but only symbolically, here and there, and dangerously, in public parks, below trees. The trenches answer the insatiable Indian need for open-air latrines. And, needless to say, supplies for the army, symbolically armed, find their way to the Calcutta open market.

*

An eastern conception of dignity and function, reposing on symbolic action: this is the dangerous, decayed pragmatism of caste. Symbolic dress, symbolic food, symbolic worship: India deals in symbols, inaction. Inaction arising out of proclaimed function, function out of caste. Untouchability is not the most important effect of the system; a Western conception of dignity alone has made it so. But at the heart of the system lies the degradation of the latrine-cleaner, and that casual defecation in a veranda which Gandhi observed in 1901.

'The moment untouchability goes the caste system will be purified.' It sounds like a piece of Gandhian and Indian double-think. It might even be interpreted as a recognition of the inevitability of caste. But it is a revolutionary assessment. Land reform does not convince the brahmin that he can put his hand to the plough without disgrace. Making awards to children for bravery does not lessen the feeling that it is unpardonable to risk one's life to save another. Reserving government jobs for untouchables helps nobody. It places responsibility in the hands of the unqualified; and the position of untouchable civil servants, whose reputations always go before them, is intolerable. It is the system that has to be regenerated, the psychology of caste that has to be destroyed. So Gandhi comes again and again to the filth and excrement of India, the dignity of latrine-cleaning; the spirit of service; bread-labour. From the West his message looks limited and cranky; but it is only that to a concerned colonial vision of India he is applying Western simplicities.

India undid him. He became a mahatma. He was to be reverenced for what he was; his message was irrelevant. He roused India to all her 'formless spirituality'; he awakened all the Indian passion for self-abasement in the presence of the virtuous, self-abasement of which the *Kama Sutra* would have approved, since it ensured a man's prospects in the other world, did not encourage him to any prolonged and difficult labour, and was withal pleasant. Symbolic action was the curse of India. Yet Gandhi was Indian enough to deal in symbols. So, latrine-cleaning became an occasional ritual, virtuous because sanctioned by the great-souled; the degradation of the latrine-cleaner continued.

The spinning-wheel did not dignify labour; it was only absorbed into the great Indian symbolism, its significance rapidly fading. He remains a tragic paradox. Indian nationalism grew out of Hindu revivalism; this revivalism, which he so largely encouraged, made his final failure certain. He succeeded politically because he was reverenced; he failed because he was reverenced. His failure is there, in his writings: he is still the best guide to India. It is as if, in England, Florence Nightingale had become a saint, honoured by statues everywhere, her name on every lip; and the hospitals had remained as she had described them.

His failure is deeper. For nothing so shakes up the Indian in order that he might be made more securely static, nothing so stultifies him and robs him of his habitual grace, as the possession of a holy man.

'Is this the train for Delhi?' I cried to a peasant group, bounding, with seconds to spare, into a compartment at Moradabad station.

'Where on earth do you think you are? Speak Hindi if you want an answer. Hindi alone here.'

This was from the head of the group. He was not a nationalist, propagating the national language. At any other time he would have been civil and even deferential. But now he was the possessor of a saffron-clad holy man, fat and sleek and oily – there is little subtlety to India – before whom the women and children of the group were abasing themselves.

It is so with Indians and Gandhi. He is the latest proof of their spirituality; he strengthens the private contract with God of all who revere him. Nothing remains of Gandhi in India but this: his name and the worship of his image; the seminars about non-violence, as though this was all he taught; prohibition, rich in symbolism and righteousness, proclaimed as a worthy goal even at the height of the China crisis; and the politician's garb.

Observe this village politician, austerely and correctly clad, speaking of the mahatma and the motherland at a country meeting.

'To get elected,' the Indian Administrative Service officer tells me, 'that man had seventeen people murdered.'

There is no inconsistency; the mahatma has been absorbed into the formless spirituality and decayed pragmatism of India. The revolutionary became a god and his message was thereby lost. He failed to communicate to India his way of direct looking. And strange: in twelve months I could find no one among his ordinary worshippers who could tell me exactly what he looked like. It was not a question to put to Indians, who have no descriptive gift, but the replies were astonishing. For some he was tiny; for one man in Madras he was six feet tall. For some he was dark; for some he was exceedingly fair. Yet all remembered him; many even had personal photographs. These did not help: the image was too familiar. So it is when legends are complete. Nothing can add to them or take away from them. The image is fixed, simplified, unalterable; witness is of no account. Nearly every word Gandhi spoke and wrote is recorded; the Gandhi bibliography is immense. But in India he has already receded; he might have lived in the days when scribes wrote on leaves and strips of brass and people travelled on foot.

# 4
# ROMANCERS

THE TITLES OF Indian films never ceased to attract me. They were straightforward, but they held infinite suggestion. *Private Secretary*: in India, where adventure of the sort implied was limited, where kisses were barred from the screen, the mind could play with such a title: the 'progressive' girl, the attractive office job (typewriter, white telephone), the mixing of the sexes; irregular love; family life threatened; tragedy. I never saw the film. I saw only the poster: a body, if I remember rightly, lay on an office floor. *Junglee* (untamed) was another title: a woman against a background of Himalayan snow. For *Maya* (cosmic illusion, vanity) a woman was shown weeping big, bitter tears. *Jhoola* (the swing) promised gaiety, many songs and dances. Then, as sinister in suggestion as *Private Secretary*, *Paying Guest*.

We were paying guests. It was in Delhi, the city of symbols, first of the British Raj and now of the independent Indian republic: a jungle of black-and-white noticeboards mushrooming out of feverish administrative activity, the Indian Council for this and Academy for that, the Ministry for this and the Department for that, the buildings going up all the time, monstrous bird's nests of bamboo scaffolding: a city ever growing, as it has been for the last forty years, a city of civil servants and contractors. We were paying guests; and our host was Mrs Mahindra, the wife of a contractor.

She sent her car to meet us at the railway station. It was an attention we were grateful for. To step out of the third-class air-conditioned coach on to the smooth hot platform was to feel one's shirt instantly heated, to lose interest, to wonder with a dying flicker of intellectual curiosity why anyone in India bothered, why anyone had bothered with India. On that platform, oven-dry, competitive activity was yet maintained. The porters, blazing in red tunics and red turbans, hustled about screeching for custom. The successful staggered beneath metal trunks sprayed with fine dust after the journey from Bombay: one trunk, two trunks, three trunks. The fans spun frenziedly above us. The beggars whined. The man from the Bhagirath Hotel waved his grubby folder. Remembering that for antarctic explorers surrender was easy and that the enduring, the going on, was the act of bravery, I reached out for the folder and, standing in the midst of noise and activity in which I had lost interest and which now seemed to swing outwards from me in waves, I read with slow concentration, in which everything was distorted and dissolving:

> *Arrive a Delhi au terme d'un equisant voyage, c'est avec le plus grand plaisir que j'ai pris le meilleur des repos au Bahgirath Hotel, dant les installations permettent de se remettre de ses fetigues dans un cadre agreable. J'ai particuliermment apprecie la gentillesse et l'hospitolite de le direction et do personnel. Je ne peploie q'ue chose, c'est de n'avoir pu arroser les excellents repos des baissens alcoolirees aux quelles nous mettent le cour en joie.*
>
> *28-7-61 Fierre Bes Georges, Gareme (Seine) France*

*Baissens alcoolirees*: yearning had glided into delirium. *Et Monsieur, qu'est-ce-qu-il peploie? Je ne peploie q'ue chose. Arrosez les excellents repos*. On the shining concrete the figures were stretched out, Indian sleepers on an Indian railway station. The unemployed porters squatted. The beggar woman, whining, even she squatted. *Arrosez les excellent repos*. But there were no fountains. The streets were wide and grand, the roundabouts endless: a city built for giants, built for its vistas, for its symmetry: a city which remained its plan, unquickened and unhumanized, built for people who would be protected from its openness, from the whiteness of its light, to whom the trees were like the trees on an architect's drawing, decorations, not intended to give shade: a city built like a monument. And everything labelled, as on an architect's drawing; every moving thing dwarfed, the man on his bicycle, with his black, black shadow; an endless, ever-spreading city which encouraged no repose, which sent people scuttling through its avenues and malls, as these scooter-rickshaws scuttled noisily in and out of the traffic, shrunk to less than human size in the presence of the monumental city.

The house was in one of the New Delhi 'colonies' or residential settlements, abrupt huddles of fantasy and riotous modern lines after the exposed austerity of the centre. It was as though an Indian village had been transformed into concrete and glass, and magnified. The houses were not yet coherently numbered; and the narrow nameless lanes were full of bewildered Sikhs seeking houses by plot numbers, whose sequence was chronological, indicating date of purchase. Dust; concrete white and grey; no trees; each Sikh attached to a brisk, black shadow.

We sat in front of an empty, unsmoked fireplace below an electric fan and rested with glasses of Coca-Cola.

'Duffer, that Bihari boy,' Mrs Mahindra said, apologizing for her chauffeur and making conversation.

She was plump, still young, with large staring eyes. She had little English, and when words failed her she gave a giggle and looked away. She said *Mm*, her eyes became vacant, and her right hand went to her chin.

The house was new and on this ground floor smelled of concrete and paint. The rooms were not yet fully decorated; the furnishings were sparse. But there were fans everywhere; and the bathroom fittings, from Germany, were rare and expensive. 'I am craze for foreign,' Mrs Mahindra said. 'Just craze for foreign.'

She marvelled at our suitcases and at what they contained. She fingered with reverence and delight.

'Craze, just craze for foreign.'

Widening her eyes, it might have been in fear, it might have been in admiration, she told us of her husband, the contractor. He had a hard life. He was always travelling about in forests and jungles and living in tents. She had to stay behind and do the housekeeping.

'Three thousand rupees a month allowance. These days cost-of-living that-is-no-joke.'

She was not really boasting. She came from a simple family and she accepted her new wealth as she would have accepted poverty. She was anxious to learn, anxious to do the correct thing, anxious for our foreign approval. Did we like the colours of her curtains? The colours of her walls? Look, that lamp bracket there was foreign, from Japan. There wasn't a thing which was not foreign except, as she confessed when we went up to her dining-room for lunch, for this brass dish-warmer.

She sat with us, not eating, staring at our plates, hand supporting her chin, widening her eyes dreamily and smiling whenever our glances met. She was new to the business, she said with a giggle. She had not had any paying guests before, and so we must forgive her if she treated us like her children.

Her sons arrived. They were in their teens, tall, and as cool towards us as their mother was demonstrative. They joined us at the table. Mrs Mahindra spooned out from the dishes into their plates, spooned out into our plates.

Suddenly she giggled and nodded towards her elder son.

'I want him to marry foreign.'

The boy didn't react.

We talked about the weather and the heat.

'The heat doesn't affect us,' the boy said. 'Our bedrooms are air-conditioned.'

Mrs Mahindra caught our eyes and gave a mischievous smile.

She insisted on taking us out with her that afternoon to do a little shopping. She wanted to buy curtains for one of the downstairs rooms. But, we said, the curtains she had shown us in that room were brand new and very elegant. No, no, she said; we were only being polite. She wanted to buy new curtains that afternoon and she wanted our foreign advice.

So we drove back into the centre. She pointed out the monuments: Humayun's Tomb, India Gate, Rashtrapati Bhavan.

'New Delhi, New Delhi,' she sighed. '*Capital* of India.'

We went from shop to shop, and I began to fade. Fading, I relapsed into mechanical speech. 'Look,' I said to the boy, pointing to a heap of slippers that were extravagantly of the orient, their tapering embroidered points curling back on themselves. 'Look, those are rather amusing.'

'They are too common for us.'

His mother was known to the shop assistants. She engaged them all in friendly conversation. They offered her chairs. She sat; she fingered; she talked. Bolt after bolt was unwrapped for her. Blandly she watched and blandly she walked away. Her movements were easy; no one appeared to be offended. She knew what she wanted, and at last she found it.

She asked us to study the fireplace that evening. It was of irregular shape and had been designed by her husband, who had also designed the irregular recesses, for electric lights, in the stone fence.

'Modern. Modern. *All* modern.'

In the morning the painters came to repaint the newly painted unused room to match the curtains that had been bought the previous afternoon.

She came into our room as we lay stripped below the ceiling fan after breakfast. She sat on the edge of the bed and talked. She examined this stocking, that shoe, that brassière; she asked prices. She lured us out to watch the painters at work; she held the material against the paint and asked whether they went well together.

She had nothing to do except to spend three thousand rupees a month. She had one especial friend. 'Mrs M. *Mehta. Secretary.* Women's *League*. Mrs M. Mehta. Air-conditioners and other electrical gadgets.' The name and the words were familiar from advertisements. Regularly Mrs Mahindra visited Mrs M. Mehta; regularly she consulted her astrologer; regularly she shopped and went to the temple. Her life was full and sweet.

A tall man of about fifty came to the house in the afternoon. He said he was answering an advertisement in the newspaper; he wished to lease the ground floor which we were occupying. He wore a double-breasted grey suit and spoke English with a strained army accent.

'Mm.' Mrs Mahindra looked away.

The man in the grey suit continued to speak in English. He represented a large firm, he said. A firm with foreign connexions.

'Mm.' Her eyes became vacant; her palm went to her chin.

'No one will sleep here.' He was faltering a little; perhaps it had occurred to him that his firm was not as desirable as the 'diplomatic' foreigners so many advertisements solicited. 'We will give you a year's rent in advance and sign a lease for three years.'

'Mm.' She said, replying in Hindustani to his English, that she would have to talk to her husband. And then there were so many other people who were interested.

'We intend to use the premises just as offices.' His dignity was beginning to yield to a certain exasperation. 'And all we would like is for a caretaker to sleep here at night. The house will remain as your home. We will give you twelve thousand rupees right away.'

She stared in her abstracted way, as though sniffing the new paint and thinking about the curtains.

'Duffer,' she said when he had gone. 'Talking English. *Barra sahib*. Duffer.'

The next morning she was glum.

'*Letter*. My husband's *father* is coming. Today. Tomorrow.' The prospect clearly depressed her. 'Talk, talk, that-is-no-joke.'

When we came back to the house that afternoon we found her sitting, sad and dutiful, with a white-haired man in Indian dress. She already seemed to have shrunk a little; she looked chastened, even embarrassed. It was our foreignness she stressed when she introduced us. Then she looked away, became abstracted and took no further part in the conversation.

The white-haired man looked us over suspiciously. But he was, as Mrs Mahindra had hinted, a talker; and he regarded himself and especially his age, which was just over sixty, with wonder. It was not his adventures he spoke of so much as the habits he had formed in those sixty years. He rose at four every morning, he said; he went for a four- or five-mile walk; then he read some chapters of the Gita. He had followed this routine for forty years, and it was a routine he would recommend to any young man.

Mrs Mahindra sighed. I felt she had taken a lot already and I thought I would release her. I tried to get the old man to talk of his past to me. He had no adventures to relate; he just had a list of places he had lived in or worked in. I asked precise questions; I made him describe landscapes. But Mrs Mahindra, not understanding my purpose, not accepting – or perhaps by duty not able to accept – the release I offered, sat and suffered. In the end it was the old man whom I drove away. He went and sat by himself in the small front garden.

'Naughty, naughty,' Mrs Mahindra said, giving me a smile of pure exhaustion.

'Summer is here,' the old man said after dinner. 'I have been sleeping out in the open for a fortnight. I always find that I begin to sleep out in the open a few weeks before other people.'

'Will you be sleeping out in the open tonight?' I asked.

'Of course.'

He slept just outside the door. We could see him, and no doubt he could see us. At four – so it was reasonable to assume – we heard him rise and get ready for his walk: lavatory chain, gargling, clattering, doors. We heard him return. And when we got up we found him reading the Gita.

'I always read a few pages of the Gita after I come back from my walk,' he said.

After that he idled about the house. He had nothing to do. It was difficult to ignore him; he required to be spoken to. He talked, but I began to feel that he also monitored.

We returned in the afternoon to a painful scene: the interviewing of another applicant for the ground floor. The applicant was uneasy; the old man, who was putting the questions, was polite but reproving; and the object of his reproof, I felt, was Mrs Mahindra, whose face was almost hidden in the top end of her sari.

We lost some of Mrs Mahindra's attentions. In no time at all she had dwindled into the Indian daughter-in-law. We heard little now of her craze for foreign. We had become liabilities. And when, attending to her father-in-law's conversation, she caught our eyes, her smile was tired. It held no conspiracy, only dutiful withdrawal. We had found her, on that first day, in a brief moment of sparkle.

We had to go to the country that week-end, and it was with a feeling almost of betrayal that we told her we were going to leave her alone with her father-in-law for a few days. She brightened at the news; she became active. We must just go, she said, and not worry about a thing. We didn't have to pack everything away; she would look after our room. She helped us to get ready. She gave us a meal and stood in the irregularly pointed stone gateway and waved while the Bihari chauffeur, duffer as we remembered, drove us off. Plump, saddened, wide-eyed Mrs Mahindra!

A week-end in the country! The words suggest cool clumps of trees, green fields, streams. Our thoughts were all of water as we left Delhi. But there was no water and little shade. The road was a narrow metal strip between two lanes of pure dust. Dust powdered the roadside trees and the fields. Once we drove for miles over a flat brown wasteland. At the end of the journey lay a town, and a communal killing. The Muslim murderer had fled; the dead Hindu had to be mourned and cremated in swift secrecy before daybreak; and afterwards troublemakers of both sides had to be watched. This occupied our host for almost all the week-end. We remained in the inspection house, grateful for the high ceiling, below the spinning fan. On one wall there was a framed typewritten digest of rules and regulations. Set into another wall was a fireplace. The winters it promised seemed so unlikely now; and it was as though one was forever doomed to be in places at the wrong time, as though one was forever feeling one's way through places where every label was false: the confectionery machine on the railway platform that hadn't worked for years, the advertisement for something that was no longer made, the timetable which was out of date. Above the mantelpiece there was a photograph of a tree standing on eroded earth beside a meagre stream; and in that photograph, in its message of exhaustion and persistence, there was something which already we could recognize as of India.

We returned to Delhi by train below a darkening sky. We waited for the storm to break. But what looked like raincloud was only dust. The tea-boy cheated us (and on this run several months later that same boy was to cheat us again); a passenger complained of corruption; one story excited another. And the wind blew and the dust penetrated everywhere, dust which, the engineers tell us, can get in where water can't. We longed for the town, for hot baths and air-conditioning and shuttered rooms.

The lower floor of the Mahindras' house was in darkness. The door was locked. We had no key. We rang, and rang. After some minutes a whispering, tiptoeing servant let us in as though we were his private friends. Everything in our room was as we had left it. The bed was unmade; the suitcases hadn't been moved; letters and leaflets and full ashtrays were on the bedside table; dust had settled on the static disarray. We were aware of muted activity upstairs, in the room with the Indian brass dish-warmer.

The sahib, the servant said, had returned from the jungle. And the sahib had quarrelled with the memsahib. 'He say, "You take *paying* guests? You take *money*?"'

We understood. We were Mrs Mahindra's first and last paying guests. We had been part of her idleness, perhaps like those men who had called to lease the ground floor. Perhaps Mrs M. Mehta, secretary of the Women's League, leased her ground floor; perhaps Mrs M. Mehta had a dazzling succession of foreign paying guests.

Dear Mrs Mahindra! She enjoyed her money and no doubt in her excitement had wished to make a little more. But her attentions had been touched with the genuine Indian warmth. We never saw her again; we never saw her sons again; we never saw her husband. Her father-in-law we only heard as, lurking in our room, we waited for him to settle down for the night. We heard him rise in the morning; we heard him leave for his walk. We gave him a few minutes. Then we crept out with our suitcases and roused one of the sleeping taxi-drivers in the taxi-rank not far off. Through a friend we later sent the money we owed.

*

The days in Delhi had been a blur of heat. The moments that stayed were those of retreat: darkened bedrooms, lunches, shuttered clubs, a dawn drive to the ruins of Tughlakabad, a vision of the Flame of the Forest. Sightseeing was not easy. Bare feet were required in too many places. The entrances to temples were wet and muddy and the courtyards of mosques were more scorching than tropical beaches in mid-afternoon. At every mosque and temple there were idlers waiting to pounce on those who did not take off their shoes. Their delight and their idleness infuriated me. So did one notice: 'If you think it is beneath your dignity to take off your shoes, slippers are provided.' At Rajghat, faced with an unnecessarily long walk over hot sand to the site of Gandhi's cremation, I refused to follow the Tourist Department's guide and sat, a fully shod heretic, in the shade. Blue-shirted schoolboys waited for the Americans among the tourists. The boys were well fed and well shod and carried their schoolbooks like emblems of their worthiness. They ran to the old ladies. The ladies, informed of India's poverty, stopped, opened their purses and smilingly distributed coins and notes, while from the road the professional beggars, denied entrance, watched enviously. The heat was unhinging me. I advanced towards the schoolboys, simple murder in my heart. They ran away, nimble in the heat. The Americans looked assessingly at me: the proud young Indian nationalist. Well, it would do. I walked back to the coach, converting exhaustion into anger and shame.

So it had been in Delhi. I was shouting now almost as soon as I entered government offices. At times the sight of rows of young men sitting at long tables, buried among sheaves of paper, young men checking slips of one sort or another, young men counting banknotes and tying them into bundles of a hundred, all India's human futility, was more than I could bear. 'Don't complain to me. Make your complaint through proper channel.' 'Through proper channel! Proper channel!' But it was hopeless; irony, mockery, was impossible in India. And: 'Don't complain to me. Complain to my officer.' 'Which is your bloody officer?' All this with a liberating sense that my violent mood was inviting violence. Yet so often it was met only with a cold, puncturing courtesy; and I was reduced to stillness, shame and exhaustion.

In Lutyens's city I required privacy and protection. Only then was I released from the delirium of seeing certain aspects of myself magnified out of recognition. I could sense the elegance of the city, in those colonnades hidden by signboards and straw blinds, in those vistas: the new tower at one end of the tree-lined avenue, the old dome at the other. I could sense the 'studious' atmosphere of which people had spoken in Bombay. I could sense its excitement as a new capital city, in the gatherings at the Gymkhana Club on a Sunday morning, the proconsular talk about the abominations of the Congo from former United Nations officials, in the announcements in the newspapers of 'cultural' entertainments provided by the embassies of competing governments: a city to which importance had newly come, and all the new toys of the 'diplomatic'. But to me it was a city in which I could only escape from one darkened room to another, separate from the reality of out of doors, of dust and light and low-caste women in gorgeous saris – gorgeousness in saris being emblematic of lowness – working on building sites. A city doubly unreal, rising suddenly out of the plain: acres of seventeenth- and eighteenth-century ruins, then the ultra-contemporary exhibition buildings; a city whose emblematic grandeur spoke of a rich and settled hinterland and not of the poor, parched land through which we had been travelling for twenty-four hours.

Yet that evening, lying in my bunk in the aluminium coach of the Srinagar Express and waiting for the train to leave, I found that I had begun to take a perverse delight in the violence of it all: delight at the thought of the twenty-four-hour journey that had brought me to Delhi, the thirty-six-hour journey still farther north that awaited me, through all the flatness of the Punjab to the mightiest mountain range in the world; delight at the physical area of luxury I had managed to reserve for myself, the separation from the unpleasant which I was yet, through the easily operated rubber-beaded windows, able to see: the red-turbanned porters, the trolleys of books and magazines, the hawkers, the frenzied fans hanging low so that from my bunk the platform appeared to be ceilinged by spinning blades: once hated symbols of discomfort, now answering all my urgency and exaltation which, fraudulent though I knew it to be, I was already fearing to lose, for with a twenty-degree drop in temperature all would subside to ordinariness.

The Punjab, intermittently glanced at during the night, was silent and featureless except for the moving oblongs of light from our train. A still hut, blacker against the flat black fields awaiting the day-long sun: what more had I expected? In the morning we were at Pathankot, the railhead – and how strange again and again to hear this solitary English word, to me so technical, industrial and dramatic, in a whole sentence of Hindustani – the railhead for Kashmir. It was cool at the station in the early morning; there was a hint of bush and, deceptive though it was, of mountains close at hand. And our passengers appeared in woollen shirts, sporty hats, jackets, cardigans, pullovers and even gloves, the woollen garments of the Indian summer holidays, not yet strictly needed, but an anticipation of the holiday that had almost begun.

At first it was only the army of whose presence we were aware on this flat scrub near the Pakistan border: signposted camps, all whitewash and straight lines, the rows of lorries and jeeps, the occasional manoeuvres of light tanks. These men in olive-green battledress and bush-hats might have belonged to another country. They walked differently; they were handsome. We stopped at Jammu for lunch. Thereafter we climbed, entering Kashmir by the road built by the Indian army in 1947 at the time of the Pakistan invasion. It grew cooler; there were hills and gorges and a broken view, hill beyond hill, receding planes of diminishing colour. We drove beside the Chenab River which, as we climbed, fell beneath us into a gorge, littered with logs.

'And where do you come from?'

It was the Indian question. I had been answering it five times a day. And now again I went through the explanations.

He was sitting across the aisle from me. He was respectably dressed in a suit. He was bald, with a sharp Gujerati nose, and he looked bitter.

'And what do you think of our great country?'

It was another Indian question; and the sarcasm had to be dismissed.

'Be frank. Tell me exactly what you think.'

'It's all right. It's very interesting.'

'Interesting. You are lucky. You should live here. We are trapped here, you know. That's what we are. Trapped.'

Beside him sat his plump, fulfilled wife. She was less interested in our conversation than in me. She studied me whenever I looked away.

'Corruption and nepotism everywhere,' he said. 'Everybody wanting to get out to United Nations jobs. Doctors going abroad. Scientists going to America. The future is totally black. How much, for instance, do you earn in your country?'

'About five thousand rupees a month.'

It was unfair to strike so hard. But he took it well.

'And what do you do for this?' he asked.

'I teach.'

'What do you teach?'

'History.'

He was unimpressed.

I added, 'And a little chemistry.'

'Strange combination. I'm a chemistry teacher myself.'

It happens to every romancer.

I said, 'I teach in a comprehensive school. You have to do a little of everything.'

'I see.' Annoyance was peeping out of his puzzlement; his nose seemed to twitch. 'Strange combination. Chemistry.'

I was worried. Several hours of our journey together still remained. I pretended to be annoyed by a crying child. This couldn't go on. But relief soon came. We stopped among pines in a lay-by above a green wooded valley. We got out to stretch our legs. It was cool. The plains had become like an illness whose exact sensations it is impossible, after recovery, to recall. The woollens were now of service. The holiday had begun to fulfil itself. And when we got back into the bus I found that the chemistry teacher had changed seats with his wife, so that he would not have to continue talking to me.

It was night, clear and cold, when we stopped at Banihal. The rest-house was in darkness; the electric lights had gone. The attendants fussed around with candles; they prepared meals. In the moonlight the terraced rice fields were like leaded panes of old glass. In the morning their character had changed. They were green and muddy. After the Banihal tunnel we began to go down and down, past fairy-tale villages set in willow groves, watered by rivulets with grassy banks, into the Vale of Kashmir.

*

Kashmir was coolness and colour: the yellow mustard fields, the mountains, snow-capped, the milky blue sky in which we rediscovered the drama of clouds. It was men wrapped in brown blankets against the morning mist, and barefooted shepherd boys with caps and covered ears on steep wet rocky slopes. At Qazigund, where we stopped, it was also dust in sunlight, the disorder of a bazaar, a waiting crowd, and a smell in the cold air of charcoal, tobacco, cooking oil, months-old dirt and human excrement. Grass grew on the mud-packed roofs of cottages – and at last it was clear why, in that story I had read as a child in the *West Indian Reader*, the foolish widow had made her cow climb up to the roof. Buses packed with men with red-dyed beards were going in the direction from which we had come. Another bus came in, halted. The crowd broke, ran forward and pressed in frenzy around a window through which a man with tired eyes held out his thin hand in benediction. He, like the others, was going to Mecca; and among these imprisoning mountains how far away Jeddah seemed, that Arabian pilgrim port dangerous with reefs over which the blue water grows turquoise. In smoky kitchen shacks Sikhs with ferocious beards and light eyes, warriors and rulers of an age not long past, sat and cooked. Each foodstall carried an attractive signboard. The heavy white cups were chipped; the tables, out in the open, were covered with oil-cloth in checked patterns; below them the ground had been softened to mud.

The mountains receded. The valley widened into soft, well-watered fields. The road was lined with poplars and willows drooped on the banks of clear rivulets. Abruptly, at Awantipur, out of a fairy-tale village of sagging wood-framed cottages there rose ruins of grey stone, whose heavy trabeate construction – solid square pillars on a portico, steep stone pediments on a colonnade around a central shrine, massive and clumsy in ruin – caused the mind to go back centuries to ancient worship. They were Hindu ruins, of the eighth century, as we discovered later. But none of the passengers exclaimed, none pointed. They lived among ruins; the Indian earth was rich with ancient sculpture. At Pandrethan, on the outskirts of Srinagar, the army camp was set about a smaller temple in a similar style. The soldiers were exercising. Army lorries and huts lay in neat rows; on the roadside there were army boards and divisional emblems.

We stopped at the octroi post, quaint medievalism, in a jam of Tata-Mercedes-Benz lorries, their tailboards decorated with flowered designs and *Horn Please* in fanciful lettering on a ground of ochre or pink. On the raised floors of shops blanket-wrapped men smoked hookahs. Skirting the town, we came to an avenue lined with giant chenar trees, whose sweet shade the Kashmiris believe to be medicinal, and turned into the yard of the Tourist Reception Centre, a new building in pale red brick. Across the road a large hoarding carried a picture of Mr Nehru, with his urging that the foreign visitor should be treated as a friend. Directly below the hoardings the Kashmiris were shouting already, with pure hostility it seemed, barely restrained by the swagger sticks of elegant turbanned policemen.

Among the shouters were the owners of houseboats or the servants of owners. It seemed scarcely conceivable that they owned anything or had anything worthwhile to offer. But the houseboats existed. They lay on the lake in a white row against floating green islands, answering the snow on the surrounding mountains. At intervals concrete steps led down from the lake boulevard to the crystal water. On the steps men sat and squatted and smoked hookahs; their *shikara* boats were a cluster of red and orange awnings and cushions; and in *shikaras* we were ferried over to the houseboats, where, mooring, and going up dainty steps, we found interiors beyond anything we had imagined: carpets and brassware and framed pictures, china and panelling and polished furniture of another age. And at once Awantipur and the rest disappeared. For here was English India. Here, offered for our inspection, were the chits, the faded recommendations of scores of years. Here were invitations to the weddings of English army officers, now perhaps grandfathers. And the houseboat man, so negligible at the Tourist Centre, so negligible as he pedalled behind our tonga, pleading with tears that we should visit his boat, himself altered: kicking off his shoes, dropping to his knees on the carpet, his manners became as delicate as the china – so rare now in India – in which he offered us tea. Here were more photographs, of his father and his father's guests; here were more recommendations; here were tales of enormous English meals.

Outside, the snow-capped mountains ringed the lake, at whose centre stood Akbar's fort of Hari Parbat; poplars marked the lake-town of Rainawari; and far away, beyond an open stretch of water, on the fresh green lower slopes of the mountains – as though the earth had been washed down through the ages to fill the crevices of rocks – were the Mogul Gardens, with their terraces, their straight lines, their central pavilions, their water-courses dropping from level to level down rippled concrete falls. The Mogul one could accept, and the Hindu. It was this English presence which, though the best known, from books and songs and those pale hands beside the Shalimar – not a stream as in my imagining, but the grandest of the gardens – it was this English presence which seemed hardest to accept, in this mountain-locked valley, this city of hookahs and samavars (so pronounced) where, in a dusty square on Residency Road, was the caravanserai for Tibetans with their long-legged boots, hats, plaited hair, their clothes as grimy-grey as their weather-beaten faces, men indistinguishable from women.

But we did not take a houseboat. Their relics were still too movingly personal. Their romance was not mine, and it was impossible to separate them from their romance. I would have felt an intruder, as I felt in those district clubs where the billiard rooms were still hung with framed cartoons of the 1930s, where the libraries had gone derelict, the taste of a generation frozen, and where on the smoking-room walls were stained engravings, difficult to see through the reflections on the dusty glass, of tumultuous horsemen labelled 'Afridis' or 'Baluchis'. Indians could walk among these relics with ease; the romance had always been partly theirs and now they had inherited it fully. I was not English or Indian; I was denied the victories of both.

# PART TWO

# 5
# A DOLL'S HOUSE ON THE DAL LAKE

HOTEL LIWARD
Prop: FLUSH SYSTEM M.S. Butt

THE SIGN CAME later, almost at the end of our stay. 'I am honest man,' the owner of the C-class houseboat had said, as we stood before the white bucket in one of the mildewed and tainted rooms of his rotting hulk. 'And flush system, this is not *honest*.' But Mr Butt, showing us his still small sheaf of recommendations in the sitting-room of the Liward Hotel, and pointing to the group of photographs on the pea-green walls, had said with a different emphasis, '*Before* flush.' We looked at the laughing faces. At least a similar betrayal could not be ours. The sign, dispelling conjecture, was placed high on the pitched roof and lit by three bulbs, and could be seen even from Shankaracharya Hill.

It seemed an unlikely amenity. The hotel stood in the lake, at one end of a plot of ground about eighty feet long by thirty wide. It was a rough two-storeyed structure with ochre concrete walls, green and chocolate woodwork, and a roof of unpainted corrugated iron. It had seven rooms altogether, one of which was the dining-room. It was in reality two buildings. One stood squarely in the angle of the plot, two walls flush with the water; it had two rooms up and two rooms down. A narrow wooden gallery went right around the top floor; around two sides of the lower floor, and hanging directly above the water, there was another gallery. The other building had one room down and two up, the second of which was a many-sided semi-circular wooden projection supported on wooden poles. A wooden staircase led to the corridor that linked the two buildings; and the whole structure was capped by a pitched corrugated-iron roof of complex angular design.

It had a rough-and-ready air, which was supported by our first glimpse of Mr Butt, cautiously approaching the landing stage to welcome us. He wore the Kashmiri fur cap, an abbreviation of the Russian. His long-tailed Indian-style shirt hung out of his loose trousers and dangled below his brown jacket. This suggested unreliability; the thick frames of his spectacles suggested abstraction; and he held a hammer in one hand. Beside him was a very small man, bare-footed, with a dingy grey pullover tight above flapping white cotton trousers gathered in at the waist by a string. A touch of quaintness, something of the Shakespearean mechanic, was given him by his sagging woollen nightcap. So misleading can first impressions be: this was Aziz. And flush was not yet finally installed. Pipes and bowls had been laid, but cisterns were yet to be unwrapped.

'One day,' Aziz said in English. 'Two days.'

'I like flush,' Mr Butt said.

We read the recommendations. Two Americans had been exceedingly warm; an Indian lady had praised the hotel for providing the 'secrecy' needed by honeymoon couples.

'*Before* flush,' Mr Butt said.

With this his English was virtually exhausted, and thereafter we dealt with him through Aziz.

We bargained. Fear made me passionate; it also, I realized later, made me unnaturally convincing. My annoyance was real; when I turned to walk away I was really walking away; when I was prevailed upon to return – easy, since the boatman refused to ferry me back to the road – my fatigue was genuine. So we agreed. I was to take the room next to the semi-circular sitting-room, of which I was also to have exclusive use. And I needed a reading lamp.

'Ten-twelve rupees, what is that?' Aziz said.

And, I would need a writing-table.

He showed me a low stool.

With my hands I sketched out my larger requirements.

He showed me an old weathered table lying out on the lawn.

'We paint,' he said.

I rocked the table with a finger.

Aziz sketched out two timber braces and Mr Butt, understanding and smiling, lifted his hammer.

'We fix,' Aziz said.

It was then that I felt they were playing and that I had become part of their play. We were in the middle of the lake. Beyond the alert kingfishers, the fantastic hoopoes pecking in the garden, beyond the reeds and willows and poplars, our view unbroken by houseboats, there were the snow-capped mountains. Before me a nightcapped man, hopping about restlessly, and at the end of the garden a new wooden shed, his home, unpainted and warm against the gloom of low-hanging willows. He was a man skilled in his own way with hammer and other implements, anxious to please, magically improvising, providing everything. The nightcap did not belong to a Shakespearean mechanic; it had a fairy-tale, Rumpelstiltskin, Snow White-and-the-seven-dwarfs air.

'You pay advance and you sign agreement for three months.'

Even this did not break the spell. Mr Butt wrote no English. Aziz was illiterate. I had to make out my own receipt. I had to write and sign our agreement in the back of a large, serious-looking but erratically filled ledger which lay on a dusty shelf in the dining-room.

'You write three months?' Aziz asked.

I hadn't. I was playing safe. But how had he guessed?

'You write three months.'

The day before we were to move in we paid a surprise visit. Nothing appeared to have changed. Mr Butt waited at the landing-stage, dressed as before and as seemingly abstracted. The table that was to have been painted and braced remained unpainted and unbraced on the lawn. There was no sign of a reading lamp. 'Second coat,' Aziz had said, placing his hand on the partition that divided bathroom from bedroom. But no second coat had been given, and the bright blue paint lay as thin and as scabrous on the new, knot-darkened wood. Dutifully, not saying a word, Mr Butt examined with us, stopping when we stopped, looking where we looked, as though he wasn't sure what, in spite of his knowledge, he might find. The bathroom was as we had left it: the lavatory bowl in position, still in its gummed paper taping, the pipes laid, the cistern absent.

'Finish,' I said. 'Finish. Give back deposit. We go. No stay here.'

He made no reply and we went down the steps. Then across the garden, from the warm wooden shack, embowered in willows, Aziz came tripping, nightcapped and pullovered. Blue paint spotted his pullover – a new skill revealed – and there was a large spot on the tip of his nose. He was carrying, as if about to offer it to us, a lavatory cistern.

'Two minutes,' he said. 'Three minutes. I fix.'

One of Snow White's own men in a woollen nightcap: it was impossible to abandon him.

Three days later we moved in. And it had all been done. It was as if all the folk at the bottom of the garden had lent a hand with broom and brush and saw and hammer. The table had been massively braced and tremendously nailed together; it was covered with an already peeling skin of bright blue paint. A large bulb, fringed at the top with a small semi-spherical metal shade, was attached to a stunted flexible arm which rested on a chromium-plated disc and was linked by incalculable tangled yards of flex – I had specified length and manoeuvrability – to the electric point: this was the lamp. In the bathroom the lavatory cistern had been put in place. Aziz, like a magician, pulled the chain; and the flush flushed.

'Mr Butt he say,' Aziz said, when the waters subsided, 'this is not his hotel. This is *your* hotel.'

*

There were others beside Aziz and Mr Butt. There was the sweeper boy in flopping garments of requisite filth. There was Ali Mohammed. He was a small man of about forty with a cadaverous face made still more so by ill-fitting dentures. His duty was to entice tourists to the hotel, and his official dress consisted of a striped blue Indian-style suit of loose trousers and lapel-less jacket, shoes, a Kashmiri fur cap and a silver watch and chain. So twice a day he came out of the hut at the bottom of the garden and, standing with his bicycle in the *shikara*, was paddled past the tailor's one-roomed wooden shack, high and crooked above the water, past the poplars and the willows, past the houseboats, past Nehru Park, to the *ghat* and the lake boulevard, to cycle to the Tourist Reception Centre and stand in the shade of chenars outside the entrance, with the tonga-wallahs, houseboat-owners or their agents, below the hoarding with Mr Nehru's portrait. And there was the *khansamah*, the cook. He was older than Aziz or Ali Mohammed, and more nobly built. He was a small man, but he was given height by the rightness of his proportions, his carriage, his long-tailed shirt and the loose trousers that tapered down to his well-made feet. He was a brooder. His regular features were tormented by nervousness and irritability. He often came out of the kitchen and stood for minutes on the veranda of the hut, gazing at the lake, his bare feet beating the floorboards.

Our first meal was all ritual. The concrete floor of the dining-room had been spread with old matting; and on the table two small plastic buckets sprouted long-stemmed red, blue, green and yellow plastic daisies. 'Mr Butt he buy,' Aziz said. 'Six rupees.' He went out for the soup; and presently we saw him and Ali Mohammed, each holding a plate of soup, coming out of the hut and walking carefully, concentrating on the soup, down the garden path.

'Hot box coming next week,' Aziz said.

'Hot box?'

'*Next* week.' His voice was low; he was like a sweet-tempered nurse humouring a spoilt and irascible infant. He took a napkin off his shoulder and flicked away tiny flies. 'This is *nothing*. Get little hot, little flies dead. Big flies come chase little flies. Then mosquito come bite big flies and *they* go away.'

And we believed him. He withdrew and stood outside below the projecting sitting-room; and almost immediately we heard him shouting to the kitchen or to some passing lake-dweller in a voice that was entirely altered. Through the windows at our back we had a view of reeds, mountains, snow and sky; before us from time to time we had a glimpse of Aziz's night-capped head as he peered through the as yet glassless window-frame. We were in the middle of the unknown, but on our little island we were in good hands; we were being looked after; no harm could come to us; and with every dish that came out of the hut at the end of the garden our sense of security grew.

Aziz, his delight matching ours, shouted for the *khansamah*. It seemed an impertinent thing to do. A grumble, a silence, a delay showed that it was so taken. When at last the *khansamah* appeared he was without his apron; he was nervous and bashful. What would we like for dinner? What would we like for dinner? 'You want scones for tea? And pudding, what you want for pudding? Tipsy pudding? Trifle? Apple tart?'

Snow White had gone, but her imparted skills remained.

*

It was only early spring, and on some mornings there was fresh snow on the mountains. The lake was cold and clear; you could see the fish feeding like land animals on the weeds and on the lake bed, and when the sun came out every fish cast a shadow. It could be hot then, with the sun out, and woollen clothes were uncomfortable. But heat presently led to rain, and then the temperature dropped sharply. The clouds fell low over the mountains, sometimes in a level bank, sometimes shredding far into the valleys. The temple at the top of Shankaracharya Hill, one thousand feet above us, was hidden; we would think of the lonely brahmin up there, with his woollen cap and his small charcoal brazier below his pinky-brown blanket. When the wind blew across the lake the young reeds swayed; on the rippled water reflections were abolished; the magenta discs of the lotus curled upwards; and all the craft on the lake made for shelter. Some pulled in at the hotel landing-stage; occasionally their occupants went to the hut to get charcoal for their hookahs or for the mud-lined wicker braziers which they kept below their blankets. And immediately after rain the lake was as glassy as could be.

The hotel stood on one of the main *shikara* lanes, the silent highways of the lake. The tourist season had not properly begun and about us there still flowed only the life of the lake. In the morning the flotilla of grass-laden *shikaras* passed, paddled by women sitting cross-legged at the stern, almost level with the water. The marketplace shifted, according to custom, from day to day. Now it was directly in front of the hotel, beyond the lotus patch; now it was farther down the lane, beside the old boat that was the pettiest of petty lake shops. Often it seemed that buyer and seller would come to blows; but the threatening gestures, the raised voices, the paddling away, abuse hurled over the shoulder, the turning back, abuse continuing, all this was only the lake method of bargaining. All day the traffic continued. The cheese man, priest-like in white, sat before white conical mounds of cheese and rang his bell, he and his cheese sheltered by an awning, his paddler exposed at the stern. The milk-lady was fearfully jewelled; silver earrings hung from her distended lobes like keys from a key-ring. The confectioner's goods were contained in a single red box. The 'Bread Bun & Butter' man called every day at the hotel; on his *shikara* board *N* was written back to front. 'Beau-ti-ful! Mar-vellous! Lover-ly!' This was the cry of Bulbul, the flower-seller. His roses sweetened our room for a week; his sweet-peas collapsed the day they were bought. He suggested salt; his sweet-peas collapsed again; we quarrelled. But his *shikara* continued to be a moving bank of bewitching colour in the early mornings, until the season was advanced and he left us to work the more profitable A-class houseboats on Nagin Lake. The police *shikara* passed often, the sergeant paddled by constables. In the post office *shikara*, painted red, the clerk sat cross-legged at a low desk, selling stamps, cancelling letters and ringing his bell. Every tradesman had his paddler; and the paddler might be a child of seven or eight. It did not look especially cruel. Here children were, as they have until recently been elsewhere, miniature adults in dress, skills and appearance. Late at night we would hear them singing to keep their spirits up as they paddled home.

So quickly we discovered that in spite of its unkempt lushness, its tottering buildings and the makeshift instincts of its inhabitants, the lake was charted and regulated; that there were divisions of labour as on land; and that divisions of water space were to be recognized even if marked by no more than a bent and sagging length of wire. There were men of power, with areas of influence; there were regional elected courts. And such regulations were necessary because the lake was full of people and the lake was rich. It provided for all. It provided weeds and mud for vegetable plots. A boy twirled his bent pole in the water, lifted, and he had a bundle of rich, dripping lake weed. It provided fodder for animals. It provided reeds for thatching. It provided fish, so numerous in the clear water that they could be seen just below the steps of the busy *ghat*. On some days the lake was dotted with fishermen who seemed to be walking on water: they stood erect and still on the edge of their barely moving *shikaras*, their tridents raised, their eyes as sharp as those of the kingfishers on the willows.

*

The hot box, promised by Aziz, came. It was a large wooden crate, grey with age and exposure. It occupied one corner of the dining-room, standing on its end at a slight angle on the uneven concrete floor. It was lined on the inside with the flattened metal of various tins, one side was hinged to make a door, and it was fitted with shelves. At mealtimes a charcoal brazier stood at the bottom. So the soup no longer came in steaming plates from the kitchen; and every morning we found Ali Mohammed squatting before the brazier, his back to us, utterly absorbed, turning over slices of bread with his fingers. A dedicated toastmaker he appeared, but he was in reality listening to the fifteen-minute programme of Kashmiri devotional songs that followed the news in English on Radio Kashmir. In the curve of his back there could be sensed a small but distinct anxiety: the toast might be required too soon, we might turn to another station, or he might be called away to other duties. Already at this time he was in his official suit; and I doubt whether, if otherwise dressed, he would have turned abruptly from his toast one morning and asked, 'You want see Kashmiri dancing girl?' His top dentures projected in a sad attempt at a smile. 'I bring here.'

Something had startled where I thought I was safest. The tourist's terror of extortion gripped me. 'No, Ali. You take me see first. I like, I bring here.'

He turned to face the hot box and the toast again. It had been a momentary impulse; he never mentioned dancing girls again.

And after the hot box, improvements came fast. Two strips of torn matting were laid down the narrow, pansy-lined path that connected the kitchen with the dining-room. The strips lay at a slight angle to one another; when it rained they looked black against the lawn. And presently – the lake giving up more of its treasures – uneven lengths of old board appeared on this matting. The polisher, a silent boy, came. He polished the 'sofa-set' in the sitting-room, and the old writing-table (stuffed with Russian propaganda: Ali brought back armfuls from the Russians he met at the Tourist Reception Centre). He polished the chairs and the bed and the dining-table; he polished day after day, saying nothing, ate platefuls of rice in the kitchen, and at last went away, leaving the furniture almost exactly as it had been. The turf-layer came; he tore and rammed and tamped on one bare bank.

It was all activity now. But there were periods of repose, especially in the afternoons. Then Aziz squatted on the kitchen veranda before the hookah and pulled; he had changed his woollen nightcap for a fur cap and had become a workaday Kashmiri, with a gift for instantaneous repose. Visitors called, boatmen, vendors; and from the hut came sounds of romping and chatter. After one outburst of gaiety we had a glimpse of Aziz running out to the veranda without his cap, and he had changed again: he was quite bald. On sunny afternoons Mr Butt and the *khansamah* wrapped themselves in blankets from head to toe and slept on the lawn.

The painters came, to give that second coat. One was purely medieval; he had the labourer's broad friendly face and he wore a dirty cotton skull-cap. The other was bare-headed and wore contemporary green overalls. But their skills matched. They painted without any preparation. They couldn't manage straight lines; they ignored the division between concrete and timber, between ceiling and walls, between glass pane and window frame. They dripped paint everywhere. Their abandon infected me. I took a brush and on an unpainted wall drew birds and animals and faces. They giggled, and drew some things of their own. The man in the overalls asked the man in the skull-cap in Kashmiri: 'Shall I ask him for *bakshish*?' Skull-cap looked at me. 'No, no,' he said. But when Skull-cap went out of the room Overalls said in English, 'I make room nice for you. You give bakshish?'

The painters left and the glazier came to complete the dining-room windows. He measured the panes by eye and hand, cut, cut again, fitted, tapped in little nails and went away. Then a new coir matting was laid down on the steps and corridors and top gallery. It was too wide for the gallery – a sewage pipe stood in the way – and it remained curled along one edge; on the steps an absence of rails made it dangerous; and after every gusty shower the matting in the corridor was soaked. Two days later a patterned green plastic tablecloth covered the dining-table. And that was not the end. Overalls turned up again. He went from green door to green door, painting numbers in chocolate, wiping out inelegancies with a rag, leaving each shaggy number in a brownish blur; then he went to the kitchen and ate a plateful of rice.

Nothing more, it seemed, could be done. And when Aziz brought me coffee one morning he said, 'Sahib, I request one thing. You write Touriasm office, invite Mr Madan to tea.'

Mr Madan was the Kashmir Director of Tourism. I had met him once, and briefly. Then, in response to my plea for help in finding accommodation, he had said, 'Give me twenty-four hours'; and that was the last I had heard. I explained this to Aziz.

'You write Touriasm, invite Mr Madan to tea. Not your tea. My tea. Mr Butt tea.'

Meal by meal, waiting on us, he pressed his case. The Liward was new; it was neither houseboat nor hotel; it needed some sort of recognition from the Tourist Office. I was willing enough to write a letter of recommendation. It was the invitation to tea that worried me; and it was this that Aziz and Mr Butt, smiling shyly behind his spectacles, insisted on. So one morning, with Mr Butt and the English-reading secretary of the All Shikara Workers Union looking over my shoulder, I wrote to Mr Madan and invited him to tea.

Mr Butt himself took the letter into town. At lunch Aziz reported that Mr Madan had read the letter but had sent no reply. Solicitous now of my own honour, Aziz added: 'But perhaps he write and wait get typewrite and send by his own *chaprassi*.'

Aziz knew the forms. But no *chaprassi* ever came with Mr Madan's reply. I had a typewriter; a uniformed army officer brought me invitations from the Maharaja; yet I was without the influence to do a simple thing like getting Mr Madan to come to tea. Perhaps it was not only language that kept Mr Butt silent. And a further humiliation awaited me. The secretary of the All Shikara Workers Union wished to get up a petition to the Director of Transport for a more frequent bus service. I drafted the petition; I typed it; I signed it. It wasn't even acknowledged. Aziz knew the forms. So when, not long after, I complained about the weakness of the bulbs and asked for one to be replaced, and he said, 'Two-three rupees. You buy, I buy – what difference?' I didn't really feel I could object. I bought.

*

The season had begun. The hotel was not recognized, but accommodation was limited in Srinagar, our prices were reasonable, and soon we began to get guests. I had been full of plans for publicizing the hotel. I had put some of these plans to Aziz and, through him, to Mr Butt. They smiled, grateful for my interest; but all they wanted me to do was to talk to those tourists in jacket and tie whom Ali brought back from the Reception Centre. When I failed I felt humiliated. When I succeeded I was miserable. I was jealous; I wanted the hotel to myself. Aziz understood, and he was like a parent comforting a child. 'You will eat first. You will eat by yourself. We give you special. This is not Mr Butt hotel. This is your hotel.' When he announced new guests he would say, 'Is good, sahib. Good for hotel. Good for Mr Butt.' Sometimes he would raise one hand and say, 'God send customer.'

I remained unhappy. Being an unorthodox hotel, we attracted the orthodox. There had been the brahmin family, the first of many, who had insisted on cooking for themselves. They shelled peas, sifted rice and cut carrots in the doorway of their room; they cooked in the broom cupboard below the steps and washed their pots and pans at the garden tap; they turned part of the new turf to mud. Others threw their rubbish on the lawn; others spread their washing on the lawn. And I believed that the idyll was at an end when Aziz announced one day, with a well-managed mixture of enthusiasm and condolence, that twenty orthodox Indians were coming to the hotel for four days. Some would sleep in the dining-room; we would eat in the sitting-room. I was beyond condolence. Aziz recognized this and offered none. We waited. Aziz became morose, almost offended, in our presence. But the twenty did not turn up; and then for a day or two Aziz looked genuinely offended.

There were other difficulties. I had had it established that the radio in the dining-room was to be turned on just before eight. As soon as we heard the pips we went down to breakfast and the news in English. One morning no pips came, only Hindi film songs and Hindi commercials for Aspro and Horlicks: the radio was tuned to Radio Ceylon. I shouted through the window for Aziz. He came up and said he had explained to the boy from Bombay about the eight o'clock news from Delhi, but the boy had paid no attention.

I had loathed the boy from Bombay on sight. He wore tight trousers and a black imitation-leather jacket; his hair was thick and carefully combed; he carried his shoulders with something of the left-hander's elegant crookedness; he had the boxer's light walk and his movements were swift and abrupt. I thought of him as the Bombay Brando; I set him against a background of swarming Bombay slum. We had not spoken. But now, leather jacket or no leather jacket, this was war.

I ran downstairs. The radio was on full blast, and Brando was sitting in a derelict wicker chair on the lawn. I lowered the volume, almost to silence at first, in my haste; and turned to Radio Kashmir. Ali was making toast; the curve of his back signalled that he wasn't going to interfere. Nothing happened during the news. As soon as it was over, however, Brando pushed violently through the curtained doorway, went to the radio, wiped out Radio Kashmir for Radio Ceylon, and pushed out again violently through the curtain.

And so now it went on, morning and evening. Aziz I knew to be neutral. Ali I thought to be on my side. He crouched silently before the hot box, deprived now of his Kashmiri devotional songs. The conflict had reached stalemate. I longed for some development and one morning I suggested to Ali that Kashmiri songs were better than the commercials from Radio Ceylon. He looked up from his toast with alarm. Then I discovered that in the few short weeks of the tourist season, of tourist transistors tuned to Radio Ceylon, his taste had changed. He liked the commercial jingles, he liked the film songs. They were modern, an accessible part of that world beyond the mountains from which the advanced, money-laden Indian tourists came. Kashmiri music belonged to the lake and the valley; it was rude. So fragile are our fairylands.

Then I went down with a stomach upset and had to stay in bed. The next morning there was a knock on the door. It was Brando.

'I didn't see you yesterday,' he said. 'They told me you were not well. How are you today?'

I said I was better and thanked him for coming. There was a pause. I tried to think of something more to say. He wasn't trying at all. He stood unembarrassed beside the bed.

'Where do you come from?' I asked.

'I come from Bombay.'

'Bombay. What part of Bombay?'

'Dadar. You know Dadar?'

It was what I had imagined. 'What do you do? Are you a medical student?'

He barely raised his left foot off the floor, and his shoulders went crooked. 'I am *guest* in the hotel.'

'Yes, I know that,' I said.

'*You* are guest in the hotel.'

'I am a guest in the hotel.'

'So *why* you say I am *medical* student? *Why?* You are guest in the hotel. I am guest in the hotel. You get sick. I come to see you. Why you say I am *medical* student?'

'I am sorry. I know that you have come to see me only because we are both guests in the hotel. But I didn't mean to offend you. I just wanted to find out what you did.'

'I work for an insurance company.'

'Thank you very much for coming to see me.'

'You are welcome, mister.'

And, leading with the left shoulder, he pushed through the curtains and left.

Thereafter courtesy was imposed on both of us. I offered him Radio Ceylon; he offered me Radio Kashmir.

*

'Huzoor!' the *khansamah* called one afternoon, knocking and coming into the room at the same time. 'Today my day off, and I going home *now*, huzoor.' He spoke rapidly, like a man with little time. Normally Aziz came with him to our room; but this afternoon he had managed to elude Aziz, whom I saw, through the window, reclining on a string bed in the kitchen veranda.

'My son is sick, huzoor.' He gave a crooked bashful smile and shifted about on his elegant feet.

It was not necessary. My hand was already in my pocket, detaching notes from a stapled wad of a hundred. It was all that the local State Bank of India had that week. It encouraged this type of protracted furtive activity: I knew how easy and dangerous it was to excite the Kashmiri.

'My son is sick *bad*, huzoor!'

His impatience matched mine.

'*Huzoor!*' It was an exclamation of pure displeasure. Three notes had stuck together and appeared as one. Then he smiled. 'Oh, three rupees. All right.'

'Huzoor!' the *khansamah* said one week later. 'My wife is sick, huzoor.'

At the door, fingering the notes I had given him, he stopped and said with sudden consoling conviction, 'My wife true sick bad, huzoor. Very bad. She have typhoid.'

This worried me. Possibly he wasn't being merely courteous. At dinner I asked Aziz.

'She not have typhoid.' Aziz's tight-lipped smile, suppressing laughter at my gullibility, was infuriating.

I had, however, betrayed the *khansamah*. He came no more with tales of sick relations. I did not like to think of his humiliation in the kitchen; and I liked to think least of all of Aziz's triumph over him. On that small island I had become involved with them all, and with none more so than Aziz. It was an involvement which had taken me by surprise. Up to this time a servant, to me, had been someone who did a job, took his money and went off to his own concerns. But Aziz's work was his life. A childless wife existed somewhere in the lake, but he seldom spoke of her and never appeared to visit her. Service was his world. It was his craft, his trade; it transcended the formalities of uniform and deferential manners; and it was the source of his power. I had read of the extraordinary control of eighteenth-century servants in Europe; I had been puzzled by the insolence of Russian servants in novels like *Dead Souls* and *Oblomov*; in India I had seen mistress and manservant engage in arguments as passionate, as seemingly irreparable and as quickly forgotten as the arguments between husband and wife. Now I began to understand. To possess a personal servant, whose skill is to please, who has no function beyond that of service, is painlessly to surrender part of oneself. It creates dependence where none existed; it requires requital; and it can reduce one to infantilism. I became as alert to Aziz's moods as he had been to mine. He had the power to infuriate me; his glumness could spoil a morning for me. I was quick to see disloyalty and diminishing attentions. Then I sulked; then, depending on his mood, he bade me good-night through a messenger or he didn't bid me good-night at all; and in the morning we started afresh. We quarrelled silently about guests of whom I disapproved. We quarrelled openly when I felt that his references to increasing food prices were leading up to a demand for more money. I wished, above all, to be sure of his loyalty. And this was impossible, for I was not his employer. So in my relations with him, I alternated between bullying and bribing; and he handled both.

His service, I say, transcended uniform. He wore none; and he appeared to have only one suit of clothes. They grew grimy on him, and his scent became riper and riper.

'Can you swim, Aziz?'

'O yes, sahib, I swim.'

'Where do you swim?'

'Right here on lake.'

'It must be very cold.'

'O no, sahib. Every morning Ali Mohammed and I take off clothes and swim.'

This was something; it removed one doubt. 'Aziz, get the tailor to make you a suit. I will pay.'

He became stern and preoccupied, a man worn down by duties; this was a sign of pleasure.

'How much do you think it will cost, Aziz?'

'Twelve rupees, sahib.'

And in this mood, catching sight of Ali Mohammed about to go off to the Tourist Reception Centre in his shabby striped blue suit, his waistcoat and watch-chain, I surrendered to the pathos of his appearance.

'Ali, get the tailor to make you a new waistcoat. I will pay.'

'Very good, sir.'

It was hard to tell with Ali. He always looked slightly stunned whenever he was addressed directly.

'How much will it cost?'

'Twelve rupees, sir.'

It appeared to be a popular price. I went up to my room. I had hardly settled down at the blue table when the door was roughly pushed open and I turned to see the *khansamah*, blue apron on, advancing upon me. He seemed to be in an uncontrollable rage. He put a hand on the jacket that was hanging on the back of my chair and said, 'I want a coat.' Then, as if alarmed by his own violence, he stepped back two paces. 'You give Ali Mohammed jacket and you give that man Aziz suit.'

Had they been taunting him in the kitchen? I thought of Aziz's tight-lipped smile, his stern look of a moment before: suppressions of triumph that had inevitably to be released. Ali had been about to go off to the Tourist Reception Centre; he must have gone back to the kitchen to break the news.

'I am a poor man.' The *khansamah* made a sweeping gesture with both hands down his elegant clothes.

'How much will it cost?'

'Fifteen rupees. No, twenty.'

It was too much. 'When I leave I will give you coat. When I leave.'

He dropped to the floor and tried to seize my feet in mark of gratitude, but the legs and rungs of the chair were in the way.

He was a tormented man; and I knew, from what I heard and saw, that there were rows in the kitchen. He was careful of his honour. He was a cook. He was not a general servant; he had not learned the art of pleasing and probably despised those, like Aziz, who prospered by pleasing. I could see that he would provoke situations with which he could not cope; and after every defeat he would suffer.

It must have been a week later. For dinner he sent across meat stew and vegetable stew. The stews were identical, apart from the shreds and cubes of meat in one. I was not a meat-eater, and I was irrationally upset. I could not touch the vegetable stew. Aziz was wounded; this gave me pleasure. He went out with the stew to the kitchen, from where the *khansamah*'s voice was presently heard, angrily raised. Aziz returned alone, walking carefully, as though his feet were sore. After some time there was a call from behind the curtained doorway. It was the *khansamah*. In one hand he held a frying-pan, in another a fish-slice. His face was flushed from the fire and ugly with anger and insult.

'Why you don't eat my vegetable stew?'

As soon as he began to speak he lost control of himself. He stood over me and was almost screaming. 'Why you don't eat my vegetable stew?' I feared he was about to hit me with the frying-pan, which he had raised, and in which I saw an omelette. Immediately after his violence, however, came his alarm, his recognition of his own weakness.

I suffered with him. But the thought of egg and oil nauseated me further; and I was surprised by the rise within myself of that deep anger which unhinges judgement and almost physically limits vision.

'Aziz,' I said, 'will you ask this person to go?'

It was brutal; it was ludicrous; it was pointless and infantile. But the moment of anger is a moment of exalted, shrinking lucidity from which recovery is slow and shattering.

Some time later the *khansamah* left the Liward. It occurred without warning. He came up with Aziz to my room one morning and said, 'I am going, huzoor.'

Aziz, anticipating my questions, said, 'This is happy for him, sahib. Not worry. He get job family Baramula side.'

'I am going, huzoor. Give me certificate *now*.' He stood behind Aziz, and as he spoke he squinted one eye and wagged a long finger at Aziz's back.

I typed out a certificate for him right away. It was long and emotional, of no use to a future employer; it was a testimony of sympathy: I felt he was as inadequate as myself. While I wrote Aziz stood by, dusting from time to time, smiling, seeing that nothing went wrong.

'I am going *now*, huzoor.'

I sent Aziz outside, and gave the *khansamah* more money than was necessary. He took it without softening. All he did was to say slowly and with passion, 'That man Aziz!'

'This is happy for him,' Aziz said again afterwards. 'Two three days we get new *khansamah*.'

So the vision of the hotel as doll's house altered.

*

'Sahib, I request one thing. You write Touriasm Office, invite Mr Madan to tea.'

'But, Aziz, he didn't come the last time.'

'Sahib, you write Touriasm.'

'No, Aziz. No more invitations to tea.'

'Sahib, I request one thing. You go see Mr Madan.'

Another plot had been hatched in the kitchen. Every week Ali Mohammed had to apply for a permit to enter the police-guarded compound of the Tourist Reception Centre. This wasted some of his tourist-catching time. What he needed was a permit for the entire season, and the kitchen felt that I could get one for him.

'Do they really give these season permits, Aziz?'

'Yes, sahib. Lotta *houseboat* have season permit.'

My lake hotel, unorthodox, unrecognized, was being discriminated against. Without further inquiry, I made an appointment with Mr Madan, and when the day came Mr Butt and I rode into town on a tonga.

And they knew about me at the Tourist Office! My previous letter had made the Liward Hotel famous. There were smiles and handshakes from several officials who were delighted, if a little puzzled, by my interest. The Indian bureaucracy has its silences and delays, but it never loses or forgets any document; and it was with pure geniality that I was hustled, as the writer of an unsolicited letter of praise, into the picture-hung office of Mr Madan, the director.

His waiting visitors, his grave expectant courtesy, almost made me change my mind. Now the greetings were over; something had to be said. So: Would Mr Madan please see that Ali Mohammed was given a permit for the season, if Ali Mohammed was entitled to such a permit?

'But permits are no longer required. Your friend, I imagine, has a British passport.'

I could not blame him for misunderstanding. Ali was not a tourist, I said. He wanted to meet tourists. He was a Kashmiri, a hotel servant; he wanted to get inside the Tourist Reception Centre. I knew that tourists had to be protected. Still. My trivialities burdened me. I became more and more earnest, anxious to get out of the encounter with dignity.

Mr Madan behaved well. If Ali applied, he said, he would consider the application.

I bade him good morning and walked briskly out with the news to Mr Butt.

'You see head clerk now,' Mr Butt said, and I allowed myself to be led into a room of desks and clerks.

The head clerk was not at his desk. We found him later in the corridor, a smiling well-built young man in a pale grey suit. He knew my letter; he understood my request. Let the hotel apply tomorrow; he would see what he could do.

'Tomorrow,' I said to Mr Butt. 'You come tomorrow.'

Hurriedly, I left him and made my way through the grounds of the Government Emporium, once the British Residency, to the Bund along the muddy Jhelum River. The elaborate Kashmiri woodwork of the Residency had decayed here and there; next to it a dingy little shack – very English, very Indian – proclaimed itself as the Emporium Café. But the chenar-shaded grounds remained grandiloquent, carefully irregular patches of daisies dramatizing the vast lawn. The Residency stood at one end of the Bund, on which, I had often been told, no Indian was allowed in the old days. Now the turnstiles were broken. Signs forbade cycling and walking on the grass bank; but there was constant cycling, and a deep path had been worn into the bank. Cows nibbled at the front gardens of buildings which, though in reality no more than an adoption of the Kashmiri style, at first sight appeared a type of mock mock-Tudor. Some old-fashioned shops survived, roomy, dark, with many glass cases; they still seemed to hold the anticipations of a thousand Anglo-Indian 'leaves'. Faded advertisements for things like water biscuits, no longer obtainable, could be still seen; boards and walls still carried the names of British patrons, viceroys and commanders-in-chief. In a taxidermist's shop there was a framed photograph of an English cavalry officer with his polished boot on a dead tiger.

One type of glory had gone. The other brightness, of the bazaar, had not yet come. But it was on the way. 'You needn't tell me, sir. I can see from your dress and your speech that your taste is English.

Step inside and let me show you my English-taste rugs. Observe. This is English taste. I *know*. Now on the other hand observe this. It is heavy, Indian and of course inferior . . .'

*Kashmirs Most Extraordinary Entertaining Rendezvous*
YAP – LET'S GO TO PREMIERS
RESTAURANT
*Hey-Fellers-Tony is At the Mike*
*With All the Five Bops*
*Fellers enjoy the 36 Varieties of Icecreams*
DRINK DRINKS
IN OUR STARLIT GOLDEN BAR

That was what the leaflets said. Now the rendezvous itself, new, contemporary – 'most gayest', according to another leaflet, 'most delicious in tours' – was before me. It was too early for Tony and the Five Bops. I had a quiet, expensive litre of Indian beer and tried to put the morning's encounters out of my mind.

Later I walked down the dusty Residency Road and talked with the old bearded bookseller. He was a BA, LLB from Bombay, and a refugee from Sind. He said he was eighty. I challenged this. 'Well, I say eighty so as not to say seventy-eight.' He told me of the Pakistani invasion of 1947 and of the looting of Baramula. In this very city of Srinagar, this city of tonga-wallahs, Ali Mohammed and Yap – Let's go to Premiers, five hundred rupees were being paid for eight-rupee bus seats to Jammu. 'Now there is nothing to do but laugh, and I often just sit here and read.' He read Stephen Leacock, and was addicted to the stories of Major Munro. Why did he say Major Munro? Well, he had read that Saki was Munro and a Major, and he felt it was a discourtesy to deny a favourite author his rank.

I was riding back to the hotel *ghat* on a tonga when I saw Mr Butt. I took him on. He was utterly wretched. I had left him too hurriedly. He had not understood my words and had spent all morning at the Tourist Reception Centre waiting for me.

Next morning I typed out the application for the season permit and Mr Butt took it into town. It was hot and it became hotter. Towards midday the sky darkened, the clouds lowered, the mountains became dark blue and were reflected in the water until the winds started to rage across the lake, kicking up the lotus leaves, tormenting the willows, pushing the reeds this way and that. Soon it began to rain and, after that very hot morning, it became quite cold. It was still raining when Mr Butt returned. His fur cap was soaked into mean, glistening kinkiness; his jacket was dark with wet; his shoulders were hunched below the turned-up collar; his shirt-tail was dripping. I watched him walk slowly down the wet boards in the garden to the kitchen. He kicked his shoes off and disappeared inside. I returned to my work, and waited for the sound of happy bare feet on the steps. But there was nothing.

And, as before, it was I who had to ask. 'Did Mr Butt get the permit, Aziz?'

'Yes, he get permit. One week.'

*

One morning some days later I was having coffee in the sitting-room when the painter in the overalls pushed his head through the doorway and said, 'You typewrite give me painting certificate sahib?' I did not reply.

# 6

# THE MEDIEVAL CITY

THE LEVEL OF the lake dropped to the last step of the landing-stage; the water became muddier and swarmed with black colonies of summer fish. The snow on the mountains to the north melted and the exposed rock looked bleached and eroded. On the cool parkland of the foothills the firs became darker blobs of green. The poplars on the lake lost their fresh greenness and the willows scattered spinning leaves in high wind. The reeds became so tall they curved, and when the wind blew they swayed and tossed like waves. The lotus leaves rose crinkled and disordered out of the water, thrust up on thick stalks. Then, like blind tulips, the lotus buds appeared, and a week later opened in explosions of dying pink. In the garden the Californian poppies and the clarkia grew straggly and were pulled out; the French marigolds, which had taken the place of the pansies, thickened and put out buds. The petunias in the shade of the dining-room wall were failing; they, like the geraniums, had been discoloured and weighted down with distemper from the painters' brushes. The godetias were at their peak: a mass of whipped colour, white and pink and pale violet. The sunflowers, seedlings when we arrived, were so tall, their leaves so broad, I could no longer look down into their hearts to examine the progress of the star-shaped buds. The dahlias put out one small red bloom, a touch of vivid colour against the green of reeds and willows and poplars.

We still had the kingfisher. But other birds appeared less frequently in the garden. We missed the hoopoe, with his long busy bill, his curved black and white wing stripes, his crest fanning out as he landed. With the heat the little flies died, as Aziz had said; and their place was taken by the house-fly. The flies I had known so far were shy of man; these settled on my face and hands even while I worked, and for several mornings in succession I was awakened before six by the buzzing of a single, Flit-surviving fly. Aziz promised mosquitoes; they would rout the flies. To him a fly was an act of God; one afternoon I saw him happily asleep in the kitchen, his cap on, his face black with still, contented flies.

I had asked for Flit, and more Flit. Now I asked for ice.

'Anybody don't like ice,' Aziz said. 'Ice is heating.'

And this reply led to one of our silences.

On very hot days the mountains to the north were hidden by haze from morning till evening. When the sun began to go down an amber light filled the valley and the mist rose slowly between the poplars on the lake. Each tree was distinct; and from Shankaracharya Hill Srinagar, smoking, appeared to be a vast industrial town, the poplars as erect as chimneys. Against this the fort of Akbar, standing on its reddish hill in the centre of the lake, was silhouetted: the sun to the left, a white disc slowly turning pale yellow, the mountains fading from grey to nothing as they receded.

*

Beyond the Bund it was a medieval town, and it might have been of medieval Europe. It was a town, damp or dusty, of smells: of bodies and picturesque costumes discoloured and acrid with grime, of black, open drains, of exposed fried food and exposed filth; a town of prolific pariah dogs of disregarded beauty below shop platforms, of starved puppies shivering in the damp caked blackness below butchers' stalls hung with bleeding flesh; a town of narrow lanes and dark shops and choked courtyards, of full, ankle-length skirts and the innumerable brittle, scarred legs of boys. Yet much skill had gone into the making of these huddled wooden buildings; much fine fantastic carving and woodwork remained, not at first noticeable, for everything had been weathered to grey-black; and there were odd effects of beauty, as when every brass and burnished copper vessel in a shop of brass and copper vessels glinted in the gloom. For against this drabness, an overwhelming impression of muddiness, of black and grey and brown, colour stood out and was enticing: the colours of sweets, yellow and glistening green, however fly-infested. Here one was able to learn again the attraction of primary, heraldic colours, the colours of toys, and of things that shone, and to rediscover that child's taste so long suppressed, which is also peasant's taste, erupting here, as in the rest of India, in tinsel and coloured lights and everything we had all once considered pretty. Out of these cramped yards, glimpsed through filth-runnelled alleyways, came bright colours in glorious patterns on rugs and carpets and soft shawls, patterns and colours derived from Persia, in Kashmir grown automatic, even in all their rightness and variety, and applied with indiscriminate lavishness on a two-thousand-rupee carpet or an old blanket which, when worked, would sell for twelve rupees. In this medieval dirt and greyness beauty was colour, equally admired in a fine rug, a pot of plastic daisies or, as once in Europe, in a fantastic costume.

As complementary as colour was gaiety. The town slept during the winter. The tourists went away, hotels and houseboats closed, and in their dark, small-windowed rooms the Kashmiris wrapped themselves in blankets and idled over charcoal braziers until the spring. The spring brought sun and dust and fairs, colour and noise and exposed food. Nearly every fortnight there seemed to be a fair in some part of the Valley. Each was like the other. In each might be found the picture-seller, his stock spread out on the ground: thin wall-scrolls with violently coloured drawings of Indian and Arabian mosques, objects of desired pilgrimage, flattened out of perspective; photographs of film stars; coloured pictures of political leaders; innumerable paperbacked booklets. There were stalls of cheap toys and cheap clothes; there were tea-tents and sweet-trays. A Hindu holy man of terrifying aspect sat in the dust behind his small dry vials that contained charms of 'eye of newt and tongue of dog'. And always there was amplified music. On the lake, too, the playground now not only of the tourists but also of the people of the town, there was music: from the *doongas*, smaller unpainted houseboats, hired complete with kitchen-women and pole-man. He walked slowly back and forth past the cabins, now carrying his pole, now leaning on it, separate from the revelry within but seemingly content; a woman, possibly his wife, bundled in dirty skirts and heavy with silver jewellery, sat solitary at the high stern, steering with a long paddle. It was movement for the sake of movement. The *doongas* went nowhere in particular and were never beyond shouting distance of gardens or houses; they called here, moored there for the night. A doonga party could last for days; people might get off at some point to attend to their affairs on land and might rejoin the boat later at another point. A dull, strenuous entertainment it seemed to me; but my winters were full. The fair in the grove at Ganderbal, a few miles to the northwest, climaxed the season. All the doongas and shikaras made their way there and moored for the night: movement for the sake of movement, crowd for the sake of crowd, noise for the sake of noise.

And in this medieval town, as in all medieval towns, the people were surrounded by wonders. About them in Srinagar were the gardens of the Mogul emperors. The pavilions were neglected but they were still whole. On Sundays the fountains of Shalimar still played, with here and there a bent or broken nozzle. But the builders had receded beyond history into legend: fabulous personages of whom little was known except that they were *very* handsome or *very* brave or *very* wise, with wives who were *very* beautiful. 'That?' said the Kashmiri engineer, waving towards Akbar's late-sixteenth-century fort in the Dal Lake. 'That is five thousand years old.' In the Hazratbal mosque on the lake there was a hair from the beard of the Prophet Mohammed. It had been brought through untold dangers to Kashmir, the medical student told me, by 'a man'. Who was this man? What did he do? Where did he come from? My student couldn't say; he knew only that once, when this man was in an especially dangerous situation, he had gashed himself in the arm and in the gash had concealed the holy hair. It was an authentic relic, there could be no doubt of that. It was so potent that birds never flew over the chapel in which it was kept and cows, sacred to Hindus, never sat with their backs to the chapel.

God watched over them all, and they responded with enthusiasm. Mohurram was the month in which for ten days they mourned Hussain, the Prophet's descendant, murdered at Kerbala. The wails and songs of the Shias came to us over the water at night. Aziz, of the Sunni sect, said with a smile, 'Shia not Muslim.' Yet on the seventh morning, when on the radio the well-known story of Kerbala was being told, tears came to Aziz's eyes, his face grew small, and he hurried out of the dining-room, saying, 'I can't stop. I don't like listen.'

There was to be a Shia procession at Hasanbad; there would be people whipping themselves with chains. Aziz, recovered from the morning's emotion, insisted that we should go, and made the arrangements. We went by *shikara*, quickly penetrating into the green-scummed, willow-hung water highways of the lake town, past the dirty yards terminating in broken concrete steps, gutters running down their sides, on which men and women and children were washing clothes, our own washerman, I was sorry to see, among them. The highways were altogether foul, smelling of the sewer; but at every yard children, miniature adults, rushed out to greet us: 'Salaam!'

At Hasanbad we moored among dozens of *shikaras*, many brilliantly canopied, walked past the foundations of a ruin of which we had never heard, and found ourselves in the middle of a dusty summer fair. The streets had been swept; water-carts laid the dust. There were awnings and stalls. The well-to-do among the women in the crowd were veiled in black or brown from head to well-shod feet; they were in groups of two or three, and through the grilled netting over their eyes we felt ourselves scrutinized. It was the poor who were unveiled; here, as everywhere else, to be conservative and correct was the privilege of the rising. We passed a father and his daughter; he was letting her play with his whip, as yet unused.

Beyond this open, almost country, road lay the narrow main street. Here the crowd was thick. Many men wore black shirts; one boy was carrying a black flag. Soon we saw some flagellants. Their clothes were stiff with blood. The procession had not yet begun and they walked idly up and down the centre of the road, between the admiring crowds, jostling those who tomorrow might once again be their betters. In the corbelled upper storeys of the narrow houses every crooked window, of Kashmiri tininess, framed a medieval picture: the intent faces of women and girls, the girls fresh-complexioned, the women, from their long seclusion, pallid, all cut out against the sharp blackness of window space. Below, in the choked road, were lorryloads of police. Some boys were tormenting the puppies below the butcher's stall; we heard the puppies kicked, a surprisingly loud sound to come from such small bodies; we heard the yelps and whines. Hawkers called; stranded cars hooted. Over it all lay the microphone-magnified voice of the mullah – the microphone an Indian inevitability – reciting the story of Kerbala. His voice held anguish and hysteria; at times it seemed he would break down; but he went feverishly on and on. He was reciting from under an awning hung across the street and was hidden by the crowd, some of whom carried coloured pennants.

More flagellants appeared. The back of one was obscenely cut up; blood, still fresh, soaked his trousers. He walked briskly up and down, deliberately bumping into people and frowning as though offended. His whip hung from his waist. It was made up of perhaps six metal chains, eighteen inches long, each ending in a small bloody blade; hanging from his waist, it looked like a fly-whisk. As disquieting as the blood were the faces of some of the enthusiasts. One had no nose, just two punctures in a triangle of pink mottled flesh; one had grotesquely raw bulging eyes; there was one with no neck, the flesh distended straight from cheek to chest. In their walk was pride; they behaved like busy men with no time for trivialities. I suspected some of the bloody garments. Some looked too dry; they might have been last year's, they might have been borrowed, or the blood might have been animal's blood. But there was no denying the integrity of the man whose nearly bald head was roughly bandaged, the blood still streaming down. The glory lay in blood; he who displayed the most was the most certain of attention.

We left the hot crowded street and made our way into the open. We sat in a scuffed, dusty graveyard, beside some boys playing an incomprehensible medieval game with pebbles. Until that morning religious enthusiasm had been a mystery to me. But in that street, where only the police lorries and the occasional motor-car and the microphone and perhaps the ice-cream sold by hawkers in shallow round tins were not of the middle ages, the festival of blood had seemed entirely natural. It was these American girls now approaching who were inexplicable and outlandish; not content with the attention they would normally attract, they wore body-accentuating garments which would have been outrageous in London. The flagellant who, ignoring them, began to get out of his blood-stained clothes on the canal steps, in full view of everyone, and was presently naked, was of a piece with the setting and the holiday mood of the day. This was his day; today he had licence. He had earned it by his bloody back. He had turned dull virtue into spectacle.

Religious enthusiasm derived, in performance and admiration, from simplicity, from a knowledge of religion only as ritual and form. 'Shia not Muslim,' Aziz had said. The Shia, he added, demonstrating, bowed in this way when he said his prayers; the Muslim, now, bowed in this. Christians were closer to Muslims than to Hindus because Christians and Muslims buried their dead. 'But, Aziz, many Christians are cremated.' 'They not Christian.' The medical student, explaining the difference between Islam and Sikhism, which he particularly detested, said that Muslims slaughtered their animals by bleeding them slowly to death, uttering prayers the while. Sikhs struck off an animal's head at one blow, without prayers. He sketched out the gesture, involuntarily shook his head with repulsion, and put his hand over his face. On the day of Id Mr Butt gave us a cake iced *Id Mubarak*, Id Greetings. The day took us by surprise; *shikara*-loads of Kashmiris, men, women and children, were ferried about the lake all morning, subdued and stiff and startling in clean clothes of white and blue. It was a day of visits and gifts and feasting; but, too, for the Kashmiri, the year's solitary day of cleanliness, a penitential debauch of soap and water and itching new cloth. Yet neither the medical student nor the engineer nor the merchant, all of whom came to visit us and offered gifts, could explain the significance of the day. It was only what we had seen; it was a day when Muslims had to eat meat.

Religion was a spectacle, and festivals, women veiled ('so that men wouldn't get excited and think bad things,' the merchant said), women bred and breeding like battery hens; it was the ceremonial washing of the genitals in public before prayers; it was ten thousand simultaneous prostrations. It was this complete day-filling, season-filling mixture of the gay, the penitential, the hysterical and, importantly, the absurd. It answered every simple mood. It was life and the Law, and its forms could admit of no change or query, since change and query would throw the whole system, would throw life itself, in danger. 'I am a bad Muslim,' the medical student had said at our first meeting. 'How can I believe that the world was made in six days? I believe in evolution. My mother would grow mad if I said these things to her.' But he rejected none of the forms, no particle of the Law; and was more of a religious fanatic than Aziz who, secure in his system, inspected other systems with tolerant interest. The sputniks had momentarily shaken some in their faith, for the upper atmosphere had been decreed closed to all but Mohammed and his white horse. But doctrine could be made to accommodate this – what the Russians had done was to send up their sputniks on the white horse – and the faith could survive because doctrine was not as important as the forms it had bred. The abandoning of the veil was more to be feared and resisted than the theory of evolution.

These forms had not developed over the centuries. They had been imposed whole and suddenly by a foreign conqueror, displacing another set of forms, once no doubt thought equally unalterable, of which no trace remained. The medieval mind could assess a building as five thousand years old, and do so casually; with like facility it buried events three and four hundred years old. And it was because it was without a sense of history that it was capable of so complete a conversion. Many Kashmiri clan names – like that of Mr Butt himself – were often still purely Hindu; but of their Hindu past the Kashmiris retained no memory. In the mountains there were cave-dwellers, thinly bearded and moustached, handsome, sharp-featured men, descendants, I felt, of Central Asian horsemen; in the summer they came down with their mules among the Kashmiris, who despised them. Of their first arrival in Kashmir there was a folk memory: 'Once, long, long ago they lived beyond the mountains. Then there was a king of Cabul who began killing them, and so they left and walked over the mountains and came here.' But of the conversion of the Valley to Islam there was no memory at all. Aziz, I know, would have been scandalized if it had been suggested to him that his ancestors were Hindus. 'Those?' the engineer said, driving past the Awantipur ruins. 'Hindu ruins.' He was showing me the antiquities of the Valley, and the ruins lay just at the side of the main road; but he didn't slow down or say any more. The eighth-century ruins were contemptible; they formed no part of his past. His history only began with his conquerors; in spite of travel and degrees he remained a medieval convert, forever engaged in the holy war.

Yet the religion as practised in the Valley was not pure. Islam is iconoclastic: the Kashmiris went mad when they saw the hair from the Prophet's beard; and all around the lake were Muslim shrines, lit at night. I know, though, what Aziz would have said if I had told him that good Muslims did not venerate relics. 'They not Muslim.' Should another conversion now occur, should another Law as complete be imposed, in a hundred years there would be no memory of Islam.

*

It was in politics as it was in religion. The analyses of the Kashmir situation which I had been reading endlessly in newspapers had no relation to the problem as the Kashmiris saw it. The most anti-Indian people in the Valley were Punjabi Muslim settlers, often in high positions; to them Kashmiris were 'cowardly', 'greedy'; and they often came to the hotel with rumours of troop movements, mutinies and disasters on the frontier. To their politics the Kashmiris brought not self-interest but their gifts of myth and wonder; and their myths centred on one man, Sheikh Abdullah, the Lion of Kashmir, as Mr Nehru had called him. He had made the Kashmiris free; he was their leader; he had been friendly to India but had ceased to be friendly, and since 1953 had been, except for a few months, in jail. From Kashmiris I could get no more; I could get no glimpse of the leader's achievements, personality or appeal. Over and over I was told, as if in explanation of everything, that when he came out of prison in 1958, there were crowds along the road from Kud to Srinagar, and red carpets everywhere.

'Listen,' said the college student, 'and I will tell you how Sheikh Abdullah won freedom for the people of Kashmir. For many, many years Sheikh Abdullah had been fighting for the freedom of the people. And then one day the Maharaja became *very* frightened and sent for Sheikh Abdullah. He said to Sheikh Abdullah, "I will give you anything, even up to half my kingdom, if only you let me keep my throne." Sheikh Abdullah refused. The Maharaja became *very* angry and said, "I will throw you in oil and make it hot." And you know what the result of that would be. That only a heap of ashes would remain. But Sheikh Abdullah said, "All right, boil me in oil. But I tell you that out of every drop of my blood will grow another Sheikh Abdullah." When the Maharaja heard this he was *very* frightened, and he gave up the throne. That was how Sheikh Abdullah won the freedom for the people of Kashmir.'

I objected. I said that people didn't behave like that in real life.

'But it's true. Ask any Kashmiri.'

It was an account of the events of 1947 that ignored Congress, Gandhi, the British, the Pakistan invasion. And this was at the high level of literacy in English. Below this there were people like Aziz, who almost daily regretted the Maharaja's repressive rule because things were so much cheaper then. Recent history was already sinking into medieval legend. Aziz and the *khansamah* had served the British; they knew them as people of certain tastes, skills and language ('padre' for priest, and to Aziz 'bugger' was an affectionate word for a dog) who had departed as unaccountably as they had come. But there had grown up a generation of students who had learned of the British only from their history books, and to them the British intervention was as remote as the Mogul glory.

Bashir told me one day that the 'East India Company went away in 1947'; and this, in our political discussions, was his sole reference to the British. Bashir was nineteen, college-educated. 'I am *best* sportsman,' he had said, introducing himself to me. 'I am *best* swimmer. I know *all* chemistry and *all* physics.' He detested the Kashmiri and Indian habit of wearing pyjamas in public; and he told me he never spat in the street. He regarded himself as educated and emancipated: he 'inter-dined' (one of the English locutions of the subcontinent) with everyone, regardless of religion or sect. He wore western-style suits, and he spoke English as well as he did because 'I come from an unusually intelligent family'.

It might be that Bashir's ignorance of history was due to his stupidity, or to his education in a language he did not fully understand (when he said *best* he only meant 'very good'), or to bad teachers and bad textbooks. (I examined one of his history books later. It was a typical Indian textbook; it was in question-and-answer form and gave the preservation of purity as one of the virtues of the caste system and gave miscegenation as one of the reasons for the decline of Portuguese power in India.) Or it might simply have been that Bashir and his friends took no interest in politics; and indeed, without newspapers and the radio, it was possible to be in Kashmir for weeks without realizing that there was a Kashmir problem. But Kashmir was being talked about on every side. All-India Radio was carrying detailed reports of the annual United Nations debate; Radio Pakistan tirelessly warned that in Kashmir as in the rest of India Islam was in danger, and Radio Kashmir as tirelessly retaliated. Mr Nehru came to Srinagar, and Radio Pakistan reported that a public meeting he addressed broke up in disorder. (He was in fact convalescing after an illness.) Whatever might be said, Bashir's ignorance of the recent history and situation of his country was startling. And he was privileged. Below him were the grimy, barefooted, undernourished primary-school boys in blue shirts who had no chance of going to college; below them were those who didn't go to school at all.

I was in bed one afternoon with an inflamed throat when Bashir brought Kadir to see me. Kadir was seventeen, small, with soft brown eyes in a square gentle face; he was studying engineering but wanted to be a writer.

'He is *best* poet,' Bashir said, interrupting his prowling about the room, sinking across my feet on the bed, and grabbing my cigarettes. He had brought Kadir to see me; but his purpose was also to show me off to Kadir, and this he could do only by this hearty familiarity which he had never before attempted with me. He could not be rebuffed. I merely wiggled my toes below his back.

'When Bashir told me I was going to meet a writer,' Kadir said, 'of course I had to come.'

'*Best* poet,' Bashir said, lifting himself off my feet and supporting himself on his elbows.

The poet's shirt, open at the neck, was dirty; there was a hole at the top of his pullover. He was small and sensitive and shabby: I yielded to him.

'He is *great* drinker,' Bashir said. '*Too* much of whisky.'

This was a proof of his talent. In India poets and musicians are required to live the part: it is necessary to be sad and alcoholic.

But Kadir looked so young and poor.

'Do you really drink?' I asked him. He said simply, 'Yes.'

'Recite,' Bashir ordered.

'But he wouldn't understand Urdu.'

'Recite. I will translate. It is not easy, you understand. But I will translate.'

Kadir recited.

'He says,' Bashir said, 'and he is talking of a poor boatman's daughter, you understand – he says in his poem that she gives colour to the rose. You get it, mister? Another man would say that the *rose* gives her the colour. He says that *she* gives colour to the rose.'

'Very beautiful,' I said.

Kadir said wearily, 'Kashmir has beauty and nothing else.'

Then Bashir, his large eyes shining, recited a couplet which, he said, I would find in some Mogul building in Delhi. He became sentimental. 'An Englishman went walking in the hills one day, you know,' he said. 'And he saw a Gujjar girl sitting under a tree. She was *very* beautiful. And she was reading Koran. The Englishman went up to her and said, "Will you marry me?" She looked up from Koran and said, "Of course I will marry you. But first you must give up your religion for mine." The Englishman said, "Of course I will change my religion. I love you more than anything in the world." So he changed his religion and they were married. They were *very* happy. They had four children. One became a colonel in the army, one became a contractor, and the girl married Sheikh Abdullah. The Englishman was very rich. *Too* much of money. He owned Nedou's Hotel. You know Nedou's Hotel? Best in Srinagar.'

'Oberoi Palace is best,' Kadir said.

'Nedou's is best. *Best* hotel. So you see, she is English.'

'Who?'

'Sheikh Abdullah's wife. *Pure* English.'

'She couldn't be pure English,' Kadir said.

'*Pure* English. Her father was an Englishman. He owned Nedou's Hotel.'

So, often and in this manner of legend, the talk turned to Sheikh Abdullah. Why had Sheikh Abdullah fallen out with New Delhi? One man said that the Indian Government had wanted to buy over the Post Office but Sheikh Abdullah wouldn't sell. The implication was clear: there had been a tussle over a demand for greater autonomy. To my informant, however, the Post Office was the post office on the Bund, a type of super-shop, doing brisk business every day, which the Indian Government wanted to steal from Kashmir. He was an educated man; and doubtless the fact of a demand for greater autonomy had undergone further distortion and simplification before it had passed down to the peasants. Propaganda needs to find its level; and medieval propaganda was as simple-clever and as fearful as any technique of hidden persuasion. Radio Pakistan could claim that the large sums of money being spent on education in Kashmir were a means of undermining Islam and the Law; and it was more effective propaganda than the Kashmir Government's boards giving development facts and figures.

'But Sheikh Abdullah was Prime Minister for more than five years. What did he do?'

'Ah, that is the beauty. He did nothing. He wouldn't take help from anyone. He wanted the people of Kashmir to learn to stand on their own feet.'

'But if he did nothing in five years, why do you think he is great? Give me an example of his greatness.'

'I will give you an example. One year, you know, the rice crop failed and the people were starving. They went to Sheikh Abdullah and said to him, "Sheikh Abdullah, we have no rice and we are starving. Give us rice." And you know what he said to them? He said, "Eat potatoes."'

Humour was not intended, and the advice was sound. Indians are willing to eat only what they have always eaten; and staples vary from province to province. In the Punjab they ate wheat. In Kashmir, as in the South, they ate rice. It was rice alone, enormous platefuls of it, moistened perhaps with a little tomato sauce, which energized Aziz's active little body. When there was no rice the Kashmiris starved; they might have potatoes, but potatoes were not food. In this lay the point of Sheikh Abdullah's advice. Needless to say, it had gone unheeded and had instead been transformed into a piece of almost prophetic wisdom, to be relished and passed on as such. *Once there was no food in the land, and the people went to the leader and said, 'We have no food. We are starving.' The leader said, 'You might think you have no food. But you have. You have potatoes. And potatoes are food.'*

Regularly white jeeps and station-wagons raced along the roads. In the afternoons they appeared to carry picnic parties of women and children in straw hats; in the evenings, bridge parties. The jeeps and station-wagons were marked U.N. in thin, square letters; they watched over the ceasefire line. In Kashmir they seemed as anachronistic as the clock in *Julius Caesar.*

*

But there was money in Kashmir, more than there had ever been. In 1947, I was told, there were fifty-two private cars in the entire state; now there were nearly eight thousand. In 1947 a carpenter earned two or three rupees a day; now he could get eleven rupees. The new wealth showed in the increased number of veiled women: for people like tonga-wallahs and fuel-vendors a new, veiled wife was a symbol of status. It is estimated that in Kashmir, as in the rest of India, one-third of development funds drains away in corruption and the exchanging of gifts. No disgrace attaches to this. The Kashmiri tailor spoke with envious admiration of his *patwari* friend, a surveyor and type of records-keeper, who in one day might collect as much as a hundred rupees; a lorry-driver had a similar admiration for a traffic inspector he knew who received monthly protection money from various lorry-drivers. From time to time there was an outburst in the press and Parliament about corruption, and here and there frenzied action might instantly be taken. In one state a minister had his doorman charged with corrupt practices: the doorman had bowed to him too low and too often, and by this had shown that he expected a tip. An architect in Delhi told me that even such token attempts to 'stamp out' corruption could be demoralizing and dangerous: the system was necessary and in India it was the only system that could work.

From the engineer I learned how the system worked in Kashmir. A contractor dug, say, one hundred cubic feet of earth. He sent in a bill for two hundred. Now it was precisely to frustrate such adventurousness that the Indian Civil Service method of checking and counter-checking had been devised. The contractor's claim had to be verified; the verification had to be endorsed; and the endorsement, to be brief, had to be approved. In the thoroughness of the system lay its equity. When verification was complete everyone, from top man to messenger, was in the know, and everyone had to be made some offering. The contractor was charged a fixed percentage of his extra profits, and this was divided, again in fixed percentages, among the employees of the department concerned. It was all regulated and above board; everything, the engineer said, smiling as he used the civil service phrase, went 'through proper channel'. It was almost impossible for any government servant to contract out, and no one particularly wanted to. Tipping was expected; the contractor who dug a hundred cubic feet and claimed for a hundred cubic feet was likely to run into trouble; and it had happened that a civil servant who objected to corruption had been transferred or dismissed for corruption. 'Even if the contractor is a relation,' the engineer said, 'he will still have to give something. It's the principle of the thing.' The top man didn't necessarily get the biggest cut of any one levy; but in the long run he made out better than his subordinates because he got a percentage of more levies.

The engineer was in his camp, at the edge of a pine forest, chill when the sun went down. Whitewashed stones lined the path to his tent. In another tent some distance away his subordinates were preparing their evening meal. There had been some trouble with them when he first came on this job, the engineer said. His predecessor had not distributed the levies fairly, and the men were rebellious. His first act had been to renounce his percentage; he had also managed to get them certain stores to which they were not entitled. This had calmed them. The engineer said he himself was against the system. If the system was worked fairly, however, it made for efficiency. It gave the men an interest in their work. Take telegraph poles. They were required to be thirty-four feet tall, to be of a certain girth; and they had to be buried five feet in the ground. Assuming that a pole of thirty-two feet was accepted – and it was only on such sub-standard poles that worthwhile tipping could reasonably be expected – it was important that the pole should be put up quickly. And who was to tell then that it was only three feet in the ground?

There was no means of checking the engineer's account. But I felt that it partly explained the illicit felling which was stripping Kashmir of its accessible forests. (To this the Kashmiris attributed the hotness of their recent summers.) And certainly the wires hung dangerously low from many of the telegraph poles in Srinagar.

*

We seemed to be in danger of losing the hotel garden altogether. First there had come the digging for the ugly telegraph pole to carry the electric wires. And now there came the digging for the poles of the awning, which was put up like lightning with the rough-and-ready carpentry of the lake, and the irruption into the hotel garden of dozens of the lake folk, variously clad in pyjamas or flapping trousers, offering advice, help or simply interest. The awning was an appanage of the houseboat; this was the reason for its appearance in the garden, where it served no purpose. It provided little shade and much heat when the sun was out, and it was taken down whenever rain threatened. It had scalloped edges, trimmed with black, and was exactly like every other houseboat awning in the area. These awnings were all made in the single-roomed tailor's shack on the water highway, where everyone, flower-sellers, grocers, red-turbanned policemen, appeared to stop for a chat and a pull at the hookah.

A day or so later Mr Butt was painting the poles of the awning a light green, and I went down to watch him. He looked up and smiled, and went on with his painting. When he looked up again he wasn't smiling.

'Sir, you ask Mr Madan to tea?'

'Mr Butt, no.'

*

The summer had seemed endless. We had put off the ruins: the Palace of the Fairies, which we could see low on the hills beyond the lake; Akbar's lake fort, Hari Parbat; the temple at Pandrethan; the sun temple at Martand; the temple at Awantipur. Now we did them all at once.

It was a cool day when we went to Awantipur, the dry fields a warm brown against the dark grey-blue mountains. We could make little of the ruins, the massive central platform, the anvil-shaped fonts of solid stone that lay among the rubble, the carvings; and the villager who attached himself to us didn't help. 'It *all* fell down,' he said in Hindustani, waving a hand. '*All?*' '*All.*' It was a type of North Indian dialogue, made possible by the stresses of the language, which I had grown to enjoy. He showed the base of a column and indicated by gestures that it was the bottom stone of a quern. That was the limit of his knowledge. No tip for him; and we walked down to the village to wait for the bus.

The blue-shirted boys had just been released from school; down a side lane we saw the young Sikh teacher organizing a ball game in the schoolyard. The boys gathered around us; they all carried enormous bundles of books wrapped in grubby, inky cloths. We made one boy take out his English book. He opened it at a page headed 'Our Pets', read out: 'Our Body', and began reeling off a text which, after a search, we found on another page. And what book was this? Urdu? They became helpless with laughter: it was Pharsi, Persian, as any child could tell. The crowd had now grown. We broke out of it, saying we wanted to get back to Srinagar; and they all then began waving down buses for us. Many buses passed, full; then one shot past, hesitated, stopped. A Kashmiri attempted to get on but was repelled by the conductor, who made room for us.

We sat in the back among some sensationally unwashed people, their cotton dhotis brown with dirt, and many Dalda tins. The man next to me was stretched out on the seat, clearly unwell, his eyes without expression, the pestilential Indian flies undisturbed on his lips and cheeks; from time to time he gave a theatrical groan, to which no one in the chattering bus paid the slightest attention. We saw that we were in a bus of 'lower-income' tourists and that we were sitting with their servants.

At the ruins the bus stopped and the khaki-clad moustached driver turned around and tried to persuade his passengers to go out and have a look. No one moved. The driver spoke again, and at length one elderly man, whom we had already recognized as the wit and leader of the bus, heaved himself up with a sigh and went out. He wore a black Indian jacket, and his top-knot proclaimed him a brahmin. The others followed.

From nowhere children appeared: '*Paisa, sahib, paisa.*' 'Oh,' said the leader in Hindi. 'You want money? Now what does a little child like you want money for?' '*Roti, roti,*' they chanted. 'Bread, bread.' 'Bread, eh?' He was only teasing. He gave; the others gave.

The leader climbed to the top of the stone steps and regarded the ruins with patronage. He made a witticism; he lectured. The others idled about dutifully, looking without interest where he looked.

A sixteen-year-old boy in white flannel trousers hurried over to me and said, 'This is Pandavas' fort.'

I said, 'This is not a fort.'

'It is Pandavas' fort.'

'No.'

He waved hesitantly towards the leader. 'He says it's Pandavas' fort.'

'You tell him no. He doesn't know what he's talking about.'

The boy looked shocked, as though I had offered him violence. He edged away from me, turned and fled to the group around the leader.

We were all back in the bus and about to start when the leader suggested food. The conductor threw open the door again and an especially grimy manservant, old and toothless, came to life. Briskly, proprietorially, he shoved the Dalda tins along the dusty floor and lifted them out on to the verge. I began to protest at the delay; the boy in white flannels looked at me in terror; and I realized that we had fallen among a family, that the bus was chartered, that we had been offered a lift out of charity. The bus again emptied. We remained helpless in our seats, while Srinagar-bound passenger buses, visibly holding spare seats, went past.

They were a brahmin family and their vegetarian food was served according to established form. No one was allowed to touch it except the dirty old servant who, at the mention of food, had been kindled into such important activity. With the very fingers that a moment before had been rolling a crinkled cigarette and had then seized the dusty Dalda tins from off the dusty bus floor, he now – using only the right hand, of course – distributed puris from one tin, scooped out curried potatoes from another, and from a third secured dripping fingerfuls of chutney. He was of the right caste; nothing served by the fingers of his right hand could be unclean; and the eaters ate with relish. The verge had been deserted; now, in the twinkling of an eye, the eaters were surrounded by villagers and long-haired Kashmiri dogs. The dogs kept their distance; they stood still, their tails low and alert, the fields stretching out behind them to the mountains. The villagers, men and children, stood right over the squatting eaters who, like celebrities in the midst of an admiring crowd, slightly adjusted their behaviour. They ate with noisier relish; just perceptibly they raised their voices, heightened and lengthened out their laughter. The servant, busier than ever, frowned as if made impatient by his responsibilities. His lips disappeared between his toothless gums.

The leader spoke to the servant, and the servant came to where we were. Busily, like a man with little time to waste, he slapped two puris into our hands, plastered the puris with potatoes, leaked chutney on the potatoes, and withdrew, hugging his tins, leaving us with committed right hands.

A family spokesman came to the door of the bus. 'Just *taste* our food.'

We tasted. We felt the eyes of the villagers on us. We felt the eyes of the family on us. We smiled, and ate.

The leader made overtures of friendship; he sought to include us in his conversation. We smiled; and now it was the turn of the boy in white flannels to look hostile. Still, all the way into Srinagar we smiled.

*

In India I had so far felt myself a visitor. Its size, its temperatures, its crowds: I had prepared myself for these, but in its very extremes the country was alien. Looking for the familiar, I had again, in spite of myself, become an islander: I was looking for the small and manageable. From the day of my arrival I had learned that racial similarities meant little. The people I had met, in Delhi clubs and Bombay flats, the villagers and officials in country 'districts', were strangers whose backgrounds I could not read. They were at once narrower and grander. Their choice in almost everything seemed more restricted than mine; yet they were clearly inhabitants of a big country; they had an easy, unromantic comprehension of size. The landscape was harsh and wrong. I could not relate it to myself: I was looking for the balanced rural landscapes of Indian Trinidad. Once, near Agra, I had seen or made myself see such a landscape; but the forlorn wasted figures reclining on string beds in the foreground were not right. In all the striking detail of India there was nothing which I could link with my own experience of India in a small town in Trinidad.

And now, unexpectedly in Kashmir, this encounter with the tourist family answered. The brief visit to the fort of the Pandavas, the gaiety of the excursion party, the giving of small coins to the begging children, the food, the rough manner of its distribution which yet concealed the observance of so many forms: I might have known that family, I could have assessed the relationships, could have spotted the powerful, the weak, the intriguing. The three generations which separated me from them shrank to one.

The encounter had done more than dislodge a childhood memory; it awakened a superseded consciousness. That food should be served in certain strict ways I at once understood. Equally I understood the mixture of strictness and dirt, the overdone casualness with which the puris and potatoes had been slapped into hands. It was partly a type of inverted asceticism, by which a necessary pleasure is heightened; it was partly the conviction, perhaps derived from a rural society poor in implements, perhaps derived from religion, that great elaboration was unnecessary, pretentious and absurd.*

* Luxury, with Indians, and especially Hindus, always seems contrived and strenuous. No people are so little interested in interiors. This lack of interest appears to be historical. The *Kama Sutra*, after laying down that the man of fashion 'should reside where he has a good chance of earning riches but should for preference select a city, a metropolis or a big or small town', prescribes the furnishings of a drawing-room: 'This outer room should contain a bed, richly mattressed, and somewhat depressed in the middle. It should have pillows at the head and the bottom and should be covered with a perfectly white clean sheet. Near this bed there should be a small couch on which the sexual act should be performed so as not to soil the bed. Over

It was above all a respect for the forms, for the way things had always been done.

Yet three generations and a lost language lay between us. This is Pandavas' fort, the boy had said. The Pandavas were the heroes of the *Mahabharata*, one of the two Hindu epics which are universally known and have something of the sanctity of holy books; the Gita is embedded in the *Mahabharata*. The *Mahabharata* is placed by some in the fourth century B.C.; the events it describes are put at 1500 B.C. Yet the ruins of what was so obviously a four-walled building, exposed on all sides, that could by no stretch of the imagination be the fort of five warrior princes, were the ruins of the fort of the Pandavas. It was not that forts were unknown; in Srinagar itself there was one which nobody could miss. The tourists in the bus went against the evidence of their eyes not because they were eager for marvels but because, living with marvels, they had no sense of the marvellous. It was with reluctance that they had got out of the bus. They had known and accepted the story of the *Mahabharata* from childhood. It was part of them. They were indifferent to its confirmation in rocks and stones, fallen into ruin and become material commonplaces which could only be viewed literally. So this was the fort of the Pandavas, this rubble, no longer of use to anyone. Well, it was time to eat, time for the puris and

---

the head of the bed there should be fixed on the wall a lotus-shaped bracket on which a coloured portrait or an image of one's favourite deity should be placed. Beneath this bracket should be placed a small table, one cubit in breadth, set against the wall. On this table the following articles, required for the night's enjoyments, should be arranged: balms and perfumed unguents, garlands, coloured waxen vessels, pots for holding perfumes, pomegranate rinds and prepared betels. There should be a spittoon on the floor near the bed; a lute, a drawing slab, a pot with colours and brushes, a few books and wreaths of flowers, too, hung from elephants' tusks let into the wall. Near the bed upon the floor should be placed a circular chair with a back for resting the head on. Boards for the games of dice and chess should be placed against the wall. In a gallery outside the room cages for pet birds should be hung from ivory tusks fixed into the wall.' (Translated by B.N. Basu.)

the potatoes. The true wonder of the Pandavas and the *Mahabharata* they carried in their hearts.

Some miles nearer Srinagar, at Pandrethan, in the middle of the army camp, a tiny, single-chambered temple, set in a hollow and shaded by a great tree, stood a little crookedly in the centre of a small artificial pool. The water was stale, leaf-littered; and the heavy, inelegant stonework of the temple was roughly patched with new concrete. The temple was in the style of the Awantipur ruin, the 'fort of the Pandavas'; but it was still in use, and it was this, rather than its age, which gave it greater meaning. Romance arose out of a sense of more than physical loss; and here, for Muslim as well as Hindu, nothing had been lost. A building might collapse or be destroyed or cease to be of use; another would take its place, of lesser or greater size or beauty. On the eastern side of Akbar's lake fort an exquisite building lay in ruin. It might have been a mausoleum. Two towers stood at one end of a small cool quadrangle whose walls were faced with black marble. The towers were broken, the flat brick dome pierced; the elegantly proportioned Mogul arches had been filled in with mud bricks, now partly disintegrated; rubble blocked the entrances and littered the high-stepped Mogul staircases which led to low dusty chambers where the fine stone grilling of the windows was broken or lost. But decay, spectacular as it was, lay only in the eye of the visitor. More important than the ruin were the corrugated-iron latrines and washing places which had been built there for the use of those who came to pray at the nearby mosque.

The Mogul gardens remained beautiful because they were still gardens; they still worked. The mausoleum, of the same period, had ceased to be of use; latrines could be set in its ruins. Out of this unexamined sense of flow and continuity the Valley was being disfigured; for if decay lay in the eye of the visitor, so too did beauty. The gardens were clearly meant by their builders to stand alone in the parkland surrounding the lake. But on one side of the green pagoda-like roof of the pavilion that rose above the trees of the

Chasmashahi Gardens there now stood, totally exposed, ten new 'tourist huts', six in one straight line, four in another. On the other side was the government Guest House, where Mr Nehru had stayed; next to this was a Milk Pasteurization and Bottling Plant; and next to this, logically enough, was the complex of a government farm. Sheep, I believe, were bred there. Their tracks scored the hillside all the way up to the eighteenth-century Pari Mahal, the Palace of Fairies – a library perhaps it had been, or an observatory, already absorbed, whatever it was, into myth – the flattened, overgrown terraces of which, sweet with wild white roses and dangerous with bees, were littered with sheep droppings. Through receding arches, cracked plaster revealing brick, the lake could be seen. And on the lake, to the delight of all the lake folk, there now increasingly appeared motor-boats. They tainted the air and water; their stutter carried far; their propellers whipped up eddies of mud; and long after they had passed, the water remained disturbed, slapping against the floating gardens, washing down their edges, rocking and swamping the *shikaras*. And this was only the beginning.

The medieval mind, which saw only continuity, seemed so unassailable. It existed in a world which, with all its ups and downs, remained harmoniously ordered and could be taken for granted. It had not developed a sense of history, which is a sense of loss; it had developed no true sense of beauty, which is a gift of assessment. While it was enclosed, this made it secure. Exposed, its world became a fairyland, exceedingly fragile. It was one step from the Kashmiri devotional songs to the commercial jingles of Radio Ceylon; it was one step from the roses of Kashmir to a potful of plastic daisies.

*

It was under the houseboat-style awning in the garden that Mr Butt ceremoniously received his guests, lake folk or tourists. And it was there one very hot Sunday morning that, looking out of my window, I saw a neatly dressed young man, pink from the awning's concentrated heat, sitting alone and self-consciously sipping tea, the hotel's best china arrayed on a metal tray in front of him.

Brisk feet pattered up the steps. There was a knock on my door. It was Aziz, breathless, grave, a serving towel or rag thrown over his left shoulder.

'Sahib, you come have tea.'

I had just had coffee.

'Sahib, you come have tea.' He was panting. 'Mr Butt he say. Not your tea.'

I went down to the young man. I had often been called upon to handle difficult 'customers' and sometimes to encourage acceptance of a price more realistic than that mentioned by Ali Mohammed at the Tourist Reception Centre.

The young man put down his cup with some awkwardness, stood up and looked at me uncertainly. I sat down in one of the hotel's weatherbeaten, shredding wicker chairs and invited him to resume his tea. Aziz, seconds before the urgent administrator, now the self-effacing, characterless servitor, deferentially poured for me and withdrew, never looking back, yet somehow – in spite of his loose flapping trousers, his tilted fur cap, the serving rag thrown rakishly over one shoulder, the soles of his bare feet flapping hard, black and cracked – communicating total alertness.

It was hot, I said to the young man; and he agreed. But it would soon cool down, I said; you had these changes of temperature in Srinagar. The lake was certainly cooler than the city, and the hotel was cooler than any houseboat.

'So you are enjoying?'

'Yes,' I said, 'I am enjoying very much.'

He had given me an opening and I made use of it. But he was not with me; he did not lose his look of embarrassment. I decided he was one of my failures.

'Where do you come from?' I put the Indian question.

'Oh, I come from Srinagar. I work in the Tourist Office. I have been seeing you around for *months*.'

Where I and my typewriter had failed, Mr Butt and Aziz had succeeded. But Aziz did not behave as though I had failed. He said that the kitchen was pleased with my handling of the young man, and a few days later he announced, as though I alone was responsible for it, that Mr Kak, Mr Madan's deputy, was coming soon to the hotel, to inspect and possibly to have tea.

Mr Kak came. I saw his *shikara* glide up to the landing-stage and I decided to hide. I locked myself in the bathroom. But no feet came tripping up the steps. No summons came. No mention of Mr Kak's visit was made that day or on subsequent days; and I learned of the outcome of his visit only when Mr Butt, accompanied by the secretary of the All Shikara Workers Union, came into my room one morning to ask me to type out the 'particulars' of the hotel for inclusion in the Tourist Office's register of hotels. I had failed; even my final cowardice was irrelevant. Mr Butt was smiling; he was a happy man. Dutifully, I began to type.

'Hotel,' said the secretary, looking over my shoulder, 'is Western style.'

'Yes, yes,' Mr Butt said. 'Western style.'

'I can't type that,' I said. 'Hotel is not Western style.'

'Flush system,' Mr Butt said. 'English food. Western style.'

I got up and pointed through the open window to a little roofed box next to the kitchen hut.

The box was perhaps six feet long, four feet wide and five feet high. And it was inhabited. By a thin, sour middle-aged couple whom we had christened the Borrowers. They were Jains. They had brought their pots and pans to Kashmir; they cooked for themselves; they washed up for themselves, scouring their vessels with mud, of which there was now a plentiful supply around the garden tap. They had at first been simple tourists, occupying one of the lower rooms. But they had a transistor radio; and often I saw them sitting under the awning with Mr Butt, all three concentrating on the transistor which, aerial up, volume up, stood on the table between them. We heard from Aziz that a sale was being negotiated; and it must have been during the negotiations that we saw one morning a brisk, brief transferring of pots and pans, bed and bedding, stool and chair, from the hotel room to the tiny box, which that evening appeared to shiver with light, escaping through cracks and gaps, and with music from the transistor. There was a window, one foot square, Kashmiri-carpentered, crookedly hinged. Through this I tried to get a glimpse of the arrangements inside. I was spotted. A woman's hand pulled the tiny, sagging window to, and closed it with a proprietorial, offended bang.

To this box I now pointed.

The secretary giggled and Mr Butt smiled. 'Sir, sir,' he said, laying his hand on his heart. 'Forgive, forgive.'

*

Srinagar was hot, and the tourists now went higher up, to Pahalgam, which we were told was 'Indian taste', and Gulmarg, which was 'English'. Presently we had the hotel to ourselves again, as it had been in the early spring. There was no washing on the lawn; no cooking parties in the broom-cupboard below the steps. The mud around the garden tap dried to black, caked earth; and in the garden the sunflowers were indeed like emblematic whirls of colour. Even the tradesmen grew torpid. Maulana Worthwhile, who sold shawls, called to ask if I had any English shoe polish, the only thing, according to him, which was good for his ringworm. The regional court held new elections under the awning and we celebrated with cake and tea. Aziz daily dropped hints about Gulmarg. 'When you going Gulmarg, sir?' He wanted us to take him there, and it was only during these slack weeks that he could leave the hotel. But we put off Gulmarg from day to day, becalmed in the summer stillness of the lake.

Then all at once stillness and peace vanished.

There was a holy man in Delhi. It happened this year that there came to Delhi from East Africa a pious family of wealthy Indian merchants. They met the holy man. He liked them; and they were so taken with him they thought they would devote their holiday to his service. The monsoon was delayed that year and, sitting in Delhi, the holy man said, 'I feel an urge to go now to Kashmir, the holy land of Hindus, the land of the holy cave of Amarnath, the purifying icy Lake of the Thousand Serpents, and the plain where Lord Shiva danced.' The merchants at once packed their American limousines with all that was necessary. 'I fear the journey will be too much for me,' the holy man said. 'You go by motor-car. I will follow by Viscount aeroplane.' They made the arrangements and then drove north for a day and a night until they came to the holy city of Srinagar. It was nearly midnight when they arrived. But the news of the arrival of twenty pilgrims spread rapidly from houseboat to empty houseboat, and wherever they went they were followed by shrieking men anxious to give them lodging. When they came to a small hotel on a plot of ground in the lake they said, 'This is what we have been looking for. We will stay here and await our holy man.' Still, through the night the houseboat men came, trying to get them on to their vessels, and there were many disputes.

This was Ali Mohammed's story.

'But they say,' he told us at breakfast, '"We don't want house-boat, we want here."'

It was the hotel's biggest kill, and Ali Mohammed was pleased. He was not Aziz; he could not sympathize with us. Nor could Aziz. He, as if recognizing the hopelessness of the situation, stayed away from us altogether.

They had come equipped for holiness. In their limousines, the wonder of the lake folk, they had brought bundles of especially holy leaves, off which they were to eat, like the sages in the days before plates were plentiful. They did not trust tap-water; they had brought special containers and early in the morning they went off to Chasmashahi, the Royal Spring, to get pure spring water. They had of course to cook for themselves; and the cooking was done, on stones placed on the lawn, by four epicene saffron-robed young men who, when their duties were done, simply idled: they had a fantastic capacity for inactivity. Holiness meant simplicity of this sort: cooking on stones, eating off leaves, fetching water from the spring. It also meant casualness and disorder. Rugs were rolled up in the hotel rooms, curtains hooked up high, furniture disarranged. Simplicity and the possession of a holy man induced arrogance. The men among the pilgrims strutted about the lawn, reducing Ali and Aziz and even Mr Butt to tiptoeing insignificance. They spoke loudly. They hawked loudly and spat with noisy repeated relish everywhere but more especially on the water-lilies, plants which had been introduced to Kashmir from England by the last maharaja and were without the religious associations of the lotus. After their meal, eaten off leaves on the very lawn on which they had been spitting, they belched. They belched thunderously but always with control: it was possible to tell, from the belches alone, who was the leader of the party. He was about forty, tall and fat; a singular element of his holy dress was the multicoloured towel he wore wrapped around his head. The young men did press-ups and other exercises. They had all lived well; this was a pious boy-scout interlude; and the Liward was their camp.

It seemed that no definite message had come from the holy man about the time of his arrival. The pilgrims took no chances. They drove off to meet every aeroplane from Delhi, leaving behind the epicene young men in saffron robes who, fatigued at last by their idleness, began to indulge in what I at first regarded as a type of child's play. Gathering whatever material they could find they constructed, with slow, silent intensity, a rough barricade around the cooking stones on the lawn. But they were not playing: they were protecting their food from the gaze of the unclean. This was not all. The turf had been trodden on by numberless unclean people: the turf had therefore to be torn up. And it was this that the squatting saffron-robed vandals were now silently doing.

I sent for Aziz. Since the arrival of the pilgrims we had not had a confrontation. His face was small. He had seen. He had done more: he had provided a plank which the saffron robes, following a logic of their own, had laid over the mud they had instantly created. What could he do? He spoke of Mr Butt's need for money; he said that God sent customers. He said that they were a holy group and that the holy man, who was expected any day, was almost a saint.

The pilgrims brought the holy man back that afternoon; and the atmosphere of arrogant, belching disorder was replaced by one of silent, self-important servitude, brisk scuttlings-about here, conspiratorial whispers there. The holy man sat in a chair below the awning. From time to time women, as though unable to hold themselves in any longer, ran to the holy man and flung themselves before his chair. The holy man barely acknowledged them. But most of the pilgrims simply sat and stared. He was, in truth, finer than any of his admirers. His saffron robe revealed a well-built body of a smooth, warm brown; there was no touch of sensuality in his firm, regular face, which might have been that of a business executive.

Behind their barricade the saffron-robed disciples were preparing their master's meal. When this was eaten, and when the pilgrims, sitting in two silent rows on the lawn, had eaten, it was dusk, and the holy man led them all in devotional song. Two men washed the holy man's robe; then, holding two corners each, they waved it in the air until it was dry.

I went over to the kitchen, for comfort, and found them all huddled and subdued around the hookah.

'To them we are all unclean,' a boatman said. 'Isn't it a cruel religion?'

I recognized the Radio Pakistan phrase. But even the boatman clearly held the holy man in awe and didn't speak above a whisper.

In the morning the lawn had been dug up some more; the area of mud had spread; and the pilgrims, blither than ever, were shelling peas and cooking and belching and spitting toothpaste on the waterlilies and bathing and washing clothes and running up and down the steps.

At breakfast I asked Ali Mohammed, 'When are they leaving?'

He misunderstood my reason for asking. He smiled, baring his ill-fitting dentures, and said, 'Big sadhu say last night, "I like this place. I *feel* I like this place. I stay here five days. I stay here five weeks. I don't know. I feel I like this place."'

'Call Aziz.'

Aziz came, limply carrying his serving rag. The rag was unclean; he was unclean; we were, indeed, all unclean together.

'Aziz, you tell Mr Butt. Either these people go or we go.'

Mr Butt came. He looked down at his shoes.

'Hotel is not Western style, Mr Butt. Not Liward Hotel now. Liward Mandir, Liward Temple. I am going to invite Mr Madan to tea *today*.'

Aziz knew an empty threat when he heard one. That last sentence had betrayed my helplessness. He at once brightened, flicked his rag about the dining-table and said, 'When you going Gulmarg, sir?'

'Yes, yes,' Mr Butt said. 'Gulmarg. You take Aziz with.'

So we compromised. We would go to Gulmarg for a few days.

'But, Mr Butt, if they are still here when we get back, we go for good.'

'That is good, sir.'

Yet I had it in my power to send the pilgrims and the holy man scuttling out of the hotel in five minutes. I could have revealed to them that that part of the lawn they had dug up for the sake of cleanliness and converted into their kitchen and barricaded lay directly over the hotel's septic tank.

*

'Hadn't we better find out about the times of the Gulmarg buses, Aziz?'

'O no, sahib. *Too* much bus.'

We got to the bus station just after eight. Aziz, unfamiliar in big brown shoes (Mr Butt's), went to buy the tickets.

'We miss eight o'clock bus,' he said, coming back.

'When is the next one?'

'Twelve o'clock.'

'What are we going to do, Aziz?'

'What we do? We wait.'

It was a new bus station. Kashmiris, emerging from the gentlemen's lavatory, wiped their hands on the curtains, which were of a contemporary fabric. A well-dressed beggar woman distributed printed leaflets which told of her tragedy. We waited.

What was it about Gulmarg that attracted Aziz? It was a holiday settlement of unpainted wooden huts about a small green meadow set in the mountains some three thousand feet above the Valley. On one side the meadow fell away to the Valley through pine forests; on the other it was bounded by higher mountains in the interstices of which, even in August, snow lay in brown drifts. We arrived in rain. At the bungalow of the friends with whom we were going to stay Aziz was at once sent off to the servants' quarters, and we saw him again only when the rain was over. He was walking back down the muddy road from such centre as the settlement had. His gait was made unusual by the weight of Mr Butt's shoes. (Mr Butt later reported, almost with emotion, that Aziz had ruined his shoes on this visit.) His smile and greeting were of pure friendliness. 'How you liking Gulmarg, sir?'

So far we had seen little. We had seen the mountains lost in black cloud; we had seen the purple flowers on the wet green meadow. We had seen the buildings and foundations of buildings looted and burned by the Pakistanis in 1947: one grand wooden building cracked open from the roof, like a toy, and left derelict, still, with its broken coloured panes and all its noises, a setting for nightmare.

Had Aziz seen more? Was there an especial friend in Gulmarg? Was there a woman? His moods had been so varied that day. In the morning he had been the efficient hotel servant. At the bus station, settling down for the long wait, he had wiped anticipation off his face, which had grown blank, almost stupefied. In the bus at last, clutching the sandwich basket, he had shown a subdued sociability. Then, as soon as he had got on to the pony for the ride through the pines up to Gulmarg, he had become animated and mischievous, bobbing up and down in his saddle, twirling the reins, making clucking noises, racing ahead, riding back, surprising the other ponies into trots. I think it was the ponies of Gulmarg he looked forward to; somewhere in him there must have been the blood of horsemen. On a pony, and even with his shoes on, he ceased to be comic; the loose tapering trousers were right; they were the trousers of a horseman. On our excursions on the following days he never walked when he could ride, even on the steepest, rockiest, nastiest paths; and as long as he was on the back of a pony he remained animated, crying out delightedly when the pony slipped, '*Oash! Oash!* Easy, easy.' He became talkative. He spoke of the events of 1947 and told of raiders who were so ignorant they took brass for gold. And he told us why he was reluctant to walk. One winter, he said, he had left the service of an employer beyond the Valley; he was without money and had had to cross the snow-covered Banihal Pass on foot. He had fallen ill, and the doctor had forbidden him ever to walk again.

He seemed to be so many persons. It was especially interesting to watch him at work on our friends, to see applied to others that process of assessment through service to which, in the early days, we ourselves had been subjected. They had servants of their own: nothing bound Aziz to them. Yet he was already taking possession of them; and already he was binding them to himself. He had nothing to gain; he was only obeying an instinct. He could not read or write. People were his material, his profession and no doubt his diversion; his world was made up of these encounters and managed relationships. His responses were acute. (How easily, how 'officially', understanding our sentimentality, he had managed the dismissal of the *khansamah*: 'This is happy for him', the *khansamah* raging impotently behind his back.) He had picked up his English by ear; he therefore avoided Indian eye-pronunciations and spoke the words he knew with a better accent than many college-educated Indians. Even his errors ('any' for 'some': 'anybody don't like ice') showed his grasp of a language only occasionally heard; and it was astonishing to hear a word or phrase I had used coming back, days later, with my very intonations. Would he have gone far if he had learned to read and write? Wasn't it his illiteracy which sharpened his perception? He was a handler of people, as in their greater ways rulers of this region, also illiterate, had been: Ranjit Singh of the Sikhs, Gulab Singh, founder of the Jammu and Kashmir State. To us illiteracy is like a missing sense. But to the intelligent illiterate in a simpler world mightn't literacy be an irrelevance, a dissipation of sensibility, the mercenary skill of the scribe?

On the way back to Srinagar I watched him prepare a face for Mr Butt. He ceased to be animated; he became morose and harassed; he unnecessarily loaded himself in the bus with bags and baskets and made himself as uncomfortable as he could. When we got off the bus his expression would have convinced anyone that Gulmarg, so far from being a holiday from hotel work, had been tedious and exhausting. He subtly overdid his glum attentions to us, as though convincing himself that we had been a great strain. It was possible, too, that he shared our anxieties about the holy man and the pilgrims and was being defensive in advance. When we were driving in the tonga along the lake boulevard he said, 'Mr Butt he say you not pay for me as guide.'

Guide! Had he been our guide? Hadn't he persuaded us to take him to Gulmarg, hadn't he dropped daily reminders? Hadn't we paid for his pony rides?

*

'Yesterday big sadhu say, "I *feel* I go Pahalgam today."'

So Ali Mohammed reported. And they had gone, leaving only the ruined lawn, mud-splashed walls and a few lentils, already sprouting in the mud, to speak of their passing. In the garden the first canna had opened, bright yellow with spots of the purest red.

I showed the sprouting lentils to Mr Butt.

'O sir,' he said. 'My shame. My shame!'

And, as if to underline this, he came to me on the following day with Aziz, and through Aziz he said, 'Sir, you ask Maharaja Karan Singh to tea. Maharaja Karan Singh come to tea here, I take down hotel sign, I sack customer, I close hotel.'

# 7
# PILGRIMAGE

IT WAS KARAN Singh, the young Maharaja of Kashmir, now the elected Head of the Jammu and Kashmir State, who encouraged us to join the pilgrimage to the Cave of Amarnath, the Eternal Lord. The cave lies thirteen thousand feet up the eighteen-thousand-foot Amarnath Mountain, some ninety miles north-east of Srinagar, and is made holy by the five-foot ice *lingam*, symbol of Shiva, which forms there during the summer months. The *lingam*, it is believed, waxes and wanes with the moon and reaches its greatest height on the day of the August full moon: on this day the pilgrimage arrives. It was a mystery, like Delphi, of the older world. It had survived because it was of India and Hinduism which, without beginning, without end, scarcely a religion, continued as a repository and living record of man's religious consciousness.

Karan Singh had gone to the cave some years before, though not with the traditional pilgrimage, and he had published a vivid account of the journey. I could not share his religious fervour, but I relished his exact descriptions of snowclad mountains, icy green lakes and changing weather. To me the true mystery of the cave lay in its situation. It was at the end of a twenty-mile track, a journey of two days, from Chandanwari, which was as far as the jeep-road went. For many months of the year this track disappeared under Himalayan snow and the cave was inaccessible; and in summer, in spite of the annual efforts of the Public Works Department, the track was difficult and in bad weather dangerous. It zigzagged up a two-thousand-foot drop; it led over a pass fifteen thousand feet high; it was a narrow ledge on a bare, curving mountainside. Beyond the tree-line breathing was not easy, and the nights were very cold. The snow never completely melted. It remained hard in sheltered gullies and canyons; it formed solid bridges over summer-slackened streams, bridges which on the surface were as brown and gritty as the surrounding land but which several feet below, just above the water, were scooped out into low, ice-blue caverns.

How had the cave been discovered? How had its mystery been established? The land was bare; it offered no fuel or food. The Himalayan summer was short, its weather treacherous. Every exploration, like every pilgrimage even today, had to be swift. And how had this mystery, so much of ice and snow, so briefly glimpsed each year, penetrated to every corner of ancient India? Himalayas, 'abode of snow': how could they be related to the burning North Indian plain and the palm-fringed beaches of the South? But they had been charted, their mysteries unearthed. Beyond the Amarnath Cave was the mountain of Kailas and beyond that the lake of Manasarovar. And legends attached to every stage of the Amarnath pilgrimage. These rocks were what remained of defeated demons; out of that lake Lord Vishnu arose on the back of a thousand-headed serpent; on this plain Lord Shiva once did the cosmic dance of destruction and his locks, becoming undone, created these five streams: wonders revealed only for a few months each year before disappearing again below the other, encompassing mystery of snow. And these mountains, lakes and streams were indeed apt for legend. Even while they were about you they had only a qualified reality. They could never become familiar; what was seen was not their truth; they were only temporarily unveiled. They might be subject to minute man-made disturbances – a stone dislodged into a stream, a path churned to dust, skirting snow – but as soon as, on that hurried return journey, they had been left behind they became remote again. Millions had made the journey, but the naked land carried few signs of their passage. Each year the snows came and obliterated their tracks, and each year in the cave the ice *lingam* formed. The mystery was forever new.

And in the cave, the god: the massive ice phallus. Hindu speculation soared so high; its ritual remained so clemental. Between the conception of the world as illusion and the veneration of the phallus there was no link; they derived from different strata of responses. But Hinduism discarded nothing; and it was perhaps right not to. The phallus endured, unrecognized as such, recognized only as Shiva, as continuity: it was doubly the symbol of India. So often on journeys through the derelict Indian countryside it had seemed that the generative force alone remained potent, separate from its instruments and victims, men. To those whom it degraded and deformed its symbol remained, what it had always been, a symbol of joy. The pilgrimage was appropriate in every way.

*

'You want a cook,' Aziz said. 'You want one man for help me. You want coolie. You want sweeper. You want seven pony.'

Each pony came with its owner. This would make fourteen of us altogether, not counting animals, with Aziz in charge.

I began pruning. 'No cook.'

'He not only cook, sahib. He guide.'

'There are going to be twenty thousand pilgrims. We don't want a guide.'

The cook was Aziz's protégé. He was fat and jolly and I would have liked to take him. But he had revealed, through Aziz, that he shared Aziz's disability; he too had been advised not to walk and he too required a pony for himself. Then he had sent word from the kitchen, through Aziz again, that he required a new pair of shoes for the journey. I couldn't afford him. I decided, too, that the coolie was unnecessary; and the sweeper was to be replaced by a small spade.

Aziz, defeated, suffered. He had known glorious establishments and he had no doubt visualized an expedition in the old style. He must have seen himself jacketed, trousered and fur-capped, trotting about on his pony and superintending. Now he saw only five days of labour. But he had never been to Amarnath and he was excited. He told us that the Muslims had been there first and that the cave, *lingam* and all, used to be a Muslim 'temple'.

He reported to Mr Butt. Mr Butt summoned an English-knowing lake scribe and a few days later, when I was in bed with yet another cold, sent in his estimate:

| | |
|---|---|
| From Srinagar to Palguime Boy Bus Rotin | 30.0.0. |
| 3 Roding Poine Rotine | 150.0.0. |
| 2 Pakige Roine Rotine | 100.0.0. |
| Tente a Kachen | 25.0.0. |
| Tabel a chare Bed | 15.0.0. |
| one colie | 30.0.0. |
| | 350.0.0. |
| Sweper | 20.0.0. |
| Extre loding and Noey Loding colie | 20.0.0. |
| | 390.0.0. |
| From 11 august up to 17 august | |
| 7 day conteri Food | 161.0.0. |
| | Rs 551.0.0. |

If you going Bus for Imri Nath then is last 17 Rs.

It was a remarkable document: an unfamiliar language, an unfamiliar script, and most of its approximations understandable. Too understandable: I was being overcharged. I was bitterly disappointed. I had known them for four months; I had declared my affection for them; I had done what I could for the hotel; I had given them a party. It must have been the depth of this disappointment; or it might have been my two days in bed. I jumped up, pushed Aziz aside, ran to the window, threw it open and heard myself shouting to Mr Butt in a strange insincere-sincere voice, the result perhaps of remembering, even while I shouted, that I had to speak clearly, as to a child, and to use words which he would understand: 'This is not *good*, Mr Butt. Butt Sahib, this is not *honest*. Mr Butt, do you know what you have done? You have *hurt* me.'

He was standing in the garden with some boatmen. He looked up, startled and uncomprehending. Then his face, still turned up to me, went blank. He said nothing.

In the silence that followed my words I felt foolish and not a little uneasy. I closed the window and quietly got back into bed. India, it was said, brought out concealed elements of the personality. Was this me? Was this the effect of India?

Whatever it was, it alarmed them at the hotel; and when, after giving me time to cool down, they gathered around my bed to discuss the estimate, they were solicitous, as though I was ill with more than a cold. Their manner also held reproach: it was as if, during all the weeks I had been with them, I had concealed my emotionalism, thereby encouraging an approach for which they could not, with justice, be blamed.

In the end many rupees were knocked off the estimate and we became friends again. Mr Butt seemed happy; he came with us to Pahalgam to see us off. Aziz was happy. He was wearing his fur cap, Ali Mohammed's striped blue suit, sandals (Mr Butt had refused to lend his shoes again), and a pair of my socks. He did not have the retinue he would have liked, but no one else on the pilgrimage appeared to be travelling in comparable style. We did, after all, have a staff; and we had a second tent for the staff. And when, at sunset, we halted at the crowded camp in the smoking woods of Chandanwari, he not only managed by his swift, intelligent arrangements to create something like luxury in the midst of restrictions, but he also managed, by his mixture of bustle, of orders sharply given to the pony man and his assistant, and of reverential exaggerated attentions to us, to hedge us around with dignity. The camp was a chaos of tents and guy-ropes and cooking stones and pilgrims defecating behind every bush. The woods were already littered with uncovered excrement; hanks and twists of excrement crowned every accessible boulder of the Lidder River, beside which we had camped. But Aziz made us feel apart; he put us on show. This was his craft, his pride. And just as that morning when we set out from the hotel for Gulmarg he could not hide his pleasure, but had to tell everyone he passed on the lake that he was off to Gulmarg, so now, pouring warm water for me to wash my hands, he said, 'Everybody asking me, "*Who* is your sahib?"' It was less a tribute to me than to himself.

His troubles began the next day. For half a mile out of Chandanwari the path ran easily between rock and the boulder-strewn Lidder River until it came to the almost vertical two-thousand-foot wall of Pissu Ghati. Here the path narrowed and zigzagged up and up between rocks, the slain demons of one legend, for two miles. The pilgrims queued for the climb, and the queue moved slowly. At Chandanwari it did not move at all. It was hours before we could get going, and then we discovered that during our morning's stupor one of our pony men had absconded. So Aziz's torment began. The ponies had to be urged up Pissu Ghati, their loads held in place – we could hear the pony men's cries all the way up and the occasional crash of tumbling loads – and there was nothing Aziz could do but to get off his pony and start pushing the abandoned, tent-laden pony up the steep path: he in his striped blue suit, his fur cap, his Terylene socks, he who had been forbidden to walk. Dignity abandoned him. He complained like a child; he cursed in Kashmiri; he swore to get vengeance; he asked me to write to Mr Madan. His whip hand flashed again and again. 'Bloody swine man!' he shouted in English, and the Terylene socks sagged down his stamping, sandalled feet. His cries grew fainter as we went ahead on our ponies. Looking down, we glimpsed him from time to time negotiating a hairpin bend, angrily dodging the tent-poles, and each time he looked tinier, dustier, more crumpled and more enraged.

We got to the top and waited for him. We waited a long time, and when at last he appeared, shouting behind his still recalcitrant pony, he was a picture of outraged misery. Ali Mohammed's blue suit had been discoloured by dust to the fawn of my Terylene socks, the tops of which had now worked their way down to his heels. Dust stuck to his small sweating face; even through his crumpled clothes I could feel the fragility of his suffering legs. My delight in his discomfiture, his abrupt transformation from major-domo to Kashmiri *ghora-wallah*, pony man, now felt like malice.

'Poor Aziz,' I said. 'Bloody *ghora-wallah*.'

This encouragement was a mistake. From now on he talked of nothing but the renegade *ghora-wallah*. 'You dock his pay, sahib.' 'You write Mr Madan Touriasm.' 'You complain Government, they take away his permit.' And he made up for his walk up Pissu Ghati by staying on his pony all the way to Sheshnag. We shouted to him to get off, to give his assistant a rest. He never heard; it was we who got off our ponies, to give the chance of a ride to the assistant, excessively burdened by Aziz after Pissu Ghati. Breathing was not easy; walking was painful, even up the gentlest slope. Aziz rode serenely on now. A pony had been provided for him; that was part of the contract. Dignity gradually returned to him. He became once again the major-domo, importantly slung with an *English* vacuum flask, which he had insisted on carrying. ('This is *beautiful* Thermos,' he had said, passing a sensuous hand over it, and throwing one of our own words back at us.) From time to time he halted and waited for us; and as soon as we caught up with him it was: 'You go see Government. They take away *ghora-wallah* permit.' He was out for blood; I had never seen him so determined.

In front and behind the pilgrimage stretched in a thin irrelevant line of movement which appeared to have no beginning or end, which gave scale to the mountains and emphasized their stillness. The path had been trampled into dust, inches thick, that rose at every step. It was important not to overtake or be overtaken. Dust overcame the dampness below wet rock; dust powdered the hard snow in gullies. Over one such gully a skull-capped Kashmiri had made himself the harassed master. He had a spade and feverishly dug up snow, which he offered, for a few coins, to pilgrims. The pilgrims, continually pressed from behind, could not stop. Nor could the Kashmiri: he frantically dug, ran with extended spade after the pilgrims already departing, did a lightning haggle, took his coins, ran back, dug again. He was all motion: it was a one-day-a-year trade.

We had passed the tree-line and now we came into sight of the milky green lake of Sheshnag and the glacier that fed it. From Karan Singh's essay I had learned that the icy waters of Sheshnag were auspicious. Some members of his party had gone down the half a mile or so to the lake, to have a lucky dip. But he had made a compromise: 'I have to admit that I used the less orthodox, though certainly more convenient, method of getting water from the lake carried up and warming it for my bath.' It would have been pleasant to dawdle here, to go down to the lake. But the pilgrimage pressed us on, and Aziz was anxious to camp.

He was right to be anxious. The camping ground, when we got to it, was crowded; the rocky banks of the turbulent mountain river were already lined with defecating pilgrims, and soon it would have been difficult to find an accessible washing spot that was unsullied. Hundreds of ponies, freed of their burdens, had been hobbled and turned loose on the mountainside, browsing on what they could find; some were to die on this journey. The evening light fell golden on the three snowy peaks above Sheshnag; it shot through the smoke which, rising above the camp, converted the tents into an extensive miniature mountain range, peak beyond white peak dissolving in evening mist; it fell on the two long rows of sadhus, more brilliant splashes of saffron and scarlet, who were being fed, at the Kashmir Government's expense, in an open area that had been spared impurity. These sadhus had been gathered from every corner of India, and their feeding, I believe, was part of the Tourist Department's public relations: officially we were all 'tourists-cum-pilgrims'.

Aziz did not cease to complain about the runaway *ghora-wallah*. I knew that he had chosen me as the instrument of his vengeance and I cannot understand why I did not rebel. His complaints and pleas wore me down; and after dinner I allowed myself to be led through the dark, cold camp, past ropes and glinting rivulets and heaven knows what other dangers, to the tent of one of the government officials accompanying the pilgrimage. I had met him the previous evening at Chandanwari, and now he greeted me warmly. I was glad for Aziz's sake and my own at this proof of my influence. Aziz behaved like a man already satisfied. He was no longer the leader; he was only my deferential servant. By his behaviour, his interruptions, he presented me as the aggrieved party, a duped tourist; then he withdrew, leaving me to get out of the situation as best I could. My complaint was half-hearted. The official made notes. We talked about the difficulties of organizing such a pilgrimage, and he offered me a cup of coffee with the compliments of the Indian Coffee Board.

I was in the Coffee Board's tent, sipping coffee, when a tall white girl of striking appearance came in.

'Hi,' she said, sitting beside me. 'I'm Laraine.'

She was American; she was thrilled by the *yatra*, the pilgrimage. Her speech abounded in Hindi words.

She attracted me. But I had grown tired of meeting young Americans in unlikely places. It was amusing, and charitable, to think that some of them were spies for the CIA or whatever it was. But there were too many of them. It seemed more likely that they were a new type of American whose privilege it was to go slumming about the world and sometimes scrounging, exacting a personal repayment for a national generosity. I had met the type in Egypt, looking for Lawrence Durrell's Alexandria, living on a few piastres a day, eating *foul* and willing to accept any Eastern hospitality that was going. In Greece for one day I had had to feed an unashamed beggar, a 'teacher', who said he never went to restaurants or hotels: 'As long as there are doors to knack on, I knack.' (He was almost certainly a spy, and he thought I was one too. 'Why is it,' he said, 'that every goddam outa-the-way place I go, I meet Indians?') In New Delhi I had met the type in its most developed form: this was a 'research student', of ineradicable grossness, who had billeted himself for six weeks in the house of a stranger, casually encountered at a wedding party. India, the world's largest slum, had an added attraction: 'cultural' humility was sweet, but 'spiritual' humility was sweeter.

So: No, I said, I wasn't thrilled by the *yatra*. I thought the *yatris* had no idea of sanitation; they polluted every river we came to; I wished they would follow Gandhi's advice about the need for a little spade.

'Then you shouldn't have come.'

It was the only reply, and it was unanswerable. My resentment had made me speak foolishly. I sought to work the conversation back to a more normal give-and-take and tried to get her to tell me about herself.

She had come to India, she said, for two weeks, and had already stayed six months. She was attracted to Hindu philosophy; when she left the *yatra* she was going to spend some time in an ashram. She was a seeker.

Her cheekbones were high; her neck was slender. But her leanness was of the sort which holds fleshy surprises; her breasts were good and full. I did not think it was the body of someone who would be allowed to remain a seeker for long. Yet in the light of the pressure lamp her eyes conveyed uncertainty. I thought they hinted at family problems and childhood distress. This, and a certain coarseness of her skin, added a disturbing edge to her good looks.

I would have liked to see more of her. But though we promised to look out for one another, we never met again during the pilgrimage.

That, however, was not the last of Laraine.

*

Ridiculously, the next morning I allowed Aziz to persuade me to complain to the government official again about the missing *ghora-wallah*. Aziz wanted blood, and his faith in the power of officials was boundless. He was almost triumphant when we started out. We had gone less than a mile, however, Aziz serene on his pony, when our bedding bundle rolled off the untended pony and tumbled down a precipice. Our cavalcade had to stop; Aziz had to walk the pony back and then down; the pony had to be reloaded and urged up again. He was raging when, half an hour later, he rejoined us. 'Swine!' he said. 'Bloody swine man!' And all the way to Panchtarni he alternately brooded and raged.

At Sheshnag we had been at an altitude of thirteen thousand feet. A gradual climb of two thousand feet brought us to the Mahagunas Pass, and a world of bleached grey stone: the snows were only temporarily absent. The mountains were grained like wood; and each mountain was grained at a different angle. From here it was an easy descent to the Panchtarni Plain, an abrupt, unbroken levelling-out between the mountains, a mile long, a quarter of a mile wide, down which a keen wind blew and shallow streams raged, white over grey rocks. Colour had grown austere and arctic, and the word 'plain' was like a definition of lunar geography.

At the edge of the wet, pale plain, and unprotected from the wind, an unburdened, unhobbled pony stood shivering to death, his Kashmiri master standing sad-eyed beside him, doing nothing, offering only his presence, both removed from the bustle of the camp, the last full camp of the pilgrimage. The talk among porters and pony men was already of the swift journey back, and even Aziz, infected in spite of his brooding, was saying like an old Amarnath hand, 'Tomorrow I go *straight* back to Chandanwari.' In that 'I' he included us all.

It was mid-afternoon when we pitched our tents. After Aziz had given us tea he left us, saying he was going to have a look round. Something was on his mind. When he returned, less than half an hour later, his look of preoccupation had disappeared; he was all smiles.

'How you liking, sir?'

'I am liking very much.'

'Pony dead.'

'Pony dead!'

'Sweeper come just now take him away.' At twelve thousand feet, and from a devout Muslim, caste. 'Why you not write Mr Butt letter, sir? Tell him how much you like. Post Office here with *yatra*. You post letter here.'

'No paper, no envelope.'

'I buy.'

He had already bought: it was an Inland Letter form that he was pulling out from one of the pockets of Ali Mohammed's jacket.

I wrote to Mr Butt, postcard sentiments. I was about to seal the letter when Aziz said, 'You put this in, sir.' It was a dirty scrap of paper, possibly an envelope flap, on which one sentence of Urdu had been written with a ballpoint pen.

'You can't put anything inside these letters, Aziz.'

At once he tore the Urdu note into tiny pieces, which he let fall to the ground, and he referred no more to it. I don't believe he posted the letter I wrote; at least Mr Butt never received it. The note was secret, that was clear. It would have been less secret if the Urdu writer had known the name of the person to whom it was addressed; the addressing was therefore my job. This must have been the plan he had been devising all day. Yet he had abandoned it so easily. Was it only a taste for mystification? Even if it was, it had very nearly enabled Aziz, an illiterate, to send a secret message to someone ninety miles away. I was disturbed. Did I fully know Aziz? Did he respond to affection like mine, or was his loyalty only to an employer?

The pilgrims, when they were on the march, could have formed a line ten to fifteen miles long. For hours, then, the line must have moved, unbroken, from camp to camp. Even as the sun was going down over the grey, whistling plain where a pony had died, where ponies every year died, the pilgrims continued to come down the mountains and across the plain, a thin wriggling line of colour rapidly merging into the darkness there, here in the lights of the camp revealed as a slow, silent march of Kashmiri pony men, skull-capped, with dusty feet in disintegrating straw sandals, Gujjars whose studded leather shoes, curiously small and elegant, curling back at the tips, matched the sharpness of their fine features, and ladies riding side-saddle muffled against the dust during the day, now muffled against the cold.

They came into a camp where the tension of adventure, so high only that morning, had already slackened. The adventure was nearly over; the restlessness was the restlessness of anticipated breaking-up and return. Many of the pilgrims had turned in early; they wished to be up for the four o'clock dash to the cave the next morning. The posters in the tent of the Indian Coffee Board were tarnished: they would be needed for only a few hours more. There were fewer wanderers about the camp than at Sheshnag or Chandanwari. No one gazed at the silver rods which for a century had been sent on the pilgrimage by the Kashmir royal house and were displayed in a lighted tent at the head of the camp; that wonder had been seen before. The crowd around the pundit in the second tent was small and settled, a sifting of the crowds of the two previous nights. From Karan Singh's essay, I imagine that during our night halts he had been reciting from the *Amarkatha*, a Sanskrit account of the pilgrimage 'believed to have been related by Lord Shiva himself to his consort Parvati in the Amarnath Cave'. He was a man of ferocious, magazine-illustration handsomeness, exactly filling his role: he had a wavy black beard, long hair, large bright eyes, and remained bare-shouldered even in the bitter cold. Tonight in his windy tent he was chanting, his eyes closed, his fingers delicately bunched on his knees. Just beyond the yellow of his pressure lamp, light was silver: the moon, almost full. Rock was as white as raging water; the wind blew; the camp went stiller.

The path to the cave was a narrow ledge cut diagonally, ever rising, ever curving, into the mountains beyond Panchtarni. Pilgrims were already returned from the cave when we started in bright sunlight the next morning; and men with red Public Works Department armbands stood at dangerous corners, controlling the two-way traffic. The foreheads of the returning pilgrims were marked with sandalwood paste. Their faces were bright with ecstasy. They had seen the god; they were exuberant and aggressive. They were unwilling to give way. They shouted, '*Jai Shiva Shankar!*' and the cave-bound pilgrims, as subdued as a cinema queue when the earlier, fulfilled audience streams out, replied softly, '*Jai Shiva Shankar!*'

'You!' a sandalwood-smeared young man shouted to me in English. 'You say, "*Jai Shiva Shankar!*"'

'*Jai Shiva Shankar!*'

My promptness confused him. 'All right. Good.' And he passed on. '*Jai Shiva Shankar!*'

Down the steep mountainside yellow flowers presently appeared in profusion, and everyone was reminded that fresh flowers were an acceptable offering to the god. Since four o'clock that morning, though, pilgrims had been passing this way: few flowers remained within easy reach, and it seemed that for many the faded flowers bought from the camp bazaar would have to serve. Then we came upon Kashmiris squatting in safe recesses before bunches of the yellow flowers, which silently, with averted eyes, they offered for sale.

We began to descend again, and from bright sunlight we turned off into the cold shadow of a long narrow valley. The valley might have been the bed of a recent river. Its base was littered with brown rubble and its sides, curving steeply, carried what looked like black tidemarks. But this was not rubble or grey shingle; this was old snow, gone the colour and texture of earth. Down one side of the valley the line of pilgrims, going and coming, stretched; and there, far away, they were crossing the ice bed, mere specks, robbed of all but the brightest colour, distinguishable only by their movement from the rubbled surface of the snow. Here was a mountain, there a valley and a river: the geography of these ranges was simple, easily grasped. But one had brought to them the scale of a smaller, managed world, and it was only at times like these, seeing a line of men swiftly diminished within what seemed a small space, that one realized what distances these Himalayas held.

Now indeed, in that valley, India had become all symbol. We on the path rode on ponies. But there, on the brown snow below, in the shadow of mountains that denied life, walked pilgrims from the plains, supporting themselves on staffs (bought from Kashmiri roadside vendors at Pahalgam): a broken line merging at the end of the valley into that other line which, across the snow-bed, no goal in sight, disappeared into the grey-brown mountains and became of their texture. The god existed: the faces and cries of the returning pilgrims carried this reassurance. I wished I was of their spirit. I wished that something of their joy awaited me at the end.

Yet a special joy had been with me throughout the pilgrimage and during all my time in Kashmir. It was the joy of being among mountains; it was the special joy of being among the Himalayas. I felt linked to them; I liked speaking the name. India, the Himalayas: they went together. In so many of the brightly coloured religious pictures in my grandmother's house I had seen these mountains, cones of white against simple, cold blue. They had become part of the India of my fantasy. It would have astonished me then, in a Trinidad achingly remote from places that seemed worthwhile and real because fully known, to be told that one day I would walk among the originals of those mountains. The pictures I knew to be wrong; their message was no message to me; but in that corner of the mind which continues child-like their truth remained a possibility. And it was partly with that sense of the unattainable given by those pictures, such as, after a lifetime it seemed, I had seen again in Indian bazaars and among the dusty stock of pavement booksellers, that I looked upon these mountains. To be among them was fleetingly, and with a truer sense of their unattainability, to claim them again. To reject the legend of the thousand-headed Sheshnag was easy. But the fact of the legend established the lake as mine. It was mine, but it was something I had lost, something on which I would soon have to turn my back again. Was it fanciful to think of these Himalayas, so well charted and perhaps once better known, as the Indian symbol of loss, mountains to which, on their burning plains, they looked back with yearning, and to which they could now return only in pilgrimages, legends and pictures?

At the end of the valley, where the ice, less protected, was partly broken, one remembered picture came to life: a sadhu, wearing only a leopard skin, walking barefooted on Himalayan snow, almost in sight of the god he sought. He held his trident like a spear, and from the trident a gauze-like pennant fluttered. He walked apart, like one to whom the journey was familiar. He was a young man of complete, disquieting beauty. His skin had been burned black and was smeared with white ash; his hair was reddish-blond; but this only made unnatural the perfection of his features, the tilt of his head, the fineness of his limbs, the light assurance of his walk, the delicate play of muscles down his back and abdomen. Some days before the pilgrimage I had seen him in Srinagar, resting in the shade of a chenar, languid genitals arrogantly exposed. He had seemed out of place, an idler, an aboriginal come to town. His ash-smeared nudity, implying an indifference to the body, had made his beauty sinister. Now he lent his nobility to all the pilgrims: his goal was theirs.

Out of the shadow of the valley the broad pyramidal slope of Amarnath burst upon us, rock-strewn, quivering white in sunlight; and the cave to which it led rose black and still, taller and wider than I had imagined it, yet now, after so much expectation, oddly obvious, like a cave in a simple religious picture. It dwarfed the pilgrims seething at its mouth; again men were needed to give scale to a too simple geography. At the foot of the slope pilgrims, preparing for the final ascent, bathed in the clear, holy waters of the

Amarvati stream and rubbed their bodies with its sand. On his own pilgrimage Karan Singh had compromised here, as he had done at Sheshnag: 'Here again I adopted the unorthodox course of getting the water carried in buckets to the tent, but this time I did not get it warmed up and bathed with the ice cold water. It was clear and warm, however, so the cold bath did not cause any inconvenience.'

Sunlight, white-rock, water, bare bodies, brilliant garments: it was a scene of pastoral at thirteen thousand feet. Just above, however, was turmoil. Beyond the stream there were few restraining khaki-clad policemen, few men with red Public Works Department armbands; and after their placid ablutions the pilgrims scrambled up to the cave and joined the purified, frenzied crowd fighting to get a view of the god and to make their offerings. The cave was about a hundred and twenty feet wide, a hundred feet high, and a hundred feet deep. It was not big enough. Within the cave, damp and dripping, a steep ramp led to the inner sanctum, the abode of the god. This was protected by a tall iron railing, with a gate that opened outwards. The crowd pressed forward; the gate could hardly be opened; whenever it was, the whole ramp seethed and there were cries from those who feared they might be pushed off the ramp: it was a long drop from the gloom of the cave to the white sunlit slope up which more and more pilgrims were coming. The newcomers, barefooted, carrying fresh or faded flowers, wedged themselves into the crowd and hoped to be taken forward by the general movement. Individual advance or retreat was impossible; a woman was sobbing with terror. I climbed up and held on to the iron railing: I could see only crowd and a low rock vault blackened by damp or incense. I climbed down again. Up the slope and from far down the ice-bed of the valley pilgrims steadily approached. They were like pebbles, they were like sand: a stippling of colour which, receding, grew finer. For hours, perhaps for all that day, there would be no slackening of the throng on the ramp.

No sight of the god, then, for me: I would sit it out. Not so Aziz. He was a Muslim, an iconoclast; but his devoutness as a

Muslim could not overcome his curiosity as a Kashmiri. He joined the crowd and instantly vanished, his fur cap alone revealing his progress. I squatted on the wet ground, in a litter of paper and wrappings and cigarette packets, beside a grimy skull-capped Kashmiri Muslim who was guarding the shoes of the Hindu devout at four annas a pair. He was doing good business. Slowly Aziz progressed. Now, at the gates, he was squeezed out of the crowd, like a pip out of an orange: fur cap, bewildered but determined face, Ali Mohammed's striped blue jacket, hands clawing at the rails. Somehow, hands working, unseen legs no doubt also working, he managed to be squeezed through the narrow opening of the gate, and then disappeared, fur cap and all, once again.

I waited a long time for him, in a ringing cave which in a few hours had been turned into a busy Indian bazaar. A bazaar: at this moment of climax there came the flatness I had all along feared. And it was like the flatness, equally expected, equally feared, of my first day in Bombay. Pilgrimages were only for the devout. I concentrated on the Kashmiri's shoes, the coins on his scrap of newspaper.

When Aziz reappeared, tarnished but awed, he reported with contradictory satisfaction, which yet held nothing of surprise – he was, after all, a Muslim – that there was no *lingam*. Perhaps none had formed this time; perhaps it had melted in the rush. Where the *lingam* ought to have been there were only offerings of flowers and money. But the pilgrims streaming through the exit were as ecstatic as any we had met on the morning's march.

'You don't come for the *lingam*,' one man said. 'It's the spirit of the thing.'

The spirit of the thing! Squatting in the cave, which rang continuously with shouts and shuffling, concentrating on the bazaar litter on the wet floor, glimpsing out of the corner of my eye the ever ascending crowd whose numbers I could less easily grasp than I could the size of the mountains and the valleys, I had grown light-headed. A physical growth, because it was extraordinary, was a spiritual symbol. The growth failed; it became the symbol of a symbol. In this spiralling, deliquescing logic I felt I might drown. I went outside into the light. Pilgrims, their offerings made, were looking up for the two rock pigeons, followers of Lord Shiva once, before they were turned into pigeons by the anger of their Lord and doomed for ever to live near Him in His cave. I did not look up. I went on down the white slope, hopping from rock to rock, and did not stop until I came to the clear stream.

*

Our return was to be swift. At Panchtarni, where the camp of the morning had already almost ceased to exist, our bundles were packed and the ponies were waiting. Aziz spoke of going straight on to Chandanwari; he wanted to be back in Srinagar on the following day, to be in time for another religious occasion: the display of the hair from the beard of the Prophet at Hazratbal mosque. I would have preferred to remain a little longer in the mountains. But no; we had to hurry; all about us there was the atmosphere of haste, almost of flight. Later, I thought. Later we would come back and spend an entire summer among these mountains. We would experience their weather – that morning in the camp at Sheshnag mist had suddenly swirled down the snow-capped mountains, adding ominousness to beauty, and had as suddenly lifted, revealing the bright sky. And in the afternoons we would have the streams to ourselves. But 'later' is always part of these moments. Already, in fact, the desolate camp at Panchtarni had affected me. The pilgrimage was over, our path was known; the journey had grown stale.

Some time in the afternoon a Kashmiri in a green cap joined our party, and a quarrel instantly blew up between him and Aziz. I was on foot; from afar I could see the gesticulating figures; and when I drew near I recognized the man in the green cap as the missing *ghora-wallah*. He was attempting to take charge of the pony he had abandoned two days before; there was nothing to stop him, but at every shout from Aziz he behaved like a man who was being restrained by physical force. Vengeance was now Aziz's;

this was the moment he had been waiting for; and his anger and contempt were frightening, except perhaps to another Kashmiri. For all its passion, in fact, the exchange had something of play. The *ghora-wallah* pleaded, but he seemed untouched by Aziz's abuse. He wept. Aziz, astride his shabby little pony, his socked, sandalled feet hanging very low, refused to be mollified. Suddenly, no longer weeping, the *ghora-wallah* ran to the abandoned pony and made as if to seize the reins. Aziz screamed; the *ghora-wallah* stopped short, as though he had been surprised in a furtive act and struck a heavy blow on the head. Finally he ceased to weep or plead; he blustered; he became abusive; and Aziz replied. He hung back; he ran forward; he hung back again. Then he didn't run forward, and gradually dwindled in the distance, a still, standing figure occasionally roused to frenzy, shaking a fist against the Himalayan skyline.

'When we reach Pahalgam you report Touriasm Office,' Aziz, perfectly calm, said to me. 'They take away his permit.'

Sheshnag camp was almost deserted; it looked trampled over and unsavoury. We passed it by and at dusk pitched our tents at a small encampment a few miles on. For hours afterwards lights came twinkling down the mountain, and went past: pilgrims hastening back to Chandanwari, puffs of dust in the light of the full moon.

The journey that remained was easy. We ourselves were in the woods of Chandanwari early next morning and by midday we were in sight of Pahalgam, back in a green world of fields and trees and earth. It was all downhill now. I got off my pony and scrambled down, avoiding the lengthy twists and turns of the jeep-track, and soon was far ahead of Aziz and the others. Aziz made no attempt to catch up with me; and even when, together again, we were on the metalled road and passing the bus station and the Tourist Office, he said not a word about the missing *ghora-wallah*. I did not remind him. He jumped off his pony to take an uninvited, and unresented, pull at someone's hookah: he had abandoned the role of the aloof major-domo. Momentarily we lost him, and when he reappeared he was carrying a quantity of peas in his shirt, the front of which was knotted to form something like a tray, which he did not need to support. The transformation from major-domo to hotel servant was complete. He was even without the vacuum flask; that, like Mr Butt's shoes, he had destroyed.

At our base, a tent in the shade of a tree, the *ghora-wallah* in the green cap was waiting for us. As soon as he caught sight of me he began to wail and weep: a formal self-abasement, a formal weeping, dry and scraping, without a hint of real distress. He ran to me, dropped to his knees and grabbed my legs with his powerful hands. The pony men gathered round with looks of satisfaction. Aziz, his shirtful of peas before him, was openly smiling down at the *ghora-wallah*.

'He is poor man, sahib.'

What was this? After all that I had heard from him about the *ghora-wallah*, could this be Aziz?

The *ghora-wallah* wept more loudly.

'He have wife,' Aziz said. 'He have children. You not report Touriasm, sahib.'

The *ghora-wallah* ran his hands down my legs and banged his forehead on my shoes.

'He very poor man, sahib. You not dock his pay. You not take away his permit.'

Holding my knees firmly, the *ghora-wallah* rubbed his forehead against them.

'He not honest man, sahib. He bloody swine. But he poor. You not report Touriasm.'

The ritual went on, without any reference, it seemed, to me.

'All right, all right,' I said, 'I not report.'

Instantly the *ghora-wallah* was up, not a trace of anxiety or relief on his broad peasant's face: he had simply been working. He dusted the knees of his trousers in a businesslike way, took out some rupee notes from a pocket, counted five and, even as I looked, gave them to Aziz.

This was the price of Aziz's intercession. Had they come to some arrangement the previous afternoon? Had it been planned days before? Had Aziz intended all his groans and complaints to lead to this, an extra five rupees? It seemed unlikely – that labour up Pissu Ghati had been real – but with Aziz I could no longer be sure. He seemed surer of me: he had taken a gift – in the long run my money – in my presence. Throughout the journey he had promoted my dignity; he must have frightened the *ghora-wallah* with my importance. But his true assessment was plain. I was harmless. Faced with this assessment, I felt my will weaken. No, I wouldn't, simply for the sake of my pride, make a scene; when all was said and done, Aziz was my servant. It would be less troublesome to preserve my character, as he had read it, until we got back to Srinagar.

The five rupees, checked, disappeared into one of Aziz's pockets. The moment for reprimand passed. I said nothing. His assessment had, after all, proved correct.

Then the *ghora-wallah*, leading his pony by the reins, came up to me again.

'*Bakshish?*' he said, and stretched out one hand.

*

The sunflowers in the garden faded and were like emblems of dying suns, their tongues of fire limp and shrivelled. My work was almost done; it would soon be time to go. Farewell visits had to be made. We went first to our friends at Gulmarg.

'We've been having our adventures too,' Ishmael said.

They always had. They attracted drama. They were interested in the arts and their house was always full of writers and musicians.

'You didn't by any chance meet a girl called Laraine on your pilgrimage?'

'An American girl?'

'She said she was going to Amarnath.'

'But how extraordinary! Was she staying here too?'

'She and Rafiq nearly drove us mad.'

This adventure (Ishmael said) had begun in Srinagar, in the Indian Coffee House on Residency Road. There one morning

Ishmael met Rafiq. Rafiq was a musician. He played the sitar. The apprenticeship of a musician in India is long and severe. And though Rafiq was nearly thirty and though, according to Ishmael, he was very good, he had not yet made a name; he was just beginning to give recitals on local radio stations. It was in order to relax before one such recital that Rafiq had come to Kashmir for a fortnight. He had little money. Ishmael, generous and impulsive as always, invited Rafiq, whom he had met that morning for the first time, to stay at his bungalow in Gulmarg. Rafiq took his sitar and went.

The arrangement worked well. Rafiq found himself with a couple who understood the artistic temperament. His music delighted them; he could never practise enough. The routine of the house was also congenial. Dinner was at midnight, after music, talk and drink. Breakfast was at midday. Then perhaps the masseur called, carrying his equipment in a small black box marked with his name. Afterwards, if it was not raining, there was a walk through the pines. Sometimes they collected mushrooms; sometimes they collected cones for the fire, to give a quick aromatic blaze.

Then one afternoon all this changed.

They were having coffee on the sunlit lawn when on the path below there appeared a white girl. She was arguing with a Kashmiri *ghora-wallah*: she had no companion and was clearly in some trouble. Ishmael sent Rafiq down to see what he could do. In that moment Rafiq's holiday was ruined; in that moment he was lost. When, a minute or so later, he returned, his hosts could scarcely recognize him as the mild, courteous sitar-player they had picked mushrooms with. He was like a man possessed. In that short time, during which he had also settled with the *ghora-wallah*, he had conquered and had surrendered: a relationship had been decided and had become explosive. Rafiq did not return alone. He had the girl, Laraine, with him. She was going to stay with them, he said. Did they mind? Could they make the necessary arrangements?

Stunned, they agreed. Later that afternoon they suggested a walk: they would show their new guest the peak of Nanga Parbat, forty miles away, on which the snow glistened like oil paint. Rafiq and Laraine soon fell behind, then disappeared. Ishmael and his wife were a little aggrieved. Self-consciously and silently, like guests rather than hosts, they continued on their walk, pausing here and there to admire the view. In time they were rejoined by Rafiq and Laraine. No fulfilment on their faces, no fatigue: they were both hysterical. They were quarrelling and their rage was real. Presently they exchanged blows. The faces of both were already marked. She kicked him. He groaned, and slapped her. She cried out, swung her bag at him, kicked him again, and he tumbled down the brambly slope. Torn, bleeding, he came bellowing up, snatched her bag and threw it far down into a valley, where it would remain until the snows came and washed it away. At this she sat down and wept like a child. His rage vanished; he went to her; she yielded to him.

He took it out on the sitar when they got back to the bungalow. He practised like a man gone mad; the sitar whined and whined. That night they had another fight. Their shouts and screams brought the police, ever on the alert for Pakistani raiders, who had made a swift looting expedition on the slopes of Khilanmarg the previous year.

Now they were both damaged and scarred; it seemed dangerous for them to be alone together. Laraine, intermittently lucid, left the bungalow more than once. Sometimes Rafiq fetched her back; sometimes she returned while he was still making the sitar cry out. For Ishmael and his wife it was too much. On the second night, during one of Laraine's absences, they asked Rafiq to leave. He put his sitar on his head and prepared to leave. His docility then, a reminder of the old Rafiq, and the sight of the musician carrying away his instrument, softened them; they asked him to stay. He stayed; Laraine returned; it began all over again.

In the end it was Laraine, bruised, fatigued, lucid and desperate, who cracked. After three days – which to Ishmael and his wife seemed like three weeks and which to Laraine and Rafiq must have seemed as long as life itself – she said she couldn't stand it; she had to get away. She would go on the pilgrimage to Amarnath; then she would go to an ashram. She was a woman and an American: her will endured long enough for her to make her escape.

'*Laraine! Laraine!*' Rafiq bellowed through the bungalow when she had gone, the name strange in his Indian mouth.

He would be practising. Suddenly he would stop and scream out: 'I must have Laraine!'

He had known passion. He was to be envied; he was also to be pitied. How often, and with what pain, he would relive not perhaps those three days but that first moment: that going down to the strange girl and that first glimpse of her answering, disturbed eyes, which would never speak in quite the same way to any other man. And it might have been while he was bellowing her name one evening in Gulmarg that I was studying her eyes in the cold tent of the Indian Coffee Board at Sheshnag, and reading in them a broken family and a distressed childhood. I was partly right, as it turned out. But I had missed the greater turmoil.

When Rafiq left Gulmarg it was with the intention of finding her. She had said she was going to an ashram. But India abounded in ashrams. Where was he to look?

*

He didn't have to look far.

I was at the blue table in my room one afternoon when I heard an American woman's voice in the garden. I looked out. It was Laraine; and before I pulled my head in I caught sight of the back of a man's head above sturdy fawn-jacketed shoulders. So she had surrendered; she had ceased to seek. They had come to the hotel for tea. I also heard them inquiring about rooms, and later heard them inspecting.

'Everything *thik*?' she asked, mispronouncing the Hindi *th*, still game for India, still spattering her speech with Hindi. 'Everything all right?'

There was a muffled male rumble as they went down the steps.

They moved in the next day. I never saw them. They remained in their room all day, and occasionally the hotel quivered with sitar music.

'I think,' Aziz said at dinner, 'that the sahib and the memsahib getting married today.'

I was awakened that night by activity in the hotel, and when Aziz came in with coffee in the morning I questioned him.

'The sahib married the memsahib last night,' he whispered. 'They mealing at one o'clock.'

'No!'

'Mr Butt and Ali Mohammed take them Mufti. She turn Muslim, get Muslim name. They get married. They mealing at *one* o'clock last night.' The lateness of the meal had impressed him almost as much as the marriage.

And now from the bridal chamber, silence: not even the sitar. No wedding breakfast, no coming out to look at the view. All morning the room remained closed, as though they were both hiding inside, awed at what had happened. After lunch they slipped out. I did not see them go.

It was not until the late afternoon, when I was having tea on the lawn, that I saw Laraine returning alone across the lake to the hotel. She was wearing a blue cotton frock; she looked cool; and she was carrying a paperback. She might have been a simple tourist.

'Hi!'

'Is it true what I hear? That you're married?'

'You know me. Impulsive.'

'Congratulations.'

'Thank you.'

She sat down; she was a little frightened; she wanted to talk.

'But isn't it crazy? Me with all this interest in Hinduism' – she showed the paperback she was carrying: it was Mr Rajagopalachari's retelling of the *Mahabharata* – 'and now overnight I'm a Muslim and everything.'

'What is your new name?'

'Zenobia. Don't you think it's pretty?'

It was a pretty name, but it had brought problems. She didn't know whether she had lost her American nationality as a result of her marriage, and she wasn't sure whether she would be allowed to work in India. She had some idea that she was now very poor and would have to live in straitened circumstances – not, I felt, fully visualized – in some Indian town. But already she was speaking of 'my husband' as though she had used the words all her life; already she was concerned about 'my husband's career' and 'my husband's recital'.

They were poorer than she had perhaps imagined. Even the Liward was too expensive for them. They were to move elsewhere the following day, and trouble about their hotel bill blew up in the morning.

Aziz reported, 'He say I overcharge. He say, "Why you tell other sahib I married?" I say, "Why you want secret? Man get married. This is for good. He give party. He invite. He not hide. And why I not tell? You wake up my sahib and he complain."'

'Are you sure you are not overcharging them, Aziz?'

'O no, sahib.'

'But he doesn't have a lot of money, Aziz. He wasn't expecting to get married when he came to Kashmir. How much did they spend on their marriage?'

'O sahib, how much they spend? Some people give Mufti five, some give fifteen, some give fifty.'

'How much did they give?'

'A hundred.'

'You are a brute. You shouldn't have let him. He couldn't afford a hundred rupees. No wonder he can't pay you now.'

'But this is for good, sahib. You get married American memsahib, you give big party. You give Parsi *khana, bangola* fireworks. You not hide. They not give party, they not give nothing.'

'The memsahib is American, but they don't have money.'

'No, sahib. They hide. Lotta people come Kashmir, feel what do here not matter. They feel Kashmir wedding not matter. But wedding paper get show in court, sahib.'

And Ali Mohammed came up with a copy of the marriage certificate, on which I saw the signatures of Zenobia, Rafiq and Mr Butt.

'They not hide, sahib,' Aziz said. 'They married good.'

It wasn't only money. They had been hurt in their pride as Kashmiris and Muslims. They had welcomed a convert; now they feared they were being made fools of.

'He not pay,' Aziz said, 'I take away sitar.'

But Rafiq chased through Srinagar and borrowed the necessary rupees. By midday he and Zenobia were ready to leave. We were having lunch when Zenobia came in to say good-bye. A man hovered behind the door curtain.

'Rafiq.'

He came in and stood a few paces behind her.

Self-possession momentarily deserted her. She knew that we knew the Gulmarg story.

'This,' she said, with acute embarrassment, 'is my husband.'

I had expected someone more tormented, more wasted-looking. He was of medium height and powerfully built, with a round, blunt-featured face. I had expected someone wild-eyed, defiant. He was dreadfully shy, with sleepy eyes; it was as if he had been caught smoking and was trying to hide the burning cigarette behind his back and to swallow the smoke without coughing. He was a musician and an Indian: I had expected long hair and a wide-sleeved white tunic, not an army-style haircut and an Indian-tailored fawn suit.

He was not the man I had imagined who would make his sitar cry out his anguish; he was only the man who would object to his marriage being known. Poor Rafiq! He had come to Kashmir for a holiday; he was going back exhausted, broke, married. I had thought of passion as a gift, a faculty with which human beings were unequally endowed. Now I felt that it was something which, in a complex conjunction of circumstances, might overtake us all.

He gave me a military handshake. He pulled out an unimpressive fountain-pen from his inside pocket and in a flowing, clerk-like hand wrote down his address, now Laraine's, now Zenobia's. 'You must come and see us,' she said. 'You must come and have dinner one evening.'

Then they went through the curtained doorway, and I never saw Rafiq again.

*

It was time for us, too, to pack up and go, to say good-bye to the mountains and the room with the two views. The reeds had turned brown; in the afternoons *shikara*-loads of cut reeds went down the water highways. The sunflower plants – so thick their stalks now, and the birds pecked at the seeds in the black, burnt-out flowers – were all cut down in one afternoon and thrown in a bundle outside the kitchen. The garden seemed exposed and ravaged, the sunflower stumps showing as white as wood.

Aziz gave us dinner one evening at his tall brick house in the lake, paddling us there himself (together with a napkin-covered pitcher of tap-water from the hotel). Night, a lantern in the *shikara*, silence, the house approached down a willow-hung water alley, and Aziz behaving with an ancient courtesy. Details were obscured; it might have been the beginning of a Venetian entertainment. We ate sitting on the floor of an upper room that had been cleared of all furniture and people, whose presence we could yet detect in close whispers and the sounds of movement; and Aziz knelt before us, talking, no longer a hotel servant but our host, grave, independent, a man of substance, a man of views and, when the women and the babies flooded in, a responsible family man. The walls were thick, comfortingly grimed, full of arched recesses; windows were small. The room promised idleness and the warmth of charcoal braziers in winter, when the lake would freeze so hard a jeep could be driven over it: we would follow the weather in Srinagar.

After our last dinner in the hotel Mr Butt assembled the servants for the tipping ceremony: Aziz, Ali Mohammed, the cook, the gardener, the odd-job boy. They had been disappointed in a wedding; I hoped I wasn't going to disappoint them further: their smiling faces carried the conviction that the age of style was not yet over. They acknowledged my gifts and typewritten testimonials with graceful Muslim gestures; they continued to smile. Perhaps they were merely being courteous; perhaps they had learned to accommodate themselves to the lesser age. But Aziz was pleased. I could tell that from the indifferent manner with which, after a lightning assessment, he thrust the money into his pocket. He became morose, active, a man harassed by duties that were never done: money was not as important to him at that moment as setting the dining-room to rights. He would relax as soon as he left the room; they would all relax. And going to the kitchen later that evening for a last pull at the hookah, I surprised them giggling over the testimonial I had written, with some care, for the odd-job boy.

We left early in the morning. Mr Butt paddled us over to the lake boulevard. It was not yet light. The water was still; on the boulevard the tonga waited. We went past the closed house-boats, the lotus beds. On the balustrade of the boulevard a man was exercising. The tonga roof sloped low: we had to lean forward to see the lake and the mountains. The town was awakening from minute to minute, and the Tourist Reception Centre, when we got to it, was infernally alive.

'Three rupees,' the tonga-wallah said.

In four months I had established among the lakeside tongas that I never paid more than one and a quarter rupees for the ride into town. But the circumstances were extraordinary. I offered two. The tonga-wallah refused to touch the notes. I offered no more. He threatened me with his whip; and I found, to my surprise – it must have been the earliness of the hour – that I had seized him by the throat.

Aziz intervened. 'He not tourist.'

'Oh,' the tonga-wallah said.

He dropped his whip hand, and I released him.

Our seats on the bus had been booked, but it was necessary to scramble, to fight, to shout. Aziz and Ali Mohammed scrambled and shouted for us, and we withdrew to the edge of the crowd.

Then we saw Laraine, Zenobia.

She was alone, and was peering short-sightedly at buses. She wore a chocolate skirt and a cream-coloured blouse. She looked thinner. She was not happy to meet us and had little news to give. She was off to her Hindu ashram after all; later she would be joining her husband. Now she was busy: she had to find her bus. It was a bus of the Radhakishun service. She turned this name to the more familiar 'Radha Krishna'; her mind still ran on the Hindu legends. Krishna was the dark god, Radha the fair milkmaid with whom he sported.

And, asking for Radha Krishna, peering at the number plates on buses, she disappeared into the crowd.

Our own seats had now been secured, our bags placed below the tarpaulin on the roof of the bus. We shook hands with Aziz and Ali and went inside.

'You don't worry about tonga-wallah,' Aziz said. 'I settle.' There were tears in his eyes.

The engine started.

'Tonga-wallah?'

'You don't worry, sahib. Correct fare three rupees. I pay.'

The driver was blowing his horn.

'Correct fare?'

'Morning fare, sahib.'

He was right; I knew that.

'Two rupees, three rupees, what different? Good-bye, good-bye. You don't worry.'

I dug into my pockets.

'Don't worry, sahib. Good-bye.'

Through the window I pushed out some rupee notes.

He took them. Tears were running down his cheeks. Even at that moment I could not be sure that he had ever been mine.

*

She wore a chocolate skirt and a cream-coloured blouse. Rafiq would remember those garments; perhaps he had seen her lay them out the previous evening. He never saw her after that morning. She went to her ashram; and then she left India. He wrote; she replied; then his letters were returned unopened. Her parents had been separated and lived in different countries. He was supported by one, rejected by the other. Still he wrote; and months later he was still grieving.

But I heard this in another season. And in the Poste Restante of another town this letter awaited me:

HOTEL LIWARD

Advance Arrangements for

Trecking, Shooting, Fishing,

Gulmarg Hut & Pahalgam Experienced Guide

Prop: M.S. Butt

My dear Sir,

I beg to acknowledge your kind favour of the 7th inst. and find that you had to face a lot of trouble en route to your destination, since the bus in which were you travelling broke. However I am pleased to find that you have reached safely your destination by His Grace.

I quite realize how the Kashmir view and other things of this place don't go out of your memory. I wish you to be here again and thus give me a chance to serve you.

In your room there was one client from Bombay and other from Delhi.

The whole family of ours send their best compliments to you.

Hoping this would find you in the best of health and cheerful spirits.

Thanking you in anticipation,

Yours sincerely,

M.S. Butt

(Mohd. Sidiq Butt).

# PART THREE

# 8

# FANTASY AND RUINS

THE BRITISH HAD possessed the country so completely. Their withdrawal was so irrevocable. And to me even after many months something of fantasy remained attached to all the reminders of their presence. I had grown up in a British colony and it might have been expected that much would have been familiar to me. But England was at least as many-faceted as India. England, as it expressed itself in Trinidad, was not the England I had lived in; and neither of these countries could be related to the England that was the source of so much that I now saw about me.

This England had disturbed me from the first, when, sitting in the launch, I had seen the English names on the cranes of the Bombay docks. It was partly the disturbance we feel – the abrupt moment of unreality in which fleetingly we lose our powers of assessment – at the confirmation of a bizarre but well-established fact. It was also for me a little more. This confirmation laid bare a small area of self-deception which, below knowledge and self-knowledge, had survived in that part of my mind which held as a possibility the existence of the white Himalayan cones against a cold blue sky, as in the religious pictures in my grandmother's house. For in the India of my childhood, the land which in my imagination was an extension, separate from the alienness by which we ourselves were surrounded, of my grandmother's house, there was no alien presence. How could such a thing be conceived? Our own world, though clearly fading, was still separate; and an involvement with the English, of whom on the island we knew little, would have seemed a more unlikely violation than an involvement with the Chinese or the Africans, of whom we knew more. Into this alienness we daily ventured, and at length we were absorbed into it. But we knew there had been change, gain, loss. We knew that something which was once whole had been washed away. What was whole was the idea of India.

To preserve this conception of India as a country still whole, historical facts had not been suppressed. They had been acknowledged and ignored; and it was only in India that I was able to see this as part of the Indian ability to retreat, the ability genuinely not to see what was obvious: with others a foundation of neurosis, but with Indians only part of a greater philosophy of despair, leading to passivity, detachment, acceptance. It is only now, as the impatience of the observer is dissipated in the process of writing and self-inquiry, that I see how much this philosophy had also been mine. It had enabled me, through the stresses of a long residence in England, to withdraw completely from nationality and loyalties except to persons; it had made me content to be myself alone, my work, my name (the last two so different from the first); it had convinced me that every man was an island, and taught me to shield all that I knew to be good and pure within myself from the corruption of causes.

Before the reminders of this England of India, then, I ought to have been calm. But they revealed one type of self-deception as self-deception; and though this was lodged in that part of the mind where fantasy was permissible, the revelation was painful. It was an encounter with a humiliation I had never before experienced, and perhaps more so to me than to those Indians who hurried about streets with unlikely English names, in the shadow of imperial-grand houses, as others might have felt for me the colonial humiliation I did not feel in Trinidad.

Colonial India I could not link with colonial Trinidad. Trinidad was a British colony; but every child knew that we were only a dot on the map of the world, and it was therefore important to be British: that at least anchored us within a wider system. It was a system which we did not feel to be oppressive; and though British, in institutions and education as well as in political fact, we were in the New World, our population was greatly mixed, English people were few and kept themselves to themselves, and England was as a result only one of the countries of which we were aware.

It was a country to a large extent unknown; a taste for English things was something a cultivated islander might affect. To the majority America was more important. The English made good tiny cars for careful drivers. The Americans made the real automobiles, as they made the real films and produced the best singers and the best bands. Their films spoke universal sentiments and their humour was immediately comprehensible. American radio was modern and marvellous and at least you could understand the accent; you could listen to fifteen minutes of news on the BBC and not understand a word. The American soldiers loved a fat backstreet whore, the blacker the better; they packed them into their jeeps and raced from club to club, throwing their money about; and they could always be enticed into unequal brawls. They were people with whom communication was possible. Beside them the British soldiers were like foreigners. In Trinidad they were incapable of hitting the right note. They were either too loud or too withdrawn; they spoke this strange English; they referred to themselves as 'blokes' (this was once the subject of a news-item in the *Trinidad Guardian*), not knowing that in Trinidad a bloke was a term of abuse; their uniforms, their shorts in particular, were ugly. They had little money and little sense of propriety: they could be seen in the Syrian shops buying cheap women's underwear. This was the England of popular conception. There was of course the other England – the source of governors and senior civil servants – but this was too remote to be real.

We were colonials in a special position. The British Empire in the West Indies was old. It was an empire of the sea and apart from a square here and a harbour there it had left few monuments; and because we were in the New World – Trinidad was virtually without a population in 1800 – these monuments appeared to belong to our prehistory. By its very age the Empire had ceased to be incongruous. It required some detachment to see that our institutions and our language were the results of empire.

The England of India was totally different. It remained an incongruous imposition. Fort St George, grey and massive and of an eighteenth-century English taste known from day trips, could not be related to the Madras landscape; in Calcutta the wide-fronted, pillared house, pointed out as Clive's, on the choked road to Dum Dum airport, appeared to require a less exotic setting. And because it was incongruous, its age, which was less than the age of the empire in the West Indies, came as a surprise: these eighteenth-century monuments ought to have appeared superficial, but now one saw that they had become part of this country of alien ruins. This was one aspect of Indian England; it belonged to the history of India; it was dead.

Distinct from this was the England of the Raj. This still lived. It lived in the division of country towns into 'cantonments', 'civil lines' and bazaars. It lived in army officers' messes, in the silver so frequently given, so reverentially polished and displayed, in uniforms and moustaches and swagger sticks and mannerisms and jargon. It lived in the collectorates, in the neat fading handwriting of those settlements which add up to a Domesday book of a continent: suggesting endless days in the sun on horseback, with many servants but few real comforts, and evenings of patient effort. ('The effort exhausted them,' a young IAS officer said to me. 'After this they just couldn't move on to anything else.') It lived in the clubs, the Sunday morning bingo, the yellow-covered overseas edition of the *Daily Mirror* in the manicured hands of middle-class Indian ladies; it lived in the dance-floors of city restaurants. It was an England more full-blooded than anyone coming from Trinidad might have thought possible. It was grander, more creative and more vulgar.

Yet it did not ring true. It had never rung true to me in Kipling and other writers; and it did not ring true now. Was it the mixture of England and India? Was it my colonial, Trinidad-American, English-speaking prejudice which could not quite accept as real this imposition, without apparent competition, of one culture on another? With one part of myself I felt the coming together of England and India as a violation; with the other I saw it as ridiculous, resulting in a comic mixture of costumes and the widespread use of an imperfectly understood language. But there was something else, something at which the architecture of the Raj hinted: those collectorates, in whose vaults lay the fruits of an immense endeavour, those clubs, those circuit houses, those inspection houses, those first-class railway waiting rooms. Their grounds were a little too spacious; their ceilings a little too high, their columns and arches and pediments a little too rhetorical; they were neither of England nor India; they were a little too grand for their purpose, too grand for the puniness, poverty and defeat in which they were set. They were appropriate to a conception of endeavour rather than to endeavour. They insisted on being alien and were indeed more alien than the earlier British buildings, many of which might have been transported whole from England. They led to the humourlessness of the Victoria Memorial in Calcutta and Lord Curzon's gifts to the Taj Mahal: a humourlessness which knew it was inviting ridicule but which derived from a confidence that could support such ridicule. It was embarrassing to be in these buildings; they still appeared to strive to impose attitudes on those within and those without.

It was all there in Kipling, barring the epilogue of the Indian inheritance. A journey to India was not really necessary. No writer was more honest or accurate; no writer was more revealing of himself and his society. He has left us Anglo-India; to people these relics of the Raj we have only to read him. We find a people conscious of their roles, conscious of their power and separateness, yet at the same time fearful of expressing their delight at their situation: they are all burdened by responsibilities. The responsibilities are real; but the total effect is that of a people at play. They are all actors; they know what is expected of them; no one will give the game away. The Kipling administrator, perpetually sahibed and huzoor-ed, hedged around by fabulous state, is yet an exile, harassed, persecuted, misunderstood by his superiors and the natives he strives to elevate; and on his behalf Kipling can rise to towering heights of mock-anger and can achieve a mock-aggressive self-pity: play within play.

> At home they, the other men, our equals, have at their disposal all that town can supply – the roar of the streets, the lights, the pleasant faces, the millions of their own kind, and a wilderness of pretty, fresh-coloured Englishwomen . . . We have been deprived of our inheritance. The men at home are enjoying it all, not knowing how fair and rich it is.

Self-congratulation coquettishly concealed by complaint to be the better revealed: it is the feminine note of the club writer who has accepted the values of the club and genuinely sees the members as they see themselves. It is the tone exactly described by Ada Leverson in her novel *Tenterhooks*, published in 1912:

> 'I feel all the time as if he [Kipling] were calling me by my Christian name without an introduction, or as if he wanted me to exchange hats with him . . . He's so fearfully familiar with his readers.'
>
> 'But you think he keeps at a respectful distance from his characters?'

To say that Kipling is a club writer is of course to use a loaded word. The club is one of the symbols of Anglo-India. In *Something of Myself* Kipling tells how every evening in Lahore he went to dine at the club and there met people who had just been reading what he had written the day before. He regarded this as a valuable discipline. The approbation of the club was important to him: he wrote about the club for the club. In this lies his peculiar honesty, his value as a poetic chronicler of Anglo-India. But in this also lies his special vulnerability, for by applying to the club only the values of the club he has exposed both the club and himself.

His work is of a piece with the architecture of the Raj; and within the imperial shell we find, not billiard-room cartoons or a suburban taste in novels, as in the district clubs, but Mrs Hauksbee, the wit, the queen, the manipulator and card of Simla. How she suffers from the very generosity which sought to bestow on her the attributes she desired! Her wit is no wit; and to us today the susceptibility of her admirers is a little provincial, a little sad. Yet the circle – queen, courtiers, jester – is so complete; something, whether we approve of it or not, has been created by which men can live in special circumstances; and it seems an intolerable cruelty to point to its falseness. A response to Kipling cannot but be personal and on this level. He is too honest and generous; he is too simple; he is too gifted. His vulnerability is an embarrassment; the criticism he invites can only seem a type of brutality. Mr Somerset Maugham has already disposed of the pretensions of Mrs Hauksbee. She once said of the voice of another woman that it was like the screech of the brakes of an underground train as it came into Earl's Court station. If Mrs Hauksbee were what she claimed to be, Mr Maugham commented, she had no business to be in Earl's Court; and she certainly oughtn't to have gone there by underground. There is much in Kipling that can be dealt with in this way. He genuinely saw people bigger than they were; they, perhaps less securely, saw themselves bigger than they were. They reacted one on the other; fantasy hardened into conviction. And to us they are now all betrayed.

*

There is a night train from Delhi to Kalka; from Kalka you continue to Simla by road or by the narrow-gauge, toy railroad that winds up the mountains. I went by road, in the company of a young IAS officer, encountered on the train to Kalka. He spoke sadly of the decay of the town since 1947. To him, as to all Indians, the myth was real. The glory of Simla was part of the Indian inheritance, which was being squandered: there were now *pan*-shops in the town. While we talked rustles came from the back of the van from the officer's pet weaver-birds. They were in a large covered cage, and when the rustles appeared to be reaching a pitch of frenzy the officer clucked and cooed and spoke soothingly to the cage. From time to time we had a glimpse of the toy train going into or coming out of a toy tunnel. It was mid-January, the air frosty, but the shirtsleeved passengers leaned passively out of open windows as though, this being India, it was always summer.

And at first it seemed that the officer was right, that Kipling's city had altogether decayed. It was wet and cold; the narrow streets were muddy; barefooted stunted men stamped uphill with heavy loads strapped to their backs; their caps recalled Kashmir and those ragged porters who ran shouting after every arriving bus at village resorts. Could glamour ever have been found here? But so it was with every Indian landscape known from books. Deception, one thought; and then, decay. But it was only that the figures in the foreground had to make their impact before fading from a vision grown as selective as when, in a dark room full of familiar objects, one's eyes have grown accustomed to the dark.

Vision contracted: Simla outlined itself: a town built on a series of ridges, a network of switchback lanes in which it was easy to get lost. In my imagination the Mall was broad and straight; it turned out to be narrow and winding. Every few yards notices warned against spitting; but the *pan*-shops were there, as the IAS man had said, and the streets were stained red with betel-juice. The photographers' windows carried faded photographs of Englishwomen in styles of the thirties. They were not relics; the shops were busy. But in India everything is inherited, nothing is abolished; everything grows out of something else, and now the Mall was given over to the offices, clamantly labelled, of the Himachal Pradesh administration, whose officers drove about the narrow lanes in green Chevrolets of the late nineteen-forties: decay upon decay. The sun sank behind the mountains; the cold grew intense. The unsettling figures disappeared, the bazaar impression faded. The ridge sparkled with electric light, and in the lamplit darkness the town centre defined itself more clearly: an English country town of fairyland, of mock mock-styles, the great ecclesiastical building asserting the alien faith, the mean-fronted shops, ornately gabled, out of which nightcapped, nightgowned men might have appeared, holding lanterns or candles: a grandiloquent assertion of a smallness and cosiness that never were. A fabulous creation, of fantasy supported by a confidence which it was impossible not to admire. But it was not what I had expected. My disappointment was the disappointment we momentarily feel when, after reading of the house at Combray, we see the photograph of the house at Illiers. The vision is correct; but it is a child's myth-creating vision. No city or landscape is truly real unless it has been given the quality of myth by writer, painter or by its association with great events. Simla will never cease to be Kipling's city: a child's vision of Home, doubly a fairyland. India distorts and enlarges; with the Raj it enlarged upon what was already a fantasy. This is what Kipling caught; this is his uniqueness.

During the night it snowed, the first snow of the winter. In the morning the hotel servant, like a magician, announced: '*Barf!* Snow.' He pulled the curtains to one side and I saw the valley white and wet with mist. After breakfast the mist cleared. The roofs dripped; the crows cawed, flapping from pine to pine, shaking down snow; the dogs barked far below and there was a sound as of revelry. On the government boards marked 'Himachal Pradesh' – sweet name: the Snow State – snow lay emblematically, as in a Christmas poster. The Mall was busy with holidaymakers, doing the morning promenade. For a long way down the snow was still thick. As we left Simla farther and farther behind, high up in the sky, the snow thinned, became like scattered cakings of salt on hard ground, then disappeared; and it was through a thick and very white Punjab fog, which delayed trains and grounded aircraft, that we crawled all the way to Delhi.

To understand the eighteenth-century England that one saw in India, it was necessary to see it as part of India. Warren Hastings can only with difficulty be read as an Englishman; as an Indian, he fits. But the Raj, though so completely of India, is part of nineteenth-century England.

*

Consider Adela and Ronny in *A Passage to India*. The sun is going down over the Chandrapore *maidan*; and they, turning their backs on the polo game, walk to a distant seat, to talk. He apologizes for his bad temper earlier in the day. She cuts into his apologies and says: 'I've finally decided we are not going to be married, my dear boy.' They are both disturbed. But they remain controlled; nothing passionate or profound is said; and the moment passes. Then Adela says:

> 'We've been awfully British over it, but I suppose that's all right.'
>
> 'As we are British, I suppose it is.'

It is an amusing exchange, still fresh after forty years. It might be said that 'British', as Adela uses it, is given point by the imperial Indian background; but the word might have been used by many of Forster's characters and its intention would have been the same. To Forster's characters their Englishness is like an extra quality which challenges, and is challenged by, all that is alien. It is a formulated ideal; it needs no elucidation. The word British, as used by Adela, can almost be spelt with a small *b*. It is difficult to imagine the word being so used in Jane Austen. In *Pride and Prejudice* it occurs once, when Mr Collins, on his first visit to Longbourn, is speaking of the virtues of his patroness's daughter, Miss de Bourgh:

> 'Her indifferent state of health unhappily prevents her being in town; and by that means, as I told Lady Catherine myself one day, has deprived the British court of its brightest ornament.'

For Jane Austen and Mr Collins the word is geographical; it is entirely different from Adela's 'British'.

Between the two uses of the word lie a hundred years of industrial and imperial power. In the beginning of this period we can sense the swiftness of change, from stagecoach to railway, from the essays of Hazlitt to those of Macaulay, from the *Pickwick Papers* to *Our Mutual Friend*. In painting it is like a second springtime: Constable discovering the sky, Bonington discovering the glory of light, of sand and sea: youth and delight that can communicate themselves to us even today. It is a period of newness and self-discovery: Dickens discovering England, London discovering the novel; newness even in Keats and Shelley. It is a period of vigour and expectation. And then, abruptly, there come fulfilment and middle-age. The process of self-discovery is over; the English national myth appears, complete. The reasons are well known: the narcissism was justifiable. But with this there was loss. A way of looking was weakened. What was English was settled; by this the world was to be assessed, and in the travel-writing of the century we can observe a progressive deterioration, from Darwin (1832) to Trollope (1859) to Kingsley (1870) to Froude (1887). More and more these writers are reporting not on themselves but on their Englishness.

At the beginning of this period Hazlitt can dismiss the English writings of Washington Irving with scorn because Irving insisted on finding Sir Roger de Coverleys and Will Wimbles in a country that had moved on since the days of *The Spectator*. Hazlitt's myth-rejecting attitude is like the attitude of those today who object to British travel advertising in the United States. ('Loverly Way to London,' says the advertisement in *Holiday* in 1962. 'Fly Sabena to Manchester. Drive right off past thatch-roofed cottages and start wending your way to London. Gradually. Beautifully.') But soon the myth becomes important; and in the new narcissism class consciousness as well as race consciousness are heightened. *Punch* in the 1880s has Cockneys talking in the vanished accents of Sam Weller. The consciousness of class in Forster is altogether different from the knowledge of class as an almost elemental division in Jane Austen. In a country as fragmented by class as England the stereotype might be considered necessary if only as an aid to communication. But, excessively cherished, it limits vision and inquiry; it occasionally even rejects the truth.

To this dependence on the established and reassuring might be traced the singular omissions of English writing in the last hundred years. No monumental writer succeeded Dickens. In the English conditions the very magnitude of his vision, its absorption into myth, precluded as grand an attempt. London remains Dickens's city – how few writers since appear to have *looked* at the city! There have been novels about Chelsea and Bloomsbury and Earl's Court; but on the modern mechanized city, its pressures and frustrations, English writers have remained silent. It is precisely this, on the other hand, which is one of the recurring themes of American writers. It is the theme, in the words of the novelist Peter de Vries, of city people who live and die without roots, suspended, 'like the fabled mistletoe, between the twin oaks of home and office'. It is an important theme, and not specifically of America; but in England, where narcissism applies to country, class and self, it has been reduced to the image of the bank clerk, always precise, always punctual, who farcically erupts into misdemeanour.

When such a theme is ignored it is not surprising that there exists no great English novel in which the growth of national or imperial consciousness is chronicled. (It is useless to look for this in the work of historians. They, more than novelists, work within the values of their society; they serve those values. It is undeniable that the possession of an empire greatly influenced British attitudes in the nineteenth century; yet G.M. Trevelyan in his *English Social History* – regarded, I believe, as a classic – devotes exactly one page and a half to 'Overseas Influences', and in this vein: '. . . the postage stamp kept the cottage at home in touch with the son who had "gone to the colonies", and often he would return on a visit with money in his pocket, and tales of new lands of equality . . .') An early novel by Somerset Maugham, *Mrs Craddock*, attempted the theme in a small way; this is the story of a farmer who strives, by a superior nationalism, to establish his claim to the superior class into which he has married. For the rest, we are presented with *stages* in the transformation, which can thus best be charted through individual books.

Osborne in *Vanity Fair* sees himself as a solid British merchant. But 'British' here is only contrasted with, say, 'French'. It is no more than the patriotism of someone like de Quincey. Thackeray's solid British merchant would dearly have liked his son to marry Miss Swartz, the West Indian Negro heiress. Mr Bumble and Mr Squeers are English; but that is not their most important feature. Twenty years later, however, what different characters begin to appear in Dickens! There is Mr Podsnap of *Our Mutual Friend*, he knows foreigners and is proud to be British. John Halifax is only a gentleman; Rider Haggard dedicates one of his books to his son in the hope that he will become an Englishman and a gentleman; it was with a similar hope that Tom Brown was sent off by his father to Rugby. By the time we get to *Howards End* even Leonard Bast can be found saying 'I am an Englishman', and meaning by this more than de Quincey ever meant; now the word is loaded indeed.

Writers cannot be blamed for being of their society; and in the novel, then, interest shifts from human behaviour to the Englishness of behaviour, Englishness held up for approval or dissection: a shift of interest reflected in the difference between the inns of the early Dickens and Simpson's Restaurant in the Strand just seventy-five years later, of which Forster in *Howards End* (1910) says:

> Her eyes surveyed the restaurant, and admired its well-calculated tributes to the solidity of our past. Though no more Old English

> than the works of Kipling, it had selected its reminiscences so adroitly that her criticism was lulled, and the guests whom it was nourishing for imperial purposes bore the outer semblance of Parson Adams and Tom Jones. Scraps of talk jarred oddly on the ear.
>
> 'Right you are! I'll cable out to Uganda this evening . . .'

Forster has made his point exactly. He has pointed at the contradiction in the myth of a people overtaken by industrial and imperial power. Between the possession of Uganda and the conscious possession of Tom Jones there is as little connexion as there is between the stories of Kipling and the novels of his contemporary, Hardy. So, at the height of their power, the British gave the impression of a people at play, a people playing at being English, playing at being English of a certain class. The reality conceals the play; the play conceals the reality.

This endears them to some and exposes them to the charge of hypocrisy from others. And in this imperialist period, when the pink spreads like a rash on the map of the world, the English myth is like a developing language. Quantities alter; new elements are added; codification, repeatedly attempted, cannot keep pace with change; and always between the projected, adjustable myth – Parson Adams in Simpson's, the harassed empire-builder in Uganda or India – and the reality there is some distance. It is long after Waterloo, in a period which begins with the disasters of the Crimea and ends with the humiliations of South Africa, that we have a period of jingoistic militarism. It is after the empire has been built that the concept arises of the merchant and administrator as an empire-builder; and, sternly, Kipling summons the rulers of the world to their pleasant duties. It is the play of puritans. At Home it creates Simpson's in the Strand. In India it creates Simla, the summer seat of the Raj where, as Philip Woodruff tells us in *The Guardians*, the 'affectation' existed among officials, at about the same time, 'of being very English, of knowing nothing at all about India, of eschewing Indian words and customs'.

*

Half-way across the world was Trinidad, a truly imperial creation. There people of many races accepted English rule, English institutions and the English language without questioning; yet England and Englishness, as displayed in India, were absent. And to me this remained the peculiar quality of the Raj: this affectation of being very English, this sense of a nation at play, acting out a fantasy. It was there in all the architecture of the Raj and especially in its faintly ridiculous monuments: the Victoria Memorial in Calcutta, the India Gate in New Delhi. They were not monuments worthy of the power they celebrated; they were without the integrity of the earlier British buildings and the even earlier Portuguese cathedrals in Goa.

In *The Men Who Ruled India* Philip Woodruff has written with sad, Roman piety of the British achievement. It was a tremendous achievement; it deserved this piety. But Woodruff's Raj is far from the Raj of the popular English imagination: the sun-helmet (which Gandhi thought sensible but which, for reasons of national pride, he could not wear), the innumerable salaaming, sahib-ing and memsahib-ing servants, and English man as superman, the native as wog and servant and clerk, specimens of whose imperfect English can be gathered into little books (still found in secondhand bookstalls) for the amusement of those who know the language well: a Raj that can be found in a thousand English books on India, particularly in children's books with an Indian setting, and can be found even in Vincent Smith's annotations, for the Oxford University Press, on the writings of the great Sleeman.

To Woodruff this side of the Raj, however established and real, is an embarrassment; it does not represent the truth of the British endeavour. But so it is with all who wish to see purpose, creative or negative, in the Raj, be it Woodruff or be it an Indian like K. M. Munshi, author of a 1946 pamphlet whose title, *The Ruin That Britain Wrought*, makes description unnecessary. There is always an embarrassment, of racial arrogance on the one hand and of genuine endeavour on the other. Which is the reality? They both are; and there is no contradiction. Racial arrogance was part of the Simpson's-in-the-Strand fantasy, inevitably heightened in the puniness of the Indian setting, the completeness of the Indian subjection. Equally heightened, and part of the same fantasy, was the spirit of service. They both issued out of people who knew their roles and knew what was expected of their Englishness. As Woodruff himself says, there is something un-English, something too premeditated about the administration of the Raj. It could not have been otherwise. To be English in India was to be larger than life.

The newspaperman in Madras presses me to attend his lecture on 'The Shakespearean Hero in Crisis'. The business executive in Calcutta, explaining why he feels he must join the army to fight the Chinese, begins solemnly, 'I feel I am defending my right – my right to –' and ends hurriedly with a self-deprecating laugh, 'play a game of golf when I want to.' Almost the last true Englishmen, Malcolm Muggeridge wrote some time ago, are Indians. It is a statement that has point only because it recognizes the English 'character' as a creation of fantasy. In India the Moguls were also foreigners, with fantasies as heady; they ruled as foreigners; but they were finally absorbed into India. The English, as Indians say again and again, did not become part of India; and in the end they escaped back to England. They left no noble monuments behind and no religion save a concept of Englishness as a desirable code of behaviour – of chivalry, it might be described, tempered by legalism – which in Indian minds can be dissociated from the fact of English rule, the vulgarities of racial arrogance or the position of England today. The Madras brahmin was reading O'Hara's *From the Terrace* and loathing it: 'You wouldn't get a well-bred Englishman writing this sort of tosh.' It is a remarkable distinction for a former subject people to make; it is a remarkable thing for a ruling nation to have left behind. This concept of Englishness will survive because it was the product of fantasy, a work of national art; it will outlast England. It explains why withdrawal was easy, why there is no nostalgia such as the Dutch still have for Java, why there was no Algeria, and why after less than twenty years India has almost faded out of the British consciousness: the Raj was an expression of the English involvement with themselves rather than with the country they ruled. It is not, properly, an imperialist attitude. It points, not to the good or evil of British rule in India, but to its failure.

*

It is well that Indians are unable to look at their country directly, for the distress they would see would drive them mad. And it is well that they have no sense of history, for how then would they be able to continue to squat amid their ruins, and which Indian would be able to read the history of his country for the last thousand years without anger and pain? It is better to retreat into fantasy and fatalism, to trust to the stars in which the fortunes of all are written – there are lecturers in astrology in some universities – and to regard the progress of the rest of the world with the tired tolerance of one who has been through it all before. The aeroplane was known to ancient India, and the telephone, and the atom bomb: there is evidence in the Indian epics. Surgery was highly developed in ancient India; here, in an important national newspaper, is the text of a lecture proving it. Indian shipbuilding was the wonder of the world. And democracy flourished in ancient India. Every village was a republic, self-sufficient, ordered, controlling its own affairs; the village council could hang an offending villager or chop off his hand. This is what must be recreated, this idyllic ancient India; and when *panchayati raj*, a type of village self-rule, is introduced in 1962 there will be so much talk of the glories of ancient India, so much talk by enthusiastic politicians of hands anciently chopped off, that in some villages of the Madhya Pradesh state hands will be chopped off and people will be hanged by village councils.

Eighteenth-century India was squalid. It invited conquest. But not in Indian eyes: before the British came, as every Indian will tell you, India was rich, on the brink of an industrial breakthrough; and K.M. Munshi says that every village had a school. Indian interpretations of their history are almost as painful as the history itself; and it is especially painful to see the earlier squalor being repeated today, as it has been in the creation of Pakistan and the reawakening within India of disputes about language, religion, caste and region. India, it seems, will never cease to require the arbitration of a conqueror. A people with a sense of history might have ordered matters differently. But this is precisely the saddening element in Indian history: this absence of growth and development. It is a history whose only lesson is that life goes on. There is only a series of beginnings, no final creation.

> It is like reading of a land periodically devastated by hordes of lemmings or locusts; it is like turning from the history of a coral reef, in which every act and every death is a foundation, to the depressing chronicle of a succession of castles built on the waste sand of the sea-shore.

This is Woodruff on the difference between European history and Indian history. He has chosen his images well. But the sandcastle is not quite exact. The sandcastle is flattened by the tide and leaves no trace, and India is above all the land of ruins.

From the south Delhi is approached through a wilderness of ruins that extend for forty-five square miles. Twelve miles away from the modern city are the ruins of the mightily walled town of Tughlakabad, abandoned for lack of water. Near Agra is the still complete city of Fatehpur Sikri, abandoned for the same reason. ('Why do you want to go to Fatehpur Sikri?' asked the travel agent in the foyer of the Delhi hotel. 'There is *nothing* there.') And listen to the guide at the Taj, talking to a party of Australians: 'So when she died he said, "I can't live here any more." So he went to Delhi and he built a *big* city there.' To the Indian, surrounded by ruins, this is a sufficient explanation of creation and decay. Consider these extracts from the first ten pages of Route 1 in the Pakistan section of Murray's *Handbook*:

> Tatta, now small, but as late as 1739 a great city of 60,000 inhabitants . . . The most remarkable sight in Tatta is the great mosque, 600 ft by 90 ft with 100 domes, begun by Shah Jahan in 1647 and finished by Aurangzeb, though now much decayed . . .
>
> 1½m farther N . . . is the tomb of the famous Nizam-ud-din . . . which some have thought was built from the remains of a Hindu temple.
>
> Excursion to Arore – formerly the very ancient Alor (Alor, Uch and Hyderabad are believed to have been the sites of three of many Alexandrias) . . . A ridge of ruins runs N.E. Reti station . . . 4m S. are the vast ruins of *Vijnot*, a leading city before the Muslim conquest: there is nothing to be seen but debris.
>
> Multan . . . of great antiquity, and supposed to be the capital of the Malli mentioned in Alexander's time . . . The original temple stood in the middle of the fort and was destroyed by Aurangzeb, while the mosque built upon its site was totally blown up in the siege of 1848.
>
> During the reign of Shah Beg Argun the fortifications were rebuilt, the fort of Alor, 6m away, being destroyed to supply material.
>
> Sukkur, pop. 77,000, was formerly famous for its pearl trade and gold embroidery. A large biscuit factory has recently been started.

Mosque on temple: ruin on ruin. This is in the North. In the South there is the great city of Vijayanagar. In the early sixteenth century it was twenty-four miles round. Today, four hundred years after its total sacking, even its ruins are few and scattered, scarcely noticeable at first against the surrealist brown rock formations of which they seem to form part. The surrounding villages are broken down and dusty; the physique of the people is poor. Then, abruptly, grandeur: the road from Kampli goes straight through some of the old buildings and leads to the main street, very wide, very long, still impressive, a flight of stone steps at one end, the towering *gopuram* of the temple, alive with sculpture, at the other. The square-pillared lower storeys of the stone buildings still stand; in the doorways are carvings of dancers with raised legs. And, inside, the inheritors of this greatness: men and women and children, thin as crickets, like lizards among the stones.

A child was squatting in the mud of the street; the hairless, pink-skinned dog waited for the excrement. The child, big-bellied, rose; the dog ate. Outside the temple there were two wooden juggernauts decorated with erotic carvings: couples engaged in copulation and fellatio: passionless, stylized. They were my first glimpse of Indian erotic carving, which I had been longing to see; but after the first excitement came depression. Sex as pain, creation its own decay; Shiva, god of the phallus, performing the dance of life and the dance of death: what a concept he is, how entirely of India! The ruins were inhabited. Set among the buildings of the main street was a brand-new whitewashed temple, pennants flying; and at the end of the street the old temple was still in use, still marked with the alternating vertical stripes of white and rust. One noticeboard about six feet high gave a list of fees for various services. Another, of the same size, gave the history of Vijayanagar: once, after the Raja had prayed, there was 'rain of gold'; this, in India, was history.

Rain, not of gold, swept suddenly across the Tungabhadra River and over the city. We took shelter up a rock slope behind the main street, in the recesses of an unfinished gateway of rough hewn stone. A very thin man followed us there. He was wrapped in a thin white cotton sheet, dappled with wet. He let the sheet fall off his chest to show us that he was all skin and bones, and he made the gestures of eating. I paid no attention. He looked away. He coughed; it was the cough of a sick man. His staff slipped from his hand and fell with a clatter on the stone floor down which water was now streaming. He hoisted himself on to a stone platform and let his staff lie where it had fallen. He withdrew into the angle of platform and wall and was unwilling to make any motion, to do anything that might draw attention to himself. The dark gateway framed light: rain was grey over the pagoda-ed city of stone. On the grey hillside, shining with water, there were the marks of quarryings. When the rain was over the man climbed down, picked up his wet staff, wrapped his sheet about him and made as if to go. I had converted fear and distaste into anger and contempt; it plagued me like a wound. I went to him and gave him some money. How easy it was to feel power in India! He, earning his money, took us out into the open, led us up the washed rock slope and pointed silently to buildings. Here was the hill of rock. Here were the buildings. Here the five-hundred-year-old marks of chisels. An abandoned, unfinished labour, like some of the rock caves at Ellora, which remain as the workmen left them one particular day.

All creation in India hints at the imminence of interruption and destruction. Building is like an elemental urge, like the act of sex among the starved. It is building for the sake of building, creation for the sake of creation; and each creation is separate, a beginning and an end in itself. 'Castles built on the waste sand of the sea-shore' not quite exact, but at Mahabalipuram near Madras, on the waste sand of the sea shore, stands the abandoned Shore Temple, its carvings worn smooth after twelve centuries of rain and salt and wind.

At Mahabalipuram and elsewhere in the South the ruins have a unity. They speak of the continuity and flow of Hindu India, ever shrinking. In the North the ruins speak of waste and failure, and the very grandeur of the Mogul buildings is oppressive. Europe has its monuments of sun-kings, its Louvres and Versailles. But they are part of the development of a country's spirit; they express the refining of a nation's sensibility; they add to the common, growing stock. In India these endless mosques and rhetorical mausolea, these great palaces speak only of a personal plunder and a country with an infinite capacity for being plundered. The Mogul owned everything in his dominions; and this is the message of Mogul architecture. I know only one building in England with this quality of dead-end personal extravagance, and that is Blenheim. Imagine England a country of Blenheims, continually built, destroyed and rebuilt over five hundred years, each a gift of the nation and seldom for services rendered, all adding up to nothing, leaving at the end no vigorous or even created nation, no principle beyond that of personal despotism. The Taj Mahal is exquisite. Transported slab by slab to the United States and re-erected, it might be wholly admirable. But in India it is a building wastefully without a function; it is only a despot's monument to a woman, not of India, who bore a child every year for fifteen years. It took twenty-two years to build; and the guide will tell you how many millions it cost. You can get to the Taj from the centre of Agra by cycle-rickshaw; all the way there and all the way back you can study the thin, shining, straining limbs of the rickshawman. India was not conquered, the British realist said, for the benefit of the Indians. But then it never had been; this is what all the ruins of the North say.

At one time the British held dances on the platform before the Taj Mahal. To Woodruff and to others this is a regrettable vulgarity. But it is in the Indian tradition. Respect for the past is new in Europe; and it was Europe that revealed India's past to India and made its veneration part of Indian nationalism. It is still through European eyes that India looks at her ruins and her art. Nearly every Indian who writes on Indian art feels bound to quote from the writings of European admirers. Indian art has still to be compared with European; and the British accusation that no Indian could have built the Taj Mahal has still to be rejected as a slander. Where there has been no European admiration there is neglect. The buildings of Lucknow and Fyzabad still suffer from the contemptuous political attitudes of the British towards its decadent rulers. Yearly the great Imambara in Lucknow crumbles into ruin. The detail on the stonework of the mausolea in Fyzabad has almost disappeared under heavy coats of what looks like PWD whitewash; elsewhere metalwork is preserved by a good deal of bright blue paint; in the centre of one garden a white Ashoka pillar, destroying symmetry and obscuring the view through the arched entrance, has been put up by an IAS officer to commemorate the abolition of *zemindari*. But of what Europe has discovered not enough care can be taken. This has become India's Ancient Culture. It is there in the comic little cupolas of the Ashoka Hotel in New Delhi, the comic little cupolas of the radio station in Calcutta, the little pillars with wheels and elephants and other devices of Indian culture that have been scattered about the zoological gardens of Lucknow, in the mock-Vijayanagar stone brackets of the Gandhi Mandap in Madras.

The architecture of nationalist India comes close in spirit to the architecture of the Raj: they are both the work of people consciously seeking to express ideas of themselves. It is comic and it is also sad. It is not of India, this reverence for the past, this attempt to proclaim it. It does not speak of vigour. It speaks as much as any ruin of exhaustion and people who have lost their way. It is as though, after all these endless separate creations, the vital sap has at last failed. Since the schools of Kangra and Basohli, Indian art has been all confusion. There is an idea of the behaviour required in the new world, but the new world is still bewildering. At Amritsar the monument honouring those who fell in the massacre is a pathetic affair of flames cut into heavy red stone. At Lucknow the British memorial of the Mutiny is the ruined Residency, preserved by Indians with a love the visitor must find strange; and just across the road is the rival Indian memorial, a white marble pillar of inelegant proportions capped by a comic little dome which might, again, represent a flame. It is like seeing Indians on a dance floor: they are attempting attitudes which do not become them. I did not see a Buddhist site that had not been disfigured by attempts to recreate India's ancient culture. Near Gorakhpur, for instance, there now stands amid the ruins of an old monastery a reconstructed temple of the period. On the flat wasteland of Kurukshetra, the scene of the Gita dialogue between Arjuna and Krishna, his charioteer, there is a new temple, and in its garden there is a representation in marble of the scene. It is less than bazaar art. That chariot will never move; the horses are dead, stiff, heavy. And this is the work of people whose sculpture is worth all the sculpture of the rest of the world, who in the South, at Vijayanagar, could create a whole 'Horse Court' of horses rampant.

Somewhere something has snapped. Where does one begin to look for this failure? One begins with that Kurukshetra temple. On it there is a plaque which says this exactly:

> THIS TEMPAL HAS BEEN BUILT THROUGH THE CHARITY OF RAJA SETH BALDEO DAS BIRLA AND HAS BEEN DEDICATED OF SHREE ARYA DHARMA SEVA SANGH IN NEW DELHI. HINDU PILGRIMS OF ALL SECTS E.G. SANATANISTS, ARYA SAMAJISTS, JAINS, SIKHS AND BUDDHISTS ETC WILL BE ENTERTAINED PROVIDED THEY ARE MORALLY AND PHYSICALLY PURE AND CLEAN
> NOTE PERSONS SUFFERING FROM INFECTIOUS OR CONTAGIOUS DISEASES WILL NOT BE ADMITTED

The crudity of the language is matched by the crudity of the self-appraisal. India may be poor, the plaque says in effect, but spiritually she is rich; and her people are morally and physically pure and clean. Self-appraisal, the crudity of the stonework and marblework, the imperfect use of the foreign language: they are all related.

*

Some Indians denied that the Indian plastic sense had decayed. Those who thought it had, rejected the view that the Moguls were partly responsible – for the quantity and extravagance of their building: Akbar exhausting experimentation, his successors taking decoration to its limit – and blamed it on the British intervention.

The British pillaged the country thoroughly; during their rule manufactures and crafts declined. This has to be accepted, and set against the achievements listed by Woodruff: a biscuit factory is a poor exchange for gold embroidery. The country had been pillaged before. But continuity had been maintained. With the British, continuity was broken. And perhaps the British are responsible for this Indian artistic failure, which is part of the general Indian bewilderment, in the way that the Spaniards were responsible for the stupefaction of the Mexicans and the Peruvians. It was a clash between a positive principle and a negative; and nothing more negative can be imagined than the conjunction in the eighteenth century of a static Islam and a decadent Hinduism. In any clash between post-Renaissance Europe and India, India was bound to lose.*

The stupefaction of peoples is one of our mysteries. At school in Trinidad we were taught that the aboriginal inhabitants of the West Indies 'sickened and died' when the Spaniards came. In Grenada, the spice island, there is a cliff with the terrible name of Sauteurs:

* If I had read Camus's *The Rebel* before writing this chapter, I might have used his terminology. Where Camus might have said 'capable of rebellion' I have said 'positive' and 'capable of self-assessment'; and it is interesting that Camus gives, as examples of people incapable of rebellion, the Hindus and the Incas. 'The problem of rebellion ... has no meaning except within our Western society ... Thanks to the theory of political freedom, there is, in the very heart of our society, an increasing awareness in man of the idea of man and, thanks to the application of this theory of freedom, a corresponding dissatisfaction ... What is at stake is humanity's gradually increasing self-awareness as it pursues its course. In fact, for the Inca and the [Hindu] pariah the problem never arises, because for them it had been solved by a tradition, even before they had had time to raise it – the answer being that tradition is sacred. If in a world where things are held sacred the problem of rebellion does not arise, it is because no real problems are to be found in such a world, all the answers having been given simultaneously. Metaphysic is replaced by myth. There are no more questions, only eternal answers and commentaries, which may be metaphysical.' (Translated by Anthony Bower.)

here the Amerindians committed mass suicide, leaping down into the sea. Stupefied communities of other, later races survive. There are the degraded Hindus of Martinique and Jamaica, swamped by Africa; and it is hard to associate the dispirited Javanese of Surinam in South America, objects of local ridicule, with the rioters and embassy-burners of Djakarta. India did not wither, like Peru and Mexico, at the touch of Europe. If she were wholly Muslim she might have done. But her Hindu experience of conquerors was great; Hindu India met conquerors half-way and had always been able to absorb them. And it is interesting, and now a little sad, to see Indians, above all in Bengal, reacting to the British as they might have done to any other conqueror, Indian or Asiatic.

The attempt at a half-way meeting is there in an early English-inspired reformer like Ram Mohun Roy, who is buried in Bristol. It is there, generations later, in the upbringing of Sri Aurobindo, the revolutionary turned mystic, whose father, sending him as a boy of seven to be educated in England, required his English guardians to shield him from all Indian contacts. It is there, a little later still, but now pathetically, in the Mullick Palace in Calcutta. Decaying already, since this is India, with servants cooking in the marble galleries, the Palace is like a film set. As we go through the tall gateway we feel that this is how a film might begin; the camera will advance with us, will pause here on this broken masonry, there on this faded decoration; there will be silence, and then the voices will come through the echo chamber, the sound of carriages on the crescent-shaped drive: for Mullick's entertainments were fabulous. Great columns of the Calcutta Corinthian style dominate the façade; fountains imported from Europe still play in its grounds; statues representing the four continents stand in the corners of the marble patio where the family now keep birds in cages; on the lower floor a large room is made small by a colossal statue of Queen Victoria; and elsewhere, below excessively chandeliered ceilings, dust has gathered on what looks like the jumble of a hundred English antique shops: a collector's zeal turned to mania:

the Bengali landowner displaying his appreciation of European culture to the supercilious European. Nothing here is Indian, save perhaps the portrait of the owner; but already we can sense the Anglo-Bengali encounter going sour.

Englishness, unlike the faith of other conquerors, required no converts; and for the Bengali, who was most susceptible to Englishness, the English in India reserved a special scorn. An imperial ideal, well on the way to a necessarily delayed realization, was foundering on the imperialist myth, equally delayed, of the empire-builder, on the English fantasy of Englishness, 'the cherished conviction', as one English official wrote in 1883, 'which was shared by every Englishman in India, from the highest to the lowest, by the planter's assistant in his lowly bungalow . . . to the Viceroy on his throne . . . that he belongs to a race whom God has destined to govern and subdue'. The mock-imperial rhetoric of the dedication of Nirad Chaudhuri's *Autobiography of an Unknown Indian* might serve as an epitaph on this unfulfilled imperial encounter. Translated into Latin, it might be carved in Trajan lettering on the India Gate in New Delhi: 'To the memory of the British Empire in India, which conferred subjecthood on us but withheld citizenship, to which yet every one of us threw out the challenge *Civis Britannicus sum*, because all that was good and living within us was made, shaped, and quickened by the same British rule.'

No other country was more fitted to welcome a conqueror; no other conqueror was more welcome than the British. What went wrong? Some say the Mutiny; some say the arrival in India afterwards of white women. It is possible. But the French, with or without their women, might have reacted differently to the francophile Bengali. The cause, I believe, has to be looked for not in India but in England where, at a time we cannot precisely fix, occurred that break in English sensibility as radical and as seemingly abrupt as that which we have witnessed in our time. The civilization to which the Indians were attracted had been replaced by another. It was confusing – the guests whom Simpson's Restaurant in the

Strand was nourishing for imperial purposes continued to bear the outer semblance of Parson Adams and Tom Jones – and many Indians, from Aurobindo to Tagore to Nehru to Chaudhuri, have recorded their bewilderment.

It is perhaps only now that we can see what a clean break with the past the Raj was. The British refused to be absorbed into India; they did not proclaim, like the Mogul, that if there was a paradise on earth, it was this, and it was this, and it was this. While dominating India they expressed their contempt for it, and projected England; and Indians were forced into a nationalism which in the beginning was like a mimicry of the British. To look at themselves, to measure themselves against the new, positive standards of the conqueror, Indians had to step out of themselves. It was an immense self-violation; and in the beginning, in fact, a flattering self-assessment could only be achieved with the help of Europeans like Max Muller and those others who are quoted so profusely in nationalist writings.

It resulted in the conscious possession of spirituality, proclaimed as in the plaque of the Kurukshetra temple. *Spiritualise Science, Says Prasad* is a newspaper headline over a report of one of the late President's almost daily speeches in retirement. It results in this, from the *Times of India*:

> A 'RETAILER' OF SPIRITUALITY
> *Santiniketan, January 16*
>
> Acharya Vinoba Bhave yesterday described himself as a 'retailer' with regard to the wealth of spirituality.
>
> He made this remark at a reception here saying that the Buddha, Jesus, Krishna, Tagore, Ramakrishna and Vivekananda were 'wholesalers of spirituality while I myself am a retailer, drawing from that inexhaustible storehouse to supply to the villagers.' – PTI

It resulted in the conscious possession of an ancient culture. At an official reception for the former governor of a state someone called across to me, as we sat silently in deep chairs set against the walls of the room, 'How is Indian culture getting on in your part of the world?' The former governor, a heavily-stockinged veteran of the Independence struggle, leaned forward and noticed me. He was reported to be keen on Indian culture; I was later to read newspaper reports of his speeches on the subject. Wishing to show that I took the question seriously and was anxious to establish a basis for discussion, I shouted back across the large room: 'What do you mean by Indian culture?' My IAS friend, under whose protection I was, closed his eyes in dismay. The former governor leaned back; silence returned to the room.

Spirituality and ancient culture, then, were as consciously possessed as Parson Adams and Tom Jones in Simpson's. But it was inevitable that with this unnatural self-consciousness a current of genuine feeling should fail. The old world, of ruins which spoke only of continuity and of creation as an elemental repetition, could not survive; and Indians floundered about in a new world whose forms they could see but whose spirit eluded them. In the acquiring of an identity in their own land they became displaced.

They acquired a double standard. Five hundred deaths from cholera in Calcutta are reported in a news-brief in an Indian newspaper. The death of twenty children merely requires to be stated.

POX IN FEROZABAD

*'The Times of India' News Service*

AGRA, June 1: Small-pox is reported to have broken out in epidemic form in Ferozabad.

Twenty persons, mostly children, are reported to have died in Jaroli Kalan village.

The death of sixteen miners in Belgium in the same newspaper is big news. The peasants in the collectorate courts attend with open mouths to the drama of debates in a language they cannot understand, while outside, in an atmosphere of the bazaar, other peasants, with all the time in the world, it seems, lounge about in the dust, and the typists sit with their ancient machines in the faint shade of trees, and the lawyers, startling in their legal subfusc, wait for custom. These collectorate bazaars function within a changed assumption of the value of man that is still only legalistic, confined to the collectorate and the courthouse, a type of make-believe, part of the complex ritual which supports the Indian through his dusty existence. Caste, another law, which renders millions faceless, is equally to be cherished. Mimicry conceals the Indian schizophrenia. India must progress, must stamp out corruption, must catch up with the West. But does it truly matter? Does a little corruption hurt anybody? Is material prosperity all that important? Hasn't India been through it all before – the atom bomb, the aeroplane, the telephone? So in conversation Indians can be elusive and infuriating. Yet I had only to think myself back to my grandmother's house, to that dim, unexpressed awareness of the world within and the world without, to understand, to see their logic, to understand both their passion and their calm despair, the positive and the negative. But I had learned to see; I could not deny what I saw. They remained in that other world. They did not see the defecating squatters beside the railroad in the mornings; more, they denied their existence. And why should these squatters be noticed anyway? Had I seen the beggars of Cairo or the Negro slums of Rio?

Language is part of the confusion. Every other conqueror bequeathed a language to India. English remains a foreign language. It is the greatest incongruity of British rule. Language is like a sense; and the psychological damage caused by the continued official use of English, which can never be more than a second language, is immense. It is like condemning the council of, say, Barnsley to conduct their affairs in French or Urdu. It makes for inefficiency; it separates the administrator from the villager; it is a barrier to self-knowledge. The clerk using English in a government office is immediately stultified. For him the language is made up of certain imperfectly understood incantations, which limit his responses and make him inflexible. So he passes his working life in a sub-world of dim perceptions; yet in his own language he might be quick and inventive. Hindi has been decreed the national language. It is understood by half the country; it can take you from Srinagar to Goa and from Bombay to Calcutta. But many in the North pretend not to understand it. And in the South the nationalist zeal for Hindi, encouraged by Gandhi, has altogether died. Hindi, it is said, gives the North an advantage; it is better for North and South to remain illiterate and inefficient, but equal, in English. It is an Indian argument: India will never cease to require the arbitration of a conqueror. And the advocates of Hindi, in their new self-appraising way, seek not to simplify the language but to make it more inaccessible. 'Radio', a universal word, will not do: it has to be rendered into the wampum-and-wigwam quaintness of 'voice from the sky'.

Indian attempts at the novel further reveal the Indian confusion. The novel is of the West. It is part of that Western concern with the condition of men, a response to the here and now. In India thoughtful men have preferred to turn their backs on the here and now and to satisfy what President Radhakrishnan calls 'the basic human hunger for the unseen'. It is not a good qualification for the writing or reading of novels. A basic hunger for the unseen makes many Indians vulnerable to novels like *The Razor's Edge* and *The Devil's Advocate*, whose value as devotional literature is plain. Beyond this there is uncertainty. What does one look for in a novel? Story, 'characterization', 'art', realism, a moral, a good cry, beautiful writing? The point hasn't been settled. Hence the paperbacked numbers of the Schoolgirl's Own Library in the hands of male university students; the American children's comics in the room of the student at St Stephen's, New Delhi; the row of Denise Robins next to the astrological volumes. Hence Jane Austen offered in an Indian paperback as a writer whose use of simile is especially to be relished.

It is part of the mimicry of the West, the Indian self-violation. It is there in Chandigarh, in that new theatre for plays that are not written, in those endless writers' conferences where writers are urged to work for 'emotional integration' or the five-year plans, and where the problems of the writer are tirelessly discussed. These problems appear to be less those of writing than of translation into English; the feeling is widespread that, whatever English might have done for Tolstoy, it can never do justice to the Indian 'language' writers. This is possible; what little I read of them in translation did not encourage me to read more. Premchand, the great, the beloved, turned out to be a minor fabulist, much preoccupied with social issues like the status of widows or daughters-in-law. Other writers quickly fatigued me with their assertions that poverty was sad, that death was sad. I read of poor fishermen, poor peasants, poor rickshaw-men; innumerable pretty young girls either simply and suddenly died, or shared the landlord's bed, paid the family's medical bills and then committed suicide; and many of the 'modern' short stories were only refurbished folk tales. In Andhra I was given a brochure of a Telugu writers' conference. The brochure spoke of the heroic struggle of the people to establish a Telugu state, to me an endeavour of pure frivolity, listed martyrs, and then gave a brief history of the Telugu novel. It seems that the Telugu novel began with Telugu adaptations of *The Vicar of Wakefield* and *East Lynne*. A little farther south I was told of a writer greatly influenced by Ernest Hemingway.

*The Vicar of Wakefield* and *The Old Man and the Sea*: it is difficult to relate them to the Indian landscape or to Indian attitudes. The Japanese novel also began as part of the mimicry of the West. Tanizaki has, I believe, confessed that in his early work he was too greatly influenced by the Europeans. Even through the mimicry, however, it can be seen that the Japanese are possessed of a way of looking. It flavours the early work of Tanizaki as it flavours the recent novels of Yukio Mishima: that curious literalness which adds up to a detachment formidable enough to make the writing seem pointless. However odd, this derives from a hunger for the seen and is an expression of concern with men. The sweetness and sadness which can be found in Indian writing and Indian films are a turning away from a too overwhelming reality; they reduce the horror to a warm, virtuous emotion. Indian sentimentality is the opposite of concern.

The virtues of R.K. Narayan are Indian failings magically transmuted. I say this without disrespect: he is a writer whose work I admire and enjoy. He seems forever headed for that *aimlessness* of Indian fiction – which comes from a profound doubt about the purpose and value of fiction – but he is forever rescued by his honesty, his sense of humour and above all by his attitude of total acceptance. He operates from deep within his society. Some years ago he told me in London that, whatever happened, India would go on. He said it casually; it was a conviction so deep it required no stressing. It is a negative attitude, part of that older India which was incapable of self-assessment. It has this result: the India of Narayan's novels is not the India the visitor sees. He tells an Indian truth. Too much that is overwhelming has been left out; too much has been taken for granted. There is a contradiction in Narayan, between his form, which implies concern, and his attitude, which denies it; and in this calm contradiction lies his magic which some have called Chekovian. He is inimitable, and it cannot be supposed that his is the synthesis at which Indian writing will arrive. The younger writers in English have moved far from Narayan. In those novels which tell of the difficulties of the Europe-returned student they are still only expressing a personal bewilderment; the novels themselves are documents of the Indian confusion. The only writer who, while working from within the society, is yet able to impose on it a vision which is an acceptable type of comment, is R. Prawer Jhabvala. And she is European.*

The Indo-British encounter was abortive; it ended in a double fantasy. Their new self-awareness makes it impossible for Indians to go back; their cherishing of Indianness makes it difficult for them to go ahead. It is possible to find the India that appears not to have changed since Mogul times but has, profoundly; it is possible to find the India whose mimicry of the West is convincing until, sometimes with dismay, sometimes with impatience, one realizes that complete communication is not possible, that a gift of vision cannot be shared, that there still survive inaccessible areas of Indian retreat. Both the negative and the positive principles have been diluted; one balances the other. The penetration was not complete; the attempt at conversion was abandoned. India's strength, her ability to endure, came from the negative principle, her unexamined sense of continuity. It is a principle which, once diluted, loses its virtue. In the concept of Indianness the sense of continuity was bound to be lost. The creative urge failed. Instead of continuity we have the static. It is there in the 'ancient culture' architecture; it is there in the much bewailed loss of drive, which is psychological more than political and economic. It is there in the political gossip of Bunty. It is there in the dead horses and immobile chariot of the Kurukshetra temple. Shiva has ceased to dance.

* 'It is possible to separate the literature of consent, which coincides, by and large, with ancient history and the classical period, from the literature of rebellion, which begins in modern times. We note the scarcity of fiction in the former. When it exists, with very few exceptions, it is not concerned with a story but with fantasy ... These are fairy tales, not novels. In the latter period, on the contrary, the novel form is really developed – a form that has not ceased to thrive and extend its field of activity up to the present day ... The novel is born at the same time as the spirit of rebellion and expresses, on the aesthetic plane, the same ambition.' Camus: *The Rebel.*

# 9
# THE GARLAND ON MY PILLOW

'I AM SURE you will never guess what my duties are.'

He was middle-aged, thin, sharp-featured, with spectacles. His eyes were running and there was a drop of moisture on the tip of his nose. It was a winter's morning and our second-class railway compartment was unheated.

'I will give you a little assistance. I work for the Railways. This is my pass. Have you ever seen one?'

'You are a ticket inspector!'

A smile revealed his missing teeth. 'No, no, my dear sir. They wear a uniform.'

'You are from the Police.'

His smile cracked into a wet laugh. 'I see that you will never guess. Well, I will tell you. I am an Inspector of Forms and Stationery, Northern Railway.'

'Forms and Stationery!'

'Indeed. I travel about, night and day, winter and summer, from railway station to railway station, inspecting forms and stationery.'

'But how did this begin, Mr Inspector?'

'Why do you ask, sir? My life has been a failure.'

'Please don't say that, Mr Inspector.'

'I might have done so much better, sir. You have no doubt observed my English. My teacher was Mr Harding. I was a Bachelor of Arts, you know. When I joined the Service I expected to go far. I was put in Stores. In those days I would take down bundles of forms and stationery from the shelves and hand them to the porter. This was, of course, after the indents had been approved.'

'Of course.'

'From Stores to the office: it was a slow business. Steady. But slow. Somehow I managed. I have remained in Forms and Stationery all my life. I have kept my family. I have given the boys an education. I have married my daughter. One son is in the army and the other is in the air force, an officer.'

'But, Mr Inspector, this is a success story.'

'O sir, do not mock me. It has been a wasted life.'

'Tell me more about your job, Mr Inspector.'

'Secrets, you are after my secrets. Well, I will explain. Let me show you, first of all, an indent.'

'It's like a little book, Mr Inspector. Sixteen pages.'

'It goes to the head of a stationmaster sometimes. Once a year these indents are sent out to our stationmasters. They prepare their indents and submit three copies. What you see now, by the way, is an elementary type of indent. There are others.'

'And when the indents are submitted –'

'Then they come to me, you see. And I pay my little visits. I get off at the station like any other passenger. It sometimes happens that I am insulted by the very stationmaster whose indents I have come to prune. Then I declare myself.'

'You are a wicked man, Mr Inspector.'

'Do you think so, sir? An Inspector of Forms and Stationery gets to know his stationmasters. They show themselves in their indents. You get to recognize them. This might interest you. It was yesterday's work.'

The indent, filled in in black, was heavily annotated in red.

'Turn to page twelve. Do you see? A hundred notepads were what he required.'

'Goodness! You've only given him two.'

'He has six children, all of school age. Ninety-eight of those pads were for those six children. An Inspector of Forms and Stationery gets to know these things. Well, here we are. I shall get off here. I believe I am going to enjoy myself today. I wish I had the time to show you what *he* has indented for.'

*

'I met one of your Inspectors of Forms and Stationery the other day.'

'You met what?'

'One of your Inspectors of Forms and Stationery.'

'There are no such people.'

'I didn't dream this man up. He had his indents and everything.'

It was a good word to use.

'It just goes to show. You can work for the Railways for years and not know a thing about it. Me, I'm exhausted by presidential tours. Our former president didn't like travelling by air. Do you know what a presidential tour means for the railway administrator? Altering time-tables. Re-routing. Going over the track inch by inch. For twenty-four hours before having men walking up and down within hailing distance of each other. And then going yourself on a decoy run a quarter of an hour ahead of the president's train. So that you get blown up first.'

*

'But where in this terrible town of yours can we have coffee?'

'The railway station is the centre of civilization in these parts. And the coffee isn't bad.'

'We'll go there.'

'Sir?'

'Two coffees.'

'No coffee.'

'Oh. Well, bring a pot of tea for two. And bring the Complaints Book.'

'Sir?'

'Complaints Book.'

'Let me talk to the manager, sir.'

'No, no. You just bring a pot of tea and the Book.'

'I am sorry about this. But we don't do the catering here. That's in the hand of a local contractor. We give him coffee and tea of a certain quality. He just sells it to somebody else. We can't do anything about it. Our contractor knows a minister. It's the Indian story. But look. Our friend is coming back.'

'Is he bringing the Complaints Book?'

'No. He's bringing two cups of coffee.'

*

Indian Railways! They are part of the memory of every traveller, in the north, east, west or south. Yet few have written of the romance of this stupendous organization which makes the Indian distances shrink and which, out of an immense assurance, proclaims in a faded notice in every railway station: *Trains running late are likely to make up lost time*. And the trains usually do. But does the romance exist? A service so complex and fine deserves a richer country, with shining cities organized for adventure. But it is only distance, or the knowledge of distance, that gives romance to the place-names on the yellow boards of Indian coaches. The locomotive will consume distance and will seem to convert it into waste. And it will do so with a speed that will presently appear as pointless as the poor, repetitive vastness of the pigmy land which, supine below a high sky, will abruptly at railway stations burst into shrill life, as though all energy had been spared for this spot and this moment: the shouts of stunted, sweating porters, over-eager in red turbans and tunics, the cries of tea-vendors with their urns and clay cups (the cups to be broken after use), the cries of *pan*-vendors and the vendors of fried or curried messes (the leaf-plates, pinned together by thin dried twigs, to be thrown afterwards on to the platform or on the tracks, where the pariah dogs, fierce only with their fellows, will fight over them – and one defeated dog will howl and howl), the whole scene – yet animated only in the foreground, for these stations are havens as well as social centres, and the smooth, cool concrete platforms are places where the futile can sleep – the whole scene ceilinged by low fans which spin in empty frenzy. The sun will rise and set, and the racing train, caught in the golden light of dawn or dusk, will throw a perfect elongated shadow from the tops of the coaches to the very rails; and distance will still not have been consumed. The land has become distance. Will the metal not ignite? Will there be no release into a land which is fruitful, where the men grow straight? There is only another station, more shouting, the magenta coaches coated with hot dust, more prostrate bodies, more dogs, the fraudulent comfort of a shower in the first-class waiting-room and a meal poisoned by one's own distress and cautiousness. And indeed people are less important to Indian Railways than freight; and less revenue comes from the first-class than from the third, the sub-standard for whom there is never enough room, even in their rudimentary coaches. The railway administrator, who knows this, can be forgiven if he fails to see the romance of his service or its brilliance. The Indian railways serve India. They operate punctually and ceaselessly because they must. They reveal more than that 'real' India which Indians believe can only be found in third-class carriages. They reveal India as futility and limitless pain, India as an idea. Their romance is an abstraction.

*

It was a third-class carriage, but not of the real India. It was air-conditioned and fitted out like an aeroplane, with rows of separate seats with high adjustable backs. Curtains were draped over the double windows; the aisle was carpeted. We were on one of the 'prestige' services of Indian Railways. These air-conditioned coaches run between the three major cities and New Delhi; for four pounds you can travel a thousand miles in comfort, at an average speed of thirty-five miles an hour.

We were travelling south, and among the South Indians, small, fine-featured, subdued at the beginning of the long journey, the Sikh was at once noticeable. He was very big; his gestures were large; he required much room. His beard was unusually thin, and his black turban, tight and low, looked like a beret: I had taken him at first for a European artist. In defiance of the many printed notices he swung his suitcase up on to the rack and wedged it into place. The action showed up his tight weightlifter's body. Turning slightly, he took in the other occupants of the carriage, from a great height, and appeared to dismiss us; his loose lower lip curled downward. He was four or five rows ahead of me and all I could see when he sat down was the top of his turban. But he had made his effect. My eyes returned to that turban again and again, and before we had travelled an hour I felt his presence as an irritant. I feared – as so often on confined journeys I have feared – that my interest was inviting his own and making inevitable a contact I wished to avoid.

The Sikhs puzzled and attracted me. They were among the few whole men in India, and of all Indians they seemed closest in many ways to the Indians of Trinidad. They had a similar energy and restlessness, which caused a similar resentment. They were proud of their agricultural and mechanical skills, and they had the same passion for driving taxis and lorries. They too were accused of clannishness, while their internal politics were just as cantankerous. But the Sikhs were of India; beyond these similarities they were unreadable. The Sikh's individuality appeared to be muffled by his beard and turban; his eyes were robbed of expression. His reputation in India did not make him easier to understand. There was his military tradition; his ferocity as soldier and policeman was known. Equally established, in spite of his adventurousness and obvious success, was his simpleness. The foolish Sikh is a figure of legend. The turban had something to do with it; it heated the Sikh's uncut hair and softened his brain. That was what the stories said; and Sikh politics – consisting of temple plots, holy men, miraculous fasts, Wild West rivalries punctuated with gunshot on the Delhi-Chandigarh road – certainly seemed both comic and fierce. There was energy, no doubt. But perhaps it was too much for India: against the Indian background the Sikhs were always a little alarming.

There had been an accident to our train the week before, and we were attached to a substitute dining-car. There was no through way from our carriage. We came to a station and I got out to transfer to the dining-car. I was aware of the Sikh getting out after me and dawdling at a bookstall. In the dining-car I sat with my back to the entrance. South Indian languages, excessively vowelled, rattled about me. The South Indians were beginning to unwind; they were lapping up their liquidized foods. Food was a pleasure to their hands. Chewing, sighing with pleasure, they squelched curds and rice between their fingers. They squelched and squelched; then, in one swift circular action, as though they wished to take their food by surprise, they gathered some of the mixture into a ball, brought their dripping palms close to their mouths and – flick! – rice and curds were shot inside; and the squelching, chattering and sighing began again.

'You don't mind if I sit with you?'

It was the Sikh. He was carrying the *Illustrated Weekly of India*. His tight black turban, slightly askew, his tight shirt and tight belted trousers gave him the appearance of a pirate of children's books. His English was fluent; it indicated a residence abroad. His mouth now seemed humorous; it curled, with amusement, I thought, as, squeezing himself between table and chair, he regarded the squelchers.

'What do you think of the food?' He gave a low, chest-heaving chuckle. 'You come from London, don't you?'

'In a way.'

'I can spot the accent. I heard you talking to the guard. You know Hampstead? You know Finchley Road? You know Fitzjohn's Avenue?'

'I know them. But I don't know them very well.'

'You know the Bambi Coffee House?'

'I don't think so.'

'But if you know Finchley Road you must know the Bambi. You remember that little fellow with tight trousers, turtle-neck sweater and a little beard?' The chuckle came again.

'I don't remember him.'

'You must remember him if you remember the Bambi. Little fellow. Whenever you went to the Bambi – whenever you went to *any* coffee-house in Finchley Road – he was always there, jumping about.'

'Did he operate the coffee machine?'

'No, no. Nothing like that. I don't think he used to *do* anything. He was just there. Little beard. Funny little fellow.'

'You miss London?'

His eyes ranged over the squelchers. 'Well, you just look.'

A woman in a sari, with blue tinted spectacles, and a baby on her knee, was lapping up *sambar*. She splayed out her fingers, pressed her palm flat on her plate, drew her fingers together, lifted her palm to her mouth and licked it dry.

The Sikh gave his deep *mm-mm* chuckle.

'At last,' he said, as the train moved off. 'I didn't want any other Sikhs to come in. Have a fag.'

'But Sikhs don't smoke.'

'This one does.'

The woman looked up from her *sambar*. The squelchers paused, looked at us and looked away quickly as if in horror.

'Punks,' the Sikh said. His expression changed. 'You see how these monkeys stare at you?' He leaned forward. 'You know my trouble?'

'Tell me.'

'I'm colour-prejudiced.'

'But how awkward for you.'

'I know. It's just one of those things.'

Enough had already occurred to warn me, but I was misled by my Trinidad training. 'I'm colour-prejudiced.' The abrupt statement was Trinidadian, and of a special sophistication: it was an invitation to semi-serious banter. I had responded, and he appeared to have taken me up neatly. I forgot that English was only his second language; that few Indians dealt in irony; and that, for all his longing for Finchley Road and Fitzjohn's Avenue, he was an Indian to whom the taboos of caste and sect were fundamental. His smoking was a flamboyant defiance, but it was guarded: he did not smoke in the presence of Sikhs. He wore the turban, beard and bracelet which his religion required; and I am sure he also wore the knife and the drawers. So the moment for declaration, and perhaps withdrawal, passed.

Waiting for our food – 'No rice,' he had said, as though stating a caste restriction: rice was the staple of the non-Aryan South – he turned the pages of the *Illustrated Weekly of India*, wetting his finger on his tongue. 'Look,' he said, pushing the paper towards me. 'See how many of these South Indian monkeys you can find there.' He showed me a feature on the Indian team at the Asian Games in Djakarta. They were nearly all Sikhs, unfamiliar without their turbans, their long hair stooked and tied up with ribbon. '*Indian* team! Tell me how this country is going to get on without us. If we sit back, the Pakistanis can just walk in, you know. Give me one Sikh division, just one, and I will walk through the whole blasted country. You see any of these punks stopping us?'

Contact had occurred and there could now be no escape. A journey of twenty-four hours still lay ahead of us. We got out and walked together on station platforms, enjoying the shock of heat after the air-conditioned carriage. We ate together. When we smoked I watched for other Sikhs. 'I don't mind, you understand,' the Sikh said. 'But I don't want to hurt them.' We talked of London and Trinidad and coffee-houses, India and the Sikhs. We agreed that the Sikhs were the finest people in India, but it was hard to find anyone among them whom he admired. I dredged my memory for Sikh notabilities. I mentioned one Sikh religious leader. 'He's a bloody Hindu,' the Sikh said. I mentioned another.

'He's a damned Muslim.' I spoke of politicians. He replied with stories of their crookedness. 'The man had lost the election. And then suddenly you had these people running up with ballot-boxes and saying, "Look, look, we forgot to count these."' I spoke of the energy of the Sikhs and the prosperity of the Punjab. 'Yes,' he said. 'The sweeper class is coming up.' We talked of Sikh writers. I mentioned Khushwant Singh, whom I knew and liked; he had spent years working on Sikh scriptures and history. 'Khushwant? He doesn't *know* anything about the Sikhs.' The only person who had written well about the Sikhs was Cunningham; and he was dead, as all the finest Sikhs were. 'We're a pretty hopeless bunch today,' the Sikh said.

Many of his stories were overtly humorous, but often, as in his references to the Sikh religious leaders, I saw humour where none was intended. Our relationship had begun in mutual misunderstanding. And so it developed. He grew more perceptibly bitter as the journey went on, but this answered my own mood. Shrill railway stations, poor fields, decaying towns, starving cattle, a withered race of men: because his reactions appeared to be like mine it did not occur to me that they were unusual in an Indian. As it was, their violence steadied me; he became my irrational self. He became more violent and more protective as the land grew poorer; he showed me that tenderness which physically big men can show to the small.

It was nearly midnight when we came to the junction where I had to leave the train. The platforms were like mortuaries. In the dim light prostrate men showed as shrunken white bundles out of which protruded bony Indian arms, shining stringy legs, collapsed grey-stubbled faces. Men slept; dogs slept; and among them, like emanations risen from the senseless bodies, over which they appeared to trample, other men and other dogs moved. Silent third-class carriages turned out to be packed with dark, waiting, sweating faces; the yellow boards above the grilled windows showed that they were going somewhere. The engines hissed. *Trains running late are likely to make up lost time.* The fans spun urgently. From everywhere dogs howled. One hobbled off into the darkness at the end of the platform; its foreleg had been freshly torn off; a raw bloody stump remained.

The Sikh helped me with my luggage. I was grateful to him for his presence, his wholeness. We had already exchanged addresses and arranged when and where we were to meet again. Now we repeated our promises. We would travel over the South. India yet had its pleasures. We would go hunting. He would show me: it was easy, and I would enjoy the elephants. Then he returned to his air-conditioned coach, behind the double glass. Whistles blew; the train moved mightily off. Yet the station remained so little changed: so many bodies remained, awaiting transportation.

My own train was due to leave in about two hours; the coaches were waiting. I changed my third-class ticket for a first-class one, picked my way down dim platforms past the bodies of dogs and men, past third-class carriages which were already full and hot. The conductor opened the door of my compartment and I climbed in. I bolted the door, pulled down all the blinds, trying to shut out the howls of dogs, shutting out intruders, all those staring faces and skeletal bodies. I put on no lights. I required darkness.

*

I did not expect it, but we met again as we planned. It was in a town where the only other person I knew was a prosperous sweet-shop-owner. I had learned to fear his hospitality. At every meeting it was necessary to eat a selection of his sweets. They were corrosively sweet; they killed appetite for a day. The Sikh's hospitality was easier. He sought to revive my appetite with drink and he gave me food. He also gave me much of his time. I felt he was offering more than hospitality: he was offering his friendship, and it embarrassed me that I couldn't respond. But I was calmer now than I had been on the train, and his moods no longer always answered mine.

'They've let this cantonment area go down,' he said. 'In the old days they didn't allow niggers here. Now the blackies are all over the place.'

The anger was plain, and was not tempered by the humour or self-satire I had seen, or made myself see, in his outbursts on the train.

'These people! You have to shout "Boy!" Otherwise they just don't hear you.'

I had noted this. At the hotel I was shouting 'Boy!' with everybody else, but I couldn't manage the correct tone. Both boys and guests wore South Indian dress, and I had already more than once shouted at the wrong man. My shouts therefore always held muted enquiry and apology.

The Sikh was not amused. 'And you know what they answer? You might think you are in some picture with American darkies. They answer, "Yes, master." God!'

In such moods he was now a strain. His rage was like self-torment; he indulged it to the pitch of soliloquy. I had completely misunderstood him. But by this misunderstanding I had encouraged his friendship and trust. We had parted sentimentally and had had a sentimental reunion. I had fallen in with all his plans. He had made arrangements for our hunting-trip. It would have been as difficult to withdraw as to go ahead. I let him talk, and did nothing. And he was more than his rages. He showed me an increasing regard. As a host he was solicitous; he placed me under a growing obligation. He was disappointed and bitter; I also saw that he was lonely. The condition of India was an affront to him; it was to me, too. The days passed, and I did not break away. He was giving me more and more of his time, and I became more and more involved with his bitterness, but passively, uneasily, awaiting release.

We went one day to the ruins of an eighteenth-century palace which had been cleaned up into a picnic spot. Here India was elegance and solidity; the bazaars and railway stations were far away. He knew the ruins well. Walking among them, showing them to me, he was serene, even a little proud. There were older temples in the neighbourhood, but they did not interest him as much as the palace, and I thought I knew why. He had been to Europe, had suffered ridicule if only in his imagination for his turban, beard and uncut hair. He had learned to look at India and himself. He knew what Europe required. The palace ruins might have been European, and he was glad to show them to me. We walked in the gardens and he talked again of our hunting trip: I would marvel at the silence of the elephants. We dawdled by the tank, ate our sandwiches and drank our coffee.

On the way back we visited one of the temples. This was at my suggestion. The derelict beggar-priest, bare-backed, roused himself from his string-bed and came out to meet us. He spoke no English and welcomed us in dumb show. The Sikh gave his chuckle and became remote. The priest didn't react. He walked ahead of us into the low, dark temple, raising his shrivelled arm and pointing out this and that, earning his fee. Carvings were scarcely visible in the gloom, and to the priest they were not as important as the living shrines, lit by oil lamps, in which there were bright images, gaudily dressed in doll's clothes, of black gods and white gods: India's ancient mixture of Aryan and Dravidian.

'This is how the trouble started,' the Sikh said.

The priest, staring at the gods, waiting for our exclamations, nodded.

'You've been to Gilgit? You should go. They're pure Aryan up there. Beautiful people. Let a couple of these Dravidians loose among them, and in no time they spoil the race for you.'

Nodding, the priest led us back into the open and stood beside us while we got into our shoes. I gave him some money and he returned silently to his cell.

'Until we came to India,' the Sikh said sadly, as we drove off, 'we were a good race. *Arya* – a good Sanskrit word. You know the meaning? Noble. You must read some of the old Hindu books. They will tell you. In those days it was unclean to kiss a very black woman on the lips. You think this is just a crazy Sikh talking? You read. This Aryan–Dravidian business isn't new. And it's starting up again. You see in the papers that the blackies are asking for their own state? They are asking for another licking. And they are going to get it.'

The land through which we drove was poor and populous. The road was the neatest thing about it. On either side there were small rectangular hollows where peasants had dug clay for their huts. The roots of the great shade trees that lined the road were exposed and here and there a tree had collapsed: pigmy effort, gigantic destruction. There were few vehicles on the road, but many people, heedless of sun, dust and our horn. The women wore recognizable garments of purple, green and gold; the men were in rags.

'They've all got the vote.'

When I looked at the Sikh I saw that his face was set with anger. He was more remote than ever, and his lips were moving silently. In what language was he speaking? Was he speaking a prayer, a charm? The hysteria of the train journey began to touch me again. And now I felt I carried a double responsibility. The Sikh's anger was feeding on everything he saw, and I longed for the land and the people to change. The Sikh's lips still moved. Against his charm I tried to pitch my own. I felt disaster close; I let reason go. I tried to transmit compensating love to every starved man and woman I saw on the road. But I was failing; I knew I was failing. I was yielding to the rage and contempt of the man beside me. Love insensibly turned into a self-lacerating hysteria in which I was longing for greater and greater decay, more rags and filth, more bones, men more starved and grotesque, more spectacularly deformed. I wished to extend myself, to see the limits of human degradation, to take it all in at that moment. For me this was the end, my private failure; even as I wished I knew I would carry the taint of that moment.

On the pedestal of a high white culvert, PWD-trim, a man stood like a statue. Rags hung over his bones, over limbs as thin and brittle-looking as charred sticks.

'Ha! Look at that monkey.' There was a chuckle in his voice, instantly replaced by torment. 'God! Can you call that a man? Even the animals, if they have to live . . . even the animals.' Words were not coming to him. 'Even the animals. Man? What does that – that *thing* have? You think he even has instinct? To tell him when to eat?'

He was reacting for me, as he had done on the train. But now I knew my hysteria for what it was. The words were his, not mine. They broke the spell.

Peasants, trees and villages were obliterated by the dust of our car.

At times it seems that to our folly and indecisiveness, and to our dishonesty, there can be no limit. Our relationship ought to have ended at the end of that journey. A declaration would have been painful. But it could have been avoided. I could have changed hotels; I could have disappeared. This was my instinct. But the evening found us drinking together. Peasants and dust were forgotten, black gods and white, Aryan and Dravidian. That moment on the road had grown out of a sense of nameless danger, and that had probably been the effect of the heat or my own exhaustion. The leaden Indian beer had its effect, and we talked of London and coffee-houses and the 'funny little fellow'.

Dusk turned to night. Now there were three of us at the glass-crowded table. The newcomer was a commercial Englishman, middle-aged, fat and red-faced. He spoke with a North Country accent. From my alcoholic quietude I noted that the talk had turned to Sikh history and Sikh military glory. The Englishman was at first rallying, but presently the smile on his face had grown fixed. I listened. The Sikh was talking of the decline of the Sikhs since Ranjit Singh, of the disaster that had come to them with Partition. But he was also talking of Sikh revenges in 1947 and of Sikh atrocities. Some of the talk of atrocities was, I felt, aimed at me; it carried on from our drive back to the town. It was too calculated; it left me cold.

Dinner, we wanted dinner; and now we were on our way to the restaurant, and the Englishman was no longer with us.

It was very bright in the restaurant.

'They are staring at me!'

The restaurant was bright and noisy, full of people and tables.

'They are staring at me.'

We were in a crowded corner.

I sat down.

*Slap!*

'These bloody Dravidians are staring at me.'

The man at the next table had been knocked down. He lay on his back, his head on the seat of an empty chair. His eyes were wide with terror, his hands clasped in greeting and supplication.

'Sardarji!' he cried, still lying flat.

'Staring at me. South Indian punk.'

'Sardarji! My friend said, "Look, a sardarji." And I just turned to look. I am not a South Indian. I am a Punjabi. Like you.'

'Punk.'

Something like this I had always feared. This was what my instinct had scented as soon as I had seen him on the train: some men radiate violence and torment, and they are dangerous to those who fear violence. We had met, and there had inevitably been a reassessment. Below all the wrongness and unease of our relationship, however, lay my original alarm. This moment, of fear and self-disgust, was logical. It was also the moment I had been waiting for. I left the restaurant and took a rickshaw to the hotel. The whole city, its streets now silent, had been coloured for me, from the first, by my association with the Sikh; I had assessed it, whether in contempt or straining love, according to the terms of his special racialism. It was as much by this that I was now sickened as by the violence I had witnessed.

I made the rickshawman turn and take me back to the restaurant. There was no sign of the Sikh. But the Punjabi, his eyes wild with humiliation and anger, was at the cash-desk with a group who appeared to know him.

'I am going to kill your friend,' he shouted at me. 'I am going to kill that Sikh tomorrow.'

'You are not going to kill anybody.'

'I am going to kill him. I am going to kill you too.'

I went back to the hotel. The telephone rang.

'Hallo, punk.'

'Hello.'

'So you ran out on me when I was in a little trouble. And you call yourself a friend. You know what I think of you? You are a dirty South Indian swine. Don't go to sleep. I am coming over to beat you up.'

He could not have been far away, for in a few minutes he appeared, knocking twice on the door, bowing exaggeratedly, and staggering in theatrically. We were both more lucid than we had been, but our conversation see-sawed drunkenly, and falsely, between reconciliation and recrimination. At any moment we could have become friends again or agreed not to meet; again and again, when we tilted to one of these possibilities, one of us applied a corrective pressure. There still existed concern between us. We drank coffee; our conversation see-sawed more and more falsely; and in the end even this concern had been talked away.

'We were going to go hunting,' the Sikh said, as he left. 'I had *plans* for you.'

It was a good Hollywood exit line. Perhaps it was meant. I couldn't say. The English language in India could be so misleading. Exhaustion overcame me: for all our coffee and play-acting talk, the break had been violent. It brought relief and regret. There had been so much goodwill and generosity there; my misunderstanding had been so great.

In the morning horror was uppermost. I had seen photographs of the Punjab massacres of 1947 and of the Great Calcutta Killing;

I had heard of trains – those Indian trains! – ferrying dead bodies across the border; I had seen the burial mounds beside the Punjab roads. Yet until now I had never thought of India as a land of violence. Now violence was something I could smell in the air; the city seemed tainted by the threat of violence and self-torment of the sort I had seen. I wanted to get away at once. But the trains and buses were booked for days ahead.

I went to the sweetshop-owner. He was soft and welcoming. He sat me at a table; one of his waiters brought me a plate of the sweetest sweets; and master and servant watched me eat. Those Indian sweets! 'Serves them in place of flesh': a Kipling phrase, perhaps altered by memory, came and stayed with me; and *flesh* seemed a raw and fearful word. For all that was soft and feeble and sweet-loving in that city I was grateful; and I feared for it.

In the sweetshop the next evening the owner introduced me to a relation of his, who was visiting. The relation started when he heard my name. Could it be true? He was reading one of my books; he had thought of me as someone thousands of miles away; he had never dreamed of finding me eating sweets in the bazaar of an out-of-the-way Indian town. But he had expected someone older. I was a *baccha*, a boy! However, he had met me, and he wished to show his appreciation. Could I tell him where I was staying?

Acrid white smoke billowed out of my hotel room when I opened the door that night. There was no fire. The smoke was incense. To enter, I had to cover my face with a handkerchief. I opened doors and windows, turned the ceiling fan on, and hurried out again to the corridor with streaming eyes. It was minutes before the incense-fog thinned. Great clumps of incense sticks burned like dying brands everywhere; on the floor the ash was like bird droppings. Flowers were strewn over my bed, and there was a garland on my pillow.

## 10

# EMERGENCY

Chinese launch massive, simultaneous attacts in Nefa and Ladakh. Newspaper headlines can appear to exult. In Madras, where I was, the waiters at the hotel read the news to one another in corridors and on staircase landings; and in Mount Road the unemployed boys and men who usually stood outside the Kwality Restaurant, offering to fetch taxis and scooters for people who had had their lunch, gathered round a man who was reading aloud from a Tamil newspaper. On the pavement women dished out cooked meals for labourers at a few annas a head; in side streets, amid buses and cars, bare-backed carters pulled and pushed at their heavy-wheeled carts, grunting, the carters between the shafts disguising their strain by a lightfooted, mincing walk. The setting mocked the headlines. India did not qualify for modern warfare. 'She, whose only peer was the Holy Roman Empire, she shall rank with Guatemala and Belgium perhaps!' So Forster's Fielding had mocked forty years before; and after fifteen years of independence, India remained in many ways a colonial country. She continued to produce mainly politicians and speeches. Her 'industrialists' were mainly traders, importers of simple machinery, manufacturers under licence. Her administration was still negative. It collected taxes, preserved order; and now to the passion of an aroused nation it could only respond with words. The Emergency was a seeking for precedents, the issuing of a correct Defence of the Realm Act, complete with instructions about gas masks, incendiary bombs and stirrup pumps.

The Emergency was suspension and cancellation; censorship which encouraged rumour and panic; slogans in the newspapers. The Emergency became words, English words. THIS IS TOTAL WAR, the Bombay weekly said on its front page. 'What do I mean by total war?' the IAS candidate said, replying to a question from the examining board. 'It is a war in which the whole world takes part.' The news grew worse. There were rumours of Gurkhas sent up to Ladakh armed only with their knives, and of men flown from the Assam plains to the mountains of NEFA clad only in singlets and tennis-shoes. All the swift violence of which the country was capable was gathered into one ball; there was a feeling as of release and revolution. Anything might have happened; if will alone counted, the Chinese would have been pushed back to Lhasa in a week. But from the politicians there came only speeches, and from the administrator correct regulations. The famous Fourth Division was cut to pieces; the humiliation of the Indian Army, India's especial pride, was complete. Independent India was now felt to be a creation of words – 'Why didn't we have to *fight* for our freedom?' – and it was collapsing in words. The magic of the leader failed, and presently passion subsided into fatalism.

*

The Chinese invasion had been with us for a week. In the house of a friend there gathered for dinner a film producer, a scriptwriter, a journalist and a doctor. Before we went in we sat in the veranda, and even as I listened to the talk I knew I could not convincingly reconstruct it. At times it seemed frivolous and satirical; then despairing; then fantastic. Its moods were always muted. The Chinese would stop at the Brahmaputra, the producer said; they merely wanted to consolidate their occupation of Tibet. He spoke coolly; no one questioned his assumption that India could not be anything but passive. From this the talk slipped to a good-humoured disputation about *karma* and the value of human existence; and before I could work out how it had done so, we were back to the border situation. The country's unpreparedness was ridiculed. No one was blamed, no plans were put forward: a comic situation was merely outlined. And where was this leading? 'A fact many people do not know,' the doctor said, 'is that it is dangerous to have an inoculation against cholera during an epidemic.' The medical analogy was overwhelming: the country had been unprepared and it was foolish, indeed dangerous, to make any preparations now. This was accepted; the film producer repeated his view that the Chinese would stop at the Brahmaputra. Gandhi was mentioned; but how did the doctor move on from this to state his belief in the occult, and why did he throw out, almost as a debating point, that 'the great healers have always used their powers to save themselves'? We remained for some time on the subject of miracles. The Tibetans, I heard, were suffering because they had forgotten the *mantras*, charms, which might have repelled their enemies. I examined the faces of the speakers. They seemed serious. But were they? Mightn't their conversation have been a type of medieval intellectual exercise, the dinner-time recreation of South Indian brahmins? Dinner was announced, and now at last a conclusion was reached. Indians too, it was said, had forgotten the *mantras*; they were powerless against their enemies and there was nothing that could be done. The situation on the border had been talked away. We went in calmly to dinner and talked of other matters.

*

Indian life, Indian death, went on.

> Wanted a Telugu Brahmin Vellanadu non-Kausiga Gotram bride below 22 years for young graduate earning Rs 200 monthly.

On the grass verge outside the hotel, next to the open refuse-heap where women and buffaloes daily rummaged among the used banana food-leaves and the hotel's discarded food, a little brown puppy lay dying. It moved about a small area, as though imprisoned, fading from day to day. One morning it looked dead. But a crow approached; and the puppy's tail lifted and dropped.

> Exquisitely beautiful, Enchanting classical Bharatha Natyam dancer, brilliant graduate, aristocratic family, broad-minded, delightful temperament, fair, slim, tall, modern outlook, aged twenty-one, wishes to marry a millowner, business magnate, well-to-do landlord, doctor, engineer, or top executive. Caste, creed, nationality no bar.

The news from New Delhi did not change. But the festival of Deepavali was at hand and the beggars were swarming into Mount Road. This boy did not at first look like a beggar. He was handsome, of a fine brown complexion; he wore red shorts and had a white cloth over his shoulders. He caught sight of me as I came out of the post office; then, behaving as one suddenly reminded of duty, he smiled and lifted the white cloth to reveal a monstrously deformed right arm. It was no arm at all; it was shaped like a woman's breast, ending not in a nipple but in a fingernail on a toy finger.

*

There was an audience of eight – not counting the secretary and the top-knotted watchman – for the lecture at the Triplicane Theosophical Society on 'Annie Besant, Our Leader'. The speaker was a middle-aged Canadian woman. She came from Vancouver. This was not as odd as it appeared, she said: according to Annie Besant, Vancouver had been a centre of the occult in far-off times. Annie Besant's Irish ancestry doubtless explained her psychic gifts, and much of her character could be explained by what she must have been in former lives. Annie Besant had been, above all, a great leader; and it was the duty of every Theosophist to be a leader, to keep Annie Besant's message alive and her books in circulation. The Theosophical Society was now encountering a certain indifference – the secretary had already said as much – and many people were no doubt asking why, if she was with us again, Annie Besant wasn't in the Theosophical Society. But there was no logic in the question. There was no reason why Annie Besant should be in the Society. Her work for the Society had been done in a previous life; she was now almost certainly, under what name we could not tell, doing equally important work in some other field. Two men in the audience were dozing.

*

Behind the high, clean walls of the Aurobindo Ashram in Pondicherry, one hundred miles to the south, they were perfectly calm. In 1950, the year of his death, Aurobindo had warned Mr Nehru of the expansionist designs of 'a yellow race'; he had prophesied the Chinese conquest of Tibet and had seen this as the first step in the Chinese attempt to conquer India. It was there in black and white in one of the Ashram's numerous publications, and must have been shown often in the last few days: the receptionist opened the book easily at the correct page.

The Master's raised, flower-strewn *samadhi*, a site now for collective meditation, lay in the cool paved courtyard of the Ashram. The Mother was still alive, though now a little withdrawn. She gave *darshan* – made an appearance, offered a sight of herself – only on important anniversaries: the date of Aurobindo's birth, the date of her own arrival in India, and so on. Of Aurobindo I knew a little. He had been educated almost wholly in England; returning to India, he became a revolutionary; escaping arrest, he fled to Pondicherry, a French territory, and there, abandoning politics, he had remained, a revered holy man in a growing ashram. But of the Mother I knew nothing except that she was a Frenchwoman, an associate of Aurobindo's, and that her position in the Ashram was special. For three and a half rupees I bought a book from the Ashram's bookstand, *Letters of Sri Aurobindo on the Mother*.

> Q: Am I right in thinking that she as an Individual embodies all the Divine Powers and brings down the Grace more and more to the physical plane? and her embodiment is a chance for the entire physical to change and transform?
>
> *A*: Yes. Her embodiment is a chance for the earth-consciousness to receive the Supramental into it and to undergo first the transformation necessary for that to be possible. Afterwards there will be a further transformation by the Supramental, but the whole consciousness will not be supramentalized – there will be first a new race representing the Supermind, as man represents the mind.

Photographs of the Mother by Henri Cartier Bresson were also on sale. They showed a Frenchwoman of a certain age, with an angular face and large, slightly protruding teeth. She was smiling; her cheeks were full and well defined. An embroidered scarf covered her head and came down to just above her darkened eyes, which held nothing of the good humour of the lower half of her face. The scarf was tied or pinned at the back of her head and the ends fell on either side of her neck.

> Q: *Pourquoi la Mère s'habille-t-elle avec des vêtements riches et beaux?*
>
> A: *Avez-vous donc pour conception que le Divin doit être réprésenté sur terre par la pauvreté et la laideur?*

Both Aurobindo and the Mother had Lights. Aurobindo's had been pale blue; his body glowed for days after he died. The Mother's Light was white, sometimes gold.

> When we speak of the Mother's Light or my Light in a special sense, we are speaking of a special occult action – we are speaking of certain lights that come from the Supermind. In this action the Mother's is the White Light that purifies, illumines, brings down the whole essence and power of the Truth and makes the transformation possible . . .

> The Mother has certainly no idea of making people see it – it is of themselves that one after another, some 20 or 30 in the Ashram, I believe, have come to see. It is certainly one of the signs that the Higher Force (call it supramental or not) is beginning to influence Matter.

The Mother was also responsible for the organization of the Ashram; an occasional impatience in Aurobindo's replies to inmates hinted at early difficulties.

> In the organization of work there was formerly a formidable waste due to the workers and *sadhaks* following their own fancy almost entirely without respect for the Mother's will; that was largely checked by reorganization.
>
> It is a mistake to think that the Mother's not smiling means either displeasure or disapproval of something wrong in the *sadhak*. It is very often merely a sign of absorption or of inner concentration. On this occasion the Mother was putting a question to your soul.
>
> Mother did not know at that time of your having spoken to T. So your conjecture of that being the cause of her fancied displeasure is quite groundless. Your idea about Mother's mysterious smile is your own imagination – Mother says that she smiled with the utmost kindness.
>
> It is not because your French is full of mistakes that Mother does not correct it, but because I will not allow her to take more work on herself so far as I can help it. Already she has no time to rest sufficiently at night and most of the night she is working at the books, reports and letters that pour on her in masses. Even so she cannot finish in time in the morning. If she has to correct all the letters of the people who have just begun writing in French as well as the others, it means another hour or two of work – she will be able to finish only at nine in the morning and come down at 10.30. I am therefore trying to stop it.

> All bad thoughts upon the Mother or throwing of impurities on her may affect her body, as she has taken the *sadhaks* into her consciousness; nor can she send these things back to them as it might hurt them.

Withdrawn though the Mother now was, her hand could still be seen in the running of the Ashram. The noticeboard carried notices about the cholera outbreak in Madras – inmates were warned against contact with people from that town – and about the annoyance of chatter at the Ashram gates; the notices were signed 'M', in a firm, stylish zigzag. And the Ashram was only part of the Aurobindo Society. Pondicherry had already melted into the rest of southern India; even the French language seemed to have disappeared. But the numerous, well-kept buildings of the Society still gave it the feel of a small French town that had been set down on a tropical coast. Walls were shuttered and blank against the light, which was intense above the raging surf; and the Society's walls were painted in the Society's colours. The Society seemed to be the only flourishing thing in Pondicherry. It had its estates outside the town; it had its workshops, its library, its printing press. It was a self-contained organization, efficiently run by its members. Their number could grow only by recruitment, from India and overseas, for the Mother, I was told, disapproved strongly of three things: politics, tobacco and sex. The children who came into the Ashram with their parents were taught trades as they grew up; the leaders among them wore distinctive uniforms, in the very short shorts of which I thought I could detect a French influence. Work was as important as meditation; the physical was not to be neglected. (I was later told by an Englishman in Madras that, running into a group of oddly dressed elderly Europeans on roller skates one day in Pondicherry, and tracing them to their source, he had come to the Ashram gates. But that might have been only a story. I saw only one European in the Ashram. He was barefooted and very pink; he wore a dhoti and Indian jacket; and his long white hair and beard gave him a resemblance to the dead Master.) By recruiting people from the world, then, the Society never became inbred; and by employing their developed talents it prospered.

The present General Secretary, for instance, was a Bombay businessman before he withdrew to the Ashram and took the name of Navajata, the newborn. His appearance still suggested the businessman. He was holding a briefcase and he seemed pressed for time. But he said he had never been happier.

'Now I must go,' he said. 'I have to go up and see the Mother.'

'Tell me. Has the Mother said anything about the Chinese invasion?'

'1962 is a bad year,' he recited hurriedly. '1963 is going to be a bad year. Things will start getting better in 1964, and India will win through in 1967. Now I must go.'

*

For weeks I had been seeing this young man. I thought he was a business executive trainee of French or Italian origin. He was tall and thin, wore dark glasses, carried a briefcase, and had a brisk, twiddly walk. He always looked self-assured and purposeful, but it puzzled me that he seemed to have much time on his hands. I saw him at bus stops at odd times of day. I saw him in museums in the afternoons. I saw him at dance performances in the evenings. We often passed one another in the street. Then – one aspect of the mystery solved when, to our mutual astonishment, we saw one another in the corridor of the top floor of the hotel one morning – I discovered that he had the room next to mine.

He puzzled and embarrassed me. But I was causing him distress, and I did not know it. In Madras they don't invite you to their homes; whatever their eminence, they prefer to call on you. So I sat for hours in my hotel room every day, receiving, with the 'boys' continually bringing in coffee for new visitors. I believe it was the convivial sounds of chatter and coffee spoons which made my neighbour break down. We came out of our rooms at the same time one morning. Ignoring one another, we locked our doors. We turned. There was confrontation. And suddenly a torrent of American speech gushed out, brooking no interjection even of greeting.

'How are you? How long are you staying here? I'm in a terrible state. I've been here six months and I've lost sixteen pounds. I felt the call of the East ha-ha and came out to India to study ancient Indian philosophy and culture. It's driving me mad. What do you think of the hotel? I think it's *creepy*.' He hunched his shoulders. 'It's the food.' Mouth working, he struck his palm against his dark glasses. 'It's sending me *blind*. It's these people. They're *crazy*. They don't accept you. Help me. You have people running in and out of your room all day. You know some English people here. Talk to them about me. Introduce me to them. They might take me in. You must help me.'

I promised to try.

The first person I spoke to said, 'Well, I don't know. Experience tells me that when people are doing inward things like answering the call of the East it is better to stay away.'

I did not try again. And now I feared to meet the young American. I did not meet him. The trains between Madras and Calcutta were running again, after the long dislocation caused by floods and the movement of troops.

*

*Ladies*, painted in yellow on some carriages. *Military*, marked in chalk on many more. It was so unlikely, this train-load of soldiers moving north through all the distress of India to the calamity on the frontiers. With their olive-green uniforms, their good looks and good manners, and their moustached, swagger-sticked officers, they transformed the railway platforms at which we stopped: they lent drama and order, and to them how comforting the familiar, receding squalor must have been! The plump little major in my compartment, carrying his water in a champagne bottle, had been so quiet after leaving his wife and daughter at Madras Central station – the three had simply sat silently side by side. Now, as the journey lengthened, he brightened; he asked me the Indian questions: where did I come from, what did I do? And the soldiers became playful. Once the train stopped beside a field of sugarcane. A soldier jumped out and began to cut stalks of cane with his knife. More soldiers jumped out, more cane was cut. The angry farmer appeared. Money passed, anger turned to smiles and waves as we moved off again.

Afternoon now, and the train's shadow racing beside us. Sunset, evening, night; station after dimly-lit station. It was an Indian railway journey, but everything that had before seemed pointless was now threatened and seemed worth cherishing; and as in the mild sunshine of a winter morning we drew near to green Bengal, which I had longed to see, my mood towards India and her people became soft. I had taken so much for granted. There, among the Bengali passengers who had come on, was a man who wore a long woollen scarf and a brown tweed jacket above his Bengali dhoti. The casual elegance of his dress was matched by his fine features and relaxed posture. Out of all its squalor and human decay, its eruptions of butchery, India produced so many people of grace and beauty, ruled by elaborate courtesy. Producing too much life, it denied the value of life; yet it permitted a unique human development to so many. Nowhere were people so heightened, rounded and individualistic; nowhere did they offer themselves so fully and with such assurance. To know Indians was to take a delight in people as people; every encounter was an adventure. I did not want India to sink; the mere thought was painful.

And it was in this mood that I walked about Calcutta, the 'nightmare experience' of Mr Nehru, 'the world's most miserable city', according to an American magazine, 'the pestilential behemoth' of another American writer, the world's last stronghold of Asiatic cholera, according to the World Health Organization: a city which, built for two million, now accommodated six million on its pavements and in its *bastees*.

'*Chuha*,' the waiter at Howrah station restaurant said affectionately, pointing. 'Look, a rat.' And the pink, depilated creature, barely noticed by the Assamese soldier and his wife, both sucking away at rice and curried fish, sluggishly made its way across the tiled floor and up a pipe. This promised horror. But nothing I had read or heard had prepared me for the red-brick city on the other side of Howrah Bridge which, if one could ignore the stalls and rickshaws and white-clad hurrying crowds, was at first like another Birmingham; and then, in the centre, at dusk, was like London, with the misty, tree-blobbed Maidan as Hyde Park, Chowringhee as a mixture of Oxford Street, Park Lane and Bayswater Road, with neon invitations, fuzzy in the mist, to bars, coffee-houses and air travel, and the Hooghly a muddier, grander Thames, not far away. On a high floodlit platform in the Maidan, General Cariappa, the former commander-in-chief, erect, dark-suited, was addressing a small, relaxed crowd in Sandhurst-accented Hindustani on the Chinese attack. Around and about the prowed, battleship-grey Calcutta trams, bulging at exits and entrances with men in white, tanked away at less than ten miles an hour. Here, unexpectedly and for the first time in India, one was in a big city, the recognizable metropolis, with street names – Elgin, Lindsay, Allenby – oddly unrelated to the people who thronged them: incongruity that deepened as the mist thickened to smog and as, driving out to the suburbs, one saw the chimneys smoking among the palm trees.

This was the city which, according to bazaar rumour, Chou En-lai had promised the Chinese people as a Christmas present. The Indian Marwari merchants, it was said, were already making enquiries about business prospects under Chinese rule; the same rumour had it that in the South the Madrasis, despite their objection to Hindi, were already learning Chinese. Morale was low; the administration in Assam had collapsed and there were tales of flight and panic. But it was not in this alone that the sadness of the city lay. With or without the Chinese, Calcutta was dead.

Partition had deprived it of half its hinterland and burdened it with a vast dispirited refugee population. Even Nature had turned: the Hooghly was silting up. But Calcutta's death was also of the heart. With its thin glitter, its filth and overpopulation, its tainted money, its exhaustion, it held the total Indian tragedy and the terrible British failure. Here the Indo-British encounter had at one time promised to be fruitful. Here the Indian renaissance had begun: so many of the great names of Indian reform are Bengali. But it was here, too, that the encounter had ended in mutual recoil. The cross-fertilization had not occurred, and Indian energy had turned sour. Once Bengal led India, in ideas and idealism; now, just forty years later, Calcutta, even to Indians, was a word of terror, conveying crowds, cholera and corruption. Its aesthetic impulses had not faded – there was an appealing sensibility in every Bengali souvenir, every over-exploited refugee 'craft' – but they, pathetically, threw into relief the greater decay. Calcutta had no leaders now, and apart from Ray, the film director, and Janah, the photographer, had no great names. It had withdrawn from the Indian experiment, as area after area of India was withdrawing, individual after individual. The British, who had built Calcutta, had ever been withdrawn from their creation; and they survived. Their business houses still flourished in Chownringhee; and to the Indians, products of the dead Indian renaissance, who now sat in some of the air-conditioned offices, Independence had meant no more than this: the opportunity to withdraw, British-like, from India. What then was the India that was left, for which one felt such concern? Was it no more than a word, an idea?

*

From the train Durgapur, the new steel town, was a spreading pattern of lights. I went out to the corridor and watched them until they disappeared. Such a small hope, and it was easy to imagine the lights extinguished. Bomdi-la fell that night. Assam lay open; Mr Nehru offered the people of the state comfort which was already like helpless condolence. Tibetan refugees got off the train at Banaras. There was smiling bewilderment on their broad, ruddy faces; no one spoke their language and they stood uncertainly beside their boxes, outlandish in their bulky wrappings, grimed to khaki, their long hair, their boots and hats. The hotel was deserted: internal air services had been cancelled. The young dark-suited manager and the uniformed servants stood silent and idle in the veranda. Something of the bazaar spirit and the spirit of wartime opportunism stirred within me. I stood on the steps and haggled. Success went to my head. 'And that is to include morning coffee,' I said. 'Yes,' the manager said sadly. 'That is to include coffee.'

Here in the cantonment area Banaras felt abandoned, and it was easy to imagine oneself a squatter. But in the town nothing hinted at tragedy. Wood was piled high on the *ghats*. Brightly shrouded bodies lay on flower-strewn litters at the water's edge, unimportantly awaiting their pyres; and above occasional blazes, oddly casual and not too visible in the reflected glare of the Ganges, family groups smiled and chattered. The steep *ghats*, platformed and stepped, their names marked in large letters, were as thronged as a holiday beach. The pious stood in the water, relaxed below beach umbrellas or gathered round an expounding pundit; young men did exercises. Above, behind the high white river front, in the twisting alleys, dark between solid masonry and enchanting but for the cowdung, hawkers offered Banaras toys, silk and brass; and in the temples the guide-priests, young, washed and combed, chewed *pan* and cursed those who refused them alms.

I went to the Nepalese Temple, 'disfigured', Murray's *Handbook* said, 'by erotic carvings; they do not catch the eye, provided that the attendant can be discouraged from pointing them out'. The attendant was a youth with a long switch; I begged him to point them out. 'Here man and woman,' he began unexcitedly. 'Here other man. He Mr Hurry-up because he say, "Hurry up, hurry up."' Tourist lore: the gloss did not please me. The pleasures of erotic art are fragile; I wished I had followed Murray's advice.

At dinner I asked the sad young manager to put on the radio for the news. It was as bad as could be expected. The manager held his hands behind his back and looked down, correct even in his growing distress. Then a reference to 'Chinese Frontier Guards' alerted me.

'But we are listening to Peking, Mr Manager.'

'It is All-India Radio. It's the station I always listen to.'

'Only the Chinese and Radio Pakistan talk of the Chinese Frontier Guards.'

'But it is in English. And the accent . . . And it sounds so close.'

It did indeed; it was coming over loud and clear. We tried to get New Delhi; we got squawks and static and a feeble, disappearing voice.

And the next day it was all over. The Chinese declared a ceasefire and promised a withdrawal. And, as if by magic, the hotel began to fill up.

*

The fighting was over but the Emergency continued, and it was the duty of this Commissioner to make tours through his Division, keeping up morale and raising funds. He had just finished one tour and had been presented with an album of photographs, mainly of himself receiving and being received. I sat in the back of his station-wagon now with some junior officers and looked through the photographs. We were travelling along an Indian road: a thin metalled strip between two lanes of earth that had been ground to fine, thick dust by the wheels of bullock-carts. This was Indian dust: it disfigured the trees that lined the road, it discoloured the fields for a hundred yards on either side. And regularly, at stations in the dust, there were reception committees, garlands, displays of calisthenics and rough exhibitions of rough local manufactures.

The Commissioner was keen on soap and shoes, and everywhere we stopped the bearded Muslim shoemakers stood beside their shoes and the soapmakers stood beside their heavy, imperfectly moulded cubes of soap. At dinner one evening the Commissioner, dressed in a dark suit, explained his interest in soap and shoes. His voice dropped to tenderness. His daughter, he said, was at school in England. Through television or some other educational medium her companions had learned that there were no towns in India, that no one wore shoes or lived in houses or washed. 'Is it true, Daddy?' the distressed child had asked. So now the craftsmen of the Division made soap and shoes. Sometimes, when he was being received, the Commissioner broke through the circle of local dignitaries to greet the children of the very poor who were on the other side of the road. Sometimes, exercising the Commissioner's prerogative, he took cakes of soap from the display and distributed them to these children, while the photographers, another album in mind, took pictures.

It was a swift tour. To me it was remarkable that an area so large and nondescript and comfortless should be capable of such organization, and that behind the clouds of dust there should be people who, with so little encouragement and such poor materials, should yet be exercising craftsman's skills. I would have liked to linger, to draw hope. But there was no time. The displays were too many. I was sitting in the back of the station-wagon and was the last to get out whenever we stopped; and it frequently happened that before I had had time to inspect the first exhibit the Commissioner and his officials were back at the station-wagon and waiting for me: since I was the last to get out I was the first to get in.

We spent more time at the meetings. Here the thin-limbed boys in white shorts and vests had been assembled in the sun, ready to go through their gymnastic exercises. Here there were arches marked WELCOME in Hindi. Here the Commissioner was garlanded. The Indian politician, when garlanded, at once removes the garland and hands it to an attendant; this acceptance and instant rejection of dignity is the stylish Indian form. The Commissioner did not remove his garlands. Hoop after hoop of marigold was hung on his bowed head, until the marigolds rose to his ears and, from the back, he looked like an idol incongruously armed: in one hand he carried his lighted cigar, in the other his sun-helmet. His attendant was not far away. He carried his master's cigar box and was dressed like a Mogul courtier: so the British had sought to degrade their predecessors.

In the decorated tent the peasants sat on mats. For the officials there were chairs and a table. Names were read out and peasants rose, came to the Commissioner, bowed and presented rupee notes for the National Defence Fund. (As the Fund rose in the area, an IAS man told me, National Savings dropped.) Some women shyly presented jewellery. Sometimes there was no response to a name, and then from all corners of the tent came explanations: a death, of man or beast, an illness, a sudden journey. The money rose in a shaky pile on the plate and was handled casually by all.

Then the Commissioner spoke. The Emergency was not over, not at all; the Chinese were still on India's sacred soil. The people of India had been preached at for too long about peace and nonviolence. Now they had to be roused. The Commissioner sought to do so first by appealing to the patriotism of the peasants and then by analysing the nature of the Chinese threat. By any Indian standard the Chinese were unclean. They ate beef: this was for the Hindus in the audience. They ate pork: this was for the Muslims. They ate dogs: this was for everyone. They ate cats, rats, snakes. The peasants remained passive, and were only roused when the Commissioner, playing his last card, invoked the Hindu goddesses of destruction.

The Commissioner had a cheer-leader, a tall elderly man in an old double-breasted grey suit. He wore spectacles and carried a sun-helmet which was the fellow of the Commissioner's. He chewed *pan* constantly; his mouth was large, with flapping red-stained lips. His face was without expression; he seemed to be doing sums in his head all the time. Clerk-like, adjusting his spectacles, he went to the microphone and stood silently before it. Suddenly he opened his enormous red mouth, revealing fillings and pieces of mangled betel-nut, and screamed: '*Kali Mata ki* –'

'*Jai!*' the peasants shouted, their eyes brightening, the smiles staying on their faces. 'Long live Mother Kali!'

'But what is this?' the Commissioner's assistant said. 'I heard nothing.' It was his line; at every meeting he used it. 'We will try again, and this time I want to hear you. *Kali Mata ki* –'

'*Jai! Jai! Jai!*'

Once, twice, three times the goddesses were invoked, to growing enthusiasm. Then abruptly the assistant turned, walked back to his seat, sat on it decisively, slapped his sun-helmet on his knees, stared straight ahead and, teeth and lips working over the *pan*, seemed immediately absorbed in mental arithmetic.

When the audience was too small, the Commissioner showed his displeasure by refusing to speak or to leave. Then officials and policemen bustled penitentially about; they summoned peasants from the fields and their homes and marched children out from the schools. But there was never any trouble in finding an audience for the evening concerts. Singers of local renown chewed *pan* and sang songs of their own about the Chinese invasion into microphones shrouded with cloth to protect them from *pan*-splutterings. There were sketches about the need to save, to grow more food, to contribute to the National Defence Fund, to give blood. Once or twice an ambitious playwright showed a local hero dying in battle against the Chinese; and it was clear that no one in the village knew what the Chinese looked like.

From the railway train and from the dusty roads India appeared to require only pity. It was an easy emotion, and perhaps the Indians were right: it was compassion like mine, so strenuously maintained, that denied humanity to many. It separated; it permitted the surprise and emotion I felt at these concerts, simple exhibitions of humanity. Anger, compassion and contempt were aspects of the same emotion; they were without value because they could not endure. Achievement could begin only with acceptance.

We were now in a region which, though physically no different from the surrounding areas, was famous for its soldiers. Was this due to some ancient mixing of bloods preserved by caste rules? To some pertinacious Rajput strain? India was full of such puzzles. The crowd here was too large for the tent. Some had put on their uniforms and decorations. The cheer-leader picked them out and seated them on a bench at the edge of the tent. But one or two preferred to walk slowly up and down the road while the Commissioner spoke. So far the Commissioner had been speaking to people who were a little irritated and resentful at having to leave their fields or the idleness of their homes. But this crowd was attentive from the first. The old soldiers gazed steadily at the Commissioner and every point he made was registered on their faces. The Chinese ate pork. Brows puckered. The Chinese ate dogs. Brows puckered more deeply. The Chinese ate rats. Eyes popped, heads lifted as struck.

The Commissioner had scarcely finished speaking when a man ran out from the crowd and threw himself at his feet, weeping.

The crowd relaxed and smiled.

'Get up, get up,' the Commissioner said, 'and tell me what you have to say.'

'You ask me to fight, and I want to fight. But how can I fight when I have no food and my family has no food? How can I fight when I have lost my land?'

The crowd began to titter.

'You have lost your land?'

'In the resettlement.'

The Commissioner spoke to his cheer-leader.

'All my good land,' the man wept, 'they gave to somebody else. All the bad land they gave to me.'

There was laughter from the old soldiers.

'I will look into it,' the Commissioner said.

The crowd was breaking up. The weeping man disappeared; the jeers at his outburst died down; and we moved on to the tea which the headman, a man of few words, had prepared for us.

There was another concert that evening. It had been organized by the local teacher. He came on just before the end and said that he had written a new poem which he would recite to us if the Commissioner gave his permission. The Commissioner took his cigar out of his mouth and nodded. The teacher bowed; then, with passionate intonations and tormented gestures, he recited. The facile Hindi rhymes tumbled out as if newly discovered, and the teacher worked himself into a frenzy as he came to his climax, which was a plea for the settled reign on earth of

. . . *satya ahimsa.*

He bowed again, anticipating applause.

'*Satya ahimsa!*' the Commissioner shouted, stilling hands about to clap. 'Are you mad? Truth and nonviolence, indeed. Is this what you are preaching with the Chinese about to rape your wife? Have I been wasting my breath all afternoon? This is a classical example of muddled thinking.'

The poet, holding his bow, cringed. The curtain fell unceremoniously on him.

Poor poet! He had devised a good evening's entertainment. He had written the anti-Chinese pieces and the songs about the Motherland; yet when it came to his own poem, the one he wished to recite himself, he had lost his head. For years he had recited, to official applause, poems about truth and nonviolence. Habit had been too strong, and had led to his public disgrace.

*

Some weeks later Mr Nehru went to Lucknow. Standing on the airport tarmac, he bowed his head forty-six times to receive forty-six garlands from the forty-six members of the State cabinet. This at any rate was the story I had from an IAS man in Lucknow, and he was a little peeved. The IAS, acting on instructions from Delhi, had taken civil defence seriously in Lucknow. They had practised blackouts and air-raid warnings; they had dug trenches; they had much to show Mr Nehru. But Mr Nehru only lost his temper. All this digging of trenches, he said, was a waste of time.

In a way, the Emergency was over.

## 11

# THE VILLAGE OF THE DUBES

THE EMERGENCY WAS over. And so was my year. The short winter was fading fast; it was no longer pleasant to sit out in the sun; the dust would not now be laid until the monsoon. One journey remained, and for this I had lost taste. India had not worked its magic on me. It remained the land of my childhood, an area of darkness; like the Himalayan passes, it was closing up again, as fast as I withdrew from it, into a land of myth; it seemed to exist in just the timelessness which I had imagined as a child, into which, for all that I walked on Indian earth, I knew I could not penetrate.

In a year I had not learned acceptance. I had learned my separateness from India, and was content to be a colonial, without a past, without ancestors. Duty alone had brought me to this town in eastern Uttar Pradesh, not even graced by a ruin, celebrated only for its connexions with the Buddha and its backwardness. And it was duty that, after a few days of indecision, idleness and reading, was taking me along this country road, infested with peasants indifferent to wheeled vehicles, to the village which my mother's father had left as an indentured labourer more than sixty years before.

When you drive through parts of western and central India you wonder about the teeming millions; settlements are so few, and the brown land looks so unfruitful and abandoned. Here wonder was of another sort. The land was flat. The sky was high, blue and utterly without drama; below it everything was diminished.

Wherever you looked there was a village, low, dust-blurred, part of the earth and barely rising out of it. Every tiny turbulence of dust betrayed a peasant; and the land was nowhere still.

At a junction we took on a volunteer guide and turned off on to an embankment of pure dust. It was lined with tall old trees. Below them my grandfather had doubtless walked at the start of his journey. In spite of myself I was held. For us this land had ceased to exist. Now it was so ordinary. I did not really want to see more. I was afraid of what I might find, and I had witnesses. 'Not that one, not that,' cried the guide, excited both by my mission and the unexpected jeep ride, as village after village died in our dust. Presently he pointed: there on our right, was the village of the Dubes.

It was set far back from the embankment. It exceeded anything I had expected. A large mango grove gave it a pastoral aspect, and two spires showed white and clean against the dark green foliage. I knew about those spires and was glad to see them. My grandfather had sought to re-establish the family he had left behind in India. He had recovered their land; he had given money for the building of a temple. No temple had been built, only three shrines. Poverty, fecklessness, we had thought in Trinidad. But now, from the road, how reassuring those spires were!

We got out of the jeep and made our way over the crumbling earth. The tall, branching mango trees shaded an artificial pond, and the floor of the grove was spotted with blurred sunshine. A boy came out. His thin body was naked save for his dhoti and sacred thread. He looked at me suspiciously – our party was large and ferociously official – but when the IAS officer who was with me explained who I was, the boy attempted first to embrace me and then to touch my feet. I disengaged myself and he led us through the village, talking of the complicated relationship that bound him to my grandfather and to me. He knew all about my grandfather. To this village that old adventure remained important: my grandfather had gone far beyond the sea and had made *barra paisa*, much money.

A year before I might have been appalled by what I was seeing. But my eye had changed. This village looked unusually prosperous; it was even picturesque. Many of the houses were of brick, some raised off the earth, some with carved wooden doors and tiled roofs. The lanes were paved and clean; there was a concrete cattletrough. 'Brahmin village, brahmin village,' the IAS man whispered. The women were unveiled and attractive, their saris white and plain. They regarded us frankly, and in their features I could recognize those of the women of my family. 'Brahmin women,' the IAS man whispered. 'Very fearless.'

It was a village of Dubes and Tiwaris, all brahmins, all more or less related. A man, clad in loincloth and sacred thread, was bathing, standing and pouring water over himself with a brass jar. How elegant his posture, how fine his slender body! How, in the midst of populousness and dereliction, had such beauty been preserved? They were brahmins; they rented land for less than those who could afford less. But the region, as the *Gazetteer* said, 'abounds in brahmins'; they formed twelve to fifteen per cent of the Hindu population. Perhaps this was why, though they were all related in the village, there appeared to be no communal living. We left the brick houses behind and, to my disappointment, stopped in front of a small thatched hut. Here resided Ramachandra, the present head of my grandfather's branch of the Dubes.

He was away. 'Oh,' exclaimed the men and boys who had joined us, 'why did he have to choose this day?' But the shrines, they would show me the shrines. They would show me how well they had been kept; they would show me my grandfather's name carved on the shrines. They unlocked the grilled doors and showed me the images, freshly washed, freshly dressed, marked with fresh sandalwood paste, the morning's offerings of flowers not yet faded. My mind leapt years, my sense of distance and time was shaken: before me were the very replicas of the images in the prayer-room of my grandfather's house.

An old woman was crying.

'Which son? Which one?'

And it was seconds before I realized that the old woman's words were in English.

'Jussodra!' the men said, and opened a way for her. She was on her haunches and in this posture was advancing towards me, weeping, screeching out words in English and Hindi. Her pale face was cracked like drying mud; her grey eyes were dim.

'Jussodra will tell you all about your grandfather,' the men said.

Jussodra had also been to Trinidad; she knew my grandfather. We were both led from the shrine to the hut. I was made to sit on a blanket on a string bed; and Jussodra, squatting at my feet, recited my grandfather's genealogy and recounted his adventures, weeping while the IAS officer translated. For thirty-six years Jussodra had lived in this village, and in that time she had polished her story into a fluent Indian *khisa* or fairy tale. It could not have been unknown, but everyone was solemn and attentive.

When he was a young man (Jussodra said) my grandfather left this village to go to Banaras to study, as brahmins had immemorially done. But my grandfather was poor, his family poor, and times were hard; there might even have been a famine. One day my grandfather met a man who told him of a country far away called Trinidad. There were Indians in Trinidad, labourers; they needed pundits and teachers. The wages were good, land was cheap and a free passage could be arranged. The man who spoke to my grandfather knew what he was talking about. He was an *arkatia*, a recruiter; when times were good he might be stoned out of a village, but now people were willing to listen to his stories. So my grandfather indentured himself for five years and went to Trinidad. He was not, of course, made a teacher; he worked in the sugar factory. He was given a room, he was given food; and in addition he received twelve annas, fourteen pence, a day. It was a lot of money, and even today it was a good wage in this part of India, twice as much as the government paid for relief work in distress areas. My grandfather added to this by doing his pundit's work in the evenings. Banaras-trained pundits were rare in Trinidad and my grandfather was in demand. Even the sahib at the factory respected him, and one day the sahib said, 'You are a pundit. Can you help me? I want a son.' 'All right,' my grandfather said. 'I'll see that you get a son.' And when the sahib's wife gave birth to a son, the sahib was so pleased he said to my grandfather, 'You see these thirty *bighas* of land? All the canes there are yours.' My grandfather had the canes cut and sold them for two thousand rupees, and with this he went into business. Success attracted success. A well-to-do man, long settled in Trinidad, came to my grandfather one day and said, 'I've been keeping my eye on you for some time. I can see that you are going to go far. Now I have a daughter and would like her to be married to you. I will give you three acres of land.' My grandfather was not interested. Then the man said, 'I will give you a buggy. You can hire out the buggy and make a little extra money.' So my grandfather married. He prospered. He built two houses. Soon he was wealthy enough to come back to this village and redeem twenty-five acres of his family's land. Then he went back to Trinidad. But he was a restless man. He decided to make another trip to India. 'Come back quick,' his family said to him. (Jussodra spoke these words in English: 'buggy' had also been in English.) But my grandfather didn't see Trinidad again. On the train from Calcutta he fell ill, and he wrote to his family: 'The sun is setting.'

Her story finished, Jussodra wept and wept, and no one moved.

'What do I do?' I asked the IAS officer. 'She is very old. Will I offend her if I offer her some money?'

'It will be most welcome,' he said. 'Give her some money and tell her to arrange a *kattha*, a reading of the scriptures.'

I did so.

Photographs were then brought out, as old to me and as forgotten as the images; and it was again disturbing to my sense of place and time to handle them, to see, in the middle of a vast land where I was anchored to no familiar points and could so easily be lost, the purple stamp of the Trinidad photographer – his address so clearly pictured – still bright against the fading sepia figures, in my reawakened memory forever faded, belonging to imagination and never to reality like this.

I had come to them reluctantly. I had expected little, and I had been afraid. The ugliness was all mine.

Someone else wanted to see me. It was Ramachandra's wife and she was waiting in one of the inner rooms. I went in. A white-clad figure was bowed before me; she seized my feet, in all their Veldtschoen, and began to weep. She wept and would not let go.

'What do I do now?' I asked the IAS officer.

'Nothing. Soon someone will come in and tell her that this is no way to receive a relation, that she should be offering him food instead. It is the form.'

So it happened.

But food. Though they had overwhelmed me, my colonial prudence remained. It had prevented me emptying my pocket into Jussodra's sad, wrinkled hands. Now it reminded me of the Commissioner's advice: 'Once it's cooked, you can risk it. But never touch the water.' He, however, was of the country. So: no food, I said. I was not very well and had been put on a diet.

'Water,' Ramachandra's wife said. 'At least have water.'

The IAS officer said, 'You see that field? It is a field of peas. Ask for some of those.'

We ate a pod of peas each. I promised to come back again; the boys and men walked with us to the jeep; and I drove back along a road that had been robbed of all its terror.

*

In the hotel in the town that evening I wrote a letter. The day had provided such an unlikely adventure. It distorted time; again and again I came back, with wonder, to my presence in that town, in that hotel at that hour. There had been those images, those photographs, those scraps of Trinidad English in that Indian village. The letter did not exhaust my exaltation. The act of writing released not isolated memories but a whole forgotten mood. The letter finished, I went to sleep. Then there was a song, a duet, at first part of memory, it seemed, part of that recaptured mood. But I was not dreaming; I was lucid. The music was real.

> Tumhin ne mujhko prem sikhaya,
> Soté hué hirdaya ko jagaya.
> Tumhin ho roop singar balam.*

It was morning. The song came from a shop across the road. It was a song of the late thirties. I had ceased to hear it years before, and until this moment I had forgotten it. I did not even know the meaning of all the words; but then I never had. It was pure mood, and in that moment between waking and sleeping it had recreated a morning in another world, a recreation of this, which continued. And walking that day in the bazaar, I saw the harmoniums, one of which had lain broken and unused, part of the irrecoverable past, in my grandmother's house, the drums, the printing-blocks, the brass vessels. Again and again I had that sense of dissolving time, that alarming but exhilarating sense of wonder at my physical self.

At the barber shop, where I stopped for a shave and begged in vain for hot water, exaltation died. I became again an impatient traveller. The sun was high; the faint morning chill had been burnt away.

I returned to the hotel and found a beggar outside my door.

'*Kya chahiye?*' I asked, in my poor Hindi. 'What do you want?'

He looked up. His head was shaved, except for the top-knot; his face was skeletal; his eyes blazed. My impatience momentarily

* 'You gave my love meaning.
You awoke my sleeping heart.
My beauty is you, my lover,
my jewels are you.'
The translation is by my friend Aley Hasan of the BBC Indian Section.

turned to alarm. Monk, I thought, monk; I had been reading *Karamazov*.

'I am Ramachandra Dube,' he said. 'I did not see you yesterday.'

I had expected someone less ingratiating, less of a physical wreck. His effort at a smile did not make his expression warmer. Spittle, white and viscous, gathered at the corners of his mouth.

There were some IAS cadets in the hotel. Three of them came to act as interpreters.

'I have spent all day looking for you,' Ramachandra said.

'Tell him I thank him,' I said. 'But there was really no need. I told them at the village I was coming back. Ask him, though, how he found me. I left no address.'

He had walked for some miles; then he had taken a train to the town; then he had gone around the secretariat, asking for the IAS officer who had taken out a man from Trinidad.

While the cadets translated, Ramachandra smiled. His face, I now saw, was not the face of a monk but of someone grossly undernourished; his eyes were bright with illness; he was painfully thin. He was carrying a large white sack. This he now humped with difficulty on to my table.

'I have brought you some rice from your grandfather's land,' he said. 'I have also brought you *parsad*, offerings, from your grandfather's shrine.'

'What do I do?' I asked the cadets. 'I don't want thirty pounds of rice.'

'He doesn't want you to take it all. You just take a few grains. Take the *parsad*, though.'

I took a few grains of the poor rice, and took the *parsad*, grubby little grey beads of hard sugar, and placed them on the table.

'I have been looking for you all day,' Ramachandra said.

'I know.'

'I walked, then I took a train, then I walked around the town and asked for you.'

'It was good of you to take all that trouble.'

'I want to see you. I want to have you in my poor hut and to give you a meal.'

'I am coming back to the village in a few days.'

'I have been looking for you all day.'

'I know.'

'I want to have you in my hut. I want to talk to you.'

'We will talk when I come to the village.'

'I want to see you there. I want to talk to you. I have important things to say to you.'

'We will talk when the time comes.'

'Good. Now I will leave you. I have been looking for you all day. I have things to say to you. I want to have you in my hut.'

'I can't keep this up,' I said to the IAS cadets. 'Tell him to go away. Thank him and so on, but tell him to go.'

One of the cadets passed on my message, involving and extending it with expressions of courtesy.

'Now I must leave you,' Ramachandra replied. 'I must get back to the village before dark.'

'Yes, I can see that you must get back before dark.'

'But how can I talk to you in the village?'

'I will bring an interpreter.'

'I want to have you in my poor hut. I have spent all day looking for you. In the village there are too many people. How can I talk to you in the village?'

'Why can't you talk to me in the village? Can't we really get him out?'

They eased him towards the door.

'I have brought you rice from your grandfather's land.'

'Thank you. It will get dark soon.'

'I want to talk to you when you come.'

'We will talk.'

The door was closed. The cadets went away. I lay down on the bed below the fan. Then I had a shower. I was towelling myself when I heard a scratching on the barred window.

It was Ramachandra, in the veranda, attempting a smile. I summoned no interpreters. I needed none to understand what he was saying.

'I cannot talk in the village. There are too many people.'

'We will talk in the village,' I said in English. 'Now go home. You travel too much.' By signs I persuaded him to edge away from the window. Quickly, then, I drew the curtains.

*

Some days passed before I decided to go back to the village. The journey began badly. There was some trouble about transport and it was not until the middle of the afternoon that we were able to leave. Our progress was slow. It was market day at the junction settlement and the road was dangerous with carts, now occupying the right-hand lane, now changing without warning to the left, their manoeuvres obscured by clouds of dust. Dust was thick and constant; it obliterated trees, fields, villages. There were traffic jams, the carts inextricably snarled, the drivers then as passive as their bullocks.

At the junction it was simple chaos. I breathed dust. There was dust in my hair, dust down my shirt, dust, nauseatingly, on my fingernails. We halted and waited for the traffic to clear. Then our driver disappeared, taking the ignition key. It was useless to look for him: that would only have meant groping about in the dust. We sat in the jeep and occasionally sounded the horn. Half an hour later the driver returned. His eyelashes, moustache and oiled hair were blond with dust, but his smile was wet and triumphant: he had managed to buy some vegetables. It was late afternoon when we got on to the embankment; and the sun was setting, converting the dust into clouds of pure gold, so that each person walked in a golden aura, when we arrived at the village. No terror attached to the land now, no surprise. I felt I knew it well. Yet some anxiety remained: the village held Ramachandra.

He was waiting for me. He was without the cloak he had worn to the hotel. He wore only a dhoti and sacred thread, and I could scarcely bear to look at his emaciated, brittle body. As soon as he saw me he held himself in an attitude of ecstatic awe: shaved shining head thrown back, eyes staring, foam-flecked mouth resolutely closed, both sticks of arms raised. We already had an audience, and he was demonstrating his possession of me. It was seconds before he relaxed.

'He says God has sent you to him,' my IAS friend said.

'We'll see.'

The IAS man converted this into a formal greeting.

'Would you like something to eat in his poor hut?'

'No.'

'You must at least have some water.'

'I am not thirsty.'

'You are rejecting his hospitality because he is a poor man.'

'He can take it that way.'

'A mouthful of food.'

'Tell him it is late. Tell him you have to investigate that embezzlement of the National Defence Fund you were telling me about.'

'He says God has sent you to him today.'

'I don't think I can keep this up much longer. Ask him what he wanted to see me about.'

'He says he won't tell you until you eat something in his poor hut.'

'Tell him good-bye.'

'He believes you might appreciate a little privacy.'

He led us through his hut into a small paved courtyard, where his wife, she who had held on to my Veldtschoen and wept, squatted in one corner, her head decorously covered, and made a pretence of scouring some brass vessels.

Ramachandra paced up and down. Then: wouldn't I eat?

The IAS man interpreted my silence.

It was really quite remarkable, Ramachandra said, that I had come to the village just at that time. He was, as it happened, in a little trouble. He was thinking of starting a little piece of litigation, but the litigation he had just concluded had cost him two hundred rupees and he was short of cash.

'But that solves his problems. He can simply forget the new litigation.'

'How can he forget it? This new litigation concerns you.'

'Me?'

'It is about your grandfather's land, the land that produced the rice he gave you. That is why God sent you here. Your grandfather's land is now only nineteen acres, and some of that will be lost if he can't get this new litigation started. If that happens, who will look after your grandfather's shrines?'

I urged Ramachandra to forget litigation and the shrines and to concentrate on the nineteen acres. That was a lot of land, nineteen acres more than I had, and he could get much help from the government. He knew, he knew, he said indulgently. But his body – he turned his long bony back to me, and the movement was not without pride – was wasted; he devoted himself to religious austerities; he spent four hours a day looking after the shrines. And there was this litigation he wanted to get started. Besides, what could be got out of nineteen acres?

Our discussion remained circular. The IAS man didn't help; he softened all my sharpness into courtesy. Outright refusal didn't release me: it only enabled Ramachandra to start afresh. Release would come only when I left. And this I at last did, suddenly, followed out to the grove by many men and all the boys of the village.

Ramachandra kept up with me, smiling, bidding me farewell, proclaiming his possession of me till the last. One man, clearly his rival, sturdier, handsomer, more dignified, presented me with a letter and withdrew; the ink on the envelope was still wet. A boy ran out to the jeep, tucking his shirt into his trousers, and asked for a lift into the town. While Ramachandra had been outlining his plans for litigation, while the letter was being written, this boy had hurriedly bathed, dressed and prepared his bundle; his clothes were fresh, his hair still wet. My visit had thrown the brahmins into a frenzy of activity. Too much had been assumed; I felt overwhelmed; I wished to extricate myself at once.

'Shall we take him on?' the IAS man asked, nodding towards the boy.

'No, let the idler walk.'

We drove off. I did not wave. The headlamps of the jeep shot two separate beams into the day's slowly settling dust which, made turbulent again by our passage, blotted out the scattered lights of the village.

So it ended, in futility and impatience, a gratuitous act of cruelty, self-reproach and flight.

# FLIGHT

To be packed, after a year's journey, before dinner; to have dinner; to be at the airline office at ten, to see the decorative little fountain failed, the wing-shaped counter empty, the tiled turquoise basin of the fountain empty and wetly littered, the lights dim, the glossy magazines disarrayed and disregarded, the Punjabi emigrants sitting disconsolately with their bundles in a corner near the weighing machine; to be at the airport at eleven for an aircraft that leaves at midnight; and then to wait until after three in the morning, intermittently experiencing the horrors of an Indian public lavatory, is to know anxiety, exasperation and a creeping stupor. There comes a point at which the night is written off, and one waits for morning. The minutes lengthen; last night recedes far beyond last night. Lucidity grows intense but blinkered. The actions of minutes before are dim and isolated, and a cause of muted wonder when remembered. So even at the airport India faded; so during these hours its reality was wiped away, until more than space and time lay between it and me.

Paper fell into my lap in the aircraft. Long blond hair and a pair of big blue eyes appeared above the seat in front of me, and tiny feet pattered against the small of my back. 'Children!' cried the American next to me, awakening from middle-aged, safety-belted sleep. 'Where do they take on all these children? Why are all these children *travelling*? What's my crazy luck that every time I go to sleep on a plane and wake up I see children? Shall I tell you a funny thing a friend of mine said to a child on a plane? He said, "Sonny, why don't you go outside and play?" "Little girl, why don't you take your pretty paper and go outside and play?"' Eyes and hair sank below the dark blue seat. 'That child behind me is going to get hurt. The little bastard is kicking my kidneys in. Sir! Madam! Will you please *control* your child? *It* . . . is . . . annoying my *wife*.' She, the wife, lay relaxed beside him, her skirt riding up above a middle-aged slackly-stockinged knee. There was a smile on her face; she was asleep.

No sleep for me. Only a continuing stupor, heightened by the roar of the engines. I made frequent trips to the lavatory to refresh myself with the airline's eau-de-cologne. The Punjabis at the rear were wakeful, in a ripe smell: one or two had already been sick on the blue carpet. Lights were low. The night was long. We were flying against time, into a receding morning. Yet light was coming; and when at daybreak we reached Beirut it was like arriving, after a magical journey, with all its attendant torment, in a fresh, glittering world. Rain had fallen; the tarmac was glazed and cool. Beyond it was a city which one knew to be a city, full of men as whole as these who, in airport dungarees, now wheeled gangways and drove up in electric lorries to unload luggage: labourers, menials, yet arrogant in their gait, their big bodies and their skills. India was part of the night: a dead world, a long journey.

Rome, the airport, morning still. The Boeings and Caravelles lying this way and that, like toys. And within the airport building a uniformed girl paced up and down the concourse. She wore a jockey-cap hat, to me a new fashion; she wore boots, also new to me. She was extravagantly made up: she required to be noticed. How could I explain, how could I admit as reasonable, even to myself, my distaste, my sense of the insubstantiality and wrongness of the new world to which I had been so swiftly transported? This life confirmed that other death; yet that death rendered this fraudulent.

In the late afternoon I was in Madrid, most elegant of cities. Here I was to spend two or three days. I had been last in this city as a student, ten years before. Here I might have taken up my old life. I was a tourist, free, with money. But a whole experience had just occurred; India had ended only twenty-four hours before. It was a journey that ought not to have been made; it had broken my life in two. 'Write me as soon as you get to Europe,' an Indian friend had said. 'I want your freshest impressions.' I forget now what I wrote. It was violent and incoherent; but, like everything I wrote about India, it exorcized nothing.

In my last week in Delhi I had spent some time in the cloth shops, and I had arrived in Madrid with a jacket-length of material in an untied brown parcel printed with Hindi characters. This was the gift of an architect I had known for a short time. Two or three days after we met he had made a declaration of his affection and loyalty, and I had reciprocated. This was part of the sweetness of India; it went with everything else. He had driven me to the airport and had put up with my outbursts at news of the aircraft's delay. We had coffee; then, before he left, he gave me the parcel. 'Promise me you will have it stitched into a jacket as soon as you get to Europe,' he said.

I did so now; and above all the confused impressions of a year, then, was this fresh memory of a friend and his gift of Indian cloth.

Some days later in London, facing as for the first time a culture whose point, going by the advertisements and shop-windows, appeared to be home-making, the creation of separate warm cells; walking down streets of such cells past gardens left derelict by the hard winter and trying, in vain, to summon up a positive response to this city where I had lived and worked; facing my own emptiness, my feeling of being physically lost, I had a dream.

An oblong of stiff new cloth lay before me, and I had the knowledge that if only out of this I could cut a smaller oblong of specific measurements, a specific section of this cloth, then the cloth would begin to unravel of itself, and the unravelling would spread from the cloth to the table to the house to all matter, *until the whole trick was undone*. Those were the words that were with me as I flattened the cloth and studied it for the clues which I knew existed, which I desired above everything else to find, but which I knew I never would.

The world is illusion, the Hindus say. We talk of despair, but true despair lies too deep for formulation. It was only now, as my experience of India defined itself more properly against my own homelessness, that I saw how close in the past year I had been to the total Indian negation, how much it had become the basis of thought and feeling. And already, with this awareness, in a world where illusion could only be a concept and not something felt in the bones, it was slipping away from me. I felt it as something true which I could never adequately express and never seize again.

*February 1962 – February 1964*

India is for me a difficult country.
It isn't my home and cannot be my home;
and yet I cannot reject it or be indifferent to it;
I cannot travel only for the sights.
I am at once too close and too far.

# INDIA:
# A WOUNDED CIVILIZATION

# PREFACE

In 1975 Mrs Gandhi, the Prime Minister of India, for no good reason suspended the constitution of her country and declared a state of emergency. This event put India, so to speak, on the world map. A request came from Knopf, my American publisher, that I should write a book on the subject; there came supporting requests from my London publisher and from the *New York Review of Books*. It was hard to refuse the blandishments. I knew that I was being asked to do something political and critical of India. I had never done that and had no wish to do it now, but the request for a new book excited me and I agreed. The money involved was small, but I hoped that it would all turn well in the end.

The book began well enough. I went to Bombay and met a surveyor. He was about to go to the rocky heartland of Maharashtra state, and thought I should come with him. This had little to do with the Emergency. I was more concerned, as I had always been, to extend my knowledge of India; and indeed it might be said that in all my writing of India so far I had been doing the same descriptive book. I went from Bombay to Poona by train, and then drove about the countryside with the surveyor. Everything was new to me; words fell into place; and what I wrote I was well pleased with. I suppose I was hoping to do the rest of the book in the same way: travel, people, and conversation. But the Emergency was real; all kinds of disagreeable things were happening in the background, and people soon became unwilling to talk to me or to be seen with me, and I saw that with my old way of proceeding I would have no book. A new way forced itself on me. It occurred to me, in the quickening panic that so often comes during the writing of a book, that I should attempt an intellectual portrait of India. To do this, I used existing material: newspapers, magazines, books, and squeezed them for their meaning.

So, after *The Middle Passage* and *An Area of Darkness*, a new method of inquiry came to me. I preferred the old way, with people, landscape and talk, but that was no longer available. The reader will note that in the prefaces to the new editions of my books I have been more concerned with the art of writing, and the related art of travel, than with what I have actually said, and that was because in different books different ways of moving and writing were forced upon me, and I had to hold myself ready for whatever might befall. There was a further very fruitful aspect of this particular piece of travel. I was writing for the *New York Review of Books*, and what came out was a series of connected pieces. So, without being trained for it or having it in my head, I was writing for serial publication. The reader will have to judge how far I was successful. I have to say, and this is true of all my books, that they fed me; I was wiser in the end than in the beginning.

Intellectually there is an idea in this book that makes a shy appearance: it is the idea that India was created by its many conquests, and that many of its attitudes come from the fact of conquest, not always acknowledged. Later I was to use this idea very openly, but I am not sure that I don't prefer the half-expressed, half-formulated adumbration that appears here. There is another result of the troubled method of composition: this is the shortest of my Indian books.

2010

# CONTENTS

# FOREWORD

THE LIGHTS OF Bombay airport showed that it had been raining; and the aeroplane, as it taxied in, an hour or two after midnight, blew the monsoon puddles over the concrete. This was in mid-August; and officially (though this monsoon was to be prolonged) the monsoon still had two weeks to go. In the small, damp terminal building there were passengers from an earlier flight, by Gulf Air. The Gulf was the Persian Gulf, with the oil states. And among the passengers were Indian businessmen in suits, awaiting especially careful search by the customs men; some Japanese; a few Arabs in the desert costumes which now, when seen in airports and foreign cities, are like the white gowns of a new and suddenly universal priesthood of pure money; and two turbaned and sunburnt Sikhs, artisans, returning to India after their work in an oil state, with cardboard suitcases and similar new shoes in yellow suede.

There is a new kind of coming and going in the world these days. Arabia, lucky again, has spread beyond its deserts. And India is again at the periphery of this new Arabian world, as much as it had been in the eighth century, when the new religion of Islam spread in all directions and the Arabs – led, it is said, by a seventeen-year-old boy – overran the Indian kingdom of Sind. That was only an episode, the historians say. But Sind is not a part of India today; India has shrunk since that Arab incursion. No civilization was so little equipped to cope with the outside world; no country was so easily raided and plundered, and learned so little from its disasters.

Five hundred years after the Arab conquest of Sind, Moslem rule was established in Delhi as the rule of foreigners, people apart; and foreign rule – Moslem for the first five hundred years, British for the last 150 – ended in Delhi only in 1947.

Indian history telescopes easily; and in India this time, in a northern city, I was to meet a young man, a civil servant, who said his Arab ancestors had come to India eight centuries before, during the great Islamic push of the twelfth century. When I asked where he lived, he said, 'My family has been living in Delhi for five hundred years.' And what in Europe would have sounded like boasting wasn't boasting in India. The family was a modest one, had always been modest, their surname, Qureshi, indicating the religious functions they had performed throughout the centuries. The entry of a member of the family into the Administrative Service was a break with the static past, a step up after eight hundred years. The young man compared his family with those of the Moslem masons and stone-cutters, descendants of the builders of the Mughal palaces and mosques, who in Delhi still sat around Shah Jehan's great mosque, the Jama Masjid, craftsmen as needy and as ragged as their ancestors had been, each man displaying the tools of the craft he had inherited, waiting to be hired, ready to build anybody a new Delhi.

India in the late twentieth century still seems so much itself, so rooted in its own civilization, it takes time to understand that its independence has meant more than the going away of the British; that the India to which Independence came was a land of far older defeat; that the purely Indian past died a long time ago. And already, with the Emergency, it is necessary to fight against the chilling sense of a new Indian dissolution.

*

India is for me a difficult country. It isn't my home and cannot be my home; and yet I cannot reject it or be indifferent to it; I cannot travel only for the sights. I am at once too close and too far. My ancestors migrated from the Gangetic plain a hundred years ago; and the Indian community they and others established in Trinidad, on the other side of the world, the community in which I grew up, was more homogeneous than the Indian community Gandhi met in South Africa in 1893, and more isolated from India.

India, which I visited for the first time in 1962, turned out to be a very strange land. A hundred years had been enough to wash me clean of many Indian religious attitudes; and without these attitudes the distress of India was – and is – almost insupportable. It has taken me much time to come to terms with the strangeness of India, to define what separates me from the country; and to understand how far the 'Indian' attitudes of someone like myself, a member of a small and remote community in the New World, have diverged from the attitudes of people to whom India is still whole.

An inquiry about India – even an inquiry about the Emergency – has quickly to go beyond the political. It has to be an inquiry about Indian attitudes; it has to be an inquiry about the civilization itself, as it is. And though in India I am a stranger, the starting point of this inquiry – more than might appear in these pages – has been myself. Because in myself, like the split-second images of infancy which some of us carry, there survive, from the family rituals that lasted into my childhood, phantasmal memories of old India which for me outline a whole vanished world.

I know, for instance, the beauty of sacrifice, so important to the Aryans. Sacrifice turned the cooking of food into a ritual: the first cooked thing – usually a small round of unleavened bread, a miniature, especially made – was always for the fire, the god. This was possible only with an open fireplace; to have to give up the custom – if I attempt now to expand on what to a child was only a passing sense of wrongness – was to abjure a link with the earth and the antiquity of the earth, the beginning of things. The morning rituals before breakfast, the evening ritual before the lighting of the lamps: these went, one by one, links with a religion that was also like a sense of the past, so that awe in the presence of the earth and the universe was something that had to be rediscovered later, by other means.

The customs of my childhood were sometimes mysterious. I didn't know it at the time, but the smooth pebbles in the shrine in my grandmother's house, pebbles brought by my grandfather all the way from India with his other household goods, were phallic emblems: the pebbles, of stone, standing for the more blatant stone columns. And why was it necessary for a male hand to hold the knife with which a pumpkin was cut open? It seemed to me at one time – because of the appearance of a pumpkin halved downward – that there was some sexual element in the rite. The truth is more frightening, as I learned only recently, near the end of this book. The pumpkin, in Bengal and adjoining areas, is a vegetable substitute for a living sacrifice: the male hand was therefore necessary. In India I know I am a stranger; but increasingly I understand that my Indian memories, the memories of that India which lived on into my childhood in Trinidad, are like trapdoors into a bottomless past.

# PART ONE
## A Wounded Civilization

# I

# AN OLD EQUILIBRIUM

## I

SOMETIMES OLD INDIA, the old, eternal India many Indians like to talk about, does seem just to go on. During the last war some British soldiers, who were training in chemical warfare, were stationed in the far south of the country, near a thousand-year-old Hindu temple. The temple had a pet crocodile. The soldiers, understandably, shot the crocodile. They also in some way – perhaps by their presence alone – defiled the temple. Soon, however, the soldiers went away and the British left India altogether. Now, more than thirty years after that defilement, and in another season of emergency, the temple has been renovated and a new statue of the temple deity is being installed.

Until they are given life and invested with power, such statues are only objects in an image-maker's yard, their value depending on size, material, and the carver's skill. Hindu idols or images come from the old world; they embody difficult and sometimes sublime concepts, and they have to be made according to certain rules. There can be no development now in Hindu iconography, though the images these days, under the influence of the Indian cinema and cinema posters, are less abstract than their ancient originals, and more humanly pretty and doll-like. They stand lifeless in every way in the image-maker's showroom. Granite and marble – and an occasional commissioned bust of someone like a local inspector of police, with perhaps a real spectacle frame over his blank marble eyes – suggest at first the graveyard, and a people in love with death. But this showroom is a kind of limbo, with each image awaiting the life and divinity that will come to it with purchase and devotion, each image already minutely flawed so that its divine life, when it comes, shall not be terrible and overwhelming.

Life, then, has to be given to the new image in the once defiled temple. A special effort has to be made. And the method being used is one of the most archaic in the world. It takes us back to the beginning of religion and human wonder. It is the method of the word: in the beginning was the word. A twelve-lettered *mantra* will be chanted and written fifty million times; and that is what – in this time of Emergency, with the constitution suspended, the press censored – five thousand volunteers are doing. When the job is completed, an inscribed gold plate will be placed below the new idol to attest to the creation of its divinity and the devotion of the volunteers. A thousand-year-old temple will live again: India, Hindu India, is eternal: conquests and defilements are but instants in time.

About two hundred miles away, still in the south, on a brown plateau of rock and gigantic boulders, are the ruins of the capital city of what was once the great Hindu kingdom of Vijayanagar. Vijayanagar – *vijaya*, victory, *nagar*, city – was established in the fourteenth century; it was conquered, and totally destroyed, by an alliance of Moslem principalities in 1565. The city was then one of the greatest in the world, its walls twenty-four miles around – foreign visitors have left accounts of its organization and magnificence – and the work of destruction took five months; some people say a year.

Today all the outer city is a peasant wilderness, with scattered remnants of stone or brick structures. Near the Tungabhadra River are the grander ruins: palaces and stables, a royal bath, a temple with clusters of musical stone columns that can still be played, a broken aqueduct, the leaning granite pillars of what must have been a bridge across the river. There is more beyond the river: a long and very wide avenue, still partly façaded, with a giant statue of the bull of Shiva at one end and at the other end a miracle: a temple that for some reason was spared destruction four hundred years ago, is still whole, and is still used for worship.

It is for this that the pilgrims come, to make offerings and to perform the rites of old magic. Some of the ruins of Vijayanagar have been declared national monuments by the Archaeological Department; but to the pilgrims – and they are more numerous than the tourists – Vijayanagar is not its terrible history or its present encompassing desolation. Such history as is known has been reduced to the legend of a mighty ruler, a kingdom founded with gold that showered from the sky, a kingdom so rich that pearls and rubies were sold in the market place like grain.

To the pilgrims Vijayanagar is its surviving temple. The surrounding destruction is like proof of the virtue of old magic; just as the fantasy of past splendour is accommodated within an acceptance of present squalor. That once glorious avenue – not a national monument, still permitted to live – is a slum. Its surface, where unpaved, is a green-black slurry of mud and excrement, through which the sandaled pilgrims unheedingly pad to the food stalls and souvenir shops, loud and gay with radios. And there are starved squatters with their starved animals in the ruins, the broken stone façades patched up with mud and rocks, the doorways stripped of the sculptures which existed until recently. Life goes on, the past continues. After conquest and destruction, the past simply reasserts itself.

If Vijayanagar is now only its name and, as a kingdom, is so little remembered (there are university students in Bangalore, two hundred miles away, who haven't even heard of it), it isn't only because it was so completely wiped out, but also because it contributed so little; it was itself a reassertion of the past. The kingdom was founded in 1336 by a local Hindu prince who, after defeat by the Moslems, had been taken to Delhi, converted to

Islam, and then sent back to the south as a representative of the Moslem power. There in the south, far from Delhi, the converted prince had re-established his independence and, unusually, in defiance of Hindu caste rules, had declared himself a Hindu again, a representative on earth of the local Hindu god. In this unlikely way the great Hindu kingdom of the south was founded.

It lasted two hundred years, but during that time it never ceased to be embattled. It was committed from the start to the preservation of a Hinduism that had already been violated, and culturally and artistically it preserved and repeated; it hardly innovated. Its bronze sculptures are like those of five hundred years before; its architecture, even at the time, and certainly to the surrounding Moslems, must have seemed heavy and archaic. And its ruins today, in that unfriendly landscape of rock and boulders of strange shapes, look older than they are, like the ruins of a long-superseded civilization.

The Hinduism Vijayanagar proclaimed had already reached a dead end, and in some ways had decayed, as popular Hinduism so easily decays, into barbarism. Vijayanagar had its slave markets, its temple prostitutes. It encouraged the holy practice of *suttee*, whereby a widow burned herself on the funeral pyre of her husband, to achieve virtue, to secure the honour of her husband's family, and to cleanse that family of the sins of three generations. And Vijayanagar dealt in human sacrifice. Once, when there was some trouble with the construction of a big reservoir, the great king of Vijayanagar, Krishna Deva Raya (1509–1529), ordered the sacrifice of some prisoners.

In the sixteenth century Vijayanagar, really, was a kingdom awaiting conquest. But it was big and splendid; it needed administrators, artists, craftsmen; and for the two hundred years of its life it must have sustained all the talent of the land and concentrated it in that capital. When it was conquered and its capital systematically smashed, more than buildings and temples would have been destroyed. Many men would have been killed; all the talent, energy, and intellectual capacity of the kingdom would have been extinguished for generations. The conquerors themselves, by creating a desert, would have ensured, almost invited, their own subsequent defeat by others: again and again, for the next two hundred years, the land of that dead kingdom was trampled down.

And today it still shows, the finality of that destruction of Hindu Vijayanagar in 1565: in the acknowledged 'backwardness' of the region, which now seems without a history and which it is impossible to associate with past grandeur or even with great wars; in the squalor of the town of Hospet that has grown up not far from the ruins; in the unending nullity of the peasant-serf countryside.

Since Independence much money has been spent on the region. A dam has been built across the Tungabhadra River. There is an extensive irrigation scheme which incorporates the irrigation canals of the old kingdom (and these are still called Vijayanagar canals). A Vijayanagar steel plant is being planned; and a university is being built, to train men of the region for jobs in that steel plant and the subsidiary industries that are expected to come up. The emphasis is on training men of the region, local men. Because, in this land that was once a land of great builders, there is now a human deficiency. The state of which the region forms part is the one state in the Indian Union that encourages migrants from other states. It needs technicians, artisans; it needs men with simple skills; it needs even hotel waiters. All it has been left with is a peasantry that cannot comprehend the idea of change: like the squatters in the ruins outside the living Vijayanagar temple, slipping in and out of the decayed stone façades like brightly coloured insects, screeching and unimportantly active on this afternoon of rain.

It was at Vijayanagar this time, in that wide temple avenue, which seemed less awesome than when I had first seen it thirteen years before, no longer speaking as directly as it did then of a fabulous past, that I began to wonder about the intellectual depletion that must have come to India with the invasions and conquests of the last thousand years. What happened in Vijayanagar happened, in varying degrees, in other parts of the country. In the north, ruin lies on ruin: Moslem ruin on Hindu ruin, Moslem on Moslem. In the history books, in the accounts of wars and conquests and plunder, the intellectual depletion passes unnoticed, the lesser intellectual life of a country whose contributions to civilization were made in the remote past. India absorbs and outlasts its conquerors, Indians say. But at Vijayanagar, among the pilgrims, I wondered whether intellectually for a thousand years India hadn't always retreated before its conquerors and whether, in its periods of apparent revival, India hadn't only been making itself archaic again, intellectually smaller, always vulnerable.

In the British time, a period of bitter subjection which was yet for India a period of intellectual recruitment, Indian nationalism proclaimed the Indian past; and religion was inextricably mixed with political awakening. But independent India, with its five-year plans, its industrialization, its practice of democracy, has invested in change. There always was a contradiction between the archaism of national pride and the promise of the new; the contradiction has at last cracked the civilization open.

The turbulence in India this time hasn't come from foreign invasion or conquest; it has been generated from within. India cannot respond in her old way, by a further retreat into archaism. Her borrowed institutions have worked like borrowed institutions; but archaic India can provide no substitutes for press, parliament, and courts. The crisis of India is not only political or economic. The larger crisis is of a wounded old civilization that has at last become aware of its inadequacies and is without the intellectual means to move ahead.

## 2

'India will go on.' This was what the Indian novelist R.K. Narayan said to me in London in 1961, before I had ever been to India.

The novel, which is a form of social inquiry, and as such outside the Indian tradition, had come to India with the British. By the late nineteenth century it had become established in Bengal, and had then spread. But it was only towards the end of the British period, in the 1930s, that serious novelists appeared who wrote in English, for first publication in London. Narayan was one of the earliest and best of these. He had never been a 'political' writer, not even in the explosive 1930s; and he was unlike many of the writers after Independence who seemed to regard the novel, and all writing, as an opportunity for autobiography and boasting.

Narayan's concern had always been with the life of a small South Indian town, which he peopled book by book. His conviction in 1961, after fourteen years of Independence, that India would go on, whatever the political uncertainties after Mr Nehru, was like the conviction of his earliest novels, written in the days of the British, that India was going on. In the early novels the British conquest is like a fact of life. The British themselves are far away, their presence hinted at only in their institutions: the bank, the mission school. The writer contemplates the lesser life that goes on below: small men, small schemes, big talk, limited means: a life so circumscribed that it appears whole and unviolated, its smallness never a subject for wonder, though India itself is felt to be vast.

In his autobiography, *My Days*, published in 1974, Narayan fills in the background to his novels. This book, though more exotic in content than the novels, is of a piece with them. It is not more politically explicit or exploratory. The southern city of Madras – one of the earliest English foundations in India, the site leased by the East India Company in 1640 from the last remnant of the Vijayanagar kingdom – was where Narayan spent much of his childhood. Madras was part of a region that had long been pacified, was more Hindu than the north, less Islamized, and had had seventy-five years more of peace. It had known no wars, Narayan says, since the days of Clive. When, during the First World War, the roving German battleship *Emden* appeared in the harbour one night, turned on its searchlights, and began shelling the city, people 'wondered at the phenomenon of thunder and lightning with a sky full of stars'. Some people fled inland. This flight, Narayan says, 'was in keeping with an earlier move, when the sea was rough with cyclone and it was prophesied that the world would end that day'.

The world of Narayan's childhood was one that had turned in on itself, had become a world of prophecy and magic, removed from great events and removed, it might seem, from the possibility of politics. But politics did come; and it came, as perhaps it could only come, by stealth, and mingled with ritual and religion. At school Narayan joined the Boy Scouts. But the Boy Scouts movement in Madras was controlled by Annie Besant, the Theosophist, who had a larger idea of Indian civilization than most Indians had at that time; and, in sly subversion of Lord Baden-Powell's imperial purpose, the Besant Scouts sang, to the tune of 'God Save the King': 'God save our motherland, God save our noble land, God save our Ind.'

One day in 1919 Narayan fell in with a procession that had started from the ancient temple of Iswara. The procession sang 'patriotic songs' and shouted slogans and made its way back to the temple, where there was a distribution of sweets. This festive and devout affair was the first nationalist agitation in Madras. And – though Narayan doesn't say it – it was part of the first all-India protest that had been decreed by Gandhi, aged forty-nine, just three years back from South Africa, and until then relatively unknown in India. Narayan was pleased to have taken part in the procession. But his uncle, a young man and a modern man (one of the earliest amateur photographers in India), was less than pleased. The uncle, Narayan says, was 'anti-political and did not want me to be misled. He condemned all rulers, governments and administrative machinery as Satanic and saw no logic in seeking a change of rulers.'

Well, that was where we all began, all of us who are over forty and were colonials, subject people who had learned to live with the idea of subjection. We lived within our lesser world; and we could even pretend it was whole because we had forgotten that it had been shattered. Disturbance, instability, development lay elsewhere; we, who had lost our wars and were removed from great events, were at peace. In life, as in literature, we received tourists. Subjection flattened, made dissimilar places alike. Narayan's India, with its colonial apparatus, was oddly like the Trinidad of my childhood. His oblique perception of that apparatus, and the rulers, matched my own; and in the Indian life of his novels I found echoes of the life of my own Indian community on the other side of the world.

But Narayan's novels did not prepare me for the distress of India. As a writer he had succeeded almost too well. His comedies were of the sort that requires a restricted social setting with well-defined rules; and he was so direct, his touch so light, that, though he wrote in English of Indian manners, he had succeeded in making those exotic manners quite ordinary. The small town he had staked out as his fictional territory was, I knew, a creation of art and therefore to some extent artificial, a simplification of reality. But the reality was cruel and overwhelming. In the books his India had seemed accessible; in India it remained hidden. To get down to Narayan's world, to perceive the order and continuity he saw in the dereliction and smallness of India, to enter into his ironic acceptance and relish his comedy, was to ignore too much of what could be seen, to shed too much of myself: my sense of history, and even the simplest ideas of human possibility. I did not lose my admiration for Narayan; but I felt that his comedy and irony were not quite what they had appeared to be, were part of a Hindu response to the world, a response I could no longer share. And it has since become clear to me – especially on this last visit, during a slow rereading of Narayan's 1949 novel, *Mr Sampath* – that, for all their delight in human oddity, Narayan's novels are less the purely social comedies I had once taken them to be than religious books, at times religious fables, and intensely Hindu.

Srinivas, the hero of *Mr Sampath*, is a contemplative idler. He has tried many jobs – agriculture, a bank, teaching, the law: the jobs of pre-Independence India: the year is 1938 – and rejected all. He stays in his room in the family house – the house of the Indian extended family – and worries about the passing of time. Srinivas's elder brother, a lawyer, looks after the house, and that means he looks after Srinivas and Srinivas's wife and son. The fact that Srinivas has a family is as much a surprise as Srinivas's age: he is thirty-seven.

One day Srinivas is reading the *Upanishads* in his room. His elder brother comes in and says, 'What exactly is it that you wish to do in life?' Srinivas replies: 'Don't you see? There are ten principal *Upanishads*. I should like to complete the series. This is the third.' But Srinivas takes the hint. He decides to go to the town of Malgudi and set up a weekly paper. In Malgudi he lives in a squalid rented room in a crowded lane, bathes at a communal water tap, and finds an office for his paper in a garret.

Srinivas is now in the world, with new responsibilities and new relationships – his landlord, his printer, his wife ('he himself wondered that he had observed so little of her in their years of married life') – but he sees more and more clearly the perfection of nondoing. 'While he thundered against municipal or social shortcomings a voice went on asking: "Life and the world and all this is passing – why bother about anything? The perfect and the imperfect are all the same. Why really bother?"'

His speculations seem idle, and are presented as half comic; but they push him deeper into quietism. From his little room one day he hears the cry of a woman selling vegetables in the lane. Wondering first about her and her customers, and then about the 'great human forces' that meet or clash every day, Srinivas has an intimation of the 'multitudinousness and vastness of the whole picture of life', and is dazzled. God, he thinks, is to be perceived in that 'total picture'; and later, in that total picture, he also perceives a wonderful balance. 'If only one could get a comprehensive view of all humanity, one would get a correct view of the world: things being neither particularly wrong nor right, but just balancing themselves.' There is really no need to interfere, to do anything. And from this Srinivas moves easily, after a tiff with his wife one day, to a fuller comprehension of Gandhian nonviolence. 'Nonviolence in all matters, little or big, personal or national, is deemed to produce an unagitated, undisturbed calm, both in a personality and in society.'

But this nonviolence or nondoing depends on society going on; it depends on the doing of others. When Srinivas's printer closes his shop, Srinivas has to close his paper. Srinivas then, through the printer (who is the Mr Sampath of Narayan's title), finds himself involved as a scriptwriter in the making of an Indian religious film. Srinivas is now deeper than ever in the world, and he finds it chaotic and corrupt. Pure ideas are mangled; sex and farce, song and dance and South American music are grafted on to a story of Hindu gods. The printer, now a kind of producer, falls in love with the leading lady. An artist is in love with her as well. The printer wins, the artist literally goes mad. All is confusion; the film is never made.

Srinivas finally withdraws. He finds another printer and starts his paper again, and the paper is no longer the comic thing it had first seemed. Srinivas has, in essence, returned to himself and to his contemplative life. From this security (and with the help of some rupees sent him by his brother: always the rupees: the rupees are always necessary) Srinivas sees 'adulthood' as a state of nonsense, without innocence or pure joy, the nonsense given importance only by 'the values of commerce'.

There remains the artist, made mad by love and his contact with the world of nonsense. He has to be cured, and there is a local magician who knows what has to be done. He is summoned, and the antique rites begin, which will end with the ceremonial beating of the artist. Tribal, Srinivas thinks: they might all be in the twentieth century BC. But the oppression he feels doesn't last. Thinking of the primitive past, he all at once has a vision of the millennia of Indian history, and of all the things that might have happened on the ground where they stand.

There, in what would then have been forest, he sees enacted an episode from the Hindu epic of the *Ramayana*, which partly reflects the Aryan settlement of India (perhaps 1000 BC). Later the Buddha (about 560–480 BC) comforts a woman whose child has died: 'Bring me a handful of mustard seed from a house where no one has died.' The philosopher Shankaracharya (AD 788–820), preaching the Vedanta on his all-India mission, founds a temple after seeing a spawning frog being sheltered from the sun by its natural enemy, the cobra. And then the missionaries from Europe come, and the merchants, and the soldiers, and Mr Shilling, who is the manager of the British bank which is now just down the road.

'Dynasties rose and fell. Palaces and mansions appeared and disappeared. The entire country went down under the fire and sword of the invader, and was washed clean when Sarayu overflowed its bounds. But it always had its rebirth and growth.' Against this, what is the madness of one man? 'Half the madness was his own doing, his lack of self-knowledge, his treachery to his own instincts as an artist, which had made him a battleground. Sooner or later he shook off his madness and realized his true identity – though not in one birth, at least in a series of them . . . Madness or sanity, suffering or happiness seemed all the same . . . in the rush of eternity nothing mattered.'

So the artist is beaten, and Srinivas doesn't interfere; and when afterward the magician orders the artist to be taken to a distant temple and left outside the gateway for a week, Srinivas decides that it doesn't matter whether the artist is looked after or not during that time, whether he lives or dies. 'Even madness passes,' Srinivas says in his spiritual elation. 'Only existence asserts itself.'

Out of a superficial reading of the past, then, out of the sentimental conviction that India is eternal and forever revives, there comes not a fear of further defeat and destruction, but an indifference to it. India will somehow look after itself; the individual is freed of all responsibility. And within this larger indifference there is the indifference to the fate of a friend: it is madness, Srinivas concludes, for him to think of himself as the artist's keeper.

Just twenty years have passed between Gandhi's first call for civil disobedience and the events of the novel. But already, in Srinivas, Gandhian nonviolence has degenerated into something very like the opposite of what Gandhi intended. For Srinivas non-violence isn't a form of action, a quickener of social conscience. It is only a means of securing an undisturbed calm; it is nondoing, noninterference, social indifference. It merges with the ideal of self-realization, truth to one's identity. These modern-sounding words, which reconcile Srinivas to the artist's predicament, disguise an acceptance of *karma*, the Hindu killer, the Hindu calm, which tells us that we pay in this life for what we have done in past lives: so that everything we see is just and balanced, and the distress we see is to be relished as religious theatre, a reminder of our duty to ourselves, our future lives.

Srinivas's quietism – compounded of *karma*, nonviolence, and a vision of history as an extended religious fable – is in fact a form of self-cherishing in the midst of a general distress. It is parasitic. It depends on the continuing activity of others, the trains running, the presses printing, the rupees arriving from somewhere. It needs the world, but it surrenders the organization of the world to others. It is a religious response to worldly defeat.

Because we take to novels our own ideas of what we feel they must offer, we often find, in unusual or original work, only what we expect to find, and we reject or miss what we aren't looking for. But it astonished me that, twenty years before, not having been to India, taking to *Mr Sampath* only my knowledge of the Indian community of Trinidad and my reading of other literature, I should have missed or misread so much, should have seen only a comedy of small-town life and a picaresque, wandering narrative in a book that was really so mysterious.

Now, reading *Mr Sampath* again in snatches on afternoons of rain during this prolonged monsoon, which went on and on like the Emergency itself – reading in Bombay, looking down at the choppy sea, and the 1911 Imperial rhetoric of the British-built Gateway of India that dwarfed the white-clad crowd; in suburban and secretive New Delhi, looking out across the hotel's sodden tennis court to the encampment of Sikh taxi-drivers below the dripping trees; on the top veranda of the Circuit House in Kotah, considering the garden, and seeing in mango tree and banana tree the originals of the stylized vegetation in the miniatures done for Rajput princes, their glory now extinguished, their great forts now abandoned and empty, protecting nothing, their land now only a land of peasants; in Bangalore in the south, a former British army town, looking across the parade ground, now the polo ground, with Indian army polo teams – reading during the Emergency, which was more than political, I saw in *Mr Sampath* a foreshadowing of the tensions that had to come to India, philosophically prepared for defeat and withdrawal (each man an island) rather than independence and action, and torn now between the wish to preserve and be psychologically secure, and the need to undo.

From the *Indian Express*:

> New Delhi, 2 Sept . . . Inaugurating the 13th conference of the chairmen and members of the State Social Welfare Advisory Boards here, Mrs Gandhi said stress on the individual was India's strength as well as weakness. It had given the people an inner strength but had also put a veil between the individual and others in society . . . Mrs Gandhi said no social welfare programme could succeed unless the basic attitudes of mind change . . . 'We must live in this age,' Mrs Gandhi said, adding that this did not mean that 'we must sweep away' all our past. While people must know of the past, they must move towards the future, she added.

The two ideas – responsibility, the past – were apparently unrelated. But in India they hung together. The speech might have served as a commentary on *Mr Sampath*. What had seemed speculative and comic, aimless and 'Russian' about Narayan's novel had turned out to be something else, the expression of an almost hermetic philosophical system. The novel I had read as a novel was also a fable, a classic exposition of the Hindu equilibrium, surviving the shock of an alien culture, an alien literary form, an alien language, and making harmless even those new concepts it appeared to welcome. Identity became an aspect of *karma*, self-love was bolstered by an ideal of nonviolence.

3

To arrive at an intellectual comprehension of this equilibrium – as some scholars do, working in the main from Hindu texts – is one thing. To enter into it, when faced with the Indian reality, is another. The hippies of Western Europe and the United States appear to have done so; but they haven't. Out of security and mental lassitude, an intellectual anorexia, they simply cultivate squalor. And their calm can easily turn to panic. When the price of oil rises and economies tremble at home, they clean up and bolt. Theirs is a shallow narcissism; they break just at that point where the Hindu begins: the knowledge of the abyss, the acceptance of distress as the condition of men.

It is out of an eroded human concern, rather than the sentimental wallow of the hippies and others who 'love' India, that a dim understanding begins to come. And it comes at those moments when, in spite of all that has been done since Independence, it seems that enough will never be done; and despair turns to weariness, and thoughts of action fade. Such a moment came to me this time in North Bihar. Bihar, for centuries the cultural heartland of India ('Bihar' from *vihara*, a Buddhist monastery), now without intellect or leaders: in the south a land of drought and famine and flood, in the north a green, well-watered land of jute (like tall reeds) and paddy and fishponds.

In the village I went to, only one family out of four had land; only one child out of four went to school; only one man out of four had work. For a wage calculated to keep him only in food for the day he worked, the employed man, hardly exercising a skill, using the simplest tools and sometimes no tools at all, did the simplest agricultural labour. Child's work; and children, being cheaper than men, were preferred; so that, suicidally, in the midst of an overpopulation which no one recognized (an earthquake in 1935 had shaken down the population, according to the villagers, and there had been a further thinning out during the floods of 1971), children were a source of wealth, available for hire after their eighth year for, if times were good, fifteen rupees, a dollar fifty, a month.

Generation followed generation quickly here, men as easily replaceable as their huts of grass and mud and matting (golden when new, quickly weathering to grey-black). Cruelty no longer had a meaning; it was life itself. Men knew what they were born to. Every man knew his caste, his place; each group lived in its own immemorially defined area; and the pariahs, the scavengers, lived at the end of the village. Above the huts rose the rambling two storey brick mansion of the family who had once owned it all, the land and the people: grandeur that wasn't grandeur, but was like part of the squalor and defeat out of which it had arisen. The family was now partially dispossessed, but, as politicians, they still controlled. Nothing had changed or seemed likely to change.

And during the rest of that day's drive North Bihar repeated itself: the grey-black hut clusters; the green paddy fields whose luxuriance and springlike freshness can deceive earth-scanners and cause yields to be overestimated; the bare-backed men carrying loads on either end of a long limber pole balanced on their shoulders, the strain showing in their brisk, mincing walk, which gave them a curious feminine daintiness; the overcrowded buses at dusty towns that were shack settlements, the children wallowing in the muddy ponds in the heat of the day, catching fish; the children and the men pounding soaked jute stalks to extract the fibre which, loaded on bullock carts, looked like thick plaited blond tresses, immensely rich. Thoughts of human possibility dwindled: North Bihar seemed to have become the world, capable only of the life that was seen.

It was like the weariness I had felt some weeks before, in the Bundi-Kotah region of Rajasthan, eight hundred miles to the west. If in North Bihar there had seemed to be, with the absence of intellect and creativity, an absence almost of administration, here in Rajasthan was prodigious enterprise. Here were dams and a great irrigation-and-reclamation scheme in a land cut up and wasted by ravines.

Imperfectly conceived twenty years before – no drainage, the nature of the soil not taken into account – the irrigation scheme had led to waterlogging and salinity. Now, urgently, this was being put right. There was a special commissioner, and he and his deputies were men of the utmost energy. The technical problems could be solved. The difficulties – in this state of desert forts, feudal princes, and a peasantry trained only in loyalty, equipped for little else – lay with the people: not just with the 'mediocrity at every level' which the commissioner said he found in the administration, but also with the people lower down, whom the scheme was meant to benefit. How could they, used for generations to so little, content to find glory only in the glory of their rulers, be made now, almost suddenly, to want, to do?

The commissioner's powers were great, but he was unwilling to rule despotically; he wished to 'institutionalize'. One evening, by the light of an electric bulb – electricity in the village! – we sat out with the villagers in the main street of a 'model village' of the command area. The street was unpaved, and the villagers, welcoming us, had quickly spread cotton rugs on the ground that had been softened by the morning's rain, half hardened by the afternoon's heat, and then trampled and manured by the village cattle returning at dusk. The women had withdrawn – so many of them, below their red or orange Rajasthani veils, only girls, children, but already with children of their own. We were left with the men; and, until the rain came roaring in again, we talked.

So handsome, these men of Rajasthan, so self-possessed: it took time to understand that they were only peasants, and limited. The fields, water, crops, cattle: that was where concern began and ended. They were a model village, and so they considered themselves. There was little more that they needed, and I began to see my own ideas of village improvement as fantasies. Nothing beyond food – and survival – had as yet become an object of ambition; though one man said, fantastically, that he would like a telephone, to find out about the price of grain in Kotah without having to go there.

The problems of the irrigation project were not only those of salinity or the ravines or land-levelling. The problem, as the commissioner saw, was the remaking of men. And this was not simply making men want; it meant, in the first place, bringing them back from the self-wounding and the special waste that come with an established destitution. We were among men who, until recently, cut only the very tops of sugar cane and left the rest of the plant, the substance of the crop, to rot. So this concern about fertilizers and yields, this acquiring by the villagers of what I had at first judged to be only peasant attributes, was an immeasurable advance.

But if in this model village – near Kotah Town, which was fast industrializing – there had been some movement, Bundi the next day seemed to take us backward. Bundi and Kotah: to me, until this trip, they had only been beautiful names, the names of related but distinct schools of Rajasthan painting. The artistic glory of Bundi had come first, in the late seventeenth century. And after the flat waterlogged fields, pallid paddy thinning out at times to marshland, after the desolation of the road from Kotah, the flooded ditches, the occasional cycle-rickshaw, the damp groups of bright-turbaned peasants waiting for the bus, Bundi Castle on its hill was startling, its great walls like the work of giants, the extravagant creation of men who had once had much to defend.

Old wars, bravely fought; but usually little more had been at stake other than the honour and local glory of one particular prince. The fortifications were now useless, the palace was empty. One dark, dusty room had old photographs and remnants of Victorian bric-a-brac. The small formal garden in the courtyard was in decay; and the mechanical, decorative nineteenth-century Bundi murals around the courtyard had faded to blues and yellows and greens. In the inner rooms, hidden from the sun, brighter colours survived, and some panels were exquisite. But it all awaited ruin. The monsoon damp was rotting away plaster; water dripped through green-black cracks in underground arches; and the sharp smell of bat dung was everywhere.

All vitality had been sucked up into that palace on the hill; and now vitality had gone out of Bundi. It showed in the rundown town on the hillside below the palace; it showed in the fields; it showed in the people, more beaten down than at Kotah Town just sixty miles away, less amenable to the commissioner's ideas, and more full of complaints. They complained even when they had no cause; and it seemed that they complained because they felt it was expected of them. Their mock aggressiveness and mock desperation held little of real despair or rebellion. It was a ritual show of deference to authority, a demonstration of their complete dependence on authority. The commissioner smiled and listened and heard them all; and their passion faded.

Later we sat with the 'village-level workers' in the shade of a small tree in a woman's yard. These officials were the last in the chain of command; on them much of the success of the scheme depended. There had been evidence during the morning's tour that they hadn't all been doing their jobs. But they were not abashed; instead, sitting in a line on a string bed, dressed not like the peasants that they almost were, but dressed like officials, in trousers and shirts, they spoke of their need for promotion and status. They were far removed from the commissioner's anxieties, from his vision of what could be done with their land. They were, really, at peace with the world they knew. Like the woman in whose yard we sat. She was friendly, she had dragged out string beds for us from her little brick hut; but her manner was slightly supercilious. There was a reason. She was happy, she considered herself blessed. She had had three sons, and she glowed with that achievement.

All the chivalry of Rajasthan had been reduced here to nothing. The palace was empty; the petty wars of princes had been absorbed into legend and could no longer be dated. All that remained was what the visitor could see: small, poor fields, ragged men, huts, monsoon mud. But in that very abjectness lay security. Where the world had shrunk, and ideas of human possibility had become extinct, the world could be seen as complete. Men had retreated to their last, impregnable defences: their knowledge of who they were, their caste, their *karma*, their unshakable place in the scheme of things; and this knowledge was like their knowledge of the seasons. Rituals marked the passage of each day, rituals marked every stage of a man's life. Life itself had been turned to ritual; and everything beyond this complete and sanctified world – where fulfilment came so easily to a man or to a woman – was vain and phantasmal.

Kingdoms, empires, projects like the commissioner's: they had come and gone. The monuments of ambition and restlessness littered the land, so many of them abandoned or destroyed, so many unfinished, the work of dynasties suddenly supplanted. India taught the vanity of all action; and the visitor could be appalled by the waste, and by all that now appeared to threaten the commissioner's enterprise.

But to those who embraced its philosophy of distress India also offered an enduring security, its equilibrium, that vision of a world finely balanced that had come to the hero of *Mr Sampath*, that 'arrangement made by the gods'. Only India, with its great past, its civilization, its philosophy, and its almost holy poverty, offered this truth; India *was* the truth. So, to Indians, India could detach itself from the rest of the world. The world could be divided into India and non-India. And India, for all its surface terrors, could be proclaimed, without disingenuousness or cruelty, as perfect. Not only by pauper, but by prince.

4

Consider this prince, in another part of the country, far from the castles of Rajasthan. Another landscape, another type of vegetation; only, the rain continued. The princes of India – their number and variety reflecting to a large extent the chaos that had come to the country with the break-up of the Mughal empire – had lost real power in the British time. Through generations of idle servitude they had grown to specialize only in style. A bogus, extinguishable glamour: in 1947, with Independence, they had lost their states, and Mrs Gandhi in 1971 had, without much public outcry, abolished their privy purses and titles. The power of this prince had continued; he had become an energetic entrepreneur. But in his own eyes, and in the eyes of those who served him, he remained a prince. And perhaps his grief for his title, and his insistence on his dignity, was the greater because his state had really been quite small, a fief of some hundred square miles, granted three centuries before to an ancestor, a soldier of fortune.

With his buttoned-up Indian tunic, the prince was quite the autocrat at the dinner table, down the middle of which ran an arrangement of chiffon stuck with roses; and it was some time before I saw that he had come down drunk to our teetotal dinner. He said, unprompted, that he was 'observing' the crisis of Indian democracy with 'interest'. India needed Indian forms of government; India wasn't one country, but hundreds of little countries. I thought he was building up the case for his own autocratic rule. But his conversational course – almost a soliloquy – was wilder.

'What keeps a country together? Not economics. Love. Love and affection. That's our Indian way . . . You can feed my dog, but he won't obey you. He'll obey me. Where's the economics in that? That's love and affection . . . For twenty-eight years until 1947 I ruled this state. Power of life and death. Could have hanged a man and nobody could have done anything to me . . . Now they've looted my honour, my privilege. I'm nobody. I'm just like everybody else . . . Power of life and death. But I can still go out and walk. Nobody's going to try and kill me like Kennedy. That's not economics. That's our love and affection . . . Where's the cruelty you talk about? I tell you, we're *happy* in India . . . Who's talking about patriotism? Have no cause to be. Took away everything. Honour, titles, all looted. I'm not a patriot, but I'm an Indian. Go out and talk to the people. They're poor, but they're not inhuman, as you say . . . You people must leave us alone. You mustn't come and tell us we're subhuman. We're civilized. Are they happy where you come from? Are they happy in England?'

In spite of myself, my irritation was rising. I said: 'They're very happy in England.' He broke off and laughed. But he had spoken seriously. He was acting a little, but he believed everything he said.

His state, or what had been his state, was wretched: just the palace (like a country house, with a garden) and the peasants. The development (in which he had invested) hadn't yet begun to show. In the morning in the rain I saw young child labourers using their hands alone to shovel gravel on to a waterlogged path. Groundnuts were the only source of protein here; but the peasants preferred to sell their crop; and their children were stunted, their minds deformed, serf material already, beyond the reach of education where that was available.

(But science, a short time later, was to tell me otherwise. From the *Indian Express*: 'New Delhi, 2 Nov . . . Delivering the Dr V. N. Patwardhan Prize oration at the India Council of Medical Research yesterday, Dr Kamala Rao said certain hormonal changes within the body of the malnourished children enabled them to maintain normal body functions . . . Only the excess and nonessential parts of the body are affected by malnutrition. Such malnourished children, though small in size, are like "paperback books" which, while retaining all the material of the original, have got rid of the non-essential portion of the bound editions.')

The prince had travelled outside India. He was in a position to compare what he had seen outside with what he could see of his own state. But the question of comparison did not arise. The world outside India was to be judged by its own standards. India was not to be judged. India was only to be experienced, in the Indian way. And when the prince spoke of the happiness of his people, he was not being provocative or backward-looking. As an entrepreneur, almost an industrialist, he saw himself as a benefactor. When he talked about love and affection, he did not exaggerate: he needed to be loved as much as he needed to be reverenced. His attachment to his people was real. And his attachment to the land went beyond that.

In the unpopulated, forested hills some miles away from the palace there was an old temple. The temple was small and undistinguished. Its sculptures had weathered to unrecognizable knobs and indentations; the temple tank or reservoir was overgrown and reedy, the wide stone steps had sagged into the milky-green slime. But the temple was important to the prince. His ancestors had adopted the deity of the temple as their own, and the family maintained the priest. It was an ancient site; it had its genius; the whole place was still in worship. India offered the prince not only the proofs of his princehood but also this abiding truth of his relationship to the earth, the universe.

In this ability to separate India from what was not India, the prince was like the middle-class (and possibly rich) girl I met at a Delhi dinner party. She was married to a foreigner and lived abroad. This living abroad was glamorous; when she spoke of it, she appeared to be boasting, in the Indian fashion: she detached herself from the rest of India. But for the Indian woman a foreign marriage is seldom a positive act; it is, more usually, an act of despair or confusion. It leads to castelessness, the loss of community, the loss of a place in the world; and few Indians are equipped to cope with that.

Socially and intellectually this girl, outside India, was an innocent. She had no means of assessing her alien society; she lived in a void. She needed India and all its reassurances, and she came back to India whenever she could. India didn't jar, she said; and then, remembering to boast, she added, 'I relate only to my family.'

Such security! In the midst of world change, India, even during this Emergency, was unchanging: to return to India was to return to a knowledge of the world's deeper order, everything fixed, sanctified, everyone secure. Like a sleepwalker, she moved without disturbance between her two opposed worlds. But surely the streets of Bombay must make some impression? What did she see at the moment of arrival?

She said mystically, blankly, and with truth, 'I see people having their being.'

## 2

# THE SHATTERING WORLD

### I

'INDIA WILL GO on,' the novelist R.K. Narayan had said in 1961. And for the prince with his ancestral pieties, the girl with her foreign marriage, the peasant of Bihar or Bundi with his knowledge of *karma*, India was going on: the Hindu equilibrium still held. They were as removed from the Emergency in 1975 as Narayan himself had been from the political uncertainties of 1961.

Narayan was then in his fifties. Living in India, writing in English for publication abroad, operating as a novelist in a culture where the idea of the novel was new and as yet little understood, Narayan had had to wait long for recognition. He was middle-aged, the best of his work done, his fictional world established, before he had travelled out of India; and when I met him in London, this late travel seemed to have brought him no shocks.

He had just been visiting the United States, and was returning happily to India. He said he needed to go again for his afternoon walks, to be among his characters, the people he wrote about. In literature itself he was not so interested. Like his hero in *Mr Sampath*, he was letting his thoughts turn to the Infinite; in the midst of activity and success, he was preparing, in the Hindu way, for withdrawal. He said he had begun to read sacred Sanskrit texts with the help of a pundit. He seemed a man at peace with his world, at peace with India and the fictional world he had abstracted from the country.

But it was in the 1930s, before Independence, that Narayan had established his fictional world: the small and pacific South Indian town, little men, little schemes, the comedy of restricted lives and high philosophical speculation, real power surrendered long ago to the British rulers, who were far away and only dimly perceived. With Independence, however, the world had grown larger around Narayan. Power had come closer; men were required to be bigger. To Narayan himself had come recognition and foreign travel; and though in the red land around Bangalore, one of the cities of Narayan's childhood, peasant life continued as it had always done, Bangalore was becoming a centre of Indian industry and science.

Narayan's small town could not easily be insulated from the larger, restless world, could no longer be seen as finished and complete, with the well-defined boundaries necessary for his kind of humour. And very soon, after the certitude of 1961, doubt seemed to have come to Narayan. As early as 1967 there appeared a novel in which his fictional world is cracked open, its fragility finally revealed, and the Hindu equilibrium – so confidently maintained in *Mr Sampath* – collapses into something like despair.

The novel is *The Vendor of Sweets*. It is not one of Narayan's better books; but Narayan is such a natural writer, so true to his experience and emotions, that this novel is as much a key to the moral bewilderment of today as *Mr Sampath* was to the sterility of Hindu attitudes at the time of Independence. *The Vendor of Sweets*, like *Mr Sampath*, is a fable, and it broadly repeats the theme of the earlier book: there is a venture into the world of doing, and at the end there is a withdrawal.

The sweet-vendor is Jagan, a rich man, conscientiously adding every day to his money hoard at home (the 'black money' of India), but a Gandhian, a faddist, a man obsessed with the idea of purity. He is fair with his customers; he cheats only the government of the country for whose sake, in the British days, he endured police beatings and imprisonment in an insanitary jail. 'If Gandhi had said somewhere, "Pay your sales tax uncomplainingly," he would have followed his advice, but Gandhi had made no reference to the sales tax anywhere to Jagan's knowledge.'

(Was Jagan then a freedom fighter, concerned about the political humiliation of his country, or was he only the disciple of a holy man, in the old Hindu tradition? Hindu morality, centred on the self and self-realization, has its own social corruptions: how many Jagans exist who, conscious only of their Gandhian piety, their personal virtue, have mocked and undermined the Independence for which they say they have worked! But Narayan doesn't raise the point. He only makes the joke about Gandhi and the sales tax; he is on Jagan's side.)

Jagan is a widower with one child, a son, on whom he dotes. The boy, though, is sullen and talks little to his father. He announces one day that he is finished with school: he wants to be a writer. And later Jagan discovers that the boy, using money from the money hoard at home, has booked his passage to the United States, to go to a school of creative writing. Jagan digests his disappointment; the boy goes away. Very quickly, the time passes; and then, almost without warning, the boy returns. He is not alone. He is with a woman, apparently his wife, who, startlingly in that South Indian setting, is half Korean, half American. Between them they have plans, and they need Jagan's money. They have come to India to set up, with American collaboration, a factory which will manufacture story-writing machines. It is an American invention; and, like Americans, the couple bustle about the ramshackle little town.

The satire is too gross, the newcomers too outlandish. Comedy fails, and the writer's fictional world collapses, for the reasons that Jagan's world collapses: they have both been damaged by the intrusion of alien elements. Shock follows shock. The boy fusses about the absence of a telephone, rides about on a scooter (Jagan is content to walk), speaks contemptuously of the sweet shop. It also turns out that he is not married to the woman, who, not being Indian, is already casteless and therefore without a place in Jagan's world. All the rules have been broken; Jagan is lost. Without a vision of the future now, he can only contemplate the sweet rituals of the recent, ordered past: his childhood, his marriage, a pilgrimage to a temple.

He feels that his home has been 'dirtied', and at last he recoils. He barricades himself against the couple; he seeks, with a 'peculiar excitement', to purify himself. He begins to sell his sweets cheaply to the poor and offends the other shopkeepers; he assembles his staff and reads the *Gita* aloud to them. Finally he decides to withdraw to a wilderness away from the town, near a ruined shrine. There, divested of possessions, he will watch a master carver, who is like a 'man from the previous millennium', complete an old, unfinished image of a five-faced goddess, 'the light that illumines the sun itself'.

Before he can withdraw, the Korean girl leaves. Jagan's son, getting nowhere with his business plans, has decided to send her away. And then the son himself is arrested for having a bottle of liquor in his car. Under the prohibition laws he faces two years in jail. For Jagan this is the final blow, not so much the threat of the jail sentence as the news that his son drinks. He weeps; he will of course pay for lawyers for his son; but he is more determined than ever to give up the world. 'A little prison life won't harm anyone,' he says. 'Who are we to get him out or put him in?' And he goes to take the bus out of town, on the way to his jungle retreat.

So, with high virtue, Jagan abandons his son, just as Srinivas, the hero of *Mr Sampath*, 'elated' by his vision of eternity, abandoned his friend. But it was only from the world of commerce and 'nonsense' that Srinivas withdrew. Jagan's flight is not like Srinivas's withdrawal, and is the opposite of the calm renunciation which Hinduism prescribes, when the householder, his duties done, makes way for his successors and turns to a life of meditation. That act of renunciation implies an ordered, continuing world. Chaos has come to Jagan's world; his act is an act of despair; he runs away in tears.

'The entire country went down under the fire and sword of the invader . . . But it always had its rebirth and growth.' This was how, in pre-Independence India, the hero of *Mr Sampath* saw the course of Indian history: rebirth and growth as a cleansing, a recurrent Indian miracle, brought about only by the exercise of self-knowledge. But in independent India rebirth and growth have other meanings and call for another kind of effort. The modern world, after all, cannot be caricatured or conjured away; a pastoral past cannot be re-established.

Bangalore, the capital city of the state which contains Narayan's fictional small town, is also India's scientific capital. In 1961 – when Narayan told me that India would go on – there were perhaps two scientists of distinction at work in Bangalore. Today, I was told, there are twenty. It was at Bangalore that the first Indian space satellite (named, typically, after a medieval Hindu astronomer) was built: more impressive as a scientific achievement, it is said, than the Indian atomic bomb, more revealing of the technological capacity that India has developed since Independence. The dedicated chief secretary of the state, a man of simple origins, sees himself and his family as the products both of Independence and of India's industrial revolution. He is committed to that revolution; the changes it is bringing about, he says, are 'elemental'.

From Bangalore there runs a five-hundred-mile highway through the Deccan plateau to Poona, the industrial town on the edge of the plateau east of Bombay. There are almost no cars on this highway, many bullock carts, many lorries. The lorries are hideously overloaded; their tyres are worn smooth; and the lorries often overturn. But, through all the old pain of rural India, the industrial traffic is constant. Change has indeed come to people like Jagan; their world cannot be made small again.

But what to the administrator is elemental change, and urgently necessary, can also be seen as violation. Narayan is an instinctive, unstudied writer: the lack of balance in *The Vendor of Sweets*, the loss of irony, and the very crudity of the satire on 'modern' civilization speak of the depth of the violation Narayan feels that that civilization – in its Indian aspect – has brought to someone like Jagan. And how fragile that Hindu world turns out to be, after all! From the outside so stable and unyielding, yet liable to crumble at the first assault from within: the self-assertion of a son to whom has come a knowledge of the larger world, another, non-Hindu idea of human possibility, and who is no longer content to be part of the flow, part of the Hindu continuity.

Some of the gestures of rebellion might seem trivial – driving in motor cars, meat-eating, drinking – but to Jagan they are all momentous. Where ritual regulates the will and so much of behaviour is ceremonial, all gestures are important. One gesture of rebellion, as Narayan seems to suggest, brings others in its train, and very quickly they add up to a rejection of the piety and reverences that held the society together, a rejection of *karma*. Such a fragile world, where rebellion is so easy, a mere abandoning of ritual! It is as though the Hindu equilibrium required a world as small and as restricting as that of Narayan's early novels, where men could never grow, talked much and did little, and were fundamentally obedient, content to be ruled in all things by others. As soon as that world expands, it shatters.

*The Vendor of Sweets*, which is so elegiac and simplistic, exalting purity and old virtue in the figure of Jagan, is a confused book; and its confusion holds much of the Indian confusion today. Jagan – unlike the hero of *Mr Sampath* in pre-Independence India – really has no case. His code does not bear examination.

Everything rests on his Gandhianism. Jagan, as we are often reminded, was a Gandhian 'volunteer' and freedom fighter in his time; and once, during a demonstration, he allowed himself to be beaten unconscious by the police. It was the genius of Gandhi: intuiting just where the Hindu virtues of quietism and religious self-cherishing could be converted into selfless action of overwhelming political force. Jagan, allowing himself to be beaten, finding in the violence offered him a confirmation of his own virtue, saw himself as a *satyagrahi*, 'fighting for the truth against the British'. The stress was on the fight for the truth rather than the fight against the British. Jagan's was a holy war; he had a vision of his country cleansed and purified rather than a political vision of his country remade.

Jagan won his war. Now, blinded by this victory to his own worldly corruption (the corruption that, multiplied a million times, has taken his country in Independence to another kind of political collapse), his Gandhian impulses decayed to self-cherishing, faddism, and social indifference, Jagan seeks only to maintain the stability of his world; he is capable of nothing else. To be pure in the midst of 'the grime of this earth', secure in the midst of distress: that is all he asks. When his world shatters, he cannot fight back; he has nothing to offer. He can only run away. Another Hindu retreat – like the Vijayanagar kingdom in 1336, like the pilgrims worshipping among the ruins of the Vijayanagar capital in 1975, like the *mantra* being chanted and written fifty million times to give life to the new image of the temple defiled during the last war.

Jagan's is the ultimate Hindu retreat, because it is a retreat from a world that is known to have broken down at last. It is a retreat, literally, to a wilderness where 'the edge of reality itself was beginning to blur': not a return to a purer Aryan past, as Jagan might imagine, but a retreat from civilization and creativity, from rebirth and growth, to magic and incantation, a retrogression to an almost African night, the enduring primitivism of a place like the Congo, where, even after the slave-trading Arabs and the Belgians, the past is yearned for as *le bon vieux temps de nos ancêtres*. It is the death of a civilization, the final corruption of Hinduism.

## 2

With the Emergency, there was a 'clean-up'. And it was on this, rather than the political crisis, that the censored press concentrated.

The former Maharani of Jaipur was then in jail, charged with economic offences and apparently without the prospect of a quick trial. The houses of the once ruling family of Gwalior were being searched for undeclared treasure. In Bombay the flats of government officials, bank officials, and businessmen – flats the newspapers described as 'posh' – were being raided, their contents assessed. Somewhere else – a touch of Hollywood India – an opium-fed cobra was found guarding (ineffectually) a four-kilogram hoard of gold and gold ornaments. Everywhere rackets were being 'busted': foreign-exchange dealings, smuggling, black-marketing, the acquiring of steel by bogus manufacturing units, scarce railway wagons shunted on to sidings and used as storage for hoarded commodities.

Panic was general, but not everyone lost his head. One New Delhi businessman (with a brother already raided), when told by his chauffeur that he was next on the list, handed over all his valuables for safekeeping to the chauffeur, who then vanished. Day by day the censored press carried communiqués about searches, arrests, suspensions, and compulsory retirements. By the third week of August, fifteen hundred smugglers alone were said to have been picked up. At this inauspicious time an expensive new jewellery shop opened in the Oberoi-Sheraton Hotel in Bombay, to big advertisements in the newspapers. Almost immediately, and as though they had been waiting for the place to open first, the authorities sealed the doors.

It was an arbitrary terror, reaching out to high and low: the divisional engineer forging issue vouchers and selling off the stores of a steel plant, the sales-tax inspector accepting a five-hundred-rupee bribe, fifty dollars, from a small businessman, the railway servant carrying rice 'illegally' in a dining car, the postman suspected of opening a foreign packet. And for the moment, after the unrest and drift of the preceding years, it brought peace to India.

But it was only terror, and it came confused with a political crisis everyone knew about. It established no new moral frame for the society; it held out no promise for a better-regulated future. It reinforced, if anything, the always desperate Hindu sense of the self, the sense of encircling external threat, the need to hide and hoard. In the high Hindu ideal of self-realization – which could take so many forms, even that of worldly corruption – there was no idea of a contract between man and man. It was Hinduism's great flaw, after a thousand years of defeat and withdrawal. And now the society had broken down. It was of that, really, that the press spoke, rather than of a clean-up, or of an Emergency, a passing crisis, which it was in the power of Mrs Gandhi or the opposition to resolve.

The Emergency, whatever its immediate political promptings, only made formal a state of breakdown that had existed for some time; it needed more than a political resolution. In 1975 the constitution was suspended; but already, in 1974, India had appeared to stall, with civil-disobedience campaigns, strikes, and student disturbances. The political issues were real, but they obscured the bigger crisis. The corruption of which the opposition spoke and indiscipline of which the rulers spoke were both aspects of a moral chaos, and this could be traced back to the beginning, to Independence.

Hindu society, which Gandhi had appeared to ennoble during the struggle for Independence, had begun to disintegrate with the rebirth and growth that had come with Independence. One journalist said that the trouble – he called it the betrayal – had started the day after Independence, when Mr Nehru, as prime minister, had moved into the former British commander-in-chief's house in New Delhi. But the trouble lay more with the nature of the movement that had brought Mr Nehru to power, the movement to which Gandhi, by something like magic, had given a mass base. A multitude of Jagans, nationalist but committed only to a holy war, had brought the country Independence. A multitude of Jagans, new to responsibility but with no idea of the state – businessmen, money-hoarding but always pious; politicians, Gandhi-capped and Gandhi-garbed – had worked to undo that Independence. Now the Jagans had begun to be rejected, and India was discovering that it had ceased to be Gandhian.

It was hardly surprising: Gandhian India had been very swiftly created. In just eleven years, between 1919 (when the first Gandhian agitation in Madras had ended with a distribution of sweets in a temple) and 1930 (when the Salt March ended with squads of disciplined volunteers offering themselves, in group after group, to sickening police blows), Gandhi had given India a new idea of itself, and also given the world a new idea of India. In those eleven years nonviolence had been made to appear an ancient, many-sided Indian truth, an eternal source of Hindu action. Now of Gandhianism there remained only the emblems and the energy; and the energy had turned malignant. India needed a new code, but it had none. There were no longer any rules; and India – so often invaded, conquered, plundered, with a quarter of its population always in the serfdom of untouchability, people without a country, only with masters – was discovering again that it was cruel and horribly violent.

In a speech before the Emergency, Jaya Prakash Narayan, the most respected opposition leader, said: 'It is not the existence of disputes and quarrels that so much endangers the integrity of the nation as the manner in which we conduct them. We often behave like animals. Be it a village feud, a students' organization, a labour dispute, a religious procession, a boundary disagreement, or a major political question, we are more likely than not to become aggressive, wild, and violent. We kill and burn and loot and sometimes commit even worse crimes.'

The violence of the riot could burn itself out; it could be controlled, as it now was, by the provisions of the Emergency. But there was an older, deeper Indian violence. This violence had remained untouched by foreign rule and had survived Gandhi. It had become part of the Hindu social order, and there was a stage at which it became invisible, disappearing in the general distress. But now, with the Emergency, the emphasis was on reform, and on the 'weaker sections' of society; and the stories the censored newspapers played up seemed at times to come from another age. A boy seized by a village moneylender for an unpaid debt of 150 rupees, fifteen dollars, and used as a slave for four years; in September, in Vellore in the south, untouchables forced to leave their village after their huts had been fenced in by caste Hindus and their well polluted; in October, in a village in Gujarat in the west, a campaign of terror against untouchables rebelling against forced labour and the plundering of their crops; the custom, among the untouchable men of a northern district, of selling their wives to Delhi brothels to pay off small debts to their caste landlords.

To the ancient Aryans the untouchables were 'walking carrion'. Gandhi – like other reformers before him – sought to make them part of the holy Hindu system. He called them *Harijans*, children of God. A remarkable linguistic coincidence: they have remained God's chillun. Even at the Satyagraha Ashram on the river bank at Ahmedabad, which Gandhi himself founded after his return from South Africa, and from where in 1930 he started on the great Salt March. *Son et Lumière* at night these days in the ashram, sponsored by the Tourism Development Corporation; and in the mornings, in one of the buildings, a school for Harijan girls. 'Backward class, backward class,' the old brahmin, suddenly my guide, explained piously, converting the girls into distant objects of awe. The antique violence remained: rural untouchability as serfdom, maintained by terror and sometimes by deliberate starvation. None of this was new: but suddenly in India it was news.

Mr Nehru had once observed that a danger in India was that poverty might be deified. Gandhianism had had that effect. The Mahatma's simplicity had appeared to make poverty holy, the basis of all truth, and a unique Indian possession. And so, for twenty years after Independence, it had more or less remained. It was Mrs Gandhi, in 1971, who had made poverty a political issue. Her slogan in the election that year had been *Garibi Hatao*, Remove Poverty. Her opponents then, fighting another kind of war, had only replied *Indira Hatao*, Remove Indira. But India had since moved fast. There was now competition in protest. And as a cause for protest the holy poverty of India was all at once seen to be inexhaustible. There seemed always another, lower level of distress.

The government now, committed by the Emergency to radical reform, decreed the quashing of certain kinds of rural debts. Two or three hundred of the moneylenders who had been terrorizing the colliers of the Dhanbad coal-fields in Bihar were arrested. And, twenty-eight years after Independence, bonded labour was declared illegal. Bonded labour! In thirteen years I had made three visits to India and had in all spent sixteen months there. I had visited villages in many parts of the country, but I had never heard of bonded labour. An editorial in the *Deccan Herald* of Bangalore suggested why: 'The system is as old as life itself . . . In the country itself, the practice of slavery had attained [such] a sophistication that the victims themselves were made to feel a moral obligation to remain in slavery.' *Karma!*

With Independence and growth, chaos and a loss of faith, India was awakening to its distress and the cruelties that had always lain below its apparent stability, its capacity simply for going on. Not everyone now was content simply to have his being. The old equilibrium had gone, and at the moment all was chaos. But out of this chaos, out of the crumbling of the old Hindu system, and the spirit of rejection, India was learning new ways of seeing and feeling.

## 3

An exponent of the 'new morality' of post-Gandhian India is the playwright Vijay Tendulkar. He writes in Marathi, the language of the region around Bombay, but he is translated into other languages. When I was there, an 'Indian English' version of his play *The Vultures* was being put on in Bombay. The title says it all: for Tendulkar industrial or industrializing India, bringing economic opportunity to small men (in the play, a family of petty contractors) releasing instincts that poverty had suppressed, undoing old pieties, has become a land of vultures.

It is the theme of *The Vendor of Sweets* again: the end of reverences, the end of the family, individuals striking out on their own, social chaos. But Tendulkar is more violent than Narayan; his India is a crueller, more recognizable place. And though

Tendulkar is Hindu enough to suggest, like Narayan, that the loss of one kind of restraint quickly leads to the unravelling of the whole system, and purity is possible only to the man who holds himself aloof, for Tendulkar there is no pure past, and religion can provide no retreat. Tendulkar, for all his brutality, is a romantic: in *The Vultures* the man who holds himself aloof is a poet, an illegitimate son, an outsider.

Tendulkar's India is clearly the same country as Narayan's. But it is a country to which change has come. The world has opened out, and men have become more various and individualistic; the will rages. Sensibility has been modified. India is less mysterious: Tendulkar's discoveries are like those that might be made elsewhere.

The hero of *Sakharam Binder* – Tendulkar's most popular play, which got him into trouble with the censors in 1972, long before the Emergency, and later ran simultaneously in four languages in four Bombay theatres – is a working man of low caste who has rejected all faith, all ties of community and family. Sakharam stands alone. His material security is the technical skill which gives him his second name: he is a binder in a printing shop. He will not marry (it isn't said, but he will be able to marry only within his caste, and so continue to be categorized and branded); instead, he lives with other men's discarded wives, whom he rescues from temples or the streets (a glimpse, there, of the Indian abyss). Sakharam is not tender or especially gifted; all he insists on being is a man, when he has closed the door on the outside world and is in his own two rooms. Hinduism, in him, has been reduced to a belief in honesty and a rejection of all shaming action. In the end he is destroyed; but he has been presented as heroic.

With Sakharam we have come far from the simple rebellion of Jagan's son in *The Vendor of Sweets*, which could be satirized as un-Indian and a mimicry of Western manners. Sakharam's rebellion goes deeper, is immediately comprehensible, and it is entirely of India. India, coming late to situations that have been lived through elsewhere, becomes less mysterious.

Some time ago Tendulkar was awarded a Nehru Fellowship, and this has enabled him to travel about India, getting material for a book on violence in India. It was news of this project – at first so startling, and then so obvious and right – that made me want to see him. I put him in his late forties, one generation younger than Narayan. He was paunchy and surprisingly placid. But the placidity was deceptive: his mother had died a few days before our meeting, and the censors had just blocked a film for which he had written the script. He said his travels about India followed no set plan; he simply, now and then, followed his nose. He had been investigating the Naxalite peasant movement, which had sought to bring about land reforms by force, had degenerated in some places into rural terrorism, and had been very quickly crushed by the government. He had been to the Telengana district in the south, and to Bihar and West Bengal in the northeast.

Bihar had depressed Tendulkar especially. He had seen things there that he had never believed existed. But he didn't speak more precisely: it was as though he still felt humiliated by what he had seen. He said only, 'The human relationships. They're so horrible because they are accepted by the victims.' New words, new concerns: and still, even for a writer like Tendulkar, the discovery of India could be like the discovery of a foreign country. He said he had travelled about Bihar by boat, down the Ganges. And it was of the serenity that came to him on this river, sacred to Hindus, that he spoke, rather than of the horrors on the bank.

So it was still there, and perhaps always would be, in the pain of India: the yearning for calm, the area of retreat. But men cannot easily unlearn new modes of feeling. Retreat is no longer possible. Even the ashrams and the holy men (with their executive jets, their international followings, and their public-relations men) are no longer what they were.

'You must go to that ashram near Poona,' the Parsi lady, back for a holiday from Europe, said at lunch one day in Bombay. 'They say you get a nice mix of East and West there.'

The young man who had been described to me as a 'minor magnate' said with unexpected passion: 'It's a terrible place. It's full of American women who go there to debauch.'

There was a risen-dough quality about the magnate's face and physique which hinted at a man given to solitary sexual excitations. He said he was 'one of the last, decaying capitalists'; he liked 'fleshly comforts'. Ashram life wasn't for him: it was possible to make money more easily in India than in any other country, barring the Arab sheikdoms. 'Sometimes at night I think about giving it all up. And then in the morning, when I think about speculations and manipulations, I wonder, what's the use of it all? Why stop?'

It was only half a joke. There are times now when India appears able to parody the old idea of itself.

Parody; and sometimes unconscious mimicry. In September this letter was featured in, of all places, the *Economic Times* of New Delhi:

> Man doesn't realize his real purpose on earth so long as he rolls in comforts . . . It's absolutely true that adversity teaches a man a bitter lesson, toughens his fibre and moulds his character. In other words, an altogether new man is born out of adversity which helpfully destroys one's ego and makes one humble and selfless . . . Prolonged suffering opens the eyes to hate the things for which one craved before unduly, leading eventually even to a state of resignation. It then dawns on us that continued yearning brings us intense agony . . . But the stoic mind is least perturbed by the vicissitudes of life. It's well within our efforts to conquer grief. It's simple. Develop an attitude of detachment even while remaining in the thick of terrestrial pleasures.

In a financial newspaper! But India is India; and the letter seems at first quite Indian, a statement of the Hindu-Buddhist ideal of nonattachment. But the writer has got there by a tortured Western route. Much of his language is borrowed; and his attitude isn't as Hindu or Buddhist as it seems. The image of the smiling Buddha is well known. He has the bump of developed consciousness on his head, the very long ears of comprehension, the folds of wisdom down his neck. But these iconographic distortions do not take away from his humanity. His lips are full, his cheeks round, and he has a double chin. His senses haven't atrophied (the Buddha tried and rejected the ascetic way); he is at peace with the senses. The possession of the senses is part of his serenity, part of his wholeness, and the very basis of the continuing appeal of this image after two thousand years. It isn't nonattachment like this that the letter-writer proposes, but something quite different, more Western: stoicism, resignation, with more than a touch of bitterness: a consumer's lament.

'"Why do you blame the country for everything? It has been good enough for four hundred millions," Jagan said, remembering the heritage of *Ramayana* and *Bhagavad Gita* and all the trials and sufferings he had undergone to win independence.'

This outburst is from *The Vendor of Sweets*. And for too long this self-satisfaction – expressed in varying ways, and most usually in meaningless exhortations to return to the true religion, and laments for Gandhianism: mechanical turns of the prayer wheel – has passed in India for thought. But Gandhianism has had its great day; and the simple assertion of Indian antiquity won't do now. The heritage is there, and will always be India's; but it can be seen now to belong to the past, to be part of the classical world. And the heritage has oppressed: Hinduism hasn't been good enough for the millions. It has exposed us to a thousand years of defeat and stagnation. It has given men no idea of a contract with other men, no idea of the state. It has enslaved one quarter of the population and always left the whole fragmented and vulnerable. Its philosophy of withdrawal has diminished men intellectually and not equipped them to respond to challenge; it has stifled growth. So that again and again in India history has repeated itself: vulnerability, defeat, withdrawal. And there are not four hundred millions now, but something nearer seven hundred.

The unregarded millions have multiplied and now, flooding into the cities, cannot be denied. The illegal hutments in which they live are knocked down; but they rise again, a daily tide wrack on the margin of cities and beside the railway lines and the industrial highways. It was this new nearness of the millions, this unknown India on the move, together with the triviality of Indian thought on most subjects– the intellectual deficiencies of the archaic civilization finally revealed during this Emergency, India stalled, unable to see its way ahead, to absorb and render creative the changes it has at last generated – it was this great uncertainty, this sense of elemental movement from below, and an almost superstitious dread of this land of impressive, unfinished ruins, that made the professional man say in Delhi: 'It's terrible to see your life's work turning to ashes.' And his wife said, 'For the middle classes, for people who live like us, it's all over. We have a sense of doom.'

# PART TWO

## A New Claim on the Land

# 3
# THE SKYSCRAPERS AND THE CHAWLS

## I

It is said that every day 1500 more people, about 350 families, arrive in Bombay to live. They come mainly from the countryside and they have very little; and in Bombay there isn't room for them. There is hardly room for the people already there. The older apartment blocks are full; the new skyscrapers are full; the small, low huts of the squatters' settlements on the airport road are packed tightly together. Bombay shows its overcrowding. It is built on an island, and its development has been haphazard. Outside the defence area at the southern tip of the island, open spaces are few; cramped living quarters and the heat drive people out into such public areas as exist, usually the streets; so that to be in Bombay is always to be in a crowd. By day the streets are clogged; at night the pavements are full of sleepers.

From late afternoon until dinnertime, on the ground floor of the Taj Mahal Hotel, which now extends over a city block, the middle class and the stylish (but hardly rich, and certainly not as rich as the foreign tourists) promenade past the hotel shops and restaurants in the mild, air-conditioned air: an elegant, sheltered bustle, separated by the hotel carport, the fierce Sikh or Gurkha doormen, the road and the parked cars, from the denser swirl of the white-clad crowd around the Gateway of India, the air moist, the polluted Arabian Sea slapping against the stone steps, the rats below the Gateway not furtive, mingling easily with the crowd, and at nightfall as playful as baby rabbits.

Sometimes, on festive days, stripped divers, small and bony, sit or stand on the sea wall, waiting to be asked to dive into the oily water. Sometimes there is a little band – Indian drums, Western trumpets – attached to some private religious ceremony. Night deepens; the ships' lights in the harbour grow brighter; the Taj Mahal lobby glitters behind its glass wall. The white crowd – with the occasional red or green or yellow of a sari – melts away; and then around the Gateway and the hotel only the sleepers and the beggars remain, enough at any time for a quick crowd, in this area where hotels and dimly lit apartment buildings and stores and offices and small factories press against one another, and where the warm air, despite the sea, always feel overbreathed.

The poor are needed as hands, as labour; but the city was not built to accommodate them. One report says that 100,000 people sleep on the pavements of Bombay; but this figure seems low. And the beggars: are there only 20,000 in Bombay, as one newspaper article says, or are there 70,000, the figure given on another day?

Whatever the number, it is now felt that there are too many. The very idea of beggary, precious to Hindus as religious theatre, a demonstration of the workings of *karma*, a reminder of one's duty to oneself and one's future lives, has been devalued. And the Bombay beggar, displaying his unusual mutilations (inflicted in childhood by the beggar-master who had acquired him, as proof of the young beggar's sins in a previous life), now finds, unfairly, that he provokes annoyance rather than awe. The beggars themselves, forgetting their Hindu function, also pester tourists; and the tourists misinterpret the whole business, seeing in the beggary of the few the beggary of all. The beggars have become a nuisance and a disgrace. By becoming too numerous they have lost their place in the Hindu system and have no claim on anyone.

The poet in Vijay Tendulkar's 1972 play *The Vultures* rebukes his tender-hearted sister-in-law for bringing him tea 'on the sly, like alms to a beggar'. And she replies, hurt, 'There wasn't any shortage of beggars at our door that I should bring it as alms to you.' But already that ritualistic attitude to beggary seems to belong to a calmer world. There is talk in Bombay of rounding up all the beggars, of impounding them, expelling them, dumping them out of sight somewhere, keeping them out. There is more: there is talk among high and low of declaring the city closed, of issuing work permits, of keeping out new arrivals. Bombay, like all the other big Indian cities, has at last begun to feel itself under siege.

The talk of work permits and barriers at the city boundaries is impractical and is known to be impractical. It is only an expression of frenzy and helplessness: the poor already possess, and corrupt, the city. The Indian-Victorian-Gothic city with its inherited British public buildings and institutions – the Gymkhana with its wide veranda and spacious cricket ground, the London-style leather-chaired Ripon Club for elderly Parsi gentlemen (a portrait of Queen Victoria as a youngish Widow of Windsor still hanging in the secretary's office) – the city was not built for the poor, the millions. But a glance at the city map shows that there was a time when they were invited in.

In the centre of the island on which Bombay is built there is a large area marked 'MILLS MILLS MILLS' and '*chawls chawls chawls*'. The mills needed, and need, workers; and the workers live or are accommodated in these chawls. These textile mills – many of them now with antiquated machinery – should have been moved long ago. Bombay might then have been allowed to breathe. But the readily available crowds of the mill area serve every kind of commercial and political interest; and the mills will stay.

Some time ago there was talk of a 'twin city' on the mainland, to draw industry and people out of Bombay. The plan fell through. Instead, at the southern tip of the island, on expensively reclaimed land, there sprang up a monstrous development of residential skyscrapers: unimaginative walls of concrete in an unlandscaped desert with, already, on the unmade roads the huts and stalls of the poor, sucked in by the new development. 'Here you are . . . QUEEN FOR YOUR STAY', says the most recent *Bombay Handbook*, published by the American Women's Association, 'Your dream of having servants is about to come true.' There isn't accommodation for the poor; but they are always needed, and forever called in, even now.

So, though every day more corrupted by its poor, Bombay, with the metropolitan glamour of its skyscrapers, appears to boom, and at night especially, from the sea road, is dramatic: towers of light around the central nightmare of the mill area.

The main roads there are wide, wet-black and clean in the middle from traffic, earth-coloured at the edges where pavement life flows over on to the road, as it does even on a relaxed Sunday morning, before the true heat and glare, and before the traffic builds up and the hot air turns gritty from the brown smoke of the double-decker buses: already a feeling of the crowd, of busy slender legs, of an immense human stirring behind the tattered commercial façades one sees and in the back streets one doesn't see, people coming out into the open, seeking space.

The area seems at first to be one that has gone down in the world. The commercial buildings are large and have style; but, for all the Indian ornamentation of their façades – the rising sun, the Indo-Aryan swastika for good luck, the Sanskrit character *Om* for holiness – these buildings were built to be what they are, to serve the population they serve. Like the chawls themselves, which in some streets can look like the solid town mansions of a less nervous time, but are newer than they look, many built in the 1930s and 1940s, and built even at that late date as chawls, substandard accommodation for factory labour, one room per family, the urban equivalent of plantation barracks or 'ranges', the equivalent, in twentieth-century Bombay, of early industrial England's back-to-back workers' terraces.

The chawl blocks are four or five stories high, and the plan is the same on each floor: single rooms opening on to a central corridor, at the back of which are lavatories and 'facilities'. Indian families ramify, and there might be eight people in a room; and 'corners' might be rented out, as in Dostoevsky's St Petersburg, or floor space; or people might sleep in shifts. A chawl room is only a base; chawl life is lived in the open, in the areas between chawls, on the pavements, in the streets. An equivalent crowd in a colder climate might be less oppressive, might be more dispersed and shut away. But this Bombay crowd never quite disperses.

The chawls, however, are provided with facilities. To be an inhabitant of a chawl is to be established. But in the nooks and crannies of this area there is – as always in India – yet another, lower human level, where the people for whom there is no room have made room for themselves. They have founded squatters' settlements, colonies of the dispossessed. And, like the chawl dwellers, they have done more: within the past ten years, out of bits and pieces of a past simplified to legend, and out of the crumbling Hindu system, they have evolved what is in effect a new religion, and they have declared themselves affiliated to an 'army', the Shiv Sena, the army of Shiva. Not Shiva the god, but Shivaji the seventeenth-century Maratha guerrilla leader, who challenged the Mughal empire and made the Marathas, the people of the Bombay region, a power in India for a century.

The power of the Marathas was mainly destructive, part of the eighteenth-century Indian chaos that gave Britain an easy empire. But in Bombay the matter is beyond discussion. Shivaji is now deified; he is the unlikely warrior god of the chawls. His cult, as expressed in the Shiv Sena, transmutes a dream of martial glory into a feeling of belonging, gives the unaccommodated some idea of human possibility. And, through the Shiv Sena, it has brought a kind of power. The newly erected equestrian statue that stands outside the Taj Mahal Hotel and looks past the Gateway of India to the sea is of Shivaji. It is an emblem of the power of the Sena, the power of the chawls and pavements and squatters' colonies, the inhabitants of the streets who – until the declaration of the Emergency – had begun to rule the streets. All shop signs in

Bombay, if not in two languages now, carry transliterations in the Indian *nagari* script of their English names or styles. That happened overnight, when the Sena gave the word; and the Sena's word was more effective than any government decree.

The Sena 'army' is xenophobic. It says that Maharashtra, the land of the Marathas, is for the Maharashtrians. It has won a concession from the government that eighty per cent of jobs shall be held by Maharashtrians. The government feels that anyone who has lived in Bombay or Maharashtra for fifteen years ought to be considered a Maharashtrian. But the Sena says no: a Maharashtrian is someone born of Maharashtrian parents. Because of its xenophobia, its persecution in its early days of South Indian settlers in Bombay, and because of the theatricality of its leader, a failed cartoonist who is said to admire Hitler, the Sena is often described as 'fascist'.

But this is an easy, imported word. The Shiv Sena has its own Indian antecedents. In this part of India, in the early, pre-Gandhi days of the Independence movement, there was a cult of Shivaji. After Independence, among the untouchables, there were mass conversions to Buddhism. The assertion of pride, a contracting out, a regrouping: it is the pattern of such movements among the dispossessed or humiliated.

The Shiv Sena, as it is today, is of India, independent India, and it is of industrial Bombay. The Sena, like other recent movements in India, though more positive than most – infinitely more positive, for instance, than the Anand Marg. The Way of Peace, now banned, which preached caste, Hindu spirituality, and power through violence, all of this mingled with ritual murder and mutilation and with homosexuality (desirable recruits were sometimes persuaded that they had been girls in previous lives) – the Sena is a great contracting out, not from India, but from a Hindu system, which, in the conditions of today, in the conditions of industrial Bombay, has at last been felt to be inadequate. It is in part a reworking of the Hindu system. Men do not accept chaos; they ceaselessly seek to remake their world; they reach out for such ideas as are accessible and fit their need.

We were going that Sunday morning to a squatters' settlement in the chawl area. We got out of the car at a certain stage, and continued by bus. I was lucky in my guide. He was a rare man in India, much more than the engineer he was by profession. His technical skills went with the graces of an old civilization, with a philosophical turn of mind, a clear-sighted and never sentimental concern about the condition of his country, a wholehearted and un-Indian acceptance of men as men.

But he was an engineer, and practical: he offered no visions of Bombay remade, of the chawls and shanty towns pulled down and the workers acceptably rehoused. India simply didn't have the resources. Its urban future had already arrived, and was there, in the shanty towns, in those spontaneous communities. All that authority could add were services, ameliorative regulation, security. The shanty towns might, in effect, be planned. It was only in this way that the urban poor could be accommodated. But the idea that the poor should be accommodated at all was not yet fully accepted in Bombay. A plan to give the poor thirty-square-yard building plots in the projected twin city had run into opposition from middle-class people who had objected on social grounds – they didn't want the poor too near – and on moral grounds – the poor would sell the plots *at a profit* and, after this immorality of profit, live where they had always lived, in the streets.

The engineer was a Bombay man, but not a man of Maharashtra, and therefore hardly a supporter of the Shiv Sena. It was his interest in housing for the urban poor that had sent him to live for a week or so among the squatters of the mill area, queuing up with them every morning to get his water and to use the latrines. He had discovered a number of simple but important things. Communal washing areas were necessary: women spent a lot of time washing clothes (perhaps because they had so few). Private latrines were impossible; communal latrines (which might be provided by the municipality) would bring about an immediate improvement in sanitation, though children might always have to use the open.

But the most important discovery was the extent and nature of the Shiv Sena's control. A squatters' settlement, a low huddle of mud and tin and tile and old boards, might suggest a random drift of human debris in a vacant city space; but the chances now were that it would be tightly organized. The settlement in which the engineer had stayed, and where we were going that morning, was full of Sena 'committees', and these committees were dedicated as much to municipal self-regulation as to the Sena's politics: industrial workers beginning to apply something of the discipline of the factory floor to the areas where they lived.

The middle-class leadership of the Sena might talk of martial glory and dream of political power. But at this lower and more desperate level the Sena had become something else: a yearning for community, an ideal of self-help, men rejecting rejection. 'I love the municipal life.' Gandhi had said that in the early days; but municipal self-discipline was one of those Gandhian themes that India hadn't been able to relate to religion or the Independence movement, and hadn't therefore required. It was the Sena now that had, as it were, ritualized the municipal need, which Independence, the industrial revolution, and the pressures of population had made urgent.

The bus stopped, and we were just outside the settlement. It was built on a small, rocky hill above a cemetery, which was green with the monsoon; in the distance were the white skyscrapers of southern Bombay. The narrow entrance lane was flanked by latrine blocks and washing sheds. The latrine blocks were doorless, with a central white-tiled runnel on the concrete floor. They were new, the engineer said: the local Shiv Sena municipal councillor had clearly been getting things done. In one of the washing sheds children were bathing; in the other, women and girls were washing clothes.

The entrance lane was deliberately narrow, to keep out carts and cars. And, within, space was suddenly scarce. The structures were low, very low, little doors opening into tiny, dark, single rooms, every other structure apparently a shop, sometimes a glimpse of someone on a string bed on the earth floor. Men and their needs had shrunk. But the lane was paved, with concrete gutters on either side; without that paving – which was also new – the lane, twisting down the hillside, would have remained an excremental ravine. And the lane and the gutters this Sunday morning looked clean. Much depended, the engineer said, on the 'zeal' of the municipal sweeper. Caste here! The pariahs of the pariahs: yet another, lower human level, hidden away somewhere!

There were eight Shiv Sena committee rooms in the settlement. The one we went to was on the main lane. It was a stuffy little shed with a corrugated-iron roof; but the floor, which the engineer remembered as being of earth, was now of concrete; and the walls, formerly of plain brick, had been plastered and whitewashed. There was one portrait. And, interestingly, it was not of the leader of the Shiv Sena or of Shivaji, the Sena's warrior god, but of the long-dead Dr Ambedkar, the Maharashtrian untouchable leader, law minister in the first government of independent India, the framer of India's now suspended constitution. Popular – and near-ecstatic – movements like the Shiv Sena ritualize many different needs. The Sena here, honouring an angry and (for all his eminence) defeated man, seemed quite different from the Sena the newspapers wrote about.

The members of the committee were all young, in their twenties. The older people, they said, were not interested, and had to be forgotten. But more noticeable, and more moving, than the youth of the committee members was their physical size. They were all so small; their average height was about five feet. Generations of undernourishment had whittled away bodies and muscle (though one man, perhaps from the nature of his manual work, had fairly well-developed arm and back muscles).

The leader was coarse-featured and dark, almost black. He worked in Air India as a technician, and he was in his Sunday clothes. His grey trousers were nicely creased, and a white shirt in a synthetic material shone over the beginnings of a little paunch of respectability. After greeting us he immediately in the Indian way offered hospitality, whispering to an aide about 'cola'. And presently – no doubt from one of the little shops – two warm bottles of the cola came. There was more whispering, and a little later two tumblers decorated with red arabesques appeared, snatched perhaps from somebody's room.

It was a chemically treated substance, the cola, calling for analysis rather than consumption. But consumption was not required. The first sip had completed the formalities; and soon we were out, walking up the lanes, understanding the Lilliputian completeness of the settlement (even a hand-operated printing machine in one of the shacks, turning out cinema handbills), every now and then coming out into the open, at the edge of the hillside, looking down at the roofs of rusting tin or red Mangalore clay tiles we had left below, beside the graveyard, and looking across to the remote skyscrapers, getting paler in the increasing heat.

The technician, the committee leader, had been living in Bombay for fifteen years and in the squatters' settlement for twelve. He had come as a boy from the countryside and had at first stayed with someone whom he knew; and that only meant, though he didn't say, that he might have had floor space in somebody's room. He had found a small job somewhere and had gone to night school and 'matriculated'. Getting into Air India afterwards as an office boy had been his big break. That airline is the least bureaucratized of Indian organizations: the ambitious office boy had been encouraged to become a technical apprentice.

This almost Victorian tale of self-help and success unfolded as we walked. But self-help of this sort was possible only in the industrial city, whatever its horrors. The technician, if he had stayed behind in his village, might have been nothing, without caste or skill or land, an occasional day labourer, perhaps bound to a master. Now, Air India and the Shiv Sena between them gave him energy and purpose. He said he had no personal ambitions; he wasn't planning to move out of the settlement. And he added, with the first touch of rhetoric, but perhaps also with truth, that he wanted to 'serve the people'. Look, here was something we should notice: the committees had placed dustbins in the lanes. And he lifted a lid or two to show that the dustbins were being used.

But the shanty town was a shanty town. Dustbins were only dustbins; the latrine blocks and the washing sheds were now not near. The twisting lanes continued, shutting out air, concentrating heat, and the small hillside, its Lilliputian novelty vanished, began to feel like a vast wasps' nest of little dark rooms, often no more than boxes, often with just a bed on the earth floor, sometimes with little black runnels of filth between the rooms, occasional enfeebled rats struggling up the gutters, slimy where steep, scum quickly forming around impediments of garbage.

It was Sunday, the technician said: the municipal sweepers hadn't been. Again! Sweepers, the lowest of the low: their very existence, and their acceptance of their function, the especial curse of India, reinforcing the Indian conviction, even here, and in spite of the portrait of Dr Ambedkar in the committee room now far below, that it was unclean to clean, and leading to the horrors we were about to come upon.

There were eight committees, and it had at first seemed too many for that small settlement. But eight were apparently not enough. There were some sections of the settlement where for various reasons – perhaps internal political reasons, perhaps a clash of personalities, or perhaps simply an absence of concerned young men – there were as yet no committees. Through these sections we walked without speaking, picking our way between squirts and butts and twists of human excrement. It was unclean to clean; it was unclean even to notice. It was the business of the sweepers to remove excrement, and until the sweepers came, people were content to live in the midst of their own excrement.

Every open space was a latrine; and in one such space we came, suddenly, upon a hellish vision. Two starved Bombay street cows had been tethered there, churning up human excrement with their own; and now, out of this bog, they were being pulled away by two starved women, to neighbourhood shouts, the encouraging shouts of a crowd gathering around this scene of isolated, feeble frenzy, theatre in the round on an excremental stage, the frightened cows and frantic starveling women (naked skin and bone below their disordered, tainted saris) sinking with every step and tug. The keeping of cows was illegal here, and an inspector of some sort was reported to be coming. A recurring drama: the cows – illegal, but the only livelihood of the women who kept them – had often to be hidden; and they were going to be hidden now, if they could be got away in time, in the rooms where the women lived.

The lane twisted; the scene was left behind. We were going down the other side of the hill now, and were soon in an area where a committee ruled. We passed through an open space, a little square. The committees were determined to keep these open areas, the technician said; but that required vigilance. A squatter's hut could go up overnight, and it was hard then – since all the huts were illegal – to have just that one pulled down. Once, when the technician was out of the settlement for only three days, a small open area had been built over. They had petitioned to have the new structure pulled down; but the offender had pleaded with the committees, and in the end, for compassionate reasons, they had allowed the structure to stand.

We were now back where we had started, at the foot of the hill, at the entrance, with the washing sheds full of women and girls, and the latrine blocks full of children: slum life from the outside, from the wide main road, but, approached from the other side, like a scene of pastoral, and evidence of what was possible.

The Sena men walked with us to the bus stop. From there the hill, variously roofed, and seemingly roofed all the way down, looked small again. The settlement was full, the technician said. They admitted no newcomers now. Sometimes, but rarely, someone left, and his hut could then be sold to an outsider. The current price would be about four thousand rupees, four hundred dollars. That was high, but the area was central and the settlement was provided with services.

The noon sun hurt; the empty Sunday road shimmered. The bus seemed a long time coming; but at last, trailing a hot brown fog, it came, a red Bombay double-decker, the lower part of its metal sides oily and dust-blown, with deep horizontal scratches, and oddly battered, like foil that had been crumpled and smoothed out.

Back through the chawls then, our red bus mingling with more and more of its fuming fellows, the main roads black and the pavements alive, the cinema posters offering fantasies of plump women and snowy Himalayan peaks, the cluttered, sunlit façades of commercial buildings hung with many brilliant signboards, past the mills and the chimneys, along the fast city highways with the more metropolitan advertisements ('butter at its buttermost') to the skyscrapers and the sea: the Bombay of the white towers, seen from that hillside, which already seemed far away.

## 2

At dinner that evening – high up in one of those towers – a journalist, speaking frenetically of many things (he was unwilling to write while the censorship lasted, and it all came out in talk), touched the subject of identity. 'Indian' was a word that was now without a meaning, he said. He himself – he was in his thirties, of the post-Independence generation – no longer knew what he was; he no longer knew the Hindu gods. His grandmother, visiting Khajuraho or some other famous temple, would immediately be in tune with what she saw; she wouldn't need to be told about the significance of the carvings. He was like a tourist; he saw only an architectural monument. He had lost the key to a whole world of belief and feeling, and was cut off from his past.

At first, and especially after my excursion of the morning, this talk of identity seemed fanciful and narcissistic. Bombay, after all, was Bombay; every man knew how and why he had got there and where he had come from. But then I felt I had misjudged the journalist. He was not speaking fancifully; his passion was real.

Once upon a time, the journalist said, cutting through the dinner-table cross-talk – one woman, apropos of nothing, mentioning Flaubert only to dismiss him as a writer of no importance; a dazed advertising man, young but nicely bellied, coming to life to wonder, also apropos of nothing, whether the temperate delights of Kashmir couldn't be 'sold' to the sun-parched Arabs of the Persian Gulf – once upon a time, the journalist said, the Indian village was self-sufficient and well ordered. The bull drew the plough and the cow gave milk and the manure of these animals enriched the fields, and the stalks of the abundant harvest fed the animals and thatched the village huts. That was the good time. But self-sufficiency hadn't lasted, because after a while there were too many people. 'It isn't an easy thing to say,' the journalist said, 'but this is where kindness to the individual can be cruelty to the race.'

It explained his frenzy. His idea of India was one in which India couldn't be accommodated. It was an idea of India which, for all its seeming largeness, only answered a personal need: the need, in spite of the mess of India, to be Indian, to belong to an established country with an established past. And the journalist was insecure. As an Indian he was not yet secure enough to think of Indian identity as something dynamic, something that could incorporate the millions on the move, the corrupters of the cities.

For the journalist – though he was an economist and had travelled, and was professionally concerned with development and change – Indian identity was not something developing or changing but something fixed, an idealization of his own background, the past he felt he had just lost. Identity was related to a set of beliefs and rituals, a knowledge of the gods, a code, an entire civilization. The loss of the past meant the loss of that civilization, the loss of a fundamental idea of India, and the loss therefore, to a nationalist-minded man, of a motive for action. It was part of the feeling of purposelessness of which many Indians spoke, part of the longing for Gandhian days, when the idea of India was real and seemed full of promise, and the 'moral issues' clear.

But it was a middle-class burden, the burden of those whose nationalism – after the years of subjection – required them to have an idea of India. Lower down, in the chawls and the squatters' settlements of the city, among the dispossessed, needs were more elemental: food, shelter, water, a latrine. Identity there was no problem; it was a discovery. Identity was what the young men of the Sena were reaching out to, with the simplicities of their politics and their hero figures (the seventeenth-century Shivaji, warrior chieftain turned to war god, the twentieth-century Dr Ambedkar, untouchable now only in his sanctity). For the Sena men, and the people they led, the world was new; they saw themselves at the beginning of things: unaccommodated men making a claim on their land for the first time, and out of chaos evolving their own philosophy of community and self-help. For them the past was dead; they had left it behind in the villages.

And every day, in the city, their numbers grew. Every day they came from the villages, this unknown, unacknowledged India, though Bombay was full and many squatters' settlements, like the one on the hill above the graveyard, had been declared closed.

# 4
# THE HOUSE OF GRAIN

## I

THE ENGINEER WHO had introduced me to the squatters' settlement in Bombay was also working on a cooperative irrigation scheme up on the Deccan plateau, some miles southeast of Poona. In India, where nearly everything waits for the government, a private scheme like this, started by farmers on their own, was new and encouraging; and one week I went with the engineer to look.

I joined him at Poona, travelling there from Bombay by the early morning train, the businessman's train, known as the Deccan Queen. There was no air-conditioned carriage; but on this rainy monsoon morning there was no Indian dust to keep out. Few of the ceiling fans were on; and it was soon necessary to slide down the aluminium framed window against the chill. Rain and mist over the mainland sprawl of Greater Bombay; swamp and fresh green grass in a land apparently returning to wilderness; occasional factory chimneys and scattered apartment blocks black and seeming to rot with damp; the shanty towns beside the railway sodden, mud walls and grey thatch seemingly about to melt into the mud and brown puddles of unpaved lanes, the naked electric bulbs of tea stalls alone promising a kind of morning cheer.

But then Bombay faded. And swamp was swamp until the land became broken and, in the hollows, patches of swamp were dammed into irregular little ricefields. The land became bare and rose in smooth rounded hills to the plateau, black boulders showing through the thin covering of monsoon green, the fine grass that grows within three days of the first rain and gives these stony and treeless *ghats* the appearance of temperate parkland.

It doesn't show from the train, but the Bombay-Poona region is one of the most industrialized in India. Poona, at the top of the *ghats*, on the edge of the plateau, is still the military town it was in the British days and in the days of the Maratha glory before that, still the green and leafy holiday town for people who want to get away from the humidity of the Bombay coastland. But it is also, and not at all oppressively, an expanding industrial centre. Ordered industrial estates spread over what, just thirteen years ago, when I first saw it, was arid waste land. On these estates there has been some re-afforestation; and it is said that the rainfall has improved.

The plateau around Poona is now in parts like a new country, a new continent. It provides uncluttered space, and space is what the factory-builders and the machine-makers say they need; they say they are building for the twenty-first century. Their confidence, in the general doubt, is staggering. But it is so in India: the doers are always enthusiastic. And industrial India is a world away from the India of bureaucrats and journalists and theoreticians. The men who make and use machines – and the Indian industrial revolution is increasingly Indian: more and more of the machines are made in India – glory in their new skills. Industry in India is not what industry is said to be in other parts of the world. It has its horrors; but, in spite of Gandhi, it does not – in the context of India – dehumanize. An industrial job in India is more than just a job. Men handling new machines, exercising technical skills that to them are new, can also discover themselves as men, as individuals.

They are the lucky few. Not many can be rescued from the nullity of the labour of pre-industrial India, where there are so many hands and so few tools, where a single task can be split into minute portions and labour can turn to absurdity. The street-sweeper in Jaipur City uses his fingers alone to lift dust from the street into his cart (the dust blowing away in the process, returning to the street). The woman brushing the causeway of the great dam in Rajasthan before the top layer of concrete is put on uses a tiny strip of rag held between her thumb and middle finger. Veiled, squatting, almost motionless, but present, earning her half-rupee, her five cents, she does with her finger dabs in a day what a child can do with a single push of a long-handled broom. She is not expected to do more; she is hardly a person. Old India requires few tools, few skills, and many hands.

And old India lay not far from the glitter of new Poona. The wide highway wound through the soft, monsoon-green land. Bangalore was five hundred miles to the south; but the village where we were going was only a few hours away. The land there was less green, more yellow and brown, showing its rockiness. The monsoon had been prolonged, but the water had run off into lakes. It was from one such lake that water was to be lifted and pumped up to the fields. The water pipe was to be buried four feet in the ground, not to hamper cultivation of the land when it was irrigated, and to lessen evaporation. Already, early in the morning, the heat of the day still to come – and even in this season of rain, the sky full of clouds, the distant hills cool and blue above the grey lake – heat waves were rising off the rocks.

The nationalized agricultural bank had loaned the farmers ninety per cent of the cost of the project. Ten per cent the farmers had to pay themselves, in the form of labour; and the engineer had computed that labour at a hundred feet of pipe trench per farmer. The line of the trench had already been marked; and in the middle of what looked like waste land, the rocks baking in spite of the stiff wind, in the middle of a vast view dipping down to the lake, a farmer with his wife and son was digging his section of the trench.

The man was small and slightly built. He was troubled by his chest and obviously weary. He managed the pickaxe with difficulty; it didn't go deep, and he often stopped to rest. His wife, in a short green sari, squatted on the stony ground, as though offering encouragement by her presence; from time to time, but not often, she pulled out with a mattock those stones the man had loosened; and the white-capped boy stood by the woman, doing nothing. Like a painting by Millet of solitary brute labour, but in an emptier and less fruitful land.

A picture of the pain of old India, it might have seemed. But it contained so much that was new: the local agricultural enthusiast who by his example had encouraged the farmers to think of irrigation and better crops, the idea of self-help that was behind the cooperative, the bank that had advanced the money, the engineer with the social conscience who had thought the small scheme worth his while and every week made the long journey from Bombay to superintend, advise, and listen. It wasn't easy to get qualified men to come out from the city and stay with the project, the engineer said; he had had to recruit and train local assistants.

The digging of the trench had begun the week before. To mark the occasion, they had planted a tree, not far from a temple – three hundred years old, the villagers said – on the top of a hill of rock. The pillars of the temple portico were roughly hewn; the three-domed lantern roof was built up with heavy, roughly dressed slabs of stone. On this plateau of rock the buildings were of stone. Stone was the material people handled with instinctive, casual skill; and the village looked settled and solid and many times built over. In the barrenness of the plateau it was like a living historical site. Old, even ancient architectural conventions – like the lantern roof of the temple – mingled with the new, unrelated fragments of old decorated stone could be seen in walls.

Four lanes met in the irregularly shaped main square. A temple filled each of two corners: and, slightly to one side in the open space of the square, there was a tree on a circular stone-walled platform. People waiting for the morning bus – luxury! – sat or squatted on the wall below the tree, and on the stone steps that edged the open raised forecourt of one temple. On this forecourt there was a single pillar, obviously old, with a number of bracket-like projections, like a cactus in stone. It was a common feature of temples in Maharashtra, but people here knew as little about its significance as they did elsewhere. Someone said the brackets were for lights; someone else said they were pigeon perches. The pillar simply went with the temple; it was part of the past, inexplicable but necessary.

The post office was of the present: an ochre-coloured shed, with a large official board with plain red lettering. On another side of the square a smaller, gaudier signboard hung over a dark little doorway. This was the village restaurant, and the engineer's assistants said it was no longer to be recommended. The restaurateur, anxious to extend his food-and-drink business, had taken to supplying some people in the village with water. People too poor to pay in cash paid in *chapattis*, unleavened bread; and it was these *chapattis* – the debt-cancellers of the very poor, and more stone than bread – that the restaurateur, ambitious but shortsighted, was now offering with his set meals. He had as a result lost the twice-daily custom of all the engineer's assistants. They had begun to cook for themselves in a downstairs room of the irrigation-project office. And a certain amount of unspoken ill-will now bounced back and forth across the peaceable little square, with every now and then, on either side, the smoke signals of independence and disdain.

The bus came and picked up its passengers, and the dust settled again. At eleven, rather late in the morning, as it seemed, the schoolchildren appeared, the boys in khaki trousers and white shirts, barefooted but with white Gandhi caps, the girls in white blouses and long green skirts. The school was the two-storied *panchayat* or village-council building in one of the lanes off the square, beyond the other temple, which had a wide, smooth, stone-floored veranda, the wooden pillars of the veranda roof resting on carved stone bases. Everywhere there was carving; everywhere doorways were carved. Outside every door hung a basket or pot of earth in which the *tulsi* or basil grew, sacred to Hindus.

Even without the irrigation scheme, improved agriculture had brought money to this village. Many houses were being renovated or improved. A new roof of red Mangalore clay tiles in a terraced lane announced a brand-new building. It was a miniature, very narrow, with just two rooms, one at the front and one at the back, with shelves and arched niches set in the thick stone walls. A miniature, but the roof had required a thousand tiles, at one rupee per tile: a thousand rupees, a hundred dollars for the roof alone. But that was precisely the fabled sum another man, just a short walk away, had spent on the carved wooden door of his new house, which was much bigger and half built already, the stone walls already rising about the inset shelves of new wood, the beautifully cut and pointed stone of the doorway showing off the wooden door, already hung: wood, in this land of stone, being especially valuable, and carving, the making of patterns, even in this land of drought and famine, still considered indispensable.

The engineer had remained behind in his office. My guide was now the sarpanch, the chairman of the village *panchayat* or council; and he, understanding that I was interested in houses, began to lead the way to his own house.

He was a plump man, the sarpanch, noticeably unwashed and unshaved; but his hair was well oiled. He was chewing a full red mouthful of betel nut and he wore correctly grubby clothes, a dingy long-tailed cream-coloured shirt hanging out over dingier green-striped pyjamas, slackly knotted. The grubbiness was studied, and it was correct because any attempt at greater elegance would have been not only unnecessary and wasteful but also impious, a provocation of the gods who had so far played fair with the sarpanch and wouldn't have cared to see their man getting above himself.

In the village it was accepted that the sarpanch was blessed: he was distrusted, feared, and envied as a prospering racketeer. Some years before, he had collected money for a cooperative irrigation scheme. That money had simply vanished; and there was nothing that anybody could do about it. Since then the sarpanch's power had if anything increased; and people had to be friendly with him, like the dusty little group scrambling after him now. To anyone who could read the signs, the sarpanch's power showed. It showed in that very full mouth of betel nut that made it difficult for him to speak without a gritty spray of red spittle. It showed in his paunch, which was as it were shaded in appropriate places by an extra griminess on his shirt. The long-tailed shirt, the pyjama bottom: the seraglio style of dress proclaimed the sarpanch a man of leisure, or at any rate a man unconnected with physical labour. He was in fact a shopkeeper; and his shop stood next to his house.

From the lane the two establishments did not appear connected. The shop was small, its little front room and its goods quite exposed. The house, much wider, was blank-fronted, with a low, narrow doorway in the middle. Within was a central courtyard surrounded by a wide, raised, covered veranda. At the back, off the veranda, and always shaded from the sun, were the private rooms. It was surprising, after the dust and featurelessness of the lane: this ordered domestic courtyard, the dramatization of a small space, the sense of antiquity and completeness, of a building perfectly conceived.

It was an ancient style of house, common to many old civilizations; and here – apart from the tiles of the roof and the timber of the veranda pillars – it had been rendered all in stone. The design had been arrived at through the centuries; there was nothing now that could be added. No detail was unconsidered. The veranda floor, its stone flags polished by use, sloped slightly toward the courtyard, so that water could run off easily. At the edge of the courtyard there were metal rings for tethering animals (though it seemed that the sarpanch had none). In one corner of the courtyard was the water container, a clay jar set in a solid square of masonry, an arrangement that recalled the tavern counters of Pompeii. Every necessary thing had its place.

A side passage led to a smaller, paved courtyard. This was at the back of the shop, which, according to a notice painted in English on the inside wall, was mortgaged – 'hypothecated' was the word used, and it seemed very fierce in the setting – to a bank. And then we were back in the lane.

A man of property, then, a man used to dealing with banks, and, as chairman of the village council, a politician and a kind of official: I thought the sarpanch must be the most important man in the village. But there was a grander: the Patel. The sarpanch was a shopkeeper, a money man; the Patel was a landowner, the biggest landowner in the village. He owned fifty good acres; and though he didn't own people, the fate of whole families depended on the Patel. And to these people he was, literally, the Master.

To the house of the Patel, then, we went, by sudden public demand, as it seemed, and in equally sudden procession. The engineer was with us again, and there was a crowd, swamping the group around the sarpanch, who now, as we walked, appeared to hang back. Perhaps the Patel was in the crowd. It was hard to say. In the rush there had been no introductions, and among the elderly turbaned men, all looking like peasants, men connected with the work of the land, no one particularly stood out.

The house was indeed the grandest in the village. It was on two floors, and painted. Bright paint coloured the two peacocks carved over the doorway. The blank front wall was thick. Within that wall (as in some of the houses in Pompeii) stone steps led to the upper storey, a gallery repeating the raised veranda around the courtyard at ground level. The floor was of beaten earth, plastered with a mixture of mud and cow dung. To the left as we entered, on the raised veranda, almost a platform, were two pieces of furniture: a bed with an old striped bedspread embroidered with the name of the village in *nagari* characters, and a new sofa of 'contemporary' design with naked wooden legs and a covering in a shiny blue synthetic fabric: the Western-style sofa, sitting in the traditional house just like that and making its intended effect, a symbol of wealth and modernity, like the fluorescent light tube above the entrance.

That part of the veranda with the bed and sofa was for receiving visitors. Visitors did not go beyond this to the courtyard unless they were invited to do so. On the raised veranda to the right of the entrance there was no furniture, only four full sacks of grain, an older and truer symbol of wealth in this land of rock and drought. It was a house of plenty, a house of grain. Grain was spread out to dry in the sunlit courtyard; and in the open rooms on either side were wickerwork silos of grain, silos that looked like enormous baskets, as tall as a man, the wickerwork plastered to keep out rats, and plastered, like the floor, with mud and cow dung.

Invited to look around, received now as guests rather than official visitors, we walked past the grain drying in the courtyard to the kitchen at the back. The roof sloped low; after the sunlight of the courtyard it was dark. To the left a woman was making curds, standing over the high clay jar and using one of the earliest tools made by civilized man: a cord double-wound around a pole and pulled on each end in turn: the carpenter's drill of ancient Egypt, and also the very churning tool depicted in those eighteenth-century miniatures from the far north of India that deal with the frolics of the dark god Krishna among the pale milkmaids. In the kitchen gloom to the right a *chulha* or earthen fireplace glowed: to me romantic, but the engineer said that a simple hinged opening in the roof would get rid of the smoke and spare the women's eyes.

Our visit wasn't expected, but the kitchen was as clean and ordered as though for inspection. Brass and silver and metal vessels glittered on one shelf; tins were neatly ranged on the shelf below that. And – another sign of modernity, of the new age – from a nail on the wall a transistor radio hung by its strap.

The woman or girl at the fireplace rose, fair, well mannered in the Indian way, and brought her palms together. She was the Patel's daughter-in-law. And the Patel (still remaining unknown) was too grand to boast of her attainments. That he could leave to the others, his admirers and hangers-on. And the others did pass on the news about the daughter-in-law of this wealthy man. She was a graduate! Though lost and modest in the gloom of the kitchen, stooping over the fire and the smoke, she was a graduate!

The back door of the kitchen opened onto the back yard; and we were in the bright sun again, in the dust, at the edge of the village, the rocky land stretching away. As so often in India, order, even fussiness, had ended with the house itself. The back yard was heaped with this and that, and scattered about with bits and pieces of household things that had been thrown out but not quite abandoned. But even here there were things to show. Just a few steps from the back door was a well, the Patel's own, high-walled, with a newly concreted base, and with a length of rope hanging from a weighted pole, a trimmed and peeled tree branch. A rich man indeed, this Patel, to have his own well! No need for him to buy water from the restaurant man and waste grain on *chapattis* no one wanted. And the Patel had something else no one in the village had: an outhouse, a latrine! There it was, a safe distance away. No need for him or any member of his family to crouch in the open! It was like extravagance, and we stood and marvelled.

We re-entered the house of grain and food and graduate daughter-in-law – still at her fireplace – and walked back, around the drying grain in the courtyard, to the front vestibule. We went up the steps set in the front wall to the upper storey. It was being refloored: interwoven wooden strips laid on the rafters, mud on that, and on the mud thin slabs of stone, so that the floor, where finished, though apparently of stone, was springy.

Little low doors led to a narrow balcony where, in the centre, in what was like a recessed shrine, were stone busts, brightly painted, of the Patel's parents. This was really what, as guests, we had been brought up to the unfinished top floor to see. The *nagari* inscription below the busts said that the house was the house of the Patel's mother. The village honoured the Patel as a rich man and a Master; he made himself worthy of that reverence, he avoided hubris, and at the same time he made the reverence itself more secure, by passing it backward, as it were, to his ancestors. We all stood before the busts – bright paint flattening the features to caricature – and looked. It was all that was required; by looking we paid homage.

Even now I wasn't sure who, among the elderly men with us, was the Patel. So many people seemed to speak for him, to glory in his glory. As we were going down again, I asked the engineer. 'What is the value of this house? Is that a good question to ask?' He said, 'It is a very good question to ask.' He asked for me. It was a question only the Patel himself could answer.

And the Patel, going down the steps, revealed himself, and his quality, by evading the question. If, he said, speaking over his shoulder, the upper flooring was completed in the way it had been begun – the wood, the mud plaster, the stone slabs – then the cost of that alone would be sixty thousand rupees, six thousand dollars. And then, downstairs, seating us, his guests, on the visitors' platform, on the blue-covered modern sofa and the bed with the embroidered bedspread, he seemed to forget the rest of the question.

Tea was ordered, and it came almost at once. The graduate daughter-in-law in the kitchen at the back knew her duties. It was tea brewed in the Indian way, sugar and tea leaves and water and milk boiled together into a thick stew, hot and sweet. The tea, in chipped china cups, came first for the chief guests. We drank with considered speed, held out our cups to surrender them – the Patel now, calm in his role as host, detaching himself from his zealous attendants – and presently the cups reappeared, washed and full of the milky tea for the lesser men.

And the Patel sat below us, in the vestibule, looking like so many of the villagers, a slight, wrinkled man in a peasant-style turban, a dhoti and koortah and brown woollen scarf, all slightly dingy, but mainly from dust and sweat, and not as studiedly grimed as the sarpanch's shirt and slack pyjama bottom. But as he sat there, no longer unknown but a man who had established his worth, our host, the provider of tea (still being slurped at and sighed over), the possessor of this house (was he boasting about the cost of the new floor?), his personality became clearer. The small, twinkly eyes that might at first, in that wrinkled head, have seemed only peasant's eyes, always about to register respect and obsequiousness combined with disbelief, could be seen now to be the eyes of a man used to exercising a special kind of authority, an authority that to him and the people around him was more real, and less phantasmal, than the authority of outsiders from the city. His face was the face of the Master, the man who knew men, and whole families, as servants, from their birth to their death.

He said, talking about the great cost of the new floor (and still evading the question about the value of the house), that he didn't believe in borrowing. Other people believed in borrowing, but he didn't. He did things only when he had the money to do them. If he made money one year, then there were certain things he felt he could do. That had been his principle all his life; that was how he intended to do the new floor, year by year and piece by piece. And yet he – like the sarpanch, and perhaps to a greater degree than the sarpanch – was almost certainly a moneylender. Many of the people I had seen that morning would have been in debt to the Patel. And in these villages interest rates were so high, ten per cent or more a month, that debts, once contracted, could never be repaid. Debt was a fact of life in these villages; interest was a form of tribute.

But it was also true that when the Patel spoke about borrowing he was not being insincere. The occasion was special. We were outsiders; he had done us the honours of his house; and now, in public audience, as it were, he was delivering himself of his proven wisdom. This was the wisdom that lifted him above his fellows; and this was the wisdom that his attendants were acknowledging with beatific smiles and slow, affirmative swings of the head, even while accepting that what was for the Patel couldn't be for them.

Now that we were on the subject of money, and the high cost of things these days, we spoke about electricity. There was that fluorescent tube, slightly askew and in a tangle of cord, in the vestibule: it couldn't be missed. The government had brought electricity to the village five years before, the Patel said; and he thought that forty per cent of the village now had electricity. It was interesting that he too had adopted the official habit of speaking in percentages rather than in old-fashioned numbers. But the figure he gave seemed high, because the connection charge was 275 rupees, over twenty-seven dollars, twice a labourer's monthly wage, and electricity was as expensive as in London.

Electricity wasn't for the poor. But electricity hadn't been brought across the plateau just to light the villages. Its primary purpose was to develop agriculture; without electricity the irrigation scheme wouldn't have been possible. Electricity mattered mainly to the people with land to work. As lighting it was still only a toy. So it was even in the Patel's house. The fluorescent tube in the vestibule, far from the kitchen and the inner rooms off the veranda, was the only electrical fitting in the house. There were still oil lamps about and they were evidently in daily use.

The fluorescent tube, like the shining blue sofa for visitors, was only a garnish, a modern extra. Sixty per cent of the village was without electricity, and village life as a whole still took its rhythm from the even length of the tropical day. Twelve hours of darkness followed twelve hours of light; people rose at dawn and retired at dusk; every day, as from time immemorial, darkness fell on the village like a kind of stultification.

The village had had so little, had been left to itself for so long. After two decades of effort and investment simple things had arrived, but were still superfluous to daily life, answered no established needs. Electric light, ready water, an outhouse: the Patel was the only man in the village to possess them all, and only the water would have been considered strictly necessary. Everything else was still half for show, proof of the Patel's position, the extraordinariness which yet, fearing the gods, he took care to hide in his person, in the drabness and anonymity of his peasant appearance.

It was necessary to be in the village, to see the Patel and his attendants, to understand the nature of the power of that simple man, to see how easily such a man could, if he wished, frustrate the talk from Delhi about minimum wages, the abolition of untouchability, the abolition of rural indebtedness. How could the laws be enforced? Who would be the policeman in the village? The Patel was more than the biggest landowner. In that village where needs were still so basic, the Patel, with his house of grain, ruled; and he ruled by custom and consent. In his authority, which in his piety he extended backward to his ancestors, there was almost the weight of religion.

The irrigation scheme was a cooperative project. But the village was not a community of peasant farmers. It was divided into people who had land and people who hadn't; and the people who had land were divided into those who were Masters and those who weren't. The Patel was the greatest Master in the village. The landless labourers he employed (out somewhere in his fields now) were his servants; many had been born his servants. He acknowledged certain obligations to them. He would lend them money so that they could marry off their daughters with appropriate ceremony; in times of distress they knew that they could turn to him; in times of famine they knew they had a claim on the grain in his house. Their debts would wind around them and never end, and would be passed on to their children. But to have a Master was to be in some way secure. To be untied was to run the risk of being lost.

And the Patel was progressive. He was a good farmer. It was improved farming (and the absence of tax on agricultural income) that had made him a rich man. And he welcomed new ways. Not everyone in his position was like that. There were villages, the engineer said later, when we were on the highway again, which couldn't be included in the irrigation scheme because the big landowners there didn't like the idea of a lot of people making more money. The Patel wasn't like that, and the engineer was careful not to cross him. The engineer knew that he could do nothing in the village without the cooperation of the Patel. As an engineer, he was to help to increase food production; and he kept his ideas about debt and servants and bonded labour to himself.

The countryside was ruled by a network of men like the Patel. They were linked to one another by caste and marriage. The Patel's daughter-in-law – who might not have been absolutely a graduate: she had perhaps simply gone for a few years to a secondary school – would have come from a family like the Patel's in another village. She would have exchanged one big house of grain for another; in spite of her traditional kitchen duties, she would be conscious of her connections. Development had touched people unequally. To some it had given a glimpse of a new world; others it had bound more fast in the old. Development had increased the wealth, and the traditional authority, of the Patel; it had widened the gap between the landed and the landless. Backed up by people like the sarpanch, minor politicians, minor officials, courted by administrators and the bigger politicians, men like the Patel now controlled; and nothing could be done without them. In the villages they had become the law.

From the *Times of India*, 2 September 1975:

> The Maharashtra chief minister, Mr S.B. Chavan, admitted on Monday that he was aware of big landlords in the rural areas using the local police to drive poor peasants off their land, particularly during the harvest season. Seemingly legal procedures were being used by the police and the landlords to accomplish this purpose, he added.

On the way back to Poona we stopped at the temple of Zezuri, like a Mughal fort, high up on a black hill. Mutilated beggar children – one girl with flesh recently scooped out of a leg – were hurried out to the lower steps and arranged in postures of supplication. Garish little shrines stained saffron and red, and their patient keepers, all the way up to the temple; archway after archway, eighteenth-century ornamented stucco crumbling over brick; bracketed pillars of varying size and age; on the stone steps, the worn carved inscriptions in various scripts of generations of pilgrims. At the top, on the windy parapet, a view through the Mughal arches of the town's two tanks or reservoirs (one collapsed and empty) and the monsoon-green plateau in a clouded sunset.

But the rain that had greened the plateau had also, the next morning, made the outskirts of Poona messy: a line of transport-office shacks and motor-repair shops in yards turned to mud. The busy Poona-Bombay road, badly made, was rutted and broken. In time, going down from the plateau, we came to the smooth, rounded green hills, like parkland, over which rain and shifting mist ceaselessly played: during the monsoon months a holiday landscape to people from the coast, at other times scorched and barren, barely providing pasture for animals. At Lonavala, where we broke our journey, a buffalo herdsman sang in the rain. We heard his song before we saw him, on a hill, driving his animals before him. He was half naked and carried an open black umbrella. When the rain slanted and he held the umbrella at his side, it was hard to tell him from his buffaloes.

But the land, though bare, offering nothing or very little, was never empty. All the way from Poona – except in certain defence areas – it was dotted with sodden little clusters of African-like huts: the encampments of people in flight from the villages, people who had been squeezed out and had nowhere else to go, except here, near the highway, close to the towns, exchanging nullity for nullity: people fleeing not only from landlessness but also from tyranny, the rule in a thousand villages of men like the Patel and the sarpanch.

## 2

In some parts of central and northwestern India, men squeezed out or humiliated can take to the ravines and gullies and become dacoits, outlaws, brigands. Whole criminal communities are formed. They are hunted down, and sometimes a district-police communiqué gets into the Indian press ('Anti-Dacoit Operation Pays Big Dividends': *Blitz*, 4 October 1975). This is traditional; the dacoit leader and the 'dacoit queen' are almost figures of folklore. But some years ago there was something bigger. Some years ago, in Bengal in the northeast and Andhra in the south, there was a tragic attempt at a revolution.

This was the Naxalite movement. The name comes from Naxalbari, the district in the far north of Bengal where, in 1968, it all began. It wasn't a spontaneous uprising and it wasn't locally led; it was organized by communists from outside. Land was seized and landowners were killed. The shaky, semipopulist government of the state was slow to act; the police might even have been ambivalent; and 'Naxalism' spread, catching fire especially in large areas of Andhra in the south. Then the government acted. The areas of revolt were surrounded and severely policed; and the movement crumbled.

But the movement lasted long enough to engage the sympathies of young people at the universities. Many gave up their studies and became Naxalites, to the despair of their parents. Many were killed; many are still in jail. And now that the movement is dead, it is mainly in cities that people remember it. They do not talk about it often; but when they do, they speak of it as a middle-class – rather than a peasant – tragedy. One man put it high: he said that in the Naxalite movement India had lost the best of a whole generation, the most educated and idealistic of its young people.

In Naxalbari itself nothing shows and little is remembered. Life continues as before in the green, rich-looking countryside that in places – though the Himalayas are not far away – recalls the tropical lushness of the West Indies. The town is the usual Indian country town, ramshackle and dusty, with its little shops and stalls, its overloaded buses, cycle-rickshaws, carts. It is there, in the choked streets, after the well-tilled and well-watered fields, after the sense of space and of the nearness of the cool mountains, that the over-population shows. And yet the land, unusually in India, is not 'old'. It was forest until the last century, when the British established tea plantations or 'gardens' there, and brought in indentured labourers – mainly from far-off aboriginal communities, pre-Aryan people – to work the gardens.

The tea gardens are now Indian-owned, but little has changed. Indian caste attitudes perfectly fit plantation life and the clannishness of the planters' clubs; and the Indian tea men, clubmen now in the midst of the aborigines, have adopted, almost as a sign of caste, and no longer with conscious mimicry, the style of dress of their British predecessors: the shirt, the shorts, and the socks. The tea workers remain illiterate, alcoholic, lost, a medley of tribal people without traditions and now (as in some places in the West Indies) even without a language, still strangers in the land, living not in established villages but (again as in the old plantations of the West Indies) in shacks strung along the estate roads.

There isn't work for everyone. Many are employed only casually; but this possibility of casual labour is enough to keep people tied to the gardens. In the hours of daylight, with panniers on their backs like natural soft carapaces, the employed flit about the level tea bushes, in the shade of tall rain trees (West Indian trees, imported to shade the tea), like a kind of protected wildlife, diligent but timid, sent scuttling by a sudden shower or the factory whistle, but always returning to browse, plucking, plucking at the endless hedging of the tea bushes, gathering in with each nip the two tender leaves and a bud that alone can be fermented and dried into tea. Tea is one of India's most important exports, a steady earner of money; and it might have been expected that the tea workers would have been among the most secure of rural workers. They are among the most depressed and – though the estate people say that they nowadays resent abuse – among the most stultified.

But it wasn't because of the tea workers – that extra level of distress – that the revolutionaries chose Naxalbari. The tea workers were, in fact, left alone. The Naxalbari district was chosen, by men who had read the handbooks of revolution, for its terrain: its remoteness, and the cover provided by its surviving blocks of forest. The movement that began there quickly moved on; it hardly touched the real distress of Naxalbari; and now nothing shows.

The movement is now dead. The reprisals, official and personal, continue. From time to time in the Indian press there is still an item about the killing or capture of 'Naxalites'. But social inquiry is outside the Indian tradition; journalism in India has always been considered a gracious form of clerkship; the Indian press – even before the Emergency and censorship – seldom investigated the speeches or communiqués or bald agency items it printed as news. And that word 'Naxalite', in an Indian newspaper, can now mean anything.

The communists, or that group of communists concerned with the movement, interpret events in their own way; they have their own vocabulary. Occasionally they circulate reports about the 'execution' of 'peasant leaders'. The Naxalite movement – for all its tactical absurdity – was an attempt at Maoist revolution. But was it a 'peasant' movement? Did the revolutionaries succeed in teaching their complex theology to people used to reverencing a Master and used for centuries to the idea of *karma*? Or did they preach something simpler? It was necessary to get men to act violently. Did the revolutionaries then – as a communist journalist told me revolutionaries in India generally should do – preach only the idea of the enemy?

It is the theory of Vijay Tendulkar, the Marathi playwright – who has been investigating this business as someone sympathetic to the Naxalites' stated cause of land reform, as most Indians are sympathetic – it is Tendulkar's theory that Naxalism, as it developed in Bengal, became confused with the Kali cult: Kali, 'the black one', the coal-black aboriginal goddess, surviving in Hinduism as the emblem of female destructiveness, garlanded with human skulls, tongue forever out for fresh blood, eternally sacrificed to but insatiable. Many of the Naxalite killings in Bengal, according to Tendulkar, had a ritualistic quality. Maoism was used only to define the sacrifice. Certain people – not necessarily rich or powerful – might be deemed 'class enemies'. Initiates would then be bound to the cause – of Kali, of Naxalism – by being made to witness the killing of these class enemies and dipping their hands in the blood.

In the early days, when the movement was far away and appeared revolutionary and full of drama, the Calcutta press published gruesome and detailed accounts of the killings: it was in these repetitive accounts that Tendulkar spotted the ritualism of cult murder. But as the movement drew nearer the city, the press took fright and withdrew its interest. It was as an affair of random murder, the initiates now mainly teenagers, that the movement came to Calcutta, became part of the violence of that cruel city, and then withered away. The good cause – in Bengal, at any rate – had been lost long before in the cult of Kali. The initiates had been reduced to despair, their lives spoiled for good; old India had once again depressed men into barbarism.

But the movement's stated aims had stirred the best young men in India. The best left the universities and went far away, to fight for the landless and the oppressed and for justice. They went to a battle they knew little about. They knew the solutions better than they knew the problems, better than they knew the country. India remains so little known to Indians. People just don't have the information. History and social inquiry, and the habits of analysis that go with these disciplines, are too far outside the Indian tradition. Naxalism was an intellectual tragedy, a tragedy of idealism, ignorance, and mimicry: middle-class India, after the Gandhian upheaval, incapable of generating ideas and institutions of its own, needing constantly in the modern world to be inducted into the art, science, and ideas of other civilizations, not always understanding the consequences, and this time borrowing something deadly, somebody else's idea of revolution.

But the alarm has been sounded. The millions are on the move. Both in the cities and in the villages there is an urgent new claim on the land; and any idea of India which does not take this claim into account is worthless. The poor are no longer the occasion for sentiment or holy alms-giving; land reform is no longer a matter for the religious conscience. Just as Gandhi, towards the end of his life, was isolated from the political movement he had made real, so what until now has passed for politics and leadership in independent India has been left behind by the uncontrollable millions.

# PART THREE

## Not Ideas, but Obsessions

# 5
# A DEFECT OF VISION

## I

IN 1888, WHEN he was nineteen, and already married for six years, Gandhi went to England to study law. It was a brave thing to do. Not the English law – which, however alien to a Hindu of 1888, however unconnected with his complicated rites and his practice of magic, could be mugged up, like another series of *mantras* – not the law, but the voyage itself. Hindu India, decaying for centuries, constantly making itself archaic, had closed up; and the rules of Gandhi's Gujarati merchant caste – at one time great travellers – now forbade travel to foreign countries. Foreign countries were polluting to pious Hindus; and no one of the caste had been to England before.

To please his mother, Gandhi had taken vows not to touch wine, meat, or women while abroad. But these vows did not satisfy everybody. One section of the caste formally declared the young man an outcaste. But Gandhi, though timid, was obstinate. For a reason which he never makes clear – he was virtually uneducated, had never even read a newspaper – he passionately wanted to go to England. He began to be afraid that the caste might prevent his going; and, two months earlier than he had planned, he took a ship from Bombay to Southampton.

And this is how, in his autobiography, *The Story of My Experiments with Truth*, written nearly forty years later, when he had become the Mahatma, Gandhi remembers the great adventure (the translation is by his secretary, Mahadev Desai):

> I did not feel at all sea-sick . . . I was innocent of the use of knives and forks . . . I therefore never took meals at table but always had them in my cabin, and they consisted principally of sweets and fruits I had brought with me . . . We entered the Bay of Biscay, but I did not begin to feel the need either of meat or liquor . . . However, we reached Southampton, as far as I remember, on a Saturday. On the boat I had worn a black suit, the white flannel one, which my friends had got me, having been kept especially for wearing when I landed. I had thought that white clothes would suit me better when I stepped ashore, and therefore I did so in white flannels. Those were the last days of September, and I found I was the only person wearing such clothes.

That is the voyage: an internal adventure of anxieties felt and food eaten, with not a word of anything seen or heard that did not directly affect the physical or mental well-being of the writer. The inward concentration is fierce, the self-absorption complete. Southampton is lost in that embarrassment (and rage) about the white flannels. The name of the port is mentioned once, and that is all, as though the name is description enough. That it was late September was important only because it was the wrong time of the year for white flannels; it is not a note about the weather. Though Gandhi spent three years in England, there is nothing in his autobiography about the climate or the seasons, so unlike the heat and monsoon of Gujarat and Bombay; and the next date he is precise about is the date of his departure.

No London building is described, no street, no room, no crowd, no public conveyance. The London of 1890, capital of the world – which must have been overwhelming to a young man from a small Indian town – has to be inferred from Gandhi's continuing internal disturbances, his embarrassments, his religious self-searchings, his attempts at dressing correctly and learning English manners, and, above all, his difficulties and occasional satisfactions about food.

Sir Edwin Arnold, known for his verse translation of the *Gita*, is mentioned, but only mentioned and never described, though Gandhi must have been dazzled by him, and the poet wasted some time as vice-president of a vegetarian club Gandhi started and ran for a short while in Bayswater. There is an entertaining account of a very brief call, with a visiting Indian writer, on Cardinal Manning. But generally English people are far away in Gandhi's London. There is no reference to plays (an account of a visit to an unnamed theatre turns out to be an anecdote about an uneaten dinner). Apart from a sentence about Cardinal Manning and the London dock strike, there is nothing about politics or politicians. The only people who come out of the void and make some faint impression are cranks, Theosophists, proselytizing vegetarians. And though they seem of overwhelming importance (Dr Oldfield, editor of *The Vegetarian*, 'Dr Allinson of vegetarian fame', Mr Howard or Mr Howard Williams, author of *The Ethics of Diet*, Mr Hills, a puritan and 'proprietor of the Thames Iron Works'), they are hardly seen as people or set in interiors. They are only their names, their status (Gandhi is always scrupulous about titles), and their convictions.

And then, quite suddenly, Gandhi is a lawyer; and the adventure of England is over. As anxious as he had been to get to London, so he is now anxious to leave. 'I passed my examinations, was called to the bar on the 10th of June 1891, and enrolled in the High Court on the 11th. On the 12th I sailed for home.'

And yet, curiously, it was again a wish for travel and adventure that two years later sent Gandhi to South Africa. He went on law business and intended to stay for a year. He stayed for twenty years. England had been unsettling only because it hadn't been India. But in England Gandhi had ceased to be a creature of instinct; out of his unsettlement there, and his consequent self-searching, he had decided that he was a vegetarian and a Hindu by conviction.

South Africa offered direct racial hostility; and Gandhi, obstinate as always, was immeasurably fortified as a Hindu and an Indian. It was in South Africa that he became the Mahatma, the great-souled, working through religion to political action as leader of the Indian community, and through political action back to religion. The adventure never ceased to be internal: so it comes out in the autobiography. And this explains the most remarkable omission in Gandhi's account of his twenty active years in South Africa: Africans.

Africans appear only fleetingly at a time of a 'rebellion', when for six weeks Gandhi led an Indian ambulance unit and found himself looking after wounded Africans. He says his heart was with the Africans; he was distressed by the whippings and unnecessary shootings; it was a trial, he says, to have to live with the soldiers responsible. But the experience did not lead him to a political decision about Africans. He turned inward and, at the age of thirty-seven, did what he had been thinking about for six years: he took the Hindu vow of *brahmacharya*, the vow of lifelong sexual abstinence. And the logic was like this: to serve humanity, as he was then serving the Africans, it was necessary for him to deny himself 'the pleasures of family life', to hold himself free in the spirit and the flesh. So the Africans vanish in Gandhi's heart-searchings; they are the motive of a vow, and thereafter disappear.

Far away, at Yasnaya Polyana in Russia, Tolstoy, in the last year of his life, said of Gandhi, whose work he followed and with whom he exchanged letters: 'His Hindu nationalism spoils everything.' It was a fair comment. Gandhi had called his South African commune Tolstoy Farm; but Tolstoy saw more clearly than Gandhi's English and Jewish associates in South Africa, fellow seekers after the truth. Gandhi really had little to offer these people. His experiments and discoveries and vows answered his own need as a Hindu, the need constantly to define and fortify the self in the midst of hostility; they were not of universal application.

Gandhi's self-absorption was part of his strength. Without it he would have done nothing and might even have been destroyed. But with this self-absorption there was, as always, a kind of blindness. In the autobiography South Africa is inevitably more peopled than England, and more variously peopled; there are more events. But the mode of narration is the same. People continue to be only their names and titles, their actions or convictions, their quality of soul; they are never described and never become individuals. There is no attempt at an objective view of the world. As events pile up, the reader begins to be nagged by the absence of the external world; when the reader ceases to share or follow Gandhi's convictions, he can begin to feel choked.

Landscape is never described. I may be proved wrong, but in all the great length of *My Experiments with Truth* I believe there are only three gratuitous references to landscape. In 1893, on the way out to South Africa, Gandhi notices the vegetation of Zanzibar; three years later, returning briefly to India, he lands at Calcutta, 'admiring the beauty' of the Hooghly River. His only important experience of landscape comes at the age of forty-five when, back in India for good, he goes to Hardwar, a place of Hindu pilgrimage in the Himalayas. 'I was charmed with the natural scenery about Hrishikesh and Lakshman Jhula, and bowed my head in reverence to our ancestors for their sense of the beautiful in Nature, and their foresight in investing beautiful manifestations of Nature with a religious significance.'

The outer world matters only in so far as it affects the inner. It is the Indian way of experiencing; what is true of Gandhi's autobiography is true of many other Indian autobiographies, though the self-absorption is usually more sterile. 'I see people having their being': the Indian girl who said that of the Bombay crowds she saw on her return from Europe was trying hard. She was in the Indian tradition; like Gandhi in Southampton in 1888, she couldn't describe what she hadn't been able to take in. In India, as she said, she 'related' only to her family. The vogue word enabled her to boast in a modern-sounding way; but the word also covered up a traditional limitation of vision and response. The deficiency that she was able to convert into boasting is an aspect of what is now being propagated as Hindu wisdom by those holy men who preach 'meditation' and expound the idea of the world as illusion.

Meditation and stillness can be a form of therapy. But it may be that the true Hindu bliss – the losing of the self – is more easily accessible to Hindus. According to Dr Sudhir Kakar, a psychotherapist at Jawaharlal Nehru University in New Delhi, who is himself Indian and has practised both in Europe and in India, the Indian ego is 'underdeveloped', 'the world of magic and animistic ways of thinking lie close to the surface', and the Indian grasp of reality is 'relatively tenuous'. 'Generally among Indians' – Kakar is working on a book, but this is from a letter – 'there seems to be a different relationship to outside reality, compared to one met with in the West. In India it is closer to a certain stage in childhood when outer objects did not have a separate, independent existence but were intimately related to the self and its affective states. They were not something in their own right, but were good or bad, threatening or rewarding, helpful or cruel, all depending on the person's feelings of the moment.'

This underdeveloped ego, according to Kakar, is created by the detailed social organization of Indian life, and fits into that life. 'The mother functions as the external ego of the child for a much longer period than is customary in the West, and many of the ego functions concerned with reality are later transferred from mother to the family and other social institutions.' Caste and clan are more than brotherhoods; they define the individual completely. The individual is never on his own; he is always fundamentally a member of his group, with a complex apparatus of rules, rituals, taboos. Every detail of behaviour is regulated – the bowels to be cleared before breakfast and never after, for instance, the left hand and not the right to be used for intimate sexual contact, and so on. Relationships are codified. And religion and religious practices – 'magic and animistic ways of thinking' – lock everything into place. The need, then, for individual observation and judgement is reduced; something close to a purely instinctive life becomes possible.

The childlike perception of reality that results does not imply childishness – Gandhi proves the opposite. But it does suggest that Indians are immersed in their experiences in a way that Western people can seldom be. It is less easy for Indians to withdraw and analyze. The difference between the Indian and the Western ways of perceiving comes out most clearly in the sex act. Western man can describe the sex act; even at the moment of orgasm he can observe himself. Kakar says that his Indian patients, men and women, do not have this gift, cannot describe the sex act, are capable only of saying, 'It happened.'

While his world holds and he is secure, the Indian is a man simply having his being; and he is surrounded by other people having their being. But when the props of family, clan, and caste go, chaos and blankness come. Gandhi in 1888, not yet nineteen, taking ship at Bombay for Southampton, would have been at sea in every way. It was about Gandhi and Gandhi's account of England that I talked to Kakar when we met in Delhi. Gandhi would have had no means of describing what he saw at Southampton on arrival, Kakar said: Gandhi would have been concentrating too fiercely on the turmoil within him; he would have been fighting too hard to hold on to his idea of who he was. (And Kakar is right: later in the autobiography Gandhi says of his first weekend in England, spent at the Victoria Hotel in London: 'The stay at that hotel had scarcely been a helpful experience for I had not lived there with my wits about me.')

'We Indians,' Kakar says, 'use the outside reality to preserve the continuity of the self amidst an ever changing flux of outer events and things.' Men do not, therefore, actively explore the world; rather, they are defined by it. It is this negative way of perceiving that goes with 'meditation', the striving after the infinite, the bliss of losing the self; it also goes with *karma* and the complex organization of Indian life. Everything locks together; one cannot be isolated from the other. In the Indian set-up, as Kakar says, it is the Western-style 'mature personality', individualistic and assertive, that would be the misfit. Which no doubt explains why, in the ashrams, while Indians appear to flourish in the atmosphere of communal holiness, Western inmates, like the hippies elsewhere in India, tend to look sour and somewhat below par.

In an active, busy country, full of passion and controversy, it is not an easy thing to grasp, this negative way of perceiving. Yet it is fundamental to an understanding of India's intellectual second-rateness, which is generally taken for granted but may be the most startling and depressing fact about the world's second most populous country, which now has little to offer the world except its Gandhian concept of holy poverty and the recurring crooked comedy of its holy men, and which, while asserting the antiquity of its civilization (and usually simply asserting, without knowledge or scholarship), is now dependent in every practical way on other, imperfectly understood civilizations.

A recent remarkable novel, however, takes us closer to the Indian idea of the self, and without too much mystification. The novel is *Samskara*, by U.R. Anantamurti, a forty-four-year-old university teacher. Its theme is a brahmin's loss of identity; and it corroborates much of what Sudhir Kakar says. The novel was originally written in Kannada, a language of South India; its India is not over explained or dressed up or simplified. The novel has now had an India-wide success; it has been made into a prize-winning film; and an English translation (by a poet, A.K. Ramanujan) was serialized over the first three months of 1976 in India's best paper, the *Illustrated Weekly of India*.

The central figure is the Acharya, the spiritual leader of a brotherhood of brahmins. At an early age the Acharya decided that he was a 'man of goodness' – that that was his nature, his *karma*, the thing he was programmed to be by his previous lives. In the Acharya's reasoning, no one can *become* a man of goodness; he is that, or he isn't; and the 'clods', the 'men of darkness', cannot complain, because by their nature they have no desire for salvation anyway. It was in obedience to the 'good' in his nature that, at the age of sixteen, the Acharya married a crippled girl of twelve. It was his act of sacrifice; the crippled girl was his 'sacrificial altar'; and after twenty years the sacrificial act still fills him with pleasure, pride, and compassion. Every day, serving the crippled, ugly woman, even during the pollution of her periods, he gets nearer salvation; and he thinks, 'I get ripe and ready.' He is famous now, this Acharya, for his sacrifice, his goodness, and the religious wisdom brought him by his years of study of the palm-leaf scriptures; he is the 'crest-jewel of the Vedanta', and the Vedanta is the ultimate wisdom.

But among the brahmin brotherhood there is one who has fallen. He drinks; he catches the sacred fish from the tank of a temple; he mixes with Moslems and keeps an untouchable mistress. He cannot be expelled from the brotherhood. Compassion is one reason, compassion being an aspect of the goodness of the Acharya. But there is another reason: the fallen brahmin threatens to become a Moslem if he is expelled, and such a conversion would retrospectively pollute, and thereby break up, the entire brotherhood. This very wicked brahmin now dies of plague, and a crisis ensues. Should the brotherhood perform the final rites? Only brahmins can perform the rites for another brahmin. But can the dead man be considered a brahmin? In his life he abjured brahminhood, but did brahminhood leave him? Can the brotherhood perform the rites without polluting itself? Can another, lower sect of brahmins be made to perform the rites? (They are willing: the request flatters them: their brahmin line got crossed at some time, and they feel it.) But wouldn't that bring the brotherhood into disrepute – having the rites for one of their own performed by a lower group?

These are the problems that are taken to the Acharya, the crest-jewel, the man of goodness. The matter is urgent. The heat is intense, the body is rotting, the vultures are flapping about, there is a danger of the plague spreading. And the brahmins, who are fussy about their food in every way, are getting hungry: they can't eat while the corpse is uncremated.

But the Acharya cannot give a quick answer. He cannot simply consult his heart, his goodness. The question of the status of the dead man – brahmin or not brahmin, member of the brotherhood or outcaste – is not a moral question. It is a matter of pollution; and it is therefore a matter for the laws, the sacred books. The Acharya has to consult the books; no one knows his way about the palm-leaf manuscripts as well as the Acharya. But this consulting of the books takes time. The plague spreads; some untouchables die and are unceremoniously burned in their huts; the brahmins are beside themselves with hunger and anxiety. And the books give the Acharya no answer.

The Acharya understands that his reputation for wisdom is now at stake; in the midst of the crisis he acknowledges this remnant of personal vanity. But a decision has to be made, and it has to be the correct one. The Acharya can only turn to magic. In the morning he goes to the temple of the monkey god and ritually washes down the man-sized idol. He puts one flower on the god's left shoulder and another on the right. And he decides how the god will answer: if the flower on the right shoulder falls first, the brotherhood can perform the rites for the dead man. But the god gives no reply. For the whole of the hot day, while the Acharya prays and anguishes (and his crippled wife becomes infected by the plague), neither flower falls. And, for the first time in his life, the Acharya, the man of goodness, has doubts about himself: perhaps he is not worthy enough to get an answer from the god.

Exhausted, tormented, he leaves the temple in the evening, to go to look after his wife. In the forest he meets the untouchable mistress of the dead man. She expresses her concern for him; she has worshipped the Acharya for his piety, and it has occurred to her that she should have a child by the Acharya. Her breasts touch him, and he is enveloped by the moment; he wakes at midnight imagining himself a child again, in his mother's lap. It cannot be said that he falls or sins. The words are too positive. As with Sudhir Kakar's patients in real life, the sexual moment simply happens. 'It was a sacred moment – nothing before it, nothing after it. A moment that brought into being what never was and then itself went out of being. Formless before, formless after. In between, the embodiment, the moment. Which means I'm absolutely not responsible for making love to her. Not responsible for that moment. But the moment altered me – why?'

The reasoning is strange, but that is now the Acharya's crisis: not guilt, but a sudden neurotic uncertainty about his nature. The earlier crisis has receded: the dead man has been cremated during the night by his mistress, with the help of a Moslem. The Acharya is left with his new anguish. Is he a man of goodness, or has he really all his life belonged to the other, 'tigerish' world? Men are what they are, what they have been made by their previous lives. But how does a man know his true nature, his 'form'?

'We shape ourselves through our choices, bring form and line to this thing we call our person.' But what has been his defining choice – the long life of sacrifice and goodness, or that barely apprehended sexual moment? He doesn't know; he feels only that he has 'lost form' and that his person is now like 'a demonic premature foetus'. He is bound again to the wheel of *karma*; he has to start again from the beginning and make a new decision about his nature. In the meantime he is like a ghost, cut off from the community of men. He has lost God and lost the ways of goodness. 'Like a baby monkey losing hold of his grip on the mother's body as she leaps from branch to branch, he felt he had lost hold and fallen from the rites and actions he had clutched till now.' Because men are not what they make themselves, there is no question here of faith or conviction or ideals or the perfectability of the self. There is only a wish for knowledge of the self, which alone would make possible a return to the Hindu bliss of the instinctive life: 'to be, just to be'.

Formless now, his wife dead from the plague, and with her death his especial act of sacrifice abruptly terminated, the Acharya decides to wander, to let his legs take him where they will. This is really an attempt to test his responses to the world; it might be said that he is trying to define his new form by negatives. What do other people see in him? Does the peasant see the brahmin still? Do other brahmins see the brahmin, or do they see a fraud? At a village fair, is he the man to be tempted by the women acrobats, the pollutions of the soda-pop stall and coffee stall, the lower-caste excitement of the cock-fight? Between the pollution-free brahmin world and this world, the 'world of ordinary pleasures', of darkness, a 'demon world of pressing need, revenge and greed', there is no middle way. All around him are 'purposive eyes. Eyes engaged in things . . . Immersed. The oneness, the monism, of desire and fulfilment.' Men are defined by the world; they are defined by the pollution they can expose themselves to.

The Acharya is terrified; he feels himself being 'transformed from ghost to demon'. But, neurotically, he continues to test himself. His caste sins mount; and he understands that by exposing himself to pollution he has become a polluting thing himself. He comes to a decision. He will return to the brotherhood and confess. He will tell them about his sexual adventure with the dead man's untouchable mistress, his visit to the common fair; he will tell them that, though in a state of pollution (partly because of his wife's death), he ate with brahmins in a temple and invited a man of lower caste to eat with him. He will speak without repentance or sorrow. He will simply be telling them about the truth of his inner self, which by a series of accidents – perhaps not really accidents – he has just discovered.

*Samskara* is a difficult novel, and it may be that not everyone will agree with my reading of it. The translation is not always clear; but many of the Hindu concepts are not easy to render in English. Even so, the narrative is hypnotic; and the brilliance of the writing in the original Kannada can be guessed. Anti-brahmin feeling (and by extension anti-Aryan, anti-northern feeling) is strong in the south; and some readers of the serialization in the *Illustrated*

*Weekly of India* have seen the novel as an attack on brahmins. This is a political simplification; but it shows to what extent Indians are able to accept the premises of the novel that are so difficult for an outsider: caste, pollution, the idea of the *karma*-given self, the anguish at the loss of caste identity.

The author, U.R. Anantamurti, is a serious literary man. He teaches English to postgraduate students at Mysore University, which has a lively English department; and he has also taught in the United States. His academic background seems a world away from the society he describes in the novel; and it is hard to assess his attitude to that society. Knowingly or unknowingly, Anantamurti has portrayed a barbaric civilization, where the books, the laws, are buttressed by magic, and where a too elaborate social organization is unquickened by intellect or creativity or ideas of moral responsibility (except to the self in its climb to salvation). These people are all helpless, disadvantaged, easily unbalanced; the civilization they have inherited has long gone sour; living instinctive lives, crippled by rules ('I didn't try to solve it for myself. I depended on God, on the old lawbooks. Isn't this precisely why we have created the Books?'), they make up a society without a head.

References to buses and newspapers and the Congress Party indicate that the novel is set in modern times. But the age seems remote; and certainly Gandhi doesn't seem to have walked this way. The Acharya's anguish about his true nature, though presented in religious terms, is bound up with the crudest ideas of pollution and caste and power. Brahmins must be brahmins, the Acharya reasons at one stage: otherwise 'righteousness' will not prevail. 'Won't the lower castes get out of hand? In this decadent age, common men follow the right path out of fear – if that were destroyed, where could we find the strength to uphold the world?' It is an aspect of this righteousness that when an untouchable woman begs for a gift of tobacco, the brahmin woman should throw it out into the street, as to a dog. In this way pollution is avoided, and righteousness and fear maintained.

'We Indians use the outer reality to preserve the continuity of the self.' Sudhir Kakar's analysis of Gandhi's stupor in England in 1888 is remarkably like Anantamurti's wonderful description of the Acharya's wanderings in the world. Gandhi is preserving his purity, his idea of the self, in the midst of strangeness. The Acharya is collecting impurities; the account he will present to the brotherhood is not an account of what he has seen, an account of the world he has decided he must enter, but an account of the pollutions he has endured. In both men there is the same limitation of vision and response, the same self-absorption.

But there is an important difference. The Acharya is imprisoned in his dead civilization; he can only define himself within it. He has not, like Gandhi in England, had to work out his faith and decide where – in the wider world – he stands. Gandhi, maturing in alien societies, defensively withdrawing into the self, sinking into his hard-won convictions and vows, becoming more obstinate with age, and always (from his autobiography) seemingly headed for lunacy, is constantly rescued and redefined by external events, the goadings of other civilizations: the terror and strangeness of England, the need to pass the law examinations, the racial pressures of South Africa, British authoritarianism in India (made clear by his experience of the democratic ways of South Africa).

When Gandhi returns to India for good, in his mid-forties, he is fully made; and even at the end, when he is politically isolated and almost all holy man, the pattern of his foreign-created mahatmahood holds. In the turmoil of Independence – the killings, the mass migrations between India and Pakistan, the war in Kashmir – he is still, at the age of seventy-eight, obsessed with the vow of sexual abstinence he had taken forty years before at the time of the Zulu rebellion in South Africa. But he is roused by the Hindu-Moslem massacres in Bengal and goes to the district of Noakhali. Sad last pilgrimage: embittered people scatter broken glass on the roads he is to walk. Seventeen years before, on the Salt March, at the other end of India, the poor had sometimes strewn his path with cool green leaves. Now, in Bengal, he has nothing to offer except his presence, and he knows it. Yet he is heard to say to himself again and again, '*Kya karun? Kya karun?* What shall I do?' At this terrible moment his thoughts are of action, and he is magnificent.

The Acharya will never know this anguish of frustration. Embracing the 'demon world', deliberately living out his newly discovered nature as he deliberately lived out the old, he will continue to be self-absorbed; and his self-absorption will be as sterile as it had been when he was a man of goodness. No idea will come to him, as it came to Gandhi, of the imperfections of the world, of a world that might in some way be put right. The times are decadent, the Acharya thinks (or thought, when he was a man of goodness). But that is only because the lower castes are losing fear and getting out of hand; and the only answer is a greater righteousness, a further withdrawal into the self, a further turning away from the world, a striving after a more instinctive life, where the perception of reality is even weaker and the mind 'just one awareness, one wonder'.

Restful to the outsider, the visitor, this ideal of diminishing perception. But India has invested in necessary change, and a changing society requires something else. At a time of change, according to Sudhir Kakar, the underdeveloped ego can be a 'dangerous luxury'. Cities grow; people travel out of their ancestral districts; the ties of clan and family are loosened. The need for sharper perception increases; and perception has to become 'an individual rather than a social function'.

This threatens everything; it unbalances people in a way outsiders can hardly understand. Caste and clan and security and faith and shallow perception all go together; one cannot be altered or developed without damaging the rest. How can anyone used from infancy to the security of the group, and the security of a minutely regulated life, become an individual, a man on his own? He will be drowned in the immensity of the unknown world; he will be lost. He will be like the Acharya in Anantamurti's novel, tormented by his formlessness. 'A piece of string in the wind, a cloud taking on shapes according to the wind. I've become a thing. By an act of will, I'll become human again.'

For the Acharya there is a sanctioned way to becoming human again; he has only to make a choice. But how does a man become an individual when there is no path, and no knowledge even of the goal? How can men learn to presume? Men can only stumble through events, holding on to the idea of the self. When caste and family simplify relationships, and the sanctity of the laws cannot be doubted, when magic buttresses the laws, and the epics and legends satisfy the imagination, and astrologers know the future anyway, men cannot easily begin to observe and analyse. And how, it might be asked, can Indians face reality without some filter of faith or magic? How often in India – at every level – rational conversation about the country's problems trails away into talk of magic, of the successful prophecies of astrologers, of the wisdom of auspicious hours, of telepathic communications, and actions taken in response to some inner voice! It is always there, this knowledge of the other, regulated world, undermining, or balancing, intellect and the beginnings of painful perception.

When men cannot observe, they don't have ideas; they have obsessions. When people live instinctive lives, something like a collective amnesia steadily blurs the past. Few educated Indians now remember or acknowledge their serenity in 1962, before the Chinese war and the end of the Nehru era, when Independence could still be enjoyed as personal dignity alone, and it could be assumed, from the new possession of dignity by so many, that India had made it or was making it. Few can interpret the increasing frenzy of the country since then, through the Pakistan war of 1965, the consequent financial distress, the drought and famine of 1967, the long agony of the Bangladesh crisis of 1971.

India is poor: the fact has only recently begun to be observed in India, with the great growth in population, the choking of the cities, the political assertiveness of industrial workers. To many Indians, however, poverty, just discovered, also seems to have just been created. It is, bizarrely, one of the charges most often made against Mrs Gandhi: her failure to remove poverty, as she promised in 1971: that very poverty which, until the other day, was regarded by everyone else as a fact of Indian life, and holy, a cause for pious Gandhian pride.

A famous Indian politician, in his time a man of great power, once almost prime minister, said to a foreign interviewer just before the Emergency: 'Here there's no rice, there's no wheat . . . Until five years ago a family used to buy at least twenty pounds of cereals a month . . . We built factories too . . . and machinery we even managed to export . . . Now we have to import everything once more.' Did he really believe what he said? No rice, no wheat, everything imported? Did he really believe in that picture of a recent richer past? The chances are that he did. He is a Gandhian, and will not consciously distort the truth. He sits at his spinning wheel every day: the Gandhian spinning wheel no longer a means of livelihood for the dispossessed, or a symbol of labour and brotherhood with the poor, but a sacred tool, an aid to thought (as with this politician) or (as with others) a yogic means of stilling the waves of the mind, an aid to mental vacuity. To know the past (when he had been a man of power) the old politician had only to consult himself, his heart. There he saw quite clearly his own fulfilment and – since the outer world matters only in so far as it affects the inner – he could claim without disingenuousness that there had been a time when things were going well with the country.

Individual obsessions coalesce into political movements; and in the last ten years or so these movements of protest have become wilder. Many of these movements look back to the past, which they reinterpret to suit their needs. Some, like the Shiv Sena in Bombay (looking back two and a half centuries to the period of Maratha glory) and the Dravidian movement in the south (seeking to revenge itself, after three thousand years, on the Aryan north), have positive regenerating effects. Others, like the Anand Marg, fusing disparate obsessions, asserting caste and violence and sexual laxity as if in an inversion of Gandhianism, are the grossest kind of Hindu cult: a demonstration, like others in the past, of the ease with which Hinduism, striving after internal continuity and calm, stripping itself of intellect and the need for intellect, can decline into barbarism.

A party which seeks a nuclear armoury for India, and combines that with a programme for protecting the holy cow (free fodder for cows, homes for old cows), might at first be dismissed as a joke. But it isn't a joke. This party is the Jan Sangh, the National Party. It is the best-organized opposition party; with its emphasis on Hindu power, it touches many Hindu hearts, and it has a large middle-class following in the cities; for some years it controlled the Delhi municipality. In the 1971 elections one of its candidates in Delhi ran purely on the cow issue.

It might all seem only part of the quaintness of India. It is in fact an aspect of the deep disturbance of India at a time of difficult change, when many men, like the Acharya in Anantamurti's novel, find themselves thrown out into the world and formless, and strive, in the only ways open to them, to become human again.

## 2

With the Emergency some of these parties have been banned and their leaders imprisoned, with many others; and people outside who are concerned about the rule of law in India have sometimes been disconcerted by the causes they have found themselves sponsoring. In India, where the problems are beyond comprehension, the goals have to be vague. The removal of poverty, the establishment of justice: these, however often stated now, are like abstractions. People's obsessions are more immediate.

One opposition pamphlet now being circulated is about the torture of political prisoners in Indian jails. The torture, it must be said, is not of the systematized South American variety; it is more an affair of random brutality. But the power of the police in India is now unlimited, and the pamphlet doesn't exaggerate. It leaves out only the fact that there has always been torture of this sort in Indian jails. Torture, like poverty, is something about India that Indians have just discovered.

There is something else about the pamphlet. It lists a number of strange things as tortures. Somebody's moustache was shaved off; many people were beaten with shoes and made to walk the public streets with shoes on their heads; some people had their faces blackened and were paraded in the bazaar in cycle-rickshaws; one university professor 'was pushed from side to side with smearing remarks'. These are not what are usually thought of as tortures; they are caste pollutions, more permanently wounding, and a greater cause for hysteria, than any beating up. Black is a colour horrible to the Indo-Aryan; the moustache is an important caste emblem, and untouchables can be killed for wearing their moustaches curling up rather than drooping down; shoes are made of leather and tread the polluted earth. Almost without knowing it, the pamphlet confuses its causes: democracy, the rule of law, and humanitarianism merge in caste outrage. Men are so easily thrown back into the self, so easily lose the wider view. In this land of violence and cruelty, in the middle of a crisis that threatens the intellectual advance India has begun to make, the underdeveloped ego is still capable of an alarming innocence.

# 6

# SYNTHESIS AND MIMICRY

## I

AT A DINNER party in Delhi, a young foreign academic, describing what was most noticeable about the crowds he had seen in Bombay on his Indian holiday, said with a giggle: 'They were doing their "potties" on the street.' He was adding to what his Indian wife had said with mystical gravity: she saw people only having their being. She was middle-class and well connected. He was shallow and brisk and common, enjoying his pickings, swinging happily from branch to low branch in the grove of Academe. But the couple were well matched in an important way. Her Indian blindness to India, with its roots in caste and religion, was like his foreigner's easy disregard. The combination is not new; it has occurred again and again in the last thousand years of Indian history, the understanding based on Indian misunderstanding; and India has always been the victim.

But this couple lived outside India. They returned from time to time as visitors, and India restored in different ways the self-esteem of each. For other people in that gathering, however, who lived in India and felt the new threat of the millions and all the uncertainties that had come with Independence and growth, India could no longer be taken for granted. The poor had ceased to be background. Another way of looking was felt to be needed, some profounder acknowledgement of the people of the streets.

And this was what was attempted by another young woman,

a friend of the couple who lived abroad. The women of Bombay, she said, and she meant the women of the lower castes, wore a certain kind of sari and preferred certain colours; the men wore a special kind of turban. She had lived in Bombay; but, already, she was wrong: it is true that the women dress traditionally, but in Bombay the men for the most part wear trousers and shirt. It was a revealing error: for all her sympathy with the poor, she was still receptive only to caste signals, and was as blind as her friend.

'I will tell you about the poor people in Bombay,' she insisted. 'They are beautiful. They are more beautiful than the people in this room.' But now she was beginning to lie. She spoke with passion, but she didn't believe what she said. The poor of Bombay are not beautiful, even with their picturesque costumes in low-caste colours. In complexion, features, and physique the poor are distinct from the well-to-do; they are like a race apart, a dwarf race, stunted and slow-witted and made ugly by generations of undernourishment; it will take generations to rehabilitate them. The idea that the poor are beautiful was, with this girl, a borrowed idea. She had converted it into a political attitude, which she was prepared to defend. But it had not sharpened her perception.

New postures in India, attitudes that imply new ways of seeing, often turn out to be a matter of words alone. In their attempts to go beyond the old sentimental abstractions about the poverty of India, and to come to terms with the poor, Indians have to reach outside their civilization, and they are at the mercy then of every kind of imported idea. The intellectual confusion is greater now than in the days of the British, when the world seemed to stand still, the issues were simpler, and it was enough for India to assert its Indianness. The poor were background then. Now they press hard, and have to be taken into account.

From the *Indian Express*, 31 October 1975:

> Education Minister Prabha Rau has urged scientists and technologists to innovate simpler technology so that it does not

> become exclusive. Mrs Rau was speaking as the chief guest at a seminar on science and integrated rural development . . . She lamented the fact that the youth were not interested in science and technology because 'it is not only expensive but the exclusive preserve of a few', and hoped that there would be more 'active participation of a larger number of people'.

The speech is not easy to understand – the reporter was clearly baffled by what he heard – but it seems to contain a number of different ideas. There is the idea that the poor should also be educated (Indian students, who are assumed in the speech to be middle-class, *are* in fact interested in science); there is the idea that development should affect the greatest number; and there is the new, and unrelated, idea about 'intermediate technology', the idea that Indian technology should match Indian resources and take into account the nature of Indian society. The first two ideas are unexceptionable, the third more complex; but, complex or simple, the ideas are so much a matter of words that they have been garbled together – either by the minister or by the reporter – into a kind of political manifesto, an expression of concern with the poor.

The poor are almost fashionable. And this idea of intermediate technology has become an aspect of that fashion. The cult in India centres on the bullock cart. The bullock cart is not to be eliminated; after three thousand or more backward years Indian intermediate technology will now improve the bullock cart. 'Do you know,' someone said to me in Delhi, 'that the investment in bullock carts is equivalent to the total investment in the railways?' I had always had my doubts about bullock carts; but I didn't know until then that they were not cheap, were really quite expensive, more expensive than many second-hand cars in England, and that only richer peasants could afford them. It seemed to me a great waste, the kind of waste that poverty perpetuates. But I was glad I didn't speak, because the man who was giving me these statistics went on: 'Now. If we could improve the performance of the bullock cart by ten per cent . . .'

What did it mean, improving the performance by ten per cent? Greater speed, bigger loads? Were there bigger loads to carry? These were not the questions to ask, though. Intermediate technology had decided that the bullock cart was to be improved. Metal axles, bearings, rubber tyres? But wouldn't that make the carts even more expensive? Wouldn't it take generations, and a lot of money, to introduce those improvements? And, having got so far, mightn't it be better to go just a little further and introduce some harmless little engine? Shouldn't intermediate technology be concentrating on that harmless little engine capable of the short journeys bullock carts usually make?

But no: these were a layman's fantasies: the bullock was, as it were, central to the bullock-cart problem, as the problem had been defined. The difficulty – for science – was the animal's inconvenient shape. The bullock wasn't like the horse: it couldn't be harnessed properly. The bullock carried a yoke on its neck. This had been the practice since the beginning of history, and the time had come for change. This method of yoking was not only inefficient; it also created sores and skin cancer on the bullock's neck and shortened the animal's working life. The bullock-cart enthusiast in Delhi told me that a bullock lasted only three years. But this was the exaggeration of enthusiasm; other people told me that bullocks lasted ten or eleven years. To improve yoking, much research had to be done on the stresses on the bullock as it lifted and pulled. The most modern techniques of monitoring had to be used; and somewhere in the south there was a bullock which, while apparently only going about its peaceful petty business, was as wired up as any cosmonaut.

I was hoping to have a look at this animal when I got to the south and – India being a land of overenthusiastic report – to check with the scientist who had become the bullock-cart king. But the man himself was out of the country, lecturing; he was in demand abroad. Certain subjects, like poverty and intermediate technology, keep the experts busy. They are harassed by international seminars and conferences and foundation fellowships. The rich countries pay; they dictate the guiding ideas, which are the ideas of the rich about the poor, ideas sometimes about what is good for the poor, and sometimes no more than expressions of alarm. They, the rich countries, even manage now to export their romantic doubts about industrial civilization. These are the doubts that attend every kind of great success; and they are romantic because they contain no wish to undo that success or to lose the fruits of that success. But India interprets these doubts in its own debilitating way, and uses them to reconcile itself to its own failure.

Complex imported ideas, forced through the retort of Indian sensibility, often come out cleansed of content, and harmless; they seem so regularly to lead back, through religion and now science, to the past and nullity: to the spinning wheel, the bullock cart. Intermediate technology should mean a leap ahead, a leap beyond accepted solutions, new ways of perceiving coincident needs and resources. In India it has circled back to something very like the old sentimentality about poverty and the old ways, and has stalled with the bullock cart: a fascinating intellectual adventure for the people concerned, but sterile, divorced from reality and usefulness.

And while, in the south, science seeks to improve the bullock cart, at Ahmedabad in Gujarat, at the new, modern, and expensively equipped National Institute of Design, they are – on a similar 'intermediate' principle and as part of the same cult of the poor – designing or redesigning tools for the peasants. Among the finished products in the glass-walled showroom downstairs was a portable agricultural spraying machine, meant to be carried on the back. The bright yellow plastic casing looked modern enough; but it was hard to know why at Ahmedabad – apart from the anxiety to get the drab thing into bright modern plastic – they had felt the need to redesign this piece of equipment, which on the tea gardens and elsewhere is commonplace and, it might be thought, sufficiently reduced to simplicity. Had something been added? Something had, within the yellow plastic. A heavy motor, which would have crippled the peasant called upon to carry it for any length of time: the peasant who already, in some parts of India, has to judge tools by their weight and, because he has sometimes to carry his plough long distances to his field, prefers a wooden plough to an iron one. My guide acknowledged that the spray was heavy, but gave no further explanation.

The spraying machine, however, was of the modern age. Upstairs, a fourth-year student, clearly one of the stars of the Institute, was designing tools for the ancient world. He had a knife-sharpening machine to show; but in what way it differed from other cumbersome knife-sharpening machines I couldn't tell. His chief interest, though, was in tools for reaping. He disapproved of the sickle for some reason; and he was against the scythe because the cut stalks fell too heavily to the ground. Scythe and sickle were to be replaced by a long-handled tool which looked like a pair of edging shears: roughly made, no doubt because it was for the peasants and had to be kept rough and simple. When placed on the ground, the thick metal blades made a small V; but only one blade was movable, and this blade the peasant had to kick against the fixed blade and then – by means the designer had not yet worked out – retract for the next cut.

As an invention, this seemed to me some centuries behind the reaping machine of ancient Rome (a bullock-pushed tray with a serrated edge); but the designer, who was a townsman, said he had spent a week in the countryside and the peasants had been interested. I said that the tool required the user to stand; Indians preferred to squat while they did certain jobs. He said the people had to be re-educated.

His alternative design absolutely required standing. This was a pair of reaping shoes. At the front of the left shoe was a narrow cutting blade; on the right side of the right shoe was a longer curved blade. So the peasant, advancing through his ripe corn, would kick with his left foot and cut, while with his right he would describe a wide arc and cut: a harvest dance. Which, I felt, explained the otherwise mysterious presence of a wheelchair in the showroom downstairs, among the design items – the yellow agricultural spray, the boards with the logos for various firms, the teacups unsteady on too stylishly narrow a base. The wheelchair must have been for peasants: the hand-propelled inner wheel of the chair, if my trial was valid, would bark the invalid's knuckles against the outer wheel, and the chair itself, when stopped, would tip the invalid forward. Yes, my guide said neutrally, the chair did do that: the invalid had to remember to sit well back.

Yet the chair was in the window as something to show, something designed; and perhaps it was there for no better reason than that it looked modern and imported, proof that India was going ahead. Going ahead downstairs, going piously backward upstairs: India advancing simultaneously on all fronts, responding to every kind of idea at once. The National Institute of Design is the only one of its kind in India; it is fabulously equipped, competition to enter is fierce, and standards should be high. But it is an imported idea, an imported institution, and it has been imported whole, just like that. In India it has been easily divorced from its animating principle, reduced to its equipment, and has ended – admittedly after a controversial period: a new administrator had just been sent in – as a finishing school for the unacademic young, a playpen, with artisans called in to do the heavy work, like those dispirited men I saw upstairs squatting on the floor and working on somebody's chairs: India's eternal division of labour, frustrating the proclaimed social purpose of the Institute.

Mimicry within mimicry, imperfectly understood idea within imperfectly understood idea: the second-year girl student in the printing department, not understanding the typographical exercise she had been set, and playing with type like a child with a typewriter, avoiding, in the name of design, anything like symmetry, clarity, or logic; the third-year girl student showing a talentless drawing and saying, in unacknowledged paraphrase of Klee, that she had described 'the adventures of a line'; and that fourth-year man playing with tools for the peasants. There are times when the intellectual confusion of India seems complete and it seems impossible to get back to clarifying first principles. Which must have been one of the aims of an institute of design: to make people look afresh at the everyday.

An elementary knowledge of the history of technology would have kept that student – and the teachers who no doubt encouraged him – off the absurdity of his tools; even an elementary knowledge of the Indian countryside, elementary vision. Those tools were designed in an institute where there appeared to have been no idea of the anguish of the Indian countryside: the landless or bonded labourers, the child labourers, the too many cheap hands, the petty chopped-up fields, the nullity of the tasks. The whole project answered a fantasy of the peasant's life: the peasant as the man overburdened by the need to gather in his abundant harvest: romance, an idea of the simplicity of the past and pre-industrial life, which is at the back of so much thinking, political and otherwise, in India, the vision based on no vision.

The bullock cart is to be improved by high science. The caravans will plod idyllically to market, and the peasant, curled up on his honest load, will sleep away the night, a man matching his rhythm to that of nature, a man in partnership with his animals. But that same peasant, awake, will goad his bullock in the immemorial way, by pushing a stick up its anus. It is an unregarded but necessary part of the idyll, one of the obscene sights of the Indian road: the hideous cruelty of pre-industrial life, cruelty constant and casual, and easily extended from beast to man.

The beauty of the simple life, the beauty of the poor: in India the ideas are rolled together and appear one, but the ideas are separate and irreconcilable, because they assert two opposed civilizations.

## 2

Indians say that their gift is for cultural synthesis. When they say this, they are referring to the pre-British past, to the time of Moslem dominance. And though the idea is too much part of received wisdom, too much a substitute for thought and inquiry, there is proof of that capacity for synthesis in Indian painting. For the two hundred years or so of its vigour, until (very roughly) about 1800, this art is open to every kind of influence, even European. It constantly alters and develops as it shifts from centre to centre, and is full of local surprises. Its inventiveness – which contemporary scholarship is still uncovering – is truly astonishing.

In the nineteenth century, with the coming of the British, this great tradition died. Painting is only as good as its patrons allow it to be. Indian painting, before the British, was an art of the princely courts, Hindu or Moslem, and reflected the culture of those courts. Now there were new patrons, of more limited interests; and nothing is sadder, in the recent history of Indian culture, than to see Indian painting, in its various schools, declining into East India Company art, tourist art. A new way of looking is imposed, and Indian artists become ordinary as they depict native 'types' in as European a manner as their techniques allow, or when, suppressing their own idea of their function as craftsmen, their own feeling for design and organization, they struggle with what must have been for them the meaninglessness of Constable-like 'views'. A vigorous art becomes imitative, second-rate, insecure (always with certain regional exceptions); it knows it cannot compete; it withers away, and is finally abolished by the camera. It is as though, in a conquered Europe, with all of European art abruptly disregarded, artists were required to paint genre pictures in, say, a Japanese manner. It can be done, but the strain will kill.

India has recovered its traditions of the classical dance, once almost extinct, and its weaving arts. But the painting tradition remains broken; painting cannot simply go back to where it left off;

too much has intervened. The Indian past can no longer provide inspiration for the Indian present. In this matter of artistic vision the West is too dominant, and too varied; and India continues imitative and insecure, as a glance at the advertisements and illustrations of any Indian magazine will show. India, without its own living traditions, has lost the ability to incorporate and adapt; what it borrows it seeks to swallow whole. For all its appearance of cultural continuity, for all the liveliness of its arts of dance, music, and cinema, India is incomplete: a whole creative side has died. It is the price India has had to pay for its British period. The loss balances the intellectual recruitment during this period, the political self-awareness (unprecedented in Indian history) and the political reorganization.

What is true of Indian painting is also true of Indian architecture. There again a tradition has been broken; too much has intervened; and modernity, or what is considered to be modernity, has now to be swallowed whole. The effect is calamitous. Year by year India's stock of barely usable modern buildings grows. Old ideas about ventilation are out; modern air-conditioners are in; they absolve the architect of the need to design for the difficult climate, and leave him free to copy. Ahmedabad doesn't only have the National Institute of Design; it also, as a go-ahead city, has a modern little airport building. The roof isn't flat or sloping, but wavy; and the roof is low. Hot air can't rise too high; and glass walls, decoratively hung with some reticulated modern fabric, let in the Indian afternoon sun. It is better to stay with the taxi-drivers outside, where the temperature is only about a hundred. Inside, fire is being fought with fire, modernity with modernity; the glass oven hums with an expensive, power-consuming 'Gulmarg' air-cooler, around which the respectable and sheltered cluster.

At Jaisalmer in the Rajasthan desert the state government has just built a tourist guest house of which it is very proud. Little rooms open off a central corridor, and the desert begins just outside the uncanopied windows. But the rooms needn't be stuffy. For ten rupees extra a day you can close the shutters, switch on the electric light, and use the cooler, an enormous factory fan set in the window, which makes the little room roar. Yet Jaisalmer is famous for its old architecture, its palaces, and the almost Venetian grandeur of some of its streets. And in the bazaar area there are traditional courtyard houses, in magnificent stone versions for the desert: tall, permitting ventilation in the outer rooms, some part of the house always in cool shadow.

But the past is the past: architecture in India is a modern course of study and, as such, another imported skill, part of someone else's tradition. In architecture as in art, without the security of a living tradition, India is disadvantaged. Modernity – or Indianness – is so often only a matter of a façade; within, and increasingly, even in remote places now, is a nightmare of misapplied technology or misunderstood modern design: the rooms built as if for Siberia, always artificially lit, noisy with the power-consuming air-conditioning unit, and uninhabitable without that unit, which leaks down the walls and ruins the fitted carpet: expense upon expense, the waste with which ignorance often burdens poverty.

There was a time when Indians who had been abroad and picked up some simple degree or skill said that they had become displaced and were neither of the East nor West. In this they were absurd and self-dramatizing: they carried India with them, Indian ways of perceiving. Now, with the great migrant rush, little is heard of that displacement. Instead, Indians say that they have become too educated for India. The opposite is usually true: they are not educated enough; they only want to repeat their lessons. The imported skills are rooted in nothing; they are skills separate from principles.

On the train going back to Bombay one rainy evening I heard the complaint from a blank-faced, plump young man. He was too educated for India, he said; and he spoke the worn words without irony or embarrassment. He had done a course in computers in the United States, and (having money) what he wanted to do was to set up a factory to build the American equipment he had learned about. But India wasn't ready for this kind of advanced equipment, and he was thinking he might have to go back permanently to the United States.

I wanted to hear more about his time in the United States. But he had little else to say about that country or – the rainy, smoky industrial outskirts of Bombay, rust, black, and green, going past our window – about India. America was as he had expected it to be, he said. He gave no concrete details. And India – even after the United States, and in spite of what could be seen through our window – he assessed only as an entrepreneur might assess it.

He was of a northern merchant caste; he carried caste in his manner. He belonged to old India; nothing had happened to shake him out of that security; he questioned nothing. From the outside world he had snatched no more than a skill in computers, as in less complicated times he might have learned about cloth or grain at home. He said he was too educated for India. But – to give the example given me by the engineer I had got to know in Bombay – he was like the plumber from the slums: a man from a simple background called upon to exercise a high skill, and exercising it blindly. Water is the plumber's business; but water is to him a luxury, something for which his wife has to stand in line every morning; he cannot then understand why it is necessary for a tap to be placed straight, in the centre of a tile. So – in spite of his own simple background, in spite of India – the computer man, possessing only his specialized skill, saw his business as the laying down of computers, anywhere.

To match technology to the needs of a poor country calls for the highest skills, the clearest vision. Old India, with all its encouragements to the instinctive, non-intellectual life, limits vision. And the necessary attempt at making imported technology less 'exclusive' – to use the confusing and perhaps confused word of the Maharashtra education minister – has ended with the school of the bullock cart, a mixture of mimicry and fantasy. Yet it is something – perhaps a great deal – that India has felt the need to make the attempt.

## 3

India is old, and India continues. But all the disciplines and skills that India now seeks to exercise are borrowed. Even the ideas Indians have of the achievements of their civilization are essentially the ideas given them by European scholars in the nineteenth century. India by itself could not have rediscovered or assessed its past. Its past was too much with it, was still being lived out in the ritual, the laws, the magic – the complex instinctive life that muffles response and buries even the idea of inquiry. Indian painting now has its scholars in India, but the approach to painting, even among educated people, is still, generally, iconographic, the recognition of deities and themes. A recently dead tradition, an unchanging belief: the creative loss passes unnoticed.

India blindly swallows its past. To understand that past, it has had to borrow alien academic disciplines; and, as with the technology, their foreign origin shows. Much historical research has been done; but European methods of historical inquiry, arising out of one kind of civilization, with its own developing ideas of the human condition, cannot be applied to Indian civilization; they miss too much. Political or dynastic events, economic life, cultural trends: the European approach elucidates little, has the effect of an unsuccessful attempt to equate India with Europe, and makes nonsense of the stops and starts of Indian civilization, the brief flowerings, the long periods of sterility, men forever claimed by the instinctive life, continuity turning to barbarism.

History, with its nationalist shrillness, sociology with its mathematical approach and its tables: these borrowed disciplines remain borrowed. They have as yet given India little idea of itself. India no more possesses Indian history than it possesses its art. People have an idea of the past and can quote approving things from foreign sources (a habit of which all Indians complain and of which all are guilty). But to know India, most people look inward. They consult themselves: in their own past, in the nature of their caste or clan life, their family traditions, they find the idea of India which they know to be true, and according to which they act.

Indian newspapers reflect this limited vision, this absence of inquiry, the absence of what can be called human interest. The pre-censorship liveliness of the Indian press – of which foreign observers have spoken – was confined to the editorial pages. Elsewhere there were mainly communiqués, handouts, reports of speeches and functions. Indian journalism developed no reporting tradition; it often reported on India as on a foreign country. An unheadlined item from the *Statesman*, 17 September 1975:

> *Woman Jumps to Death:* A woman jumped to death after throwing her two children into a well at Chennaptna, 60 km from Bangalore recently, according to police – PTI.

Recently! But that is all; the police communiqué is enough; no reporter was sent out to get the story. From the *Times of India*, 4 October 1975:

> An 'eye-surgeon', who had performed 70 eye operations here in February resulting in the loss of eyesight of 20 persons and serious injuries to many others, has been arrested in Muzaffarnagar, the police said there yesterday. The man, apparently an Ayurvedic physician with no knowledge of surgery, had promised patients in Jalgaon that he would perform the operations at concessional rates.

That is all; the story is over; there will be no more tomorrow.

A caste vision: what is remote from me is remote from me. The Indian press has interpreted its function in an Indian way. It has not sought to put India in touch with itself; it doesn't really know how, and it hasn't felt the need. During its free years it watched over nothing; away from the political inferno of its editorial pages it saw few causes for concern. Its India was background, was going on. It was a small-circulation left-wing paper, the *Economic and Political Weekly* of Bombay, that exposed the abuses on the coalfields in the Dhanbad district of Bihar, where workers were terrorized by moneylenders and their gangs. Shortly after the Emergency, the government announced that two or three hundred of the moneylenders had been arrested. That, too, was a simple agency item in the Indian daily press. No paper related it to what had gone before, or seemed to understand its importance; no one went out to investigate the government's claim. Only, some time later, the Calcutta *Statesman* carried an account by a reporter of what it felt like to go down a pit at Dhanbad: a 'colour' piece, cast in terms of personal adventure, an Indian account, with the miners as background.

Since the Emergency the government – for obvious reasons – has decreed that newspapers should look away from politics and concentrate on social issues. It has required newspapers to go in for 'investigative reporting' – the borrowed words are used; and it might be said that the news about India in the Indian press has never been so bad as it is now. Recent numbers of the *Illustrated Weekly of India* (adventurously edited, even before the Emergency) have carried features on bonded labour, child labour, and child marriage. The Indian press has at last begun to present India to itself. But it does so under compulsion. It is one of the paradoxes of India under the Emergency that make judgement about the Emergency so difficult: the dangers are obvious, but the results can appear positive. The press has lost its political freedom, but it has extended its interpretative function.

The press (like technology, eventually) can be made to match Indian needs. But what of the law? How can that system, bequeathed to India by another civilization with other values, give India equity and perform the law's constant reassessing, reforming role? From the *Times of India*, 5 October 1975:

> The Prime Minister, Mrs Indira Gandhi, said today that the Indian legal system should assume a 'dynamic role' in the process of social transformation, shaking off the 'inhibiting legacy of the colonial past' . . . She said: 'Law should be an instrument of social justice.' Explaining the 'dynamic role' of the legal system, Mrs Gandhi said it should assist in the liberation of the human spirit and of human institutions from the straitjacket of outdated customs. She said the people's respect for law depended on the extent of their conviction that it afforded them real and impartial protection. 'Our ancients realized this when they stated that society should uphold dharma so that dharma sustains society,' she added.

But how can the imported system assume its dynamic role in India? The difficulty, the contradiction, lies in that very concept of *dharma*. The *dharma* of which Mrs Gandhi speaks is a complex word: it can mean the faith, pietas, everything which is felt to be right and religious and sanctioned. Law must serve *dharma* or at least not run counter to it; and that seems fair enough. Yet *dharma*, as expressed in the Indian social system, is so shot through with injustice and cruelty, based on such a limited view of man. It can accommodate bonded labour as, once, it accommodated widow-burning. *Dharma* can resist the idea of equity. Law in India can at times appear a forensic game, avoiding collision with the abuses it should be remedying; and it is hard to see how any system of law can do otherwise while the Indian social system holds, and while *dharma* is honoured above the simple rights of men.

A.S.R. Chari is a famous Indian criminal lawyer. He has written a book about some of his cases; and in October 1975 *Blitz*, a popular left-wing weekly of Bombay, retold this story from the Chari book. In Maharashtra, in the 1950s, a marriage was arranged between the daughter of a cloth-seller and the son of a lawyer. The lawyer turned up for the wedding ceremony with 150 guests, all to be fed and lodged at the cloth-seller's expense. The cloth-seller objected; the lawyer, angered by the discourtesy and apparent meanness, threw two thousand rupees in notes at the feet of the cloth-seller in a gesture of insult. Yet the marriage went ahead: the lawyer's son married the cloth-seller's daughter. Only, the lawyer forbade his son to have anything more to do with his wife's family, and forbade his daughter-in-law to visit her parents. The girl suffered. ('She seemed to have been a highly strung girl,' Chari writes.) She suffered especially when she was not allowed to visit her sister in hospital. Her husband was firm when she asked his permission. He said: 'You know the position. I cannot allow this. Do not be too unhappy over it.' Waking up that night, the young man found his wife dead beside him.

Cyanide was detected in the viscera of the dead girl; and the young man was charged with her murder. The prosecution argued that she could not, by herself, have obtained the cyanide in Bombay; it must have been administered by her husband, who, as a photographer, had chemicals of various kinds in his laboratory. But the police hadn't found potassium or sodium cyanide in the laboratory; they had only found potassium ferricyanide, not a poison. This gave Chari – arguing the young man's appeal against conviction for murder – his clue. 'Potassium ferricyanide, though not ordinarily a poison, would act as a poison when taken by a person who had hyper-acidity – that is, a person who secreted too much hydrochloric acid in the stomach.' So the girl had committed suicide. Her husband was acquitted.

Justice was done. But the injustice to the dead girl was hardly commented on. The Supreme Court, hearing the appeal, spoke of 'false ideas of family prestige'; but in Chari's legalistic account, as rendered in *Blitz*, full of technicalities about the admissibility of evidence, the punishment of the cloth-seller by the suicide of his daughter is made to appear just one of those things. 'Oh yes,' one of the appeal judges said, 'you have to make arrangements so thoroughly that you satisfy every demand made by any one of the bridegroom's party.' And in this acknowledgement of the traditional demands of family honour the tragedy of the girl is lost: writing letters to the family she is not allowed to see ('God's will be done'), so quickly accepting that her young life is spoiled and has to be ended.

The law avoids the collision with *dharma*. Yet it is this *dharma* that the law must grapple with if the law is to have a 'dynamic role'. That is the difficulty: to cope with the new pressures, India has in some ways to undermine itself, to lose its old security. Borrowed institutions can no longer function simply as borrowed institutions, a tribute to modernity. Indians say that their gift is for synthesis. It might be said, rather, that for too long, as a conquered people, they have been intellectually parasitic on other civilizations. To survive in subjection, they have preserved their sanctuary of the instinctive, uncreative life, converting that into a religious ideal; at a more worldly level, they have depended on others for the ideas and institutions that make a country work. The Emergency – coming so soon after Independence – dramatizes India's creative incapacity, its intellectual depletion, its defencelessness, the inadequacy of every Indian's idea of India.

# 7

# PARADISE LOST

## I

'WE ARE LIKE a zoo,' the melancholy middle-class lady said in Delhi. 'Perhaps we should charge.'

She lived in India: I was a visitor. She intended a rebuke, possibly an insult, but it was easy to let it pass. India was like a zoo because India was poor and cruel and had lost its way. These were things about India that, with the Emergency, she had just discovered; and they were more than intellectual discoveries. Once – like other middle-class people, like other people secure in their caste world – she might have been able to detach herself from the mess of India; now she felt she was going down with it.

Her husband was connected with the opposition; his career was suddenly jeopardized; he lived in fear of arrest. In the pre-Emergency days – when the students were rioting, the unions were striking, and it seemed possible to get rid of Mrs Gandhi's government and give India a fresh start – he had been a figure. Now all his political boldness had turned to hysteria. Action had ceased to be possible; the revolution at whose head he thought he was marching had vanished, leaving him exposed.

'Thousands of us will surround her house to prevent her going out or receiving visitors. We'll camp there night and day, shouting to her to resign. Even if the police arrest us, beat us up, slaughter us. How many can they slaughter? And what will they do with the corpses?' This was what old Mr Desai, a famous Gandhian and once deputy prime minister, had promised a foreign interviewer. But then, just a few hours later, Mr Desai had been arrested, no doubt to his own surprise ('I prefer to believe that before committing such a monstrosity Mrs Gandhi would commit suicide,' he had told the interviewer, unwittingly showing up the vanity and shoddiness of his Gandhian posture). And there had been no uprising, no corpses in front of Mrs Gandhi's house in New Delhi.

Jaya Prakash Narayan, the most respected opposition leader, had been wiser. In his last public speech, in New Delhi, the evening before his arrest, he asked the students in his audience: 'Will you go to classes or to prison?' 'Prison!' they had replied. And he had said, 'Let us see.' And the students, when the time came, had done nothing; they had become part of the great peace of the Emergency.

The revolution had turned out to be no revolution. And India, which only a few weeks before had seemed capable of renewed Gandhian fervour, had become like a zoo. The sad lady sat forward on her chair, knees apart below the wrappings of her sari, and looked down at the floor, shaking her head slowly from side to side, as though contemplating the depth of the Indian tragedy; while her husband, speaking above the traffic noise that came through the open windows, offered visions of the repression to come.

He extended his personal anxieties to the country: he foresaw that the British-built 'garden city' of New Delhi, now inherited by the Indian rulers of India, would soon be barricaded against the poor and guarded by machine guns. I thought he was exaggerating, but he said that the expulsion of the poor had already begun. A squatters' settlement in the Diplomatic Enclave had been levelled, and people and their possessions thrown out in the rain.

Many weeks later this municipal event was to appear in a London newspaper as hot news from the new India: the overthrow of socialism, the beginning of the assault on the poor: Indian events given a South American interpretation, and thereby made easier for everyone. The report was to catch the very hysteria with which the news had been given to me. But I remembered, that evening in Delhi, that such expulsions of illegal squatters were not new. In 1962, at the time of my first visit to the Indian capital, while Mr Nehru still ruled, a similar kind of settlement had been bulldozed in the middle-class Defence Colony area. For days the collapsed brown-black spread of thatch and sacking and mud had remained beside the highway – it was as though the people who had lived there had been snuffed out, blown away. There had been a photograph in the newspaper; but not many people came to watch; there had been no outcry.

But that was in 1962, the last year of Mr Nehru as father figure, the last year of post-Independence glory for the Indian middle class, when (until the Chinese war blew away the fantasy) India seemed to have made it and Independence was still seen mainly as a matter of personal dignity, an Indian voice abroad, 'Indianization' at home, a new kind of job, a managership, an appointment in the new diplomatic service, a new glamour, a conscious display of national costume and 'culture'.

The lady who in 1975 was so sad, contemplating the tragedy of India, resenting visitors as voyeurs, would in those days have dismissed the subject of Indian poverty; she would have spoken – as middle-class ladies did then – of the happiness of the poor (greater than the happiness of others), their manners, their dignity, the way they kept their hovels clean; she would have contrasted the Indian poor with the unspeakable slum-dwellers of foreign countries. Times had changed. 'Indianization' no longer meant a redistribution of jobs, a sharing-out of the British legacy. It was the slogan of an opposition party, a populist-religious appeal to Hindus, a word of threat to minorities, part of the intellectual confusion, the new insecurity, the blind dredging up of dormant fantasies and obsessions, the great enraged stirring from below.

The lady looked down at the floor, and while her husband walked about and talked, she shook her head slowly, saying 'Mmmm'. In that position her cheeks drooped; and they aged her, adding to her air of melancholy. She knew a family in the demolished settlement. Poor people, simple people. The man had come down to Delhi from the hills. He had found a job and built his little house on this piece of land. He had brought down his wife, and they had since had four children. He was only thirty. But, poor fellow, what other pleasures did he have? *He* didn't have TV. He had brought down his brother as well, and the brother had brought down his wife, and they had begun to have their own children. Now that life had been smashed. They had all been thrown out in the rain. In the rain: the government couldn't even wait until the monsoon was over.

But had they really been thrown out just like that? Hadn't they been given notice of some sort? Yes, a year's notice. But what could poor people do? It was also true that those who had registered at that time had been given building plots of their own somewhere else. But what did poor people know about registering? Who was there to help them? And, besides, the new plots were ten miles away. How would people get to work? Buses? Yes, there were buses, but I didn't know the Delhi bus service. It was all melancholy and terrible, especially for the family she knew. Who were they? The man worked for her; he was her servant. She had lost her servant; he had lost his job.

It had taken some time to pull the story out, through the lady's melancholy and her husband's hysteria; and neither the lady nor her husband seemed to understand how depressing it was for a visitor, at a time of a real crisis, to have this personal loss (not yet an established loss: the servant could have got a bicycle) presented as an aspect of national tragedy.

'I come upon people, both men and women, who seem to enjoy being ill-treated by others. It is an emotional luxury for them to dwell on and speak about their grievances and wallow in self-pity. Among such people conversation means relating what they suffer at the hands of official superiors or inferiors, relatives near or distant.' This is what the seventy-nine-year-old Bengali writer Nirad Chaudhuri wrote in 1970, in *To Live or Not to Live*, a handbook for Indians on 'living happily with others'. Chaudhuri, beating his own way out of the thicket of Indian attitudes, believes that Indians do not *live*, that they live 'unsoundly', to no purpose. 'Do we live at all? This would seem an absurd question, for none of us commit suicide, though, to be honest, I would confess that I have come to feel that a large majority of the persons I know should do so, because I cannot see any point in their remaining alive.'

It was the effect on me of that Delhi evening. I had gone to that apartment expecting ideas, discussion. I had found no ideas, only obsessions, no discussion, only disingenuous complaint and an invitation to the wallow, the sweet surrender to tragedy.

The traffic noise came through the windows and I had to strain to hear what was being said. The lights were very dim and I had to strain to see. It was a government apartment in a suburb far from the central 'garden city' of New Delhi. It hadn't been easy to find because, like many places in the suburbs of New Delhi, where streets can be nameless, it had a number rather than a guiding address. And it was numbered like a civil-service file, and had that quality of being worn and much handled and about to be passed on. Our host, a civil servant, high in the service but embittered, connected with a department which was without the resources to do what its name suggested, had very soon detached himself from us. He left his plain wife and bespectacled adolescent son – old error, new hope – to sit with us while, standing in gloomy corners, shielding his prey of the evening from our sight, like an animal eating in secret, he worried and importuned a minor – and exceedingly stupid – provincial politician. The ambition was like despair; it shrieked more than the hysteria of the opposition man who feared arrest and the wallow of the woman who had lost her servant.

My taxi-driver that evening was a Sikh. He had been a sportsman in his time and still had the sportsman's presence. He knew foreign countries by the sportsmen they produced, and he spoke English well; he was a diligent reader of the newspapers. He owned his taxi and had a place in the taxi rank of the hotel. I thought he was better off than most people in India. But his thoughts were of migration. He wanted to go to one of the Arab gulf states. He had paid a large sum of money to a middleman, a 'contractor'. His papers were almost in order now, he said; all he was waiting for, from the contractor, was his 'no objection' certificate. Yet the thought of the large sum he had paid to the contractor worried him. He spoke like a man who knew he had waited too long and had begun to fear that he had been cheated.

For so many people India seemed to have gone wrong; so many people in independent India had become fugitives or sought that status. And this was in Delhi, a migrant city in the better-off north, where people were awakened and energetic, and for whom India ought to have gone right. The land stretched a thousand miles to the east and the south, through the overpopulated Gangetic plain and the rock plateau of the Deccan. At the end of that bad evening it seemed barely imaginable – the huts of the landless along the Poona-Bombay road, the child labourers of Bihar among the blond hanks of jute, the chawls and squatters' settlements in central Bombay, the starved squatters in bright cotton slipping in and out of the stone ruins of Vijayanagar, the famine-wasted bodies just outside Jaipur City. It was like a calamity that no one could come to terms with. I was without the Indian defences, which were also the attitudes that contributed to the calamity. I could only wait for the morning.

## 2

An immovable government, one-party rule, a democratic system which engaged only a fraction of the population, a decadent Gandhianism expressed in the white homespun of the Congress politician, no longer the sign of service but the uniform of power, the very sight of which could enrage, and now the Emergency, a censored press, secret arrests: it was easy to enter into the hysteria of the opposition man.

But it was also easy to understand why the revolution had evaporated. The leaders, offering what they saw as unassailable Gandhian truths, offering themselves as so many Gandhis, were misled by the apparent answering fervour of the crowds. But the India of 1975 was not the India of 1930 and the Dandi Salt March. Political action couldn't be concentrated in a single symbolic act (picking up a handful of salt from the shore at Dandi), a religious act, a ritual cleansing of a subject and defiled land. The needs of 1975 were more worldly and difficult. India wasn't to be cleansed again; it was (as Mrs Gandhi intuited) to be cleaned up and got going; it was to be seen to be offering worldly opportunities. The very fierceness of the Emergency answered the public mood, assuaged old frustrations. The crowds went home in peace.

And the Gandhianism of a man like Mr Desai was as exhibitionist and hollow as the Gandhianism of the men he opposed; it offered nothing. The sacrifice was for others (those corpses outside Mrs Gandhi's house); Mr Desai (according to that interview he gave to the foreign journalist) saw himself as secure, immune even from arrest. The revolution was an expression of rage and rejection; but it was a revolution without ideas. It was an emotional outburst, a wallow; it would not have taken India forward; and the revolutionary crowds knew that. At its core, absurdly elevated to a political programme, was a subtle distortion of the old Gandhian call to action. At its core were the old Indian attitudes of defeat, the idea of withdrawal, a turning away from the world, a sinking back into the past, the rediscovery of old ways, 'simplicity'.

Simplicity: it was the obsession that evening in Delhi of the opposition man, and it made discussion impossible. Simplicity was the old India and Gandhi. It was the opposite of everything that independent India had committed itself to, and as a motive for political-moral protest was inexhaustible. Everything that had been done was wrong; nothing was right. The opposite of simplicity was the power politics that had come to India; the opposite of simplicity was repression, concentration camps, Hitler. This was the direction in which India was going, and it was better for this India to be smashed into little bits. Czechoslovakia was a small country: had Czechoslovakia suffered? This view of recent history was startling. But he was a wounded man; and his Gandhian simplicity – like Mr Desai's – had become indistinguishable from a primitivist rage.

His simplicity was something that could be defined only by negatives. It was a turning away from the idea of the modern state. (Defence? Who would or could conquer India? And this from a responsible man, a maker of opinion, in just the twenty-ninth year of full Indian Independence, after a thousand years of invasions and conquests!) Simplicity was, above all, a turning away from the idea of industrial development, the idea of the machine. The Gandhian spinning wheel and the handloom would have saved the peasantry and kept India secure in its villages. (Such engineering effort, though, such a need of electrical power, such organization, such a network of brick-lined canals, to take drinking water for the first time in history to the desert villages of Haryana in the north: and not water for every dwelling – that was impossible – but one or two standpipes per village.)

But perhaps this idea of simplicity – though backed up in the Indian way by quotations from Western sources, and presented as a basis for political action – was something more debilitated, something older. Perhaps it was no more than a turning away from the difficulties of a development that had been seen to be impossible, a consequent intellectual surrender, a religious giving up, a yielding to old Indian fantasy: the mystical sense of the Indian past, the idea of eternal India forever spontaneously having its rebirth and growth, the conversion of the destitution and serfdom of rural India (and the heavy-footed vultures squabbling in the rain over the bloated carcasses of dead animals) into a memory of pastoral: a memory of the time, so recent, just out of reach, when people knew the undefiled gods, and the gods gave brahmins all the answers, and the bull drew the plough and the cow gave milk, and the manure of these animals enriched the fields, and the stalks of the harvest thatched the simple huts of the pure.

That Indian past! That fantasy of wholeness and purity, confusing the present! Indian opposition groups in London have circulated a text of the speech Jaya Prakash Narayan delivered the evening before his arrest. It is quite different in tone from the pious venom of Mr Desai's interview that same day with a foreign journalist. The Narayan speech explains and informs; it is the speech of a constitutionalist who has assembled his facts and references; it quotes the Indian Supreme Court judges and Sir Ivor Jennings. But it is also the speech of an Indian political campaigner addressing a mass audience; and there is a philosophical-historical passage which has to be quoted in full.

> The youth, the peasants, the working class, all with one voice must declare that we will not allow fascism to raise its head in our country. We will not have dictatorship in our country. We will carry on our people's government. This is not Bangladesh. This is not Pakistan. This is Bharat. We have our ancient tradition. Thousands of years ago we had small village republics. That sort of history is behind us. There were village Panchayats in virtually every village. In the times of the Mauryas, Gupta, the Pathan, the Mughals, the Peshwas, we had our Panchayats. The British deliberately broke this tradition in order to strengthen their own hold on the country. This ancient tradition was in Bangladesh and in Pakistan, but they seem to have given it up. But our leaders sought a reawakening. Gandhiji always said that *Swaraj* means *Ramraj*. Swaraj means that every village will have its own rule. Every village, every mohalla and town will manage its own affairs. What they must not do is just hand over the lot to their representatives to get it all done at a 'higher level'.

The passage that begins with an antifascist call (and gives India a working class, almost as if to equip it for that modern struggle) quickly becomes less straightforward. India becomes the ancient and sacred land of Bharat, and its past is mystically invoked: leaping the defilement of the British period, the speaker looks back to the eighteenth-century Maratha bandit kings, glances at the Moslem conquerors (the Mughal, the Pathan), jumps a thousand years to the purely Indian Guptas (AD 320–600), and goes back a further five hundred years to the Mauryas (322–185 BC). Through all this – empires, achievement, chaos, conquest, plunder, the steady loss of Indian territory to the world of Islam – India is said to have kept her soul, to have preserved the democratic ways of her village republics, her 'people's government'. Democracy hasn't come to India from an alien source; India has had it all along. To rediscover democracy, India has only to rediscover herself.

But then Narayan turns this rediscovery into something more mysterious. 'Gandhiji always said that *Swaraj* means *Ramraj*.' *Swaraj* means self-rule, self-government; it was the word used in the British days for Indian Independence. *Ramraj* is something else. It is Rama's rule, a fantasy of bliss. Rama is the hero of the *Ramayana*, the sacred Hindu epic. This epic echoes events of 1000 BC, was composed or set down (by a named poet) at about the same time as the *Aeneid*, but (unlike the *Aeneid*) has always been a living poem, more than literature, possessed by all Hindus, however illiterate or depressed, from childhood. Rama incarnates all the Hindu Aryan virtues; he is at once a man and God; his rule – after exile and sorrow – is the rule of God on earth. The narrative of his adventures fills the imagination of the child; and no Hindu can forget that early closeness to figures and events he later learns to be divine, to be legend and not legend.

*Ramraj* is something the Hindu always knows he has lost: in one way remote, impossible, just a word, in another way only as remote as childhood, just out of reach. From *Punjabi Century* (1963), the autobiography of one of India's most distinguished business administrators, Prakash Tandon, we can get a fuller idea of the *Ramraj* Gandhi offered in 1919, at the start of his Indian agitation, and of the political effect then, at a time of high emotion, even on a professional family. 'These visitors,' Tandon writes,

> spoke about the freedom of India, and this intrigued us; but when they talked in familiar analogies and idiom about the Kal Yug, we saw what they meant. Had it not been prophesied that there were seven eras in India's life and history: there had been a Sat Yug, the era of truth, justice, and prosperity; and then there was to be a Kal Yug, an era of falsehood, or demoralization, of slavery and poverty . . . Gandhi rechristened India Bharat Mata, a name that evoked nostalgic memories, and associated with Gao Mata, the mother cow . . . He . . . spoke about the peace of the British as the peace of slavery. Gradually a new picture began to build in our minds, of India coming out of the Kal Yug into a new era of freedom and plenty, Ram Rajya.

Nearly sixty years later, in 1975, Jaya Prakash Narayan's appeal is the same. '*Swaraj* means *Ramraj*.' We have gone far beyond the Indian 'working class' and the anti-fascist struggle, beyond political systems and the contemplation of the past; we have gone back to the beginning of the Hindu world, to 'nostalgic memories'. We have gone back to the solace of incantation, and back to Gandhi as to the only Indian truth. As though Britain still ruled in India; as though Gandhi hadn't been created by specific circumstances; as though the Indian political situation remains unchanging, as eternal as India itself, requiring always the same ideal solution. The irony is that the Indian tyranny against which Jaya Prakash Narayan is protesting, and the sterility of contemporary Indian political life – immovable power on one side, and on the other side frustrated and obsessional 'Gandhian' protest, mixing political and historical fantasy with religious exaltation – the irony is that both tyranny and political sterility were ensured by the very success of Gandhi.

It was Gandhi who gave the Congress Party a mass base, a rural base. Four out of five Indians live in villages; and the Congress remains the only party in India (except for certain regional parties) which has a rural organization; it cannot lose. The opposition parties, even a revivalist Hindu party like the Jan Sangh, the National Party, are city parties. In the villages the Congress is still Gandhi's party; and the village tyrannies that have been established through nearly thirty years of unbroken Congress rule cannot now be easily removed. In the countryside the men to watch for are the men in white Gandhian homespun. They are the men of power, the politicians; their authority, rooted in the antique reverences of caste and clan, has been ennobled by Independence and democracy.

Like the two who were introduced to me, late one afternoon, at a great irrigation scheme in the south, as 'farmers'. I had asked – after lunch and visits to offices and viewing points – to visit fields and see farmers; and the irrigation administrator, in spite of his jacket and tie (emblems of his high administrative rank), became nervous, like a man fearful of trespassing. The ragged men gathering silently around us, obviously connected with the work of the land, were not farmers, as I had thought. What were they? They were labourers, less than labourers, nothing; the administrator seemed not to see them. A government jeep was sent to get the two farmers the administrator said he knew; and we waited for a long time in a damp timber yard, in the dying light of a rainy, overcast day, the crowd around us growing, until the farmers arrived, men in their early fifties, hopping nimbly off the jeep in full Congress uniform of white Gandhian homespun, one man freshly bathed and speaking fluent English and with a big wristwatch, the other man tall and pale and paunchy, with a Gandhi cap: not farmers at all, but landowners and politicians, rulers of the district, acting out for the visitor the democratic charade of being farmers and living each man off the income of six acres of land: taking me, after all that waiting, just across the road from the timber yard to a small, over-irrigated field, now in darkness, where their white homespun yet glowed: around us the serfs, underfed, landless, nothing, less than people, dark wasted faces and dark rags fading into the dusk.

To make democracy work, Jaya Prakash Narayan suggests, to undo tyranny, it is only necessary for India to return truly to itself. The *Ramraj* that Gandhi offered is no longer simply Independence, India without the British; it is people's government, the reestablishment of the ancient Indian village republic, a turning away from the secretariats of Delhi and the state capitals. But this is saying nothing; this is to leave India where it is. What looks like a political programme is only clamour and religious excitation. People's government and that idea of the ancient Indian village republic (which may be a fanciful idea, a nationalist myth surviving from the days of the Independence struggle) are not the same thing. Old India has its special cruelties; not all the people are people. And (though Narayan doesn't seem aware of the contradiction) it is really against that old India that, later in his speech, he protests.

> She [Mrs Gandhi] speaks of the welfare of the Harijans [untouchables]. Does she not feel any shame for all the misdeeds done recently to the Harijans? In U.P. [Uttar Pradesh, Mrs Gandhi's home state] and in Bihar [Narayan's home state] whole Harijan villages have been put to the torch. One Harijan was burnt alive. She does not have any right to speak on behalf of the Harijans. Those poor people, they do not understand all the sophisticated talk. Recently I was in the Bhojpur area. How many Harijans were mercilessly butchered!

India is to be returned to itself, to surrender to its inmost impulses; at the same time India is to be saved from itself. The synthesis of Marxism and Gandhianism which Jaya Prakash Narayan is thought by his admirers to have achieved is in fact a kind of nonsense; he offers as politics a version of an old religious exaltation; and it has made him part of the sterility he is protesting against.

A passionate Marxist journalist – waiting for the revolution, rejecting all 'palliatives' – told me that the 'workers' of India had to be politicized; they had to be told that it was the 'system' that oppressed them. After nearly thirty years of power the Congress has, understandably, become the system. But where does the system begin and end? Does it take in religion, the security of caste and clan, Indian ways of perceiving, *karma*, the antique serfdom? But no Indian cares to take political self-examination that far. No Indian can take himself to the stage where he might perceive that the faults lie within the civilization itself, that the failure and the cruelties of India might implicate all Indians. Even the Marxists, dreaming of a revolution occurring like magic on a particular day, of tyranny swept away, of 'the people' then engaging in the pleasures of 'folk' activities – the Marxist journalist's word: the folk miraculously whole after the millennia of oppression – even the Marxists' vision of the future is not of a country undone and remade but of an India essentially returned to itself, purified: a vision of *Ramraj*.

An extraordinary feature of Indian opposition right-wing parties in exile has been their insistence on the antiquity and glory of India. In April 1976, in London, at an 'International Conference on Restoration of Democracy in India', the audience heard that Alexander the Great, on his march into India (327 BC), had not defeated King Porus of the Punjab. Western histories had lied for two thousand years: Porus had defeated Alexander and compelled him to retreat. Half true about Alexander in India; but the topic, in the circumstances, was unexpected. Yet it was in character. In the programme booklet for the conference an Indian merchant in the Dutch West Indies (secure in someone else's economy and political system, the creation of another civilization) had taken space to print this quotation from Swami Vivekananda, the Vedantist who at the turn of the century exported Hinduism to the United States.

> Our Punya-Bhumi and its Glorious Past. If there is any land on this earth that can lay claim to be blessed Punya-bhumi, to be the

> land to which souls on this earth must come to account for Karma, the land to which every soul that is wending its way Godward must come to attain its last home, the land where humanity has attained its highest towards gentleness, towards calmness, above all, the land of introspection and of spirituality – it is INDIA.

Protest! The restoration of democracy!

'To be critical and not be swept away in a flood of archaic emotions is a much greater effort for us Indians (and I include myself),' Dr Sudhir Kakar, the psychotherapist at Jawaharlal Nehru University in New Delhi, writes in a recent letter. 'The Indian intellectual's struggle is on two fronts – inner and outer – for it has been our developmental fate that, in contrast to say France or Germany, it has always been earliest childhood that was seen to be the golden period of individual life history, just as the remotest past is considered to be the golden age of Indian history.'

So, in all the distress of India (now a fact of life, and immutable), protest looks back to the past, to what is thought to have been violated, what is known to be lost. Like childhood, this golden Indian past is not to be possessed by inquiry; it is only to be ecstatically contemplated. The past is a religious idea, clouding intellect and painful perception, numbing distress in bad times. And it is into this past – achingly close in the heart – that Gandhi has been absorbed. He too has become part of what India has lost; he is himself the object of nostalgic memories. To possess him, or to act in his name, is to have the illusion of regaining purity and the past; and in order to possess him, men have only to look inward. Everyone in India is Gandhian; everyone has his own idea of Gandhianism, as everyone has his own intimation of the *Ramraj* he offered.

## 3

In 1971, after she split the Congress, Mrs Gandhi called a midterm election. I followed this election in one constituency, Ajmer, in the semidesert state of Rajasthan. The candidate standing against Mrs Gandhi's man was a blind old Congressman who had taken part in the Independence struggle and had gone to jail. He was a little vain of having gone to jail, and spoke as though the young people coming up who hadn't gone to jail (and couldn't have, because the British had gone away) couldn't be said to have 'a record of service'.

He was a Gandhian and he wore his elegant homespun and he was honoured and he was a man of the utmost probity, and quite rich too, as a lawyer specializing in land-revenue cases. He told me that poor peasants sought him out from all over the state. His record as a legislator after Independence was blameless but null, though he thought that his stand on matters like cow-protection could bear examination by anyone; and he said he had also been connected with a campaign for the correct labelling of certain cooking oils. If he hadn't done more, it was perhaps because he didn't see that there was more for him to do; his main duty was, as it were, to keep the Gandhian prayer wheel turning.

Rajasthan is a state of famine and drought, and it had just been scourged by an eight-year drought; part of the state had been stripped of trees and turned to desert. But during his campaign (or what I saw of it) the old Congressman made no promises to anybody, and offered no ideas; all he offered was himself and his Gandhianism and his record of service. (There were, it should be said, many complex caste matters to be straightened out.)

I asked him one day, as we were racing across the desert in his campaign jeep, what it was about Gandhi that he particularly admired. He said without hesitation that he admired Gandhi for going to Buckingham Palace in 1931 in a dhoti; that act 'put the picture of poor India before the world'. As though the world didn't know. But to the old Congressman India's poverty was a special thing, and I got the impression that, as a Gandhian, he didn't want to see anyone spoiling it. The old man disliked machines; he told me he had heard that people in the West had begun to turn against them as well; and – though in a famine region, and though asking people for votes – he strongly disapproved of having piped water and electricity taken to the villages. Piped water and electricity were 'morally bad', especially for the village women. They would be denied valuable 'exercise' and become 'sluggish', and their health would suffer. No more fetching 'healthy water from the well'; no more corn-grinding with the old-fashioned quern. The good old ways were going; everything was being Westernized.

The old Congressman lost the election, and lost it badly. The reason was simple. He had no organization; the local Congress organization (which he had once manipulated) was solidly behind Mrs Gandhi and her candidate. The old man had forgotten about that. On the afternoon the results were announced I went to see him. He was sitting on a string bed in his drawing room, dressed in white, grieving, supported in his loss by a few silent followers sitting flat on the terrazzo floor. After decades of power, he had been overthrown. And in his defeat the old Congressman saw the death of Gandhian India, the India where, as he defined it, people believed that 'means should be as fair as the end'.

'There are no morals now,' the old man said. 'The Machiavellian politics of Europe have begun to touch our own politics and we will go down.'

Blind to his own political nullity, the idle self-regard of his own Gandhian concept of service, he was yet half right about India, for a reason he would not have understood.

'Archaic emotions', 'nostalgic memories': when these were awakened by Gandhi, India became free. But the India created in this way had to stall. Gandhi took India out of one kind of *Kal Yug*, one kind of Black Age; his success inevitably pushed it back into another.

# 8

# RENAISSANCE OR CONTINUITY

## I

GANDHI LIVED TOO long. Returning to India from South Africa in 1951, at the age of forty-five, holding himself aloof from the established politicians of the time, involving himself with communities and groups hitherto untouched by politics, taking up purely local causes here and there (a land tax, a mill strike), he then very quickly, from 1919 to 1930, drew all India together in a new kind of politics.

Not everyone approved of Gandhi's methods. Many were dismayed by the apparently arbitrary dictates of his 'inner voice'. And in the political stalemate of the 1930s – for which some Indians still blame him: Gandhi's unpredictable politics, they say, his inability to manage the forces he had released, needlessly lengthened the Independence struggle, delayed self-government by twenty-five years, and wasted the lives and talents of many good men – in the 1930s the management of Indian politics passed into other hands.

Gandhi himself (like Tolstoy, his early inspiration) declined into a long and ever more private mahatmahood. The obsessions were always made public, but they were personal, like his – again almost Tolstoyan – sexual anxieties in old age, after forty years of abstinence. This period of decline was the period of his greatest fame; so that, even while he lived, 'he became his admirers'. He became his emblems, his holy caricature, the object of competitive piety. Knowledge of the man as a man was lost; mahatmahood submerged all the ambiguities and the political creativity of his early years, the modernity (in India) of so much of his thought. He was claimed in the end by old India, that very India whose political deficiencies he had seen so clearly, with his South African eye.

What was new about him then was not the semi-religious nature of his politics; that was in the Indian tradition. What made him new was the nature of the battles he had fought in South Africa. And what was most revolutionary and un-Indian about him was what he left unexpressed and what perhaps, as an Indian, he had no means of expressing: his racial sense, the sense of belonging to a people specifically of the Indian subcontinent, that the twenty years in South Africa had taught him.

The racial sense is alien to Indians. Race is something they detect about others, but among themselves they know only the subcaste or caste, the clan, the gens, the language group. Beyond that they cannot go; they do not see themselves as belonging to an Indian race; the words have no meaning. Historically, this absence of cohesiveness has been the calamity of India. In South Africa, as Gandhi soon saw, it was the great weakness of the small Indian community, embattled but fragmented, the wealthy Gujarati Moslem merchants calling themselves 'Arabs', the Indian Christians claiming only their Christianity, both separating themselves from the indentured labourers of Madras and Bihar, all subjected as Indians to the same racial laws.

If it was in London as a law student that Gandhi decided that he was a Hindu by conviction, it was in South Africa that he added to this the development of a racial consciousness, that consciousness without which a disadvantaged or persecuted minority can be utterly destroyed and which with Gandhi in South Africa was like an extension of his religious sense: teaching responsibility and compassion, teaching that no man was an island, and that the dignity of the high was bound up with the dignity of the low.

'His Hindu nationalism spoils everything,' Tolstoy had said of Gandhi in 1910, while Gandhi was still in South Africa. It is obvious in Gandhi's autobiography, this growing, un-Indian awareness of an Indian group identity. It is there in his early dismay at the indifference of the Gujarati merchants to proposed anti-Indian legislation; in his shock at the appearance in his office of an indentured Tamil labourer who had been beaten up by his employer; and the shock and dismay are related to his own humiliations during his first journey to Pretoria in 1893, when he was twenty-three. Gandhi never forgot that night journey to Pretoria; more than thirty years later he spoke of it as the turning point of his life. But the racial theme is never acknowledged as such in the autobiography. It is always blurred over by religious self-searching, 'experiments with truth', attempts at the universal; though for twenty years, until early middle age, he was literally a racial leader, fighting racial battles; and it was as a racial leader that he returned to India, an oddity among the established politicians, to whom 'Indian' was only a word, each man with his own regional or caste power base.

Indians were not a minority in India; racial politics of the sort Gandhi knew in South Africa would not have been understood. And at least some of the ambiguities of his early days in India can be traced back to his wish to repeat his South African racial-religious experience, to get away from the divisive politics of religion and caste and region: his seemingly perverse insistence that India was not ready for self-government, that India had to purge itself of its own injustices first, his mystical definitions of self-government, his emphasis on the removal of untouchability, his support of trivial Moslem issues in order to draw Moslems and Hindus together.

He had no means, in India, of formulating the true racial lessons of South Africa; and perhaps he couldn't have done so, any more than he could have described what he had seen as a young man in London in 1888. The racial message always merged into the religious one; and it involved him in what looked like contradictions (against untouchability, but not against the caste system; a passionate Hindu, but preaching unity with the Moslems). The difficult lessons of South Africa were simplified and simplified in India: ending as a holy man's fad for doing the latrine-cleaning work of untouchables, seen only as an exercise in humility, ending as a holy man's plea for brotherhood and love, ending as nothing.

In the 1930s the Moslems fell away from Gandhi and turned to their own Moslem leaders, preaching the theory of two nations. In 1947 the country was partitioned, and many millions were killed and many more millions expelled from their ancestral land: as great a holocaust as that caused by Nazi Germany. And in 1948 Gandhi was killed by a Hindu for having undermined and betrayed Hindu India. Irony upon irony; but the South African Indian had long ago been lost in the Hindu mahatma; and mahatmahood in the end had worked against his Indian cause.

Jamnalal Bajaj, a pious Hindu of a northern merchant caste, was one of Gandhi's earliest financial backers in India. He gave the land and the money for the famous ashram Gandhi founded at Wardha, a village chosen because it was in the centre of India. Bajaj died in 1942; and his widow, honouring his memory, gave away a lot of money to cow-protection societies. Ved Mehta recently went to interview the old lady for his book *Mahatma Gandhi and His Apostles*. After Gandhi's death in 1948, Mrs Bajaj said, she had transferred her loyalty to Vinoba Bhave, the man recognized as Gandhi's successor. 'I walked with Vinobaji for years,' Mrs Bajaj told Mehta. 'Ten or fifteen miles a day, begging land for the poor. It was very hard, changing camp every day, because I never eat anything I haven't prepared with my own hands. Everyone knows that Moslems and Harijans have dirty habits.' And the old lady, who had been chewing something, spat.

But the end was contained in the beginning. 'For me there can be no deliverance from this earthly life except in India. Anyone who seeks such deliverance . . . must go to the sacred soil of India. For me, as for everyone else, the land of India is the "refuge of the afflicted".' This passage – which is quoted by Judith M. Brown in her study of Gandhi's entry into Indian politics, *Gandhi's Rise to Power* (1972) – comes from an article Gandhi wrote for his South African paper in 1914, at the very end of his time in South Africa, just before he returned to India by way of England. After the racial battles, the South African leader, with his now developed antipathy to Western industrial civilization, was returning to India as to the Hindu holy land: even at the beginning, then, he was already too various, and people had to find in him what they wanted to find, or what they could most easily grasp.

Judith Brown quotes a letter to a relative, written a few months before the newspaper article: 'The real secret of life seems to consist in so living in the world as it is, without being attached to it, that *moksha* [salvation, absorption into the One, freedom from rebirth] might become easy of attainment to us and to others. This will include service of self, the family, the community, and the State.' This declaration of faith, apparently a unity, conceals at least four personalities. The Hindu dreams of nonattachment and salvation; the man exposed to Western religious thought thinks that the conduct of the individual should also make salvation easy for others; the South African Indian preaches the widest social loyalty (the community, the Indian community); the political campaigner, with his respect for (and dependence on) British law and institutions, stresses service to the state.

It was too much. Something of this complex South African ideology had to go in the holy land of India; and many things went. The racial intimations remained unexpressed; and what was utterly consumed – by holiness, the subjection of India, the lengthening of the Independence struggle, and the mahatma's hardening antipathy to the machine, at once the symbol of oppression and the West – what was utterly consumed was that intrusive and unmanageable idea of service to the state.

For Vinoba Bhave, Gandhi's successor in independent India, the Gandhian ideal is the 'withering away' of the state. Or so he said many years ago. What does it mean, the withering away of the state? It means nothing. It means this: 'Our first step will be to get Gram-Raj [government by the village]: then lawsuits and disputes will be judged and settled within the village. Next it will be Ram-Raj [the Kingdom of God]: then there will no longer be any lawsuits or disputes, and we shall all live as one family.' Bhave said that more than twenty years ago (the quotation is from an admiring biography by an Italian, published in London in 1956). And something like that is still being said by others today, in the more desperate circumstances of the Emergency. 'Wanted: a Gandhian Constitution' is the title of a recent article in the *Illustrated Weekly of India*, which, since the Emergency, has been running a debate about the Indian constitution. The writer, a former state governor and ambassador, merely makes the plea for village government; he also takes the occasion to talk about his acquaintance with Gandhi; and the article is illustrated by a photograph of the writer and his wife sitting on the floor and using a quern, grinding their daily corn together in pious idleness.

It is what Gandhianism was long ago reduced to by the mahatmahood: religious ecstasy and religious self-display, a juggling with nothing, a liberation from constructive thought and political burdens. True freedom and true piety are still seen to lie in withdrawal from the difficult world. In independent India, Gandhianism is like the solace still of a conquered people, to whom the state has historically been alien, controlled by others.

Perhaps the only politician with something of Gandhi's racial sense and his feeling for all-India was Nehru, who, like Gandhi, was somewhat a displaced person in India. At first they look so unalike; but only twenty years lay between the mahatma and the English-educated Nehru; and both men were made by critical years spent outside India. In his autobiography Nehru says he was infected by the prevailing, and fashionable, anti-Semitism at Harrow School; he could hardly have failed there to have become aware of his Indianness.

The irony is that in independent India the politicians who have come up are not far removed from the men whom Gandhi – short-circuiting the established Western-style politicians of the time – began to draw into politics in 1917. They are small-town men, provincials, and they remain small because their power is based on the loyalties of caste and region. The idea of all-India is not always within their grasp. They have spoken instead, since the 1960s, only of India's need for 'emotional integration'; and the very words speak of fracture. The racial sense, which contains respect for the individual and even that concept of 'the people', remains as remote from India as ever. So that even Marxism tends to be only its jargon, a form of mimicry: 'the people' so often turn out to be people of a certain region and of a certain caste.

Gandhi swept through India, but he has left it without an ideology. He awakened the holy land; his mahatmahood returned it to archaism; he made his worshippers vain.

## 2

Vinoba Bhave, Gandhi's successor, is more a mascot than a mahatma. He is in the old Indian tradition of the sage who lives apart from men, but not so far from them that they are unable to provide him with a life-support system. Before such a sage the prince prostrates himself, in order to be reminded of the eternal verities. The prince visiting the sage: it is a recurring theme in Indian painting, from both Hindu and Moslem courts. The prince, for all his finery, is the suppliant; the sage, ash-smeared or meagre with austerities or bursting with his developed inner life, sits serenely outside his hut or below a tree. There is no particular wisdom that the sage offers; he is important simply because he is there. And this is the archaic role – one or two centuries away from Gandhi in South Africa in 1893, Gandhi in India in 1917 – that Bhave has created for himself, in contemporary India, as Gandhi's successor. He is not a particularly intelligent man and, as a perfect disciple of the mahatma, not original; his political views come close to nonsense. But he is very old; something of the aura of the dead mahatma still hangs about him; and he is the man the politicians would like to have on their side.

For some time in the 1950s Bhave was associated with Jaya Prakash Narayan, who later became one of the opposition leaders. And there was some anxiety, when the Emergency was declared in June 1975 and Narayan was arrested, about what Bhave would say. But, as it happened, Bhave wasn't talking at the time. It was the mahatma's custom, in later years, to have a weekly day of silence. Bhave, in emulation of the mahatma, but always overdoing things, had imposed a whole year's silence on himself; and there were still some months of this silence to go. Eventually, however, it was reported that various statements had been shown the old man – in the manner of those questionnaires that call for the ticking of boxes – and he had made some signs to indicate his support for the suspension of the constitution and the declaration of the state of Emergency.

When, later, he fell ill, Mrs Gandhi flew to see him; and her personal physician gave him a check-up. It was Mrs Gandhi who, under heavy security, spoke at the meeting held in Delhi to honour Bhave's eightieth birthday; and it was in deference to Bhave – or so I heard it said – that, in all the uncertainty of the Emergency, Mrs Gandhi reproclaimed the prohibition of alcohol as one of the goals of the government. Six doctors in the meantime were looking after the old sage; thus cosseted, he lived through his year of silence and at last, in January 1976, he spoke. The time had come, he said, for India to move from rule by the majority to rule by unanimity. Which was quite astute for a man of eighty. The actual statement didn't mean much; but it showed that he was still interested, that India was still protected by his sanctity.

Bhave in himself is nothing, a medieval throwback of whom there must be hundreds or thousands in India. But he is important because he is now all that India has as a moral reference, and because for the last thirty years he has been, as it were, the authorized version of Gandhi. He has fixed for India the idea of the true Gandhian way. In spite of the minute documentation of the life, in spite of the studies and the histories, it is unlikely that in the Indian mind – with its poor historical sense, its capacity for myth – Gandhi will ever be more than Bhave's magical interpretation of him.

When the politicians now, on one side or the other, speak of Gandhi or Gandhianism, they really mean Bhave. By a life of strenuous parody Bhave has swallowed his master. Gandhi took the vow of sexual abstinence when he was thirty-seven, after a great struggle. Bhave took the same vow when he wasa child. It has been his way: in his parody all the human complexity of the mahatma has been dimmed into mere holiness. Bhave has from the start looked for salvation in simple obedience alone. But by obeying what in his simplicity he has understood to be the rules, by exaggerating the mahatma's more obvious gestures, he has become something older even than the mahatma in his last phase.

Gandhi was made by London, the study of the law, the twenty years in South Africa, Tolstoy, Ruskin, the *Gita*. Bhave was made only by Gandhi's ashrams and India. He went to the Ahmedabad ashram when he was very young. He worked in the kitchens, in the latrines, and sat for such long hours at the spinning wheel that Gandhi, fearing for the effect of this manual zeal on the young man's mind, sent him away to study. He studied for a year in the holy city of Banaras. Lanza del Vasto, Bhave's Italian biographer (*Gandhi to Vinoba: the New Pilgrimage*, 1956), gives some idea of the magical nature of these studies:

> It is . . . certain that he consulted some hermit on the banks of the Ganges on contemplation and concentration, the suspension of the breath, the rousing of the Serpent coiled up at the base of the spine, and its ascension through the chakkras to the thousand-petalled lotus at the top of the head; the effacement of the 'I' and the discovery of the Self.

At Banaras one day a literature student asked Bhave about *Shakuntala*, the late-fourth-century Sanskrit play by the poet Kalidasa. It was a good subject to raise with someone who knew Sanskrit, because *Shakuntala*, which in translation reads only like a romance of recognition, is considered one of the glories of Sanskrit literature, and comes from what is thought of as a golden age of Indian civilization. But Bhave was fierce with the inquirer. He said, 'I have never read the *Shakuntala* of Kalidasa, and I never shall. I do not learn the language of the gods to amuse myself with love stories and literary trifles.'

For Bhave's biographer this is part of Bhave's perfection. It is how Indian spirituality, taken to its limits, swallows up and annuls that very civilization of which Indians boast, but of which, generally, they know little. Bhave, in the vanity of his spiritual perfection, is more than a decadent Gandhian. His religion is a kind of barbarism; it would return men to the bush. It is the religion of poverty and dust. And it is not extraordinary that Bhave's ideas about education should be like those of Mr Squeers. Get the children out into the fields, among the animals: it was, after all, the only education that the god Krishna received.

Bhave's Italian biographer, holidaying away from Europe, can at times get carried away by the Oriental wisdom of his subject, so suited to the encompassing physical wretchedness; and the book is padded out with the master's sayings. (Bhave, though he has published, doesn't believe in writing books: he has to be savoured in his sayings.) This is the political Bhave: 'The will of the people by itself equals 1. The state by itself equals 0. Together these make 10. Does 10 equal 10 because of 1 or because of the 0?' And this is Bhave (pre-1956) on the wickedness of the machine: 'Are the richest crops gathered in America, where the sowing is done from the air, or in China, where all the land is cultivated by hand on miniature allotments?'

It is hard to imagine now, but in 1952, when newly independent India was taken at its own valuation in many countries, Bhave appeared on the cover of *Time* magazine. The successor to the mahatma, and almost a mahatma himself! This was not long after Bhave had started his 'Land Gift' scheme. It was his Gandhian attempt to solve the problem of the Indian landless, and it is the venture with which his name is still associated. His plan was to go about India on foot, to walk and walk, perhaps forever, asking people with land to give some to the landless. The *Time* cover was captioned with a Bhave saying: 'I have come to loot you with love.'

The idea of the long walk was borrowed from Gandhi. But it was based on a misunderstanding. Gandhi's walks or marches were purely symbolic; they were intended as gestures, theatre. In 1930 Gandhi had walked in slow, well-publicized stages from Ahmedabad to the sea, not to do anything big when he got there, but just to pick up salt, in this way breaking an easily breakable law and demonstrating to all India his rejection of British rule. In 1947, in Bengal, he had walked in the Noakhali district, just to show himself, hoping by his presence to stop the communal killings.

These were fairly long walks. But Bhave – as usual – intended his own walk to be much, much longer, to be, it might be said, a career; and he didn't intend it to be symbolic. He was aiming at nothing less than land-redistribution as he skittered through the Indian villages, hoping, by the religious excitement of a day, to do what could (and can) be done only by law, consolidating administration, and years of patient education. It was like an attempt at a Gandhian rope trick: the substitution of spirituality for the machinery of the state. It tied in with Bhave's avowed Gandhian aim of seeing the state 'wither away'. India, released by Gandhi from subjection, was now to regenerate itself by the same spiritual means. All the other 'isms' of the world were to be made obsolete. It was an open, breathtaking experiment in Gandhian magic; and the interest of *Time* magazine, the interest of the West – always important in India, even at its most spiritual – kept the excitement high.

It became fashionable to walk with Bhave. It became, in the words of Lanza del Vasto, 'the new pilgrimage'. For a few weeks early in 1954 Lanza del Vasto walked with Bhave; and Vasto – Gandhian though he was, with a best-seller about Gandhi under his belt, and hoping to do something with Bhave too – Vasto found the going rough. Even in his awestruck account a European-accented irritation keeps breaking in at the discomforts and disorder of the Bhave march: the bad food, peppery and oversalted; the atmosphere of the circus, the constant noise, the worshipping crowds chattering like aviaries, easily distracted, even in the presence of the master; Bhave's own followers, incapable of talking in anything but shouts, constantly publicly belching and hawking and farting. Vasto tries hard to understand; a prisoner of his pilgrimage, he tries, by a natural association of ideas, to find in the torment of the nightly camp 'the innocence of the fart . . . the sportings of a lovable people which loves to communicate'.

And every day there is the next village, and the hard clay roads of Bihar. Always, Bhave strides ahead, in the lead. No villager, however worshipping or rapturous, must run across his path or walk in front of him. It is permitted only to follow– sainthood, and the salvation it offers (contained in the mere sight of the saint), has its stringencies. At one stage Bhave, for no apparent reason, seems to have his doubts and seems to be dropping hints of a fast against the 'laziness' of some of his staff (which includes a press officer) and the 'meanness' of some other people. Clearly, things have been going on behind the scenes that Vasto doesn't know about. But long before then it has occurred to the reader that, in spite of all the sermons, this walk is just a walk; that nothing, or very little, is being done; that none of those chattering villagers may be either giving or getting land; that everybody is just declaring for God.

In the early days there had been talk of a university to serve the special needs of the movement, and someone had given land for it not far from the site of the Buddha's Enlightenment. Bhave was asked about the university one day. He said, 'The ground is there and I've had a well dug on it. The passer-by will be able to draw a bucket of water and drink his fill.' But the questioner wanted to know about the university. 'What will be its aims, statutes, and syllabuses?' Bhave said: 'The ground is there, the well is there. Whoever wants to drink will drink. What more do you want?'

Even for a saint, this was living dangerously. But Bhave was Bhave, and it was seven more years before he gave up the long walk and settled down quietly as a sage, sinking into the stupor of meditation.

Magic hadn't worked; spirituality hadn't brought about land-redistribution or, more importantly, the revolution in social attitudes that such a redistribution required. The effect, in fact, had been the opposite. The living saint, officially adulated, preceded by magical reports, offering salvation to all who cast eyes on him, was a living confirmation of the rightness of the old ways, of the necessity for old reverences. Bihar, where Bhave did much of his walking, remains – in matters of land and untouchability – among the most backward and crushed of the Indian states.

Bhave, even if he understood Gandhi's stress on the need for social reform, was incapable of undermining Hindu India; he was too much part of it. The perfect disciple, obeying without always knowing why, he invariably distorted his master's message. Once, on the march, he said that untouchables did work human beings shouldn't do; for that reason they should be given land, to become tillers. This might have seemed Gandhian; but all that the words could be taken to mean was that latrine-cleaners were latrine-cleaners, that untouchables were untouchables. The whole point of Gandhi's message was lost.

Hindu speculation can soar high; but Hindu religious practices are elemental, and spirituality for most people is a tangible good, magic. Bhave offered spirituality as just such a good; and he could offer it as a commodity in which, as Gandhi's heir, he was specially licensed to deal. At a public meeting in 1962 – at Shantiniketan, the university founded by the poet Tagore to revive the arts in

India – Bhave described himself as 'a retailer of spirituality'. At Shantiniketan! Such was Bhave's security in India; to such a degree had the rational thought of a man like Tagore been chewed up by the cultural primitivism of Gandhian India.

Some years before, in a memorable statement made during the great days of the long walk, Bhave had described himself as the fire. It was his duty simply to burn; it was for others to use his fire. Humility, once it becomes a vow, ceases to be humility, Gandhi said in his autobiography; and Bhave's interpretation of his function in India is as vain and decadent as it appears. It was a perversion of the *Gita*'s idea of duty, a perversion of the idea of *dharma*; it was the language of the magician.

Bhave, with his simplicity and distortions, offered Gandhianism as a kind of magic; and he offered himself as the magician. Gandhi, the South African, was too complex for India. India made the racial leader the mahatma; and in Bhave the mahatma became Merlin. He failed, but that did not tarnish his sainthood. He had failed, after all, only because the times were bad; because, as so many Indians say, offering it as the profoundest wisdom, since the death of Gandhi truth has fled from India and the world. In a Black Age, Bhave had virtuously attempted old magic; and on his eightieth birthday he was honoured in New Delhi. Paunchy Congressmen in crisp white homespun sat on the platform and some made speeches. Mrs Gandhi, after a little fumbling, carefully garlanded his portrait.

The latest – censored and incomplete – news about Bhave is that in June 1976 he started a public fast. In this fast, which he must have considered his last public act, there is still the element of Gandhian parody. Gandhi, too, did a famous last fast. But Gandhi's fast – his last expression of pain and despair in partitioned India – was against human slaughter in the Punjab and Bengal. Bhave's last fast, if the reports are correct, was against cow-slaughter.

It seems to be always there in India: magic, the past, the death of the intellect, spirituality annulling the civilization out of which it issues, India swallowing its own tail.

## 3

With the dismantling, during the Emergency, of its borrowed or inherited democratic institutions, and with no foreign conqueror now to impose a new order, India for the first time for centuries is left alone with the blankness of its decayed civilization. The freedoms that came to independent India with the institutions it gave itself were alien freedoms, better suited to another civilization; in India they remained separate from the internal organization of the country, its beliefs and antique restrictions. In the beginning it didn't matter. There were development plans. India industrialized, more effectively than is generally supposed; it more than doubled its production of food; it is now the world's fourth largest producer of grain. And out of this prodigious effort arose a new mutinous stirring, which took India by surprise, and with which it didn't know how to cope. It was as though India didn't know what its Independence had committed it to.

The population grew; the landless fled from the tyranny of the villages; the towns choked; the restlessness created by the beginnings of economic development – in a land immemorially abject – expressed itself in the streets, in varying ways. In this very triumph of democracy lay its destruction. Formal politics answered less and less, became more and more formal; towards the end it had the demeanour of a parlour game, and became an affair of head-counting and floor-crossing. And the Indian press, another borrowed institution, also failed. With its restricted view of its function, it matched the triviality of the politics; it became part of the Indian anarchy. It reported speeches and more speeches; it reduced India to its various legislative chambers. It turned into national figures those politicians who were the least predictable; and both they and the freedom of the press vanished with the Emergency.

The dismantled institutions – of law and press and parliament – cannot simply be put together again. They have been undone; they can be undone again; it has been demonstrated that freedom is not an absolute in independent India. Mrs Gandhi has given her name to the Emergency, and impressed it with her personality. It is unfortunate that this should be so, because it has simplified comment on one side and the other, and blurred the true nature of the crisis. With or without Mrs Gandhi, independent India – with institutions of government opposed to its social organization, with problems of poverty that every Indian feels in his bones to be beyond solution – would have arrived at a state of emergency. And the Emergency, even with Mrs Gandhi's immense authority, is only a staying action. However it is resolved, India will at the end be face to face with its own emptiness, the inadequacy of an old civilization which is cherished because it is all men have but which no longer answers their needs.

India is without an ideology – and that was the failure of Gandhi and India together. Its people have no idea of the state, and none of the attitudes that go with such an idea: no historical notion of the past, no identity beyond the tenuous ecumenism of Hindu beliefs, and, in spite of the racial excesses of the British period, not even the beginnings of a racial sense. Through centuries of conquest the civilization declined into an apparatus for survival, turning away from the mind (on which the sacred *Gita* lays such stress) and creativity (Vinoba Bhave finding in Sanskrit only the language of the gods, and not the language of poets), stripping itself down, like all decaying civilizations, to its magical practices and imprisoning social forms. To enable men to survive, men had to be diminished. And this was a civilization that could narrow and still appear whole. Perhaps because of its unconcealed origins in racial conquest (victorious Aryans, subjugated aborigines), it is shot through with ambiguous beliefs that can either exalt men or abase them.

The key Hindu concept of *dharma* – the right way, the sanctioned way, which all men must follow, according to their natures – is an elastic concept. At its noblest it combines self-fulfilment and truth to the self with the ideas of action as duty, action as its own spiritual reward, man as a holy vessel. And it ceases then to be mysterious; it touches the high ideals of other civilizations. It might be said that it is of *dharma* that Balzac is writing when, near the end of his creative life, breaking through fatigue and a long blank period to write *Cousine Bette* in eight weeks, he reflects on the artist's vocation:

> Constant labour is the law of art as well as the law of life, for art is the creative activity of the mind. And so great artists, true poets, do not wait for either commissions or clients; they create today, tomorrow, ceaselessly. And there results a habit of toil, a perpetual consciousness of the difficulties, that keeps them in a state of marriage with the Muse, and her creative forces.

And Proust, too, killing himself to write his book, comes close to the concept of *dharma* when, echoing Balzac, he says that in the end it is less the desire for fame than 'the habit of laboriousness' that takes a writer to the end of a work. But *dharma*, as this ideal of truth to oneself, or living out the truth in oneself, can also be used to reconcile men to servitude and make them find in paralysing obedience the highest spiritual good. 'And do thy duty, even if it be humble,' says the Aryan *Gita*, 'rather than another's, even if it be great. To die in one's duty is life: to live in another's is death.'

*Dharma* is creative or crippling according to the state of the civilization, according to what is expected of men. It cannot be otherwise. The quality of a faith is not a constant; it depends on the quality of the men who profess it. The religion of a Vinoba Bhave can only express the dust and defeat of the Indian village. Indians have made some contribution to science in this century; but – with a few notable exceptions – their work has been done abroad. And this is more than a matter of equipment and facilities. It is a cause of concern to the Indian scientific community – which feels itself vulnerable in India – that many of those men who are so daring and original abroad should, when they are lured back to

India, collapse into ordinariness and yet remain content, become people who seem unaware of their former worth, and seem to have been brilliant by accident. They have been claimed by the lesser civilization, the lesser idea of *dharma* and self-fulfilment. In a civilization reduced to its forms, they no longer have to strive intellectually to gain spiritual merit in their own eyes; that same merit is now to be had by religious right behaviour, correctness.

India grieved for the scientist Har Gobind Khorana, who, as an American citizen, won a Nobel Prize in medicine for the United States a few years ago. India invited him back and fêted him; but what was most important about him was ignored. 'We would do everything for Khorana,' one of India's best journalists said, 'except do him the honour of discussing his work.' The work, the labour, the assessment of the labour: it was expected that somehow that would occur elsewhere, outside India.

It is part of the intellectual parasitism that Indians accept (and, as a conquered people, have long accepted) while continuing to see their civilization as whole and possessed of the only truth that matters: offering refuge to 'the afflicted', as Gandhi saw it in 1914, and 'deliverance from this earthly life'. It is as though it is in the very distress and worldly incapacity of India – rather than in its once vigorous civilization – that its special virtue has now to be found. And it is like the solace of despair, because (as even Gandhi knew, and as all his early political actions showed) there is no virtue in worldly defeat.

Indian poverty is more dehumanizing than any machine; and, more than in any machine civilization, men in India are units, locked up in the straitest obedience by their idea of their *dharma*. The scientist returning to India sheds the individuality he acquired during his time abroad; he regains the security of his caste identity, and the world is once more simplified. There are minute rules, as comforting as bandages; individual perception and judgement, which once called forth his creativity, are relinquished as burdens, and the man is once more a unit in his herd, his science reduced to a skill. The blight of caste is not only untouchability and the consequent deification in India of filth; the blight, in an India that tries to grow, is also the over-all obedience it imposes, its ready-made satisfactions, the diminishing of adventurousness, the pushing away from men of individuality and the possibility of excellence.

Men might rebel; but in the end they usually make their peace. There is no room in India for outsiders. The Arya Samaj, the Aryan Association, a reformist group opposed to traditional ideas of caste, and active in north India earlier in the century, failed for a simple reason. It couldn't meet the marriage needs of its members; India called them back to the castes and rules they had abjured. And five years ago in Delhi I heard this story. A foreign businessman saw that his untouchable servant was intelligent, and decided to give the young man an education. He did so, and before he left the country he placed the man in a better job. Some years later the businessman returned to India. He found that his untouchable was a latrine-cleaner again. He had been boycotted by his clan for breaking away from them; he was barred from the evening smoking group. There was no other group he could join, no woman he could marry. His solitariness was insupportable, and he had returned to his duty, his *dharma*; he had learned to obey.

Obedience: it is all that India requires of men, and it is what men willingly give. The family has its rules; the caste has its rules. For the disciple, the guru – whether holy man or music teacher – stands in the place of God, and has to be implicitly obeyed, even if – like Bhave with Gandhi – he doesn't always understand why. Sacred texts have to be learned by heart; school texts have to be learned by heart, and university textbooks, and the notes of lecturers. 'It is a fault in the Western system of education,' Vinoba Bhave said some years ago, 'that it lays so little stress on learning great lines by heart.' And the children of middle schools chant their lessons like Buddhist novices, raising their voices, like the novices, when the visitor appears, to show their zeal. So India ever absorbs the new into its old self, using new tools in old ways, purging itself of unnecessary mind, maintaining its equilibrium. The poverty of the land is reflected in the poverty of the mind; it would be calamitous if it were otherwise.

The civilization of conquest was also the civilization of defeat; it enabled men, obeying an elastic *dharma*, to dwindle with their land. Gandhi awakened India; but the India he awakened was only the India of defeat, the holy land he needed after South Africa.

## 4

Like a novelist who splits himself into his characters, unconsciously setting up the consonances that give his theme a closed intensity, the many-sided Gandhi permeates modern India. He is hidden, unknown except in his now moribund Bhave incarnation; but the drama that is being played out in India today is the drama he set up more than sixty years ago, when he returned to India after the racial battles of South Africa. The creator does not have to understand the roots of his obsessions; his duty is merely to set events in motion. Gandhi gave India its politics; he called up its archaic religious emotions. He made them serve one another, and brought about an awakening. But in independent India the elements of that awakening negate one another. No government can survive on Gandhian fantasy; and the spirituality, the solace of a conquered people, which Gandhi turned into a form of national assertion, has soured more obviously into the nihilism that it always was.

The opposition spokesmen in exile speak of the loss of democracy and freedom; and their complaints are just. But the borrowed words conceal archaic Gandhian obsessions as destructive as many of the provisions of the Emergency: fantasies of *Ramraj*, fantasies of spirituality, a return to the village, simplicity. In these obsessions – the cause of political battle – there still live, in the unlikeliest way, the disturbance of Gandhi's blind years in London as a law student and the twenty years' racial wounding in South

Africa. They are now lost, the roots of Gandhi's rejection of the West and his nihilism; the failure of the twenty years in South Africa is expunged from the Indian consciousness. But if Gandhi had resolved his difficulties in another way, if (like the imaginative novelist) he hadn't so successfully transmuted his original hurt (which with him must have been in large part racial), if he had projected on to India another code of survival, he might have left independent India with an ideology, and perhaps even with what in India would have been truly revolutionary, the continental racial sense, the sense of belonging to a people specifically of India, which would have answered all his political aims, and more: not only weakening untouchability and submerging caste, but also awakening the individual, enabling men to stand alone within a broader identity, establishing a new idea of human excellence.

Now the people who fight about him fight about nothing; neither he nor old India has the solutions to the present crisis. He was the last expression of old India; he took India to the end of that road. All the arguments about the Emergency, all the references to his name reveal India's intellectual vacuum, and the emptiness of the civilization to which he seemed to give new life.

In conquered India renaissance has always been taken to mean a recovery of what has been suppressed or dishonoured, an exalting of old ways; in periods of respite men have never taken the opportunity, or perhaps have been without the intellectual means, to move ahead; and disaster has come again. Art historians tell us that the European renaissance became established when men understood that the past was not living on; that Ovid or Virgil could not be thought of as a kind of ancient cleric; that men had to put distance between the past and themselves, the better to understand and profit from that past. India has always sought renewal in the other way, in continuity. In the earliest texts men look back to the past and speak of the present Black Age; just as they look back now to the days of Gandhi and the fight against the British, and see all that has followed as defilement rather than as the working out of history. While India tries to go back to an idea of its past, it will not possess that past or be enriched by it. The past can now be possessed only by inquiry and scholarship, by intellectual rather than spiritual discipline. The past has to be seen to be dead; or the past will kill.

The stability of Gandhian India was an illusion; and India will not be stable again for a long time. But in the present uncertainty and emptiness there is the possibility of a true new beginning, of the emergence in India of mind, after the long spiritual night. 'The crisis of India is not political: this is only the view from Delhi. Dictatorship or rule by the army will change nothing. Nor is the crisis only economic. These are only aspects of the larger crisis, which is that of a decaying civilization, where the only hope lies in further swift decay.' I wrote that in 1967; and that seemed to me a blacker time.

*August 1975 – October 1976*

# INDIA:
# A MILLION MUTINIES NOW

# PREFACE

## About fiction and non-fiction: some words about *India: A Million Mutinies Now*

INDIA: A MILLION Mutinies Now is a long book, one of my longest. Long books (it has to be said) are harder to write than short books, and I have more than a certain regard for this one. Twenty years after the writing I still have a clear memory of the labour and the ambition.

I thought when I began to write that I would do fiction alone. To be a writer of the imagination seemed to me the noblest thing. But after a few books I saw that my material – the matter in my head, the matter in the end given me by my background – would not support that ambition.

The ambition itself had been given me by what I knew of the great nineteenth-century novels of Europe, or what I thought I knew of them. I put it in that cautious way because before I began to write I actually hadn't read a great deal. I saw now – something I suppose I had always sensed but never worked out as an idea – that those novels had come out of societies more compartmented, more intellectually ordered and full of conviction than the one I found myself in. To pretend that I came out of a society as complete and ordered would in some ways have made writing easier. The order I am talking about is, to put it at its simplest, the order, the fenced-in setting, that underpins the television situation comedy. The rules of the fenced-in world are few and easily understood; the messy outside world doesn't intrude to undo the magic. I could have tried to write like that. But I would not have got very far. I would have had to simplify too much, leave out a lot. It would have been to deny what I saw as my task as a writer.

I had to be true to my own world. It was more fluid, harder to pin down and to present to a reader in any accepted, nineteenth-century way. Every simple statement I could make about myself or my family or background had to be qualified in some way.

I was born in 1932 on the other side of the Atlantic in the British colony of Trinidad. Trinidad was an outcrop of Venezuela and South America. It was a small island, essentially agricultural when I was born (Trinidad, like Venezuela, had oil, which was beginning to be developed). It had a racially mixed population of perhaps half a million, with my own immigrant Asian Indian community (finely divided by religion, education, money, caste background) about a hundred and fifty thousand. (I have rehearsed these matters elsewhere, but I feel they should be stated here again, for this occasion.)

I had no great love for the place, no love for its colonial smallness. I saw myself as a castaway from the world's old civilisations, and I wished to be part of that bigger world as soon as possible. An academic scholarship in 1950, when I was eighteen, enabled me to leave. I went to England to do a university course, with the ambition afterwards of being a writer. I never in any real sense went back.

So my world as a writer was full of flight and unfinished experience, full of the odds and ends of cultures and migrations, from India to the New World in 1880–1900, from the New World to Europe in 1950, things that didn't make a whole. There was nothing like the stability of the rooted societies that had produced the great fictions of the nineteenth century, in which, for example, even a paragraph of a fairytale or parable by Tolstoy could suggest a whole real world. And soon, as I have said, I saw myself at the end of the scattered island material I carried with me.

But writing was my vocation; I had never wished to be anything but a writer. My practice as a writer had deepened the fascination with people and narrative which I had always had, and increasingly now, in the larger world I had wanted to join, that fascination was turning into a wish to understand the currents of history that had created the fluidity of which I found myself a part. It was necessary for me as a writer to engage with the larger world. I didn't know how to set about it; there was no example I could follow.

The practice of fiction couldn't help me. Fiction is best done from within and out of great knowledge. In the larger world I was an outsider; I didn't know enough and would never know enough. After much hesitation and uncertainty I saw that I had to deal with this world in the most direct way. I had to go against my practice as a fiction-writer. I had to use the tools I had developed to record my experience as truthfully as possible. So there came this divide in my writing: free-ranging fiction and scrupulous non-fiction, one supporting and feeding the other, complementary aspects of my wish to get to grips with my world. And though I had started with the idea of the nobility of the writer of the imagination, I do not now rate one way above the other.

In the practising of this new way I had to deal first of all with my ancestral land, India. I was not an insider, even after many months of travel; nor could I consider myself an outsider: India and the idea of India had always been important to me. So I was always divided about India, and found it hard to say a final word. In all I have written three books about India. They are non-fiction, as they had to be, but they are as personal and varied and deeply felt as any work of fiction could be. *India: A Million Mutinies Now* was the third of those Indian books. It was written twenty-six years after the first. It had taken the writer all that time to go beyond personal discovery and pain, and analysis, to arrive at the simple and overwhelming idea that the most important thing about India, the thing to be gone into and understood, and not seen from the outside, was the people.

The book was dedicated to a further idea: that India was, in the simplest way, on the move, that all over the vast country men and women had moved out of the cramped ways and expectations of their parents and grandparents, and were expecting more. This was the 'million mutinies' of the title; it was not guerrilla wars all round. Nearly every English-speaker would have some idea of the brief Indian Mutiny of 1857 when some mercenary Indian soldiers of the British East India Company, confused and angry, but with no clear end in view, mutinied against the British. The million mutinies of my title suggests that what is happening now is a truer and more general way ahead.

This seems a reasonable thing to say now, in 2010, at the time of an acknowledged Indian boom. It was different in 1988, when I began the book. India was full of a pietistic Gandhian gloom, self-satisfied and rather happy as this kind of gloom often is in India. The talk among the talkers in the towns was of degeneracy, a falling away from the standards of earlier times: politics were being criminalised, and there was corruption everywhere. Standard stuff, not profound, not based on any real knowledge of the country; but it could undermine one. It was the background against which I worked out my idea of the mutinies.

The idea didn't come to me out of the air. I had done a lot of hard travelling in India in the past twenty-six years. As a writer, a free man, I had picked up a more varied knowledge of the country than most Indians, who were bound to their families and jobs. I had spent many weeks in the districts, away from the big towns. With the help and hospitality of Indian friends and officials I had been able in various places to enter, if only for a week or two at a time, the life of the bare and sometimes forbidding Indian countryside. I had been granted some knowledge of small-town life. I had not always written of what I had seen. So my experience had banked up, and the idea now came to me of expanding on that experience and doing a large book, full of people, an Indian panorama which (since I believe that the present, accurately seized, foretells the future) would contain or explain in a broad way most of what might happen in the country for the next twenty or thirty years. This was what I told my English publishers. They liked the idea; they bought it after ten minutes, quite literally; and not many days after that I found myself in the Taj Mahal Hotel in Bombay, marvelling at my ambition, and not really sure how I was to come to a human understanding of the enormous city (such an apparently impenetrable afternoon crowd just outside, moving about the Gateway of India, beside the tarnished Arabian Sea). And, of course, behind the city there was the country: memories for me, alarming now, of endless sunstruck journeys by road and rail.

I had four blank, frightening days in the glamorous hotel, during which I did the dispiriting thing of keeping a self-conscious journal with nothing to say. I didn't like the journal form; it blurred vision. I preferred distance, and the sifting of memory. The comparison that comes to mind now is that of Ibsen, still more poet than playwright, struggling to keep a journal on his trip to the opening of the Suez Canal in 1869. Momentous days, fabulous sights: made for a journal, one would have thought; but it must have fatigued Ibsen to be on the outside, dealing only with the externals of things; and he simply stopped. In some such way in Bombay I broke down and gave my dour journal up; and looked around to make another kind of start.

A big board in the hotel lobby advertised a resident or 'in-house' fortune-teller; I was often tempted in those four days to go for a reading, to find out whether I would do the book. I didn't have to do that. One does more in anxiety than one suspects. The book did get started – 'Bombay is a crowd' is the opening line I alighted on – and then it moved fast.

Ideas are abstract. They become books only when they are clothed with people and narrative. The reader, once he has entered this book and goes beyond the opening pages, finds himself in a double narrative. There is the immediate narrative of the person to whom we are being introduced; there is the larger outer narrative in which all the varied pieces of the book are going to fit together. Nothing is done at random. Serious travel is an art, even if no writing is contemplated; and the special art in this book lay in divining who of the many people I met would best and most logically take my story forward, where nothing had to be forced.

I had to depend on local people for introductions, and it was not always easy to make clear what I was looking for. Many people, trained in journalistic ways, thought I was looking for 'spokesmen' for various interests. I was in fact looking for something profounder and more intrusive: someone's lived experience (if I can so put it) that would illuminate some aspect, some new turn, in the old country's unceasing adjustment to new thought, new politics, new ideas of business. So in this book one kind of experience grows out of another, one theme develops out of another.

Part of my luck was the decision, made for no clear reason one day in the Taj Mahal Hotel in Bombay, to do the religiously inauspicious Indian thing and travel round India in an anti-clockwise direction. To have gone the other way, north, to Delhi and Calcutta and the Punjab would have been to get to the meat of the book too quickly, to leave the rest of the country hanging on, in a kind of anti-climax. To go south first, as I did, was to deal in a fresh way with important things like the influence of caste on the development of Indian science, the little-known century-long caste war of the south, the dispossession of the Brahmins. This could be said to prepare the reader (and the writer) for the disturbances of the north: the British in Calcutta, Lucknow, Delhi: all the history of the past century, just below the present.

I have often been asked about my note-taking method during the actual time of travel. I used no tape-recorder; I used pen and notebook alone. Since I was never sure whether someone I was meeting would serve my purpose I depended in the beginning very often on simple conversation. I never frightened anyone by showing a notebook. If I found I was hearing something I needed I would tell the person I wanted to take down his words at a later time. At this later time I would get the person to repeat what he had said and what I half knew. I took it all down in handwriting, making a note as I did so of the setting, the speaker, and my own questions. It invariably happened that the speaker, seeing me take it all down by hand, spoke more slowly and thoughtfully this second time, and yet his words had the rhythm of normal speech. An amazing amount could be done in an hour. I changed nothing, smoothed over nothing.

Ambitious and difficult books are not always successful. But it remains to be said that in paperback in England this book has been reprinted thirty-five times. I marvel at the luck.

2010

# CONTENTS

# I

# BOMBAY THEATRE

Bombay is a crowd. But I began to feel, when I was some way into the city from the airport that morning, that the crowd on the pavement and the road was very great, and that something unusual might be happening.

Traffic into the city moved slowly because of the crowd. When at certain intersections the traffic was halted, by lights or by policemen or by the two together, the pavements seethed the more, and such a torrent of people swept across the road, in such a bouncing froth of light-coloured lightweight clothes, it seemed that some kind of invisible sluice-gate had been opened, and that if it wasn't closed again the flow of road-crossers would spread everywhere, and the beaten-up red buses and yellow-and-black taxis would be quite becalmed, each at the centre of a human eddy.

With me, in the taxi, were fumes and heat and din. The sun burned; there was little air; the grit from the bus exhausts began to stick to my skin. It would have been worse for the people on the road and the pavements. But many of them seemed freshly bathed, with fresh puja marks on their foreheads; many of them seemed to be in their best clothes: Bombay people celebrating an important new day, perhaps.

I asked the driver whether it was a public holiday. He didn't understand my question, and I let it be.

Bombay continued to define itself: Bombay flats on either side of the road now, concrete buildings mildewed at their upper levels by the Bombay weather, excessive sun, excessive rain, excessive heat; grimy at the lower levels, as if from the crowds at pavement level, and as if that human grime was working its way up, tide-mark by tide-mark, to meet the mildew.

The shops, even when small, even when dingy, had big, bright signboards, many-coloured, inventive, accomplished, the work of men with a feeling for both Roman and Sanskrit (or Devanagari) letters. Often, in front of these shops, and below those signboards, was just dirt; from time to time depressed-looking, dark people could be seen sitting down on this dirt and eating, indifferent to everything but their food.

There were big film posters on billboards, and smaller ones repeating on lamp-posts. It was hard, just at this moment of arrival, to relate the romance the posters promised to the people on the ground. And harder to place the English-language advertisements for banks and airlines and the *Times of India* Sesquicentennial ('Good Times, Sad Times, Changing Times'): to the stranger just arrived after a night flight, the city suggested by those advertisements was like an almost unimaginable distillation – a special, rich liquor – of the humanity that was on view.

The crowd continued. And then I saw that a good part of this crowd was a long queue or line of people, three or four or five deep, on the other pavement. The line was being added to all the time; and though for stretches it appeared to be standing still, it was moving very slowly. I realised I had been driving past the line for some time; perhaps, then, the line was already a mile long. The line was broken at road intersections: policemen in khaki uniforms were keeping the side roads clear.

What were these people waiting for? What was their chance of getting what they wanted? They seemed peaceable and content, even in the sun and the brown smoke of exhausts. They were in good clothes, simple, Indian-style clothes. People joining the line came almost at a trot; then they became patient; they seemed prepared to wait a long time. I had missed the beginning of the line. I didn't know what lay there. A circus? I believe there had been posters for a circus earlier on the road. An appearance by film stars? But the people in the line didn't show that kind of eagerness. They were small, dark, patient people, serious, and in their best clothes; and it came back to me that somewhere along the line earlier there had been flags and emblems of some sort.

I was told, when I got to the hotel in downtown Bombay, that there was no public holiday that day. And though the crowd had seemed to me great, and the line quite remarkable, something the newspapers might have mentioned, the hotel people I spoke to couldn't tell me what the line might have been for. What had been a big event for so many thousands somewhere in mid-town Bombay had sent no ripple here.

I telephoned an acquaintance, a writer. He knew as little as the hotel people. He said he hadn't been out that morning; he had been at home, writing an article for *Debonair.* Later, when he had finished his article, he telephoned me. He said he had two theories. The first theory was that the people I had seen might have been lining up for telephone directories. There had been trouble about the delivery of new directories – Bombay was Bombay. The second theory was something he had had from his servant woman. She had come in after I had telephoned, and she had told him that that day was the birthday of Dr Ambedkar, and that there was a big celebration in the suburb I had passed on my way from the airport.

Dr Ambedkar had been the great leader of the people once known in India as the untouchables. He had been more important to them than Mahatma Gandhi. In his time he had known honour and power; he had been law minister in the first government of independent India, and he had drafted the Indian constitution; but he had remained embittered to the end. It was Dr Ambedkar who had encouraged the untouchables – the *harijans,* the children of God, as Gandhi called them, and now the Dalits, as they called themselves – to abandon Hinduism, which had enslaved them, and to turn to Buddhism. Before his thought could change or develop, he died, in 1956.

No leader of comparable authority or esteem had risen among the castes for whom Dr Ambedkar spoke. He had remained their leader, the man they honoured above all others; he was almost their deity. In every Dalit house, I had been told, there was a photograph of Dr Ambedkar. It was a photograph I had seen many times, and it was strange that a better photograph hadn't been used. The Ambedkar icon was like a grey passport photograph reproduced in an old-fashioned newspaper process: the leader reduced to a composition of black and white dots, frozen in an image of the 1940s or 1950s, a plumpish man of unmemorable features, with the glasses of a student, and in the semi-colonial respectability of jacket and tie. Jacket and tie made for an unlikely holy image in India. But it was fitting, because it went against the homespun and loincloth of the mahatma.

The Dr Ambedkar idea seemed better than the idea about the telephone directories. There had, indeed, been a religious stillness about the people in the line. They had been like people gaining merit through doing the right thing. The Dr Ambedkar idea made sense of the flags and the emblems of which I had had a memory. The people I had seen were honouring their leader, their saint, their deity; and by this they were honouring themselves as well.

Later that day I talked to an official of the hotel. He asked for my impressions of Bombay. When I told him about the Ambedkar crowd, he was for a moment like a man taken aback. He was at a loss for words. Then, irritation and unhappiness breaking through his well-bred hotel manner, he said, 'The country's going from bad to worse.'

It was a version of what I had heard many times about India; India had changed; it was not the good and stable country it had once been. In the days of the freedom movement, political workers, honouring Gandhi, had worn homespun as an emblem of sacrifice and service, their oneness with the poor. Now the politician's homespun stood for power. With industrialization and economic growth people had forgotten old reverences. Men honoured only money now. The great investment in development over three or four decades had led only to this: to 'corruption', to the 'criminalization of politics'. In seeking to rise, India had undone itself. No one could be sure of anything now; all was fluid. Policeman, thief, politician: the roles had become interchangeable. And with money – the money of which the crowded, ugly skyscraper towers of Bombay spoke – many long-buried particularities had been released. These disruptive, lesser loyalties – of region, caste, and clan – now played on the surface of Indian life.

The Dalits, for instance. If they had still been only the mahatma's harijans, children of God, people for whom good things might be done, objects of sentiment and a passing piety, an occasion like the morning's Ambedkar anniversary wouldn't have given anyone thoughts of a world about to undo itself. But a certain amount of money had come to the people once known as harijans, a certain amount of education, and with that there had also come the group sense and political consciousness. They had ceased to be abstractions. They had begun to do things for themselves. They had become people stressing their own particularity, just as better-off groups in India stressed their particularities.

And the Dalit particularity was perhaps not the most important one in the city of Bombay. Just outside the hotel was the Gateway of India. This was a British monument: a high, magnificent arch, commemorating the arrival in India in 1911 of the King-Emperor, George V. The imperial associations of the arch were now absorbed into the poetic idea of the gateway; and the paved open area around it was a popular afternoon promenade. On either side of that imperial monument simple and quite small signboards had been put up, with one word in the Devanagari script, black on white – giving the name of the city as *Mumbai* rather than 'Bombay'.

Those *Mumbai* boards spoke of an internal fight. Bombay was a cosmopolitan city. That was how it had been from the start, and that was how it had developed; it had drawn people from all over the sub-continent. But, in independent India, Bombay had found itself in the state of Maharashtra; and in the mid-1960s a Maharashtrian regional movement had started. This movement wanted Maharashtra to be for the Maharashtrians. In the beginning the movement's hostility had been aimed mainly at poor migrants from South India; but other people had felt threatened as well. The movement was known as the Shiv Sena, the Army of Shiva, taking its name from Shivaji, the 17th-century warrior-leader of the Maratha people. The newspapers had been critical; they called the Sena 'fascist'. But the Sena had not ceased to grow. Two years before, it had won control of the Bombay Municipal Corporation.

The corporation building was in the confident Victorian-Gothic style of British Bombay. A wide, solid staircase, with Victorian metalwork below a polished timber banister, led to the council chamber. The walls there were half-panelled in a rich red-brown wood, and the desks and chairs were set in arcs and semi-circles around the mayoral chair. The councillors' chairs were upholstered in green. But the mayoral chair had a saffron cover. Saffron is a Hindu colour, and here it was the colour of the Shiv Sena. Saffron satin filled the Gothic arch below the gallery on one end wall of the chamber. In front of the saffron satin was a bronze-coloured bust of Shivaji; above the bust, on the satin, were a round shield and crossed swords, also in a bronze colour.

High up on the wall at the back of the mayoral chair, and above the Gothic arches (springing from grey marble columns), were portraits of famous old Indian mayors of Bombay from colonial days. The men in the portraits were dignified; they wore wigs or Parsi caps or Hindu turbans or Muslim turbans. The dignity of those men, and the nationalist pride their dignity would once have encouraged, had now been superseded.

The council chamber was so perfect in its way, so confident, its architectural details so considered, it was hard to imagine that it had all been negated by the simple saffron of the Sena. It made me think of the Christian cathedral in Nicosia in Cyprus, taken over by the Muslims, cleansed of much of its furniture, and hung with Koranic banners. It made me think of the Marathas of the 17th century, in the vacuum between the Moguls and British, raiding as far north as Delhi, as far east as Bengal, and setting Maratha rulers on the throne of Tanjore in the far south.

The visitor, coming into Bombay from the airport, might see only small dark men in an undifferentiated crowd, and dust and fumes; might see, between the concrete blocks, a mess of makeshift huts and the parasitic shelters those huts spawned, one kind of dependence leading down into another; might see what looked like the unending smallness of men. But here in the corporation chamber, in the saffron and crossed swords of the Sena, were the emblems of war and conquest.

It made the Independence struggle seem like an interim. Independence had come to India like a kind of revolution; now there were many revolutions within that revolution. What was true of Bombay was true of other parts of India as well: of the state of Andhra, of Tamil Nadu, Assam, the Punjab. All over India scores of particularities that had been frozen by foreign rule, or by poverty or lack of opportunity or abjectness, had begun to flow again. And it was easy to see how someone like the man in the hotel, who had grown up with another idea of India and its development, could feel alienated and insecure.

Some such feeling of alienation I had known myself when I had first gone to India, in 1962. That had been a special journey for me: I had gone as the descendant of 19th-century indentured Indian emigrants. Such emigrants had been recruited from the 1860s on, mainly from the eastern Gangetic plain, and then sent out from depots in Calcutta to work on five-year indentures on plantations in various parts of the British Empire and even elsewhere. People like my ancestors had gone to Fiji in the Pacific; Mauritius in the Indian Ocean; South Africa; and to some of the territories in the

West Indies, principally the Guianas (British Guiana and Dutch Guiana) and Trinidad. It was to Trinidad that my ancestors went, starting some time in the 1880s, as I work it out.

These overseas Indian groups were mixed. They were miniature Indias, with Hindus and Muslims, and people of different castes. They were disadvantaged, without representation, and without a political tradition. They were isolated by language and culture from the people they found themselves among; they were isolated, too, from India itself (many weeks away by steamboat from Trinidad and the Guianas). In these special circumstances they developed something they would never have known in India: a sense of belonging to an Indian community. This feeling of community could override religion and caste.

It was this idea of an Indian community that, near the end of the last century, the thirty-year-old Gandhi – at that time hardly with a political or historical or literary idea – discovered when he went to South Africa and began to work among the Indian immigrants there. And it was during his 15 years in South Africa that intimations came to Gandhi of an all-India religious-political mission.

I was born in 1932, 15 years before the Independence of India. I grew up with two ideas of India. The first idea – not one I wanted to go into too closely – was about the kind of country from which my ancestors had come. We were an agricultural people. Most of us in Trinidad were still working on the colonial sugar estates, and for most of us life was poor; many of us lived in thatched, mud-walled huts. Migration to the New World, shaking us out of the immemorial accepting ways of peasant India, had made us ambitious; but in colonial and agricultural Trinidad, during the Depression, there were few opportunities to rise. With this poverty around us, and with this sense of the world as a kind of prison (the barriers down against us everywhere), the India from which my ancestors had migrated to better themselves became in my imagination a most fearful place. This India was private and personal, beyond the India I read about in newspapers and books.

This India, or this anxiety about where we had come from, was like a neurosis.

There was a second India. It balanced the first. This second India was the India of the Independence movement, the India of the great names. It was also the India of the great civilization and the great classical past. It was the India by which, in all the difficulties of our circumstances, we felt supported. It was an aspect of our identity, the community identity we had developed, which, in multi-racial Trinidad, had become more like a racial identity.

This was the identity I took to India on my first visit in 1962. And when I got there I found it had no meaning in India. The idea of an Indian community – in effect, a continental idea of our Indian identity – made sense only when the community was very small, a minority, and isolated. In the torrent of India, with its hundreds of millions, where the threat was of chaos and the void, that continental idea was no comfort at all. People needed to hold on to smaller ideas of who and what they were; they found stability in the smaller groupings of region, clan, caste, family.

They were groupings I could hardly understand. They would have given me no comfort at all in Trinidad, would have provided no balance for the other India I carried as a neurosis, the India of poverty and an abjectness too fearful to imagine. Such an India I did now find, in 1962; and, with my idea of an Indian identity, I couldn't be reconciled to it. The poverty of the Indian streets and the countryside was an affront and a threat, a scratching at my old neurosis. Two generations separated me from that kind of poverty; but I felt closer to it than most of the Indians I met.

In 1962, in spite of five-year plans and universal suffrage, and talk of socialism and the common man, I found that for most Indians Indian poverty was still a poetic concept, a prompting to piety and sweet melancholy, part of the country's uniqueness, its Gandhian non-materialism.

An editor of an economic weekly, a good and dedicated man who became a friend, said to me in Bombay, when we talked of the untouchables, 'Have you seen the beauty of some of our untouchables?' India was the editor's lifelong cause; the uplift of the untouchables was part of his cause; and he was speaking with the utmost generosity.

There was a paradox. My continental idea of an Indian identity, with the nerves it continually exposed, would have made it hard for me to do worthwhile work in India. The caste or group stability that Indians had, the more focussed view, enabled them, while remaining whole themselves, to do work – modest, improving things, rather than revolutionary things – in conditions which to others might have seemed hopeless – as I saw during many weeks in the countryside, when I stayed with young Indian Administrative Service officers.

Many thousands of people had worked like that over the years, without any sense of a personal drama, many millions; it had added up in the 40 years since Independence to an immense national effort. The results of that effort were now noticeable. What looked sudden had been long prepared. The increased wealth showed; the new confidence of people once poor showed. One aspect of that confidence was the freeing of new particularities, new identities, which were as unsettling to Indians as the identities of caste and clan and region had been to me in 1962, when I had gone to India only as an 'Indian'.

The people once known as untouchables lined up for more than a mile on a busy road to honour their long-dead saint, Dr Ambedkar, who in his icon wore a European-style jacket and tie. That proclamation of pride was new. It could be said to be something Gandhi and others had worked for; it could be said to be a vindication of the freedom movement. Yet it could also be felt as a threat to the stability many Indians had taken for granted; and a middle-class man might, in a reflex of anxiety, feel that the country was going from bad to worse.

*

The Bombay stock market had boomed. Papu, a twenty-nine-year-old stockbroker, had made more money in the last five years than his father had made in all his working life. Papu's father had migrated to Burma during the British time, when Burma was part of British India. When Burma had become independent, and had withdrawn from the Commonwealth, Papu's father, like other Indians, had been made to leave. In India, Papu's father had gone into trading in stocks and shares on his own account. He read the financial pages carefully and he made a modest living. 'On the stock market,' Papu said, 'if you succeed seven times out of 10, you are doing well.' Papu's father, not a formally educated man, had done well according to his own lights.

Papu, better educated, and operating in a far larger economy, had done very well, even by his own standards. The last five years, he had said, had been exceptionally good; and he felt that the next ten years were going to be pretty good as well.

But Papu had become anxious. He didn't know where the new aggressiveness of Indian business was going to lead, and he wasn't certain how far, with the strong religious feelings he had, he would be able to fit into the new scheme of things. He had also grown to fear something his father had never thought about: Papu, at the age of twenty-nine, lived in dread of revolution and anarchy. The fear was partly a fear of personal loss; but it was also an extension of Papu's religious concerns.

Papu came of a Jain family. The Jains are an ancient, pre-Buddhist offshoot of Hinduism, and they aim at what they see as absolute purity. They don't eat meat; they don't eat eggs; they avoid taking life. Every morning a Jain should bathe, put on an unstitched cloth, and walk barefooted to his temple to pray. And yet the Jains are famous in India for their skill as businessmen.

Papu's office was in the stock market area of Bombay. At road level it was not easy for the visitor to distinguish this area from other areas in central Bombay. The lobby of the tall building where Papu's office was had a special Indian quality: you felt that every day, in the name of cleaning, someone had rubbed the place down with a lightly grimed rag, and – in the way that a fresh mark of sandalwood paste is given every day to an image – given a touch of black grease to the folding metal gates of the elevators. Roughly painted little boards gave each elevator a number; and there was a little zigzag line for each elevator, so that in the lobby people created a floral pattern.

On the upper floor where we got off the walls still hinted at the lightly grimed rag. But in this upper lobby, which was much quieter, people clearly didn't have the anxiety they had downstairs about being seen or about giving offence, and they had spat out gritty red mouthfuls of pan-juice, sometimes in a corner, sometimes broadside, in great splashing arcs, on the walls.

After this informality there was an office. Desks, clerks, office equipment. There were framed colour pictures of Hindu deities on the walls, and some of the pictures were garlanded. Papu's chamber was a small inner room. Computer screens blinked green. On one wall were three pictures of deities side by side. The goddess Durga, riding on her tiger, was on the right; a garland of marigolds hung over the glass.

I asked Papu about Durga. He didn't answer directly. He began to talk about his Jain faith and its application to what he did.

He said, 'Basically, we are without the killer instinct, which is what businessmen should have.'

I said, 'But you do so well.'

'We are traders.' The distinction was important to him. 'The killer instinct is required in industry, not in trading. Which is why the Jain community is not involved in industry. If I'm trading on the stock exchange now, and I cannot get some money out of a guy, I wouldn't hire a mafia guy to get it out of him. Which is what happens here in something like the building industry – if I'm a builder, I have to have my own mafia connections.'

'How long has it been so?'

'It's growing in the cities. After 1975' – the time of Mrs Gandhi's Emergency – 'all the mafia dons gave up smuggling and took up building. They will "encourage" people, for instance, to vacate land, so that the land can be used for building.'

It was what many people spoke about. It was part of the 'criminalization' of Indian business and politics.

Papu said, 'It is a problem. I don't know how long this' – he indicated his own room, with the computers, and the outer office – 'is going to continue. We're doing well right now. We're vegetarians, but I don't know how long we can go on without going out there to fight.'

It was strange, this stress on vegetarianism just there. But vegetarianism was fundamental to Papu's faith. In the mess and flux and uncertainty of life, vegetarianism, the refusal to be impure, was something one could anchor oneself to. It was an exercise of will and virtue that saved one from other kinds of excess, including the excess of 'going out there to fight'.

Papu was of middle height. His vegetarianism and his sport – which, unexpectedly, was basketball – had given him a fine, slender physique. He was strong, without pronounced muscular definitions; he was curiously like one of the smooth marble figures of Jain sculpture. His eyes were serene; his face was squarish and well-defined, his skin smooth and unmarked.

He thought that if the nature of trading changed, if the killer instinct entered it, Jains would have to fight or give up. From what he said, it seemed that so far Jains had preferred to give up. They had left the building industry. In Bombay, as in Delhi, they had given up those trades which required them to carry cash or valuables.

He began to speak again of his faith, and when – taking his own time to come back to my early question – he spoke of the goddess Durga, he didn't speak of her as a deity with special attributes. He spoke of her simply as God.

'I have to think of God whenever some things happen. I lost my father in the beginning of this year. My father died of a heart attack. At a time like that the feeling comes that there is some external factor I can't do anything about.

'I am now using computers, the way they are doing in the developed countries. There is a time that there is a feeling in me that if I'm able to beat the market, it's because I'm able to take on these developments. But then – when something like this happens: my father, his death – I get the feeling that my intelligence or my aggression is worth nothing. Here I am, in this business. I forecast stock movements, price movements. There is an obsession about the work, as you know. And then suddenly this feeling – that I can't foresee my life. That is the time I feel there is something like God, and I wish to have faith.

'In the last year that feeling has been coming any time I'm excited or very sad. Earlier, if I had been excited, I would have expressed my excitement. You would have been able to see it. But now I know that at the end of the day, after the excitement, something sad might happen. So why get excited?'

'I can understand older men having these thoughts. But you are not old.'

'We have this saying on the Bombay stock exchange: "How many *Diwalis* have you seen?"' Diwali, the Hindu festival of lights. 'Which is a way of saying, "How old are you?" The friend of mine who owns this firm is only thirty, and he's been very successful these last five years. He's encountered two income-tax raids, and several ups and downs. Things which my father would have taken a lifetime to experience, he's done in five years. So we say it isn't the number of Diwalis you've seen, it's the number of crackers you've burst. For me the same is true, not only in business, but in life. I go to the temple every morning. I basically pray to have control over certain feelings.'

'Grief?' I was thinking of his father.

He misheard me. He thought I had said 'greed', and he said, 'Greed and fear. The two feelings associated with my business. I walk into the temple, hold my hands together, and wait there for five minutes.'

'Who do you address when you do that?'

'Something you think of who's controlling the world.'

'You don't think of a particular deity?'

'If you're doing business, the picture you would have would be of the goddess Lakshmi. On other occasions it would be Saraswati. Lakshmi is the goddess of wealth, Saraswati is the goddess of wisdom. And when I think of the children in the slums, I have to think of God. That is the time I think there is a certain womb I came out of – which is why I'm here today, and not there. Now, why am I here, and not there, in the slums? Nowhere in the organized learning I received at school and college do I get an answer to this question. The answer is: God. A couple of times a day I think these thoughts.'

'Did your father think these thoughts as well?'

'My father was a self-made man. He was only a matriculate. He had to be more involved with his work. Basically, a man thinks of these other things when he's taken care of food and shelter. Although my father must have been having the same thoughts, he had to be doing his duties to his family. I'm a little more comfortable at a younger age. That is one of the reasons why this comes up.'

'Can anyone be successful in business without some aggression?'

'Aggression creates a vicious circle. I'll give you an example. We have a man called Ambani here. He's going to become the largest industrialist in India in a couple of years. This man would really give you the true picture of how business success works in India. He is a good administrator and a good manipulator. Those are different words. An administrator organizes his business, a manipulator manages the world outside. Ambani's got the foresight, and finally he's got the aggression. If you compare him to old industrialists like Tata and Birla, he's one generation ahead. Birla had the licences. He put up industries, he's manufacturing goods. This man Ambani goes one step ahead. He makes and breaks policies for himself. Now he sees a demand for polyester. It's shiny and it lasts and lasts. It's perfect for India, where people can't afford to buy too many clothes. So he gets into polyester, and he makes sure that nobody else is involved in it. After this he takes the next step – making the raw material for polyester. Then he wants other people to make polyester so they can use his raw material. This backward integration will get him to a situation where he will control the textile industry in India. Polyester will be the largest market.

'If I want to go out into any business in India, that is what I would have to do. Something like that.

'But there is another side. There is a firm here called Bajaj. They are the second largest scooter-manufacturer in the world. Three years ago, when the Japanese entered India, we thought that Bajaj would soon be out. He's not only able to stay, but he's grown much more than all of them. He's a Harvard graduate. But it's a conventional family, with all the culture and conventions of Indians. They've gone through personal taxation at 97 per cent and inheritance tax as high as 80 per cent, and yet today they are still very large. This gives me confidence that it can still work.'

By 'it' he meant the traditional Indian way, the way that fitted in with 'all the culture and conventions of Indians'.

Papu said, 'The important point here is your asking me how to be sucessful without aggression. The problem is discipline. I don't find my non-vegetarian friends have the will-power and discipline and character that the vegetarians have. When we started out being vegetarians we never thought of these things. But now, looking back at life, we find the non-vegetarians have a problem.'

Papu had a plan of sorts for his own future. He wanted to work for the next ten years, to exercise the business faculties with which he had been endowed. He wanted in those ten years to make enough money to live on for the rest of his life. And then he wanted to devote himself to social work. But he had doubts about his plan. He had doubts especially about the wisdom or efficiency of giving up. If he personally went out and did social work, wouldn't that be a waste of his natural talent? Wouldn't he serve his social cause better if he continued in business and devoted his profits – which would grow – to his social work?

These ideas were worrying him. He was uncertain about his promptings, and that worried him even more. He thought that, living the kind of life he did, the concern he felt for the poor was at the moment only 'hypocritical'.

'If I say I should be doing social work, why should I be here in an air-conditioned office? If I have a genuine feeling, I should be out there in the slum, working. But up to the age of forty I may have to continue to live like a hypocrite. And then I would do what I want. Today I am getting so great a return for my input. This makes me feel I should be working harder. This makes me feel I should not be entitled to these luxuries.

The earlier generation of Jains, when they thought of social work, used to build marble temples. We find that to be not very right, maybe because there are already so many temples. We think of orphanages and hospitals. Our generation thinks more of social work than of religion.'

'Are you really as nervous of the poverty as you say?'

'I am sure there's going to be a revolution. In a generation or two. It cannot last, the inequalities of income. I shudder when I think of that. I am very sure that the Indian mind is religious, fatalistic. Even after all the education I've had, I still think that destiny will take me – I'll get there whatever I do. This is why we haven't had a revolution. Now, with the growing frustrations, even if people are religious there is going to be a revolution. The tolerance is being stretched too far.'

'What form do you think the revolution will take?'

'It won't be *anything.* It will be totally chaos.'

*

For some, like the Shiv Sena, the revolution had already started. Nikhil, a young magazine journalist I had got to know, took me on a Sunday morning to meet a Sena 'area leader' in the industrial suburb of Thane. The Sena had 40 units in Thane – 40 units in one suburb – and each unit had a leader like Mr Patil, the man we were going to see.

Thane was one hour north of downtown Bombay by train. The coaches were broad and roomy and basic, built for the heavy duty of Bombay suburban travel, no-nonsense affairs of undisguised metal poles and brackets and bolts. A prominent metal label in each coach gave the name of the builders: Jessop and Co., Calcutta, once British, now Indian.

We passed blocks of flats, mildewed and grimed; swamps, drains; browned patches of field; dust, children; and, always, the shacks and the rag-roofed dependent shelters they encouraged, the existing shack or hut or shelter providing one ready-built wall for the newcomer, the tide after tide of human beings that came into Bombay all the time, sometimes undoing in a night the rehabilitating effort of years. The Shiv Sena, in its early days, had wanted Maharashtra for the Maharashtrians; it had campaigned against immigration into Bombay from other states. What could be seen from the train was explanation enough.

Even in Thane, one hour out, there was a feeling that living space was still immensely valuable. In a working-class lane near the railway station – just past the bright stalls, some with fruit, some with cheap watches, some with Sunday-morning fripperies, shiny fairground goods – a simple apartment could cost two and half lakhs of rupees, 250,000 rupees, about £10,000.

The entrance to Mr Patil's house was off this lane, in a passageway between two two-storey houses. Mr Patil lived upstairs in the house to the right, an old house; the house to the left, which was still being built, and had unexpected architectural style, was going to be substantial. The yard at the end of the passageway was like an old Port of Spain backyard, with a busy outdoor life; though the crumbling brick dependencies against the back wall had the Bombay constriction, and spoke of people making do with very little room.

In the plot or yard on the other side of the back wall, and not far from that wall, was the weathered concrete frame of a projected building of some size that looked as though it had been abandoned.

If that building had gone up, it would have blocked out some of the light from Mr Patil's yard; the yard would have felt hemmed in. As it was, with the openness at the back, there was, curiously, no feeling of oppression in Mr Patil's yard, even with the crowd and the general noise – many scattered sounds, many varied events, running together to make something like a sea sound.

The wooden staircase up to Mr Patil's floor was steep (saving space), and called for care. The construction was interesting, with each thick plank mortised into the side boards. In the little verandah or gallery at the top there were taken-off shoes and slippers, but we were not asked to take our shoes off.

There was a visitor before us in the room inside. He was a police inspector in khaki uniform, and he was sitting in an arm chair next to Mr Patil. The inspector hadn't taken off his boots either. They were quite splendid boots, and must have been personal, not part of his police issue. They were ankle-high, of soft leather, with nice indentations and ridges, and they were ox-blood in colour.

The inspector was in his late thirties or early forties. He was serious and respectful, but also self-respecting. Mr Patil was frowning; the frown could be read as an expression of his authority. He was small and had begun to get plump. He was young, in his late twenties, and the way he was sitting gave prominence to his little paunch. The paunch looked new, something he was still learning to live with, like the roundness of his thighs, which was causing his trousers noticeably to tighten. He was barefooted in his sitting room. That was custom; but it was also a mark of his privilege: the local dignitary, receiving at home.

The police inspector had come that Sunday morning to ask for the Sena's help with a local 'Eve-teasing' problem. The sexual harassment of women in public places, often sly, sometimes quite open, was a problem all over India. The particular incident the inspector was worried about had caused two groups in the area to square off against each other. In that crowd and closeness it didn't take much for nerves to tear; trouble came easily.

The sitting room was pink-washed, and it had a terrazzo floor. In its furnishings and decorations it was, making allowance for period details, like rooms I had known in Trinidad in my childhood, the rooms of people who had begun to feel they were doing well and had begun to respect themselves. There was a Sony television set, with a video. A patterned lace cloth covered the Sony, and there was a doll on the cloth. On the pink walls there were plastic hibiscus sprays on sections of plastic trellis-work. A double bed occupied one corner of the room; two bolsters in faded pink were set symmetrically on it at an angle one to the other; and some clothes of Mr Patil's hung on a hook of some sort.

Mr Patil's mother was sitting flat on the terrazzo floor in the open doorway to the left. The room beyond must have been the kitchen. I fancied that a smell of frying fish was coming from that room, but I might have been wrong. Perhaps the Patils didn't eat fish; in India such details were important, and could be serious caste matters. There was at any rate a smell of cooking; and it must have been this which – while the police inspector and Mr Patil talked – drew a little tiger-striped ginger cat across the sitting room to the doorway where Mr Patil's mother was sitting. The cat was a surprise: I thought Indians didn't care too much for cats. This was an Indian cat, lean in neck and limbs, heavy only in belly, more scrawny and desperate than the chubby cats of England.

Mr Patil's mother was wearing a red or pink patterned sari, tied in a way which enabled the legs to be wrapped separately. She was very short, with much slack, tired-looking flesh, and she wore thick-lensed glasses. She was sitting in the doorway to enjoy the Sunday-morning company; though it was also plain from her manner that she didn't want to intrude into any of the serious business her son might have to deal with.

The serious, impressive police inspector rose at last. He said he was glad that Mr Patil had been so understanding. Both groups in the Eve-teasing affair had enough supporters to cause real trouble in the locality, he said; and in these matters it was the policy of the police to try to reconcile people. Then he left, and he could be heard picking his way lightly down the steep steps in his boots.

Mr Patil frowned harder, set his mouth, and waited to hear what I had to say. He had no English, only Marathi. Nikhil translated for me. I said I wanted to know first of all about the locality, and about Mr Patil's family.

Mr Patil said his family had spent their entire life right there, in that locality. His father had worked in the tool room of a factory in central Bombay for 40 years. What did the factory make? Neither Mr Patil nor his mother knew. The factory was closed down now, finished. But what was important was that his father had been in regular work. Because of that the family had not known hardship when they were children. They knew hardship as a family only when their father died, in 1975. In India there were no pensions.

Mr Patil had a dark, square face. He wore a moustache. His hair was getting thin.

He went out to work after his father died. He found a job in the packing department of a company that made transistors. A girl cousin told him about the job. She worked in the factory; in fact, she still worked there. He didn't get much in the packing department, 300 rupees a month, working eight hours a day. He didn't like what he had to do, but it was a job. He had made a lot of friends in the factory; many of them had remained friends.

He never thought of himself and his family as poor. He never thought of himself as rich or poor. He always felt he was middle class – using that word in the Indian way. And what he said carried an echo of what Papu, the Jain stockbroker, had said: a man has to take care of food and shelter before he can notice other things. Just as Papu's success had given him the social concerns that his more harassed father had never had, so, though the Shiv Sena spoke of the deprivation of Maharashtrians, that idea could come to people only when they had ceased, in fact, to be absolutely deprived.

How, growing up in that locality, had ambition come to Mr Patil? Had he been ambitious as a child? He had. He wanted to be famous. He didn't want to be famous for any particular thing; he just wanted to be famous. At one time he thought he would like to be a famous cricketer. But now he wasn't ambitious in that way; he had scaled it down. He just wanted to do what the Supreme Leader of the party wanted him to do.

He was ten years old when he had first seen the leader. He had seen him right here, in this locality. That would have been in 1969 or 1970. He saw a poster one day announcing a visit by the leader. At that time he had never heard of the leader: the Sena was only three years old, and the leader wasn't as famous as he became later. But Mr Patil noticed the poster about the leader's visit. This was during the festival of Ganpati. And now, in Mr Patil's talk, religion and Sena politics began to run together.

Ganpati, Ganesh, the Hindu elephant god, with his long, friendly trunk, his bright eyes, and big, contented belly, was adored in Maharashtra. He was very important in the Patil house: the family kept a Ganpati image in the house. Every year there was a festival dedicated to Ganpati. The festival lasted nine days, and there was a big event on each of those days. Mr Patil as a boy would go to the big event on all the nine days of the festival; he did that every year.

He said, in Nikhil's translation of his Marathi, his mother (much paler in complexion than he) nodding while he spoke, 'Everything good that has happened to me has come through the grace of Ganpati. Every month there is one day devoted to the worship of Ganpati. I travel then 110 kilometres to worship at the huge shrine of Ganpati at Pali.'

On the wall at the back of the Sony television there was a colour photograph or picture of this image at Pali: the broad, spreading belly of the deity a violent, arresting red, not altogether benign.

I asked whether this idea of Ganpati as the bestower of good luck had always been in his family. He said yes. What had been the first time in his own life he had associated Ganpati with something good?

He scratched his thin hair. The tiger-striped ginger cat or kitten was now sitting below the chair on which the police inspector had sat, and was looking delicately around. Mr Patil's mother, sitting on the terrazzo floor in the doorway, which appeared to be her own place of sitting, lifted her head, as if thinking herself of the first time her son had been blessed by the god; the thick lenses of her glasses created pools of light over her eyes.

On the wall above the bed with the symmetrically set bolsters was a fluorescent electric tube; fluorescent tubes were used in India because they were cheap. There were two little windows in that wall. In one window the iron bars were set vertically; in the other window – for the variation and the style – the bars were set horizontally. Both windows had similar curtains, each curtain gathered up with a sash in two places.

The little pink-walled room was really quite full of things to look at: much thought here, much pride. There was a wardrobe, and there was also a black-framed glass case or cabinet about three feet high. On top of the cabinet was a very big multi-coloured candle, to balance the doll on the Sony. Among the things on the shelves were a set of stainless-steel tumblers and eight china cups with a flowered pattern. The glass cabinet and the things in it – leaving aside the aluminium tumblers – were like things I had known in my childhood. They were still here in a kind of wholeness: my heart went out to them.

Mr Patil said at last, 'I never used to go to school. I used to just roam around, play cricket. I was finally told that I would be thrown out of the school. So I prayed to Ganpati. I was about fifteen or sixteen at this time. I told Ganpati that if I wasn't thrown out of the school, I would make the pilgrimage to Pali. And I wasn't thrown out. The headmistress had a change of heart. When she called me she said she was only going to warn me that time.'

Having remembered that, he remembered other occasions of Ganpati's grace. 'Three or four years ago my mother fell ill. High blood pressure. She went to hospital. She was on oxygen.

She couldn't talk. I went to Pali to the Ganpati shrine and I made an offering of a garland and a coconut. When I came back, my mother was much better.'

And his mother – sitting in the doorway, not flat on the floor, as I had thought, but on a thin piece of wood, perhaps an inch high – put her palms together while her son spoke, and said, in Nikhil's translation, that she folded her hands in gratitude to Ganpati.

Even at his birth there was some element of mercy and blessing. This was in 1959. There were very bad riots in the locality. People were throwing stones. Taxis were not easy to get, but his father managed to find a taxi-driver who said he would try to take Mrs Patil to the hospital. The taxi had to drive five kilometres through the riots to the government hospital. It got there safely, and as soon as his mother went in, she was delivered of him.

Mother and son told the story in relay, and the mother, sitting on the floor, again put her palms together and said that it was Ganpati's mercy.

And then, two years or so ago, there was a serious crisis for him. The crisis was in his political life, and it lasted nine days. That was a very long time to be on the rack. He made a pilgrimage to Pali, and vowed to Ganpati that if he came out of his crisis, he would make an offering of 101 coconuts:

Wasn't that like trying to buy something from the god?

'My faith is rooted in reality. I am not in the habit of offering 101 coconuts and asking to be made prime minister of India.'

Was this faith in Ganpati something deep in himself, always there? Or did he, after he had prayed, look for some sign from the deity?

He said, in Nikhil's translation, 'Even when things look bad I hear a voice inside. I suppose you can call it self-confidence.' Nikhil gave the Marathi word he had used for 'self-confidence': *atma-vishwas.* That was Ganpati's greatest gift.

I said, 'How did you take 101 coconuts up to the shrine?'

'You can buy the nuts at the shrine itself.'

He told me more about the Ganpati festival. Every year you had to get a new image from the image-maker. You kept the image at home for as long as you wanted, but at the end of the festival you had to throw away or immerse the image. It was the tradition in their family to keep the image for one day and a half; then they took it to a lake not far away and immersed it. It had been his mother's ambition all her life to bring the Ganpati image home from the image-maker's with a musical band. Recently, she had been able to do that. Her other son had got a very good job, and the family had hired a band and brought the image to the house, and they had had the band again when they had taken the image out of the house to the lake.

With this talk of Ganpati, of shrines and pilgrimages and vows and offerings, I began to get some idea of the mysteries the earth held for people like the Patils, the glory that sometimes touched their days, the wonders they walked through. There was more to their world than one saw. Thane was an industrial suburb. But the land itself was very old; it had its sanctity; and the same people could live naturally with many different ways of feeling.

It was during this auspicious festival of Ganpati – right here, in this locality, in these lanes I had walked through seeing only the surface of things – that Mr Patil, when he was ten, had seen the poster about the visit of the leader of the Shiv Sena. He had gone to the meeting, to look at the leader. The leader at that time was running his own weekly magazine and was better known as a cartoonist. The young Patil boy didn't find the leader physically impressive when he saw him. He saw a thin man, with glasses, in a buttoned-up long coat. But as soon as the leader began to speak the boy's blood began to 'boil'. The leader's speech lasted 30 to 35 minutes, and at the end people like the young Patil, whose blood had boiled at the thought of all the injustices the true people of Maharashtra had to endure, began to shout their acclamation of the leader.

'Weren't you too young to understand talk about discrimination against Maharashtrians?'

'No. I used to hear a lot about how the Muslims and outsiders were creating problems for Maharashtrians. I used to hear it at home and on the streets. My elder brother used to tell me about it.'

'Your father?'

'He had no interest in it at all.'

The father didn't have the security of his sons. It was as with Papu's father.

And though for a long time after this the ten-year-old boy had heard no more big Shiv Sena speeches, he began to lend a hand when the party wanted people to put up posters and banners. Later, when his father died, and he had gone out to work with the transistor company, he began to do political work for the party in the evenings. He continued to do that party work even when he found a new job. In the new job he was concerned with exporting manpower to Dubai and the Middle East. He got 950 rupees a month, as against 300 with the transistor company. He took people for interviews.

Didn't he want to go to the Middle East himself, to make some money?

'I didn't pass my matric at school. So if I'd gone I would have had to do some menial work.'

'You didn't think there was anything wrong in sending people from here to a Muslim country?'

'Not all Muslims are enemies.'

His work for the party at that time was to sit in the Sena office in the evenings and listen to people's complaints. The Sena always believed in the social side of things. There was a lot to be done that way. People needed help. Some people had water for only four hours a day. In many buildings water didn't rise above the first floor. Even after he had been appointed area leader of the Sena – that appointment had come three years before – he still did that kind of social work. When we had arrived, for instance, there was a lady in the kitchen with his mother. She had come to complain about a water-connection. She had paid somebody 1000 rupees for the connection, and so far she had had no connection and no water. The area leader had to interest himself in the problems of the people; it was good for the party politically.

Did his blood still boil? Or had he become calmer, with the success of the Sena, and his own position as area leader?

His blood still boiled. 'There is a place called Bhiwandi, about 25 kilometres from here. When India lost a cricket match to Pakistan, they used to let off crackers in the marketplace, the Muslims there. When I was small I could do nothing about it. But now I can't bear it. There used to be groups of Muslims who used to come over from Bhiwandi to Thane here. The local people were so full of resentment against those Muslims that they had clashes with them in 1982, and they broke open the Muslim shops and sold the goods to the people. They sold towels for two rupees. The Muslim shops have come back now, but they live in fear. The Shiv Sena is very powerful. I will tell you: the Muslims even give donations to the Shiv Sena.'

Nikhil said on his own, 'But isn't this extortion?'

Mr Patil didn't think so.

I wanted to know – thinking of his adoration for Ganpati – what was more important for him: religion or politics? In Nikhil's Marathi translation this came out as: *dharma* or *rajnithi?*

Mr Patil said, 'Dharma.' Religion. But this wasn't the personal faith in Ganpati he had talked about. With the Sena's success and growth, the Sena's ideas had grown bigger: the religion that Mr Patil meant was Hinduism itself. 'There is a plot to wipe Hinduism off the face of the earth.' It was a Muslim plot, and that was why it was vital to keep Hinduism alive.

Two more thin Indian cats or kittens had come into the sitting room – a tabby, and another ginger-coloured cat – and they were walking about inquiringly. Some friends or relations of the Patils had also dropped in, to listen to what Mr Patil had to say to his visitors.

I asked whether Hinduism could be kept alive, if Indian business and industry kept on growing as it had been growing.

He didn't see any contradiction. 'If you want to survive, you have to make money.'

'That isn't the Gandhian attitude.'

'I have contempt for Gandhi. He believed in turning the other cheek. I believe that if someone slaps you, you must have the power to ask him why he slapped you, or you must slap him back. I hate the idea of non-violence.'

This was in keeping with his Maratha warrior pride. I wondered how much of Maratha history he knew. What ideas of history were afloat in this locality, in all these narrow lanes? Did he know Shivaji's dates?

He did. He said, '1630 to 1680. I know all that. Shivaji saved the Maharashtrians from atrocities. But then the English came, and they committed atrocities on everybody else.'

I could understand the larger communal mood here, the conflict between Hindus and Muslims. But I wondered about the meaning caste would have in an industrial area like this, where people lived so close together. What were the Sena's relations with the Dalits? From the little I had seen, the Dalits had developed the beginnings of that self-confidence, the *atma-vishwas,* which had been part of Ganpati's gift to Mr Patil. Did that touch some chord in him? Did his concern for Hinduism lead him to some fellow feeling for them?

He was rigid. 'We have no differences with them. They don't consider themselves Maharashtrians or Hindus. They are Buddhists.'

Hadn't they been driven out of Hinduism by caste prejudice? Was there no sympathy for them? When he was a boy, his blood had boiled when he had heard his leader speak of the discrimination against Maharashtrians. Didn't he think that Dalits had cause to feel like that too?

He didn't think so. Dalit anger was something the Dalit leaders and the people called the Dalit Panthers – in imitation of the Black Panthers of the United States – were encouraging for political reasons. 'They have no reason to be angry. They've not suffered as much as they say. And the present Dalit organizations are linked to Muslim groups.'

I asked Nikhil whether that was so. He said yes. 'Both those sections, the Dalits and the Muslims, are alienated. And someone thought it would be a good idea to bring them together.'

Alienation: it was the common theme. Mr Patil was triumphant now; but his blood still boiled. Even now he felt that his group might sink, and that others were waiting to trample on them. It was as though in these small, crowded spaces no one really felt at home. Everyone felt that the other man, the other group, was laughing; everyone lived with the feeling of siege.

The time had now come to go with Mr Patil to the Sena office. We said goodbye to his mother; and she, still sitting, lifted her head, her eyes lost below the concentric circles of her thick glasses, and brought her palms together again. Together with some of the people who had come to hear Mr Patil talk, we went out of the pink room to the verandah, past the taken-off slippers and shoes at the door.

We went first to the end of the verandah to look at the view at the back: the brick sheds against the back wall, the abandoned structure next door, with rusty reinforcing iron rods coming out of the concrete. One of the men with us said in English, 'Unauthorized.' So, in spite of the apparent haphazardness all around, there was some kind of municipal regulation.

We went down the steep staircase to the passageway between the two houses, and then out into the sunlight of the paved lane. A little way to the right was the local Sena office, Mr Patil's domain. Structurally, it was a concrete box, a one-roomed shed; but it had been decorated on the outside to look like a fort, with a formal and very simple kind of crenellation at the top, and with the concrete wall painted to suggest blocks of grey stone with white pointing. It was quite startling in the dust and dirt and crumble of the lane. It looked like a stage set or like something from a fairground. But it was a reminder of the warrior past of the Marathas. The past was real; the present power and organization of the Sena was real.

We hadn't been asked to take off our shoes before we went into Mr Patil's sitting room. But we had to take them off now before we stepped from the lane into the Sena office: this, though it was dustier than his sitting room, was Mr Patil's true shrine. The inside walls were painted blue. The floor was paved with stone flags – the people of Maharashtra build naturally and well in stone.

There was a desk against the far wall, with a high-backed chair, like a throne. As soon as we entered, Mr Patil went and sat on the high-backed chair, as though this was part of the formality of the place. In front of the desk were nine folding metal chairs; they were for visitors, and they were painted in the same blue colour as the wall. On the back wall, above Mr Patil's chair, there was a picture of a tiger: the tiger was the Sena's emblem. The only other picture on that wall was of the leader of the Sena. On the desk there was a bronze-coloured bust of Shivaji, and there was another, similar bust on a pedestal set at an angle in the corner away from the desk. The busts were of plaster of Paris, and each carried a fresh mark of sandalwood paste, which was a holy or sacred mark, on the forehead. There was a tall dark-green iron cabinet near the door, and the lighting was by fluorescent tube. A cuckoo clock on a wall – a reminder of Mr Patil's sitting room – was the only decorative thing in the little cell.

The Sena office was a Sena fort, and there were 40 like it in Thane. In one way, it was martial make-believe; in another way, it was perfectly real. There were constant group fights in the locality. Some of the fights were between the Sena and the Dalits, especially those of the Dalits who called themselves Panthers; and there were also fights between the Sena and some Congress groups. The fights were serious, and sometimes deadly, with swords and acid-bulbs as weapons. The Sena also fought to protect its supporters against criminals and thugs. Some of the Sena supporters were stallholders such as we had seen on the way from the railway station; there were always people trying to extort money from them.

While we were talking in the office, Mr Patil leaning back in his high-backed chair, Nikhil and I leaning forward on our blue metal chairs (the blue scratched down to rust at the edges), there was a sound of tramping in the lane. It sounded almost like a little approaching disturbance, a little event. And we saw, passing in the sunlight in front of the door, a number of handcuffed young men, roped together with what looked like new rope, roped together upper arm to upper arm. The roped-up men were in two files, and they were being marched or led, without shouts or haste or roughness, by a squad of policemen in khaki uniform.

Nikhil said, 'But that's unconstitutional. People can't be handcuffed just like that. The Supreme Court has handed down a ruling.'

The men being led away seemed to have dressed for Sunday. Their shirts were clean and stylish; the shirt of one man had broad vertical black and silver stripes. They were very young men, all slender, some thin.

The man who had said, of the unfinished concrete structure at the back of the Patil house, 'Unauthorized' – that man now again spoke one word, with the Indian affirmative shake of the head, to explain what we had seen. He said, 'Without.'

Without what?

Railway tickets – everyone around me knew, everyone was ready to explain.

What did Mr Patil think of what we had seen?

He was easy about it. 'It's an everyday occurrence. They are being taken to prison, and they will have to stay there for three or four days. Some are poor people. But some do it for the kicks.'

We went out of the office into the lane. The policemen and their prisoners had almost gone out of sight. The little disturbance had passed; the life of the lane was closing over it.

In a canal (or worse) off the lane I saw an animal of some sort parting the dark green-brown water. A dog? A cow – one of the small Indian variety of cow? A calf? It was hard to see the dark creature against the dark water. But then a round snout rose flat and pink above the surface: a pig. And, vision established now, I also saw, paddling on ahead, their irregular white markings looking from a distance like light on the dark canal, or foam, a number of little black-and-white piglets, paddling and bucking about in the murky water.

The man who had said 'Unauthorized' and 'Without' now said, 'Dalit pigs.'

What did he mean by that? Many Indians, Hindus and Muslims, considered the pig unclean; some could hardly bear the sight of the animal. Was there some Dalit intention to provoke – in these pigs (that few dared touch) being turned loose in a crowded area?

That wasn't so.

The man who had said 'Dalit pigs' said, 'The Dalits eat them on Sundays.' So the pigs were not only part of the Dalit separateness; there was also a formality about Dalit pig-eating. The man added, 'They also sell pigs.'

Just a little way up the lane – where the policemen had passed – many small boys were playing cricket with an old, smooth, grey tennis ball. The Sena fort; the slender young men in their nice shirts handcuffed and roped up; the cricket, the gentlemanly, stylish game from halfway across the world – everything was open for inspection here. And so much more was innocently on view: just below the surface, human emotions and needs, and ideas of mystery and glory, ran riot.

*

On a white wall somewhere near Mohammed Ali Road in downtown Bombay I had seen this slogan painted in tall black letters: LIBERATE HUMANITY THROUGH ISLAM.

Mohammed Ali Road had a reputation. It was the main thoroughfare of the Muslim area of downtown Bombay. The area was spoken of as a 'ghetto', and it was so often in the news, in such worrying ways, that people tended to use newspaper language to describe it. It was 'volatile', a 'flashpoint'; it was where communal riots could begin and, having begun, could spread like fire.

It was dreadfully crowded, with every kind of smell and noise. The brown-black smoke from cars using kerosene-adulterated fuel was like a hot fog in the sunlight. It burned the skin and felt jagged in the lungs. It was part of the general feeling of oppression; and the slogan about Islam, seen through this smoke, had the effect of a scream. The slogan was in letters as high as the wall on which it was painted, and it was in English. It wasn't for the people of the ghetto; it was for people outside, people like the Shiv Sena, who might think of making trouble.

Nikhil knew a young man who lived in the Mohammed Ali Road area. The young man's name was Anwar. Early one evening, after he had finished his work, Anwar took us to see where he lived. Anwar was very small and frail, with a suggestion of some inherited debility. But he had a compensating passion about his Muslim faith, and he was full of fight.

The early evening traffic on Mohammed Ali Road was very slow. The shops and the pavements were as jammed as the road. The electric lights created the effect of a ceiling or canopy and appeared to press down on everything, adding, with the hot smoke, to the feeling of crowd and abrasion and life lived at an extremity. It was too noisy to talk in the taxi.

At a certain point we got out of the taxi, and then we followed Anwar away from the lights and the smoke to an area of sudden smallness. Narrow lanes opened into narrower, and they were lined with little low houses. Some way off, Mohammed Ali Road glowed and roared; but the lights here were dim, the lanes were full of shadows, and the near noises were domestic and subdued. We were not in unregulated slum. The lanes were straight and paved, and – though the scale was very small – there was a regularity of lay-out and building that suggested an official housing project. Anwar said that this was so; we were in a municipal settlement.

His house was a narrow section of a wire-netting and concrete row. For two or three feet from the ground the walls of the front room were concrete; above that they were wire netting. A white sheet stretched over the wire netting screened the front room of Anwar's house from his neighbour's on one side; the screen was on the neighbour's side of the wire netting. Anwar's house, his section of the row, was perhaps no more than nine feet wide. The wire netting and concrete were painted blue. The front room might have been six feet deep. It had a passageway on one side, with shoes and slippers on shelves built into the concrete wall. This passageway led to the main, middle room. Beyond that, Anwar said, was the kitchen.

Somewhere in the upper space of the middle room was a sleeping loft. The sleeping loft was important. Without it houses like this wouldn't work, wouldn't be able to provide space for whole families. This was the first I had heard of the Bombay sleeping loft. I heard a good deal more about it in the days that followed; and I began to understand how large families – not always slum-dwellers or pavement-sleepers – managed to live in one small room. At night all over Bombay sitting rooms changed their function; the various portions of a house like Anwar's (essentially that main middle room) became simply a place for sleeping in. A sleeping loft utilized to the full the space, the volume, of a room.

We had been talking in the lane outside Anwar's house. We hadn't yet gone inside the house. Our talk encouraged a young man from the adjoining house or section to come out to have a look at us. He was of medium height, with a good physique, and he was freshly dressed, as if for relaxation, in a singlet and khaki shorts. It was momentarily astonishing to me that someone of normal size and so reasonably turned out should have come out of such a restricted space. We fell silent when he came out and stood in the lane in the dim light, in his patch of territory, saying nothing; and, as though we felt we had been indiscreet or discourteous talking in the open about the houses of the settlement, we went then, almost as if for the privacy, into the wire-netted front room of Anwar's house. The young man came back into the front room of his own house and stood about for a while. In the dim light there he or his pale shadow, changing size, could be seen against the white-sheet divider or screen – the sheet fixed to the wire netting on his side – like a figure in a puppet play.

Someone in Anwar's family had made preparations for our visit. A clean sheet had been spread on the string bed in the front room, as a courtesy to Nikhil and me. At Anwar's invitation, we sat there. Anwar's father then came out from somewhere in the middle room. He was our host now; and Anwar was sent to buy cold lemonade.

Anwar's father, a small man, though not as small as Anwar, looked frail and unwell; and I thought that some of the son's apparent debility would have come from the father. He was very dark, with a very thick, silver beard. That beard was like the old man's only physical vanity: it was expertly trimmed and combed, and it rippled and shone. And more than physical vanity was there: in India different groups wear different styles of beard, and Anwar's father's spade-shaped beard was a Muslim beard. That was the beard's forthright message.

He said he was sixty-four. And before Nikhil and I could say anything, he said he knew he looked much older – and that was true: I had thought of him as close to eighty. Europeans didn't look as old as Indians, he said. He knew; he had once worked in an Italian firm, and he had seen Europeans of seventy looking healthy and working hard. Indians aged as they did because of the conditions they lived in. Here, for instance, they didn't just have traffic fumes; they also had mill smoke, from a cloth mill. Still, he was sixty-four. That was something; his father had died at forty.

Anwar came back with some chilled bottles of lemonade. This was formally offered, bottle by bottle. We drank a little – the lemonade was very sweet, and seemed to have some chemical tincture – and we tried to make general conversation, though we were really too many in the space, and voices and sounds came to us from all directions, and that white screen (pinned to the other side of the wire-netting divider) began to seem ambiguous in its intention, not wholly friendly.

I asked the old man whether there were thieves in the settlement. It had occurred to me that the very openness of life there, and the communality of it (as of a commune), might have offered people a kind of protection.

The old man said there were thefts every day. And there were quarrels every day. The quarrels were worse. A lot of the quarrels came about because of the children. People hit other people's children, and the parents became angry.

He had lived under every kind of pressure. So had Anwar. Perhaps – if, in circumstances like these, there could be said to be a scale in such matters – it had been harder for Anwar, who was more sensitive, better educated, and, in the outside world, had a harder fight in the technical field he had chosen.

Playing with the lemonade, considering the old-fashioned courtesies of father and son in that setting, the humanity that remained to them, the old man's calm acknowledgement of the better health and strength of others, the better conditions of life of others, I began to feel an affection for them both. I felt that if I had been in their position, confined to Bombay, to that area, to that row, I too would have been a passionate Muslim. I had grown up in Trinidad as a member of the Indian community, a member of a minority, and I knew that if you felt your community was small, you could never walk away from it; the grimmer tilings became, the more you insisted on being what you were.

With the old man as our host in the front space of his house, the wire-netted enclosure, and with Anwar being only his father's son there, our talk could only be formal. I didn't feel that difficult questions could be pressed. For the talk to go beyond the part-time job the old man had been lucky enough to find, for Anwar to talk more freely, and without the worry about being overheard, we had to go somewhere else.

So, gently, trying to avoid accident, we laid our lemonade bottles down on the blue concrete wall against the wire netting; and the old man, who had been getting a little restless himself, read the sign well. He stopped talking, created a pause, and we said goodbye.

We went out again to the narrow lanes, where dim lights threw big shadows. Around the corner, a child was defecating in a patch of light. In somebody's front room a big colour television set on a low stand flickered and flashed away, without anyone watching. Anwar said they had no television in their own house. His father said that television was against Islam.

We came to where the low-roofed settlement ended, and Bombay proper began again. Beyond a boundary lane or road was a tall block of flats. The enemy were there. That was a Shiv Sena building, Anwar said. When there was trouble the people who lived in those flats threw bottles at the people who lived below.

Past that building, we came to the roaring main road. We went to a small milk bar Anwar knew: fluorescent tubes, ceramic tiles, grey marble, a sink, tumblers of glass and stainless steel.

I said to Anwar, 'So you live constantly on your nerves?'

Nikhil interpreted the reply. 'It plays havoc with his nerves.'

As worn-away as his father, his dark face thin and tremulous, he sipped at the milk he had ordered.

He said, Nikhil translating directly for him now, 'Those children. You have these clashes between children which turn into blood feuds with adults, and I feel helpless to do anything about it. Fights take place between neighbours all the time. When they are Hindus and Muslims – Hindus are in a minority here – it turns into a communal riot. It gets very bad during cricket matches. When there was the World Cup last year – the one-day cricket matches – people became nervous about the India-Pakistan matches. But then neither India nor Pakistan went into the finals. When Pakistan lost the first semi-final to Australia, the Hindus went wild, and they threw stones and broke the asbestos roofs of the huts.'

How those fights troubled him! Both he and his father had spoken with special dread of fights between neighbours, and I wondered whether they had been talking about themselves. I tried to find out. I asked him about the blood feuds – was his family affected in some way?

His reply was unexpected. 'My brothers have the reputation of being *goondas,* thugs. They're not the right kind of people. Because of this reputation, neighbours think twice before starting anything.'

Tough brothers – they would, for some reason, have been physically quite different from Anwar and his father. Tough brothers, not the right kind of people – yet they enabled Anwar to talk tough himself. Did that little house contain them all?

I asked Anwar, 'That man next door, the man who came out to look at us – how do you get on with him?'

'He's studying at a college outside Bombay. You can just imagine the kind of brothers I have – I have six brothers, and my father still has to work.'

Some family split here. Perhaps the brothers Anwar was talking about, the toughs, might have had a different mother.

He said, 'I don't think of them as my brothers.' But then immediately he softened that. 'The environment has made them what they are. They had to become thugs, to survive. I will tell you this story about the foolhardiness of my brothers. You've been reading in the papers recently about the don who's become the new king of the Bombay underworld. Some time ago, when this don got a contract to kill someone in the locality, he came on a reconnaissance to our area. And – you wouldn't believe – one of my brothers picked a fight with him.'

'What sort of man did the don have to kill?'

'The man the don had to kill was in the business of sending people to the Middle East – manpower export – and he must have cheated someone. But my brothers saw this don as someone intruding on their turf. They exchanged insults and abuse, my brothers and the don, and each side said they would see what the other did. My brother got an Ambassador car and they packed it with weapons. They were planning to attack the don's area, but someone tipped the police off, and my brothers were caught. They were released in a couple of days. Someone here bailed them out.'

'Your brothers have money, then?'

'They make money and then they start gambling.'

'You would say that they, too, are living on their nerves?'

'They don't have the mental make-up I have. If the occasion arises, they will give their lives without a thought. It's the environment.'

In that talk of his thuggish brothers ready to give their lives there was, now, a kind of inverted pride, as when he had spoken of the fear his brothers inspired in the neighbours.

I asked him about the riots of 1984. People spoke of them as a fearful Bombay event, historical, a marker.

He seemed to blow at his milk, as if to cool it. But the milk wasn't warm. That constant parting of his lips, that seeming expulsion of breath, was only a trick of the muscles of his thin face, part of the tremulousness of his face.

He said, 'That was when the will to fight came to me. I was in the final year of the matriculation. There is a Muslim cemetery near Marine Drive, and there is a day near the Ramadan period when it is necessary to visit that cemetery. A group from this area went. At two o'clock in the morning we were walking back home. Some of us were wearing skullcaps, Muslim caps. We passed a Shiv Sena stronghold. We were pelted with stones. We complained to some policemen. They didn't listen. In fact, they followed us for two miles. They thought we were the troublemakers. That was the first sign we had of the riot. Before that night there had been no sign of any trouble. Actually, the real trouble was very far away, about 25 kilometres from here.'

It became hard in the milk bar to hear what Anwar was saying. Above the noise of traffic in the road, there were now querulous voices in the bar itself, Indian voices, specially edged to cut through most sounds of man and machine – above all, the rising and falling cicada sound of motor-car hooters.

Anwar said, 'We returned to this area about three o'clock in the morning. Some of us were bleeding from the stones, and people asked us what had happened. I should tell you that on that night, *shab-e-baraat*, Muslims stay awake right through.

'The next day I had forgotten about the incident. But when I went with a friend to a house near here, I found it full of weapons. That was the doing of one of the big dons. His men had stocked up, to retaliate. Soon after, firing began in the locality. There was curfew throughout the day, and then they banned gatherings of more than five people. In the colony itself' – the area where he lived – 'police infiltrated to check whether people had weapons.'

'Did the presence of the police calm people down?'

'I have no confidence in the police. I will tell you. You can't kill cows in public here – there's an abbattoir you have to take your cows to. But you can pay a policeman, and kill a cow in public. When goats have to be sacrificed at the festival of Id, most Muslims take their goats to the abbattoir to have them slaughtered. But there are some local hoods who insist on killing the goats in public. It's a macho act, to challenge the police. When the police come, the hoods say, "If you interfere, you won't leave here alive."'

He had slid away from the subject of the riots of 1984; he had gone back to the subject of the toughs.

I said, 'These fights with the police excite you?'

He said, with some solemnity, 'It is exciting. I like it. It happens because the police discriminate against the Muslims, and the Muslims have contempt for the police.'

'But what's the point of the game?'

He didn't answer directly. He said, 'There are very few sensible people among the Muslims.' He spelt out the Urdu word he had in mind for 'sensible': *samajdar.* 'There are few educated Muslims here. People who are educated will never get involved in that kind of fighting.' He seemed slightly to have changed his attitude to the fighters.

'So it will just go on?'

He said, with his curious mixture of melancholy and acceptance, 'I see no end to it. I don't see how it can end.'

'How did the riots end that time?'

'Mrs Gandhi came and asked people to try to settle things. But things get settled and then – they burst out again.'

I thought of the narrow lanes and the low wire-netting dwellings, with sleeping lofts below the fragile asbestos roofs. 'What was life like during the riots? Did people sleep?'

'When there are riots, you don't know the meaning of sleep. You can't sleep. It's a big sin if someone of your faith is assaulted and you do nothing about it.'

'Don't you think that someone like you should be trying to live somewhere else?'

'I can't take such a step.' It was what I thought he would say. 'There are so many family ties. It is mandatory for a Muslim to honour those ties.' Family, faith, community: they made a whole. 'What advice would you give a younger brother, or someone coming up?'

The advice wasn't about going away or breaking out. It was more immediate. It was about surviving, here. 'I would tell him that he should think of retaliating and fighting back only if the person in front of him has made a mistake.'

'Mistake?'

'If someone abuses you, for instance.'

Abuse, quarrels, fights within and without: that was the world he lived in, and, physically, was so little equipped for.

I mentioned the slogan I had seen: LIBERATE HUMANITY THROUGH ISLAM.

He said, 'I agree with it totally.'

'When did you learn about Islam?' How, living where he did, would he have had the time, the privacy, the calm?

'I learned from my parents. And I've also read the Koran.'

'There are so many people in Bombay who feel they know the way to liberate humanity.'

He appeared to change his point of view. 'It's the nature of the world. When people gather in groups, each one will say that his is better than the others.'

I thought again of the family with the big colour television set near his house. I asked about them.

'They have a business, making ready-made clothes. They make a little money.'

People in business, making money, and yet living here: it was proof again of what people said, that all you required in Bombay was accommodation. Once you had a place to sleep, anywhere, on a pavement, in a hut, in a corner of a room, you could get a job and make money. But – did the people with the television set show off a little?

The people with the TV and the tailoring business didn't show off, Anwar said. But my question had touched something. He said, 'They know that TV is forbidden in their religion.' Then, as often, Anwar softened what he said. 'But they don't want their children to go to other houses to watch TV, and to be turned away. That can cause trouble.'

'Why do you think so many of the dons in Bombay are Muslims?'

'I've told you. There are few educated people among the Muslims. They go off the rails when they're young.'

'Are they religious people, these dons?'

'They are all loyal adherents of Islam.'

'Defenders of the faith?'

'It is inevitable that they will fight for Islam. It is a contradictory role. They will continue their criminal activities, but at the same time they will read the Koran and do the *namaaz* five times a day. The community does not admire these people. But the people are enchanted by the way the dons behave with the common Muslims.'

'They are the community's warriors?'

'They organize our underground. *Tanzeen-Allah-ho-akbar* – that's what it's called. It is organized by a don. It was created after the riots. We have meetings and decide strategy. We meet every month, even if there is no trouble.'

'What do you think will happen to the children in your colony?'

'The future is awful for them. All those children see murder, assaults.'

'Have you seen murders?'

'Yeh, yeh.' It was an Indian affirmation, rather than American or English, and it was spoken with a side-to-side swing of the head in the Indian way.

The bar-owner had begun to talk loudly to the bar in general about the people at the far end – he meant us – who had been occupying a table for too long. I was going to leave a fair sum for him, but he wasn't to know that. I had my back to him, and I thought I shouldn't turn around to look at him; I thought that if our eyes met he might be driven to a deeper rage. Nikhil, who had been facing him all the time, and occasionally reporting on his mood, ordered *gulab jamun* for everybody; and Anwar, who had already worked his way through two tumblers of milk, began – appearing all the while to blow at it – to eat a portion of that rich milk sweet, steeped in syrup.

He said, 'I saw my first murder when I was ten. We were playing badminton in the colony. There was a hut close by, and there were two men who began to quarrel. These two men usually slept on the same hand-cart at night. They were both about thirty. They had begun to quarrel, and then I saw one of the men running away. We went to see what had happened, and we saw that the man on the hand-cart had had his head nearly severed. He wasn't dead. He was in the throes of death.'

'What clothes?'

'Underwear. Shorts and a singlet. And the body in the throes of death caused the hand-cart to capsize.'

'People ran up?'

'Only children. About six or seven of us. And as the body fell to the ground, it spurted blood on us. I was very frightened.' He began to laugh, eating his sweet, sucking at the thick syrup in his aluminium spoon. It was the first time he had laughed that evening. 'We were still children. It didn't occur to us that this was a police matter. Our first reaction was to go and wash the bloodstains off our shirt.'

'How many murders have you seen since then?'

'Ten or twelve.'

'Why do you laugh?'

'It's part of everyday life to us here. The reasons for those murders are very small. For instance, one day two men with umbrellas had a little collision. One man went to hit the other man, and the other man ran into a house, and the man chasing him ran in after him. I was talking to a friend just there, and I saw it. The man doing the chasing pulled out a knife and killed the other man, just like that. Eighty per cent of people in this locality carry weapons.'

The bar-owner hadn't been pacified by the extra orders for gulab jamun; he had continued to complain. And when Anwar finished his sweet, we prepared to leave. My thoughts went back to the people with the big television set.

'The people with the TV – are they very religious?'

'They are devout people. They are more religious in some ways and less religious in others.'

'In what ways more religious?'

'They offer namaaz five times a day. I offer namaaz only once.'

Formal prayers five times a day – and yet, to Anwar and his father, that faith, obsessive as it was, was flawed.

'Can you see yourself living without Islam?'

'No.'

'What does it give you?'

'Brotherhood. Brotherhood in everything. Islam doesn't teach discrimination. It makes people help people. If a blind man is crossing the road, the Muslim doesn't stop to find out what creed he belongs to. He just helps.'

'What do you think will happen to your colony?'

'I don't see any solution.'

'It will just go on as it is? You really think it will be the same when you reach your father's age?'

'Yes.'

'You don't ever think of going away?'

'At the moment I have no intention to do so.'

'Are you a Sunni?'

He looked surprised. He didn't think that I would know about Sunnis. To him his faith was something secret, something outsiders couldn't really know about.

I wanted to know whether there were other Muslim groups or sects in his colony. I asked whether there were Ismailis or Ahmadis among them. He said he had never heard of those groups. Were there Shias?

'There are no Shias in the community.'

'Isn't that strange?'

'I don't find it strange.'

His orthodox faith was the one pure thing he had to hold on to. He couldn't imagine life without it. It was a stringent faith. It shut out television; it had no room for heretics. All the many rules and celebrations and proscriptions were part of the completeness of Anwar's world. Take away one practice, and everything was threatened; everything might start to unravel. It was correct, for instance, for Muslim men to pee squatting; and I heard later, from someone who worked with Anwar, that Anwar insisted on doing this at the modern urinals in his place of work, though it created problems for him.

Many of the people one saw on the streets and in offices lived in a small space. From small spaces, every morning, they came out fresh and clean and brisk. Whole families, not slum-dwellers or pavement-dwellers, lived in one room; and they might live in the same room for a generation.

Mr Raote had grown up in a family like that. He was one of the earliest members of the Shiv Sena; he had been among the 18 people, no more, at the very first Shiv Sena meeting in 1966. Now, with the victory of the Sena in the municipal elections, he was a man of authority, chairman of the Standing Committee of the Bombay Corporation. He had his own little office in the Victorian-Gothic Corporation building, with a waiting room and a secretary and straight-backed chairs for people with petitions and needs. But he had lived for the first 28 years of his life in the one room where he had been born, in the suburb of Dadar, in mid-town Bombay.

In Dadar Mr Raote now lived in the top flat of a tall block he had built himself, after he had turned developer in his thirties. But the tenement with the one room which had been his home for more than half his life was within walking distance, and he took me to see it one morning.

We took the lift to the ground floor of his building, went out to the sandy front yard, went from the front to the back through a passage in the building, between shops with stylish signboards; and from the back walked to the next main road. Mr Raote was very well known; his walk created a little stir; people were respectful. It couldn't have been open to many people to have the past (and a triumphant return to it) so accessible, just at the end of a short walk.

We turned off, very soon, from the footpath of the main road into a yard with an old two-storey building. We went round to the back and went up the steps at the side of the building to a verandah or gallery at the top. This verandah (like the one on the lower floor) ran the length of the building, and the floor was laid in the Maharashtrian way with slabs of stone. Separate rooms opened into the verandah. The room at the end was where Mr Raote's family had lived.

We looked in from the doorway, and saw new carpentry and paint, in contemporary styling and colours. 'It's been done up,'

Mr Raote said. The room next to it was darker and plainer; it was more like the room Mr Raote had known. It was about 15 feet deep by 10 feet wide, with a kitchen at the back and with a loft for storage and sleeping. All the rooms on that upper floor had a common bathroom and toilet.

Before we had come over, Mr Raote had said, 'My father made us study. You will recognize the difficulty when you visit the spot.'

And now, standing in the verandah where he had walked and run thousands of times, looking down at the yard which would have been shared with all the people from all the rooms in the building, I wondered how life had been lived in that small space, how five brothers and two sisters and father and mother had managed. How did children sleep and play and get ready for school?

Mr Raote said his father and mother used to awaken the children at four in the morning. Between four and seven they did their exercises – running, push-ups – and they studied. They had to do it all before seven. What made it difficult after that? The crowd in the building and yard, the noise? Mr Raote said, 'The atmosphere.'

As a top Shiv Sena man, Mr Raote had a reputation for roughness. And he had been a little rough with me when I was taken to his office to be introduced to him. When he understood that I wasn't looking for material for another hostile interview, that I was more interested in his background and development, his manner changed. He was interested in his own story; his idea of himself was of a man who had struggled.

He was now chairman of the Standing Committee of the Corporation, he said; but his first job in the Corporation had been as a clerk, in 1965, when he was twenty-one, and his salary then had been 218 rupees a month, £16. He offered that fact almost as soon as we began to talk seriously. And then he offered another: when he was a boy, he said, he used to help his father make coffins.

I liked that detail. He liked it too. He wanted to tell the rest of the story. He asked me to come to his flat in Dadar, and he sent his Ambassador car for me early one morning. The windows of the car had the dark tinting that had become fashionable in Bombay; there were two small plastic fans that made for fair comfort; and on the dashboard there was a little picture of Hanuman, the deity who stood for strength.

When I was taken up to the flat, Mr Raote was still doing his puja. Waiting, I went out to the terrace and looked at the view north and south, all the great length of Bombay, unexpectedly green from this height. When Mr Raote had finished his puja, I went into the sitting room, and he began to talk.

'When I was born, my father was working as a mechanic in All-India Radio, AIR. This was in 1944. He was getting 300 rupees a month. It was sufficient. I grew up thinking of myself as lower middle class. We had no luxuries, but we had enough to eat. We used to have a kind of soaked-wheat cereal in the morning, *satva*. You become very strong if you eat that. It takes two hours to prepare.

'I studied up to 11th standard in Marathi. Then I joined the college. About this time my father retired from AIR, and he became a jack of all trades. There was a big drop in his earning. He used to earn 75 to 90 rupees a month as a carpenter in the film studio, working for many hours at a time.

'He also used to go as a carpenter to prepare coffins. I used to go with him sometimes. Making coffins is a very specialized thing. It isn't easy to get that bend at the shoulders. The plank has to be one; it mustn't be cut. And you have to have a very good bottom in a coffin, because the whole pressure of the body falls on that bottom. We would get four annas, a quarter of a rupee, for a coffin for a small child. Twelve annas for a medium-size coffin. For a bigger-size coffin, six feet or six feet five inches, we used to get one rupee and a quarter. That was just for the labour. In a day we would be able to prepare five or six coffins. Normally a person wouldn't go to make coffins. It's a casteless occupation – not for a person of caste. But we did it for the cash.

'My father wanted to see at least one of his children become a doctor. My sister was admitted to the college for science. I completed my own Inter Science studies. My first choice after this was for the military. I wanted to be an officer, but I had no one to advise me. I joined the Indian Navy training course in 1962, and went to the exams and all. But I was a month too old, so I had to come back again. Then I tried to become an engineer. It was hard to get into a school in Bombay. I got admission to the Sholapur Polytechnic – that's far away from here. My father said he couldn't pay the expenses, and he couldn't. The expenses in Sholapur would have been 200 rupees a month. So I had to give that up too. That was in 1964. The next year I put my name down at the state employment exchange. We were still living in that one room. I joined St Xavier's Technical Institute for evening classes.

'So already there were these two or three failures in my life – not getting into the military, being too old for the navy training course, and not getting into an engineering school. It's a frustration at that age. That's the age when boys can develop ambition. If they don't develop ambition, they start to drift.

'My mother and father gave me encouragement, and my intention to do something in life was always there. I had the confidence.'

I remembered what Mr Patil, the Shiv Sena area leader in Thane, had said about confidence, *atma-vishwas:* it had been given him by Ganpati. I asked Mr Raote whether he thought he had got his confidence from Ganpati.

He said he had got his confidence from religion in the larger sense, rather than from Ganpati in particular. 'He is not a special deity. Everything in India begins with Ganpati or Ganesh. No Hindu puja starts without him. The religion we have is from childhood. It is part and parcel of our life. No Hindu family will give up the morning puja. We have a special garment for the puja. Religion definitely gave us confidence. It built our character.

'We are coming now to the most important aspect of my life. I've told you about my failures and frustration, and how I gave up and put my name down at the state employment exchange.

In 1965 I took a job as a clerk in the Bombay Corporation. The salary was 218 rupees. Was that a good wage? To the man who has no earnings, whatever he earns is good. And my main ambition at this time was that my sister should become a doctor, as my father wanted. We did secure her admission to a medical college. And she was offered three scholarships – from the British Council, Tata's, and somebody else. We chose Tata. They gave the complete tuition fee. The books we got from other people.'

Mrs Raote had been in and out of the sitting room, but in a self-effacing way. Now, smiling, she came up to us with an open photograph album. She had heard us talking about religion, and the photographs she wanted to show were of a religious occasion: the thread ceremony for one of her sons. This prompted Mr Raote to go and bring out the unstitched length of cotton – mauve, with a band of another colour – which he wore when he did his puja. Mrs Raote was a pale-complexioned, handsome woman; and, as so often in Indian homes, the simple and apparently artless devotion of the wife to her husband was something that made an impression.

Mrs Raote withdrew. The open album rested on the sofa. And Mr Raote went on with his story.

'I should add something else at this point. In 1962, three years before I had taken the job with the Corporation, and at the beginning of the time of my failures and frustration, I had come across a weekly called *Marmik*. This was a cartoon weekly, the first in the Marathi language. It was edited by Bal Thackeray. He and his brother and his father wrote the whole paper. *Marmik* always had a big cartoon on the front cover. It was this that caught my eye. The circulation of the paper was about 35 or 40 thousand at that time.

'And now, in 1965, with my sister in the medical college, and me in the Corporation as a clerk, and my father working as a carpenter in the film studio, *Marmik* really began to work on my mind. Every week the magazine spoke about the injustices done in Bombay and Maharashtra to the sons of the soil. And I found I was terribly attracted to the emotional personality of Bal Thackeray and his father, as expressed in the magazine. I even tried to meet Bal Thackeray. He was living in Shivaji Park.'

Mr Raote waved to the west, to an area of green: Bombay from this height all clear before us, from the Gateway of India and the Fort area in the south, to the hills and suburbs of the north: the great city, from this height all its squalor lost below the green of trees, now truly Mr Raote's own.

'There was an announcement in *Marmik* in May 1966 about a youth organization that was to be founded. It was to be called the Shiv Sena. I started visiting Bal Thackeray's house. Actually, the coconut was broken on the 19th of June 1966 at his house.' The breaking of a coconut at the start of an important venture is with Hindus a kind of puja or religious act. 'Eighteen people were there. At 8.20 in the morning.'

'Was that time chosen by a pundit?'

'No. It just happened. I was one of the 18 people there. Four of the 18 were from Bal Thackeray's own house: Bal Sahib himself, his father, and his two brothers. The first meeting lasted about half an hour. It was in the main room of their small house. Their father occupied that room, being an old man. He wrote everything on a Marathi typewriter. It is still there in the house, as a memorial of him. It was Bal Thackeray's father who gave the name Shiv Sena.' Shiva's Army. 'It just seemed natural and right. And we pledged ourselves at that meeting to fight the injustices done to the sons of the soil.

'That was how the Sena began. Bal Sahib used to hold small meetings here and there. Four months after the founding of the Sena he announced a public meeting on the issue of injustice. That meeting was to be on the 30th of October 1966. It had a tremendous response. Four to five lakhs.' Between 400 and 500 thousand people. 'And a number of gymnasiums in the town began to be attracted.'

What were those gymnasiums? I had never heard of them before.

'The gymnasium is a Maharashtrian institution. My father was too poor to send us to a gymnasium. But, as I told you, he made us run and exercise in the mornings. The gymnasium has been a Maharashtrian institution since the time of our great saint, Ramdas Swami. He was the guru of Shivaji.' Shivaji, the warrior leader of the Marathas in the 17th century, the founder of Maratha military glory. 'Ramdas was a very practical guru. His message in part was that you should exercise and keep your body fit. One of Ramdas's famous sayings is, "Don't talk. Act."'

And now again Mrs Raote came to us, this time with a big, thick book in Marathi. It was a book of Ramdas's verses, a well printed modern edition, with a dust jacket. This made Mr Raote go and bring out some other big Marathi books: the verses of other classical Maratha teachers, Dineshwari, Tukaram, Eknath. These names were not really known to me. The books all looked new, and were well printed and well produced; but they were too bulky to handle easily, and I felt they were sacred household objects rather than books to be physically read. They were passed to me one by one, and I held them for a little and passed them back. They were then laid out on the sofa, next to the open photograph album with the snaps of Mr Raote in his puja cloth at the thread ceremony for his son.

I wondered how, in the conditions of Bombay, in the conditions Mr Raote had grown up in, people had kept in touch with their sacred books.

He said there had been no problem. 'In a traditional Maharashtrian household the elders would recite, morning and evening, *slokas* or verses from the writings of the famous gurus, so that a child, whether he had actually read the texts or not, would be aware of those verses. Nowadays it's done by tapes.'

There was a small shelf of such tapes in Mr Raote's sitting room, in a corner which seemed, from the objects laid out in it, to be a kind of holy or sacred corner.

He said, 'Maharashtra is a land of saints.' He played a part of a tape with a chanting or singing of Ramdas's verses – and the rhythms took me back 40 years and more to the *Ramayana* singing

I had heard in my childhood. Ramdas's verses had endured, Mr Raote said, because of their rhythm. 'Ramdas's slokas have a special, simple, repetitive rhythm.' They were not musical for the sake of being musical. 'They are addressed to the mind. Each and every Maharashtrian, even if he lives in a hutment, has a culture.'

He stopped the tape, and returned to the story of the early days of the Shiv Sena. The Sena, the army of the land of saints, had caught on fast. But even as the Sena grew, Mr Raote's personal life declined. Between the founding of the Sena, in June 1966, and the big public meeting four months later which established it as a power in Bombay, Mr Raote's father died.

'The whole family was now on my head, and I had to continue as a clerk in the Corporation. I've told you that my first choice was always for the military, and I applied at this time for the Air Force pilot aptitude test. I got through the preliminary test in Bombay. Out of 1500 in my centre, only 12 were selected for a further interview at Bangalore. I was one of the 12. I went to Bangalore, and I got through all the aptitude tests of the Air Force. But the most delicate test – the machine test – was the one I failed. As part of that test, 100 questions had to be answered in five minutes. The speed of the questions baffled me. I had had no guidance in these matters. You need to practise to answer 100 questions in five minutes. There are schools today training people for examinations like that. But not then. And this failure was added to my frustration at having to serve in the Corporation, although I was never interested in service.'

I had noticed in other people this Indian use of the word 'service'. In one way it was related to 'civil service'; in another way it was related to the old-fashioned English use of 'service', meaning domestic service. The meaning of the word in India lay somewhere between the two. 'Service' in India stood for employment; but it also meant working for somebody else, working for wages, being dependent. (Mr Patil of Thane, for instance, speaking of his father who had worked for 40 years in the tool room of a factory, had said that his father had been 'in service'.)

'But I had to serve in the Corporation until my sister had got her M.B.S. degree. And I got married in 1968. My father-in-law and mother-in-law made me get married. I was doing the evening classes at St Xavier's Technical Institute, and I would have preferred to get married after I had finished my studies. It was a love-match.'

He used the English words, 'love-match', running them together and making 'love' rhyme with 'how', so that the words seemed to have become Marathi words.

'We belonged to different castes. I used to give lessons at that time. She was one of my students. That was how this affair came up.' This giving of lessons was unexpected, another side of the Corporation clerk. 'She used to live over there, in that house.'

From the top of the block where we were he waved to an area of green and roofs not far away: Bombay, from here, an immense city, but the spaces he had moved in always small, village-like.

'There was opposition to our association from both sides. The castes were different, but they were not all that different. Caste wasn't the reason for the opposition. In our family we didn't want love-match. Our tradition is the proposed marriage.' The arranged marriage. 'It was the same on her side. So my in-laws, or the people who became my in-laws, compelled me to get married. And this marriage became another burden.

'To reduce this burden, I asked my wife to give up her studies and go into service. She gave up her studies and became a telephone operator. This was a government job, in the state secretariat. She got between 171 and 180 rupees a month, about £9, after the rupee devaluation. This was in 1969. We had a child in 1970. But, with my wife in service, I was not much worried by this.

'Then at last, in 1972, my sister got her M.D. She informed me on the phone at 12 o'clock one day that she had got through. And that same day I resigned from the Corporation. Eight years I had been in service – while my sister was becoming a doctor, as my father wanted. The day she became a doctor, I resigned. I had no job to go to, but I resigned. All that we had was my wife's job.

Her job in the state secretariat had been a temporary one, but then fortunately she got a job as a telephone operator in the Corporation. It was an accident that she joined the Corporation when I left it.'

During the later years of service there had been Mr Raote's parallel life with the Sena. The Sena had risen, had begun to march, had become feared. In 1968 it had won more than a third of the seats in the Corporation. It had launched an agitation about the borders of Maharashtra; it had called a strike that had brought Bombay to a standstill for four days. Immigrants from South India had grown especially to fear the Sena. And Dadar, the suburb where we were – with a view of Shivaji Park, near where Bal Thackeray's house was, and with a view of the two-storeyed tenement where Mr Raote and his family were still living at that time in their one room – Dadar, as Mr Raote said, was 'the epicentre' of the Shiv Sena earthquake.

I had a memory myself of that early Sena time, from the other side. This was in 1967, a year after the Sena had been founded. I had been visiting a Parsi acquaintance. He was a 'boxwallah', as the word was in those days. A boxwallah was an executive in a big firm, usually a firm with foreign affiliations; and in those days, before the Indian industrial boom, to be a boxwallah was to be secure, even exalted. The man I knew had married a Hindu woman of a well known family; and it was surprising to hear now, from people who should have been far above the day-to-day stresses of Indian life, that this 'mixed' marriage had made them both liable to physical attack from the Sena in their area.

It was evening; we were high up; there were lights below, some pale and yellow in the shanties. My vision of Bombay began to change: the 'poor', the people down there, were acquiring individuality and had begun to stake their own claim to the city; piety (or rage at their condition, or disgust) was no longer a sufficient response. The man I knew – speaking in 1967 with something of the passion I was to find this time in Papu, the young Jain stockbroker – said, of the dangers of mob attack, 'I try not to worry about it. I tell myself that, if I find something starting to happen, I must think it's like being in a nasty road accident.'

Yet at that time, 1967, and for years afterwards, Mr Raote, one of the original 18 of the Sena, had been working as a clerk in the Corporation, his salary rising over eight years from 218 rupees a month to 272 rupees and 50 paise (100 paise make a rupee), travelling back and forth on those crowded suburban trains between the Victorian-Gothic building where he worked and the tenement in Dadar where he had been born and where he had continued to live, in the same one room: carrying the grief for his father, the high ambition for his sister, his own frustrations at not being an officer, then an engineer, then something in the Indian Navy, daily feeling his clerkship in the Corporation, his 'service', as a humiliation.

Outside, he was unknown. But as the Sena had grown, he had risen in the Sena. All the time he had left over from work he gave to the Sena. He thought that in those days, between the Corporation and the Sena, he was working for 20 hours a day. He found himself running 22 Sena areas in central Bombay; he became close to the top leaders; he was put in charge of the Sena's election organization. He began to be known; his name began to get into the papers.

Yet, when he resigned in 1972 from the Corporation, all they had was his wife's telephone-operator salary. Then he appeared to have some luck. Just two days after he left the Corporation, he found a job as a shop supervisor in the tube-well section of one of the most highly regarded engineering firms in India. His salary was to be 750 rupees a month, nearly three times what he had been getting in the Corporation. This was a great piece of good fortune, but it hardly lasted. His Sena reputation undid him.

The Maharashtrian workers began to treat him as a Sena organizer rather than a shop supervisor. They wanted him to start a union. This kind of excitement couldn't be kept secret from the management. The works manager called him in one day – the works manager was an old army officer: the kind of man Mr Raote had longed to be – and began to question him. Had he come to work, or had he come as an activist?

Mr Raote couldn't endure the questioning. 'I am a hot-tempered man. I resigned that very day. I had been with the firm for one month and 22 days.'

Mr Raote paused here. He was coming now to the part of his story he especially wanted to tell; this was the period of his life he had wanted me to know about almost as soon as he had decided to talk seriously to me, in his office in the Corporation.

So, sitting at home now, after his morning puja, with the open photograph album and the sacred Marathi books laid out on the sofa, he paused. Then he said, 'That was when my starving started. That was my most difficult time.'

Though it was the time of his glory in the Sena.

'I began to work the whole day for the Sena. My wife used to feed my family with what she got from her job. And now – since it was a love-match – there began to be trouble in our family. My mother and my wife couldn't get on.'

Whether arising out of a love marriage or an arranged marriage, it was the eternal conflict of Hindu family life, a ritualized aspect of the fate of women, like marriage itself or childbirth or widowhood. To be tormented by a mother-in-law was part of a young woman's testing, part, almost, of growing up. Somehow the young woman survived; and then one day she became a mother-in-law herself, and had her own daughter-in-law to torment, to round off a life, to balance pain and joy.

'I decided at last to leave my place.' To leave, at last, the one room at the end of the upper verandah. 'I left with my wife and children. We went to stay at my mother-in-law's place.'

That wasn't far away. Like the tenement he had left, the building he moved to could be seen from the flat where we were. He would show both places to me later from the roof terrace: the drama of small spaces and short distances, the settings themselves always accessible afterwards, never really out of sight, and perhaps for this reason cleansed (like stage sets) of the emotions they had once held.

'If my mother-in-law gave me food, I had food. If they didn't give me food there, I would starve for the day. In those days I didn't have a penny in my pocket, not even for a cigarette. But, being a proud person, I have never gone down in front of anybody for anything. I prefer starving. And those were my starving days. Since that time, you know, I have only one meal a day. That meal is at night. I never eat in the mornings. I have only coffee.

'One of my maternal uncles used to visit me at that time. Twice or thrice a week. He was absolutely poor, but he used to take me to a hotel.' The word 'hotel', as used by Mr Raote, and pronounced *ho-tal,* was more of a Marathi or Hindi word than an English word, and meant a restaurant, usually of a simple sort. 'He would give me a meal. Poor food. And a cup of tea, and a cigarette.

'One day my father-in-law didn't come home. He didn't come home the next day either. We began a long search for him. After four days he came back on his own. We found him in the road. He had had a road accident, and he had been discharged from the hospital. After this he became "psychiatric". He used to harass everybody. So I had to stay away from my mother-in-law's place during the day. I was quite homeless. I used only to sleep at my mother-in-law's place.

'Then one of my father-in-law's friends offered me a place in East Dadar. We went there, and it was there that my second son was born. During all this tormented time my wife was pregnant. In East Dadar I got settled nicely. I had a peaceful life. I used to get there at 11 in the evening, after my work for the Sena. This was in 1973–1974.

'This period of my life lasted four years. I used to walk kilometres to take the Sena meetings. I never grumbled then. When, later, I was elected to the Corporation, and began to talk there, all that I poured into the speeches came from these years I've been telling you about.'

What had supported him? Had he felt 'guided'?

He had felt guided. He had a guru. In what I had thought of as the holy corner of the sitting room there was – not far from the small shelf of devotional cassettes – a large, perhaps more than life-size picture of a handsome, bearded man, just the face. I had seen the picture as I had come in; but with the feeling I had had that the corner was holy, and private, I hadn't looked at the picture more closely. That man – with features of almost unnatural regularity and beauty, in the picture – had been Mr Raote's guru.

It was of religion that now, near the end of the morning, Mr Raote wished to talk. He took me to his puja room. It was next to the sitting room. The shrine was a deep, chest-high recess in a wall. The images were freshly garlanded; there was a husked coconut with a tuft of fibre or coir at the top. Right at the back of the recess, and fitting the back, was another picture of the guru, perhaps trimmed to fit the space, but similar to the picture in the sitting room: the devotee, and the shrine, would be held in the gaze of the guru. Fresh flowers were placed on the shrine every day; the coconut was changed every month. Mr Raote spent an hour and a half every morning on his puja. He sat on a deer skin. The skin was then rolled up and placed on a high shelf.

Some days later, when I went to see Mr Raote again in his flat, I got the rest of his story.

At the end of that four-year period of starvation, good fortune came to him quite suddenly. In the garage of a friend, right here in Dadar, he began to make furniture. It was a new turn for him; but he wasn't absolutely a novice. At school he had done woodwork and furniture-making as a special technical subject. Now, in the friend's garage, he began to make sofas, tables and chairs; and he sold the pieces he made. He discovered he had talent.

He had made much of the furniture in his flat. Against one wall was a special table he had designed. It was like a Pembroke table, with two fold-down flaps on either side of a central plank.

But in this design the central plank was very narrow, about eight inches, making it ideal for the small, multi-purpose spaces of Bombay dwellings. The design found favour; it was adopted by all the leading furniture-manufacturers of Bombay. Mr Raote also specialized in study units that doubled as room-dividers. The pieces he made were all his own designs: the ideas just came to him. 'The moment I started working in the furniture business I thought of these things.' He also made doors. He had made all the doors in his flat, and designed and made all the decorated teak architraves. The flat was a special kind of triumph for him, a proof of his success and a demonstration of his talent. There was much in it I had taken for granted and only now, with his help, began to see.

His success grew. He began to do woodwork for big buildings on subcontract; and then he thought he would go into the building business itself. Two years after he had started making furniture, he put up his first big building in partnership. Though his journey had seemed long to him, he was at that time only thirty-three. Since then he had done 15 or 16 big projects.

'But in all my business I have tried, as a member of the Shiv Sena, to accommodate the middle-class Maharashtrian. So, instead of becoming a multi-millionaire as a builder, I prefer to follow the path of the leader, to follow the principles he has laid down.'

This devotion to the Shiv Sena and its leader was like an aspect of Mr Raote's religion. He had always had courage, and confidence, the gift of religion, the *atma-vishwas* of which Mr Patil of Thane had spoken.

'In my rise, my falls, whatever the problems, I faced them boldly, whether as a businessman or social worker or head of a family. Up to the time of my college days I had my father pushing me on. Then in 1964 I came across the great saint who had set up his ashram at Alibagh.'

This was the guru whose picture was in the corner of the sitting room and at the back of the shrine in the puja room. Mr Raote, from what he said now, had come in contact with him in the year he had had the great disappointment of not being able to go to the engineering college at Sholapur.

'I used to go to see him for his blessing. I never asked anything of him. I went to him only for his blessing, to serve him because he was a saint, and I feel he changed my entire life. He died in 1968. But I feel he is still blessing me whenever I need his blessing. Though he is not here physically, in the actual body, he always gives me and my family his presence. Look,' Mr Raote said, taking me to the teak front door of his flat. 'My door has no latch. It is always open.'

I had caught Mr Raote just in time to get the end of his story. Though when we were making our arrangements, he had told me nothing about it, it turned out now that I had caught him, that second morning, on the very day he was going off to his ashram for nine days. He was going alone, without his wife.

'I go every year, without fail. These nine days of my year I cannot give to anybody else.'

He had done other pilgrimages. He and his wife had been six times to the cave of Amarnath in Kashmir, 13,000 feet up in the Himalayas, where – an ancient miracle of India – every year in the summer an ice phallus formed, symbol of Shiva, waxing and waning with the moon.

He said, 'I love that Himalayan place.'

The worldly man who wanted to be an officer and an engineer, the Sena worker, the devout Hindu: there were three layers to him, making for a chain of belief and action.

Papu, the young Jain stockbroker, speaking of the Shiv Sena, one of the many components of the threat around him, said, 'All our problems are economic. We wouldn't have a problem if we didn't have an economic problem.'

He was taking me that afternoon – after trading on the stock exchange had ceased – to see where he lived, and especially to see the slum by which he was surrounded. Dharavi, as its name was,

was a famous slum. There were people in Bombay who claimed, with a certain amount of pride, that it was the largest slum in Asia.

We were in a yellow-and-black taxi, and moving slowly: sunlight and crowd and hooter-din, the hot exhausts of buses billowing black, grit resting on the skin. And then, in the middle of this, a glimpse of purity: a group of thin young boys in white loincloths, walking fast on the other side of the road.

The boys were Jains, Papu said, *munis,* aspirants to the religious life, and they would have been the disciples of a guru. Munis didn't have a fixed abode; they were required to move about from place to place and to live off charity. There were places attached to temples where they might spend a night; they asked at Jain houses for their food.

How would they know that a house was a Jain house?

'Normally there is a board at the entrance, or an emblem of some sort, or some kind of tile. Nowadays you can even get stickers. But usually there is an attendant with the young munis. He takes them round and shows them the houses. It is said that the purpose of this discipline is to control the ego. In Jainism knowledge is very important. A brahmin is supposed to be the most intellectual person; he is the person to whom everyone listens. It is to become someone like that that the munis go around asking for their food. To gain knowledge, they have first to keep the ego under control.'

But the rituals and traditions came from a more pastoral time. Did they serve their purpose when they were acted out now in the streets of Bombay?

Papu's attitude was that rituals had to be constantly adapted. Jains, for instance, were supposed to bathe every morning and walk barefooted in an unstitched garment to the temple. In Bombay many Jains could still do that; Papu's mother did it in the suburb where she and Papu lived. But Papu himself couldn't do it. He might walk to the temple after his bath, but he couldn't walk barefooted and he couldn't go in an unstitched cloth, because nowadays he went to the temple on his way to work.

I told him about my visit to the Muslim area and my talk with Anwar.

He said, 'The aggression can be made creative. We used to play basketball with a Muslim team from that area. The aggression of the young Muslim boys made them good basketball players. It gave them the killer instinct.' The killer instinct which Papu saw in the Indian industrialist, but which traders like himself didn't yet have. 'If I hit them, they hit back. And they play to win. Whereas I come back home satisfied with a good game. If they hit me, I wouldn't hit back. I suppose I might complain, that's all.'

He talked again about his wish to retire at forty to do social work. I knew, from what he had said before, that he had doubts about the idea, doubts especially about the possible waste of his God-given talent, which, if properly used, might produce more funds for his welfare work. Now – sitting in the taxi, in the dust and afternoon glare, at the end of his working day – doubts seemed to have taken him over and enervated him. He wasn't even sure about the social work he was doing on Sundays among people of the slum in his area.

'Every Sunday a group of us, mainly Jains, feed the slum people. We feed perhaps 500 of them. We start at about 10.30 in the morning. For many of the people we are feeding it may be the only big meal in the week. It may keep them going. I am doing it to help them – there can be no doubt about that. But there is also in me a feeling of relief from the guilt which I always have. Whatever I do for them, I know there are limitations. Perhaps I should try to help them to help themselves. My father's idea about this was: "I would like to teach them fishing, and not give them fish." If I'm giving them a square meal, it ends there. What I think I would like – even if it means helping only five kids rather than 500 – is that the five I help should be able to make a living.'

He was obsessed by the idea of charity, of what he, with his blessings, might do for others. Charity was like an expression of the religious life, the prudent life, the pure life.

We came at last to Sion. This was the name of the suburb where he lived. He asked the driver to drive round the area of 'quarters'. His spirits, low during the drive out, went lower. He spoke of prostitution and despair in the back streets; but he didn't look at what we were driving through. The 'quarters', though, were only government quarters, apartment blocks for government employees. As a piece of urban development, it was depressing – Indian architecture at its most ignorant and inhumane, concrete block after concrete block set down in scarred, bare land looking in places like a rubbish dump – but it wasn't the slum I had been preparing myself for.

That slum, the famous one, was, in fact, on the other side of Sion. Papu had, however, stopped talking about it. And I began to feel that, though the idea of showing me the slum had been Papu's, his mood had changed during the drive out, and he couldn't face it now.

We went to the street where he lived. It was in the middle-class area of Sion, some way from the quarters, and on the other side of a thoroughfare. It looked a well-to-do and established street; there were big trees; and well dressed men and women, office workers, were waiting for buses. The flat Papu had bought on that street had cost the equivalent of £100,000 – and we were an hour away from central Bombay, and close to a very big slum. That gave an idea of what had happened to property prices here. It explained why the big problem for most people in Bombay was the problem of finding room, a place to stay, a place to sleep; and why the huts and shanties and rag-structures filled so many of the city's nooks and crannies.

The sandy yard of Papu's block was swept and clean and bare. In another city it might have seemed a drab yard. But here it was noticeably clean, noticeably bare; and it was as though the emptiness of the yard was an aspect of its cleanliness.

Papu said, 'This is a co-operative block. That means that the people here are vegetarians. The people in the other building' –

the neighbouring block, architecturally similar – 'are mixed vegetarian and non-vegetarian. Property values are higher here because this building is vegetarian. If you cook fish, there is a smell that it generates. If there is a non-vegetarian in a building, you may sometimes see a goat tied up in the yard for a couple of days, and then one day you won't see the goat, and you'll know it's been killed and eaten. But it's changing for young people in our community. When they go out they feel that the rest of the world eats meat, and they can get the feeling that they might be feeble, without manhood. Everybody tries to change things to suit himself.' That was also what Papu thought about rituals: they were being adapted all the time.

We took the old-fashioned lift to his flat. He showed the distinguishing Jain sticker above his front door, and the Hindu marks on the front doors of other flats. His sitting room, looking out on to the street and the school across the street, was big and uncluttered. It was of a piece with the yard: the emptiness of the space was like luxury. The walls were clean, the terrazzo floor gleamed.

I asked about my shoes. He said it wasn't necessary to take them off. But later he said something which made me feel I should have taken them off without asking. We were talking about ritual acts; and he said that a Punjabi friend had said that the floor of the sitting room where we were was truly a floor one could walk barefoot on. What the friend meant was that normally the ritual of taking off shoes – before entering a temple, for instance – meant walking on filth, getting your clean feet dirty in the name of a ritual cleanliness.

Papu said, 'I like the concept of purity. I like it as a way of life.'

His mother came out and was introduced: a grave, silent lady, part of whose life had been spent in Burma, until, with the independence of the country, the Indians had been expelled. She brought her palms together in the Hindu gesture of greeting – and I remembered that she walked barefooted every morning to her temple.

'In India religion enters every sphere of activity,' Papu said. He opened a drawer. 'These are company reports.' He took one out.

'This is the annual report of a South Indian company.' He showed the photographs at the front of the report. They recorded the visit of a holy man to the company's headquarters, and showed him standing in the middle of the board of directors, all the directors standing stripped to the waist and in puja garb.

'They are one of the most efficient cement plants in the country,' Papu said. 'At the back of our minds we always have this idea that following religion or rituals is not going to harm us at all. So why not do it? There was the father-in-law of one of my friends. He told me one time that to succeed in a certain tiling you've got to feed a cow every day with certain things. Say, wheat. Feed a cow every day with wheat. Well, at that stage in my life, if I'm working towards a goal, I don't want to leave a single stone unturned. And I know that by doing this thing I'm not going to harm myself. So why not do it?

'There are certain places of worship in Bombay – temples, mosques, even churches – where people go on certain days. On Tuesdays they go to Siddhi Vinayak Temple, devoted to Ganesh. Why Tuesday? No one really knows, but all the people there are probably doing it for the same reason, and on the same principle: Why not do it?'

'A materialist attitude?'

'Certainly. Ninety per cent of us call to God when we need something. There is a church here that Hindus go to. It's something they believe in, but it isn't their religion. If you're a Hindu, how can you go to a church?'

On the sloping middle shelf of the wall unit there was a copy of *Fortune* magazine and a book, *Elements of Investment*. Papu was aware of the oddity: those practical books and magazines, his own Jain faith, his need for a comprehensive purity, the setting, the other faiths around him.

Tea was brought out, on small stainless-steel trays. It was a Jain tea, vegetarian, nothing prepared with eggs. There was a puri, and various fried things made from flour and ground lentils.

I thought that Papu had given up the idea of the visit to the great slum of Dharavi. But his spirits had revived in the sitting room of his flat, and after our tea he took me to a back room, to show me the view. The slum was closer than I thought. It lay just beyond the railway tracks that ran at the back of the street on which Papu's block stood. Papu's middle-class area, so established-looking when one came to the street, was contained in a narrow strip between the area of the quarters and the area of the great slum.

He said, of the slum, 'You wouldn't be able to stand the stink.'

A little later, with the determination and suddenness with which people go out into bad weather, he said we should be going.

We set out on foot. The slum was only a short walk away. We began to cross the busy, dusty bridge over the railway lines. The afternoon traffic was hectic. We had barely got down the hump of the railway bridge, when Papu, losing a little of his resolution, said we should take a taxi.

To stress the extent of the slum, he said, 'Look. No tall buildings from here to there.' It was a good way of taking it in. Otherwise, moving at road level, one might have missed the extent of the flat ragged plain, bounded by far-off towers.

And then, in no time, we were moving on the margin of the slum, so sudden, so obvious, so overwhelming, it was as though it was something staged, something on a film set, with people acting out their roles as slum dwellers: back-to-back and side-to-side shacks and shelters, a general impression of blackness and greyness and mud, narrow ragged lanes curving out of view; then a side of the main road dug up; then black mud, with men and women and children defecating on the edge of a black lake, swamp and sewage, with a hellish oily iridescence.

The stench was barely supportable; but it had to be endured. The taxi came to a halt in a traffic jam. The jam was caused by a line of loaded trucks on the other side of the road. The slum of Dharavi was also an industrial area of sorts, with many unauthorized businesses, leather works and chemical works among them, which wouldn't have been permitted in a better regulated city area.

Petrol and kerosene fumes added to the stench. In this stench, many bare-armed people were at work, doing what I had never seen people doing before: gathering or unpacking cloth waste and cardboard waste, working in a grey-white dust that banked up on the ground like snow and stifled the sounds of hands and feet, working beside the road itself or in small shanties: large-scale rag-picking.

Papu said he hardly passed this way. In the taxi he sat turned away from the slum itself. He faced the other side of the road, where the loaded trucks were idling, and where, in the distance, were the apartment blocks of the middle-class area of Bandra, on the sea.

The traffic moved again. At a certain point Papu said, 'This is the Muslim section. People will tell you that the Muslims here are fundamentalists. But don't you think you could make these people fight for anything you tell them to fight for?'

The stench of animal skins and excrement and swamp and chemicals and petrol fumes, the dust of cloth waste, the amber mist of truck exhausts, with the afternoon sun slanting through – what a relief it was to leave that behind, and to get out into the other Bombay, the Bombay one knew and had spent so much time getting used to, the Bombay of paved roads and buses and people in lightweight clothes.

It had been hard enough to drive past the area. It was harder to imagine what it was like living there. Yet people lived with the stench and the terrible air, and had careers there. Even lawyers lived there, I was told. Was the smell of excrement only on the periphery, from the iridescent black lake? No; that stench went right through Dharavi. Even more astonishing was to read in a Bombay magazine an article about Papu's suburb of Sion, in which the slum of Dharavi was written about almost as a bohemian feature of the place, something that added spice to humdrum middle-class life. Bombay clearly inoculated its residents in some way.

I had another glimpse of Dharavi some time later, when I was going in a taxi to the domestic airport at Santa Cruz. The taxi-driver – a Muslim from Hyderabad, full of self-respect, nervous about living in Bombay, fearful of sinking, planning to go back home soon, and in the meantime nervously particular about his car and his clothes – the taxi-driver showed the apartment blocks on one side of the airport road where hutment dwellers had been rehoused. In the other direction he showed the marsh on which Dharavi had grown and, away in the distance, the low black line of the famous slum.

Seen from here, Dharavi looked artificial, unnecessary even in Bombay: allowed to exist because, as people said, it was a vote-bank, a hate-bank, something to be drawn upon by many people. All the conflicting currents of Bombay flowed there as well; all the new particularities were heightened there. And yet people lived there, subject to this extra exploitation, because in Bombay, once you had a place to stay, you could make money.

And people could be made by the conditions in which they lived. As animals could be made by the conditions in which they were reared: as chickens (to call up a Trinidad memory of 40 years before), reared in a small cage, found it impossible to walk when they were released, and half hopped, half flew, as they had done in their cage. So people who lived in the little spaces of Bombay dwellings got used to those spaces; got used to the communal life of those spaces, and could find the other life, the life of privacy, emotionally disturbing.

Mr Ghate was a high Sena official. He had grown up in the mill area, in one room in a chawl or millworkers' tenement; and he still lived in a chawl, though it was open to him, as a man of position, to live in better accommodation in a better area. He had tried to do that some years before, but it had ended badly. His wife had suffered in the comparative seclusion and spaciousness of the self-contained apartment they had moved to. This was more than moodiness; she had become seriously disturbed. Mr Ghate had moved back to a chawl, to the two rooms he had now, back to the sense of a surrounding crowd and the sounds of life all around him; and he was happy again.

I went to Mr Ghate's chawl in the company of Charu, a young Maharashtrian brahmin. Without Charu, I might not have been received by Mr Ghate. Mr Ghate, Charu said, was one of the 'brash' men of the Sena; and 'brash' was Chant's brahminical word for someone rough and aggressive.

Mr Ghate lived at the top of his chawl block. Without Charu, I don't think I would have made it even to the internal staircase of the place – I was so demoralized, so choked, driven so near to a stomach-heave, by the smell at the entrance, with wet mangled garbage and scavenging cats and kittens in a little patio, and then, in the suddenly dark passage, by the thick warm smell, catching at my throat, of blocked drains. It was Charu, with his brahmin's sense of duty, with his feeling that an appointment should be kept, who (constantly looking back at me, and sometimes even stretching out a hand, like a father leading his child from sand to sea for the first time) led me on and on, up the chawl steps, past open doors giving glimpses of family living spaces.

Hot air should have risen; but at the upper level the air was fresher. A tiger emblem outside a door, the Shiv Sena emblem, identified Mr Ghate's room or apartment. It overlooked the main road. The little windows, frosted glass in green-painted frames, were open behind their wire-netting burglar-proofing; the traffic fumes they let in were even refreshing.

Mr Ghate had two small rooms. One, beyond a curtained doorway, was the kitchen. The room we were received in, where people would have slept at night, doubled in the day as a kind of Sena office. It was full of papers. They were in a fitted cupboard against the side wall – an unexpected modern touch. Among other decorations on one wall was a poster, perhaps originally from an oil company, with a colour photograph of a tiger and the English words, *You observe a lot – by watching.*

Mr Ghate's father had been a millworker. He earned 400 rupees a month, a little over £30. The family had been large, five brothers and two sisters. There had been four sisters, but two had died. The one room they had all lived in was the standard chawl room, 10 feet by 10 feet; and it had worked out quite nicely when they were children. In the mornings they just had tea for breakfast, no cooked food. From seven in the morning till one in the afternoon the children went to school. This meant that in the mornings, for a month or so at a time, Mr Ghate's father would have had a certain amount of room for himself. Mr Ghate's father did shift work at the mill; every month the shift changed.

I remembered what Mr Raote had said about the culture every Maharashtrian had, and I asked Mr Ghate whether he had gone to the gymnasium as a child. He said no; but the question had some meaning for him, because he added immediately that he had taken part in sports. I asked about religion. How, growing up in his chawl, had he learned about religion and the teaching of the saints? He said he wasn't himself a religious man – so there had been a kind of break with the past. But, he said, his father had done the puja at home; though neither his father nor his mother was educated, and until he went to college his family had never owned a book.

It sounded a basic life, a hard life. But everyone had rubbed along. Things changed when he got married. His wife left her family chawl for Mr Ghate's chawl; and then there was a child. The time came when 10 people were living in the 10 feet by 10 feet room. There were 'differences', and constant quarrelling. So Mr Ghate had taken his wife and child to 'staff quarters' – a self-contained apartment in an apartment block – in a suburb 30 or 40 minutes away by train.

It should have meant a new life – the distance from the family, the end of the quarrelling, and the space: after 100 square feet for 10 people in the chawl, they had 300 square feet for three people in the new apartment. But it had led to calamity. Mr Ghate's wife had lived all her life in a chawl. Now, left alone for much of the day in her self-contained 300 square feet, not seeing anyone, not having anyone to talk to, she had become frightened. She had begun to suffer seriously from claustrophobia, and she had been taken close to breakdown.

So they had come back to the mill area, where they had grown up, and Mr Ghate had had the good fortune to find a place in a chawl. The two-roomed suite or apartment such as he had was called in Bombay a 'one-roomed kitchen'. The main room was actually a little bigger than the standard 10 feet by 10 feet chawl room. Five of them lived there now, and there was no space problem.

He had bought the rooms in 1985, and the mechanics of the purchase were like this. The chawls, many of them decades old, from the very beginnings of the Indian industrial revolution, were originally attached to mills, and were meant to accommodate millworkers. Technically, the millowners still owned the chawls; but (because of rent-control laws) the millowners no longer looked after the chawls, had virtually abandoned them; and tenants were nowadays free to sell the lease of the rooms they held. A buyer paid a premium to the sitting tenant, and then the buyer paid rent to the millowner. In 1985 Mr Ghate had paid a premium of 35,000 rupees for his two rooms, about £1400. But now all he paid to the mill-owner in rent was 12 rupees a month, 50 pence – which no doubt explained why the millowners had stopped looking after the chawls.

Mr Ghate was now a protected tenant; he said he could stay in his two rooms forever. And from the way he talked, that was what he intended to do now, after having tried to break away. Not everyone was like him, he said. Many people who didn't have the means dreamed of moving to an apartment. He had the means; he could get a loan from the bank; but he was perfectly happy where he was.

Reviving in the fresher air of his room, I began to see it a little with his eyes. I noticed the amenities. There was a ceiling fan; there was a sturdy step-ladder for climbing up to the loft. Below the loft was a utility area, with various conveniences: a clothes cupboard, a wooden stool, a clothes-horse (now hung with towels), a length of hose pipe, and a rubbish bin in blue plastic with a pedal-worked cover. The utility area was at Mr Ghate's back, near the open window. The area at the front of the room was more the office part of the room, and it had that big fitted cupboard. Mr Ghate, as though apologizing for the extravagance, said he had bought the cupboard last year, because with his Sena work he had many papers to deal with.

There were more than papers behind the glass doors of the cupboard. On a top shelf were tumblers and plates in plastic and stainless steel. On other shelves were photographs, and a gold-coloured plaque with the new Marathi slogan of the Sena I had heard about: *Say it with pride: 'I'm a Hindu'*. The Sena, as it had become more powerful, was trying to be less regional. It was appealing now to a more general Hindu sentiment, and some people found this as worrying as its earlier call of Maharashtra for the Maharashtrians.

I wanted to hear a little more about chawl life. Charu and Mr Ghate talked for a while in Marathi, and then Charu summed up.

'He likes the life here. He grew up in this atmosphere. He doesn't feel a bigger room or apartment would make any difference to him. He doesn't envy or hate other people's wealth. He values people for their mind alone.'

'What is it about the life here that he likes?'

Talking in Marathi to Charu, Mr Ghate seemed to get carried away as he described the advantages of chawl life.

Charu said for him, 'In a chawl you always know what's happening everywhere. You know what's going on in all the other families. You hear everything, you see everything. In this way people live life together, sharing one another's problems. There is no *life* in an apartment.'

There was a lot of life in this chawl. On the upper floor alone, where we were, there were 40 rooms. Five toilets served those 40 rooms. You saw people all the time.

'Doesn't he want privacy?'

Charu's reply was emphatic. '*He doesn't want privacy.* He says that those who want privacy can always move out to a block.' There was a touch of sharpness in that, after what he had said earlier about people who didn't have the means but wanted to move to apartment blocks. 'If you need some privacy for reading and writing, it's always available here after one o'clock in the morning.'

'Does he often stay up?'

'Yes. He often reads until 2.30, three o'clock in the morning. Otherwise there is no chance of reading and writing here.'

'Doesn't he believe that a little more privacy would lead to better education?'

'Your intelligence, or the reading you do, doesn't depend on whether you live in a block or a chawl. It is more your tendency – your aptitude, your character.' And he referred to a famous recent case where a local boy from a slum came first in a Maharashtra state examination.

'Shouldn't he be offering a better life to his followers?'

The reply, in Charu's direct translation, was severe. 'I don't want to help anybody to a luxurious life. This is a millworkers' area.'

'He wants people to remain millworkers?'

The question was slightly altered in translation. Charu seemed to have put it as a personal question, and he got a personal reply.

'He himself has a job in a bank. One brother works in a state corporation. Another, younger brother works in a mill. But that brother is not too educated; he didn't have the intellectual capacity. That brother now gets 1000 rupees a month. That isn't a good wage. To live in Bombay satisfactorily, you need a minimum of 2000 rupees.'

I tried to go back to the question, in a different way. 'What ambition does he have for people in this chawl?'

I missed again. The question seemed to have been put as a question about the future of the chawl, and Mr Ghate gave a literal reply.

'This chawl is ninety years old. It's of sound construction, and it will last for another 50 years. But I have my doubts about its future. The families here are poor. If this chawl is damaged they will not be able to rebuild or to buy their own places somewhere else. They will have to leave Bombay, if anything happens to this chawl.'

On the wall at his back, just below the loft, were Sena pictures and emblems. In addition to the poster with the tiger, there was a big bronze-coloured plaque of Ganesh against a saffron-coloured backing, and there was a framed picture of the coronation of Shivaji: an idea, like something from the Indian cinema, of power and glory and glitter.

That idea would have been full of meaning for Mr Ghate. I wondered how it squared with the work he actually did for the Sena, and the conditions of the chawl. When he considered the chawl, what did he actually see? Who looked after the chawl now, and cleaned the common parts?

Mr Ghate said the tenants themselves cleaned the chawl. I asked why they hadn't done anything about the blocked drains and the rotting garbage at the entrance.

He said, 'Bombay will never be beautiful. There are certain inherent defects. The drains were cleaned some time back, but they got choked up again. There are also problems with people. *Absence of civic sense*.' The last words were in English.

Shouldn't the Sena, with its special social philosophy, do something about that?

'It's a perennial problem. You have to start with the children. It's not an economic problem. These people throw rubbish out of the window.'

I asked about his own background. His family came from a village near Goa, he said. He still had relatives there, and they came to stay every year for 10 or 15 days. They felt attracted to Bombay and would have liked to live there. But they knew that a decent life in the city would be hard to come by, and so they went back.

There were women's voices in the kitchen, beyond the curtained doorway. Mrs Ghate, who had been in the kitchen all along, pulled the curtain back, and said that there had been an accident somewhere in the chawl. An old woman had just come with the news and wanted to know whether Mr Ghate would see her.

He said he would. The old woman was a little frantic. She stood in the doorway and said with tears that two of the children in her room had got burnt. Their father was at the mill, and there was no one who could help.

Mr Ghate said immediately that he would send the children to the hospital in his car. He hurried out to attend to that, and Charu and I were left alone in the room.

Charu told me some more about the communal life of people in Bombay. He said that the love of the communal life stemmed from the life in the joint or extended family: that was a full life, of a constant crowd, and shifting, passionate relationships between the various groups or sections of an extended family. Charu said his own wife, who was doing an M.Sc. degree in child development, couldn't read if she was alone; she preferred to read when there was someone talking near by. Even now, his wife liked staying with her family in their old flat, for the company, the warmth, the constant reassurance of human voices.

Since Mrs Ghate had pulled it, the curtain in the kitchen doorway had remained pulled back. I could see that there was a puja box in the kitchen, something quite basic, nothing like Mr Raote's recessed wall-shrine. Mr Ghate had said that he was not a religious man; the puja box in the kitchen must have been for his wife's sake.

When he came back to us, Mr Ghate looked troubled. He had got the children to the hospital. But he was now worried about his wife. She fell easily into depressions. She knew the affected family, and the accident to the two children was already having a bad effect on her.

Still, the incident showed how important it was for the Sena to have a representative in a place like the chawl. The Sena was known for its social work, and people felt they could approach him.

I asked whether the communal life of the chawl and of other packed areas made political organization easier.

'The chawl is like a bigger family. The area is an even bigger family.'

And other groups could be organized easily as well?

He didn't answer.

He was a stern, dark man. His concern for his wife, which he talked about so openly, was like the one soft thing in him. He had got married in 1970. He was twenty-one then, and his wife was eighteen. The love story he had to tell was in some ways like Mr Raote's in far-off Dadar. The girl who became his wife lived in another chawl. He began to go to that chawl to give lessons to a friend who was weak in mathematics. He had got to know the girl's family; he had begun to give lessons to the girl as well; an attachment had developed.

The girl's father was a teacher. (Mr Ghate's millworker father had never owned a book.) He didn't like it when Mr Ghate dropped out of his engineering college. At that time, too, the Shiv Sena had a bad and violent reputation. The girl's family thought Mr Ghate was an idler. It was this family opposition to Mr Ghate that first threw his wife into a depression.

Mr Ghate said, 'She's extremely sensitive.'

One day they were sitting together, Mr Ghate and the girl, in a hotel. A *ho-tal*, a simple restaurant. The girl's sisters and her brother saw them. Mr Ghate felt that it would be difficult after this for the girl to go back to her family room. So he took her to an uncle's place in an apartment block. The next day they got married. That hadn't been his intention at all when he took the girl to his uncle's. But he saw that it was the only thing he could do; the decision to get married was entirely his own. The marriage was done with Vedic rites, simpler than the traditional Hindu marriage rites.

So his marriage had been a love marriage. Had other members of his family followed his example?

He said a sister had made a love marriage a year or so before. 'It's happening more and more, you think?'

'Yes.' But then, in spite of the romantic story of his own marriage, he became stern. He was clearly unhappy about his sister's marriage. 'Love marriages don't last, unless there is an understanding of minds. A marriage doesn't survive if it's based on physical attraction.'

'Was there opposition to your sister's love marriage?'

His reply was ambiguous. 'There was no opposition. She got married purely out of physical attraction.'

'What was the man's job?'

'Ayurvedic doctor.' *Ayurveda,* traditional Hindu medicine.

'Well off?'

'Fairly well off, but not independent. That's why I wanted my sister to get a job. They're staying at Sion. Just recently I got her a job.'

Sion was Papu's suburb. Was Sion a euphemism for Dharavi? I asked, 'Staying in quarters in Sion?'

'They're staying in a proper block. But I don't really know. I have nothing to do with my sister now. I've got her a job, and that's all I want to know about her.'

'But why?'

'The boy is not on his feet.'

'How much is she getting in her job? The job you got her.'

'About 900 rupees.'

'You don't want to go and see how she's getting on?'

'No, no. I've given her a job. They have a child. But no. My sister is not on the same wavelength, and I don't like that. Her way of life is very cheap. She has cheap expectations. To her, I am not too educated. But I believe that my way of thinking is superior to my sister's. Her thinking is: "You must have your own block. You must have a lot of money." But she doesn't have the capacity.'

The translation was Charu's, and I wasn't sure what Mr Ghate meant. He had said earlier that he valued people only for their mind, and perhaps he was saying now that his sister's material ambitions outran her education and made her absurd.

'And she doesn't adjust to people,' Mr Ghate said. 'My wife is adjustable. But my sister can't adjust with my wife.' Perhaps the trouble lay there.

'Is your sister a good-looking girl? Handsome?'

'*Not totally*.' He spoke the words in English. With the affirmative Indian side-to-side swing of the head, he added, in English again, '*Fair*.' Then he restated his position. 'I don't value much the blood relation. My relatives never helped me. Only my friends helped me. Now that I've got a name and position, a lot of my relatives come to me. But I don't give them too much attention.'

'Why do you say that your sister's ambition is cheap?' He didn't reply.

I put it directly to Charu: 'Shouldn't he, as a Sena man, be encouraging people like himself to have ambition?'

They talked, Charu and Mr Ghate, and Charu gave Mr Ghate's reply. 'What is important is for a person to know whether he is really suited to have that ambition. People come to me all the time to ask for help. But I don't think they deserve help by rights. They should be worthy.'

I asked him about the tiger poster on his wall. He said a friend had given it. He spoke the English words, '*You observe a lot – by watching*.' He spoke the words in an awkward, fractured way, but he seemed to load them with a special, even mysterious, meaning. I asked about the Shivaji coronation or durbar in the other picture. What year was that? He didn't know the year.

His sister had tried to break away. He hadn't forgiven her, for that and for the love marriage which, in his own life, he considered part of his strength and character. He was a hard man, made by the chawl life from which he could now never separate himself. Perhaps, with the Sena pride that was his anchor, he felt – with everything else – that old ideas of honour and correctness had been violated by his sister.

Perhaps the sister was going to be all right; perhaps she would be able to stand alone, without the supports of family and clan and caste. But this was also no doubt how, in Bombay, people fell through the cracks into the abyss, and some – the lucky ones – were cast up again in places like Dharavi, not far from where, with the ambition that in her brother's eye was so absurd, inviting trouble, the girl now had an apartment 'in a proper block', almost certainly something in one of those characterless 'quarters' that had thrown Papu into a gloom a few days before.

It was said by people one met, and by columnists in the newspapers, that Indian society was being 'criminalized'. What was meant was that, with all the frustrations of India, political parties and business people were using gangsters to get their work done or to speed things up: to deter political defections, to encourage political donations; to enforce payment of a debt, to compel adherence to an unwritten 'black-money' contract.

Crime now paid very well. The gangs fought like politicians for territory, and the gang wars of Bombay were in the news. The newspapers and magazines were running articles about the wars that were like accounts of the opaque political disputes in many of the states of the Indian Union. They were opaque for the reason that the politics were opaque: there were no principles or party line, there were only personalities. People only had enemies or allies, and the relationships of both gangsters and politicians were constantly shifting. The killings in the crowded Bombay streets were, like the politics, about power and leadership. And, as the dust cleared, the newspapers and magazines began, competitively, to feature profiles of the don emerging as the king of the Bombay underworld.

This don was like a politican in another way: he was so written about, so interviewed (though he was based outside India, in the Gulf, in Dubai), that all the articles about him were like one another. Like many people in the public eye, the don had become his newspaper profiles; he had nothing new to say.

I thought it would be better for me to meet someone lower down, not of don status, someone not so interviewed, someone who had not formalized his experience to such a degree, and might still have something to say. I didn't really believe that such a meeting could be arranged – I was a visitor, passing through, with nothing to offer – but the gangsters of Bombay loved their publicity, and were especially interested in people who wrote in English. They wanted to be known abroad as well.

My contact was Ajit. Late one afternoon we took a taxi out to Dadar; it was a drive I was getting to know well. After we left the taxi, we walked a little way, through the relaxed late-afternoon crowd, to a pan-shop next to a cinema. We waited there for a while, among the cinema dawdlers, until someone greeted us; and then someone else came. We followed this second man. We turned into various rich-looking residential streets, and finally entered a tree-shaded house by a side door, losing what remained of the daylight when we went in.

It was a new apartment house. The ground-floor apartment we went into was well furnished in an Indian bourgeois, furniture-shop way. And it was strange, there, among those feminine furnishings, and in a very dim electric ceiling light, in an atmosphere still of Indian decorousness (shoes taken off at the entrance and left inside the front door), to be looking at Indian faces expressing Indian welcome and civility, and to hear in Indian-English voices, relishing the moment of theatre, that I was among gangsters.

There were about six or seven men in the small sitting room. They were young men, in their late twenties, and all of them, except for the leader, the man who now began to do the talking, had faces one would have expected to see on university teachers or men working in banks. Many of the men were standing when we came in, and they remained standing.

The leader was sitting alone on a fat, over-stuffed sofa. Like a prince showing favour, he asked me to sit beside him. He was dark, with a well-formed mouth with a full and curved lower lip, and with prominent eyes with well-defined eyelids – the kind of features that were stressed by the artists of some Rajput courts.

And I didn't know what to talk to him about. I had expected to meet one man alone; I hadn't expected a roomful. I was further put out by the sudden loss of daylight and its replacement by a dim ceiling bulb that made me stare hard and was like a physical irritant.

I had been hoping, in whatever talk I had had, to take things slowly, to approach the subject of crime and the gangs with some circumspection, and to light on my material on the way. But it became clear, from what the leader said, that he wanted to start *in medias res*. He wanted to talk right away about the gang wars that were going on, and to stake a claim for his gang and his group. But I knew very little about the Bombay gangs. I didn't know about the personalities and rivalries and famous battles; and I couldn't take advantage of the openings the leader was giving me.

He seemed at last to understand my difficulty. He must have been disappointed, but he didn't show it. He began, instead, to help me with the beginner's story he must have thought I was writing. He said he knew he was going to die sooner or later from a policeman's bullet. I felt he wanted that to be quoted. And then, as though letting a novice reporter into the sensational material he thought such a reporter needed, he told me what his group did by way of crime.

They did a certain amount of protection; in that line they 'worked with' stall-keepers. They did the numbers game. They had recently broken new ground: they had done a kidnapping for a political party, snatching and holding a student leader of another party at the time of the students' union election. A profitable and growing business for them was encouraging people to give up controlled tenancies, releasing land or a building for redevelopment. They also did a certain amount of 'biscuit' work – stealing melted-down gold 'biscuits', which was one way in which people liked to keep their black money. What was nice about that was that when someone lost his biscuits he couldn't complain to the authorities. The biscuit business was a nice business; all you needed was information, and you could get good information from the police. At one time, when they were younger, and money wasn't as plentiful as it now was in Bombay, they used to do black-market theatre tickets. A neat little business, really: you bought up all the seats for a popular film, and had touts sell them at a premium. But that was in the old days; it wasn't worth their while now. The one thing they didn't do was contract killing; they couldn't kill a man they had nothing against.

His manner was confidential. He leaned close to me on the overstuffed sofa and talked without raising his voice. He was like a businessman outlining his services, giving a prospectus. He didn't move or gesture a great deal; his tone was even; the energy and unreliability were all in his eyes.

The other men in the room were not still. They were moving about all the time, looking through the iron-barred window: the light of the street lamp now falling on the trees just outside. Someone gave a whistle, two or three times. And then – Indian courtesy – a man came in, with cold cola drinks for the visitors.

The leader – with the dark, perfect face – disturbed me more and more. He was acting, of course: the physical stillness, his quiet, confidential manner, the absence of gesture, were studied. But even when his words had the effect of humour, he didn't intend humour; he meant what he said; he believed in power and physical authority.

And there was another man in the room who was beginning to disturb me. He had remained standing, alert, sometimes looking out of the window. He had a bandaged hand. At first I had seen breeding and Indian civility in his face; but then his face had begun to seem empty, and I had found it harder to read. He was a brahmin, or a man of a caste not much lower, gone wrong.

That hand of his was bandaged, I now heard, because it had been slashed by someone from another gang: part of the current gang war. As the leader spoke of that attack, the man began to undo the bandage, to display the fearful wound, the twisted fingers: however strong the will, flesh was only flesh.

'He's all right,' the leader said, in his even way. 'Vithal's all right. That hand can still hold a knife.'

And I wasn't to go away and worry about the wound: the blow had been avenged already. The leader himself had avenged it. He had been sitting in a restaurant in the neighbourhood – not a *ho-tal,* but a proper restaurant, a famous one frequented by gangsters – when he had seen the slasher in a car outside. He had run out of the restaurant and – just like that, without any thought for the consequences – he had fired at the slasher in the car. The slasher had fallen to his knees then, and he had cried and embraced the leader's feet and begged to be spared. (That was the way the story was told: at one moment the slasher was in the car, then he was out of it.) The leader, exchanging the gun for a knife (to give logic to the story as it was told), began to work the knife over the slasher's shoulders as he kneeled, giving the man repeated shallow stabs, and he had said to him, 'You are crying. I don't have to kill you now. You cry and you hold my knees. Why should I kill you?'

The leader, telling the story, repeated those words two or three times. He hadn't made many gestures so far; but now he acted out the small, back-and-forth stabs over the kneeling man's shoulders.

It was a big moment for the gang, that moment of revenge, with the slasher embracing the leader's feet. Vithal and another man seconded what the leader said, and they and others stressed the sequel. The slasher, after that incident, had ceased to be a man. He became ridiculous; no one was afraid of him; he had to be dropped from his gang, and was now a nobody in Bombay, with no one ready to take him in.

'Vithal is all right,' the leader said. 'That hand is all right. It can use a knife.' And then, as though we were colleagues and he was talking to me in an allusive way of things we both knew (and also to explain a gap in his story), he said, 'I like a knife. It's surer. You can't be sure with a gun. You fire, you think the man is dead, but the bullet hits the ribs.'

He told a story of an attack they had made on a rival gang one Christmas at a funeral. They had gone among them with their knives. They had taken the other people by surprise, and they had done a lot of damage before the other mourners even knew what was happening.

One of the things that had thrown me at the beginning – apart from the light and the number of people in the room – was the idea I had had, perhaps from a misunderstanding of something Ajit had said, that the people I was among were Muslims. I had begun to talk to them as though they were Muslims, and had then found out that they were Hindus, with their own ways of communal feeling.

So far, the leader had done most of the talking. But when I asked about the Muslims in the gangs, Vithal said he didn't trust the Muslims in his own gang and preferred not to work with them. The Muslim gangsters came from poor areas. They, the people in the room, were 'middle-class people'. They came from this middle-class suburb of Dadar, like the great Indian cricketers, Gavaskar, Patil, Shastri. Vithal, slowly bandaging up his mangled hand again, looking down at it without apparent emotion, said, as though making an old joke, 'It's something to do with the water.'

The Muslims turned to crime, Vithal and the others said, because their values were lower. The Muslims had more than one wife and they had very large families. And, in a curious inversion of pride, the men in the room said that while Muslim gangsters were heroes to the Muslim community, Hindu gangsters like themselves were outcasts.

Though outcasts, they were religious. They felt protected by the deity of a temple, Santoshi Mata. She was a version of Durga or Kali, the goddess of power.

The leader said with perfect seriousness, 'She's the goddess of the victory of good over bad.'

They were religious people: they wanted that known. It was their policy, for instance, never to harass the poor.

The leader said, 'If you do that, the poor will curse you. And the curse of the poor is a very damaging thing.'

They slept in different places every night; they had their safe houses, like the one we were in now. No one knew where the other slept. They met in different places every day. They had ways of communicating. Every day when they got up they waited for news, of the gang war, of the way certain jobs had gone. And the leader said he had recently got married. The girl had been dazzled by the glamour of the life.

Before we left, the leader asked Ajit for 15 copies of a newspaper of a certain date. There was an article about him, or an article in which he was mentioned, in the issue he wanted.

Publicity like that, recognition like that, was precious to him; it was his link to the world outside. As a Hindu outlaw, still deep in his faith, with his Hindu community still a focus for some of his pride, he was really a lost man. Things were desperate for him and Vithal and many of the others. They couldn't withdraw from the life; they couldn't hide. To do so, they would have to go far away, to the other side of India, beyond the reach of the gangs. Everyone among them now had something to answer for. What the leader had prophesied for himself held for them all: they would all die from police bullets.

It was early evening when Ajit and I went out into the streets again. The street lamps in the residential area fell yellow on trees and cast multiple shadows. The well-stocked shops and stalls in the main roads were brightly lit. From what we had heard, some of the stalls were receiving protection; it gave a new character to the scene.

The men we had been among had an almost cinematic idea of their roles, and had perhaps modelled themselves on certain film stars. It was hard, while they talked, and while one was in their presence, absolutely to believe in what they said, it was so much like something out of a film or a book about gangs and crime and murder. They had been boasting. But, according to Ajit, much of what they said was true. The men in that room had been responsible for eight killings. Vithal, with the chopped hand, was especially deadly.

And they were all doomed. The gangsters at the top, the men the newspapers and magazines called the dons, could be famous public figures, could be courted by political parties and film people, could put their money into the making of films, could be absorbed into the glamour of Bombay. But the men below, the men in the middle, like the men we had been among, were doomed.

They had fallen as children for the life of crime. As children, Ajit said, they would have been attracted by the glamour of the famous criminals in their area, who might have a meal in a restaurant and not pay, who might stop at a fruit stall and choose a fruit and walk away without paying: gestures of style. It was a Bombay-given idea of style for which those men had thrown away their lives: an idea of style with elements of pathos to the outsider, style that was like an expression of the stress and nerves of the city of small spaces: style, a human need, which Anwar felt in his colony, and Mr Ghate's sister had felt in her chawl.

The gangsters made offerings to the temple of Santoshi Mata. Mr Ghate's sister – though expelled from her family for having gone against custom and contracted a love match – had married an ayurvedic doctor, someone, that is, who was full of traditional lore. However much they had to be modified in the city, the rituals of the past adhered to many people, and there was a need in Bombay for men who knew about rituals.

That was why the pujari, the professional performer of pujas, had come to Bombay. He came from the state to the south of Maharashtra. He belonged to the priestly group of the Chitrapur Saraswat brahmins. More particularly, he belonged to one of the seven priestly families attached to a famous temple where there was a deity that had been revered for more than 300 years.

It could be said that the pujari had grown up in an ashram. The pujari's father had been a pujari, and his father before him – that was as far as the pujari could trace his ancestry. The pujari had lost his father at the age of ten, but it had been a joint family, and the ten-year-old boy had been instructed in pujas and rituals and texts by his father's brothers.

To belong to a priestly family was to have distinction in the community, but it didn't mean having money. Very little hard cash came the way of the pujaris attached to the temple, and the boy had never gone away for a holiday. His boyhood had been spent almost completely in the temple, and his studies there had been only of religious matters. Towards the end of his time of study, a secular modern college had been started in the town, but the pujari had gone there for only one year. So he really hadn't had much modern education; and when the time came for him to start earning a living, there was no modern job he could do.

Like his father and grandfather, he could only be a pujari. It was hard. The seven priestly families – joint families – had produced a lot of pujaris, and there simply wasn't the work for all of them locally. Matters were made worse because very many people of the local Saraswat brahmin community had migrated to Bombay.

The young pujari decided to follow them, to see what might come his way in Bombay. Bombay was an unwelcoming city, but the pujari had some luck. He had an aunt in the city, and he was able to stay with her for a year. That couldn't be regarded as a fixed arrangement, though, because the aunt had a son who was close to the age of marriage; this son would be bringing home his bride when he got married, and the pujari would have to go somewhere else. Still, for the time being, there was a place to stay.

And there was also work. Since the temple from which the pujari had come was famous in the community, and since, in fact, the pujari's family was known to people who had made pilgrimages to the temple, and there were people in Bombay who had known the pujari as a child, there was no question – as with a new lawyer, say, waiting for a brief – of the pujari having to hang around and wait for people to come and ask him to do the rites to bless a new flat or cleanse it of its former spirits. He began to do little pujas almost as soon as he arrived in the big city.

He was a shy young man of twenty-four, still with country ways and temple ways. When he did pujas for people in those early days, and they asked what the fees were, he would brush aside the subject of money and say he left it to them. People took advantage of this, but in the beginning he didn't know. When he realized what was happening he decided to standardize the fees. When he left it to people to pay what they thought fit, they would give him as little as 350 rupees for a wedding – which meant chanting verses solidly for six hours, and doing complicated things all the while. Nowadays his fixed charge for a wedding was 1000 rupees, and there were no complaints.

So he settled into Bombay, built up his practice, and when after a year or so his aunt's son did get married, the pujari was able to move out without suffering hardship. He became a 'paying guest'. This was a special Bombay condition: it meant he rented sleeping room or space in somebody's apartment, in a room or loft. It was enough for him.

He discovered that, as a professional pujari in Bombay, he had certain advantages. There were five pujaris from the community in Bombay. Two were older men; a third had learned the business in Bombay from his father. The young pujari, still fresh from the temple source, as it were, had a certain appeal for the old-fashioned or conservative folk. Only one pujari was younger.

There was a sixth pujari in Bombay, but he was so famous and established, so grand, his methods so modern, that he could be considered to be in quite another category. This pujari had so adjusted old ritual to the pace of Bombay life that he could recite the complete wedding verses – which normally took six hours – in three and a half hours. This pujari was sixty-three years old, and because of his speed with the verses he was known as 'The Electric

Pujari'. This man had also taped certain pujas – taped the verses connected with the pujas – and marketed them to the community abroad, in various oil states in the Persian Gulf, mainly. He was said to charge 1000 rupees for a wedding tape, and proportionate sums for shorter pujas. He had done so very well that – according to the story – he and his wife (an officer in a bank) had gone on a long holiday trip to London and the United States; and even on this trip – success attracting success – the Electric Pujari had performed three marriages and three thread ceremonies. He was so important in Bombay now, he had become a Shiv Sena leader, and had put money into a Marathi-language film.

Of the Electric Pujari the young pujari said, 'He's an enterprising fellow.' But the young pujari didn't want to compete with this old lion. He didn't want to do puja tapes. He was content doing things in the old-fashioned way he did them. He thought there were people who appreciated this way. Because of the Bombay traffic – he could spend hours every day just getting from place to place – he could do no more than three pujas a day, and that was enough for him.

He made on an average 1000 rupees a month (on an average: weddings didn't come every month), and he was content. There were also the food gifts: the rice and coconuts and fruit and pulses, things needed in pujas as consecrated offerings: a portion of the too-abundant store laid out by the devotee used up in the ritual itself, the rest given to the pujari to take away. So, going from house to house every day (living the kind of life the Jain *munis* lived in traffic-ridden Bombay, finding food at the homes of the faithful), it must have seemed to the pujari that in Bombay the world had been made whole again for him, after the scarcities of the far-away temple.

He was a small, even dainty man of thirty, not much above five feet. He was sweet-faced, with a little moustache and the pale skin of his community, and he was dressed in white. His dhoti had a light-brown edging. He wore a necklace of sandalwood beads, and he had a white nylon shopping bag for his belongings. His voice was as soft as his smile and his eyes. He was the picture of the serene and gentle brahmin: he looked as content and unfussed as he said he was.

His talk of pujas and gifts of food – and that nylon bag or sack to take away offerings, no doubt – brought back memories. There had been so many pujas in my grandmother's family in Trinidad when I was a child, so many ritual readings from the scriptures and the epics. They had given us less the idea of what we were than the idea that in Trinidad we were apart. These readings – sometimes going on for days – had been in a language I didn't understand. I remembered them as holiday occasions, punctuated – at certain stages of the ritual, when clarified butter and raw brown sugar fed and sweetened the sacrificial fire – by the ringing of bells, the blowing of conches, the play of cymbals.

These occasions had fixed in me the idea of the privilege of pundits. They were the star performers on these occasions, and everything was done to pamper them. The best blankets or sheets were spread for them to sit on; the best food was kept for them, and served to them in state at the end. Afterwards, when the religious moment had ceased, had turned to ashes, as it were, and the pundits were no longer strictly on show, it remained their privilege discreetly to go and gather up the coins that had been thrown on the sacred fire on the decorated shrine, as well as the coins that had been thrown on the brass plate with burning camphor – emblem of the sacred fire – that had been taken around the people watching the ceremony: you threw your coin on the plate, passed your fingers through the camphor flame and took your fingers to your forehead.

To me, they were memories from far back, almost from another life. And here they were whole, in an unlikely setting. I met the pujari in Nandini's apartment. Nandini was a journalist who worked for an advertising magazine. She was of the community of the pujari. She herself had no belief in rituals and no need of them, but the pujari seemed still to be called upon on certain occasions by her family. The apartment was in the neighbourhood of Dadar. It was an apartment in a block – four floors, 10 apartments on each floor – and we were on an upper floor: a respectable middle-class Bombay apartment: verandah, front room, back room.

With a memory of the excitement I had felt as a child at the idea of money being raked out from the warm ashes of the shrine, and coins being picked up warm from the plate with the burning camphor, I asked the pujari whether people in his community put money on the plate with the burning camphor. He said the custom didn't exist in his community. But sometimes people from outside the community put money on the plate when the sacred fire was taken round, and then even people in the community, not wishing to be outfaced, followed suit – and all that money was his.

He told me about the deity of the temple-and-ashram, the *math,* where he had grown up. The deity there was the Lord Bhavani Shankar. Who was he? The friend of Lord Shiva. What were his attributes? The pujari behaved as though I was testing him. Bhavani Shankar, he said, was a reincarnation of Yama, the Lord of Death.

He said, 'You pray to him so that the soul may rest in peace.'

'Isn't that a Christian idea?'

It wasn't the Christian idea; he didn't seem to know the Christian idea. He talked on in his soft way, with his smile and his bright eyes, and Nandini interpreted.

'Our community believes in the soul, the *atma,* that merges with the Lord.' And almost at once – he was a pujari, a performer of ritual, rather than a guru or philosopher or theologian – he outlined, again as though he felt he was being tested, the ritual that had to be performed after a death. 'On the 14th day after a person dies you have a ceremony where you have to prepare all kinds of food – certain dishes in addition to the dishes the dead person liked – and there is an elaborate puja. After the puja you put all the dishes on a plantain leaf and you leave it out in the open. The expectation is that a crow will come and peck at what is laid out on the plantain leaf' – Indian crows are rapacious and swift and watchful – 'and we take that as a symbol of the soul merging with the infinite.'

That was the kind of thing he had studied at the temple. It was an immense course of study. There were rituals at death; there were rituals at birth.

'There is a cradling ceremony. You have then to refer to the *Panchang.* That's an ancient text; it's printed now in various Indian languages. You refer to that text to cast a horoscope and find a name. That's common Hindu practice. It isn't restricted to our community. I had to learn that, and I had to learn the details of all the other ceremonies. Let's suppose you move into a new apartment. You have to exorcize the spirits that are there. The new apartment should be pure. To achieve that, again you have to go through quite an elaborate puja. When a child is eight there is a thread ceremony. And there is the wedding ceremony, of course – six hours, with the pujari chanting all the time.'

I wanted to know whether the details of the rituals were absolutely fixed, or whether there were disputes between pujaris – as, long ago in Trinidad, there were disputes between pundits, sometimes about small things: the correct form of Hindu salutation, for example.

The pujari said, 'In recent times the pujaris have been taking shortcuts, especially with the marriage ceremony. They think a six-hour ceremony is too long.' He didn't like the shortcuts. 'There is no meaning to it. I feel that once you start taking shortcuts it all goes down the drain.'

That was another point. How much of that complicated Hindu theology – evolved layer upon layer over millennia – had already gone down the drain in Bombay? For me, in Trinidad, only two generations away from India – though the Hindu epics still had a charge – whole segments of Hindu theology had been lost; later, parts of it were to be recovered, but only as art-history. Without its setting and its earth, Hindu theology seemed to blow away, as it had blown away after centuries from the cultures of Java and Cambodia and Siam: irrecoverable now, the emotions and the elaboration of belief that had supported the building of Angkor.

The pujari said he always took care to explain the verses he chanted. He had also bought some books published by the Arya Samaj – the reforming Hindu movement, more active earlier in the century than now. The Arya Samaj books explained the significance of some of the ceremonies he performed, and helped him to explain them to devotees.

Did he himself sometimes have trouble with the theology?

'I've grown up with it. It's part of me.'

'Bhavani Shankar. The friend of Shiva, the reincarnation of Yama. These are difficult ideas by themselves. When you run them together, they become harder.'

He said again, 'You pray to Bhavani Shankar so that the soul merges with the Lord.' Speaking then of the various deities, he said, 'To understand God, each one has his own way. In our *math* we have given him that persona, Bhavani Shankar. The math has been there for 300 years, and the deity has been there for centuries.'

'Is the deity there very different from Ganpati at Pali?' This was Mr Patil's deity, the bringer of good fortune, the bestower of confidence.

The pujari said, 'In my eyes all deities are the same. Ganpati is actually the deity I like most, because Ganpati is the Lord of Learning.'

'Isn't that Saraswati?'

'Ganpati's other name is Vidia-Dhiraj. The Lord of Wisdom. When it comes to God, there is no end to learning. You probe deeper, and you always get more. Once you are in the profession, you don't feel like giving it up. It is my livelihood, but at the same time through it my search for knowledge goes on. My faith has been so built up over the years, is so strong, that it wouldn't be the same if I did something else, if I was working in a bank, for instance.'

The pujari's younger brother worked in a bank. This brother had been trained as a pujari, too, but he had also gone to the local college. This was what was happening now to young men of the pujari class, the pujari said. They were turning away from their traditional work. One man, for instance, a fully trained pujari from the temple, was writing the accounts in a hotel in Bombay, near the airport. The younger generation didn't want to go into the profession. The pujari didn't blame his brother for working in a bank. Everybody didn't have the same kind of faith; and even if the brother had decided to come to Bombay and be a pujari, he would have had a lot of trouble finding accommodation.

'How much does your brother get in the bank?'

'Twelve hundred rupees a month.'

'That's about what you get.' And perhaps a good deal less, if the pujari's daily gifts of food, and other things like cloth, were taken into account.

In the beginning, the pujari said, it had depressed and worried him that he hadn't had a chance to study properly at the modern college in his temple town. He used to feel he was going to have a hard time making a living. But he no longer worried about the education he had missed, especially now that he was earning almost as much as his younger brother, who had gone right through the college and had ended up in a bank. Sometimes kindly people told him he should be thinking of some additional, modern occupation, just in case. Even if he was earning almost as much as his brother, that still wasn't a great deal in Bombay.

'But,' the pujari said, 'the first thing people ask you if you go for a job is, "Are you a graduate? Have you done this course or that course? Do you have any job experience?" So the best thing for me is to continue in this profession.'

'You talk as though you've looked for other jobs.'

'I haven't. But I've seen a lot of graduates sitting at home because they have no employment.'

Even if he didn't want to think of a back-up profession, it must have occurred to him that travelling in Bombay was going to get worse, and that it would take him longer and longer to get from puja to puja. Shouldn't he, then, be thinking of doing something on the lines of the Electric Pujari, to safeguard his future?

He talked as though he had considered it. 'I don't believe in that.' He meant preparing his own puja cassettes. 'You are too busy *fast-forwarding* and *rewinding*.' He used the English words. 'Your concentration is disturbed. The whole purpose of doing the puja is lost.'

I said that in a temple ashram a pujari could be poor, and not lose dignity. Even now, it was probably all right in Bombay, being a poor pujari. Was it always going to be like that? Bombay was changing all the time; there was a lot more money around now. Wasn't there the risk that, as a poor pujari, he might start to fall in people's esteem?

'Let others have material wealth. I have peace of mind.' In fact, he said, smiling, he wasn't doing badly. He wasn't a paying guest nowadays. He had just bought an apartment of his own, a 'one-roomed kitchen', as they called it in Bombay, an apartment like the one where we were talking. Three hundred and ninety-three square feet, 75,000 rupees.

I made a simple calculation. He had been in Bombay six years, and he said he made 1000 rupees a month. So the apartment cost more than his entire earnings for the six years. Did he have a mortgage?

He said, with his sweet smile, 'No. Savings.'

Savings! So he had been living more or less on the gifts he got as a pujari, and had hardly been spending what he picked up in puja fees.

He said, 'I paid by instalments. Because I am a pujari, the contractor gave me special consideration. He is a man of my community.'

'Not many people have that kind of luck in Bombay.'

He said simply, 'I accept it as a divine favour.'

It turned out that he had even begun to think of getting married. It wasn't going to be easy for the woman he married, since he would be out all day travelling to do his pujas. So he was thinking that it would be nice if he could have a *working wife* – he used the English words – and that, of course, would help with the expenses and all that side of life which I appeared to be so concerned about.

Did he have pleasures?

It wasn't a good question. There was no division in his mind between work and pleasure. He was a pujari; he served God; that wasn't a matter of work and hours. Still, he set himself to thinking. And his gentle black eyes were bright and smiling as he thought. Pleasure, pleasure – what might pass as pleasure?

He said, 'I like decorating the shrine.'

He looked inwards always. But – we were in Bombay, a city of many faiths and races and conflicts. How did he see the city? What did he feel when, for instance, he saw the tourists around the Gateway of India and the Taj Mahal Hotel? What did he feel about the crowds, the people among whom he – in his pujari's garb – would almost certainly stand out?

'I'm indifferent to it. I have my work. It keeps me busy. I don't have the time to go visiting. I don't have the time to look around me.'

He had been in Bombay six years, and was going to be there as far ahead as he could see. But the only person he still looked up to and revered was the head of the Chitrapur Saraswat brahmin community.

He looked inwards and was serene; he shut out the rest of the world. Or, as might be said, he allowed other people to keep the world going. It wasn't a way of looking which his fellows in the community had (some of them in the Gulf, among Muslims). But it made him a good pujari.

Subroto – who came from Bengal, and worked in Bombay in the art department of an advertising agency, but was reconciled to living in the city as a paying guest, the buying or renting of an apartment of his own being too far beyond him – Subroto took me one afternoon to meet a friend of his, a film writer who had fallen on hard times. Hard times in Bombay meant hard times. For the film writer it meant a fall almost to the level of his potential audience, the people who (as the writer himself was to say) filled the sweaty, broken-down cinemas, and looked to the screen for release.

The writer lived in an apartment block in Mahim in mid-town Bombay, near a vegetable market that gave off warm rotting smells. In this apartment block there were 10 apartments to a floor, as in Nandini's block; but the block wasn't as well kept as Nandini's. As Subroto and I went up the concrete steps we had glimpses, through open doors, of clutter in small rooms, and sometimes of figures stretched out in afternoon rest on beds or on the floor; and my fancy was ready – in the general atmosphere of the place – to work up these figures and postures into more sinister tableaux.

We came to the floor we wanted, and followed a verandah or gallery, very bright in the afternoon sun, to where it opened into a room freshly painted and almost bare. This room, of slanted sunlight and shadow, had two beds against opposite walls, two folding chairs, and three pieces of basketwork on one wall as the chastest kind of decoration, a touch of home, perhaps a touch of Bengal. In that setting, with its clear and sharp details, the details almost of improvised stage properties, there was my host the writer, a tall man in white Bengali costume, a man in his forties, handsome, ironic, with the hint of a suppressed rage, a man to whom my heart at once went out.

I realized a little while later that the room, so plain and without disorder, would have been specially prepared for our visit. It was the only room in the apartment. Two people lived and slept in that room. There was an adjoining kitchen area, beyond a doorway with a curtain.

The writer said: 'Calcutta is where I studied. I keep on drifting back. It's my home town, mentally. It's where I feel comfortable.

That's where I feel things are happening all the time, and that's where I acquired the ambition of being a film writer. It is difficult for a film writer to survive – I knew that, and for 11 years I was a cost accountant. That was the time efforts were being made to make India a very big industrial country. A lot of building was going on in many parts of the country, and I was a cost accountant in the construction industry. I got shifted from one place to another and went all over the country, and often stayed in wild and empty places. I became a nomad, and have remained that way since.

'One fine day I just got up and went away from my job. It happened here, in Bombay. I had come to Bombay with my firm. Bombay was becoming a very industrial city at that time, in the late 60s. And I went away from my job here and I got involved in a lot of theatre activity. I used to read a lot in my time off when I was with the building industry; in some of the places where we were you had nothing else to do. And when I came to Bombay I found that a lot of the friends I had here, people I had met elsewhere, were theatre people.

'In the 70s a lot of theatre people became film people. There was a government Film Finance Corporation. Money was up for grabs. So a lot of my friends grabbed this money and joined the movement, and a lot of good films were made. But then these good films didn't get released. They made the seminars, they made the festivals, and a lot of very long articles were written about them. But unfortunately the films themselves were never seen because they were never released.

'I will tell you how I managed when I left the building firm. I was living on the roof of a high-rise building with two friends, under the water-tank. We bribed the watchman. That's how we lived for one year. The best view in town, and free. This was in 1969. I was twenty-seven. The only thing we could afford was country liquor. The deal with the watchman was like this: we would bring a bottle one night, and he would bring a bottle the next night. The result was that we became drunkards up there. We had no option. The watchman wouldn't allow us a free evening to ourselves – that was part of the deal.

'The watchman was from Nepal, and he told us frightening stories about Nepal. He told us he walked for 27 days to get from his village to the Indian border, and he was starving for those 27 days. He came here to get a job, and when he got his first pay packet he went to a restaurant and ate so much food he came down with dysentery. When he got drunk he used to say, "Everybody should be shot!" And we would agree with him.

'We were making up stories, trying to write screenplays. Then one of our friends got some money. And he made a film. Three of us had collaborated on the screenplay, and when the film came out my name was not on the credits. This was my first lesson in art cinema. We were very emotional and foolish. Instead of beating the hell out of the director, we said, "I'm not going to work with you again." Which suited him.

'Let me tell you how I got into the commercial side.

'At that time whole villages in the Punjab were migrating. Many of them were being smuggled into England. Very few of them had valid passports and what not. There was a very famous actor in the commercial cinema who said he wanted to make a film about these Indian emigrants. The actor was very famous. In fact, he was at his peak.

'By that time I had left the top of the high-rise and the Nepalese watchman, and I was staying in a boarding house. Two of us were sharing a room. We never had a room to ourselves in those days. My friend was working for this famous actor, and this actor was looking for a bright young man. And that's something else you'll learn: they're *always* looking for bright young men. I apparently fitted the slot. I was young enough, and the famous man thought I was bright enough.

'The only other option I had at that time was to go back to construction work. The Gulf was opening up at that time, and my old firm were threatening to send me to the Gulf. I was actually still under contract to that company, and had been under contract when I walked out on them – for this great freedom to be a writer.

'So word got to the actor, and the great man sent for me. His office was in Santa Cruz, near the airport. Santa Cruz was part rich, part very slummy. The actor's office had become part of the slums. In the 30 years since he'd built his offices there, the green had gone and the slums had come. Slum all around, and in the middle there was this ramshackle office building. And I found that the interior of the building had nothing to do with what was outside – it was plush, carpeted, centrally air-conditioned. Nothing to do with the outside. I had walked into the dream factory.

'The office was big – colossal. I had to walk through two rooms to get to the actor's private chamber. And that was huge. What struck me were the books on the walls. Those editions of the Nobel prizewinners in 30 volumes. The *Encyclopaedia Britannica* was on the other side, and there were marvellous globes and expensive coffee-table books about animals and flowers. The screenplays of all the so-called film classics of the West were on the other side. Right above his head, in fact.

'He started talking about this film about Indian emigrants. He gave me the outline of the plot. I said –'

I broke in to ask the writer, 'What was the outline?'

'Two lines. Just two lines. I said, "It's a very brilliant idea." He looked at me with sparkling eyes and he said, "That's a very intelligent remark to make."

'Let me tell you a little about this famous actor. He was perennially young. He *is* perennially young. He was about fifty then, perhaps fifty-one, fifty-two.

'"So," he said. "Let's try to do the line-up."'

I asked, 'He wanted that straight away?'

'He wanted it right off. That was my first lesson in this new course. How to write a film script for commercial films.

'I was very excited. I thought it was the biggest thing to happen to me, as I picked my way back through the slums outside. I went back to my boarding house. That was in the middle of one of the ugliest slums in Bombay, one of the ugliest of those so-called fishing villages. I burned the proverbial midnight oil that night. Luckily, my roommate was a Punjabi. He knew what the emigrants were like, and he gave me some ideas of their characteristics. I wrote a couple of scenes.

'I took them in to the office the next day. The actor read the scenes in front of me – four scenes in seven pages – and he clapped his hands and said, "This is wonderful! Let me just look at these pages. I will work out some 'lines' and we will talk about it tomorrow."

'The next day came, and he said, "I've thought out everything." And for three hours he told me a story – the story of the film we were supposed to be working on. It was a horrifying experience. It had nothing to do with the village or the humiliations of the emigrants. It was like every other commercial story – it was about spies and shootouts and gangs. It was pretty awful.

'So I looked at him. And at that moment it flashed through my head: "If I tell him it's a very good story, I've got a job." So I told him, "It's a very good story." And he paid me on the spot. Advance money. A contract was made. It was quite favourable to me. He gave me 5001 rupees that morning. It's an Indian custom, that extra one rupee. Even if it's a million rupees, they will pay you that extra one rupee. It's for good luck. Though actually I think the one rupee was my payment for saying it was a good story, and the other 5000 rupees was for my good luck in thinking I should say it. So I thought, "Keep on saying it's a good story."

'It took two years to make that film. And I wrote nothing. Not one single line. I will swear by anything you want that I didn't write a single line. I just kept listening to his rubbish every second day, and I kept saying, "Wonderful!"

'I was making 10,000 rupees a month for saying yes to him. That was what everybody else was saying to him. This great man used to live in a very strange world. If you are a star you live in a very strange world. You manufacture a world where everyone keeps on saying yes to everything you say. If you say no, you are out of that world. And permanently. The rejection is like Jehovah's revenge or something. They live in this world, and they lose touch with reality, with the audience, with the audience's taste. That's why so many films fail. And when they don't run, there's always a fall guy.

'He would call me into his office apparently for a story session, and I would listen to him talking about the wonderful films he was going to make. These people, their heads are like a bubbling kettle. I would listen to him for anything from two hours to seven hours, eight hours. And this went on for two years.

'The film came out. My name was on the credits. But I hadn't written anything, I swear to you. Because there was no *written* script. This was what I learned: that films can be made from scraps that come out, scraps of conversation. In fact, a writer was looked down on. A film writer was supposed to *talk* – to be a talker of scenes, rather than a writer. So that they could get a *feel* of the scenes without having to read. Because reading is something *nobody* in the film world does. The writer is the odd man out.

'They *talk* about stories. They talk about scenes. Even if you write a scene, they shoot it differently. They change while editing, while shooting. And all actors here fancy themselves to be writers. An actor may come and, if he's got clout, he may change a line.

'This was in 1972. I was thirty, and everybody thought I was a brilliant young man. Until the film came out. And it flopped. It didn't run at all. And I learned another lesson: that when a film doesn't run, invariably the writer has to take the blame.'

'How much had been spent on the film?'

'Close to nine million rupees. It was extraordinary. Huge houses would be erected for the village scenes. Places where even maharajas wouldn't stay, and those houses were supposed to be village huts. The hero was an unemployed village youth. The clothes he wore in the film had been stitched at a cost of a lakh of rupees. And he would stand in those lovely clothes, and employers would tell him, "This job is not for you." The man saying that – playing the employer, the owner of the factory – he would be an extra, earning 30 rupees a day in those days. And he would be wearing shabby clothes of his own – because you don't have to find clothes for an extra.

'I hated every moment of it. I hated myself for doing it.'

I said to the writer, 'But you knew what Hindi films were like.'

'Yes and no. I saw Hindi films, but I didn't know how they were actually made. And they're still being made the same way. How can it be otherwise? Nobody who made a film went to see a cinema show with the audience. In those days they would have this private viewing theatre. They never saw the film with the sweaty audience. The halls are terrible. They are advertised as air-conditioned, but the air-conditioning often doesn't work, and it's hot and humid and sweating and it's packed.

'So I took the blame, and I went away from Bombay. And I drifted around for a while, mostly in Calcutta and Bengal. I didn't want to return to the film industry at all.

'But it's hard to leave the film industry. A friend wanted to make a film in Bombay. So I came back, and started up again. At that time I had the reputation of being a very good script-writer, without having written a script. Many of the things I had worked on had remained at the ideas stage, and ideas can be brilliant. Then this friend, with four disasters behind him, wanted to make a quick, cheap film. He wanted to make it just to survive – a film which we could make quickly.

'There was a well-known actress who was a friend of the group. We thought we could cash in on her name. So we started shooting without knowing where the next day's money was going to come from. After eight days the money ended, and the shooting stopped. We didn't know what to do. And then – you wouldn't believe – a man came and said he wanted to back the film. He was acting for somebody, and I actually believe we got the backing because the person for whom the man was acting liked the story of the film.

'It was the story of a husband's adulterous affair. In Hindi films the standard treatment of this kind of story is that at the end, after the affair, the husband cries and goes back to his wife, and she cries and takes him back. In our film, when the adulterous man came back crying to his wife, she sent him away. This was the story, and for some reason it appealed to someone and they wanted to back it.

The film was made. It ran – to our surprise, and the surprise of everybody else. At the end of the film, when the wife kicked the husband out, women would stand up and clap. This wasn't only in Bombay; it was in some smaller cities as well.

'We made two other films. Both were very great successes. We became quite famous, in fact. And at that point my friend wanted to cash in on the fame – he wanted to make big-budget films. Offers were coming.

'So it was back to square one. The commercial cinema – saying yes to distributors and stars. And yet at that time we had the clout to keep on making good films.

'So I gave up, and I left Bombay again. But there is something you should know. A film writer gets used to working with a particular director. He knows the director's style, and the director knows the writer's ways. It isn't easy, after this kind of relationship, for a writer to team up with another director.

'So after four years I came back – to team up with the same man, after he'd had another four disasters. Much bigger disasters than the four he'd had when we met and did the quickie. I've been here for a year now.

'How did I manage during those four years? I starved. I did odd jobs. Ghost-writing. I became involved in projects that didn't take shape. And here I am back. And while I was starving I got married – I thought it was just the right time.'

His silent Bengali wife, in a fresh green sari, brought out tea from the kitchen area behind the curtain – where she had been for much of the time – and she laid the tea on a little side table.

Subroto was lounging on one of the beds – there was no other place for him in the room.

I asked the writer to describe the apartment where we were. He said, 'We are in an apartment in Mahim. It's a rented apartment, in a standard four-storeyed Bombay block. We have one room. It's 10 feet by 10 feet. It's a one-roomed kitchen apartment, as they call it.'

He stood up and raised both arms – in his loose cotton tunic – and looked at the ceiling. The gesture filled the little room.

He said, 'This is my room. This is my only room under the sun.'

The room faced west. It was full of light. The verandah was so dazzling that Subroto at one stage thought of closing the door to it.

The writer said, 'I'm working on three films now. It's very difficult in India to survive on one film. This time I've discovered that although they don't follow a screenplay, they have more respect for it. I hope it will last.'

'You think you're a better writer now than you were at the beginning?'

'When I first came I had great notions of what a film writer should be. I was wrong then. I thought that a screenplay was close to a novel or a play. I really thought it was a novel that got shaped up into a play. What I've realized is that a film writer has to know a lot about film technique – the limitations, for instance, and where you can do away with words totally. We write *visuals* – that's what a screen writer is supposed to do. The screen writer is actually a link between all the crafts of film-making, and I'm talking of the actors as craftsmen also. Much of it is in technical shorthand – it's much better if you write it like that. The technicians understand the technical shorthand. They understand it emotionally. The cameraman understands not only the visual of a close-up, but also the emotion. To the layman that kind of writing might be boring – it's like reading the blueprint of a bridge, but that blueprint is full of meaning for an engineer. A script-writer had better learn that part of the technique. Or he's wasting his time, and other people's time. The writer's contribution is really to give a conceptual vision of the whole film – because the technicians can only work one shot at a time. Actually, it's a director-writer team that makes a film.

'So now I've been back for a year. The first six months were hard. People were indifferent, because I'd left the club.'

'Looking back now at your first experience, with the actor, don't you think that something might be said for talking a film – as he used to do?'

The writer was unforgiving. 'That is the enemy. That complacent attitude – that is the enemy.' He jumped a thought or two and said, 'I think I will make money this time. I've got enough for the next month, from the film work I've been doing. At the moment I'm clearing debts.'

'Who are the nice people in the film business?'

'Everybody and nobody. It's totally success-oriented. They worship success. And the success is very concrete, you see. A film opens on a Friday, and by Monday you know the fate of the film. You know the box-office figures. There's nothing abstract about that. It's all there in cold figures. And if the film runs, people are very nice to you.'

At the beginning he had seemed full of rage, with an irony that sometimes threatened to turn to bitterness and self-pity. But he had grown softer as he had talked. When he had talked about the nature of film writing, he had become contemplative, working through to the right words, and he had seemed then to be even at ease with himself.

I felt his attitude to the film industry might have changed.

He said, 'I'm losing my cynicism about it.'

I said, 'It may be because you have a new feeling for the art.'

'People make bad films or good films. But one can't say there is no such thing as screen-writing. There is. And one thing you do learn is that life goes on. There is no such thing as failing in life. You fail at a particular point. The joy of an artist is not to think of success or failure, but to just go on.'

I asked about his way of working.

'We rent a hotel room for five days or seven days. And we talk out the film. Then I'm left alone, and I'm given four weeks or six weeks to write the treatment – basically, scenes without dialogue, in sequence. And then we get together for another three days. And then I'm left alone again. This time it comes out with dialogue, and it takes about two weeks.'

He then said something which made me wonder whether, in spite of what he had said about making money this time, he hadn't with one part of himself given up ideas of succeeding again in the cinema. He said his thoughts had been turning to real writing, the writing of prose, for the printed page. And he wanted to know whether he could send me things he had written or might write.

I said my judgement would be worthless. I had given all my adult life to writing; I had thought about it every day. I wrote, and experienced, in my own way; the two things were linked. My judgements were good only for myself.

He smiled. 'My judgements on other people's screenplays are worthless too.'

Subroto and I left soon after. We went down the narrow, twisting concrete staircase, half-walled on one side and rubbed to shininess. We saw again through open doors the life of single rooms: the people, and the great amount of clothes that in those small spaces couldn't be put away or stored. The smells from the rooms became stronger lower down, the grime more perceptible.

When we stepped out into the bright, dusty yard, there was a call from above, and we looked up at the writer and his wife in her green sari looking down at us from their balcony, one of the 40 balconies of the apartment block: like theatre boxes, from where we were. The sun fell on their heads and faces. Like people suddenly playful, they both smiled and gave small waves.

At the end of the dusty yard there was a tree with a circular, concrete-walled, earth platform at its foot. On this platform, against the trunk of the tree, was a small black image garlanded with marigolds, and there appeared to be a man watching over it. The image was a living deity, and it had fresh holy marks, of sandalwood paste, on its forehead. Past that, we were in the dusty street.

We began to walk to Dadar railway station. It was only a short walk, and Subroto apologized more than once for not taking a taxi. Outside the vegetable market, where the smells were high, boys were lifting wet vegetable rubbish with their bare hands into Ashok Leyland garbage-compacting trucks. Dadar station – with its high, gloomy platforms, its crowd, the echoing sound of the crowd, the stalls, the shoeshine boys and men, the twist of slow-burning rope tied to a metal pillar for people to light their cigarettes from – gave a feel of the big city: as though trains and the constant movement of people had the power, by themselves, to generate excitement.

I asked Subroto, 'Do you think he is going to make it this time?'

'He isn't going to make it.'

We went over the footbridge to the platform on the other side of the rails. Everything in that footbridge was worn, without identifiable colour, years and years of dust seeming to have eroded and dulled metal and to have got into the heart of every piece of timber.

Subroto said, 'He's not positive.'

By that Subroto meant that the writer, in spite of what he had said about making money now, was as he had always been: he didn't really want money or possessions. Even if, with marriage, the writer had changed, Subroto said, the writer's old reputation was now working against him. He had been too scornful of people in the business; he had made too many enemies. There was an influential man, influential in films and in politics, the kind of two- or three-sided figure who was now appearing in Indian public life, who had wanted the writer to do a treatment of a particular story. The writer, Subroto said, had read the outline in the great man's office and then, in a rage at having been asked to work on such rubbish, quite literally thrown the sheets of paper with the story outline in the great man's face.

All the way back to downtown Bombay, against the metallic clatter of the big, open coaches, Subroto talked of art and design and the work he hoped to do. He lived in Bombay only as a paying guest; he didn't think that would ever change. But his talk of his vocation and what he might do was selfless; what he had said about the unworldliness of the writer seemed to be true about him as well.

The shacks and shanties beside the railway lines went by; the dusty light turned golden. I thought of Subroto, and I thought of the writer in his apartment: such a setting for a man who talked of his craft with so full a heart and mind, such refining of his artistic experience: such a mismatch between dreams and setting. It was what had struck me on that first morning in Bombay when, on one side of the road, I had seen the long, patient line of people waiting to honour Dr Ambedkar, and, on the lamp standards on the other side of the road, the small, repeating posters for a new film, a product of the Bombay commercial cinema.

I had heard, vaguely, some years before, of the Dalit Panthers. I had got to know little of them beyond the name, which had been borrowed from the Black Panthers of the United States. It was a romantic borrowing; it encouraged the – too simple – belief that the Dalits (or scheduled castes or harijans or untouchables, to take the wounding nomenclature back through its earlier stages) were in India what black people were in the United States.

I heard now, from Charu, in our many taxi-rides up and down Bombay, of the man who had founded the Dalit Panthers. He was Namdeo Dhasal; he had a parallel reputation in Bombay as a Dalit poet. He was now about forty-seven, though he wasn't sure of the exact year of his birth. He had been born in a village 100 miles or so inland, and he had migrated to Bombay 30 years before. He had lived for a long time in the brothel area, among criminals and prostitutes. Golpitha was the name of that area, and it was the name of Namdeo's first book of poems, written in Marathi, and published in 1974, when he might have been twenty-seven. In that same year Namdeo had founded the Dalit Panthers, and he had immediately become a man of some political standing in Bombay.

The poetry side was a surprise to me. It was surprising that, in the small spaces of Bombay, and with the crowd and frenzy, there was a living Marathi literature, with all the high social organization that such a literature implied: the existence of publishers, printers, distributors, critics, buyers. It was as surprising to me as the idea of the Maharashtrian gymnasium had been, when I had heard about it from Mr Raote.

Namdeo had not been the first Dalit to write. There had been earlier Marathi voices from the depths. But they had written in received, literary Marathi. Namdeo's great originality was that he had written naturally, using words and expressions that Dalits and no one else used. In his first book of poems he had written, specifically, in the language of the Bombay brothel area. That had caused the sensation; he had been praised and condemned.

Charu, who was a Maharashtrian brahmin, and quite learned in Marathi writing, said there were a number of words in Namdeo's poems that he couldn't understand. He gave me this translation of a poem called 'The Road to the Shrine', from Namdeo's first collection.

*I was born when the sun became weak*
*And slowly became extinct*
*In the embrace of night.*
*I was born on a footpath*
*In a rag.*

[And the 'crude', Dalit word used for 'rag' was *chilbut*.]

*On the day I was born I was an orphan.*
*The one who gave me birth went to God.*
*I was tired of this ghost*
*Haunting me on the footpath.*

*I spent most of my life*
*Washing away the darkness in that sari.*

[But the word used for 'sari' was not an elegant one: it was *luggude*, and it referred to the way village women tied their saris, wrapping the garment around each leg separately, creating a kind of sari-breeches]

*I grew like a person who has lost his fuse.*
*I ate excrement and grew.*
*Give me five paise, give me five paise,*

[there are 100 paise in a rupee]

*And take five curses in return.*
*I am on my way to the shrine.*

Even in that rough translation, improvised by Charu in a busy hotel lobby, the poem was moving. It was much more moving to Charu. He said that the voice was absolutely new in Marathi; and he told me that Vijay Tendulkar, the contemporary Marathi playwright, had compared Namdeo to Tukaram, the 16th-century Maharashtrian poet-saint, whom I had heard about for the first time from Mr Raote.

In the poem Charu had translated, the mingled suggestions of sex and degradation were harsh and undermining, and the ideas of untouchability and brothel-area sex, childbirth and rags, all coming together, were like an assault. This was the passion that Namdeo had put into his politics and the Dalit Panthers.

But that name, which he had borrowed from the Black Panthers, was like a foreshadowing of what was to come. Like the Black Panthers, the Dalit movement, with its success, began to fragment. That pitch of passion couldn't be sustained; there was the temptation to many to make their peace with the wider society.

And though Namdeo became famous and courted, he began to lose his followers. Soon even his literary reputation began to recede. He had done a fair amount of work; he had written two novels, in addition to his poetry; but his most recent book had been published in 1981, seven years before. He wasn't writing so much now; and he had contracted a debilitating illness.

He had no telephone. But Charu knew where his house was, and we went there one afternoon to leave a message for him. The house was not far from the Golpitha area he had written about. It was a house, though, not an apartment; and it was in a reasonably wide and clean lane. Just across the lane from the front door of the house an old open jeep had been parked or abandoned and was now, mysteriously, bleaching away, its tires squashed and perished, its metal body almost bare, yet still looking whole.

Charu called from the lane. After a little while a dark young woman, bright-eyed, fine-featured, opened a leaf of the front door. She and Charu spoke in Marathi, and we went up the concrete steps that were set against the front wall of the house and led directly from the lane to the front door.

The room we entered ran the width of the house. It was the main room of the house. The walls were a lilac colour, and recently painted, in an eggshell finish. There were white-painted rattan chairs with dark-green cushions; and from one of the sturdy beams of the ceiling a basket chair hung by a chain. A feature, this hanging chair, a touch of luxury; and a plump young woman in a blue georgette sari, a visitor, was sitting in it, with her feet on the floor and moving with deliberation back and forth.

The dark woman who had welcomed us was Mallika, Namdeo's wife. She was stylishly dressed, in a kind of long peasant skirt in lightweight material. The skirt swung as she walked about the terrazzo floor on her small bare feet, and her tinkling Marathi voice filled the room as she welcomed Charu and me.

There was a very large colour photograph of a white baby on one wall. On another wall were small colour snapshots of Namdeo:

full-cheeked, paunchy, but with a face that was still strong. On the opposite wall was a photograph of Mallika's own father. He had been famous, a folk singer, a member of the Communist Party, and a Muslim. A small red flag hung on the wall behind the television set at the far end of the room, not far from a framed copy of the famous grey-toned photograph of Dr Ambedkar in a jacket and tie.

The woman in the blue sari in the basket chair had not been introduced to us. We had addressed no word to her; and she, as private as always, and seemingly quite content, had continued with small movements of her feet to move the basket chair back and forth. Now, without social disturbance, she got up and went inside.

Mallika herself then went inside, skirt swinging, and after some time brought out tea for us on a kind of woven tray, very pretty. I was beginning to understand that very little Mallika did was casual, that in everything she did, or had some control over, she aimed at prettiness or elegance: in her dress, her walk, the colours of the room, the big colour photograph of the white baby, and even in her dogs, a pair of white, fluffy, combed Pomeranians, slightly listless in the Bombay heat, that she had bought four years before, for their beauty.

We left our telephone numbers with her. She said she would ask Namdeo to get in touch with us. Abruptly, then, with no intermediate atmosphere, we were out of the front room or hall into the lane where the abandoned jeep squashed its rotted tires. And at the end of that short lane we were back in a more familiar Bombay.

Charu told me later that the story of that marriage – Mallika's and Namdeo's – was famous. Mallika had written an autobiography in Marathi, *I Want to Destroy Myself,* and the book had been a bestseller. In Marathi that meant a sale of 10,000 copies.

Mallika's book was a story not only of love, but also of disillusion and pain. Almost as soon as she and Namdeo had married, things had begun to go badly for the Dalit Panthers, and Namdeo's behaviour had changed. She had suffered. She had been introduced to shocking things. Namdeo had a venereal disease; he continued to go with women from the brothel area. But she was tied to Namdeo, by the child they had had, and by her love for him. She was passionate about the freedom of women; but in her own life, because of her love for Namdeo, she found that she had lost some of her autonomy. After 10 years of love and torment she had written her book.

The book was sexually frank; and though that kind of writing was not unknown in Marathi women writers, Mallika's created a sensation, because it offended many people's caste sensibilities. Though Mallika's father had been a Muslim, her mother was a Hindu, of a caste just below the brahmin caste; and people had been upset and wounded by Mallika's story of her love for Namdeo and her later turbulent life with him.

No message came from Namdeo, and late one morning Charu and I went back to the house. Mallika wasn't there, but someone let us in. Before we could leave a note, Mallika came. She had been out shopping, and was wearing a light chiffon sari that billowed about her, a small, rust-red motif on white; and she was carrying in her hands, almost as part of her dress, just a few turnips or carrots with their green: the vegetables looking in her hands like emblems in a kind of Italian renaissance painting.

And then Namdeo himself appeared, with a friend. Namdeo was sturdy, paunchy, dark, unexpectedly avuncular. He would not have stood out in a crowd. I saw suggestions of forcefulness only in his eyes and forehead; but that might have been because I knew who he was. It was hard to see in him the poet or the Panther. There was a curious placid quality to him; it was as though his inner fire had burned out. And then I remembered what Charu had said about his illness. It was his illness, that other external enemy, that had finally weakened him, and given him the easy, affable, and yet somehow distant manner he now showed us.

He spoke no English. Yes, he said to Charu in Marathi, he would like to meet us. Tomorrow. Yes, come for lunch. No? Well, come after lunch. From two to five. Come then.

He went inside then with the man who had come with him, and Charu and I said goodbye to Mallika and left. It seemed easy enough, arranging that meeting, now that we had met Namdeo. But Charu thought it had been too easy. He had his doubts about the appointment. And I learned later – from other people – that in the matter of time-keeping and appointments Dalits had a poor reputation.

And it was as Charu feared. When we went to the house the next day, Namdeo wasn't there. This was Mallika's news when we went up the concrete steps from the lane to the front room or hall. And just as, the first time we had gone to the house, there had been a young woman in the basket chair, to whom we had not been introduced, so now there was someone in the front room who was not mentioned: a thin dark woman sleeping on a mat on the floor, just like that.

We followed Mallika to the kitchen at the back, and then through a side door to a small room at the side of the house, with a high, deep-embrasured, iron-barred window. This was the room Mallika had prepared for our meeting with Namdeo. It had two of the painted rattan chairs, a table with a table-cloth, and, in one corner, an old-fashioned, pretty electric table lamp with a draped woman in bronze-coloured metal, holding a torch.

Waiting there for Namdeo, I talked to Mallika. I asked her about the house. I could see that it was unusual, but I felt I wasn't in a position to see it correctly. I brought too many outside ideas to it. I asked her to describe the house for me, so that I could begin to see it as people in the area might have seen it.

Something of what I intended got lost in the interpreting, and Mallika said, 'This is my parents' house.' The house, therefore, of one of the most famous folk singers of Maharashtra, the house of a successful man. 'It is the house where I grew up. It's nice to stay in a house where you've been since your childhood.'

She and Namdeo had done a certain amount of renovation. They painted the house every two years. As for the area, it was an area of working people; but middle-class people also lived on the street. She knew everyone there. When her father was alive their family had been looked up to.

But her parents had had a mixed marriage. Her father was a Muslim, her mother a Hindu. Had that made for problems?

'I didn't know my father was a Muslim. My mother was a Pathari Prabhu. A little lower than brahmins. These Patharis eat fish. Pathari Prabhus are the original Bombay people, and that is how they have been eating fish.' Eating fish, that is, though they were very nearly brahmins, because they were a coastal people.

She had learned about the Pathari Prabhus from her mother's mother, when she used to go and stay there. She hadn't been particularly interested in her mother's relatives; she hadn't gone out of her way to make inquiries about them because they were the kind of people they were. What she knew about that side of her origins was more a kind of 'idle knowledge' that had come to her as she had grown up.

I asked her about her book. Had she intended it to be as daring as it had turned out?

'I didn't think like that. It was necessary for me to write that book. I had no choice. It wasn't open to me to separate one side of my life from the other side.'

She was wearing a lightweight sari, a simple pattern on a pink ground. She was sitting on one of the white-painted rattan chairs. In the room was a steel wardrobe, olive-green, with a long mirror on one door – it was a kind of wardrobe I had been seeing in Bombay. On top of the wardrobe was a tarnished little globe. The masonry or plaster of the window-sill was nicely bevelled; the eggshell finish of the paint, added to that bevelling, made me want to run my hand over it.

In her book – sections of which Charu had translated for me at great speed, before we had come out – she had said, talking of her love for Namdeo, that she felt 'a blank' at the thought of leaving him. I told her I had been taken by that.

She said, 'Even now I love Namdeo, and am willing to give him everything. Even though he has some negative points. There is a kind of thread running through our relationship. Even when I don't want him, I want him. Even now, whatever is good in me, whatever is creative in me, I would suppress for his sake. I know that if I do certain things he will go out of my life. I don't want that. Then there is my child. We are in a kind of vicious triangle. I love Namdeo. The child loves me. Namdeo loves the child.' The child was thirteen.

The book hadn't been flattering of Namdeo. Some people thought it had even damaged him politically. Had Namdeo read the book while she was writing it?

'If I hadn't written the book, I would have gone mad. Namdeo didn't read it. He used to read my poems. But he wouldn't read my prose. I showed him the manuscript of the book, but he didn't read it. It was only when the book was published that he read it. But then for a year before he had been suffering from his nervous illness.'

She was smaller than her erect posture and her hips suggested. Her dark arms were slender, even thin. She had a big red spot between her pencilled eyebrows. She had a watch and bangle on her right wrist, and eight or nine thin silver bracelets on her left arm.

'He didn't say anything about the book, but there was a change in his behaviour. He has never mentioned the book to me to this day. But I know that when other people have said to him that he should write a rejoinder, he has defended my book. His argument then is that this woman who has lived with him all these years, and has seen it all with her middle-class eyes' – there it was, the social comment, the comment on her family house perhaps, the comment on the way Mallika saw herself in relation to Namdeo, and the way he saw her – 'his argument is that this woman has every right to express what she feels about the marriage.'

Now, Mallika said, a little of the earlier relationship, when she had first loved him, had revived. He was still under treatment for his illness, and he had stopped drinking. His drinking had caused many clashes between them, and he used to beat her. But she felt that much of that had been due to his political frustration, witnessing the quick decay of the Dalit movement he had started.

Her understanding didn't make it less hard for her. 'I would get angry. I would cry. I would shout. I would find it extremely humiliating. I loved the man, but I never thought my life would be so degraded – after I had gone against everybody and married him. Because I had gone against everyone, I felt I couldn't give up on the marriage just then and tell people what a failure the marriage had been. I also felt that if I kept quiet I would have to bear it forever, and that was not my nature. Everybody reacts to a situation in a way which comes most naturally to them, and I turned to writing.

'I wrote the book straight off, within a month. I wrote it sometimes in the front room, and sometimes here, at this table. Sometimes I wrote in the kitchen also.' The kitchen, seen through the doorway, with a door to the right leading to the front room or hall. 'There was no fixed time for writing. I wrote whenever I could.'

'Was Namdeo in the house when you were writing?'

'He was very much in the house.'

'Did he have any idea what you were writing? You weren't nervous?'

'I didn't know what he would do. I thought he would beat me up or throw me out, and go to the court.' To get custody of their child. 'I think a mother should have a right to her child. But according to Indian law the father can have custody of the child after the child's seventh birthday. So, even if I left, I had no guarantee that one day Namdeo wouldn't come and take away the child.'

A good half of the book she wrote in those tormenting circumstances was a reliving of her early love for Namdeo.

It had begun 14 years before. She was sixteen, and she had gone to the resort town of Lonavala, between Bombay and Poona, to do some studying. She had gone with her brother-in-law Anil, who had leftist leanings, and with a famous Marathi film-actor and director. Anil was writing a film-script.

On the fourth or fifth day of this Lonavala interlude Namdeo appeared. He came late one night with another man from the Dalit movement. Mallika had already met Namdeo. She had met him in her family house – the house where we now were. Namdeo used to come to the house to hide. This was in 1974, when the Dalit movement was at its peak, and there were riots in the Bombay district of Worli.

'He had never paid much attention to me. This surprised me, because the boys here found me attractive. But he never paid me much attention. I read his poems, and I realized he had leftist leanings. I gave him my poems to read.

'He came now to Lonavala. At that time Lonavala had a very poetic atmosphere, a pre-monsoon atmosphere. It looked as though it was about to rain, but it never rained. There were quite a few similarities between us. He liked rain and I liked rain. He liked poetry and I liked poetry. Our literary opinions more or less matched, and even now, in literature, we have very many things in common. I was at the age when you really fall in love with somebody.'

She laughed. And when I said I thought that that time in Lonavala was still romantic to her, she laughed again and lifted her thin arms with the thin bracelets, and clapped her hands.

'Then he would talk about politics, and how the police were harassing him and beating him, and I would find it very thrilling. I felt I wanted to be close to him. This wasn't a sexual feeling. I felt compassion. I felt I wanted to put my hand on his head.'

'You had no caste feeling about the man?'

'I had no caste prejudices. I didn't know about his caste, and I didn't think it was essential to know that.'

Perhaps her communist father, the folk singer, had trained her that way. Yet caste would have been in everything Namdeo did. He was a caste leader, and caste still attached to him. In the house that afternoon, in the front room or hall, which Mallika had decorated with such care, there was a thin dark woman in dark clothes sleeping on a mat. That woman, I now learned from Mallika, was Namdeo's mother.

'She is seventy. Because of Namdeo's politics and the ups and downs of his career, she's had a nervous breakdown. Namdeo was her only son. She always had the fear in those days, in the 70s, at the height of the movement, that somebody would beat him up and kill him. Whenever she put on the TV she felt that somebody was going to read out that news. That pressure was always on her, and led to her breakdown.'

But – going back to the earlier point – the fact was that, at sixteen, Mallika had no caste feeling about Namdeo.

'Practically everybody at Lonavala knew we were getting close to one another. We had been together for about 15 days. Anil, my brother-in-law, would joke about it. It was he who asked one day whether I liked Namdeo, and he said we were quite suited to each other. So that same night, after we had had dinner, all of us who were staying in the bungalow – it hadn't begun to rain, but it was cool: Lonavala is cool – I called him into an inner room, away from the people sitting outside, and I said to him, "What do you think of me?" And he said, "Do you want me to put it in words?"'

She raised her hands and the eight or nine thin silver bracelets slipped down her thin arm.

'After this my brother-in-law talked to him. He asked him some questions about his background and his feelings. Namdeo didn't like this. My brother-in law said to him that I had come to Lonavala to do some studying. "Since you've come she hasn't read a single word. She is still at page 153."'

'What book was that?'

'A history book. So my brother-in-law said to Namdeo, "You better leave." The next day Namdeo left.'

But hadn't her brother-in-law encouraged Namdeo? Yes, Mallika said; but when her brother-in-law had spoken to Namdeo about his intentions, he wasn't speaking in anger or in rebuke; he was only speaking formally. Namdeo, though, hadn't like being questioned at all; so he had been asked to leave.

'Just before Namdeo left Lonavala, he took my hand. He called me "comrade" and he gave the "red salaam", the communist salute. This excited me. Before he went he taped something by me – it was a song I used to sing night and day. I heard later that he would play that tape to his friends in Bombay.'

They were married four months later. After the schoolgirl romance, the sexual side of marriage had been disagreeable for her. That was one of the things she had written about openly in her book. 'The pleasure came when the routine started. It was then that I started getting the pleasure. The psychological pressure lessened with the experience.' She hadn't had any idea of the sexual give-and-take in a relationship. And it amazed her, it enchanted her, to be able to give her body and herself to someone she loved. She wrote of this in her book, and people reacted in different ways to her frankness. Some people 'threw themselves at her feet' in admiration; some people abused her.

The marriage itself came under another strain almost at once. 'Within two months of our marriage the Panther movement started breaking up. Dalits stay in small settlements and pockets, little groups. Each pocket and settlement began to have its own leader, and poisonous things began to be said about Namdeo in those settlements. His marriage to me added to his troubles. I was the daughter of a well-known communist, and the Dalits don't like communists. The reason for that is simple. Dr Ambedkar, the hero of the Dalits, didn't like communism. Every Dalit has Dr Ambedkar's picture in his house. So the Dalits hate communists.

'The next year, 1975, there was the Emergency. There were something like 350 court cases against the Dalit Panthers – speeches, fighting, etc. The government withdrew all those cases when the Panthers supported the Emergency. That wasn't really what Namdeo wanted to do. And though he never said anything about it, I feel that was when he began to feel compromised. But that was when I, too, needed him most – in July of that year I had had my child. I needed Namdeo, and I felt he was neglecting me.'

'Because of political pressure?'

'His setbacks and frustration. That helped to send him away from me. So his political life had an effect on his personal life.'

'Do you still find him an attractive man?'

'Much water has flowed down the Ganges, but if he were to come in this room now, I would feel like a young girl. I would feel I had just fallen in love with him. Nothing has really changed in that. There are many other men who may be physically more attractive or intellectually superior. But I don't want them.'

I asked her about the 'five-star life' that – according to his critics – had come to Namdeo as a Dalit Panther, a man in the news.

Mallika said, 'This downward journey began right at the Emergency.'

Namdeo's mother had got up from her mat in the front room. Through the doorway I saw her in the kitchen, a thin dark figure in dark clothes, moving silently, like a shadow.

Mallika said, 'Namdeo is a born politician. If he decides tomorrow to write his autobiography, there would be just a page for me. That is why his political ups and downs had its repercussions on his private life. This is one of the questions I asked in my book. Why should this affect me? Why isn't he helping me with my life?

'After the Emergency he became unpredictable. His friends in the underworld began giving him money. One day he would have 10,000 rupees. The next day he wouldn't have a rupee. And we both had a common trait – money never stuck to us. Namdeo used to say it was middle class to keep money in the bank. So whatever money he had he spent – and on high living.'

Ever since 1975, just a year or so after its time of glory (and a year or so after Mallika's Lonavala romance), the Dalit movement had been in decay. She used an English word: *numb.* The movement fragmented and fragmented again, and there were allegations and counter-allegations about money being taken by various people from various sources. The Dalits, as a result, had lost faith in the people who had been their leaders.

It was now five o'clock. We had been with Mallika for three hours. And at this moment – when our meeting would have been ending, if he had been there for it – Namdeo appeared. His mother was still in the kitchen.

And it was as Mallika had said: Namdeo was in the house; she was aware of his presence; her thoughts were of him. She began to speak to us with only half a mind – speaking simple pieties about the Dalit movement – but then she calmed down again.

I asked about the violent sexual imagery in some of Namdeo's poems, the conflation of sex and excrement and degradation. When she had married Namdeo, her thoughts had been all of romance; even the sexual side of marriage had shocked her. Had she, after that first shock, become wholly accepting? Wasn't she still unsettled, just a little, by certain things in Namdeo's poetry?

No; she wasn't unsettled in any way. What she felt, more than shock at some of the words and images, was Namdeo's great power as a poet. 'It's quite true and pure poetry. It's not just an imitation. I look upon him as one of the greatest poets in Marathi. We've had people who've changed the course of poetry. He's one of them. *He's a milestone.*' She spoke the last words in English.

Namdeo came in from the kitchen to the little room where we were. His glasses were on his forehead. He smiled and was polite. He made no reference to the meeting he hadn't come for. He said only that there were people waiting for him, and he couldn't stay to talk.

He was busy that day with his political work. He was organizing a demonstration by prostitutes in the Golpitha district, he said. He showed the black-and-white posters he had just picked up from the printers. He asked whether I would like to come to that demonstration. I said yes. He gave me a copy of the poster, and we arranged to meet at the house the day after the demonstration, when he would have more time. And then he was out of the room.

I asked Mallika, 'Does he show you his poems?'

'If he writes something here, he will show it to me. If he writes it somewhere else, he will show it to the person nearest him, whether that person understands poetry or not.'

All the shocks of her relationship with Namdeo appeared now to lie in the past – the discovery, for instance, in the first year of their marriage, that he had a venereal disease. She had written about that, and about other discoveries she had made. She lived more easily now with the things she had written about; and she thought her life with Namdeo could go on forever as it was going on now: 'a middle-class family state'. She was not, besides, in a position to do anything extreme: she always had to think of her child.

'I want the child to become my friend. I don't want the child to grow up like his father – the negative aspects.'

'What negative aspects?'

'Raging, cursing. The movement is the first thing Namdeo thinks about. So, whatever our relationship, he will never break his ties to the movement.'

The movement was now stalled. People might come together on certain issues; they might shout slogans and march. But people no longer had a direction or a purpose.

I told her about the long line of people I had seen on the way in from the airport. What would their mood have been, waiting to pay tribute to the long-dead Ambedkar?

'Emotional. Dalits will sacrifice anything and everything for Ambedkar. He is not an extra god for them. He is God. They would slaughter their wife. Anything for Ambedkar.'

Charu added on his own, 'Like Christ to the Christians.'

Mallika agreed.

I asked whether she had been supported by any religious faith during these years.

'Whenever things were bad I turned to myself.'

'No faith?'

'I have faith in myself. I have faith only in my own existence.'

The first part of Mallika's book had ended (in Charu's spoken translation): 'Male ego is the most hideous thing in our present society. Women find quite a pleasure in boosting it. It reminds me of a story in which the tree itself gave its branch to a woodcutter who had only an axe-blade and no handle . . . I do not believe that for anybody called Namdeo I should surrender my entire life.' But the book was also an account of her obsession with the man and his poetry and his cause, and her consequent loss of freedom. The second part of the book ended: 'This has been the journey of a defeated mind.' And though what she had done had been done for the sake of a man, she had always been alone. 'There was nobody with me.'

Charu and I got ready to leave. And now many of the details of the house had a fuller meaning: the photographs of Mallika's father and mother, the colour snaps of Namdeo, the red flag (made by Mallika's son) in the front room, the dark, shadow-like, silent figure of Namdeo's mother who had had a breakdown many years before (and was about to die now), the framed certificate to Namdeo from the Bombay Russian House of Culture, the icon-picture of Dr Ambedkar, the poster for the prostitutes' meeting Namdeo was planning. On one wall, above the very big colour photograph of a white baby (Mallika said she simply liked the picture) there was a framed drawing by her son: brown rocks, black boulder, red sun, black birds. In the up-and-down scratching of the brown crayon, which had given volume and solidity to the rocks, I had seen a great subtlety, and had thought that the picture was a contemporary Chinese print.

The prostitutes' meeting that Namdeo was organizing in Golpitha was to be on Tuesday. On Sunday there was an item in a newspaper that I was to be the 'chief guest' at the meeting. Other newspapers picked up the item the next day; and though people I knew in Bombay began to telephone me, some with worry, some with amusement, I didn't think the newspaper story was of any consequence. I thought that misconceptions or exaggerations of that nature would blow away.

From the impression of busyness Namdeo had given, and from the serious-looking black-and-white Dalit Panther poster, I expected the meeting to be quite an event. But when Charu and I went we found hardly anything. There were Dalit Panther banners across some lanes; there were many policemen and police vehicles about; but there seemed to be no extraordinary stir.

We had gone early, to get something of the atmosphere of the brothel area. We went walking in the narrow lanes: the lights, the signboards, the booths, the people sitting out, some on string beds, in the shadows at the side of the lanes; the piles of wet rubbish, the smell of drains; prostitutes and their 'mistresses' and moneylenders and prostitutes' clients all part of the same display, the mixture of sex and innocence and degradation as undermining as in the poems of Namdeo's that the area had inspired.

The evening life of the area was going on. The prospect of Namdeo's Dalit Panther meeting – to protest against what was seen – was hardly causing a tremor. The meeting was to take place at the end of one of the lanes, dark and without motor traffic, but full of activity, with a walking space only in the middle, between the booths and stalls and the string beds. In bright light at the end of the lane, on a platform spread with white sheets, seated musicians were playing country melodies.

No one seemed to be attending. But as Charu and I got nearer, men with cameras, and men and women whom Charu recognized as newspaper reporters, came out from the shadows. And Charu and I understood that, for that evening, so far as the newspapers were concerned, we were the story.

I thought we should go away. Charu and I turned and walked back to the other end of the lane. The newspaper people followed us. When we were at the end of the lane, and near a brighter main road, Charu said it would be wrong to leave just like that. We would anatagonize the newspaper people, who had given up their evening for this event; and they might go away and write hostile stories. He thought it would be better for him to go and talk to the newspaper people – he knew them: some were his friends – and explain matters to them.

He led me to a cigarette stall, and asked me to stand there and wait for him. He went back down the lane, and was soon lost in the darkness and the crowd. But the photographers didn't go away. They stayed a few feet from me, keeping their eyes on me (in case I tried to run off), while the musicians, their white platform bright and distant at the end of the dark lane, played their rocking country rhythms. All at once a photographer took a picture; and at that flash all the photographers began to click and flash away, creating the effect of dud fireworks around me.

At last Charu came back. He had news. Namdeo had arrived, and – unusually – Mallika had come with him. It was essential now for me to go back and be with them for a little, Charu said. If I didn't do that, they might feel that I was letting them down. Already, Charu said, even if I wasn't aware of it, and couldn't understand the reason for it, a certain amount of caste hostility was building up in the people of the lane, who had witnessed our coming and going. It would take just one little spark for there to be trouble. There was another reason, Charu said, why I should go and be with Namdeo and Mallika. Mallika, after all the time she had given me, had gone to the further trouble of writing me a long letter in Marathi; she had given him the letter to pass to me.

A length of matting covered by some kind of cloth, a version of a red carpet, had been laid down the middle of the wet, dirty lane. Down that we walked, back towards the musicians, who were playing on. We turned into a little room: Mallika was there, welcoming, smiling, in a fresh sari, and Namdeo. I was glad to see them, glad that Charu had made me come back. Women of the area garlanded me. It was what the photographers wanted; and it was those happy pictures – rather than the furtive ones in the dark lane – that made the newspapers the next day.

In the taxi back, Charu translated Mallika's letter: many sheets of foolscap in a beautiful, stylish script. She was concerned that I might not have understood the two sides of her way of feeling: her love of freedom, her love for Namdeo. But she had, in fact, said it all when we had met.

We went to see Namdeo the next day at the house. That was the arrangement we had made some days before. But Charu was nervous, and even worried. We hadn't stayed for Namdeo's meeting; he might have felt that we had walked out on him. He might have felt that we had damaged him politically, and there was no knowing what he might do. He was an unpredictable man.

When we got to the house Mallika told us that Namdeo was there. He was inside, eating. He came out and greeted us and right away went back in. We saw all the day's newspapers in the front room: they had been unfolded and looked at. I hadn't read the stories that had accompanied the photographs. Charu had; and out of a wish to make peace for both of us (and rebuking me for not having accepted Namdeo's offer of lunch when it had been made some days before), he settled down, at Mallika's invitation, and with Mallika serving him, to eat an enormous meal in the front room. He ate all she gave him, and then he asked for more.

But Charu had been too nervous. Mallika was happy with the way the evening had gone. She even wanted me to know that the musicians at the meeting had been part of her father's folk-song troupe. Namdeo was very happy. He was eating at the back, but that didn't mean anything. When the eating was over, Charu's in the front room, and Namdeo's in the back room, we all met in perfect amity in the back room, with the olive-green metal wardrobe with the tall mirror, and the bronze-coloured lamp stand; and Namdeo made it clear that he was ready, as he had promised, to give me the whole afternoon.

Still, bearing in mind what Charu had said, I didn't think I should talk right away about the prostitutes' meeting. I thought I would begin with his poetry. I told him about the early poem

Charu had translated for me, 'The Way to the Shrine'. I asked about the sexual violence of that poem and other, later poems of his I had got to know.

He replied at great length. Charu, perhaps out of a continuing nervousness, and perhaps also out of his interest in literary matters, allowed Namdeo to talk for a long time before he translated or summed up; and Namdeo talked slowly, reflectively.

In the middle of Namdeo's Marathi I caught the English words *not sexual.* He said 'The Way to the Shrine' was not one of his best poems. He gave this interpretation of the poem. The poet was like an orphan in the land of his birth. The shrine that the poet was going towards was a real place, a famous sea-side mosque in Bombay; but Bombay was a cosmopolitan city, and the shrine of the poet's pilgrimage could be any of the city's sacred places. The 'darkness in the sari' and 'the ghost in the footpath' was the social system into which the poet had been born. The darkness in the sari was not a sexual image – even the lowest woman would have her own code. The darkness in the sari meant ignorance: the poet had spent much of his life washing away this darkness, this ignorance.

But he had written better poems. He wished I had got to know some of those. He had written a poem about water. It was quite a well-known poem.

*Water is taught caste prejudices . . .*

That idea about water was important to him. He referred to it more than once. It came from his memories of the strict untouchability that prevailed in the village near Poona where he had grown up. The upper castes used the river upstream; the scheduled castes used the river downstream; and the upper castes used the river first.

He had a memory of something that had happened when he was in the second standard. The village children didn't have caste prejudices; they would play together. One day he went bathing in a pond with some upper-caste boys. The guard spotted him and threw stones at him. He had defiled the pond. He was chased and stoned. He ran bleeding back to his own settlement and hid there. His mother was abused, and afterwards his mother beat him for defiling the pond and causing trouble.

He thought he was born in 1940, but he couldn't be sure. Even at school – this would have been in 1951 or 1952 – the scheduled-caste boys would have to sit outside the school-room. They weren't allowed to touch any source of water; water had to be poured into their cupped hands. A teacher couldn't touch a scheduled-caste child. When a teacher wanted to punish a child from one of those castes, he threw things at the child.

His family was of the Mahar caste. They lived in a joint family: the wives and children of three brothers, about 25 people in all, lived in one house. Namdeo's father didn't live in the house; he had migrated to Bombay, leaving his family behind. The family had land. They lived by farming, and also by the traditional duties of their caste.

As Namdeo was talking of the traditional duties of the Mahars in his native village, we were joined in the small inner room by a man I had seen in the house before, one of those silent, unintroduced, unexplained people who appeared to have the freedom of the house. This small, dark man, with a thick moustache and an orange-coloured tunic, stood beside Namdeo's chair, and listened with especial attention now, shaking his head in solemn affirmation as Namdeo spoke of the duties of Mahars.

Mahars had to summon people to the revenue department. That was an official duty, for the government, and in the old days it could mean travelling long distances in all kinds of weather. Other duties were more traditional. When someone in the village died, it was the Mahars who were entrusted with the task of informing all the relatives of the dead person. Mahars also disposed of dead bodies. In return, the Mahars were given an allowance of grain three times a year by the upper-caste villagers.

The friend of the house solemnly swung his head from side to side, staring down at a point half-way to the floor, so that it was as if, while Namdeo spoke, the friend of the house was nostalgically remembering the old ways.

He repeated now, 'Three times a year.'

Mahars had another privilege. This was like a daily ritual, and Namdeo spoke long about it, and the friend of the house listened and looked down at the floor and shook his head.

Mahars, Namdeo said, had the right to call on the upper-caste houses every day and ask for bread. If there were 10 Mahar households in a village they would divide the upper-caste households among themselves, and each Mahar household would be allotted certain caste households to call on. The Mahar who had that task would leave his house early in the morning with a woven basket or a metal basket on his head. When he got to the upper-caste house he would make his obeisance and ask for bread. He would ask for bread twice. If the bread wasn't given then, it was the right of the Mahar absolutely to demand it. The Mahars did this every morning. And the upper-caste people would give bread, letting the bread fall into the basket, without themselves touching the basket.

'Without touching,' the friend said.

This was the way the caste system worked when it was still strong, before 1955. After that it began to break down. Instead of grain and certain rights, Mahars could be offered money for what they did; but sometimes they weren't offered anything. So while their duties in the village remained the same, such rights as they had had began to diminish. Ambedkar was powerful at that time; and Mahars and other scheduled-caste people began then to make political demands.

Among the scheduled castes in that area, Mahars were the only ones with the right to own land. That was why Namdeo's family had land and made a certain amount of money from farming. That right of the Mahars, to own land, had come about for an interesting reason.

Once upon a time, there was a raja of Bidar. He wanted to send his daughter to a certain place. The Mahars were the people who traditionally carried the palanquins, and the raja ordered the local Mahars to carry his daughter to where she had to go. The Mahars understood the seriousness of what they had been asked to do; as a precaution, to avoid accident or misunderstanding, they castrated themselves before setting out. The raja's enemies started to spread a story that the raja's daughter had been carnally used by the Mahars. The raja summoned the Mahars and questioned them. They displayed themselves to him, and said they had castrated themselves before taking the princess. The raja was so pleased he gave the Mahars land. That was how the Mahars became the only scheduled caste in the area to own land.

Namdeo had seemed to take much pleasure in the romantic tale; just as, earlier, encouraged by his friend, he had seemed, with something like nostalgia, to call up the caste practices of his village. I asked Charu to ask him about this nostalgia: I thought I might have missed something.

Namdeo spoke for a long time, and his friend in the orange-coloured tunic was as encouraging as always.

Finally Charu reported: 'He's fully aware of the pain he's undergone. But there is also a poet and writer in him, and as a poet and writer he wishes to search out his own roots. Pain has always been part of his psychology. There was no question in the old days of complaining. You were a Mahar and you did your duties, and that was that.'

It wasn't all pain for him in the village. The village teacher had the prejudices of his caste, and he neglected Namdeo. But this neglect gave Namdeo some freedom as a child. He enjoyed taking the cattle out to graze; he went swimming in the river.

In 1958, when he was seventeen or eighteen, and in the fourth standard, he left his village and came to Bombay. He remembered that *Mother India,* with the actress Nargis, was showing in the cinemas. He stayed in a slum area with one of his uncles, who had two rooms in a chawl. The chawl was called 'Dhor Chawl', after the Dhor caste, a caste who disposed of dead cattle and ran the tanneries. Only people of that caste were living in the chawl. So Namdeo didn't leave caste behind in his village; caste followed him to Bombay.

He didn't go out to work. He went to school. In the school in the village he had been a failure in the fourth standard; in Bombay, in the same standard, he stood first. It was then, too, that he began writing poetry.

All his poems came straight out, 'in a flow'. He had read about Bob Dylan and Eldridge Cleaver. And he had read some Negro poets; and Leroi Jones. He had read them in English. He understood English, though he couldn't speak it. There was no direct influence, but he was aware of those poets. He also knew Allen Ginsberg, Rimbaud, Rilke, Baudelaire, Lorca, the last four in English translations. He'd read all the major mid-20th-century poets.

And though, from a distance, his career seemed to be like the careers of a number of Black Power people in the United States – he had become someone the newspapers and magazines wrote about, and in the end he had become more famous than his cause – yet, talking to him in this little room of the Bombay house, I felt that he was the prisoner of an Indian past no one outside could truly understand. It had been harder for him to break out, to reject the past, than it had been for black people in the United States. And now Namdeo was again, if in a different way, a prisoner of India, with its multiplicity of movements and desperate needs; he could easily sink again. It wasn't really possible for him, as it might have been possible for a black activist in the United States, to withdraw, to settle for ease.

I asked whether he was now more a poet than a politician.

'The roles are not separate. I am against this caste system. I express it in my politics and in my poems. Poetry is a political act. Politics is part of my poetry.'

Only now I thought I could refer to the adventure of the previous night.

'You will keep on working with the prostitutes?'

'I will keep on working on various problems. Prostitutes are a major problem.'

'Are there Dalits who are jealous of you?'

'There is a jealousy of me. There are allegations that I am a communist.'

When he had first come out to greet us, before going in again to continue eating, he had seemed casually dressed, a man at home, with a brownish shirt and a many-coloured dhoti. In fact, he had dressed carefully. The shirt was elegant, fawn-coloured, thick and textured; and his dhoti had a plaid pattern. He fitted into the room, with its walls in an eggshell finish, and the plastic flowers in a vase on the window-sill in front of the vertical iron bars: a lot of Mallika's taste here.

I said, 'Mallika says your poetry is a milestone.'

'I feel surprised when people say things like that. Marathi literature is so poor. There were nice poems like Tukaram's, and then there was nothing for hundreds of years.'

His life was very public now. Was it possible for him to write poetry while living such a public life?

He misunderstood the question. 'I'm not really troubled. I don't expect to be praised.'

'Mallika said you defended her right to publish her book.'

He didn't make a direct comment. 'It's a conflict between two cultures, two backgrounds. Mallika's mother was a traditional Hindu. Though her father was Muslim, her culture was traditional Hindu middle-class culture.'

'You defended her book.'

'Her book was damaging to me, it is true. My image outside was that of a progressive, and Mallika's picture was damaging. But Mallika was right. I've always been an Ambedkarite. That's been part of my being, and I feel that Mallika has a right to say what she feels about her husband.'

Then, explaining himself, not waiting for me to ask questions, he began to speak of some of the things I might have heard about him or wanted to know about him.

'My political rise started in 1971–1972. Before that I was living in that Kanthipura area in the underworld. Money was easy to come by. It was a red-light area, full of ignorance and the mafia and cruelty. It's a cruel area, and that had an effect on me. It had a tremendous impact on my character. When you are young, you are tough and militant. Your energy can take you on to a good path or a wrong path. If I didn't have my special past, and if I wasn't aware of Ambedkar's movement, I might have been one of the big men of the underworld, and I mightn't have gone into politics. Because of the way I had been brought up, I was full of anger and ready to fight at the slightest provocation. Some of the fights I got into came close to murder. Everybody in the Bombay underworld knew me.'

The afternoon had gone; dusk was almost upon us. Our talk had taken a long time, because Namdeo had always spoken at length, and I had had to wait for Charu's translation or summaries. I was tired. Charu was tired, and he had missed the visiting Russian circus to which he had been hoping to take his wife that evening. I got up, ready to leave. But Namdeo didn't want it.

He said, 'You haven't asked me about my personal life.'

And then, like a man doing what was expected of him, giving full value, he spoke the things people said about him and sometimes used against him.

'I used to be a taxi-driver. From 1967 to 1971. I used to go with prostitutes. I have tried all kinds of vices. *Now I'm too much normal and gentleman.*' The last sentence was in English. 'Even after I got married, I used sometimes to go to prostitutes. When the Dalit Panthers split, I used to drink very heavily. I started the Panthers, and then they put me in a minority. It was a great blow. It saddens me still.'

'Why do you think you lost your power?'

'I was ahead of my time. I tried to expand the definition of Dalits – to take in all the oppressed, not just the scheduled castes. If you really want to break untouchability, you have to get into the mainstream. I wanted to be in the mainstream. That was why I wanted to expand the definition of Dalits. But the reactionaries among the Dalits didn't want to be in the mainstream. Their feeling was that, to break communal feelings, you have to be communal yourself. And those were the people who put me in the minority.'

Then there was his illness. That came in 1981; that was also the year he had published his last book. He had spoken in a cool, open way of his life and failings, while the friend of the house with the thick moustache and the orange or saffron tunic (looking more and more like a religious garment of some kind) had listened and looked down at a point half-way to the floor and shaken his head affirmatively from time to time. And Namdeo spoke now of his illness in the same way. It was as though he was detached from his life, and observing it from a distance. He was no longer looking for praise or approval: he spoke of Mallika's right to publish her critical book as though the other possibility, of anger and suppression, had never entered his head.

He had spoken of his own past violence. But he was calm now: it might, after all, have been something he had inherited from the Hindu culture around him.

'What does Ambedkar mean to the Dalits?'

'There was a time when we were treated like animals. Now we live like human beings. It's all because of Ambedkar.'

So, just as greater meaning could be read into the house with the eggshell lilac walls and the white-painted rattan chairs, so a greater understanding became possible of the long, patient line of dark men and women on one side of the road on the morning I had arrived: not just the poor of India, but an expression of the old internal cruelty of that poverty: people at the bottom, full of emotion, with no politics at that moment, just rejecting rejection.

## 2

# THE SECRETARY'S TALE
## Glimpses of the Indian Century

NIKHIL SAID ONE day, 'I know a man here called Rajan. He is the private secretary of an influential politician and businessman. He says he met you in Calcutta in 1962.'

I couldn't remember, and I still didn't remember even when Nikhil took me one afternoon to Rajan's office. Rajan was a small, sturdy man of the South with a square, dark face. His office – or the suite of which it formed part – was one of the most spacious and stylish offices I had seen in Bombay. It was in the international style, in cool, neutral colours, and it was beautifully air-conditioned. Rajan was clearly a man of authority in that office. He wore a fawn-coloured, short-sleeved Mao outfit, which might also have passed as a version of Indian formal clothes, or might simply have been a 'safari' suit.

He said, 'You came to Calcutta in 1962, during or just after the China war. You were with some film people. In those days I myself took a great interest in films and the arts – it was the most hopeful period of my life. Someone from the Film Society at the end of one evening introduced me to you. My duty was to take you back to the drug-company guest house where you were staying.'

The painful war in the background, the mingled smoke and autumnal mist of Calcutta, the small, ceiling-lit rooms of the Film Society, full of old office furniture: one or two moments of the vanished evening began to come back, but they were the merest pictures, hard to hold on to. And nothing remained of the end of the evening.

'I was twenty-two,' Rajan said. 'I was working in an advertising agency. I was a kind of clerk. My salary was 315 rupees a month. I was tipped to be an assistant account executive, but that wasn't to be.' Three hundred and fifteen rupees, £24, a month.

'When did you leave Calcutta?'

'It's a long story,' Rajan said.

And later that afternoon – while we sat outside the club house in Brabourne Stadium, the old international cricket ground of Bombay, and had tea, and watched the young cricketers practising at the nets (at the other end of the ground: the high, scaffolded back of the big stage built for the Russian ice show, part of the visiting Festival of Russia) – and on another day, in a hotel room not far from his office, beginning after his office work, and talking on until late in the evening, Rajan told me his story.

'I was born in Calcutta in 1940. Our family came from the South, from what in British times was known as the province of Madras and today is the state of Tamil Nadu. My grandfather used to be some kind of petty official in one of the law courts near the town of Tanjore. He was respected by people for his honesty and courage. Courage in the sense that if something wrong happened, or if someone asked him to do something his heart wouldn't let him do, he would turn violent or resist it in any form he thought fit.

'A Britisher was above him. He wanted my grandfather to be a witness in a lawsuit and say what was not true. I know only that it ended up in a kind of fracas, and my grandfather took off his footwear and hit the Britisher. He realized that after that life would be difficult for him in Tanjore. He decided to migrate to the North with his only son, who was a student at that time. This would have been early in the century, between 1900 and 1905. He chose to move to Calcutta, which was the British headquarters. He could make a living there and have some kind of life.

'In Calcutta he stayed with some friend or distant relation till he found his feet. He got his son to learn stenography. South Indians, brahmins especially, had a better grasp of English because they were more exposed to it, and they would get jobs as secretary, stenographer, or even typist. These were probably the most widely followed professions for the South Indian or Tamil brahmins in British times – and this is something that has changed only in very recent years. Otherwise, as a class, South Indian brahmins worked as teachers or as priests or as petty clerks. Or, if they were lucky enough, they would take up a job in one of the government departments. These were the days when a 10-rupee-a-month government job was a most prized thing – it was the ultimate aspiration of the bulk of the Tamil brahmins who had done some schooling. And quite a few of them migrated to the North, to the big cities, Bombay, Calcutta, Delhi.

'After he settled, my grandfather lived in Howrah, on the other side of the river from Calcutta city. It was one of those typical Calcutta residential houses – a *pucca* house, a proper house, not *kaccha,* something unfinished or improvised, and it was in a respectable middle-class locality. These places could be rented. It was a locality where there were other people from the South who had similarly migrated, and it gave them some security to live among their own kind. There was no ill-feeling at that time towards South Indians in Calcutta – those times were different. In fact, South Indians were widely respected by the Bengalis. It's quite different today. Since the 1960s South Indians in Calcutta feel they don't belong, in spite of their having been there for many decades. Which is perhaps one reason why I left Calcutta and moved to Bombay – but that was many years later.

'My father became a stenographer when he was seventeen or eighteen. This would have been about 1909, and he would probably have worked in one of the British companies. He was a capable stenographer, and he told me he had twice won the 50-rupee government prize for speed in English shorthand and typing. He continued to live in Howrah, in my grandfather's dwelling, which was a portion of a residential house. In Calcutta there were no such things as flats or apartments or tenements. There were just parts of houses – with the landlord occupying a part of the house, and renting out the rest with little adjustments here and there.

'In a few years both my grandfather and grandmother passed away, not leaving much by way of money or property. But my father moved to better jobs over the years. A stage came, in the decade between 1915 and 1925, when he was quite well paid. He had enough money not only to look after his family more than comfortably, but also to acquire some status symbols, like horses and phaetons. He had a few Arab horses driven by Muslim coachmen. Why Muslim? In those days they were the most widely available for those jobs. In those days, for certain trusted jobs, Hindus wouldn't mind having Muslims around them.

'I myself don't have any memory of this period of my father's life. These are all versions narrated to me by my eldest sister, without me asking for it. And narrated also by people who used to know my father very closely. Some of them would come out with remarks like: "Rarely have South Indians lived in Calcutta in such status or style as your father did." When I was a kid, when I was thirteen, fourteen, fifteen, when I was at school, I heard this when I ran into them at some social gathering. There would be talk then of someone doing well in life, or of someone having failed, and there would be talk of my father's past glory. When I heard these stories I felt a mixture of both pride and sadness.

'My father, during this time of well-being, took to the typical British style of dressing – complete with top hat, the suit, the waistcoat, double-toned shoes, the tie. And he also spent his leisure hours playing tennis. He started a tennis club close to his house. As a South Indian, his living expenses were meagre. All South Indian or Tamil brahmins were vegetarians without exception in those days, of course. So 200 rupees a month was quite a sizeable salary. An average family could make do with 30 or 40 rupees.

'He was a deeply religious man, as most of the South Indian brahmins were. Apart from tennis, the only thing on which he would spend his time were his pujas and *bhajans,* devotional songs. He was quite recognized for his singing of bhajans. He became a leader of the community in the locality. With this result: he kept new migrants from the South, young men coming in search of a livelihood, in his house. He fed them and clothed them and trained them in shorthand and typing. There was almost a regular stenography class in our house. And he helped them into jobs with British firms.

'My father used to respect the British. His ability to get along with the British people, and his love for the English language itself, probably did not make him look at them only as some kind of people to be hated. He never had a bent for politics of any kind.

'My father got married three times. He lost his first wife, and then he married a second time, so that his second wife could look after his first two children. When his second wife died, leaving in turn two or three children, he was forced by his relations to marry a third time. In those days such marriages were not difficult. Despite their impecunious situation, the Tamil brahmins were invariably good breeders. They would be happy to give away their daughters to anyone who wanted to marry them, so long as they were sure of the basics – that the man belonged to the same community, and the man was capable of supporting his wife and family.

'In 1935, when my father married for the third time, he was forty-three. His third wife, my mother, was eighteen. There was a child in 1937, a boy, but he barely lived six months, largely because of my mother's poor health. I was born in 1940.

'By this time my father had married off his first two daughters, and he had one more daughter to marry off. He also had a son from his second marriage still going to school. These were the uncertain war years. My father at that time was a godown or warehouse keeper. It was a responsible job – most of the items in the godown were imported. The godown was owned by the Japanese firm of Mitsui. My father had taken this job with the Japanese in

1936, after he had married my mother. And he continued with it until, with the war, these Japanese operations in India were closed down. When this happened, my father moved to the newly created government department of the DGMP, the Directorate-General of Munitions and Production.

'When the war ended, my father gave up this job. About this time Mahatma Gandhi's Independence movement was taking on more serious proportions, and the Muslims too were becoming agitated. In 1946 there were very bad Hindu-Muslim riots in Calcutta.

'But before this, my mother had fallen seriously ill. When my mother was close to death, she asked my elder stepsister – who had married a former army man – to bring me up. So when my stepsister and her husband left Calcutta, I went with them. I was six. My mother died a month later.

'Almost at the same time the big Hindu-Muslim riots took place in Calcutta. In the riots, the house in which we had been living was burned down. We had left Howrah long before and had moved to the city proper. When my father lost his job with the DGMP at the end of the war, we had moved to a single-room tenement in a large building. This was the building that was set on fire during the riots and burned down – with the room where my mother had died, and where we had stored almost everything that had belonged to us.

'My father was forced during the riot to get into a jeep and leave everything behind, paying all that he had, several thousand rupees, to save himself, paying that to the people who transported him. They dumped him and others like him in Howrah railway station, leaving them to take trains to their chosen destinations away from the city.

'I was with my sister and her husband far away, where my sister's husband was working as a food supply inspector for the state government. He had been discharged from the army, Auchinleck's army, in 1945. He had been one of the Viceroy's Commissoned Officers, as they were called, and when he left the army he had the rank of *jemadar.* These people, the VCOs, had been drafted into the army before the war, at a time when the British felt they would soon be facing a war situation. As a kid I used to admire him. I used to look forward to seeing him. In my eyes he was some kind of a hero. He was always well turned out. He had a lot of gifts for us – chocolates, canteen supplies. The only thing I didn't like about him was the smoking.

'I realized what was happening to my father in Calcutta. I used to see the photographs in the papers, and people talked about the horrors. This sequence – of my having seen my mother dying slowly over many months in one room, with my aged father nursing her; and then my being handed over to my sister's charge, and moving with her and husband to an altogether new place, on the other side of India, where people spoke another language, Marathi, which I couldn't understand – this sequence put me into a spell of utter gloom and depression.

'I look at it as depression now. At the time what I did was just sit outside the house, on the steps, just crouching, leaning my head on my arms, sitting all by myself on the steps outside my stepsister's house. I spent hours like that, confused, not knowing what to think.

'Suddenly one morning my father landed, and I suppose he restored me to a certain amount of life. Then he left again, promising to take me away, back with him, after things settled down. This was just before Independence.

'My brother-in-law started playing truant from his job. He would leave us, and go away for weeks on end, and not tell us where he was going. My sister wrote to my father for help. But my father was yet to settle down himself. He was almost fifty-five at this time. After various moves with my sister and her husband – who kept on changing jobs, and in every job kept going off, as he had been used to doing – my father came and took me and my sister away to Calcutta, where he had at last found a place to stay. He had also found a job, in an import company. This was in January 1948, the month when Mahatma Gandhi died.

'I spent some time with my father. Then my grandmother came and took me back to her village in the South, and put me in a school there. But this village life didn't suit me, and in 1950 I returned to Calcutta, to my father. He began to educate me at home. It was only in 1952, when I was eleven, that I actually entered a school. My father couldn't come with me. So I went to the school myself and got myself admitted after a test, in Class 8.

'My father was teaching me mainly English. He didn't attach much importance to the other subjects. Because of his love for the English language, and because he was now aged, he would get me to read out the editorials and leading articles from the *Statesman,* although often I didn't follow what I was reading. He would ask me to underline the difficult words and phrases, and leave me to write down the meanings as my home work for the afternoon.

'My father's income had gone down, and the place where we were living was in a locality where the rents were low. The locality had a sprinkling of leftover Britishers in the mansions around us, a sizable number of Muslims, and an equally large number of Anglo-Indians and Christians. The whole family – there were six of us now: my father, my stepbrother, my stepsister and her two children, and myself – had one very large room. About 20 feet by 16 feet or 18 feet. We had to share the common tap and toilet.

'There were few South Indians in that locality. The family didn't quite fit in. So my father decided to shift over to a place where mixing would be more easy, and my school would be closer. I had joined a South Indian school.

'I studied there for three years. I had problems every year at exam times with various minor ailments, and it was really only my general good performance that saw me through from one class to the other.

'We had moved to a three-room flat. My brother had started earning by then.

'I completed school in March 1955. My father passed away two months later, in a street accident very close to our house. My father was an early riser. He had gone to the market to buy flowers for the morning puja; and, as he was returning, a motorcycle on the wrong side of the road, with three people on it, dashed against him, and he fell unconscious. We found him in a pool of blood, with the vegetables and the flowers he had purchased strewn all over.

'We took him to the hospital by taxi, together with one of the men from the motorbike, the other two having vanished. This man wasn't injured. He was only pretending; and when he saw it was only my brother and me holding our father, he opened the taxi door at a street corner, and ran away. My father stayed in the hospital for three days. Three painful days. He never regained consciousness. He passed away.

'The whole family now had to live on my brother's 150-rupees income, £14 a month. He was working as a secretary to a British factory-manager, the factory being located in one of the suburbs. So we had to leave the three-roomed flat. We moved to a smaller place near to my brother's factory.

'I couldn't think in terms of going on to a college. I didn't want to be a burden on my brother. And I wanted to be on my own in any case. So I decided to learn the most obvious thing – typing, to begin with. There was a typing school not far off from our new place. The fees were four rupees a month. My brother paid in the beginning, but then I was able to earn some money to pay the fees myself. I did odd typing jobs at the institute. I was on the lookout then for any kind of employment, but things were not easy. Often I used to walk 10 or 12 miles to look up a friend, in the hope of finding a job through his help. I was about sixteen at this time.'

Rajan, though sturdy, was a short man. I wondered what his physical condition was like at the time he was talking about.

I asked him, 'Did you feel strong or weak?'

'I didn't feel physically energetic enough all the time. But what kept me going was the determination to be on my own. I'll tell you something I did one day. I even approached a Britisher in my brother's factory. He said, "You're too young. You should be at school." Another person I approached said, "But you haven't even grown a moush." A moustache.

'I suffered spells of gloom and melancholia. It was almost what I felt when I used to sit on the steps of my sister's house. I often even thought of ending my life. There were the suburban trains. And there was always the Hooghly River. But the counsel of a close friend of mine changed my mind.

'I had no adolescence. I stepped directly from childhood into adulthood. And I felt undernourished. Our food had gone down after my father's death, because my brother had to feed so many mouths on his meagre income. An added dimension to my none too happy life at this time was my relationship with my stepbrother, who was supporting us all. We could never get along. He was almost nine years senior to me, and he would always beat me up badly. It was on one of those occasions, when he had beaten me up badly, that I was driven to thinking in terms of ending my life.

'Things brightened up the next year, 1957, when I ran into a friend who said he could fix me up in a job in a Marwari concern. The Marwaris were taking over from the British in Calcutta, and were then the principal business people in the city – and they continue to be so. They were taking over the jute mills, the tea gardens, the coalmines, etc.

'I took a job with one of those family concerns as a typist. The salary was to be 90 rupees a month, seven pounds. I was just about able to get myself a second pair of trousers and a shirt. It was a long journey to the office and a long journey back. In that month I spent no more than 10 rupees on myself, and I handed over the rest of what I earned to my brother as my contribution to the family expenses. I travelled on the second-class train. I didn't go to a movie. I didn't spend more than two annas, one-eighth of a rupee, a penny, on my lunch.

'A month after I joined, I was summoned by one of the directors. I had put the carbon in the wrong way when I was typing out a statement. I was sacked. Luckily, within seven days, I ran into another friend – we were on the same tram – and he took me to another employer. This was also a Marwari. He interviewed me in his house. His company was a newspaper company, which is today India's largest.

'I was to work in their newly opened advertising department. I typed out advertising reports. I got 125 rupees. So I was doing slightly better. I contributed a full 100 rupees to the family, and spent 25 rupees on myself, including the tuition fees at an evening college I had just joined, doing Intermediate Commerce.

'We could now afford to shift back to the old locality in South Calcutta. We lived in a flat shared between two families. My relations with my brother continued as before. But he had stopped beating me, after I had one day returned a slap he had given me.

'I stayed for a year with the newspaper group. Then I left and went to Lipton's for a salary of 10 rupees a day. The manager there recommended me to his own advertising agency, and for six years, from 1958 to 1964, I worked with that advertising agency. That was when I met you. It was a good time for me. I was a member of the British Council. My love for the English language drew me to people proficient in the English language – journalists, film-makers, copywriters, and advertising people generally.

'I liked the advertising profession. It was different. It made me think. It was not drudgery. My other jobs had been drudgery. And I particularly liked the people in the profession – the artists, the account executives, the printers, the copywriters. I joined the advertising agency on 270 rupees. The senior director liked my English, and I worked for him. He liked the interest I showed in the work. He promoted me to assist him in various campaigns. Soon I was tipped to be an assistant account executive. I got on with other people in the firm as well, because I was the youngest of the lot, and could converse fluently in their language, Bengali. Bengalis appreciate that. I got an annual increment of 15 rupees. In 1964 I was getting 330 rupees. I was promised promotion, to be an assistant account executive. And finally, when it didn't come, I resigned in a huff.

'I became an assistant to an advertising and short-film producer who had taken a liking to me. I picked up the basics of filmmaking. He paid me 350 rupees. I even shot certain sequences on my own. But the Pakistani war of 1965 put an end to that kind of film-making company, and I had to find another job. During this time I met important people in the Calcutta creative world. That made me very happy. I always thought I had a creative urge in me, which hadn't found expression because I hadn't had a settled life and a proper foundation.

'Somebody told me I should go to England. It was because of that I took a job with Air India, for the free flight to England. At the end of my first year I went to England for a visit. But I had to return, because of that recurring problem in the family about my stepsister and her husband. At the end of my second year with Air India I made a trip to the United States.

'The Air India salary was 350 rupees. It was too low – the rupee had been devalued in 1967. I even had to do a part-time job in the evening. At last, I answered an advertisement from a manufacturing company. On the strength of my experience I was given a job in the management cadre, for thrice the Air India salary. The bosses soon promoted me and put me in charge of a purchasing department.

'So, after all these years, I found myself on the other side. But I couldn't identify myself completely with the management, because I knew too well what life was like for others. But then the political situation in Bengal was becoming turbulent. Labour was unruly. The leftists had more or less gained control of the unions and the state. And the physical conditions in the city also started deteriorating. More and more firms were coming under the control of the Marwari capitalists. And then there was the oil crisis of 1973. I was in charge of procurement of oil for the factory. I really faced a rough time. Plus the power shortages, the difficult transport, and the labour militancy I had to put up with as part of the management staff. You might say I had found the right kind of job, but at the wrong time. I hated going to work in the mornings.

'At the end of 1973 I quit – the problems in the job, the conditions of life in Calcutta. These things were compelling me to move out of Calcutta. I could only think of Bombay as the alternative, because my occasional trips to that city earlier – because of my job with Air India – had impressed me with its cosmopolitanism and its opportunities.

'So, without having a job in my hand, I moved to Bombay with my little savings. In Bombay I stayed with a relative almost my own age who was running a photographic studio in a distant suburb. He had no room. But I used to live in the studio, sharing the common toilet with other tenants in the building, and an open space for my bath. We used to store water for our photographic needs, and out of this I used to bathe.

'And I slept in a kind of loft that I specially made for myself. It was almost twice or thrice the size of an average coffin. It was just below the roof, and above the false ceiling of the front portion of the shop. I would climb into it by using the window bars as steps, and then I would slide myself into the small opening. I was comfortable. The air would come through the opening around the roller shutter. Often I would find this little loft to be the most convenient place for doing my reading and occasional writing – of letters, not articles.

'I was earning a meagre sum, having started working in the studio. I would send most of this back to my people in Calcutta, because the four children of my sister were growing, and my step-brother now had his own family to look after.

'Initially I thought I would be able to build up the photography business with my relative, as I knew a little bit of photography as an amateur. But after a while, my savings having dried up, my relation turned out to be none too helpful. When I needed money he wouldn't give it, and when I asked for the money I had already spent on the studio he wouldn't return it.

'So it was a strained relationship, although, helplessly, I continued to live there, sleeping and reading in my cubby hole, because accommodation of any kind was one real problem in Bombay. As the situation worsened, I decided to give up the idea of any photography business and having to depend on my relation.

'As a first step, I put an ad in the classified pages of the *Times of India*. That must have cost me about 14 or 15 rupees – the paper charged concessional rates for job-seekers. I got 40 replies.

'The advertisement I wrote read something like this: "South Indian secretary with over 10 years' experience, with impeccable English, seeks interesting position in advertising, public relations, travel, etc." I shortlisted the replies by choosing not to respond to companies located in the suburbs on the Central Railway, especially factories. The travelling conditions there were difficult and would involve a change of trains half-way from where I was living with my relation – that was an hour and a half away on the Western Railway line.

'I decided to attend only four interviews, all of which were to take place around the Victoria Terminal in Churchgate, and were in offices rather than factories or workshops. Nothing happened the first day. I didn't come to accept the jobs for varying reasons – salary, office atmosphere, and the interviewer himself. In fact, I told off one of the interviewers when he asked a very absurd question. "Why did you leave Calcutta after all these years? Those beautiful women there – you should have stayed at least for the *rasgolla*-like women there.' I thought that was too degrading to women. Probably he found I was more than he required. It was a trading company, and he was one of those uncouth characters who had suddenly come into money.

'The four interviews I had arranged were to last two days. Two a day. At the end of the first day I was somewhat despondent. I didn't want to return to Calcutta. On the other hand, I didn't want to make my life more miserable by being without much money and continuing to live with my relation. So I decided that if I didn't get a job the next day, I would have to return to Calcutta, from where my sister had been persistently writing to me.

'The following day I came all the way from the photographic studio to Churchgate. On arrival at Churchgate station I went to Satkar Restaurant opposite the station. The board said: "Tea and Snack Bar". I ordered myself an idli and a coffee – idli was about 60 paise and coffee was 40 paise – because I thought that was all I could afford, with my money touching the bottom.

'As I was finishing my coffee, I looked through the papers, the letters from the firms I had shortlisted, to see who were the people I still had to look up. And there I found this call from a man who described himself simply as "Municipal Councillor". His address was on "A" Road. I asked the waiter where "A" Road was. He said, "You are sitting on the very same road." I found that the address the municipal councillor had given was just a stone's throw away.

'I made for it, and discovered it was an office within a residence. After I had waited for a while, a gentleman came in. This was my first sight of the man with whom I was to work for the next 14 years. He was a tall man – no, average, five foot seven, five foot eight. Very fair, not heavily built. He looked well groomed, well dressed.

'He took me inside his office, and after a very brief conversation, 15 minutes, he straight away asked me to join him. Although I was readily impressed by the man, by his speed and quick decision, I did not accept his offer straight away, as I had to ponder over the salary offer he had made, which was 900 rupees. But he made no secret of his keenness to engage me. It looked almost as though he had guessed my situation, decided how much I should get, and made me an offer. To this day I don't know whether he knows much about me, my background, my life away from the office.

'He asked me to ring him back as soon as I had made up my mind, and he hoped he wouldn't have to wait too long, because he had made up *his* mind that I was the kind of man he was looking for. I went back to the restaurant – it was a different waiter – and, after weighing the situation, had very nearly come to the conclusion that a job in hand was better than none. I phoned him up the next day, and joined him the Monday following.

'When I got this job, there was an effort on the part of my relation in the photographic studio to patch up our relationship. But I didn't want it. I stayed for three months after that in the cubby hole in the studio. Then I continued to move from place to place as a paying guest with various families – with problems of their own, of all kinds. I had a suitcase of clothes and another suitcase of books and knick-knacks. Two suitcases of possessions – that was all I had.

'In my work for my employer I began to know people of importance. I enjoyed that. He was a civic leader and I could see that he was an ambitious man. I thought I would have opportunities of rising with him. And, indeed, he has risen in all directions. He is more famous and powerful and wealthy now than when I first went to work for him.

'People who deal with me in my office might say that I have risen with him. But I feel it hasn't been exactly in the manner I had hoped for. For a long time, while I worked here, my nomadic life as a paying guest continued, with my two suitcases, until I met a very kindly family – very hard to think of in a place like Bombay – who were generous enough to offer me a room all to myself, although in an old building. This was in 1980. I was forty years old. At that age, for the first time in my life, I had a room of my own. This was a dream in a place like Bombay, where people have to sleep on the pavement and in drainpipes – and it was perhaps the best thing to have happened to me.

'Until three years ago I lived on this charity, in a single room in that old house, with a common privy shared by 40 people. I couldn't think of marriage then. My salary, though very good by Bombay standards, couldn't have bought me a dwelling of any kind. But I've since been lucky, despite the odds, to acquire a flat or apartment of my own.

'And then a friend of mine felt I should settle down. This friend knew that I had seen my responsibilities to my sister's family through. He put an ad on my behalf in the matrimonial pages of the paper. It's the classified ad which has brought me things, and now again the ad came into my life and changed the course of events for me.

'Among the people who responded to the advertisement my friend had inserted for me was my prospective father-in-law. I had given my background and age in the ad. I had hidden nothing. I said I wanted a lady who would look forward to a simple life. I got about 90 replies, perhaps 100. They were from various parts of India. I think I got so many replies because I had said in the advertisement: "Caste, community, widows, divorcees, no bar." I wanted a lady, though, who was already in Bombay, because that would settle many problems. Bombay life is so hard – there are language problems for people not knowing Hindi – and transport is hard, and generally the style of life is hard here. It isn't an easy thing to get acclimatized to.

'In about half an hour with my prospective father-in-law he was able to understand my basic character. The meeting took place in the coffee shop of the Ritz Hotel. He had come over to my office, but I had to keep him there for a couple of hours, this seventy-year-old man, because I wasn't free when he came. He is a Keralite, but a brahmin. An average-sized man, bald, quiet-spoken, with the real stamp of patience on his face and in his demeanour. He was a retired electrical engineer in charge of purchase for a public-sector undertaking – part of industrializing India. He had been all over the country, and his children were broadminded.

'About a week after this meeting I went to their house at about 10.30 at night, after a full day's work. She was in bed. Her father woke her up. I spoke to her. She had been working for a nationalized bank for 10 years, took interest in yoga, and was not given to speaking much. She was average in her looks. She wasn't fat, but because of her height she didn't look lean. She was about four foot ten. She wore specs.

'And after conversing more or less through her father and her mother, I felt I should meet her again and let her speak her own mind in a private talk, without the parents. After three days I met her once again in her cousin's place. The cousin appreciated this attitude of mine, and made all appropriate arrangements, for privacy, etc. Over a cup of coffee we talked for a little over half an hour – she had just come back from her office in the bank. She wasn't a great dresser. I had the impression she didn't worry much about her attire.

'After three days I telephoned her at her office, and this time we met in a restaurant. And by and large we agreed that we should get married. We got married in about 40 days. I wanted a civil marriage – no dowry, no give, no take; no crowding around with relations and friends; no party, no feasts, no gifts. But they didn't want a civil marriage. So I called my cousin to perform the rites. I was totally without religion myself; I had never made a special effort to understand Hindu theology or principles.

'I am happy at last in having a purpose in life, now that I have a family of my own. I've put an end to my otherwise unsettled life. Marriage came to me when I was forty-five. My wife was thirty-nine. We both had to wait a long time for this mercy. And God has blessed us with this added happiness that – at this late stage – we have had a child.

'I am still left with the feeling that I might have risen much higher, given a little more understanding and sympathy. Or perhaps in another country. What keeps haunting me all the time is the feeling that I am doomed to rise no more than I have risen, Even in this job I have been like a ship's ladder. The sea rises, the ship rises, and the ladder rises with it. But the ladder cannot rise on its own. I cannot be independent of my employer and rise in life.

'And yet I have, positively, a sense of fulfilment. When my father died, we were almost penniless, despite our earlier well-being. My sister brought me up early. And when my brother-in-law deserted her, it became my turn to take care of her and rear her children. I was able to do it. Today they are all well placed. I look upon them as symbols of my achievement.

'And yet, too, I thought I would be some kind of creative person – like the persons I knew in Calcutta, when I first met you in 1962. But that kind of life and companionship has always eluded me. I started off as a secretary, and am still a secretary, and shall probably end as a secretary. I haven't risen beyond what my father and grandfather could rise to, at the beginning of the century. The only consolation is that, even as a secretary, I am not as badly off as most other secretaries are. And perhaps, even, I no longer believe I am just a secretary.'

## 3

# BREAKING OUT

As soon as I got to the airport at Santa Cruz, the airport in Bombay for internal Indian flights, I felt like a refugee. There was a crowd at the entrance; and criminally inclined young men of the neighbourhood were trying to extort money from passengers for moving luggage a few feet from taxis to the doorway.

Policemen were guarding the doorway against the young men, but they seemed not to be offering protection to people outside, even when they were almost at the door; and the young men, understanding this, ran two or three at a time to people just arriving, fell shouting on suitcases and bags, and tried to create an unbalancing atmosphere of frenzy. They were small and thin, these young criminals of the neighbourhood, and they were in tight milk-chocolate-coloured trousers of some synthetic fabric that showed up their frailty in hip and thigh. Their faces were small and bony, and their necks looked as though they might easily snap. Their wretchedness of physique didn't make them less threatening: they called up the very thin, fawning-sinister figures of some of the Cruikshank illustrations for Dickens.

Crowd and noise and threat and urgency outside, taxis coming and going in the mid-afternoon sun. Crowd inside as well, and noise, but it was a different kind of noise: it was more stable: it was the noise of people going nowhere. There was only one internal airline in India; it was a state airline, and it was in a mess. It was said by various spokesmen that the flights of this airline had to be late because many of them originated in Delhi, and there was fog in Delhi on many mornings. There were other problems. The airline had never had enough aircraft, and in the last few weeks a number of aircraft had been withdrawn for one reason and another. Services were now in chaos. But air travel remained a necessary badge and privilege for important people, scientists and administrators and business executives; and for weeks a fair portion of the country's most eminent men and women was, at any given moment, becalmed in the country's airports, as if by an act of enchantment. Items in the newspapers regularly told of depleted conferences on important subjects in this town and that town. Yet the demand for seats, especially at this holiday season, was greater than ever, and I had been able to get a ticket for this flight to Goa only through the intercession of an influential friend.

In the airport hall the information screens flashed news of ever more flights delayed or abandoned. It was as though there had been some national emergency or disaster. The many grey-and-white screens gave constant, silent electronic jumps, delivering the bad news above the heads of the crowd, who were going nowhere but were not still, were in constant, very slow movement. My own flight to Goa had been delayed for five hours already. Now the screens, whenever (as in a lottery) the number of the Goa flight came up, promised a further delay of four hours. But some people had been waiting in the hall all that day.

From time to time there were the sounds of aircraft taking off. They were tormenting sounds: the planes taking off were the actual planes people were waiting to board, but at that moment different flight numbers were attached to them, and they were starting on roundabout journeys, with many stops, before coming back to Santa Cruz.

My own flight to Goa would be in a plane that was coming from an unlikely town. This was told me by an athletic-looking man from Delhi, who went five times a year to Goa on business and knew the ways of the airline. This was all the information I had to hold on to; since after a certain time of night there appeared to be no airline officials anywhere, not even the young girls at the quaintly named Facilitation Desk. The advice of the man from Delhi was to watch out for the announced arrival time of the flight from the unlikely town he had told me about. If I added an hour's turn-around time to that, I would have the time of my flight to Goa.

I wasn't to give up hope, the man from Delhi said. He knew for sure that the flight wasn't abandoned. He had a cousin in the catering business – or he might have said that his in-laws did some of the catering for the airline – and he knew that his cousin or his in-laws had distinctly received orders for a plane-load of food-boxes for the Goa flight that day. This meant, he said, that the flight might even leave before midnight. This was the way of privilege in India: to know someone who knew someone who had a connection, even a tangential one, with an important organization.

All this while – the bright light of mid-afternoon giving way to late-afternoon smokiness, to dusk, to undeniable night, to a dim fluorescent evenness in the hall – an elderly American lady had been standing next to the barrow or cart with her luggage. She wasn't relaxed; she didn't lean on the cart; her aged body was rigid as if with the fear of theft and the need to protect her goods. Her eyes were now blank, as though, not through tantric excess or meditation (which she might even have come to dabble in), but only by waiting in an Indian airport hall, she had arrived at the inner calm the famous gurus had the secret of. She had been waiting since morning and would have to wait several hours more. She was now mentally so far away that even when the pretty, plump Indian Muslim woman (herself waiting since the previous evening) got up from her chair and offered it to her, it was some time before the American lady understood she was being spoken to. When she understood that she was being asked to separate herself from her cart, her old lady's face filled with alarm, and, speaking no word, she stood more rigidly in a protective posture beside her goods.

She was standing not far from the check-in counter. The air-conditioning in that corner was very cold. I hadn't felt it at first. But then I was glad I had a thickish jacket. Even with that jacket I began to feel stiff after a few hours. I gave up the chair I hadn't wanted to leave, and I joined the very slow refugee movement in the hall. I discovered a bookshop. I bought two Indian paperbacks, a book of cartoons by the cartoonist Laxman, and *Khushwant Singh's Book of Jokes,* and discovered in five minutes (what I might have guessed) that humorous books require a full life and a contented mind; that where empty time stretches on without limit, the short joke, requiring only a few seconds' attention, can be wearisome to the spirit, and can make a bad situation worse. Better simply to endure.

There was a restaurant. It was on an upper floor. It was comfortingly warm after the frigid conditions near the check-in counter. It took about half an hour, a plateful of cashew nuts I didn't need, and a pot of tea I didn't need, for me to realize that the musty, tainted smell of the restaurant was more than the smell of warmth, was the smell of an enclosed and airless room; that the air-conditioning there had broken down.

Cold downstairs, hot and dusty and choking upstairs. Outside, in the night, was the fresher, un-conditioned air; but to get at that somebody would have had to break the sealed glass.

And just as, according to some people, you can empty your mind in a meditation chamber by focussing on a single flame, so – among the becalmed travellers moving about in slow whorls in the aqueous fluorescent light, people increasingly like people in an allegory, darkly reflected in the glass that sealed them in, conversation now fled from most of them – so, thinking only of my flight number, I found that with every passing quarter of an hour I was taken more and more out of myself. I was taken far away from the man I had been earlier that day, and was becoming more like that American lady I had seen (when I had been more in command of myself), standing rigid beside her goods on a barrow:

Indian architecture and air travel giving me, as it had given her, the Hindu idea of the illusion of things.

There was no escape. With every passing hour, the possibility of a return to the hotel in Bombay (would there be room?), and the hiring of a car for the 12- or 14-hour drive to Goa (where a hotel booking had to be taken up, or lost forever), became less and less a practical proposition. So between heat and cold I moved, withdrawn, living feebly on rumour.

But the man from Delhi was right. There was a plane to Goa; and when – time having ceased to matter – we swarmed and bumped aboard, there were the food-boxes of the Delhi man's story, the grey cardboard boxes (with white-bread sandwiches and a pastry of some kind and an apple from the North) that his friends or relations had prepared for the airline for that day's Goa flight. The plane felt over-used. The airline in-flight magazine was dog-eared. A piece of the overhead trim had shaken loose; every time the stewardess tapped it back in, it quivered out again. But there was Goa at the end of the very short flight. And it was interesting, getting out into the clean night air, at last, to see the name of the place spelt out in the Hindi Devanagari characters: *Go-wa*.

It was now well past midnight. We got into a cramped tourist bus. There was very little space between the seats, and the glass was tinted: it was like a continuation of the constraints of Santa Cruz. After some time we came to the Mandovi River. And there, literally, was a break in the journey. There was no bridge over the Mandovi River. There had been a bridge, a new one, until quite recently. But after standing for 10 years or so, the bridge had fallen down one day, and the Mandovi was now crossed by ferries, rough contraptions that looked as old as the century, but had been built only after the bridge had fallen down. Luggage was manhandled down from the roof of the bus on to Indian earth and then into the ferry, and then, at the other bank, out of the ferry and up on to the roof of a second bus: technology giving way (furtively, in the Indian night) to the India of many feeble hands doing simple small tasks.

And when, two days or so later, I saw the collapsed bridge in daylight, only the mighty piers standing, the linking pieces not there, it seemed to sum up the experience of that long day and night, the fracture in reality.

Nikhil, talking to me one day in Bombay of his religious faith, which was profound, had told me of his devotion, especially in times of crisis, to two figures: Sai Baba (not the current figure with the Afro hairstyle, but the original turn-of-the-century teacher), and the Image of the Infant Jesus.

Nikhil came of a Hindu family, and his choice of Jesus – which at first was what I thought he meant – seemed unusual. But Nikhil had a particular image in mind, and he told me of the reason for his faith. He had once had some worrying legal problem in connection with his work. In this anxiety he had come across a leaflet about the Image of the Infant Jesus. The leaflet recommended that in times of special need prayers should be offered up to the Infant Jesus every nine hours. This was what Nikhil had begun to do. It meant getting up at a difficult time every two or three days, but it also meant that his days were built around the act of prayer. Nikhil lived with this devotion to the Image of the Infant Jesus over many weeks, and at last the legal problem that had been worrying him disappeared. Nikhil remained grateful. It was irrational, he said; he knew that; but he couldn't help it.

Nikhil must have told me about the whereabouts of this image, but I hadn't taken it in. At the hotel in Goa one morning I saw, at the entrance, a new, well-cared-for minibus with the words INFANT JESUS painted above the windscreen. I asked the driver about it. He pointed to a cream-coloured plastic figure – like a toy from a corn-flakes box – on his dashboard. The driver was a Christian Goan. He told me that the original image was in a church in Old Goa.

It was a famous image, of tested efficacy. The plastic image on the minibus dashboard was the merest symbol of the real thing.

The church the minibus driver spoke of was, in fact, the famous cathedral of Old Goa, where Saint Francis Xavier was buried.

This cathedral, and the other Portuguese buildings of Old Goa, some way inland on the Mandovi River, were quite staggering in the setting. So far from Europe (six months' sailing even in the 18th century); so bright the light; the white beaches speaking more of the empty islands of the New World (but empty only after they had been 'dispeopled': they would have been populated and busy at the time of the discovery) rather than the crowded villages and towns of old India, with its tangled past. Part of that Indian past was right there, in Old Goa: in the Arch of the Viceroys, which had been created out of an arch of the – barely established – Muslim ruler the Portuguese had dispossessed. Through that arch, it was said, every new viceroy of Goa ceremonially passed when he arrived.

In another old building, now the museum, there was a gallery with portraits of all the viceroys of Goa. The portraits had been done in batches. One portrait was of Vasco da Gama. A fabulous name, but the portrait of him, as of the other viceroys, was clumsy, a kind of poor shop-sign art. The art of the colonisers didn't match their venturesomeness. This deficiency fitted in with what one knew of the brief period of Portuguese vigour; and it perhaps explained why, outside Old Goa, so little remained of Portugal, adding to the unreality of the damp-stained rococo ecclesiastical buildings of Old Goa.

Still, it was the early date of the Portuguese empire in India that continued to astonish. Every day I was reminded of it when – far from Old Goa on the Mandovi, and just with a sight of the remains of great red-stone military fortifications, all circles and straight lines, on a tropical beach – I sat down to eat in the hotel, and saw an old European print of Goa reproduced on the paper place-setting. The engraved legend gave the year of the arrival in India of the fierce and victorious Portuguese viceroy, Albuquerque: 1509. He conquered Goa the next year. Just 18 years after Columbus had discovered the islands of the New World, and before that discovery had proved its worth; nine years before Cortes started on his march to Mexico. In India itself, before the great Mogul emperor Akbar was born.

Haters of idolatry, haters of all that was not the true faith, establishers in Goa of the Inquisition and the burning of heretics, levellers of Hindu temples, the Portuguese had created in Goa something of a New-World emptiness, like the Spaniards in Mexico. They had created in India something not of India, a simplicity, something where the Indian past had been abolished. And after 450 years all they had left behind in this emptiness and simplicity was their religion, their language (without a literature), their names, a Latin-like colonial population, and this cult, from their cathedral, of the Image of the Infant Jesus.

Nearly everything else of Portugal had been swallowed up in the colonial emptiness. There had been a statue of the poet Camoens in the main square of Old Goa – Camoens, the author of the *Lusiads* (1572), the epic of the expansion of Portugal, and the true faith, overseas. But the statue was taken down (and placed in the museum) after Goa had been absorbed into independent India; and a statue of Mahatma Gandhi was put up in that 16th-century Portuguese square.

Camoens knew Goa and East Africa and Malaya and China; he was like Cervantes in Spain, an old adventurer in imperial wars. He was the first great poet of modern Europe to write of India and Indians; and he wrote out of the hard-won knowledge of a decade and a half of 16th-century wandering. There is a wonderful living sense of south-western India in his poem, not only in its account of kings and castes and religion and temples (the great Hindu kingdom of Vijayanagar, destroyed by the Muslims seven years before Camoens published his poem, is felt to be in the background), but also in dozens of smaller things: the Indian ruler, for instance, who receives the just-arrived Vasco da Gama, chews part to the 16th-century Portuguese rhythms of Camoens's verse.

It might have been thought that Goa would have been as proud to claim Camoens as it was proud to claim Saint Francis Xavier.

But the statue had been taken down; and though the hotel place-setting repetitively proclaimed the antiquity of Portuguese Goa, there was no copy of his poem in the hotel bookshop, and no one there even knew his name. India had its own priorities and values. The tourists who came in coaches to the square of Old Goa came less for the architecture (and the statue of Mahatma Gandhi) than for the Image of the Infant Jesus in the cathedral. They bought bundles of wax tapers and lit them in a cloister.

Old Goa was very old. Almost as many years separated it from the present as separated the final Roman defeat of Carthage from the fall of Rome itself. And Portugal (though it lived on in 20th-century Europe) had become the museum here. A new middle-class India had become the tourists. That was an astonishing twist in history. Portugal had arrived in 1498 and triumphed in 1509–10. Just over half a century later the great Hindu empire in the South, the empire of Vijayanagar, was defeated and physically laid waste by a combination of Muslim rulers; almost at the same time, in the North, the Mogul power was entering its time of glory. It might have seemed then that Hindu India, without the new learning and the new tools of Europe, its rulers without the idea of country or nation, without the political ideas that might have helped them to preserve their people from foreign rule – it might have seemed then that Hindu India was on the verge of extinction, something to be divided between Christian Europe and the Muslim world, and all its religious symbols and difficult theology rendered as meaningless as the Aztec gods in Mexico, or the symbolism of Hindu Angkor.

But it hadn't been like that. Through all the twists and turns of history, through all the imperial venturings in this part of the world, which that Portuguese arrival in India portended, and finally through the unlikely British presence in India, a Hindu India had grown again, more complete and unified than any India in the past.

History in Goa was simple. In the long colonial emptiness the pre-Portuguese past had ceased to matter; it was something to be picked up from books; and then the 450 years of Portuguese rule was like a single idea that anyone could carry about with him. To leave Goa, to go south and west along the narrow, winding mountain road into the state of Karnataka, was to enter India and its complicated history again.

Just as Portuguese rule had given a great simplicity to the history of Goa, so British rule gave a direction to later Indian history and made it easier to grasp. Events, at a certain stage, could be seen to be leading up to British rule; and, thereafter, events could be seen leading to the end of that rule. To read of events in India before the coming of the British is like reading of many pieces of unfinished business; it is to read of a condition of flux, of things partly done and then partly undone, matters more properly the subject of annals rather than narrative history, which works best when it deals with great things being built up or pulled down.

Historical names were on that road down through Karnataka. Bijapur was one such name. It was the name of a Muslim kingdom, established almost at the same time as the Portuguese in Goa (Goa had, in fact, been taken away from Bijapur). The name was associated in my mind not with Goa or Old Goa, but with a fine, Persian-influenced 17th-century school of miniature painting: the very name brought the faces and the postures and the special colours and costumes to my mind. But how did Bijapur fit into the history of the region? What were its dates, its boundaries? Who were its rulers and enemies? It was hard to carry all of that in the mind: I would have to look it up in the books, and even then (though I would learn that it had lasted two centuries) I would get no more than the bare bones of dates and rulers. Its achievements, after all, hadn't been that great; there was nothing in its history to catch the mind, as there was in the art (and the architecture, from my reading: a certain kind of dome). And so that name of Bijapur, and the other historical names on the road south, were like random memories in an old man's mind.

There had been too many kingdoms, too many rulers, too many changes of boundaries. The state of Karnataka itself was a new creation, post-British, post-Independence, a linguistic state, answering the new pride, the new sense of self, that the nationalist movement had fostered.

The land was sacred, but it wasn't political history that made it so. Religious myths touched every part of the land outside colonial Goa. Story within story, fable within fable: that was what people saw and felt in their bones. Those were the myths, about gods and the heroes of the epics, that gave antiquity and wonder to the earth people lived on.

All the way south through Karnataka there were buses full of young men strangely dressed, in black tunics and black lower cloths. They looked like young men on a holiday excursion, but the black they wore was unsettling. When I got to Bangalore I learned that the men in black were on a pilgrimage. They were going to a shrine in the southernmost state of Kerala. The shrine honoured Ayappa, a Hindu ruler and saint of days gone by. The pilgrimage was essentially a Hindu affair; but the pilgrims to Ayappa were also required, in an unlikely way, to do honour to Vavar, an Arab and a Muslim, who had been a friend and ally of Ayappa's.

Only men could go on that pilgrimage, and for 40 days they had to live penitentially. No meat, no liquor, no activity conducive purely to pleasure; and they had to stay away from women. The last stage of the pilgrimage was a 25-mile walk up a hill to the shrine of Ayappa. There, on a particular day in January, a divine light appeared. Not everyone who went on the pilgrimage went for the light; most people walked up to the shrine on days when there was no light.

I learned all this from a young man who befriended me in Bangalore. His name was Deviah; he wrote about science for a daily newspaper. He came from a farming family; produce from the family land was still sometimes sent to him in Bangalore by the night bus. Deviah had been on the pilgrimage for the first time eight years before. He had gone when he was feeling low, and was oppressed by thoughts that he had done very little in the five years since he had left college. He thought he had been changed by the pilgrimage – the discipline of the 40 penitential days, the long walk up to the shrine, the companionship on that walk, and seeing the way people had begun to help one another. He also felt he had had professional luck afterwards; and he had gone almost every year since then. Deviah didn't believe in the divine light. He thought it might be only burning camphor, and the work of a human agency; but it didn't lessen his faith. It didn't lessen his wonder at the story of Ayappa.

This was the story Deyiah told.

'Ayappa was a real figure, about 800 years ago. He was born in interesting circumstances. Raja Rajashekhar didn't have children. He and his queen did penance to Shiva and asked for the gift of a son. One day when Raja Rajashekhar was out hunting on the banks of the River Pampa – which in Kerala is as holy as the Ganges in the north: it can wash away your sins – he found a boy child with a bell attached to its neck. The raja began to look for the parents of the child. A *rishi*, a sage, appeared – in fact, the rishi was Lord Shiva himself – and told the raja that the child was meant for him. The raja, the rishi said, was to take the child to the palace and bring him up as his son. "But whose child is he?" Raja Rajashekhar asked. The rishi said, "You will find out on the boy's twelfth birthday."

'So Raja Rajshekhar took the foundling to the palace and looked after him. That palace is still there, by the way. It is not like the maharajas' palaces you see today. It is quite a small house. The raja looked after the child as his own, and it began to be understood that the boy would succeed Raja Rajashekhar when the time came.

'The raja's chief minister didn't like that. During all the years of the raja's childlessness the chief minister had grown to believe that his own son would one day inherit the kingdom. So, from the very start, the chief minister hated Ayappa.

'When Ayappa was ten years old, something unexpected happened. The queen gave birth to a son. But Raja Rajashekhar had grown so attached to Ayappa, the foundling, the gift of the gods, that he made it clear that Ayappa was still to succeed him on the throne.

'The queen and chief minister now began to conspire. Their plan was this. The queen was to pretend to fall ill. She would say she had a headache. The palace doctor – who was also in the conspiracy – would make a show of doing everything he knew. The queen's headache wouldn't go away, and at last the doctor would say, "There is only one thing that can save the queen's life. She must be given the milk of a tigress."

'That was what the queen, the chief minister, and the doctor plotted to do, and that was what they did. Raja Rajashekhar was driven to despair. How could the milk of a tigress be obtained? How could anyone milk a tigress? The queen and the chief minister, however, knew very well what would happen. They knew that Ayappa was valorous, and they knew that, though he was only ten, as soon as Ayappa heard of the queen's need, he would undertake to go out and bring back the milk of a tigress. And that was what Ayappa said he intended to do. Raja Rajashekhar knew it would be suicide for Ayappa to try to milk a tigress, and he forbade the boy to leave the palace. But Ayappa used a trick and got out, deceiving the raja in order to save the queen.'

That was how the first part of the story ended. When Deviah began the second part, he said, 'So far we've been dealing with history. Now we enter the realms of mythology. In order to understand why Ayappa was born, we have to go back 3000 years.'

And, slipping easily down the aeons, we began to travel back to the time of the gods.

Deviah said, 'Ayappa was really the son of Shiva and Vishnu.' They were both male deities, but for the purposes of the story Vishnu had to be considered to be in a female incarnation: Deviah had no trouble with these transformations. So the Ayappa who went out into the forest to get the milk of a tigress was not the mere boy the queen and the chief minister thought. He was the son of two of the gods of the Hindu trinity.

Deviah said, 'When he was wandering in the forest he came across a demon, and he killed the demon.' There was a story attached to this demon. Deviah was quite ready to break off the main narrative and give the inset story. I asked him not to.

He said, 'All right. To cut a long story short, the monster or demon Ayappa killed in the forest was a female monster, and she had been terrorizing the *devas*.' They were the gods – residing and having their councils in the place where gods reside. (Ayappa must have killed the monster by some means not available to the gods. There would have been another story here, and Deviah almost certainly knew it.) When the monster was killed, there was rejoicing among the gods. They, of course, knew what Ayappa's predicament was. 'So,' Deviah said, 'out of gratitude, the gods turned themselves into tigers and tigresses, and Ayappa came back to Raja Rajashekhar's palace riding a tiger. The tiger was believed to be Brahma.' The son of Shiva and Vishnu, riding Brahma: completing the Hindu trinity.

Deviah said, 'This forest expedition of Ayappa's had lasted two years. The queen's headache had long been cured. In fact, she had lost her headache as soon as Ayappa had left the palace to go and milk a tigress. And the day Ayappa returned to Raja Rajashekhar's palace, he was twelve years old.'

The identity of Ayappa – coming back riding a tiger – was now clear, to everyone. It was what the rishi, who was Lord Shiva himself, had prophesied: that on the foundling's twelfth birthday his parentage would be known. And now all enemies, all the conspiring of queen and chief minister, vanished like morning mist, and Ayappa in due course entered into his inheritance.

The wicked chief minister, who had wanted his own son to rule, fell ill with an incurable disease – a real disease. One night Ayappa appeared to him in a dream and told him to go and wash away his sins in the River Pampa. So he did, and was cured; and then, calling Ayappa's name, the chief minister ran all the way to the temple which Ayappa had been divinely guided to build at the top of a hill. He, the chief minister or former chief minister, thus became the first of Ayappa's pilgrims.

What about the Arab in the story? He belonged to the historical Ayappa figure, Deviah said. He would have been a raider or a pirate. He had been defeated by Ayappa, and then he had been an ally. No attempt had been made to get him to give up his religion; when he died, a mosque had been built over his grave. This mosque stood at the start of the 25-mile walk up the hill to the temple of Ayappa, where the divine light flared every year on the 14th of January. All pilgrims had to pay their respects to the mosque. That was why there were many Muslims among Ayappa's pilgrims. This was something else that attracted Deviah. He liked the mixture of the two religions.

I had never, before this journey, heard of the Ayappa pilgrimage. And perhaps if I hadn't got to know Deviah I might have taken the black-clad figures for granted, part of the crowded Indian scene, and might not have thought to ask about them. The appearance of the divine light at the shrine coincided with a harvest festival in the South, and with a great religious fair in the North; the pilgrimage, the walk up the sacred hill, had perhaps been grafted on to something quite ancient, something to do with the change of the seasons. As the pilgrimage to Ayappa and Vavar, it had been going on for centuries, Deviah said; but in recent years, for some reason, and in spite of the 40 days' penance and the long walk up to the shrine, it had become very popular. A million and a quarter men were expected to be at the shrine at the time of the appearance of the divine light; and some newspapers said that during the year 25 million men might have made the pilgrimage – though, even for India, that figure seemed rather high.

Perhaps the popularity of the Ayappa cult had to do with the fact that people now had a little more money; that roads were better, travel easier, and more buses were available; that more men, young and old, could now, for the best of reasons, get away from their families for a little and become tourists. The Ayappa buses could be like tourist buses; they sometimes took the pilgrims to some of the sights on the way – though this was wrong, Deviah said, since sightseeing was a pleasure; and an Ayappa pilgrim should do nothing that could be construed as a pleasure.

People had a little more money now. It showed in the Karnataka countryside on the road south from Goa. Indian poverty was still visible, the middens, the broken-down aspect of houses and lanes. But the fields, of sugar-cane and cotton and other crops, looked rich and well-tended; the village houses were often neat, with plastered walls and red-tile roofs. There was nothing like the destitution I had seen 26 years before, when I had travelled through on a slow, stopping bus. There were none of the walking skeletons, with their deranged eyes. The agricultural revolution was a reality here; the increased supply of food showed. Hundreds of thousands of people all over India, perhaps millions of people, had worked for this for four decades, in the best way: very few of them with an idea of drama or sacrifice or mission, nearly all of them simply doing jobs.

No corner of this land was without its connection with the gods: mocking when it was a land of scarcity and famine, but more fitting now. Tractors pulled trailers loaded with cotton in big, fat, hessian-wrapped bundles, the cotton forcing its way, like a kind of strained liquid, through the brown sacking. At the same time people in village yards were engaged in biblical-looking tasks, threshing, winnowing. The land was almost beautiful, almost without pain for the beholder.

It was a kind of regeneration that could have come only slowly. There would have been false moves, failures, wasted labour. As there seemed to be even now: a forest department had been at work, planting eucalyptus trees in blocks beside the road. The planting had been successful; for mile upon mile there had been something like shade on both sides of the road, refreshing to look on. But all of that, the work of years, might have to be levelled now, the land stripped again, a fresh start made: the latest word about the eucalyptus was that it was a killer tree, greedy of moisture, desiccating rather than protecting the field it stood beside.

The road was very busy, reflecting the agricultural activity. But the trucks, though decorated with love, were overloaded in the Indian way, and were driven fast and close to one another, as though metal was unbreakable and made a man a god, and anything could be asked of an engine and a steering wheel and brakes. Between Goa and Bangalore that day 10 or 12 trucks had been wrecked, and some people had almost certainly been killed, in seven bad truck accidents. Trucks had driven off the road into ponds; trucks had driven into one another. Driver's cabs had crumpled, glass had shattered. Axles had broken, wheels had splayed at odd angles; and sometimes trucks, like vulnerable, soft-bellied animals, had turned upside down below their cruel loads, showing the wretchedness and rustiness of their metal underbellies and the smoothness of their recapped tires.

Through this old, new land we came to the town of Bangalore. It was 5000 feet above sea level, and was known in the old days for its rain and mild climate, its race course, its Simla-like civilities. Bangalore – though it had a British cantonment or garrison area – had been part of the princely state of Mysore, one of the largest princely states in British India. It had a palace. The royal family of Mysore had been known not only for their great wealth, second only to the fabulous but idle wealth of the Nizam of Hyderabad, but also for their responsibility as rulers, their pride in their state and their people. They had been known as builders of colleges and hospitals and irrigation systems, planters of roadside trees and big public gardens. Bangalore had been a place to which people retired or withdrew from the steamier India of business and work.

Since Independence Bangalore had changed. The climate that had attracted retired people began to attract industry, and Bangalore had grown. It was the centre of the Indian space research programme; it was one of the more important centres of the Indian aircraft industry. Every kind of scientific institution was in

Bangalore. The tree-lined roads of the garden city of the maharajas was now full of the noise and smell and fumes of three-wheelers and cars. It was no longer a city for walking in.

The development of Indian science and technology interested me. What sort of people had made the move, and given India an industrial revolution in 50 years?

In Bombay I had fleetingly talked to Dr Srinivasan, chairman of the Indian Atomic Energy Commission, at a social gathering at his apartment. He had told me then that his grandfather had been a *purohit,* a priest, a kind of pujari. His father, now eighty-six, and living in Bangalore, had been a schoolteacher.

Late one afternoon, a day or so after I arrived, I went to call on Dr Srinivasan's father. The old man was in a dhoti; he had a thin red caste-mark down the centre of his forehead. He was an extraordinarily handsome man, small, slender, fine in every way. He had the face of a man with a deep internal life. He showed an old passport-sized photograph of his father, Shadagopachar, the purohit. Shadagopachar was in his purohit garb, one shoulder bare. His eyes were bright, focussed on the camera, but his appearance was masked by his caste-marks: the thin red line down the middle of the forehead, and two much thicker marks going up from the eyebrows. Those thick white marks were of mud, a refined mud that was still sold in little cakes in the shops. The white mud on the forehead was the symbol of the feet of the Lord.

The family had migrated to Bangalore in the 1890s from a town 40 miles or so away. In Bangalore Shadagopachar had been taught Sanskrit and instructed in all the Vedas by his uncle. But purohits earned very little – four annas, a quarter of a rupee, for a puja – and Shadagopachar also had a job in the maharaja's government as a lower division clerk. He collected files, filed them, and bound them, and in this job he earned between 11 and 15 rupees a month. Graduates at that time earned from 25 to 30 rupees, around two pounds; but Shadagopachar was only a matriculate.

Shadagopachar wanted his son to pass the university examination because graduates could get good jobs with the government, and make much more than they could make as purohits.

'But we were all taught Sanskrit. We were all taught to do the morning and evening prayers. There was a midday prayer as well, but because we had to go to school we would do that prayer in the morning before we went to school. When I graduated, I applied for a job in the education department. This was in 1925.'

That was how the schoolteaching career had begun. But the knowledge of Sanskrit and the general religious training he had received from his father had also stayed with him. Out of that confluence – the new education, the purohit or brahmin's difficult, abstract learning, the concern with the right performance of complicated rituals, the stillness that went with the performance of some of those rituals – there had come a generation of scientists. The old Hindu Sanskrit learning – which a late 18th-century scholar-administrator like Sir William Jones had seen as archaic and profound as the Greek, and had sought, in a kind of romantic, living archaeology, to dig up from secretive, caste-bound brahmins in the North – that old learning had, 200 years later, in the most roundabout way, seeded the new.

*

It might have been coincidence, but the two scientists I met later in Bangalore – men of different disciplines and from different parts of the country – also had purohit or priestly grandfathers.

Subramaniam's family came from a small village which, with the post-Independence reorganization of Indian states, was now in the neighbouring state of Andhra.

'My ancestors lived for a long time in that area. There is a small spot not far from the village – this spot's out in the middle of the jungle – and there is a small shrine in that spot. Our family say that the deity there is our deity.

'The first ancestor I know about is my great-great-great-grandfather. There is a strange legend about him. The legend is that there was this tiger who was making a nuisance of himself in the area. This ancestor decided to tackle it. He wrapped himself in blankets, took a machete, went to the place where the tiger attacked people, and stood there, inviting the tiger, so to speak, to attack him. The tiger did, and my ancestor hacked it to death. I heard the story as a child. It was just this story of physical valour. Perhaps exaggerated. And that's about as far back as I can go.

'My family considered themselves to be part of Mysore State, the maharaja's state. My grandmother – she survived until the 1960s – divided the world into three parts. The first part was the Raja's Land, *Raja Seemay.* That was Mysore State, where things were nice and good and pleasant, and where people who were fortunate like ourselves lived. The second part of the world was what she called *Kumpani Seemay*, the Company's Land. At the time I didn't connect the words – the Company was the East India Company, and the word was still used by her in the 1950s. The Company's Land was part of India, but it wasn't as nice as the Raja's Land. It was true that some of our relatives lived in the Company's Land, but you had to have sympathy for people who lived there. Beyond these two areas was the rest of the world. This way of thinking was something that was just natural to my grandmother.

'We are a family of brahmins. In a way we are priestly, but my grandfather was not a priest. He was a small landowner, and he was also a minor government official. As a village official he would have been paid 10 rupees, perhaps five rupees. The village would have considered him comfortable, but not rich. He was comfortable socially rather than economically. There were many in the village richer than him.

'My grandfather realized that education in English was essential, and he made sure his son got that education. And so my father, who was born in the 1900s, was the first man in our family who went to schools where English was the medium. My father just applied to a school and got in. Nowadays it's a rat-race to get your child into schools; the demand is great. But then my father just applied. He probably walked to school. Our village didn't have a high school. Many people walked long distances to school. I myself – and this was in the 1940s – walked several miles to school.

'I don't know what led my father to science. I personally feel that the scientific tradition is not alien to India. I think that science comes naturally to Indians. Many Indians like to think of themselves as having a tradition of pursuing knowledge, and science is knowledge as it was understood by Bhaskara, one of our old or ancient scientists. Today in India you can buy Bhaskara's treatise on astronomy of 600 or 700 AD, and there is extant a famous medical treatise of about the same time. I must make it clear that I don't for a moment believe all these other people who run around saying that everything – atom bombs, rockets, aeroplanes – was invented by ancient Indians.

'But Indian knowledge became out of date. The measure of that is that what Newton wrote in 1660 was not understood or appreciated in India until the middle of the 19th century. On the other hand, in 1000 AD, and for a century or two after that, there was a knowledge that India had which would have surprised Europe. Especially in mathematics. In 1000 AD Indians were confident in their knowledge. We have evidence for that. But by 1800 that confidence had vanished. Raja Ram Mohun Roy was the first man who publicly acknowledged that the fact of the matter was that there were many things we knew nothing about.'

Ram Mohun Roy came from Bengal. He campaigned against the burning of widows on their husbands' funeral pyres. He sought, more generally, to purify Hinduism, and to bring the new learning of Europe to India. He was India's first modern reformer, and his dates are astonishing: he was born about 1772, and died, during a mission to England, in 1833.

I told Subramaniam what I had read somewhere about the Mogul emperor Jehangir (who succeeded the great Akbar, ruled from 1605 to 1625, and loved the arts): Jehangir had scoffed at the notion of a New World on the other side of the Atlantic.

Subramaniam said, 'And Aurangzeb' – ruling from 1650 to 1700, a period of rapid Mogul decay – 'referred to England with contempt. He said it was a tiny island, its king like a minor raja in India. This was late in the 17th century.

'In my own family that realization – that our knowledge was out of date – came to my grandfather. But it was too late for him to do anything about it. He was born in the 1880s and died when he was fifty-five. But, as I said, he was determined that his son should have the new education.

'After high school, my father came to Bangalore, to the university. And then he wanted to do research. At that time in India one of the biggest names in research was Meghnad Saha, a Bengali. He was professor of physics at Allahabad. He had made a name for himself a few years earlier with a paper that showed how ionization was related to temperature. This paper of Saha's was in 1922, and his formula, Saha's formula, is still the basis for understanding the composition of the stars. Saha, incidentally, was a great nationalist.

'My father decided he would like to go and work with Saha. And he actually did. For a man who was a first-generation college student it would have been a bit of an adventure for him. I think my father would have been financially supported in Allahabad by his father and father-in-law. My father kept a journal in Allahabad, and one of my projects is to look at that journal.'

The science, the venturesomeness, and then the journal: the longing for new experience, and then the wish to put order into that experience – that was impressive, in a man not long out of a village.

Subramaniam, with his own wish to categorize and define, said, 'I think it's a demonstration of the two points I've made. The first is that the tradition of science is not new. And the second is that I don't think that in my father's mind there was any feeling that he was doing something entirely alien when he was doing science. I think a feeling for that – science and mathematics – was central to many Indian minds.

'My father came back and taught physics in high schools in Bangalore and in other places in Mysore State. Mysore State was in many ways advanced. In a quiet way. The maharajas, and the ministers they had, were quite often in a peculiar way liberal and forward-looking. One side of them was conservative, but there was another side which looked to the future. Have you heard of Visweswaraiah? He was an engineer who was appointed *diwan* or chief minister in 1910 or thereabouts. He was responsible for many projects in the state which made it the model state in the country. Mr Gandhi, in the 1930s, when he came to Mysore, said it was *Rama rajya*.'

It was something many people in Bangalore had mentioned to me. *Rama rajya,* Rama's rule or kingdom – it was the highest Hindu praise: Rama the hero of one of the two great Hindu epics, the embodiment of goodness, universally loved, the man who in any situation could be relied upon to do the right thing, the religious thing, the wise thing, a figure at once human and divine: to be ruled by Rama's law was to know bliss.

Subramaniam said, 'There was a tradition in the state of benevolent rule. And Visweswaraiah was ahead of his time. He made a five-year plan in the 1920s or 30s. The same man set up the University of Mysore. And Mysore was the first state where electric power was available. The rulers had a lot of local pride.

'My father settled in Bangalore, and then my grandfather also came here. We grew up in an Indian joint family, a large family. My grandfather was a man who took his religious life seriously. He headed his family, and he did his pujas. I don't think he was doing anything else at that time. He died in the latter part of the 1930s.

'The feeling grew in my father that there might be conflicts between the science he knew and practised, and the way he lived. It did produce conflicts in the house, especially in a house which was very religious, as my grandfather's house was. My father had the feeling that many things we were doing didn't make sense. Rituals, for example. Caste barriers.

'He tried to reconcile the two. He developed a certain outlook of his own – Hindu or brahminical, as he saw it, rooted in a certain respect for ancient Indian scholarship and philosophy. But it tried to be free of all the things he associated with prejudice. There was one thing he did – at that time it was an improper thing to do, and not so minor. All brahmin children go through an initiation ceremony – it's a serious affair, and usually it's done when the boy is young, six, seven, eight. My father had a very good friend, not a brahmin, and he insisted that his friend join in this function that was being performed for his own child – me, as a matter of fact. That raised eyebrows. This was in the 1940s. But my father was very clear in his mind about this matter.

'About rituals, I think my father went through a stage when he rejected them, and then finally he accepted them in a certain modified form. So, in his later years, he used to perform puja, but in a very unobtrusive way. I remember arguing with him about the puja he performed, and he said it was sufficient that it gave him a certain mental peace and privacy for a part of the day. He can be described without paradox as a man who was conservative in one way and liberal in another. In matters of caste, etc., he was liberal. But he was not westernized at all.'

I asked Subramaniam, 'Do you perform pujas?'

'I don't perform pujas. But I still have a feeling for the small shrine in the jungle, with the family deity.'

'How does a family get a deity like that?'

'A family deity is something given to you. It might have been adopted at some stage. Some event fixed it. Some teacher perhaps. It may be that a person asks a favour of some temple and is granted the favour, and becomes a follower of a deity of that temple.

'My father remained a teacher almost all his life. After he retired as a teacher he worked in a mental-health institute, mainly helping with the electronics on an electro-encephalogram, to measure "brain waves". And, by the way, one of the bits of research they did was on a sadhu. They put electrodes all over his head and tried to find out how these brain waves were behaving when he went into a trance. They did find that he was in fact very calm.

'My father spent the last 20 years of his life writing books on science in the local language. He saw that that was the way things were going to be changed – that you speak of science in the language of the people, and not in English. Those books were pretty good. Some very good. He wrote on energy long before energy-conservation became a topic. He wrote on astro-physics. He wrote a little book about sound. This talked about the physics of sound, and then it tried to tell the reader how this physics was related to the music he heard, the local music. This book was written in the 1940s. It's a small book. It used to be sold for two annas.' One-eighth of a rupee, less than a penny.

'How did you think of yourself when you were growing up? Poor? All right?'

'I felt we were middle class.' Middle class in the Indian way, meaning not poor, but with a suggestion of simplicity and making do, not middle class in the European or American way. 'Not rich. A strained middle-class house. There was never money to spare. Never. I would say that this was something which was taken as part of life, not something we went around thinking about all the time. There are certain advantages in the big joint families: things are taken care of. It's like a little state: you have friends, you carry on.

'The fact that my father had done science influenced me. And my father had literary friends, because he had written books in the local language. Quite often there would be arguments in the house about science, religion, literature. It was a very educated atmosphere, very cultured, very stimulating. The background was simple only in an economical sense. Not at all in a cultural sense. And this is quite important in an old country like India.'

I understood what he meant. It was what I felt – in a lesser or different way – about my own Indian family background in far-off Trinidad. I felt that the physical conditions of our life, often poor conditions, told only half the story: that the remnants of the old civilization we possessed gave the in-between colonial generations a second scheme of reverences and ambitions, and that this equipped us for the outside world better than might have seemed likely. But I also recalled something else: the shoddiness of the Indian books we bought, sometimes out of piety towards the ancestral land. I remembered the poor paper, the broken type, the oily ink, the sloping lines, the uneven margins, the rusting metal staples. The idea of India was part of our strength, and it received part of our piety; yet there was this other idea of the Indian reality, of poor goods, of poor machines poorly used.

Subramaniam said, 'If I go back to the time the British were here – and my recollections are vague: I was born in the 40s – we saw then that things made in England or Europe – there was little of U.S. goods – we saw them as good things. We saw Indian things as not so good quality. I think that people of my father's generation must have had a remarkable mental or intellectual strength to preserve their souls in the middle of all this Indian shoddiness. People knew that things were not very good. But they had some inspiration they drew from a real or imagined greatness. They had some innate feelings of old cultural strength, which preserved them. So you would see people admiring things from Britain, but at the same time we were going to say, "That's great, but we're not going to capitulate to that."'

'Didn't it give you some doubts about the possibility of an Indian industrial revolution, and the capacity of Indians to manufacture things that would feel finished and real?'

'I never had any doubt about that. Never. We saw that as a matter not of whether, but when. We complained that it was too slow.'

'You don't think the shoddiness had a psychological effect on people?'

'I felt a little ashamed. There was certainly a feeling that a lot of businessmen were making money without making quality goods, and that gave a feeling of ill-gotten wealth. One looked forward to a pretty distant future when things wouldn't be so. We saw that the answer was to have a strong science in the country. My own feeling was compounded of shame, ignorance and hope. I think these attitudes would not have been widely shared. On the hope there would have been widely different views.

'Quite a few Indians at that time felt that the British Raj would last forever – not a large number, but quite a few. One of my most vivid recollections was of an argument between my father and my mother's father. He was a doctor.'

'A doctor!'

'As I told you, the background was simple only in an economic sense. The argument – during the war – was about what the future might be. My grandfather, the doctor, thought that Europe, the West, was very powerful, and that it was almost impossible for India to get rid of the British. And even if the British lost the war, the Germans would be there. So he saw the future as still dominated by the West for a considerable time. And he also thought that Indians were incapable of taking care of the country – running it, ruling it.'

That sent me back to another set of early feelings about my ancestral culture. In Trinidad, in the late 30s and early 40s, I used to see poor Indian people sleeping in the squares of Port of Spain. These people were peasant emigrants from India; they had served out their indentures 20 years or so before, had not been given their passages back to India, and had then become destitute, abandoned by everybody. In the colonial city they were further isolated by their language; and they were to live on the streets until they died out. The idea came to me, when I was quite young, seeing those destitutes, that we were people with no one to appeal to. We had been transported out of the abjectness of India, and were without representation. The idea of the external enemy wasn't enough to explain what had happened to us. I found myself at an early age looking inwards, and wondering whether the culture – the difficult but personal religion, the taboos, the social ideas – which in one way supported and enriched some of us, and gave us solidity, wasn't perhaps the very thing that had exposed us to defeat.

Subramaniam said, 'I felt that, but in a different way from you. The foreigner was here. The country had become slaves and had been plundered. But that wasn't just because of the culture. It was because over the centuries we had become weak and stagnant.'

He began to talk of the pattern of Indian history.

'I go back to Alberuni's comments about the Hindus.' Alberuni, the Arab historian of about 1000 AD at the court of Ghazni, in what is today Afghanistan. Subramaniam had mentioned Alberuni at the beginning of our talk. Alberuni's book was one of the sources for what was known about ancient Hindu science and learning; but Alberuni had also written some famous words about Hindu arrogance in that learning.

'We became complacent. A system had been evolved here whereby the preservation of the country's culture and its social organization was independent of the military masters who ruled the country. The country was run on principles that assumed that kings would change, that wars would be fought, but that society would go on, pretty much undisturbed by those events.

'Up to a point that is why Hindus are a-historical. If you look at what Indian culture remembers – we preserve our books on mathematics, astronomy, grammar. We preserve Bhaskara and Charaka.' Seventh-century scientists. 'Among the things which are preserved are not the names of kings or their battles – that is not part of our tradition. We know Bhaskara and Shankaracharya.' Shankaracharya, a ninth-century philosopher who travelled all over India, revitalized Hindu philosophy, set up religious foundations (which still exist) in certain places, and is thought to have died at the age of thirty-two. 'But if you ask, "Who ruled this part of the country in 1700?" people wouldn't know, and basically they wouldn't care.

'That, however, has been the weakness of the country, and it has brought on us military defeat. But it changed with the British. When the British came here, it slowly became clear to Indians that these political and military defeats were things they couldn't ignore. What in other places would have been a natural reaction, a natural assumption, in India had to be an intellectual conclusion. It took a long time. The realization came very late, in the 19th century.

'It was a widely shared feeling. That is why people went to English schools. I went to an English-medium school. But it was a very Indian school. It was run by people who were orthodox Hindus, but convinced that we had to learn English, science, technology. It was very stimulating. I remember lots of disagreement among my teachers about the future. Even Gandhi was a subject of controversy. Looking back on it, I am astonished that there were some people there, teachers, maybe half a dozen – and their wages would have been very low – who were actually driven by the desire to get people to learn. You got a feeling of mission. I remember one of my teachers who, for no reason I can imagine now, took a great deal of interest in me, gave me a book on the lives of great scientists, and did so out of his own pocket.'

'Was he a brahmin?'

'He was a brahmin. It was a brahmin-inspired school.'

I thought of the brahmin contribution to the Independence movement, and the regenerative social ideas that had come with that movement. I thought of the brahmin contribution afterwards to science.

I said, 'So the brahmins have in a way paid their debt back?'

'I'm not sure they've paid it back yet. They're responsible still for many things on our social landscape.' Subramaniam broke off here, to continue on a related theme. 'A great social revolution took place in this state after Independence, and it was as a consequence of Independence. The social revolution was that the identity of the politically powerful classes changed in a few years. It was a bloodless revolution, but it was a revolution, though people outside India don't know about it. Before Independence, the administration in the state was in the hands of brahmins. A few years after Independence, power changed hands – and I mean the way power changed hands in other parts of the world. The people who now sit in the offices are of a different social class.

'The prime minister's science adviser was saying the other day that the trouble with Indian science is that it is too much a brahmin science, and that we needed a more lower-caste kind of science. But the fact that so many brahmins are in science is only a development of history.'

'Do you feel threatened?'

'No doubt about it. Entrance to universities is not based strictly on merit. There are quotas for different classes. Many brahmins feel now that even education has become difficult. There are the quotas, and private colleges are expensive. It may partly be responsible for the large number of Indian professionals abroad.'

My thoughts, as I had driven down from Goa, through the untidy but energetic towns, full of the signs of growth, and then through the well-tilled fields at harvest time, had been of the Indian and, more specifically, Hindu awakening. If Subramaniam was right, there was a hidden irony in that awakening: that the group or caste who had contributed so much to that awakening should now find itself under threat.

Education and ambition by themselves would have taken people nowhere without an expanding economy. Perhaps, even, the expanding economy explained the shift in Indian education. For Pravas, an engineer, the expansion had started some time before Independence, when the old British emphasis on law and order (especially after the Indian Mutiny of 1857) had been modified by the idea of development.

'Many people were sucked into that process. There was an explosive growth in India around 1930. It built momentum around 1947, had a big growth thereafter, and is now slowing down. In

1962, when I was thinking of universities and a career, I had a choice of professions and institutions. People today have to struggle hard. But these things have a positive side.

'The average aspiration of the Indian is to grow under a shadow – and this is all right as long as someone else throws the shadow. In concrete terms, this means you look for employment, you try to get into structures created by other people. That's how we got governed in the first place. The attitude is: "As long as the local environment is the same, I don't care who is running things at the top." I read something in a paper some time ago. It was to the effect that, before the British came to India, the Indians were like bees in a garden. And that's fine, as long as someone else looked after the garden. And then of course the Britishers became both the owners of the garden and the gardeners, the *malis* – with those other guys, the bees, going happily from flower to flower.'

'What about the positive side of the struggle today?'

'That shadow area I talked about is becoming congested now. It is forcing people to go out on their own. It is forcing them to be entrepreneurial.'

Pravas came from far away, from the east of the country. His grandfather had been a priest, and his father entered government service as a clerk.

'It is almost the standard Indian success story. My father would have got into the service in the mid-40s, the time at which the administration was just beginning to pick up. There was still not a lot of science and industry, or anything like that. But the structure was expanding. This was a precursor of development. When the real development came, there was non-traditional administration. Traditional administration would need police, soldiers, clerks and lawyers. Non-traditional administration needed industrialists, artisans, engineers, doctors, scientists, entrepreneurs. Because my father entered the service at the precursor stage, he wasn't a scientist.'

'What sort of things did your father read?'

'He retained quite a lot of tradition. He chanted *mantras.* My grandfather was a good old classical ritualistic purohit, according to what I've heard. Performing the rituals was his profession. Whereas with my father, if you want to trace the transition, the mantras were chanted out of familiarity, reverence, a way of expressing your gratitude to God – you had these mantras reverberating in your head since childhood. I make no difference between that and the young man today in a video or audio surrounding who chants, formally and informally, Hindi film songs.

'My father is taller than I, and he makes a good sight sitting there cross-legged, chanting, with his back straight. I think the posture is beautiful. My father is seventy-six, and his back is still straight. But with my father the chanting of the mantras has been, in quotes, "degraded" from a livelihood to pleasure. Oral pleasure, if you like; nostalgia; a protection against fears. A gamut of feeling – all this I call pleasure, since it's done out of volition.

'We lived in a small princely state in the east. My grandfather was one of the priests of the royal family. Not really a big king: it was a feudal kingdom of maybe 100 or 200 square miles.'

A small princely state in the east, a priest serving the ruling family. I said, 'That is really old India.'

Pravas said, 'The degree of cultural change that I have personally gone through and digested would break a person elsewhere. When I was a child, and we went to visit my ancestral place, we would go in bullock carts – it was the only mode. Or walk. That was as recently as 1960. You wouldn't have what we think of as a bathroom. You would go down to the river.'

'Were you aware of hardship?'

'At the time it seemed normal. Everybody did that in the village. And for years, going back to the village after I had left it, going back for a day or so, it was more like a picnic. Before you recognized you were deprived, you were out.

'Most of the kings in those days had a policy of encouraging a certain amount of intellectualism. It was a cause for pride. In direct terms that meant they made sure that their people, the priestly caste, the intellectuals, didn't have to depend on other people for their security. So they gave a piece of land to the purohits. A gift of land to a purohit or anybody else couldn't be taken back. It was a gift in perpetuity. It would have been considered a sin of the lowest order to recover a gift. In that kingdom there were between five to 10 priestly families. The religious rituals were very specialized. Some purohits did certain things, and other purohits other things.'

'They were privileged people?'

'Yes and no. The piece of land wasn't much. It was a subsistence piece. It was only to see that the person didn't die. It was something to fall back on, but nothing more than that. The purohits didn't have a lot of clothes. They had two dhotis or something like that. Compared to the tradesmen, people selling grain or timber or oilseeds or oil, they would be poor. Compared to the beggars, they were well off.'

'So the brahmins were kept by the kings in an ambiguous position?'

'If you look at it from the economical point of view, then of course it looks incongruous. But it had a logic of its own. The brahmins had status and royal protection. The king would deal severely with any act of aggression against the priests. And the kings would encourage intellectual exchanges. Debates, chanting, *yagnas* or big pujas, with brahmins from other kingdoms as well, perhaps – everybody competing, or co-operating in a competitive sense, to show their own excellence. Sometimes you would have a thousand brahmins sitting and chanting, but with each man keeping an ear for who was singing well or badly. It's precisely what happens at scientific or intellectual conferences today.

'The internal factor is that the priestly community was born and brought up with the psychology that they didn't expect more. It's so much part of the internal system that it's gone down to the folk level. The Lord Vishnu has two wives – Lakshmi, the goddess of wealth, and Saraswati, the goddess of wisdom. The two wives would naturally be at loggerheads – a depiction of the fact that the intellectual life seldom goes with wealth: you have to choose one of them. So, by a combination of circumstances, this priestly class didn't look for riches, and they wouldn't be given riches. A perfect matching of interests.

'In my father's life the balance was of a different kind. He didn't have an assured security, like my grandfather. He had to work to provide for his family. His life was half ritual, half the struggle for survival. The balance was between the two.

'In certain communities you are supported by the scaffolding of the society. If you are in a merchant caste, dealing in oilseeds or cotton straw, and you wish to graduate to dealing in radios, the scaffolding is the same. You only change the commodity. There is a group movement there. Whereas, in a case like my father's, he wasn't moving with the society – the society wasn't moving in a co-ordinated way. Quite a lot of young men were doing the same thing at that time, but all of them were doing it individually. Not only did my father have the difficulty of clearing the way, but every time he moved back, to my grandfather's house, there would have been conflict. It would have been like moving between a hot and a cold room.'

'What sort of conflict?'

'In the older society, you would keep your purity both genetically and externally. You would only marry certain people, and you wouldn't have contacts beyond a certain point with people of a lower caste. You wouldn't be able to eat food cooked by someone of a lower caste. Eating was considered a sacred activity. Food was looked upon as a sacrifice to the gastric juices. There were rigid prescriptions about the time you could eat, in what direction you faced while eating, who served, and how much you ate. Food was dissected to the last detail. Different classes of people ate different amounts. For instance, in the scriptures it is prescribed that for intellectuals doing very little physical work the right amount of food would be the rice cooked from a handful of rice grains held in the fist.

'Hinduism is a trinity-based religion – there are three options for everything. So food was of three kinds – *sattvik, rajasik, tamasik*. Sattvik foods encouraged intellectual pursuits, clarity of mind, purer thoughts. Sattvik foods were very light – most grains, a certain amount of clarified butter, the lighter vegetables. Rajasik food is work-oriented.'

(From Deviah I later had a more comprehensive list of sattvik foods: leafy greens, milk, curds, butter, rice, wheat, most sprouts, most pulses (except a kind of dal), sweet potatoes (but not potatoes), fruit. From Deviah I also learned that rajasik food was more than work-oriented. Rajasik food encouraged both valour and passion, and Deviah gave this list: *urad* dal, meat, wine, spices (true brahmins don't get on with spices). As for tamasik food – which Pravas with apparently brahminical scruple didn't go into (and about which, fearing the worst, I didn't press him, not wanting him to go off on this detour) – Deviah said it encouraged sloth. Strangely, though, the tamasik list that Deviah gave seemed quite subtle, with some elements of the rajasik; and some of its vegetables seemed to be light enough for the sattvik diet. This was Deviah's tamasik list: onion, garlic, cabbage, carrot, aubergine, potatoes, urad dal, meat. Urad dal and meat were both on the rajasik list.)

Pravas said, 'The sattvik is mind-oriented. Such people were expected to do what they did because it should be done, and not because you get a reward. Such people did what they did out of an internal motivation. Brahmins were identified with the sattvik tendency. Therefore they couldn't eat certain foods.

'The whole thing was ritualized in every way. For example, if your father was alive, you shouldn't face south when you ate. This wasn't an all-India prohibition, but it was more than local. So it was a serious matter if the shadow of a lower-caste person fell on your food. If it happened while you were eating, that was that. You stopped eating. The food became impure. And I forgot: nobody should touch you while you were eating, and you had to eat in a certain posture. Some people were so "orthodox", in inverted commas, they couldn't even hear the voice of a lower-caste person while they ate. These people ate deep within their houses.'

'Would they get angry if they had to stop eating because of the shadow or the voice?'

Pravas said with a smile, 'Brahmins are not supposed to get enraged. They would just stop eating. Rage is not considered a brahminical quality. Though a large number of the brahmins I know, 80 per cent, say, are very short-tempered.

'So my father moved between these hot and cold rooms, as I've called them. It was a perpetual struggle for him. He had to face a lot of questioning when he went back to my grandfather's. Had he been eating food cooked by non-brahmins? Or wearing the right kind of dress? That was important in those days. My grandfather never wore long trousers; he wore the dhoti. My father wore half and half – dhoti and trousers. But the food business wasn't a joke for them. In that value system it was sacrilege to break any of the rules.

'Because of his background my father was philosophically oriented. Even within that his reading was different from my grandfather's. My grandfather would practise the hard-core Sanskrit, the original mantras as written in the Vedas or Puranas. It is the hallmark of ritualism that you don't necessarily understand the deeper meanings of everything you do, and my grandfather didn't necessarily understand what he chanted. Ritualism is perhaps, though not very crudely, a show-act.

'My father wasn't a performer; he didn't have that pressure. So he tried to understand what he read. He read a lot of interpretations by newer philosophers. This led him to read in many languages. He read modern philosophical works in Bengali, and he read in English. I grew up with volumes and volumes of his books in Devanagari and English. He made relatively small forays into other topics. The core was philosophical.

'And there was something else. In addition to the old Puranic values, my father had the diffusion from nationalistic values, essentially Gandhian. Gandhianism was almost a mass hysteria in India, but of a healthy kind. It was the good old values, but packaged in a modern-looking way, very mass-based. The old values looked intellectual and were intellectual, and therefore maintained a distance from the masses. Gandhi found a way of making old truths appear simple. And I grew up with quite a few of those Gandhian slogans. "Work more, talk less."

'In my house the continuity of the brahminic value system remained, and then I also made my own change from an old world to a new world, from a hot room to a cold room. But this time the change was different. Nobody asked me, "Why are you wearing long pants?" Or, "Did you eat food cooked by a brahmin?" But, like my father in his government job, I didn't have a scaffolding. I had, so to speak, to break down the door myself.'

'Why did you go in for science?'

'There's the milieu and the current value system. The third factor is a sense of mystery.'

'Mystery?'

'It's one of the strongest motivating forces. All religions are replete with miracles. Mystery attracts, and science has that mystery. I felt that mystery, subconsciously. Put two chemicals together and the colour changes – that's the simplest mystery. Or make a machine like an electric fan which runs apparently without any motive force.

'I have made one more level of transformation than my father did from his father's time. I am more liberal in outlook than my father. I've probably become more questioning, because of what we may call "science". I'm less knowledgeable about rituals. My father got a part of what his father had, and I have only a part of the rituals my father had.

'I grew up in my intimate family surroundings up to the age of fifteen or sixteen. That's the time you pick up the rituals, because you are not allowed to perform certain rituals before a certain time. For example, there are some rituals that only married men can do. But at that age I went away from home, going back only for a few days a year. So I missed a lot of the ritual side. And now I have only half the faith in it.

'I don't do it, but I have a nostalgia for it. My roots are in it. It is not alien to me. If someone says to me that I shouldn't eat rajasik food – eggs or something – I don't find it strange. I understand, unlike a modern nutritionist. And, in the philosophy line, I have done more of what my father did. I diversified, even more than him, into other schools of Indian philosophy and schools of other philosophies. My father had gone from the basic Vedic to the broader Indian philosophy. I have gone from that to a more global approach.'

I said, 'With your scholarly approach, you probably actually know more about Hinduism than your grandfather.'

Pravas said, 'Probably I can articulate it better in a Western sense, but I cannot say I know more than my grandfather.

'Change is a continuous process. You can discern a change only once in a generation. Because once you discern it, you are already there. So in these last 50 years I can discern only two changes, but they are large because a continuing process is being focussed at two or three points. The next big change will come with my son. There are spans of transition. There are much bigger spans with the succeeding generations.

'My son will go through a very large change in circumstances in many ways. In the family, in the school surroundings, in the job market, everywhere. I grew up in a half ritualistic background. My son will have no ritualistic background. But if my son loses the rituals even further, he could still be rooted locally, within his peer group. There will be many like him. Society is moving that way.

'The food restrictions and so on that I talked about are known to some, but not known to most in my generation. They don't know that such things existed and exist. And yet they are perfectly at balance in the local surroundings. If you get too attached to your roots in the old sense, you might actually become unrooted, fossilized. At least in form, at least in style, you must get into the new stream, get the new roots. More of India is doing that. Style becomes substance in one generation. Things that one starts to do because other people are doing it – like wearing long pants, in my father's case – become natural for the next generation.'

I thought that the changes he was talking about might have been in some way like the changes that had come a generation or two earlier to the Indian community in Trinidad, the peasant India that my grandfathers had taken with them, an apparently complete world, with language and rituals and social organization: an India that had, in its New-World setting, even during my childhood, begun to disintegrate: first the language going, then the reverence for the rituals and the need for them (the rituals going on long after they had ceased to be understood), leaving only a group sense, a knowledge of family and clan, and an idea of India in the background, an idea of India quite different (more historical, more political) from the India that had appeared to come with one's ancestors.

Pravas said, 'For you the change was not subversive.'

The word was arresting.

He said, 'The change wasn't from within. It was external. Here change is gradual. It's happening all around me – in my father, my brother, everybody. I cannot distinguish any longer what is alien.'

And (extending what Pravas said) there was a further, and fundamental, difference between the new generations in India and our immigrant community far away. For people of that community, separated from the Indian earth, Hindu theology had become difficult (as it had become difficult for people of formerly Hinduized areas of south-east Asia); the faith had then been half possessed by many, abandoned by many. It had been part of a more general cultural loss, which had left many with no strong idea of who they were. That wouldn't happen in India, however much ritualism was left behind, and however much the externals changed.

Pravas said, 'There will remain a few primordial principles. People will lose all the details about individual behaviour – eating and sleeping and so on. All these things will go away. But in the group memory some streams will remain perennial. Faith and its expression is one of those primordial streams, though the details may get blurred.

'Recently there has been on TV the serials of the epics, the *Ramayana* and the *Mahabharata*. Most of the people on the streets of Bangalore haven't actually read those epics. They haven't read them in the original or in an English version or in any version. They take them for granted; they're there. They would have known the main characters and the broad theme. They wouldn't have known the details; they wouldn't know the inside characters. But the TV serials were an instant success.'

And now, for Pravas, there were all the frustrations of modern Indian life. As he described them, they were like the frustrations of the visitor: the difficulty of travel by air or train or road; the crowded, dangerous city streets; the poisonous fumes; the difficulty of doing simple things, the difficulty of arranging the physical details of day-to-day living, which the industrial revolution was meant, after all, to simplify.

Pravas said, 'Sometimes even I despair. And it is perhaps only something in my make-up that stops me going to the mafia.' To straighten people out, to get things done. 'There are no rules in the Indian streets.' That wasn't a simple or frivolous matter. Pravas rode a motor-scooter; he arrived always, when he came to see me, like a kind of spaceman, with his big helmet. 'You feel a little bit like being in a jungle, and this can transfer to a larger view of things. It can, and does. It actually translates into a loss of productivity. I am a far less productive person than I ought to be. A lot of energy goes into these things, those traffic jams, that chaos. Friction in society is like friction in the machine.'

I thought of his grandfather, one of the five or 10 priests of the king of a small state in the east. He lived on very little; he had only his subsistence piece of land to keep him from absolute want, if the king withdrew his favour. He had no other skill – the little state at that time didn't require many skills. That was an arbitrary world, where change could come suddenly and overwhelmingly to a man. It was like the India which had been overrun again and again by this army and that; it was the India of unfinished monuments, of energy going to waste, creating an impression of randomness. That was a jungle, too. Did Pravas's grandfather live with something like that idea?

'I never knew my grandfather. He died when my father was twelve or thirteen. I have no memory of his world, but I can reconstruct it. He was part of a static society. He was not different from his father or grandfather. So, even if there was friction, he wouldn't discover it, because he didn't have the bike.'

The bike – Pravas had been talking of the Bangalore traffic and his own motor-scooter. I liked the metaphor: it made the static past understandable.

I began to wonder whether many of the frustrations Pravas spoke about were not rooted in the past, whether they hadn't been created by the smallness of Indian expectations, the almost pious idea – like the idea behind Gandhian homespun – that a country so poor needed very little. I wondered whether there wasn't deep in India even now a psychology of shoddiness, an extension of the idea of holy poverty, the old religious-political feeling that it was wrong, wasteful, and provoking to the gods (and the ruler) to get above oneself. And I asked Pravas, as I had asked Subramaniam, about the psychological effects on him, as he was growing up, of the shoddiness of Indian manufactured goods.

He said, 'I didn't have much to compare with when I was growing up. I might have seen my grandfather's watch, but I never saw an Indian watch and had nothing to compare. So I didn't feel bad. I didn't grow up with too many imported goods. The things we used were made locally, or we simply didn't have them. We used a lot of the products of Indian artisanship – metal plates, not china, and metal plates have been made for thousands of years. Textiles had been made long before I was born. So the basic needs were met by local goods. When you are small, besides, your needs are very small.'

About the shoddiness of Indian goods he saw now he was philosophical. 'Compared with contemporary goods elsewhere, they are bad. Compared with the nothing we had 50 years ago, it is something. It only means we have started late. Japanese goods 50 years ago were shoddy.'

The new world was so new: it had begun for some people with their grandfathers, and for most with their fathers. And people had travelled so far so fast that many active people had a success story to tell, their own sometimes, or that of someone in their family.

I had got to know Kala. She was of Tamil brahmin origins. She did the publicity for a big organization. She was in her twenties, and unmarried. She was diligent and methodical; she had a reputation as a worker. She was grave, self-possessed, educated. But I didn't know enough of India, and especially of that brahmin South from which she came, to guess at her background.'

And then, at lunch one day, speaking of it as of a fairy story, she said that her grandfather had started from nothing, had been so poor as a child that he had studied by the light of street lamps.

(Hadn't that been said of many other people? Hadn't there been another very poor boy somewhere – without paper or pencil or slate – who had had to work out sums on the back of a shovel with a piece of charcoal? I thought of Kala's story as a piece of romance. And then, some weeks later, in a small brahmin 'colony' in Madras, I saw a small boy one evening actually sitting with a book below a street lamp. The lamp was too dim to read by, but the brahmin boy was there cross-legged with his book, acting out ambition and struggle and self-denial, doing the virtuous thing he and his parents had heard about.)

I asked Kala the name of this ancestor. It was the name of a princely-state administrator; it was a name famous in pre-

Independence India. The boy who had studied by the street lamps had risen to power and wealth.

From Kala's manner, I might have expected someone like that grandfather in her background. What was unexpected – and yet a little thought would have shown that it was in keeping with that brahminical background – was that, on Kala's mother's side, there was a *sanyasi* ancestor, an ascetic, someone who had renounced the world to go and meditate on the river-steps or ghats of Banaras, among the pyres and temples beside the Ganges.

Such strands of old India did Kala carry in her make-up. She knew she was part of the movement out of old India that Pravas had spoken about; but she didn't know it in the same analytical way. When Kala meditated on her family past, as she did with something like obsession, her thoughts were of her mother, who had been caught by that movement forward, had been trapped between the generations, and had had her life distorted.

Kala took the story about her grandfather reading under the street lights seriously. She had heard the story when she was nine or ten from her mother, and then later on in more detail from her grandfather himself. She said, in her grave way, 'When there is a power failure, and the lights go off, and one becomes irritated, then I think of this man, this boy, who didn't have lights at all in his house.' It was probably so. 'This was in Madras in the early 1900s. His parents had sent him to his grandmother's house in Madras to live.' And though Kala didn't say, I thought that this would have been part of the brahmin migration to the cities that occurred in so many people's stories. In Madras, Kala's grandfather lived in a brahmin area near an important temple.

'My grandfather has told me about having to wait at the temple every evening to collect *parsad,* the consecrated food offerings. That food was his evening meal, and his grandmother's meal as well. We visited that temple recently, the temple of Kapaleshwar, one of the two famous old temples of Madras. My grandfather showed me a stone lion on which he used to lean or sit while he waited for the evening puja to be over, to collect his food and go home. The pundits used to scold him: "Can't you even stand and wait respectfully while the puja is going on?" This time, when he went back as a very old man, the priests were standing outside to receive him.

'When he finished the school in Madras, he came to Bangalore, to go to the college here. He stayed with a relative, and he went on his own and got himself admitted to the college.' It was interesting, how that recurred in stories of the past: the child going on his own, without a parent or adult, to get enrolled in a school. 'While he was in college, he married my grandmother. He was a teenager, and she was eleven, if I remember right. In those days, when children were married, they stayed in their parents' house until they grew up. I should tell you that, as I knew them, my grandmother and grandfather were a romantic and devoted couple. I asked him about those early days of his marriage, and he told me that sometimes after his classes at the college he would go down to the market and pick up things for the home, including sometimes beads and coloured threads for my grandmother, his wife.

'The father of that eleven-year-old bride was the sanyasi I told you about. He was a boy sanyasi, and he was in Banaras. The man who became his father-in-law is supposed to have heard in some way of this sanyasi far away in Banaras – Banaras is many hundreds of miles from here – and he had heard that this sanyasi was destined to marry his daughter.' Sanyasis are renouncers of the world; they have no households; they don't marry. So this idea of the destiny of the sanyasi was a strange one.

Kala said, 'They, the people who became the in-laws of the sanyasi, would have been religious people. They must have been in touch with astrologers; they must have had their daughter's horoscope read. So the man of the family went to Banaras, or he sent someone, to look for this boy sanyasi who had appeared in his daughter's horoscope. They went to Banaras, and they looked among all the holy men there, and they found the boy sanyasi. They put this proposal of marriage to him. But he was firm; he didn't want to re-enter the world. So they came back. But then various things happened, and then they went again to Banaras, and somehow they said certain things, and they persuaded the sanyasi to give up his ascetic life and to leave Banaras and to come here and get married. Not long after this marriage, the sanyasi's wife had an accident, and she began to lose her sight. She was sixteen when she got married.'

'Didn't the astrologer see that?'

Kala said, 'I don't know.' The story that had been handed down to her was like myth: it was full of wonders, but it had its gaps.

'Do you have any story of what the sanyasi said after his wife lost her sight?'

'There are no reports of the sanyasi's reaction.'

'How did he make a living?'

'The sanyasi became a priest at Palani, and in time a high official there. Palani is a famous temple town. The deity of Palani is a manifestation of Shiva. I go there almost every year with my mother. She believes in the temple.'

'What does that mean?'

'She believes in the power of that temple.'

'Do you believe in it?'

'I love my mother, and I believe in her. My mother was very close to her grandmother, the wife of the former sanyasi, and I believe there would have been some family feeling for the Palani temple. Though I go every year with my mother, it doesn't mean much to me. I'm not a particularly religious person myself.

'Palani is a rich temple. There are temples that are richer, but Palani is pretty rich, and many pilgrims go there. Temples are rich from the lands they have, and from the offerings the devotees make. One of the richest temples in the South is the temple at Tirupati. There is a story about it. The deity of that temple, Srinivasa, took a large debt from Kubera, the Lord of Wealth. The goddess Lakshmi gives wealth; Kubera owns it or hoards it, or lends it out. And the story at Tirupati is that the money that people give to the temple is being saved by Srinivasa, the temple deity, to repay the debt to Kubera. Many people believe in that story and that deity. There is a huge *hundi,* a huge cloth bin, and you throw the money in that. You throw anything – gold, silver, diamonds. I believe there have been people who have thrown in revolvers and bloodstained knives, hoping to be forgiven for the crimes they have committed with those weapons. And it is said that the very big offerings of money come from people who have made it illegally. Palani doesn't get anything like the offerings at Tirupati, but it gets.'

'So the sanyasi became a man of power?'

'The impression I get is that he was a very saintly man, and that he wasn't interested in things like power. He died when his daughter, my grandmother, was quite young. She was about fourteen. She had already been married, but she was living in her own parents' house – that was the custom. Before his death, the sanyasi had said to his wife, "If ever you have to depend on anybody, go and stay in the house of the husband of our eldest daughter." So my grandmother went to live in her husband's house, the house of my grandfather, and the whole family went with her.'

'How had that marriage been arranged – between your grandfather and grandmother?'

'We are a fairly small sub-sect of Tamil brahmins, and I guess that people were more sub-sect-minded in those days. Possibly everybody was distantly related. People kept records, or remembered, or kept track of everybody else – somebody's cousin's mother-in-law or something. This clannishness exists today in vestiges. People still keep track of distant kinspeople – which doesn't make sense to me.'

But Kala was in a position to make her own life. She had been educated; she had her job; she was free to come and go. Fifty years before, there would have been no job for her; the publicity job she did wouldn't have existed; even the kind of company she worked for mightn't have existed. People 50 years before would have thought and felt differently; the idea of the clan would have been comforting.

Kala said, 'Perhaps two generations ago the world didn't seem so small a place as it seems now.

'After his time in the college, my grandfather passed an examination, and he joined the government service. He rose. He was very dynamic. He had the reputation of being bold and honest. He went abroad many times.'

This was how Kala told the story, lingering over the boyhood and the street-lamp studying, and then racing away to the great success. It was almost like a proof of what Pravas had said, that with the development of the Indian economy, people had been sucked in and taken upwards.

'In the course of his life he had nine children. He also had his mother living with him, and his mother-in-law, and his sister-in-law. My grandfather was the only earning person in that house. There wasn't much money going around, but all his children were taught horse-riding, swimming and music, and they went in for trekking. I am sure this was a consequence of his career in administration.

'It's all like a story to me. As I knew my grandfather's place, there were no horses, no stables, no swimming. I've also heard of a palace the family lived in, when he served a princely state. There were peacocks in the garden. The stories are true. But those were different times. I feel no nostalgia; I just think it would have been a nice place to visit.

'By the time my grandfather was having this palace life, my mother had been married. So she didn't live in the palace. She just visited it. She had a baby daughter whom she took for a speedboat ride, when the baby was a month old or something. She said she knew the baby wouldn't remember the ride, but she wanted to share everything she knew with her daughter.'

And though Kala didn't say, I thought that the month-old baby girl might have been Kala herself.

'This part of the story, the story of my mother's marriage, is the most painful part. It is not pleasant and not easy for me to talk about it. My mother went to British schools, convents. She was very good in everything she did – music, sports, academic work. She was very bold and confident.' It was noticeable, Kala's approving emphasis on boldness. 'She wanted to do a lot of things. She thought she would like to be a doctor. She enjoyed going to school and wanted to study further. She was still very much a child at heart. She used to read a lot, English novels. Marriage was not on her mind at all. She was a child, a schoolgirl, almost like a British schoolgirl.' Kala, always grave, was now close to tears. 'She says she wasn't a very beautiful child, but I know that she was a very beautiful woman.

'She got married when she was fourteen, and there was nothing she could do about it. She said she would have just liked to be left alone. She was very distressed, and her elder brother and her boy cousins were also distressed. They, the boys, told her that she could run away – and they would take care of her.'

'Whose idea was this marriage?'

'It was her father's idea. My grandfather's idea.'

'Have you talked to him about it?'

'No.'

'Why not? You know him.'

'I know him pretty well. But he is no longer the man he was then, and I am sure that if he had been the man he is now, he would not have done what he did.

'My mother was in the 10th standard. I don't ask her too many questions about that. I find it too painful, and there is nothing I can do about it, sitting here now. Maybe it's a cowardly attitude on my part, not wanting to know more. She completed school – after her marriage she stayed on for a few more months. It was all quite embarrassing for her, the last few months. People kept asking her whether she was married – many of her friends were British girls or Anglo-Indians. All of them were a good deal older than her. Many of them had boy friends. There were a lot of Tommies around in Bangalore. This was in 1946.'

It was unsettling, this glimpse of 1946 and the real world, in what had up to then been like a far-off story: 1946, the British still in India, still in that cantonment area of Bangalore, but with independence coming, and with the deadly Hindu-Muslim riots about to happen in Calcutta.

I said, 'That year sounds very recent to me. It was just a year or so after Somerset Maugham had published *The Razor's Edge* – about sanyasis and people looking for self-realization.'

Kala said, 'That was a book she liked. She continued to read a lot. It was all wrong, that marriage,' Kala said, carefully using restrained language. 'They should have let her be. She would have become a far greater woman if they had left her alone.'

'Didn't your mother tell her father that the whole thing had become very embarrassing for her at school, after the marriage?'

'I don't think my mother would have told her father that.

'The next bit I don't find easy to talk about. She couldn't study any further. For a few years after her marriage she was virtually a chattel, working for the large joint family of her husband. Hard physical work – washing clothes and scrubbing vessels. She had no time to herself, no freedom. She wasn't allowed to go and visit her people when she wanted to. She could make no decisions as to what she would like to do with her own life. Somebody always decided for her.'

'What did your father think about all this?'

'My father was a quiet, easygoing, peaceable sort of person. His family was ruled by the older women in it.'

'Your grandfather was a distinguished man. How could he have married his daughter into that kind of family?'

'They were well thought of. They were an aristocratic family. They were considered to be philanthropists. They probably didn't practise what they preached. Many of the women of the family were in social welfare organizations. They were far better formally educated than they permitted my mother to be. It all comes down to double standards, a lack of sensitivity, a touch of cruelty.'

Cruelty, yes: it was in the nature of Indian family life. The clan that gave protection and identity, and saved people from the void, was itself a little state, and it could be a hard place, full of politics, full of hatreds and changing alliances and moral denunciations. It was the kind of family life I had known for much of my childhood: an early introduction to the ways of the world, and to the nature of cruelty. It had given me, as I suspected it had given Kala, a taste for the other kind of life, the solitary or less crowded life, where one had space around oneself.

But I didn't think that what Kala said about double standards was appropriate. Hindu family life was ritualized. Just as there were rituals for every new stage in a person's life, so there were roles that people were required to fill as they progressed through their allotted years. Mothers-in-law were required to discipline the child brides of their sons, to train the unbroken and childish girls in their new duties as child-bearers and household workers, to teach them new habits of respect, to introduce them to the almost philosophical idea of the toil and tears of the real world: to introduce them, in this chain of tradition, to the kind of life and ideas they had been introduced to by their own mothers-in-law. Such a disciplining of a child bride would have been considered virtuous; the cruelty, however willed, however voluptuous, would have been seen as no more than the cruelty of life itself. The social work the women of the family did would have been directed to people several layers below, many times more abject. The very wish to do social work would have issued out of an idea of virtue and correctness at home. The concept of double standards came from another world, came from Kala's world today.

Kala said, 'It was a total shock for my mother. She was the only daughter-in-law. She would be the last person considered for any kind of treat or outing. There wouldn't be room in the car for her. And she was still so much a child herself. Everyone was so much older. She was hit sometimes.' This was too painful for Kala to talk about. 'Both her mother-in-law and her husband hit her. Somehow, suddenly, as soon as she was married she was expected to turn into an adult.'

'Have you talked to your father's family about this?'

She hadn't. 'By the time I knew about it, everyone was so much older. There was no point in picking a quarrel. This life went on for five years.'

'Your grandfather was a man of such dignity and honour. Didn't he do anything for his daughter?'

'Hindu parents were not supposed to question what was being done to their daughters after they had been married. It wasn't that they didn't know; they were not supposed to question. They would, nowadays.

'In these five years my mother talked a lot to my father. She talked to him, and eventually they decided that they shouldn't live in that house any longer. My father applied for a job in a tea plantation in the Nilgiris. He got the job, and they moved there.

'That was where I grew up until I went to my boarding school. It was a nice colonial town. As I knew it, there were just the vestiges of colonialism – a Christian culture, parties. It didn't matter what religion you practised. There were no visible British people living there; there were lots of Anglo-Indians. The houses were colonial in design – high ceilings, wooden floors, big gardens, porticoes, servants' quarters some distance away from the house. It felt normal to live there.'

To Kala's mother it might also have been a version of, it might have echoed, the convent life from which she had been snatched five or six years before.

'The happiness began for you in the Nilgiris?'

'I think so. But the marks are still there. What might have been. It's all been a tremendous waste, the waste of potential in a woman nobody considered important. I value freedom a great deal now. My mother has always taught me how important education and financial independence are.'

'You aren't married?'

'I have nothing against the institution, but I don't see it as a goal.'

'Does your mother worry about that?'

'She would like me to get married. But not with any specific time limit. She wants me to be happy. And I feel that, compared to what she went through, anything I go through would appear trifling.'

She was still part of the story she had told me, over two or three meetings. She was full of the emotions of it, and unable to see in it the historical progression that I thought I saw.

She said, on another day, 'I do think about the individuals involved, all of them, and I sometimes wonder what they really felt at certain moments. I think all of them were very courageous people. Each of them displayed some kind of courage in making the changes that they did make. I wonder whether I would be able to display the same sort of courage, if I were put in a difficult or trying situation.'

'I don't think any of us can really know how our grandfathers and grandmothers thought or felt.'

Kala said, 'The world they lived in was very different.'

Prakash, a minister in the non-Congress state government of Karnataka, invited me to breakfast one Sunday morning. The minister's house was near the hotel, and Deviah came and walked there with me.

We had to walk carefully, picking our way over broken or unmade footpaths. Level or fully made footpaths are not a general Indian need, and the Indian city road is often like a wavering, bumpy, much mended asphalt path between drifts of dust and dirt and the things that get dumped on Indian city roads and then stay there, things like sand, gravel, wet rubbish, dry rubbish: nothing ever looking finished, no kerbstone, no wall, everything in a half-and-half way, half-way to being or ceasing to be.

Deviah and I would have liked to talk while we walked, but it was hard. We were being kippered all the time by the gritty smoke from cars and scooters. The dust these vehicles kicked up took a long time to settle down, so we walked in dust as well. By the time we reached the minister's house we had become part of the Bangalore road scene, with dust and fumy grit on skin and clothes and shoes and hair and glasses.

This invitation to breakfast gave a touch of the specialist industrial fair, of drama and American rush, to the politician's life. And, in fact, this early-morning time was when ministers and politicians of importance were very busy. Suppliants (with their own idea of the drama of the occasion), rising and getting ready in darkness, went at dawn to wait outside a great man's house – just as, in ancient Rome, a client's first duty in the morning was to run to the house of his patron, to add to the crowd there, for the sake of the great man's dignity. As in old Rome, so in modern Bangalore: the more important the man, the greater the crowd at his door.

Prakash wasn't among the top crowd-pullers. He had a more sedate reputation as an educated and competent minister, a shrewd and serious politician, yet capable of detachment: someone a little out of the ordinary in state politics.

He lived in one of the houses built by the Karnataka government for state ministers. These houses stood together in an area or park of their own. They were two-storey concrete houses, light-ochre in colour, and they were on biggish plots. There wasn't a crowd outside Prakash's house, such as I had seen at other people's houses, but there was a fair enough press of suppliants – patient, almost idle – to establish the man's importance. There were parked cars and security people in the yard. The parked cars suggested privilege: they looked as though they belonged to people with easy access to the minister.

Deviah and I were in that category that Sunday morning. Nothing was said, but the fact seemed to be known; and, road-stained though we were, the suppliants yielded as we approached, and a path to Prakash's front door opened between them. From the outside, the house had looked only like a house. It wasn't so.

We walked through a number of grimy, official-looking rooms that might have been the much used offices of some government department, and appeared to be staffed by government clerks. We came then to a more personal sitting room, more personal but still with an official feel, with many low armchairs around a low centre table. The day's newspapers, flat and new and undisturbed, were neatly laid out on the table in two staggered rows, each paper showing only its masthead. Some of the mastheads were in English or Hindi; others were in regional scripts.

Prakash, true to his character, didn't keep us waiting. Almost as soon as he had been told we had arrived, and before I could pick up one of the papers, he came in from an inner room to greet us, a small, brisk, confident, humorous-looking man in his forties; and he immediately led us to the room adjoining, a dining-room – this part of the house now quite private and personal, quite different in its atmosphere even from the sitting room – where a big table was laid for a most serious kind of Indian breakfast. And almost as soon as we had sat down at the table, Mrs Prakash appeared, in a fresh blue sari, and began serving us: the ritualized duty of the conservative Hindu wife, personally to serve food to her husband: a duty, but also now, considering what her husband was, a high privilege. How many of the people waiting outside would have envied her that familiarity with the minister, that attending on him; to how many would she have appeared blessed.

I asked about the men he had been seeing that morning, the men who had been waiting outside the front door, and had made way for us as people infinitely more privileged. The most important one among them, Prakash said, was a village accountant in government service. He had been charged with misappropriating 5000 rupees, about £200, from the land revenue which it was his duty to collect. This man had been suspended from his job, and he had travelled all night on a bus, making a journey of 200 miles, to see the minister that morning. Prakash had seen him for seven or eight minutes. The man said he had paid back the 5000 rupees, and he wanted Prakash to help him to be reinstated in his job. Prakash had told him that he could do nothing; the departmental inquiry would have to take its course. And that was it: after the 200-mile night journey, and the morning wait at the minister's house, and the seven or eight-minute audience, the village accountant would just have to take the bus back to his village.

Prakash's wife kept on bringing little side dishes, and serving us from dishes that had already been placed on the table. She brought from time to time fresh hot puris, crisp and swollen.

Prakash, eating away elegantly with his fingers, said, 'Now that fellow will take the matter to the High Court – after the departmental inquiry.'

I said, 'So it will become like a career to him?'

Prakash said, 'If the High Court finds there has been a technical flaw in the departmental inquiry –'

'And most often there is,' Deviah said, also eating, picking at this and that.

Prakash said, 'If there's been that technical flaw, he will get his reinstatement, and his back wages. During his suspension – he has been suspended – he will be getting a subsistence allowance of 75 per cent of his salary.'

I said, 'What sort of background for that kind of man?'

Prakash said, 'Such a man will be the son of a farmer or a local artisan. In government service he will be getting about 1200 rupees a month.' About £48. 'That's why everybody in a village tries for a government job – unless they have good land. If he loses his case, he will go back to nothing. He will have to depend on agriculture.'

The man we were talking about was thirty-six. He had three children. He had come to see Prakash because he belonged to Prakash's constituency. This was in the Bellary district, and agriculture there would have been very hard. Bellary was known in the state as a 'hot area', with summer temperatures of 105 degrees.

Prakash said, 'He might have misappropriated this sum of 5000 rupees over one or two years. People come to pay their land revenue, and he takes their money. Small sums, 25 rupees or so at a time. He gives bogus receipts. And then one day a superior officer asks why farmers here and there are not paying their land revenue. He makes some simple inquiries; he sees the bogus receipts; and the foolish fellow is caught.'

Deviah said, 'He might even think it's unfair, when so many bigger people all around him are taking and getting away.'

I asked Prakash, 'Did the man cry? Did he drop to the ground and hold your legs?'

Prakash, with his witty way of talking, said, 'He might have cried the first night, after he'd been caught. But after a year he's become hardened.'

I liked that 'hardened'. Prakash, in real life or civilian life, the life before politics, had been a country lawyer, and he knew his people.

'But now he's grown fatalistic. He talks of *karma,* fate. It is the Hindu way.'

'Would people in his village look down on him or ostracize him now?'

'At his level people wouldn't bother with that kind of theft. I don't think they would even know about it. The upper class in India take theft for granted. It's only the middle class who are still maintaining these values, and worrying about theft and corruption. It's in the social fibre. It's everywhere. At an appointments board someone will jump up and say, "I'm sorry, I can't interview the next candidate. He's my brother-in-law. You must excuse me." Perfectly nice and correct, but it is also an indication to the panel that the candidate in question is the man's brother-in-law.'

He broke off and, lifting a side dish, said, 'Everything in this house has been provided by the government. Every cup, every plate. How can a man give up this life?' He was referring not to himself, but to others. 'It's in the social fibre, as I say. In the old days the maharajas used to get their land revenue. But in addition to that people would go and offer them gifts – gold, ornaments, fruits, coconuts. They would offer it on a plate, and the plate would be of brass or silver, according to your status. The present-day maharajas are the ministers. Indira Gandhi was a maharani.

'Buying religious favours is another equivalent. There again you have different levels of gifts. Some people might give only a coconut. Do you know the story about the temple at Tirupati?'

It was the story I had heard from Kala.

Prakash said, 'You give money there to help Lord Venkateshwara to repay his loan from Kubera. He borrowed the money to get married.'

Kala had left out the last detail. Perhaps it was so, detail added to detail, that difficult mythological stories grew in the minds of people here.

We got up from the breakfast table then, to go to the State Guest House. Prakash had thought we would have more privacy there, and not be troubled by suppliants.

A fresh batch was waiting outside the front door. One small, smiling fellow, in sandals, was neatly dressed in tight brown trousers and a clean beige-and-yellow Polyester shirt in a check pattern. He was a driver. He was pining for a job with the government. He wasn't unemployed, but he was working for a private firm, and the pay there wasn't as good as it would have been with the government. Prakash had given the man a recommendation some months before, but the man hadn't got a government job; so he had made this morning trip to Prakash again, to complain and plead.

And as royalty, moving among a welcoming crowd, finds a word or two for a selected few, so Prakash, moving among his breakfast suppliants – but not strictly like royalty, more like a medical professor in the ward of a teaching hospital – found words to say to a few, but the words apparently spoken to the suppliant were really words spoken to Deviah and me about the suppliant, and were spoken as though the suppliant wasn't absolutely with us, as though Deviah and I were medical students making the round of a hospital ward, and Prakash, our professor, was talking about people prostrate on their beds or with bandaged limbs in slings and pulleys.

One man did look like a hospital case, and he was showing a very dirty, very creased official form in the local Kannada script which seemed to say – Prakash knew about this man, had met him earlier that morning – that his wife was a cancer patient in a Bangalore hospital. The man's story was that he had come to Bangalore to put his wife in the hospital; he wanted now to go back to his village, but he didn't have any money; he wanted 42 rupees for the bus fare.

The fellow looked quite spectacularly broken down. He was thin and half-starved, with a worn tunic made from some kind of commercial hessian sack, with the commercial lettering on the sacking only half washed out. The top of his nose was skinned, down to the red flesh, and he was carrying a baby and a feeding bottle.

As soon as we came within prostrating distance, this fellow, holding the baby in one arm, made a dive with his other hand for Prakash's feet, in an exaggerated gesture of respect – taking care, during his downward sweep, first to set the feeding bottle upright on the concrete surround of Prakash's house. Prakash made a gesture to the wretched man to get up. The man got up, bent down again to pick up the feeding bottle, dandled the shaken-up baby a little, put the bottle in the baby's mouth, and fixed wild eyes on Prakash. Prakash looked at the man, not really returning the gaze, looking more with something like social or academic distance, and – seeming to assess the man while he spoke – gave Deviah and me a little lecture about the man's condition.

People who were taken into the hospital could have their spouses stay with them, Prakash said. It was a legal provision. If this fellow said he wanted the fare to go back to his village, it was because he chose not to take advantage of that facility. The fellow was probably making the rounds of ministers and other people that morning. Prakash himself had already that morning issued instructions to someone on his staff to give the fellow a couple of rupees, though he wasn't sure that the fellow was genuine.

'And if he does get the 42 rupees for the ticket back,' Deviah said, 'he will probably travel without a ticket.'

The presentation of need was extraordinary. Perhaps it was too much of a production, with the baby and the bottle and the sacking tunic. But the wild-eyed man looked a genuine wreck, genuinely ill and wasted.

Prakash was cool. Leading us now to his car, as though the lecture was almost over, he said that people like that didn't come from the traditional begging groups or castes. They fell into the way of life by accident, or example, or encouragement; they were surprised by the rewards. And then, Prakash added, with an alliterative flourish, 'They become addicted and adjusted.'

(And Prakash was right. More than a week later, when Deviah and I were talking to a state legislator in his room at the legislators' hostel, this wretched man appeared, with the baby and the milk bottle, but without the sacking tunic, and without the official-looking form that said his wife was in the cancer hospital. The legislator's assistants drove the man away immediately, and he went off without a word. He wasn't as wild-eyed as he had been at Prakash's; his skinned nose had begun to heal, and he looked curiously rested. He was as careful with the baby as he had been at Prakash's; perhaps he had borrowed it against a deposit of some kind.)

We went on in Prakash's car through the dusty roads to the State Guest House. Minister at home, minister here too: people jumped about at his appearance. I began to feel the range of his power, began a little to see Karnataka through Prakash's eyes; though the room we were shown into, for our private talk, was a rough little hostel bedroom with a high urine smell, and with the one table in it too low for me to write on.

We went to the main guest house. It was a big stone building in the centre of the tawny grounds. When we were settled in the wide verandah on the upper floor, I asked Prakash about political power in India. How did people come by it? What were a man's qualifications for power?

Caste, he said, was the first thing of importance. A man looking for office or a political career would have to be of a suitable caste. That meant belonging to the dominant caste of the area. He would also, of course, have to be someone who could get the support of his caste; that meant he would have to be of some standing in the community, well connected and well known. And since it seldom happened that the votes of a single caste could win a man an election, a candidate needed a political party; he needed that to get the votes of the other castes. So the whole parliamentary business of political parties and elections made sense in India. It encouraged co-operation and compromise; the very multiplicity of Indian castes and communities made for some kind of balance.

Power achieved here, Prakash said, was very great, in the surroundings of Indian life, the surroundings of struggle and making do. And the fall, the loss of power, was equally great, and could be very hard to bear.

The chairs in the stone verandah were heavy and ugly, government chairs, bleached and dulled by sunlight; and there were very many of them. The verandah, not yet in direct light, was nevertheless full of glare. The trees in the brown-grass grounds were few; the shadows emphasized the light and the dryness. The big rolled-up green blinds were the only decorative touch in the verandah, and they added to the bare, dull, official feeling of the State Guest House.

Prakash said, 'When the average politician falls he will have nowhere to go, and no cushion. He may be an advocate in a country area, or a son of a peasant or landlord, or son or brother of a petty merchant; but not a man with a lot of money. And many may not come from a movement.'

'Movement?'

'Movement would be the Independence movement, or the movement against Indira Gandhi's Emergency, or the peasant movement here in this state, or the labour movement, or any people's movement. When you don't come from such a movement, and you have nothing to fall back upon when you lose power, you are in a hurry to make money.

'The power gives so much of comfort, perks, and status – a bungalow, all fully furnished, all personal attendants and secretarial staff. A chauffeur-driven car, and facilities to stay in government bungalows and guest houses when you travel out, and air tickets – you can fly around at the expense of the government. But when you come out of power, if you have no means, you may have to go back to the semi-urban area from where you came. There you can hardly afford to have a secretary or servants. You may have one servant, but not the bunch of servants you had as a minister. Or the free telephone calls.'

Prakash appeared to be speaking against these things, but I thought I could detect a certain lingering over the details of privilege. He had been a minister for six years, and now his government, from what I could decipher in the newspapers, was in some trouble.

I said, 'Servants. You talk a lot about servants. Are servants very important to these men from the country areas?'

Prakash was a lawyer, ironic, bright: he detected my drift. He said, 'In the good old days too many servants, for the big landlords, the zamindars, and the feudals, gave a status. Today it is the power. Servants are there to make your life comfortable. If you are a minister, and you travel on an aeroplane, there will be somebody to buy you a ticket. There will always be a block of seats for the government, and these will be kept till the last minute; so there is always a chance that you will get a ticket. And your P.A., your personal assistant, will come right up to the airport to see you off' – Prakash again lingering over the details, savouring the things he still enjoyed – 'and at the destination somebody will come and receive you. There will be a vehicle at your disposal, and your reservation of accommodation has already been made.

'But as a man without power' – and now, as a preacher painting a picture of purgatory, to balance the heaven of success, Prakash began to darken the details of Indian air travel – 'many a time you will not know where to buy a ticket, where to stand in a queue, how to get your baggage checked. In a western society, which is so very orderly, between a man with privileges and a common man there won't be a big gap in the physical arrangement of life, arrangement of travel and comforts and stay.

'Even in western countries it is an innate thing in a man to look to be in power. And it is all the more so in India, because the power means everything here. When an American president leaves the White House, it makes no difference as far as his lifestyle is concerned, and his physical comforts. Many a time in India it wouldn't be like that, unless you have a will to live in austerity, like the old gods of the Gandhian era.

'Our new-generation politicians don't have that spiritual power, and they feel the difference. They try for a while, after they have fallen, to capitalize on their so-called contacts with the authorities. They undertake certain commissions for people who want things done. But those contacts very soon go away. And the industrialist who courted you drives by in his big car to his rich house in his nice area, and he doesn't even look at you.

'Because of industrialization, and the green revolution in the rural areas, a new class of nouveau-riche persons are emerging, and these people are being exposed for the first time to university education, comfortable urban life, stylish living, and western influences – materialistic comforts. During this transition period, we are slowly cutting from the moral ethos of our grandfathers, and at the same time we don't have the westerner's idea of discipline and social justice. At the moment things are chaotic here.'

I would have liked him to talk more personally. But it wasn't easy. The political crisis in his government, the glimpse of the possibility of the end of things, was encouraging him to put a distance between himself and the delights of power. It was at the same time bringing out his political combativeness. It was making him moralize in an old-fashioned way (almost as though he had already left office) about Gandhianism, materialism, and the dangers to India of the super computer the people in Delhi were talking about.

At last he said, 'I wasn't rich, but I wasn't poor. My family could live in comfort and with security. This was in Bellary. I have land there, and much of what I needed was produced on my land – millet, rice, tamarind, chili, vegetables, and fuel. I can go back any time. But after six years in office here I can notice a change in my children. Their formative years have been spent in this opulence and status, and people giving so much concern and attention to them. Now they don't wish to go back to the village. For me it's nothing.

'Bellary is very hot. And many of these relatives and friends of mine feel a little awestruck when they come here. The friends may have a little jealousy, friends from the village, or people who worked along with me in the old days and have seen me walking the streets of a small place. Now they feel I've become all-important, and there is a jealousy – and this is apart from the ruthlessness of the system, where my own colleagues are pulling down my legs when I am climbing up fast. This is innate in the system, but the jealousy is different.

'Even my voter, he will be more comfortable to talk to me when I am there, in my abode. But when he comes here and sits on a sofa' – it was interesting, getting this idea of the world as it appeared to Prakash's voter, seeing even the drabness of the State Guest House transformed – 'when he sits here, with this big garden, lawn, police people, attendants, it makes him ill at ease, and immediately he feels I am too far away, and that personal equation goes away or changes.'

Car doors banged outside the Guest House. Someone, or some party, had arrived. Very quickly after the banging of the doors a briskly moving group of men in coloured robes came up the steps and walked through the inner room: big men in big shoes, taking firm strides. I saw this only at an angle; I was sitting slightly turned away from the inner room. And then Prakash, lowering his voice, told me it was the Dalai Lama who had arrived.

It was a little unlikely, but I was half prepared. I knew that the Dalai Lama was on tour in India. In Bombay I had read in the newspaper one day that the Dalai Lama was coming to the city to visit Buddhists there. I wasn't sure what was meant by that. When people in Bombay spoke of Buddhists they didn't mean Tibetans; they were more likely to mean Dalit neo-Buddhists. But I hadn't asked further about the Dalai Lama's visit to Bombay. And now, without any announcement I had heard of, with only a few cars, and few state policemen, he had come even further south, and was really far from home.

The Dalai Lama moved so fast that, almost as soon as Prakash had told me who it was, the figure had gone through the inner room, half hidden by an assistant walking close to him, swinging a briefcase. The end of a stride, the swing of the assistant's briefcase – that was all I had really caught.

Afterwards, monks came out to the wide verandah where we were sitting. After the rush of their arrival, they were calmer. From the bareness of the verandah they looked down at the scorched lawn and gardens. Their heads were shaved, and they wore sweaters below their dark-red robes. It seemed at first that they were only staring at the strange aspect of the Indian South. But they were looking for their followers.

Prakash told me there was a Tibetan 'camp' near Mysore City, about 100 miles to the south. There, on land that had been given them by the Indian government, the Tibetans grew maize, did dairy farming, and knitted their distinctive sweaters. There had been no Tibetans in the grounds of the State Guest House when we had arrived. But gradually, in small informal groups, the Tibetans from the Mysore City camp – who had been waiting in the streets outside – began to appear on the burnt lawn, the women in traditional Tibetan dress, the men in jeans, bright-faced, handsome people, who perhaps now, after more than a generation away, were beginning to lose touch with home: another Asian dispossession, part of the historical flux.

My thoughts for some time were with those people. The monks remained on the verandah, looking out, as though they wanted to fix their gaze for a while on each person in the small, scattered, waiting groups. And even when Prakash began to speak again, I felt we were continuing to be part of that wordless Tibetan scene.

Prakash said, 'Our people, because of the long tradition of the rajas and maharajas and feudal lords, they always look with awe and fear on the seat of power, and at the same time they nourish a dislike and hatred towards the seat of power. But there is a dichotomy. They like an accessible, simple, compassionate, benevolent man in the seat of power. But at the same time they have a mental picture of power – of pomp, pageantry, authority and aristocracy. These things don't go together many times.

'In a case like me, they would like to see me as their good old humble country lawyer – as before 1983, when I came to power and became a minister. But they will respect my authority only if I'm surrounded by a group of officers, and if I myself assume postures.

'On the 16th of February 1983 I took the oath of secrecy and office as a minister at Bangalore. On the same day there was a communal disturbance at Bellary – with a police firing, seven deaths, arson and looting. I immediately that night left for Bellary by car, 200 miles down. And I immediately assumed the authority there, and started directing the District Inspector of Police, the Deputy Commissioner of Bellary, and other officers. And I was able to control the disturbance in a day.

'As a lawyer, I had appeared before the Deputy Commissioner of Bellary in several cases, where I used to address him as "Your Honour". But, as a minister, there was a transformation. I suited giving him commands. Within a day there was a change in me. And people wouldn't have liked it, and the situation wouldn't have been controlled, if I had just been a *mofussil* lawyer. It's a very strange society we've created. Democracy has made it possible for people like us to have a different role.'

And his government had cut down on ministerial pomp. There had been a lot more in the Congress days: police escorts, red lights flashing to warn off cars, sirens. In those days people couldn't just turn up at the ministers' houses; they had to have an appointment.

Power came from the people. The people were poor; but the power they gave was intoxicating. As high as a man could be taken up, so low, when he lost power, he could be cast down. So the legislators were in a frenzy from the start, and in constant movement, like a group of penguins in an Antarctic blizzard, the ones at the outer rim seeking to work their way through the seething mass to the warm centre. The politics of the state, the comings and goings which filled the local newspapers, were the politics of alignment and realignment. When a majority became shaky, a politician's vote in the chamber became an asset: it could be sold any number of times. Recently (I heard this from another politician), there had been 10 very difficult men who required a lakh of rupees, 100,000 rupees, £4000, for every vote they cast in the chamber. The government and opposition parties had to raise funds to meet these expenses; the ways they chose to raise those funds could be controversial.

The politics of the state, as reported in the newspapers, were opaque to the visitor. In the politics of alignment and realignment there were no principles or programmes. There were only enemies or allies: penguin politics. What was true of this state, Karnataka, was true of other states as well. There were very many columns of the newspapers that one could ignore, or take as read. Political knowledge didn't come from learning the names, just as computer skill didn't come from trying to learn a computer programme by heart. The programmes could be changed or abandoned; the politicians could disappear, or move about very fast.

It seemed miraculous that there was government at all. But, with the growth of the Indian economy, active governments generated the greatest profit for all. And out of the political frenzy there had come a kind of balance: for the first time in the history of India, perhaps, most people felt that they or their representatives, someone of their group, had a chance of getting to the warm centre of power and money.

Prakash was that day in the midst of yet another crisis of some sort, which was taking up a lot of space in the newspapers. We walked down to the asphalted area around the Guest House, where four or five middle-aged men, chewing pan, in fresh cream-coloured homespun tunics and dhotis, with an air about them of sweet conspiracy, were waiting for him in the bright light – a little distance away from the cars and khaki-clad policemen of the Dalai Lama's party. Legislators were being asked that day to sign a loyalty statement, and there was much of the eternal counting of Gandhi-capped heads. Homespun clothes, once the clothes of the poor, now no longer worn by the poor, worn only by the men to whom the poor had given power.

People of all conditions spoke with respect of the days of the old maharajas, and there was a reminder of old Mysore glory in the three-mile-long wall of the palace park in the centre of Bangalore. The palace there had been only the summer palace of the maharajas. It stood deep within the park and couldn't be seen from the road. The park itself, immensely valuable as land alone, was now the subject of litigation, and was closed to the public.

The main palace was in Mysore City, 100 miles to the south. I heard from Deviah that there was still a barber in Mysore City who had been in the service of the 25th and last maharaja. There was also a brahmin who had acted as a pundit of some sort to the maharaja. The barber was said to be full of stories; but Deviah and I went to Mysore one day to see the brahmin.

The road was good, one of the roads of the old Mysore State. It was shaded for long stretches by the big rain trees that had been planted in the time of the maharajas, and were now looked upon almost as part of the continuing bounty of the maharajas. And there were rich green fields that had come into being because of the irrigation works undertaken by the famous chief minister of the 24th maharaja.

Mysore City was built around the palace. We had a glimpse of part of the grounds as we entered the city. Tempting; but that spaciousness and splendour were for later. Our business that morning lay in the city itself, in a small concrete marriage hall, which the former pundit of the maharaja was now supervising. The marriage hall was new and quite ordinary-looking, but it belonged to a foundation that had been set up by the ninth-century philosopher Shankaracharya. So the pundit, though he might appear to be doing commercial work, was still close to religion.

He was a small man of seventy-two. Three broad bands of white ran horizontally across his forehead, and there was a red-and-sandalwood dot between his eyebrows. He had a gold-set ruby earring in each ear. His white tunic was buttoned over a small belly, and this belly was curiously narrow and long; so that, buttoned in the tunic, the pundit appeared to have the shape of a cucumber. The white holy marks on his forehead came from the ash of burnt cowdung. The cowdung was burnt for that purpose on a special day, Shiva-ratri, Shiva's Night. Deviah told this story about Shiva-ratri: every day Shiva watches over the world, but there is one day when he falls asleep, and Hindus on that day (or night) have to stay awake, to watch.

We met the pundit in the office room of the marriage hall. It was a small plain room, with cream-coloured walls, and with an iron chest in one corner and some bedding on the red concrete floor. A red telephone stood on a shelf in another corner, next to a board with four keys. One wall had inset shelves, painted green. Old fluorescent light tubes with attached electric wires (no doubt meant for use in the marriage hall, and stored here as a precaution against theft) were on one shelf; loose electric bulbs were on another shelf; a stack of thin booklets of some sort, together with a number of old-looking paper-wrapped parcels, were on a third shelf. From a nail or a hook at the side of the green inset shelves a woven bag hung flat against the wall. The wall was like a piece of furniture: it was a place for putting things or hanging things.

The pundit was born in 1916. His father was not from Mysore, but from Tamil Nadu; he acted as agent for an absentee landlord, and he was also a dealer in grain. The pundit's mother came from Mysore. Since women return to their parents' house for the birth of their children, the pundit was born in Mysore. He was then taken to Tamil Nadu by his parents; but when he was ten his father died, and his mother's father brought him back to Mysore and put him in the Sanskrit College in Mysore City.

He had a Mysore government scholarship to the Sanskrit College. Anybody who wanted to study Sanskrit was given a scholarship. He started with a scholarship of two rupees a month, about 16 pence. Two rupees were quite enough for a boy of ten in 1926; the salary of a first-division clerk at that time was 30 rupees.

The pundit was not a fluent talker. He waited for questions, and Deviah translated his replies.

Deviah translated: 'It was my grandfather who put me in the college. He was a cook in the palace, and I don't know whether he knew about the scholarship when he put me in the college. We weren't living in the palace; we were living in a rented house outside the palace. My grandfather used to cook for the palace pujas. He cooked the food that was consecrated. He earned 18 rupees a month. Though he was a cook at the palace, he never ate there. He ate at home – this was his custom as a brahmin. He lived for 92 years.'

The pundit studied at the Sanskrit College for 20 years, from 1926, when he was ten, to 1946. Over those years the two-rupee scholarship he had started with was increased, bit by bit.

One of the important things he studied was astrology. He studied that for five years. He had a teacher who was a very famous astrologer.

'There is no end to learning as an astrologer. Just as science keeps on developing, with new discoveries, so I've not stopped learning about astrology.'

On the desk at which the pundit sat was a little dark-blue or grey plastic bag – plastic, not leather, which was the skin of an animal and unclean. On the wall above his head was a framed colour picture of Shiva and his consort. Light had bleached the colours. Both figures had been given as much beauty as the artist could give: a feminine beauty, of an almost erotic nature.

The pundit said, 'We can tell a person's blood group by the day he was born. We have three blood groups, and we can say whether people are compatible or not. They don't have to take a blood test. There is no difference between astrology, medicine, and *dharmashastra*.' Deviah translated this as 'traditional learning'. 'To learn astrology, you first have to learn all the other sciences. Before you prescribe certain medicines, you have to look for certain planetary conditions, because certain medicines work only under certain circumstances. Certain medicines work only under the rays of the sun, or the moon, or Mars or Mercury.'

He could predict the future. 'If you give the correct time of birth – but it has to be down to the minute – I will tell you everything correctly. If there's a minute's error, it makes a world of difference. The place is also important.'

In 1946, after 20 years, he came to the end of his studies at the Sanskrit College. He had lived for all this time on his scholarship from the state government. In his last year at the college this scholarship was 15 rupees a month. He was now thirty, and he was at last free to get married. He married the daughter of a man who worked as a clerk in the palace. He also found a job; he became librarian at the same Sanskrit College, at a salary of 45 rupees a month. He stayed in that job for 16 years.

One of the projects he worked on as librarian of the Sanskrit College was the translation of all the Puranas, the sacred old texts of Hinduism, into Kannada, the local Mysore language. This project was sponsored by the maharaja, and the pundit's work on it came to the maharaja's notice. The maharajas in India had lost their titles in 1956, but they still had their privy purses; and in Mysore the maharaja still had considerable ceremonial standing as state governor, *raja pramukh*.

One afternoon in 1962, on a day of the full moon, the pundit had finished his puja and was sitting at home, when a servant came from the palace. The servant had been sent by the maharaja's secretary, and the message was that the pundit was wanted at the palace by the maharaja. The maharaja would have told his A.D.C., and the A.D.C. would have told the secretary, and the secretary would have told his servant.

The pundit must already have had some idea of what the maharaja wanted, or he must have been given some idea by the servant. Because, when this call from the palace came, the pundit straight away sent word to the palace, to both his father-in-law and his grandfather, the one a palace clerk, the other a cook.

The grandfather hurried home. He was happy for his grandson's sake, but he was also nervous. He said to the pundit, 'You have been trained as a scholar, a *vaidhika*. But the work you are going to do now is that of a *loukika* – worldly work. You may not fit in. Think of that.' He also gave his grandson detailed instructions about how he was to behave when he came into the maharaja's presence.

At about three in the afternoon, when it would have been very hot, the pundit left his house to walk to the palace. He was dressed as a brahmin, in his dhoti, and with a shawl over his shoulders. Otherwise he was bare above the waist. He was barefooted. It was his way; he had never worn footwear of any kind; to this day he never wore anything on his feet – and, indeed, when I looked below the desk or table at which the pundit sat, I saw his bare feet flat on the red concrete floor, the skin dark and thickened at the soles, padded and cracked. It was no trouble either to walk barebacked in the afternoon sun; the pundit was used to that.

It was about half a kilometre to the palace. He met the secretary in one of the inner rooms, and the secretary sent him in directly to the maharaja, who was in the palace library. The library consisted of three rooms, each about 40 feet long by 25 feet wide. They were all full of books, with hardly a place to sit down. The books were in all languages.

In one of those rooms the maharaja was sitting. The pundit went up to him and did the obeisance his grandfather had trained him in, bringing the palms together and bowing low. The maharaja was wearing a djibba and a dhoti, and he was in a 'social' mood.

'What did he look like?'

'He was a tall man, built like a king. Hefty.' He wasn't thinking only of the seated figure he had seen that day in the library; he was thinking of the man he had later got to know. 'In the morning, after his puja, when he came out with his holy marks on his forehead, he looked like God.'

The maharaja – but that wasn't the word the pundit used: he used the English word 'Highness', pronouncing it in a way that made it sound part of the local language – the maharaja, Highness, told the pundit that he had been chosen to work in the palace.

'I hadn't applied for the job or anything. So bravely I told Highness what my grandfather had told me, that I had lived all my life as a vaidhika, and couldn't now live as a loukika. And Highness said, "I am using you here only for vaidhika work. I want you to be *mukhthesar*."

'I knew what the duties of a mukhthesar were. They were to organize all the pujas of the palace, to choose the purohits or priests, and to supervise what they did, to make sure that the pujas and rituals were correctly carried out.'

The maharaja spoke to the pundit for half an hour. He told him what he would have to do. There were 10 permanent purohits in the palace; the pundit would have to supervise them, and all the additional purohits who might be called in on special occasions. The pundit would also have to look after the jewels of the palace temple. People who worked in the palace were given a special allowance of 20 rupees a month, and the maharaja told the pundit that he would be getting this allowance. The allowance was given because palace staff were on call all the time and had no leave. The salary itself would be 150 rupees; as librarian at the Sanskrit College the pundit was getting 45 rupees a month.

'It was my duty to do it. Whatever Highness said, I had to do. I was already an employee of Highness, because the Sanskrit College belonged to Highness.'

After his audience in the library the pundit walked back to his family house. He told his father-in-law and grandfather the news, and his grandfather was pleased. He said, 'We've all got good names in the palace. You should do your work well and keep our good name there.'

As someone working in the palace the pundit had to have a uniform. He immediately went to the palace tailor to be measured. He ordered two suits, and the charge was 200 rupees, more than a month's salary. But for some reason the maharaja wanted the pundit to start working in the palace right away. So the pundit was in a quandary about what to wear – the uniforms he had ordered from the tailor weren't going to be ready for some days.

The pundit said, 'I did a mad thing. I borrowed my father-in-law's uniform. We were the same build.' And that was a mad thing to do, because a brahmin shouldn't wear other people's clothes: it was as unclean as drinking from a vessel used by someone else. 'For three days I wore my father-in-law's uniform. Then I had my own from the palace tailor, the two suits. I got them on credit. I didn't have 200 rupees. I paid with my salary, and paid it off in three or four instalments.'

He wore white trousers and a long coat. The coat was white for the mornings, black at night. He wore the Mysore turban, white with a gold band; and he got a white sash. No shoes: inside the palace no one wore shoes, not even the maharaja. The maharaja wore shoes only outside the palace.

On the cream-coloured wall of the marriage-hall office where we were talking there were finger-prints of grime, the eternal grime of India. The floor was dark red, and some inches up the wall were skirting areas in the same colour. Pale-green doors led to other rooms; over a padlocked door – leading perhaps to the marriage hall itself – was a gay *No Admission* sign in a wavy scroll. And, as in an Indian city street, where nothing was absolutely clean or finished, there was in this room, in the corner with the iron chest, a lot of half-swept-up dust and old fluffy dirt, together with the rags and the broom that might have done the sweeping and the wiping. The desk at which the pundit sat was of steel, and painted grey.

The pundit's working hours, as palace mukhthesar, were long. They were from six in the morning to two in the afternoon. He would go home then for an hour, and go back to the palace and stay till seven. That was on ordinary days. On certain days, like the days of the Dussehra festival, the pundit could stay at the palace until midnight. This was because at Dussehra the temple jewels were on display, and the pundit would have to stay and see that the jewels were put back in the palace vault.

When the maharaja was away, 'on camp', the pundit was free and could rest. The maharaja went away on camp four or five times a year, for 15 days or so at a time. Sometimes he went abroad; then he was away for a month.

'Highness used to go on pilgrimages. Highness had this habit, that if he read in an old text, a Purana, about a certain temple – in any part of the country – he would say, "Let's go there." The next day he would be ready, and about 25 people would go with him. He had one or two special railway coaches, which would be attached to the scheduled trains. He used to take cooks, bodyguards, a purohit, an astrologer. Sometimes he used to take his family. Highness had a "craze" for visiting temples. There is no temple that he didn't see – he was such a devotee.'

In 1965 the pundit, as mukhthesar, was allowed quarters: a small house with two rooms and a 'hall'. The rent was 10 per cent of his salary. Three years later, in 1968, he was given a special ceremonial uniform. He didn't have to pay for this uniform; it was a gift of the maharaja. The long coat was red, with gold facings and gold buttons. The buttons had a phoenix symbol and the letters *JCRW,* which were the initials of the maharaja: Jaya Chama Rajendra Wodeyar. The trousers were of silk, and biscuit-coloured.

I wondered whether it wasn't too gaudy for him, as a brahmin.

'I was proud of it. When I wore that dress, nobody could stop me anywhere, in the street or in the palace.' He even had himself photographed in that uniform.

He rose in the service. The maharaja called him *Shastri Narayan,* 'Lord of the Shastras', 'Great Scholar'. But then there began to be signs of things going bad outside. In 1971 the maharajas of India were 'de-recognized' by Mrs Gandhi's government, and the maharaja lost his tax-exempt privy purse of 2,600,000 rupees, worth at that time (after the devaluation of 1967) £130,000. Still, the maharaja continued to promote his mukhthesar. In 1972 the mukhthesar was appointed assistant secretary; there were two assistant secretaries in the palace. The pundit had entered the palace at a salary of 150 rupees; over the years this had doubled to 300; now, as assistant secretary, he was getting 500.

'Highness received the catalogues of various booksellers. He ordered 300 to 400 books a month. The palace secretary bought them for him. Highness bought Penguins and books of the Oxford University Press. I had to read or look over or taste the new books, and give a summary to him of books I thought might interest him. He was interested in philosophy and history. He talked about philosophy with me and with others. Highness liked to have a scrapbook. I knew the sort of thing that interested him, and would point certain passages out to him. Certain passages he would want typed out, for his own speeches and writings.

'Highness had two crazes, two madnesses. Temples. Second, books – buying them and reading them. He used to read throughout the night. I was associated with both his madnesses.

In his reading room he allowed no one. He had his own system of arranging or storing books. He kept them on the floor. No one was to touch them while they were there. When he had finished with a book, he brought it to me and asked me to catalogue it and put it on the library shelves.'

I wanted to know what English books the maharaja read and discussed with his mukhthesar, his Shastri Narayan. I was expecting to hear the names of Aldous Huxley, Bertrand Russell, Christopher Isherwood. But the pundit couldn't help me; he couldn't remember the name of any English writer.

In 1973, two years after the maharajas had been de-recognized, there was a strike by the palace staff for better pay. At one time there had been 500 workers in the palace. At the time of the strike there were 300. The maharaja gave the strikers the increases they asked for. It was too much for him. The next year everybody on the palace staff was given a gratuity and sent away. The pundit himself was given 19,000 rupees, nearly £1000. But not long afterwards the maharaja sent for him, and five or six others, and took them back. He continued to be mukhthesar and assistant secretary, and the work was just as hard as it had been.

'For some people,' the pundit said, 'Highness never changed.' But there had been a price for the maharaja's favour. Because of his irregular eating habits, the pundit said, he had developed an ulcer. As a brahmin it wasn't possible for him to eat outside his own house. He couldn't eat at the palace; even his grandfather, who had been a cook at the palace, had never eaten there. And because of the long hours the pundit had had to work in the palace, his digestion had become disorganized.

One day in 1974, when he was fifty-eight, he began vomiting blood. He was taken to the hospital. He stayed there for eight days. He was about to be discharged when the news came that the maharaja had died. That was how it had happened – as suddenly as that. The doctors advised him not to think about the maharaja's death; it would be bad for him. They postponed his discharge from the hospital; they kept him in for two more days. So, after all the years of personal attendance as mukhthesar, superintendent of pujas, he had not been present for the death of the maharaja, and the important rites afterwards.

The pundit said, 'To this day I try not to think about Highness's death.'

I didn't think he was exaggerating. The story we had heard had come out with much trouble; it had taken many hours. For nearly 50 years, as student, librarian, mukhthesar, he had lived on the bounty of the maharajas; and for 12 years he had personally served the maharaja. But the story of his life and his service with the maharaja existed in his mind as a number of separate stories, separate little stories. He had never before, I think, made a connected narrative out of those little stories.

After he left the hospital, he stayed home for a year. And then he saw this job as manager of the marriage hall advertised, and he took it.

'It's a job.'

Had he really succeeded in putting such an important part of his life out of his mind? Did no feelings now remain in him for the palace?

'No feelings. The times are not suitable for that kind of living any more. Times have changed.' He said the words simply, without any stress. There was still a royal family, but there was no maharaja now. The son of the former maharaja was a member of parliament on the Congress side.

Four times a year now he went to the palace, to make offerings to the head of the royal family. He went as a brahmin, as he had always gone: bare-backed, with a dhoti and shawl, and barefooted. But now he didn't go as an employee or palace servant. He went as a man in his own right. He went as a representative of a great and ancient religious foundation – though he just managed a marriage hall for them – and the gifts he took were not a retainer's gifts, but priestly offerings: a garland, two coconuts, and kumkum for the red holy marks on the forehead.

Nothing in the former mukhthesar's account had prepared me for the extravagance of the maharaja's palace. A fire in the last century had destroyed the old palace; the one that now existed, the palace where the pundit had gone for his first interview with the maharaja, had taken 15 years to build, from 1897 to 1912; just after – to think of comparable extravagance – the Vanderbilt château at Biltmore in Tennessee. A European architect had designed the palace, and it answered every kind of late-19th-century British-Raj idea of what an Indian palace should be. Scalloped Mogul arches; Scottish stained glass made to an Indian peacock design; in the main hall, hollow cast-iron pillars (painted blue), made in England, to a decorated pattern – the guide still knew the name of the manufacturers; marble and tile floors, Mogul-style pietra dura, white marble inset with coloured stones in floral patterns, and Edwardian tiles.

Many of the sightseers in the palace – everyone still required to be barefoot – were young men in black, pilgrims to Ayappa. Busloads of them had come, and there was a touch of vanity and even boisterousness about them, a touch of the visiting football crowd. Deviah didn't like it, The days before the pilgrimage should be days of penance, he said, days of doing without pleasure; Ayappa pilgrims shouldn't be breaking their journey to walk through a palace.

There was a very wide, shadowed, cool gallery where the maharaja in the old days would have shown himself to his subjects. The scalloped arches framed the very bright, brown gardens outside; the vistas here had the scale of the vistas through the arches and gateways of the Taj Mahal. And here especially – feeling the cool marble below my feet, in the deep recess of the pillared gallery, with the heat and the harsh light outside, like a complement of privilege – I thought of the pundit and his employer: privilege and devotion meeting in mutual need.

Among the palace treasures displayed was a gallery of Hindu deities. Some of those deities seemed to have been touched, like the palace itself, by a mixture of styles: the increasing naturalism of Indian art in the 20th century had turned ancient Hindu icons into things that looked like dolls.

Deviah thought so too. He didn't like the 'calendar' ideas of Hindu gods which were now widespread. 'The gods look like girls, women. I can't accept the idea of gods being made to look like women. Rama was a brave man, when you get to know about him.'

The palace design, with its garishness and mixture of styles, its European interpretation of Indian princeliness, expressed – paradoxically – a kind of Indian self-abasement before the idea of Europe. The gallery with the deities, speaking of a Hindu faith that was like something issuing out of the earth itself, expressed the opposite. The doll-like quality of some of the deities – modern-looking and camera-influenced though they were – even added to the mysteriousness.

The royal family of Mysore had taken a special interest in the festival of Dussehra. For the 10 days of the festival the jewels of the palace temple were on display until midnight, watched over by the mukhthesar; and on the last day of the festival the maharaja himself had taken part in the procession in the city. It was a great sadness for the people of Mysore, the guide said, when – after his derecognition – the maharaja had to stop appearing in the Dussehra procession. His place had thereafter been taken by a large image of the family deity – and the image was there, in the deities' gallery.

In a gallery around the main hall of the palace was the 24th maharaja's celebration of the festival. There were panels all the way around with sections of a continuous, realistic oil painting, based on photographs, of almost the entire Dussehra procession of 1935. The faces of everyone, the guide said, could be identified. The uniforms of all the courtiers and the various grades of attendants were as they had been – the bare feet unexpected, but not immediately noticeable. The painters had taken delight, too, in rendering the details of the street, the buildings and shops and cars, the shop signs and advertisements. The painting hadn't absolutely been finished. Nine painters had worked for three years, from 1937 until the death of the 24th maharaja. The 25th maharaja, whom the pundit served, hadn't been interested in art; and the Dussehra picture sequence – like many old Indian monuments, and for the same reason: the death of a ruler – was left unfinished. There were a few blank panels at the very end of the gallery.

There had been no hint of that dereliction in the pundit's account of his master. Nor had there been any hint of what was to be seen in the trophy room: the 25th maharaja had travelled in many countries, and shot wild animals. The towering neck and head of a startled-looking giraffe was among the trophies. It had been killed in Africa, and stuffed in Mysore; one of the world's most accomplished taxidermists lived in Mysore at that time. Another trophy was the lower, curving half of an elephant's trunk, made rigid and converted into an ash-tray or ash-bin, with an iron grille at the top for stubbing out cigarettes and cigars.

People spoke readily of the days of the maharajas. But no one I met seemed to possess the whole story of the end of the 25th and last maharaja of Mysore. Various people had various pieces, which sometimes didn't match. He had borrowed far too much from local businessmen – that was one story. Another was that he had had unsuitable favourites. A third story was that he had been involved in a lawsuit; and the prospect of having his ancient name – naked, without its titles – shouted three times by a court usher, in a place where his word had once been law, was so tormenting to him that he had taken an overdose of sedatives.

One version of the death was that he had swallowed a crushed diamond. Kala said that the swallowing of a diamond to commit suicide was a recurring piece of business in local Kannada-language films: people in extremity bit at the diamonds on their rings, and then began writhing in agony. So the story of the swallowing of the crushed diamond gave appropriate grandeur to the tragedy of the last maharaja, which remained mysterious.

I was told that he was fifty-five when he died. This made him three years younger than the pundit, though the pundit had said nothing of the maharaja's age, had left all that side of the man vague. Even after his death, misfortune followed the maharaja, someone said. The people around him began to pull off the rings from his fingers, and they had to pull hard, because the maharaja was very fat – that was what was contained in the pundit's respectful description of him as 'hefty', 'like a king', 'like God'. And, in this story, that bad death was followed by an unhappy cremation. The pyre was of sandalwood. Sandalwood is expensive (it was a monopoly of the old Mysore State). People began to pillage the pyre of half-consumed sandalwood pieces; and the next day it was discovered that the body had been incompletely burnt.

Folk tales had been generated by the idea of the tragedy of the last maharaja, de-recognized, impoverished, and finally hopelessly in debt. But nothing of that had entered the pundit's memories. He remained true to the man he had found: his memories were of the pure and devout man he had served indirectly and directly for 18 years.

In Bangalore three miles of wall enclosed the 500 acres of the summer palace grounds. The big and very valuable site was the subject of litigation; the public were not allowed in; special permission was required. The grounds were unkempt; films were sometimes shot in them. The palace was in red-grey Bangalore granite, and it was said (fancifully) to be modelled on Windsor Castle. The grass was burnt brown; the paths were of red laterite; sometimes in the grass were red anthills three or four feet high, like some melting-down spire top from the architectural imagination of Gaudi. The lamp standards were broken, one or two leaning, many of the white globes broken or vanished. And all around was the traffic and the smoke and the cicada sound of the car horns of Bangalore, a city now of business, science and industry.

On the road between Bangalore and Mysore City was the river-island fort of Tippu Sultan, who had in the late 18th century ruled here. He had been defeated by the British, by Wellington. Old history, not known to everyone in England now, its place in the imagination having been taken over by later wars, later villains. The British had installed the Mysore maharajas in place of Tippu. They were not upstarts; in the 14th and 15th centuries the Wodeyars had been satraps of the mighty Hindu kings of Vijayanagar. By an unlikely twist they had been restored to power. Now they were receding fast into the difficult Indian past, beyond the reach of the imagination – like so many of the historical names on the road down from Goa.

# 4
# LITTLE WARS

*Aqui a cidade foi, que se chamava*
*Meliapor, fermosa, grande e rica;*
*Os idolos antigos adorava,*
*Como inda agora faz a genu inica.*
Camoens: *The Lusiads* (1572)

Here was the beautiful, great and rich city called Mylapore, where the unregenerate heathen worshipped their ancient idols, as they still do.

SOMEWHERE IN THE Himalayas, one day in August 1962, when I was part of the great annual pilgrimage to the ice lingam, symbol of Shiva, in the cave of Amarnath, 13,000 feet up, I met 'Sugar'. He was from the South, from Madras, a biggish, soft-featured man. We had become friends then, and two months or so later, when I was in Madras, I saw a lot more of him. He was a brahmin, and lived in the brahmin area called Mylapore, near the famous old temple. He was a melancholic, withdrawn man: so he had appeared to me in the Himalayas, and so he appeared to me in Madras, in his home surroundings. He didn't have much conversation. What he offered, with a full heart and without any apparent kind of second judgement, was his friendship, which was of the most undemanding sort. He was always ready to see one; he was always pleased to be with one. He was in his late thirties, but he hadn't married. He lived with his mother and father in their comfortable, middle-class, Mylapore house.

I was spending a whole year in India that time. Some weeks after I had arrived I had gone north to Kashmir. I had done some work there for some months, and then I had begun to move down south. Sometimes, in country areas, I stayed with young government officers I had got to know. Sometimes I stayed in government bungalows and rest houses, bare shells of places offering the barest facilities – though those facilities, in the Indian countryside before the green revolution, were like luxury.

In the towns I stayed in such hotels as I could afford. Before I had gone to India I had had the idea that, with the many hands available, hotels in India would have been cheap and good, like the hotels in Spain in the early 1950s. It wasn't like that. In India at that time there was hardly a tourist trade, and hotel-keeping wasn't yet a profession. The people who ran modest hotels in small towns could only offer a version of the accommodation they themselves had; the staff they employed would have been like their own ragged house servants.

And then in Madras it was different. The restaurants and hotels that were vegetarian were clean (though the popular non-vegetarian or 'military' places, as they were quaintly called, were as bad as anything in the North). The cleanliness and the vegetarianism were connected; they were both contained in the southern idea of brahminism. At the Woodlands Hotel I stayed in a clean room in an annexe, and ate off banana leaves (for the sake of the purity, and the link with old ways) on marble tables in the air-conditioned dining-room. There were gardens and an open-air theatre or stage in the hotel grounds.

If I had known nothing of the brahmin Hindu culture of the South – if I had known nothing of the arts of music and dance, in both of which brahmins were pre-eminent – I would have begun to get some idea of it there: an idea of caste, like the Elizabethan idea of 'degree', acting as a check on the disorder – cultural, social, physical – which in India could easily come.

But with this idea of a protective culture there also came a feeling of strangeness. It was there, in the dining-room of the Woodlands, in the vegetarian food of the South. This wasn't at all like the vegetarian food, the dal and the rati, I had grown up thinking of as essential Indian food. This vegetarian food of the South – which drew the crowds to the Woodlands – was too subtle, too light; it made no impression on my stomach; it never left me feeling fed.

And the religion was as strange as the food. Sugar wanted me to get to know the Mylapore temple; he worshipped there. But the idea of the temple had played almost no part in the Hinduism I had grown up with in Trinidad. I knew about pujas; they were done at home; my Indian-born grandfather had built a puja room at the very top of the house he had built in Trinidad in the 1920s. What I was most familiar with were the occasional ceremonial readings from the epics and the scriptures. The devotee faced the pundit across a specially made and decorated earthen shrine, laid with a sweet-smelling sacred fire of resinous pitch pine. At intervals during the reading the fire was fed with clarified butter and sugar; and then a bell was rung, a brass gong was struck, and sometimes a conch was blown. Words, with a kind of tolling music – that was the Hinduism I had grown up with, and it had been hard enough for me to understand. The idea of the temple to which Sugar tried to introduce me – the idea of the sanctum, and the special temple deity at its centre – was very far away, even a little unsettling.

With all its welcome and restfulness, in Madras I always had the feeling that I was in a strange place. The sculptured pyramidal temple towers, the palm trees, the bare-backed brahmins among the old stone pillars, the big and beautiful water-tank at Mylapore, with internal stone steps all around – they were like things in old European prints. Because of those temple towers, especially, I again and again had a little visual shock and felt that I was seeing the place afresh; that the culture was still whole and inviolate; that I was seeing what the earliest travellers had seen.

Travellers, the sea: my Madras memories were mixed up with memories of dawn walks to the city beach, which was very long and very wide. At sunrise people washed their cattle in the sea. The sun came up from the sea; the flat wet sand shone red and gold; the ribby, bony-rumped, horned cattle stood on their blurred reflections; and then the heat of the day began.

Less than five years later I was in Madras again for a few days. There had been a state election (but it wasn't for that that I had gone); and the atmosphere in the Woodlands Hotel on the day of my arrival was like the atmosphere in a colonial territory after the election of the party that was going to rule after Independence. Motor-cars, music, new clothes, the political heroes of the day recognizable by the extra excitement their arrival caused. And the open-air stage or theatre area of the Woodlands was festooned and decorated, as for a carnival.

Twenty years after the Independence of India, this colonial-style celebration. After my introduction to the brahmin culture of the South, this was my introduction to the revolt of the South: the revolt of South against North, non-brahmin against brahmin, the racial revolt of dark against fair, Dravidian against Aryan. The revolt had begun long before; the brahmin world I had come upon in 1962 was one that had already been undermined.

The party that had won the state election in 1967 was the DMK, the Dravidian Progressive Movement. It had deep roots; it had its own prophet and its own politician-leader, men who were its equivalents of Gandhi and Nehru, men whose careers had run strangely parallel with the careers of the mainstream Indian Independence leaders. Until that moment I had hardly heard about them, and had hardly known about the passion of their cause. And what that victory in 1967 meant was that the culture to which I had been introduced by Sugar less than five years before, the culture which had appeared whole and mysterious and ancient to me, had been overthrown.

Sugar appeared, in his brahmin way, not to pay attention to what had happened. He was still living in the house of his parents in Mylapore, still going to the ancient temple, still doing with apparent contentment the modest business job he had always done.

His friendship after five years was as warm as ever. He was still as melancholy as I had remembered him, still with that deep, internal nagging. Perhaps now he was a little more withdrawn. I don't think we talked politics. Instead, in an upstairs room of his parents' house, we talked of certain Tamil books of prophecy he had become interested in. He told me they were ancient books; they had now been published, in many volumes, by the state government.

He couldn't say why he had become interested in the prophetic books, whether he was interested in finding out about his own future, or whether his interest in the books was that of a student. There was an ambiguity: he was clearly fascinated by the books, yet he appeared to be warning me off them, telling me that the priests who read and interpreted those holy books could take a lot of money off people.

He read other books as well. They were in his room. He brought them out: romantic feminine fiction from England, books to pass the time, he said, as though for him the matter of a book was not important, as though in his solitude what mattered was simply the act of reading, keeping the mind going.

Now, more than 20 years later, I was in Madras again; and, again without intending it, I had come at a political time. Another state election was about to take place. The posters of the various parties, and the party emblems, and the pictures of the leaders were everywhere. Some of the posters were enormous, like the cinema posters of Madras; and that was fitting, because the leaders the Dravidian movement had thrown up, after the original Dravidian party had split, had been Tamil film stars. In the posters all the politicians had the round plump faces of Southern film stars, and even people known to be dark were given pink cheeks: it was part of the iconography of leadership.

The film star who had been chief minister for much of the past decade, and whose death had led to the present state election, was shown with dark glasses and a white fur cap. The glasses and the cap had been his trade mark both as a star and a politician. He had been a famous stunt man, a kind of local Errol Flynn figure, and to his admirers he had been almost divine. He had been more interested in being a ruler and a star rather than in the business of governing. It was said that at his death some 18,000 files were waiting for his attention. One of the things he had done was to abolish the Madras Corporation. So Madras was in a mess, with mounds of rubbish everywhere. It was as though this, too, was part of the revolt of the South, this violation of the old ideas of purity.

The politics of colonial revolt in Tamil Nadu had followed a colonial course: theft, waste, stagnation, words, the eternal appeal to old grievances. But those grievances were real. The original Dravidian revolt had not been gone back on, had not been rejected by the people of the state: the election fight now was between factions of the original DMK, and what had remained of the DMK itself.

It was the DMK, the winners of 1967, who won again this time. A few days after my arrival the black-and-red flags of the party were everywhere – black the colour of caste revolt, red the colour of revolution. The flag fluttered in celebration from three-wheeler scooter-taxis; from bicycles. Sometimes in open vans or jitneys raised hands held the flag aloft, the raised hands symbolizing the rays of the rising sun, which was the DMK's election emblem.

I looked up Sugar's name in the telephone directory late one evening. I found a name that was like his, but the address was new. I telephoned. A Tamil voice was at first totally rejecting, totally refusing to understand. But then, as the owner of the voice made the adjustment to my English, his own English began to surface, became quite clerk-like and precise. Sugar was asleep, he said; he couldn't be disturbed now; he had 'retired' for the night; it was his habit to 'retire' at nine. When did he get up? He got up at five. I left my name.

The next day there was a message from Sugar. A woman's voice answered when I telephoned, and after a while Sugar came on the telephone. He sounded ill. I asked him how old he was; I said it was something I had never known.

He said, 'Sixty-four. Not too young.'

'So you were thirty-seven when we met in Kashmir?'

'I was a young man. Like you.'

Now Mr and Mrs Raghavan looked after him. It was Mr Raghavan I had spoken to the previous night, and this morning it was Mrs Raghavan who had taken the call. The telephone was theirs; they kept it upstairs; he lived downstairs; it wasn't easy for him to climb steps now. He had retired from 'service'. His mother had died; his father had died. He had left the family house I had seen him in. He had moved from Mylapore. He lived in a little apartment in the Raghavans' house. He wanted me to come right away. He gave the address and said – curiously, I thought – 'Everybody knows my house.' He spoke with something like urgency. His voice began to break; I thought he was very ill.

He was waiting for me, and when the taxi stopped he ran up to me, calling me by my name – I was about to go through a gate to the wrong house. He was in a yellow singlet and dhoti. He was not as tall as I had remembered. In the Himalayas he had been dark, burnt by the mountain sun; he was paler now. The melancholy of his expression had merged into his invalid's appearance. The flesh on his face and his exposed shoulders had grown softer, suggesting the man who couldn't climb steps.

He led me through the correct gate to the house where his apartment was. The apartment was on the ground floor, and we stepped directly from the garden path to his sitting room. He said, 'Drawing-sleeping,' meaning that the room was his sitting room as well as his bedroom. 'Attached bathroom.' He pointed, but didn't offer to show it. There was also a kitchen, and a room that was his temple. That was his great news for me: his temple. He had set up his own temple in his apartment. There were images there of the three most important deities, the deities of wisdom, strength, and money.

'Come, let me show you. Take off your shoes.'

The last command was friendly but firm, without the diffidence with which the request was usually made, the suggestion that if one didn't want to, one didn't. But friendship was uppermost in his mind: he was offering me this sight of his temple as a gesture of friendship.

I took off my shoes and stood before the black, garlanded, unreadable images.

He watched with me. He had always been tolerant of my lack of faith. Then he took me to the room that was his kitchen. He made a show of hanging his head and letting his drooping shoulders droop a little more. He laughed and said, 'Please don't write about my kitchen.' He knew it wasn't clean, he said. But there was no running water. All the water he used in the kitchen had to be fetched in jars. It wasn't easy for him now to lift a full jar; he gave a demonstration, to show how his body could no longer do some of the simple things he wanted it to do. He became ill if he lifted things that were heavy; so he couldn't keep his kitchen clean. The kitchen was grimy. Dirt and cooking grime had caught on the wire netting over the window, and on the ledges and shelves just below. He was looking after himself now, he said; he was dispensing with things. A girl came in to sweep for him. But (though he didn't say) he couldn't as a brahmin allow that girl into his kitchen.

He was sixty-four now. He was dispensing with things. In the front room, the main room of the apartment, the drawing-sleeping, he had a number of small pieces of furniture pushed together in a jumble at one end. He was going to get rid of that furniture; he didn't need it.

'I want a plain room.'

I asked why he hadn't married.

'Why? Why? How can I answer? I didn't feel like it.'

And that was the kind of reply he gave when I asked him about the temple and how the idea had come to him. The idea had just come to him, he said.

I remembered his interest in 1967 in the prophetic books. I asked him about that. Had that interest left him now? And, again, I wanted to know how that interest had come to him.

He said; 'Why? Why? These are your sort of questions. How can I answer?' The wish had simply come to him. But I was right about one thing: that wish, to delve into the books of prophecy, was now in the past.

And, considering his new solitude, his stained dhoti and singlet, for the first time since I had known him I asked him directly about his life.

He had worked in the same firm all his life, starting when he had left college. Towards the end he had run the office, been a kind of office manager. He had looked after the files of all the employees. He loved the firm still. At the time of his retirement he was earning 2000 rupees a month, £80. That was enough for a single man. The firm was now giving him a pension of 1000 rupees a month. From some money that the firm had invested for him he was getting a further 1300 rupees. It was enough.

The concrete floor of the drawing-sleeping where we were was decorated with white floral patterns, such as exist on the threshold of many Indian houses. They are usually done with flour, and done afresh every day, but the pattern on Sugar's floor was a plastic stick-on. The walls were blue, tarnished from the rubbing of backs and hands and, above the back of the chairs, from oiled heads. All the pictures on the walls were religious pictures. There was a hanging two-shelf wall cupboard with sliding glass doors; inside, medicine bottles and candles and tablets in foil-covered cards were mixed up with papers and household bric-a-brac. I had never felt this kind of desolation in his parents' house in Mylapore.

I asked whether he had had a happy life.

'A plain life. A plain life.'

Then he began to receive people. They came in through the open front door. The first man to come in was a dark man with fresh holy marks on his forehead: he had done his morning puja, or had been to the great temple.

'He's a landlord,' Sugar said, when the man went into the temple room. 'A moneyed man.'

The second visitor was younger; his features were finer. He greeted Sugar and then, with no further word, went into the temple room. This man wore a formal, reddish-brown long tunic. Sugar said the man was an executive in a big company.

'People come,' Sugar said, as though explaining his visitors. The first man, the landlord and moneyed man, came out and sat against a wall in the drawing-sleeping. When the man in the reddish tunic came out, he sat on a chair that was part of the furniture jumble at one end of the room.

This second man, the executive, was the production manager in his company. It seemed rather late in the morning for him to be here, but he said he came every morning to Sugar's temple, to meditate, and to be calm. They didn't talk a lot when they were together. On Sunday evenings he came for three hours; he had a lot of time on Sundays. Once, during a power failure, he had sat with Sugar for nearly four hours, and they had hardly talked during that time. To come and sit in the room where we were, with the tarnished blue walls, and with a glimpse of the dark kitchen, was a form of meditation. Meditation, which implied the emptying of the mind, wasn't easy, the production manager said: the beginner's thoughts ran too easily to family, job, and things like that. It took years to learn to meditate. He wasn't like Mr Sugar.

This was news to me: that Sugar had this reputation, as a sage, a holy man.

I asked him, 'Can you empty your mind?'

He said, playing it down, yet pleased that – without his saying anything – I knew, 'I have achieved little.'

The production manager said, 'With most god-men you go to get something.' It wasn't like that with Sugar. He came to Sugar just for the peace; he wanted nothing from him.

The brahmin world of Mylapore had been turned upside down. But in Sugar's little blue sanctuary the politics of the streets outside were far away: the red-and-black flags, the 80-foot painted cut-outs of the new heroes (against rough wooden scaffolding). In the little apartment in the Raghavans' house Sugar kept a kind of court and had his own circle, and was perhaps more protected, more looked-up to, than he had ever been in the family house where he had grown up. He was holy, offering peace. It explained one of the things he had said on the telephone: 'Everybody knows my house.'

He said, when I was getting ready to leave, 'You must come and eat with me. I will cook for you myself. I will cook pumpkin for you.'

'Pumpkin?'

'You ate pumpkin every day at Woodlands in 1962.'

There were other things he had remembered that I had forgotten. He remembered that in his family house in 1962, and again in 1967, I had had long, serious talks with his father about books and India.

It was flattering to be remembered in this way, in these details, after so long. I felt it also spoke of a life plain to the point of tears. Yet this plainness had in the end brought its reward. His gifts had become known. Perhaps the very qualities that had made him memorable in the pilgrim throng in the Himalayas – his solitude, his stillness, his melancholy, the feeling of incompleteness and search that he gave off – had attracted others.

Only 33 or 34 per cent of the voters had voted for the victorious DMK party; but the red-and-black flags of the party so multiplied in the city, it began to seem that nearly everyone had voted for the DMK. On walls where it had been painted before election day, the party's election emblem, of the sun rising above hills, was now lovingly reworked and decorated, a little more and then a little more again, seeming further to mock the open palm and the two doves, emblems of two of the defeated parties, emblems until a few days before of great hope and jauntiness, but now abandoned, neglected, no loyal or happy hand adding a celebratory touch of extra colour.

Within a day or so of the election result very big painted signboards began to appear in some places in the city with very big portraits of the three heroes of the party. There were no names, no words; you had to know who the heroes were. They were shown in profile, in a staggered line, each profile like a royal head on a coin; and each hero was done in a different colour. The current leader of the party was done in a kind of brown; the man who had led the party to its first election victory in 1967 in a slatey-blue or grey; and the profile behind these two was that of the old, pink-cheeked man with a long wavy beard who had been the prophet of the party.

The prophet was known as 'Periyar'. It was a Tamil word, meaning a sage or a wise man. I knew the name Periyar, but only just; I knew nothing about the man. I began to learn now, and I was astounded as much by what I learned as by the fact that, with all my reading about the Independence movement in India, I had read or registered so little about this prophet of the South.

He was an atheist and a rationalist, and he made two or three speeches a day over a very long life. He ridiculed the Hindu gods. He cruelly mocked caste Hindus, comparing the poverty of their scientific achievements with the achievements of Europe. And then, having it both ways, he also said that the Hindus had copied their gods ('some selected animals, a few birds, a few trees and creepers, a few mountains and some rivers') from the gods of ancient Egypt and Greece and Persia and Chaldea.

This was the first surprise: that someone who – at least in the English translation of his often disorganized Tamil discourses – came over as a humorist and a satirist should have been received by the people of Tamil Nadu as a prophet, and at a moment of political triumph so long after his death should have been freshly honoured. But Periyar had never intended humour when he spoke against Hinduism and caste Hindus. He had once been a believer; and he was as obsessed with the religion and its propounders as only a man once a believer could be.

There was a place in Madras called Periyar Thidal. It was on the site of a former bus or tram depot. Periyar himself had bought the place in 1953, for a lakh of rupees, 100,000 rupees, worth then about £7,500. It was the place from which his organization still operated.

A garlanded black statue of Periyar stood in the middle of the big sandy plot, with this inscription on the plinth: PERIYAR THE PROPHET OF THE NEW AGE THE SOCRATES OF SOUTH EAST ASIA FATHER OF THE SOCIAL MOVEMENT AND ARCH ENEMY OF IGNORANCE; SUPERSTITIONS; MEANINGLESS CUSTOMS AND BASELESS MANNERS. Periyar's grave was in a corner of the plot. All around the grave were polished grey granite slabs engraved with some of Periyar's sayings. One of those sayings, virtually an incantation, was very famous: *There is no God. There is no God. There is no God at all. He who invented God is a fool. He who propagates God is a scoundrel. He who worships God is a barbarian.* This was how Periyar began all his discourses.

It was hard to imagine anything so blunt and bitter being accepted in any part of India, if something else wasn't being offered with it. And what Periyar offered, with his 'rationalism' and his rejection of God, was his rejection of the brahmins and their language; his rejection of the North; his rejection of caste; his rejection of the disregard the fair people of the North had for the dark people of the South.

There was importance, too, in the fact of that grave in the Periyar Thidal. Hindus are cremated; Periyar insisted on being buried. He was more than the rationalist: to the people who listened to him and liked what he said, he was the anti-Hindu.

He was born in 1879, 10 years after Gandhi was born, and 10 years before Nehru was born. His political life began in 1919, and continued until his death in 1973. And that was the second big surprise of Periyar: that he should have lived so long, that his career should have for many years run parallel with that of Gandhi, and that Gandhi, through many of the later years of his struggle and search, should have had at his back this figure of the anti-Hindu who finally became the anti-Gandhi, a man whose life and career echoed and reversed much of Gandhi's own.

Gandhi was a vegetarian. Periyar made a point of eating beef. Gandhi struggled to control the senses. Periyar ate enormous quantities of food, and was enormously fat. One of Periyar's admirers told me, 'He was a *glutton*.' And, in this reversal of values, the word was intended as praise. 'He always had a *biriyani* – rice and mutton, beef, pork. He was never *fussy* about food.' Gandhi was always fussy about his food.

He was different from Gandhi, opposed to him, and yet in some ways – in his discovery of his cause, his working out of ways to serve it, his lifelong adherence to it, and, above all, in his practical business sense – he was like Gandhi. Like Gandhi, Periyar was born into a Hindu merchant caste. Gandhi came from a family of small-scale administrators. Periyar came from a family of well-to-do merchants. Periyar was not as well educated as Gandhi, and it could be said that he was more devout and traditional. Gandhi went against the principles of his caste and travelled to London to study law. Periyar, in his mid-twenties (while Gandhi was in South Africa, fighting hard battles), went to Banaras, to live the life of a sanyasi, to live naked, on the alms of the devout, in the hope of finding some kind of spiritual illumination.

The illumination never came, and he left Banaras and went back to his family business in his own town. He also went into local municipal politics, and then in 1919, when Gandhi had been back in India for some years, Periyar joined the Indian National

Congress. He supported its handloom campaign and took part in the non-cooperation movement.

Then came the break. It had to do with the caste prejudices of the brahmins in the South. Non-brahmins were not allowed free entry to temples. They were absolutely barred from the inner sanctum where the temple deity was; they had to be content with a view from a distance. Sometimes non-brahmins were not even allowed to walk on the lane in front of a temple.

This last prohibition caused an especial commotion in the neighbouring state of Kerala in 1924. Kerala was at that time a princely state, with its own maharaja, and the brahmins of Kerala were even stricter about caste prohibitions than the Tamil brahmins of Madras. Within the compound of the royal palace there was a temple, and there was also a law court. One day, when a sacred temple fair of some kind was going on, the temple lane was closed to non-brahmins. The temple lane was also the lane to the law court. A lawyer called Madhavan, a non-brahmin, had to appear in a court case that day; but (fame comes to people in unlikely ways) Madhavan was not allowed to walk past the temple. Some non-brahmins in Kerala protested and started an agitation; they were jailed by the maharaja. They appealed to Periyar. He came to Kerala and campaigned for a whole year, until the temple lane was opened to non-brahmins.

There was another crisis soon after. It was discovered that, at a Congress school for propagating Gandhian thought, brahmin children were fed separately from non-brahmin children. And then it turned out that the school, though run by a brahmin, was being financed by non-brahmins. The matter was reported to Gandhi; but his response was ambiguous and light-hearted.

Periyar at that moment broke with Gandhi and the Congress. (There is a – brahmin – story in Madras that the break really came because Periyar had been asked to account for money connected with the handloom campaign.) In 1925 Periyar founded the Self-

Respect Movement, and it was his brilliant idea then to symbolize his cause by wearing a black shirt. Black-shirted, he campaigned for the rest of his life, for nearly 50 years, against brahminism, caste, Congress, the Hindu religion, the disabilities of women. He established the idea of Self-Respect marriages for non-brahmins, marriages conducted without priests or religious vows. And he preached a crude kind of socialism.

'In the world of the future, there will be no men without character and culture . . . The depravity of modern character is founded on culture, justice and discipline being used for maintaining caste and class differences among men . . . When these capitalist and individualist conditions are absent, the need for depraved character will not arise.'

He offered a vision of a future bright with the fruits of science, and without the need for the idea of God.

'Communications will mostly be by air and of great speed . . . Radios may be fixed in men's hats . . . Food enriched with vitamins will be encased in pills or capsules sufficient for a day's or week's sustenance. The average life may stand at 100 years or more . . . Motorcars may weigh about one hundredweight and will run without petrol . . . Electricity will be everywhere and in every house, serving the people for all purposes . . . No industry or factory will run for the private profits of individuals. They will all be owned by the community at large, and all inventions will cater for the needs and pleasures of all people . . . When the world itself has been converted into a paradise, the need to picture a paradise in the clouds will not arise. Where there is no want, there is no god. Where there is scientific knowledge, there is no need for speculation and imagination . . . The struggle for existence needs to be changed into a life of happiness.'

With this preaching, reiterated day after day, this vision of the pain of caste disappearing together with the idea of God, there went his inherited feeling for the practical side of things. He had been born into a business family, and he remained concerned with money all his life, never denying its value, seeking always to keep himself and his movement independent and free of pressure. His movement was never short of money; the trust he left behind to look after his cause was rich.

His relics were in a big room in the main building at the Periyar Thidal. On a four-poster bed in the front part of the room there was a life-size photographic cut-out (the cinema-advertisement style and election-campaign style transferred to this private museum) of Periyar, very old, with a big beard, sitting cross-legged, in a writing posture. There was a patterned pink blanket on the bed, and the cut-out leaned against a bolster. The poles of the four-poster were white; there was no canopy. A tall revolving bookshelf stood at one side of the bed, with small busts of Buddha and Lenin, souvenir-shop objects, and a statue of a horse, a gift. The horse had no significance; it had been kept by Periyar for its beauty, and as a memento of the giver.

More symbolical gifts were in a glass case: silver implements of iconoclasm: two silver mallets, and two silver sticks, in shape like the stick the aged Periyar used.

The leadership of the Periyar movement had passed to Mr Veeramani. He was the keeper of Periyar's memory, and the guardian of his relics. When he showed me the mallets and the sticks, he reminded me with a laugh of what he said was an old Sanskrit saying: 'The poison of the cobra is in his tongue alone. The poison of the brahmin is from head to foot.' That saying led to another, which Mr Veeramani said was a well known Hindi saying: 'If you see a brahmin and a snake, kill the brahmin first.' (I had heard that years before in a different version, and I had been told then that it was a household saying of the people of south-east Asia: 'If you are in the forest and you see a snake and an Indian, kill the Indian first.')

After the emblems of iconoclasm, the emblems of kingship. Periyar had often been called the white-bearded king of Tamil Nadu. A town in the South had given the old man a decorated silver throne, and that throne was in a glass case, with a silver crown, the gift of followers in another town. Another gift was a silver sceptre, with small heads of Periyar and Buddha at the top; and in yet another glass case were curving silver swords.

Right around this big museum room, at the top of the walls, just below the ceiling, was a set of 33 oil paintings depicting the stations of Periyar's long life. It was as with Bible pictures: you had to know the story. And once you knew, it was all there: Periyar as a naked sanyasi in Banaras in 1904, eating such food as he could find; Periyar 10 years later in municipal politics in his home town; Periyar with the Congress in 1919; Periyar campaigning in Kerala in 1924 for the rights of non-brahmins to enter temples; Periyar campaigning not long after for the abolition of caste distinctions in the Congress school; Periyar founding his Self-Respect Movement in 1925, and wearing his black shirt for the first time; Periyar in Germany in 1932, in the company of 'German atheists'; Periyar in Russia the same year with Russian sanatorium employees; Periyar in 1943, discussing the break-up of India after Independence with Mr Jinnah (campaigning for a Muslim Pakistan), Dr Ambedkar (wanting a scheduled-caste state called Dalitstan), Periyar himself hoping for a southern, Dravidian, non-brahmin state called Dravidstan. Later paintings showed Periyar, after Independence, painting out the Hindi names of railway stations in the South, in 1952; breaking idols of Ganesh, Ganpati, the elephant god, in 1953, to show that they were only of clay, and quite harmless; in 1957 painting out 'Brahmin' from a signboard saying 'Brahmin Hotel', 'brahmin' meaning vegetarian, as opposed to 'military', non-vegetarian; and in the same year burning the Indian Constitution. He had been single-minded and unwearying through a long life. In the centre of the room a collection of his personal relics had been laid out by Mr Veeramani in another glass case: his flashlight, his magnifying glasses, his unusually stout stick, his watch, his spectacles, his stainless-steel food tray, his bedpan and syringe and other medical paraphernalia. Almost like Gandhi's relics; and they would have been Gandhian, if Periyar had left nothing else behind. But the property he had left in his trust, including the large city site of the Periyar Thidal, was worth many millions; and this worth had multiplied many times over in the 15 years since his death.

In spite of his love of food and his meat-eating, there was, in his single-mindedness and obsession, something like purity, and it was this quality that made him the anti-Gandhi. But that figure, of the anti-Gandhi, had meaning only because the real Gandhi existed. Gandhi developed and grew; for the first 40 years of the century, from his thirtieth year to his seventieth, he was constantly searching for new political and religious ways. His search made him a universal figure; people to whom the politics were far away could yet refer their own search to his. Periyar was a local figure; he never outgrew his cause. Without Gandhi and the Congress and the Independence movement his cause wouldn't have had the power it had; he was riding on the back of something very big. That might have been why I hadn't heard of him.

It was Sadanand Menon, a writer living in Madras, who had taken me to the Periyar Thidal and had given me the background necessary to an understanding of Periyar's life and movement.

Towards the end of the 19th century, with British rule, Sadanand said, the brahmins became dominant in a way they hadn't been for some time. They were dominant in Indian social life, the professions, and in the beginnings of the nationalist movement. But Madras Province (taking in Tamil Nadu and other areas) was very large; Madras was a port; and, as the economy of the province grew, other middle castes began to produce their own prominent personalities. Many of these middle-caste people were well-to-do – like Periyar's own family; many were landlords; some could send their sons to Oxford and Cambridge. As soon as such people had emerged from the middle castes, the antique brahmin caste restrictions would not have been easy to maintain. What Periyar did was to take this mood of rejection to the non-brahmin masses.

Sadanand said, 'His mode of communication was cultural. The Self-Respect Movement began three or four newspapers simultaneously. They laid great emphasis on education. In the 1930s one of the methods of the movement was the method of social discourse – not lecturing down. An educated volunteer would go to a slum area in a city, or to the village square, and he would start reading aloud from a paper. In no time he would have a crowd around him. And he would interpret what he was reading according to the Self-Respect Movement's ideology. This has remained a form till today. It has remained the backbone of the DMK, this direct contact between the party cadre and the people. The other parties don't have this. They haven't even attempted it. I remember in the 1960s going to a place near where I was living, and observing a DMK party worker. He would come on the dot at 6.30 in the evening, carrying the party newspaper, together with an English paper and any other Tamil paper. He would have a hurricane lantern. He sat in a shed, just four poles and a roof, and he read aloud, and he would have an audience of 150 people.'

How deep, or important, was the rationalist side of the movement? How far had people been able to reject God or the gods?

Sadanand said that the rationalist movement as such had become a parody of itself over the years. But political power had come to the DMK, which was the political offshoot of that movement, and there had been an upheaval.

Sadanand said, 'The DMK came to power in 1967' – the year I had come to Madras for the second time, and I had gone to see Sugar and his father in their two-storey house in Mylapore, and Sugar had told me about the books of prophecy – 'and they created a ministry, the Hindu Religious and Charitable Endowments, the HR&CE. The HR&CE minister controlled the enormous resources of the Hindu temples and trusts. Land, fixed assets, jewelry – every temple has enormous amounts of jewelry: the idols themselves, and the daily donations. The donations to a temple are anonymous; there is no means of accounting for them. The temple wealth was unassessable. How could you put a value on a 10th-century Shiva? After this – and this was quite separate from what the government was doing – the idols began to be stolen and were replaced by replicas. Archaeologists have recently pointed out large-scale replacement of temple icons by fakes. The originals have ended in private collections around the world.'

'Didn't the DMK mind about that? Isn't it their art too?'

'The DMK didn't think twice about that. They were dealing with the enemy. At the same time the new government started on a policy of distributing temple lands to the landless. But this was a notional thing. The names of 200 people could be produced who had been given one acre of temple land each, but actually that land might all belong to one man or the party. The people didn't get anything out of it.'

Sadanand spoke of this as the 'looting' of the temples, using that word – originally a Hindi word, and this fact reflecting something of the history of India – in the Indian sense. Had the brahmins been impoverished as result?

'In most of the temples the brahmins became simply the conductors of rituals, the purohits, and certainly there was impoverishment.' But more important, in Sadanand's account, was the downgrading of the temples. 'The temples as originally conceived were largely social institutions. Each temple had schools, granaries, facilities for large-scale water-storage – the origin of the temple tank – hospitals, stalls for cows. They were also patrons of the arts. But the DMK made crude equations. The temple became equated with oppression of a certain sort, and then the whole thing was vandalized, without discrimination.'

The movement claimed to have a link with the non-brahmin past of Tamil Nadu, and especially with the Chola emperors of the eighth to the 10th centuries. But this again, according to Sadanand, was glib and unhistorical.

'The Cholas were democrats, if you can imagine democracy within a feudal structure. But they were also the imperialists of the area, and the Chola symbol of the movement is the symbol of Tamil imperialism, nothing else. The Cholas were known to be learned people, to have written books on astronomy, and to have been patrons of the arts. The DMK Chola symbol stands for none of this. The Chola kings developed fascinating systems of irrigation in the Tanjore area. The DMK never bothered to look at irrigation.'

Out of their narrowness, their regionalism, their caste obsessions, other things suffered. The English language suffered. The number of people from the state holding positions in the central government declined; many of the central government officers in Tamil Nadu now came from outside. The Tamil language itself deteriorated.

'The movement is not creative any more. Tamil has become a language which is incapable of expressing one modern idea. It's a fosssilized language, and this is reflected in the quality of Tamil journalism. Much of it is frivolous, inane.

'The movement still has a place. But what it keeps reproducing nowadays is this parody. Out of it there has come an impoverished iconography. You saw that flat cut-out of Periyar on the bed. That idea was extended later to the politicians of the movement, the leaders of the DMK and its successor parties. They were projected as giants in 80-foot cut-outs – a substitute for what they have lost. And religious or neo-religious movements have become stronger in Tamil Nadu.

'The current neo-religious movement here is the Adi Parashakti cult. You'll find it at a place half-way between Madras and Pondicherry. It's a cult of the primal mother – the Dravidian religion, as opposed to the Aryan religion, was mother-centred. From that has emerged this new cult. Just this one man, a schoolteacher, claimed one fine day that he had had a dream of this Mother or Shakti coming to him and ordering him to propagate her name. He claims that when he woke up there was an idol of Adi Parashakti growing out of the earth in front of him. The followers of this cult have a uniform, red and red. This is one of the paradoxical fall-outs of the rationalist movement.'

There was a deeper irony. The anti-brahmin movement was not a movement of all the non-brahmin castes. It was a movement mainly of the middle castes. There was, as ever in India, a further lower level, a further level of disadvantage. For these people at the very bottom the DMK offered no protection.

Sadanand said, 'The DMK came to power in 1967, talking of the oppression of the lower castes. In fact, the most brutal attacks on the scheduled castes have happened post-1967. In 1969 40 harijans were burnt alive in a hut. The caste known as the Thevars was responsible. They are a middle caste, a backward caste who have in the last 100 years come up socially and are now powerful, with their own caste association. They are one of the most militant castes. They call themselves the *kshatriyas,* the warriors, of the Tamil hierarchical order. The Dravidian Movement had been founded by the middle castes. When their government came to power, they became the oppressors.'

Sadanand's analysis of the cultural impoverishment brought about by the movement was almost certainly true. It was there in the iconography; it was there in the exaggerations and simplicities and contradictions of Periyar's speeches, where words seemed to have been loved for their own sake, and where speeches, in order to be relished, had to be spun out, conceit upon conceit. But, equally, there was the passion of the followers of Periyar. Periyar had touched something in these people, something deeper than logic and a regard for historical correctness; that also had to be taken into account.

Mr Gopalakrishnan was the proprietor of Emerald Publishers, publishers of school textbooks and books about the rationalist movement. He told me this story.

'My father was a very small businessman. He was of the Mudaliar caste. We were lower middle-caste people. He kept a stall. He sold cigarettes, aerated water, little things like that.

'I became a rationalist in the early 1940s, when I was ten or thereabouts. I was a student at the Sri Ramakrishna High School in Madras. It was a brahmin-dominated school. Even the peons and the watermen, four or five of them, were brahmins. We were only a few non-brahmins in each class. Every day we got sermons from some of our teachers that we were only fit for grazing cattle. We heard that from three teachers in particular. They thought that non-brahmins shouldn't study, and the words they oft repeated were: "Go and graze the cattle."

'We had to go to the prayer meeting in the prayer hall every morning. The prayers were in Sanskrit. They were the same prayers every day; they were boring. I had a non-brahmin classmate who didn't go to the prayer meetings; he would get beatings very often for that. All the boys would come with their caste mark. I used to use a piece of chalk, instead of the so-called sacred ash, to make the horizontal marks on my forehead. My friend never did it, and he was beaten for that, too. He was a creative boy. Ten years later he wrote a play and acted in it – a play with rationalist views.

'One day, when I was at the school, I had a chance of attending one of Periyar's meetings. The meeting was in Saidapet, where we were living, and many people, non-brahmins, were going. At that meeting for the first time I was able to understand why the brahmin teachers were so prejudiced against us. Till then I couldn't understand why they were so prejudiced. I started reading literature published by Periyar's movement, and the magazines they published. It took me four years to become a complete rationalist.

'First of all, in 1947 I stopped going to the temple. Until then I used to go with devotion. It was something I had got in babyhood from my mother and my sisters – the environment was like that. In those days the brahmin priests treated their non-brahmin devotees with contempt. The devotees took it for granted: it was the tradition. I used to take it for granted too, in my early days. The priest used to throw the sacred ash with contempt at the non-brahmin devotees, from a distance, whereas the brahmins were allowed to go to the sanctum sanctorum, where the idol actually stands. The non-brahmin devotees could see the idol only at a distance.

'My stopping temple-going was a gradual process. In my college days I used to read Shaw, Wells, and Russell. Their writings made a big impact, and I had the courage to face the believers in my family and in my society.

'My mother continued to be ritual-minded. She became worried, many years after, that when she died I might do no ritual for her. But then, three months before she died, she called me to her and told me that I wasn't to do any ritual for her.

'Now I ignore the Hindu religion. I don't waste my time discussing it. I never did any ritual for my mother when she died. That was two years ago. What I do every year on that day is to give new dresses to every granddaughter. That's all. There's no community lecture. No flowers. I just have my mother's portrait, that's all.'

More obsessed, with a passion that nothing could assuage, was Mr Palani. He was a small, dark man of sixty-three. He was born in Coimbatore district, and he had fresh memories of the discovery of caste prejudice at his school more than 50 years before.

'I on my own did not have anything like this anti-brahmin feeling. My brother got admitted to the school where I was. I was doing my fifth standard. My brother was in the fourth standard. One recess, being a fresher, he just followed the other boys to a hotel to drink water. He did what the other boys did. He took a brass tumbler and dipped it in the bowl of water and started drinking it. It was a brahmin hotel – a hotel where people don't stay, but take their meals. It was a middle-class hotel. The proprietor was terribly angry when he saw my brother putting his hand in the brass bowl and taking water. He emptied the whole bowl outside, and started shouting at my brother.

'My brother came back weeping to me at the school, and I told him that as we are non-brahmins we are not supposed to take water directly ourselves from the bowl. He should have asked some brahmin boy to take a glass of water and give it to him. Brahmins are lighter in complexion comparatively than we are. My brother said, "Why?" He refused to reconcile with this thing. I started thinking myself. I had just been following the custom that was there. I was eleven; my brother was ten. I had been at the school for a year.

'We went home and talked to our father. He was a government clerk. He was earning 35 rupees a month. In those days this was supposed to meet the requirements of a small family. My father's father had been a weaver. We were of the weaver caste, the *sengunthar* caste. But my father had been educated up to the school-leaving certificate, up to the age of sixteen. He was now thirty.

'When he heard our story, my father said, "This is a custom in these places. So even though it is unfair, you must reconcile." He followed the rules himself – not wholeheartedly, but he followed. In brahmin hotels he wouldn't go into the space reserved for brahmins. In those days there were two compartments in any brahmin hotel, one for brahmins, one for the others. So my father wouldn't trespass into the brahmin compartment.

'We were living in a small tiled house, a house with brick walls and a tiled roof. It was a rented house. We were paying about five rupees a month for it. It was not electrified. We had a servant girl whom we fed and paid about three rupees a month.'

'Did she eat with the family?'

'She wouldn't eat with us. She would eat after us. It wasn't a social discrimination; she was just serving us. She slept in the house. She slept in the adjacent room. We slept – all the children – in the big room. There were three rooms in the house, our parents' room, the children's room, and the servant's room. She came from the village. We knew her family. We had requested them to spare a girl for our house. We were middle-class people.'

'Was that why your brother reacted as he did?'

'I'm not sure. It might have been just a human reaction.' He returned to the story of his political development. 'Then there was the anti-Hindi agitation in 1938. There had been state legislative assembly elections in 1937 on a limited franchise, and a Congress government had come in. This government proposed to introduce Hindi compulsorily in the schools. There was an agitation started by Tamil scholars and educationists, and by Periyar and his group.

'Periyar came to talk one evening. It was still daylight when he began, and when the darkness came the Petromax pressure lamps were lighted. He was a stout man, medium height, with a beard. He was wearing a Tamil dhoti and a black shirt, with a shawl over one shoulder. He was a fair-complexioned man. He was a Naicker by caste – merchant community.

'He explained how Hindi was going to eliminate English, and how this elimination of English was going to be a disadvantage for Tamil Nadu. Tamil would become secondary to Hindi in the course of time. Once the language got downgraded, everything related to the culture and the society would also be downgraded. Everybody in the audience agreed with this.

'This speech was followed by others made by Periyar's lieutenants. They were young men and middle-class men. One of them was Mr Annadurai. He later founded the DMK, and led it to victory in the state elections in 1967. He was very eloquent. He swayed the people when he started talking. Schools were picketed on this issue of Hindi, and these leaders undertook a march from the southernmost tip of Tamil Nadu to Madras.'

Seven years before, Gandhi had arrived at the idea of the nonviolent political march. After a long period of thought in his ashram at Ahmedabad, Gandhi had hit on the idea of walking from there to the sea, to make salt: wonderful theatre, with a definite physical goal, and an uncertain outcome; and a wonderful symbolic act of civil disobedience as well, since salt – so cheap, so necessary, and used by even the poorest – was a monopoly of the foreign government. Gandhi's 1931 salt march lasted many days; it revived and gave new vigour to the national cause. And in 1938 the anti-Hindi march through Tamil Nadu served the

Dravidian cause: the Congress state administration dropped the idea of making Hindi compulsory in schools. But Mr Palani didn't make the Gandhian reference.

He said, 'Five years after that agitation, in 1943, I joined engineering college. That again was a very big thing for me. In my old school I had been an outstanding student. I had won scholarships and all that, and my teachers recommended to my father that I should be put in a college. So I did a two-year arts course in an arts college. A professor in that college, when I finished the arts course, insisted I should do engineering. So I applied to the engineering college. I would not have got admission in the open competition, because the brahmin boys scored much higher marks. But fortunately for me – and for people like me, who came from backward, non-brahmin communities – thanks to another agitation of Periyar, some additional seats were reserved for such backward communities. Had this reservation for the backward communities not been there, I wouldn't have been an engineer. That is what I mean when I say that my joining the college was a big thing.

'Now let me tell you this. When I joined the engineering college, I found that in the mess in the hostel the brahmin boys were fed in the nearest enclosure to the kitchen, and their enclosure was separated from the rest of the mess by a wooden partition. All the cooks in the mess happened to be brahmins. So brahmins had a lion's share of the advantages of the mess. This upset us. We started going earlier and sitting in that enclosure. Because there were more of us than brahmins, they finally agreed to remove the partition, and there was a common mess afterwards. You see, they will try to do something so long as we are dumb. Once we start asserting our rights, they wouldn't have the temerity to oppose that.'

'What about the national cause? 1943 was an important time. Did you take part in the national movement?'

'The national movement was going on. But at the same time, within that, we wanted our self-respect to be recognized.'

'Was your brother as active as you?'

'He was in another college. He was a sympathizer with the cause, but he didn't come out in the open as much as I did. He left everything to me.'

'What did your father and mother think of the rationalist side of Periyar's message?'

'They didn't bestow much thought on that side of things. They sympathized more with the linguistic issue and the reservation of places for non-brahmins. In 1943, while we were not at one with the atheistic aspect of Periyar's philosophy, we were very much with him in his fight for the eradication of superstition and rituals.

'This Tamil civilization of ours is a very old one. Say, about 5000 years old. The cities of Mohenjo-Daro and Harappa – Mohenjo-Daro now in Sind in Pakistan – are Dravidian cities. They go back to 5000 BC. That's what historians say. Till about 2000 years back, the society was a casteless society. What happened at that time was that this foreign civilization came from the north, and they started differentiating among classes. Every century since then there has been a protest by some Tamil intellectuals against the caste system. These intellectuals have always in different degrees been resisting rituals and superstition. But they didn't decry the entire system. They said that religion was necessary and God was necessary. But the Aryans were introducing superstitions.'

'You were religious when you were young?'

'I was a regular visitor to temples when I was very young, with and without my parents. We would go and see, and walk around, and go to the deity, and we would pray for prosperity and education and wealth. I was a believer. Up to my twelfth year. After hearing Periyar, I slowly withdrew myself. After twelve, I was a believer, but not a temple-goer. I started disbelieving the ritual part of the religion. In my younger days I read a lot of mythology, but when I started understanding it was all exploitation, I stopped being interested.'

He went back to his personal story. 'I left engineering college in 1948. I was twenty-three. This other thing happened then. I joined the government service, and I was posted as a junior engineer to a small town. My parents were very happy about my becoming an engineer and joining the government service.

'In the small town where I was posted I had to take over from a brahmin officer. On the day of my taking over he gave me a dinner at his house. He was living in a rented house. After the dinner the servant maid took back the vessels inside. I could hear the wife of that brahmin officer telling the servant maid not to take the vessels I had used inside the kitchen, but to put them in the back yard for further washing and cleaning, because those vessels had been touched by me. This upset me.'

'What did you do?'

'I didn't say anything at the time.'

'Had you and the officer eaten together?'

'We had eaten together, sitting on the ground, eating with our hands. That experience left a dent. I pocketed the insult. I didn't do anything. They were giving me the dinner, and it wasn't courteous to shout or rebel or say anything.'

'Your grandfather was a weaver. Your father was a clerk. You became an engineer when you were twenty-three. Isn't your story also the story of a rise and of opportunity?'

'I became an engineer because of reservation. And I resolved to fight for similar privileges for others in similar fields. I wanted to devote myself full-time to that cause. I did whatever I could in my official capacity – allocating funds to backward areas, setting up facilities in remote places. The DMK was founded by Mr Annadurai in 1949. But, being an official, I couldn't join.'

'India became independent in 1947. You've left that out of your story.'

'Periyar hadn't bothered too much about the national movement and Independence. He was solely concentrating on caste and religion.' And Mr Palani, treating my question as an interruption, went on, 'The DMK emerged as a political wing out of his social movement and began to involve itself in the political life of the state and the country. The Congress was dominant at that time.

In 18 years the DMK took power from the Congress. From being a secessionist movement, the DMK had become a party looking for regional autonomy. Many of my friends, people of my own age group, happened to occupy positions of responsibility in the administration. So I could use their goodwill to see that many social-justice programmes could be introduced.'

In this small dark man were locked up generations of grief and rage. He was the first in his line to have felt the affront; and, from what he had said, he was still the only one in his family to have taken up the cause. His passion was very great; it had to be respected. But I also began to wonder whether so great a rage left any room for a private life, the play of simpler emotions.

'When did you get married?'

'In 1951.' This was three years after that dinner with the brahmin officer.

'What caste was she?'

'Same weaver caste. From a neighbouring town.'

'Why the same caste?'

'It was more to please the parents. And also the girl chosen by my parents appeared acceptable to me.'

'Educated?'

'Moderately educated. Up to school-leaving standard. It was an arranged step.'

'In some ways a backward step?'

'Yes.'

'Dark girl?'

He showed the back of his hand. 'My colour.'

'A religious wedding?'

'Yes. But we didn't have a pundit. We had a senior man from our community who conducted the rites. He just prayed to God to bless the couple. It was a *via media*. Not a brahmin marriage, nor a marriage of Periyar's Self-Respect type.'

'You're still a Hindu? You haven't thought of becoming Buddhist?'

'It's not necessary. So long as you're allowed to propagate your own views, there's no need to go to another religion.'

'How do you arrange the various ceremonies?'

'When my children were born I had no ceremonies. In our forefathers' time there was a religious ceremony connected to each individual event in a man's or woman's life – birth, ear-piercing, puberty for a girl, marriage, pregnancy. All these things we don't have now.'

'What happened to your younger brother?'

'He also became an engineer. He married an educated girl in Coimbatore. Same weaver caste. Again out of deference to parents.'

'How did you marry your own daughters?'

'My first daughter's marriage was conducted in the presence of a very small number of most intimate relatives and friends. My second daughter's marriage was a Self-Respect marriage. It was a Periyar marriage, and it was conducted by a well known academic, a man from our movement.'

He was unrelenting in his cause, though his own need for religious faith involved him in contradictions and compromises; though the caste structures in his own family remained in place; and though, in the garbage of Madras, the broken roads, the absence of municipal regulation, the factionalism and plunder of the DMK administration and its successor administrations, something close to chaos could be seen.

Sadanand Menon had spoken of the 'looting' of the ancient temples of the city. And the great tank of Mylapore temple was indeed sad to see, empty, seemingly about to fall into ruin, with its beautiful internal steps buckled in parts.

I asked Mr Palani about the temple.

He said, 'I would like Mylapore temple and tank to continue and uphold their architectural and cultural part of our heritage. But still at the same time I am against these institutions being used to create differences among people. They say that brahmins alone can take water from the tank and use it in the sanctum sanctorum. Only brahmins can go there. People have tried to go into the sanctum in other places, but they have been prevented by law. About 10 years back, Mr Karunanidhi, the DMK chief minister then – he's chief minister again now, after the election – introduced a law that non-brahmins should be entitled to become priests. The brahmins took the matter up, and the law was struck down by the Supreme Court of India on the grounds that Hindu law as it is today required priests to be brahmins.'

That was where we always came back: brahmin prejudice. It was the fount of his passion. To that passion he was always loyal, however much the way of protest might lead to the undoing of his world. And, really, that brahmin cause, part of the apparent wholeness of the world of the South in 1962, was indefensible.

I asked, 'The servant girl who worked in your parents' house – what happened to her?'

'She got married.'

'Weaver-caste man?'

'Same weaver caste, and they've started a little weaving business. They're just making a living.'

I asked what his feelings were about the various Dravidian governments since 1967.

'The DMK government was very good at the beginning. But power corrupts, and the brahmins are intelligent people. They have their own means of diluting the devotion of these people to social reforms. They promise things from the centre in Delhi – in return for which they want concessions locally. They are preeminent in the cultural field. There again they tone down the efforts and intensity put forward by the state government.'

His cause made his world complete, left no room for doubt, supplied explanations for everything. And I wondered again whether there was really no part of him that was private, no part not touched by his cause.

I said, 'You can't withdraw into yourself a little, like the rest of us? You can't shut out the world sometimes and be with yourself alone?'

'My wife complains very frequently that I don't care for the family and the children, that I'm always interested in others and their welfare. I'm afraid she's almost right. I've defaulted in some respects. I've not lived a balanced life or a full personal life. I feel obsessed by my cause. It's the state of affairs that made me live this life.'

I went to see Sugar again one morning. He was always in his little ground-floor apartment in the Raghavans' house when he wasn't asleep. He was always available. He received people all the time, except for a period in the middle of the day. He was a local seer; he counselled; and sometimes he just listened.

The furniture pushed together at one end of the drawing-sleeping had disappeared; the room was almost as plain as he had said he wanted it.

His visitors that morning were a middle-aged brahmin group. And perhaps – it must have been something I had always known, but hadn't really thought about – all his visitors were brahmin. The group that morning looked grave but content. The reason for their content was that they had arranged the marriage of a girl in the family; and they were talking, with excited joyful sadness, about the wedding expenses.

The topic of wedding expenses was in the news: for some time the newspapers had been carrying reports from different parts of the country about Hindu brides being done to death by their husbands' families – often by fire – for not bringing a sufficient dowry or valuable enough gifts. These days a boy's family often required modern gifts, motor-scooters, or expensive electronic goods.

However, thoughts of bride-burning were far away from the group in Sugar's drawing-sleeping. They were just ticking off the expenses of the great day, one by one, and it was as though the ceremony was being savoured, in all its details, in advance.

Sugar said to me, with an air of finality, and with the authority of his position, 'They will have to spend a lakh and a half. I've told them. A lakh and a half.'

That was 150,000 rupees, £6,000. But a fairer measure of the cost was to be had if it was set against the salary of the girl's father, on whom all the expenses were going to fall. He was a middle-rank executive, and he earned between 7000 and 8000 rupees a month. The marriage of his daughter was going to cost him 20 months' of his salary.

I had arrived almost at the end of the calculations, and the man and the women of the party, and Sugar, were quite happy to go through it again, for my benefit.

The first expense was the *choultry,* the wedding hall. The cost of that, for the two days you needed to hire it, was going to be 6000 rupees. And that was a modest choultry; there were choultries in Madras that cost 10 and 20 times as much. You had to add to that the cost of the electricity, and the cleaning-up afterwards.

'And the sundries,' Sugar said, using a word from his old, office life.

With the sundries, the maintenance of the choultry wasn't going to come to less than 2000 rupees. Then the cook was going to charge 4000 rupees.

'At the very least,' Sugar said. 'Preparing food for 500 people four times a day for two days – that's not cheap. The cook will have to have 10 assistants.'

'Vegetables,' one of the women said.

'Three thousand,' the man said.

Sugar said, 'Provisions. Provisions will be 10,000 rupees.'

I asked about the word. 'Provisions', as Sugar used it, seemed to be quite distinct from vegetables.

Sugar said, 'Rice, condiments, Bengal gram, green gram, rice flour, tamarind, chili, pepper, salt – that's provisions.'

'Saris for the bride,' one of the women said. 'And clothing gifts for relations on both sides. Ten thousand.'

Sugar said, 'I don't see how you could do it for less. And clothes for the groom.'

The man of the party said, 'Five thousand.'

'Jewelry,' Sugar said. 'Fifteen 24-carat sovereigns at 3000 apiece.'

One of the women said, 'Plus 12,000 for diamond ear-rings.'

'Two k.g. of silver vessels,' the man said. 'Fifteen thousand. Stainless steel and brass vessels for the household. That will be another 5000.'

'Honeymoon expenses,' one of the women said.

Sugar said firmly, 'Ten thousand there.' He explained to me: 'Furniture for the first night – cot, mattress, sheets, pillows, two or three vessels full of sweets. Dresses for the occasion for bride and groom.'

The man said, 'And you have to give gifts during the first year of the marriage. You have to give dresses, and clothes for the groom. You also have to give the groom a ring or a watch. The request will be made after the marriage. If you give a diamond finger-ring, the Diwali gifts will come to 5000.' Diwali, the festival of lights towards the end of the year. 'There are four or five other festivals. You have to give 2000 each time during the first year. Add it up.'

Sugar, shaking his dhoti-covered legs very slightly, said, 'One and a half lakhs.' A hundred and fifty thousand rupees.

I said, 'I get a figure of 129,000.'

Sugar said, 'It will be one and a half, by the time you actually start spending.'

I said to the man in the party, 'Yet you look so happy.'

He said, 'It's a happy occasion. We know the boy. He's a nice boy.'

'How do people manage if they have two or three daughters?'

The man said, 'That is why middle-class brahmin ladies are not marrying. They go for jobs instead. In our brahmin community, all our savings go to our daughters' marriage. It gets balanced out if you have a son and a daughter. If you've got only sons, you're lucky.'

'How can people make these high demands nowadays?'

The parents of the boy – who's getting all these things – his parents say, "We've educated him, and now he's earning lucratively." So, as a compensation for what they've spent on him, they want to make capital.'

Things were not easy for brahmin boys nowadays. Places in educational institutions and jobs with the government were reserved for backward communities, and scheduled castes, and scheduled tribes, and physically handicapped ex-servicemen. Fifty per cent of places were now reserved for backward communities, and there was talk of raising that figure to 70 per cent. That would mean that only five per cent of places would be filled in open competition: that meant that only five per cent of places would be open to brahmins.

The man said, 'That's why we are migrating to other places, greener pastures.'

Mylapore was once famous as one of the two or three brahmin areas of Madras. Now only 40 per cent of the people in Mylapore were brahmins. The others were non-brahmins, including even some scheduled castes. Houses had come up for sale in the normal way, and the people with the money – not necessarily brahmins – had bought the houses. In the villages at one time there used to be brahmin *agraharams,* separate streets for brahmins, where no one else was allowed to walk. Now all of that was gone. Brahmins had moved out of the villages, to better themselves. They had left those village agraharams, and other people had bought the houses. There had been an upheaval, but brahmins were not people who fought back or demonstrated or complained, and people outside didn't know about the upheaval that had taken place.

I said, 'So Tamil Nadu is going to be a *shudra* place.'

I had spoken in innocence. But the man looked startled, and Sugar made a show of covering his face with his hands.

Sugar said, 'Don't write that. If you write that, they will come and burn your house. Don't say "shudra" here. Say "Dravidian".

You know how they call us? In Tamil the correct word for a brahmin is *parpannan*. When they want to mock us they say *papain*. To say "shudra" is like them saying "pa-paan".'

The people with the wedding on their minds got up to go. The joy of the wedding in prospect made them talk of the position of brahmins (middle class though they were, and vulnerable) with something like light-heartedness.

When they went away, Sugar looked tired.

He said, 'You see. They come all the time. I heal people. Did you know that? I heal people by faith. I have seen about 1000 or 2000 people. Every day I see two or three or four or five people. Every day.'

His dhoti didn't look fresh; nor did his yellow singlet. There was a slight dampness to the skin on his soft shoulders. He looked unexercised, unwell.

'How do you heal them?'

'You give them burnt cowdung, and chant mantras, and solace them by kind words.'

I was puzzled: he seemed to be setting himself at a distance from what he did for people. He sounded tired.

He said, 'They come for marriages.' He meant they came for advice about the marriage of their children or other relations. 'I have to predict them.'

'How do you do that?'

'Something occurs in my mind, and I tell them.'

He crossed from the low seat where he had been sitting, facing me, and he sat down in the chair just beside mine, against the wall. We both had our backs to the door. We looked at the blue wall of the drawing-sleeping, with the religious pictures, and the centrally placed hanging shelves, cluttered behind the sliding glass panels.

He said, 'Cent per cent correct.' He was referring to the predictions he made for people, and again it seemed that he had changed his attitude to what he did for other people. 'If I say 15th of the month, it may occur on the 10th or 20th – a few days this way or that way.'

'When did this gift come? You didn't have it in 1967.'

'It suddenly came. In 1970. I don't know how it came. One Mr T. told me I'd got this gift. And he said to me, "Use it in a proper way, so that you can be useful to many people." From that day onwards I'm doing these things. I used to go to Mr R.'s house often. It was in Madras. A small house, a poor man. I cannot say he is my guru. He likes me, and I like him, that's all. Birds of the same feather flock together, and he has these gifts as well. I can't do miracles like Sai Baba – I don't want you to think that.

'What happened was this. A friend of mine, a businessman, a middle-class man, a good friend, a man about fifty at the time, he came to tell me that his brother is very sick, is running a 104-degrees temperature. "Sugar, give me something for my brother, to reduce his fever." And other symptoms he's got as well, like fits and other things. And this friend came to my house, and I received him, and asked him to sit for a while, and I took some cow-dung ashes and chanted *Sudarsan* mantra, and I gave it to him.'

'What made you do that?'

'Something. Some forces asked me to do it. At that moment, when I'm doing it, I'm not Sugar. I'm not myself. After a few seconds, I gave that ashes to my friend. He went home and gave it to his brother, and smeared it on his forehead. The brother was all right the next morning. He went to office. I was working myself at that time in an office.

'After that, I cannot sleep for two days. I went to Mr R.'s place and asked him about this. "There is something wrong with me. I cannot sleep. I'm seeing some black figures in front of me. Human figures. Black figures." He asked me, "What did you do yesterday?" I narrated the whole story. He scolded me. "Who asked you to give ashes and other things to your friend? In future don't do it." And he asked me to do the same Sudarsan mantra again. I'm all right in a day or two.

'From that day onwards, I'm not doing anything like that, without getting permission from elsewhere. I see those black figures now, even as I am talking to you. Two figures. Horns on their head. *Madan* – cow-headed man. It is a malevolent figure. He may do so many things. At the moment he is very friendly with me. I have to get permission from him whenever anybody comes to ask for this or that. I will hear it in my head, his permission.

'I want to get rid of this gift. I want to get rid of all these things. Temple, everything. I want to get rid of all these things. I want peace. People are coming and worrying me about their horoscope, and about not getting jobs for their sons, and not getting marriages for their daughters, and lost property. And: "I'm sick, Sugar. Do something for me." I don't know how to get rid of these things. I don't like these things. You come and tell me your daughter is not well. "Do something for me." What am I gaining?

'You've not seen these people. It is for those people I've put up a sign on my door asking them not to come at a certain time – that's when I have my rest.

'It is only on account of these things I'm not well. I get a poor blood flow to the brain. I get giddiness often. I can't climb stairs. Slowly I'm stopping these things, but I'm not telling them.'

I said, 'What will you do when you stop?'

His life in the little apartment seemed built around receiving visitors, waiting for them. It was hard to see how he would occupy himself if he stopped seeing people.

He said he thought he would read. 'Even today I'm reading books. Jack Higgins, Wilbur Smith. Haley, the *Airport* man. So many others. To while away my time I'm reading these things. Any book – whether it is *Gita* or trash.'

Twenty years before, I had noted that about him: his ability to read popular romantic fiction from England – so far away, in every sense, from his life and experience in Mylapore.

He said, 'I want some books to while away my time. It keeps my mind occupied. Sometimes I chant mantras. Some mantras I chant 2000 times, 3000 times, the same mantra throughout the day.'

We were sitting side by side.

I said, 'You will have to get rid of this gift.'

'I will. I have confidence. I know myself. I will do it. I have no peace here. I want to go away from the city to some far-off place, but the doctors won't permit. I must be within kilometres of my doctor.'

He pointed to a chair against the opposite wall, below the hanging glass-fronted shelves.

'I can sit there and read your face, give full details, if you sit before me. But after that I will get a headache. I will suffer for two days.'

But the talk I had heard, the previous time I had come to the little apartment, was of the peace people found with him. One man had talked of emptying his mind, of spending four hours in the darkness with Sugar, during a power cut, and hardly saying a word.

Sugar said, with something like irritation, 'They come here not for peace, but to hear what I may blab about them. It's very good for them, to hear about their difficulties and how to get rid of those things. They say they want peace. But they want advice.'

I remembered the landlord, the 'moneyed man', as Sugar had said, sitting patiently in his chair; and I remembered the young business executive, with his fine brahmin face, and the fresh holy marks on his forehead, sitting forward, his feet below his chair, the palms of his hands on the edge of his chair.

Sugar said, 'But I'll keep my mouth shut. And they'll sit here, and talk about politics and other things, and then they'll go away.

'Mr R. knows what I'm going through. He himself is suffering. He is an old man of eighty-six. He will predict accurately. He will tell you about your house in London, how you keep your home. He will tell you all these things with you sitting here in front of him.'

I asked, 'Why did you like me in 1962?'

We had met late one afternoon, at the end of the day's march, after the tents had been pitched, not far from a mountain river. The temperature, even in August, was dropping fast; the colours of the mountain were grey and brown. And he had been there in the twilight, muffled up in his coarse woollen pullover. We had begun to talk just like that.

Sugar said, 'In my last birth we both had met. You might have been my brother, friend, and father. I felt something up there in the Himalayas. I won't forget your name. I will always remember your name.'

'I thought you were a sad man. Were you sad?'

'No sadness then. Nothing. My father was alive. My mother was alive. I liked seeing places in the Himalayas. I was the first in my family to go to the Himalayas.'

'Is there anything I can do for you?'

'God will look after me. I have faith in him. Raghavan charges me little for the apartment. I spend all day here, so you might say I look after the house for them, in a way. We have a mutual understanding.'

'Tell me about this burnt cowdung you give people. Where do you burn it?'

'I buy it.'

So it was a common item, on sale in shops dealing in puja goods. It wasn't something special, something he had made himself.

'It's called *vibudhi*. You can buy it in bags, one kilo, two kilos a time. Mine is not scented. I give three rupees a kilo. Scented, they are selling for one rupee, or one rupee 50 paisa, for a packet of 100 grams. How to make it I don't know.'

A slender young girl in dark clothes came in through the front door. No words passed between her and Sugar. She began to clear up and sweep in the middle space, the space between the temple and the kitchen, both of which places would have been barred to her, since she would not have been a brahmin.

There had been a revolution. The temples had been 'looted'. The streets and walls were ragged and scrawled with election slogans and emblems. Mylapore was said to be only 40 per cent brahmin. But in the little space that was still Sugar's the old world seemed to continue.

In Bangalore Kala had told me of her brahmin ancestor who had left his village and had come to the city of Madras, and had been so poor there that he and his mother had lived on the consecrated food of the great temple of Mylapore. That story – old gods, old temples, poor brahmins – had seemed to me to come from a far-off, fairy-tale time. But the story was of the new world, of a countryside becoming overpopulated, and of the dispersal of the brahmins. The story I had heard in Sugar's apartment of the breakup of the brahmin agraharams or village settlements told of the same dispersal, the scattering of people from their ancestral homes.

But on this kind of journey knowledge can sometimes come slowly; the traveller can sometimes listen selectively; and certain things – because they appear to fit the country or the culture – can be taken too much for granted. When at the beginning of my stay in Madras I met Kakusthan, and heard that he was a brahmin who was trying to live as a full brahmin, I didn't understand how unusual and even heroic this resolve of his was.

He lived in a brahmin colony or agraharam near one of the old temples of Madras. His father had been the one to move there; before that, for many generations, the men of Kakusthan's family had been priests of a temple in a village, now two hours or so away from the city by bus. Kakusthan belonged now, by his profession, to the modern world. He worked for a big business company, and he wrote economic reports and project-assessments of various kinds for them. But the guardianship of the family temple had fallen to him. His acceptance of the responsibility was part of his resolve to live as a full brahmin; and so, while sitting at his office desk and while travelling about on his office work, Kakusthan was dressed as a brahmin priest. He wore the caste-marks on his forehead; his head was shaved; he wasn't bare-backed, but he wore the long cream-coloured brahmin's tunic.

To me, India was a land of caste costume. (Though it was a good deal less so than a country like England, where a whole ritual of costume and colour, marking different jobs, groups, social ranks, sports, leisure activities, gradations of meals, different times of day and year, kept many people in a constant pacific frenzy: in India everyone just had his one costume.) And Kakusthan's antique appearance, when I first met him, made less of an impression than it ought to have done. As for living as a full brahmin, I thought this meant that Kakusthan was the purest kind of vegetarian, not eating fish or eggs or garlic or onions; that he followed the basic laws of ritual cleanliness, not eating or drinking from vessels someone else used; that he used the right hand for clean activities, the left for unclean; and that generally he strove to avoid pollution.

But Kakusthan's brahminism went far beyond that. The purity he aimed at forbade him to eat food he hadn't first offered to his god at home, forbade him even to drink water he hadn't consecrated in this way. In the great heat of Madras this meant that for him every working day was full of hardship. And, in fact, the brahminical restrictions he had imposed on himself were also a kind of private penance, an act of piety and expiation towards his father and his ancestors.

Kakusthan had been a poor brahmin. As a child in Madras he had been made to suffer because of the brahmin observances his father had forced on him. Periyar's anti-brahmin ideas had gone right down to the children of Madras, and Kakusthan had been so tormented at school and in the streets that he had broken faith with his past. He had wanted to turn his back on his brahmin duties; and he had quarrelled with his father. He had succeeded in breaking away; he had made a life for himself elsewhere. But then in early middle age he had been eaten up by remorse; and he had come back to Madras, to live in the very agraharam or brahmin colony, and the very house, where he had grown up. He lived there now with the determination to be as pure a brahmin as was possible.

The colony Kakusthan lived in was in the Triplicane district of Madras. As a brahmin area, it was second only to Mylapore; and the Parthasarathy temple, which was about 1000 years old and was at the heart of the Triplicane district, was in the eyes of its devotees the equal of the Mylapore temple.

The colony was in a lane at the side of the temple. From the lane the temple wall was unexpectedly high. The stonework was beautiful and precise, and the lower section of the wall was painted in broad vertical bands of rust and white, sacred temple colours. Facing this temple wall, and almost in the middle of the lane, was the entrance to the colony: a gateway like a screen, not very high, with wooden doors, and with the symbol of Garuda, the bird 'vehicle' of Lord Vishnu, painted above the doors.

To the left of the gateway, as you entered, was the stone-walled temple garden, separated from the temple by the lane. The garden was old, possibly as old as the temple itself – and that enclosed formal space, with its own symbolical *gopuram* or temple-tower, seemed to take one back to old, superseded ways of feeling. The colony (though clearly on a sacred site) was not itself old. It had been established as a colony towards the end of the last century or at the beginning of this; and the land had been given by a charitable resident of Triplicane to provide for brahmins who had come from the villages, and were either serving in the temple or simply serving as pundits in the city.

The doors of the colony were closed at night, from 10 to five in the morning; only residents could enter then. The colony was closed at all times to people deemed unclean: smokers, drunkards, cobblers, scheduled-caste people generally, and Muslims. Such people were not allowed to pass through the doorway. Some people had to be let in to service the colony, but they were not allowed to enter the houses.

Past the doorway, a paved path led between low small houses to the central yard. There were wells in the yard, with winches and ropes. Women and girls were drawing water when I went; and the pastoral scene was surprising in the middle of a crowded town. Kakusthan, who was my host and guide, said that brahmins could use only well water for drinking, because well water had a direct connection with the earth. (I didn't know about this brahmin rule. It cleared up an old mystery for me. In 1971 I had gone to India to follow the election in a drought-stricken desert constituency in Rajasthan, in the north-west. One of the candidates, a God-fearing old Gandhian, much admired, had repeatedly spoken, on the grounds of morality, against the taking of piped water to the desert villages. 'Good old water from the well', he kept on saying, was good enough; piped water would 'tell on the health and morals' of women in the villages. He hadn't explained why he had said that; but – going by what Kakusthan now said – his audience would have understood his caste shorthand.)

Over the years, with the increase in the population of the colony, the level of water in the well had gone down 30 feet, Kakusthan said. Years ago you could just dip your 'vessel' by hand and get your water. Now there was rationing, six pots per family in the morning, six pots in the evening. 'Pots', 'vessels' – these were the correct words, because brahmins didn't use buckets. I didn't know about that either, but the explanation was simple. Modern buckets were made of galvanized iron, and brahmins had to use pots made of brass or earthenware, since these materials had a direct connection with the earth. And there, at the colony well, were the women and girls with their awkward, handle-less pots – and one might have seen only the city pastoral, and missed the caste regulation.

Near the well was a hand-pump. The water got from this was strictly for use in the latrine – though, clearly, its source was the same as the drinking water in the well. The rule about the hand-pump and the latrine seemed fierce and brahminical; in fact, it showed how difficult it was nowadays absolutely to live as a brahmin. The very idea of the latrine was a non-brahmin idea: to enter such a polluted place was itself pollution. No old-time brahmin would have even contemplated the idea. Good brahmins, traditional brahmins, used open-air sites, a fresh one each time. So there was a compromise there, as well as in a number of small things the visitor mightn't have noticed or thought about: the wearing of stitched garments like shirts, the wearing of leather sandals, and even the buying of bundles of food-leaves from the market.

Leaves, to eat your food off, were brahminically more correct than plates. Leaves were used once and thrown away; plates were used more than once and were technically always polluted, however much you washed them. There was a special quality of ritual, and romance, to eating off a leaf. It was something that had survived with us even in far-off Trinidad. After special religious occasions in my grandmother's house, when I was a child, people were fed on banana leaves (as they were in the Woodlands Hotel in Madras as late as 1962). A fresh banana leaf was a beautiful thing to eat off: dark green, with a hollow spine of a paler colour, the leaf itself smooth yet with grip, ribbed, with a slight sheen, impermeable, with no intrusive smell or taste. To eat off a leaf like that not only marked a special occasion; it became associated, in the most romantic way, with religion, making one think of one's remote origins, and of the forests through which the Hindu epic heroes, divinities, wandered during the years of their exile. Even in small Trinidad, though, the forests were far away, and banana leaves were not things you just went out and picked. They had to be brought from miles away; they had to be brought fresh; and they weren't always to be had. It was a wasteful and expensive way of serving food. In Madras, now, the Woodlands Hotel no longer used banana leaves. People like Kakusthan who needed to eat off leaves bought bundles of a smaller, rounder kind of dried leaf in the market. They were not fresh, not particularly clean, and they had no aesthetic quality. The idea of cleanliness had been overlaid by ritual; what was really being honoured was the idea of the leaf, the natural thing used once and thrown away.

In the colony there was a restriction about women I hadn't known about. Menstruating women and girls were segregated during their periods. There was a special room for them in a corner of the colony. This room had two doors, and both were kept closed, so that people walking outside wouldn't be polluted. Kakusthan told me that a menstruating woman was polluting at a distance of 10 to 15 feet: if for some reason you had to talk to a menstruating woman, that was the distance you should keep her at. The women in this separate room had their own latrine and bathroom. They did absolutely nothing for the three days of their period. For them, Kakusthan said, it was a time of 'a full and complete rest'. They read books or listened to music. The room could accommodate 10 women, and in the old days the room was always full; but nowadays, modern life being what it was, with girls going out to work (and with other girls slipping out to the cinema and so on: there was a wicket gate at the back of the colony that menstruating women used), at any given time there would be only five or six women in the room. This segregation made women hate the idea of menstruation, Kakusthan said; yet at the same time they welcomed the segregation, because it gave them the kind of regular little holiday they might never otherwise have.

Only five of the houses in the colony had an upper sleeping room; and these houses were in a row down one side, against a boundary wall. All the other houses were single-storeyed and low, built flat to the ground. So the central yard, all the life around the well, was overlooked by the higher buildings at the back. I wondered whether that didn't raise problems of pollution for the brahmins of the agraharam, being gazed down at by people of other castes, or having the shadows of those taller houses fall on their colony. Kakusthan said the high buildings at the back were no problem. The people who lived in them were of the cowherd caste, *yadavas,* Lord Krishna's caste; between yadavas and brahmins there was mutual regard.

The other immediate neighbours of the colony were Muslims. It might have seemed that the 53 families of the colony were vulnerable, and could easily be overrun in a riot; but for some reason there had never been any communal trouble at all between the Muslims and the brahmins. The Muslims might even – though Kakusthan didn't say this – have acted as a buffer against unfriendly non-brahmins. So, between the temple and the yadavas and the

Muslims, the colony enjoyed a kind of security: the houses, Kakusthan said, had no locks on their doors.

The colony – with its wooden doors closed every night, and standing next to the enclosed temple – made one think of some old foundation in Europe, alms-houses, say, in a cathedral close; and there was something of that in the way the colony was run. There was a trust; it collected the rents, did building repairs and general maintenance, and paid the man who watched the gateway. Tenancy of the houses passed down from one generation to the other; most of the families in the colony had been there for decades. Kakusthan's father had got into the colony in the early 1940s.

Kakusthan said that penniless brahmins migrating – in the old days – from the villages to the towns were attracted to the areas around the temples not only because it was easier for them to make a little money by being pundits or mendicants, but also because the temple had tanks and wells, and offered water direct from the earth. The temples were also near the sea. This nearness to the sea was important, because during the lunar and solar eclipses, and on some other occasions as well, traditional brahmins liked to have a dip in the sea.

It wasn't easy, being a good brahmin! The more Kakusthan went into it, the more he came up with needs and observances; and the more awkward the whole business appeared. Perhaps an absolute brahmin way wasn't possible. Perhaps it had always been like that; perhaps at all times brahmins would have had to compromise in one thing or another.

Kakusthan's father had come to make his way in Madras in 1932 or 1933. He was twenty-two then, and married, but he didn't bring his wife with him. Not only did he not have the money; it was also not quite right, at that time, for a husband and wife to break away, as a couple, from the joint-family house.

Kakusthan's father was the first in his family to have gone to an English-medium school. He got only as far as the 10th standard; but he later became a teacher. He was especially good in mathematics, and he gave private lessons in the subject. As with other brahmins of his generation, he was hard to categorize. It could be said that he was a half-educated village man; at the same time, so far as mathematics went, he was gifted and unusual. And there was, in addition, his Hindu and brahmin learning. This was considerable.

In the family village there was an old temple. For 700 or 800 years, since the time of the Chola emperors, Kakusthan's father's family had had special rights and privileges in that temple. They did the pujas for the temple deity, and everything offered to the deity in that temple went first to the deity and then to Kakusthan's father's family. In that temple the privilege of Kakusthan's father's family exceeded that of emperors.

His breeding and ancestry made Kakusthan's father the equal of anyone; yet when he left his village, all that he and his family could raise was the train fare to Madras. He left six people behind in the village: his wife, his parents, the family of his elder brother. None of them had an income; all of them depended on the young man who had gone to Madras on the train.

Having no money at all, Kakusthan's father stayed with relatives in Madras. For some time he lived on charity as a young brahmin, eating at different brahmin houses on different days. But then he began to make a little money from his learning. He knew by heart all the 4000 verses of the Vedas in Tamil. The fact got around, and at pujas the young man would be called upon to recite the 4000 verses. He would get a rupee or two for that, and his food as well. With the money for the verses, and then his fees for the private lessons he gave in mathematics, and his salary as a teacher, he was able in the end to have a decent income. He would have made about 40 to 45 rupees a month, enough to keep himself and the six people he had left behind in the village.

Some time in the early 1940s, after 10 years of this life, Kakusthan's father finally brought his wife to Madras. They found a room for 10 rupees a month, about 75 pence. Children were born. And then, with the help of friends, Kakusthan's father got a place in the brahmin colony, paying more or less what he had been paying outside. He would have been in his early thirties; security of a kind had at last come to him. He moved twice within the colony; some people did that. In 1943 Kakusthan was born.

It was like the beginning of a success story. There had been a good deal of movement – but had there been success? Forty-five years later Kakusthan was showing me round the place where he had spent all his childhood and adolescence, and where he had come back to live for good; and Kakusthan was dressed as a brahmin. He was almost certainly the richest man in his little community. But the community was poor; historical though the setting was, with all its promptings to religious pastoral, with the enclosed temple garden at the front, the well and the winch in the central yard (and with the people of Lord Krishna's cowherd caste in the high buildings at the back), many of the women and girls at the well, filling up their pots of rationed water, looked pallid and undernourished.

The brahmin colony was a little urban slum, lower in energy than the Muslim community on the outer limit of the temple area. And the colony was under pressure. Its already compromised brahminical ways were being steadily more compromised. The most dreadful compromise had been made when the sweepers, the cleaners of latrines, had begun to ask for sums the community couldn't afford. Then, to show the sweepers, and to deter further blackmail, the brahmins had cleaned their own latrines. Kakusthan himself had rallied the young men of the community. He told them that every day every person touched excrement, even if it was his own; and that it was therefore all right for them to clean their own latrines and sewers. At any other time what Kakusthan proposed would have been regarded as a form of caste suicide; but Kakusthan spoke of it as a moral, caste triumph.

He was a small man, an inch or two above five feet, warm-complexioned, well made. His eyes were bright and steady. It was his eyes that gave away his passion – at one time the passion of the renegade, the man who wished to break out at whatever cost, now the passion of the man wishing to honour what he felt to be the true way.

He lived in one of the five houses which had an upper floor, with a sleeping room off an open terrace. The room to which he led me when I first went to his house was at the far end downstairs. It was perhaps against the boundary wall; it was dark and airless, with a slight smell of drains, a little cell, where everything, paint and walls and cupboards and fittings, showed age and use in the fluorescent light, but where no doubt everything was ritually clean. Cleanliness – like pollution – could come easily to a brahmin: a finger flick of water could be deemed to purify a room.

Since I was a visitor, and this was India, Kakusthan wanted me to eat something in his house – though having a stranger in his house wasn't strictly what he should be doing as a man trying hard to live as a good brahmin. Of course, he wasn't going to eat with me; but he wanted me to eat something from his kitchen. That was why we were downstairs. We had passed by the kitchen when we had gone through to the little room at the back; and I had seen, on a table or a stand or a half-wall next to the kitchen doorway, a black image, with a flame burning before it in a tall, sooty oil lamp of bronze or silver. The lamp was of a style that took one back to the ancient world: the wick burned in the mouth of a shallow oil container shaped like a curling leaf, and this oil container was attached to a vertical pole. The black image was of Kakusthan's deity; everything that Kakusthan ate had first to be offered to this deity.

I had my own scruples, too, about eating far from home – far, at any rate, from the Taj Coromandel Hotel. But I felt ashamed of those scruples, and I accepted a little food from Kakusthan's kitchen, and put my lips to the glass of coffee, though the breaking of bread (or a puri) in Kakusthan's back room did make my writing fingers oily. This became hard to ignore; it called for a more than ritual washing outside – Kakusthan pouring for me, not complaining, wasting precious water from the well, one of the six evening pots he was allowed. (And there had been no need for me to feel ashamed, or to feel that I had to eat. Kakusthan was a man of the world. When I next visited him at the colony, some days later, I told him straight out that I was like him, too, and didn't eat away from home. He accepted that immediately. He laughed and said, 'All right, I'll be the untouchable this time.')

That first afternoon, in the dark, fluorescent-lit room at the back of his house, he talked in a matter-of-fact way of his neighbours.

He said, 'It is a poor community. Almost the entire community is poor. The first generation largely consisted of purohits, pujaris, cooks, and a few office-goers. The second generation is somewhat better. There are more boys and girls in the family earning money, with jobs.'

'What kind of jobs?'

'Jobs which were not dreamt of by traditional brahmins. Like operating machines, working as mechanics, and all other industrial manual labour. My neighbour on this side is a cook.'

Fifteen people lived in the cook's room. This wasn't as bad as it sounded: the 15 didn't sleep in the room at the same time. In fact, they had their own reserved sleeping places in the central yard: in the summer, which lasted the better part of the Madras year, everyone slept in the yard or in the open. The cook made the greater part of his money at weddings; but he had to employ so many assistants that the profit on a 1000-rupee wedding job was really very small.

The neighbour on Kakusthan's other side was a 'peon' or office boy. He worked in a government office. There was another boy in the colony who drove a mechanized rickshaw. His father had been a Sanskrit scholar, an authority on the Vedas and Hindu rituals.

'It's really sad,' Kakusthan said. 'The boy himself says, "What can I do, when there is no other means for me? I'm not educated. Nor did I follow in my father's footsteps."'

I said, 'That sounds unusual.'

'He wasn't educated because of lack of parental care.'

And when Kakusthan and I next met, in the hotel where I was staying, it was of the poverty of the brahmin colony beside the great temple of Parthasarathy that he continued to talk.

Kakusthan said, 'The situation today is many times better than what it was in the 1950s, when I was growing up there. I felt the need for better comforts. The people I knew at school dressed better, looked better, were stronger, and more modern in their appearance. I looked more like a village boy – with my dhoti, my religious marks on my forehead, and my *churki*.'

It was, barring the churki, the way he looked now. The churki, the long, uncut tuft or lock of hair at the back of the head, was an antique brahmin badge. Kakusthan no longer had a long churki; the one he wore was just an inch and a half long, but it served his purpose. (Four or five times a year, on an auspicious day, as part of his revived brahminism, Kakusthan had all his body hair shaved – eyebrows, everything, except for the hair under his arms and the churki. He was between shaves when we met; the hair on his head looked like a crewcut, and the short churki wasn't particularly noticeable.) When he was a child he had been made to wear the churki by his father. It wasn't something that many brahmin boys wore in the 1950s; it had been at the root of his torment at school.

Kakusthan said, 'All these things brought contempt and ridicule by other boys, which even today continues. I used to react violently if the boy who ridiculed me was weak, and used to ignore the boy who was strong. I complained to my father about my social plight at school, and his reply would be, "Go and report to the headmaster." He would also say that it was to uphold the family tradition that I had to wear those religious marks and have the churki – without which the entire family in the village would be looked down on by other families, particularly as our family as brahmins were serving the deity there.

'My father himself was suffering from the same kind of ridicule in his own school and elsewhere in the city – on the buses, on the streets. The whole brahmin community was suffering at that time from that kind of ridicule, due to anti-brahminism, let loose by the so-called Dravidian Movement.' The *Dravidar Kazagham,* the Dravidian Movement, started by Periyar. 'This was in the mid-1950s, when there was widespread movement against brahmins and their practices. This took the form of breaking idols, cutting off brahmins' churkis and sacred threads, and rubbing off the religious marks on the forehead. In Madras most of the vegetarian restaurants used to boast themselves as "brahmin hotels" – and the Dravidian people would erase the word "brahmin". Now hotels do not have these words in the city. In those days you would have the "brahmin hotel" and the "military hotel".'

The 'military hotel' still existed when I first travelled in the South. It meant a place where meat was served; and – as though accepting the brahmin prejudice against such places, as though revelling in the difference and absolute freedom such a prejudice gave – the military hotels in the South were really very dirty and unwashed.

Somewhere on the bus route between Bangalore and Madras in 1962, somewhere on the red earth of that region, I had my first sight of the military hotel. It was a shack on bare earth, part of the informal bus-stop area. The English words on the signboard – in that old-looking landscape of simple colours, like an exotic view in an English 18th-century print – seemed to go back to the British East India Company's wars against Tippu Sultan. The quaint words seemed to hold something of Indian history, something of the 18th-century Indian anarchy, when armies, of Indian hired troops, fought over the land, without reference to the people who worked in the villages or in the fields.

From one kind of war to another, one kind of consciousness to another: in the main museum room of the Periyar Thidal, among the 33 paintings of the stages or stations in the life of Periyar, was one showing the great man in 1957, when he was nearly eighty, painting out 'Brahmin' from a hotel or restaurant signboard. Periyar in this painting was white-bearded and very grand. He had a whitewash brush in one hand; he stood on a bench or stool to reach the signboard; and he was calmly going about his business, without interference from anyone, policeman or politician or hotel-owner or hotel customer. The colours of the painting were simple, the details curiously literal (the signboard, the stool or bench on which Periyar stood, the painting brush edged with white), as though they were illustrating a well known text; and the effect was that of the calm world of a children's comic strip.

Kakusthan, talking of the humiliations he had to put up with as a boy because of his traditional brahmin dress, said, 'I resisted whenever I could, and I got beaten, even while I was telling my parents that I had to switch to the new ways of life – particularly removing the churki, and wearing trousers. We suffered from the churkis. That was the thing we suffered from the most. When I used to go to school sports, there used to be a lot of amusement when I took part in running-races and the sport known as *kabbadi*. When I ran, my churki would get loose and fall down, and that got a lot of laughs. In kabbadi my opponents would seize me by the churki, hold me by that long strand of hair, and they would win the game.

'I stayed at school until 1958. I joined a college then on a pre-university course, and the irony is that I got into that college only because of my churki and caste-marks. The man who recommended me was a brahmin, and he cherished the same values we had in our family. But I was in that college for only six months. I was subject to more intense ridicule from my college mates. And they were adults now, not boys.

'All this made me very sad. I started feeling entirely different from my father, and begged him to spare me these agonies. But he was firm. He said that family respect and tradition were more important than these passing experiences. I was not convinced. I dropped out of college. I felt I had to be independent.'

Independent – it was a strange word.

Kakusthan said, 'Independent of these practices. I was sixteen. I felt I must be as modern as anybody else.'

'Weren't you frightened when you left the college?'

'I wasn't frightened. I was full of hope that I would be able to do what I wanted once I was away from home. I told my mother these things in confidence. She partly agreed with me, and partly didn't. She understood my feelings.'

I tried to set that family drama of 30 years before in the colony I had seen. In the yard around the well the people would have been more obviously brahminical in their dress and restrictions: people once of authority, now safe only in this little area of theirs. I tried to think of the passions of father and son exploding in the small private space the family had in the colony: the dark small room at the back of the kitchen on the lower level, the sleeping room off the common terrace above, with a view – as you climbed the narrow stone-and-concrete steps at the side of the house-row to that terrace – of the overgrown temple garden, memorial of a calmer time.

'For a few days I stayed at home. My father was very angry. He didn't talk to me. He didn't want me in the house. I had betrayed the family and let down his prestige. He wanted me to be a graduate and a bank employee or a central government employee, even while adhering to my religious pursuits at the temple in our village – where we had much honour as brahmins. He would cite several examples of people who did the two things – wear the long tuft, the churki, and at the same time did good, secure, modern jobs.

'Through friends in the colony, friends of my own age or a little older, I got a job with an electric-bulb dealer as an office boy on a salary of one rupee a day. This was in 1959. But since the father-and-son relationship was extremely strained, there was no peace at home. There was also a mother-father tussle, with mother and father quarrelling, and with occasional beatings for me from both father and mother. So I left home.

'I decided to go to my married sister. She lived in the town of Vellore, 100 kilometres west of Madras. Her husband had become a schoolteacher after retiring from the army. I went to Vellore by bus. I got the fare out of the old college books. My father had bought them new. I sold them to a hawker for a throw-away price.

'It was a Saturday when I left home. Every Saturday and Wednesday I had my traditional oil bath, and my mother used to soap my long hair. She did so that Saturday. I had my morning meal around 10.30, and immediately afterwards I slipped away to the bus stop, not telling any soul I was leaving for Vellore. I had very little money, just enough for the bus fare to Vellore, and I walked from Triplicane to Parry's Corner. Five miles, in the scorching heat. It took about an hour.

'There was a lurking fear in me. Was I doing the right thing? What would be my mother's reaction? This agitated me all through my travel to Vellore. Mid-way I even thought of returning home. But then the other half of my mind compelled me to go on – and I told myself I was only going to my sister's place, after all.

'For a few days I was a welcome guest there in Vellore, at my sister's. But then their sympathies were more with our parents than with me, after I had explained why I had come to them. My sister wrote to my parents that I was with her. My father had been quietly looking for me, but he had been pretending not to be concerned about my disappearance.

'My brother-in-law tried to get me a job in Vellore. But Vellore is a predominantly Muslim town, and I was handicapped by my Hindu-brahmin appearance. Whenever I went with my brother-in-law to get a job, the first question would be: "Why don't you wear pants and become more modern, if you want a job?" But even though I'd left home, I wasn't courageous enough to remove the churki or put on trousers. I was in a dilemma. I had no job, and I couldn't go home. I spent some sleepless nights, even while putting a brave face on things.

'I must have stayed a month at my sister's. And then, reluctantly, I went back to Madras. I didn't go back to my own home. I went to the house of a friend of my mother's. This house was outside our brahmin colony.

'The son of this friend of my mother's also wore the churki and the caste-marks and was obedient to what his parents told him. He was an extraordinarily brilliant boy, in mathematics and statistics. He is today a professor in a big American university. And even then, when I went to his house – he was two years older than me – he was an admirer of the genius Ramanujan, whose mathematical work he and his equally brilliant colleagues would discuss and debate for hours together. They especially discussed the unsolved mathematical problems of Ramanujan's. These boys were college students. I couldn't follow the discussions, but I could admire the deep commitment to the studies they were pursuing – commitment which I didn't have.

'What impressed me most was the way in which the father of the boy took interest in these discussions, and encouraged them by supplying coffee. You must imagine these discussions going on in a house as poor as my father's in the agraharam, the colony. There was an irony. My mother's friend's husband was a Sanskrit teacher, and yet his son was a mathematical genius. My father was a mathematics teacher, and I was a mathematical zero.

'The mathematical debate went on past midnight. I felt sorry I couldn't participate, and I literally wept that night that I had had to disappoint my father.'

Tears came to Kakusthan's eyes. He tried to ignore the tears, to go on talking. But then he began to cry at those memories of 30 years before. He stood up and said, 'Let me take five minutes off.'

He walked to the rear of the hotel lobby and began to walk up and down, a small figure in his brahmin clothes, noticeable, five feet one or two, walking up and down, wrestling with his grief, looking down, in his abstraction like a monk or holy man in his cloister, indifferent to the hotel setting.

Were the tears for himself, for what he might have made of himself if he hadn't been pushed into rebellion? Or were the tears for the unhappiness he had caused his father 30 years before? The tears were for both things: he said when he came back and sat down and collected himself that it was the difference between the two families that had upset him all over again.

'I spent 10 to 15 days in that atmosphere, and was full of guilt that I had left home and studies. This boy I have mentioned would teach me mathematics, and console me that nothing was lost, that even now I could pick up the threads. That gave me encouragement to go back to being a student.

'I went home to the agraharam. I settled there. But I couldn't get back into college. It was the middle of the year. I took a job. I needed the money, to satisfy my social cravings – taking friends to hotels, going to movies, etc. None of these things would have been available to me, if I had to depend on my father. In fact, they were forbidden. At home we never even drank coffee – it was a foreign item, an item invented by the British. And even today in strict brahmin homes coffee is not drunk, because of its intoxicating effects – the caffeine.

'I went back to my job with the bulb-dealer. I got 26 rupees a month. I gave my family 20 rupees, and I kept six – to fulfil all my cravings, without the knowledge of my father. I stayed in that job for a year. And having tasted money power, I was reluctant again to take up studies. So I went back to my old ways again.

'The work was hard. I literally had to hawk the bulbs around the city, sometimes on a bicycle, sometimes walking, when the cycle was punctured. It used to be so hot that sometimes the tires used to burst. Even my father was moved by the arduous nature of my job, which was telling upon my health. I became very lean, with the irregular food. So he got me a job with an engineering consulting firm, making blueprint copies, at 65 rupees a month – a big jump.' Sixty-five rupees, £5 a month, in 1960.

'One day I burnt a blueprint. The engineer slapped me, and went away without saying a word. I was at fault. I didn't blame him. I told my father when I went home. He advised me to take it in my stride as part of life. I was surprised – I thought my father might also want to beat me for the mistake with the blueprint.

'I did the blueprints for the company for nine months. Then I was posted to one of the company's construction sites. Work was going on at that site on behalf of one of the big industrial concerns of the South. It was here again, for the second time in my life, my traditional brahmin appearance and approach came to my aid or advantage.

'The managing director of the company we were working for was very pleased with my strict adherence to the brahmin way of life. He was so pleased to see a brahmin boy in churki in charge of a building site, being a *maistry* – especially at this time, when anti-brahmin feeling was at its height. This was in 1961.

'I did not know how important this managing director was, how many businesses he controlled. He asked me about my father, and he sent a message through me asking my father to meet him. I was a little nervous. So also was my father. We didn't know what the managing director wanted or who he was. They met, and the managing director got on well with my father immediately. After hearing about my father's background, and especially his versatility in the 4000 hymns of the Tamil Vedas, he asked my father to be his teacher in the Tamil Vedas. Which my father did. This happy meeting with one of the very great industrialists of the South made my father so happy he wondered how I could have pleased an outsider, when I couldn't please people at home.

'On completion of the job which our construction firm was doing for him, the great man offered me a job in his own organization. He wanted me to begin as an "attender", on a salary of 97 rupees, 52 rupees basic and 45 rupees allowance. "Attender" is another word for office boy. But to get into that organization in any capacity would be today like getting into IBM. I did more typing than office-boy work. So at last I began to rise, and I never stopped – with God's grace. I was seventeen.

'The company opened a branch in Vellore. I got transferred there – to be with my married sister, and to be independent. When the Chinese war came in 1962, I became politically active – which I'd never been before. I gave my rings and ear-rings – things given me by my uncle on the occasion of my thread ceremony – to the war effort. This outraged my parents, and it also outraged my sister, because the things I had given had belonged for some generations to the family.

'A visitor came one day from Delhi. He was a first cousin. He worked in the Delhi office of an American concern. He was shocked to see me in my traditional appearance – and also shocked by the paltry salary I was getting. He asked me to leave the job I was doing and to come to Delhi. He said that, for the same effort I was putting into the firm in Vellore, he would get me twice the salary in Delhi. It was a fascinating offer for me. I immediately decided to accept his offer. But I wasn't sure how my father would react.

'As I expected, my father was reluctant to let me go to Delhi, lest I should deviate further. For four months there was a lot of debate, and many heated exchanges, between me and my father. But in the end it was my father who bought the ticket for me. It cost about 42 rupees, and he gave me some pocket money as well. For the journey itself my family gave me *idli* and *dosas* and fried eatables. They gave me too much. I had to throw away the surplus. Their thinking was that the train might get stranded, and they didn't want me to suffer if that happened. It is even today the normal South Indian family way with travellers.

'Finally, on the third of May, 1963, I charted an entirely new course in my life. I left by Grand Trunk Express from Madras Central railway station at 7.30 p.m. I arrived 40 hours later in Delhi, at 11.30 in the morning on the fifth of May – according to the Gregorian calendar, my birthday.

'The very first thing I did in Delhi – as instructed by my cousin – was to drive straight from the railway station to the barber saloon and remove the churki. That was a moment of great anguish and pain. For 18 full years both my mother and my sister used to rear it – as they would do their own child. They were proud of it. They were jealous of it. I had unusually long hair, longer than my sister's. It used to hit my calf when I undid it. They would wash it and oil it and comb it and knit it together.

'My agony was deeper as the barber, a young man, a real thin-looking man with a moustache, started making probing questions – whether I was sure I wanted what I said. He gave me three chances. He said in Hindi, "Are you sure? Are you sure? Are you sure?" I repeatedly said, "Yes," though in my heart of hearts I was trembling and worried about what my father would say. The barber was so kind and considerate he started cutting it slowly, from below, instead of killing it at one blow – to give me another chance to think again. That was the day I lost all my religious fervour – as Samson lost his physical power.'

That was where the story should have ended, with the flight to Delhi, the cutting off of the tresses at the back of the head, and the start of a new life. But Kakusthan had returned for good to the colony from which he had fled. His story was of a double transformation; and it was of the second transformation that he told me on another day.

Kakusthan said, 'In New Delhi I found myself, and for the next 16 years I lived there. I did a small job for the American firm for which my cousin worked. I also worked as a stenographer for a trade union journal.'

Stenography: the old South Indian brahmin vocation, the vocation that followed on from the doing of rituals, and was the other side of the talent for mathematics and physics.

'I got 50 rupees a month from my cousin's American firm. I got 200 rupees from the trade union paper. And it was during my time on the trade union paper that the second transformation began to take place.

'The trade union movement in India based itself on the principles of Gandhian philosophy: truth and non-violence, duty before right: you produce before you make demands. That is precisely what the Gita tells us, and those were the principles of the Indian National Trade Union Congress. Our day's work at the paper was started with a prayer meeting. That had an effect on me. So did the daily religious column on the back page of the *Hindu* newspaper of Madras. And I also read the writings of Mahatma Gandhi, especially his autobiography.

'In the office there was this religious and spiritual atmosphere. Outside, there was the allurement of Delhi life, the life of money, beauty, everything. For some time it attracted me, that Delhi life. And it worried me – because I didn't have the money. But then the religious books I was reading began to have more pull. So over a period of time I changed again, and I embraced the religious life.

'In this period I took a degree from Delhi University; and I married. I had been attracted by my sister's daughter in Vellore, and I had determined to marry her as soon as I could. The family agreed, but I told them that she should graduate first. I met her educational expenses, and on the last day of her final examination the marriage process started.

'Other editorial jobs with papers and magazines followed after I left the union paper. One such job took me to the town of Ahmedabad in 1980. I was thirty-seven. My father came to see me there, for the birthday of my second son. He was extremely pleased that I was in a good position at last – even though I was minus my churki. He would have been doubly delighted if I had still had the churki.

'The first morning he was there he saw me doing the morning puja. It was something I routinely did, but he was taken aback. We talked for a while about the puja I had done that morning, and the texts connected with the puja. He mentioned some error I had committed in doing the puja, and he hinted that if I had studied better when I was young, the mistake would not have happened.

'I apologized for that mistake. And I apologized for everything that had happened earlier.

'I asked him to induct me into our traditional rituals. I asked him also to teach me the 4000 verses of the Tamil Vedas, and all the other mantras that I would need to know for the rituals in the temple in our ancestral village.

'He said he would teach me. He started that day itself, since it was a Friday and an auspicious day. After 15 days he left Ahmedabad for Madras. Before he left, he promised he would teach me every day for two or three years. But he never came back. He died six months after he left Ahmedabad.

'For 11 days after his death there were elaborate rituals. All those who came, relatives, Vedic pundits, recalled the greatness of my father, my grandfather, my uncle, and the religious way of life of our family, especially in the service of the village deity. I heard that my grandfather had died after a religious argument with the temple pujari about a particular ritual that had not been carried out properly. My cousin had also died in similar circumstances. He had objected to certain rituals that had been introduced at the temple, and then he had lain down in the temple doorway; and people had walked over him. He died a few days afterwards of grief and shock.

'I thought, when I heard these stories, that if my grandfather and other relatives could lay down their lives for the sake of the family deity, shouldn't I at least follow their example? 'I decided to move back to Madras.

'I got a job here. It was easy now, with my experience. And my condition with the firm I approached was that they should have no objection to my external form – no objection to my wearing religious marks on the forehead, having the churki, and wearing the traditional brahmin attire: all the things I hadn't understood when I was younger. It was important for me to get this condition agreed to, since I was coming back to Madras primarily to continue my family's temple obligations.'

I asked him, 'Why this stress on external form? Isn't devotion something you carry in your heart?'

Kakusthan said, 'Perhaps if there had been no temple obligation and honour in our family life and tradition, our life would have been a little more flexible, as in many other normal brahmin families. In all the temple rituals external forms come first, because without the external form I will not be entitled to serve the deity. The external form is as important as the internal. The purer the external form, the purer the internal.'

He had suffered because of the external form. He was entitled to speak as he did.

'I had left the agraharam in 1963. I returned in 1981. I returned to my family house in the colony, and I returned a quite different man, a brahmin fully committed, fully realized. On the first anniversary of my father's death, at the end of the rituals conducted at that time, there was a total break from the past for me: from *loukika* to *vaidhika,* from being in the world to being of the spirit.' They were words I had heard for the first time in Mysore City, from the brahmin who had been master of religious ceremonies for the last maharaja of Mysore. In the palace where the brahmin had served there had been splendour and extravagance beyond human need, almost as though in the Hindu scheme one of the functions of great wealth was to remind men of the vanity of the senses. But the ruler's great wealth had formed no part of the brahmin's story. The physical needs of men were limited: that was the message of the small plain room where the brahmin told his story.

That was the message, too, of the agraharam or colony where Kakusthan lived, in the set of small rooms he had known as a child. In Christian thinking the eternal opposites are the forces of good and evil. In Hindu or brahmin thought the opposites are worldliness and the life of the spirit. One can retreat from one to the other. When the world fails one, one can sink into the spirit, the idea of the world as the play of illusion.

Kakusthan said, 'I became then, one year after my father's death, what I now am, the man you see. I decided then to live the vaidhika life as far as is possible, to live with all the rigours and discipline that go with it.'

'What are the rigours?'

'I shall not eat outside. I shall eat only what I offer the god at home.' So the oil lamp burned always in front of the image of the god, just next to the kitchen area. 'I shall not even drink water outside. Nor mix with people unchaste. Because, if I don't observe these things, I will be polluting the god of our temple.

'I now live in the colony as a full brahmin. People respect me for the sudden change in my life, and the strict observances now. My family was poor, and this colony is also poor – lower-middle-class people with limited income. Though I am well off, due to the grace of God and the blessings of my forefathers, I want to live nowhere else. Living among these people I know gives me a tremendous happiness and peace.'

We had met over many days, in my hotel and in the colony. Sometimes Kakusthan had met me at the hotel and taken me back to the colony; sometimes he had sent his teenaged son to fetch me. The son was many inches taller than his father, but he was without his father's sturdiness; his eyes were softer.

Kakusthan, whatever he had chosen for himself, was ambitious for his son and wanted the boy to do well at school. And just as, many years before, Kakusthan's father might have asked someone to talk to Kakusthan, so now Kakusthan asked me, the last time we met, to talk to his son and to put to the boy the need for doing well, for getting on with the school books.

The boy, Kakusthan said, was too fond of play. He had gone out that morning, for instance, to play cricket. But that was good,

I said. All right, Kakusthan said. But then the boy had gone out again in the afternoon to play cricket.

We were going back to the colony, and Kakusthan had a simple plan for getting me to have a private talk with his son. We – Kakusthan and I – would go up to the terrace overlooking the colony yard directly in front and the walled temple garden to one side. The boy would bring up tea for me, and then Kakusthan would excuse himself and go down to the bathroom.

So, in the colony, the boy brought up a tumbler of tea to me on the terrace; and we began to talk, while down below – in this area where he was king – Kakusthan in his brahmin clothes walked confidently, without hurrying, across the crowded afternoon yard, past the well, to the bathroom in the corner.

The boy loved cricket. He said he loved both batting and bowling. I liked his seriousness about the game. And I couldn't find it in my heart to give him the lecture Kakusthan wanted me to give, about sticking to the books: I couldn't see how, in the conditions of the colony, anyone could do any serious reading or study there. One evening, on the dimly lit paved path leading in from the gateway, I had seen a young boy sitting cross-legged outside his little house, in the dark, before an open book: acting out virtue for his parents' sake, the brahminical love of learning reduced to this ritual form.

I asked the boy, Kakusthan's son, what sort of job he hoped to do. His soft eyes became startled. He knew the question; he was dismayed to hear it from me. He might become a stenographer, he said; he might get a job in an office; it depended on 'fate'.

I was surprised by his talk of fate. Kakusthan had never done so. But Kakusthan had been a rebel all his youth. His son was now very much a young man of the colony, with ideas and ambitions not above those of other young men there. Kakusthan, I believe, would have liked his son to be more forceful. But I didn't want to press the boy. He was years away from getting his degree and taking a job; his world, his way of looking, was going to change before then.

And I told Kakusthan, when he came back up to the terrace, that the boy was going to be all right; that his seriousness about cricket spoke of something spirited and reassuring in him; and the books side and the career side would fall into place when the time came. It was half what Kakusthan wanted to hear; he looked pleased. We began to talk of other things.

It was a late Sunday afternoon, still the Madras winter. The sun was mild; the atmosphere in the agraharam without tension; everyone in the yard seemed to be at play.

The terrace was shaded by an old tree, and Kakusthan and I were sitting in this shade, on the concrete half-wall in front of his sleeping room. I asked him to talk to me about what we were seeing in the yard.

Had I noticed the TV aerials? There were 20 of them, he said. In the colony there were even some colour television sets. People were not as cut off from the rest of the world as they had once been.

'And look at those girls over there,' he said. 'Skipping.'

It would have been easy to miss the significance of that. But 20 years or so ago, he said, those girls wouldn't have been allowed to play like that, in an open yard. Those girls were close to puberty, and 20 years ago the shades of the prison house would have already begun to fall on them.

And, Kakusthan said, I had spoken of the pallor and debility of some of the people in the colony. But some of the brahmin boys now did exercises. That boy, for instance, across, the yard, two houses or so away from where the long-skirted girls were skipping – that boy did exercises. The boy was a young man, bare-backed, elegant of posture, not tall. He had the physique found in many kinds of Indian sculpture: broad-shouldered, slender-waisted, smooth-bodied, strength and tension lying within, not expressed in the ripple or indentation of muscle.

Kakusthan approved; he was concerned with physical fitness. He was a small man; his father had been a small man; they had both been subjected to ridicule and physical torment in the town.

From our perch on the terrace we considered both the young man who did exercises, and his father. Where did the young man do his exercises? Right there, in the busy yard; no one minded. He came from a family of 10. Those 10 people lived in that one room whose door we could see. The father was a peon or office-attender. The son who spent so much time perfecting his body was only a clerk.

I said to Kakusthan, 'He's got a good brahmin face.'

'And the colour,' Kakusthan said, with a nod.

He looked abashed then, and lowered his voice: a woman had come up to the terrace, he said, and I was in her way. I was sitting on the half-wall in front of Kakusthan's upper room, and my legs were sticking out into the passage that ran along the edge of the terrace. If the woman had tried to pass she might have touched me, and that would have been wrong; it would also have been wrong for her to talk to me directly. I stood up. Without a word, the woman passed; three or four paces down she turned off into her own little space.

The evening light became softer and yellower. Women and girls went to the well to fill their pots.

When I had first gone to the colony, I had thought, from the way Kakusthan spoke, that the community was fading away, making too many accommodations with the world outside. I realized now that he meant the opposite. The community was learning to adapt: that was its strength.

He said, 'As long as the world exists, brahmins will always survive. Brahmins are indispensable to the society.'

Mr K. Veeramani, a short, brisk man in a long-tailed black shirt, worn in the Indian way, hanging out, not tucked in, looked after the Periyar Thidal and kept the Periyar flame alive in Tamil Nadu.

Periyar had died in the last week of 1973, at the age of ninety-four; and Periyar's second wife had suceeded to the leadership of the movement. She had died five years later; and then Mr

Veeramani had become the leader. The movement at that time appeared to have lost its way, to have ceased to matter politically or socially. But now, with the election victory of the original Dravidian political party, the movement appeared once again to be at the heart of things.

Mr Veeramani, as Periyar's philosophical heir, travelled about the state, making speeches, and conducting Periyar-style Self-Respect marriages. In Tamil Nadu, where many people couldn't read and write, speeches were important. People enjoyed speeches, the sound of words; and Mr Veeramani said he could speak for up to two hours at a time, if there was the need. As for the Self-Respect marriages, he did only about eight or 10 a month, about 120 to 150 a year. Not many; but the rationalists, Mr Veeramani said, were only a 'microscopic' element in the state. He didn't think it lessened the importance of his work. This was to preserve as much of Periyar's message as possible. So he looked after the relics – the bed, all the various gifts to Periyar; he explained the iconography of the 33 paintings in the room, showing the stations of Periyar's long life; he published pamphlets; and he led visitors round the grave, reading out the more famous sayings of Periyar's that were carved in grey granite around the grave. Without this work of his over the years, Mr Veeramani said, Periyar's message would have been distorted.

Mr Veeramani was born in 1933, in the town of Cuddalore. His father was a tailor. Tailoring was an 'imported' profession (the way coffee was 'an imported item'), and so it wasn't associated with a particular caste, like weaving. Cuddalore was a port, and Mr Veeramani's father, in addition to his local trade, did a certain amount of tailoring for foreign sailors. Mr Veeramani's father was as a result quite well off; but much of his money went first on a court case (he was an expert in stick-fighting and wrestling, trained people in these arts, and in a roundabout way he found himself dragged into a serious local feud); and then the rest of his money went on medical expenses when he fell ill with filarial fever, caused by infected water.

One of Mr Veeramani's school-teachers was an admirer of Periyar, and important in the Self-Respect movement. This teacher, a man of about twenty-eight or thirty when Mr Veeramani got to know him, had changed his name from Subramaniam (the name of a Hindu deity) to Dravidarmani, which meant 'an important Dravidian person'. He got Mr Veeramani to change his name as well: from Sarangapani, the name of a god, to Veeramani, 'brave man', 'hero'.

When he was about ten or so, Mr Veeramani acted in a school play, and Mr Dravidarmani was so impressed by the boy's talents that he began writing speeches on the Self-Respect theme for the boy to deliver at public meetings. In 1944 in Cuddalore there was a Dravidian Conference. Periyar came to that. There also came a famous atheist Tamil poet who was a disciple of Periyar's. The poet's name was Bharathidasam. He was forty-seven, originally of the weaver caste, and he lived in great poverty in the town of Pondicherry (then a French colonial enclave in British India). He was thought of as the Shelley and the Whitman of the movement. There was a poem of Bharathidasam's that was regularly quoted in Self-Respect speeches. Mr Veeramani gave me this translation of the poem:

*The world is still in darkness.*
*Even people who believe in caste are allowed to live.*
*The persons who frighten people by religion are still thriving.*
*When will all this trickery come to an end?*
*Unless and until this kind of trickery comes to an end,*
*Freedom and liberty are to be equated with evil only.*

Unlike Periyar, who was short and very fat, an avuncular-looking old man, Bharathidasam was forbidding. He was tall and very big. He wore a dhoti, a shirt, and a red shawl – red for the revolution. He lost his temper easily and had the reputation of always speaking his mind.

It was in the presence of this man, and Periyar, that the ten-year old Mr Veeramani acted out the speech his teacher had written for him to deliver at the Dravidian Conference. The speech was in Periyar's broadest anti-brahmin, anti-Hindu style. It was about the absurdity of the Hindu myth that brahmins had sprung from the head of Brahma, kshatriyas or warriors from his arms, banias or merchants from his thighs, and shudras from his feet. How – the ten-year-old asked the conference – could someone not a woman give birth to people from so many parts of the body from which birth couldn't take place?

Periyar was impressed by the speech, and after that Mr Veeramani became one of the recognized speakers for the Self-Respect movement. He used to be billed as the ten-year-old rationalist, and soon he began to write (or at any rate to make up) his own speeches.

In 1949, five years after the Cuddalore conference, there was a split in the movement. It was caused by Periyar's decision, at the age of seventy, to marry for the second time.

The woman he wanted to marry was the daughter of a timber merchant in Vellore. The family were supporters of the movement, and Periyar used to stay in their house when he went to Vellore. The daughter was training to be a teacher; but her mother, though she was a follower of Periyar, was yet sufficiently influenced by traditional ways to want her daughter to give up the idea of teaching and to get married. The daughter was twenty-five; that was thought to be very old. When the daughter got to know what her mother's plans for her were, she left the family house in Vellore and went to stay in a far-off place in a school-teacher's house.

Periyar knew the daughter. When he heard what had happened, he called the daughter away from the school-teacher's house and he put her up in his own house in the town of Erode. He refused to let her go back to her mother's house. He made the young woman his secretary; she also became his nurse; and six years later they were married. She was thirty-one then; Periyar was seventy.

This was the story Mr Veeramani told me, and he was anxious for me to understand why Periyar had married at this late age. Periyar had accumulated a lot of property. He didn't want this property to pass to his relatives. He wanted it to be used for the movement, and he thought that this could be best done by leaving it to his secretary-nurse. Under Hindu law, however, he could make her his legal heir only by marrying her.

Not everyone understood the motives, and an important section of the movement broke away to form their own group. Mr Veeramani, however, at this stage a fifteen-year-old rationalist, remained loyal to Periyar. He remained loyal when he went to the university; he remained loyal when he began to study law. And then, while he was still doing his law studies, something important happened.

In 1957 Periyar was sentenced to six months' imprisonment for burning the Indian Constitution. (There was an illustration of this episode, literal, clear, and cool, in the relic-room of the Periyar Thidal.) Up to this time Mr Veeramani had just been a propagandist for the movement, energetic and with a reputation, but still at a distance from Periyar. Now, with the great man in jail, Mr Veeramani found himself touring the state with Periyar's wife, Mrs Manyammai – as Mr Veeramani called her.

When Periyar came out of jail, he sent for Mr Veeramani. Periyar was in the town of Tiruchy. Mr Veeramani went there immediately.

Periyar said to him, 'What about your future? Are you going to get married?'

It was a surprising question, because Periyar was against early marriages; he thought they worked against the uplift of non-brahmins. Mr Veeramani at this time was twenty-five, and he still had more than a year to do at Madras Law College.

Mr Veeramani said, 'Sir, I don't think marriage is a necessity at this stage. I don't have my own economic independence, and I would like to give my most to the party.'

Periyar said, 'But it's only in the interests of the party that I'm suggesting marriage to you.'

The girl or young woman whom Periyar wanted Mr Veeramani to marry was the eldest daughter of a couple for whom, in 1933, Periyar had performed a Self-Respect marriage. That Self-Respect marriage had become politically famous, because in 1952 its validity had been challenged in the courts. But – sentiment apart – Periyar's real reason for wanting Mr Veeramani to marry the daughter of that couple was that the family was well-to-do, the father belonging to a merchant community, the mother coming from a landowning family; and marriage to the daughter would enable Mr Veeramani to work full time for the movement.

When Mr Veeramani understood this, he said to Periyar, 'If it is in the largest interests of the party, I will obey your command.'

Mrs Manyammai then went to Mr Veeramani's parents to give them the news that their son was going to get married, and after this she took Mr Veeramani to the girl's house in Tiruannamalai. They went by train and bus and finally arrived at the farm-house where the girl and her mother were staying. There was a lot of fertile land attached to the farm-house – rice fields and groundnut fields. After the usual preliminaries the girl came out and served some food (a curious remnant of old ritual), and then went back inside. But, in fact, she knew Mr Veeramani well, from his appearances in public meetings.

Six months later the marriage took place. Periyar and Mrs Manyammai sent out the invitations in their own names, so the wedding gathering was like another Dravidian conference. The wedding itself took place on a Sunday afternoon at five. The time was chosen quite deliberately, because orthodox Hindus considered it an especially inauspicious time. The atheist poet Bharathidasam, the Whitman-like figure of the movement, read out a poem he had composed for the occasion.

There was a curious sequel: in his final law examination, Mr Veeramani found himself having to answer a question about the 1933 Self-Respect marriage of his in-laws.

The marriage had worked out as Periyar had hoped. Mr Veeramani had been free to do his work for the Dravidar Kazagham, the Dravidian Movement, and had kept Periyar's name and message alive. And now, after all the ups and downs of the last 30 years, Periyar's more-than-life-size portrait was to be seen in many places in Madras, and Mr Veeramani, keeper of the flame, moved through Madras like a hero.

The house in which Mr Veeramani lived belonged to his wife. It was in the Adiyar area of Madras, near the Theosophical Society. It was a big concrete house, fifteen years old. It was on three floors, and the Veeramanis occupied one floor.

High up on a wall in the drawing-room was a big black-and-white photograph of Periyar and Mrs Manyammai. Periyar was seated, holding his stout stick with the curved handle. The other components of his appearance were now well known to me: the big, wavy beard, the dhoti, the shawl, the black shirt. Mrs Manyammai, steady-eyed, stood plump and firm in a black sari at the side of his chair, and her right hand rested on the back of the chair.

It seemed fitting for that photograph to have a place of honour in Mr Veeramani's drawing-room: that marriage of Periyar's was like a forerunner of Mr Veeramani's.

Mrs Veeramani served tea and withdrew: dutiful and correct, saying little, and still like someone serving a cause. Though, if one didn't know what that cause was, one might never have guessed, so traditional and demure and self-effacing was her manner.

In that family atmosphere, below Periyar's photograph, Mr Veeramani told me about the practical side of Periyar. He had come from a rich merchant family, and he had made himself richer.

'He was very careful. He was a custodian not only of human rights, but of the party property rights. He multiplied those rights by investing in mills and banks. In 1973 his worth, or his party's worth, was more than two crores.' Twenty million rupees, a million pounds. 'Now the property is worth about 10 crores.' Four million pounds.

'People would give him money. And when, say, he had got 99 rupees, he would take a rupee from Mrs Manyammai, and he would convert those 100 rupees into a 100-rupee note, so that he wouldn't easily spend it. Mrs Manyammai would laugh.' Mr Veeramani laughed too. '"Frugality, thy name is Periyar!" The whole of Tamil Nadu knows it. Even for his signature he used to charge. Instead of garlands, he asked people to give him two rupees.'

He charged for his speeches, and he made two or three a day, travelling an average of 200 miles a day in the van his supporters had given him. His last speech was made five days before he died, at the age of ninety-four. He had married Mrs Manyammai when he was seventy, so that she would inherit his property; but their marriage lasted 24 years, and she outlived him by only five years. Then the mantle had passed to Mr Veeramani.

Mr Veeramani's eldest son was an engineer, studying in Boston. His second son had a degree in commerce, and was now in plastics. And the first daughter was also in the United States, doing a master's degree in information systems. Mr Veeramani's father had been a tailor in the town of Cuddalore. The world had opened out for his grandchildren in a way he could not have imagined.

On the wall opposite the one with the photograph of Periyar and his wife there was a 1989 Tamil Tigers calendar, hanging above a bookcase. The calendar had a big colour photograph of the two Tamil Tiger leaders, Pirabhakaran and Mathaiya. They were shown in sun-struck, hot-looking woodland, and they were in camouflage guerrilla garb. They were both fat and big-bellied, and smiling, as though at the absurdity of the uniform they had put on for the calendar photograph. But they were not clownish at all. They had brought chaos to Sri Lanka. And their calendar for 1989 was here, in Mr Veeramani's drawing-room. The rationalist movement of Tamil Nadu, the anti-brahmin movement, also contained this idea of Tamil glory, past and present.

Until this trip to Madras, Periyar had been barely a name to me; and I had never heard of Mr Veeramani. But for 40 years

Mr Veeramani had been at the centre of an immense local revolution, which, with all the economic and intellectual growth that had come to independent India, had taken on the characteristics of a little war; and so far Mr Veeramani had been on the winning side.

The same could not be said of Kakusthan. A good half of his story had been of retreat and flight – until family feeling and filial piety had made him turn back and consciously embrace an archaic way. But perhaps the comparison of Mr Veeramani with Kakusthan wasn't just. Perhaps a better comparison would have been with those brahmins who had moved from old learning to new, from temple rituals to science, the brahmins who (almost in the manner of Mr Veeramani) had broken out of old ways more radically.

Madras, with the sculptured towers of its temples, its special foods, the idlis and dosas, its music and its dance, the museum with the great bronzes, could appear to the visitor to be still a whole culture. It took time to understand that a usurpation had taken place, that brahmins were on the defensive, though they were still the musicians and dancers, still the cooks, still the priests in the temples.

It was hard not to feel sad at the undoing of a culture. But the brahmin cause – if such a cause existed – could not be isolated from all the other Indian causes. It was better to see the undoing of a culture – the rise of Mr Veeramani, the flight and transformation of the brahmins – as part of a more general movement forward.

Bharathidasam, the atheist poet of the Dravidian Movement, wore a red shawl – red for the revolution. The flag of the DMK, the political party that had grown out of the Dravidian Movement, was red and black – red for the revolution, black for the Dravidian cause. The two colours, taken together, might have been thought to stand for all the insulted and injured of Tamil Nadu, all the people whom the especial brahmin rigidity of the South had put outside the pale. But the Dravidian Movement represented only the middle castes – Periyar himself was a man of a merchant caste – who, in other parts of India, had a fairly honourable place in the caste system. Below those middle castes, now triumphant, there were, as always in India, others. They, too, had been shaken up; they too had begun to stake their claim.

Seven or eight years before, in the north of Tamil Nadu, there had been a peasant rebellion – or a Maoist rebellion. It had been destroyed. In the 40 years or so since Independence the Indian state had had to deal with many kinds of insurgency, in many parts of the country. The state had learned how to manage, when to stamp hard, when to lay off.

There were survivors of that peasant rebellion. They had been restored to civilian life, and were probably doing better now than they had ever done. The police were still in touch with these men; and it was through the police that a meeting was arranged for me with two of them.

They had been summoned from a district far away, and the meeting took place in my hotel room. A plain-clothes police officer came with them. On my side were two newspapermen, one a crime reporter, to interpret, the other a sports writer, to observe. So there were six of us in the hotel room. The number made for formality. The hotel's tea and biscuits, and the solicitous room-service waiter, made everyone a little stiffer.

I didn't know what to make of the former rebels. They were very dark, solidly built, and in something like a uniform: long dhotis and loose-hanging cream-coloured shirts. Their hair was thick and long and well oiled, combed back from the forehead and from the sides, and cut at the back in a straight line just above the shirt collar.

The older of the two was the spokesman. He had a heavier build, a chunkier nose, and a shinier skin. He said his brother had been a communist, and it was this brother – later killed by a landlord – who had indoctrinated him. He, the speaker, had indoctrinated the second man, who was younger, and was his brother-in-law. It had been easy to indoctrinate the brother-in-law. His father worked in the Railways, in the canteen. One day the father's toes were cut off in an accident in the railway yard. The son then applied for a job in the Railways. He should have got a job: there was a tradition in the Railways that when a man was injured and had to retire, a member of his family was given a job, for compassionate reasons. But the son didn't get a job, because other people had bribed the assistant station-master or some official of that standing.

The police officer nodded: that was the way it was, at that level – and the officer's compassion was interesting. The newspapermen agreed. It was like that with those jobs.

There were very few brahmins in their village. It was an area of backward castes and *Adi-dravids,* the first Dravidians, aborigines, tribal people. These people were exploited by the big landlords or zamindars. A big landlord here was anyone who owned more than 50 acres. Many of the zamindars were people of the Reddiar community who had come from the neighbouring state of Andhra Pradesh. But there were also Adi-dravid zamindars.

The zamindars employed women for three rupees a day and men for five rupees a day. The minimum wage at that time was five rupees for women and nine for men. The aim of the Maoists was to create enmity between the workers and the landlords. They did this by telling the workers about the minimum wage, and encouraging them to ask for it. The landlords often refused, and brought in workers from other villages. Sometimes the landlords became rougher. The older man's brother had been killed by a zamindar. After that, it was war: that zamindar had to be killed.

Three attempts were made to kill the zamindar. He was shadowed, and one day, when he was on a bus, six of the Maoists got on the bus. But nothing happened. The rebels became indecisive, thinking of the other passengers; and in the confusion the zamindar got away. The second time they waited for the zamindar early one morning in a field. He came; they shot at him; they missed. The third time they got their man. A party of eight assaulted the zamindar's house and threw pin-grenades. They killed three people: the zamindar, his mistress, and a baby. They didn't know about the baby; the death of the baby upset them.

After that they did only two more killings. They were just following orders at this stage. The orders were more like decisions: these decisions were made at group meetings. Their wish was to overthrow the government, and their aim, when they were dealing with people whom they had decided were 'enemies', was simply to kill them.

Then the police began to move in. They threw a vice, a 'wrench', around the area where the Maoists were operating, and the wrench was gradually closed. Thirty Maoists were killed. The two men in the hotel room were lucky. They had surrendered to the police some time before, and were in prison, charged with the murder of the zamindar and his mistress and the baby. (This was how the story was told: it was blurred and unsatisfactory at this point. But because of the formality of the occasion, because of the time gap between what the speaker said and what came out in translation, because of the compression of the translation, it didn't occur to me to ask further questions at the time. It was only later that the blurring became apparent.)

The police could make no case against the two men. They couldn't find witnesses, and the reason was that a warning had been sent out by the two men, 10 days before the hearing, that if anyone came forward to give evidence, he wouldn't be alive the next day. This was said quite coolly in the hotel room; and the plain-clothes police officer, nodding, sucking in his breath, took it coolly too, as though it was all part of the game.

Eventually the two men were released. Since their group had been wiped out, they had nothing to go back to – and here, though the question hadn't been asked, they both said they had betrayed no one in their group. The younger man, the brother-in-law, said that the police had cut the 'nerves' on one of his feet. He showed a dark scar, like a burn mark, on the top of his sandalled foot. But even after that, the younger man said, he hadn't given anyone away. The police officer didn't look put out and didn't try to interfere in what was being said; it was as though that, too, that wretchedness about the nerves and the foot, was part of the game, and everyone knew it.

With the help of the police – and no doubt as part of the state policy of rehabilitation – the two men went into business. Neither did well. The older man went into the tomato business, deciding for some reason to ship his tomatoes all the way to Calcutta. He lost 25,600 rupees, about £1000. The brother-in-law started making *beedis,* cheap leaf cigarettes; he said his employees ran away with the money. Neither man looked cast down by his business failure; they both seemed quite content.

I didn't know what to make of what I had heard. There were so few word-pictures in what they had said, so few details. That might have been because of the translation, or because of the formality of our meeting, or because they had spoken their stories too often. There was an obviousness about them. I was reminded of the obviousness of the gangsters I had met in Bombay; they, the gangsters, were obvious because their lives were, after all, very simple. And perhaps the foot soldiers of a revolution, such as these men might have been, had to be simple people too, receiving messages simple enough for their capacities and needs.

I asked them what they knew about Periyar. And at once, even in the crime reporter's translation, they seemed to say more than they had done up till then – and it might have been because it wasn't a question they were expecting.

They honoured Periyar, the older man said. His father had been a follower of Periyar. But Periyar had struggled against caste alone; he hadn't thought of class. 'He shook us up, but he wasn't relevant to our kind of struggle.' That was the crime reporter's first translation. Later he amended it. What had been said was, in a more literal translation, 'We had no connection.' And that hinted better at the caste gap between the Dravidian Movement and the Maoists.

I asked them about the anti-religious side of Periyar's message. The older man said they weren't religious, but their women were. Though even the women had begun to do without brahmins in their ceremonies.

This sounded genuine. So, right at the end, I began to feel that the two men, whatever their relationship with the police, might have been what they said they had been.

Before they left, the brother-in-law asked to use the bathroom. I had my misgivings, but the police officer waved the man into the bathroom. We waited. There was no sound of a flush. Then the man came out; and carefully closed the door behind him.

Later, opening that carefully closed bathroom door, I found the toilet bowl unflushed, and the seat and floor pissed over. Was it social inexperience alone? Or was there also – in this man who had fought the class war – some very deep caste feeling about the uncleanliness of latrines: places so unclean they were beneath one's notice, places for other people to notice, other people to clean?

I talked this over with Suresh, the sports writer, a day or so later. He said the two men were among the lowest of the low. However little I might have been aware of it, they would have stood out in the hotel lobby. They were far below the shudras, and quite outside the reach of the Dravidian Movement. Would they have had any idea of what was religiously clean and unclean? At that level, Suresh said, though caste and community distinctions might not be easily visible to people above, they were nevertheless rigidly followed.

The shirt and long dhoti and oily long hair of both men had probably been modelled on some star of the popular Tamil cinema. This care with their appearance was a sign that they had moved forward, had been shaken out of their village ways. The little paunches were also an aspect of the self-respect that had come to them with their rehabilitation. They had said that they had given up the revolution, and wanted now only to look after their families. And that, Suresh said – whatever other ambiguities there might have been in their stories – felt true.

I went to say goodbye to Sugar. He was always there in his little ground-floor apartment, a prisoner of his reputation.

I found him giving advice to a man who had brought a computer print-out of two horoscopes. A marriage was being considered, and Sugar was giving an opinion about the horoscopes. He was being firm. The girl's horoscope was not suitable; in six months or so the boy would find someone more suitable. The inquirer, a high-up civil servant, didn't seem to mind. He was from the boy's side. In this business of match-making boys had the whip hand; girls and their families were the suppliants.

I said, 'Does the girl have a bad horoscope?'

'Not bad,' Sugar said. 'Not suitable.'

It was strange, finding him, with his own melancholy, so ready to play the tyrant as a seer. I felt that, in spite of what he had said about the selfishness and falsity of the people who came to see him, and what he had said about giving it all up, he took pleasure in his holy man's work and reputation.

Then he must have felt he had to make me some offering. He made it in the way that was now natural to him.

He looked at me across the little room and said, 'When I saw you in the Himalayas in 1962, your face was *bright*. It was one of the things that attracted me to you. Now you look troubled. Has it to do with your life? Your work?'

I said, 'I was more troubled in 1962. But I was younger. Like you.'

'Will you be coming back to Madras again? Come and see me. Come and see me before two years.' He was exercising his gifts of prophecy on himself. 'After two years –'

He shook his head and, slumped in his chair, his illness and solitude now like pure burdens, he let his glance take in the little space that he had made his own – the drawing-sleeping, without the furniture jumble I had first seen there, with the holy pictures on the wall and the hanging shelves with his headache tablets, the adjoining hall between the kitchen, which he couldn't clean himself and which he could allow no one else to clean, and the temple room with its forbidding images – the little space he was soon to vacate.

# 5

# AFTER THE BATTLE

IN INDIA IN 1962 I took much of the British architecture for granted. After what I had known in Trinidad and England, British building in India seemed familiar, not a cause for wonder. Perhaps, too, in 1962, just 15 years after Independence, I didn't allow myself to see British Indian architecture except as background. I was saving my wonder for the creations of the Indian past. Even Lutyens's great achievement in New Delhi I saw in a grudging way, finding the scale too grand, looking in his ceremonial buildings for the motifs he had got from the Mogul builders, and finding in his adaptations further evidence of vainglory.

I looked in this partial way even at the lesser architecture of the British, the bungalows and houses built for officials in the country districts. They were pleasant to stay in; with their porticoes and verandahs, thick walls, high ceilings, and sometimes additional upper windows or wall-openings, they were well suited to the climate. But they seemed too grand for the poverty of the Indian countryside. They seemed also to exaggerate the hardships of the Indian climate. So that, though absolutely of India, these British buildings, by their exaggeration, seemed to keep India at a distance.

But the years race on; new ways of feeling and looking can come to one. Indians have been building in free India for 40 years, and what has been put up in that time makes it easier to look at what went before. In free India Indians have built like people without a tradition; they have for the most part done mechanical, surface imitations of the international style. What is not easy to understand is that, unlike the British, Indians have not really built for the Indian climate. They have been too obsessed with imitating the modern; and much of what has been done in this way – the dull, four-square towers of Bombay, packed far too close together; the concrete nonentity of Lucknow and Madras and the residential colonies of New Delhi – can only make hard tropical lives harder and hotter.

Far from extending people's ideas of beauty and grandeur and human possibility – uplifting ideas which very poor people may need more than rich people – much of the architecture of free India has become part of the ugliness and crowd and increasing physical oppression of India. Bad architecture in a poor tropical city is more than an aesthetic matter. It spoils people's day-to-day lives; it wears down their nerves; it generates rages that can flow into many different channels.

This Indian architecture, more disdainful of the people it serves than British Indian architecture ever was, now makes the most matter-of-fact Public Works Department bungalow of the British time seem like a complete architectural thought. And if one goes on from there, and considers the range of British building in India, the time span, the varied styles of those two centuries, the developing functions (railway stations, the Victoria Memorial in Calcutta, the Gateway of India in Bombay, the legislative buildings of Lucknow and New Delhi), it becomes obvious that British Indian architecture – which can so easily be taken for granted – is the finest secular architecture in the sub-continent.

Calcutta, more than New Delhi, is the British-built city of India. It was one of the early centres of British India; it grew with British power, and was steadily embellished; it was the capital of British India until 1930. In the building of Calcutta, known first as the city of palaces, and later as the second city of the British Empire, the British worked with immense confidence, not adapting the styles of Indian rulers, but setting down in India adaptations of the European classical style as emblems of the conquering civilization.

But the imperial city, over the 200 years of its development, also became an Indian city; and – being at once a port, a centre of administration and business, education and culture, British and Indian style – it became a city like no other in India. To me at the end of 1962, after some months of Indian small-town and district life, Calcutta gave an immediate feel of the metropolis, with all the visual excitement of a metropolis, and all its suggestions of adventure and profit and heightened human experience.

Twenty-six years later, the grandeur of the British-built city – the wide avenues, the squares, the attractive use of the river and open spaces, the disposition of the palaces and the public buildings – could still be seen in a ghostly way at night, when the crowds of the day had retreated to their nooks and crannies, to rest from the restless vacuity and torment of the new Calcutta day: the broken roads and footpaths; the brown gasoline-and-kerosene haze adding an extra sting to the fierce sunlight, mixing with the street dust, and coating the skin with grit and grime; the day-long cicada-like screech, rising and falling, of the horns of the world's shabbiest buses and motor-cars. The British-built city could still be seen, even in this ghostly way, because so little had been added since Independence; so little had been added since 1962.

Energy and investment had gone to other parts of India. Calcutta had been bypassed, living off its entrails, and giving an illusion of life. Certain buildings in central Calcutta seemed to have received no touch of paint since 1962. On some walls and pillars – as on the walls and pillars of buildings awaiting demolition – old posters and glue had formed a tattered kind of papier-mâché crust; you felt that if you tried to scrape off that crust, you might pull away plaster or stucco. The famous colonial clubs – the Bengal Club, the Calcutta Club – were in decay, and Indians now moved in rooms once closed to them. Decay within, decay without: Calcutta in some places had a little of the feel of an abandoned Belgian settlement in central Africa in the 1960s, after Africans had moved in and camped. Camped: it was the word. At Independence, with the partition of Bengal into Indian West Bengal and Pakistan East Bengal, there had been a very big movement of refugees from the east. They had camped, where they could; they had clogged up large areas in and around the city. And since then the population of the city had doubled.

There was no room by day on the streets or in the large sunburnt parks. There was no place to go walking. You could drive very slowly along a dug-up road and through the crowds to the Tollygunge Club, and there you could go walking on the golf course. But the drive was exhausting; and the drive back, in the kerosene-and-gasoline fumes, undid the little good you might have done yourself. People told you that up to 15 years ago the streets of central Calcutta were washed every day. But I had heard that in 1962 as well. Even then, just 15 years after Independence, 16 years after the great Hindu-Muslim riots which had marked so many memories, people were looking back to a golden age of Calcutta.

The British had built Calcutta and given it their mark. And – though the circumstances were fortuitous – when the British ceased to rule, the city began to die.

One of the people I met in Calcutta in 1962 was Chidananda Das Gupta. He worked at the time for the Imperial Tobacco Company, later known less provocatively as the ITC. Because he worked for such a grand British company, Chidananda was one of the select and envied group of Indians known as 'boxwallahs'.

These boxwallahs represented in their own eyes a synthesis of Indian and European culture. They were admired and envied by Indians outside the group because their boxwallah jobs were secure, in addition to being, with the British connection, a badge of breeding. The salaries were very good, among the best in India; and – to add to the boxwallah superfluity – there were company cars and furnished company apartments. And the work was not hard. Any firm a boxwallah worked for more or less monopolized its particular field in India. All that was required of a boxwallah was that he should be a man of culture, and well connected, an elegant member of the team.

Chidananda had another interest. He loved the cinema, and was one of the founders of the Calcutta Film Society. It was at the Calcutta Film Society that I met him one evening. And 26 years later I was to be reminded – by Rajan, the secretary, who had told me his story in Bombay – that at the end of that evening Chidananda had entrusted me to him, asking him to see me safely back to the guest house of the drug company where I was staying. No memory had stayed with me of Rajan, to whom this easy intercourse with film people and Bengali men of culture at the Film Society had come as a joy, a glimpse of a Calcutta far sweeter than the one he knew. Of the society office I had the merest impression: a dim ceiling light in a small room full of old office furniture. Of Chidananda I carried away a boxwallah picture: a slender moustached man of forty in a grey suit.

Chidananda didn't last at ITC. He became a film-maker and writer; that became his career, and it took him away from Calcutta. Twenty years or so later, as a semi-retired man, he had come back to Calcutta. He worked for half the week as editor of the arts pages of *The Telegraph* newspaper. The rest of the week he lived at Shantiniketan, the university founded by Rabindranath Tagore, the poet and patron saint of Bengal.

Shantiniketan was two and a half hours away by train from Calcutta. Chidananda was building a house there, living in the house while it was being built around him. I went to see him there one Sunday.

What did I know of Shantiniketan? I thought of it as a poet-educationist's version of Gandhi's Phoenix Farm in South Africa: something connected with the Independence movement, and at the same time a protest against too much mechanization: some idea of music, of open-air classes, of huts as lecture halls: something Arcadian and very fragile, depending on a suspension of disbelief and criticism, and something which – since I hadn't heard about Shantiniketan for a long time – I thought had faded away.

I travelled up in the air-conditioned lounge car of the Shantiniketan Express. It was arranged like a drawing-room with sofas and arm-chairs. Its decorative motifs were Buddhist, and one railed-off part of the car might even have contained a shrine area: a reminder of the Buddhist faith in the regions to the north. I was the only passenger in the lounge car; this explained the fearful price the bell captain of the Calcutta hotel had paid on my behalf. But the effect of luxury was absent: the lounge car was used as a sleeping room by lower railway staff, and three of them were snoring away on sofas.

The land was rice land, the level, treeless land of a delta, with green and brown fields. The green fields were full of water, with rice plants in different stages of growth in different fields. In some fields seedlings stood in the water in bundles, like little stooks, before being planted out in rows. The fields that had been reaped were brown and dry; sometimes stubbled, sometimes cleared and ploughed; sometimes with spaced-out mounds of darker, new earth, to revive the soil, waiting to be ploughed in. Water was being lifted in many different places from field to field, sometimes by electric pumps, sometimes by means of a long, flexible sleeve, lowered by hand into a field with water, then lifted and poured into the other field. Every kind of activity connected with the growing of rice was to be seen on this wide, flat delta: this went on for mile after mile, and it was hard to understand how there could ever have been famine here. But then, near Shantiniketan, the land began to dry out, began to look like flat desert, and unfriendly.

Chidananda was at the station to meet me. Twenty-six years on, we were like actors coming on in the third act of a play, exiting young at the end of act two, and reappearing with powder or flour on hair and eyebrows. He was in casual Indian clothes (and not in the grey boxwallah suit my memory had fixed him in), and he had an old Ambassador car. It was far cheaper to run here than in

Delhi, he said; that was one consideration when he had decided to move to Shantiniketan.

The short lane leading out of the station was a tangle of cycle-rickshaws. The car was the intruder here, Chidananda said. There actually was a special railway stop for Shantiniketan, but the people of Bolpur, the stop before, insisted that everyone going to Shantiniketan should get off at Bolpur, to give their trade to the local bazaar.

We got out into the open after a little. There were trees. Many had been planted by the university, Chidananda said, and they had helped to increase the rainfall. The shade, too, was nice; but still it was dusty, very dusty. There were no university mud huts now, just ochre-washed concrete houses. We passed the Shantiniketan temple. It was a hall of pleasing proportions, self-consciously unecclesiastical. But it was of its period. It had pierced walls and panes of coloured glass, and from the road it looked Edwardian, and a little gaudy.

Chidananda showed some of the houses Tagore lived in when he was at Shantiniketan. Tagore, Chidananda said, became bored very quickly with a house, and liked to move from house to house: the poet's privilege, the founder's privilege, and perhaps also the self-indulgence of the Bengali aristocrat. I had some feeling as well of the great man licensed or at play in Shantiniketan: there were some university buildings that Tagore had designed himself, attempting a blend of Asian motifs, Hindu, Indian, Chinese. Strange to consider now, the romanticism and self-deception behind that pictorial idea; yet at the time there would have been passion mixed up with the play, the need – against the old and apparently enduring glory of the British Empire and Europe – to assert Asia.

Chidananda's unfinished house was at the edge of the university area. The house, of brick, was to be on two floors. The ground floor was almost complete; about three months' work remained to be done on the upper floor. The land around the house was open on three sides. Chidananda had chosen the spot for the privacy and the silence and the fresh air, none of which could now be had in Indian cities. But the main reason why Chidananda had come to Shantiniketan was that – with all its changes: it was now a university like any other in India – it was connected with the special Bengali culture he had grown up in. The soil was sacred to him, as it was sacred, though in a different way, to the simple Indian tourists who came. These tourists came, not because they knew the poetry or the work of Rabindranath Tagore, but because they had heard of him as a holy man, and it was good to visit the shrines of such people.

Chidananda's father had been a preacher for the Brahmo Samaj all his life. The Brahmo Samaj was a kind of purified or reformed Hinduism which the father of Rabindranath had elaborated in the 19th century. It was an attempt to synthesize the New Learning of Britain and Europe with the old speculative Hindu faith of the Vedas and the Upanishads. It was a direct development of the ideas of Raja Ram Mohun Roy of Bengal (1772–1833), the first modern Indian reformer and educationist. The quality of men like Roy and the elder Tagore cannot be easily appreciated today, when the goods and inventions of Europe and America have changed the world, and simple people everywhere have to make some accommodation to the civilization that encircles and attracts them. In the late 18th and early 19th century Europe, in India, was less a source of goods. In the static conditions of Indian civilization at the time – with all its pressures towards old ways, old virtues – it required exceptional intellectual power to recognize the new gifts of Europe.

Chidananda said, 'The Brahmo faith brings together the essence of the Upanishadic teaching and some Christian forms. Such as a form of service – a service on Sunday morning and Sunday evening. You would sit in pews in the larger churches, and there would be a pulpit. The service would alternate between spoken rituals and prayers, and hymns, many of which were written by Rabindranath Tagore, some by his father. It was Rabindranath's father who devised the mode of the service. The Brahmo separated

Upanishadic monotheism and the thought of a universal spirit, which was formless, from Puranic Hinduism – idolatry, many deities, mixed with animism, casteism. It believed in the education of women and the ideals of democracy, and the abolition of the caste system.'

This was the faith that Chidananda's father served all his life. The decision to do so came to him at an early age.

'My grandfather used to take my father to the Sunday service of the Brahmo Samaj from the time he was ten years old. This was in the town of Chittagong, now in Bangladesh.' Chittagong: now associated with the poverty and natural disasters of Bangladesh, but to the Portuguese poet Camoens 400 years ago one of the fairest cities of rich and fertile Bengal: *Chatigão, cidade das milhores de Bengala.*

'At fourteen my father decided he wanted to become a Brahmo. My grandfather had never foreseen such an outcome, and he was outraged. My father left home one night. He literally walked and – to use a modern term – hitchhiked, on bullock carts and boats, to reach Shillong up in the hills, 500 miles away. In those days there was still quite a living tradition of wayside hospitality. My father told me he would walk or go by bullock cart all day, and at evening he would go to the nearest house and ask for shelter for the night, and it would be given.

'He went to Shillong because he knew some Brahmos there. They then helped him with his education, and he went to college with a lot of well-known people, among them Satyajit Ray's father, Sukumar Ray, a great humorist and publisher.

'My father never graduated. He did what in those days was called "First Arts", the first two years of college, and he became a missionary of the Brahmo and was paid a small allowance. Quite soon thereafter he met my mother and fell in love with her – in Ganga, in Bihar, where my mother's father was a well-established doctor. When my father asked for his daughter's hand, the doctor agreed. And my father remained a poor preacher all his life.'

For someone of this background – and perhaps for all devoted Brahmos – Shantiniketan was holy ground, for a special reason.

'Rabindranath's father was travelling through this area in the 1840s. It was like a desert, and he liked the place very much. There was one tree, and he sat under it, and that day he decided to found an ashram on the spot. It was to be modelled on the ancient *brahmacharya* ashram – where you practise celibacy during your student days and learn at the feet of your guru. He did found the ashram, and a long time afterwards Rabindranath founded the university, *Vishwa-Bharati,* India's World University. There is a raised platform under the tree where Rabindranath's father sat. That is considered the most sacred spot at Shantiniketan.

'What Raja Ram Mohun Roy began as a reform movement early in the 19th century Devendranath Tagore made into a religion. It transformed the Bengali middle class. Rabindranath Tagore expanded that religion into a culture. And that culture became Nehru's politics. Because Rabindranath channelled it into a culture, and didn't restrict it to religion, it was soon absorbed by the wider middle class. Today the Brahmo Samaj is still technically there. But the life has gone out of the institution – and into the wider society.'

Chidananda first saw Shantiniketan in 1940, when he was nineteen. He was living with his family in the neighbouring province of Bihar, and his father suggested that he should go and spend a holiday there. He stayed in the guest house. He shared a room with an Indonesian teaching batik at the university. It excited Chidananda to be with someone from abroad, and he was also excited by the Indonesian's name, which was Prahasto. This was a name straight out of the Hindu epic, the Mahabharata. Chidananda immediately had a greater idea of India and Asia; and he felt – what Tagore intended students at his university to feel – that in going to Shantiniketan he had gone to a place that was part of the world, not just of India.

A few days later Rabindranath made a speech at the temple.

'It was very early in the morning, December, quite cold – there were few houses in Shantiniketan then, much more open ground – and we sat on the cold marble floor in the glass temple, with pieces of glass of various colours. When the sun came up it threw all kinds of colours on the faces and clothes of the people. We all sat there and waited for Rabindranath.

'He was wheeled in. Then he got up from the wheelchair. He was very tall, but bent with age. He walked in on his own. He was in a white dhoti and koortah and shawl. I was impressed by that sight. It was like an evocation of ancient India, a romantic feeling of encountering a sage from olden times. He sat on a very low stool. Everyone else was seated on the marble, without any spread.

'Then the singing began. No modern instruments, all traditional instruments. No harmonium, though – Rabindranath disliked it because it has a fixed scale, a western scale, and it is impossible with it to sound the semi-tones or micro-tones which are important to the Indian system of classical music. Then they sang a hymn, one of Rabindranath's hymns.

'He read from a prepared text, in Bengali, with Sanskrit quotations. He was a very big man, six foot two, and he looked very *strong*, and I was struck by the contrast between his voice, which was thin and high, and the largeness of the man. I had expected a deep, rich voice. It took a few minutes to overcome that feeling. But very soon the spell of what he was saying took over. This was December 1940, and the war was very much with us. The subject of his address was the crisis in civilization – he was concerned about the movement towards self-destruction.'

So Chidananda was introduced by Tagore to a way of thinking about the world. It was one of the blessings of the Indian Independence movement, that many of its leaders should have been men of large vision, capable of looking beyond their Indian cause.

*

That first visit of Chidananda's to Shantiniketan lasted two weeks. Less than a year later Rabindranath died. Chidananda, like many Bengalis, felt that Shantiniketan without Rabindranath was nothing; and it was 46 years before he went back again. He went back, in fact, only after he had decided to go and live there. To make that return journey, he did what I had just done: he took the train from Howrah station in Calcutta, and got off at Bolpur two and a half hours later.

'That station lets you into the very worst of the Bengali small-town atmosphere – ugly, noisy, crowded, full of the kind of deprivation I see in the style of urbanization in our country, the deprivation of mind, of basic needs. The station had changed much more than Shantiniketan had changed.

'I went through the chaos of Bolpur. I knew I was going to Shantiniketan, where there would be open spaces and quiet surroundings and trees. It didn't trouble me too much – because you can't wish away the reality of your country. It was good to know it had a hidden heart beyond all this chaos. I've been practising yoga for about 15 years now, and it's helped me tremendously to arrive at this mental state – in which I could take an enormous amount of chaos and confusion around me, for a while, without losing my own peace of mind.

'So even on that first visit I found I liked the place. Some months later I bought some land, as much of it as I could afford, and I began to build right away. An old architect friend, a retired man, a Bengali, drew the plans. He knew the area, the climate, the wind direction.

'It's a changed place. I don't expect it to be what it was. You can't go back to the old days when people here lived in mud houses and went about barefooted by choice. But I feel that, coming back here, I have come back to more free ways of thinking, living, acting. It doesn't make me feel shut in. I've been reading the Upanishads again – a renewed inclination. Formally, I'm an atheist, but I've reached a state where I separate spirituality from theism and religion. To me the Upanishads represent man's effort to understand the universe and himself at the very highest level of spirituality.

'Here it's only two and a half hours away from Calcutta, but I feel I've come a very long way from my previous incarnation. The boxwallah incarnation which you saw in 1962 was quite far away from the roots of my culture and upbringing.'

Chidananda had wanted, when he was a young man, to be a teacher. At one stage he had even wanted to be a Brahmo missionary, like his father. But then his wish to prove himself in the world had led him to advertising and then to the tobacco company.

When the news came that he had got the job, everyone congratulated him. But his wife said, 'Why do you want to take this job? Don't you realize we will become a different kind of people?'

Chidananda said, 'In 1962, when you met me, I was looking after the company's advertising, which was one of the biggest advertising operations in the country. The company itself was a kind of tobacco monopoly dating from the British times. Anything that was made was sold, almost regardless of its quality. I will give you this idea of the complacency of that boxwallah world. There was a highly paid staff manager who spent a large part of his time measuring the carpet that a particular category of officer should get, and discussing the colours of curtains with the wives.

'The boxwallah was manufactured into a highly peculiar animal. The system was created to answer the needs of the British, their life-style, their ways of eating, sitting, sleeping, shitting. The Britishers who came out here for the company looked upon their time in India as a stay in a hotel, where everything was provided – down to the last towel and last spoon – in preparation for the time when they would go back home and buy themselves a house and wash their own clothes. Even servants were provided.

'Within six weeks of joining, I wrote a report saying that the name of the company should be changed from the Imperial Tobacco Company to the ITC. All it caused at the time was laughter.

'Like the administration of the British Empire itself, the commercial empire, which was an extension of the first, separated a handful of Indians from the rest and made them into an integral part of the system of governance. The object was to make them identify more with British interests than with Indian interests. This was done in a very subtle way. The British would unhesitatingly serve Indian officers whether in political administration or commercial administration. I don't think this happened with other empires, and it still doesn't happen with foreign companies operating in India. French or American or Japanese companies almost never have one of their nationals serving under an Indian.

'The company was highly hierarchical. There were two distinct classes, officers and men. We, the officers, would have chauffeur-driven cars, and our wives would be provided with separate cars to go out shopping – choosing carpets and curtains. There were colleagues of mine who would straighten their tie if the chairman telephoned, or send the car home to get a fresh jacket if they were going out to lunch. And, of course, at work the officers had separate lavatories.

'My wife got quickly used to the comforts and loved them. I enjoyed the luxury of the life – it would be hypocrisy to say otherwise. And I must say that way of living left a mark on the nature of our needs in later years.

'My problem was that because of my interest in literature and the cinema I was constantly associating in my private life with people who were utterly different. At the end of the day's work I would go to the office of the Calcutta Film Society. I had founded that along with Satyajit Ray in 1947, the year of Independence. Our main work was sticking envelopes and writing addresses. We were lucky to have a fan over our heads – in a dingy office of a film distributor. Here we discussed the greatness of world cinema.

'Ray was closely associated with our work. With his enormous height and his wide shoulders, he came to remind me a great deal of Tagore, and I now see him as the last great representative of the Tagore era. But, unlike Tagore, he has a big, booming voice. He is swarthy; Tagore had fair, delicate skin. In his culture, his Indianness, his universality (not to be compared with fashionable cosmopolitanism), his honesty, Ray has some very Brahmo virtues.

'So I was living a Jekyll and Hyde existence. Western clothes, quite formal, during the day, and the Film Society in the evening. Occasionally a colleague would become curious about my leisure pursuits. He would come to the Film Society to see a French or German film, but he would be repelled by the smell of sweat on the bodies of my close associates, who'd travelled long distances on buses, trams, or walking, and worked all day in offices that were not air-conditioned, and didn't have the means to go back home to change their clothes.

'A very acute illustration of the kind of spiritual disquiet that the Jekyll and Hyde existence caused me came in the shape of something very material: I remember going with my colleagues to the wedding of a British executive of our company with an Indian girl, something that had caused a great deal of consternation in the higher echelons of our management.

'Perforce I was in a western lounge suit, along with my colleagues. Or perhaps it was a lack of strength of will on my part. I found, on that extremely hot and sultry evening, the place full of Bengalis in their comfortable thin poplin koortahs and dhotis. As I was sweating inside my completely unsuitable clothes I suddenly realized which side I belonged to, and I said to myself in disgust, "What have I done to myself?" This incident crystallized a lot of things inside me. I began to consider leaving the company, giving up the style of existence it imposed on its executives.

'I would say there was a lot of underemployment of intelligence in those jobs. Many of us, in sales, went out to the bazaars in Calcutta and in small towns all over the country, but their main job there, I found, consisted in picking up random packets of cigarettes to check the code numbers at the back, which told you how fresh or how stale the cigarettes were.

'So people drifted from breakfast to office to lunch to an outing at the bazaar and then to the club and a late night every night. There was air-conditioning in the office and at home and in the club, so one wouldn't have to spend more than half an hour or an hour without air-conditioning.

'The main virtue of this style of existence was that it prevented you from thinking. If you started thinking it could cause you discomfort. It damaged some of the Indians, permanently affecting their ability to be themselves, and printing on them a kind of pretence. I've seen a fair number of people who've become incapable of holding their own without this protective umbrella. And I've seen people go through an infernal amount of humiliation within the organization.

'These jobs were more or less sinecures. So they would humiliate you by taking away certain visible symbols of authority and leaving you without any work. I've seen people go day in, day out to the office and just sit there, and then go back home – Oxford and Cambridge graduates who, if they had gone into other jobs, might have used their capacities better. The whole office would know about this humiliation. It was made very visible. But for many people resignation was unthinkable. It would have been like being thrown out of a warm and well-lit room into the middle of a winter in northern Sweden.

'At that time Indian business had not expanded that much, and opportunities were very limited. In any case, Indian businesses wouldn't have given the boxwallahs the kind of life-style they had become used to. Nowadays Indian business will give you certain facilities and very expensive life-styles – provided you deliver the goods. They make certain of that: there are no sinecures left in Indian business.

'By the mid-60s the new movement in business had begun. The realities were closing in on the beleaguered boxwallah regiment. The tobacco company changed. It transformed itself over a short period, 10 years – which is quite short for a change of culture. This transformation was brought about by Indians. The British trained their men, but they didn't try to run the business themselves. Today ITC has diversified and is coping very well with the slow-down in the tobacco business.'

That transformation was proof of the positive side of the boxwallah culture; that positive side had to be remembered.

'The work ethic was very high. There was a lot of drive and discipline, though they didn't always know what they were driving at. They were at heart good Indians, patriotic Indians. In 1962, at the time of the China war, about the time we met, I remember there was a meeting of the finance committee. The finance director said, "Well, gentlemen, do you think the next meeting of the committee will be held in Peking?" I answered, "Sir, not unless our prime minister takes to wearing an umbrella under his arm." And I will say this for the British, they liked this kind of repartee, and respected you for it.'

Ashok was 25 years younger than Chidananda. Ashok worked for an old British boxwallah company. The company itself had now been bought over by one of the new generation of super-rich Indian financiers and industrialists, much of whose business activity lay outside India.

Ashok hadn't wanted to go into business for the privileges and position Chidananda had described. He had been more excited by the idea of 'marketing' – modern-sounding, active, up-to-the-minute. (I thought that marketing was just another word for selling, and didn't ask Ashok to define it for me. Many weeks later, in Delhi, it was defined for me by a former advertising man in this precise way: 'Marketing is the identifying and satisfying of an unmet need.' Not the creating of needs – that would have been considered devil's work in a poor country. Just the identifying of unmet needs.)

Ashok's first story – he told me three stories in all – was of his attempt to get into marketing.

'I made a number of false starts. The first was when I did commerce at the university. That was what my parents wanted me to do. I knew commerce wasn't for me, but I gritted my teeth and went ahead with it. I just scraped through the final exams, and that dented my self-confidence. Then I applied to join a management institute. I did that because everybody else was doing it. Inevitably, I didn't get in.

'At that stage my father fixed me up with a chamber of commerce in Delhi. I was there for a year and a half. I came into contact with a number of the industry barons for whom the chamber had been set up; but you also had a number of rustic individuals. It gave me a fair idea of the half-and-half way things were in India. I was drawing a pittance, 300 rupees a month, £15, but I was living in the house of an uncle, and didn't have many expenses.

'One day, at a middle-class party in Delhi, in Defence Colony, I met a Dr Malhotra. He was a portly man of middle height, in a dark-brown suit. I asked him what he did, and he said in an offhand way that he was the director of IMBA. I asked him what IMBA was, and he said it was the Institute of Management and Business Administration. It sounded familiar, but that was because many of these places have names that sound like that. Anyway, I was terribly impressed. He was a man in his mid-forties. I was in my early twenties. He looked very prosperous, and talked that way too. He was indifferent to me initially, no doubt seeing me as just another young man working somewhere.

'But then the conversation led to the fact that my father was an influential businessman in Calcutta, and Dr Malhotra's attitude to me changed. He became quite interested in what I did, how much I earned, and then he gave his opinion that I was made for much better things. My own gullibility took me along on the wave of his interest. His approval of me was total.

'It was beyond him why someone of my obvious talent should be wasting his time drawing 300 rupees in a nondescript chamber of commerce, when I could have the world at my feet. I said,

"Have you anything better to suggest?" He said, "Boy, do I!" He described his IMBA institute. From the way he told it, IMBA was set up to propagate the discipline of marketing to as many people as possible in the country. And he now had plans to expand from Delhi to the other metropolitan centres.

'The way he told it, his own marketing acumen was sought by the large corporations of India, and he had had something to do with the success of quite a few well-known brands. Just listening to him excited me, opening my eyes to the wonderful world of marketing, of which I had heard so much.

'I thought I wanted to go into marketing. Partly this was because lots of my friends and colleagues were applying to these institutes of management, in which marketing was an important discipline, or they were joining large corporations as management trainees in the marketing division. I didn't understand what the thing was about, but it seemed to me the thing to do. It had a certain glamour, a certain aura.

'I agreed with Dr Malhotra that I was wasting my time where I was. He invited me over to his office the following day, where, as he implied, I might learn something to my advantage. I trotted off the next morning. Before I knew it, Dr Malhotra was offering me a job, at double the salary I was getting at the chamber, and with the enticing prospect of going back and working in Calcutta.

'When I asked him why an obviously successful marketing man like him was interested in a raw beginner like me, someone who had failed to get into the management institutes, he said the way he saw professional qualifications was like this: B.S., M.S., and Ph.D. Bullshit, More Shit, and Piled High and Deep. Which again made a deep impression on me. Even in my school reports they used to say: "His marks are not a true indication of his ability." So I was ready to fall in with what Dr Malhotra said.

'"It's work experience that counts," he said. And he said he preferred, having the views he had, to pick up raw people like me and make them blossom.

'He asked me to look after the Calcutta branch or, as he called it, the "Calcutta Bureau" of IMBA – I think he liked the modern sound of the word "bureau". The job, as he described it, would mean setting up courses, and enrolling corporate and individual members at fairly high fees.

'I had the presence of mind to ask him how this was going to help me learn about marketing. I saw that the job meant selling IMBA rather than learning the marketing skills for which IMBA was apparently famous. He said this would be only one aspect of my work. IMBA itself would be deeply involved in marketing research and counselling for clients. This impressed me. I saw myself developing into a marketing whizz-kid.

'I overrode my father's doubts, and I accepted Dr Malhotra's offer. The day I joined IMBA he gave me a box of visiting cards with my name and my grandiose designation as Bureau Executive. I had never had a visiting card before. I was very pleased.

'I was hoping to spend a week or so in Delhi, learning about the workings of IMBA, but it was apparent that Dr Malhotra was in a bit of a hurry to see me off to Calcutta. He wanted me to go there and start enrolling the big corporations as members. He said I was to get the help of my father. This gave me a little pause: I began to feel that he was interested in my father, and that something was amiss.

'He packed me off to Calcutta. He paid the train fare. He had indicated to me that he had an office in Calcutta, and that a friend was looking after the office. Shortly after I arrived, this friend telephoned and invited me over. The office was in a congested part of North Calcutta, and when I went I found a dingy little place in an old, ill-kept multi-storeyed block.

'When I asked this gentleman, Dr Malhotra's friend, where my IMBA office would be, he pointed to a broken small table in one corner of the room, and he said I could work from there. He went on to add that while in an absolute emergency he could consider some typing work, he would prefer it if I used a carbon and wrote my own letters and reports by hand. He said I could also use the telephone – the only one in the office that worked. But every time I made a call I should make a note of it, and these costs would be debited to IMBA.

'And from that desk I actually attempted to run my first marketing training course. Dr Malhotra told me I should negotiate with a hotel for a conference hall, and lunch and dinner and so on for the participants. I was to try to get a good price – he was particular about that – and I actually did so.

'He told me more than once that he was getting a reputed American professor down to Calcutta for the training course. That was the point I had to push. The American idea was important. The management scene in the country was heavily influenced by the management boom that was taking place in America, and Dr Malhotra was certainly sensitive to that.

'I did as he said, and was quite successful in enrolling the 25 candidates or so he wanted for the course. I did this primarily because I met a number of senior corporation people who were family friends. That gave me an entry point, and I found that the rest was quite easy. I went to see them, and they were happy to nominate someone in their firm to attend the course for 2000 rupees a head. I should say that a lot of these senior people expressed surprise and dismay that I was associated with such an outfit – of which they hadn't heard.

'The course itself passed off without incident – except one. The American professor and his wife did come down. He wasn't really well known. He came from some obscure university, and in fact he was running a somewhat similar outfit somewhere in the vast North American continent. He was a cartoon American tourist, paunchy, late forties.

'This professor and his wife were put up in the hotel Dr Malhotra had made me negotiate with, for the conference hall and so on. It wasn't the best hotel in town. It was a couple of rungs below. The professor and his wife didn't like what they saw, but

Dr Malhotra told them that this was India, a very poor country, that standards were lower, and that service in these less pretentious hotels was often better than in the five-star hotels, which could sometimes be all show.

'Just when it seemed that the Americans were getting reconciled to their quarters, a rat appeared and scurried across the room. The lady screamed and said, "I can't stand *slithery* things." And, to the chagrin of Dr Malhotra, the Americans insisted on being taken to the very best hotel in Calcutta. This was the Grand Hotel. It was infinitely more expensive. I myself had to make the arrangements.

'The course was seen as a feather in my cap. But then, as soon as it was over, Dr Malhotra said I should start preparing for another – going through the whole thing again. And I myself wasn't happy about the course I had just arranged, because it seemed to me on reflection that it hadn't done anything for me in the marketing way.

'I also wasn't being successful in enrolling members in IMBA. Dr Malhotra was greatly interested in this, since each corporate member would bring in some 7000 or 8000 rupees, and an individual member about 1000 rupees. Most people simply didn't know about IMBA. Dr Malhotra thought I should be able to enrol them simply because I belonged to an influential family. But I didn't feel I had anything to offer the big corporations. It's hard enough to sell a good product without being pushy. To sell a dud product was well nigh impossible to me at that time, when I was young and shy. And my father's friends were becoming a little more vocal in their protests about my requests to them for 8000 rupees for corporate membership of IMBA.

'My weekly, carbon-copied, ballpoint-penned IMBA reports to Dr Malhotra made less and less impressive reading. And Dr Malhotra was becoming more and more impatient. He also began to feel that there was some danger that I might leave IMBA.

'He flew down to Calcutta and wanted to know why I wasn't producing results. I put it to him that I had joined IMBA to develop knowledge and skills in the discipline of marketing, in the classical sense. And what I had been doing in the last couple of months was selling or marketing IMBA itself, which had helped neither my knowledge nor my reputation. I suggested to him that what IMBA needed in Calcutta was some indigent retired army officer with organizational ability, and not an idealistic twenty-three-year-old man on the threshold of a career. It came to me to say at that point that I hoped we could part amicably.

'We didn't part amicably. He became angry. He said he had invested a lot of money and time in me. I ignored that: I thought he was going to ask for some kind of money back. He became very angry, and said he was going to remove my name from life membership of IMBA. It was news to me that I was a life member of IMBA, but apparently branch executives or "bureau executives" became that automatically.'

The burnt-out Maoists I had met in Madras had been on the periphery of a much larger peasant movement. This movement had its centre in Bihar and Bengal, almost 1000 miles to the north-east; and it had been at its most active in the late 60s and early 70s. Communism in Bengal had a long history. It was another colonial import, one of the things that had come after the New Learning of the 19th century, and the mixed culture. Even now, in the dead British-built city, and almost as an aspect of its death, there were frequent, solemn communist marches through the litter and rubble and hopelessness. Even now, while a communist party ruled in the state, people could still be moved by the poetry of red flags and revolution.

Dealing in poetry and passion, never really persecuted, at times even hostile to the idea of Indian Independence, fighting its own sometimes remote wars, the communist party had split and split. There had been the Communist Party of India; then there had been the Communist Party of India (Marxist); then there had been the Communist Party of India (Marxist-Leninist). It was this last, Maoist faction that had got the peasant revolt going. The revolt had been crushed. But the movement, while it lasted, had attracted and consumed many thousands of educated people in Bengal and other parts of India.

There were survivors. One of them was Dipanjan. He was now a science professor in a college in central Calcutta. It was a real, working college, but physically it was in a state of decay, Calcutta decay.

The signboard was peeling; the windows of the two-storey building were broken. But there was a gate-man, guarding the double gate. He sent me upstairs to Dipanjan, up a narrow, half-walled concrete staircase at the far end of the main building, to a broken-down room with tables with pieces of simple equipment. The uneven floor was unswept, or swept up to a certain wavering line, where the swept-up dust and the broom that had done the sweeping had both been abandoned, just like that. Dust adhered to all the mouldings or extrusions of the tall dun-coloured doors; the plaster on the wall was broken in many places. The room gave one no sense of applied colour, no sense of surfaces made even or lines made straight.

Dipanjan was a small, slender man with glasses. He wore a short-sleeved beige-coloured shirt and trousers. We went to a tall, cupboard-like room just off a central doorway. A desk and two chairs and some tall metal cupboards took up most of the space. The little bit of wall that could be seen between the cupboards was stained: something brown and oily had dripped down from the window.

I asked Dipanjan, after we had talked for a while, 'Do you see what I see here?'

He said in his soft, steady, precise voice, 'It's like other colleges. It's India.'

But he didn't see all that I saw. He said he could see the equipment on the lab tables: he could ignore what surrounded it. What he did see in a special way, what upset him and worked on his nerves far more than it did on mine, was the unswept dust on the floor.

The college was for drop-outs, he said, 'defeated soldiers' (though they looked active enough and healthy enough in the small college yard). They were people who couldn't get into other colleges. Their chances of getting a job were small – a B.Sc. degree didn't get you a job anyway – and they were not motivated. The girls at the college were better motivated. They didn't have the great need to achieve that the boys had; they didn't have that pressure; and, paradoxically, they made better students. The college wanted more girls. The fees were 30 rupees a month, £1.20, which even in India wasn't a great deal.

In that cramped space off the lecture room we talked that afternoon of his background. In physique and voice, and features and manner, he was a gentle man, a mild man. He would not have stood out in any Calcutta gathering. It wasn't easy to see in him the revolutionary who, 20 years or so before (he was now forty-five), had gone out into the countryside to live among the peasants, preaching the idea of revolution and then, in accordance with the party directive, calling for the annihilation of certain people, class enemies.

His mother had been from a well-to-do family. Her father had been high up in government service, a member of the IES, the Indian Educational Service. Before that, he had been 'a minor scientist', Dipanjan said. He had devised one of the early instruments for measuring radioactive particles, and had made a name for himself.

I said, 'I don't see how you can call him a minor figure.'

Dipanjan, not losing his evenness of manner, said, 'In Calcutta minor scientists are quite common. This is the city of M.N. Saha, S.N. Bose, J.C. Bose, and P.C. Ray. The first three were Fellows of the Royal Society. It is only recently that Calcutta has become a backwater. Even in the 1960s, Presidency College of Calcutta had a congregation of physics teachers which could hardly have been excelled anywhere else in the world at that time. So you must understand why I cannot look upon my maternal grandfather as anything but a minor scientist.'

In the South, science had grown over two or three generations out of the brahminical tradition of abstract learning. In Bengal, in the British-built city of Calcutta, science had come with the New Learning; scientific achievement had come out of colonial competitiveness and the wish of Indians to prove themselves.

On his father's side, Dipanjan came from the Bengali gentry. It was only on this trip that I had heard this word in India. I had thought of 'gentry' as an English word, suggesting people rooted and attached to ancestral land, and protective towards it. And the word here in Bengal was in fact an English word, from the early 19th century. Dipanjan said, 'The British made the gentry hereditary. From their point of view, they were creating a class of hereditary farmers of revenue.'

Dipanjan's father's family came from the Faridpur district. In 1947 this became part of East Pakistan. The gentry of Faridpur were in the main upper-caste Hindus. They rented out their land; the cultivators were Muslims and Hindus of the scheduled castes. During the Hindu-Muslim massacres in Bengal in 1946–47, the Hindus of Faridpur had to flee: not only the upper-caste landowners, but also the scheduled-caste cultivators. But long before that flight from Faridpur, Dipanjan's father's family had become impoverished. The ancestral land of the family had been so divided that all that had come to Dipanjan's grandfather (and his dependents) was one room in the big ancestral family house.

This grandfather, when he was twenty, joined the government service, in the Accountant-General's Office of Bengal. He was helped by the joint-family system. His son, Dipanjan's father, went to live in an apartment owned by a relation in Calcutta. It was in this apartment that Dipanjan was born.

In 1940 or thereabouts, while he was studying in college, and when he was seventeen or eighteen, Dipanjan's father became a communist. Dipanjan never thought to ask his father later why he had become a communist: he took it as normal. Membership of the party was a serious affair. When, in 1943, Dipanjan's father wanted to get married, he had to get the permission of the party, because his prospective bride came from a family that was in government service. The party gave its permission on condition that Dipanjan's prospective father-in-law (the minor scientist, the IES officer) made out a cheque – for any sum – payable to the Communist Party of India.

After the war, in 1946, when Dipanjan was two and half years old, the party advised Dipanjan's father and mother to go to Hungary for their higher studies. Dipanjan was left behind with his grandparents. Dipanjan's father and mother returned in 1950 – after all the upheavals of Partition and Independence. Dipanjan's mother had done a teacher-training course in Hungary; she was able to get a job soon after she came back to Calcutta. But Dipanjan's father, who had become a Ph.D. in biochemistry, couldn't get a proper job. He moved from one unsatisfactory position to another until 1955, when he found something in his own field; and then he left the Communist Party. And just as Dipanjan had never asked his father why he had become a communist, so he never thought later to ask his father why he had left the party: it wasn't in the Hindu or Indian tradition, this questioning of elders by young people. There was an odd relic of that Hungarian interlude of his parents: they had both learned Hungarian, and in Calcutta it became their private language, when they wanted to keep things from Dipanjan.

Dipanjan developed asthma when he was seven, in 1951. His mother became protective; the boy lived a retired life, drawing sustenance from books. There were many books in the apartment. There were his father's communist books. There were also the books of the father's uncle, to whom the apartment belonged. This uncle was a nationalist; he had books that took the nationalist side. But Dipanjan at that time was not too interested in politics.

He was getting, though, some ideas about the world. In 1952 he had gone with his mother to a slum, where she was teaching children the alphabet: this was party work. He had also gone sometimes to see some of his grandfather's relatives who had fled from Faridpur in East Bengal. These relatives were living in one of the refugee colonies around Calcutta. Dipanjan didn't understand at the time; but later, when he began to read about the events of 1947, he remembered the refugee colonies he had gone to as a child, and the events had more meaning for him. But he didn't think that his generation had been influenced politically by Partition.

He was good at his studies. 'My mother slowly became ambitious for me. And now, with hindsight, I think that must have taken up a lot of my mental space. In 1960, when I was sixteen and about to leave school, my major preoccupations were shining academically and writing poetry. I had become interested in literature, and was writing in Bengali and English.'

He was romantic, but in that setting there was no opportunity for him to meet girls. What was open to him, though, was the city of Calcutta. 'I was fond of the city even then, and even now I am fond of it. My roots are only in Calcutta. I have no village in Bengal to which I can lay claim. I felt Calcutta as a very living city, because Bengali poetry had become really modern in Calcutta, after Rabindranath and after the revolt against him.'

What about the crowds and dirt of Calcutta? Did he see that, or react to it?

'Calcutta has always been like this. It was even worse in British times. To a Calcuttan it is the perennial challenge – to rise above the all-absorbing task of just keeping yourself clean, which is time-consuming, energy-consuming. The challenge is how to do that and find time for other more significant things. That is the challenge faced by the ivory-tower intellectual and the rickshaw-puller.

'In J.C. Bose's time there were not many underground drains in the Indian areas of Calcutta. The drains would have been ditches.

'We are cursed with a corrupt corporate life. Cleaning the streets is a corporate act, and they will never be cleaned. Corruption here is a way of life, and it has existed here from the time of the East India Company.'

It was now the end of the working day. The motor-car horns and hooters were shrieking a little more exuberantly or impatiently in the streets outside. The college attendant who had brought tea and sodas – adding wet rings to the little stained table at which we sat – now came to close up, and to padlock doors.

Dipanjan took me down to the staff room on the lower floor. No one was there. The room had an enclosed, damp, musty smell, which not even the ceiling fan could blow away. In one corner there was a small, rough, chalk-faded blackboard, crookedly hung. No piece of woodwork or joinery was elegant or finished. What would have been the effect on the teachers? And on the students, the defeated soldiers?

High up on the wall, just below the ceiling, was a large framed photograph. It was a photograph of J.C. Bose, the scientist whose name Dipanjan spoke with reverence. There was an intention of honour; but, in that setting, whatever work the great man might have done seemed to have led to nothing.

The next day was Dipanjan's day off from the college, and he thought I should come to where he lived. This was in South Calcutta, in a lane so hard to find he drew a detailed map for me to give to the car-driver. Someone whom I consulted thought the journey might take up to an hour, depending on the traffic. So I started early.

The traffic was easy that morning, but after some time the city thoroughfare appeared to shrink, to collapse in on itself from its increased human density. The roadway narrowed; roadside huts and lean-tos, without pronounced colour, just a mish-mash of brown and black and grey, appearing to encroach on space meant for vehicles, hid the solider concrete buildings behind them, and gave the impression of a very long village road set in dirt, such freshness as had come with the morning already burnt up here by brown traffic fumes and sun-shot traffic dust. What seemed to threaten in many places in central Calcutta appeared to have happened here:

it was like witnessing the creation of a ruin: a large inhabited city was reverting to earth.

In spite of all the instructions, we overshot the meeting place that Dipanjan had decided on, and we had to go back through the hectic little road and look for it. Dipanjan's map was so detailed that both the driver and I had exaggerated its scale. Dipanjan had said that at one corner of the lane where we were to meet there was the playing field of a sports club. I had been looking for something the size of a football field: the playing field in question turned out to be the size of a small building plot, about a third of an acre, a square of concrete in a field of dust. He had said that there was a furniture shop on the other side of the lane. I had been looking for an emporium of fair size; but the Nufurnico shop was a small one-storey concrete shed. In this part of Calcutta – where needs and activities had contracted – there was a compensating inflation of nomenclature. In the 'playing field', which had a few basketball boards, there was also a sign for Sunny Green Creche, Green Park. Nufurnico described itself as 'Dealers of Foam Matters, U-Foam Matters and Pillow'. Foam matters: it made sense, in a way.

I had time to think about these things – and also to note the very dusty palm trees, which for some time I had failed to see – because I had arrived about half an hour too early. Out of the crooked lane between the furniture shop and the playing field (Dipanjan had thought I might have lost my way if I had gone into that lane on my own) reasonably well dressed people began to appear, walking briskly, some even with briefcases, Calcutta folk somehow with a day's work to do. And then Dipanjan appeared, with the deliberate tread of the other walkers in the lane, but he was sandalled now and in a dhoti: home clothes, for his day of rest.

Forty years before, he said, all this area was rice land. This was one of the areas outside Calcutta where refugees from East Pakistan had settled after 1947; everything here had been built in the last 40 years by people trying to remake their lives. And, indeed, away from that main road, the atmosphere of the little lane (perhaps by contrast) appeared pleasant. There was drainage, and electricity. But here too the numbers of people had grown and grown; even in the last 10 years many of the open spaces Dipanjan had known had been filled in.

Dipanjan's apartment was the lower floor of a small two-storey house. His landlord lived upstairs. Dipanjan made me take my shoes off in the little verandah, which was just a few feet away from the lane. The front room was a combined bedroom and sitting room. It was 10 feet by 10 feet. 'And, what is worse,' Dipanjan said, 'by 10 feet.' He meant that the room was 10 feet high as well: an absolute little cube.

There was a big bed in one corner. There was also a cane-bottomed settee; bookcases full of books and papers in apparent disorder; and some red box files in another corner. The apartment had another room, for the children; and there was also a space – it was the word Dipanjan used: he didn't say 'room' – with the kitchen at one end and the bathroom and W.C. at the other end.

The two children had been waiting to see their father's guest. The elder was a girl of nineteen, who was studying to be an engineer at the university of Jadavpur, not far away. She was smiling, open, handsome, with glasses; there was an outgoing quality about her which I had not seen so far in her father. She said mischievously of her plump brother, who was thirteen and was clearly going to be physically bigger than his father: 'He wants to go to America.' It must have been partly true, partly teasing; but the brother took it well. And then they were both off, into the little verandah, and then a few steps down into the lane.

Dipanjan had moved into the apartment in 1980. They were quite cramped there now; but they didn't think so in 1980. The children felt cramped, though. The little apartment cost 600 rupees a month, £24. There were some neatly kept houses around. There was a nice small house next door, with a hibiscus shrub against the ochre-coloured wall, really quite close to the windows of the room in which we were. That house belonged to an ayurvedic doctor, someone practising traditional Hindu medicine.

They had nice neighbours in the lane; they couldn't complain about that; but the house was terribly dusty. That was why Dipanjan was so particular about getting me to take off my shoes: to keep out the dust which my shoes might have brought in. Trucks often went down the narrow lane; when they did, dust blew straight into the house. And there were mosquitoes.

Dipanjan said, 'That reminds me. I should put on a coil.'

He went to the inner 'space' – his long dhoti was brown or beige, with a plaid or check pattern – and he came out after a while not with the green mosquito coil I was expecting, but with a plastic blue Japanese 'gadget' – Dipanjan's word – that had to be plugged into a power point. The chemical in the plastic container was released by heat.

A sweeping woman, speaking no word, looking at no one, bending down low from the waist, her legs quite straight, passed through the front room, flicking her little broom at those small areas of the terrazzo floor that were not covered by furniture or the red box files.

Dipanjan's wife came in. Her name was Arati. She was of Dipanjan's age. She wore a dark-coloured sari with a small pattern, and a black bodice. She, too, was a teacher: her classes started very early in the morning, and finished at 10.

She wanted to know about lunch. She said that Dipanjan couldn't eat wheat. 'Rice, rice, rice – that's what he wants, three times a day, as often as I give him. He can't digest wheat.' That was an aspect of Dipanjan's 'post-political' life. It had been brought about by Dipanjan's illnesses during his life underground in the villages, and by the badness of water in the delta.

'Amoebiasis,' Arati said. 'It's a chronic condition. Does it occur in your place? It's in most of the third world.'

It was the first time, since I had been talking to Dipanjan, that reference had been made to his life as a guerrilla. And it was unexpected that it should have come in this direct, unheroic way, with this emphasis on his personal frailty – the tormenting things he had known before the dust and mosquitoes of the lane.

Dipanjan sat on the bed. The three small windows of the room, with iron bars and green shutters, lit him from different angles. There were three old photographs on the blue walls, and one small portrait in colour. The photographs were of Dipanjan's father and mother, his father's father, and his father's maternal uncle, in whose rent-controlled apartment Dipanjan's father and then Dipanjan had lived until 1969. This relative had been a nationalist and a journalist; he had edited a proscribed Gandhian journal and had gone to jail in 1942. He was a man of culture, a Brahmo, a man of the Bengal Renaissance. But Dipanjan's greatest admiration was for his father's father, who was an orthodox Hindu. He had gone into the Accountant-General's Department because there had been no money for his higher education, and he had devoted nearly all his working life to looking after his brothers and sisters – which wasn't easy, especially after the calamities of 1947.

The photograph of this grandfather was big. Dipanjan had had it made from a damaged original. Other prints of lesser intensity had been made, but he liked the one he had on the wall.

'He had penetrating and dazzling eyes. I prefer this print because of the eyes. We have all inherited our preoccupation with ethics from him. He was a man of principle. People say he never did a wrong thing in his life.'

The other photograph, in colour, quite small, was of the young Mao.

Dipanjan said, 'You don't recognize him. It was presented by a Dr Bose, who was sent by Nehru to Chiang Kai-Shek in 1939, and ended up with Mao. The photograph is there because it was a gift. You mustn't read too much into it, though I have a strong and healthy respect for the man.'

Among the newspapers on the bed was a financial paper. Dipanjan liked to follow the economic news. The Indian economy was fragile, and he said there could be another depression like the one in 1965, which had led to food riots and given an impetus to the peasant movement.

Arati brought out tea. Dipanjan poured a cup for the driver of the car that had brought me, and took it out to him; he was parked in the yard next door.

Arati said, 'Are you staying for the summer?' She hardly waited for my reply. 'The heat is unbearable. There are so few trees now.'

I said, 'Why do they cut them down?'

'It's because of the people. There are too many people. You can't have people and trees. They've cut down so many trees, the weather is changing. We have colder winters and hotter summers.'

A woman neighbour called conversationally, across the short distance from the lane, 'Arati?' and almost immediately came in. At the same time a cycle-rickshaw went by in the lane, with many young children sitting on two facing benches below a little roof – young children going home from school in a toy-like contraption, reminding me of the baker's cycle-vans I used to see as a child in Port of Spain.

Arati and her neighbour talked in the kitchen space at the back of the front room. Their words were very clear through the open door.

Dipanjan, when he came back from looking after the car-driver, settled himself on the bed, among the newspapers, and began to talk.

'When I went to Presidency College I was not politically active. I sided with the left because of my upbringing, but the political activity in the college at that time was at a low level. Towards the end of my second year, when I was driving myself very hard academically, and it was becoming quite a strain, I began to wonder why I was doing it. I was also dabbling in poetry. My father never read my poems – I didn't show them to him. My mother wasn't interested. They thought it was perhaps a harmful diversion. They never encouraged me. I began to question why I was writing. Quite a few of us at college were assailed with similar problems and doubts, both boys and girls.

'From this time I suddenly became aware of the poverty and misery around me. Until then I hadn't been aware. I saw things and I accepted it as part of the scenery. I will tell you a little story. One day – I still remember – we were going, a friend and I, to see a showing of a picture made from a play of Bernard Shaw. I was about to go there. I had just left my house. And I saw this person – I wouldn't say he was a beggar: he was in no position to beg.

'He was lying on the curb. He was about to die, and fully conscious and silent. He was lying in front of a pathological laboratory. I asked the lab people to phone for an ambulance. The ambulance came, and I found that nobody was willing to accompany the person to hospital. So I had to accompany him. I wasn't very eager to do it, but I accompanied him. He was indifferent. Absolutely. He didn't talk.

'We drove to a hospital. Doctors examined him and on his ticket they wrote that he should be admitted, and they stamped the ticket with a prepared seal: "There is no accommodation in this hospital. Try somewhere else." The driver had to take him back in the ambulance. The driver asked me whether I knew this person. When I said I didn't, the driver said, "We can take him to another hospital, but the same thing will happen there."'

I asked Dipanjan, 'What did the man look like? You haven't mentioned that.'

'He was in rags, caked with dirt. The most striking thing about him was that he had hydrocel, an inflammation of the scrotum, caused usually by filariasis, a tropical parasitical disease. And when he walked he had to carry his scrotum in his hands, it was so heavy.

'I asked the ambulance-driver how often this kind of thing happened, and the driver said often. He said that when they were asked to pick up people like that, they did, without making a fuss. But no one accompanied the person, so their practice was to deposit him on some other street, because they knew that no hospital would accept them.

'Seeing that I felt in some way responsible for the man, the driver said, "There is one place I know where he might be accepted. I'm not sure, but let's go." He drove to this place near the temple of Kali, and there was this little space – just a long dark corridor, with perhaps just a tiled roof, and on both sides destitute people lying on beds waiting for death. So we left him there, and we placed the medical ticket near his head, and we came out.

'This place was the beginning of the place Mother Teresa was building up for such people, and she was quite unknown at the time. I should make it quite clear that I am not making any comment on the utility or validity of Mother Teresa's outlook or work. But I must say that even today there is no other place in Calcutta where a dying destitute will be accepted.'

At this point the electricity failed, as it often failed in Calcutta. Dipanjan's first thought was for the Japanese mosquito-repellent, which depended on heat. Without that repellent, he said, we simply wouldn't be able to sit and talk. He got up and got an oil lamp, lit it, and placed the blue gadget on top of the glass chimney. Almost at once the power came back, so he turned the oil lamp off. We also changed places. I sat on the bed; he sat on the cane-bottomed settee.

He said, 'It was a Sunday morning. A fine day, but it rained in the afternoon, after we had placed the man at Kalighat. I missed the cinema show. I spent about three to four hours ferrying that man around.

'This is just an example. Don't think this is my road to Damascus. It stands out in my mind, but it didn't mark my conversion. It was one of a host of things which were happening around me to which my eye was being opened for the first time. And I began to wander about the streets of Calcutta, sometimes alone, sometimes with friends.'

Sitting on the cane-bottomed settee, thinking of the past, his eyes unfocussed, he raised his slender bare arms against the blue-washed wall.

'From 1964, 1965, onwards, the way I was leading my life started appearing futile and meaningless. I retained a strong attachment to physics and poetry, but began to devote less time to it.'

In 1964 Dipanjan took his first degree from Presidency College, and began to do post-graduate work at Calcutta University Science College. At the same time there was a development in his personal life. He had met and proposed to Arati, and there was opposition from her family. Arati came from a distinguished brahmin family. Dipanjan was of the *kayastha* caste. Of this caste Dipanjan said, 'The kayastha caste is technically a shudra, but in West Bengal and elsewhere their possession of land had effectively Sanskritized them. They are a clerkly caste, scribes since the Mogul times or even before.'

Parallel with this turbulence, there was the economic crisis he had spoken about at the start of the morning.

'Since 1965 prices of rice and other foodstuffs had soared to unheard-of heights. Kerosene disappeared. Factories closed. Retrenched workers committed suicide. Even qualified engineers and doctors couldn't find jobs. In West Bengal there was a great uprising. This movement of the people between 1965 and 1966 completely changed the outlook of our generation.

'The people started off by confronting retailers in markets and insisting that they take their prices down. In places they looted godowns where grain was being hoarded illegally. When the government used the police against them, there was resistance by the demonstrators. From stone-throwing to setting public places and transport on fire – this has been a hallowed tradition of protest since British times. When someone sets a bus on fire, you know that now he means business.'

'Was your family affected by the rise in prices?'

'We personally – my family – could afford it. People were always talking about it – the prices, the crisis, the food riots, the failure of the government, the police firing. The movement was always called the Food Movement.'

It was organized by the ordinary political workers of a communist faction, and not by any of the big men of the party. Then in 1966 the students of Presidency College, Dipanjan's old college, formed a pro-communist movement for the first time. The leaders of this movement were expelled, and there was a six-month student agitation against their expulsion.

One night Dipanjan was coming back from South Calcutta by bus. He saw a crowd in the grounds of Presidency College. He got off the bus to see what it was about. He didn't find anyone he knew, but the next day, when he went back, he discovered that the leaders of the student movement, and others, were his friends. He began to spend more and more time with those friends, in Presidency College, in the coffee house opposite, and in the college hostel.

He began to do political work among those students who were not committed. 'There was a vocal minority who felt they had come to the college to study and build their careers. And we had to persuade them.' There was a feeling that the activists organizing the students and the Food Movement were Chinese agents. Dipanjan had to do a lot of reading to deal with these accusations. He started reading Marxist literature.

'This was the time of the Cultural Revolution in China, and it had tremendous influence in Calcutta – what the Chinese students were doing, and why they were doing it, and why there had to be a cultural revolution after a revolution proper.

'I was very excited. I thought that now I could start making my life meaningful. I had no consciousness of my father's political past in the party, or his uncle's past as a nationalist and a Gandhian. My father had by that time become an ordinary householder; he kept no contact with the party. My mother had also stopped being a communist. My father's nationalist uncle had become a bitter critic of the whole Indian polity. He never voted in his life, declaring that under no circumstances would he enter a process of choosing the least harmful among scoundrels.

'But I still lacked an ideology or philosophy, though all my time was being taken up by politics. I didn't return home some nights. Arati was getting extremely worried. My parents had almost written me off.'

'What were you doing at nights?'

'We would be talking with boys at the hostel until 11. We would then talk among ourselves until 12 or one. Then we would sleep on the lawn of Presidency College.'

This was how he was living in 1967, when he took his M.Sc. and got a job; and when – after all the turmoil with Arati's family – he and Arati were married, four years after he had proposed to her.

'It was a packed and exciting time, emotionally, intellectually. It was the start of my education in the world. I had been leading a sheltered life. I was academically minded. My mother was over-protective – I had this asthmatic condition. My mother cried a lot. It was her ambition for me that suffered greatly. My father, having been once bitten himself, was worried about the direction our movement would take.

'In Presidency College we slowly developed one central idea. We felt that the Indian communist movement had failed because the leadership, which was composed of middle-class intellectuals, had made itself into a bureaucracy. The initiative of the masses had never been developed. And then in April 1967 the Naxalbari incident occurred.'

This was the incident, in West Bengal, after which the Naxalite movement was named.

'I was reading the paper in the morning. I read this item on the front page. Peasants had surrounded a police party with bows and arrows and had shot down a police inspector, in the course of a struggle to occupy the lands monopolized by landlords, illegally for the most part.

'This was a dramatic incident. I just couldn't believe it – that this thing, which we had been reading about in our books, in Marxist literature, in history books, could really happen: that the toiling people could take up arms, and they could fight for their rights. And my mind was made up, and that of most of our friends at Presidency College: that this was the struggle with which we were going to link our lives. In Calcutta the first posters in support of the Naxalbari uprising were put up by us, on the wall opposite Presidency College.'

'Who were your friends?'

'Some had backgrounds like mine. Many of them were sons of impoverished gentry on this side of the border. We were all middle-class people.

'We immediately decided to go among the toiling people. Some of us went back to their villages. And some of us went to the industrial slums. There was a major involvement with the workers of the Guest Keen Williams factory in southern Howrah. A trade union leader there had sought us out. Soon in the villages and in the factories the news began to spread that students were coming from Calcutta to talk to people about how to change their conditions.'

'How did you fit this in with your work?'

'I was working in a morning college. So the afternoon and evening were free.'

'Weren't you nervous about knocking on people's doors?'

'I wasn't nervous about the industrial Workers. I could tune to their wavelength. But later, when I left my job – I changed many jobs – and went to the villages, my experiences were traumatic. But that was much later, in 1969.

'In 1967 we were still building up the student movement. I had to run to many places, taking political classes and having group discussions with students, equipping them with propaganda to fight the official party propaganda *against* the Naxalite movement. The party saw it as a threat to their organization.

'For the year or two after that I spent much time in Guest Keen Williams. Arati went with me at times. My life at that time would be something like this. At 2 a.m. I would return home walking, because the last bus or tram had passed. Or I would spend the time on Presidency College lawn, or in the building or the hostel if it rained. I would have to go back to work by 6.15, 6.30. Classes began then. At 10 I would be back at Presidency College. We would start discussions with the students of the college and with students who had come from colleges all over Calcutta and West Bengal to learn of the movement.

'The police were keeping an eye on us. They sent spies to the college. We caught one and gave him a beating up. There were frequent street fights with the police.'

'What was that like?'

'Whenever you go into a fight, whether it's a private fight or a fight with the police, you are nervous to start with. Then the tension slowly drains out, and excitement takes its place, and finally you are quite ready even to risk your own life. Traditionally in Calcutta you fight the police with brickbats. That is the ordinary kind of fight. A serious fight would involve home-made bombs and country-made guns. But such fights are rare, and only occur at the height of important political movements.'

I found this strange: his ability to talk of disturbances and fights in this academic, Aristotelian manner.

I said, 'You talk of these fights with the police as though you were protected in some way.'

Dipanjan said, 'The communists were then sharing power. We understood their dilemma. We knew that the police wouldn't be able to cross certain limits. This was the first time the communists were sharing power in West Bengal, and they couldn't throw themselves against the students and the workers. The very fact that the police had fired on the peasants at Naxalbari caused a division within the party, and brought over some senior communists on to the side of the Naxalite movement.

'In the evenings, after being with the students, we would go to the factories and the slums, or take political classes and conduct group discussions. We were slowly learning the classical Marxist political ideas – Marx, Lenin, Mao, all of them.

'And then, in 1969, we went to the villages. The communist party in West Bengal is pretty old, even in many of the rural areas, and grassroots leaders who wanted the struggle started helping the students who had come to their areas.

'We had a rule. You must have with you only a *lungi,* a cloth, a vest or singlet, and a towel. You went to the villages, identified the huts of the agricultural labourers or poor peasants, and you told them directly why you were there. You started talking immediately about the political aims – seizure of power by the toiling people. We called this Red Guard Action.

'The pioneers faced a lot of trouble getting their message across. But by the time I went to the villages, this fact was well known among the peasants. We kept just the fare back to the urban centre from which we had come, and no other money. And we kept a dhoti, a shirt, and pair of slippers for use in transit between the villages and towns.

'The peasants fed us when they could. In some new places sometimes they wouldn't, at the beginning. But on the whole everywhere they gave us a patient hearing. We slept in their huts. Usually, if they had only one room, and the hamlet was safe, composed only of poor people, we would sleep on the verandah. But this was a rare luxury. Usually we had to sleep concealed in a loft. As the state increased its repression, we would have to remain concealed the whole day. One or two of us had the experience of having to relieve themselves in pots.'

'Repression' – this, too, was strange: that after all he had gone through he should use this abstract word, and make it sound like something from a political textbook.

He went on: 'Two problems crept up. Amoebiasis, because drinking water is uniformly bad. And scabies. Because we had to bathe hurriedly, and on many days not at all. We lacked the know-how of keeping oneself clean in an Indian village. All the villagers know how to clean themselves with a little oil, a little alkaline ash, a little water – which we didn't. But this didn't really trouble us. This was the most exciting and the most interesting and fulfilling part of our political work: when we were moving among the villagers.

'The major problem at the beginning was that I felt that there was an invisible partition between us and the villagers, that we were talking two different languages. It took a long time to get accustomed to the silences and obliquities of rural India.'

'Make that a little more concrete.'

'Suppose I've come to a village where they're afraid to keep me. They won't tell me that outright. When I went to one such village in the evening, the people suggested to me that I should go with the boys to a nearby *jaira,* a whole-night theatrical performance, a high spot in the annual life of a village. They were hinting to me that I couldn't stay in any of their houses that night.'

'You haven't told me what it was like in the villages.'

'The quality of life was better than in the urban slums. Apart from a lepers' village, where – before harvest time – they had a little wheat, but so little they couldn't make chapattis. They made paste of the flour and served that in very small quantities. Children couldn't digest that paste. Hunger – getting one full meal a day – that was the major determining factor of the quality of village life for five months of the year at that time.'

And I was struck again – as I had been when he was telling of the dying man he had picked up from the Calcutta street – by the way he spoke of the distress of India: as though it was a personal idea, a personal observation, as though his group observed it better than others and with more understanding, as though this distress was something they were entitled to refer to, to explain their actions.

It was now well past midday, well past the normal lunch hour. He was tired. He said he wanted to have a shower. Arati had prepared the lunch, and when Dipanjan went to the back space to have his shower, she brought out the food and set it on a little stool for me: simple food, two pieces of fried fish, peas, puris. The fish was bony, not easy to pick at, but Arati said that if I used my fingers I could feel the bones better and get rid of them.

Standing in the little room while I ate, she talked again of the heat of the summer in Calcutta; and again she asked whether I was staying for that. She talked again of the trees that had been cut down. I asked her whether Indians hated trees, whether there was some idea that trees sheltered or encouraged bad spirits. She said no, Indians loved trees; but now there were simply too many people, and the trees had to be cut down.

Dipanjan had left her during her first pregnancy, she said – when he went to live in the villages. She had gone to stay with his parents. That was the Indian way, the custom here: the wife stayed with her in-laws. In order to write about India, she said, you had to spend a lot of time in India. There were so many things of India that were different.

She said she had been sympathetic to the cause in the beginning. But she didn't like that idea of going to the villages, taking revolution to the people. She thought it was foolish. The poor here in India believed in their fate. That going out to the villages had set the revolution back by 40 years. And she didn't like it when the murders began. She didn't like that at all.

Dipanjan and I hadn't got to that yet: Dipanjan had promised that for another day, perhaps tomorrow.

Perhaps, I said to Arati, the flaw had lain in that very idea of revolution, that idea of a particular moment when everything changes and the world is made good, and men are made anew.

She didn't take the point up.

Turgenev had written a novel about that, I said. He had written a novel about middle-class people in Russia in the late 1860s taking revolution to the workers. Perhaps if people had read that book without prejudice they mightn't have made the misjudgement that the people in the novel had made. But she hadn't read Turgenev;

she didn't know *Virgin Soil.* Her Russian reading didn't go back so far; her Russian reading appeared to have gone back only as far as the classical political texts.

Standing sideways in the doorway, looking out at the verandah and the white early-afternoon light in the lane, the light that was still only the light of spring, she said reflectively that people in other countries seemed to be withdrawing from Marxism.

She wasn't a tall woman. But she was sturdy; and she was still shapely.

She said she had spent some time in England, when Dipanjan had gone there to do higher studies in physics, after all that business was over. And what she had seen in England, and especially what she had noted about the position of women in England, had further shaken her up. Perhaps, she said, Marx was wrong. And I found it moving: such passion, in that tiny cluttered room, with the threat of the summer to come.

At dinner that evening, in a large apartment in central Calcutta, I met someone who had known Dipanjan as a fellow student at Presidency College. Dipanjan had been a talented and even brilliant student, I heard. Then this Naxalite business had occurred, and there had been the dreadful time when it seemed that Dipanjan, married to someone from a very distinguished Calcutta family, might have been hanged. Since that Naxalite business they hadn't met, Dipanjan and the man who was talking to me.

The man said, 'He was a better student than I was. Now he teaches physics. I do physics – that's the difference between us. The college he teaches at is awful. He must know that. He is wasting his talent there. He should return to the mainstream.'

But that wasn't a subject he felt he would be able to raise with Dipanjan, if they were to meet. The matter was too embarrassing. All that Naxalite, communist involvement – in which, from his own account, Dipanjan for the first time in his sheltered life appeared to have found community, drama, and purpose – now lay like an embarrassment between Dipanjan and the other world he had known.

Perhaps, the man said, Dipanjan was too ashamed to meet the people he had once known. So he lived where he did, and taught in that poor college. It was the same when he had gone to England: he had lived in the simplest kind of bedsitter.

Someone else at the dinner said that this kind of disappearing, this hiding away, was a very Bengali thing to do.

And I thought of Dipanjan coming out of the lane early that morning to meet me – in his cloth and shirt – coining after all those other people from the poor settlement with their respectable fronts, their briefcases and dispatch-boxes. From what he had said at our first meeting, I had got the impression that he taught at his college out of a fellow feeling with the students, 'defeated soldiers'. And my first idea was that some similar feeling of social responsibility had made him live where he lived. But no; it wasn't like that. He lived where he did because he couldn't do better. In the villages he had suffered; in the town now he suffered almost as much, from the dust and the mosquitoes, and his wife suffered from the heat. He had chosen a hard way; and neither he nor his wife was used to harsh conditions.

*

I went to see him the next morning at the college, and took in again the details of the two-storey building, with its Calcutta-style classical ornament, its pediment, and the columns in pairs inset in the walls on both storeys. The green shutters were coated with the grainy black grime of fumes and dust – you could write in that grime. The small trees in the small college yard were discoloured with dust; only the fresh shoots of the spring showed green and clear. Slowly burning mounds of old, flattened, garden rubbish sent pungent smoke into the air, not unpleasant, a gentler smell of autumn in the Calcutta spring. It was a Calcutta custom, this burning of garden waste even in the centre of the city, and it added to the brown haze. Many broken brown classroom tables and chairs had been placed that morning in a jumble on the small untended lawn of the college yard, where weeds grew out of litter mounds.

Upstairs, broken window panes and door panes had been replaced by wire netting of various meshes. The tarnished label, *Department of Physics,* done with screw-down metal letters, looked incongruous. The wavering line of dust on the red floor – the dust Dipanjan and I had spoken about two days before – was still there. In the choked room or cell at the side, the rings made by the soda bottles and the saucers of two days before had not been wiped.

Dipanjan made a half wave at the rings on the table, a half nod at the dust in the room with the lab tables, and said, 'It will *never* be cleaned.'

We sat in the cell, he in his old chair, I in the one I had sat in, facing each other across the little table. The table was really quite multifariously stained. A narrow strip of white-tiled wall showed behind the olive or khaki-coloured metal cupboards and between the cupboards. Brown drips, from some unknown source, had coagulated on the tiles.

I told him that there were certain things I hadn't found in what he had told me. He had talked of going to the Guest Keen Williams workers in Calcutta. How had he done that? Who was the first worker he had talked to? I hadn't got many pictures from his narrative. He had gone to the villages – how had he done that? Had he just taken a bus or a train to a particular village? Could he go beyond certain abstractions – 'workers', 'villages', 'peasants', 'repression'?

He accepted what I said. He offered to fill in details. He talked first of the time in 1967 when he had gone among the Guest Keen Williams workers in Calcutta.

'One of my friends had been living in the Guest Keen Williams slum for some time, and he had met this second-rank communist leader. My friend asked me to come over to judge whether this man was a genuinely revolutionary man. I took a bus from Presidency

College, crossing Howrah Bridge. I got off at Howrah station and caught another bus, and that went through the crowded streets of Howrah to the Guest Keen Williams gate.'

(A week or so later I made the same journey myself, with someone from the Guest Keen Williams company. A year-long company lockout had just come to an end, and the inactivity of a year showed in the yard, in the tropical weeds and the post-monsoon rust. The company was one of those lumbering former British companies that had grown slack during the times of near-monopoly; it couldn't adapt easily to new conditions. The company's troubles of 1966–67 had been the beginning of its long decline. In 1966, when the Indian economy was in a bad way, Indian Railways, on which Guest Keen Williams was more or less traditionally dependent, cut their orders by more than half. For six or seven months in 1967 the points and crossings department, and the crossing-sleepers department, had no work. The bolt and nut department was also affected. Workers got their wages, but they got only the minimum. This was what I was told by the company: this was the background to Dipanjan's story.)

Dipanjan said, 'My friend and I waited for a long time at the gate. We looked at the union shack. We talked to the people there. Workers were coming out of the gate. I saw the variety of the people – Muslims, Hindus, Biharis, Bengalis. I was exhilarated, but the man my friend wanted me to see unfortunately didn't turn up.

'The next visit I remember was this. The company was bringing in some new machines, and some workers were going to be laid off on half pay. The role envisaged for us by the organizer of the splinter communist union was that we should go to the slums inhabited by non-Bengali workers, whom the unions hadn't succeeded in recruiting. These workers were anti-communist.

'Late one afternoon many of us had entered the slums. I found myself in a room in one of the huts, and here is this Bihari sitting on a string bed in the space outside his hut.'

'How old?'

'Middle-aged. Reticent at first. But he smiles, and then I start talking about the machines that were going to come. I talked in Hindi, which I didn't know well at that time. He was friendly but non-committal.

'And here is another scene I remember – some time later. I began to go to this slum in the evenings. I had been asked to speak to the workers about Marxism. By that time the splinter union had a large following. This was a Muslim hut, and I was waiting with one of the workers. I had still not got used to the conditions of their life, and what I remember most after 20 years is that there was a public drain running through the room. That is the main thing I remember. Then I went to the class, to talk on Marxism. I don't think I got my meaning across. They were tired, and I was speaking at too abstract a level, as I now understand.

'I was in this euphoric world. I was very young, and some of the Muslim workers – I am talking now about workers in the docks, where I went later – were telling us to go back home to our parents, who were crying for us, and to go back to our studies. I remember I asked one of these workers, "Why should I go back? And why aren't you coming forward and helping me with my work?"'

'How old was he?'

'This chap was middle-aged. I still remember what he said in his Hindustani: "We have come here to make money." It occurred to me that I was being too theoretical. But the party had said that workers in the town were "backward" compared to the peasants, and I had that rationalization to fall back on.'

I said, 'Arati didn't like you going to the villages.'

'In mid-68 I told her I would be going. When I actually had to go, she was pregnant. She cried. She didn't think it was a great thing to do, but she didn't think it was a foolish thing to do at that time. She felt I was betraying her. To some extent I felt that myself.'

'How did you go to the villages?'

'It was another anti-climax, at first. We had certain well-developed urban centres outside Calcutta. I took a train and went to one of them. It was a two-and-and-a-half-hour journey. I went to a factory-worker's house. I knew the house. I had gone there before on certain errands. He was a refugee from East Bengal. He had built a small house of his own, in a ramshackle and dirty part of the town.

'That same day I met one of the village comrades. He was expecting me. We leave the next day by bus. I have a canvas bag, but with nothing in it, only a dhoti. We get down in the late afternoon. My clothes don't stick out, but my glasses do, and my Calcutta accent. We walk for half an hour and reach the village centre, where all the people support us. That night there is a meeting to decide upon a course of action. I don't attend the meeting.

'At night we go to eat in someone's hut. The village people have arranged collectively for the food. The rice is wet. It's not been strained at all, because that rice-water itself is food, and there is a lot of that wet rice. And I can't eat it. It's a strain for me, because I can't throw it away either. My city stomach is just too small for it. And there is nothing else to eat, and nobody is going to eat a real meal again until the next night.'

'What are you eating off? Plates? Leaves?'

'Metal plates. It's a thatched hut. We are eating outside, in an open space. No lights except for the sky, and quite a lot of mosquitoes. I am disconcerted.'

'Why?'

He switched tenses. 'I was afraid of what I had to face the next day – communication-wise. We slept on a string bed outside the hut – two of us to a bed, and that was pretty uncomfortable, because a string bed sags in the middle. I had a sense of forlornness and apprehension. In the villages there are no lavatories. There are certain fields – with nearby pools of water – that are set aside for the purpose.

'Next morning a better-off peasant (he had a radio) gave us tea – which is not common in the villages: the villagers at that time didn't have hot drinks. In the afternoon we were given another meal – again of rice – because we were going off on another journey on foot. A journey of three to four hours.

'I found it hard to keep up with the peasant guide. We reached our destination in the evening. I was charged up with my politics, but they were going slowly and calmly about their everyday tasks. I noticed that, and I felt like a fool. In the cities everyone was boiling, and here were these peasants, who were supposed to be the main force of the revolution, quite impassive. I felt let down, and I began to feel homesick for Calcutta.

'The next afternoon I began to walk back to the nearest party centre, which was in a very small town. I don't remember any of the physical stress, and I don't think it made any impact on me. All I remember is that I had to walk about six hours, because I had no money – we were not supposed to take any. While I walked, buses were plying.

'This was how I began my Red Guard Action. And then I felt I was doing my work at last.'

I said, 'You know I don't want any names. But none of the people you are talking about have any faces. I can't see them.'

Dipanjan said, 'There are faces. But when we began with the Guest Keen Williams workers we were following the communist tradition in which people are objects, not living subjects making their own lives – and history in that process. Our interaction at the human level was mainly within our own political set. Which is why when that Muslim dock-worker asked me why I didn't go back to my family, it made such an impression on me. Even today I believe that conversation was on a different level.

'I would like to make a further comment. The faces of my friends are with me. But most of them are still active politically, and I want to make no comment on them.'

An event then occurred, on 1 May 1969, which called Dipanjan back from the villages to Calcutta. On that day, at a public meeting on the Calcutta Maidan, the great central park of Calcutta, the communist faction that had been organizing the Naxalite peasant movement announced its separate identity as the Communist Party of India (Marxist-Leninist).

Dipanjan said, 'My parents rejected the new party. Arati was not pleased at all. At this stage she would have liked me to leave politics. Our daughter was to be born in October. I stayed on in Calcutta, working politically in the docks, until the end of 1969. And then I returned to the villages.

'The earlier comrades had been asking the peasants to form their own organizations, to seize political power and, in the process, to confiscate landlords' lands and, later, guns – to harvest forcibly the produce of their lands, to take the produce of the landlords' lands. And build centres of peasants' power, as opposed to landlords' power, in the villages.

'And, in fact, there had been a big peasant uprising in the region in the harvest season. I was too late for that. It was during this uprising that the party line about individual killing arrived. The killings were to be carried out by conspiratorially constituted squads. And this time, when I began my Red Guard Action, I had to ask the peasants to form annihilation squads, as they were called.

'This time, for me, the first trauma about the villages and noncommunication was over. I had learned a little. I began this Red Guard Action with more conviction and less nervousness. This was an extensive journey, lasting many months, six months to a year. I moved from village to village, community to community, tribals and non-tribals, untouchables and farmer castes. I really learned about India.'

'What did you feel about the new directive?'

'Many of the comrades before had succeeded in forming squads and carrying out annihilations, mainly in the area covered by the old uprising of the harvest season, based on land and harvest – occupation of land, and forcible harvesting.'

'Were you shocked by the directive?'

'No, no. Indians are basically a very violent people. I was doing Red Guard Action in new areas, and in spite of my best efforts I could not persuade the peasants to carry out a single annihilation – which was a cause of great remorse to me, and led to a feeling of inadequacy.'

'Do you remember how you did the asking?'

'Oh, yes. I asked a peasant in whose hut I was staying. I remember that hut very well. They had a new-born baby, and she was being fed rice-water instead of milk – in a bottle – something which appeared quite shocking to me. These people were like others we talked to. They had very little land, enough for perhaps three months' sustenance. The party had asked us all to concentrate on these people.

'I asked this man, "Who is the most hated landlord of the area?" He named the landlord. I told him, "Why don't you kill him off?" He brings another peasant that evening, and asks me to broach the subject with him. The two of them agree that that landlord should be killed off, but they refused to do it themselves.'

'Did the idea shock them?'

'The idea didn't shock them. As I keep on telling you, we are a very violent people. I tried to convince them, coming and going, for about two months.

'My life was a concealed life in that hut. If the landlord knew of my presence he would have killed me or handed me over to the police. I knew it was dangerous. I knew I had exceeded the law. But killing a man is nowhere considered contrary to any ethical code. You must understand that the *Ramayana* and the *Mahabharata* rule the everyday religious code of the Hindus, just as the Koran does for the Muslims, and these are books which extol killing for a greater purpose. I should think that, like any other Indian, I had no sense of ethical outrage in advocating killing for a cause.'

'Gandhi?'

'Of the many ideals of Gandhi which the Indians didn't accept, *ahimsa,* non-violence, stands out most.'

'The Jains?'

'They're a strange sect. But it's the wrong perspective of India you have, when you mention these religions – Buddhism, Jainism, and Gandhi. I point to what happened in Kampuchea, Ceylon, Burma, China – all countries ostensibly under the umbrella of Buddha and Confucius. All these peoples are very violent.'

'Let's go back to the villages.'

'As I said, I began to feel inadequate. In late 1970 and early 1971 the movement as a whole faced a setback, and many of my friends started re-thinking.

'In the last few months, before my arrest, I had become involved with tribal people. I got to like them very much. I felt at home with them. I understood their political aspirations. For the first time I had come across a section of peasants who thought and acted politically. I used to talk a lot to a schoolmaster among them. These months were very satisfying, the most satisfying of my life in the villages, more so because the doubts that my friends in the movement had developed about the line of individual killing – these doubts gave me the latitude to talk freely without the party trammels, which I was beginning to find impractical.'

'How many people were annihilated in your area?'

'More than 10 people were killed in the area because of this line. Most of them were landlords.'

But now the police were closing in.

'Our friends had to break off from the party, and many of us had to keep on the move, in Bihar and Bengal. One night, at about eight or nine, we were at a food shop by a railway station in north Bihar. There were some policemen in plain clothes there, shirts and trousers. They were from the Bengal Police, and they were in search of some other Naxalites. They had come to the railway food shop to buy some cooked meat for themselves. One of my friends was recognized, and we were arrested.

'At that time the police had started killing off Naxalites, and my first reaction was that they would kill us off. This reign of terror was by this time six months old, and I had accustomed myself to such a fate – just to keep myself going.

'The policemen at the food stall were older than us. They were not abusive. They took us to the police station. There we immediately tried to influence the Bihari police officer in charge of us to prevent these policemen from Bengal from killing us.

'The Bihari officer, an educated man, said, "I do respect you. You work for the country. But my duty as a police officer places me against you." We laughed at him. "Why are you mocking us? These Bengali police officers will kill us in a few minutes' time."

'They tied us with some ropes, and on the way the policemen gave us some blows, harping on the fact that we were Bengalis. The Bihari police officer was shocked, and immediately informed the whole police circuit of Bihar by radio of our arrest, so the Bengali policemen couldn't kill us, if that had been their intention.

'Most of us were never tried. Only a few were tried and convicted. The rest of us were kept under detention without trial until the amnesty of 1977 in West Bengal.

'I was in prison until October 1972, in Calcutta. In prison I found two things which disheartened me. The first was the quality of the Naxalite prisoners from Calcutta. We had been hearing that they had been killing individual policemen, even traffic constables, and suspected spies. The prison was full with Naxalites, especially young boys, and they were not politically oriented at all. What had happened was that there had been an upheaval against the school system – boys and girls forced into the school system, who had then dropped out, and had been recruited by the party for urban violence.

'The party had fragmented. My own ideas were not clear. I felt there had been maladies within the movement. I felt that my political search had reached a dead end, and I would have to begin anew. And for some time I could not think of myself as a political worker any longer.

'After I came to the Calcutta prison I could meet my parents and Arati regularly. No case could be proved against me. I remained in preventive detention. Finally, I wrote the government that if they released me, I would go abroad for further studies in physics.'

The petition was granted. He was accepted by London University, and his father paid his fare to England. The police went with him right up to the plane. He completed his Ph.D. in London, and then came back to Calcutta. This was in September 1974.

I asked him, 'What do you think now?'

He fingered his glasses, squinted, and looked out through the window. I was sitting across the narrow table from him, in a chair with arms, between the two tall metal cupboards. Behind him was an empty room, with patches of new, level plaster on the walls.

He said, 'The major mistake, the basic misunderstanding of the Marxist position – I feel the people must liberate themselves. The intellectuals can only hand them the equipment for doing so.'

He now did civil rights work, and taught in the slums. 'I see no discontinuity with my earlier political search. Between going to the urban slums, and this teaching in the slums.' He leaned back against an olive-green metal cupboard, and considered the sky. 'Society is so structured that the toiling people can never find their own voice, their own view of the world, their own identity.'

I asked about Arati, and her time in England.

'It altered her world. Because she found for the first time that a woman was not merely or at all the appendage of a some man. I was very happy to come back here. Arati cried for days, and her friends who were brought up never to show their emotions in public were unhappy for her. Given the choice, she would have continued to live in England – this feeling of freedom, and recognition of her as an individual.

'I had this running fight with her from 67 to 72 – I could not convince her that if we stayed with my parents we would always be dominated by them. She did not recognize the domination as such. And only when we went to England she realized what I was saying.

Until then she regarded that as part of my eccentricity – which, for example, had led me into the Naxalite movement. I used to say, "Let's take an apartment." Or: "Why don't you stand up to my mother? Why do you carry out everything my father says, even when it is hurting you?" She never knew there could be a different way of life. Nowadays things have changed, and are changing, but in the 1960s she was in no way an exception in her view of life.'

This gave an added point to what Arati had said at her house the previous day, when Dipanjan was having his shower. When Dipanjan had gone to live in the villages, Arati said, she had gone to live with Dipanjan's parents. In India a wife stayed with her inlaws; you moved from your parents' house to your husband's parents' house. India was different from other places; you had to know many things in order to write about India.

But now they lived by themselves.

I asked Dipanjan, 'Are you happy in the little house?'

'Yes. As far as Arati and I are concerned, the material side of life has never been important. Both of us are capable of hard physical toil.'

'What about the disorder of your bookcase there – tilings just thrown together? And the dust – can I mention the dust? You were saying that the college is a corporate place, and that is why it will never be cleaned.'

He said, 'I am ashamed of that, in my house. Both of us are overworked and can't find the time. Arati works as a teacher of physics in a morning college. She works there from 6.30 to 10 – and you have to add an hour to go there, and two hours to come back. But I am ashamed of that disorder in my house. And say "dust", if you like. My grandfather would have taken me to task. But *no one* is ashamed of this place. That's the difference.'

'Do you feel that the most active part of your life is over?'

'Not at all. My life so far has been the first part of the search.'

'May I ask this? You have spent so much time thinking of others. Isn't that arrogant? Shouldn't you have also thought of developing your own talent? You don't have to answer. If you don't want to answer, I'll withdraw the question and not refer to it.'

'I'll answer. The most brilliant boy of the year before me at Presidency College is now a renowned professor in the U.S.A. He asked me the same question. Not the arrogance part. In physics the questions which interested me I found were beyond my ability to answer. I worked on them; I thought about them. I still work on them – or, I should say, I still read about them. But less difficult questions cannot hold my interest. In poetry I am never satisfied with what I write, and especially because the type of poetry I write can only appeal to a few people like myself. But I find helping others is something I can tackle, although I make mistakes. I keep on learning from them.'

Ashok's first story had been about his attempt to get into marketing, and his entanglement with IMBA, the Institute of Management and Business Administration, run by Dr Malhotra of Delhi. His second story was about his marriage, his break with the past.

He said, 'I eventually went into an advertising agency, and was immediately happy. My career righted itself from here. I grew in my job; I learned a lot about the real world of marketing; it was the most productive five years of my career.

'But this went with an upheaval in another aspect of my life. I came from a traditional South Indian brahmin household. My father had travelled on various postings all over the world and had settled in Calcutta. And I had a public-school upbringing in India. Yet so ingrained was the traditional outlook of the family that I had never thought of dating girls, although I was popular, and sang pop songs and Indian classical songs. In this Indian classical side I had been trained at home by a private tutor; it was part of one's traditional upbringing.

'A number of my friends were leading an active social life, but I myself didn't see this as either necessary or indeed desirable. Other people did it, had girl friends, but I felt that wasn't for me. I suppose it was deeply in my subconscious that I would get married in the traditional arranged way – until I actually went to participate in a ceremony of "viewing" a girl with the object of marriage.

'My family had arranged it in the standard way, through the exchange of horoscopes. The girl lived in Bangalore, and I went all the way down there to see her. There were hordes of my relatives there, and her relatives. We were told to arrive at the appointed place, which was of the girl's parents' choosing, at a certain time.

'It was in the evening. The occasion itself involved everybody sitting round in a circle. I was introduced only to the girl's father, and we sat round in a circle in the hall. Savouries and sweets were passed around. And everyone was dressed for the occasion. So peculiar were the arrangements, I wasn't sure who the girl was. There were other girls from her side, and I hadn't been introduced to the girl herself, and the girl's father kept up a constant chatter, asking me a whole host of questions about what I did, and what I liked, and what I disliked, and so on.

'Alarmingly, he also started talking about possible marriage venues. So I found responding in a normal way difficult. He would say, "I would rather hold the wedding in Sholapur than in Bangalore, because I have better facilities in Sholapur. What do you think?"

'And you couldn't say no and you couldn't say yes. If you said no, it would have been rude. If you said yes, it would have been nonsense. So one indulged in a series of diplomatic half-volleys. One smiled vaguely. I was relieved when the hour was over. When people asked me what I thought, I kept saying I didn't know.

'One was supposed to make up one's mind about a girl whom one did not actually get to meet, with whom one did not exchange a word, and who was just about surreptitiously pointed out by one of my relatives. One was supposed to make up one's mind at the end of the occasion.

'It also disturbed me that the girl apparently had no say in the matter. Certainly everybody – all the 20, 30 people there – was anxiously waiting to know whether I had given the green signal. On these occasions it's all weighted in favour of the boy, and the girl's family occupies the inferior position.

'Many years later a feeling of shame crystallizes around the memory. But at that point the feeling was one of embarrassment, though even today boys and girls get married in the way I chose not to then. In fairness to them, I should say they have no choice. It's not fair for me to tell anyone to follow my example. Perhaps if it had been handled differently, I might have been less embarrassed.

'At the end, while we were trooping out, saying goodbye, it occurred to me – in a trice – that I wouldn't like to go through this again.

'We went back to our family house. I was confused. In the car were my brother, his wife, my father, and I. I was quite silent, and remained silent. They knew I was unhappy. I pushed off to a friend's house and stayed there till late. I was scheduled to leave Bangalore the next day. What was worrying me was that my family had given the girl's parents the promise that they would revert to them the next day.

'When I went back home later that night, my father and my brother asked me what I had decided to do – did I want to marry the girl? I said no. My father said, "No problem. We'll find another girl."

'I told my father I wasn't saying no because I didn't like the girl's face – that would have been unfair: I hadn't had a chance to talk to the girl. I was saying no to the process, not to the girl. And I didn't want to talk about it any more.

'My elders thought that time would heal things, that this was my first time, and that the next time round would be different.

'I became less and less communicative. It's in the situation that parents and children don't talk openly about these things. Nobody ever asks you what your views on marriage are. It just happens that one fine day somebody presents you with a proposal.

'And it was at this time that, spurred on by the thought that I would have to go through with that viewing process once more or many times more, my mind gradually turned towards the principle of making up my own mind who I wanted to marry.

'There was someone I had known, a marketing executive. Marketing – it's always been marketing for me. But this girl I knew came from another community. I declared myself to her. We agreed that it could be a workable proposition. We knew each other socially. We spoke the same language. But she was of a different community. And when I finally broached the subject to my parents, they were as opposed as I thought they would be. They went into a shell, withdrew – as I had withdrawn after the viewing ceremony at Bangalore. It was difficult to communicate with them, because in a situation like this they had a certain crude logic on their side: in a matter like this there could be no half-way compromise. For them I was about to break the family link with history, tradition, and they could have no vision of the future. For them everything appeared to become black.

'I was on test, too, because the person I wanted to marry wanted to see how I would react to pressure. So it was important to me to stand up. I told my parents I wasn't going to change my mind, but I wasn't in a hurry. They could take their time. It was very hard for them, but slowly they came round. They were counselled by some people in the family and by friends. Our wedding was held in the traditional grand manner.

'Today we are physically apart, in different cities, my wife and I in Calcutta, my parents elsewhere. This distance has helped us to adjust to each other. We meet once in a while, a couple of times a year, and we have a cordial relationship. My brothers and sisters have married in the traditional way, and they live with my parents in the same city. But there is no great bonhomie among them. It is my view that the South Indian brahmin cannot let himself go; everything is restrained.

'Among the younger generation of the family, I became a hero. Quite a few members of the family have done what I have done. And it's not now quite the shock that it had been. But one also has to accept – what my parents felt but couldn't express, what made them go into their shell – that something indefinable has snapped. We've been brahmins for untold generations.'

Fifteen years or so had passed since the end of the Naxalite rebellion, but Debu – who was now a high executive in a big company – still looked forward to a new, true revolution. Debu had taken part in the rebellion in its early stages. He had then fallen out ideologically with some elements of the leadership, and had had to hide from both police and former associates. He could chart, precisely and convincingly, how the revolution of love and compassion had turned into simple nihilism, with people talking of revolution and peasant power, but never actually taking on the state, or the powerful or the protected, concentrating instead on the weak and the exposed. But there was still in Debu some idea that a fresh and better start might be made.

He said, 'The only change – a big change – between then and now is that at that time, in the late 60s, I thought I would be a part of the revolution, and now I know that I shall be a *witness* to it. A supportive witness. I don't think the need for revolution has changed.' And going on from there to talk of his involvement, he dropped a half-thought: 'Once you've tasted blood –'

Tasting blood – strange metaphor.

Debu said, 'Organizing large masses of people.' And he meant something else as well: experiencing the love the people offered to those who were trying to do something for them. 'Love is a trite word. You cannot describe the thing I mean – it was something welling up and touching you. At that time I thought this was to do with loyalty to the party. Now I feel that the party always is the person. That is what I mean by the taste of blood: the people give you a million times more than what you might ultimately give them.'

He was born in the late 1930s, into the Calcutta middle class. But when Debu was young, his father, a professional man, had a serious illness that lasted for some years; and the family became poor. They were helped by friends, but isolated by their own relatives.

Some of those relatives, when they came to visit, said things like: 'When you want to sell those chairs, you must let us know. We might want to buy them.' The chairs were real, not just a figure of speech. When I met Debu again, and he took me to his large apartment, after a little tour of middle-class central Calcutta, and the once British clubs, I saw the chairs in his drawing-room: low, old-fashioned, ebony or black-lacquer Bengali chairs, a complete set. They would have reminded him every day of those hard years of his father's illness; they would have confirmed him every day in the distrust of the class from which he had come.

He had thought for so long about those years that the story came out easily, like a simple fable, together with the political moral he drew from it. There were four components of the Bengali middle class, he said: caste, education, family history, and money. The first three stayed with his family when they fell, but lack of money took them to the outer limit of the class.

He couldn't forget that. Even when his family circumstances improved, he remained an 'achiever', passionate to do well at school and college. Even when he was playing cricket – at which he was good – that passion to achieve, to do well at his school, was with him. He punished himself. He said that for six years he worked 16 hours a day. Finally, when he was twenty-two, he had his reward. He became an executive in one of the boxwallah companies, at a time when the Calcutta boxwallah world still had 10 years or so to go.

It was only then that he could look around. He read a book about President Kennedy, and decided, with some young accountants, to do social work in the slums. The group had vague political ideas; they were not connected with any political party. Their primary idea was the old Bengali idea of the Motherland, the idea that Bengal had given to the rest of India, Debu said: the idea that India had to be a country one could be proud of. The idea had decayed in Bengal since Independence, Debu said. 'In my class the idea is still there, but it is a remnant of the past – considered an anachronism – and in the class above, the industrialists and businessmen, the idea exists more or less as a negative quantity.'

The slum work became serious. Debu was giving it three evenings a week and two mornings a week. He already had a distrust of his middle class. Now he saw, close to, the injustices of society lower down. He saw how the middle classes were responsible; and he saw also the *chain* of injustice.

'You had Sir So-and-so, the landlord of a slum. He would do whatever he was doing to the widowed housewives of that particular slum through his lower-middle-class agent. The agent would have his own agents among the lower class in the lumpen proletariat. This was the chain. If you disposed of the landlord, he would be replaced by someone else. The chain itself would go on.'

After three or four years with his firm, Debu went to the United States on a one-year business fellowship. As part of the deal, he gave lectures on India. He found the experience unexpectedly humiliating. At the end of every lecture there would always be some questioner asking, 'How come you're starving and begging for food, if you're so great?' And there would always be someone making a shaming comparison between India and China.

He started to study Marxism and Indian history, and he decided that when he went back to Calcutta at the end of the year he would join the more radical of the communist parties. This was the time of the Food Movement, when India was going through its worst food crisis. Sixty people had been shot by the police in West Bengal, and people were eating 'milo'.

'This was a derivative of maize which the Americans fed their pigs, and which they had sent over as charity, and the Government of India were dishing out in their ration shops to feed the village poor. I was very ashamed and angry. To me it wasn't the *poor* who were eating it. It was Indians and Bengalis.'

He joined the Communist Party (Marxist) and began to work in the villages. He lived with the peasants. In the main he did propaganda. He also tried to stop black-marketing in rice. He and his fellow workers did this by stopping the movement of rice out of the villages. They also worked to prevent the eviction of share-croppers.

Debu began to rise in the party. The Bengali *bhadra-lok*, the middle class, loved what was foreign, and Debu found that being a foreign-returned person and an English speaker was helping him up even in the Communist Party (Marxist). This was unsettling, but it was also the time when Debu began to have the almost mystical experience of receiving the love of the people. He placed no limit on the time he wanted to give to the cause, no limit on the risk he was prepared to take; and the people in return gave him love.

'People I didn't know at all – peasants, labourers – no one among them ever said, "You can't stay here. We can't give shelter to this friend of yours."'

He formed a committee to fight revisionism in the party, but then he himself became disenchanted with the party. He found that at the lower levels of the party leadership there was a lot of minor corruption: people were stealing fish or rice that had been collected for the party. When he complained to a higher-level committee, he was accused by them of being a CIA agent. He began to feel that some people were trying to push him out of the party.

But he had also begun to write articles about the peasant movement, and these articles had got the attention of the people who were later to form the Naxalite faction of the party. Some of these articles were read out on Peking Radio; to the Naxalites, as bhadra-lok as any in their love of the foreign, this was the highest recognition. Debu became important in the councils of the faction. The leader of the faction, when he came to Calcutta, began to stay in Debu's house.

'I had come into this movement through indignation felt abroad at the position of India. And since most of the people of India were poor and lived in villages, this indignation focussed on the poor. I was convinced you needed an *overturning* brought about by the poor, since my class and the class above stank, and no redemption could even begin to come from them. And this is where the abstract part comes: the entire concept of *overturning* came from Marxism as interpreted by Lenin and particularly by Mao. At this time there were two classes of books about Russia and China. On one side were the cold warriors. And on the other were the starry-eyed – Han Suyin, Felix Greene, Edgar Snow. One rejected the cold warriors. I say this with hindsight.

'When the Naxalite movement started – with its attempts to inform and involve the mass of the people – it was quite different from what the other communist parties had been doing. And I want to tell you that I started believing it could be done, it could happen here now. It was the transformation of desire into belief.

'The Naxalites were not using quotations only from Marx, but from Rabindranath and Vivekananda and Romain Rolland. In their wall posters they gave *facts* about poverty, the amount of food available, the wage scales. And one could see people reading them, and even the illiterates understood them when somebody read them out to them. And above all there was the business of not wanting office, staying away from the electoral process – which had become quite filthy, a matter of money and compromise.

'And now comes the agony, for someone like me. If you have to do something big, you have to be organized in a big way. To be organized in a big way, you needed a command structure. And with a command structure you had battles between individuals for positions in that command structure.

'In communist parties you fight your inner party battles with a thesis and a programme for revolution, and then there are debates, accompanied by expulsions and counter-expulsions, until in the end you have a small group of people or an individual left in supreme command. The style in which this takes place varies from country to country – that grows up from the soil, the culture, the traditions.

'In Bengal we were heavily struck by several things. There was the bhadra-lok tradition I've told you about – not in the sense that it led to any gentlemanliness in the struggle, but in the sense that the bhadra-lok is upper caste and Hindu, and has a fixation with the foreign. The upper-caste Bengali is governed by certain laws of inheritance which make internecine war a way of life. That informed our actions very much. We forgot the other political groups, even the extreme communalists. The fight among ourselves was bitter. In this fight you might say that the people became secondary. The level of our intensity was very great; our quarrels were correspondingly bitter. It wasn't at all an abstract ideological war. It was like a family conflict which had strong overtones of violence.

'A second, later development was parallel: the sanction of individual killing.' This went with other things, which Debu now outlined. "The seizure of college and school buildings, the destruction of laboratories and libraries – since it was considered that this educational system created enemies of the people. The rewriting of our history. The destruction of the statues of people like Raja Ram Mohun Roy and Vivekananda.' Ram Mohun Roy, out of whose teachings the Brahmo Samaj and the Bengali Renaissance had arisen, which had given so much to India and the nationalist cause, and which still remained dear to people like Chidananda Das Gupta. Vivekananda, the religious teacher – quotations from whose writings had appeared on the first Naxalite wall posters. 'They were considered people who had compromised with imperialism, and served the interests of the landlords and the then ruling classes. Along with this came the slogan: "China's chairman is our chairman."'

Stage by abstract stage, from a raw, humiliated concern with the poor and India, to cultural and economic suicide, new compulsions and violations, and a cause far removed from the peasant's hunger.

The leader of the Naxalite faction was called Charu Mazumdar. Debu knew him well.

Debu said, 'I was present at the small meeting in Calcutta when Charu Mazumdar first unveiled that policy, of individual killing. He had already spoken of this in the villages, and had sent out letters to individual units. This was the first time he was talking about it in Calcutta, and I actually went with him to the meeting.

'It was in North Calcutta, in a lower-middle-class home. I remember a short corridor and a small room. The corridor was full of slippers left by those sitting on the floor in the small room. It was a late-evening meeting, a local meeting.

'I had tremendous admiration for Charu Mazumdar then, and I have admiration now. He was the most intense person I had ever met. And he truly believed in what he spoke about. He put tremendous faith in the young and the new. He truly loved the peasant – *much,* much more than the love I felt for them. My love was different. He *believed* in the Indian peasant. He admired them.

'His sense of Indian history was really startling – the essence and dynamics of Indian history. He had no greed, none at all. No sense of personal comfort. There were many thousands of people, at that point, who were prepared to give their lives and follow his command. And he had developed that power without coercion. The only other organization I have known with the kind of power he possessed is the army, and in the army there is a great deal of coercion.

'He was a thin, short man with glasses. His glasses had very powerful lenses. He generally dressed in shirt and dhoti, or bush shirt and trousers. The clarity of his speech and expression was very great. And this was duplicated in his movements.' Debu meant that Charu Mazumdar's movements were economical and precise, without too many gestures. 'He had enormous energy, his movements were swift. And, by God, he could inspire.

'He never ever raised his voice, but he could speak with great emphasis. And in that small room in North Calcutta he started speaking. There were two windows at the back of the room, and they were both open. I noticed those windows, because I was worried that people outside would be listening. There was very little in that room. I remember an unpainted wooden table with lots of books on it, and a radio. The radio was important. Do you know why? That was the link to Peking Radio. All Naxalites gave enormous importance to the radio – "where-yesterday-we-were-mentioned-on-Peking-Radio" sort of thing. There was something wrong with me. In my whole life I have never listened to Peking Radio more than twice.

'There was also a small bare bench at the back. I noticed that no one was willing to sit on it, in spite of the crowd in the room. But ultimately the room became so packed that people had to sit on the bench. Charu Mazumdar was sitting on the floor – that was why people were reluctant to sit on the bench: they didn't want to be higher than he was.

'People were smoking. That was why the windows were open. I was smoking myself. The atmosphere was still free and easy. I think some tea was brought in, but not for everybody – it couldn't get to everybody in the room.

'Charu Mazumdar started by mentioning certain successes the group had had in Bengal and in certain other parts of the country. "You are doing very good work here, I know. And they are frightened of us. You can expect them to attack. Our experience has proved that killing individual oppressors helps to mobilize the people, because the people then perceive that the oppressor can be *destroyed.* Therefore I have just issued this letter." He read out the letter from a handwritten script. It was the letter calling for individual killing. Then he called for questions.

'I was shocked. But I think my own roots came into play then – as it always does. I was shocked, but simultaneously thrilled. The thrill was: "Have we at last found the way?" It didn't enter my mind to question what had been given as fact: that killing had generated large-scale enthusiasm among the poor.

'My shock was on two counts. One, it was so close to murder. But this I rationalized: it's not murder, it's execution. People weren't going to be killed just like that. The individual killings were going to be discussed and agreed upon by the group. The second shock was that virtually all the gurus of Marxism had warned against terrorism. And this sounded like terrorism.

'The questions that came were essentially like this: "What do we do in the cities?" "What happens if the landlord is supplanted by another oppressor?" There were many tactical questions. I was one of the last to ask a question, and I asked it in a very humble way, I must tell you, because, compared to the fellows there, I was from the wrong class, and the fellows sitting there were more active in the field than I was. The question I asked was about Mao and Lenin having warned against terrorism. So how, theoretically, could we support this?

'Charu Mazumdar answered us all. Very quietly, convincingly. We were all convinced.'

I said to Debu, 'Tell me a little more about him.'

'He was about fifty-eight. Wizened, fair. He was from a landlord's family in North Bengal, and his father was a famous doctor, well-to-do. He was very bright in his studies and did well. He was pulled into the swadeshi movement' – the nationalist movement – 'and from there he transferred to the peasant movement, and made a name for himself. He became a member of the Communist Party. What he did was to transform a militant reform movement – protecting the sharecropper – into the beginning of a revolutionary movement. He did that by deciding that the battle would be carried on against the *state*.'

'Didn't it occur to you that it was madness?'

'At the time I didn't think it was madness. I don't think it is madness now. If there is to be revolution, it has to take on the state.

'That meeting in North Calcutta lasted for three hours. Charu Mazumdar's initial statement was for about an hour and 15 minutes. The discussion was about another hour. Afterwards, little groups would talk to him about their local problems, and leave.

'Up to that time the Naxalites had been occupying schools, defacing statues, etc. Isolated incidents. These things I objected to rather seriously. Up to about April 1970 Charu Mazumdar and others assured me that they were the result of over-enthusiasm. I remember now with hindsight that it was the lower-middle-class and rural schools that were made targets. There was no attempt at touching the elite schools.

'When the directive came that "China's chairman is our chairman", I became very angry, and went to see him. I said, "If the Chinese start coming I will be one of the first with a gun in my hand to stop them." On that topic he immediately kept quiet. But I think that the personal equation we had built up since 1968 – he had stayed in my house, and we had had long discussions – that equation snapped. Later I wrote him a letter. It was a long letter, full of theoretical backing to things I opposed. He didn't reply. At that time the killings had started. The party had moved underground, and all communication was cut.

'That was how I left the movement. From 1970 to 1972 I was involved with a parallel organization. We were mainly doing propaganda. We were hunted by the police. We had to hide from both sides.

'The first policeman was killed in Calcutta in early May, 1970, in a bomb attack. After mid-1970 the action became more general. Traffic policemen were being killed, because they were easy game. There was a funny side. The traffic police were issued arms. The Naxalites snatched the arms, so the traffic policemen chained the arms to themselves. Simultaneously there began the killing of informers.

'And when you start killing *informers*, then you really open the can of worms. You do not refer to his class – you cannot refer to his class, because he has to be within your own ambit to be an informer. Again, with hindsight, I also see that there were no attacks against big targets, the big industrialists, the big landlords.

'And further divisions appeared in the Marxist-Leninist camp. More groups left. By 1973 the Marxist-Leninist camp was divided into 20 factions. The police and their gangs had killed several thousands. By 1973 the movement – that phase of it – was finished.

'I came out of hiding in 1972. The police knew about my break with Charu Mazumdar. The last time I was questioned in detail was in 1972. My great luck was that my last arrest had been in April 1970 – before the first policeman was killed in Calcutta. Then I had gone underground.

'I am doing nothing now. I think in some ways our country has more respect and honour in the world than at that time. From beggars we have become borrowers. I am exercised by the gap between rich and poor, exercised by the lack of patriotism amongst the power-brokers, exercised by the number of industries going sick. And I am exercised by the fact that borrowers generally end up begging.'

Debu didn't tell me about the end of Charu Mazumdar. That I heard from someone else. He was arrested in Calcutta in 1972, and died soon afterwards. He was an asthmatic, and when he was arrested he had a tube of oxygen with him. He must have suffered continuously in the damp and heat of Bengal.

Ashok's first story had been about his attempt to get into marketing. His second story had been about his marriage, his break with the past. His last story was about his life in advertising, and his sighting of the Calcutta boxwallah world, just when that world was about to disappear, giving way to the cruder, richer business world of post-Independence India.

Ashok said, 'My first experience of the Calcutta boxwallah was when as a trainee account executive in an advertising firm I was taken to my first client meeting, and was introduced to this very senior executive in the marketing division of the company. The man was portly and appeared to be quite jovial. He was smoking an imported brand of cigarette, and – this was the middle of May, which is something in Calcutta – he was wearing a suit. His office was air-conditioned. The general atmosphere was of a man in a plush office with a leisurely approach to life.

'He appeared to be in no great hurry to discuss the business in hand. We were going into all kinds of trivia about life in general, the cricket series, a little office politics. All kinds of things were being talked about from 11 or so until 12 or 12.15. And then there was this long pause, and it seemed almost a pity that we had to set aside the general discussion.

'My boss broached the subject of business, and this was gone through with great dispatch. I was just observing; I was only a trainee. The business side of things was finished in a quarter of an hour. It was now about 12.30. Lunch was looming. The client asked my boss if he had a luncheon engagement. My boss said no. The client said, "Perhaps we ought to discuss a little more business over lunch."

'My boss instructed me to run to the office and take out an IOU for 500 rupees, and join them at a five-star hotel. The client wasn't inviting us – it wasn't known for clients to invite advertising agency personnel to lunch. The lunch was to be on us. I suppose I was quite excited at that moment. I had heard a great deal about client entertainment, but I hadn't done any, or been part of it, at that time. The lunch that day started at 12.45 and finished at 3.30. Everybody was happy at the end.

'This way of doing things went on till the early 70s. The big companies had more or less a monopoly in their respective fields. They didn't have to sell. They merely allocated. There was never enough to meet the demand.

'That's changed now. There are a lot more companies making the products, and companies are having to battle it out – to meet production volumes, to place them in the market, to persuade the customer. So all of a sudden companies had no room for people who merely dressed well, could talk to the boss's wife, could play a round of golf, and hold their drink. The country itself had started setting up business schools. To a large extent they tended to be textbook American models, and this created problems for companies. But these institutes enabled companies to get a shortlist of candidates. It became a status symbol to recruit an MBA.

'People who in earlier days would have gone up the ladder now began to flounder, because they didn't have the talent to hold down their job. Whereas, before, office life was a pleasant interval between the company apartment and the club house, now, in my firm, if I want to rise, I have some sacrifices to make. For example, I might have to travel 20 days a month. If you're an all-India organization, you can travel to monitor what's happening in the field. You're also doing it because your colleagues are doing it, and it can be seen as a sign of your commitment to your organization.

'In the old days, if an executive went to the wedding of, say, the niece of a dealer, that would have been seen by the dealer as a most enormous favour, and the executive would have been suitably rewarded by the dealer. Today the executive goes to that wedding to keep in with the dealer. So the whole thing now changes. These dealers most of them speak Hindi, and the older social accomplishments – speaking English, dressing well, playing golf – no longer matter. If you're travelling 20 days a month, and you're the sales manager, you're spending all those days in the company of the dealers and your field staff, and almost every evening is a fairly heavy drinking evening.

'I can't say that when I started I had any idea that marketing would be the way it is now. But in my company I am specifically on the advertising side, and this gives me creative satisfaction. Social graces are still a bonus for an executive; they can add sheen to an executive's profile. But what the executive is really expected to have are qualities of a hard-nosed entrepreneurial businessman – which is the kind of man he is dealing with. In his company he has to be a sophisticated communicator; and when he is sitting in a poky little dealer's shop somewhere he has to speak a different kind of language. He is probably drinking tea out of a dirty tumbler – and yet that dealer probably makes infinitely more than the executive.

'Traditionally in India the dealer network is a very potent force. They're a breed apart. They may even be different from dealers in other countries. To a very large extent people in the dealer community have not been educated. But they are naturally talented at making money. They take pleasure in making money, and more money. It's a family business, handed down from generation to generation. They will sit from 10 to 10 at night in their little shops and think nothing of it – that's their life. They keep rolling the money they make into more and more profitable ventures. And they like to show that they have money. The dealers' houses might have chandeliers and wall-to-wall carpeting, quite unnecessary, imported TV colour sets, and curtains and cushions in the most garish colours.

'But these people are important to companies. So you have these sophisticated organizations with their trained manpower from management institutes, who then have to learn to deal with people who are semi-literate but extremely savvy when it comes to money matters. We need them more than they need us, at this moment in our country's development.

'The strength of a dealer's shop or "counter" – that is how it is referred to: So-and-so is a good counter or a poor counter or a reliable counter – comes from his having been, or his family having been, in business for generations. He knows what his market will take.

'The targets are worked out on a counter basis for each town. We might say of a dealer: "He's a good 500-TV-set counter, and I must get him to sell 200 of mine." That's the kind of thinking that's taking place in an executive's mind. And once he returns to his base city or town, with his head muzzy with too much drink and travel, he's on to his computer, feeding it with all this information. No sales manager worth his salt can be found without his strips of Alka-Seltzer – they all have stomach problems – along with their calculators. They're drinking till 11 or 12 at night, and they're up again at 8.30 or 9, to face the new day.

'The boxwallah of the bygone era was really, typically, a shallow fellow, interested in appearances and the good life. We've swung the other way today. Professionally, the executive today is superior to his counterpart of 15 years ago, but his development as a human being is retarded. He is becoming more of an automaton. He physically has little time to think about anything except the turnover and collection targets for the month.

'If I had known that marketing was going to turn out to be like this, I probably wouldn't have wanted to go into it when I was young. I've turned down requests from the company to move into direct selling jobs. I don't want to pay that kind of price. I prefer to stay on the advertising side. And I don't have to do the extra things the sales executives have to do – going to the airport to meet this boss and that boss and take them home and spend an evening with them. I don't have to do that at all.

'Life is hard now for the executive, and the city of Calcutta adds to this pressure, by offering so little in return to a person who's putting in so much effort. After a hard day's work you can find yourself stranded in a car for hours on end, and when you return home there is no power. There are generators, but they make a dreadful din, and are limited. Apart from visiting one of Calcutta's clubs, if he's fortunate enough to be a member, an executive has little choice of places to go. He cannot go out walking because the pavements and the roads don't allow it. The parks are overcrowded. Most of these parks are infested with rich young men and women who take their cars and turn up their car stereos and eat all evening – junk food from hawkers – and throw the litter around.

'The infrastructure of the city is crumbling. The drainage system is perhaps the worst in the world. In the monsoon, major areas of the city are waterlogged for anything up to 72 hours at a time. One year the water never drained away. Carcases of animals appeared, and we were afraid of an epidemic.

'The only section of people here who seem to be thriving in Calcutta are the Marwaris. They came from parts of Rajasthan a couple of hundred years ago. They thrive by being middlemen, buying and selling. This is what they were good at, and they continue to be. They were never known for cultural or technical skills. And they just grew as a community. They have been the only ones, in the last 15 or 20 years, who are able to buy properties in the posh areas where previously only the rich Bengalis or expatriate executives lived. They have participated in the property boom. Today in these areas you have multi-storey buildings coming up – one more nail in the coffin of the city: more cars, more sanitation problems, etc. – with the Marwaris themselves occupying most of the apartments.

'The other aspect is that some of the very rich Marwaris keep buying up companies after buying just enough shares to gain control. And so a number of old firms are now in the hands of Marwaris. Most of them do not nurture or invest in these companies. They strip the assets. They are quite happy to let the company become more and more sick. It is also true that in the earlier era the British didn't bother very much about growth. Their main concern was repatriation of a certain amount of profits in foreign exchange to the parent company, and most British managing directors came here for a short-term period of three or five years.

'At the other end of the spectrum you have the red-flag-waving unions constantly playing cat-and-mouse with the management. The union leaders themselves don't do any work at all. The unions represent what ultimately the true Bengali is like: he is indolent, doesn't want to work, but he wants something for nothing, and he must protect his dignity at all costs. He will publicly despise the Marwari trader, but he wouldn't be able to do the same job himself.

'We put in a great deal of effort. We draw a monthly pay cheque. And for people like us, who are not businessmen, we feel that the city in which we live must offer us something in return. We must at the end of the working day have more than the prospect of just coming back home. You can't go to any cinema house, because most of them have poor sound systems and virtually non-functioning air-conditioning systems – they don't renovate them. I haven't been to a cinema hall in Calcutta for five or six years.

'I have told you how as a young man I longed to break into the world of marketing. I have done that, and I can say that professionally I have done well. But that profession hasn't turned out to be what I thought, and now I feel that those of us in Calcutta who are in the middle between the Marwaris and the trade-union Marxists – the executive class, who used to be an influential part of the city – are slowly being squeezed out of existence.

'The fact is that the problems of Calcutta are of a magnitude that cannot be endured. My wife and I feel now that we won't see improvements in our lifetime. We feel we should be trying our luck somewhere else, and saying goodbye to Calcutta.'

My own days in Calcutta had been hard. When I had first come to Calcutta, in 1962, I had, after the early days of strain, settled into the big-city life of the place; had had the feeling of being in a true metropolis, with the social and cultural stimulation of such a place. Something of that life was still there. But I was overpowered this time by my own wretchedness, the taste of the water, corrupting both coffee and tea as it corrupted food, by the brown smoke of cars and buses, by the dug-up roads and broken footpaths, by the dirt, by the crowds; and could not accept the consolation offered by some people that in a country as poor as India the aesthetic side of things didn't matter.

My feelings went the other way. In richer countries, where people could create reasonably pleasant home surroundings for themselves, perhaps, after all, public squalor was bearable. In India, where most people lived in such poor conditions, the combination of private squalor and an encompassing squalor outside was quite stupefying. It would have given people not only a low idea of their needs – air, water, space for stretching out – but it must also have given people a low idea of their possibilities, as makers or doers. Some such low idea of human needs and possibilities would surely have been responsible for the general shoddiness of Indian industrial goods, the ugliness and unsuitability of so much of post-Independence architecture, the smoking buses and cars, the chemically-tainted streets, the smoking factories.

'Everybody is *suffering* here,' a famous actor said at dinner one evening. And that simple word, corroborating what Ashok had said, was like an illumination.

For years and years, and even during the time of my first visit in 1962, it had been said that Calcutta was dying, that its port was silting up, its antiquated industry declining. But Calcutta hadn't died. It hadn't done much, but it had gone on; and it had begun to appear that the prophecy had been excessive. Now it occurred to me that perhaps this was what happened when cities died. They didn't die with a bang; they didn't die only when they were abandoned. Perhaps they died like this: when everybody was suffering, when transport was so hard that working people gave up jobs they needed because they feared the suffering of the travel; when no one had clean water or air; and no one could go walking. Perhaps cities died when they lost the amenities that cities provided, the visual excitement, the heightened sense of human possibility, and became simply places where there were too many people, and people suffered.

Calcutta had had a left-wing or Marxist government for years, and I was told that the money nowadays was going to the countryside, that the misery of Calcutta was part of a more humane Marxist plan. But things are often as they appear, and it is possible that this is one of the ways cities die: when governments are dogmatic or foolish, killing where they cannot create, when people and governments conspire to frighten away the money and the life they need, when, in a further inversion, the poetry of revolution becomes its own-intoxication, and Marxism becomes the opiate of the idle people.

Perhaps when a city dies the ghost of its old economic life lingers on. So, in Calcutta, old firms with famous names are taken over and their assets are broken up; and people invest in real estate, since people always have to live somewhere; and there is an illusion of an economic life. Every few days, in a further illusion of activity, there is a political demonstration; and idle young men, morose and virtuous-looking, take their red flags and slogans through the self-perpetuating misery of the streets; and money and ambition and creativity go elsewhere in India. Without the rest of India to take the strain, the death of Calcutta might show more clearly, and Bengal might show as another Bangladesh – too many people, too little sanitation, too little power.

At the back of the hotel was a market: I looked down on its low, spreading roof. Buzzards perched on the ledges of the hotel, waiting. The ledges were black with an accumulation of blown dust and the grit of brown traffic smoke. The style of the British-built red-brick building opposite the market – the formality, the symmetry, the elegance, the thought, the confidence, the reference to classical ornament – was now oddly at variance with the life of the street, and seemed to come from a dead age.

The sticky-looking asphalt of the cambered street lay between wide, irregular drifts of dust that had hardened to earth in the gutters at the side; the streets would be washed now only by the monsoon. The once paved footpath outside the market had crumbled and in places merged with the earth in the gutters. People went about minute tasks. Men pulled rickshaws. In 1962 this had been offensive to see, but it was said that the poor needed employment. Twenty-seven years on, the rickshaws were still there. The same thing was said about employment for the poor; but the Calcuttans, with their low ideas of human needs and possibilities, appeared genuinely to enjoy the man-pulled rickshaw as a form of transport; and many of the rickshaws looked nice and new, not like things on the way out. Minute tasks: one man walked by carrying a single, limber, dancing sheet of plywood on his head. Other people went about perfectly seriously carrying tiny loads on their heads, no doubt for very small fees.

On important days big circular baskets of trussed white chickens appeared outside the market, and one or two men seemed idly engaged for some minutes throwing trussed chickens from one basket to another. Then one noticed that the basket from which the chickens were being thrown was full of movement, and the basket into which the chickens were being thrown was still. And then one saw that the gesture of chicken-throwing also contained another, the wringing of the chicken's neck: two jobs combined in a single, fluent, circular gesture.

One man might then be seen taking away his own little load of dead white chickens: the chickens artistically arranged into a big feathery ball hung on the handle of his old bicycle, the feathers of the stiff dead chickens hanging down the other way and showing brown-yellow rather than white, with the stiff brown claws and legs like spokes in the feathery ball, like sticks in candyfloss. The man had trouble arranging the load on his bicycle. When he first tried to get on the bicycle and ride away, the chickens got in the way of his knees.

At the end of the day a little green pick-up truck came, and the wide circular baskets, empty now, were stacked in the truck in two piles. When the truck went away, there remained – in this city where rubbish was seldom cleared – only a few scattered white feathers in the dust of the broken and silted-up street.

The British were in Calcutta for a long time. It might be said that the Anglo-Bengali culture – out of which modern India grew – is as old as the United States. Raja Ram Mohun Roy, the first exponent of that culture, was born in 1772, four years before the Declaration of Independence. From Raja Ram Mohun Roy there is a direct line to Rabindranath Tagore, whom Chidananda Das Gupta saw in 1940 when he first went to Tagore's university at Shantiniketan.

On that visit Chidananda heard Tagore, nearly eighty, deliver a talk in the Shantiniketan temple on 'Crisis in Civilization'. In that talk – a famous talk, published a few months after Chidananda heard it – Tagore said he had always believed that 'the springs of civilization' would come out of 'the heart of Europe'; Now, with the war and the coming cataclysm, he could no longer have that faith. But he couldn't lose faith in man; that would be a sin. He lived now in the hope that the dawn would come from the East, 'where the sun rises', and that the saviour would be born 'in our midst, in this poverty-shamed hovel which is India'.

It was an old man's melancholy farewell to the world. Five years later the war was over. Europe began to heal; in the second half of the century Europe and the West were to be stronger and more creative and more influential than they had ever been. The calamity Tagore hadn't foreseen was the calamity that was to come to Calcutta.

In 1946 there were the Hindu-Muslim massacres. They marked the beginning of the end for the city. The next year India was independent, but partitioned. Bengal was divided. A large Hindu refugee population came and camped in Calcutta; and Calcutta, without a hundredth part of the resilience of Europe, never really recovered. Certain important things were in the future – the cinema of Satyajit Ray, especially – but the great days of the city, all its intellectual life, were over. And it could appear that the British-built city – its grandeur still ghostly at night – began to die when the British went away.

# 6

# THE END OF THE LINE

ONE OF SATYAJIT Ray's few films to be set outside Bengal is *The Chess Players.* It is an historical film about the annexation of the kingdom of Oude by the British in the 1850s. Oude was one of the provinces of the Mogul Empire; in the mid-18th century it became one of the successor states of that empire. The city of Lucknow was the capital of Oude, and it was the setting of the Ray film: a work of subtlety, looking at the events of the 1850s as they might have seemed to people at the time. The film was more than a comment on 19th-century British imperialism. It also considered – with understanding and melancholy and humour – the decadence or blindness or helplessness of a 19th-century Indian Muslim culture at the end of its possibilities: where the rulers play chess and conduct petty affairs, while their territory (and its people) pass into foreign rule.

The British annexation of Oude was one of the things that led to the Indian Mutiny of 1857. In colonial times, and for a period afterwards, this was called by some the First War of Indian Independence. But this was a 20th-century view, 20th-century language, and a kind of mimicry, seeking to give to old India something of the socialist dynamism the Russians found in their own history. The Mutiny was the last flare-up of Muslim energy in India until the agitation, 80 years or so later, for a separate Muslim state of Pakistan.

Lucknow was the end of the line for Muslim India. The city is the capital of the state of Uttar Pradesh, which is the largest state in the Indian Union. In its historical heart it is like a graveyard from the days of the Nawabs of Oude, full of the ruins of war. The city was shelled and fought over during the Mutiny; afterwards the British preserved the ruins as a memorial, and passed them on to independent India.

The hunting lodge of the Nawabs, *Dilkusha*, 'Heart's Delight', is roofless. Much of its plaster has gone, revealing the layers of thin bricks that make up the mass of the walls. It was a local way of building; but the style of the – palatial – lodge, with what remains of the stables, is of European inspiration: the Nawabs of Oude employed Europeans in many capacities. Even in ruin, the hunting lodge remains wonderfully suited to the climate. To stand in the shade of its thick walls, even on a bright and warm day, is to feel cool and relaxed. The climate – that elsewhere in Lucknow, amid the concrete and glass, seems altogether unfriendly – here, a short distance away, becomes quite benign, almost a perfect climate. So, almost certainly, it would have appeared to the designers of the lodge. Among these shattered old walls, one can even think of the Lucknow climate as part of the luxuriousness of the days of the Nawabs.

A more extensive ruin, in a similar kind of style, is the Residency. The British Resident, originally an ambassador or agent, became in time the effective ruler of Oude; and the Residency was built by the Nawabs, over some decades, for this powerful figure. It was a settlement, a little town, not simply a building on its own. It was where, at the beginning of the Mutiny, the British people of the area were gathered together, with Indian servants and Indian soldiers loyal to their cause (or fearful of the mutineers' cause). There were 3000 people in all in the Residency, and they were besieged for three months by the mutineers. When the siege was lifted, 2000 of the 3000 had died. The British among them had been buried in a corner of the Residency; later, fine tombstones were put up in their memory in that corner.

And just as the ruins of the Nawabs' hunting lodge were left as a reminder of the end of the power of the Nawabs of Oude, so the damaged buildings of the besieged Residency were preserved as a monument of British courage. The hunting lodge – blown up after victory by the relieving British forces (mainly Scots and Sikhs) – was the more complete ruin. The buildings of the Residency carried very many little dints caused by rifle bullets, with occasional larger excisions caused by non-explosive cannonballs. Perhaps the siege had failed because the mutineers didn't have the weapons for it. Both the hunting lodge and the buildings of the Residency showed, below plaster, the flat thin Lucknow bricks that made up their mass.

The Residency was one of the famous monuments of the British Raj. Now, after the withdrawal from India, and the wars of this century, there is hardly room for it in the British memory. But it remains important in Indian history. Independent India inherited the monument, and has kept it up. The Residency is now a public garden, with trees and flowers and paths between the shot-up, weathered buildings.

Rashid, who came of an old Lucknow Muslim family, walked with me in the Residency on my last day in Lucknow. He had in the beginning been neutral, talking of history, pleased to show the famous sights of the famous city, and pleased, too, to show that in Lucknow (unlike other Indian cities) there were still places to go walking in. But in the museum building, with its trays of pathetic mutineers' cannonballs, and other carefully tended imperial relics, its tarnished photographs and engravings with faded captions, Rashid's mood changed. His Muslim sentiments flared up; he became quite agitated at the events of 130 years before, full of rage about the powers of the British Resident and the humiliations of the Nawab, full of rage and grief at the siege that had failed, the chance of Muslim victory which, though so near, had not come. He said, 'Bastards! Bastards!' And he was referring not to the besiegers but the besieged, whose heroism and general predicament, lucky escapes and cruel deaths, were the subject of the museum display.

Not far away, and visible from the ruins of the Residency, was a white marble pillar with a twist at the top, to symbolize the flame of freedom. Independent India had put that monument up, to counter the British Raj's monument to itself. It was a feeble thing, the equivalent in marble of Rashid's rage. Its symbolism was quite crude beside the real, bullet-marked buildings of the Residency, and it was historically invalid: the Indian Independence movement didn't grow out of the Mutiny.

No monument of independent India could have solaced Rashid, because, in Rashid's view, Independence – 90 years after the Residency siege – had come as another kind of Muslim defeat. Independence had come with the partition of the subcontinent into India and the two wings of Pakistan, so that the Muslims of undivided India had found themselves, as Rashid said, under three roofs.

Many of the middle-class Muslims of Lucknow had migrated to West Pakistan. The Muslim culture for which Lucknow had been known – the language, the manners, the music, the food – had disappeared. Where once Muslims had ruled, there now remained, after what could be seen as 300 years of a steady Muslim decline, the cramped, shut-in, stultifying life of the Muslim ghetto of the old town. There were other Muslims still, middle-class people like Rashid, and upper-class people as well, people sometimes of princely antecedents. But the predominant feature of Muslim Lucknow was that life of the ghetto, where people were ill-equipped and vulnerable, withdrawn and highly-strung.

Lucknow still had something of its old Muslim legend and aura when I went there for the first time, in 1962. Certain frivolities still seemed to speak of the past. People flew kites; special toys were made; special perfumes (including a clay perfume, meant to give the monsoon scent of rain falling on parched earth) were made with a medium of sandalwood oil, so as not to offend the Muslim religious law. Though there were no longer any singing girls, the intricately worked screens on the upper floors of buildings in the *chowk* or bazaar area seemed to speak (like a 19th-century oil portrait of a Nawab, baring one plump breast) of old Lucknow indulgences.

There was no legend now. The upper-class Muslim community, which had been at the centre of the legend, had shrunk; while the general population of the city had doubled or trebled. Shabby, post-Independence concrete had spread everywhere; certain thoroughfares had become hellish. The city of the Nawabs had become an administrative city, Rashid said, a district city: an Indian mofussil town.

The hotel, part of the new concrete city, was like a parody of a five-star hotel. It had its 'logo'. It had various cards in the rooms, offering this and that, listing services and asking for comments. It had its door-knob breakfast menus, very difficult to fill in rationally. It had it all. All the best hotel forms had been borrowed; only the services were missing. The 'Do Not Disturb' light didn't function. The red telephone was more or less a dummy, sometimes releasing a faint, seemingly cavern-lost voice, hardly decipherable. The towels, perhaps because of some violent bleach, had turned a pale fluorescent blue, with a thin but thorny nap. The lampshade was broken; the lights were dim and strained one's eyes. A full half of the wall that faced west was of glass. Even now, and it was still only spring, it became quite oppressive in the afternoons, and it was necessary to use the weak-metalled window catch (weak-metalled: the catch seemed ready to bend between one's thumb and finger) to open the window, to let in a lot more hot air, together with the full roar of the traffic and the horns and the hooters.

But, miraculously, out of that window, there was a view that took one back to the past, gave one the illusion of looking at the original of one of the large views done by Thomas and William Daniell in late 18th-century India, and later published in London as aquatints. The view was of the River Gumti – or its lower channel, full, placid, not wide – between its tawny and dusty-green banks.

The Daniells' views were often taken with the help of the camera oscura, and they can suggest immense distances; close to, an Indian aquatint of the Daniells is full of literal detail, full of human figures, some very small. There was that kind of distance, that kind of minute busyness, to this view of the River Gumti from the hotel room.

Along the top of the bank to the right there was a path, and figures were walking on it down all its length, small, separate figures, the colours of their clothes not easy to catch at this distance. Trees at the back of this path concealed the residential streets on that side of the river bank. More in the foreground, above the full lower channel of the river, but well below the path on the right bank where people walked, there was a wide, irregular, tree-less shelf. Far to the left, black water buffaloes, small, moving black specks, gave a touch of the African or American wilderness to this river shelf. To the right, and closer, washermen in the mornings spread out their washed sheets and clothes to dry. In the middle of the shelf, at the edge of the flowing river channel, were widely spaced huts, with distempered walls, pink or white, some with advertising copy in Hindi: single-roomed huts with sloping roofs, reflected in the smooth water. These huts belonged to swimming clubs. At the weekends boys swam in the river, keeping close to the bank and the huts.

On the left bank of the river, directly below the hotel, there were Hindu temples. Far away, on the same bank, were the minarets of old Lucknow, reminders of the mosques and *imambaras* in which in 1962 I had looked for the glory of old Lucknow. Below, hidden by trees, were the lanes of the chowk or bazaar, which in 1962 still had a touch of the *Thousand and One Nights,* but which now, Rashid said, showed the final tragedy of the Muslim city to someone who knew how to look.

I went looking with him one morning. It was so crowded and cramped and repetitive in the lanes, the visitor might have seen the area as the expression of a single culture; and he might have missed the distinctions that Rashid saw.

The shops or stalls, as in the usual Indian bazaar, were narrow little boxes, fully open to the road or lane, and set side by side, with hardly a gap between. The floors were a few feet above the lane. Gutters at the side received water and waste from the drains that ran between or under the stalls. This waste water didn't run off to some larger drain, Rashid said. It just stayed there, in the open gutter, and evaporated.

All the shops and stalls had metal shutters; every shop and attached house was built like a fortress, for the days of riot. From time to time, where there should have been a shop, there was a moraine of rubble, as though – out of age, fragility, or rot – the shop and the house with it had fallen inwards, a small demonstration of how the ground level of cities might rise, layer upon layer.

Had there always been a bazaar here? Was it possible to think of a time when this site was bare, a field? Rashid and I walked through a ceremonial gate, an archway, called after the great Mogul emperor Akbar. He ruled from 1556 to 1605. Perhaps the gate had been built in the late 16th century to mark a visit of the emperor's; so the outlines of the bazaar would have been then (in Shakespeare's time) what it was now. There were glimpses of a more recent past – 18th-century or 19th-century – in the small flat Lucknow bricks that could be seen below the broken plaster on some old buildings. The bricks were set in lines that echoed the lines of the structure – in arches, for instance, they were set in concentric arcs – so that they looked like iron filings demonstrating the lines of magnetic force around a magnet.

The outer bazaar was mixed. The shopkeepers were Hindu; the artisans were Muslim. Both groups had their history and special traditions. The artisans did simple work. They beat thin ribbons of silver into very thin, half-crumbling silver leaf or silver foil. They made cheap shoes; they did a local kind of embroidery called *chikan*;

they did bead embroidery. The shopkeepers, Hindus, were either merchant-caste people from Uttar Pradesh, or Punjabi *khatris* who had come to the area 200 or 300 years before and had stayed as moneylenders and traders.

One shop out of five was supplying goods for bigger shopkeepers in the same area: thread for chikan embroidery, gold and silver spangles for brocade work, wooden printing blocks for stamping designs on chikan work, the very wide ledgers used for the single-entry style of Indian book-keeping. Some shops sold kites: Lucknow still had that tradition of kite-flying. Some shops sold goldsmith's equipment; some sold fresh flowers, for Hindus to take to the temple. Generally, Rashid said, the shops in this outer bazaar sold basic, everyday items connected with traditional ways of living, Hindu and Muslim.

Very small boys sat cross-legged on the floor of their narrow stalls, at the front, above the gutters, and filed away at the needles which were used in the bigger establishments for doing brocade work. These needles looked like the plastic ink-refills of ballpoint pens; they were of that size, and they had a similar kind of point. They were sold for a rupee each: a boy had to prepare a lot of needles before he made anything like money.

There were many mosques, and some of them might have been built on the rubble of old stalls and houses: the mosque here was like a kind of folk art, over-ornamented, weak in design, painted with love. While Rashid and I walked there came, above the bazaar noise, the amplified, breaking voice of a mullah. There was such passion in that trained voice: he might have been reciting something from the Koran. In fact, Rashid said, the man with the loudspeaker was only saying: 'Give money for the mosque, and have a palace of gold in heaven.'

The simplest kind of faith: though the outer bazaar was mixed, not purely Muslim, the bazaar life was like an expression of the faith of the book and the mosque, and it was possible to feel that everything here served the faith. The most glittering and spangled stalls were the Koran stalls. They were hung with feathery paper tassels of gold and silver. In the general drabness of bazaar goods, those tassels, which were for braiding girls' or women's hair, caught the eye. These Koran stalls not only sold the book; they also sold boxes to keep the book in; bookstands to place the book on while it was being read; incense sticks to go with the reading; and caps to wear while you read the book, since it was forbidden to read the book with your head uncovered. The reading caps were in bright orange, red, or green; there were also crocheted skullcaps.

The shops didn't open before 11, Rashid said. The reason was that, though they didn't live far from their work, the shopkeepers didn't go home for lunch. Once they went to their shops and sat on the floor, on sheets or sacking or carpets or durries, they were there for the whole working day. They were as much prisoners of the bazaar as the artisans who worked for them. The entrances to the shopkeepers' houses were in the narrow passageways off the main bazaar lane; the living conditions in those hidden spaces were not too different from what could be seen of working conditions in the lane.

There was a point in the bazaar when you crossed over from the mixed Hindu-Muslim area to the area that was purely Muslim. The cross-over point was clear enough to Rashid; it wasn't so clear to me. The crowds beyond that point were denser, Rashid said, and the people were smaller; they were undernourished and stunted. And I did see, when I had got my eye in (or thought I had), that many of the children in this part of the bazaar were thin and wizened, with staring eyes, and often had some kind of skin infection.

There were small private schools here and there, but generally the Muslim children of the bazaar were not educated in the modern way. Their parents didn't see how that kind of education could lead to anything for their children. They also felt, in a profound way, that that kind of education was for other people. Education and learning were, of course, good things; but for them as Muslims that good learning, pure and untainted, was to be had only in the Koranic school or the seminary. Nothing outside the faith was for the people of the faith, the people in these squashed passageways and shops. The smallness of the spaces added to the feeling of comfort and protection within, added to the sense of the corruptions without.

Many children – boys – went to the seminary (a big, new building) or the Koranic schools in the bazaar. But most were apprenticed by their parents to various simple bazaar trades when they were eight or seven or six or even five. And if some of the children serving in the stalls or working in the shops looked frightened, it was because, Rashid said, they knew they were going to be 'bashed up' by the shopkeeper to whom their parents had apprenticed them, or the overseers of their employers.

Rashid said, 'It's an unfed world. And what can be more cruel than an unfed stomach?'

And yet, in the purely Muslim area, where Rashid was teaching me to see only gloom, I thought there was a greater feeling of festival and shopping joy than in the drab, workaday stalls of the mixed outer bazaar. Watches were repaired here; kites were sold (kite-selling common to both Hindu and Muslim shops); photographs were framed; people sold kebabs; there were other cook shops; there were even firework stalls.

And always, licensed and provocative, hanging around the stalls, like a decayed reminder of Lucknow's past, were the transvestites and eunuchs of the ghetto, in women's clothes and with cheap jewelry, making lewd jokes and begging: the darkness of the sexual urge finding this ritual, semi-grotesque, safe public expression – in this lane where few women were to be seen, and those who were seen, thin, tiny figures, were clad in black from head to toe. These eunuchs and transvestites sold their bodies; they had a market.

'They are sexual objects,' Rashid said. 'Can you imagine?'

They sat on their haunches at the side of the lane, near the gutters, below the floors of the shops, these sacrificial women-men of Lucknow. Their faces, half male, half female, were worn and lined and crudely rouged; but they had men's teeth, big and blackened and spaced out.

Hammer sounds, muffled and competitive, came from stalls where boys or young men, four or five or six to a stall, sat or squatted and hammered thin ribbons of silver into very fine sheets of silver foil. This foil was placed on sweets or other delicacies, to suggest luxury; it had no other purpose. The silver ribbon was placed between goatskins and beaten with a mallet. About a dozen pieces of ribbon were beaten at the same time, the silver ribbon interleaved, one piece at a time, between the goatskins – I read later that intestines, being more pliable, were most suitable for this kind of work. It took two to three hours to hammer out a piece of ribbon into foil. A sheet of foil was sold for half a rupee or a rupee, according to its size. A young man's working day, therefore, might produce silver foil that could fetch from 18 to 36 rupees. Take away the cost of the silver, and the cost of the stall, and there wasn't much that a young man could earn in a day, from that incessant banging, companionable or competitive, in a small space. The silver foil hammered out in this way was fragile, shredding at the touch of a finger. Almost without purpose as a commodity, it was stored between the leaves of discarded books.

Rashid said, 'All the jobs here have this soul-destroying quality. They are doing it only because their fathers did it before them. They've probably never stepped out of the area. They listen to cassettes of film songs and religious songs, turned up loud, to distract themselves from the deadening labour, whether it's beating out silver foil or doing embroidery or brocade work. They drink a lot of tea in glasses. There is a reason for the tea-drinking. It kills the appetite. When they want to pee, they just go down and pee in the streets.

'It's so basic. The level of education is so low, and so are the needs and the skills. Apart from the transistor and the occasional electric fan, they could be living in another age. Their leisure life is like this. They hire a television set and three video cassettes for

100 rupees. A number of them club together to pay the 100 rupees. And they sit through the night, 40 or 50 of them, watching those three films. There are about 60 firms hiring out TVs and VCRs in this area, and they're all doing good business. There is a little exploitation here, too. Someone with spare cash books a TV for a certain slab of time in the evening – the man doing that will do it every day – and then he sells that time (and the TV) for a premium of 20 rupees or so.

'At the most the only education the children get is the Koran. The women are not educated. They inbreed a lot. First cousins get married. That explains some of the physical degeneracy. The boys marry young, at fifteen or sixteen or seventeen. At forty a man is a grandfather, and burnt out. They eat badly. Meat and bread and no vegetables. They have poor sanitation. Most of them never meet a Hindu or non-Muslim in their lives. The people who go to the Gulf and make money stay in the ghetto when they come back. They build big houses there, to enjoy the regard of their fellows.

'Most of them are Shias. The highlight of their year is the Mohurram.' The period of mourning for Hussain, the son of Ali, the Shia hero. 'Elsewhere Mohurram runs for 12 days, or 40 days. Here in Lucknow it runs for two months and eight days. One of the Begums of Oude made a pledge once that if a certain wish of hers was fulfilled, Mohurram in the kingdom of Oude would last for two months and eight days. This Mohurram has given the Shias here a shared identity. For those days you cry, you beat your breast, you knife yourself, you moan. It helps them to bear their misery, and it gets them out of the house. This Mohurram has led to tensions with the Sunni majority. With this result: Lucknow has never had a Hindu-Muslim clash, only a Sunni-Shia clash.

'There are any number of mosques in the area, and the call to prayer on microphones and amplifiers comes regularly from all quarters. The words for the Sunni and the Shia are the same, but there is a slight difference in the timing. So you hear 10 calls a day instead of five.

'And then there is Ramadan for a month, when you fast during the day. In that month restaurants close during the day and stay open at night. That gives a real casbah effect.'

In a purely Muslim country people might have been less tense about the faith, and nerves might have been less raw. But here it was known that what lay outside the lanes and passageways of the chowk was outside the faith, and from this world outside there came threats and provocations.

Near the end of my time in Lucknow Rashid told me what the most worrying recent threats had been. There was the man from Bangalore who had petitioned the court to ban the Koran in all its languages and editions in India, on the ground that the Koran preached sedition. The petition was a form of provocation, and should not have been taken seriously. Instead, Rashid said, the judge, a woman, rather too legalistically agreed to consider the petition. This caused rioting. The petition was thrown out later by another judge, who ruled that the Koran, like the Bible, was 'a basic document', and couldn't be the subject of that kind of legal petition.

Then there was the affair of a mosque in the town of Ayodhya, 300 miles away, which the Hindus had turned into a temple. Ayodhya was important, even sacred, to Hindus. It was the birthplace of Lord Rama, the hero of the Ramayana; and there were Hindus who said that after their invasion the Muslims had built a mosque on the site of Rama's birthplace. With Independence, Hindus wished to claim the site again. In 1949, Rashid said, the mosque was closed down, because of the danger of rioting. Then, four years or so ago, there had been a development. A Hindu petitioned the district judge for permission to pray there. The petition was allowed; the locks of the place were opened; Hindus took possession, and were still in possession. There had been riots; people had been killed; the bitter squabble was still going on.

The third threat had to do with Muslim personal law. A wealthy Muslim lawyer divorced his first wife and married again. He gave the first wife the lump sum stipulated in their Muslim marriage contract. The divorced wife then went to the Indian courts and asked for a monthly maintenance allowance as well from her husband (this was how Rashid told the story). After 20 years the case reached the Indian Supreme Court. The judge spoke of the deficiency in Muslim personal law, and granted maintenance to the divorced wife. There was an outcry from Muslims at this interference with their personal law, which was part of their faith; and the Indian government, responding to the protests, passed legislation that overturned the decision of the Supreme Court.

Parveen lived in an old-fashioned, spacious, enclosed Muslim house in the old quarter of Lucknow. The front room was the sitting room; the private rooms were at the back. Two years before, Parveen had decided to go into politics. There had been jealousy from other women, Muslim and non-Muslim; but Parveen had begun to make her mark politically, and a little time before she had led a delegation of Muslim women to the prime minister. There were photographs of this occasion on the ochre-coloured walls of Parveen's sitting room.

Parveen was a handsome woman of upright carriage. There were lawyers and landowners and high government officials in her background, and she had the confidence of her class, which had once been the ruling class here. She was a world away from the Muslims in the chowk or bazaar, and the small black-veiled figures who occasionally flitted about the lanes there. She wore no veil; she spoke forcefully and well; and yet there were in her unexpected moments of feminine reserve which reminded you that she came from a special culture, that this Muslim house with its areas of feminine seclusion represented an important part of her nature.

She wanted to go into 'secular' politics; and she meant that she wanted to go, as a Muslim woman, into the politics of the state. This ambition in no way diluted her religious faith. Certain aspects of the Muslim faith were 'the law', she said: they couldn't be discussed. Such an aspect was the aspect of women's rights.

Women enjoyed many rights under Islam. They didn't need to have their rights – which were in any case 'the law' – amended by the state. They enjoyed the right, for instance, of inheriting property from their parents; Hindu women had no such right. Whatever was given to a Muslim wife during marriage was hers to keep; that wasn't so with western women. When a marriage was arranged a man undertook to pay a woman a certain sum if he divorced her. That was enough; the idea of maintenance was repugnant to a Muslim woman. When a woman became a wife, it didn't mean that she had become a servant. After a divorce a husband became a stranger, and there was no question of a woman taking money from him afterwards. Other countries or communities could think of modifying the rights of people according to the needs of the time. But the Koran had laid down the law for Muslims for all time.

The words were strong, but Parveen spoke them easily, when – with Rashid to help with her English – she came to the hotel to talk of her political work. She was a defender of the faith. But the faith – complete, fully formulated – sat lightly on her. At her social level it was even part of her certainty and strength, and seemed to equip her for the public life she wanted to enter.

She had a talent for organizing. She was off that day to meet – informally – a young woman who had been suggested as a prospective bride for her brother. She would go to this far-off town; she would call on a friend. In the friend's house – and apparently quite by chance – there would be the young woman her brother wanted her to meet.

Life was going on for Parveen. She didn't have Rashid's dark vision. Rashid was a bachelor. He was a reader, a solitary. He brooded; his mood changed easily. He loved his apartment; he loved retreating to it.

As for the Muslims of the chowk or bazaar – of course, Parveen said, they were trapped in their ignorance, and it was hard to get through to them. But though people spoke of this ignorance and constriction as a specifically Muslim problem, many other groups in India were in a similar position – people in the rural areas, the scheduled castes.

Perhaps it was that comparison that depressed Rashid. Muslims had once ruled here, set the tone. Now they had been depleted by the middle-class migration to Pakistan; and, in spite of the esteem in which individuals were held, as a group they ranked low.

Rashid was of an old Shia Muslim family. An ancestor in the mid-18th century had been a trader, with seven ships plying out of Bombay. Perhaps they hadn't really been ships, Rashid said; perhaps they had been only dhows. But that ancestor had done well. He had even built an *imambara*, a replica of one of the Shia mausoleums erected in Iran and Iraq for descendants of the Prophet. It was the practice in those days for a Shia who had done well to put up an imambara, as a place where religious discourses might take place.

In the 19th century an ancestor had served at the court of the last Nawab of Oude. When this ruler was exiled to Calcutta by the British, Rashid's ancestor had gone with him, and this ancestor had lived in Calcutta until his death in the 1880s. Rashid's mother's father was an administrator in one of the bigger princely states. He looked after everyone in his family; he wrote poetry; and he dressed like an Edwardian gentleman. Rashid thought – going only by photographs – that this grandfather looked a little like Bertrand Russell.

Rashid's father's father was the first one in his family to learn English. He worked in the railways, in what was then the new railway station of Lucknow – and it is still one of the more impressive buildings of Lucknow. Rashid's father, when he was of age, thought he would go into the police service. At that time upper-class Muslims, landowners, went into the professions; they did law and medicine. People like Rashid's father went into the police service or the administration. Rashid thought that his father was a handsome man. He was five feet eight, which made him an inch or two taller than Rashid. He was slightly marked by smallpox; but at that time nearly everybody had pock-marks.

In those days, if you were someone like Rashid's father, it was easy to join the police service. Somebody took you to the English officer and offered you for the service. The officer would say, 'Send him from the day after.' This happened to Rashid's father. He joined the force as an assistant superintendent; this was the starting officer-rank. But he lasted only three days. He didn't like the drills, and he couldn't bear the abusive language of the instructors. He couldn't see it as just part of the game, part of the toughening-up process; he wanted to get out right away.

He decided after that to go into business. He and his brother opened a shop in Lucknow that sold cameras and photographic equipment. This was in 1911, the year of the coronation of the King-Emperor George V: the high-water mark of the British Empire, and the British Indian Raj. The camera shop that Rashid's father started in that year did well in imperial India. It suited the place; it developed with photography itself, and became one of the best shops of its kind. Branches were opened in other Indian cities, mainly the hill resorts, where people went for their summer holidays. The Lucknow shop was in the main shopping street called Hazratgunj. In those imperial days Hazratgunj – now crowded and a mess – was sprayed with water every evening by a municipal van.

The other shops in Hazratgunj were owned by Englishmen and Jews and Parsis. Rashid especially remembered the shop of a Jew called Landau. Landau had a very big corner shop, and he sold watches. The walk-way outside his shop was roofed or canopied by the floor above. There were wrought-iron pillars downstairs; the residence part of the building was upstairs, with a verandah with slender pillared arches, echoing the solider pillars below. Anderson Brothers were tailors; they closed after Independence in 1947. Another tailor was MacGregor. He didn't leave in 1947; he stayed on in Lucknow and died there. MacGregor had Indian royalty and Englishmen among his customers, and men from the Indian Civil Service. 'You could tell that a coat had been made by "Mac",' Rashid said. 'People wore them 30 years on.'

Rashid, who was born in 1944, remembered his father's shop as having showcases in Burma teak. They had been made in Lucknow by Muslim artisans, working to his father's designs. The shop was like a club; outsiders and idlers were nervous of going in. 'Money wasn't the main thing. People came to meet my father and their other friends there.'

Rashid's family house was in old Lucknow. It had a separate section for the women. Guests couldn't go into the main house. They stayed in the drawing-room, which was right at the front of the house and had a separate entrance. The furniture in that drawing-room was in the English style, made in Lucknow: enormous pieces, very uncomfortable. At the back of the drawing-room were a few other rooms, and then there was the courtyard of the main house. In summer the family slept out in the courtyard. Water was first thrown on the courtyard to cool it. The servants then laid out the string beds in rows, and put up mosquito nets on bamboo poles. There was a stand for pitchers in which drinking water was kept, to cool for the next day. A big square table was in a corner of the courtyard; it was covered by a white cloth and had a coloured tablecloth in the centre. Food was put on that square table. Dinner was at nine, when Rashid's father came back from the shop.

Almost as soon as Rashid had got to know this ordered middle-class family life, the family fortunes began to change. When independence came in 1947, Rashid's father wanted to migrate to Pakistan. He had a nephew who was looking after the branch in the hill town of Mussoorie; he asked this nephew to take the stock from Mussoorie to the shop in Karachi, which was now in Pakistan. The nephew did so; but, in the chaos of those days, the nephew got the Karachi shop transferred to his own name.

'So my father was left high and dry. He gave up the idea of moving to Pakistan.'

'What happened to your cousin?'

'He lost his leg in a motorcycle accident. He mucked up the shop, and was reduced to bringing provisions for the school his wife ran. You might say that he was punished. But that brought no joy to us.'

Hindu and Sikh refugees from Pakistan began to come to Lucknow.

'They were strange to us. The people behind our house, though not very rich, were an educated Muslim family. In 1947 they went to Pakistan. Their house was then assigned to a refugee family. One memory that stays in my mind was how the mother of the new family used to make their children defecate on pieces of paper and throw it over the common wall into our courtyard. We made a fuss, and they understood, and stopped. They probably came from the Punjab, although I don't know.

'Slowly you could see new signboards coming up in the town. The old shops belonged to Muslims. Now on the new boards you saw different names. Instead of the staid, English kind of shops you saw garish shops, brightly lit, with music. In Aminabad, old Lucknow, the Sindhis put up rows and rows of cloth shops. The first thing they started doing was shouting and asking you to come into their shops. "Come in, sister. Come and see." This was unheard-of among us. No glass cases there. Rickety little boxes. But a lot of those people who came then have now put up enormous shops full of chrome and glass.

'They were better businessmen than we were. They were better salesmen. They would sell smuggled goods – we never touched them. They would work on turnover rather than a decent margin. And our stocks began to get old and shop-soiled, and less in demand.'

In 1951 the *zamindari* system of land tenure was abolished. 'Land holdings were reduced. Hereditary rights were taken away from the major portion. The zamindari system had been established by the British in 1828. It replaced the Mogul *mansabdari* system, whereby land rights were given to people and they were required to supply a certain number of horses when required – in the mansabdari system your status depended on the number of horses you were assigned. So, in 1951, a lot of the zamindars or big landlords who had big houses in Lucknow – absentee landlords – had to adjust to changing times. A lot of them left for Pakistan. The abolition of zamindari removed our clientele in one fell swoop. All of a sudden the economy changed. And the English customers left. Our shop was "by appointment" to several governors of the province – it was that respected.

'Hazratgunj stopped being whitewashed. The roads were dirtier. You found a lot of pavement shops. It became impossible to walk on the footpaths. The whole atmosphere changed.'

With this calamity in business, there was a family tragedy. The family had a summer house in Mussoorie, and there one summer Rashid's elder brother was drowned. Altogether, the years just before and after Independence had brought blow after blow for Rashid's father: the very bad Hindu-Muslim riots in Calcutta in 1946, the Partition in 1947 and the loss of the Karachi shop, the abolition of zamindari, and now the loss of the elder son.

It was harder for the old than the young. Rashid was at the famous Anglo-Indian school in Lucknow, La Martinière, and he was very happy there. La Martinière had been founded by an 18th-century French adventurer, Claude Martin, who, having come to India, had taken service with the Nawabs of Oude. He had an Indian wife or wives, and at his death he left part of his great fortune, to set up schools for Eurasian children. A hundred and fifty years on, La Martinière at Lucknow still had a mixed, cosmopolitan atmosphere; and Rashid, during this time of family stress, was able to grow up with a certain amount of security, and almost in a kind of political innocence.

'We had boys from every community in the school, all from the same middle-class background. The families knew each other. I took my world for granted. It was there, the family was there, the extended family, the cousins. Religion was just part of life. It wasn't a burden. A lot of things helped there – the school, and the friends who came to call at my father's house: they were people of all religions. We were made to read the Koran with a succession of moulvis, but we never got beyond the first chapter.

'Our father never forced us to go to the mosque, and I personally have never been. It was my temperament: there was no death-of-God attitude in that. We would go to the *majlis*, at the imambara or at friends' houses, ostensibly to listen to religious discourses about the battle of Kerbala and the death of Hussain, the son of Ah. But, really, it was a social thing. This was the Shia side, as against the purely Islamic part, of our upbringing. The one thing my father was absolutely firm about was that on the 10th day of Mohurram we would go barefoot to Taalkatora-Karabala, a graveyard with an imambara where Shias were buried. This was an opportunity to visit the family graves also.'

Inevitably, as he grew up, Rashid became aware of all that Independence and Partition meant.

'It was a foregone conclusion that my sister would marry a Pakistani boy, because Muslims in India weren't doing so well, and the Pakistanis themselves wanted to marry a girl from the old country. Muslims in India weren't doing well, because after Partition there were no jobs for them, and a general lack of opportunity. There was the resentment of the majority community. It was but natural. First you fight to get a country, and then you refuse to go.

'It was also the survival of the fittest working. Every Muslim house split after Partition. There wasn't a family that wasn't affected. Parents stayed back, sons went away. The ones who stayed back were not ready to face the jungle. A lot of them were landlords, and they lacked the competitive spirit. My brother did brilliantly in his studies, in India and then in the United States. When he came back to India he couldn't get a job for six months. He went to Pakistan and got a job right away.

'Then the language started changing. Children over here were learning Hindi, and Muslim parents did not teach their children Urdu. We literally murdered Urdu. There was no preservation, such as the Armenians did for their language or the Jews did for Hebrew. Next to the religion, the language was dearest to the Muslim heart, because that was the essence of his identity. Urdu was not far from Hindustani, the lingua franca of the elite of the north-west. But Hindustani started changing, started to be more Sanskritized, became Hindi.'

In 1971 Rashid's parents went to Pakistan for the wedding of the brother who had migrated a few years before. While they were there, the second Indo-Pakistan war, the war over Bangladesh, occurred. Rashid's father, now very old, died in Pakistan at that time; his mother stayed on with the married son.

'Another strand was broken in my relationships. Up to this time I had been apprenticed to my father's shop. But when he passed away in Pakistan – and since the business was collapsing anyway – I closed it down.'

The shop had been started 60 years before, in the year of the coronation of the King-Emperor George V; it was closed down in the year the state of Pakistan broke into two. The whole life of the shop – though Rashid didn't make the point – had been contained between those two historical moments.

Rashid began to drift. He went to England and did odd jobs there. He sold six-month accident insurance for two pounds and five pounds from door to door. He had to knock and say, 'Good morning, are you the proprietor? My name is Rashid, and I believe this will interest you.' He hated the business of knocking on doors. One day – memories of Landau, the watch-seller, in the very big corner shop in Lucknow came to Rashid – a Jewish antique dealer from France opened to him, and told him, with some concern, that he wouldn't make it as an insurance salesman in London and he should go back to India. Rashid went to work in a pancake house. He worked in a Kentucky Fried Chicken shop. He learned to cut a chicken into nine equal pieces with an electric saw and to deep-fry the pieces for 11 minutes. He cut up 120 chickens a day.

He left England after two years. He went to Pakistan. He found they had no 'identity crisis' there; religion was not a man's distinguishing feature. But he didn't like the Pakistan money culture, the business aggressiveness of people who, when they had been in Lucknow, had been more easy-going. He didn't like the boasting about money and possessions; in Lucknow that simply wasn't done. He left, and went back to India, to Bombay, and worked for three years in an export company.

He was waiting for an inheritance. He was hoping to use that to go into the real estate business. But then he ran into a communal-minded official, and he began to find all kinds of obstructions thrown in his way. The litigation he had started then had gone on and on. He was near the end now, and the chances were that he was going to get what was his; but he had wasted many active years.

'I had never faced a communal problem before. Communal riots were something that happened to the lower classes. It's like the ethnic trouble you hear about in Pakistan. When I read or hear about it, I know that my brother won't be involved, that his house will be far away from the trouble. So, here, I mixed with my Hindu friends and never gave the matter a thought – until I had to face the wrath of a communal officer. That did shake me – that a man, just by the flick of his pen, could change my life so much.

'The Indo-Pakistan war of 1971 was a watershed not only in Muslim lives, but also in Hindu-Muslim relationships. The myth of Muslim superiority was all finished. Here was India playing a decisive role in the sub-continent. Every Muslim had a soft corner in his heart for Pakistan, and everyone was sad that the experiment had failed after less than 25 years. The dream had died. Then the

Pakistani soldiers were prisoners of war for two years. That was a constant reminder.

'I would feel a change taking place in personal relationships. My Hindu friends started lecturing. "What are Muslims doing with themselves?" They started becoming reformist about the Muslim faith and what they saw as our archaic practices. "How long are you Muslims going to carry on like this? How long are you going to be so dependent on your mullahs, your *mokallas?*" The sad fact was that there was a lot of truth in what they said. I was hurt, but we had to take it.'

The main palace of the last Nawab of Oude, the Kaiserbagh Palace in Lucknow, was nearly all destroyed by the British during the Indian Mutiny of 1857. In 1867, when British power seemed secure again, unchallenged, the surviving wing of the Kaiserbagh was given to the Raja of Mahmudabad as a city residence.

Almost 70 years later, the descendant of the Raja became the treasurer of the Muslim League, and campaigned for the formation of a separate Muslim state of Pakistan. Pakistan came into being 10 years later. And then – as though he hadn't fully worked out the consequences of the creation of Pakistan: Lucknow was in India, and many hundreds of miles away from Pakistan – the Raja found that he had made himself a wanderer. It wasn't until 1957 that he committed himself to the state for which he had campaigned. In that year he became a Pakistani citizen; with the result that, during the Indo-Pakistan war of 1965, all the Raja's property in Lucknow, the palaces and land, were taken over by the Indian government as enemy property.

The family property was still alien (rather than enemy) property. But petitions had been made to the Indian government, and the Raja's son, Amir, now lived in the Kaiserbagh Palace that had been granted by the British to his ancestor 120 years before.

I had met Amir in Parveen's drawing-room. He was in Indian evening dress, the long coat, the tight trousers. He was a small man, delicate in visage, sturdy in body, and he had the manner of a prince. An English public school and some years at Cambridge had given him an English style. But when I next met him, in the library of his palace, he was to tell me that when he spoke another language, Urdu, say, and when he was with people – Muslims, Shias – who might have looked up to him as a prince and a defender of the faith, he was quite different. Recent history had given him many styles, many personalities; had imposed strains on him such as his ancestors hadn't known.

Amir was now in state politics, and for three years or so had been a member of the Legislative Assembly in the Congress interest. His father had belonged to the Muslim League, which in the 1930s and 1940s had been opposed to the Congress. But now in India the Congress was the party that best served the interest of Muslims; and, in a further twist, as a politician Amir used the title, Raja of Mahmudabad, to establish the link with his forebears, and to give 'a focus of identification' to the local Shia and Muslim community.

His father's association with Pakistan could have been politically damaging; but Amir said that the people of Mahmudabad, 80 per cent of whom were Hindu, had never shown him or his family any hostility. And Amir honoured his father's memory. His father was a deeply religious man, with streaks of mysticism. He hated his caste, Amir said.

'My father never wanted to be a ruler. He couldn't bring himself to be a raja. He was most uneasy about benefiting from it. He thought income earned from property was tainted, since it wasn't earned by the sweat of one's brow.'

That idea had come to Amir's father when he was a child. It was an idea he had got from his mother. She, Amir's father's mother, came from a family of poor Muslim scholars who considered learning to be superior to wealth.

'My father's father was a maharaja, a man of personality, but not a socialist. He married for a second time, and relations between him and my father became strained. This was no doubt when my father developed his attitude to his caste. One of the first things I heard from my father – which I later understood to be one of the teachings of Ali – was: "You will not find abundant wealth without finding by its side the rights of people that have been trampled." And: "No rich morsel is eaten without there being in it the hunger of those who have worked for it."'

I said that such statements applied to poor or feudal countries. They couldn't apply to all countries.

Amir said, 'People in England may not be able to understand the kind of destitution and misery that exists in India.'

Though Amir didn't say so directly, it might have been his father's religious nature that made him campaign for a separate Islamic state of Pakistan – not merely a homeland for Muslims, but a religious state. Amir's father began wearing homespun when he was very young. When, in 1936, at the age of twenty-one, he joined the Muslim League, he gave up music, which he and the rest of the family had loved – Indian classical music, western classical, Iranian classical.

Amir was born in 1943. When he was two years old, his ears were pierced. It was the custom in Muslim countries for slaves' ears to be pierced; and the piercing of Amir's ears meant that he had been sold to the Imam: the child had been pledged to the service of the Shia faith. This service began soon. When India and Pakistan became independent in 1947, Amir, then aged four, started on a wandering life with his father and mother.

'After Partition my father left India. He was a very committed man, but he wasn't a politician. Just before Independence we were in Baluchistan, in Quetta, in what had become Pakistan. On the day of Independence we crossed the border into Iran. We went to Zahedan, and from there we went in two buses to Mashhad, and then to Tehran. We went on to Iraq by air. The convoy followed by road. This was in 1948.'

Although they were now living this wandering life, Amir's father had transferred no money out of India. All he had taken with him were books and carpets.

'My father was invited to return to India on certain conditions – that he took no part in public life, that he condemned the Nizam of Hyderabad, and that he spoke out against cow-slaughter. These conditions were not acceptable to my father. He said he was willing to give an undertaking not to eat beef personally, but he couldn't speak out against cow-slaughter, because beef was the cheapest food for Muslims.'

They went, in Iraq, still with Indian passports, to Kerbala. This was the site of the battle where Hussain, son of Ali, had died; it was sacred ground to Shias. On this sacred ground there arose in Amir's father's mind – perhaps it had been there all along – some idea of having his son become an ayatollah, a Shia divine. In 1950 Amir, aged seven, was sent to a religious school in Kerbala. He stayed at the school for two years. And then his father – who had begun to earn a livelihood by importing tea and jute from India – changed his mind, and decided that Amir should have a secular education, after all. This didn't mean, Amir said, a turning away from the religious side of things. Ali himself had said, 'The best form of worship is reflection and thought, and there is no form of worship that is better than reflection, thought and knowledge.' Before Ali, the Prophet had said, 'Acquire knowledge if you have to go to China.'

I asked Amir, 'What did they mean by knowledge?'

He said, 'Ali was once asked, "What is knowledge?" He said, "Knowledge is of two kinds. One is the knowledge of religions." And that is interesting – the plural, *religions,* rather than religion. "The other is the knowledge of the physical world."'

The first idea was that Amir should be sent to a Jesuit school outside India. But then it was decided to send Amir and his mother back to Lucknow; and in Lucknow Amir, now in his 10th year, was enrolled at the Anglo-Indian school of La Martinière. This was when Amir – who had seemed so English in Parveen's drawing-room – began to speak English; until then his languages had been Urdu and Persian.

Culture upon culture now: because the boy who went to La Martinière felt, after his time in Iraq, that part of him was Arab or Iranian. After his classes at La Martinière there were special religious lessons at home every day, in the very room of the palace where we were now sitting – cool, with the solid brick-work of old Lucknow, with a terrazzo floor, and with bookshelves inset in the damp-marked, whitewashed walls.

The Muslim and Shia festivals were also constant reminders of the faith. Amir took 12 days off for Mohurram – 'The principal of La Martinière was most disapproving' – and a further four days for the 40th day after the martyrdom. At the end of Mohurram there were another eight days off, and there were four days more in Ramadan – the month of purification, and of the martyrdom of Ali, and of the beginning of the revelation of the Koran.

During his time at La Martinière Amir was living in the palace with his mother, his two aunts, and his father's brother and his wife. To protect him from untoward influences, he was not allowed to visit other boys or to become involved with their families. He had his own guardian, a childless man, who stayed in the palace day and night. This man – who also had a knowledge of Urdu and Persian which Amir found remarkable – followed Amir 'like a shadow', even when the boy went to the cinema or a restaurant. At La Martinière he would wait in the car, or just outside it, sitting on a carpet on the ground, while Amir was at his classes.

'As a result of this I became a reticent person, extremely withdrawn. I had difficulty in talking. If there were outsiders, I found it impossible to open my mouth.

'I used to wear philacteries underneath my shirt, and boys at school would feel them and tease me. The other thing I used to wear were ear-rings, in my pierced ears. I used to wear an emerald in my right ear, and a ruby in the left. This looked very strange, and I would twist both my ears and hide the stones behind the ear lobe. I took these off – I was permitted to take them off – when I went to England, after the end of my schooling here.'

All this time the Raja, Amir's father, had been living in Iraq. But then in 1957, 10 years after the creation of Pakistan, he took the step which was to cause his family a good deal of hardship: the Raja went to Pakistan, and changed his Indian passport for a Pakistani one.

Amir said, 'My mother became very ill when she heard the news, right here. My mother is a rani in her own right, a woman of great pride. She never tried to take anything from my father. She was also religious. She lost both her parents when she was nine. She was ill when she heard the news about my father in Pakistan, because she felt that the great crises of 1947 had passed – not one voice had been raised in Mahmudabad against my father. Nehru met my father and asked him to think again, and to keep his Indian passport. Nehru said, "You've always acted impulsively. We all would be happy if you return and take your passport back." My father said, "One cannot change one's nationality like one's clothes."'

And Pakistan didn't work out for the Raja. He had had the idea of going into politics, but then he discovered that it wouldn't do for him. He was a Shia, in a country with a Sunni majority; he didn't have a local language in Pakistan; and he was a *mohajir,* a foreigner. His political ideas had also changed. In the 1930s and 1940s, when he was very young, he had wanted Pakistan to be a religious state. He thought now that it should be a secular state. He didn't believe that the Pakistan army would stand for that kind of politics. So he left Pakistan and began to travel again. He spent much time in the old imperial capital, London.

It might have seemed from this account that, in his young man's agitation for the creation of Pakistan, the Raja had been irresponsible; that he hadn't foreseen the political convulsions or worked out the human consequences; that other people had been asked to pay for his Muslim and Shia piety, while he himself had been keeping his options open for as long as possible. Iraq, Pakistan, England, India – these were all countries to which he might have gone, as a man of standing.

But people have their own ideas of their predicament. Of this wandering stage of his father's life Amir said, 'I think it was almost like a penance, you see. I feel it was necessary for him to undergo the same process of homelessness that other people had gone through when they left India and went to Pakistan.

'I used to visit him every year. One of the books he made me read was Pearey Lai's *Gandhi: the Last Phase.* He was greatly moved by the fact that at the time of Independence Gandhi was nowhere to be seen. He wasn't in Delhi. He was in Calcutta, mourning and grieving for the tragedies of that city.' The tragedies of the religious riots of 1946, which marked the beginning of the end for the city of Calcutta. 'In the Shia way of feeling, if there is grief and mourning on one hand, and celebration on the other, the Shia tilts to the grief.'

After Amir had finished his schooling at La Martinière his parents didn't know what to do with him, and he lost some time. At last, in 1961, when he was eighteen, he was taken by his father to England and placed in a public school. That was when he was allowed to take off his earrings. On the way to England they stopped off in Lebanon, where the Raja had many friends; and later they did a tour of Europe. In Paris they went to a casino and a night-club: the Raja wanted his son to see what these places were like, and he wanted his son to see them first with his father as his companion.

At eighteen, Amir was somewhat old for a public school. But he spent three years there, until he got into Cambridge, to do mathematics.

'I wasn't treated too badly at school. I was still withdrawn. I was friendly with a few boys. I cherished my faith. For me it was a sort of armour. For me the fact that something is secret and personal and internalized gives it a new dimension and a strength. The fact that you can't perform or express it, what you feel, heightens the experience, the power of that.'

Amir was to enter Pembroke College, Cambridge, in 1965. Before that, he was taken by his father on a tour of Pakistan and the Middle East. They met Shia divines, and in Lebanon they stayed with Sayed Musa Sadr.

'I heard world affairs discussed between my father and him in language and idiom which later became part of the Iranian revolution and the uprising in Lebanon. They talked of the presence of the western powers in Lebanon, the kind of regime that existed in Iraq – oppressive, anti-religious. They talked about the Shah in Iran. They talked about the need for bringing about a revolution on the principles of Ali – which I thought most Utopian, and said so to my father.'

After this Shia exaltation, this talk of revolution and the rule of Ali, there was calamity. So far, the Raja's political actions and gestures had been without great personal consequences. Now, overnight, everything changed. In September 1965, a few weeks before Amir went up to Pembroke College, Cambridge, there was war between India and Pakistan, and all the Raja of Mahmudabad's property in India was declared enemy property. Had the Raja foreseen that consequence when he became a Pakistani citizen in 1957 – or when, 30 years before, he had started to agitate for a separate Muslim state?

Amir said, 'Our palace in Mahmudabad, the Qila, was totally sealed – the place where I had grown up, and my father and his forebears. None of my family was permitted to enter it. All the income was taken by the Government of India through the Custodian of Enemy Property. The Cambridge term was about to begin. I got letters from home, saying how the Armed Constabulary had come and surrounded the Qila and sealed every door. Although there was this terrible blow, my family *never* thought of moving to Pakistan.

'The Qila was sealed for a year and a half, during which time there were two big robberies. An enormous amount of very valuable things was taken away. During this period my uncle and my mother petitioned the government to permit them to observe Mohurram in the Qila – that had been our family tradition. Permission was eventually given, with the condition that they were confined to two rooms and one bathroom. They accepted the condition, and they went and lived in verandahs. The imambaras were open, though – that was where the Mohurram ceremonies actually took place.

'I was in Cambridge all this time. I was very distressed. My work suffered. A lot of people didn't know all the background. I talked to my tutor. I used to read the life of Ali, for consolation. And certain chapters and verses of the Koran.'

I asked what the verses of the Koran were.

Amir said, reconstructing a verse from memory, '"I give good tidings to those who are not weak but have been weakened." Let me get the actual verse. I know it very well. I will have no trouble finding it.'

He got up from the white-covered table at which we were sitting, went to the next room, and came back with a small blue-covered book. But he couldn't find the verse in that book. He went to shelves on the opposite wall, took down a bigger book, came and sat again at the table. While he looked in the book he said, 'This verse occurs again and again in the Irani revolution.' He sometimes, said 'Irani' for 'Iranian'. At last he found the verse. He read it to himself first of all. I could see that he was moved. Then he read it aloud to me.

'"And we wished to be gracious to those who were being oppressed in the land, to make them leaders, and to establish a firm place for them in the land, and to show Pharoah and Haman and the hosts at their hands the very things against which they were taking precautions."' He paused, and said, 'This gives an understanding of the Shiites right from the time of Imam Ali onwards. The "oppressed" here doesn't mean someone inherently weak, but those who have been made weak by circumstances, and have latent in them the power of faith and action.

'I used to read this at Cambridge. It's a promise, you see, a promise of God's. This is actually about the children of Israel, but it has been used throughout the history of the Shiites as a promise of deliverance.'

Amir read further in his big book, read the fine print of notes, and said, 'It's one of the Meccan revelations. Before the flight to Medina. The Meccan revelations are noted for their poetry.'

I said, 'While the Prophet was still only a prophet?'

Amir said, 'That might suggest he stopped being a Prophet, and would be blasphemous.'

'Before he became a ruler? While he was still without temporal power?'

'That would be better.' He said again, 'The Meccan revelations are well known for their poetic quality.'

While Amir was trying in this way in Cambridge to reconcile himself to the loss of the family property, his father was in Pakistan again. But the next year the Raja came to England, to work at the Islamic Institute in Regent's Park; and he stayed there while Amir did his studies. It was now open to the Raja, as someone working in England, to become a British subject again. If he had done so, he would have ceased to be an 'enemy' or an 'alien', and the Indian government would have released his property in Lucknow and Mahmudabad. But the Raja preferred to carry the cross of his Pakistani citizenship, though it was still bringing hardship to his family.

Amir's academic work developed. After he had done his Cambridge degree, he went to Imperial College in London; and then he went back to Cambridge, to the Institute of Astronomy.

'Things quietened down. I reconciled myself to the situation at home, and resolved to undo some of the problems. But the problems remain. The Qila at Mahmudabad is open now. I use it and maintain it, but it is still not our property. Were it not for my mother's investments and so forth, it would be impossible to live there.'

In 1971 there was the Indo-Pakistan war over Bangladesh.

'It was a blow from which my father never recovered. He died two years later. He was very unhappy when he died – this unparallelled bloodshed by the Pakistan army in Bangladesh, and the materialistic crassness of Pakistan itself. He was very unhappy about the types of rulers and the classes that had come up.'

Amir took his father's body to the shrine of Mashhad in eastern Iran. The Raja had hoped, when Amir was a child, that Amir might have become a famous ayatollah, in the Iranian tradition. This hadn't happened; but Amir was greatly moved by the journey to Mashhad with his father's body.

'Some of the ulema, the religious teachers who had known my father, made the announcement that the body of an *aim,* a Shia divine, a servant of the faith, had come from London. And my father was buried just outside the shrine, in a cemetery where many eminent theologians had been buried. The burial was intended to be temporary – the final burial was to be in Kerbala in Iraq. In 1976 I heard from the Iranians that the Shah had given orders for the cemetery to be turned into a park, and that there was a danger that my father's grave might have been obliterated. But when I went to Mashhad I found that, owing to the intervention of Mr Bhutto' – the prime minister of Pakistan: the Raja had died a Pakistan citizen – 'my father's body had been reburied within the inner shrine.'

So in death the devout Raja had found a kind of fulfilment. His political and religious passion had bequeathed many languages, many cultures, many modes of thought and emotion to his son. He had had his son's ears pierced, to pledge him to the service of the faith; and Amir had indeed inherited something of his father's passion. But with that – his academic work in Cambridge and London had been in astronomy – Amir had also developed religious doubts.

'These doubts began at school and continued at university, and at periods became intense. But the totality of my experience –

which is of an historical or cultural nature – is so deep and ingrained in my being that it's now indelible. It's a sort of dialectical process, in which religion, and the concerns of the real world, unfold for me a path in a dialectical manner. I veer towards religion to seek support in worldly matters. And that brings me back to doubts, and then back again to religion. I move back and forth between both worlds.'

(He had arrived, it seemed, at the Hindu idea of opposites: the worldly life, the life of the spirit: *loukika, vaidhika.* But that idea didn't interest him.) At Cambridge he had been attracted by some aspects of Marxism. He was especially attracted by the Marxist attempt to analyse history scientifically. But it was his Shia faith that made him receptive to the larger Marxist idea.

'There are a great number of elements and contradictions in my way of thinking. The aspect of Marxism which drew me was its concern with bringing about a just and more equitable society, especially for the oppressed, the insulted and the injured. My instinct was to go to Trotsky and Che Guevara, neither of whom succeeded, though their message lived. Kerbala, you see.' Kerbala, where Hussain, son of Ali, had perished. 'So the world picture given me by Marxism ran into my own religious picture.'

It was this mixture of historical and religious ideas that reconciled him to the long Muslim decline here in Lucknow.

'I find solace in both ways of thinking. The historical way shows me that human destiny is above this – our sufferings, our little problems. This idea of human destiny shows me that we are really moving towards a better world, in spite of all the trouble and conflagration. The religious way teaches me endurance, reconciliation with the divine plan of which this is a part, but with hope and belief in a better future. The Koranic verse I read out to you has been the sustenance of so many peoples throughout the world.

'I felt in my own case it was a great help I was a Shia, because from childhood I was acquainted with people who had fought for ideals and had been vanquished, ostensibly by earthly power, and yet had left such a profound imprint on history. I feel proud that most of my ancestors didn't care about material success so much as about what they believed in. I am very proud of my father's life.' His father admired Gandhi. 'The fact that his possessions were spectacles, sandals, a staff, a few changes of clothes, and books, brought him nearer to the ideal of the Shia ruler, as Ali was. The link between my father and Gandhi was that he realized that religion could be used to bring about a great change of consciousness – about the world and the place of men in it – and also to bring men to action.'

I asked him what the Kaiserbagh Palace meant to him.

'One has a kind of bond with it – all the changes, all the things that have happened, all the forebears. It's almost as if it, the house, is an organic, living thing.'

The wing in which he lived was 400 feet long by 100 feet wide, and it was on two floors. The whole wing was occupied. I asked about the number of servants.

He said, 'Goodness, I haven't counted. Certainly three figures for the retainers and their families. In my mother's kitchen upstairs meals are cooked *every day* for about 40 people, on an average. A great expense. At times I wonder whether it's worth it. But I know I can't leave it. I have a pied-à-terre in London, in Hampstead. That's a refuge. No servants.'

He had returned from the Astronomy Institute in 1978, and had been living in Lucknow more or less permanently since that time. Then, three years ago, he had gone into state politics. After the 1985 elections, he had written to Rajiv Gandhi, reminding him of the links between their two families, and offering to serve. It was suggested to him that he should contest a seat in the state elections. He didn't think he would get the nomination; he thought that there might have been hostility towards him because of his father's past. But he did get the nomination; the hostility he did attract was that of the man he had displaced.

'He grew up here in the palace. His family served our family for three generations. I knew him very well. It's like a film, like something in a novel. Before the elections, he used to come here every day. He's now doing everything he can to finish me off in every way. He's immensely rich now.'

Amir was smiling.

I said, 'You appear to be managing.'

He laughed. 'After all the things we've been talking about – to come down to *this! This:* the rage of a political rival.

We had been talking for a long time, sitting at a big table covered with a white tablecloth. Behind him were inset bookshelves, part of his library. From time to time during the day Amir's very young son, Ali, had appeared, and idly gone in and out of various doors. We had had lunch, sandwiches and fried fish, not from the kitchen upstairs, but from the Kwality restaurant in Lucknow. (I heard this later from Rashid. He knew the palace servants, and he had seen them at Kwality's when they had gone to get the take-away lunch.)

It was cool in the library–sitting-room of the palace. Wajid Ali Shah, the last Nawab of Oude, had planned the palace on Versailles lines, it was said; but perhaps what was meant by that was only that he had planned to build a lot. The walls were thick; they were made of the thin Lucknow brick and the special mortar of lime and ground-stone. The temperature was so benign that I had stopped thinking about it. But warmth and dazzle were outside all the time, and they made themselves felt as soon as we were out of the library, and in the dust of the drive.

Outside, too, were some of the palace servants Amir had spoken about, thin men standing up and, whether noticed or not, making constant gestures of obeisance and keeping their eyes fixed on their master: men quite unlike the waiters of restaurants or the staff of hotels, or even the staff of the main Lucknow club: men made by the security and idleness and antique etiquette of palace life.

We were going to the Legislative Assembly. Amir wanted to show it to me. But we were delayed for a while. A car came down the drive. It held a constituent. He jumped out of his car; Amir got out of his. The two men shook hands, and Amir told his constituent that he would be back in half an hour or 40 minutes.

He said he saw about 20 people a day. At any rate, 20 people came to see him. It was the side of political life he didn't care for. The people who came to see him often had impossible requests, about jobs or their dismissal from jobs, or about the fixing of tribunals of inquiry. They sometimes even wanted Amir, as their elected representative, to bribe people on their behalf. Amir wasn't like Prakash, the minister, in Bangalore. Amir wasn't amused, as Prakash was, by this aspect of the human comedy; he didn't enjoy the theatre of the morning crowd of suppliants and downright beggars at his door. Amir didn't like being badgered. He had discovered, he said, that people were never grateful for what you did for them; they always felt you could have done more.

The legislature was not in session. We looked at the chamber through the glass door. The formality and ritual of the chamber appealed to Amir. But he was enervated by the pettiness of much of political life. The vendetta of the man he had displaced, however much he appeared to laugh at it, was emotionally draining, an entanglement and irritation he could have done without.

'Politics costs a lot of money, and I feel guilty squandering – if the word can be used – money on politics. I have doubts about continuing.' But to someone of his ancestry there was a special appeal in public life. 'My political life has renewed and revived the link between my family and the people of Mahmudabad which had atrophied since 1936. That was the year my father became a member of the Working Committee of the Muslim League.' And his election victory from Mahmudabad wasn't something he could easily turn his back on. 'It was a moving experience, because the people of Mahmudabad – 80 per cent Hindu – voted overwhelmingly in my favour, in spite of my father's politics. It was an unprecedented majority in the district of Lucknow. My mother was very touched. She said – on election night in the

Qila – that she hadn't seen the Qila filled with so many people since her childhood.'

The Hindu spring festival of Holi, which had emptied the Legislative Assembly, had also emptied the school of La Martinière. The buildings were famous: a late 18th-century French or European extravagance in far-off India. The grounds were immense; and, as so often in such settings, one thought with something like envy of the man who, 200 years or so ago, had had the foresight or the luck to buy so much land. The school was important to people who had grown up in Lucknow. It figured in the memories of Rashid and his friends. It figured in the memories of Amir, and in a printed memoir by his father.

It was still a private school: the money available was not enough to keep it absolutely in repair. To approach the school from dusty scrub at the back, to see the weeds sprouting out of the masonry, taking root on ledges, was like seeing something about to become a ruin. It was in better order at the front, more impressive. There were well-watered green gardens there, full of colour.

On this quiet day, with the great expanse of the sunstruck grounds, and their burnt colour, it was again – as with the view of the Gumti River from the hotel window – like being in the original of one of the late 18th-century prints of the Daniells. The Daniells would have been of the period of the self-styled General Martin, would have been of that period when a European soldier of fortune could have sold some of the skills of Europe to an Asian ruler for vast sums.

Some such thought must have been going through Rashid's head as well. His memories of La Martinière had been entirely happy; and an old boy's school pride had made him bring me here. Yet the sight of the Oude cannon cast by the general, still with the general's name in big raised letters, polished to a shine by the innumerable hands that had caressed them – the sight of that on the wide terrace at the front of the school had stirred up old ideas of Muslim and

Indian helplessness and defeat; and, quite unexpectedly, Rashid had begun to be enraged by the thought of European and American experts of today, the successors of General Martin, travelling regally about the poorer countries.

He was overcome by his mood. He stayed in the shade in the pillared front loggia, and sent me out into the sun to look at the names of old boys carved on the wide stone steps at the front of the terrace.

Some other idea of loss was working on him, something to add to all that had been lost since the 18th century.

He said later, 'All the masters here used to be Anglo-Indians, except for the Hindi master. They were very respected. Their families have now gone to Australia. Their families had been in Lucknow for generations. The Anglo-Indians had been mostly in the railways, teaching, and the police. The railways were absolutely their show. And their colonies, the areas where they lived, were outside the city – lovely, clean places. After 1947 they packed their bags and left.'

Something of that melancholy attached also to Hazratgunj, the main shopping street of Lucknow in the old days, where Rashid's family had had their camera shop, and where Landau the watch-maker had had his big corner shop. Landau's corner was now Ramlal and Sons, a cloth and sari shop, with the slogan, 'Our Collection is Your Selection'. Not far away was the house where MacGregor, the old Hazratgunj tailor, who had made clothes for princes and IAS men and Raj Englishmen, had lived until his death.

The melancholy of the recent past, there. Elsewhere, the memories of the defeats of 130 years before, in the ruins of the Residency and of the Nawab's palace and hunting lodge. Before that, and just as painful now, the reminder of the glory of the older Nawabs: especially in the monument known as the Great Imambara, built as famine relief work in the late 18th century: over-decorated, weak, but impressive by its sheer scale. No great architecture in the old princely city, but many parks, many places to walk in: not many cities in India had this kind of style. But these walks saddened Rashid, as they were saddening him that afternoon, bringing out the tragic Shia side of his nature, the side that dealt in defeat, grief, and injustice.

He said, 'Lucknow is me. It's not the river or the buildings or anything. You don't like your father because he's six feet two inches, and handsome. He's your father. In this way, Lucknow is me. We've been here for generations, on both sides.'

What did it mean, being a Lucknow Muslim?

'It's like the Buddhist idea of "Not this, not this". I'm an Indian, but the temple is not for me. I'm a Muslim, but in its details my faith cannot be the same faith as the one in Afghanistan or Iran or Pakistan. I speak Urdu. I greet people in the Lucknow Muslim way. I say "My respects to you" instead of "Peace be upon you". I derive my sustenance from Lucknow. It gives me my sense of identity – the buildings, the monuments, the culture, the relationships.'

There was a new white palace that could be seen above the greenery from many places in the city. It was called the Butler Palace, and the story was that it had been built by Amir's father as a palace of pleasure for a British official, Sir Harcourt Butler. It was part of the property that Amir had lost. It was still in the possession of the Custodian of Alien Property, and it had been rented out for 38,000 rupees a year to the Indian Council of Philosophical Research. The palace, so far as as some of its motifs went, was in the Lucknow style. It wasn't a distinguished building: all that gave it a palace feel were the four many-sided towers at the corners.

In one of those towers an elevator had been installed. Upstairs was a very large philosophical library; many of the volumes were new, and looked unused. No finer or more respectful use could have been made of the building. But, from what Rashid said, that didn't assuage Amir's grief. Amir, Rashid said, had never set foot in the Butler Palace since it had ceased to be his.

I asked Rashid afterwards – at the end of our tour of old Lucknow, the city of schools and palaces – about his visits to

Pakistan. I wanted him to tell me a little more. I wanted more concrete details.

He said, 'In India the beggars asked for small change. In Pakistan they asked for a rupee. The customs officers in Pakistan were taller and better built than on the Indian side, and this was the first time I'd seen a Punjabi Muslim. But then I thought – and I wonder whether you'd understand this – "What's the use of their being Muslims, if they speak this crude Punjabi, and not chaste Urdu?" You see, I had associated Muslims with Urdu and culture.

'When I went to Lahore I thought it was a better version of Lucknow: a whitewashed Lucknow, where all the people had had a bath and changed their clothes. It was pleasing to see. There was a funny thing: you looked at the cinema advertisements, and, because they were making copies of Indian pictures – the Pakis can't make a picture to save their lives – you saw the names of pictures you knew, but with new stars, different faces. In Lahore you feel at first you are in a different city of India which you are visiting for the first time. But slowly the differences become apparent. You meet a person, you get to talking. You think he is a Punjabi, tall, well-built, speaking Urdu in a crude Punjabi accent. You ask him where his father is from, and he says Lucknow – and you are left amazed, because you are now so different from each other after 40 years.

'I stayed for two months, but I knew I couldn't belong there, in spite of the wealth. Even the relatives I met had changed. They were more worldly-wise; they were more aggressive. They had become like the refugees who had come from the Punjab and Sind to Lucknow. I had a cousin who was a trader. He had a finger in every pie; he could bribe every officer; he knew that the main thing was to move and make money. He had been made homeless twice, the first time in 1947, at Independence, and then in 1971, in Chittagong in Bangladesh. He knew he could depend on nothing but money. Other values didn't matter. He was quite different from the person I remembered.

'Another thing I found over there was that there was no living in the past, as with us here. They had a healthier attitude to Partition than the Indian Muslim. What was done was done. They'd started a new life – they'd forgotten the people they'd left behind, even the people who still remembered them and thought of them and had sent messages through me.

'After my two months I was glad to leave. I felt relief to be back in India, after the claustrophobia of an Islamic society. I liked seeing women again on the streets. The dirt and filth of India didn't seem to matter. The people in Pakistan were relaxed enough about their religion. It was just the wretched laws, hanging like a cloud over one: the call to prayers, the moulvi coming to my friend's house and asking why he hadn't seen us at the mosque recently. The thought police. Islam on wheels.

'I felt relief to be back here. That sense of belonging, which I had in India, I knew I couldn't find anywhere else. Yet I also know that I can never be a complete person now. I can't ignore Partition. It's a part of me. I feel rudderless. If there had been no Partition I might have been a married man with all the paraphernalia of a middle-class Muslim existence. But I've lived all my life so far as a bachelor, and it's now too late for me to change. The creation and existence of Pakistan has damaged a part of my psyche. I simply cannot pretend it doesn't exist. I cannot pretend that life goes on, and I can have the normal full emotional life, as though what had been here before is still around me.'

# 7
# WOMAN'S ERA

Some weeks later, when I had left India, and was among my own things again, I looked at a book I had bought many years before but hadn't read in any connected way. The book was *My Diary in India in the Year 1858–9*. The author was William Howard Russell; he was described on the title page as the special correspondent of *The Times*. It was as correspondent of *The Times* that Russell had made his name in the years immediately before, during the Crimean War: his reports about the hospital conditions of the British expeditionary force had caused Florence Nightingale to be sent out to the Crimea. It was with that reputation, and no doubt with the hope of repeating something of that success, that, nine months after coming back to England, he had gone off again, to the Mutiny in India.

Train and ship and train to Paris; train to Marseilles; steamer to Malta and Alexandria; train to Cairo and Suez; three weeks in a steamer to Ceylon and Calcutta. And then by cart and rail and cart to the front.

Russell was thirty-six. He was the only correspondent who had been sent out by a British newspaper to report on the Mutiny 'and the revolt which followed it'. The 'letters' he sent back to *The Times* were duly published in the paper. Then the diary, which supplied the letters, was prepared for the press, 800 pages in all, with yellow-tinted lithographs and an engraved map. It was published in 1860 in two volumes by the firm of Routledge, Warne, and

Routledge: Victorian energy making a great effort – a hard journey, and a sustained literary labour – appear effortless.

The Russell of the Crimea was famous enough to enter the history books. I learned about him at school in Trinidad; he was the first foreign correspondent I ever knew about. The Russell of the Indian Mutiny I didn't know; I had never heard of his Indian book until I saw the two volumes in the antiquarian bookshop. They would have been handsome, authoritative-looking volumes when they were new, with an angular decorative pattern stamped on the hard covers bound in purple cloth. Light had bleached the purple colour to a pale brown on the back of both volumes, had caused a fade at the top edge and the bottom edge of the covers, had cracked the purple cloth down one hinge of the binding, and had nibbled away at the brittle top.

I found the book hard to read. I thought the writer took too long to get to India; and what engaged him on the way didn't seem very interesting. When I looked at the later pages I found the tactical military details hard to follow. At the time of the writing those details would have been the hot news from India; they didn't hold me now. There were other things in India in 1858 and 1859 that I found myself looking for.

But after this trip to India, and especially after my walks in Lucknow with Rashid, the *Diary* became a different book. The long journey to India that Russell described was in fact a journey to the battle for Lucknow. The engraved fold-out map at the beginning of the text was labelled 'Plan of the Operations against Lucknow March 1858'. On that map I saw a number of the places Rashid had shown me.

The British army had encamped in the Dilkusha park, the park of 'Heart's Delight'. The hunting lodge of the Nawabs, not yet in ruin, and to Russell's eye like a French château, was the British commander-in-chief's headquarters. It was annoyed by one of the Nawab's cannon at La Martinière. Among the people firing on the British positions from La Martinière were some of the Nawab's

African eunuchs – strange that such people still existed in India in 1858. I wonder what Rashid would have made of that detail in Russell's book. Perhaps the detail would have been obliterated by the rage and grief he would have felt at the defeat, and by the sacking of the Kaiserbagh Palace afterwards – in the surviving wing of which I had met and talked to Amir, whose ancestors had been given the palace by the British nine years after that sacking.

One of the yellow-tinted lithographs was entitled 'The Plunder of the Kaiserbagh'. It had been done, later in England, and was an illustration of Russell's text: 'It was one of the strangest and most distressing sights that could be seen; but it was also most exciting . . . Imagine courts as large as the Temple Gardens, surrounded with ranges of palaces, or at least buildings well stuccoed and gilded, with fresco-paintings on the blind windows . . . From the broken portals issue soldiers laden with loot or plunder. Shawls, rich tapestry, gold and silver brocade, caskets of jewels, arms, splendid dresses. The men are wild with fury and lust of gold – literally drunk with plunder . . . I had often heard the phrase, but never saw the thing itself before. They smashed to pieces the fowling-pieces and pistols to get at the gold mountings and the stones set in the stocks. They burned in a fire, which they made in a centre of the court, brocades and embroidered shawls for the sake of the gold and the silver . . . Oh, the toil of that day! It was horrid enough to have to stumble through endless courts, which were like vapour baths, amid dead bodies, through sights worthy of the Inferno . . . suffocated by deadly smells of rotting corpses, of rotten ghee, or vile native scents; but the seething crowd of camp followers into which we emerged in Huzrutgunj was something worse. As ravenous, and almost as foul, as vultures . . .'

Two days before, Russell had got 'a small bit of loot of very little value': a portrait of the King of Oude, which he had cut out of its frame. He had taken the portrait from a room in the Badshahbagh, 'a large walled garden and enclosure, amid one of the finest of the King of Oude's summer palaces'. A small piece of loot, after horrors: the protective ditch around the Badshahbagh 'was filled with the bodies of sepoys, which the coolies were dragging from the inside and throwing topsy-turvy, by command of the soldiers; stiffened by death, with outstretched legs and arms, burning slowly in their cotton tunics . . . We crossed literally a ramp of dead bodies loosely covered with earth.' More dead soldiers were being burned in the rooms inside. 'It was before breakfast, and I could not stand the smell.'

A more substantial piece of loot came to Russell from the Kaiserbagh: 'a nose-ring of small rubies and pearls, with a single stone diamond drop.' He had a chance that time of getting an armlet of emeralds and diamonds and pearls as well, but the soldier who had looted it wanted 100 rupees in ready cash, there and then, and – 'Oh, wretched fate!' – all Russell's money was with his Indian Christian servant, Simon, who was in the camp. Russell heard later that a jeweller – whether in England or India is not said – had bought the armlet from an officer for £7,500, a very large sum in 1860.

The ruins of the Residency still had the power to enrage Rashid; he would have found it hard to bear this account of the looting of his beloved Lucknow. And harder perhaps to bear Russell's accounts of Lucknow before its destruction, 'more extensive than Paris and more brilliant'. From the top of the hunting lodge in the Dilkusha, this was the view: 'A vision of palaces, minars, domes azure and golden, cupolas, colonnades, long facades of fair perspective in pillar and column, terraced roofs – all rising up amid a calm still ocean of the brightest verdure. Look for miles and miles away, and still the ocean spreads . . . Not Rome, not Athens, not Constantinople, not any city I have ever seen appears to me so striking and beautiful as this . . .'

Of the Kaiserbagh, which even in that 'wilderness of fair architecture' Russell saw as 'vast . . . a blaze of gilding, spires, cupolas, domes', there remained only the wing where Amir and his mother lived with their establishments. Rashid had told me more than once that in the old days there were no streets around the palace, only gardens, and it was only from Russell's book that I began to understand to what an extent royal Lucknow had been a city of palaces and gardens.

Across the river from my hotel – beyond the higher dry shelf in the channel with the huts now of the swimming clubs, the black buffaloes on some mornings, the sheets and the many-coloured clothes spread out by the washermen to dry, where I had seen the deep perspective views of an aquatint by the Daniells – on that bank there would have been the Badshahbagh, the Royal Garden.

'Such forests of orange-trees, such trickling fountains, shady walks, beds of flowers, grand alleys, dark retreats and summer-houses . . . in which were now revelling some of the Welch Fusileers.'

There was a similar – perhaps French-inspired – elegance in the many courtyards of the Kaiserbagh, the main palace.

'Statues, lines of lamp-posts, fountains, orange-groves, aqueducts, and kiosks with burnished domes of metal . . . Lying amid the orange-groves are dead and dying sepoys; and the white statues are reddened with blood. Leaning against a smiling Venus is a British soldier shot through the neck, gasping . . . Court after court the scene is still the same. These courts open one to the other by lofty gateways, ornamented with the double fish of the royal family of Oude, or by arched passageways, in which lie the dead sepoys, their clothes smouldering on their flesh.'

It is ironical that – as with Bernal Díaz del Castillo's account of Montezuma's city of Mexico in 1520 – the first account of the splendours of 10th-century Lucknow should also be an account of its destruction. It is ironical, yet not unexpected: the history of old India was written by its conquerors.

What was pain for Rashid was also pain for me. I couldn't read with detachment of the history of this part of India. My emotions ran congruent for a while with those of Rashid; but we grieved for different things. Rashid grieved for the wholeness of the Lucknow world he had been born into, the world before Partition. This world would have had elements of old Muslim glory: the glory of the Kings or Nawabs of Oude, and before them the glory of the Moguls. There was no such glory in my past. Russell's journey from Calcutta to Lucknow lay in part through the districts from which, about 20 or 25 years later, my ancestors migrated to Trinidad, to work on the plantations there.

That was the lesser India I was looking for in Russell's book. It was the India only glancingly referred to, always assumed: the India that, in Russell's pages, went on working during this time of war, working in the fields, constructing fortifications, clearing away corpses, looking for positions as servants: an India engaged, without ever knowing it, in subduing itself. On the Grand Trunk Road near Benares long lines of cotton-laden country carts creaked one after the other to Calcutta: trade and business going on in the British-run city. The human groups on the road, indifferent to the terrible war, gave the impression of being at a fair. The people who worked the fields were separate from the war; they took no part in the wars of the rulers.

From Russell's book I learned that the British name for the Indian sepoy, the soldier of the British East India Company who was now the mutineer, was 'Pandy'. 'Why Pandy? Well, because it is a very common name among the sepoys – like Smith of London . . .' It is in fact a brahmin name from this part of India. Brahmins here formed a substantial part of the Hindu population, and the British army in northern India was to some extent a brahmin army. The Indians who were now being used to put down 'Pandy' were Sikhs, whom the British had defeated less than 10 years before.

With that British army marching to Lucknow to put down the mutineers was a host of Indian camp-followers. Russell said they were mostly Hindu. The Muslims among them were domestic servants; the Afghans sold dried fruit. Among the Hindu camp-followers were merchants and their wives and families, travelling with their store-tents. There were drovers, looking after the sheep and goats and turkeys for the army; and there were any number of porters, 'whole regiments of sinewy, hollow-thighed, lanky coolies' carrying chairs and tables, 'hampers of beer and wine, bazaar stores, or boxes slung from bamboo poles'.

Russell, as special correspondent of *The Times,* was attached to the staff mess of the British headquarters, and the mass of army servants ensured that dinner on the march was as formal as ever.

'It was about 5 p.m., when a wheeling multitude of kites and vultures soaring above the dust, announced that we were near an encampment, and very soon the joyful sight of a plain full of tents met our eyes . . . Our servants came out to meet us, and I alighted at my tent door . . . On entering everything was in its place just as I left it. Our mess-dinner was precisely the same as at Cawnpore; and it was hard to believe we were in an enemy's country.'

Russell noted the 'high delight' with which these Indian camp-followers – making life so comfortable for the British army – 'were pouring towards Lucknow, to aid the Feringhee' – the foreigner – 'to overcome their brethren'. He saw a parallel with the spread of ancient Roman power. Even the mixed speech of the camp-followers he saw as a symbol of conquest.

None of this was easy for me to read. I had had trouble with *My Diary in India* when I had first tried to read it. I had trouble with it now. I made three or four attempts at it, and found myself rejecting it, for literary reasons. I found it Victorian and wordy. I thought the writer too much of an imperial figure, travelling too easily through a world made safe, and taking that world for granted, almost as much concerned with himself and his dignity and his character as a special correspondent as with the country he had travelled to see, and the people he found himself among.

But these judgements, arrived at from scattered readings, always foundered on the quality of Russell's descriptive writing. The trouble I had with Russell's book was like the trouble I used to have, when I was a reviewer, with good books with which I was nonetheless out of sympathy. Such books were hard to write about; they could make one twist and turn, until one acknowledged their quality. So it took time for me to yield to the Russell book, to take it at its own pace, to accept its purpose; and then I found it very good. His aim, he said, was 'to give an account of the military operations', and also 'to describe the impressions made on my senses by the externals of things, without pretending to say whether I was right or wrong'.

The trouble I had with the book was a trouble with history, a trouble with the externals of things he described so well. There was such a difference between the writer and the people of the country he was writing about, such a difference between the writer's country and the country he had travelled to. The correspondent's job for *The Times;* the British army telegraph, which he used to send his 'letters' to the paper; the talk of railways and steamers – Russell's world is already quite modern.

He had been on *The Times* since 1843, when he was twenty-one; and the first war he had gone to have a look at was the Danish War of 1848. Now – calm, experienced, going out to this Indian war – on the steamer from Marseilles to Malta he finds himself among English people going to many places. 'To trace their destinations from Malta would be to cover the East with a wide-spreading fan. There were men for Australia, for China, the dominions of the Rajah of Sarawak, for Penang, Singapore, Hong Kong, Java, Lahore, Aden, Bombay, Calcutta, Ceylon, Pondicherry . . .' For these people much of the world had already been organized; and many of them were equipped, like Russell himself, to understand and to move into new parts of the world.

That impression of an energetic, spreading civilization is heightened by Russell's careful modesty, the character he gives himself as an observer who is conscious of his special reputation but at the same time knows his limitations. He will not compete with other experts; he will not describe again what he knows others have described. So he refuses to say anything about the wonders of ancient Egypt, or to say one word about the 'much-vexed' Mediterranean. Until he sets out on his march from Calcutta, his tone is allusive; he is writing for his equals; he is an imperial traveller, travelling in a well-charted world.

Yet days out of Calcutta, moving at first in a horse-drawn covered cart, he seems to have gone back a century or two. Just days away from the comforts of Calcutta, he is among people to whom the wider world is unknown; who are without the means of understanding this world; people who after centuries of foreign invasions still cannot protect or defend themselves; people who – Pandy or Sikh, porter or camp-following Hindu merchant – run with high delight to aid the foreigner to overcome their brethren. That idea of 'brethren' – an idea so simple to Russell that the word is used by him with clear irony – is very far from the people to whom he applies it. The Muslims would have some idea of the unity of their faith; but that idea would always be qualified by the despotism of their rulers; and the Muslims would have no obligations to anyone outside their faith. The Hindus would have no loyalty except to their clan; they would have no higher idea of human association, no general idea of the responsibility of man to his fellow. And because of that missing large idea of human association, the country works blindly on, and all the bravery and skills of its people lead to nothing.

It is hard for an Indian not to feel humiliated by Russell's book. Part of the humiliation the Indian feels comes from the ambiguity of his response, his recognition that the Indian system that is being overthrown has come to the end of its possibilities, that its survival can lead only to more of what has gone before, that the India that will come into being at the end of the period of British rule will be better educated, more creative and full of possibility than the India of a century before; that it will have a larger idea of human association, and that out of this larger idea, and out of the encompassing humiliation of British rule, there will come to India the ideas of country and pride and historical self-analysis, things that seem impossibly remote from the India of Russell's march.

Nine years after Russell's book was published, Gandhi was born. Twenty-one years after that, in 1890 (when Russell would have been sixty-eight years old, with three more *My Diary* war-books to his name, one in 1861, *My Diary North and South,* about the American Civil War, another in 1866 about the Austro-Prussian War, and a third in 1870 about the Franco-Prussian War), in 1890 Gandhi was a law student in London, coping as best he could with the bewilderment of a cultural journey the opposite of Russell's Indian journey in 1858. Ten years after that, in 1900 (five years after Russell had received a knighthood), Gandhi was in South Africa, campaigning for the rights of Indians who, 20 or 25 years after the Mutiny, had been sent out as indentured immigrants to many of the former slave colonies of the British Empire, to work on the plantations. And then in 1914 (seven years after Russell's death: the 86 years of the newspaperman's life entirely contained within the period of imperial glory), Gandhi was getting ready to go back to India, wondering how to get started there, how to make use of the political-religious lessons he had learned in South Africa.

From 1857 to 1914, from the Indian Mutiny to the outbreak of the Great War – it isn't long, and great things are seeded in that time. But look back over the 100 years before the Mutiny: right through this period there is an unvarying impression of a helpless, trampled-over country, never itself since the Muslim invasions, wealth eternally squeezed out of it, with a serf population always at work, in the fields, building fortifications, for kings that change and kingdoms with fluid, ever-shifting borders.

'I shall never cease thinking, that rational liberty makes men virtuous; and virtue, happy: wishing therefore ardently for universal happiness, I wish for universal liberty. But your observation on the Hindu is too just: they are incapable of civil liberty; few of them have an idea of it; and those, who have, do not wish it. They must (I deplore the evil, but know the necessity of it) they must be ruled by an absolute power; and I feel my pain much alleviated by knowing the natives themselves . . . are happier under us than they were or could have been under the Sultans of Delhi or petty Rajas.'

The words are by a great 18th-century British scholar, Sir William Jones. They come from a letter he wrote in 1786 from Calcutta to an American friend at the other end of the world, in Virginia. Seventy-five years before William Howard Russell's journey to India, Sir William Jones – at the age of thirty-seven – had gone to Calcutta as a judge of the Bengal Supreme Court. There were no railways or steamers then, no short cut through Egypt; the journey to India was around the Cape of Good Hope, and could take five months; one out of three letters between India and England was lost. Sir William Jones wanted to make his fortune in India. For five years he had angled for an Indian appointment, for the great money it offered. He hoped, once he was in India, to make £30,000 in six years; he was obsessed by that figure. Such were the sums to be made out of the servility and wretchedness of India – trampled over, but always working blindly on.

His talk – to his American correspondent – of liberty and happiness was not disingenuous. William Jones loved the idea of civil liberty, and was a supporter of American independence. He had made three visits to Benjamin Franklin in Paris; and at one time he had even thought of going out to settle in Philadelphia. He was of modest middle-class origins (one grandfather a well-known cabinet-maker). Though he was a lawyer and a fellow of an Oxford college, and famous as an extraordinary scholar of eastern languages, he always in England needed the support of an aristocratic patron. That was why he wanted the £30,000 from India: for his own freedom. And he was unusual: he gave back to India as much as he took. In Bengal, while he did his important and original work on Indian laws, and regularly sent back his money to England to add to his growing hoard, he was also – for no money, for love, learning, glory – going deep into Sanskrit and other languages, talking with brahmins, recovering and translating ancient texts. He brought many of the attitudes of the 18th-century enlightenment to India. In the cultural ruins of much-conquered India he saw himself like a man of the Renaissance in the ruins of the classical world.

This is from a very long journal-letter he sent back to his patron, the second Earl Spencer, in 1787, towards the end of his fourth year in Bengal: 'To what shall I compare my literary pursuits in India? Suppose Greek literature to be known in modern Greece only, and there to be in the hands of priests and philosophers; and suppose them to be conquered successively by Goths, Huns, Vandals, Tartars, and lastly by the English; then suppose a court of judicature to be established by the British parliament, at Athens, and an inquisitive Englishman to be one of the judges; suppose him to learn Greek there, which none of his countrymen knew, and to read Homer, Pindar, Plato, which no other Europeans had even heard of. Such am I in this country; substituting Sanscrit for Greek, the *Brahmans* for the priests of *Jupiter* . . .'

William Jones made more than the £30,000 he had set his heart on; he amassed nearly £50,000. It took him almost 11 years to do so. The thought of the money would have comforted him; but the money itself did him no good. His wife went back a sick woman to England. The year after, when he was getting ready to follow her, he died, and was buried in Calcutta. He was forty-eight.

He, and people like him, gave to Indians the first ideas they had of the antiquity and value of their civilization. Those ideas gave strength to the nationalist movement more than 100 years later. And those ideas travelled very far. In Trinidad, in colonial days, and before India became independent, those ideas about our civilization were almost all that we had to hold on to: as children we were taught, for instance, what Goethe had said about *Shankuntala*, the Sanskrit play that Sir William Jones had translated in 1789.

What luck that bit of knowledge should have come our way! Sanskrit was considered a sacred language; only priests and brahmins could read the texts. William Jones had to get the help of a Hindu medical man to translate the play; and even in our own century pious people could get fierce about the sacredness of the language. Nearly 200 years after William Jones had translated the play, someone in independent India asked Vinoba Bhave, an imitation-Gandhi, seen by some as a kind of spiritual lightning-conductor for the country, what he thought of *Shakuntala.* The idle fellow replied angrily, 'I have never read the *Shakuntala,* and never shall. I do not learn the language of the gods to amuse myself with trifles.'

It is a wonder that, with this internal destructiveness, the play survived; that some knowledge of our cultural past should have come down to us. For every Indian the British period in India is full of ambiguities. For me, with my background – the migration from that overpopulated Gangetic plain 20 or 25 years after William Howard Russell had crossed it in imperial, *Times*-correspondent style, with servants and tents and access to the staff mess of headquarters; and the darkness which for so long blocked my own past as a result of that migration – for me there are special ambiguities.

It fills me with old nerves to contemplate Indian history, to see (perhaps with a depressive's exaggeration, or a far-away colonial's exaggeration) how close we were to cultural destitution, and to wonder at the many accidents which brought us to the concepts – of law and freedom and wide human association – which give men self-awareness and strength, the accidents which have brought us to the point where we can in a way meet William Howard Russell, even in those 'impressions made on my senses by the externals of things', not with equality – time cannot be bent in that way – but with something like lucidity.

*

So I could go only part of the way with Rashid in this contemplation of the recent past. I had no idea of a state of glory from which there had been a decline or a break; and I had no easy idea of an enemy.

Growing up in far-off Trinidad, I had no idea of clan or region, none of the supports and cushions of people in India. Like Gandhi among the immigrant Indians of South Africa, and for much the same reasons, I had developed instead the idea of the kinship of Indians, the idea of the family of India. And in my attempt to come to terms with history, my criticism, my bewilderment and sorrow, was turned inward, focussing on the civilization and the social organization that had given us so little protection.

People in India didn't feel as I did. Perhaps – being in India, and having to order their day-to-day lives there – they couldn't feel or allow themselves to feel like that. But in Delhi this time I met a publisher whose sorrow went beyond mine. His name was Vishwa Nath. He was in his seventies. His family had lived in Delhi for 400 years. There was a story in his family that during the Mutiny, at the time of the British siege, they had had to abandon the family house and take refuge somewhere else. One episode out of many: Vishwa Nath's thoughts, as a Hindu, went back much further than the Mutiny, went back centuries.

He said, 'When I read the history of India, I weep sometimes.'

He was fourteen at the time of Gandhi's salt march in 1931. Ever since then he had worn Indian homespun.

He said, 'Gandhi made us a nation. We were like rats. He made men out of us.'

Rats!

But he was speaking almost technically. 'Man as a species has been trying to kill off rats all through his existence on the earth, but he has never succeeded. Even in New York they haven't succeeded. Similarly, we have been subdued, subjected to torture, conquest – but nobody has been able to kill us off. That has been the strong point of our civilization. But how do you live? Just like rats.'

He hated the idea of caste: 'the main reason why we are slaves'. And he had what I had never had: a clear idea of the enemy. The brahmins were the enemy – yet again, and more than 1000 miles north of the anti-brahmin politics of the South.

'The brahmins let the country down, during all those dreadful invasions by the Mohammedans. All through, they went on chanting their prayers, their *havans:* "God will protect us."'

With his homespun and his nationalism, his sense of history, and his reverence for Gandhi, there was his – seemingly contradictory – rejection of religion. The mixture made for a special passion, and Vishwa Nath's passion came out in the magazines he edited and published in four languages. His women's magazines were especially successful. *Woman's Era* was a fortnightly in English. It had been started 15 years before, and it had damaged the older English-language women's magazines. It sold about 120,000 copies now; it was the best-selling women's magazine in English. Vishwa Nath thought he could take it up to half a million.

I don't believe I had ever looked at an Indian women's magazine. I had taken them for granted. I had been aware of them, knew some of the names. It had never occurred to me that in India they would have had a unique evolution. As soon as the idea came to me, I saw that it couldn't be otherwise, in a society still so ritualized, so full of religious rules and clan rules, where most marriages were arranged, and the opportunity or need for adventure was not great.

I had heard about *Woman's Era* in Bombay. Its success was spoken of as something extraordinary; but people I met didn't care for the magazine itself. It was thought uneducated and backward-looking – in spite of what I was to learn later in Delhi of the editor's iconoclasm and reforming mission. The magazine was extraordinary because it had found a new kind of working-woman reader. A reader of that sort who spent scarce rupees on an English-language magazine might have been thought to have social and cultural ambitions. But that wasn't true of the *Woman's Era* reader; and that was part of her oddity. She was content with her old, shut-in world.

The editor of a rival magazine, one of those damaged by *Woman's Era,* said, '*Woman's Era* is naive right through. It is the first magazine of its kind in India to cater for this new group.'

How did she define this new group?

'It has now acquired a bit of affluence, embraced consumerism. It has a bit of education. But this education has been circumscribed by their traditional thinking and by their family's old beliefs – it's a kind of non-education, a kind of parrot education.'

The bookshop in the Bombay hotel didn't stock *Woman's Era*. The woman assistant made it clear that she didn't like even being asked for it. I bought a copy from a pavement magazine-seller. My first impression was that the magazine was dull. If I hadn't been looking for it, I might have missed it in the pavement seller's display. It was well produced but undistinctive, with an unprovocative young woman's face on the glazed-newsprint cover: carefully made up but unprovocative, a woman's view of a woman. And if, without knowing the magazine's reputation, I had looked through its pages, almost nothing would have stayed with me.

The main article, six pages long, with posed colour photographs, was about 'bride-seeing'. This is the custom whereby, before a marriage is finally arranged, a party from the boy's family visits the girl's family house, and the girl is shown to the visitors and put through her paces. Ashok, the business executive I had got to know in Calcutta, had felt so humiliated by his own experience of bride-seeing that he had decided not to do it again. He had done his own courting and made his own proposal, and kept his family out of it. Ashok could do that; he could look after himself. Not many readers of *Woman's Era* were in that position, and the attitude of *Woman's Era* to bride-seeing was quite different. Most marriages were arranged, the writer of the article said. As long as this was so, bride-seeing was the best way of introducing the girl to the boy; and it was not as demeaning as some people said.

The article was, in fact, an article of advice to girls and their families about the best way of dealing with the occasion. In the first place, a girl shouldn't feel rejected, the writer says, if after a bride-seeing a boy says no. It may be only that the 'demand' – the financial demand – of the boy's family is too much for the girl's family. To prevent that kind of misunderstanding, it is important for the girl's parents to check out the boy and his family thoroughly, before the invitation to view. The girl's parents should visit the boy several times. One tip the article-writer gives to the girl's parents is to see, when they are in the boy's house, whether servants, children, and pets like the boy.

For the bride-seeing occasion itself, the girl shouldn't wear too much make-up or jewelry. She shouldn't boast, and she shouldn't say she can do things which she can't do. Nor should the parents try to appear better-off than they are; some families, the writer says, even borrow furniture to make a show. Then there is the question of dignity. The girl and her family are the suitors on such occasions; the boy and his family have to be won over. But: 'The girl's parents should not behave in an ingratiatingly humble and servile manner.' Easy enough to say; but how, in the circumstances of a bride-seeing, can the girl's family keep their dignity? The writer makes one suggestion. 'Some families insist that the girl touch the feet of every boy and his parents who come to see her. This practice is deplorable, goes against the basic human dignity, and is best avoided.'

Still, the unfairness of the procedure remains. '"Why can't the boy sit in *his* drawing-room, nicely groomed and smelling of aftershave, with his head bent and his academic qualifications, job certificates, etc., in his hands?"' To that complaint of a girl, which the writer of the article quotes, there is no reply. Except this: if a girl doesn't want to go out husband-hunting on her own – 'and believe me, in our society it is an extremely difficult game' – then the girl has to put up with the bride-seeing visits. 'If the boy's people put on airs and act uppity, they can be forgiven, for tradition and thousands of years of social behaviour have gone into it.'

Later, after I had met Vishwa Nath in Delhi, I could see a little of his passion and iconoclasm in that last sentence. But without that knowledge, the sentiment appeared simply archaic, an acceptance of old ways because they were the old ways and the best ways. And, with that acceptance stated or implied (sometimes with a take-it-or-leave-it tone), the article got on with its business, which was to give the kind of instruction that might come from some worldly-wise person within the family. Dress modestly for the bride-seeing; mind what you say; watch out for trap questions from the boy's family; be respectful towards older members of the boy's family, and affectionate with the children.

Instruction, instruction of the simplest sort – that appeared to dictate the tone of the magazine. That appeared to be the need the magazine was meeting. The customs, like bride-seeing, might be old; but the world in which they were being practised was new; and in this world the readers of the magazine appeared to be starting almost from scratch.

'Personal Hygiene' was a long article in the same issue of the magazine. It was illustrated with a photograph of a girl bending over a sink and throwing water at her face, and the advice it offered was of the most elementary kind. There was a little flick of irreligion at the very beginning of the text, but to spot it you had to be in the know. 'Today, of course, whether one believes in godliness or not is not a matter of such grave concern, as is the fact that many of us fail to adopt cleanliness and personal hygiene as our chosen religion.' Cumbersome, even imprecise; but the point of the article was the clear and simple hygiene lesson.

'There is no harm in getting dirty, but the problem arises only when we like to stay dirty . . . The importance of keeping our body and our surroundings clean and orderly cannot be stressed over much. Their direct result is good health, peace of mind and happiness.' To be clean, to be 'tidy', was to avoid infections, and that meant spending less on doctors and medicines: it was, therefore, to avoid a certain amount of financial worry.

Stage by stage, then, taking nothing for granted, the writer took the reader through the problems, in India, of personal hygiene. 'An orderliness of the surroundings is the first and essential step.' 'Orderliness' – a euphemism. 'Surroundings' – a strange word, but clearly 'house' or 'apartment' wouldn't have suited everyone's living space. So we begin to understand that the living conditions of the people for whom this article is meant are not always good. Some of the readers of this article would be at the very margin, would just be making do.

Water is important, the article says; enough of it should be available. India is a warm country, and a bath once or twice a day is necessary, 'accompanied by a thorough and strong but gentle scrubbing, using soap and lukewarm water'. After the washing of the body, the washing of clothes. 'Clothes which have once become wet with perspiration should be washed well before they are worn again . . . Cleanliness of the undergarments is extremely important as these are worn next to the skin. If they are used continuously without changing, they are likely to cause irritation of the skin, or more serious conditions.' A full-page advertisement opposite the last page of text is for an anti-lice treatment. Daughter embraces mother; they both smile at the camera. 'She trusts me with all her problems . . . and I trust only Mediker with her lice problem.' (Lice! No wonder the young woman in the hotel bookstore made a face when I asked for *Woman's Era*.)

Simple instruction – it made for dullness, if you were on the outside. And the stories – there were five in the issue – were like fables. A fat woman goes with her husband on a posting to Korea. She is nervous of the hotel food. She fancies that the mutton is really dog-meat and the noodles are worms. She eats salad and yoghurt and a little rice for two months; she loses weight and becomes another, better person. The rich young Indian businessman, back in India to look for a wife, is frightened away by the flashy girl he had been expected to marry; instead, he chooses the humble, orphaned cousin who has been living with the girl's family as a kind of servant. In another story the rich husband is completely won over by the simple goodness of the poor-relation aunt whom his wife is trying to hide. Simple goodness – it is the quality most people in these *Woman's Era* stories turn out to have. There are references in the magazine to women reading romances, especially the English romances published by Mills and Boon. But the love that matters in these stories is family love rather than romantic love.

Family love, articles of simple instruction on unglamorous subjects, advertisements for a Procter and Gamble lice-treatment, advertisements for antiseptic creams, water-heaters: there was nothing here to exercise the fantasy, to encourage longing. Who would ever have thought that this was the formula for a best-selling women's magazine?

Gulshan Ewing was one of the most famous women's magazine editors in India. She became the editor of *Eve's Weekly* in 1966, and took it to its great success in the late 1970s.

At dinner in Bombay one evening, speaking informally of the *Woman's Era* phenomenon, before she knew (or I knew) that I was going to take a greater interest in the subject of women's magazines, Mrs Ewing described the kind of new reader women's magazines in India had to reach out to. This reader did a job. She got up early, looked after her family, got them off to school and work, and then went out to work herself, in an office, perhaps. At half-past five she left her office. On the way to the bus stop or railway station she bought the vegetables for the evening meal, and cut them up on the way home.

I was attracted by that detail of the cutting up of the vegetables on the train home. But it took only one or two suburban train journeys for me to understand that in Bombay the detail was romantic, a vision of pastoral, that suburban trains were so crowded that, far from cutting vegetables on her train, the woman office worker would have had to fight – hard – to get on the train. Later I read a whole story in *Woman's Era* about a girl becoming separated from her sister during a scrimmage to get on a suburban train.

Mrs Ewing admitted the fantasy when I went to see her some days later in her office. She had simply wanted, she said, to describe the position of the Indian working woman in the cities. I might have thought that she was being merely witty in her description; but the life of the working woman was not funny.

'We've talked to these people, and friends of these people. We've had feedback. And what generally happens is that she – the working woman – she's up at the crack of dawn, about five, to fill the water for the day. We don't have 24-hours' running water in most houses. Water comes on early in the morning, goes off all day, and returns in the late evening for an hour or under a couple of hours. That's in the lower-middle-class areas. So when she gets up – tubs, barrels, whatever she can get hold of, she fills. Then she does the morning chores, filling the tiffin-carriers for husband and children, after giving them tea, breakfast, whatever. It's mainly she who does it. Then she's off to work herself. A very long train journey in a crowded train, usually. She hardly gets a seat.'

'What kind of job would her husband have?'

'A clerk, a bank employee. A middle-level job in a factory, earning about 1000 to 1500 rupees. Her job would be anything from 600 to 1000.'

'That sounds hard.'

'Very hard. It's not funny at all. She's away from the children the whole day. She gets off from her office at 5.30 or six. She might first take a bus to the station. Or – this is more harrowing – she might have to take a bus all the way home. There are mile-long queues for the bus sometimes. When I pass I often wonder when they are ever going to get a bus. Before getting to the bus or station she would buy her vegetables or whatever she needs. Her vegetables are there, in her little *thela,* a carrier bag.

'And then she gets home. And before having her own cup of tea, she has to give one to her own lord and master, who's probably sitting with his feet up, already at the television. Ten to one, in spite of the low earning, they have a television. Then the dinner, then a bit of the children's homework – if she's capable of doing that. Her day would end late. She would have to do the washing up. Then she has to think of the water again.'

'How do they keep going?'

'This is their lot, their destiny. They believe this is how it has to be for them. I'm not necessarily describing the reader of *Eve's Weekly* or *Woman's Era*. I'm just making the point of how sad such women can be with so much drudgery in their lives.'

Women in such circumstances needed special magazines. Simple mimicry of European or American magazines wasn't what was required. The idea of glamour might even be wrong.

Mrs Ewing said, 'The only difference between the middle readership of *Eve's Weekly* – which might be secretaries – and the readership of *Woman's Era* is language. *Woman's Era* uses more simplistic language and talks down to the woman. A fascinating explanation of the success of *Woman's Era* was given to me the other day. The women who read *Woman's Era* are really intimidated by magazines. They'd rather pick up magazines like *Woman's Era* that don't make them feel uncomfortable. But I'm optimistic that that kind of reactionary woman's journalism will be on the way out. When we' – she meant *Eve's Weekly* – 'write about bride-inspecting, we get all het-up. And we tell the woman, the girl, that she doesn't have to go through this. But she can only revolt if she is educated enough to be economically independent at some later stage.'

That was the point: that for a girl or woman from that background, with that education, living in those 'surroundings', the idea of revolt was fantasy. *Woman's Era* was addressed to those women. And so the magazine which had at first appeared so characterless to me, so dull, began to say more, began to create a whole new world of India, a whole new section of urban Indian society which wouldn't have been easy for me to get to know.

There were no Indian women's magazines before Independence. Middle-class Indian women read the two popular British magazines, *Woman's Weekly* and *Woman's Own*. When the British went away these magazines ceased to be available. Even a middle-class Indian woman would have found them too expensive to subscribe to from India. I was told this by Nandini Lakshman. She was a journalist specializing in media and advertising matters. From her I got a short history of Indian women's magazines.

'When the *Times of India,* a British paper, was Indianized, they started *Femina*. This was in the early 50s. In the early issues they had a British hangover. The editor was a Parsi lady. In those days modelling wasn't considered a good profession in India. So in *Femina* you had pictures of a lot of these foreigners posing in these Indian outfits. The Indian women who modelled came from affluent Indian families who were not so bound by custom and traditional norms. Then unfortunately within a few years the first editor committed suicide. Nobody knows the reason why. She must have been in her late forties. Then you had an Indian editor for the first time.

'*Femina* wanted then to reach out to more women. So they started this Miss India contest. They had contests all over the country – in the major metros, Bombay, Calcutta, Madras, Delhi – and then all the winners had a Miss India competition. Not really middle-class – it was quite a society affair: the affluent, the moneyed, the influential, people who frequented social parties. The contest had a kind of snob appeal. Initially there weren't too many girls who participated, because again a beauty contest was considered below their dignity, even for many of the snob people – because not everybody wins. I suppose it was the fear of being rejected. And, moreover, the chosen Miss India had to participate in the Miss Universe contest. And there, in one session, she had to wear a swimsuit and parade herself. This would have been shocking to all Indians. So in the early days we had Parsi girls and Christian girls as Miss Indias. But even though the middle-class

Indian woman couldn't participate, she began to aim towards that. It was something new to her – the glamour, the image. She was partly shocked, partly fascinated.

'*Eve's Weekly* came along at about this time, and they also started a beauty contest. The circulation of both papers then would have been about 15,000. Much later, they started carrying articles about how to drape your sari, how to look good. It was the editor of *Femina,* a man, who began to do that. I suppose he had a more open view of women's expectations.

'In those days you didn't have too many women working. The magazines carried stories like "The Experiences of a War Widow" – or the experiences of people who had lost their husbands during the Partition of India.

The creation of Indian women's magazines was a gradual process – with a growing readership and a wider market, because of growing education and more awareness. *Femina* touched 90,000 in the late 70s; *Eve's Weekly* also. *Woman's Era,* the star today, was launched in 1973. As *Woman's Era* has risen, *Femina* has dropped – to 65,000 today. And now there's a new magazine, *Savvy,* which is the opposite of *Woman's Era. Savvy* is three years old, and it already has a circulation of 50,000. It's a monthly. *Femina* is for the older woman. *Savvy* is for the city-bred woman, from eighteen to thirty.

'*Savvy* is a scandalous magazine. It carries a cover story, a personality story, about a woman. She is known as the "*Savvy* Woman of the Month". She has to be a divorcee, or she can have affairs, or she can have her husband beat her up, or she can leave her husband and kids for somebody, or he can leave her for somebody else, or she can have a husband and a lover. And at the end of it all she can still emerge victorious. She manages to have her cake and eat it too. Every month. *Savvy* women are fairly famous, but not always. If I have a gory life, if I want to dare all and bare all, *Savvy* will make a heroine out of me. They have found a market for this: I think they did some kind of research. An Indian woman may not admit that she reads *Savvy,* but she still reads it. *Savvy* is for the metro areas. *Femina* and *Woman's Era* you will find in the small towns, like Nasik and Nagpur. *Savvy* did something on rape a couple of months ago – with photographs – and the women's organizations said it was too blatant, and there was a court injunction, and they had to withdraw all the issues.'

We talked about *Woman's Era*. I told Nandini what Gulshan Ewing had said about the working woman to whom *Woman's Era* was reaching out.

She said, 'That's glamorizing the *Woman's Era* reader a bit. It's the elite voice talking.' Nandini herself was just a generation or two from traditional and small-town life. 'Every day I change two buses and take a train to come to office. And I get up early. But I don't read *Woman's Era*. I cook at home and I come to work, and I don't find it a drudgery. That's a skyscraper view. The person who says that probably has a lot of servants at her fingertips.'

Nandini didn't see *Woman's Era* as appealing to the working woman. 'It aims at the traditional middle-class housewife. I don't mean illiterate. It is the only magazine that carries five stories, fiction, in every issue. All about: they lived happily ever after. The husband comes back to the wife. *Woman's Era* is very biased towards women. The woman can do no wrong. She is always a good person. She may be a grandmother, or a wife, or a mother-in-law; she is always a good person. Even when the husband is an alcoholic, in the story the wife with her good nature helps him give up the bottle. To the magazine it may not matter why the husband has hit the bottle. They don't tackle that angle. The situations are from everyday life. The readers can identify with each and every situation. In the 1950s, in *Femina* and *Eve's Weekly* the stories would have been remote.'

I said that the *Woman's Era* stories seemed to me to be fables, to be hardly stories.

Nandini said, 'They are badly written. I fail to understand that in spite of such bad presentation and packaging the magazine has such a wide readership.'

Was there an element of instruction? Did women turn to the magazine for simple basic advice?

'The stories are meant to *entertain*. The reader sees the situation as one that may befall her. Mother-in-law and daughter-in-law problems. Or the boy studying abroad. He is engaged to a girl in India, or he is married to her, and he has affairs abroad, but ultimately he comes back to the wife, and they live happily ever after. *Woman's Era* doesn't tackle social problems. They tackle *personal* situations. The editors know what they are doing.'

We talked about the 'bride-seeing' article. It had caused a certain amount of offence. Many people talked about it, and from the journalistic point of view it had to be considered a success.

Nandini said, 'I would condemn bride-seeing. But they don't. Their article has the sub-title, "A Positive Look at the Custom". And they carry photographs like this.'

A posed colour photograph, occupying the top half of the first page of the article, showed a girl bringing tea on a tray to a viewing party. The room in the photograph was small and cramped (perhaps one of the standard 10 feet by 10 feet Indian rooms), and there was almost no space between the furniture: a matching three-piece 'sofa set', a coffee table, and a side table with a big lamp and with marigolds in an earthen pot. Four people of the visiting party were on the sofa; and two of the visiting women were staring hard at the girl, who was standing with the tea tray, in a new sari, her hair freshly done, looking with something like wretchedness at the camera.

Nandini didn't have my outsider's eye. She saw nothing humorous in the photograph; her feelings were absolutely with the young girl. 'It is horrendous. At the end of the article they say that a get-together between the boy and the girl is advisable – they don't say it's a must – and they have a photograph of a boy and a girl facing each other across a table, but not looking at each other and not talking. "Be respectful and affectionate" is a sub-heading.' She read out from the article: '"The boy's sisters and nieces and nephews should be treated with friendly affection."' She was irritated by what she read. She said, 'If a battalion comes to see you, you are not on parade. You are not being bought. In the article they try to take a liberal step. But the arguments justifying the custom are so strong, the liberal step is nullified. They are not appealing to the new woman. They are appealing to the traditional woman.

'My sister is educated, but she went through an arranged marriage. She hadn't fallen in love with anybody, and there was this proposal from these people. So my parents asked her. There wasn't this kind of exhibition. She just met the boy. He is a merchant-navy captain. Both of them liked each other.'

'Would *Woman's Era* readers suffer when they have to go through something like that bride-seeing?'

'They are conditioned to the fact that they have to go through all this. Some women do find it a torture, but they have to go through with it. However educated or affluent a woman is, you have her saying, "Ultimately I would like to get married and have children." But there are also women who accept *Savvy* magazine. There are the two strands now, and these two papers are leaving *Femina* and *Eve's Weekly* far behind.

'When you come to the advertising, you will find food ingredients and certain cosmetics in *Woman's Era* and *Femina*. But not a winter skin-care lotion costing 50 rupees for 200 ml. That would be advertised in *Savvy*. It's not such an easy market in India. It has to be studied.'

From time to time on my journey I bought an issue of *Woman's Era*, and my regard for its journalistic and social achievement grew. I felt it deserved its success. I thought its merit lay in something Gulshan Ewing had mentioned: it did not intimidate its readers.

A recurring theme of its stories was the discovery by a woman – usually a new bride – that the great shame she feels about her poor relations is misplaced. And *Woman's Era* never shamed its readers. In its stories, its recipes, its photographs of interiors (like the cramped small room which illustrated the bride-seeing article), it acknowledged the conditions in which its readers lived; and it never went beyond those conditions. Perhaps that recognition in itself was a kind of glamour; perhaps in no other form – not cinema or television – did women of that group find that recognition.

With that recognition, there was always reassurance. It could be said that reassurance was the dominant tone of *Woman's Era*. In the stories (the themes usually connected with family love) people always turn out to be better and more human than they appear. And there was reassurance again in the articles of instruction or advice. Nothing was taken for granted there. *Woman's Era* will tell you everything about how to pay a visit: don't go unannounced, don't let your children touch things, don't let them jump in their muddy shoes on your host's sofa and cushions. In another number *Woman's Era* – turning the tables, as it were – will tell you how to deal with an unexpected caller: 'Not immediately after their arrival, but some time during their stay, you can give them a tip by saying tactfully, "Had I known you were coming for a stay, I would have provided you with more comforts and adjusted our own schedule." Unless the guest is extra thick-skinned, this should serve to carry the message across.'

*Woman's Era* will tell you how to write a letter: don't use a crumpled or grease-marked sheet, don't tear a sheet from your daughter's notebook, don't use big words, don't write only about yourself, don't slap the stamps on all over the envelope. The magazine will even tell you how to go to the cinema: don't take food, don't comment on the plot, don't take your baby and walk it up and down the aisle when it begins to cry.

People who don't need this kind of advice don't need *Woman's Era*. And the people who need the advice are never rebuked or ridiculed. The faults are never written about as the reader's faults. They are other people's faults, faults the reader might have observed; there is always some story or fable to soften the correction. *Woman's*

*Era* invites its readers to a special, shared world. The editorial tone is one of concern, almost love.

And when I got to know the editor, Vishwa Nath, I found that this tone fairly reflected his idea of a mission.

He was seventy-two, and he was still very much in control of his printing and publishing business. He was of middle size, brisk, with no great fat on him, looking cool and ready for business in his white trousers and short-sleeved shirt – Indian homespun, but I wouldn't have known if he hadn't told me.

He gave the impression of not being used to talking about himself. He had no personal anecdotes, and didn't draw moral lessons from his experience. He was still engaged in the world; ideas still held him; he was engrossed by his work and it made him look outwards. He loved the idea of magazines; he loved everything to do with print. He was proud of the new Heidelberg presses on the ground floor. At the same time, out of his love of print, he kept, in a caged room on the upper floor, trays and boxes of movable type, Hindi and English, from older days.

His family had first set up a printing press in Delhi in 1911. So in the printing business he had something like an ancestry. As with Indians in other fields, the talent that had appeared to flower after Independence had been maturing over a generation or two. His family had been in Delhi for 400 years, but he could trace it back only as far as his great-grandfather, in whose house he had been born in 1916, and where he had lived until 1934. This great-grandfather had been born just before the Mutiny, perhaps in 1854; he was the man who had passed on the story of the family abandoning the house during the British siege and sacking of Delhi in 1857.

There was a more tangible record of that ancestor. At some time in the 1870s he had been employed by a British lexicographer, Dr Fallon. Dr Fallon was preparing a Hindi-Urdu-English dictionary; and Vishwa Nath's ancestor had travelled about North India with Dr Fallon, recording the words and phrases they heard.

At Vishwa Nath's back, in his office, there was a glass-doored bookcase that rose from the cupboard to the ceiling. Dr Fallon's *Dictionary* – re-bound – was on a shelf in that bookcase. It was 1200 pages long, the pages almost quarto size, 10 inches by seven: *A New Hindustani-English Dictionary, with Illustrations from Hindustani Literature and Folk-Lore,* by S.W. Fallon Ph.D., published in 1879 by Trubner & Co., London, and E.J. Lazarus & Co., Banaras. Every entry appeared in the three languages, in the three scripts; the pronunciation of the Hindi or Urdu word was given an English approximation.

So, just 20 years after William Howard Russell's journey, there had been this other English journey, through some of the same districts, and there had been this other labour, that couldn't possibly have been adequately rewarded. And there, in Dr Fallon's preface, was the acknowledgement of Vishwa Nath's scholarly ancestor: 'Munshi Thakur Das of Delhi.'

Thakur Das, in fact, 30 years or so later, bought the copyright of the *Dictionary* from Dr Fallon. His intention was to reissue the book. That was one reason why he bought a printing press in 1911 – the coronation year of the King-Emperor George V, as Vishwa Nath said: the year when the capital of British India was shifted from Calcutta, and the foundation was laid for New Delhi. But Thakur Das didn't reissue the *Dictionary.* He died almost as soon as he had bought the press. Vishwa Nath's grandfather had then to see to the setting up and commercial working of the press. The *Dictionary* would have been a very heavy labour; and it wouldn't have paid its way. Vishwa Nath said, 'Every single letter, in Hindi, English, and Urdu, would have had to be set by hand. So the press did other work to keep going.' The *Dictionary* was set aside, surviving in the family only in that copy in the glass case in Vishwa Nath's office.

Vishwa Nath said, 'It's now out of copyright, and there are stories that someone has brought out a photo-offset edition.'

Vishwa Nath's grandfather died in the influenza epidemic of 1917. That was when his father and grand-uncle took over the press. They were an orthodox Hindu family. 'A joint family, living together and working together.' But there was friction. 'There was a division in the family. By 1939 the press was almost finished. I wanted to work in the press, but I saw they were quarrelling. So I came out and qualified as a chartered accountant. I never practised, though. I started a new press, on my own, without the rest of the family. I was twenty-two.'

I asked him what Delhi was like then.

'Easy-going, before the war. For six months the city slept. The Government of India used to go out to Simla from April to September – the summer exodus. New Delhi was almost completely deserted. Everybody took it easy, sleeping in the day, doing things leisurely.'

Politics? Gandhi?

'I became interested in 1930.' He was fourteen. 'I wanted to go to prison, but I was a minor. They wouldn't arrest me. That was during the time of the salt march. Gandhi was noted for his stunts. I call it a stunt. The salt march was a stunt, but it was necessary. We had no arms. He went out to the villages and roused the masses. The salt march actually electrified the whole country. I remember the day Gandhi reached Dandi on the sea, we in our street in Delhi prepared salt from a brackish well, and we said, "We have broken the salt laws." From that day of the salt-making I started wearing the *khadi,* the homespun. And I still do.

'The time of the salt march we had processions every day. It was the first time women came out of their houses, came out of purdah in Delhi and all over North India. Some of our relatives courted arrest. My uncle was imprisoned for six months; he later became a minister in Nehru's government.'

It was at that time, too – 'The whole country was in ferment' – that the idea of publishing began to come to him. He liked reading; he spent all his pocket money on books and magazines.

'I used to go to the press, and set type by hand – for play. My father loved printing, and I also loved printing. When I was in the eighth class, when I was eleven, I had decided that I would publish magazines.'

I felt he was speaking for me. In colonial Trinidad, at about the same age, I had developed – largely through my father, a journalist – a love for print, the shapes of letters, the variety of typefaces, a wonder at the way words were transformed when handwriting turned to type. Out of a love for that process I had decided to be a writer, with perhaps less idea of what I was going to write about than Vishwa Nath – in the ferment of India in the 1930s – had of the magazines he was going to publish.

We talked for a while about printing. I asked about Hindi typefaces. I liked them very much. They seemed strong and elegant and logical, and at the same time true to the written script. I asked Vishwa Nath if he knew who had designed the first Hindi typeface. I felt sure that the designer would have been someone from India. Apparently I was wrong.

'Drawings were sent from India to England. The Devanagari script' – the Hindi script, derived from the Sanskrit – 'was cut over there. All the type we used – for Fallon's *Dictionary,* for everything – was imported from England. We kept on importing Devanagari type from England until the 1920s, when type-foundries were set up in India. The paper we used was imported. The machinery was imported. The ink was imported. It was only when Gandhi started this swadeshi movement – the movement for using India-made goods – that there was a quest for producing things in India.'

There was a side of imperialism that had nonetheless to be acknowledged. 'Actually we owe a great deal to those British officers and men and scholars who went deep into our literature, to translate the texts which the brahmins didn't want known outside their own coterie.' That point about the brahmins was something Vishwa Nath wouldn't let go: it still made him bleed, and still drove him on. But always, too, there was his professional side, and it was with a printer's enthusiasm that he spoke of the Hindi type.

'The Sanskrit script is essentially a script for handwriting. It has ascenders, descenders, the letters move right and left, and there are many contractions. It was really a marvellous job to make it – the typeface – in movable type. In English we have 26 letters and two cases, upper case and lower case. In printeries there were literally two cases, one with the capital letters, one with the small letters. When you are setting Hindi you have to have four cases.' For the contractions, the half letters, the vowel indicators. He drew a plan on a sheet of paper, and said, 'No. You will need five to six cases.'

Two rooms away from his office – empty rooms now, at this time of evening, the tables clear, the many chairs unoccupied – was where he kept the trays of old type. He pulled out a few trays and showed them: formes still set, the movable type worn at the edges, shiny. From a gallery on this top floor you could look down at the Heidelberg machines on the ground floor, and the stacks of printed sheets. There was a smell of ink and warm paper.

In his white homespun, walking briskly through the empty rooms, he was – even without the deference of employees to underline his status – the owner, the man who knew where it all was, because he had arranged for it to be as it was.

When we were back in his big office – the big desk, the swivel chair upholstered in brown velvet, the glass-doored bookcase rising to the ceiling, the books on the shelves, the file copies of his magazines, the black Shiva statue on the cupboard, an old copy of American *Cosmopolitan:* all the varied attributes of his personality – he talked of history and his anti-brahmin obsession.

'When I was young the freedom movement was at its height. We had been slaves for centuries, and when the Independence movement started we had to have some tonic – that we were not as bad as the British had called us. To gain our self-respect, we started thinking we had a very ancient civilization – and of course there's some truth in that. But then it also had its weaknesses, and it was those weaknesses that made us slaves for a long time.

'When I started my own press in 1939 – and soon after that began bringing out my own magazines – I started reading our old scriptures. I wanted to find out for myself how great or grand our civilization was. And when I looked into our ancient literature I found that we were lacking something very vital. The more I went into the scriptures the more my mind was turned – and then this thing started.' The thing: the reformist slant of his magazines.

'The Hindu religion is a conglomeration of faiths, 500 religions or faiths. We've had reformist movements from the very beginning. From the dawn of civilization we've had reformist movements against orthodoxy. What happens is that every reform movement degenerates into a sect – the Lingayats, the Arya Samajists, everybody. Buddha rebelled. Mahavir, the founder of the Jains, rebelled. Guru Nanak, the founder of the Sikhs, rebelled. It's a long list. They rebelled and degenerated into sects, and became as orthodox as the previous orthodox people. So I didn't put on those saffron robes and start going about to those conferences, or preaching in public. I published my magazines.'

His first magazine, *Caravan,* in English, was started in 1941. In 1945 he started *Sarita,* for women, in Hindi. Both magazines had a circulation of about 15,000.

'A substantial circulation for that time. There was a big uproar when I published an article that stray cows should be eliminated. They came out in procession. There were posters all over the city. This was in 1950 or thereabouts.'

But there wasn't much rebellion in *Woman's Era*. People even thought of it as a conservative magazine.

He said, 'Rebellion isn't in *Woman's Era*. It's in *Sarita,* our Hindi magazine, which sells three times what *Woman's Era* sells. *Woman's Era* is more for social affairs. It's educative. Teaching women the simple things nobody bothers to tell them about.'

His idea of social affairs was different from Nandini's. She had said that the magazine dealt in personal situations rather than social problems. Their differing uses of the word came from differing world-views, differing assumptions and levels of education. And Vishwa Nath had his own ideas of rebellion.

'In *Sarita* we go full blast, preaching against gods and goddesses, even God itself. Last month we had an article in *Woman's Era*, "Prayers Breed Selfishness and Sycophancy".'

He took a file copy from the bookcase and showed the article. I thought that only *Woman's Era* could have used so heavy a title. It was, though, a fair description of the article, which railed against the prayer practices of people of all faiths. The article was shot through with Vishwa Nath's rage about Indian history. People who abased themselves before God, the article said, could also abase themselves before a despotic ruler. This touch of historical judgement, this mention of a despotic ruler, seemed to remove the contemporary scene, and gave an antique flavour to the article, which, for all its passion and boldness, and its contemporary photographs, came out as curiously inoffensive, a criticism not so much of religion as of foolish individuals trying to make a contract with God.

Was he a religious man? Only a religious man, I thought, could be so obsessed with religion. Only someone of true Hindu inclination could have spent so much time with difficult, speculative Hindu texts. I remembered Chidananda Das Gupta in Shantiniketan: not a theist, Chidananda had felt a 'renewed inclination' in his semi-retirement to read the Upanishads, and – only a few years younger than Vishwa Nath – had found in them the highest level of spirituality, and rewarding.

Vishwa Nath said, 'I am not a religious man at all.' The Upanishads? 'Play of words. The Upanishads are just a play of words. *Atman,* Brahma – the whole exercise is to prove that atman is part of Brahma, and Brahma is atman. Some say yes, some say no, some say it's half-and-half. The Hindu philosophers spend all their lives hair-splitting.'

The Dancing Shiva was in his office as a work of art, not as a living icon.

'I think religion is the greatest curse of mankind. It has killed more people, destroyed more property, than any other thing. Even today – Northern Ireland, the Middle East. Hindus, Muslims, Sikhs, all fighting each other in India. The oldest profession is not prostitution. It is the priesthood.'

Yet, with this iconoclasm, there was in Vishwa Nath something that was like its opposite: a concern for the family. In India this concern was like a wish to preserve the old social order; and perhaps, like the iconoclasm, it came out of some personal need. This seeming contradiction was at the heart of *Woman's Era*.

Vishwa Nath said, 'The family is the hinge of civilization. My stress is that the family should be strengthened, not destroyed. Woman's Lib is responsible for quite a good deal of the disintegration of the family.'

He saw himself as a man made not only by Gandhi and the Independence movement, but also by his family past. Perhaps, with his family past, the family stories of the siege and sacking of Delhi at the time of the Mutiny, and with his reading of Indian history, the invasions and the cruelties which could make him cry, the pillaging and destruction by the Muslim invaders of the great Hindu temples of North India – perhaps there was with him some dread of chaos which younger people – who saw him only as conservative – didn't have.

One reason why he had started *Woman's Era* – the very name a counter-blast to Woman's Lib – was to fight for the sanctity of the family. It was important to do such a paper in English.

'I had to reach women who don't read Hindi. It is the English-reading, English-speaking people who control things in this country. All this feminist Woman's Lib movement is conducted by English-speaking people. You don't find it so much in Hindi or the Indian languages.'

Nandini had said of *Woman's Era,* 'The editors know what they are doing.' The words had suggested that, in India's professional and competitive magazine business, the people who ran the magazine had done 'research' of some sort, like the research the people at *Savvy* were said to have done. But Vishwa Nath, I felt, moved by instinct; no amount of research could have led to his formula.

The *Woman's Era* formula couldn't be copied, because the personality of the editor couldn't be copied, with its many ambiguities: the tears for the past, the iconoclasm, the fear of chaos coming again, the strong nationalist feeling, the homespun, with the over-riding love of print that had come down from the ancestor who, less than 20 years after the Mutiny, had worked on Dr Fallon's *Dictionary,* applying a new kind of scholarship to the everyday India he knew.

In the beginning, at Independence, women's magazines (as Nandini had said) had been a borrowed idea, appealing to a few at the top. *Woman's Era* was an expression now of a purely Indian social order much lower down, offering instruction and reassurance, and a subtle transformation of the hard real world, to women just emerging, women whose lives were a tissue of ritual and given relationships, and didn't want to rebel or dream.

The formula couldn't be copied, or transferred. Vishwa Nath himself had tried to apply the *Woman's Era* formula to a general magazine, *Alive. Alive* hadn't found a public. What made sense in the shut-in woman's world came out in the general magazine as quirky and insubstantial.

# 8

# THE SHADOW OF THE GURU

To awaken to history was to cease to live instinctively. It was to begin to see oneself and one's group the way the outside world saw one; and it was to know a kind of rage. India was now full of this rage. There had been a general awakening. But everyone awakened first to his own group or community, every group thought itself unique in its awakening; and every group sought to separate its rage from the rage of other groups.

Every day the newspapers carried plain official accounts of events in the Punjab: so many killed by Sikh terrorists; so many people arrested for harbouring terrorists; so many terrorists killed by police; so many 'intruders' from across the Pakistan border killed.

In the wide streets and roundabouts of New Delhi there were reminders of the trouble in the north. At night there were road-blocks. At places below the trees there were sandbags, guns, and policemen. In some areas there was a policeman every 100 yards or so. In the city which Vishwa Nath remembered as being empty and sleepy when he was a child (and where the trees would have been little more than saplings: still only a dream of a new Delhi) terrorism had led to the creation of this new and effective police apparatus.

The British forces the correspondent William Howard Russell had seen at the siege of Lucknow had been made up principally of Scottish Highlanders and Sikhs. Less than 10 years before, the Sikhs had been defeated by the sepoy army of the British. Now, during the Mutiny, the Sikhs – still living as instinctively as other Indians, still fighting the internal wars of India, with almost no idea of the foreign imperial order they were serving – were on the British side.

During the assault on Lucknow an incident took place that sickened Russell, who was a tough man, and a hardened relisher of war. One of the Lucknow palaces – the 'yellow house' on the racecourse – was being attacked by Sikh soldiers. The defenders fought back with spirit; at one stage they shot and killed one of the Sikhs' British officers. When it was clear that the defenders intended to fight to the end, the attacking soldiers were withdrawn, artillery was brought up, and the yellow house was blasted with shot and shell. The defenders were brave men, Russell said; they should have been sung in ballads. But no mercy was shown them in Lucknow. Those who had survived the shelling were bayoneted by the Sikhs and quickly killed – all but one man. For some reason this man was dragged out by the feet, bayoneted about the face and chest, and then placed on a fire. The tormented man struggled; half burnt, he managed to get up and tried to get away; but the Sikhs held him down in the fire with their bayonets until he was dead. Russell, in a footnote, said – a characteristic touch – that he saw the charred bones on the ground a few days later.

Russell was told that during the Punjab war the Sikhs mutilated all the prisoners they took. So this bayoneting and burning of the man who – possibly – had killed their officer might have been no more than their practice. Perhaps it was part of the barbarity of the country; or simply the barbarity of war. Russell loved war, but he had no illusions about it. 'Conduct warfare on the most chivalrous principles,' he wrote, 'there must ever be a touch of murder about it.'

In the Sikh fierceness at the battle of Lucknow there would have been a wish to get even with the 'Pandies' who had helped to defeat them less than 10 years before. There would have been a more general wish as well to get even with the Muslims. And it was historically fitting that the Sikhs should have helped to bring about the extinction of Muslim power in Lucknow and Delhi, because it was out of the anguish caused by Muslim persecution of Hindus that the Sikh religion had arisen, in 1500 – at about the time of Columbus's last voyage to the New World.

People within the Hindu fold had always been rebelling against brahmin orthodoxy, Vishwa Nath had said; and everyone who had rebelled had started a sect with its own rigidities. Buddha had rebelled; Guru Nanak, the first Guru of the Sikhs, had rebelled. Two thousand years separated the rebellions, and they had different causes. Buddha's rebellion had been prompted by his meditation on the frailty of flesh. Guru Nanak's rebellion or breaking away had been prompted by the horrors of the Muslim invasions – the horrors to which at that time no one could see an end.

Guru Nanak's illumination was the quietist one that there was a middle way: that there was no Hindu and no Muslim, that there could be a blending of the faiths. Islam had its fixed articles of faith, however, its fixed, pervasive rules – no room there for Nanak-like speculation and compromise. The full Islamic 'law' could be asserted at any time; and 100 years later, at the time of the fifth Sikh Guru, the persecutions and the martyrdoms at the hands of the Moguls began. Nearly 100 years after that, at the time of the 10th and last Guru, the religion was given its final form, and Sikhs were given their distinctive appearance: the hair not to be cut, and to be wrapped in a turban, a kind of underpants to be worn, and a steel bracelet, and a knife – so that every day, with these intimate emblems, a man would be reminded of what he was.

As the Mogul power declined in the first half of the 18th century the power and numbers of the Sikhs grew. In the ravaged north of India, in the interim between the collapse of the Moguls and the coming of the British, there was for a short time the Sikh kingdom of Ranjit Singh. This was the kingdom that the British defeated with the help of 'pandy' in 1849. But there was no great humiliation with that defeat; it might even be said that that defeat propelled the Sikhs forward.

The British, at the height of their empire, had a general disregard for all Indians. Even in 1858, while the Mutiny was going on, Russell noted this slighting British attitude towards the Sikh soldiers who were fighting on the British side. But by being incorporated into British India the Sikhs were immeasurably the gainers. They were granted a century of development. Without the British connection, north-west India – assuming that there had been no more regional or religious wars – might have been no more than Iran until oil, or Afghanistan: poor, despotically ruled, intellectually disadvantaged, 50 or 60 or more years behind the rest of the world.

Independence and the Partition of India in 1947 damaged the Sikhs; millions had to leave Pakistan. But again, as after their defeat by the British, they quickly recovered. With the expanding economy of an industrializing independent India, with a vast country where they could exercise their talents, the Sikhs did very well; they did better than they had ever done. They became the country's best-off large group; they were among the leaders in every field. And then in the late 70s their politics, always sectarian and clannish and cantankerous, became confounded with a Sikh fundamentalism preached by a young man of a simple village background, a man born in the year of Partition. There began then the train of events which were to lead to the daily budget of terrorist news in the newspapers; and the khaki-clad policemen with guns in the green streets of New Delhi.

For 150 years or more Hindu India – responding to the New Learning that had come to it with the British – had known reforming movements. For 150 years there had been a remarkable series of leaders and teachers and wise men, exceeded by no country in Asia. It had been part of India's slow adjustment to the outside world; and it had led to its intellectual liveliness in the late 20th century: a free press, a constitution, a concern for law and institutions, ideas of morality, good behaviour and intellectual responsibility quite separate from the requirements of religion.

With a group as small as the Sikhs, where distinctiveness of dress and appearance was important, there couldn't be this internal intellectual life; even the idea of such a life wasn't possible. The religion had reached its final form with the 10th Guru, and he had declared the line of Gurus over. Such a religion couldn't be reformed; reform would destroy it. A new teacher could only restate its fixed laws and seek to revive old fervour. So it happened that India's most advanced group could be called back by a village teacher to a simpler past.

The preacher's name was Bhindranwale, after the name of his village. His first name was Jarnail; this was said to be a corruption of the English word 'general'. At his first appearance he was encouraged by the Congress politicians in Delhi, who wished to use him to undo their rivals in the state. This seemed to have given him a taste for political power. The word used most often – by admirer and critic – for Bhindranwale in this incarnation is 'monster'. The holy man became a monster. He moved into – effectively, occupied – the Golden Temple of Amritsar, the Sikhs' holiest shrine, built by the fifth Guru (who was more or less Shakespeare's contemporary). He fortified the Temple, making use of its immunity as a sacred place; and, with a medieval idea of the scale of things, perhaps a villager's idea of a village feud, he declared war on the state. To serve Bhindranwale and the faith, men now went out with the mission of killing Hindus. They stopped buses and killed the people in them. Riding pillion on motor-scooters, they gunned down people in the streets. The resulting shock and grief would have confirmed the terrorists in their idea of power, would have confirmed them in their fantasy that it was open only to them to act, and that – as in some fairytale – an enchantment lay over everyone else, rendering them passive.

Eventually the army assaulted the Temple. They found it better fortified than they knew. The action lasted a night and a day, and there were many casualties, among soldiers, defenders, and Temple pilgrims. Hindus as well as Sikhs grieved for the violation of the holy place; Hindus also offered prayers there. Police officials were later to show that there was another, cleaner way of isolating the Temple. But at the time – to deal with a novel situation: a murderous insurrection conducted from the sanctuary of a holy place – the army action, heavy-handed though it was, seemed to be the only way.

The damage was done. Stage by stage, then, the tragedy unfolded. To avenge the desecration, Mrs Gandhi was murdered by some of her Sikh bodyguards. And, again, it is as though the men who planned the murder didn't sufficiently understand that their action would have consequences, that by doing what they did they would be putting their community at risk: Sikhs were settled all over India. There were riots after the murder. The most dreadful were in Delhi, where hundreds died. Out of that great fire in 1984, these terrorist incidents in the Punjab, on the frontier with Pakistan, were the embers.

To most people what had happened in the Punjab was a pure tragedy, and not easy to understand. From the outside, it seemed that the Sikhs had brought this tragedy on themselves, manufacturing grievances out of their great success in independent India. It was as if there was some intellectual or emotional flaw in the community, as if in their fast, unbroken rise over the last century there had developed a lack of balance between their material achievement and their internal life, so that, though in one way so adventurous and forward-looking, in another way they remained close to their tribal and country origins.

Something went wrong with a tire of my hired car on the road to Chandigarh. It wasn't only a puncture. The much-used, much-recapped tire had also split in an arc half-way down the wall. Chandigarh was more than three hours away, and the other tires didn't look too good. There was no question of taking a chance; the ravaged tire had to be mended before we went on. Help was at hand, though. There was a Punjabi truck stop just a short way down the road – we could see it from where we were – and after we had changed the wheel we went there.

The truck stop was a dusty yard with brick sheds on three sides. Some of the sheds were walled, some open. Advertisements for Apollo tires nailed to a wall gave a reassuring technical feel to the place. At the back and sides of the yard were fields of ripe wheat; down one side was a ditch of stagnant, blackish water. Drivers turbanned and unturbanned sat above the dust on string beds in the open sheds and drank tea. The tea was prepared in an open kitchen at the back (a lot of blue smoke over black earthen fireplaces), and served by two boy waiters in long trousers and very dirty (and now perhaps uncleanable) long-tailed Indian shirts.

While the driver of my hired car manhandled the wheel with the split tire, traffic roared and rasped by, the brown smoke from unmuffled exhausts mixing with roadside dust. Within the split tire there was, surprisingly, an inner tube. I hadn't seen one for years. Over this tube the driver, an unturbanned Sikh, then squatted with the repair man, and after they had pumped the tube up they passed it through water in a red plastic basin. (There was another red plastic basin in which glass tumblers and heavy china cups were soaking on a stand outside the cooking shed.) The flaw in the tube was found, the spot was dried and rasped, some adhesive solution was applied, and a bandage was stuck on. The procedure sent me back to my childhood; it made me think of the way we used to mend bicycle punctures; I had thought it was something that had passed out of my life forever.

Stepping down from the greasy brick platform, where they had been working on the tube, the driver and the repair man selected, from a small collection, a tire so worn it had been finally abandoned. They cut two sleeves out of this tire, one sleeve out of the thin part of the tire, the other out of the thicker part. Both sleeves were then fitted into the tire where it had split; the mended inner tube, pink and deflated and flabby, was also fitted in; and then somehow the driver and the repair man hammered and malleted the whole thing together, pumped the tire up, and bumped it up and down professionally a few times on the grease-blackened earth. Finally, like a man more fulfilled than irritated by the accident, Bhupinder the driver set the nose of his car towards Chandigarh, and we didn't stop until we got there.

The traffic was of all sorts: buses, trucks with towering loads, packed three-wheeler taxi-buses with about 20 people each (I counted), mule carts, tractors with trailers, some of the trailers carrying very wide loads of straw in sacking, or carrying logs placed crosswise, so that they occupied a good deal more of the width of the road than you thought from a distance. There seemed to be no limit to a load. Metal, being metal, was deemed to be able to carry anything that could be loaded onto it. Many bicycles carried two or three people each: the cyclist proper, someone on the cross bar, someone sitting sideways on the carrier at the back. A motor-scooter could carry a family of five: father on the main saddle, one child between his arms, another behind him holding on to his waist, mother on the carrier at the back, sitting sideways, with the baby.

Always in India this feeling of a crowd, of vehicles and services stretched to their limit: the trains and the aeroplanes never frequent enough, the roads never wide enough, always needing two or three or four more lanes. The overloaded trucks were often as close together as the wagons of a goods train; and sometimes – it seemed to depend on the mood or local need of drivers – cars and carts came in the wrong direction. Hooters and horns, from scooters and cars and trucks, sounded all the time, seldom angrily. The effect was more that of celebration, as with a wedding procession.

Chandigarh, when I first saw it in 1962, was a brand-new city. It had been built as the capital of what was then the state of Punjab. It was an empty, still artificial-feeling city in 1962. It was full of Punjabi tourists, running up and down the modern concrete towers Le Corbusier had built for the state assembly, the high court, and the secretariat. The city was now full, built up. It was squabbled over by the two states into which Punjab had split.

Le Corbusier's unrendered concrete towers, after 27 years of Punjab sun and monsoon and sub-Himalayan winter, looked stained and diseased, and showed now as quite plain structures, with an applied flashiness: megalomaniac architecture: people reduced to units, individuality reserved only to the architect, imposing his ideas of colour in an inflated Miroesque mural on one building, and imposing an iconography of his own with a giant hand set in a vast flat area of concrete paving, which would have been unbearable in winter and summer and the monsoon. India had encouraged yet another outsider to build a monument to himself.

Grass grew now between the blocks of the paving. Armed policemen guarded the buildings in the evenings; visitors were driven off. The people of Chandigarh, following a more natural Indian inclination, promenaded in the afternoons on the lakeside, far from the dreadful public buildings. The city over which people squabbled was without a centre and a heart.

But the air was clean. It was still cool; in the evenings it was cold. The hotel garden was full of flowers, and the big shaved lawns, soaked by a fat hose every day, were bright green.

Gurtej Singh was famous as a Sikh who had resigned from the Indian Administrative Service – the highest branch of the Indian civil service – because of his commitment to the Sikh cause. He was represented to me as someone who would give me some understanding of the Sikh alienation. On a number of mornings he came to the hotel, after he had taken his sixteen-year-old daughter to her school in Chandigarh, and we talked. I didn't know then that he had been acquainted with Bhindranwale; that he had gone underground for four years after the army assault on the Golden Temple in June 1984; that he had been charged with sedition, and was still technically on bail.

He was forty-one, tall, just over six feet, slender, with sombre, intense eyes. He was carefully dressed, in pale colours. There was an elegance about his manner as about his physique – nothing of the big-eating Sikh or Punjabi there. It was hard to imagine that he had come from a farming family and a village background, and that he was the first in his family to have received anything like a formal education.

He wanted, the very first time he came, to talk about the importance of water. Punjab depended on the water of its rivers; it didn't like sharing its water with other states. Since 1947, he said, more people had died quarrelling over water than had died during the upheavals of Partition. 'The water problem is the crux of the matter.'

But I could hear about water from many other people. I felt, too, that it was a simplification, something to be put forward at a first meeting. Fundamentalism and alienation would have had other promptings as well; and I was more interested, at this first meeting with Gurtej, in understanding how his ideas of religion had come to him.

The first ideas, he said, had come to him from his grandfather. From his grandfather he had also got the idea of 'gentlemanliness'.

'We don't have many rituals. My grandfather taught me the simplest form of prayers. It's just a simple prayer for the well-being of the entire world. It lasted from half an hour to 45 minutes. Every morning my grandmother would get up for the household chores – and that included churning the morning milk – and she would keep on repeating the prayers while at work. She was not an educated person, and she remembered only those things she had heard, the simplest of couplets from the scriptures.

'She got up at four. After she had got up I couldn't sleep, and then I gradually got interested in those prayers of hers. My grandfather would pray in a more formal manner. He would wash himself in the morning and sit with the holy book in his hand. We have a small version, with the daily prayers, and he would carry that with him all the time. The last thing would be the *ardas,* the conclusion of the prayer, the supplication.

'My parents were living in a different village. There was no school in that village, so they had sent me to my grandparents' village, where we had a school next to the house. I went to that school until I was big enough to go away to Dehra Dun, to a boarding school.'

I wanted to hear more about the 'gentlemanliness' of the grandfather.

Gurtej thought. He began to remember; his intense eyes softened. 'He always dressed properly, in clean clothes, and a white turban. He always had his watch with him. He was conscious of time, which no one else in the village was. He was a progressive man. He was the first man to get a radio, the first man to buy a jeep in the village. And he kept a daily diary. He had a contact with some saint, who had taught him to make anti-snakebite medicine. This he religiously used to make before the onset of the rainy season every year, and he would distribute it to the neighbouring villages. People used to come to ask for that medicine whenever there was a case of snakebite.

'Sometimes I used to go with him on a camel to the neighbouring market town. When we passed through a place where the village elders used to sit he would ask me to greet them loudly. And I never heard him shouting at anybody. When he thought the worst of a person he would say '*Dusht!*' – 'Wicked man!' – and then we knew he was very angry.

'He used to give pocket money to me and to his son – who was my uncle – wanting us to be on our own, not depending on him for anything. He would help anybody who came. He was the only person to have a horse carriage, and when people wanted it – for a wedding or to go to hospital – he let them have it. He was widely respected. He was one of the better-off farmers.'

From this protected life Gurtej was taken away when he was sent to the boarding school in far-off Dehra Dun.

'I was in a different sort of culture, and there must have been a yearning in my heart to be in touch with my land, my culture, my people. I began to read the poems of Sohan Singh Seetal. He's a poet and a writer. He is still living in Ludhiana. The books I read at that time were ballads, concerned with Sikh history in the Mogul period and the British period.

'I still remember several poems – which were full of the suffering of my people. One poem was about the general order of massacre given by two or three Mogul governors – that every Sikh should be hunted down. And the mothers from whom the children were snatched, to be cut up to pieces. Young boys being murdered. Women being incarcerated, tortured. The torture of the companions of the ninth Guru – that was in 1675. They were killed in front of his eyes. One was set on fire. This was in Delhi, in Chandni Chowk. Another was sawn alive – put into a wooden casket and cut into two. You see the helplessness and anguish of people at that time. They were doing no wrong. They were just following God according to their own lights.'

His eyes misted over. He found it hard to bear the details of physical pain, which he was yet stressing. Then he related what he had said – almost mythical suffering, but with real, historical dates – to the problems of the present.

'Consciously or unconsciously, a Sikh is all the time trying to avert a situation like this.' Religious persecution. 'And this is what made me support this agitation for justice in the Punjab. It was more of an emotional identification with my people – in the days of the Punjabi Suba, 1957 to 1960.' The agitation then by Sikhs for a Punjabi-speaking state: Gurtej was ten in 1957. 'The intellectual reason came afterwards. What I recall is that as soon as a Punjabi Suba was formed, Hindus started agitating against it. They burnt a gurdwara' – a Sikh temple – 'in Karnal. They attacked a gurdwara in Delhi. Stoning took place. And all over the Punjab towns there was a bit of a commotion.'

So present suffering linked to past suffering. The heroic past ennobled or gave a different quality to the trials of the present.

Gurtej said, 'The fifth Guru was burnt to death.' In 1606, by the order of the Emperor Jehangir, Akbar's son. The fifth Guru, the organizer of the faith, the founder of the Golden Temple. 'The best human being I can conceive of is the Guru' – the singular or the collective noun is used by Sikhs for all the 10 Gurus – 'and I believe them to be motivated sincerely by the good of all the community. Why should they suffer like that?'

'Did you ask your grandfather? Did you talk to him about this problem of suffering?'

'I don't remember having asked him. I think the first time I talked about these things was with Sardar Kapur Singh in 1965–66.'

This man, Kapur Singh, was important to Gurtej. He was born in 1911 to a farming family. A gifted and unusual man, he completed his education at Cambridge, and he gained entrance to the Indian Civil Service, the ICS, the predecessor in British times of the Indian Administrative Service. But then at Independence in 1947 there was some trouble about money meant for refugees and also trouble about buying an expatriate's car, and Kapur Singh was dismissed from the service. Kapur Singh claimed that he had been wrongly dismissed, and it might be said that for the rest of his life Kapur Singh fought and refought his case; mixing this grievance with regional Sikh politics, the writing of poetry, and the writing of difficult books about the Sikh religion. This was the man who became Gurtej's mentor. He opened Gurtej's eyes to the position of Sikhs in India.

I wondered whether, before this meeting with Kapur Singh in 1965 (when Gurtej was eighteen), Gurtej had noticed any discrimination against him as a Sikh. He said yes; he remembered that once, when he was queuing up to buy a railway ticket, the booking clerk had been rough with him.

'When you first talked, what did Kapur Singh tell you about suffering?'

'He told me it was an eternal fight between good and evil, and by their suffering the Gurus have only shown that people should identify themselves with good causes. He used to say that a measure of man is the sense of commitment he has. It's the only thing important in man. Otherwise, it's an animal existence. And he would say it's the only way to salvation, serving mankind. And Sardar Kapur Singh's words carried conviction because he had suffered much, and he had no regrets.'

In this way Gurtej had arrived at some idea of the Sikh religion: a special idea of the Gurus, a special idea of the Sikh God.

Of Guru Nanak, the first Guru, who had had the illumination that there was no Hindu and no Muslim, Gurtej said, 'I see him as a man who's conscious of the sufferings of his people, and having an intense desire to change the situation.' He didn't see Nanak simply as another rebel against Hinduism. 'He's not a reformer, he's not a philosopher, he's not a poet – though he expressed himself in poetry. He's a prophet of God.' This idea of the prophet – a Muslim idea, a Christian idea, a Jewish idea – was not held by every Sikh. But Gurtej was firm. 'There's no doubt in the minds of Sikhs. We look upon all the Gurus as *one*.' In this account, therefore, over the first 200 years of their history the Sikhs had a line of 10 God-sent prophets.

Why the emphasis on suffering? How could a believer live from day to day with this idea of suffering?

Gurtej said, 'The stress on suffering is like this. The world is an unhappy place to live in, and unhappiness has to be eliminated. There are only two ways. Either you make somebody else suffer, or you suffer. And I think a man of God must suffer himself, rather than pass it on to somebody else. I regard myself as a man of God. I always have, and always hope to. The very idea of attaining salvation by serving mankind is unusual in this subcontinent. In the other religions here the stress is on monasticism, renunciation, a personal salvation. At crucial times in my life I have found that I would like to decide a thing as the Guru might have decided it.'

This idea of the Sikh prophet went with a particular idea of God. 'For Sikhs he is the fountainhead of all virtues, a living God manifesting himself through his prophets. Of all the prophets, if you ask me who is the prophet nearest to the Guru, I would say Mohammed. Our idea is different from Islam in only one aspect: the dominant element in our concept of godhead is justice and kindness. The Islamic God appears to me to be a little harsh – if you see the punishment renegades got at the hands of Mohammed himself. And when you see the manifestation of sovereign power in Islamic states, there is an element of cruelty, a bit of oppression. We view God as a liberator. Ranjit Singh ruled the Sikh kingdom for 40 years, and he never sentenced anyone to death. This, I think, is the spirit of Sikhism. This is our concept of God as kindness.'

I said, 'There is no such conception of God in Hinduism.'

'Everything is violent in Hinduism. Do you see the Devi strung with skulls around her neck? If you ask me, Hinduism is the most violent of religions.'

Some years before, in England, listening to the radio one day – when Bhindranwale and Sikh fundamentalism and his fortification of the Golden Temple were still far away, and I knew little about them – I had heard an interview with Bhindranwale in the Golden Temple. Sikhism, Bhindranwale had said, was a revealed religion; the Sikhs were people of the Book. I was struck then by the attempt to equate Sikhism with Christianity; to separate it from its speculative Hindu aspects, even from its guiding idea of salvation as union with God and freedom from transmigration. I had thought of Bhindranwale's statement as an attempt, by a man intellectually very far away, to make his cause more acceptable to his foreign interviewer.

So I pressed Gurtej now about his idea of the prophet.

He said, 'If we get bogged down in Darwinian ideas of evolution, and see everything as evolving from something else, we cannot see a finished product right at the beginning. And this is what the prophets do: they present you with a finished product.'

I felt then, from his language and imagery ('Darwinian', 'product'), that his ideas had been worked out and studied; and I had the feeling that he might have been put on to this way of thinking by his mentor, Kapur Singh.

One of the pamphlets Gurtej gave me was entitled 'The Trial of a Sikh Civil Servant in Secular India'. It was an English translation of Kapur Singh's account of his fight for justice after his dismissal from the Indian Civil Service, his '30 years of persecution by the state authorities without an income and without an occupation'.

The story as presented in the pamphlet was fragmented and not easy to follow; the translation, besides, was poor and the roughly printed pamphlet was full of printing errors. But it seemed that he had been dismissed on a charge of embezzling government money meant to be given out to refugees from Pakistan at the time of Independence. He had been suspended in 1949, and dismissed after a departmental inquiry by the Chief Justice of the Punjab. Kapur Singh's defence was that he had given out the money in question to refugees, but he had thought it 'neither possible nor wise', in the circumstances of Partition, to get receipts from refugees who couldn't be identified and had no addresses. The government itself, he said, had directed that 'cumbersome formalities' like the obtaining of receipts should be ignored in dealing with refugees.

One of the points of his pamphlet was that the charge of embezzlement had been brought against him only because he had been protesting against a directive issued in 1947 to all deputy commissioners in the Punjab that 'the Sikhs in general . . . must be treated as a criminal tribe. Harsh treatment must be meted out to them to the extent of shooting them dead so that they wake up to political realities'. Mr Nehru himself had been behind that directive. (Mr Nehru had also been behind a directive Kapur Singh had heard about in 1954, from a Sikh major in the army, that Sikhs in the army were to be 'constantly threatened, terrorized, insulted and kept in subjugation'.) Mr Nehru's mind had been poisoned against Kapur Singh by 'compulsively malignant Hindus and Sikhs with tainted conscience', who had told exaggerated stories about Kapur Singh's Sikh-oriented politics. As a result, Mr Nehru and his home minister 'were on the lookout of an oppportunity for liquidating me'.

The departmental inquiry into the embezzlement charge against Kapur Singh was conducted by the Chief Justice of the Punjab. He was an Englishman – this was in 1950, just three years after Independence. He ruled that Kapur Singh was guilty. 'The British Government was requested to Knight him in recognition of his valuable service to the people of the Punjab during his tenure as Chief Justice. Accordingly he was Knighted by the Queen. Most of his time as Chief Justice was spent in enquiring against me.'

As for Kapur Singh: 'I was dismissed from service and thrown from pillar to post for 12 long years.' He took his case to the Public Service Commission, and after that to the Supreme Court, 'I was driven from pillar to post for another four years . . . Then in accordance with the Guru's exalted words "The ultimate test of truth is to the fighting for it," I started a serious legal battle. I filed a detailed writ against the high-handedness of the government in the High Court at Chandigarh.'

Some months before, in Bangalore in the south, Prakash, the minister, had told me at breakfast about one of his morning petitioners. This man, a village official charged with embezzling a portion of the land revenue he collected, had been suspended from his job; and he had travelled all night on a bus to wait at dawn outside Prakash's door and to plead for the minister's help. Prakash had seen the man for seven minutes, had said that the departmental inquiry had to take its course; and the man had then to go back all 200 miles to his village. It seemed hard, all that travel for so little. But Prakash, in his witty way, had described how someone like that suspended official, after a day or two of tears and fright at his situation, might find, as it were, a second wind in the idea of *karma,* fate, might become quite calm and lucid, and, supported by that idea of fate, might devote the rest of his life to litigation and action for the cause abruptly granted him.

Kapur Singh's religious support was of another kind. '"Irreligiousness is the root cause of all misery" is our ancient thought,' he wrote in his pamphlet. And in his long legal fight he was both consoled and encouraged by the example of the Sikh Gurus who had been persecuted by the Moguls. He began to see his own persecution as 'the destiny of a Sikh in consequence of the power falling into Hindu hands'. When his case was at the Supreme Court, his lawyer told him one day (the account is full of this kind of hearsay), 'All around me I hear it being said that total demoralization of Kapur Singh is necessary to contain the Sikhs, and he must be liquidated in spite of law and regulations.' When his writ was at the Chandigarh High Court he happened one day to be in a shop and there he heard one of the judges say to the shopkeeper, 'He is a dangerous Sikh – a poisonous snake.'

His sufferings linked him to the persecuted warrior Gurus of the Mogul time, and their sufferings had led to his present political predicament. In the 17th and 18th centuries Mogul governors and generals 'got Guru Arjun imprisoned and executed after unbearable torture, conspired to kill Guru Hargobind, attempted to do away with Guru Harkrishan, got Guru Teg Bahadur beheaded, got the infant sons of Guru Gobind Singh bricked alive in a wall, caused a fatal wound on the person of the Tenth Master, inspired the Imperial edict of the genocide of the Sikhs, were responsible for butchering Banda Singh Bahadur and his companions, became the preceptors of the Great Holocaust, and in the 19th century raised the flag of Jehad against the Sikh political power. Their activities ultimately culminated in the . . . formation of Pakistan.' So the litany of religious pain ran together with history and contemporary politics and Kapur Singh's personal calvary. The identification was complete: 'The Mogul king Bahadur Shah had ordered, "Followers of Nanak [should] be executed on sight." I, being a declared Sikh, fell a victim to this Mogul firman.'

It was as though the faith called up this identification with the torments of the Gurus; and as though this identification created in the believer the feeling of injustice and persecution, and perhaps even the wish to be persecuted.

What I would never have guessed from that pamphlet – what I learned from another book of Kapur Singh's that Gurtej gave me later – was that, with that obsession about his case, Kapur Singh had had a full and fruitful life in independent India. He had done his writing; he had been professor of religion at a Sikh college in Bombay; and he had been active in Punjab politics, being both a member of the state assembly and the central parliament in Delhi. He and Gurtej met in 1965. Kapur Singh was fifty-four, and quite famous in Chandigarh. Gurtej was eighteen, a student at the university in the town. The two men became close. Kapur Singh would begin his letters to Gurtej, 'My dear son'. He bequeathed his books and papers to Gurtej.

One of the titles that Kapur Singh claimed was 'Decorated National Professor of Sikhism'. Gurtej, on his card, described himself as 'Professor of Sikhism'. There was clearly in Gurtej some wish to honour Kapur Singh; and – after reading the pamphlet of Kapur Singh's that Gurtej had given me – I wondered whether in his own career in the Indian Administrative Service Gurtej didn't have before his eyes Kapur Singh's martyrdom in that role 30 years or so before.

Kapur Singh had been dismissed, but he said he had really fought a point of principle, objecting to an anti-Sikh directive. Gurtej, who had joined the service in 1970, had resigned in 1982, also on a point of principle. He had become worried, he said, about serving the ends of justice. 'You can only serve as long as the state remains just.' In the Punjab in 1977, during Mrs Gandhi's Emergency, his doubts had grown. 'I see my people running from pillar to post. They are humiliated, though they don't feel it. They feel it's the normal way in this country.'

It was about his government service that we began to talk when he came the second time to the hotel, early in the morning again, with the shaved hotel lawn shining in patches from its flooding by the big hose, and with the banks of flowers still in shadow.

In 1969, when he was twenty-two, he had got married. It was an arranged local marriage. The following year he joined the Indian Police Service. It was at school – in Dehra Dun, away from home – that his thoughts had turned to that kind of career: quite a change for someone from a farming background. A friend of his was the son of an Indian Administrative Service officer; that first put the idea in Gurtej's mind. Then he heard someone say that the only worthwhile services were the Indian Administrative Service and the Indian Police Service. So he had written the examination. 'I made no special preparation. I just studied hard. After having done my M.A. in history I sat for the Indian Police Service.' He was successful; only a handful of people got in every year.

He shifted the next year to the sister service, the IAS. And, even after all that had happened, he still thought highly of that service. 'It was a good service, and if I were inclined to serve in adminstration, this would be the service I would like to join.'

The IAS was an all-India service, and Gurtej's first posting was in the South, in the state of Andhra. He became disenchanted almost at once.

'I was able to detect one case of death in police custody due to torture. And instead of the police officer concerned being punished, he was actually rewarded – so that he would avoid the punishment. The man killed was a small peasant; his wife appeared very poor to me. I was an S.D.M., sub-divisional magistrate. It's mandatory for an S.D.M. to conduct a divisional inquiry into any death in police custody. I was told to set the matter aside – it had been pending for three years.'

But he couldn't set the matter aside, and the case still worried him. 'After 18 years I still remember the names of the people. It was a pathetic case. I felt very bad about it. The wife had been hunted out of the district so that she couldn't give any evidence against the police. There had been a quarrel between the man – the dead man – and some landlord in the village. The man had probably become a source of irritation to the landlord. People like that don't feel confident enough to attack a landlord.'

I asked Gurtej why he had stayed on in the service, after that experience.

'I thought the time would come when I could do more. But that time didn't come. I started realizing that the corruption has set into the administrative machinery, and that people are really pawns. Whenever politicians are interested in a case, whenever they have a vested interest, it's impossible to take any action.

'In the same year, 1971, a whole family had died of starvation in Andhra Pradesh. It was in one of the revenue sub-divisions. A question was asked in Parliament. I was asked to inquire into it. The district magistrate contacted me later to ask what I thought of the case. I said it was a starvation death. The D.M., the revenue collector, said, "No, no, we can't write that. It will cause a commotion. It will be a bad advertisement in the foreign press." And again, as often with Gurtej, the thought of suffering brought tears close to his sombre eyes. 'It was a family of poor people. The old man died first. They had no means of subsistence. No one offered them food. And then the wife died; and then the children died. Harijans, scheduled caste. The case was taken out of my hands.'

'But you say the IAS was a good service. Weren't there good things?'

'There were good things. I was in the drought-prone area programme. We tried to provide relief to people in drought-prone areas. We provided wells, sources of irrigation. That was a good thing. Though there again I ran into trouble. With the *zilla parishad,* the district council. That's an elected body, and the chairman wanted all the minor irrigation works to be entrusted to his relative. And that relative was sub-contracting it out to others, and he made money on that. The chairman had a big clout in the administration. But I didn't help him. He wanted to humiliate me. He called me to a meeting of the zilla parishad. But that time the democratic process worked – very unusual. The other elected members supported me, and rebuked the zilla parishad chairman for harassing an honest officer.'

Even that didn't reconcile Gurtej to the administrative service. But wasn't politics the art of the possible? And couldn't that be said with greater force of the civil service? Wasn't there – going only by what he had said – an intention of improvement and service to the people?

Gurtej didn't see it like that. He had gone into the service with the highest expectations: they allowed of no worldliness or compromise. He said. 'I am not somebody's minion. I am serving the law, the country's constitution. Why should I play to the whims of some corrupt man? As an officer, if you can't act impartially, there is no meaning in remaining in service. Even for self-respect it is essential that you should feel you are doing what is right.'

Though he was far away in the South, his association with Kapur Singh continued. In 1974 he formally took his vows as a Sikh, going through the ritual which the 10th Guru had laid down. He took *amrit,* drank the consecrated nectar, a mixture of sugar and water stirred with a double-edged sword. Not every Sikh went through this ceremony and made his formal vows.

Gurtej said, 'I had doubts until then whether this sort of ceremony was necessary. Sikhism is committed to ideas; ritualism has no place. I had been following all the tenets of the religion, but had not formally taken this amrit. Sardar Kapur Singh said that it was a formal ceremony that must be gone through, to declare that you are openly committed.'

The actual ceremony was carried out in the Punjab, where he had gone on two months' leave. And it was carried out at the town of Anandpur, where the 10th Guru, Guru Gobind Singh, had performed the first baptism of Sikhs in 1699.

Gurtej said, 'The amrit was stirred with the sword of Ali.'

This was quite bewildering. Did he mean the Ali of the Muslim Shias, the cousin and son-in-law of the Prophet Mohammed?

He did. He said, 'The caliph.'

How had this sword survived more than 1000 years? How had it come into the possession of Guru Gobind Singh?

'It was presented to him by the Mogul Emperor Bahadur Shah.'

So again, in this version of the Sikh faith that Gurtej propounded, there was an Islamic twist, a non-Hindu, non-Indian aspect, a separateness of the faith from the land of its origins.

'During this period in Andhra Pradesh I continued my studies in Sikhism. I wrote an article in 1975 about the martyrdom of the ninth Guru. He was beheaded in Delhi by the Emperor Aurangzebe, in Chandni Chowk. Then I wrote some articles for the *Encyclopaedia of Sikhism*.'

He was encouraged in his studies and writing by his wife, 'a double graduate'. Together they visited important Sikh temples in the South. 'Every year we went to the gurdwara established in the memory of the 10th Guru near the spot where he had been cremated.' The 10th Guru had died in 1708, killed, it is said, by one of his own Muslim followers. The Guru had travelled down to the South – the episode has its ambiguities – to help the Emperor Aurangzebe's successor in a dynastic war.

In 1977, when he was thirty, and after six years in the South, Gurtej went back to the Punjab. His father was ill, with Parkinson's disease; he was soon to die. It was still the time of Mrs Gandhi's Emergency, and there was an agitation against it by the Sikh political party. The agitation was going on from the Golden Temple.

'It kept on nagging people that they were not free. It's all right to make two ends meet and have an animal existence, but there's more to life. We have in India two absolutely opposed ideas about government and politics. The Hindu idea is that government must have every right to do as it pleases. This is how the violations of the constitution are tolerated by everybody. The Hindu idea is that whatever the government does is the law. It is more susceptible to dictatorship. The Sikh idea is that God is the only true sovereign, and that governments have a mandate to govern on the condition that they do justice. I was very happy that my people were resisting this subversion of the laws and constitution during the Emergency.'

Gurtej didn't go back to Andhra Pradesh. 'In 1979 I joined the Punjab government – an IAS transfer, on deputation – and worked until 1980. It was a good experience. The chief minister was known to me. He was not a crookish man. We worked on a big process of decentralizing certain powers. It was good for democracy.'

He also began at this time to be politically active. 'Bhindranwale was in the air.' This was the fundamentalist or revivalist preacher who was to become the 'monster' of Sikh politics. 'Since 13 April 1978' – the 13th of April is a date that recurs in Sikh affairs: it is the date of the harvest festival, and is chosen as the date of great events: the first Sikhs were baptized on this date by the 10th Guru – 'since 13 April 1978 he had shot into prominence. He was a young man who had recently become the leader of a seminary.' The immediate cause of Bhindranwale's fame was a dispute with a Sikh sect called the Nirankaris. 'The Nirankaris are as old as Independence. They were a reform movement started in Sikhism in the late 19th century. And then one Buta Singh took over that movement, and he was supported by the government to create a schism in the Sikh body.' It wasn't clear from this account whether the government that encouraged the Nirankaris was the British Indian government, or the government of independent India. 'In a demonstration against the Nirankaris on the 13th of April 1978, 13 of Bhindranwale's followers were shot.'

In this atmosphere of excitement, Gurtej took up political work. He began to help Sant Longowal in the Punjab water problem. Longowal was another religious leader; he was to be murdered in 1985, the year after Bhindranwale and many others were killed in the army action at the Golden Temple.

Gurtej, explaining his association with Sant Longowal, said, 'The Sikh idea is the service of mankind. And here was a representative of my people asking me to be with him in this agitation. Everybody must serve his people first, and through them serve humanity.'

He resigned from the IAS in 1982. 'My deputation was over, and there was trouble over a paper I read about the Sikh problem. I thought that people didn't want me in the service. I think that the administration was objecting to my religious activities.'

He had told me the day before that at the boarding school in Dehra Dun, far from the atmosphere of home, he had read ballads about the suffering of 'my people'; and that Kapur Singh had later talked to him about the persecution of the Sikhs. It didn't seem to me a sufficient explanation of the way he had developed. It occurred to me now to ask him again about his childhood.

How had his family heard of this boarding school in Dehra Dun? Was he sent off alone, or were there other boys from the village with him?

'Three of us were sent. A brother and a cousin and I. Somebody in my grandfather's village was already studying there. The school was run by the Irish Brothers, the order of St Patrick.'

'How often did you go back home?'

'We just came home for the holidays. It has taught me a lesson. I will never send my children to a boarding school.'

'When did you go?'

'1951. From 1951 to 1961.'

'But in 1951 you were just four.'

'Every day I used to sit up in bed and pray that the term should come to an immediate end. We were allowed to go home once in six months, for a month or so.'

An exile from four to fourteen: so the memories he had spoken of the day before, of the camel rides with his grandfather, so gentlemanly with his clean clothes and white turban and watch and horse carriage, and the making of the snakebite serum at the start of the rainy season – all those memories would have been like memories of a lost paradisal life, something far removed from the India to which he would have been awakening over the 10 years in Dehra Dun.

It also occurred to me – but this was two or three months later – that it might have been at that Irish Catholic school, with the example of the Irish brothers for 10 whole years, a school term running for six solid months, and this was in the 1950s, still close to colonial times, in the decade before the discovery by the hippies and others of a spiritual and romantic India, it occurred to me that in his solitude over those 10 years some idea of the greater seriousness or modernity of revealed religion, and some wish to touch his own faith with this non-Indian magic, might have come to Gurtej.

But that idea, about revealed religion, didn't come to me until much later; I couldn't put it to Gurtej. At the time I was too taken with the idea of the four-year-old child sent away from home.

How had he managed? Did he think he had gained anything from the separation and the loneliness?

He said, 'I think if I hadn't gone to the boarding school I wouldn't have been able to appreciate the basic nature of things, and I would never have tried to analyse why certain things function as they do.'

I asked him to talk about the changes that had come about in the village he knew.

'There has been a revolution. Attitudes have changed – towards the joint family system, to begin with. Agrarian relationships have changed. My paternal grandfather at one time had about 3000 acres of land. Every year he would buy some.'

An idea came to him. He broke off what he was saying and added, as if in parenthesis, 'And yet my father wasn't an educated man. He stayed at school until the fourth standard. My grandfather' – the gentlemanly figure of Gurtej's childhood – 'didn't believe in education. When I was doing my M.A. I heard my grandfather, my paternal grandfather, say to my father one day, "Why don't you take this boy out of school?" He still thought I was going to the secondary school. And my father, not wishing to show disrespect, said, "What can I do? He doesn't listen."' And, for the first time since we had met, Gurtej laughed.

'My grandfather was greatly *disturbed* to see me reading. He said I was reading *all* the time. I was the first in the family not to be a farmer, and perhaps the first in the family to be a graduate. In my village there are now 16 people who have their M.A. When I was born there was only one person – and he had done his B.A. and was a teacher. The people are greatly concerned now about what is happening. There is this craze for education. People are paying through the nose to send their children to better institutions.'

He returned to the subject of his grandfather's 3000 acres. 'There's no one with so much land now. There has been fragmentation of holdings. Intensive cultivation, with high-yielding varieties. It's a revolution. I used to go sometimes to see my grandfather in the field, carry his lunch and sometimes buttermilk – he was very fond of buttermilk. The agricultural practices which I saw then are totally extinct today. The cutting of the crops was in April. In most of the land then we had only one crop a year. April was a very hot month. And my grandfather would take about 40 people as labourers, give them sickles, and they would go out to the fields at about four in the morning, to avoid the heat. They would be cutting until 11 o'clock – a whole big row of people sitting in the field and going at it with gusto, holding the stalks in the left hand and cutting with the right, and then moving on, in a competitive spirit.'

After Gurtej the theoretician, the man with ideas about religion and history, this was like another man.

'It was a sort of celebration, this harvesting. The cutters would rest in the afternoon, and go back again in the evening, from 4.30 to 6.30, seven. Now it is impossible to see this sight in any village. Nobody gets up at four in the morning to go to the fields. I think the adoption of machinery has changed the attitude and life. It has given people the education required to handle such complicated machinery, and to that extent they have become more modern. This again is one of the causes of the Punjab problem, which the Hindus in other areas don't understand.'

I said that what he was saying about machinery was true of other parts of India as well, in villages and cities. It was an aspect of the Indian industrial revolution.

He appeared to agree, but went on, 'Agricultural man comes in touch with several aspects of administration very early in life. Because of water, he understands the hierarchy of officials. Because of seeds, he gets to know the universities. He understands the functioning of government much better than people in towns do.'

He went back to the subject of change. 'We used to have sharecroppers. That's gone. The dependence on labour is no more to the same extent. During the harvest the common scene in the evening used to be the sickles being sharpened. The poor carpenter would be at it the whole night, because the sickles were required again in the morning. Today I have several people in my village who make and repair the new agricultural implements. In small towns in the Punjab you now have a long row of repair shops on both sides of the road.'

He thought of something else that had changed. 'Nobody in the village is paid in kind any more. And there is the position of the harijans, the scheduled castes. That has changed. One day, when I was a child, I had water from a well in the village. I didn't know it was the harijan well. My uncle didn't allow me to enter the house. I had to sit there in the entrance, and the village *granthi* – the reader of the Sikh scriptures – was called, and he gave me some water, to purify my misdeed. Today the same uncle has harijans working in his kitchen. They cook for him.

'This has taken place in the Punjab, but it is going to be extended to the entire country. The attitudes of the people are going to change everywhere, and they are going to expect more and more of their government. The government is deteriorating fast. It will not be able to come up to the expectations of the people, and therefore I see a deep-rooted chasm in the country. Utter chaos. Our government has become a sort of mafia – the politician, the government servant, and the trader, none of them primary producers. They are going to come into conflict with the producers.'

Gurtej gave me copies of some of the papers he had written on the Punjab and Sikh issue. One of the papers, written for a university seminar at the beginning of 1982, might have been the one that had got him into trouble with the administration. It was called 'Genesis of the Sikh Problem in India'. It reminded me of Kapur Singh's writing; it was academic in tone, with long sentences and difficult words, and with quotations from the Sikh scriptures in the footnotes. Its primary theme was the separateness of the Sikh faith and ideology from the Hindu; its further theme was that the Punjab was geographically and culturally more a part of the Middle East than of India. The great enemy of Sikhism and the Sikh empire of Ranjit Singh had been – again – brahminism.

'With nothing more tangible than unflinching faith in the Guru, the Sikhs built up an Empire on the foundations laid by the Guru. They planted the saffron flag' – saffron also the colour of the Shiv Sena in Bombay, with material in that colour draped on the wall panels of the Bombay Municipal Corporation, and decorated with crossed swords – 'in the heartland of the customary invaders, humbled the might of China and reduced the god-king of Tibet. Then they turned to liberating India from the English.' But they were frustrated. 'The Brahminically oriented forces within and without the Punjab cooperated in destroying the Sikhs who alone held out a promise of the early redemption of India.'

So, with his pastoral memories of his grandfather's village, the enchantments of harvest and celebration, there was this other dream of glory, based on Ranjit Singh's short-lived 19th-century kingdom. It was a partial view. But that was to be expected; people all over India, awakening to history and new knowledge of their place in the scheme of things, refashioned history according to their need.

What was unexpected in Gurtej's account of his life and beliefs was how much he took for granted. The constitution, the law, the centres of education, the civil service with its high idea of its role as guardian of the people's rights and improver of their condition, the investment over four decades in industrial and agricultural change – in Gurtej's account, these things, which distinguished India from many of its neighbours, were just there. There was no acknowledgement that generations of reformers and wise men – refusing to yield to desperate conditions – had created those things that had supported Gurtej in his rise from the village.

With his pastoral memories, his dream of Sikh glory, there was also his idea of religious purity. He applied this idea to the affairs of men, and rejected what he found. Like Papu the Jain stockbroker in Bombay, who lived on the edge of the great slum of Dharavi and was tormented by the idea of social upheaval, Gurtej had a vision of chaos about to come. Papu had turned to good works, in the penitential Jain fashion. Gurtej had turned to millenarian politics. It had happened with other religions when they turned fundamentalist; it threatened to bring the chaos Gurtej feared.

To be baptized was to take nectar, amrit. The Golden Temple was at Amritsar, the pool of nectar. It was said that there had been a pool here known to the first Guru. Sacred sites usually have a history: it was also said that the place was mentioned in a version of the Ramayana, and that 2000 years and more before Guru Nanak, the Buddha had recognized the special atmosphere of the Golden Temple site. The Emperor Akbar, the great Mogul, gave the site to the fourth Guru, and the first temple was begun by the fifth Guru in 1589, the year after the Spanish Armada. In the chaos of the 18th century the Temple suffered much from the Muslims. The Sikh king Ranjit Singh rebuilt it in the 19th century. He gave the central temple its gold-leaf dome. This gold leaf, reflected in the artificial lake, has a magical effect. Even after the battle-marks of recent years the Temple feels serene.

Bhindranwale came to the sanctuary of the Golden Temple in 1982, and he turned it into his fortress and domain. He was thirty-five. Four years before, he had been only a preacher and the head of a Sikh seminary; now he was a politician and a warrior. He was also an outlaw: pursuing a vendetta against the Nirankari sect, whom he considered heretics, he had been accused of murder.

He was a proponent of the pure faith; he was persecuted; he offered his followers a fight on behalf of the faith. He incarnated as many of the Sikh virtues as any one man could possess. He and his followers controlled the Temple. The guns were smuggled in from Pakistan. From the Temple, killings were planned, and bombings, and bank robberies. Not all of these things were done with Bhindranwale's knowledge; there would have been a number of free-lance actions: the seeds of chaos were right there. The Temple provided sanctuary; it was the safe house. It was not physically isolated from the town; the old town went right up to its walls. Guns and men could come and go without trouble.

In that atmosphere some of the good and poetic concepts of Sikhism were twisted. One such idea was the idea of *seva* or service. When terror became an expression of the faith, the idea of seva altered.

This is the testimony of one man: 'Inderjit was a close adherent of Bhindranwale. He was involved in the murder of Sandhu. Inderjit used to come to Darbar Sahib [the Golden Temple] and ask for any seva from Bhindranwale. He had once come to me also and had offered his services for any action. Since I hardly knew him, and he had come on his own to see me, I did not place any trust in him. He was, in fact, a very suspicious-looking character. He had developed friendship with [some people] who used to go out of the Golden Temple complex for committing terrorist actions. Two days after the assassination of Sandhu, Inderjit came to Darbar Sahib. By his exuberant behaviour and boastful talks he made it quite clear that he had a hand in the killing of Sandhu, and that he prided about it.' Sandhu, in fact, was Inderjit's next-door neighbour. Inderjit's service or seva was to give information about his neighbour's movements to the seven-man killer team. Neighbourliness had no place in this idea of the faith.

Bhindranwale's military adviser in the Temple was Shabeg Singh. He had been a major-general in the army, and had served with distinction in the Bangladesh war of 1971. Then something had gone wrong: he had been cashiered from the army for embezzlement, but allowed to keep his rank. Revenge had become his religion; Bhindranwale's cause had become his.

From the witness quoted above, there is this story of how preparations were made to take on the state: 'As the events were taking place at a very fast pace, it was appreciated that the police entry into the Golden Temple had become imminent. It was decided that the Sikh youth should be mobilized . . . The decision was taken in March–April 1984. Groups of Sikh youth numbering 30 to 50 came to the Golden Temple for the purpose. In the car-parking space in the Ram Dass Langar' – one of the Temple kitchens – 'wooden partitions were erected to lodge them there. In one of the rooms Shabeg Singh used to impart theoretical training about firearms. Demonstrations were given by him and sometimes by a few of us . . . These groups were treated to inflammatory sermons . . . The groups used to stay for two or three days. In all, about 8000 to 10,000 youth would have been covered.'

In this way Bhindranwale made himself politically powerful, and he might have made himself more powerful if he had had more time. But the freelance terrorist actions continued, and in June 1984 the army moved in. The army had underestimated the strength of the defenders: about 100 soldiers died. This was not the end of the matter. Bhindranwale's followers, and others, occupied the Temple again and made it again a terrorist base. In 1986 the police went in once more; and again after that the terrorists came. In May 1988 the police did what they should have done at the beginning: they cut off water and electricity and laid siege to the terrorists within the Temple. Many of the terrorists occupied the central gold-domed sanctum in the middle of the pool. Police marksmen outside the Temple fired at those who tried to get water from the pool. It was the Punjab summer, and very hot. Nearly 200 terrorists surrendered. During the siege the central temple had been defiled, used as a latrine, by the terrorists. Elsewhere in the Temple bodies were discovered of people who had been killed by the terrorists before the police action.

The men who had defiled the central temple had not fought to the end. A Sikh journalist who witnessed the siege was shocked by their surrender. He had been brought up to have another idea of good Sikh behaviour. This idea had already been confounded by some of the terrorist actions. He hadn't believed that people of his faith would kill women and children; he hadn't believed that they would stop a bus and kill all the passengers. He had thought, at first, that these stories had been made up by the authorities. And there were people who continued to believe that the men who had surrendered during the siege of the Temple were not Sikhs at all. A pamphlet written by a retired army officer said that the men were 'government-sponsored . . . criminals . . . given Sikh form and apparel and taught rudimentary knowledge of the Sikh traditions.'

The establishing of a Sikh identity was a recurring Sikh need. Religion was the basis of this identity; religion provided the emotional charge. But that also meant that the Sikh cause had been entrusted to people who were not representative of the Sikh achievement, were a generation or so behind.

Bhindranwale had spent most of his life in a seminary in the country town of Mehta Chowk, not far from Amritsar.

At the entrance to the town there were small shops set in bare earth yards on both sides of the road. One shop had this sign, as spelt here: UNIVERSIL EMPLOYMENT BEURO *Overseas Employment Consultant.* All around were fields of ripe dwarf wheat, due to be harvested in a few days. There were also fields of mustard, and fields of a bright-green succulent plant, grown as animal fodder.

Lines of eucalyptus marked the boundaries between fields, adding green verticals to the very flat land: line standing against eucalyptus line all the way to the horizon suggested woodland in places.

Fields went right up to the seminary. The flat land, spreading to the horizon below a high sky, seemed limitless; but every square foot of agricultural earth was precious. The gurdwara or temple attached to the seminary had white walls, and the Mogul-style dome that Sikh gurdwaras have, speaking of the origin of the organized faith in Mogul times. The dome looked rhetorical; it stressed the ordinariness of the Indian concrete block which it crowned. The window frames of the white block were picked out in blue. The main hall of the gurdwara was quite plain, with big-bladed ceiling fans, and a wide railed upper gallery. Coloured panes of glass in the doorways were the only consciously pretty touch.

The seminary building was just as plain. On the upper floor, in a concrete room bare except for two beds, the man who was the chief preacher talked to the visitors. There were no more guns at the seminary, he said; and they took in only children now. Some of those children, boys, came to the room, to look. They wore the blue seminarian's gown that went down to mid-shin. It was bright outside, warm; the gowned and silent small boys in the bare room, come to look at the visitors, made one think of the boredom of childhood, of very long, empty days. Some idea of sanctuary and refuge also came to one. Many of these children were from other Indian states; some – solitaries, wanderers – seemed to have been converted to Sikhism, and to have found brotherhood and shelter in the seminary. That idea of welcome and security was added to when a big blue-gowned boy brought in a jug of warm milk and served it to the visitors in aluminium bowls.

The chief preacher said he had come to the seminary when he was about the age of the boys in the room. He had left his family home to stay in the seminary: that was more than 20 years ago.

It was in some such fashion that Bhindranwale had come to the seminary. He had come when he was four or five. Twenty-five years later he had become head of the seminary; and five years after that – after he had taken on the heretics among the Sikhs – he had moved to the Golden Temple. There, two years later, he had died.

He was from a farming family, one of nine sons, and he had been sent to the seminary because his family couldn't support all their children. What could he have known of the world? What idea would he have had of towns or buildings or the state? In these village roads, that ran between the rich fields, there were low, dusty, red-brick buildings, with rough extensions attached, sometimes with walls of mud, sometimes with coverings of thatch on crooked tree-branch poles. Straw dried on house roofs. Shops stood in open dirt yards.

After 25 years in the seminary, he began to call people back to the true way, the pure way. He would go out preaching; he became known. One man heard him preach in 1977 – a year before his great fame – in the town of Gayanagar in Rajasthan. Three thousand people, perhaps 5000, had come to hear the young preacher from Mehta Chowk, and Bhindranwale spoke to them for about 45 minutes. 'He held them spellbound, talking the common man's language.' What was said? 'He asked people not to drink. He said, "Drinking does you harm, and you feel guilty. Everybody wants to be be like his father. Every Sikh's father is Guru Gobind Singh. So a Sikh should wear long hair, and have no vices." There were many references to the scriptures.'

In this faith, when the world became too much for men, the religion of the 10th Guru, Guru Gobind Singh, the religion of gesture and symbol, came more easily than the philosophy and poetry of the first Guru. It was easier to go back to the formal baptismal faith of Guru Gobind Singh, to all the things that separated the believer from the rest of the world. Religion became the identification with the sufferings and persecution of the later Gurus: the call to battle.

The faith needed constantly to be revived, and there had been fundamentalist or revivalist preachers before Bhindranwale. One such was Randhir Singh. The movement he had started in the 1920s was still important, still had a following, could still send men to war against heretics and the enemy. The head of the movement now was Ram Singh, a small dark man of seventy-two, who had been a squadron-leader in the air force.

He said of the founder of his movement, 'He saw the light. His skin was dark, but when he saw the light he started glowing. He could see the future and also all the things about the past. His skin glowed more than English people's. He had rosy cheeks – the light emanated from his cheeks. He saw the light when he was twenty-six. He revolted against the British government. This was the Lahore conspiracy case of 1920. He was imprisoned for life.

'In the jail one day a padre asked him, "You look healthy. You must have good food." Sant Randhir Singh said to the padre, "I have the worst food." The padre said, "You look happy. Do you have someone with you, or do you stay alone?" The sant said, "I'm never alone." The jailer said to the padre, "The man is telling lies. We never put two prisoners together." So the padre asked the sant again, "Who stays with you?" And the sant said, "Almighty."

'When the sant came out in the 1930s – after 16 years in prison – he began to devote his life to singing religious verses, and reading, and administering amrit to others.'

I asked Squadron-Leader Ram Singh, 'Why is the amrit necessary?'

He said, 'God is hidden within us. He is a name only – in every human being. When you take amrit, only then you become aware of it – that name comes automatically on your tongue.'

He started on a discourse about amrit. 'It's a mixture of pure water and white sugar. The sugar is created out of white sugar and baking soda. It's heated, so that it swells and foams up, so that, solidified, it forms sugar buns. It is mixed with the water in iron containers, and an iron double-edged sword is moved backward and forward in the mixture. This was initiated by the 10th Guru, Guru Gobind Singh. You give amrit to render the receiver deathless. Iron is a magnetic metal. In that iron vessel in which you mix the amrit you have the greatest concentration of lines of magnetic forces. When a conductor moves across the line of magnetic forces you get an electro-magnetic force. That energizes the sugar buns and water, and to a small extent dissolves the iron in it. So it's a little iron tonic as well.'

We were talking in his sitting room. There was a carpet on the floor, and a cloth on the centre table, and knick-knacks on hanging shelves: a clock, a small statue of a rearing horse, a china jar, a colour snapshot of a child, a small silver salver (a souvenir of London), and some small painted flower-pieces.

Squadron-Leader Ram Singh was born in 1916. His father was a farmer, and he had gone to some trouble to give his son an education. Ram Singh joined the air force in British times, in 1939. In 1957 he had taken amrit.

Why had he felt the need? Had there been some personal crisis? He said no. He had read books by Sant Randhir Singh, and he had discovered that without amrit one just couldn't reach God.

He spoke clearly. I felt he wished to be friendly. He had the tone and manner of a reasonable man, a man at peace. He was in a fawn-coloured costume, with a milk-chocolate-coloured cardigan. He wore what looked to me like a head-tie rather than a full turban; it was of a saffron colour. The knife, one of the five emblems of Sikhism, hung in a sheath from a big black cross-band, and it made him look less like a warrior than a bus conductor. His beard was a yellowish grey.

The movement aimed at creating pure Sikhs, and amrit was necessary. 'After you take amrit, you don't eat food not cooked by *amritdharis.*' People who have taken amrit. 'That helps to control the five evils: lust, anger, covetousness, ego, family attachments.'

It would also have created the idea of brotherhood. Was that why some people in the movement had become suspect to the government?

He said they had had trouble with a reformist Sikh group who believed in living Gurus: they believed, that is, that the line of Gurus didn't end with the death of the 10th Guru in 1708. They were a small group, but they were a great and constant irritant. In 1978 one person from his movement had been killed by people from that group, and some people of the movement had gone underground.

But he spoke as one for whom violence was far away. His life was consumed by his faith. He got up – his day began – at midnight. He had a bath, and said his prayers till four. From four till 5.30 he read from the Sikh scriptures. Then he slept until 8.30. That was his life. That was the life that had come to him with the pure faith he had turned to when he was forty-one. It clearly had given him peace.

Just before we left, his son came in. He was a handsome, light-eyed man. He had overcome polio, and was a doctor. He was sweet-visaged; he radiated gentleness; he had all his father's serenity. He was in government service; he said with a smile that they were currently on strike. The silver salver on the hanging shelf, the souvenir of London, was something he had brought back after a trip to England.

The terrorists lived now only for murder, the idea of the enemy and the traitor, grudge and complaint, like a complete expression of their faith. Violent deaths could be predicted for most of them: the police were not idle or unskilled. But while they were free they lived hectically, going out to kill again and again. Every day there were seven or eight killings, most of them mere items in the official report printed two days later. Only exceptional events were reported in detail.

Such an event was the killing by a gang, in half an hour, of six members of a family in a village about 10 miles away from Mehta

Chowk. The two older sons of the family had been killed; the father and the mother; the grandmother, and a cousin. All the people killed were devout, amritdhari Sikhs. The eldest son, the principal target of the gang, had been an associate of Bhindranwale. But a note left by the gang, in the room where four of the killings had taken place – the note bloodstained when it was found – said that the killers belonged to the 'Bhindranwale Tiger Force'.

The North Indian village tends to be a huddle of narrow angular lanes between blank or pierced house walls. Jaspal village, where the killings had taken place, was more open, simpler in plan, built on either side of a straight main street or lane. It was a village of 80 houses, and was a spillover from a neighbouring, larger village. Eight years before, some of the better-off people of that village had begun to build their farmhouses at Jaspal, on big, rectangular plots on either side of the main lane.

When we arrived, in mid-afternoon, the people at work on the edge of the village were cautious. We – strangers arriving in an ordinary-looking hired car – could have been anything, police or terrorists: two different kinds of trouble. They frowned a little harder at their tasks, and pretended almost not to see us. It was strange to find that there was no policeman or official in the village, and that less than 48 hours after the murders the village had been left to itself again.

The central lane was wide and paved with brick, and it was strung across with overhead electric lines. The farmhouse walls on either side were flat and low, some of plain brick, some plastered and painted pink or yellow. In an open space below a big tree there were short poles or stakes for tethering buffaloes, and there was a high mound of gathered-up, dried buffalo manure. At various places down the lane – as though the lane also served as a buffalo pen for some of the villagers – there were flat, empty, propped-up carts with rubber tires, and buffaloes and feeding troughs and heaps or pyramids of dung-cakes for fuel. The village ended where the bricked lane ended. Beyond the lane – half in afternoon shadow now, and dusty where not freshly dunged – there was a narrower dirt path, sunstruck, going through very bright fields of mustard and ripe wheat, with tall eucalyptus trees with their pale-green hanging leaves, and crooked electricity poles.

We didn't have to ask where the house of death was. About 15 women with covered heads were sitting on a spread in the wide gateway. The gateway was painted peppermint green, with diamonds of different colours down the pillars. The two big metal-framed gates had been pulled back: a wrought-iron pattern in the upper part, corrugated-iron sheets fastened to the criss-crossed metal frame on the lower part, the resulting triangles painted yellow and white and blue and picked out in red. At the far end of the farmyard – the vertical leaves of the young eucalyptus trees hardly casting a shadow – the men sat in the open on the ground, white-turbanned most of them, their shoes taken off and scattered about them, a string bed near by. The buffaloes were in their stalls, against the low brick wall, over which the gang had jumped two nights before. Such protection at the front, metal and corrugated-iron; such openness at the back, next to the fields.

We were taken to the farmhouse next door. It seemed a much richer place. The yard was not of beaten earth, but paved with brick, like the lane. It was one of the few houses in Jaspal to have an upper storey. This upper storey was above the entrance. It was decorated with a stepped pattern of black, white, green and yellow tiles, and at the corners there was a regular pattern of half-projecting bricks, for the style. The trailer in the courtyard was to be attached to a tractor: it carried the mysterious, celebratory words that all Indian motor-trucks have at the back: OK TATA. And there was something like a flower garden in one corner of the courtyard: sunflowers, bougainvillaea, nasturtiums, plants that loved the light.

We sat on string beds in the open, bright room at the left of the entrance. The brick ceiling, which was also the floor of the upper room, rested on wooden beams laid on steel joists. The concrete pillars were chamfered, with bands of moulded or carved decoration, and painted in many colours – an echo here of the pillars of Hindu temples before the Muslim invasions. Everything in this courtyard spoke of the owner's delight in his property.

People began to come to us. They sat on the string beds, their backs to the light, or leaned against the painted pillars. The Punjabi costume – elegant in Delhi and elsewhere – was here still only farm-people's clothes, the smeared and dirty clothes of people whose life was bound up with their cattle. A sturdy woman in her thirties, in a grey-green flowered suit, grimy at the ankles, came with a child on her hip and sat on the string bed. The woman's eyes were swollen, almost closed, with crying.

The child who now sat on her lap and held on to her was the seven-year-old son of the eldest brother. The boy had been in the room when his father was killed; he had been saved from the burst of the AK-47 only because another brother had hidden with him under a cot. The boy was still dazed, yet still able from time to time to take an interest in the strangers; occasionally, while people talked, tears appeared in his eyes. He had been put into a clean, pale-brown suit, and his hair had been done up in a topknot.

The uncle who had saved him was a handsome, slender man of twenty-three. He had dressed with some care for this occasion, all the visitors coming: a blue turban, a stylish black-and-grey check shirt. He began to tell of the events; while he did so a girl cousin came and unaffectedly rested her head on his shoulder.

The farming day went on. The buffaloes came home, through the front gateway. The heavy chains they dragged rang dully on the bricked yard, and their hooves made a hollow, drumming sound. And village courtesies were not forgotten: water was brought out for the visitors, and then tea.

Joga was the name of the man in the black-and-grey check shirt. What he said was translated for me then by the journalists with me, and amplified the following day by Avinash Singh, a correspondent of the *Hindustan Times.*

The family had had dinner, Joga said, and a number of them were in the room on the living-quarters side of the courtyard. (The opposite side was for the cattle or buffaloes.) Some of them were 'sipping tea'. A little after nine there was a commotion in the courtyard, and someone called out from there: 'The one who has come from Jodhpur, and poses as a religious man – he should come out.'

Joga thought at first that some villagers were calling, but then the tone of the voices convinced him that they were 'the boys', 'the Singhs'. 'The Singhs': the word here wasn't simply another word for Sikhs. It meant Sikhs who were true to their baptismal vows; and in these villages it had grown to mean men from one or other of the terrorist gangs. 'Singhs' was the word Joga used most often for the men who had come that night. The other word he used was *atwadi,* 'terrorists'. Only once did he say *munde,* 'the boys'.

Joga was holding Buta's son on his lap. As soon as he decided that the men who had come were Singhs, he hid with the child below the cot.

Buta, the eldest brother, went to the door of the room. The men outside had called for the man who had come 'from Jodhpur'. Jodhpur had a meaning: Buta, with 200 or 300 others, had been detained in the fort at Jodhpur as a suspected terrorist for more than four years, from June 1984 to September 1988 – just eight months before. Buta had been detained because he had been in the Golden Temple at the time of the army action, and he was known as a religious follower of Bhindranwale's. Buta admitted being a follower; but he said he wasn't a terrorist. He was in the Golden Temple that day, he said, because he had taken an offering of milk for the anniversary of the martyrdom of the fifth Guru, executed on the orders of the Emperor Jehangir in 1606.

This was the man, only thirty-two, but already with many years of suffering, his life already corrupted, who went and stood at the door and looked out at the many muffled men in the courtyard.

The leader said, 'Who is Buta Singh?'

'I am Buta Singh.'

'Come with us. We want you. We have come to take you.' And the man who spoke said to one of his Singhs, 'Tie his hands.'

Some of the men made as if to seize him by the arms. Buta said, 'I won't, I won't.' There was a scuffle, and two of the Singhs fired. A bullet hit Buta just below his ribs on the right side, and he fell backwards into the room. Buta's mother threw herself on her son, saying to the men, 'Please don't kill.' Buta's brother Jarnail and Buta's wife Balwinder also fell on Buta. The Singhs pulled away Balwinder by her hair from her husband, and they fired again with their AK-47s. Buta hadn't been killed yet; but he was killed now, with his mother and his brother. Buta's grandmother was wounded, and was to die in a few days.

Buta's father ran out from his room at the front of the courtyard, the street side. He ran across the courtyard to where the men with the guns were. He tried to grab one of the guns. He was killed with a shot to the head.

After this, the Singhs – there were eight or nine of them – went out of the gateway to the main village lane. Opposite, a little to the right, was the house of Natha Singh, Buta's uncle, the first cousin of his father. They wanted Natha Singh. When the front gate of Natha's house wasn't opened for them, they went around to the back, climbed over the low wall, and they called for him. Natha had five children; the eldest was a polio-stricken girl of fourteen.

Natha came out when he was called. The gang took him out to the lane, and asked him to take them in his tractor to the house of Baldev. They very much wanted Baldev as well. They had a case against him: Baldev, they said, was an amritdhari Sikh, but Baldev had gone against his vows and had been having dealings with a temple priest in the town of Jalandhar. They didn't find Baldev when they got to his house, which was just at the end of the lane, next to the fields. Baldev had heard the gunfire and had slipped away; he had had threatening letters before because of his religious practices. So they had driven back in the tractor with Natha, and in the lane, just outside his house, they had shot Natha Singh dead.

The Singhs had been in the village for half an hour, not more. Then they were gone. It wasn't until eight hours later, at about 5.30 in the morning, that someone of the family picked up the note the terrorists had left behind – now bloodstained and hard to read. The note said that Buta Singh and Natha Singh had been killed because they had been responsible for the deaths two months before of two terrorists just half a kilometre from the village. There was a price of 30,000 rupees on the head of one of the terrorists killed then.

The police said that the gang in question wanted Buta to join them. Buta, as a man who had been close to Bhindranwale until 1984, would have given the group some 'credibility'.

There was another story as well that the villagers told. Shortly after his release from Jodhpur, Buta – who had taken a B.A. degree while in detention – had applied for a minibus permit. This was part of the government's plan to rehabilitate people like Buta. Buta went one day to the town of Jalandhar to see about his permit. He didn't come home at the time he should have done. People in the village made inquiries, and they found that Buta had been arrested by the Central Reserve Police Force in Jalandhar. He was held for nine days.

Buta never told anyone what he had been arrested for, or what had happened during the nine days of his detention. All they knew was that Buta was very frightened when he came back, and never wanted to be alone when he went out of the village – to the tubewell or the local market. (Some said that Buta was afraid of being caught by the police again. But this didn't seem logical. Buta could have been picked up by the police whether he was with a companion or not. A companion, on the other hand, might have deterred an assassin from the gangs.)

We went at last next door, to the house of death, picking our way past the women sitting in the gateway. They were not keening now; they were sitting as silent as the men in the sunstruck yard – no shade there from the vertical eucalyptus leaves, the afternoon sun seeming in fact to catch the leaves in a kind of glitter. The plastered courtyard wall of the living quarters was painted pink, the pierced ventilation concrete blocks above doorways and windows were peppermint green, like the entrance walls: Mediterranean colours. The doors and windows and the vertical iron bars over the windows were a darker green.

The bedrooms were at the front of the building, on either side of the gateway. The doors opened into the courtyard, and the back wall (with iron-barred windows) was also the wall of the lane. There were two rooms on the left. In addition to being used as bedrooms, Avinash told me, they would have been used as store-rooms, with wheat and rice in gunny sacks. Buta Singh's father had been sleeping in the room at the corner of the courtyard; it was from there that he had run out.

The bedroom to the right of the gateway was the principal room of the farmhouse. It was where Buta Singh and his wife slept. It was also the drawing-room. There were no chairs now. The chairs and the centre table, Avinash said, had been removed, because it was known that after the murders visitors were going to come. There were two beds side by side. The bedclothes on them were in disorder. There was an extra bed in the room, together with tin trunks and chests. There was a souvenir of the Golden Temple on a shelf, and Sikh religious calendars on the wall. In Sikh popular art the Gurus are shown with the pupils of their eyes half disappearing below the upper lid, so that more white than usual is seen in the eyeball; this way of rendering the eyes suggests blindness and an inner enlightenment. In this room the pictures made an unusual impression.

There was a photograph of Buta's father-in-law, and there was one other photograph, of Buta himself: a studious-looking young man in glasses. The studiousness and the glasses were a surprise, in this setting of the farmhouse and the village. Buta might have cultivated the scholarly appearance; he would almost certainly have been the first man in his family to have received higher education. Buta's wife, Balwinder, was the only graduate in the village; and no doubt it was her example that had made Buta study for a B.A. degree while he had been in detention in Jodhpur.

Two or three generations – not only of work, but also of political encouragement, political security, development in agriculture, the growth of a national economy – had led Buta's family to where it had got. Two or three generations had led to the beginning of an intellectual inclination in Buta Singh. Awakening to knowledge, he would have seen with a special clarity what he had come from. Ideas of injustice and wrongness would have come more easily to him than ideas of the steady movement of the generations; and the fundamentalism of someone like Bhindranwale would have seemed to answer every emotional need, would have appeared like a programme: ennobling complaint and the idea of persecution, offering history as an idea of glory betrayed, and offering for the present the twin themes of the enemy and redemption. That idea had trapped him and swept him away.

The police said he had been killed because he had refused to join the gang. The note left by the Singhs said he had been responsible for the deaths, by police bullets, of two important terrorists. There might have been truth in both statements. It was part of the wretchedness of the situation, where men had to be blooded into the cause, and, once blooded, couldn't turn away. He must have suffered. Everyone said that he was a very religious man. He had bought religious primers for his two young sons; he went twice a day to the gurdwara to pray. Such devoutness! In the beginning it might have met an emotional and intellectual need; later, perhaps, it had become just a praying for protection.

It had ended for him in the next room. The room was at the side of the courtyard. It faced south. The door was open; but, against the pale glare of the dung-plastered courtyard and the sunlit pink-distempered wall, the doorway looked very dark. Inside, in the shadows, brass pots and steel pots glinted on shelves. There were scuff-marks on the floor where Buta and his family had fallen. Not more than 42 hours had passed since then. But the marks might have been made by the people who had come to look. The note left by the killers, when it was found, was soaked in blood. The ground now was black with flies, barely moving.

Only three days before the killing, Avinash told me later, Buta Singh's wife, the graduate, had opened an English-medium school in the neighbouring village. It was something she had wanted to do for a long time. 'I thought my dream had come true,' she told Avinash. 'I didn't know my husband's return from Jodhpur would spell doom for the family.'

Across the lane was the house of Natha Singh, Buta's uncle. His wife couldn't read. She had five children, the eldest with a disability. She told Avinash, 'I don't know what to do. My world is finished.'

It was for Natha Singh that a new spasm of mourning began when we went outside. To the right of the peppermint-green entrance with the multi-coloured diamond pattern, women were now sitting, now throwing themselves down, on the spot where Natha had been killed, when he had driven the tractor back from Baldev's house. On both sides of the dung-dropped lane farming life went on: buffaloes held their heads down to the troughs at the side of the lane, against the walls of houses. Taking out these animals, bringing them back, milking them or unyoking them, feeding them, bedding them down – these things gave rhythm and correctness to a day and were followed like religion.

Two other men from the village had been detained in Jodhpur. While the women keened, and the buffaloes ate, we heard one man's story. On the very day Ranjit was released from Jodhpur, his brother was killed. Ranjit didn't say who his brother had been killed by; this suggested that his brother had been killed by 'the boys'. His brother's body was found 20 kilometres away from Amritsar – not far from where we were. And so it happened that on the day Ranjit returned home, after four and a half years in Jodhpur, his brother's body also came home. That had happened just a month before.

How could they talk so calmly of grief? They had to some extent been prepared by the faith; but they could talk like that because many hundreds had suffered like them. Avinash said that he and other correspondents had seen more than 50 mass killings such as we had heard about that afternoon. Exactly a year and a week before, 18 members of a Rajasthani clan, half of whom were Sikhs, had been killed. The AK-47 was a weapon of pure murder. It could empty a magazine of 32 bullets in two and a half seconds; the bullets sprayed out at many angles, and could kill everyone in a room in those two and a half seconds. In one night in one subdivision of Amritsar 26 people had been killed, including a thirty-day-old baby girl and the ninety-one-year-old head of a family.

We drove back to Amritsar through by-ways and village-ways, looking at the rich, well-cultivated land. It was still afternoon and bright, still safe. After some time we felt we had lost our way. We were on a dirt road between irrigated fields. We saw two men on a bicycle, one man doing the pedalling, one man on the carrier. The man on the carrier was sitting elegantly, sideways, feet together, but not dangling or hanging down. His shoes were locked together and they were lifted, as though above the dust. When we stopped to ask the way, he slid off, with a practised movement, and offered to come with us, to set us on the road to Amritsar.

He was as handsome as his posture on the bicycle had suggested. He was a Sikh, with a trimmed beard. The trimmed beard had a meaning: it meant he had not taken amrit. He had heard about Buta Singh's death, and the other murders, and he thought it dreadful. He himself didn't belong to any of the purely Sikh political groups. He was in business in a small way and he considered himself successful. He enjoyed his success. He had built a house, he said, with toilets and flush system and everything. He had spent four lakhs on this house, £16,000. But he was thinking now that he might have to give up his house and leave the area. He hadn't taken amrit, and he didn't intend to. He didn't think he would be able to live by the strict amritdhari rules, and he didn't want to get into trouble with the boys, as other people had done.

In the Sikh catalogue of the torments and martyrdoms of its founding Gurus, the bricking up alive of the two sons of the 10th Guru has a special place. The story – with its echoes of *King John* and *Richard III* – has some of the quality of myth.

The man who orders the execution of the children – boys aged nine and ten – is the Mogul governor of the town of Sirhind. Only one person objects to the cruelty: he is a Muslim nobleman of Afghan ancestry, the Nawab of Malerkotla. Then he pleads for the bodies to be honourably cremated: Muslims are buried, Sikhs and Hindus are cremated. The governor says, 'All right. We'll grant you a cremation site. But it will be only as big as what you can cover with gold sovereigns.' The Nawab agrees. He lays out part of his treasure on the ground, and the two bodies are cremated there. So two sacred places come into being: the place where the boys were bricked up, and the place where they were cremated. And the anniversary of the martyrdom is marked by a ritual procession from one place to the other.

Where there isn't a sense of history, myth can begin in that region which is just beyond the memory of our fathers or grandfathers, just beyond living witness. This story of the bricked-up children might have occurred 2000 or 200 or 100 years ago. The events can, in fact, be dated. The 10th Guru gave amrit, baptized the first Sikhs, established the Sikh martial order, in 1699, in the town of Anandpur. Two years later he was besieged in the town by the Mogul forces. The siege lasted for three years. The Guru escaped with two of his sons; but the Guru's mother and his two other sons were captured. They were taken to Sirhind. In 1710 Sirhind fell to the Sikhs.

Events which can be dated and analysed, and placed at a proper distance, from the present, can also at some stage begin to appear far away; can fade. Myths are fresh; they never lose their force. Though at Malerkotla in 1762 the Sikhs were massacred by an invading Afghan army, in Malerkotla in 1947, at the time of the Partition of India and the population exchange between India and Pakistan – the flight of Muslims to Pakistan, and Sikhs and Hindus from Pakistan – in Malerkotla in 1947, because of that Afghan nobleman who laid down gold sovereigns over the cremation site of the two sons of the 10th Guru, no Muslim was harmed. In the 1960s the Sikh political party, the Akali Dal, nominated the Nawab of Malerkotla as their candidate, and he got the Sikh vote in three elections.

I was told this by Amarinder Singh. Amarinder was the head of the house of Patiala. Informally – because the titles of princes have been abolished, and the princes 'de-recognized' – he was the Maharaja of Patiala. All Sikhs are 'Singhs'; in the common surname differences of caste and rank were intended to be submerged. The ideal remains; but almost from the start Sikh chieftains arose, and Patiala was one of the grandest. After Sirhind – where the two boys were bricked up – was incorporated into Patiala territory, it became the family tradition to mark the martyrdom of the Guru's sons with a ritual procession.

'Sirhind was the seat of the Mogul governor. When the Sikhs eventually captured the fort, there was nothing on the spot. No Sikh emblem had survived. The Moguls had destroyed it all. The sites were located where the bricking was done, and the first gurdwara was built. It was subsequendy rebuilt. The rebuilding was done by my father in the early 1950s. The tradition was that, on every anniversary, from the site where they were bricked up to the site of the cremation the Guru Granth Sahib was carried on a bier.' A mimic funeral procession, with the Sikh scriptures – as finally established by the 10th Guru – standing in for the Guru's two sons. 'This went on till the 1960s, when the Akali party acquired control of the gurdwara, and they took over the ceremony.'

The family had a special obligation to the faith. 'We are the only family to have been blessed twice by the Guru.' Amarinder was using the collective form of the word 'Guru', as Sikhs often do. The first blessing was given by the sixth Guru, Hargobind (1606–1644), who comforted the crying son of the family: 'What is he crying for? His horses will drink water out of the River Jamuna.' This was the Guru's way of prophesying that Patiala territory would eventually stretch to that river.

A later ancestor was one of those baptized by the 10th Guru. It was to this ancestor that, at the battle of Chamkaur, not long after the disaster of Anandpur, the 10th Guru wrote for help.

'The Guru was surrounded by the Mogul forces in the fort, but he managed to get a message out. In that letter he says, "My home is your home. And I am in danger. Come." But by the time my ancestor arrived, the battle was over.' In that battle the Guru's two other sons died. 'This was the first generation into the Khalsa.' Later, when the Guru was on his way to the South, where he died in 1708 (two years before the Sikhs managed to capture Sirhind), he made a prophecy about the Patiala family and the eventual size of their state.

That letter of the Guru's from Chamkaur was especially precious to the family. It was from that letter that Amarinder's father or grandfather had derived the current Patiala family motto: 'My House Is Your House'. The earlier motto had been 'Heaven's Light Our Guide'; it could still be seen on old Patiala crockery.

On the roof of the palace there was a gurdwara. The only object of Sikh worship is their holy book, assembled over the years by the various Gurus, and given finally the status of a Guru. But in this gurdwara there were also relics of the 10th Guru. After I had washed my hands and covered my head, I was shown some of these relics: a sword of the Guru, in its velvet-covered scabbard; some spears; a letter, the actual transcription of which must have been done by a secretary or scribe.

On the roof of the palace, old pieties: the historical events of 300 years ago absorbed into religion (the 10th Guru died two years after Benjamin Franklin was born). The palace itself spoke of more recent transformations. It was a new palace, built in the 1930s, sumptuous, but without the oriental motifs such as the European architect of the Maharaja of Mysore had lavished on the Mysore City palace of 1912. This new Patiala palace was like a grand European country house, international or neutral in its feel, built for comfort, using the Indian climate well, converting it into an amenity. In its various reception rooms were signed photographs, such as the visitor sees on open days in grand houses in other countries. But here the photographs – of rulers – marked a changing world, a changing vision, an emerging India: the Kaiser, Victor Emmanuel, the Belgian royal family, Tito, Nehru, Indira Gandhi.

There were many pictures, most of them apparently bought in Europe; but few were notable. There had been a school of Sikh painting, developing just before the British time. The works of this school had been small-scale, on paper, a private court art, records of faces for the most part, the sheets assembled in albums or wrapped up in bundles and stored in palace libraries. The taste or judgement hadn't carried over to the art of Europe, larger, in oils, meant for display on walls and serving a purpose that wouldn't always have been clear. So, though there had been an abundance of money, Amarinder's father and grandfather had bought neither old masters nor any of the great names of the century.

The most striking painting was a larger-than-life full-length portrait of Amarinder's father. The Maharajas of Patiala were famous for their great height. The Raja of Patiala whom William Howard Russell met in Patiala in 1858 was more than six feet tall, and heavily built. The exaggeration, in the painting, of Amarinder's father's size, with his regal stance, was monumental in its effect, and breathtaking. Of a piece with that was a large salon-style painting, hung above the wide staircase, of the Silver Jubilee thanksgiving celebration of the King-Emperor George V in London in 1935, with Amarinder's grandfather and other Indian princes, notably Kashmir and Bikaner, shown with the Prince of Wales, the future George VI and Queen Elizabeth, and their daughters Elizabeth and Margaret.

Amarinder said, 'My grandfather was an autocrat through and through. He came to the throne when he was nine years old. He became a full-fledged ruler when he was eighteen, in 1907. From 1907 to 1938 he was a full-fledged ruler. He put Patiala on the map. He picked an able team to run the state. He was a patron of sports, and music. But he was an autocrat.'

His idea of what he owed himself was shown in the palace where he had lived: the old Patiala palace, on the other side of Patiala city.

'It had 1000 rooms and 400 acres. It is now a sports college. It was three-quarters of a mile from my father's room to mine. We actually measured it one day, taking account of all the steps. It was far too big. So my father built this palace in the 1950s. This is still enormous, but at the time it seemed to the family, after the old palace, that it was a little cramped.'

And, before that old palace – the kind of Indian palace that established the idea of the extravagant wealth of the maharajas at the time of the British Raj – there had been the Patiala fort.

'The old fort was used when people had to fight. There is a tower from which people could fire down.'

The fort began to be built in 1714, on the site of the hermitage of a Muslim fakir or holy man. The fakir's fire was lifted into the fort that was built at the time, and that fire had been kept going ever since.

It was in the fort that in 1858 the then Maharaja (or Raja) of Patiala and his courtiers, all in their best clothes and jewels, had ceremonially received William Howard Russell, showing honour to an important representative of the paramount, and now triumphant, Indian power. It is unlikely that the Raja of Patiala would have understood what Russell's job was, but he would have known that Russell's opinion mattered, and he did all that he could to make a good impression. He went out some way from the fort, on his caparisoned elephant, to meet Russell. He offered Russell an elephant as well, and he ceremonially offered a hand – all this ritual of courtesy and welcome in something like dumb show.

The fort was now half in decay. It was in the middle of the bazaar area in Patiala city, with whole streets, or large sections of them, selling shoes, or certain food dishes, or embroidered garments – Patiala specialities. The first courtyard, where Russell had entered on his elephant, was now used as a urinal by some people. A house built at a later date for important visitors, a house with classical columns, was falling down. Squatters lodged there; and someone had chalked, roughly, *UNSAFE*.

Within, the fort quickly became a maze of small courtyards and passages and steps. There was a small Mogul-style garden, restful, even in its semi-ruin, after brick and plaster. In the late 19th and early 20th centuries ideas of elegance came to Patiala from Britain and Europe. In the 18th century elegance was provided by the Mogul. There is an irony, though, in the 18th-century Sikh borrowings from the Mogul enemy: today, long after the disappearance of Mogul power, the decorated 18th-century Mogul dome lives on in the Sikh gurdwara, as much an emblem of the Sikh place of worship as the spire is of the Christian church.

Apart from this garden, the fort was built up, all paved, no earth showing. Passages, courtyards, terraces, roofs: crumbling brick and plaster, more perishable than wood. Here and there were small, oppressive, over-decorated, dark rooms, with dark mirrors on the walls and carved ceilings. Here and there a ceiling had collapsed, and it could be seen that the village way of building a brick roof, as in the farmhouses at Jaspal village – the bricks set on end on timber beams – had also been the way of the men who had built for the rajas and rulers. Impossible to restore or preserve the old fort: it was in the nature of this brick to crumble. A palace like this could last only while it was lived in. Here and there small attempts at restoration – concrete patching, whitewash – added to the feeling the fort gave of having been built over many times, grown room by room and space by space to its limit, and then finally abandoned.

In some rooms at the top, even with all the decay, the religious rites connected with the foundation of the town and the Patiala fort – blending Muslim and Hindu and Sikh piety – were going on. It was necessary here to take off shoes, because the site was still consecrated. The fire of the Muslim fakir that had been lifted up into the original fort of 1714 was kept going: it was one of the wonders of Patiala. Only oak was used for this fire, and the ash was offered to make a holy mark (a Hindu form). Hindu images of Krishna and Kali were tended in an adjoining room. In another room, opening on to a roof patio, a dark-complexioned reader was chanting from the Sikh scriptures, with a barefoot attendant swinging a whisk over the holy books, which were covered with very fine silk cloths. So, at the very top of the abandoned fort, as at the top of the contemporary palace, there was a reminder of the beginning of clan or family things.

It would have been touch-and-go for the clan in the early part of the 18th century. But the Mogul power declined; the Afghan invasions and raids ceased; the Sikhs came into their own. Patiala state at the end had territory of nearly 7000 square miles. A fair amount of this came in the early 10th century.

'In the 1830s the Gurkhas decided to take the entire mountain range. In 1830 they marched and attacked our hills. All the hill rajas got together and asked for help, and we sent our troops. It was a six months' war. The Gurkhas were defeated. The head of the Nepalese general hung on the Patiala gate until it disintegrated.'

Patiala never got on with the great Sikh ruler, Ranjit Singh. 'When Ranjit Singh threatened, Patiala entered into a treaty with the British. Patiala stayed neutral in the Anglo-Sikh wars.' Even before the Sikhs were defeated in 1849, two battalions of Sikh irregulars were recruited by the British in Patiala. When the Mutiny broke out eight years later Patiala remained loyal to its treaty with the British. That support was crucial; without it the British might have been defeated in North India.

'In our family archives there is a letter from the last Mogul emperor, Bahadur Shah. In our archives we keep rulers' personal documents; the other documents have gone to the state. In the palace we have a librarian looking after our archives. The mutineers pressed Bahadur Shah into being their titular ruler, and he wrote letters to all the Indian states asking for their support. But at that time his domain wasn't even Delhi. His domain was literally only the Red Fort. The letter was in English, very flowery, probably written by a scribe. It was a scroll two feet long. But we had this mutual defence pact with the British, and it was that which we had to honour.'

In June 1858, when the Mutiny had been more or less suppressed, William Howard Russell went 'with a party' to look at the defeated emperor in the Red Fort at Delhi. The Red Fort was occupied by British soldiers and Gurkhas (recruited now, like the Sikhs, to replace the soldiers from other mutinous communities). The emperor was squatting on his haunches in an empty passage off a small roof patio. He was a small, withered man of eighty-two, barefooted, in a dirty muslin tunic and thin cambric skullcap. He was vomiting into a brass basin; Russell didn't ask why. The old man was mentally far away from the people who had come to stare at him. He had a habit of poetry, and Russell said that a day or so before he had composed a poem, writing 'some neat lines on the wall of his prison by the aid of a burnt stick'. This didn't arouse Russell's wonder or compassion, only his mockery. He never thought to find out what the words meant.

British people in India at this time were talking of blowing up the Jama Masjid in Delhi, as earlier someone had talked of destroying the Taj Mahal and selling the marble. Even the Raja of Patiala had become suspect to the British, and Russell heard complaints that he had been in communication with the Emperor Bahadur Shah.

It seemed from what Amarinder said that there was some truth in the story. He said, 'A brother of the maharaja was very fond of Bahadur Shah, because he was a poet. And he went to offer help to the emperor. After the Mutiny he came back to Patiala, and the British then asked for him to be handed over to them. Patiala refused, and the British couldn't push it because there were few loyal rulers left.

'So a compromise was reached. The maharaja's brother left Patiala. And he eventually renounced the world, living first in Rishikesh in the Himalayas, one of the Hindu centres of learning and pilgrimage, and then in the early part of the century he moved south to Bangalore.' Bangalore was in the princely state of Mysore, somewhat removed from British jurisdiction. There he died in the 1950s, well over a hundred. He became a teacher and a sadhu kind of figure. His wife continued to live in the old Patiala fort. Theirs had been a child marriage. She had come as a child to the fort, and was left by her husband when she was nine. And she continued living in the fort, refusing to leave, until the 1930s. She had never seen anything outside the fort. There was strict purdah in those days. She had never seen a car, a train, people outside the palace, a forest, a field. My grandfather wanted her to take drives. He insisted and insisted, and – it must have been in the early 1930s or late 1920s – my grandfather forcibly took her out in the car to see the things she hadn't seen before. While she lived in the fort she refused to let anyone draw her water from the well. This was because she wanted to live the difficult life she thought her husband was enduring.'

It was hard to believe in this story. If, say, the brother of the Raja of Patiala was sixteen when he had gone to offer his help to Bahadur Shah, he would have been born in 1840 or 1841. To have died in the 1950s would have made him over one hundred and ten at the time of his death. And his child bride would have died at the age of ninety or thereabouts. Still, the story as Amarinder told it contained many of the great transformations that had come to

India from Mutiny to Independence. The lifetime of those people would have contained not only the transformation of the Sikhs from ruffianly frontiersmen to farmers and businessmen; it also contained the transformation of their rulers from warrior chieftains to Raj-style maharajas.

Amarinder said, with a wave of his hand, 'My grandfather wouldn't have been able to *understand* this.' And by 'this', Amarinder meant independence, parliament, universal suffrage. 'Do you know, my grandfather kept my maternal grandfather in prison, and kept them out of Amritsar for nine years, for being a member of the Praja Mandal. That was what the people involved in the freedom struggle called the Congress in the princely states. My maternal grandfather was a man of character, too. He didn't climb down. All the family's confiscated property was returned only when my parents got married.'

Two generations lay between the jewelled ruler William Howard Russell saw in the Patiala fort in 1858, and the maharaja who ruled absolutely in the 1000-roomed Motibagh Palace from 1907 to 1938. One role followed on from the other: the British connection enhanced the ruler's glory. It was altogether different for Amarinder's father.

'My father had a difficult life. He took over in 1938 when his father died. He was twenty-five. There was the war in 1939, and then from 1945 there was the Independence movement. My father was chancellor of the Chamber of Princes. So he lived with instability. With Independence he was the first to sign the instrument of accession, and Patiala merged with all the Punjab states. It was a decline for my father personally. From being a ruler he became a governor of a state. Patiala was being considered as the possible capital of Indian Punjab. But the chief minister at the time got it scotched. He thought that Patiala would always have an influence in state matters, so he cooked up the idea of building a brand-new city at Chandigarh. And then in 1958 the Punjab States Union merged with the Punjab, and my father became a *nobody*.' He stood for the Punjab assembly, but he didn't like politics. He became an ambassador; it didn't assuage his grief. 'He was an introvert. He kept the problems inside. When he died in 1974 – he was only sixty-one – the doctors said his heart was like that of a man of eighty-five.'

Amarinder himself had no problems of adaptation. He was born in 1942; he was five when Independence came. 'I've been brought up in a modern environment.' There was a palace education: an English nanny, a German kindergarten tutor, and training by 'a great master' in Sikh scriptures, legends and folklore. There was also a full education outside the palace, in preparatory schools in Simla and Kasauli, in a famous Indian public school, and then in the Indian Military Academy at Dehra Dun. He joined the army, enlisting in the oldest Sikh regiment, directly descended from the two battalions raised in Patiala in 1846. He loved army life, and would have liked an army career. But he had to leave the army to look after the affairs of the family. He later 'grew into politics' – exercising, perhaps, something of the skills of his 18th-century ancestors during the early days of the Patiala state.

Then the preacher Bhindranwale appeared. There was a terrorist crisis; and the army that Amarinder loved was ordered to move on the Temple he held sacred.

'When the chips were down I couldn't let 300 years of history go. It was the Sikhs who made Patiala. The two Gurus have blessed us. I had to stand with our people.'

When I went back to Chandigarh I saw Gurtej again. It was then that he told me – what I suppose was common knowledge – that after Operation Bluestar, the code-name for the army action at the Golden Temple, he had gone underground for more than four years. For the first time he spoke in some detail about Bhindranwale. Kapur Singh, the dismissed ICS officer, had been Gurtej's first hero and mentor; Bhindranwale was the second.

'He was always a religious man. To the very end. He was the son of a small farmer in Faridkot district. The district was named after Farid, a Muslim Sufi saint of the 13th century; his couplets appear in our scriptures. Bhindranwale was born in 1947. He was one of nine sons. He was the son of a second wife. The father had seven sons from the first wife, two sons from the second wife. The father couldn't support all the sons, and at an early age, four or five, Bhindranwale was sent to the seminary.'

Gurtej was also born in 1947. He, too, had been sent away to a boarding school when he was four or five. And he too came from a farming family, though his grandfather had been rich, with 3000 acres.

'The father had a little land, and there was no intensive agriculture at that time. One son went to the army; he is retired now as a captain. Another son went to Dubai and is now back, well-to-do, still farming. Others are also farming.

'Bhindranwale spent all his years in the seminary, and we never heard anything about him until 1976. By then he was married, with two sons. His wife would have stayed in the village; it was an arranged marriage. Bhindranwale was known as a contemplative man, totally unconcerned about the world around him. Sometimes he would go to work in his family fields, and he was known as a very hard worker. Cutting starts on the 13th of April. It's a very hot period; the sun shines harshly. Bhindranwale would start cutting in the early morning and go at it right until the evening, without food or drink. He was a very determined man. This was told me by one of his brothers.'

And not for the first time Gurtej, talking about the life of the village, the life of the fields, fell – easily – into a lyrical strain.

'In 1977 the head of the seminary died. He had nominated Bhindranwale to succeed him. The head of the seminary died during the Nirankari controversy.' The Nirankaris: reformist Sikhs to some, heretical to others. 'His legacy to Bhindranwale was the continuation of this struggle.'

The following year, on the day of the spring or harvest festival, an important day in the Sikh religious calendar, there was a clash between the two groups in Amritsar, and a number of Bhindranwale's followers were killed. With this event Bhindranwale became a figure.

Gurtej said, 'I got to know him in 1980. The high priest who had given me amrit in 1974 had died, and I went to his village for the last rites. And there I met Bhindranwale. He was a very truthful man, a man of his word. He never went back on what he said. He was a man of God. He had unbounded faith in God. While taking decisions he only consulted his conscience. He lived the life of a mendicant.

'In 1980 the head of the Nirankaris was killed in his own place in Delhi – just like Indira Gandhi later – and he was allegedly killed by somebody who had been employed as a carpenter there. The Arya Samaji press blamed Sant Bhindranwale for the killing and demanded his arrest. Shortly after that, the head of the Arya Samaji press was killed near Jalandhar, and it was in this connection that warrants were issued for the arrest of the Sant.

'The Arya Samajis control the Hindu press of Punjab. The history of Punjab in this century is full of controversies between Arya Samajis and Sikhs, the essence of the trouble being that the Arya Samajis were attacking the separate identity of the Sikhs. At the beginning of this century the Arya Samajis publicly converted some *chamar*' – untouchable – 'Sikhs back to Hinduism at Jalandhar. And their hair was cut off, plaited together into a rope, and the rope was sold at a public auction. The idea was to ridicule Sikhism and Sikhs.

'At the time the warrants were issued for the arrest of the Sant he was preaching in a village in Haryana. This information was given to him there, perhaps by the Haryana administration, who didn't want any trouble in their area. The Punjab police party arrived after the Sant had left, and they became so angry they burnt his buses and destroyed his holy books. After this, his arrest was enforced at Mehta Chowk, at the seminary. A big crowd had collected on the day of his arrest. After he had been taken away he appealed to the people to be peaceful. The police resorted to firing – at the town itself – and 34 people were killed. The police claimed they had been attacked with swords.

'These three things upset him: the burning of his buses and holy books, his being accused as a conspirator, and the killing of his people. He was in jail for some months. Then he was released unconditionally. In 1982 he went to the Golden Temple. The circumstances were like these. Two or more of his followers had been arrested. And then the people he sent to supervise the legal protection of these men were themselves arrested. That was when he decided to launch an agitation.

'He was a tall man, six feet one inch, as tall as I am, and a lean man. A very forthright man, outspoken. He had very simple habits. He ate very little. In this he was unlike Sardar Kapur Singh, who liked his food. He had an incisive mind. You could discuss things with him. He knew, for instance, that I ate meat, but he didn't mind. He never asked me to stop eating meat. I had a long argument with him about whether it was according to the tenets of Sikhism to eat or not to eat meat. This was in January 1983 at the Akal Takht in the Golden Temple. The discussion lasted two hours. He kept on telling me in a good-humoured way, "You prove it to me that it is according to the tenets of Sikhism to eat meat, and I will polish off one and a half kilos in no time."

'He used to call us for discussions several times, sometimes just for the interpretation of passages in the scriptures. The seminary supported the traditional interpretation. The seminary interpretation is nearer to the Hindu understanding of the scriptures, and it is all expressed in Hindu terminology. Most of the examples are from Hindu mythology. I used to support the more recent, scientific interpretation, established in 1960 or so.'

I asked about this scientific interpretation.

'It was by Sahib Singh – the interpretation of the scriptures according to the grammar of the language. He was a saintly man, a teacher.'

This statement – I took it down without understanding it fully, and considered it only many weeks later – cast a little light on a difficult sentence on the first page of Kapur Singh's pamphlet, 'The Trial of a Sikh Civil Servant in Secular India': 'The basis of grammar and language are certain metaphysical postulates, cultural patterns and human propensities, the logical demonstration of which may not be possible, but without acceptance of which, neither language nor grammar can be properly studied or understood . . .'

And I wondered whether, in these religious discussions in the Golden Temple, Kapur Singh's ideas might not have filtered through Gurtej to Bhindranwale, and encouraged him to go against his seminary training and to say to the BBC radio correspondent, when the Golden Temple crisis was worsening, that Sikhs were not like Hindus but were more like Jews and Muslims and Christians, people of a prophet and a book.

In that interview Bhindranwale also said – in English, in a voice breaking with passion – that Sikhs were subject to such persecution in India they had to 'give a cup of blood' to get a cup of water. This kind of exaggeration from a religious leader had puzzled me; but at that time I hadn't yet begun to enter the Sikh ideas of the torment and grief of their Gurus.

What Gurtej went on to say now gave me some idea of Bhindranwale's state of mind in the airless, imprisoned atmosphere of the Golden Temple during the last days.

Gurtej said, 'He was most enamoured of the personality and sacrifices of Guru Gobind Singh. The last days of Guru Gobind Singh he remembered by heart. He remembered the day-to-day doings of the Guru. He really lived it out. If you met him in December on a certain day he would say, "On this day the Guru was doing such-and-such." In fact, he would remember it by the time of the day. It was very remarkable. He would look at his watch and say, "In another two hours the Guru would have been getting his sons ready for the battle." And so on. In the month of December the Guru's sufferings began, because that was when he left his fort at Anandpur Sahib.' Anandpur: the town where the Guru's mother, and the Guru's two young sons – to be bricked up later – were captured by the Moguls.

Shut up in the Golden Temple, Bhindranwale must have begun to see himself as the 10th Guru besieged in Anandpur.

Gurtej said, 'People didn't go to him to talk about history or scriptures. His family rarely visited him. Whenever they came, they came as devotees. He had no time for his family in this period.

'I used to go to see him at the Temple once a month. Never less than two hours. There was some degree of mutual understanding between us. Once he said, "You should come to see me more often." I said, "I have to look after my family." He said, "How many children do you have?" I said, "Two." He said, "I have two children too. God looks after children." And he quoted a passage from the scriptures about migrating birds who leave their offspring behind. He said, "They fly for thousands of miles, and God sustains them."'

I asked Gurtej about the killings done in Bhindranwale's name, and the killings he was said to have given orders for.

'They were made-up stories. The purpose was to defame him.'

After Operation Bluestar – the army assault on the Temple, in which Bhindranwale and many of his followers died, and many soldiers as well – it was given out officially that Gurtej was among the people killed. This alarmed Gurtej. 'A case of sedition had been registered against me in connection with a booklet about Sikh human rights. The meaning of giving me out as dead was that instructions had been given to the forces to eliminate me.' So Gurtej went underground, and stayed in hiding for more than four years.

'My obituary also appeared in the *Indian Express.* It was flattering by and large. But it said that I didn't eat with Muslims –

which is wrong, totally. I wrote a letter to the *Indian Express* saying, "Let any Muslim prepare a tasty vegetarian meal and invite me."' Vegetarianism wasn't the issue. Gurtej wasn't a vegetarian. 'But I don't eat meat killed in the Muslim or Jewish fashion. It's a commandment of the 10th Guru, when we take amrit. Such taboos in religion often have a deeper meaning.'

The point about the *Express* obituary must have been that Gurtej adhered strictly to his Sikh vows. Kapur Singh had written a big book about the significance of Sikh vows; Gurtej had given me a copy of the book. And now – leaving to one side the question of his life underground after Bluestar – he told a story to explain the 10th Guru's injunction to his followers against having relations with Muslim women.

'One of the stories appearing in one of our Sikh texts, *The Fundamentals of Sikhism* by Sewa Dass, relates to a person who had been forcibly converted to Islam in the 1700s. He went to the Guru, who was presiding over the congregation, and said, "I have been forcibly converted." "How have you been converted?" "I've been made to eat cow's meat." "That doesn't make you a Muslim." "I've been circumcised." "That can't make anybody a Muslim." "I've been made to repeat the Kalma." "That's the name of God. It doesn't make you a Muslim." Somebody in the congregation was surprised. He asked the Guru, "How does one become a Muslim then?" And the Guru said, "By marrying a Muslim woman, or having such relations with her." The implication is that marriage is a voluntary act. "If you *accept* that you are a Muslim, then alone you become a Muslim." This is how the Guru comforted the man.'

As much as any story of martyrdom, this story from the final years of the last Guru speaks of the persecution and anguish and violation out of which the Sikh military brotherhood was born. Though that wasn't the point Gurtej made: Sikhism, in his interpretation, was a religion of prophecy and revelation.

When I asked him what had supported him during his time underground, he said, 'I was thinking I was suffering with my people. There was another consolation: this was the period I turned most to my scriptures. The main theme of the scriptures is that one lives in the world in such a fashion that one becomes acceptable to God. And I thought I was doing that. I did a lot of reading and writing. So my time underground was instructive. One could contemplate the nature of things.'

'That was what you said about your Roman Catholic boarding school, your schooldays away from home. So your time underground was like a repeat of your childhood?'

Gurtej said, 'I don't know whether character is destiny or destiny is something in its own right. But things do develop which put you in situations that develop you in a definite direction.'

One cause of grief during this time underground was the death of Kapur Singh, at the age of seventy-five. Gurtej had known and loved Kapur Singh for 20 years. The cantankerousness which had irritated Gurtej at their very first meeting was something he now smiled at, as he smiled at other quirks of the man: his liking for his food, his love of ice cream. He could eat a pound at a time. He used to say to Gurtej, 'You must eat ice cream. It's good for your liver.'

Gurtej said, 'He was a rather stout man, not very tall, with thick-rimmed glasses. Always a pen or two with him, looking every bit a scholar, with a book or magazine tucked under his arm, always.'

Kapur Singh had carried his grievance about his dismissal from the ICS for embezzlement for nearly 40 years; he had kept it fresh. The grievance hadn't fatigued Gurtej or raised any doubts in him. He said, 'The idea of injustice is there in every Sikh.' And he was still ready to fight that particular side of Kapur Singh's case. Gurtej had become like a member of Kapur Singh's family; it distressed him that he couldn't be with the old man at the end.

'Finally I was able to get some sort of protection from the High Court. I had applied to the High Court saying that the sedition case against me was false, and the intention of the government was to harass me and harm me physically. The court granted me seven days' time to appear in the lower court and sign my petition and ask for bail. And I did that. I am still technically on that bail.'

This was why, a few months before, Gurtej had been able to visit Kapur Singh's brother, when that brother was dying. The family, Gurtej said, belonged to a sect of Sikhs who, since the days of the first Guru, traditionally became mendicants and teachers – and this was perhaps one factor in Gurtej's admiration of Kapur Singh.

'His father was a small landowner – about 20 acres or so. The other son was totally uneducated. He remained a farmer all his life – while Kapur Singh was educated at Cambridge University. In lieu of this, the younger son got 10 more acres of land. The younger brother was on his death-bed when I met him last year, and he complained that Kapur Singh's relatives were trying to snatch those extra 10 acres from him.'

Gurtej, Kapur Singh, Bhindranwale: they were all men of farming families. Great events had claimed them; but below all the passions – about faith and purity – there were elemental things that could take men further back: to a deathbed anxiety about 10 acres of land.

Sanjeev Gaur, the Amritsar correspondent for the *Indian Express,* was attacked and stabbed one day in Febuary 1984 just outside the Golden Temple.

'There was an old pickpocket of Amritsar who had become a political activist, first for the Indira Congress, and then as a member of the All-India Sikh Students Federation. I wrote a story about this pickpocket for the *Express.* The day the story was published I went to the Golden Temple, and he gave me a very dirty look. My source told me I should be careful.

'A fortnight later I was stabbed by two young boys, one wearing a saffron turban. They asked my name first, and then they started hitting me. Five times they stabbed me in the thigh. And I heard another voice saying, "Drag him inside." I thought that was the moment of death, because I had been reporting for the last month or so about the discovery of five bodies in gunny sacks in the gutters of the Golden Temple – people killed by the terrorists inside the Temple. The people killed were mostly Sikhs – suspected by the terrorists to be police informers.

'The two men who attacked me left me. I began to walk to a clinic. People were looking at me. Blood was oozing out of my trousers. The people who were looking were helpless. If they had helped me, they would have incurred the wrath of the terrorists. And then I asked a cycle-rickshaw-wallah – a lot of them there, outside the Golden Temple – to take me to a doctor, and then two Sikhs helped me. I later learned that the two men who had helped me were communists.

'But I should also mention that Bhindranwale condemned the attack. He told some journalists that he didn't believe in daggers – he believed in guns. And two of his main aides telephoned me at home to express their regrets. They said they were not behind the attack.

'Then I was posted to the East by my paper, but deviously, for my safety.'

Dalip, another reporter, told of what happened after the Golden Temple had been occupied by Bhindranwale.

'People stopped going to the Golden Temple. Both my neighbours stopped going, though they wanted to. People were angry about what was happening in the Temple, but the Sikh political party never condemned the desecration of the Temple by Bhindranwale and his guns. The Sikh political party were fighting a joint agitation with Bhindranwale from the Golden Temple, and they were afraid of him. He was a killer. He didn't worry about Hindu or Sikh – once you opposed him, you would be on his hit list.

'I was witness to one killing he ordered. I was sitting in Room 47 on the third floor of the Guru Nanak Niwas. This was one of the rest houses in the Temple where he used to stay with his followers.

There were armed men sitting all around, eight, 10 people. This was in the middle of 1983. Suddenly one guy entered. He was a middle-aged Sikh, in shirt and pyjamas, and he was looking glum. His hair was cut and his beard was cut awkwardly. He started talking to Bhindranwale: "Santji, this is what Bichu Ram, a police inspector, has done to me. He took me to a police station and desecrated me. He cut my hair and my beard."

'Bhindranwale immediately asked one of his aides to take down all the details. Fifteen days or so later this Bichu Ram, in charge of one of the police stations, was shot dead.

'The second way of operating, of ordering killings, was to pronounce the names of people whom he wanted killed from a public platform. He did this from the 19th of July 1982 till June 1984. He would make a speech. Always against Mrs Gandhi, Giani Zail Singh [the Indian President], and Darbara Singh, the chief minister of Punjab. And he would say these people should be taught a lesson for having harmed the Sikhs. Afterwards he would talk against some local police officers. And many of the people whose names he spoke would be later killed. Bachan Singh, a senior police officer of Amritsar, was killed, together with his wife and daughter.

'I used to talk to Sikhs. But by and large Sikhs did not come forward to condemn the happenings in the Golden Temple. They were blaming New Delhi – everything was being done by New Delhi. They were never criticizing Bhindranwale and his men. Whenever terrorists were killed the Sikhs were very upset – they spoke of fake encounters. Whenever the terrorists killed innocent people, I never heard my neighbours expressing regret.'

Dalip had Sikh connections; this explained some of his passion.

I said, 'Someone who knows Sikhs well has told me that there was something wrong with the way Bhindranwale and his followers looked. They had the eyes of disturbed people. Was it a kind of communal madness, you think?'

'It's the minority fear, the persecution complex, the death wish. It's a new religion. It has produced great generals and great sportsmen. But it hasn't produced great religious thinkers to strengthen the religion. Nothing happened after Guru Gobind Singh set up the Khalsa in 1699. Since 1699 it has produced no great thinkers.

'It's madness, it's fanaticism. It can't really be explained. It's the tragedy of the Sikh religion that in the post-Independence era a man like Bhindranwale has come to be accepted as the most important Sikh leader since Guru Gobind Singh. He was called in his lifetime by many Sikhs the 11th Guru. And he really was a product of Mrs Gandhi. She built him up to fight the Sikh party, the Akalis.'

'Why did educated people give their support to Bhindranwale?'

'Frustration.'

'When did you first see him yourself?'

'The 24th of July 1982. In the Golden Temple. The famous Room 47. I was checked by his bodyguard. Guns in the Temple were seen for the first time in 1982, and it's a perversion of the religion.

'He arrived in the Golden Temple on the 20th of July 1982. He left it dead on the sixth of June 1984. He harmed the Sikhs the most, the Sikh religion the most. He harmed Punjab, and he harmed India.

'The aides questioned me, and when I told them I was a journalist, they smiled and were very happy, and they immediately escorted me inside.

'I greeted him. He was sitting on a string bed, and he was nicely dressed up, wearing that long white cotton gown going down to his knees, and that blue turban. And his revolver hung from a belt around his waist. He had angry eyes – you asked about the eyes. He looked lean and hungry, the type of people who are dangerous. He said, "Who are you?" Very dictatorial. I said, "I'm a journalist." I gave him the name of the weekly I worked for, and I mentioned that I was also the correspondent for a Canadian paper. "Do you want to interview me?" "No, I've just come for your *darshan*."'

Darshan is what a holy man offers when he shows himself: the devotee gets his blessing merely from the sight, the darshan, of the holy man.

'He was very flattered. He smiled and he laughed. He had been very serious when I entered.

'I found an old lady handing over to him bundles of currency notes, and she also removed one or two of her gold rings and handed them over to him. Standing over the old lady was an old man, who I learnt later was General Shabeg Singh.' Major-General Shabeg Singh: cashiered in his mid-fifties for embezzlement, and now acting as Bhindranwale's military adviser.

'Shabeg was lean and thin, middle height, very fair, wearing spectacles, flowing beard, white beard, white pyjama and kurta. He was smiling. I shook hands with him. He said, "I'm General Shabeg Singh. I led the Mukti Bahini in the Bangladesh war." I said, "Sir, you are a general. How did you get attached to Bhindranwale?" I needed copy for a colour story – my first day in Amritsar. His reply was, "I see spirituality in his eyes. He is like Guru Gobind Singh."

'I came out of the Golden Temple a sad man, wondering about the fate of the community, wondering about the general's reply, comparing Bhindranwale with Guru Gobind Singh. I was very sad when I sat at the typewriter. Because I was not impressed by Bhindranwale. I knew he was not Guru Gobind Singh. I knew he was just being used by the Indira Congress to harm the rival Akali party in Punjab. He was an ordinary man on whom greatness was being imposed. Why should the community accept him? Why should General Shabeg Singh not judge him as a man? Why were people just impressed by his angry looks and the armed men around him? He was not an intellectual, not a thinker, and he was not a pious man.'

Dalip meant, I suppose, that Bhindranwale wasn't really a man of God. But what were the noticeable religious aspects of the man? There must have been many.

'He was a vegetarian, a lover of music. He would go to the Golden Temple water tank every morning at three and listen to the music played by the blind musicians from inside the main shrine. They play on the harmonium and recite the scriptures. That music is soothing, divine – and I give him full marks for wanting to be part of that. You feel the presence of God when that music is played in the silence, and there are no people around. He did that every morning for one hour. And he was not a womanizer.'

The vegetarianism, the love of music, the early rising, the sexual control, were run together in this account to give an idea of the austerity of the man that so impressed people in the early days, when he went out preaching and urged people to be like their father, the Guru.

Dalip said, 'He made himself a monster.' Monster: it was the word people used of the later man. 'He began to think he would rule the country or rule Khalistan. He wanted to rule something. He accepted the compliment when people told him he was like Guru Gobind Singh. Subconsciosly, Bhindranwale began imagining himself to be Guru Gobind Singh – a reincarnation of the 10th Guru.

'I will give you two more pictures of him. The first is from the middle of 1983. A colleague on an Indian daily did a big story saying that Naxalites had entered Bhindranwale's camp. I checked out my colleague's story and found it was all right, and I extended it with inquiries from my own sources. Bhindranwale hated the story in the daily, but I learned about that only later. The day after my own story came out, I went to see Bhindranwale. That was my practice, to go and see him after things about him by me were printed.

'The same room in the Temple. Room 47. Now I can open the door and go in coolly – everybody knows me now. I took along a friend with me, someone from the medical college. The moment I open the door of Room 47, I see the angriest look in his blood-shot eyes. They were red eyes when he was angry, which often he was. And I got the message. There were eight or nine of his armed admirers in the room, and two journalists were interviewing him.

'He started shouting at me, in crude Punjabi, at the top of his voice: "How dare you compare me with thieves and scoundrels and lumpens?" That is what he thought Naxalites were. He continued shouting at me in this way for three minutes, and then he ordered one of his men to bring the copy of the magazine with my story. And I, the magazine's correspondent, stood in front of him like a schoolchild who has offended the teacher. I couldn't utter a word – I was so afraid: I could see the guns around, and I knew he could kill me if he wanted to.

The magazine arrived. He handed it to me. He had cooled down a bit, but he was still very angry. He asked me to translate what I had written into Punjabi. I pleaded that I wasn't good at translating from English into Punjabi. He cooled down more. And then, to my amazement – I realized how shrewd he was – he signalled to me, while he was sitting on his string bed – I was no more than four feet away – to come closer to him.

'He wanted me to come closer to him, and when I went closer to him on his string bed, he pulled my head down and he whispered into my ears. "You are like a younger brother to me," he said in Punjabi, whispering, "and still you write against me."

'The meeting ended, and I came out of the room with my friend, the man from the medical college. He had wanted to see Bhindranwale, and had asked me to take him, because as a journalist I could go in and out of Room 47. I apologized to my friend for the shock treatment.

'I didn't meet Bhindranwale for a couple of days after that. I felt most uncomfortable. I didn't know how to report him. I knew one had to be critical of him, but it was so difficult to be sitting in Amritsar and to attack him. For a few months I kept quiet.

'But the magazine wanted stories, and in October 1983 I did a story saying that Bhindranwale was losing his popularity, that not many people were coming to see him. The magazine played it up:

'The Sant in Isolation', a full two pages, with a big photograph of that big man in his white cotton gown, half smiling, half frowning. And, as usual, after my story appeared, I went to see him.

'He was having a walk on the terrace of the rest house, the Guru Nanak Niwas. Not many people were there – 40, 50, mostly his followers. He started walking with me. Obviously he didn't know about the story. That was the last time I had a friendly chat with him. The next day I went again to see him, accompanying a Canadian TV team as an interpreter. He had learnt about the story by then, and in full public view, on the same terrace of the Guru Nanak Niwas where he had walked with me alone the day before, he told me that if I didn't stop writing against him, then I wouldn't be alive. He said this in Punjabi, in symbolic language. *Sannu uppar charana anda hai*. "We know how to take you up."

'After this I stopped seeing Bhindranwale. I didn't report on him. I didn't do any critical story. I was afraid. On the 23rd of December 1983 he shifted from the Guru Nanak Niwas to the Akal Takht, from the rest house to a sacred building. I went with some local journalists to see him. He was sitting on the floor – 50, 60 people with him. Some fruits and sweets lying near by. He gave me a piece of sweet and a banana, and he made some sarcastic remark, which I don't recall. Obviously he didn't like me any more. Some weeks later a colleague was stabbed outside the Temple. This didn't have anything to do with Bhindranwale, but in the atmosphere of fear nobody went to the aid of the stabbed man. They just stood and watched him bleed. I asked my paper to move me somewhere else.'

Just as Gurtej, talking of the fields and harvest, fell into a kind of lyricism, so I felt that Dalip, talking of the morning music in the Golden Temple, had spoken with a special reverence for the sacredness of the old site. I asked how shocking Operation Bluestar, the army action at the Temple, had been to him.

'Bluestar itself was not shocking to me. What was shocking was the manner in which it was done. It was a very bad operation. I thought Bhindranwale and his men could have been caught easily without bloodshed. I felt sorry for the 93 soldiers who were killed. They chose such a bad day to catch Bhindranwale. And they didn't even catch him.'

He was killed on 6 June; and General Shabeg was killed. Many other people with him managed to leave the Temple before the army action. They lived.

Kuldip was one of those who had been with Bhindranwale right up to the end, but had somehow lived. He had been in hiding for five years. 'It's a hard life, an ascetic life, moving from place to place. The police always get to find where you are, and then you have to move.' He had been active in the All-India Sikh Students Federation: a strange name, because the group was known for its violent inclinations, and the prominent people in it were not really young, and could be considered students only in the broadest way.

Kuldip was about fifty, but he looked older. His face was creased and lined, with a further network of thin worry-lines, speaking of internal stresses even below those stresses connected with his life on the run. He dressed in the palest colours – his turban was of the palest brown – as though he wished not to draw attention to himself. Those colours, the lined face, and the small, quiet eyes suggested a deeper withdrawal.

He came an hour earlier than we had arranged, and he came straight up to my hotel room. He had to wait while I finished a long telephone call. He didn't seem to mind waiting. He sat quietly in the armchair, and I found it hard to believe that the quietly dressed man sitting in the hotel room was the 'activist' I had been told he was. It even occurred to me that he might have been from the police. When we began to talk, I asked him about his life on the run.

He said, 'So many people who are with me have been tortured to death and killed. Hundreds have been killed in false encounters. They are being killed for the freedom of the human race.'

The freedom of the human race?

He meant that. The current Sikh movement was intended 'to undo the political and social injustice of the world.' The goal was 'political power guided by Sikh religious principles and Sikh religious force'. The ultimate goal was 'a universal religious system, a universal spiritual system, universal humanistic values'.

'This is just the microcosmic experiment in the Punjab. Already we had in the time of the kingdom of Ranjit Singh this experiment in Punjab. We would like to recover the Sikh system of that time, the Sikh system of the 19th century, before the annexation of the Punjab by the English. And we want to apply that system to the whole of the world.'

I wasn't prepared for the language. Perhaps, then, he was or had been a student, exposed to the language and views of someone like Kapur Singh.

How did he define the Sikh 19th-century system?

'A secular system, a socialistic system also, a Sikh socialistic system. The main point is having the Sikh religious and political system along with the socialism. Religion and spirituality are intrinsically inseparable parts of the human personality. Similarly, the urge to dominate, to have political power, is also part of the human personality. This is so in animals, in birds also. And why not in human beings? Animals have got their leaders, the birds have got their leaders. Similarly, Khalsa [the Sikh brotherhood, as established by Guru Gobind Singh in 1699] wants to be the leader of the world, as it has got the inseparable elements of that leadership in its character.'

He thought that the goal would be reached in 10 or 15 years. At the moment the struggle was going badly. 'There is no discipline. There is no central leadership. We have lost control, and this thing is now going in favour of the government. Some of these anti-social elements are semi-religious people attracted by the emotional aspect of the movement. They are not deeply read, and they don't have regard for the deeply read and educated people, because these deeply read people don't believe in killing people aimlessly. No doubt there are some government agents also involved, and the blame is being put on the Sikhs. But our group' – the Sikh Students Federation – 'has not so many bad elements, comparatively.'

He had been born in a part of the Punjab that had gone to Pakistan in 1947, at the time of the Partition. 'My great-grandparents were generals in the army of Ranjit Singh. My ancestors fought in both Anglo-Sikh wars, 1843, 1849. One was commander of 300 men, and so was the other. Around 1900 half the family got converted to Islam. They fell in love with some Muslim girl, and got converted. Our parents felt bad about it.' In 1947 the Sikh part of the family came over to India, to a part of the Indian Punjab that later became part of the state of Haryana. They had about 80 acres there. 'One-tenth of what we had in Pakistan. This was the price of our sacrifice for freedom.'

I asked whether it was irrigated land. Water was such a talking point in the Punjab: there was such resentment (in spite of the Punjab's own green, rich fields) of the water of the rivers of the Punjab going to other states.

'Irrigated land, but not so rich.' One brother farmed the family land; one had become a teacher, another wanted to be a lawyer. It was the Sikh pattern: all the middle-class people I met had their connection with the land still, and many could think themselves back easily into old peasant passions. 'Now we've got used to Haryana,' Kuldip said. 'But we are not so well-to-do. We're just hand-to-mouth.'

I asked him about his career.

'In the early days I wanted to become an engineer, just out of love of the word "engineer". But I failed in mathematics. Then I wanted to become a lecturer in chemistry or physics. The life of a lecturer seemed to me very easy, very peaceful.'

I understood him. His words took me back to my own beginnings, to my own uncertainties, when (just the second person in my family to go to a university) the life of the university did seem to me peaceful and protected, and I wanted to prolong my time there.

Kuldip said, 'But I failed there too. I got poor marks. At that time I was twenty-five. I was teaching practical science in a college. Then I wanted to be an advocate, but that line I didn't like. Then I got attracted to English literature. I was now thirty. This study of literature fascinated me. I did an M.A. in English literature at a university. It took two years. I got a job as English lecturer in a college.'

'How did you support yourself when you were doing all that studying?'

'At first my parents were giving me money.' This would have been money from the land. 'Then I supported myself, and then for some time I supported my brother who was younger to me.'

For some years, since his mid-twenties, he had been in touch with a well-known holy man, whom he thought of as his 'revered father'. 'I used to listen to him. Other people were also there around him. This was in the town of Sirsa. Then I got attracted to the study of religion. But I liked the study of literature better than the study of religion. Literature is real. Religion is obscure. The Sikh Gurus made the study of religion like the study of literature.' I thought he meant by that that the Sikh scriptures were like literature: the important Gurus were also poets.

When he was nearly forty, then, he got another job, as a research fellow in a college department. That was when he was claimed first by politics and then by Bhindranwale's movement. 'He promised to bear the whole expenses of the English daily which we were planning to start in Chandigarh.'

When I had asked Dalip what he thought attracted people to Bhindranwale, he had said, 'Frustration.' I hadn't absolutely understood what he meant. But now, from what Kuldip told me about his wandering, stop-and-start, and still unresolved career, I began to understand a little more about these men from farming communities who had been cut loose from one kind of life, and were without conviction or vocation in the new world.

I asked him, 'What attracted you to Bhindranwale?'

'His magnetic personality.'

'Did you think he had angry eyes?'

'No, spiritual eyes. Of course, he had the anger of a lion – when he got angry. The movement was very well under control until Bluestar, and this worried the government.'

'Was he a tyrant? Did he want to be a ruler?'

'He wasn't a tyrant. He followed the principles of the Guru. The Gurus gave orders in battle to kill the enemy. But I shouldn't put it like that. The Gurus had no enemy: enmity was thrust on them. Similarly, enmity was thrust on that man.'

What about storing guns in the Golden Temple? Wasn't that contrary to the religion?

'In Sikhism nothing is wrong with guns in the gurdwaras, provided they are not used unjustly. Guru Gobind Singh sometimes personifies God Almighty with the mystical names of weapons. There are so many verses where he praises the strength of arms as he praises God Almighty.'

'I've heard that Bhindranwale began to think he was Guru Gobind Singh.'

'Sometimes in congregations he used to recall the doings of the Guru. He was close in spirit to the Guru. In the Sikh religion anyone who truly follows the edicts of the Guru is said to become so close to the Guru that he becomes the Guru, and the Guru becomes he.'

He told me about Bhindranwale's last days.

'I was living with him in the Temple from the 29th of March 1984 to the sixth of June 1984. I last saw him on the fifth of June. In the evening. We talked about the situation. He was firm. He inspired me with courage. Everybody there was prepared for anything. General Shabeg was standing outside. He sent me to Santji.

'I remember the last words of Shabeg: "The best place to die is the highest place of your religion, and a place connected with your ancestors." And he further said, "The place where we are standing has got both of the highest qualities. So it is best to die here." We were in the Akal Takht.' The council building, it might be said, of the Golden Temple: the Chapter House. 'To bring food from the langar' – the communal kitchen of the Temple: the communal kitchen in the place of worship is an important Sikh idea – 'was very hard. So food was brought over the Temple wall by the people, over the roofs of the adjoining houses. This went on for only one day. We had parched channa in quantity' – chick-peas – 'and that was distributed to us. Water was stored in buckets.

'Four of us were stationed behind the two flags on the first floor. Nobody was worried. We were all happy. Kirtan was going on.' Hymn-singing, from the central gold-domed temple in the pool. 'And they were singing a couplet: "Nobody can kill one whose God is almighty." *Jisda sahib dada hué usnu marna koi*. This inspired us.'

'Did you know about the bodies stuffed into the drains?'

'I didn't know.'

'Does it upset you now?'

'No. All is fair in love and war.'

He became restless all at once, and said he had to go. He said he would telephone me in Delhi in a few days. I walked down the steps with him. He didn't walk towards the hotel desk. He turned smartly about and walked at the side of the flowerbeds on the front lawn, stepped over a low border into the drive, and walked out of the hotel gate.

A day or so later the police announced that a terrorist bombing campaign might be about to start in Delhi. This gave a new twist to what Kuldip had told me about his movements, though it remained hard for me to associate the man with the lined face and subdued eyes, who had sat so stilly in my room, with violent acts.

Gurtej had said at the beginning of my time in Chandigarh, when I had asked him about the emphasis on suffering in Sikhism: 'This world is an unhappy place for many, and it [unhappiness] has to be eliminated. There are only two ways. Either you make somebody suffer, or you suffer.'

On the day Kuldip had mentioned, the telephone operator in the Delhi hotel rang my room and said, 'There is a man on the telephone who wants to talk to you, but he will not give his name.'

Before I could decide what to do, the caller had rung off. No further call like that was made; I never heard from Kuldip again. I was relieved in a way; because the news about the bombing campaign had put me – like the people in Jaspal village, and other villages – in a quandary.

# 9
# THE HOUSE ON THE LAKE
## A Return to India

INDIA WAS FULL of visitors; the number rose year by year. In all the big towns I went to – except Amritsar and Lucknow – the hotels were packed: trade fair following trade fair, one kind of public or holiday occasion following another, foreign delegations of various sorts treading on one another's heels.

The India I had gone to in 1962 was like a different country. India was not yet a place to which many people went to do business. It was not yet a place to which tourists wanted to go. Hotels of any standard were few and far between. Away from the main centres travel was hard. In some places you spent the night in a room in the railway station; in some places, if you could get the official permission that was required, you stayed at a 'dak bungalow', a post house. It was a lovely name, suggesting old-fashioned travel, and old-fashioned attentions. But when you got to the sunstruck, mildewed, colonial bungalow, with perhaps a few zinnias or thin-stalked roses or nondescript shrubs in its sandy garden, you had to shout for the watchman; and eventually some barefoot ragged fellow appeared and offered to cook for you in the kitchen of his own quarters the kind of meal he cooked for himself, which, when it came, might smell of woodsmoke or the cowdung cakes over which it had been cooked. In the sparsely furnished bedroom the coarse-napped 'bedding' would smell of the brackish or tainted soapy water in which it had been washed; the floor would feel sandy or gritty underfoot; the mosquito net would have tears and holes; the ventilation gaps at the top of the wall would leave one feeling exposed. The night could feel long.

The India I had gone to in 1962 had been like a place far away, a place worth a long journey. And – almost like William Howard Russell a century before – I had gone by rail and ship from London: rail to Venice; ship to Athens; ship to Alexandria; ship to Karachi and Bombay. Twelve years before, I had travelled to London from the island of Trinidad. There, as the grandson and great-grandson of agricultural immigrants from India, I had grown up with my own ideas of the distance that separated me from India. I was far enough away from it to cease to be of it. I knew the rituals but couldn't participate in them; I heard the language, but followed only the simpler words. But I was near enough to understand the passions; and near enough to feel that my own fate was bound up with the fate of the people of the country. The India of my fantasy and heart was something lost and irrecoverable.

The physical country existed. I could travel to that; I had always wanted to. But on that first journey I was a fearful traveller.

I had planned to spend a year in India; and – though I had no clear idea for a book – I hoped that for part of that year I would settle down somewhere and do some writing. I arrived in Bombay some time in February. Early in April I went north to Kashmir: train to Delhi; night train to Pathankot; and then by bus for a day and a morning (with a halt for the night: moonlight on the terraced rice-fields of Banihal) up into the mountains and then down into the vale of Kashmir.

I put up in a gloomy, mildewed hotel in the town. In its rooms you had no idea of the setting, no sight of lake or mountains or fresh snow; you just had a cluttered backyard town view. I didn't see myself staying there for three or four months. There were the houseboats on the lake, relics of the Raj. But the well-equipped ones – like white barges on the water, echoing the fresh snow on the dark mountains all around – were too expensive for me. These were the ones with the good china and the hand-carved old furniture and the old-fashioned English menus (and still, here and there, the photographs and sometimes the recommendations of English guests of 30 years before – before Independence, before the war). The smaller houseboats were shabby. But even if I could have afforded the better ones, I didn't think I would have been able to write and live in one room on a houseboat. It would have been constricting not to be able to walk out when one wanted; I would have felt it as a kind of imprisonment.

It began to look as though, after the long trip north, Kashmir wasn't going to work out. But then, on the second or third day, looking all the time for a good place to stay, I allowed myself to be led by a small man with a big blue jacket and a black fur cap to what he had said was a hotel on the lake itself, with its own garden.

It was hard to credit, but it was as Ali Mohammed, the man with the black cap, had said. I was to get to know him very well. For many weeks I was to see him leaving his hotel base, morning and afternoon, getting into a lake boat with his big bicycle, being paddled to the lake boulevard, and then cycling to the bus station or the tourist department or any other place where he might win a visitor, as he had won me. Though he wasn't pushy or talkative, was really a shy, subdued fellow, liking nothing better than a little smoke on the hookah with his friends in the hotel kitchen at the end of the garden.

The hotel was like a little house. It was called the Hotel Liward – that was the way the word was spelt, and that was how I thought of it. It had two storeys and a pitched corrugated-iron roof. It stood in its own garden in the lake, not one of the floating gardens, thick mats of lake weeds and earth, which could be towed about, but a fixed plot of earth. I rented an upper-floor bedroom at one end of the house. This section of the house had just been built for the new season – the Liward expanded every few years – and the way the building was designed, this bedroom had no immediate neighbour. It had windows on two sides, with views of the lake and the mountains and the snow. It had its own brand-new bathroom. Bathroom and bedroom smelled agreeably of new wood and new concrete. The small sitting room of the hotel was adjacent to the bedroom; I rented that as well, so that I could almost say that I had my own little wing of the Liward.

It was an extraordinary piece of luck for me. The Liward, my time in Kashmir, became a point of rest in my Indian year, a point of rest in my fearful travelling; and perhaps it enabled me to go through with my Indian venture. I had uprooted myself from London, and invested all the money I had in this Indian journey; it would have been hard if it hadn't worked, and I hadn't been able to last.

I stayed at the Liward for more than four months. I got to know all of them who worked and smoked in the kitchen shack at the end of the garden. Ali Mohammed – so important at the very beginning – soon became a figure in the background. Mr Butt owned the hotel, but English was beyond him; we communicated only by smiles and gestures. Mr Butt's right-hand man was Abdul Aziz. He couldn't read or write. But he had an acute social sense and could read faces and situations; he had a prodigious memory; and he spoke an idiomatic English, picked up purely by ear. It was with Aziz that I dealt during those four months at the Liward. It was with Aziz that I made my excursions to the higher valleys. Aziz and Mr Butt planned my expedition to the cave of Amarnath, at the time of the great pilgrimage there in the month of August; and Aziz came with me on that as well, to exercise some control over the retinue they had hired for me.

And I wrote my book. What had been a mere idea, an impulse, a series of suggestions, what at the start of the writing had felt unreal, began to have its own life and to exercise its own power in that room with the two views. That had also been part of the comfort and reassurance of that season, that feeling of a book growing day by day. Aziz and Mr Butt had knocked up a table for me to write at. They had also given me a table lamp.

The next year, in an oppressive furnished flat in south London, I began to write my book about India. I had intended to write one, but after my early weeks I had begun to give up the idea. Travel writing was new to me, and I didn't see how I could find a narrative for a book about India: I was too overwhelmed by the distress I saw. I had kept no journal, made few connected notes. But money had been spent, and a book had to be written. A full two to three months after my return, I began to write. In the writing, the Kashmir interlude became what it had been the year before in India: a point of rest. Calling up events day after day, I found a narrative where at the time there had appeared to be none.

After the book was written – order given to memories, a narrative found, Indian emotions faced and written out – the details began to fade. The time came when I no longer read the book. Kashmir and the Hotel Liward – and Mr Butt and Aziz – remained a glow, a memory of a season when everything had gone well. It was open to me after that to go back to Kashmir at any time. Air travel had simplified the world, had simplified our ways of dealing with sections of our past. Sometimes people wrote me about the hotel; someone sent me a photograph to show the changes that had come to the building. But I never felt the need to go back.

This time I went back. I went by air. So I saw the airport which, 27 years before, I had never seen or been near. There had been stringent security checks at Delhi airport, because of the situation in the Punjab. There was security at Srinagar: the Kashmir valley was restless. It had been restless in 1962 as well. But all over India people lived more on their nerves now, and had a different attitude to authority.

The road to the town was being improved. It led past many big new houses; I hadn't seen that kind of private wealth in 1962. The city centre was as mud-coloured and medieval-looking as I had remembered: as though all the colours of Kashmir, by themselves as vivid as the colours in a paint-box, had run together and created the effect of mess and mud. The brick and timber of old buildings – or buildings that looked old – were both the colour of mud. Mud was also the colour of the streets, the colour-effect of the variegated clothes of the people; and mud – with here and there a green algae patch or crust – was the colour of the turgid, steep-banked river that ran through the town. An arm or canal of this river was choked with small unpainted houseboats side by side: and there the houseboats showed very clearly as a slum row, little floating houses permanently moored to the bank, each with its outhouse on the bank.

Some memory stirred, at the grey-brown colour of the houseboats; but the feeling of crowd and constriction was new. Some memory also came to me of someone telling me in 1962 that in the days of the British (though Kashmir was a princely state, with its own ruler) Indians were not allowed to walk on the Bund, the main avenue in the town. That was now far in the past. The Kashmiri-Indian town had burst its bonds and had spread a long way down the lake boulevard. This new development was not the colour of mud. It was a roaring Indian bazaar of concrete and glass and new paint, hotels and shops and signboards. And facing it, on a section of the lake where in 1962 there had been only water, was a long row of tourist houseboats, each houseboat with its signboard: the Kashmiris and the visitors semingly lined up and facing one another like two sports teams, the visitors handicapped in their houseboats, denied movement and manoeuvre, the Kashmiris nimble on the shore, ready to deal with any landing party, with their irregulars paddling about on the lake, appearing from nowhere, their shallow low boats capable of nosing into the smallest opening. All down this stretch of the lake boulevard was a roar of human voices, as in a market or bazaar.

At the far end of the lake boulevard, and some way beyond this new development, was the Palace Hotel, in its own spacious grounds. I was staying there this time. The hotel had been the summer palace of the Maharaja of Kashmir. It was a big but plain building of the 1930s, low and wide, set well back from the lake and boulevard. The apple orchards planted by the last maharaja but one were in blossom; so were the almond trees. After the mud colours of the town, the colours here were of the freshest spring-green.

I knew the palace as a palace. In 1962 Karan Singh, the maharaja, had been in residence; his official position in the state had been that of governor, *sadr-i-riyasat;* and I had been invited to the palace more than once for dinner. On one occasion I had gone in a tonga, a horse-drawn cart. The horse had laboured and slipped up the long, hard incline of the drive. I could have walked faster. It felt absurd to be sitting in the tonga, but I didn't know what to do. The whole procedure had seemed undignified to the officials watching: they had finally come up in a jeep to rescue me.

No memory remained to me of palace entrance or rooms. The carpet was worn in the corridor downstairs. Upstairs, outside my room, there were warm kitchen smells; and there was a glimpse, through a concrete screen, of the staff quarters. My room was big; the furniture felt inadequate; the coarse-tufted carpet was bright green. No sense of glory or comfort or holiday: just a feeling, in the spring-damp air, of a big building running down, with too many things to put right now, a building too big for those of us who were in it, a building just opened up for the season, needing summer and a holiday life, which, with the religious and political restlessness in the valley, it perhaps wasn't going to get.

The gardens the windows looked out on were in good order, though. The grass had been cut low, the two big trees freshly pollarded, the flower-beds bright with bulbs and seed-packet colours. Two Japanese girls in jeans, having their photographs taken, posed one for the other, squatting in front of the red tulips and giving tinkling little squeals. Beyond and below, seen through spring growth, the new sprays of poplars and the soft lime-green fronds of willows, was the lake. The far-off mountains had fresh snow at the top. It was a privileged, palace view: no sight, from the window, of the new building on the lake shore to the right, the terracing of the lower mountainside; no sight of the houseboat rows to the left.

Somewhere there, to the left, was the Liward Hotel. And it was towards that that very soon, not wanting to delay the moment, I went. I took a hotel taxi. There was a minimum charge. For that charge I could have gone two or three times the distance I did go; I could even have walked. Old Kashmiri irritations began to revive, telescoping the years.

Misled by the crowd I saw ahead on the boulevard, not able with the new clutter on the lake to gauge where the Liward might be, I got off too soon, at the wrong boating steps, and became involved in a haggle with the boatman in charge about the fare to the Liward. The boatman had the height of a child; and, below his brown gown, he had the physique of a child. Pale, marked skin, discoloured in patches; a cadaverous small face on a thin neck; light-coloured hair, bright eyes. His appearance spoke of winter starvation; but his eyes, like his haggling voice, were full of rage. I hadn't seen anyone like that on the boating steps in 1962; but neither had there been the crowd, and the human roar.

We settled for 25 rupees for the crossing to the Liward, a pound: far too much, five times too much.

The water of the lake, streaming through my fingers, was cool. And even with all the traffic, the lake still had its spring-time clarity. It was full of little fish, a delight to see, and the ferns at the lake bottom tossed slowly in the current. (Later, in high summer, the water would cloud.) Where there had been openness in 1962 there was now a long row of houseboats, each with its signboard and steps; and some of the boats seemed to be linked by a railed timber walk, supported on stilts.

We paddled past that; made for a water lane with shop-boats and service boats. And soon – the crossing certainly not worth 25 rupees – there was the Leeward, in that corrected spelling, according to its big signboard. Not the modest cottage and lake garden I had lived in, but an establishment dominant even in the new commercial clutter: solid, concrete-walled, many-winged, many-gabled.

The photograph of the Leeward I had been sent some years before had shown a building two storeys high. I felt that the roof had been raised since then, and a third storey added. The gables were oddly splayed at the bottom ends, thicker, and almost with the curve of hockey sticks. With the steep pitched roof, the effect was Tibetan or Japanese.

I had remembered flat lotus leaves on the lake beside the Leeward garden. A few were still there, bui they were not as noticeable as the tall, litter-trapping grass that grew about the landing stage. The hotel had always been at an intersection of water lanes; but now it was as though a residential area had become a business area. Houseboat shops moored to ragged remnants of black islets, rough timber and corrugated-iron shops on stilts, and handcrafts emporia faced the Leeward across all the lanes. The Leeward had its own grocery shop in one corner, with a large wall advertisement; and next to that was an emporium of Kashmir leather and wool goods.

From the landing stage a railed path led between two rectangles of garden. It was (apart from the bath-tub jardinière in one corner) a little like the garden I knew. But it was impossible to reconstruct the site, to work out where my sitting room had been, and where the bedroom with the two views. The hotel island, the plot of earth, must itself have been added to.

At one end of the building, opposite the hotel shops, was the office, a small white-walled room with glass windows. A high counter; a brown keyboard; a calendar on the wall; Kashmir tourist folders opened out. There were also posters of Mecca: the kaaba stone, and a dome. There had been no decorations with that religious twist in the old Leeward. Clearly someone had made the pilgrimage to Mecca, or wished to show his allegiance.

There was no one in the office. A little boy hanging around outside seemed to be connected with the hotel. I sent him to look for Aziz or Mr Butt. It was Mr Butt who came. I hardly had to wait. After 27 years, it was as simple as that. He had a white fringe of beard, the beard of a man who had made the pilgrimage. Perhaps in a crowd I might not have spotted him. But here, in his own setting, he was immediately recognizable: the fur cap, the dark colours he liked to wear, the thick-lensed glasses, the slenderness.

He behaved like a man who was unsurprised. We were indeed both like actors in a play, who had rehearsed this moment. In 1962 there had been nine rooms in the hotel, he said; now there were 45. The charge now was 125 rupees per night, five pounds, eight dollars, to include bedding and hot water. He knew precisely how long I had stayed in the hotel in 1962. I didn't have to ask him; he reminded me. I had stayed four months and 15 days. Just as writing, the ordering of events and emotion, made things manageable for me, helped me as it were to clear the decks, so it seemed that putting numbers to things, finding the right numbers, helped Mr Butt to file things away and put a pattern on events.

After the hotel news, which he had given very quickly, the most important thing he had to tell me was that he had made the pilgrimage to Mecca. There was his health. 'But I am good, sir.' And, to prove it, he held my hand and gripped it hard.

I asked how old he was. He had trouble translating the numerals. He said eighty-six first of all, then seventy-six, then sixty-six. Perhaps he was sixty-six; that would have made him thirty-nine in 1962, one year short of forty – that would have seemed to me old then.

He told me about the others. Ali Mohammed, who had brought me that lucky day to him, had gone away. The *khansamah,* the cook, tormented and temperamental, creating all kinds of crises in the cook house and quarters at the end of the garden, had died. But Aziz was still there, very much so. At the moment he was in his own house; he would be back at the hotel in the afternoon.

I said I would come back at about four to see Aziz. Language – or the absence of a common language – lay between Mr Butt and me, as it had always done. Having come to the end of such language as we had in common, we had come to the end of things to say just then. And I took the lake boat back to the boat steps and the small, angry-eyed man.

On the shore there was a hill known as Shankaracharya Hill. There was a Hindu temple at the top; in 1962 Karan Singh used to maintain the brahmin there. Many afternoons I walked up the hill. I got to know the brahmin. He was a jovial hermit, with a woollen cap. When it rained, or was misty or cold, he kept himself warm in the Kashmiri way, hugging a small clay brazier of burning charcoal below a blanket. There had been so many new things to take in: it was only now – going back to the boating steps through this echoing bazaar roar from lake and boulevard – that I saw that on the small hill next to Shankaracharya there was a big television transmission mast; and I wondered about the temple and the brahmin.

I went back to the Leeward at about four. Taxi again from the Palace Hotel; lake boat again from the 25-rupee steps. A small handsome young man was waiting for me in the office. He had a sleeveless blue padded jacket in some synthetic material, as stylish as his haircut. He said he was 'Aziza's' son – 'Aziza' was what he said: it was, as I remembered, the affectionate form of Aziz.

Aziz's son! He was eighteen. He was a student at a college in Srinagar. He was studying accountancy. Accountancy! But, of course, with all the activity in the lake and the town, there was a need.

And Aziz appeared, coming out of that corridor from which, in the morning, Mr Butt had appeared. Mr Butt had remained slender; Aziz had become broad and paunchy and round-faced. He was wearing many garments: loose trousers, long-tailed shirt, a pullover stretched tight over his paunch, a kind of unbuttonable waistcoat (more back than front), and a lightweight, full-skirted jacket. Strangely, his size made little difference: he remained the man I had known. There was still the energy, the lightness of step, the neutrality of expression, the assessing intelligence, the slight blink, as though he was shortsighted.

What news? Well, he said, the boy – he meant his handsome son – had wanted to become a doctor. But they had talked him out of that. There was no business like the hotel business. And Mr Butt, joining us, chuckled and said, after Aziz, that there was no business like it.

I asked Aziz about Mr Butt's fur cap. I had, in my earlier book, described the effect one day of heavy rain on the fur: having found those words, and having never forgotten them, I had remembered the cap. I wondered now whether the cap, like the white beard Mr Butt wore, had a religious significance; or whether it meant that Mr Butt belonged to a particular clan.

Aziz said, 'You can pay 1000 rupees for that cap.'

That seemed to be all. It was only then I noticed that Aziz was himself wearing a fur cap; and then memory – in a dozen vivid pictures – told me that Aziz had always worn a fur cap, that the cap had been part of his appearance, and that I had seen him bareheaded only once – after some horseplay in the kitchen, which had sent him out laughing and dishevelled into the garden. But I hadn't had to find words for his cap; it hadn't acquired importance for me.

I told Aziz about my trouble at the boating steps, and the charge of 25 rupees. The boatman was waiting with his boat to take me back. Aziz made a gesture and called the boatman over. I felt the boatman didn't like being called: he appeared not to notice.

Aziz himself appeared to forget the boatman. He brought out a box of photographs and he and Mr Butt began to look for old ones. They found one of the hotel in 1962, showing the garden and my sitting room. And they found another, an over-exposed one, of the staff of that time. Mr Butt was there, and Aziz; and Ali Mohammed, blunt-featured and earnest, who had now gone away; and the dead khansamah. The khansamah was tall and really rather fine, with a face more tormented than I remembered. Perhaps his rages hadn't been due just to temperament; perhaps he had been ill sometimes, and in pain.

There had been no more than five or six people in that old group. Now the hotel employed 20 people, and there was even a manager.

What did Aziz do, then?

Aziz's son said: 'He is the commander-in-chief.' And Mr Butt, understanding, smiled.

I asked Aziz about Mr Butt's health. Mr Butt had hinted in the morning that he wasn't absolutely well. Aziz said that Mr Butt shouldn't be smoking, but he smoked his hookah in secret; he couldn't give it up. And Mr Butt, not smiling, made a grave gesture of helplessness.

I reminded Aziz about the boatman, and the 25-rupee crossing charge.

Aziz said, 'You pay *twenty-five* rupees this morning?'

And when I said yes, he looked grave, like a doctor coming upon a bad and unexpected symptom. But then, like a doctor, he was willing to do what he could. He called the boatman over again, and this time the boatman came. Aziz and Mr Butt talked to him. Aziz said later that he had told the boatman that I was an old friend of the hotel's, not 'a three-day tourist'. And more than once during this talk with the boatman Mr Butt said, 'Four months and 15 days.' At the end the boatman smiled and Aziz said that I was to pay the boatman what I wanted. I didn't think this was good enough. Aziz knew that; he suggested that I pay 15 rupees.

Memory had brought back that picture of a skittish, bareheaded Aziz in the garden of the old Leeward – a rare skittishness then, and hard to imagine now in the dignified, successful man in front of me. How old had he been then? To me at the time he had been a mature, ageless kind of man.

'How old are you, Aziz?'

'Forty-eight, fifty.'

That was far too young. But he didn't seem to know; and perhaps, not being able to read and write, having to depend only on his own memory, his ability to relate events in his own life to events outside, he had no means of knowing.

We talked about the Himalayan pilgrimage to the cave of Amarnath that they had arranged for me, with muleteers, tent-pitcher, a cook, and Aziz in general command. Helicopters went to Amarnath now, Aziz said; and there were immense numbers of pilgrims, four lakhs, five lakhs, 400 thousand, 500 thousand.

Aziz said, 'You remember *ghora-wallah?*'

He was talking about one of the muleteers in our party. I would have written about him; the details would have been there in my book; but the man himself, and events connected with him, had slipped my memory. But Aziz remembered, and a memory came back to me of a muleteer who had abandoned us high up in some pass and who, before that, had caused some of our baggage to roll down a hillside – and Aziz had had to do the retrieving.

I would have liked in 1962, after the Amarnath journey, to dawdle for a few more days in the high Himalayas, with the Leeward team and their equipment. But Aziz hadn't wanted that. He had hurried me back to Srinagar, for another – Muslim – religious occasion. In the Hazratbal mosque at the far end of the lake there was a famous relic, a hair of the beard of the Prophet. It was displayed once a year, and Aziz was passionate to get back for that.

He liked big religious occasions, a mingling of faith and fair and holiday; and his news now was that, like Mr Butt, he had gone on the pilgrimage to Mecca. He had gone twice. The pilgrimage took three months. The Indian government made the travel arrangements. You went first to Jeddah; and then you took taxis and buses to Mecca. There were toilets everywhere between Jeddah and Mecca. It wasn't like Amarnath. Everything was clean in Mecca. He spoke like a man of the faith; he also spoke like a man who knew a thing or two about hotels and accommodation.

Two pilgrimages to Mecca: that meant money, leisure, success of a substantial kind. It wasn't what I would have prophesied for Aziz in 1962. And, really, it was extraordinary that Aziz and Mr

Butt, with their different talents and natures, should have worked together in the same way for all these years. They had supported one another; Mr Butt had allowed Aziz to grow; and the business had grown beyond their imagining.

I asked Aziz about the fancy gables on the hotel.

He said, 'A style, a style. You should see the new buildings here.'

He had a story to tell about my book. After the book came out the hotel had been called up by the Tourism Department. They said they hadn't liked what they had read about the Leeward. They had read that hotel guests spread their clothes to dry on the Leeward's lawn and hung clothes out of the windows. The Tourism Department didn't like that. Aziz said he had had to tell the government man very firmly: 'You don't *understand* the book.' An old fight, but clearly a fight: Aziz told the story twice.

Success; but the lake was crowded. All India was crowded, Aziz said, as though this was something people now had to live with. Forty years before, you could drink water from the lake (and I remembered people in excursion boats even in 1962 using lake water to make the special Kashmiri tea). Now, Aziz said, and Mr Butt shook his head in agreement, the flush systems of some houseboats emptied directly into the lake.

Then, abruptly – as though explaining the stillness or the flatness of the occasion, and the absence of hospitality – Aziz told me it was Ramadan. They were not supposed to talk much. They were going to break their fast at 7.10 that evening.

Aziz's son, Nazir, went with me in the boat back to the boulevard. He said that Mr Butt had told him and other people about the time I had sat out with them in the garden and smoked the hookah. I remembered the occasion. The smoke of the coarse-chopped Kashmiri tobacco, pleasant to smell, enticing, had turned out to be fierce and gripping in the throat and the lungs, stronger than any tobacco I had tasted, the hot charcoal-and-tobacco smoke barely cooled by the water in the bowl of the hookah.

I didn't think that anyone at the Leeward would have time for that kind of playfulness now. The mood felt different. The lake here was too built up, too busy.

From the lake and the boulevard and the boating steps there was now a late-afternoon roar. An amplified, quavering, nerve-stretching voice was part of the roar. It was the amplified voice of a mullah in the mosque on the boulevard – new to me, that mosque, a plain small building, part of the new development, many houses deep, on the boulevard, below Shankaracharya Hill. The very plainness of the mosque seemed to speak of the urgent need of the new lake crowd.

Aziz had said, after his talk with the boatman, that I was to pay 15 rupees for the crossing. The boatman himself had smiled and had appeared amenable to whatever was decided. But it wasn't the boatman I had to pay. It was the small, angry-eyed, angry-voiced man at the boating steps; and he absolutely insisted on 25 rupees. Nazir, who had come with me partly to protect me against this demand, was abashed. I noticed, though, that he didn't argue with the boating-steps man; he simply offered to pay the extra rupees himself. The lake clearly had its own rules, its various territories and spheres of influence. The Leeward's writ, and Aziz's, didn't run here. I paid what was asked. And then, solicitously, Nazir put me in a taxi and sent me back to the Palace Hotel.

There was more than an hour of daylight left. The view of the lake from the hotel garden beckoned me out again. I walked down to the Palace Hotel steps and took a boat for half an hour. Almost as soon as we had put out, two very small children, in a boat of their own, came alongside and threw mustard flowers into my boat. The gesture took me by surprise. I smiled, the children smiled back and asked for *baksheesh*. They were perfect little beggars: the smile, the whine, the aggression.

And then it was the turn of the salesmen. One by one they came, and besieged my boat. One man said, 'We will do it one after the other.' I thought he was making a joke, commenting on my situation; but he was speaking quite seriously. And they stayed with me, two on one side, three on the other, so that I was at the centre of a little flower-pattern, a daisy-pattern, of lake boats. They showed their goods in detail: saffron, stones, cheap jewelry, and all kinds of pointless things in papier mâché. The salesmen's boats were paddled by little children. The salesmen themselves reclined on pillows and cushions, and gave an impression of following one of the lake's more luxurious occupations. One or two were covered in blankets from the neck down; below those blankets they would have had little charcoal braziers.

Nazir and I went on a tour of the lake. We had hardly pushed off from the Leeward landing stage – we were still in front of the hotel – when the little begging children appeared, paddling fast, throwing sprigs of mustard flowers into our boat, and saying, in a sibilant whisper at once demure and penetrating, 'Baksheesh, baksheesh.' Nazir gave them one or two rupees each. He said, 'If you don't give them money, they won't go away.' He was as tender with the salesmen, allowing our boat to be delayed just long enough to give offence neither to the salesmen nor to me.

After we had passed the long row of houseboats we were in open water, and no one came near. We passed what I had remembered as the maharaja's lake pavilion. A memory came to me of a poplar-lined causeway between the lake boulevard and the lake pavilion: there was no causeway now.

In 1962 I had had tea in the lake pavilion one day with Karan Singh and his wife. Karan Singh had a great appetite for Hindu thought, and at that tea he had talked of the ninth-century Hindu philosopher Shankaracharya, who, born in the South, had, in a short life of 32 years, walked to the four corners of India (while India was still itself, before the Mohammedan irruptions), preaching and setting up the religious foundations that still existed. The hill beside the lake where we were was named after the philosopher; Karan Singh took a personal interest in the temple at the top.

The setting for our tea was spectacular: the pavilion, the lake all around, the mountains, the poplar-lined causeway, the long drive rising between orchards and gardens to the palace. I asked who had designed it all. I was expecting to hear the name of an architect. Karan Singh, looking around, simply said, 'Daddy.'

That had fixed the moment for me. But now there was no royal causeway, no tall poplars, only openness, a breeze picking up strength across the water, and blowing our boat against the rough poles and the slack, rusting strands of barbed wire around the pavilion island, where the buildings looked damp and closed, awaiting summer and people.

Nazir and the boat-boy between them poled and pulled the boat around the pavilion island. The lake was still choppy; but it became calm beyond a causeway laid with a big black pipe that took drinking water to the city. In the distance was the Hazratbal mosque. It had a white dome and minaret, and that whiteness stood out against the brown-black cluster of two-storey and three-storey houses.

The dome and minaret were new. Hazratbal had been a plain mosque. There had been riots one year in Srinagar when the famous Hazratbal relic, the hair of the beard of the Prophet, disappeared. I asked Nazir about it.

He said, 'It was found in Srinagar, in a private house.' (I was told later by someone else that a well-connected woman, who had fallen ill, had expressed a wish to see the relic, and it had been brought to her.)

Nazir, talking of this and that, said that he was corresponding with an English girl who had stayed at the Leeward. They wrote once a month.

He said, with unexpected seriousness, and without prompting from me, 'It's in God's hand whether I marry a Kashmiri or a foreign girl. Only God knows the future.' And that mention of

God was serious, not idiomatic. Kashmiri girls, Nazir said, were nice, but foreign girls were more 'experienced' – and I didn't ask what he meant by that.

I asked him about religion. He said he went to the mosque every day. He went alone for half an hour or so, to pray for 'everybody'. On Fridays he went for two and a half hours, to pray with everybody else. He had been religious ever since he was ten.

We saw fishermen, scattered, still, almost emblematic against the open bright water, standing or lying on their low boats. We moved slowly towards them, coasting in the calm water after each paddle stroke: it was a wonderful moment of quiet just minutes away from the hubbub around the houseboats and boating steps of the boulevard.

One fisherman cast a small net where he had previously laid bait – a tin can marked the spot. The fisherman, having cast his net, used a long pronged stick, held within the net, to stir up the fish hiding in the reeds and ferns. As the fish rose they were caught within the weighted net; the net was hauled aboard, and the fish caught were kept in a covered, water-filled section of the boat's hull. Two other men were spearing fish: holding a spear, each man crouching a little way beyond the edge of his flat boat, with a dark cloth thrown over his head, the better to see through the water to the fish below. So for minutes they crouched, looking like small unmoving bundles at the edge of a boat, until they attempted to spear a fish, the spear held still until that moment of thrust.

From the openness we moved to the gardens, fixed or floating. The fixed gardens were planted at their edges with willows, whose roots made a cage that kept the soil from being washed away. Just a few hundred yards away from the tourist lake, and as though no middle way was possible, was this old agricultural life of the lake people: weeds and ferns being twirled loose from their lake-bed roots by means of a curved stick, and lifted dripping, mixed with black lake mud, into the flat-bottomed boats, and then taken to fertilize the gardens, where weeds and mud and water were shovelled off all in one with broad wooden shovels.

Women squatted and worked in spinach beds, and children worked with them, as children worked with adults everywhere in the lake, in gardens and on boats. Between the strips of gardens the algae-covered water lanes were lined with low-hanging willows. The houses were of timber and pale-red brick. People washed themselves on one side of a narrow plot; and on the other side young girls used the water to wash pots and pans. Some men, meeting among reeds, stayed in their boats and talked, as they might have done on a street. Some men and boys fished with rod and line. A boat passed with a cottage-cheese seller. Slowly – women and girls paddling their own boats, women and girls more visible here, among the gardens – we came back to the busy highways of the lake, behind the houseboats.

We passed a settlement among willows, rough houses of dusty red brick set in timber frames. A one-roomed shop-stall, with a platform a few feet above the water, had a large picture of the Ayatollah Khomeini of Iran (of whom it was said in Iran, by his enemies, that he was really Indian and Kashmiri).

Nazir said in a whisper, speaking with something like awe and nervousness and distance, as though he was speaking of people who were very strange, 'All this is Shia.'

Aziz had spoken in that way of Shias in 1962. He had spoken of them as people different from himself; once he had even said that Shias were not Muslims. I had barely understood then what he had meant. One afternoon, not really knowing what I was being taken to see, knowing only that it was a Shia occasion, I had gone by boat with some hotel people to see the Mohurram procession in the old town. I had remembered the occasion as a series of medieval pictures: remembering especially the pale, half-covered faces of secluded women, framed in small timber-framed upper windows, looking down at the bloody scene of self-flagellation below.

It had been hard for me, emerging from the soft lake world of willow-hung waterways and lotus and vegetable gardens, to believe what I had so suddenly come upon: bloodied bodies, blood-soaked clothes, chains, whips tipped with knives and razor blades, the exalted, deficient faces of the celebrants, and their almost arrogant demeanour. They pushed people out of their way. I was ready to believe, what I was told then, that much of the blood on display was really animal blood. I hadn't understood the religious-historical charge of the occasion, the undying grief it sought to express. I had only been alarmed by it, and glad to get away from it, glad to return to myself and what I knew.

Nazir said he had been told by his father that I had complained about the Shia drumming during Mohurram. And I felt now that the distance with which Nazir (and his father before him) had spoken of the Shias had contained some wonder that the apparently peaceable lake people we were paddling by had this other, ecstatic side.

It had become cloudy. Clouds came down over the mountains to one side of the lake. A strong breeze began to blow just as we were coming out of a water lane to the open water at the back of the houseboats and the Leeward Hotel. It began to blow us back, and dislodged the awning of our boat. This wind also kicked up the dark-red or russet underside of the flat round lotus leaves, revealing where – among the reeds and the tall grass and the litter around houseboats and service boats – the lotus were. I had been looking for the lotus. The pink flowers came out in June and July; I remembered them as one of the glories of the lake. But the lotus was also a crop here: even in the wind a man in a boat could be seen collecting lotus roots, using a special rod or tool for breaking them off under water and pulling them into his boat – endless, this loading and unloading of boats.

Becalmed, having trouble with our awning, we were 'boarded' by two begging children, throwing mustard flowers, keeping their boat glued to ours, and asking for baksheesh.

Nazir drove them away. It was the first time I had heard him raise his voice; and they respected his voice. He explained, 'They're a bad family.'

Perhaps in some way they had broken the code of the lake. They were thin-faced and very small, starvelings of the lake (like so many others), yet with something predatory and disturbing in the thin-armed frenzy with which, indifferent to wind and rain, having spotted us, they had paddled towards us.

The long row of big tourist houseboats gave us shelter. We moved in their lee, beside the railed timber walk that appeared to link them all. And then, the wind having dropped, we turned into the main river lane, back into the clutter of shops and sheds on stilts or stone walls, service boats with walls of old corrugated iron, timber and corrugated-iron structures on sodden bits of black, nearly bare earth: J&K Unique Stores, Manufacturers of Kashmir Arts and Crafts; a grocery shop; a butcher's stall with cases of bottled soft drinks on the wooden platform in front; the New Pandit Shawl House and the Mir Arts Emporium facing the Leeward's own handicrafts emporium and corner grocery shop; and, side by side on one narrow service boat moored to its own little island, a fur and leather-goods shop, a grocery, and the Sunshine Haircutting Saloon.

And, in this area, what could be heard when the rain stopped, what became noticeable, was the roar of human talk from many directions, as in a covered market, regularly pierced by the cries of children.

It was said that there were now 2000 houseboats in the lake. Every houseboat needed a service boat, or an attached garden. And what people said was that the lake, by which everyone in lake and city lived, the lake which drew the tourists, and was not very large, was shrinking.

*

The rain returned in the afternoon. Clouds hid the mountains and the lake misted over. The Palace Hotel felt unaired and desolate.

There were few visitors; the tourist season was not starting well. The hotel staff, formally dressed, outnumbering the visitors, were subdued; the formality of their dress added to the gloom. The Harlequin Bar was empty; it was serving no liquor. It was a big bar, and there was no crowd now to hide its shabbiness: the carpet, or carpet-like material, that was tacked to the front of the counter was ragged in places. A secessionist Muslim group had been setting off bombs in public places in the city. The group had also made a number of demands. It wanted no alcohol in the state; it wanted Friday and not Sunday to be the day of rest; and it wanted non-Kashmiri residents expelled. The hotel people, while they waited for the authorities to take action, had met among themselves and decided to avoid trouble. That was why the Harlequin Bar of the Palace served no alcohol, and why – until some Japanese visitors insisted – not even beer was served at dinner in the dining-room.

In the afternoon, in all the rain, a Muslim holy man, a *pir,* turned up at the hotel, and it woke the place up. The pir was a very small, very thin, dark man, with something like a crew cut. He was in his sixties. He wore a dark-grey gown which came down to a few inches above his frail-looking ankles, and he was barefooted. He came to the hotel in a three-wheel motor-scooter, and when he got out he was carrying a telescopic umbrella. Six cars, full of people, were following his scooter. The pir appeared to be in a rage. He began to shout as he got to the desk. Shouting, waving his umbrella, seizing the arm of a foreign woman tourist, letting her go, he raged down the corridor, knocking down or hitting things in his way.

The staff didn't object. The holy man's curse was to be feared. Equally, his blessing was to be sought. He behaved as he did because he was holy, and because, as someone told me, he was 'in direct line' with God. His movements and his moods couldn't be predicted; but clearly, at this moment, during this extraordinary visit to the Palace Hotel, he was in a state of high inspiration. That was why the six cars were following him. With all the risks, people were anxious to get in his way. A waiter told me that if you had the chance, if you were lucky enough, to sit in front of the pir, you didn't have to tell him of your problems. He knew about your problems right away; and – always if you were lucky – he began to talk about them.

And then he was gone, with his gown and umbrella, and in his scooter, and the cars chased after him, leaving the hotel staff to return to themselves.

At 7.11 – one minute later than the day before – the mullahs' calls from the mosques around the lake announced that the sun had set, and believers could break their day-long Ramadan fast.

Religion, faith: there seemed to be no end to it, no end to its demands. It was like part of the nerves of the over-populated, over-protected valley.

While the maharajas ruled, Hindu sentiment had been protected in the valley. The killing of a cow, for instance, was a criminal offence, punishable by 'rigorous imprisonment'. The portraits of the maharajas, Karan Singh's ancestors, were still there on the main staircase of the building, beyond the main dining-room.

Some of the worn carpets in the hotel now had been in the palace in 1962. They had been specially woven; there had been some talk about them one evening. On a subsequent evening the burning head of a guest's cigarette had fallen on a carpet we had talked about and created a scorch spot. Karan Singh had not flinched, had not expressed, by a hesitation in speech, or a glance, that he was concerned or had even noticed.

His family had ruled for more than a century here; his princely ways were instinctive. It was also interesting for me to see how rulers managed more everyday things. We went to the cinema in Srinagar one evening. We went late and left early, before the lights came up; and then we raced back to the palace. I asked Karan Singh's wife one day whether they stopped at foodstalls, roast sweet-corn stalls, for instance, at sweet-corn time. She said they did; and their practice was to pay more than was asked – leaving me wondering even now whether, with that tradition, the ruler was asked less than his subject, or more.

I wanted to get a shawl, and I asked Aziz and Mr Butt to help me. I went to the Leeward one morning, and for form's sake – with Nazir standing with me – I looked through the stock of the hotel shop. There was nothing there that I wanted, and then – to wait for Mr Butt's real shawl-man – Nazir took me to the Leeward's sitting room. They had all wanted me to see this sitting room; they were proud of it. It was a big room in bright colours on the upper floor; it had tall sliding glass windows; and it overlooked the busy water-lanes in front of the hotel. There was a photograph of the Golden Temple – perhaps this was a political gesture of some sort on somebody's part. There was also a bleached picture of a Kashmiri girl. The girl was famous in legend, Nazir said; she was poor, a peasant girl, but by her singing she had won a king's heart.

Aziz came up to the sitting room. He ordered tea, and had a cup with me when it came. Tea was permissible in Ramadan in certain conditions: Mr Butt, for instance, who was not well, could have tea. Aziz had brought some photographs of himself in Mecca: cheerful, relishing the pious adventure. What a taste he had for life!

I asked him, 'Aziz, do you remember how often I went to the maharaja's in 1962?'

After 27 years, he knew precisely. He said, 'You went to have dinner three times. One time you went for tea.'

Then I thought to ask him what I had never asked in all the months we had been together. Where had he been born? He said here, on the lake. His father had been a Kashmiri, and his grandfather too; he was a pure Kashmiri. His father had been in business. A little shop. Up to 15 years ago, he said, people in Kashmir were poor. Now people were better off; now people were 'good', though – as both he and Nazir agreed – there were so many more of them. But that, Aziz said, speaking now as a man who had travelled, was also the problem of Bombay, Calcutta, Delhi.

I wondered why in 1962 I had asked Aziz so little about himself. Shyness, perhaps; a wish not to intrude; but also perhaps derived from the idea of the writer that I had inherited: the idea of the writer as a man with an internal life, a man drawing it all out of his own entrails, magically reading the externals of things.

Aziz went down, and shortly afterwards I saw the shawl-merchant's boat pull up at the Leeward's landing stage. The merchant came up alone. His loose baggy trousers, of thin brown cotton, were tucked into thick woollen socks pulled up high. He was a man of middle age, slender, sharp-featured and impressive. With his black, kinky-curled fur cap (like Mr Butt's), his black shoes and his black Indian-style jacket, long-skirted, hooked at the top (the top hook was visible), he looked Central Asian rather than Kashmiri. His name was Sharif.

Two lake boys brought up his small tin trunk, carrying it like a palanquin. He took off his shoes, spread a sheet on the carpet of the Leeward's sitting room, below the tall sliding glass windows, kneeled down, took out some embroidered tunics and laid them aside, and then, reverentially, took out the small bundle of his better-quality shawls, wrapped in white cotton. I had absolute faith in Mr Butt's management of this affair; and Mr Sharif's reverence for his goods confirmed what I felt. His stuff was good, thin, light, very warm, suggesting, at certain angles, a kind of ripple in the weaving. He took off his fur cap, showed the needle stuck into the crown, and said – pointing to his somewhat inflamed eyes – that he was more than a seller. He was a maker of shawls.

He wanted 8,600 rupees. I asked for a better price. He said 8,500, and he was firm. I asked Nazir to go and call Mr Butt. Nazir dutifully began going down the steps. On the landing (overlooking the water my bedroom had looked out on: now stagnant, with all the new building and boats, and attracting bottles and wrapping and other litter) Nazir stopped and called me. He wanted to know where I was – how serious I was. He said that Mr Butt knew Mr

Sharif very well, and had told Mr Sharif to show me good pieces and give me a good price.

Aziz reappeared. We left Mr Sharif upstairs, and went down to the office. Nazir brought down the shawl I had liked. Aziz felt it and said he would guarantee it for two years: it was what Mr Sharif had said. Mr Butt came, walking in from the front garden. And then Mr Sharif himself came down the steps. So there was a general meeting in the office around the milk-chocolate-brown shawl.

Aziz said 8,500 was too much. Mr Sharif disagreed. Aziz said I wasn't a three-day tourist. Saying nothing, Mr Sharif left the office, and walked down the marble-floored verandah to the hotel shop. I thought he had been offended in some way.

But Nazir said, 'He's going to pray.'

Mr Sharif got a mat from the shop, set it down on the white marble verandah just outside the office, and, while it rained, began to bow and pray. In the office we continued to debate the issue.

Mr Butt said that Mr Sharif was a good man. They had gone to Mecca together. Nazir said that Mr Sharif led the prayers in the mosque. He was not only a man of authority, but also a man of his word.

And Mr Sharif bowed and prayed, the rain pattering on the white marble just inches away from him.

Aziz said, 'Offer 7,500.'

That was how it was settled. The offer was apparently made and accepted without further reference to me. Mr Sharif finished his prayers, rolled up the mat, took the mat back to the shop, came back to the office, picked up an Urdu newspaper that was a couple of weeks old, began to read from it to Mr Butt (whose spectacle lenses were very thick now). Slowly, after he had finished his reading, he folded the finger-ring shawl; and then, with a similar deliberation, he wrapped the folded shawl in a sheet of the Urdu newspaper he had been reading.

While this was going on, Aziz showed me a third photograph of his trip to Mecca, and I asked Mr Butt what I had never asked him in all the months in 1962. What had he done before starting the Leeward? He said he had been a contractor; he had started the hotel in 1959, with five rooms. Thirty years later, the hotel had 45 rooms.

Much money had come to the valley; many people had risen; there was a whole new educated generation. But a good deal of that improvement had been swallowed up by the growth in the population.

The new wealth showed in the new middle-class building on the north shore of the lake, and on the lower slope of the hill with the Hari Parbat fort. At the same time, behind the houseboats, the stultifying old lake life went on (picturesque in sunlight, less so in the wet and the cold after the rain); and the lake was now more populous. More boys than ever shouted and competed for custom at the boating steps. The effect, though the setting was quite different, was like that of the Muslim ghetto of the old bazaar area of Lucknow.

An older style of life, again, seemed to go on in the centre of the old city, where small covered boats choked the canals, where the brick and timber shops were as I had remembered them, and where very quickly after rain the streets became dusty – with the dust from dried mud. At the rim of that old city, though, there were many important-looking new buildings, among them the university and a government building connected with animal husbandry. But then again, in the villages beyond this, as though the two styles of life were quite separate, was the immemorial world of rice-planting.

In small flooded fields people worked with their hands alone or with wooden ploughs. The houses were basic, brown-red brick between timber uprights, on two or more floors. The pitched roofs of corrugated iron were open at the gable ends, and in this space (and sometimes in a dormer window in the roof) were stored firewood, straw or fodder, or grain. Water ran down the hillsides in many channels; willow and poplar cast cold shadows; and boulders and tree-branches made crude and crooked fences in wet yards. And here as elsewhere wood and brick and the clothes of people were the colour of mud.

Even with this wretched-looking village life – people sitting on the platform-floor of open one-room shops, wrapped in grey-brown blankets or gunny sacks – there were the signs of big public works, as though a great effort was needed to support even that style of life, to provide electricity, to build a road, to offer some kind of transport. And always, the children: very small, in smiling groups, outnumbering the adults. The abiding memory was of the children.

Above a certain altitude it seemed that people lived in treeless mud. There were little ploughed plots of sodden earth around low houses of stone or timber, with people sitting or squatting at the edge of the mud. Safe above mud and water, straw was hung in bundles on the branches or in the forks of dried or dying trees. Even here there were children, wearing loose grey or brown gowns that made them look like little adults and made it hard, from a distance, to judge their size.

I saw this on a drive to Sonamarg with Nazir. Sonamarg was on the road to Ladakh in the north-east. It was new to me; it might have been that in 1962 the road wasn't good or wasn't open to visitors. The road was closed in winter; it had just been opened for the season. At higher altitudes it ran between walls of snow – melting from below, creating little caverns and snow overhangs; and the just-cleared asphalt surface was being abraded and dug up by runnels of melting snow.

At Sonamarg we were surrounded by thin, shouting boys who wanted us to toboggan down the snow slopes. 'Thirty rupees, 30 rupees.' The boys wore caps and had blotched complexions. From the roadside signs, Sonamarg seemed to mark a kind of boundary between Kashmir and Ladakh. It was no more than a collection of government huts and tourist lodges and shops. There were no fields or houses; the boys must have come from a village some distance away.

Nazir would have liked me to take a slide, to do the holiday thing, and to give the boys some work. Nazir's father was a successful man. He himself, with his nice haircut, his jeans and trainers, his dark-blue anorak (I asked him about it: it was Taiwanese, and cost 500 rupees, £25), was the picture of a young man of the middle class. But here, as on the lake, he had this feeling of solidarity with the Kashmiri children.

Going back down, back to the softer valley, getting an idea of its comparatively restricted size, returning quickly to crowds and small spaces (on the outskirts of Srinagar Nazir pointed out a little orchard that belonged to Mr Butt, but we didn't stop), I felt again, as I had felt at some of the boating steps, that even in this setting of mountains and snow-fed rivers, people had become as hemmed in and constrained as they were in the narrow ghetto lanes of Lucknow.

At the Leeward the next day I said goodbye to them all in the late afternoon, about half an hour or so before they broke their fast at the end of the Ramadan day: goodbye to Mr Butt, Aziz, the man who ran the hotel shop (from whom I had bought nothing), and the slender young man who was the manager of the Leeward. They were all in the little white glass-walled office downstairs, with the key-board and the calendar and the two posters of Mecca showing the kaaba and a golden dome. And just before I left they asked, just for the courtesy, whether I wanted tea.

Mr Butt's last news – the news he wanted me to take away and remember – was that he had made the pilgrimage to Mecca. He didn't speak of it as a penance; he spoke of it as a joy and fulfilment. It made him smile and laugh at the moment of farewell.

With Aziz my last talk was about money. His son Nazir had spent much time with me, and on our excursions had sometimes spent his own money. What would be a good recompense? There was no question of payment, Aziz said. Baksheesh was another matter: that could be one rupee, fourpence, or a lakh, 4000 pounds. That was no help to me at all, but Aziz didn't go beyond that.

When I suggested a figure, Aziz's face remained unreadable – and that was how I left him.

In the boat going back to the boulevard, feeling the end of the Ramadan day pressing on us, I made my offering to Nazir. He took what I offered, but it was immediately clear that he had done so only out of courtesy. His face altered; he looked away. I felt I had mishandled the moment: Nazir, though he had done tourist things with me, had perhaps been treating me as a friend. I felt again, but more acutely now, what I had sensed from the beginning: that my relationship with Nazir, an unexpectedly handsome young man with his own new ideas of elegance and self, couldn't but be more complicated than my relationship with his father.

I wanted to save the moment. I said that the gesture I had made had been made out of friendship for him and Aziz and Mr Butt. I said that twice. He softened; some recognition seemed to come to him that he too had to do something to save the moment – so soon to end, at the boating steps, and before the sunset call from the mosques.

The stiffness went out of him. And as we slipped down the busy waterway, past the small houseboat with the leather and fur-goods shop, the grocery, and the Sunshine Haircutting Saloon, we talked about his studies. In a few months he was going to get his school-leaving certificate. For two years after this he would study commerce at a college – preparing for his career in accountancy and, as his father and Mr Butt hoped, his life in the hotel business – and then he would go to the university.

From his grandfather's little shop in the lake, to his father's successful hotel career, to his own prospects as a graduate and accountant – there had been a step-by-step movement upwards. Would it continue?

He had never been out of Kashmir. At the moment the valley (and the mountains around it) was all the world he knew. He was still part of it. Twenty-seven years after I had got to know him, Aziz had remained more or less the same. It wouldn't be like that with Nazir. Already he had intimations of a world outside. Already, through that monthly exchange of letters with a foreign girl, there had come to him the idea of the possibility – always in Allah's hands – of a foreign marriage. In 27 years – hard for me now, in late middle age, to imagine that stretch of time, that boundary in the shades – Nazir wouldn't be the same. New ways of seeing and feeling were going to come to him, and he wasn't going to be part of the valley in the way he was now.

In 27 years I had succeeded in making a kind of return journey, shedding my Indian nerves, abolishing the darkness that separated me from my ancestral past. William Howard Russell, in 1858, had described (and commented on) a vast country physically in ruins, even away from the battles of the Mutiny. Twenty-five years or so later, from a part of the country Russell had travelled through (in such style as was available), my ancestors had left as indentured servants for the sugar estates of Guyana and Trinidad. I had carried in my bones that idea of abjectness and defeat and shame. It was the idea I had taken to India on that slow journey by train and ship in 1962; it was the source of my nerves. (It was the idea that surfaced again, to my surprise, during the writing of this book, when I first tried to read William Howard Russell's *Diary,* and I found myself rejecting the book, the man, and even his great descriptive talent.)

What I hadn't understood in 1962, or had taken too much for granted, was the extent to which the country had been remade; and even the extent to which India had been restored to itself, after its own equivalent of the Dark Ages – after the Muslim invasions and the detailed, repeated vandalising of the North, the shifting empires, the wars, the 18th-century anarchy. The twentieth-century restoration of India to itself had taken time; it could even seem like a kind of luck. It had taken much to create a Bengali reformer like Ram Mohun Roy (born in 1772); it had taken much more to create Gandhi (born in 1869). The British peace after the 1857 Mutiny can be seen as a kind of luck. It was a time of intellectual recruitment. India was set on the way of a new kind of intellectual life; it was given new ideas about its history and civilization. The freedom movement reflected all of this and turned out to be the truest kind of liberation.

In the 130 years or so since the Mutiny – the last 90 years of the British Raj and the first 40 years of Independence begin increasingly to appear as part of the same historical period – the idea of freedom has gone everywhere in India. Independence was worked for by people more or less at the top; the freedom it brought has worked its way down. People everywhere have ideas now of who they are and what they owe themselves. The process quickened with the economic development that came after Independence; what was hidden in 1962, or not easy to see, what perhaps was only in a state of becoming, has become clearer. The liberation of spirit that has come to India could not come as release alone. In India, with its layer below layer of distress and cruelty, it had to come as disturbance. It had to come as rage and revolt. India was now a country of a million little mutinies.

A million mutinies, supported by twenty kinds of group excess, sectarian excess, religious excess, regional excess: the beginnings of self-awareness, it would seem, the beginnings of an intellectual life, already negated by old anarchy and disorder. But there was in India now what didn't exist 200 years before: a central will, a central intellect, a national idea. The Indian Union was greater than the sum of its parts; and many of these movements of excess strengthened the Indian state, defining it as the source of law and civility and reasonableness. The Indian Union gave people a second chance, calling them back from the excesses with which, in another century, or in other circumstances (as neighbouring countries showed), they might have had to live: the destructive chauvinism of the Shiv Sena, the tyranny of many kinds of religious fundamentalism (people always ready in India to let religion carry the burden of their pain), the film-star corruption and racial politics of the South, the pious Marxist idleness and nullity of Bengal.

Excess was now felt to be excess in India. What the mutinies were also helping to define was the strength of the general intellectual life, and the wholeness and humanism of the values to which all Indians now felt they could appeal. And – strange irony – the mutinies were not to be wished away. They were part of the beginning of a new way for many millions, part of India's growth, part of its restoration.

When I went back to Bombay I got in touch with Paritosh, the film writer. Paritosh worked in the commercial cinema, and he loved the film form: it was his vocation, almost his faith. But he didn't care for the people who made films in India. They made him suffer; they enraged him; and he had had his ups and downs.

When I had met him, five months before, he had just come out of a bad period. During this period he had turned his back on Bombay and films and had gone back to his own city of Calcutta to rest and recover. But then – having married in this period – he had come to the end of his mood of rejection, and he had come back to Bombay to start again. He was living in a mid-town area in a bare one-roomed apartment. 'This is my only room under the sun,' he had said, throwing up his arms, looking at the ceiling, making the room feel very small. But he had prospects: he had come back to Bombay to work on a film with a once successful producer he had known. Every now and then they met in a neighbourhood hotel and discussed the script.

Paritosh was determined to stay the course and to succeed this time. He said he felt he was going to make some money. But his cousin, who had taken me to see him, and had sat in the room with us, was gloomier. Paritosh's temperament would get in the way; he would quarrel with someone, or something would happen; and Paritosh would be back where he had always been. I listened to what the cousin said as we walked back through the crowded streets near a market to the suburban railway station; and I had become depressed, thinking of the fine-looking writer in his bare room. Now, five months on, I wanted to know what had happened.

I didn't have to make a journey to see Paritosh – no overcrowded suburban train, no choking taxi ride through the brown smoke of the Bombay highways. He came to have a coffee with me in the hotel. He was a busy man; he had things to do. His face was suffused now with the pleasure he felt in his busyness; some of the rage had been ironed away.

He had written his film. And the producer had found a backer. They had been able to start shooting, and to show rushes of early scenes to distributors. The distributors had bought the film. The backer had got an almost instant return on his investment, and he had put up money for a second film – Paritosh seethed with ideas. Paritosh had already got his writer's fee for the first film; it was a substantial fee; he had, already, bought a bigger apartment in a better area. In five months his fortunes had changed; this was the kind of thing that was possible in rich, energetic, squalid Bombay; this was why the city drew people all the time.

He had retained a bigger financial share in the second film. This film, Paritosh said, was to be more for himself. The first one, the one that had bought him his apartment, was commercial, popular – but he wasn't using the words to criticise his work: he was only describing a particular kind of film.

What was it about? What kind of story and characters had been filling his head when I had met him in his little room? What was the material he had been banking on? The film was set in a Bombay slum, one of the many shanty towns of the city. The hero was a young slum-dweller; he was a man of possibilities, but he was corrupted by a gangster. A commercial film, but topical, and strong. (And also, as fictions often do, carrying an unconscious echo of the creator's predicament.)

To make the film, Paritosh said, they had had to build their own slum or shanty town. For legal reasons they couldn't use a real place. They had taken photographs of various real places, and they had created a kind of composite Bombay slum. While the film was being shot, they had all lived in the various huts of the set. Just the day before, Paritosh said, they had begun to dismantle the make-believe slum they had lived in for many weeks. It had given him a pang.

*December 1988 – February 1990*

# ACKNOWLEDGEMENTS
## [for *India: A Million Mutinies Now*]

When you travel for a book like this, you often don't know what you are looking for until you have found it. You need a lot of help on the way. On this journey many people helped. They shared their knowledge; they gave names and introductions. Three people, all of them newspaper editors, helped especially, from beginning to end: Nikhil Lakshman, Vinod Mehta, Rahul Singh. Vinod Mehta and Rahul Singh each did a part of the journey with me; but I must stress that I alone am responsible for what I have written. There are a number of other people I would like to remember here. In Bombay: Charu Deshpande; Ajit Pillai. In Bangalore: T.J.S. George. In Madras: K.P. Sunil. In Calcutta: Shekhar Bhatia; Vir Sanghvi; Sunanda Datta Ray; Satyabrata Bose. In Delhi: Rekha Khanna Mehta. In Chandigarh: Kanwar Sandhu. Other people who helped are mentioned in the text; sometimes, for obvious reasons, their names and circumstances are changed.